ELECTORAL COLLEGE VOTES IN THE 2008 ELECTION

THE UNITED STATES
A political map showing the number of electoral votes per state

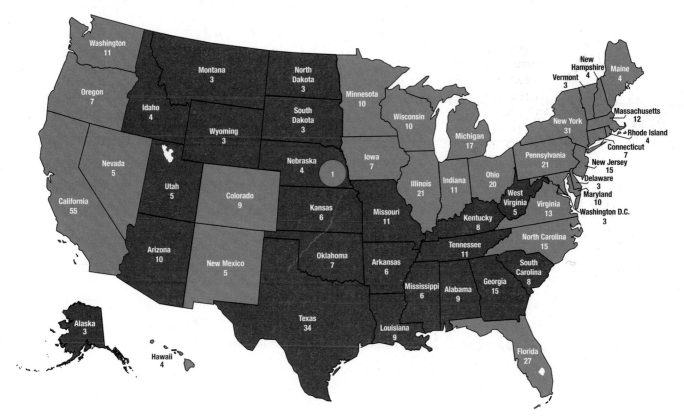

A political map with states drawn in proportion to the number of electoral votes

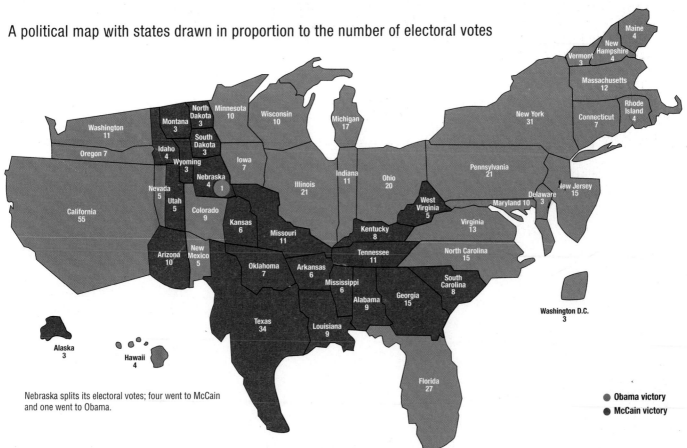

Nebraska splits its electoral votes; four went to McCain and one went to Obama.

● Obama victory
● McCain victory

GOVERNMENT IN AMERICA

PEOPLE, POLITICS, AND POLICY

A P* EDITION

FOURTEENTH EDITION

GEORGE C. EDWARDS III
Texas A & M University

MARTIN P. WATTENBERG
University of California, Irvine

ROBERT L. LINEBERRY
University of Houston

Longman

New York   Boston   San Francisco
London   Toronto   Sydney   Tokyo   Singapore   Madrid
Mexico City   Munich   Paris   Cape Town   Hong Kong   Montreal

Editor-in-Chief: Eric Stano
Assistant Development Manager: David B. Kear
Development Editor: Terri Wise
Marketing Manager: Lindsey Prudhomme
Assistant Development Editor: Donna Garnier
Media Supplements Editor: Regina Vertiz
Production Manager: Denise Phillip
Project Coordination, Text Design, and Electronic Page Makeup: Pre-PressPMG
Cover Design Manager: John Callahan
Cover Designer: Maria Ilardi
Cover Images: Ron Sanford/Corbis and Stockbyte/Getty Images
Photo Researcher: Julie Tesser
Senior Manufacturing Buyer: Roy Pickering
Printer and Binder: Worldcolor/Dubuque
Cover Printer: Phoenix Color Corporation

For permission to use copyrighted material, grateful acknowledgment is made to the
copyright holders on pp. 776-778, which are hereby made part of this copyright page.

Library of Congress Cataloging-in-Publication Data

Edwards, George C.
    Government in America : people, politics, and policy / George C. Edwards,
    Martin P. Wattenberg, Robert L. Lineberry.—14th ed., Advanced placement ed.
        p. cm.
    ISBN-13: 978-0-13-715159-2
    ISBN-10: 0-13-715159-4
    1. United States—Politics and government—Textbooks.   I. Wattenberg,
Martin P., 1956-   II. Lineberry, Robert L.   III. Title.
    JK276.E39 2009
    320.473—dc22

                                                        2008048832

Copyright © 2009 by Pearson Education, Inc.

Advanced Placement Program and AP are registered trademarks of The CollegeBoard,
which was not involved in the production of, and does not endorse, this book.

Longman
is an imprint of

4 5 6 7 8 9 10—WCD—11 10

AP* Edition ISBN-13: 978-0-13-715159-2
AP* Edition ISBN-10:   0-13-715159-4

PEARSON

www.PearsonSchool.com/Advanced

BRIEF CONTENTS

DETAILED CONTENTS

PART 2 PEOPLE AND POLITICS

PART 3 THE POLICYMAKERS

AP* CORRELATION GUIDE

UNITED STATES GOVERNMENT AND POLITICS: AP* TOPICS CORRELATED TO *GOVERNMENT IN AMERICA*, FOURTEENTH EDITION

AP* TOPICS	*GOVERNMENT IN AMERICA*, FOURTEENTH EDITION
I. Constitutional Underpinnings of United States Government	**Chapters 1, 2, 3**
Considerations that influenced the formulation and adoption of the Constitution	pp. 31–55
Separation of powers	pp. 49–50
Federalism	pp. 51–52, 71–96
Theories of democratic government	pp. 14–17
II. Political Beliefs and Behaviors	**Chapters 1, 6, 7, 8, 9, 10, 11**
Beliefs that citizens hold about their government and its leaders	pp. 3–8, 198–205, 210–211
Processes by which citizens learn about politics	pp. 191–195
The nature, sources, and consequences of public opinion	pp. 10–13, 195–201, 347–348
The ways in which citizens vote and otherwise participate in public life	pp. 206–210, 305–325
Factors that influence citizens to differ from one another in terms of political beliefs and behaviors	pp. 201–205, 317–325
III. Political Parties, Interest Groups, and Mass Media	**Chapters 7, 8, 9, 10, 11, 12, 13, 17, 19, 20**
Political parties and elections	Chapters 8, 9, 10
Functions	pp. 248–251
Organization	pp. 253–256
Development	pp. 258–267
Effects on the political process	pp. 248–251, 257–258, 268–271, 388–391, 416–419
Electoral laws and systems	pp. 278–300, 305–307, 322–323, 367–373, 21.8–21.15
Interest groups, including political action committees (PACs)	Chapters 11, 12, 17, 19, 20
The range of interests represented	pp. 336–342, 348–355, 562, 613–614
The activities of interest groups	pp. 342–348
The effects of interest groups on the political process	pp. 333–348, 391, 613–614, 20.7
The unique characteristics and roles of PACs in the political process	pp. 292–298, 341–342, 345–347, 350–352, 355–356, 371–372
The Mass Media	Chapters 7, 9, 13
The functions and structures of the media	pp. 218–235
The impact of media on politics	pp. 223–245, 287–291, 427–435
IV. Institutions of National Government: The Congress, the President, the Bureaucracy, and the Federal Courts	**Chapters 3, 7, 9, 11, 12, 13, 14, 15, 16, 21**
The major formal and informal institutional arrangements of power	Chapters 3, 12, 13, 15, 16
Congress	pp. 363–385
The presidency	pp. 406–427
The bureaucracy	pp. 471–494
Federal courts	pp. 75–80, 509–533
Relationships among these four institutions, and varying balances of power	pp. 385–388, 415–427, 495–503, 518–526
Linkages between institutions and the following	Chapters 6, 7, 9, 11, 12, 13, 15, 16, 21
Public opinion and voters	Chapters 6, 12, 13, 15, 16
Congress	pp. 367–373, 389–391
The presidency	pp. 419–421, 427–432

AP* FEATURES

The AP* Edition of *Government in America* includes additional features that will be helpful to AP* students. The AP* Correlation Guide includes a detailed list of Government and Politics: United States AP* topics correlated to *Government in America*. By following the page references in the second column, students can find the discussion of each of the six major topic areas, and their more-specific details, in the pages of *Government in America*. This AP* Correlation Guide will help students study and review for exams.

The AP* Edition also includes for each chapter a selection of multiple choice and free response questions. These practice drills replicate actual AP* exam questions, tied specifically to each chapter of *Government in America*. The answers to the questions are also included for both the multiple choice and free response questions, and include explanations for the answers, to further guide students. The AP* Exam questions and answers are at the back of the book.

PREFACE

Politics matters. The national government provides important services, ranging from retirement security and health care to recreation facilities and weather forecasts. The national government may also send us to war or negotiate peace with our adversaries, expand or restrict our freedom, raise or lower our taxes, and increase or decrease aid to education. In the twenty-first century, decision makers of both political parties are facing difficult questions regarding American democracy and the scope of our government. AP* students need a framework for understanding these questions.

We write *Government in America*, 14e, AP* Edition to provide AP* students with a better understanding of our fascinating political system. This fourteenth edition of *Government in America* continues to frame its content with a public policy approach to government in the United States. We continually ask—and answer—the question, "What difference does politics make to the policies governments produce?" It is one thing to describe the Madisonian system of checks and balances and separation of powers or the elaborate and unusual federal system of government in the United States; it is something else to ask how these features of our constitutional structure affect the policies governments generate.

We do not discuss policy at the expense of politics, however. We provide extensive coverage of five core subject areas: constitutional foundations, patterns of political behavior, political institutions, public policy outputs, and state and local government, but we try to do so in a more analytically significant—and interesting—manner. We take special pride in introducing AP* students to relevant work from current political scientists, such as the role of political action committees (PACs) or the impact of divided government—something we have found AP* teachers appreciate.

To render the policy focus in concrete terms, two important themes appear throughout the book: the nature of democracy and the scope of government. Each chapter begins with a preview of the relevancy of these themes to the chapter's subject, refers to the themes at points within the chapter, and ends with specific sections on the two themes under the heading "Understanding . . ." that show how the themes illuminate the chapter's subject matter.

The first great question central to governing, a question every nation must answer, is *How should we govern?* In the United States, our answer is "democracy." Yet democracy is an evolving and somewhat ambiguous concept. In Chapter 1, we define democracy as a means of selecting policymakers and of organizing government so that policy represents and responds to citizens' preferences. As with previous editions, we continue to incorporate theoretical issues in our discussions of different models of American democracy. We try to encourage AP* students to think analytically about the theories and to develop independent assessments of how well the American system lives up to citizens' expectations of democratic government. To help them do this, in every chapter we raise questions about democracy. For example, does Congress give the American people the policies they want? Is a strong presidency good for democracy? Does our mass media make us more democratic? Are powerful courts that make policy decisions compatible with democracy?

The second theme, the scope of government, focuses on another great question of governing: *What should government do?* Here we discuss alternative views concerning the proper role and size for American government and how the workings of institutions and politics influence this scope. The government's scope is the core question around which politics revolves in contemporary America, pervading many crucial issues: To what degree should Washington impose national standards for clean air or speed limits on state policies? How high should taxes be? Do elections encourage politicians to promise more governmental services? Questions about the scope of government are policy questions and thus obviously directly related to our policy approach. Since the scope of government is *the* pervasive question in American politics today, AP* students will have little problem finding it relevant to their lives and interests.

We hope that AP* students—long after reading *Government in America*—will employ these perennial questions about the nature of our democracy and the scope of our government when they examine political events. The specifics of policy issues will change, but questions about whether the government is responsive to the people or whether it should expand or contract its scope will always be with us.

NEW TO THIS EDITION

Government in America, 14e, AP* Edition has been substantially revised and updated to reflect recent, and often historic, changes in politics, policy, and participation. All figures and tables include the most recent data available. Approximately 30 percent of the photos and their captions are new to this edition.

The Fourteenth Edition also includes

- a new feature called **My State**, which shows students how their state ranks in relation to other states on a dimension of politics or policy relevant to the chapter in which it appears; topics include immigrants as a percentage of state populations, the number of visits Clinton and Obama made to different states during the 2008 primary season, state and local spending on public education, and abortion laws for minors.
- chapter tests at the end of each chapter—including multiple choice, true/false, and short answer—giving students an opportunity to test their retention and understanding of key chapter concepts
- questions to encourage critical thinking in boxed features, as well as photo and figure captions
- expanded and updated coverage of immigration in Chapters 6 and 18 to reflect the policy's prominence in American politics
- added coverage of Hispanic civil rights issues in Chapter 5
- extensive coverage of the rise of the new media, particularly the Internet, and the declining role for newspapers and network nightly news in Chapter 7
- extensive quotes from the 2008 Democratic and Republican Party platforms in Chapter 8, which clearly outline the differences between the two major parties
- material on Democratic Party superdelegates in Chapter 9 in light of their high profile role in 2008
- new material on campaign finance in Chapter 9 in light of 2008 developments
- a new in-depth section on the historic 2008 election in Chapter 10
- more detail on the lobbying process, particularly who spends the most and how much, in Chapter 11
- a new focus on why there are not more women in Congress in Chapter 12
- material on the Bush presidency, its legacy, and presidential power in Chapter 13
- a section on the privatization of public policies in Chapter 15
- new material examining the state of the economy and the government's intervention
- new material on the War in Iraq and the War on Terrorism in Chapter 20
- a substantial number of new figures to increase the visual appeal of the book and make data more accessible and understandable to students

Politics **Matters**

In its relevant, balanced treatment of politics and policymaking, *Government in America* refers to two key themes throughout: *the nature of democracy* and *the scope of government*. Each chapter begins with a preview of the two themes, establishing them as a context for the discussion to follow.

PUBLIC OPINION AND POLITICAL ACTION

POLITICS IN ACTION:
A RARE MOMENT OF CONSENSUS IN PUBLIC OPINION

American public opinion about the events of September 11, 2001, and the subsequent war in Afghanistan reflected a unanimity that is rarely seen. Normally, analysts find a great diversity of views among the American public, and public opinion surveys usually reveal many conflicting attitudes that frequently reflect ambivalence. But such was not the case in this instance. Hundreds of millions of Americans responded with remarkably near-unanimous opinions. Most everyone agreed that this was an act of war that demanded an immediate response by force. Partisan differences, racial differences, and regional differences mattered little in understanding attitudes about the events of September 11 and the war against terrorism.

A CNN/*USA Today* poll conducted on September 11, 2001, found that 86 percent felt that the attacks that day had been an act of war. A *Washington Post*/ABC poll conducted on September 13 found 93 percent favored military action when asked, "If the United States can identify the groups or nations responsible for the attacks, would you support or oppose taking military action against them?" The same poll found that 85 percent favored striking at Afghanistan if Osama bin Laden was found to be culpable and Afghanistan refused to turn him over. Support for military action dropped a bit when people were asked if it meant innocent civilians might be hurt or killed

183

**Every chapter concludes with a section titled "Understanding . . ."
which reviews the chapter's content in light of the two themes.**

UNDERSTANDING PUBLIC OPINION AND POLITICAL ACTION

In many third-world countries, there have been calls for more democracy in recent years. One often hears that citizens of developing nations want their political system to be like America's in the sense that ordinary people's opinions determine how the government is run. However, as this chapter has shown, there are many limits on the role public opinion plays in the American political system. The average person is not very well informed about political issues, including the crucial issue of the scope of government.

PUBLIC ATTITUDES TOWARD THE SCOPE OF GOVERNMENT

Central to the ideology of the Republican Party is the belief that the scope of American government has become too wide ranging. According to Ronald Reagan, probably the most admired Republican in recent history, government was not the solution to society's problems—it was the problem. He called for the government to "get off the backs of the American people."

Reagan's rhetoric about an overly intrusive government was reminiscent of the 1964 presidential campaign rhetoric of Barry Goldwater, who lost to Lyndon Johnson in a landslide. Indeed, Reagan first made his mark in politics by giving a televised speech on behalf of the embattled Goldwater campaign. Although the rhetoric was much the same when Ronald Reagan was first elected president in 1980, public opinion about the scope of government had changed dramatically. In 1964, only 30 percent of the population thought that the government was getting too powerful; by 1980, this figure had risen to 50 percent.

DEMOCRACY, PUBLIC OPINION, AND POLITICAL ACTION

Remember, though, that American democracy is representative rather than direct. As *The American Voter* stated many years ago, ¡The public's explicit task is to decide not what government shall do but rather who shall decide what government shall do."⁴⁰ When individuals under communist rule protested for democracy, what they wanted most was the right to have a say in choosing their leaders. Americans can—and often do—take for granted the opportunity to replace their leaders at the next election. Protest is thus directed at making the government listen to specific demands, not overthrowing it. In this sense, it can be said that American citizens have become well socialized to democracy.

If the public's task in democracy is to choose who is to lead, we must still ask whether it can do so wisely. If people know little about where candidates stand on issues, how can they make rational choices? Most choose performance criteria over policy criteria. As Morris Fiorina has written, citizens typically have one hard bit of data to go on: "They know what life has been like during the incumbent's administration. They need not know the precise economic or foreign policies of the incumbent administration in order to see or feel the results of those policies."⁴¹ Thus, even if they are voting only according to the nature of the times, their voices are clearly being heard—holding public officials accountable for their actions.

Illuminating **Themes**

Several times in each chapter's margin, **Why It Matters** insets encourage AP* students to think critically about an aspect of government, politics, or policy and to consider the impact—usually on themselves—if things worked differently. Each **Why It Matters** feature extends the book's policy emphasis to situate it directly within the context of students' daily lives.

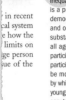

? Why it Matters
Political Participation
Inequality in political participation is a problem in a representative democracy. Public policy debates and outcomes would probably be substantially different if people of all age groups and income groups participated equally. If young adults participated more, politicians would be more inclined to work on ways by which the government could help young people get the training necessary to get good jobs. And if the poor participated at higher levels, government programs to alleviate poverty would likely be higher on the political agenda than they are today.

...y in recent ...cal system ...e how the ...limits on ...ge person ...sue of the

...scope of ...d Reagan, ...as not the

YOU ARE THE Policymaker

Should We Impose Term Limits on of Congress?

In the late 1980s, many reformer... incumbency advantage enjoyed b... lifetime tenure, which served as ... encouraged ethics abuses. To inc...

YOU ARE THE Judge

The Case of the Drive-in Th...

Almost everyone concedes that *sometimes* obscenity should... banned by public authorities. One instance might be when a... person's right to show pornographic movies clashes with another's right to privacy. Presumably, no one wants hard-cor... pornography shown in public places where schoolchildren m... see it. Showing dirty movies in an enclosed theater or in the privacy of your own living room is one thing. Showing them in public is something else. Or is it?

You Are the Policymaker asks AP* students to read arguments on both sides of a specific current issue—such as whether we should prohibit PACs— and then to make a policy decision. In Chapters 4 and 5 (Civil Liberties and Civil Rights), this feature is titled **You Are the Judge** and presents the AP* student with an actual court case.

The **America in Perspective** features examine how the United States compares to other countries on topics such as tax rates, voter turnout, and the delivery of public services. By reading these boxes and comparing the United States to other nations, AP* students can obtain a better perspective on the size of our government and the nature of democracy.

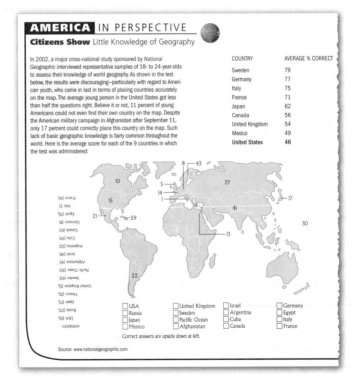

AMERICA IN PERSPECTIVE
Citizens Show Little Knowledge of Geography

In 2002, a major cross-national study sponsored by *National Geographic* interviewed representative samples of 18- to 24-year-olds to assess their knowledge of world geography. As shown in the test below, the results were discouraging—particularly with regard to American youth, who came in last in terms of placing countries accurately on the map. The average young person in the United States got less than half the questions right. Believe it or not, 11 percent of young Americans could not even find their own country on the map. Despite the American military campaign in Afghanistan after September 11, only 17 percent could correctly place this country on the map. Such lack of basic geographic knowledge is fairly common throughout the world. Here is the average score for each of the 9 countries in which the test was administered:

COUNTRY	AVERAGE % CORRECT
Sweden	79
Germany	77
Italy	75
France	71
Japan	62
Canada	56
United Kingdom	54
Mexico	49
United States	46

Correct answers are upside down at left.

Source: www.nationalgeographic.com

Politics **Matters**

How the Under-30 Crowd Learns from Different Media Sources Compared to Older Americans

In December of 2007, the Pew Research Center asked a representative sample whether they regularly learned about the presidential campaign from a variety of media sources. This table shows the results, broken down by age. Notice that young people are substantially more likely to learn from the Internet and comedy TV shows. In contrast, older people are more likely to learn from the traditional sources of newspapers and network TV news (NBC, CBS, and ABC). Because so many young people are bypassing these sources, both newspapers and network news are facing the likely prospect of declining audiences for some time to come.

Cable TV news—CNN, MSNBC, and the Fox News Channel—have seen their audiences expand in recent years, as Americans of all ages have come to rely on them fairly heavily. However, given how little time most people stay tuned to these channels, one has to be skeptical that people are getting much more than basic headlines from them. In theory, the Internet offers all the details about public policy and government that anyone could want. Whether people who learn about politics via the Internet take advantage of the opportunities offered there remains to be seen. Comedy shows, on the other hand, offer very limited chances for learning about politics. Commenting on this survey finding, Jon Stewart of *The Daily Show* at first dismissed out of hand any notion that young people were turning to his comedy show to learn about political events. Subsequently, his show has adopted the slogan of "Keeping America Informed—Unintentionally."

% SAYING THEY REGULARLY LEARN SOMETHING ABOUT THE PRESIDENTIAL CAMPAIGN FROM:	AGE 18-29	AGE 30-49	AGE 50+
Cable news networks	35	36	41
Nightly network news	24	28	40
Daily newspaper	25	26	38
Comedy TV shows	12	7	6
Internet	42	25	15

Source: December 2007 survey by the Pew Research Center for the People and the Press, *http://people-press.org/reports/questionnaires/384.pdf.*

QUESTIONS FOR DISCUSSION

▶ How much do you think can really be learned about politics from the comedy shows that one out of eight young people say they learn from?

▶ Why do you think young people are so much less likely to learn from the traditional major news sources—TV network news and newspapers?

The popular **Young People and Politics** feature illustrates how policies specifically impact young adults, how their political behavior patterns are unique and important, and how their particular policy desires are being met or ignored by public officials.

MyState | A Nation of Minorities

The country's minority population has now reached over 100 million, including about 45 million Hispanic Americans and 40 million African Americans. Minorities comprise approximately a third of all Americans.

This map shows the percent of non-Whites in each state. Hawaii has the largest minority population at 75 percent, followed by the District of Columbia (68 percent), New Mexico (57 percent), California (57 percent), and Texas (52 percent).

Source: U.S. Census Bureau, News Release, May 17, 2007.

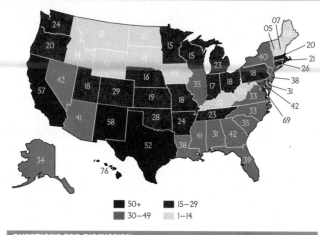

Legend: ■ 50+ ■ 15–29 ■ 30–49 ■ 1–14

QUESTIONS FOR DISCUSSION

▶ How does your state rank in terms of minority population?

▶ Why do you think some states have much larger minority populations than others?

▶ How have these groups impacted the nature of politics in your state?

NEW! MyState features bring the lessons of national politics home to the state level, putting important political issues in the students' own backyards. Figures on issues—ranging from the percentage of a state's population made up of immigrants, to spending on public education—both inform readers about political circumstances in their own states and illustrate their state's position on the topic in relation to the rest of the country.

Making Politics Matter to **Students**

A GENERATION OF CHANGE

The Shrinking Gap Between Men's and Women's Wages

Over the past generation, the gender gap between the earnings of a typical American woman and that a typical American man has narrowed. In 1985, women's median weekly earnings were 68 percent of that of men. As you can see in the graph below, the most recent data show that this disparity is no longer as great, with women now earning about 81 percent of what men earn.

QUESTIONS FOR DISCUSSION

▷ Do you think the gender gap in earnings will continue to shrink as your generation moves into the work force? Why or why not?

▷ Some people think that the government should take steps to promote pay equity between men and women. For some proposals along these lines, see http://www.pay-equity.org/cando.html. What do you think? Is this the sort of area where the government should take action, or is this a matter best left to private enterprise?

WOMEN'S EARNINGS AS A % OF MEN'S

YEAR

Source: U.S. Department of Labor, Bureau of Labor Statistics, *Women in the Labor Force: A Databook* (2007 edition), Table 16.

Because AP* students often have little idea of just how much things have changed in their lifetimes (an 18-year-old student in 2009 was born in 1991, when President George H. W. Bush was in office), the A Generation of Change feature provides AP* students some historical perspective—based on their very own life spans. Topics include changes in network news broadcasts, partisan re-alignment in the South, and the increase in polarization of Democratic and Republican voters.

Get Connected

Public Opinion and SLOPs

Public opinion polls play an important role in American politics and government. Some observers even argue that policymakers keep an eye on polls when trying to develop policy, a practice that may be to the detriment of our system of government. Some polls are conducted scientifically and provide useful information about what Americans are thinking. There are other polls called self-selected opinion polls, or SLOPs, that may provide biased or misleading information. You may have seen SLOPs on an interest group's Web site or even on the local news. How are scientific polls conducted, and how do they differ from SLOPs?

Search the Web

The Gallup Organization is one of the oldest public opinion polling firms in the country. Go to the "How Polls are Conducted" page at the Gallup Web site, *http://media.gallup.com/PDF/FAQ/HowArePolls.pdf*. Now review the National Council on Public Polls' "Statement About Internet Polls," *www.ncpp.org/?q=node/3.1* While the National Council on Public Polls' statement is about Internet polls, this type of public opinion poll could have the same shortcomings as the self-selected opinion poll you might see on television or find on an interest group's Web site.

Questions to Ask

• What are the important characteristics about Gallup's polling methods that allow people to have confidence in the findings revealed by the organization's polls?

• Why does the National Council on Public Polls think it is important to know if people were able to participate in the poll more than once?

• What are the shortcomings of any public opinion poll?

Why It Matters

The people are able to voice their opinions through public opinion polls, but polls may cause problems for our political system if they are not conducted correctly. It is important for the consumers of public opinion polls, including policymakers and voters, to have confidence in the information such polls present.

Get Involved

Find the results of an Internet poll at the CNN Web site, *www.cnn.com*; Fox News Channel's Web site, *www.foxnews.com*; or in your local media. Evaluate the poll using the National Council on Public Polls' "Statement About Internet Polls." Contact the person or group who published the poll and ask them to answer the questions on the statement if the poll doesn't provide the answers directly. Consult this issue brief from the Pew Research Center for the People and the Press, *http://people-press.org/commentary/display.php3?AnalysisID=20*, to offer suggestions on how to improve the poll. For more exercises, go to *www.longmanamericangovernment.com*.

Chapter Test

Multiple Choice

1. Which of the following groups tends to be undercounted in the national census?
   a. Senior citizens
   b. College students
   c. Women
   d. Minorities
   e. Working adults

2. The second great wave of immigration, during the late nineteenth and early twentieth century, was primarily characterized by an influx of immigrants from all but which of the following countries?
   a. Italy
   b. Poland
   c. Russia
   d. Eastern Europe

5. What happened to California's Proposition 187, which called for illegal immigrants to be denied access to public services?
   a. It won at the ballot box and has been implemented since then
   b. It won at the ballot box, but there have been practical obstacles to its implementation
   c. It won at the ballot box, but there have been legal obstacles to its implementation
   d. It did not win at the ballot box
   e. It has not been voted on yet

6. Which of the following is not generally true of women's political beliefs compared to men's?

8. All else being equal, the chance of a sampling error is the highest in a poll that questioned:
   a. 500 people
   b. 800 people
   c. 1,000 people
   d. 1,500 people
   e. 2,000 people

9. Assume that Gallup conducted an opinion poll in which 2,000 randomly selected individuals were asked whether they approved or disapproved of the Congress. The results show that 58 percent of respondents approved. Knowing what you know about the science of polling, you now know with 95 percent certainty that the

NEW! End-of-chapter Chapter Tests enable AP* students to assess their understanding of key points before they move on to the next topic.

Get Connected involves AP* students in the study of politics and government via the Internet. These user-friendly exercises appear at the end of every chapter, asking AP* students to research a particular topic covered in the chapter by visiting one or more related Web sites. Each exercise draws students' attention to the relevance of the topic in the context of their own lives.

PRINT AND ONLINE RESOURCES

For Qualified AP* Adopters

Most of the teacher supplements and resources for this book are available electronically on the Instructor Resource Center. Upon adoption or to preview, please go to PearsonSchool.com/Advanced and click "Online Teacher Supplements". You will be required to complete a one-time registration subject to verification before being emailed access information to download materials.

NAME OF SUPPLEMENT	AVAILABLE IN PRINT	AVAILABLE ONLINE	TEACHER OR STUDENT SUPPLEMENT	DESCRIPTION
American Government Study Site		✓	Both	Online package of practice tests, Web links, and flashcards organized by major course topics and arranged by *Government in America's* table of contents. Visit www.pearsonamericangovernment.com
AP* Test Prep: U.S. Government and Politics 0137153252	✓		Student	This student study tool, created for use specifically with *Government in America*, AP* Edition, contains a wealth of resources for students, including practice test questions with answers and applications for each chapter, and sample AP* practice exams with answers. Available for purchase.
Study Guide 020568436X	✓		Student	Contains learning objectives, chapter summaries, and practice tests. Available for purchase.
Study Card for American Government 0321291859	✓		Student	Course information is distilled down to the basics, helping AP* students quickly master the fundamentals, review a subject for understanding, or prepare for an exam. Laminated for durability. Available for purchase.
Instructor's Manual 0205684343	✓	✓	Teacher	Offers chapter overviews and outlines, teaching ideas, and discussion topics and Web activities incorporating recent political news.
AP* Test Bank 0205684351	✓	✓	Teacher	Contains over 200 questions per chapter in multiple-choice, true-false, short answer, and essay format. Questions address all levels of Bloom's taxonomy and all multiple-choice test questions have five answer choices, conforming to the format of the AP* exam.
PowerPoint Presentation 0205684378		✓	Teacher	This rich battery of slides includes a lecture outline of the text along with graphics from the book. Available on the Instructor Resource Center*.
Digital Transparency Masters 0205684440		✓	Teacher	These PDF slides contain all maps, figures, and tables found in the text. Available on the Instructor Resource Center*. AP* teachers can download the transparency masters by registering for access as an adopter at *www.phschool.com/advanced* and clicking on the Online Teacher Supplements link for directions.
Instructor's Resource CD 0137153244		✓	Teacher	Contains the Instructor's Manual, PowerPoint Presentations, Digital Transparency Masters, Test Bank. The CD also contains the TestGen Computerized Testing System, which allows teachers to edit existing questions and add their own items. Tests can be printed in several different formats and can include features such as graphs and tables.

IMPROVE RESULTS WITH mypoliscilab

Designed to amplify a traditional course in numerous ways or to administer a course online, **MyPoliSciLab** combines pedagogy and assessment with an array of multimedia activities—videos, simulations, exercises, and online newsfeeds—to make learning more effective for all types of students. Now featuring the combined resources, assets, and activities of both Prentice Hall and Longman Publishers, this new release of **MyPoliSciLab** is visually richer and even more interactive than previous iterations—a quantum leap forward in design with more points of assessment and interconnectivity between concepts.

TEACHING AND LEARNING TOOLS

✓ **Assessment**: Comprehensive online diagnostic tools—learning objectives, study guides, flashcards, and pre- and post-tests—help students gauge and improve their understanding.

✓ **E-book:** Identical in content and design to the printed text, an e-book provides students access to their text wherever and whenever they need it.

✓ **UPDATED! PoliSci News Review:** A series of weekly articles and video clips—from traditional and non-traditional news sources—recaps the most important political news stories, followed by quizzes that test students' understanding.

✓ **NEW! ABC News RSS feed: MyPoliSciLab** provides an online feed from ABC News, updated hourly, to keep students current.

✓ **ABC News Video Clips:** Over 60 high-interest 2- to 4-minute clips provide historical snapshots in each chapter of key political issues and offer opportunities to launch discussions.

✓ **UPDATED! Roundtable and Debate Video Clips:** These video clips feature professors discussing key concepts from ideologically diverse perspectives and debating politically charged issues.

✓ **Student Polling:** Updated weekly with timely, provocative questions, the polling feature lets students voice their opinions in nationwide polls and view how their peers across the country see the same issue.

✓ **Political Podcasts:** Featuring some of Pearson's most respected authors, these video podcasts present short, instructive—and even entertaining—lectures on key topics that students can download and play at their convenience.

✓ **NEW! Student Podcasts:** The new **MyPoliSciLab** allows students to record and download their own videos for peer-to-peer learning.

INTERACTIVE ACTIVITIES

✓ **New and Updated Simulations:** Featuring an appealing new graphic interface, these role-playing simulations help students experience political decision-making in a way they never have before—including new "mini activities" within the simulations that prepare students to make the right decisions.

✓ **NEW! Debate Exercises:** These provocative new exercises present classic and contemporary views on core controversies, ask students to take a position, and then show them the potential consequences of taking that stand.

✓ **More Focused Comparative Exercises:** These exercises have been revised in scope to concentrate on a more specific issue when comparing the US to other political systems, giving students a more concrete foundation on which to analyze key similarities and differences.

✓ **More Interactive Timelines:** With redesigned media and graphics, these timelines let students step through the evolution of some aspects of politics and now include more interactive questions throughout.

✓ **More Dynamic Visual Literacy Exercises:** These revised exercises offer attractive new graphs, charts, and tables and more opportunities to manipulate and interpret political data.

✓ **Expanded Participation Activities:** Reflecting our county's growing political interest, these expanded activities give students ideas and instructions for getting involved in all aspects of politics.

Icons in the margins of this book direct students to the activities on MyPoliSciLab related to the topics they are studying.

ONLINE ADMINISTRATION

No matter what course management system you use—or if you do not use one at all but still wish to easily capture your students' grades and track their performance—Pearson has a **MyPoliSciLab** option to suit your needs. Contact one of Pearson's Technology Specialists for more information or assistance.

High school teachers can obtain teacher and student preview or adoption access in one of two ways:

- By registering online at www.pearsonschool.com/access_request.
- Through the use of a physical pincode card. High school adopters will receive an adopter access pincode card (ISBN 0130343919) with their textbook order.

Preview access pincode cards may be requested using ISBN 0131115989. Both adopter and preview pincode cards include follow-on directions and provide teacher and student access.

For questions concerning access, please contact your local Pearson sales representative or email PHwebaccess@pearsoned.com.

ACKNOWLEDGMENTS

We greatly appreciate the guidance and feedback provided by the following reviewers of the AP* Edition: Pamela Lamb, Del Rio High School; Nick Liston, Fremont Christian High School; Darin Maier, St. Andrew's Episcopal School; Lisa Puccetti, Southern High School; Rebecca Small, Herndon High School; and Christopher Smith, Herndon High School.

Many colleagues have kindly given us comments on the drafts of the fourteenth edition of *Government in America:* Phillip J. Ardoin, Appalachian State University; Richard Bilsker, College of Southern Maryland; Karen Callaghan, Texas Southern University; Gregory K. Culver, University of Southern Indiana; Robert De Luna, St. Philip's College; Andrew Dowdle, University of Arkansas; Gialisa Gaffaney, Cerritos College; Yolanda Garza Hake, South Texas College; Manoucher Khosrowshahi, Tyler Junior College; Richard Kiefer, Waubonsee Community College; Geoff Peterson, University of Wisconsin–Eau Claire; James Rhodes, Luther College; John Roche, Palomar College; Gregory Schaller, Villanova University; Heather Wyatt-Nichol, Stephen F. Austin State University; Kathryn Yates, Richland College.

There are also many reviewers of previous editions to whom we owe our continued gratitude: Donald Aiesi, Furman University; David Gray Alder, Idaho State University; Shari Garber Bax, Central Missouri State University; Craig Bauer, Our Lady of Holy Cross College; Valentine J. Beliglio, Texas Woman's University; Nancy L. Bednar, Del Mar College; Jeffrey C. Berry, South Texas Community College; William Biano, Pennsylvania State University; Richard Bilsker, College of Southern Maryland; Allison Calhoun-Brown, Georgia State University; Myles L. Clowers, San Diego City College; Sara Trowbridge Combs, Virginia Highlands Community College; Don Cothran, Northern Arizona State University; Jim Cox, Georgia Perimeter College; Malcolm L. Cross, Tarleton State University; Donald Kent Douglas, Long Beach City College; Herbert Gooch, California Lutheran University; Forest Grieves, University of Montana; Martin Gruberg, University of Wisconsin; Dick Hernandez, Orange Coast College; Martin James, Henderson State University; E. Terrence Jones, University of Missouri, St. Louis; Haroon A. Khan, Henderson State University; Ashlyn Kuersten, Western Michigan University; Lisa Langenbach, Middle Tennessee State University; Michael Leuy, Southeast Missouri State University; Cecilia G. Manrique, University of Wisconsin–La Crosse; Nancy Marion, University of Akron; Thomas R. Marshall, University of Texas, Arlington; Craig Matthews, Fullerton College; Derrick Moffitt, Georgia Military College; Michael K. Moore, University of Texas at Arlington; Amy S. Patterson, Elmhurst College; Joseph Romance, Drew University; Robert Speel, Pennsylvania State University, Erie; Bruce Stinebrickner, DePauw University; Glen Sussman, Old Dominion University; William R. Thomas, Georgia State University; R. Mark Tiller, Houston Community College, Northwest; Reed Welch, West Texas A & M University; Harry L. Wilson, Roanoke College; John Wood, Oklahoma State University.

A number of editors have provided valuable assistance in the production of this edition of *Government in America.* Editor-in-Chief Eric Stano provided valuable guidance. Terri Wise was a superb Developmental Editor, coordinating every aspect of the book. We are grateful to both of them. Finally, we owe a special debt of gratitude to Professor Donald Haider-Markel of the University of Kansas, who did an outstanding job drafting Chapter 21.

George C. Edwards III
Martin P. Wattenberg
Robert L. Lineberry

ABOUT THE AUTHORS

George C. Edwards III is Distinguished Professor of political science at Texas A&M University. He also holds the Jordan Chair in Presidential Studies in the Bush School and has served as the Olin Professor of American Government at Oxford and the John Adams Fellow at the University of London and held senior visiting appointments at Peking University, Hebrew University in Jerusalem, Sciences Po in Paris, and the U.S. Military Academy at West Point. He is an Associate Member of Nuffield College at the University of Oxford and was the founder and from 1991 to 2001 the director of The Center for Presidential Studies.

When he determined that he was unlikely to become shortstop for the New York Yankees, he turned to political science. Today, he is one of the country's leading scholars of the presidency, he has authored dozens of articles, and he has written or edited 23 books on American politics and public policymaking, including *At the Margins: Presidential Leadership of Congress, Presidential Approval, Presidential Leadership, National Security and the U.S. Constitution, Implementing Public Policy,* and *Researching the Presidency.* He is also editor of *Presidential Studies Quarterly* and consulting editor of the *Oxford Handbook of American Politics* series. Among his latest books, *On Deaf Ears: The Limits of the Bully Pulpit* is a study of the effectiveness of presidential leadership of public opinion, *Why the Electoral College Is Bad for America* advocates direct election of the president, and *The Strategic President* focuses on the nature of presidential leadership.

Professor Edwards has served as president of the Presidency Research Section of the American Political Science Association, which has named its annual dissertation prize in his honor and awarded him its Career Service Award. A member of Phi Beta Kappa and a Woodrow Wilson Fellow, he has received the Decoration for Distinguished Civilian Service from the U.S. Army and the Pi Sigma Alpha Prize from the Southern Political Science Association. He is also a member of the Council on Foreign Relations. He has spoken to more than 200 universities and other groups in the United States and abroad, keynoted numerous national and international conferences, given hundreds of interviews with the national and international press, and can often be heard on National Public Radio. Grants from the National Science Foundation, the Smith-Richardson Foundation, and the Ford Foundation have funded his work. He has served on the Board of Directors of the Roper Center, the Board of Trustees of the Center for the Study of the Presidency, and on many editorial boards.

Dr. Edwards also applies his scholarship to practical issues of governing, including advising Brazil on its constitution and the operation of its presidency, Russia on building a democratic national party system, Mexico on elections, and Chinese scholars on democracy, and authoring studies for the 1988 and 2000 U.S. presidential transitions.

When not writing, speaking, or advising, he prefers to spend his time with his wife Carmella, sailing, skiing, scuba diving, traveling, or attending art auctions.

Martin P. Wattenberg is Professor of political science at the University of California, Irvine. His first regular paying job was with the Washington Redskins, from which he moved on to receive a Ph.D. at the University of Michigan. He is the author of *Is Voting for Young People?*, part of Longman's Great Questions in Politics series. In addition, he is the author of several books published by Harvard University Press: *Where Have All the Voters Gone?* (2002), *The Decline of American Political Parties* (1998), and *The Rise of Candidate-Centered Politics* (1991).

Professor Wattenberg has lectured about American politics on all of the inhabited continents. His travels have led him to become interested in electoral politics around the world. He has coedited two books published by Oxford University Press—one on party systems in the advanced industrialized world and the other on the recent trend toward mixed-member electoral systems.

Robert L. Lineberry is Professor of political science at the University of Houston and has been its senior vice president. He served from 1981 to 1988 as dean of the College of Liberal Arts and Sciences at the University of Kansas in Lawrence.

A native of Oklahoma City, he received a B.A. degree from the University of Oklahoma in 1964 and a Ph.D. in political science from the University of North Carolina in 1968. He taught for seven years at Northwestern University.

Dr. Lineberry has been president of the Policy Studies Section of the American Political Science Association and is currently the editor of *Social Science Quarterly*. He is the author or coauthor of numerous books and articles on political science. In addition, for the past 35 years he has taught regularly the introductory course in American government.

He has been married to Nita Lineberry for 43 years. They have two children, Nikki, who works in Denver, and Keith, who works in Houston. They have six grandchildren—Lee, Hunter, Callie, Arwen, Elijah, and Eleanor.

GOVERNMENT
IN AMERICA

INTRODUCING GOVERNMENT IN AMERICA

POLITICS AND GOVERNMENT MATTER—that is the single most important message of this book. Consider, for example, the following list of ways that government and politics may have already impacted your life:

- Any public schools you attended were prohibited by the federal government from discriminating against females and minorities and from holding prayer sessions led by school officials. Municipal school boards regulated your education, and the state certified and paid your teachers.
- The ages at which you could get your driver's license, drink alcohol, and vote were all determined by state and federal governments.
- Before you could get a job, the federal government had to issue you a Social Security number, and you have been paying Social Security taxes every month that you have been employed. If you worked at a relatively low-paying job, your starting wages were determined by state and federal minimum-wage laws.
- As a college student, you may be drawing student loans financed by the government. The government even dictates certain school holidays.
- Even though gasoline prices have risen substantially in recent years, federal policy continues to make it possible for you to drive long distances relatively cheaply compared to citizens in most other countries. In many other advanced industrialized nations, such as England and Japan, gasoline is twice as expensive as in the United States because of the high taxes their governments impose on fuel.
- If you apply to rent an apartment, federal law prohibits landlords from discriminating against you because of your race or religion.

Yet, many Americans—especially young people—are apathetic about politics and government. For example, before his historic return to space, former U.S. Senator John Glenn remarked that he worried "about the future when we have so many young people who feel apathetic and critical and cynical about anything having to do with politics. They don't want to touch it. And yet politics is literally the personnel system for democracy."[1]

Stereotypes can be mistaken; unfortunately, this is one case where widely held impressions are overwhelmingly supported by solid evidence. This is not to say that young people are inactive in American society. As Harvard students Ganesh Sitaraman and Previn Warren write in *Invisible Citizens: Youth Politics After September 11*, "Young people are some of the most active members of their communities and are devoting increasing amounts of their time to direct service work and volunteerism."[2] It is only when it comes to politics that young people seem to express indifference about getting involved. Whether because they think they can't make a difference, the political system is corrupt, or they just don't care, many young Americans are clearly apathetic about public affairs. And while political apathy isn't restricted to young people, a tremendous gap has opened up between the young (defined as under age 25) and the elderly (defined as over age 65) on measures of political interest, knowledge, and participation.

An annual nationwide study of college freshmen in 2007 found that only 37 percent said "keeping up with politics" was an important priority for them. As shown in Figure 1.1, since the terrorist attacks of September 11, there has been some resurgence of political interest among college students, but nevertheless it remains far below the level researchers found in the 1960s. Furthermore, political interest among young people as a whole is quite low. In 2004, the National Election Study asked a nationwide sample about their general level of interest in politics. Only 52 percent of young people interviewed said they followed politics most or some of the time compared to 86 percent of senior citizens. Yet there was no generation gap in terms of political interest when 18- to 20-year-olds first became eligible to vote in the early 1970s. Back then, 69 percent of young people expressed at least some interest in politics compared to 65 percent of the elderly.

Because they pay so little attention to public affairs, American youth are less likely to be well informed about politics and government compared to senior citizens. The current pattern of political knowledge increasing with age has been well documented in recent years. But it was not always that way. The 1964 and 2004 National Election Studies each contain a substantial battery of political knowledge questions

FIGURE 1.1

The Political Disengagement of College Students Today

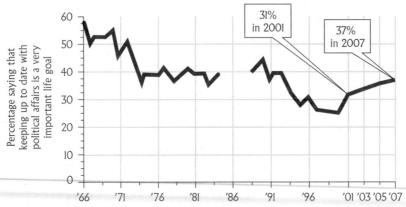

Source: UCLA Higher Education Research Institute.

FIGURE 1.2

Age and Political Knowledge: 1964 and 2004 Compared

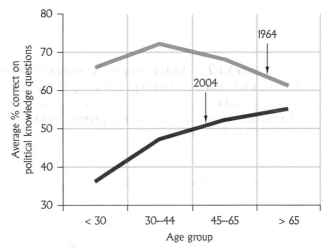

Source: Authors' analysis of 1964 and 2004 National Election Studies.

that enable this point to be clearly demonstrated. Figure 1.2 shows the percentage of correct answers to eight questions in 1964 and six questions in 2004 by age category.[3] In 1964, there was virtually no pattern by age, with those under 30 actually scoring 5 percent higher than senior citizens. By contrast, in 2004 young people provided the correct answer to only one out of every three questions, whereas people over 65 were correct more than half the time. Regardless of whether the question concerned identifying current U.S. or foreign political leaders or partisan control of Congress, the result was the same: young people were clearly less knowledgeable than the elderly.

Thomas Jefferson once said that there has never been, nor ever will be, a people who are politically ignorant and free. If this is indeed the case, write Stephen Bennett and Eric Rademacher, then "we can legitimately wonder what the future holds" if young people "remain as uninformed as they are about government and public affairs."[4] While this may well be an overreaction, there definitely are important consequences when citizens lack political information. In *What Americans Know About Politics and Why It Matters*, Michael Delli Carpini and Scott Keeter make a strong case for the importance of staying informed about public affairs. Political knowledge, they argue, (1) fosters civic virtues, such as political tolerance; (2) helps citizens to identify what policies would truly benefit them and then incorporate this information in their voting behavior; and (3) promotes active

The Internet has opened up a new world of opportunities for computer-savvy young people to learn about politics. But with so many Web sites for so many specific interests, it remains to be seen whether many people will take advantage of the wide range of political information now available.

participation in politics.[5] If you've been reading about the debate on health care reform, for example, you'll be able to understand proposed legislation on managed care and patients' rights. This knowledge will then help you identify and vote for candidates whose views agree with yours.

Lacking such information about political issues, however, fewer young Americans are heading to the polls compared to previous generations. This development has pulled the nationwide voter turnout rate down in recent years. In 1996, presidential election turnout fell below the 50 percent mark for the first time since the early 1920s, when women had just been granted suffrage and had not yet begun to use it as frequently as men. Young people have always had the lowest turnout rates, perhaps the reason why there was relatively little opposition in 1971 to lowering the voting age to 18. But even the most pessimistic analysts could not have foreseen the record-low participation rates of young people in recent years.

Why does voter turnout matter? As you will see throughout this book, those who participate in the political process are more likely to benefit from government programs and policies. Young people often complain that the elderly have far more political clout than they do—turnout statistics make it clear why this is the case. As shown in Figure 1.3, in recent years the voter turnout rate for people under 25 has consistently been much lower than the corresponding rate for senior citizens. Whereas turnout rates for the young have generally been going down, turnout among people over 65 years of age has actually gone up slightly over the same period. Political scientists used to write that the frailties of old age led to a decline in turnout after age 60; now such a decline occurs only after 80 years of age. Greater access to medical care because of the passage of Medicare in 1965 must surely be given some of the credit for this change. Who says politics doesn't make a difference?

Of course, today's youth have not had any policy impact them the way that Medicare has benefited their grandparents or the way that the draft and the Vietnam

FIGURE 1.3

Presidential Election Turnout Rates by Age, 1972–2004

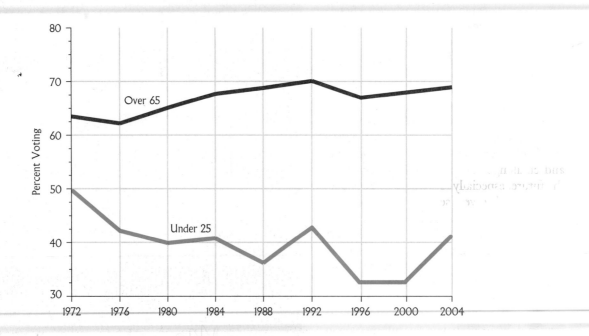

Source: U.S. Census Bureau Current Population Surveys. Data can be found at *www.census.gov/population/www/socdemo/voting.html*.

War affected their parents. However, the cause of young people's political apathy probably runs deeper. A broader reason is that today's youth have grown up in an environment in which public affairs news has not been as readily visible as it was in the past. It has become particularly difficult to convince a generation that has channel surfed all their lives that politics really does matter.

Major political events were once shared national experiences. Consider how nearly everyone in America was glued to their television to follow the events of September 11, 2001. For many young people, this was the first time in their lives that they closely followed a major national event along with everyone else. With this lone exception, the current generation of young people has been the first to grow up in a media environment in which there are few such shared experiences. Growing up in a fragmented media environment with hundreds of TV channels and millions of Internet sites has offered today's youth a rich and varied socialization experience but also one that has enabled them to easily avoid political events.

In contrast, when CBS, NBC, and ABC dominated the airwaves, their blanket coverage of presidential speeches, political conventions, and presidential debates frequently left little else to watch on TV. As channels have proliferated over the past two decades, though, it has become much easier to avoid exposure to politics altogether by simply grabbing the remote control. While President Nixon got an average rating of 50 for his televised addresses to the nation (meaning that half the population was watching), President George W. Bush averaged only about 30 between 2001 and 2006.[6] Political conventions, which once received more TV coverage than the Summer Olympics, have been relegated to an hour per night and draw abysmal ratings. The 2008 presidential debates drew a respectable average rating of 35, but this was only about three-fifths of the size of the typical debate audience from 1960 to 1980. In sum, young people have never known a time when most citizens paid attention to major political events. As a result, most of them have yet to get into the habit of following and participating in politics. Initially, there was some hope that September 11 might get more young people to follow national affairs. But to date there has been little evidence of this taking place. For example, a May 2008 Pew Research Center survey revealed that 33 percent of young adults said they enjoyed keeping up with the news compared to 61 percent of senior citizens.

The revolutionary expansion of channels and Web sites presents both opportunities and challenges for political involvement in the future, especially for today's youth. Some optimistic observers see these developments as offering "the prospect of a revitalized democracy characterized by a more active and informed citizenry."[7] Political junkies will certainly find more political information available than ever before, and electronic communications will make it easier for people to express their political views in various forums and directly to public officials. However, with so many media choices

TIMELINE

Major Technological Innovations that Have Changed the Political Landscape

The narrow 537-vote margin by which George W. Bush carried the state of Florida in 2000 proved the old adage that every vote counts. Here, an election official strains to figure out how to interpret a voter's punch in the tedious process of recounting ballots by hand.

for so many specific interests, it will also be extraordinarily easy to avoid the subject of public affairs. Thus, groups that are concerned about low youth turnout are focusing on innovative ways of reaching out to young people to make them more aware of politics.

It is our hope that after reading this book, you will be persuaded that paying attention to politics and government is important. Government has a substantial impact on all our lives. But it is also true that we have the opportunity to have a substantial impact on government. Involvement in public affairs can take many forms, ranging from simply becoming better informed by browsing through political Web sites to running for elected office. In between are countless opportunities for everyone to make a difference.

GOVERNMENT

government

The institutions and processes through which **public policies** are made for a society.

The institutions that make authoritative decisions for any given society are collectively known as **government**. In our own national government, these institutions are Congress, the president, the courts, and federal administrative agencies ("the bureaucracy"). Thousands of state and local governments also make policies that influence our lives. There are roughly 500,000 elected officials in the United States, which means that policies that affect you are being made almost constantly.

Because government shapes how we live, it is important to understand the process by which decisions are made as well as what is actually decided. Two fundamental questions about governing will serve as themes throughout this book:

How should we govern? Americans take great pride in calling their government democratic. This chapter examines the workings of democratic government; the chapters that follow will evaluate the way American government actually works compared to the standards of an "ideal" democracy. We will continually ask, "Who holds power and who influences the policies adopted by government?"

What should government do? This text explores the relationship between *how* American government works and *what* it does. In other words, "Does our government do what we want it to do?" Debates over this question concerning the scope of government are among the most important in American political life today. Some people would like to see the government take on more responsibilities; others believe it already takes on too much and that America needs to promote individual responsibility instead.

While citizens often disagree about what their government should do for them, all governments have certain functions in common. National governments throughout the world perform the following functions:

In the United States, the transfer of power is achieved through peaceful means. In 2007, the Democrats gained control of the House of Representatives for the first time in 12 years. Here, Republican leader John Boehner symbolically passes the gavel to the new Democratic Speaker of the House, Nancy Pelosi.

Maintain a national defense. A government protects its national sovereignty, usually by maintaining armed forces. In the nuclear age, some governments possess awesome power to make war through highly sophisticated weapons. The United States currently spends over $500 billion a year on national defense. Since September 11, the defense budget has been substantially increased in order to cope with the threat of terrorism on U.S. soil.

Provide public services. Governments in this country spend billions of dollars on schools, libraries, hospitals, and dozens of other public institutions. Some of these services, like highways and public parks, can be shared by everyone and cannot be denied to anyone. These kinds of services are called **public goods**. Other services, such as a college education or medical care, can be restricted to individuals who meet certain criteria but may be provided by the private sector as well. Governments typically provide these services to make them accessible to people who may not be able to afford privately available services.

Preserve order. Every government has some means of maintaining order. When people protest in large numbers, governments may resort to extreme measures to restore order. For example, the National Guard was called in to stop the looting and arson after rioting broke out in Los Angeles after the 1992 Rodney King verdict.

Governments provide a wide range of public services, including providing a national defense. When President George W. Bush judged that the danger of Iraq using weapons of mass destruction was a threat to U.S. security, he ordered an invasion of Iraq in 2003 to topple the regime of Saddam Hussein. Getting rid of the regime proved only the beginning of America's efforts in Iraq, however. Here we see army soldiers in 2008 attempting to flush out al Qaeda extremists and weapons smugglers operating near Baghdad.

Socialize the young. Most modern governments pay for education and use it to instill national values among the young. School curricula typically offer a course on the theory and practice of the country's government. Rituals like the daily Pledge of Allegiance seek to foster patriotism and love of country.

public goods
Goods, such as clean air and clean water, that everyone must share.

Collect taxes. Approximately one out of every three dollars earned by an American citizen is used to pay national, state, and local taxes—money that pays for the public goods and services the government provides.

All these governmental tasks add up to weighty decisions that our political leaders must make. For example, how much should we spend on national defense as opposed to education? How high should taxes for Medicare and Social Security be? We answer such questions through politics.

POLITICS

Politics determines whom we select as our governmental leaders and what policies these leaders pursue. Political scientists often cite Harold D. Lasswell's famous definition of politics: "Who gets what, when, and how."[8] It is one of the briefest and most useful definitions of politics ever penned. Admittedly, this broad definition covers a lot of ground (office politics, sorority politics, and so on) in which political scientists are generally not interested. They are interested primarily in politics related to governmental decision making.

politics
The process by which we select our governmental leaders and what policies these leaders pursue. Politics produces authoritative decisions about public issues.

Pro-life and pro-choice groups are single-minded and usually uncompromising. Few issues stir up as much passion as whether abortion should be permitted and, if so, under what conditions.

political participation

All the activities used by citizens to influence the selection of political leaders or the policies they pursue. Voting is the most common but not the only means of political participation in a **democracy**. Other means include **protest** and **civil disobedience**.

single-issue groups

Groups that have a narrow interest, tend to dislike compromise, and often draw membership from people new to politics. These features distinguish them from traditional **interest groups**.

policymaking system

The process by which policy comes into being and evolves over time. People's interests, problems, and concerns create political issues for government policymakers. These issues shape policy, which in turn impacts people, generating more interests, problems, and concerns.

The media usually focus on the *who* of politics. At a minimum, this includes voters, candidates, groups, and parties. *What* refers to the substance of politics and government—benefits, such as medical care for the elderly, and burdens, such as new taxes. *How* people participate in politics is important, too. They get what they want through voting, supporting, compromising, lobbying, and so forth. In this sense, government and politics involve winners and losers.

The ways in which people get involved in politics make up their **political participation**. Many people judge the health of a government by how widespread political participation is. America does quite poorly when judged by its voter turnout, with one of the lowest rates of voter participation in the world. Low voter turnout has an effect on who holds political power. Because so many people do not show up at the polls, voters are a distorted sample of the public as a whole. Groups such as the elderly benefit by having a high turnout rate, whereas others, such as young people, lack political clout because of their low likelihood of voting.

Voting is only one form of political participation. (See Chapter 6 for a discussion of other forms of participation.) For a few Americans, politics is a vocation rather than an avocation. They run for office, and some even earn their livelihood from holding political office. In addition, there are also many Americans who treat politics as critical to their interests. Many of these people are members of **single-issue groups**: groups so concerned with one issue that members cast their votes on the basis of that issue only, ignoring a politician's stand on everything else. Groups of activists dedicated either to outlawing abortion or to preserving abortion rights are good examples of single-issue groups.

Individual citizens and organized groups get involved in politics because they understand that the public policy choices made by governments affect them in significant ways. Will all those who need student loans receive them? Will everyone have access to medical care? Will people be taken care of in their old age? Is the water safe to drink? These and other questions tie politics to policymaking.

THE POLICYMAKING SYSTEM

Americans frequently expect government to do something about their problems. For example, the president and members of Congress are expected to keep the economy humming along; voters will penalize them at the polls if they do not. The **policymaking system** reveals the way our government responds to the priorities of its people. Figure 1.4 shows a skeletal model of this system. The rest of this book will flesh out this model, but for now it will help you understand how government policy comes into being and evolves over time.

FIGURE 1.4

The Policymaking System

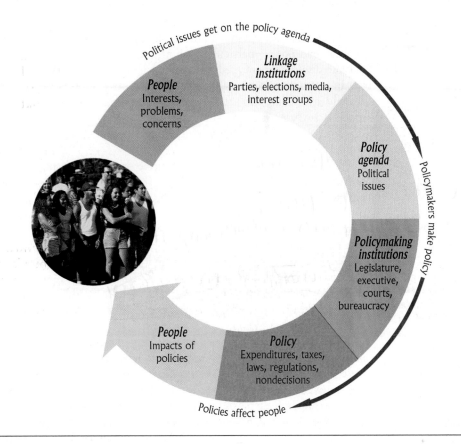

PEOPLE SHAPE POLICY

The policymaking system begins with people. All Americans have interests, problems, and concerns that are touched on by public policy. Some people may think the government should help train people for jobs in today's new technological environment; others may think that their taxes are too high and that the country would be best served by a large tax cut. Some people may expect government to do something to curb domestic violence; others may be concerned about prospects that the government may make it much harder to buy a handgun.

What do people do to express their opinions in a democracy? There are numerous avenues for action, such as voting for candidates who represent their opinions, joining political parties, posting messages to Internet chat groups, and forming interest groups. In this way, people's concerns enter the **linkage institutions** of the policymaking system. Linkage institutions transmit Americans' preferences to the policymakers in government. Parties and interest groups strive to ensure that their members' concerns receive appropriate political attention. The media investigate social problems and inform people about them. Elections provide citizens with the chance to make their opinions heard by choosing their public officials.

All these institutions help to shape the government's **policy agenda**, the issues that attract the serious attention of public officials and other people actively involved in politics at any given time. Some issues will be considered, and others will not. If politicians want to get elected, they must pay attention to the problems that concern voters. When you vote, you are partly looking at whether a candidate shares your agenda. If you are worried about rising health care costs and a certain

linkage institutions

The political channels through which people's concerns become political issues on the policy agenda. In the United States, linkage institutions include elections, political parties, interest groups, and the media.

policy agenda

The issues that attract the serious attention of public officials and other people actually involved in politics at any given point in time.

candidate talks only about America's moral decay and ending legalized abortions, you will probably support another candidate.

A government's policy agenda changes regularly. When jobs are scarce and business productivity is falling, economic problems occupy a high position on the government's agenda. If the economy is doing well and trouble spots around the world occupy the headlines, foreign policy questions are bound to dominate the agenda. In general, bad news—particularly about a crisis situation—is more likely than good news to draw sufficient media attention to put a subject on the policy agenda. As they say in journalism schools, "Good news is no news." When unemployment rises sharply it leads the news; when jobs are plentiful, the latest unemployment report is much less of a news story. Thus, the policy agenda responds more to societal failures than successes. The question politicians constantly ask is, "How can we as a people do better?"

People, of course, do not always agree on what government should do. Indeed, one group's concerns and interests are often at odds with those of another group. A **political issue** is the result of people disagreeing about a problem or about the public policy needed to fix it. There is never a shortage of political issues; government, however, will not act on any issue until it is high on the policy agenda.

Policymakers stand at the core of the political system, working within the three **policymaking institutions** established by the U.S. Constitution: Congress, the presidency, and the courts. Policymakers scan the issues on the policy agenda, select those they consider important, and make policies to address them. Today, the power of the bureaucracy is so great that most political scientists consider it a fourth policymaking institution.

Very few policies are made by a single policymaking institution. Environmental policy is a good example. Some presidents have used their influence with Congress to urge clean-air and clean-water policies. When Congress responds by passing legislation to clean up the environment, bureaucracies have to implement the new policies. The bureaucracies, in turn, create extensive volumes of rules and regulations that define how policies are to be implemented. In addition, every law passed and every rule made can be challenged in the courts. Courts make decisions about what policies mean and whether they conflict with the Constitution.

political issue

An issue that arises when people disagree about a problem and how to fix it.

policymaking institutions

The branches of government charged with taking action on political issues. The U.S. Constitution established three policymaking institutions—Congress, the presidency, and the courts. Today, the power of the bureaucracy is so great that most political scientists consider it a fourth policymaking institution.

public policy

A choice that **government** makes in response to a political issue. A policy is a course of action taken with regard to some problem.

POLICIES IMPACT PEOPLE

Every decision that government makes—every law it passes, budget it establishes, and ruling it hands down—is **public policy.** There are many types of public policies. Table 1.1 lists some of the most important types.

TABLE 1.1

Types of Public Policies

TYPE	DEFINITION	EXAMPLE
Congressional statute	Law passed by Congress	No Child Left Behind Act
Presidential action	Decision by president	U.S. troops invade Iraq
Court decision	Opinion by Supreme Court or other court	Supreme Court ruling that individuals have a constitutional right to own a gun.
Budgetary choices	Legislative enactment of taxes and expenditures	The federal budget resolution
Regulation	Agency adoption of regulation	Food and Drug Administration's approval of a new drug

Policies can also be established through inaction as well as action. Doing nothing—or nothing different—can prove to be a very consequential governmental decision. Reporter Randy Shilts's book traces the staggering growth in the number of people with AIDS and reveals how governments in Washington and elsewhere did little or debated quietly about what to do.[9] Shilts claims that because politicians initially viewed AIDS as a gay person's disease in the 1980s, they were reluctant to support measures to deal with it, fearful of losing the votes of antigay constituents. The issue thus remained a low priority on the government's policy agenda until infections started to spread to the general population, including celebrities like basketball star Earvin "Magic" Johnson.

Once policies are made and implemented, they affect people. **Policy impacts** are the effects that a policy has on people and on society's problems. People want policy that addresses their interests, problems, and concerns. A new law, executive order, bureaucratic regulation, or court judgment doesn't mean much if it doesn't work. Environmentalists want an industrial emissions policy that not only claims to prevent air pollution but also does so. Minority groups want a civil rights policy that not only promises them equal treatment but also ensures it.

Having a policy implies a goal. Whether we want to reduce poverty, cut crime, clean the water, or hold down inflation, we have a goal in mind. Policy impact analysts ask how well a policy achieves its goal—and at what cost. The analysis of policy impacts carries the political system back to its point of origin: the concerns of the people. Translating people's desires into effective public policy is crucial to the workings of democracy.

DEMOCRACY

AIDS was relatively low on the political agenda until well-known celebrities started to die from the disease. AIDS activists have found, however, that getting the problem on the agenda is only half the political battle. Getting the government to take aggressive action to find and approve new treatments has proved to be at least as difficult.

In 1848, Karl Marx and Friedrich Engels published *The Communist Manifesto,* one of the most famous political documents ever written. It began with these words: "A specter is haunting Europe. It is the specter of communism." Today one could write, "A specter is haunting the world. It is the specter of democracy." In recent years, democratic forms of governments have emerged in Eastern European countries that were formerly communist, in Latin American countries that were controlled by military dictatorships, and in South Africa, where apartheid denied basic rights to the Black majority. Yet despite this global move toward democracy, not everyone defines democracy the way Americans do—or think they do.

policy impacts
The effects a policy has on people and problems. Impacts are analyzed to see how well a policy has met its goal and at what cost.

DEFINING DEMOCRACY

Democracy is a means of selecting policymakers and of organizing government so that policy reflects citizens' preferences. Today, the term *democracy* takes its place among terms like *freedom, justice,* and *peace* as a word that seemingly has only positive connotations. As you can see in Figure 1.5, currently most people in most democracies around the world believe that although democracy may have its faults it is the best form of government. Yet the writers of the U.S. Constitution had no fondness for democracy, as many of them doubted the ability of ordinary Americans to make informed judgments about what government should do. Roger Sherman, a delegate to the Constitutional Convention, said the people "should have as little to do as may be with the government." Only much later did Americans come to cherish democracy and believe that all citizens should actively participate in choosing their leaders.

democracy
A system of selecting policymakers and of organizing government so that policy represents and responds to the public's preferences.

FIGURE 1.5

Most citizens in most democracies believe that democracy is the best form of government

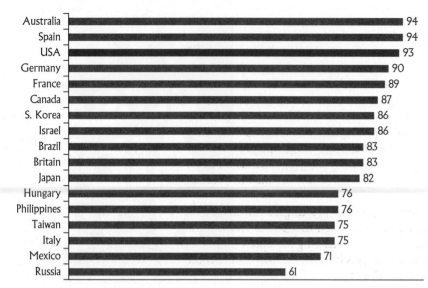

Country	Percent
Australia	94
Spain	94
USA	93
Germany	90
France	89
Canada	87
S. Korea	86
Israel	86
Brazil	83
Britain	83
Japan	82
Hungary	76
Philippines	76
Taiwan	75
Italy	75
Mexico	71
Russia	61

Question wording: Please tell me how strongly you agree or disagree with the following statement: "Democracy may have problems but it's better than any other form of government." Do you agree strongly, agree, disagree, or disagree strongly with this statement? [Percent responding that they "strongly agree" or "agree" displayed in the figure].

Percent who believe democracy is the best form of government

Source: Authors' analysis of the Comparative Study of Electoral Systems, module 2 (2001-2006).

Most Americans would probably say that democracy is "government by the people." This phrase, of course, is part of Abraham Lincoln's famous definition of democracy from his Gettysburg Address: "government of the people, by the people, and for the people." How well each of these aspects of democracy is being met is a matter crucial to evaluating how well our government is working. Certainly, government has always been "of the people" in the United States, for the Constitution forbids the granting of titles of nobility. On the other hand, it is a physical impossibility for government to be "by the people" in a society of over 300 million people. Therefore, our democracy involves choosing people from among our midst to govern. Where the serious debate begins is whether political leaders govern "for the people," as there always are significant biases in how the system works. Democratic theorists have elaborated a set of more specific goals for evaluating this crucial question.

TRADITIONAL DEMOCRATIC THEORY

Traditional democratic theory rests on a number of key principles that specify how governmental decisions are made in a democracy. Robert Dahl, one of America's leading theorists, suggests that an ideal democratic process should satisfy the following five criteria:

Equality in voting. The principle of "one person, one vote" is basic to democracy. Voting need not be universal, but it must be representative.

Effective participation. Citizens must have adequate and equal opportunities to express their preferences throughout the decision-making process.

Enlightened understanding. A democratic society must be a marketplace of ideas. A free press and free speech are essential to civic understanding. If one group monopolizes and distorts information, citizens cannot truly understand issues.

Citizen control of the agenda. Citizens should have the collective right to control the government's policy agenda.

If particular groups, such as the wealthy, have influence far exceeding what would be expected based on their numbers, then the agenda will be distorted. Thus, the government will not be addressing the issues that the public as a whole feels are most important.

Inclusion. The government must include, and extend rights to, all those subject to its laws. Citizenship must be open to all within a nation if the nation is to call itself democratic.[10]

Only by following these principles can a political system be called "democratic." Furthermore, democracies must practice **majority rule**, meaning that in choosing among alternatives, the will of over half the voters should be followed. At the same time, most Americans would not want to give the majority free rein to do anything they can agree on. Restraints on the majority are built into the American system of government in order to protect the minority. Basic principles such as freedom of speech and assembly are inviolable **minority rights**, which the majority cannot infringe on.

In a society too large to make its decisions in open meetings, a few must look after the concerns of the many. The relationship between the few leaders and the many citizens is one of **representation**. The literal meaning of representation is to "make present once again." In politics, this means that the desires of the people should be replicated in government through the choices of elected officials. The closer the correspondence between representatives and their constituents, the closer the approximation to an ideal democracy. As might be expected for such a crucial question, theorists disagree widely about the extent to which this actually occurs in America.

THREE CONTEMPORARY THEORIES OF AMERICAN DEMOCRACY

Theories of American democracy are essentially theories about who has power and influence. All, in one way or another, ask the question, "Who really governs in our nation?" Each focuses on a key aspect of politics and government, and each reaches a somewhat different conclusion.

Pluralist Theory   One important theory of American democracy, **pluralist theory**, states that groups with shared interests influence public policy by pressing their concerns through organized efforts.

The National Rifle Association (NRA), the National Organization for Women (NOW), and the United Auto Workers (UAW) are examples of groups of people who share a common interest. Because of open access to various institutions of government and public officials, organized groups can compete with one another for control over policy, and yet no one group or set of groups dominates. Given that power is dispersed in the American form of government, groups that lose in one arena can take their case to another. For example, civil rights groups faced congressional roadblocks in the 1950s but were able to win the action they were seeking from the courts.

Pluralists are generally optimistic that the public interest will eventually prevail in the making of public policy through a complex process of bargaining and compromise. They believe that rather than speaking of majority rule we should speak of groups of minorities working together. Robert Dahl expresses this view well when he writes that in America "all active and legitimate groups in the population can make themselves heard at some crucial stage in the process."[11]

majority rule
A fundamental principle of **traditional democratic theory**. In a democracy, choosing among alternatives requires that the majority's desire be respected. See also **minority rights**.

minority rights
A principle of **traditional democratic theory** that guarantees rights to those who do not belong to majorities and allows that they might join majorities through persuasion and reasoned argument. See also **majority rule**.

representation
A basic principle of **traditional democratic theory** that describes the relationship between the few leaders and the many followers.

pluralist theory
A theory of government and politics emphasizing that politics is mainly a competition among groups, each one pressing for its own preferred policies. Compare **elite and class theory**, **hyperpluralism**, and **traditional democratic theory**.

Group politics is certainly as American as apple pie. Writing in the 1830s, Alexis de Tocqueville called us a "nation of joiners" and pointed to the high level of associational activities as one of the crucial reasons for the success of American democracy. The recent explosion of interest group activity can therefore be seen as a very positive development from the perspective of pluralist theory. Interest groups and their lobbyists—the groups' representatives in Washington—have become masters of the technology of politics. Computers, mass mailing lists, sophisticated media advertising, and hard-sell techniques are their stock in trade. As a result, some observers believe that Dahl's pluralist vision that all groups are heard via the American political process is more true now than ever before.

On the other hand, Robert Putnam argues that many of the problems of American democracy today stem from a decline in group-based participation.[12] Putnam theorizes that advanced technology, particularly television, has served to increasingly isolate Americans from one another. He shows that membership in a variety of civic associations, such as parent-teacher associations, the League of Women Voters, and the Elks, Shriners, and Jaycees, have been declining for decades. Interestingly, Putnam does not interpret the decline of participation in civic groups as meaning that people have become "couch potatoes." Rather, he argues that Americans' activities are becoming less tied to institutions and more self-defined. The most famous example he gives to illustrate this trend is the fact that membership in bowling leagues has dropped sharply at the same time that more people are bowling—indicating that more and more people must be bowling alone. Putnam believes that participation in interest groups today is often like bowling alone. Groups that have mushroomed lately, such as the American Association of Retired Persons (AARP), typically just ask their members to participate by writing a check from the comfort of their own home. If people are indeed participating in politics alone rather than in groups, then pluralist theory is becoming less descriptive of American politics today.

Elite and Class Theory   Critics of pluralism believe that it paints too rosy a picture of American political life. By arguing that almost every group can get a piece of the pie, they say that pluralists miss the larger question of how the pie is distributed. The poor may get their food stamps, but businesses get massive tax deductions worth far more. Some governmental programs may help minorities, but the income gap between African Americans and Whites remains wide.

Elite and class theory contends that our society, like all societies, is divided along class lines and that an upper-class elite pulls the strings of government. Wealth—the holding of assets such as property, stocks, and bonds—is the basis of this power. Over a third of the nation's wealth is currently held by just 1 percent of the population. Elite and class theorists believe that this 1 percent of Americans controls most policy decisions because they can afford to finance election campaigns and control key institutions, such as large corporations. According to elite and class theory, a few powerful Americans do not merely influence policymakers—they are the policymakers.

At the center of all theories of elite dominance is big business. Few presidents in American history tried harder to help big business than Ronald Reagan, and many elite theorists believe that he succeeded beyond all expectations. As Kevin Phillips wrote in his best-seller *The Politics of Rich and Poor*, "The 1980s were the triumph of upper America—an ostentatious celebration of wealth, the political ascendancy of the richest third of the population and a glorification of capitalism, free markets and finance."[13]

Since George W. Bush assumed the presidency, many scholars have argued that the political deck has become increasingly stacked in favor of the superrich. For example, political scientists Jacob Hacker and Paul Pierson wrote in 2005

elite and class theory
A theory of government and politics contending that societies are divided along class lines and that an upper-class elite will rule, regardless of the formal niceties of governmental organization. Compare **hyperpluralism**, **pluralist theory**, and **traditional democratic theory**.

Elite theorists often point to the power of the big oil companies as evidence that big economic interests prevail in American politics. The executives of the oil companies routinely deny any collaboration to set prices artificially high, as they did in this recent appearance at a congressional hearing.

that "America's political market no longer looks like the effectively functioning market that economics textbooks laud. Rather, it increasingly resembles the sort of market that gave us the Enron scandal, in which corporate bigwigs with privileged information got rich at the expense of ordinary shareholders, workers, and consumers."[14] A report on rising inequality issued by the American Political Science Association in 2004 concluded, "Citizens with lower or moderate incomes speak with a whisper that is lost on the ears of inattentive government officials, while the advantaged roar with a clarity and consistency that policymakers readily hear and routinely follow."[15]

The most extreme proponents of elite theory maintain that who holds office in Washington is of marginal consequence; the corporate giants always have the power. Clearly, most people in politics would disagree with this view, noting that it did make a difference that Bush was elected in 2000 rather than Gore. According to Gore's promises in 2000, for example, the wealthiest Americans would have received no tax cuts had he become president, whereas under President Bush the wealthy and the middle class alike were granted tax cuts.

Hyperpluralism   A third theory, **hyperpluralism**, offers a different critique of pluralism. Hyperpluralism is pluralism gone sour. In this view, groups are so strong that government is weakened, as the influence of many groups cripples government's ability to make policy. Hyperpluralism states that many groups—not just the elite ones—are so strong that government is unable to act.

Whereas pluralism maintains that input from groups is a good thing for the political decision-making process, hyperpluralism asserts that there are *too* many ways for groups to control policy. Our fragmented political system made up of governments with overlapping jurisdictions is one major factor that contributes to hyperpluralism. Too many governments can make it hard to coordinate policy implementation. Any policy requiring the cooperation of the national, state, and local levels of government can be hampered by the reluctance of any one of them.

According to hyperpluralists, groups have become sovereign, and government is merely their servant. Groups that lose policymaking battles in Congress these days do not give up the battle; they carry it to the courts. Recently, the number of cases brought to state and federal courts has soared. Ecologists use legal procedures to delay construction projects they feel will damage the environment, businesses take federal agencies to court to fight the implementation of regulations that will cost them money, labor unions go to court to secure injunctions against policies they fear will cost them jobs, and civil liberties groups go to court to defend the rights of people who are under investigation for possible terrorist activities. The courts have become one more battleground in which policies can be effectively opposed as each group tries to bend policy to suit its own purposes.

Hyperpluralists contend that powerful groups divide the government and its authority. Hyperpluralist theory holds that government gives in to every conceivable interest and single-issue group. When politicians try to placate every group, the result is confusing, contradictory, and muddled policy—if politicians manage to make policy at all. Like elite and class theorists, hyperpluralist theorists suggest that the public interest is rarely translated into public policy.

hyperpluralism

A theory of government and politics contending that groups are so strong that government is weakened. Hyperpluralism is an extreme, exaggerated, or perverted form of **pluralism**. Compare **elite and class theory**, **pluralist theory**, and **traditional democratic theory**.

CHALLENGES TO DEMOCRACY

Regardless of which theory is most convincing, there are a number of continuing challenges to democracy. Many of these challenges apply to American democracy as well as to fledgling democracies around the world.

Increased Technical Expertise   Traditional democratic theory holds that ordinary citizens have the good sense to reach political judgments and that government has the capacity to act on those judgments. Today, however, we live in a society of experts whose technical knowledge overshadows the knowledge of the general population. What, after all, does the average citizen—however conscientious—know about eligibility criteria for welfare, agricultural price supports, foreign competition, and the hundreds of other issues that confront government each year? Years ago, the power of the few—the elite—might have been based on property holdings. Today, the elite are likely to be those who command knowledge, the experts. Even the most rigorous democratic theory does not demand that citizens be experts on everything; but as human knowledge has expanded, it has become increasingly difficult for individual citizens to make well-informed decisions.

Limited Participation in Government   When citizens do not seem to take their citizenship seriously, democracy's defenders worry. There is plenty of evidence that Americans know little about who their leaders are, much less about their policy decisions, as we will discuss at length in Chapter 6. Furthermore, Americans do not take full advantage of their opportunities to shape government or select its leaders. Limited participation in government challenges the foundation of democracy. In particular, because young people represent the country's future, their abysmal voting turnout rates point to an even more serious challenge to democracy on the horizon.

Escalating Campaign Costs   Many political observers worry about the close connection between money and politics, especially in congressional elections. Winning a House seat these days usually requires a campaign war chest of *at least* half a million dollars, and Senate races are even more costly. Candidates have become increasingly dependent on Political Action Committees (PACs) to fund their campaigns because of the escalation of campaign costs. These PACs often represent specific economic interests, and they care little about how members of Congress vote on most issues—just the issues that particularly affect them. Critics charge that when it comes to the issues PACs care about, the members of Congress listen, lest they be denied the money they need for their reelection. When democracy confronts the might of money, the gap between democratic theory and reality widens further.

Diverse Political Interests   The diversity of the American people is reflected in the diversity of interests represented in the political system. As will be shown in this book, this system is so open that interests find it easy to gain access to policymakers. Moreover, the distribution of power within the government is so decentralized that access to a few policymakers may be enough to determine the outcome of public policy battles.

When interests conflict, which they often do, no coalition may be strong enough to form a majority and establish policy. But each interest may use its influence to thwart those whose policy proposals they oppose. In effect, they have a veto over policy, creating what is often referred to as **policy gridlock**.

policy gridlock
A condition that occurs when no coalition is strong enough to form a majority and establish policy. The result is that nothing may get done.

In a big city, gridlock occurs when there are so many cars on the road that no one can move; in politics, it occurs when each policy coalition finds its way blocked by others. This political problem is magnified when a president of one party has to deal with congressional majorities of the other party, as has often been the case in recent years.

Democracy is not necessarily an end in itself. For many, evaluations of democracy depend on what democratic government produces. Thus, a major challenge to democracy in America is to overcome the diversity of interests and fragmentation of power in order to deliver policies that are responsive to citizens' needs.

AMERICAN POLITICAL CULTURE AND DEMOCRACY

The key factor that holds American democracy together in the view of many scholars is its **political culture**—the overall set of values widely shared within American society. As Ronald Inglehart and Christian Welzel argue in their book on cultural change and democracy, "Democracy is not simply the result of clever elite bargaining and constitutional engineering. It depends on deep-rooted orientations among the people themselves. These orientations motivate them to demand freedom and responsive government. . . . Genuine democracy is not simply a machine that, once set up, functions by itself. It depends on the people."[16]

Far more than most countries, the political culture of the United States is crucial to understanding its government, as Americans are so diverse in terms of ancestries, religions, and heritages. What unites Americans more than anything else is a set of shared beliefs and values. As G. K. Chesterton, the noted British observer of American politics, wrote in 1922, "America is the only nation in the world that is founded on a creed. That creed is set forth with dogmatic and even theological lucidity in the Declaration of Independence."[17] Arguing along the same lines, Seymour Martin Lipset writes that "the United States is a country organized around an ideology which includes a set of dogmas about the nature of good society."[18] Lipset argues that the American creed can be summarized by five elements: liberty, egalitarianism, individualism, laissez-faire, and populism.[19] We will review each of these aspects of American political culture briefly on the following pages.

> **political culture**
> An overall set of values widely shared within a society.

Comparing Political Landscapes

Liberty One of the most famous statements of the American Revolution was Patrick Henry's "Give me liberty or give me death." During the Cold War, a common bumper sticker was "Better Dead Than Red," reflecting many Americans' view that they would prefer to fight to the bitter end than submit to the oppression of communist rule. To this day, New Hampshire's official state motto is "Live Free or Die." When immigrants are asked why they came to America, by far the most common response is to live in freedom.

Freedom of speech and religion are fundamental to the American way of life. In the Declaration of Independence, Thomas Jefferson placed liberty right along with life and the pursuit of happiness as an "unalienable right" (that is, a right not awarded by human power, not transferable to another power, and which cannot be revoked).

Egalitarianism The most famous phrase in the history of democracy is the Declaration of Independence's statement "We hold these truths to be self-evident that all men are

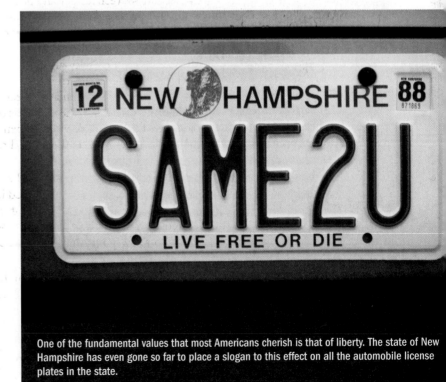

One of the fundamental values that most Americans cherish is that of liberty. The state of New Hampshire has even gone so far to place a slogan to this effect on all the automobile license plates in the state.

What Are American Civic Values?

created equal." As the French observer Alexis de Tocqueville noted long ago, egalitarianism in the United States involves equality of opportunity and respect in the absence of a monarchy and aristocracy. Americans have never been equal in terms of condition. What is most critical to this part of the American creed is that everyone has a chance to succeed in life.

Tocqueville accurately saw into the American future that the social equality he observed in American life in the 1830s would eventually lead to political equality. Although relatively few Americans then had the right to vote, he predicted that all Americans would be given these rights because, in order to guarantee equality of opportunity, everyone must have an equal opportunity to participate in democratic governance. Thus, another key aspect of egalitarianism is political equality, which involves equal voting rights for all adult American citizens.

Today, about three out of four Americans say they are proud of the fair and equal treatment of all groups in the United States. As you can see in Figure 1.6, this level of pride in the country's egalitarianism is extremely high compared to other democracies.

Individualism   One of the aspects of American political culture that has shaped the development of American democracy has been individualism—the belief that people can and should get ahead on their own. The immigrants who founded American society may have been diverse, but many shared a common dream of America as a place where one could make it on one's own without interference from government. Louis Hartz's *The Liberal Tradition in America* is a classic analysis of the dominant political beliefs during America's formative years. Hartz argues that the major force behind limited government in America is that it was settled by people who fled from the feudal and clerical oppressions of the Old World. Once in the New World, they wanted little from government other than for it to leave them alone.[20]

FIGURE 1.6

Americans rank very highly in terms of being proud of their country's fair and equal treatment of all groups

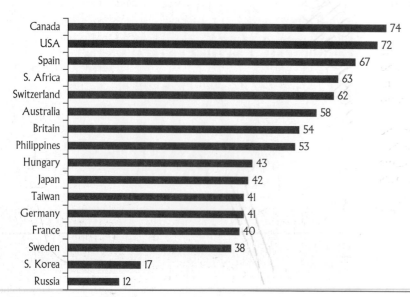

Question wording: How proud are you of [country] in each of the following—its fair and equal treatment of all groups—very proud, somewhat proud, not very proud, not proud at all? [Percent saying "very proud" or "somewhat proud" displayed in the figure].

Percent proud of equal treatment of all groups in their country

Source: Authors' analysis 2003 International Social Survey Program surveys.

Another explanation for American individualism is the existence of a bountiful frontier—at least up until the start of the twentieth century. Not only did many people come to America to escape from governmental interference, but the frontier allowed them to get away from government almost entirely once they arrived. Frederick Jackson Turner's famous work on the significance of the frontier in American history argues that "the frontier is productive of individualism."[21] According to Turner, being in the wilderness and having to survive on one's own left settlers with an aversion to any control from the outside world—particularly from the government.

Laissez-faire   An important result of American individualism has been a clear tendency to prefer laissez-faire economic policies, which promote free markets and limited government. As John Kingdon writes in his book *America the Unusual*, "Government in the United States is much more limited and much smaller than government in virtually every other advanced industrialized country on earth."[22] Compared to most other economically developed nations, the United States devotes a smaller percentage of its resources to government. As we will see in Chapter 14, the tax burden on Americans is small compared to other democratic nations.

Further, most advanced industrial democracies have a system of national insurance that provides most health care; the United States does not, though Bill Clinton unsuccessfully tried to establish such a system. In other countries, national governments have taken it on themselves to start up airline, telephone, and communications companies. Governments have built much of the housing in most Western nations, compared to only a small fraction of the housing in America. Thus, in terms of its impact on citizens' everyday lives, government in the United States actually does less than the governments of similar countries.

Populism   Abraham Lincoln summarized American democracy as a "government of the people, for the people, and by the people." Such an emphasis on *the people* is at the heart of populism, which can best be defined as a political philosophy supporting the rights of average citizens in their struggle against privileged elites. As Lipset writes, American populist thought holds that the people at large "are possessed of some kind of sacred mystique, and proximity to them endows the politician with esteem—and with legitimacy."[23]

In America, being on the side of the ordinary people against big interests is so valued that liberal and conservative politicians alike frequently claim this mantle. Liberals are inclined to argue that they will stand up to big multinational corporations and protect the interests of ordinary Americans. Conservatives, on the other hand, are likely to repeat Ronald Reagan's famous promise to get big government off the backs of the American people. A populist pledge to "put the people first" is always a safe strategy in the American political culture.

Former Prime Minister Tony Blair of Great Britain and President George W. Bush worked closely together as allies during the 2003 Iraqi war and formed a close friendship. But the two leaders had extremely different views regarding the proper scope of government in domestic policy. Blair was first elected to the British Parliament as a self-declared socialist, and in his position as prime minister he strived to strengthen Britain's national health care system. In contrast, President Bush favored free-market policies and opposed the idea of establishing a national health care system in the United States.

A CULTURE WAR?

Using the Census to Understand Who Americans Are

Although Americans are widely supportive of cultural values like liberty and egalitarianism, some scholars are concerned that a sharp polarization into rival political camps with different political cultures has taken place in recent years. James Q. Wilson defines such a polarization as "an intense commitment to a candidate, a culture, or an ideology that sets people in one group definitively apart from people in another, rival group."[24] Wilson believes that America is a more polarized nation today than at any time in living memory. He argues that the intensity of political divisions in twenty-first-century America is a major problem, writing that "a divided America encourages our enemies, disheartens our allies, and saps our resolve—potentially to fatal effect."[25]

Other scholars, however, believe that there is relatively little evidence of a so-called culture war going on among ordinary American citizens. Morris Fiorina concludes, "There is little indication that voters are polarized now or that they are becoming more polarized—even when we look specifically at issues such as abortion that supposedly are touchstone issues in the culture war. If anything, public opinion has grown more centrist on such issues and more tolerant of the divergent views, values, and behavior of other Americans."[26] Wayne Baker outlines three ways in which America might be experiencing a crisis of cultural values: (1) a loss over time of traditional values, such as the importance of religion and family life; (2) an unfavorable comparison with the citizens of other countries in terms of values such as patriotism or support for moral principles; and (3) the division of society into opposed groups with irreconcilable moral differences. Baker tests each of these three possibilities thoroughly with recent survey data from the United States and other countries and finds little evidence of an ongoing crisis of values in America.[27]

PREVIEW QUESTIONS ABOUT DEMOCRACY

Throughout *Government in America* you will be asked to evaluate American democracy. The chapters that follow will acquaint you with the development of democracy in the United States. For example, the next chapter will show that the U.S. Constitution was not originally designed to promote democracy but has slowly evolved to its current form. Much of America's move toward greater democracy has centered on the extension of civil liberties and civil rights we review in Chapters 4 and 5. Probably the most important civil right is the right to vote. Upcoming chapters will examine voting behavior and elections and ask the following questions about how people form their opinions and to what extent they express these opinions via elections:

- Are people knowledgeable about matters of public policy?
- Do they apply what knowledge they have to their voting choices?
- Are American elections designed to facilitate public participation?

Linkage institutions, such as interest groups, political parties, and the media, help translate input from the public into output from the policymakers. When you explore these institutions, consider the extent to which they either help or hinder democracy.

- Does the interest group system allow for all points of view to be heard, or do significant biases give advantages to particular groups?
- Do political parties provide voters with clear choices, or do they intentionally obscure their stands on issues in order to get as many votes as possible?
- If there are choices, do the media help citizens understand them?

It is up to public officials to actually make policy choices because American government is a representative democracy. For democracy to work well, elected officials must be responsive to public opinion.

- Is Congress representative of American society, and is it capable of reacting to changing times?
- Does the president look after the general welfare of the public, or has the office become too focused on the interests of the elite?

These are some of the crucial questions you will address in discussing the executive and legislative branches of government. In addition, the way our nonelected institutions function—the bureaucracy and the courts—is crucial to evaluating how well American democracy works. These institutions are designed to implement and interpret the law, but bureaucrats and judges often cannot avoid making public policy as well. When they do so, are they violating democratic principles for policy decisions, given that neither institution can be held accountable at the ballot box?

All these questions concerning democracy in America have more than one answer. A goal of *Government in America* is to offer different ways to evaluate and answer these questions. One way to approach the preceding questions is to address one of the most important questions facing modern American democracy: Is the scope of government responsibilities too vast, just about right, or not comprehensive enough?

THE SCOPE OF GOVERNMENT IN AMERICA

In his first presidential address to Congress in 1993, Bill Clinton stated, "I want to talk to you about what government can do because I believe government must do more." Toward this end, President Clinton put his wife Hillary in charge of developing a comprehensive government program to require businesses to provide a basic level of health insurance for their employees. Congressional Republicans lined up solidly against Bill and Hillary Clinton's plan for national health insurance, arguing that government intervention in the affairs of individual citizens and businesses does more harm than good.

Those who are inclined to support government involvement in matters such as health care argue that intervention is the only means of achieving important goals in

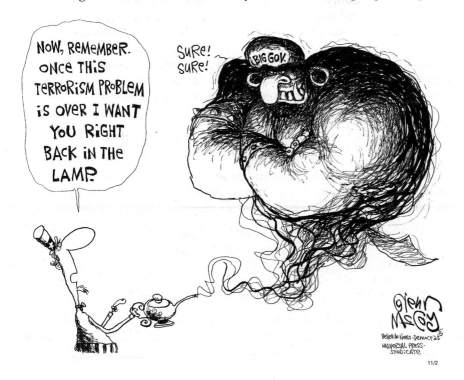

American society. How else, they ask, can we ensure that everyone has enough to eat, clean air and water, and affordable housing? How else can we ensure that the disadvantaged are given opportunities for education and jobs and are not discriminated against? Opponents of widening the scope of government agree that these are worthwhile goals but challenge whether involving the federal government is an effective way to pursue them. Dick Armey, who served as the Republicans' majority leader in the House from 1995 to 2002, expressed this view well when he wrote, "There is more wisdom in millions of individuals making decisions in their own self-interest than there is in even the most enlightened bureaucrat (or congressman) making decisions on their behalf."[28] Or, as President George W. Bush regularly told supporters during the 2000 presidential campaign, "Our opponents trust the government; we trust the people."

HOW ACTIVE IS AMERICAN GOVERNMENT?

gross domestic product
The sum total of the value of all the goods and services produced in a nation.

In terms of dollars spent, government in America is vast. Altogether, our governments—national, state, and local—spend about 29 percent of our **gross domestic product**, the total value of all goods and services produced annually by the United States. Government not only spends large sums of money but also employs large numbers of people. About 18 million Americans work for our government, mostly at the state and local level as teachers, police officers, university professors, and so on. Consider some facts about the size of our national government:

- It spends about $3.1 trillion annually (printed as a number, that's $3,100,000,000,000 a year).
- It employs over 2.2 million people.
- It owns one-third of the land in the United States.
- It occupies 2.6 billion square feet of office space, more than four times the office space located in the nation's 10 largest cities.
- It owns and operates over 400,000 nonmilitary vehicles.

How does the American national government spend $3.1 trillion a year? National defense takes about one-sixth of the federal budget, a much smaller percentage than it did three decades ago—even with the recent increase after September 11. Social Security consumes more than one-fifth of the budget. Medicare is another big-ticket item, requiring a little over one-tenth of the budget. State and local governments also get important parts of the federal government's budget. The federal government helps fund highway and airport construction, police departments, school districts, and other state and local functions.

When expenditures grow, tax revenues must grow to pay the additional costs. When taxes do not grow as fast as spending, a budget deficit results. The federal government ran a budget deficit every year from 1969 through 1997. The last few Clinton budgets showed surpluses, but soon after George W. Bush took over the government was running a deficit once again. In fiscal year 2009, the deficit for the year was over $400 billion. No doubt the events of September 11 contributed to the reappearance of deficit spending due to the negative impact they had on the U.S. economy as well as the added security expenses the government suddenly encountered. But opponents of President Bush have placed much of the blame on the large tax cut the president proposed in the 2000 campaign and then delivered early in his presidency. In any event, years of deficits have left the country with a national debt of over $9 trillion, which will continue to pose a problem for policymakers for decades to come.

Whatever the national problem—pollution, AIDS, hurricane relief, homelessness, hunger, sexism—many people expect Congress and the president to solve it with legislation. Thus, American government certainly matters tremendously in terms of dollars spent, persons employed, and laws passed. Our concern, however, is less about the absolute size of government and more about whether government activity is what we want it to be.

PREVIEW QUESTIONS ABOUT THE SCOPE OF GOVERNMENT

Debate over the scope of government is central to contemporary American politics, and it is a theme this text will examine in each chapter. Our goal is not to determine for you the proper role of the national government. Instead, you will explore the implications of the way politics, institutions, and policy in America affect the scope of government. By raising questions such as those listed in the next few paragraphs, you may draw your own conclusions about the appropriate role of government in America. Part 1 of *Government in America* examines the constitutional foundations of American government. A concern with the proper scope of government leads to a series of questions regarding the constitutional structure of American politics, including the following:

- What role did the Constitution's authors foresee for the federal government?
- Does the Constitution favor a government with a broad scope, or is it neutral on this issue?
- Why did the functions of government increase, and why did they increase most at the national rather than the state level?
- Has bigger, more active government constrained freedom, or does the increased scope of government serve to protect civil liberties and civil rights?

Part 2 focuses on those who make demands on government, including the public, political parties, interest groups, and the media. Here you will seek answers to questions such as the following:

- Does the public favor a large, active government?
- Do competing political parties predispose the government to provide more public services?
- Do elections help control the scope of government, or do they legitimize an increasing role for the public sector?
- Are pressures from interest groups necessarily translated into more governmental regulations, bigger budgets, and the like?
- Has media coverage of government enhanced government's status and growth, or have the media been an instrument for controlling government?

Governmental institutions themselves obviously deserve close examination. Part 3 discusses these institutions and asks the following:

- Has the presidency been a driving force behind increasing the scope and power of government (and thus of the president)?
- Can the president control a government with so many programs and responsibilities?
- Is Congress, because it is subject to constant elections, predisposed toward big government?
- Is Congress too responsive to the demands of the public and organized interests?

The nonelected branches of government, which are also discussed in these chapters, are especially interesting when we consider the issue of the scope of government. For instance:

- Are the federal courts too active in policymaking, intruding on the authority and responsibility of other branches and levels of government?
- Is the bureaucracy too acquisitive, constantly seeking to expand its budgets and authority, or does it simply reflect the desires of elected officials?
- Is the bureaucracy too large and thus a wasteful menace to efficient and fair implementation of public policies?

The next 20 chapters will search for answers to these and many other questions regarding the scope of government and why it matters. You will undoubtedly add a few questions of your own as you seek to resolve the issue of the proper scope of government involvement.

SUMMARY

Evidence abounds that young people today are politically apathetic. But they should not be. Politics and government matter a great deal to everyone and affect many aspects of life. If nothing else, we hope this text will convince you of this.

Government consists of those institutions that make authoritative public policies for society as a whole. In the United States, four key institutions make policy at the national level: Congress, the presidency, the courts, and the bureaucracy. Politics is, very simply, who gets what, when, and how. People engage in politics for a variety of reasons, and all their activities in politics are collectively called political participation. The result of government and politics is public policy. Public policy includes all the decisions and nondecisions made by government.

The first question central to governing is, "How should we govern?" Americans are fond of calling their government democratic. Democratic government includes, above all else, a commitment to majority rule and minority rights. American political culture can be characterized by five key concepts: liberty, egalitarianism, individualism, laissez-faire, and populism. This text will help you compare the way American government works with the standards of democracy and will continually address questions about who holds power and who influences the policies adopted by government.

The second fundamental question regarding governing is, "What should government do?" One of the most important issues about government in America has to do with its scope. Conservatives often talk about the evils of intrusive government; liberals see the national government as rather modest in comparison both to what it could do and to the functions governments perform in other democratic nations.

Chapter Test
Multiple Choice

1. Currently, there are roughly _____ elected officials in the United States.
   a. 50,000
   b. 100,000
   c. 200,000
   d. 500,000
   e. 700,000

2. Most political scientists consider _____ a fourth policymaking institution.
   a. The media
   b. The bureaucracy

   c. Political parties
   d. Public opinion
   e. Lobbyists

3. According to Robert Dahl's traditional democratic theory, an ideal democratic process should satisfy all but which of the following criteria?
   a. Equality in voting
   b. Effective participation
   c. Enlightened understanding
   d. Citizen control of the agenda
   e. Equal participation

4. Seymour Martin Lipset argued that all of the following are elements of America's creed EXCEPT:
   a. Egalitarianism
   b. Traditionalism
   c. Populism
   d. Laissez-faire
   e. Individualism

5. Roughly how much of the United States' gross domestic product (GDP) is spent on national, state, and local government?
   a. One-tenth
   b. One-fourth

c. One-third
d. One-half
e. Two-thirds

6. Which of the following is NOT an example of a single-issue group?
   a. The National Rifle Association (NRA)
   b. People for the Ethical Treatment of Animals (PETA)
   c. Mothers Against Drunk Driving (MADD)

d. American Association of Retired Persons (AARP)
e. National Right to Life Committee (NRLC)

7. Which of the following are NOT considered linkage institutions?
   a. Political parties
   b. Interest groups

c. The courts
d. The media
e. Political elections

True/False

8. A public good is a service that is provided by the government and is available to individuals who meet certain criteria.
   True_____   False_____

9. The theory of hyperpluralism is based on the assumption that input from interest groups is a good thing for the political decision-making process.
   True_____   False_____

10. The federal government ran a budget deficit every year from 1969 through 1997.
    True_____   False_____

11. The American national government spends more money annually on national defense than it does on Social Security.
    True_____   False_____

12. Compared to other nations around the world, U.S. taxes are relatively high.
    True_____   False_____

Short Answer

13. Please name and explain at least three of the functions that national government performs, according to the textbook.

14. What are the three policymaking institutions established by the U.S. Constitution?

15. Explain in your own words three of the four types of public policies introduced in the textbook. What is an example of each?

16. What are the three ways in which Wayne Baker argues that America might be experiencing a crisis of cultural values? Do you agree or disagree, and why?

Short Answer/Essay Questions

17. Imagine that you are the campaign manager for one of the candidates in an upcoming presidential election. The candidate you are working for is hoping to draw the younger voters in particular. What strategy would you use in order to reach your target audience and get young people interested in your candidate's campaign?

18. Please interpret the data shown in Figure 1.1. What are possible factors that explain these results? How are the numbers shown in this figure related to the results summarized in Figure 1.3?

19. What are the four continuing challenges to democracy mentioned in the textbook? Of those, which do you believe is currently the most significant challenge to American democracy, and why? How would you attempt to resolve this problem?

20. The data in Figure 1.6 indicate that only Canadians rank more highly than Americans in terms of being proud of their country's fair and equal treatment of all groups. What are some of the factors that explain why this is so important to Americans? Why do you think this is not the case in some of the other countries listed?

21. Please compare and contrast the basic assumptions of pluralist theory, elite and class theory, and hyperpluralism. Based on what you know about American government, which of these three theories best explains politics in this country, and why?

22. In your opinion, does the expansion of TV channels and Internet sites offering political information positively or negatively affect the political involvement of young people? Why?

Answer Key

1. D	4. B	7. C	10. True
2. B	5. C	8. False	11. True
3. E	6. D	9. False	12. False

Key Terms

government (8)
public goods (9)
politics (9)
political participation (10)
single-issue groups (10)
policymaking system (10)
linkage institutions (11)
policy agenda (11)

political issue (11)
policymaking institutions (12)
public policy (12)
policy impacts (13)
democracy (13)
majority rule (15)
minority rights (15)
representation (15)

pluralist theory (15)
elite and class theory (16)
hyperpluralism (17)
policy gridlock (18)
political culture (19)
gross domestic product (24)

Internet Resources

www.policyalmanac.org
Contains a discussion of major policy issues of the day and links to resources about them.

http://thomas.loc.gov/home/histdox/fedpapers.html
The complete collection of the *Federalist Papers*.

www.tocqueville.org
Information and discussion about Tocqueville's classic work *Democracy in America*.

www.bowlingalone.com
A site designed to accompany Robert Putnam's work, which contains information concerning the data he used and projects he is working on to reinvigorate American communities.

www.yahoo.com/government
A good place to go to search for information about government and politics.

GetConnected

The Policymaking System

Americans frequently want government to enact specific policies in order to address various problems. However, not all problems are the same. In addition, not all Americans agree on which problems government should solve or on how government should solve them. As Figure 1.4 illustrates, the policymaking system in the United States is complex, involving many actors and institutions. Political parties—one of the many linkage institutions within the policymaking system—play a key role because they bring the people's concerns to the policy agenda. In order to examine this part of the policymaking system up close, let us take a look at a concern shared by many Americans—Social Security insurance and its continued availability—and the proposed policies of key political parties to address this concern.

Search the Web

Go to the Web sites for the platforms of the Green Party, *www.gp.org/platform/2004/socjustice.html#1000939*; the

Republican Party, *http://security.gop.com/GroupPage.aspx?/*; the Democratic Party, *www.democrats.org/a/national/secure_retirement/*; and the Libertarian Party, *http://www.lp.org/issues/social-security*. Review the portion of each platform that relates to Social Security. Get a sense of each party's position on Social Security reform. Write down the key terms and phrases each platform uses.

Questions to Ask

- Based on what you have read, do you think the different political parties have different views on Social Security insurance?
- Which party appears to propose the least significant changes in the Social Security program?
- Which party appears to propose the most significant changes in the Social Security program?
- After reading each party's position, which do you most agree with?

Why It Matters

Everyone who works pays Social Security taxes and it is hoped that we will all have a chance to collect it when the time comes. However, there are many proposals to change the Social Security system. Some of the proposals might make it more difficult to collect. Others might make it more costly. Still others might make it possible for citizens to invest part of their Social Security in the stock market. It is important to understand these proposals and to support the party that best reflects your view on what should happen to Social Security insurance.

Get Involved

Go to the Web and try to find your major state political party Web sites. See how each of the parties proposes solving the problems you think are most pressing in your state. For instance, how do the parties propose paying for education or roads? Or, what are their positions on the environment and declining population in rural areas? If you find that you agree with one of them, you might want to consider sending an e-mail asking about how you can become involved with that party. *For more exercises, go to www.longmanamericangovernment.com.*

For Further Reading

Alesina, Alberto and Edward L. Glaeser. *Fighting Poverty in the US and Europe: A World of Difference*. New York: Oxford, 2004. A multi-faceted analysis of how and why the scope of government is smaller in the United States than in Europe.

Bok, Derek. *The State of the Nation: Government and the Quest for a Better Society*. Cambridge, MA: Harvard University Press, 1996. An excellent analysis of how America is doing, compared to other major democracies, on a wide variety of policy aspects.

Dahl, Robert A. *Democracy and Its Critics*. New Haven, CT: Yale University Press, 1982. A very thoughtful work by one of the world's most articulate advocates of pluralist theory.

de Tocqueville, Alexis. *Democracy in America*. New York: Mentor Books, 1956. This classic by a nineteenth-century French aristocrat remains one of the most insightful works on the nature of American society and government.

Hartz, Louis. *The Liberal Tradition in America*. New York: Harcourt, Brace, 1955. A classic analysis of why the scope of American government has been more limited than in other democracies.

Kingdon, John W. *Agendas, Alternatives, and Public Policies*. 2nd ed. New York: HarperCollins, 1995. One of the best efforts by a political scientist to examine the political agenda.

Macedo, Stephen, et al. *Democracy at Risk: How Political Choices Undermine Citizen Participation, and What We Can Do About It*. Washington, DC: Brookings, 2005. An insightful review of many aspects of political participation in America.

Putnam, Robert. *Bowling Alone: The Collapse and Revival of American Community*. New York: Simon & Schuster, 2000. Putnam's highly influential work shows how Americans have become increasingly disconnected from one another since the early 1960s.

Schuck, Peter H. and James Q. Wilson, eds. *Understanding America: The Anatomy of an Exceptional Nation*. New York: Public Affairs, 2008. An excellent set of readings about various policy topics, with an emphasis on how American policy differs from that of other established democracies.

Sitaraman, Ganesh, and Previn Warren. *Invisible Citizens: Youth Politics After September 11*. New York: iUniverse, Inc., 2003. Two Harvard students examine why today's youth demonstrate a commitment to community service while at the same time largely neglect involvement in politics.

Stanley, Harold W., and Richard G. Niemi. *Vital Statistics on American Politics, 2007–2008*. Washington, DC: Congressional Quarterly Press, 2008. Useful data on government, politics, and policy in the United States.

THE
CONSTITUTION

POLITICS IN ACTION:
AMENDING THE CONSTITUTION

Gregory Lee Johnson knew little about the Constitution, but he knew he was upset. He felt that the buildup of nuclear weapons in the world threatened the planet's survival, and he wanted to protest presidential and corporate policies concerning nuclear weapons. Yet he had no money to hire a lobbyist or to purchase an ad in a newspaper. So he, along with some other demonstrators, marched through the streets of Dallas, chanting political slogans and stopping at several corporate locations to stage "die-ins" intended to dramatize the consequences of nuclear war. The demonstration ended in front of Dallas City Hall, where Gregory doused an American flag with kerosene and set it on fire.

Burning the flag violated the law, and Gregory was convicted of "desecration of a venerated object," sentenced to one year in prison, and fined $2,000. He appealed his conviction, claiming the law that prohibited burning the flag violated his freedom of speech. The U.S. Supreme Court agreed in the case of *Texas v. Gregory Lee Johnson*.

Gregory was pleased with the Court's decision, but he was nearly alone. The public howled its opposition to the decision, and President George H. W. Bush called for a constitutional amendment authorizing punishment of flag desecraters. Many public officials vowed to support the amendment, and organized opposition to the amendment was scarce. However, an amendment to prohibit burning the American flag did not obtain the two-thirds vote in each house of Congress necessary to send a constitutional amendment to the states for ratification.

Instead, Congress passed a law—the Flag Protection Act—that outlawed the desecration of the American flag. The next year, however, in *United States v. Eichman*, the Supreme Court found the act an impermissible infringement on free speech.

After years of political posturing, legislation, and litigation, little has changed. Burning the flag remains a legally protected form of political expression despite the objections of the overwhelming majority of the American public. Gregory Johnson did not prevail because he was especially articulate, nor did he win because he had access to political resources such as money or powerful supporters. He won because of the nature of the Constitution.

Understanding how an unpopular protestor like Gregory Lee Johnson could prevail against the combined forces of the public and its elected officials is central to understanding the American system of government. The Constitution supersedes ordinary law, even when the law represents the wishes of a majority of citizens. The Constitution not only guarantees individual rights but also decentralizes power. Even the president, "the leader of the free world," cannot force Congress to act, as George Bush could not force Congress to start the process of amending the Constitution. Power is not concentrated efficiently in one person's hands, such as the president's. Instead, there are numerous checks on the exercise of power and many obstacles to change. Some complain that this system produces stalemate, while others praise the way it protects minority views. Both positions are correct.

Gregory Johnson's case raises some important questions about government in America. What does democracy mean if the majority does not always get its way? Is this how we should be governed? And is it appropriate that the many limits on the scope of government action, both direct and indirect, sometimes prevent action desired by most people?

constitution

A nation's basic law. It creates political institutions, assigns or divides powers in government, and often provides certain guarantees to citizens. Constitutions can be either written or unwritten. See also **U.S. Constitution.**

A **constitution** is a nation's basic law. It creates political institutions, allocates power within government, and often provides guarantees to citizens. A constitution is also an unwritten accumulation of traditions and precedents that have established acceptable styles of behavior and policy outcomes. As the body of rules that govern our nation, the U.S. Constitution has an impact on our everyday lives. Our theme of the scope of government runs throughout this chapter, which focuses on what the national government can and cannot do. A nation that prides itself on being "democratic" must evaluate the Constitution according to democratic standards, the core of our other theme. To understand government and to answer questions about how we are governed and what government does, we must first understand the Constitution.

THE ORIGINS OF THE CONSTITUTION

In the summer of 1776, a small group of men met in Philadelphia and passed a resolution that began an armed rebellion against the government of what was then the most powerful nation on Earth. The resolution was, of course, the Declaration of Independence; the armed rebellion was the American Revolution.

The attempt to overthrow a government forcibly is a serious and unusual act. All countries, including the United States, consider it treasonous. Typically, it is punishable by death. A set of compelling ideas drove our forefathers to take such drastic and risky action. Understanding the Constitution requires an understanding of these ideas.

THE ROAD TO REVOLUTION

By eighteenth-century standards, life was not bad for most people in America at the time of the Revolution (slaves and indentured servants being major exceptions). In fact, White colonists "were freer, more equal, more prosperous, and less burdened with cumbersome feudal and monarchical restraints than any other part of mankind."[1] Although the colonies were part of the British Empire, the king and Parliament generally confined themselves to governing America's foreign policy and trade. Almost everything else was left to the discretion of individual colonial governments. Although commercial regulations irritated colonial shippers, planters, land speculators, and merchants, these rules had little influence on the vast bulk of the population, who were self-employed farmers or artisans.

FIGURE 2.1

European Claims in North America

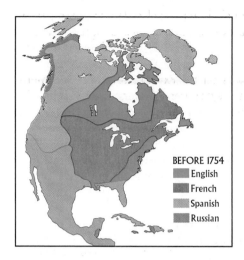

BEFORE 1754
- English
- French
- Spanish
- Russian

AFTER 1763
- English
- French
- Spanish
- Russian

Following its victory in the French and Indian War in 1763, Britain obtained an enormous new territory to govern. To raise revenues to defend and administer the territory, it raised taxes on the colonists and tightened enforcement of trade regulations. (Britain also gained Florida from Spain as a result of the war.)

As you can see in Figure 2.1, Britain obtained an enormous new territory in North America after the French and Indian War (also known as the Seven Years' War) ended in 1763. The cost of defending this territory against foreign adversaries was large, and Parliament reasoned that it was only fair that those who were the primary beneficiaries—the colonists—should contribute to their own defense. Thus, in order to raise revenue for colonial administration and defense, the British Parliament passed a series of taxes on newspapers, official documents, paper, glass, paint, and tea. Britain also began tightening enforcement of its trade regulations, which were designed to benefit the mother country, not the colonists.

The colonists lacked direct representation in Parliament and resented the legislature imposing taxes without their consent. They protested, boycotted the taxed goods, and as a symbolic act of disobedience even threw 342 chests of tea into Boston Harbor. Britain reacted by applying economic pressure through a naval blockade of the harbor, further fueling the colonists' anger. The colonists responded by forming the First Continental Congress in September 1774, sending delegates from each colony to Philadelphia to discuss the future of relations with Britain.

DECLARING INDEPENDENCE

As colonial discontent with the English festered, the Continental Congress was in almost continuous session during 1775 and 1776. Talk of independence was common among the delegates. Virginia, as it often did in those days, played a leading role at the Philadelphia meeting of the Congress. It sent seven delegates to join the serious discussion of repudiating the rule of King George III. These delegates were joined later by a last-minute substitute for Peyton Randolph, who was needed back in Williamsburg to preside over Virginia's House of Burgesses.

The substitute, Thomas Jefferson, was a young (only 33), well-educated Virginia lawmaker who had just written a resolution in

COMMON SENSE;

ADDRESSED TO THE

INHABITANTS

OF

AMERICA,

On the following interesting

SUBJECTS.

I. Of the Origin and Design of Government in general, with concise Remarks on the English Constitution.

II. Of Monarchy and Hereditary Succession.

III. Thoughts on the present State of American Affairs.

IV. Of the present Ability of America, with some miscellaneous Reflections.

Man knows no Master save creating HEAVEN,
Or those whom choice and common good ordain.
THOMSON.

PHILADELPHIA;

Printed, and Sold, by R. BELL, in Third-Street,

MDCCLXXVI.

Thomas Paine's *Common Sense* encouraged the colonists to declare independence from Britain.

the Virginia legislature objecting to new British policies. Jefferson brought to the Continental Congress his talent as an author and his knowledge of political philosophy. He was not a rabble-rousing pamphleteer like Thomas Paine, whose fiery tract *Common Sense* had appeared in January 1776 and fanned the already hot flames of revolution. Jefferson was steeped in the philosophical writings of European moral philosophers, and his rhetoric matched his reading.[2]

In May and June 1776, the Continental Congress began debating resolutions about independence. On June 7, Richard Henry Lee of Virginia moved "that these United States are and of right ought to be free and independent states." A committee composed of Thomas Jefferson of Virginia, John Adams of Massachusetts, Benjamin Franklin of Pennsylvania, Roger Sherman of Connecticut, and Robert Livingston of New York was formed to draft a document to justify the inevitable declaration. On July 2, the Congress formally approved Lee's motion to declare independence from England. The Congress adopted the famous **Declaration of Independence**, written primarily by Jefferson, two days later, on July 4.

The Declaration of Independence quickly became one of the most widely quoted and revered documents in America. Filled with fine principles and bold language, it can be read as both a political tract and a philosophical treatise. (It is reprinted in the Appendix of this book.)

Politically, the Declaration was a polemic, a political argument, announcing and justifying a revolution. Most of the document— 27 of its 32 paragraphs—listed the ways the king had abused the colonies. The delegates accused George III of all sorts of evil deeds, even though he personally had little to do with Parliament's colonial policies. They even blamed the king for inciting the "merciless Indian savages" to make war on the colonists. The delegates focused blame on King George because they held that only he, not Parliament, had authority over the colonies.

The Declaration's polemical aspects were important because the colonists needed foreign assistance to take on the most powerful nation in the world. France, which was engaged in a war with Britain, was a prime target for the delegates' diplomacy and eventually provided aid that was critical to the success of the Revolution.

Today, we study the Declaration of Independence more as a statement of philosophy than as a political call to arms. In just a few sentences, Jefferson set forth the American democratic creed, the most important and succinct statement of the philosophy underlying American government—as applicable today as it was in 1776.

Declaration of Independence

The document approved by representatives of the American colonies in 1776 that stated their grievances against the British monarch and declared their independence.

John Adams (from right), Roger Sherman, Robert R. Livingston, Thomas Jefferson, and Benjamin Franklin submit the Declaration of Independence to Continental Congress President John Hancock. Legend has it that Hancock remarked, "We must be unanimous; there must be no pulling different ways; we must hang together," to which Franklin replied, "We must indeed all hang together, or, most assuredly, we shall hang separately."

THE ENGLISH HERITAGE: THE POWER OF IDEAS

Philosophically, the Jeffersonian pen put on paper ideas that were by then common knowledge on both sides of the Atlantic, especially among those people who wished to challenge the power of kings. Franklin, Jefferson, James Madison of Virginia,

Robert Morris of Pennsylvania, Alexander Hamilton of New York, and other intellectual leaders in the colonies were learned and widely read men, familiar with the works of English, French, and Scottish political philosophers. These leaders corresponded about the ideas they were reading, quoted philosophers in their debates over the Revolution, and applied those ideas to the new government they formed through the framework of the Constitution.

John Locke was one of the most influential philosophers read by the colonists. His writings, especially *The Second Treatise of Civil Government* (1689), profoundly influenced American political leaders. His work was "the dominant political faith of the American colonies in the second quarter of the eighteenth century. A thousand pulpits thundered with its benevolent principles; a hundred editors filled their pages with its famous slogans."[3]

The foundation on which Locke built his powerful philosophy was a belief in **natural rights**—rights inherent in human beings, not dependent on governments. Before governments arise, Locke held, people exist in a state of nature in which there are no formal laws or governments. Instead, the laws of nature govern people, laws determined by people's innate moral sense. This natural law brings natural rights, including life, liberty, and property. Natural law can even justify a challenge to the rule of a tyrannical king because it is superior to man-made law. Government, Locke argued, must be built on the **consent of the governed**; in other words, the people must agree on who their rulers will be. It should also be a **limited government**; that is, there must be clear restrictions on what rulers can do. Indeed, the sole purpose of government, according to Locke, was to protect natural rights. The idea that certain things were beyond the realm of government contrasted sharply with the traditional notion that kings had been divinely granted absolute rights over subjects.

Two limits on government were particularly important to Locke. First, governments must provide standing laws so that people know in advance whether their acts will be acceptable. Second, and Locke was very forceful on this point, "the supreme power cannot take from any man any part of his property without his consent." To Locke, "the preservation of property was the end of government." The sanctity of property was one of the few ideas absent in Jefferson's draft of the Declaration of Independence. Even though Jefferson borrowed from and even paraphrased Lockean ideas, he altered Locke's phrase "life, liberty, and property" to "life, liberty, and the pursuit of happiness." We shall soon see, however, how the Lockean idea of the sanctity of property figured prominently at the Constitutional Convention. James Madison, the most influential member of that body, directly echoed Locke's view that the preservation of property is the purpose of government.

Locke argued that in an extreme case people have a right to revolt against a government that no longer has their consent. Locke anticipated critics' charges that this right would lead to constant civil disturbances. He emphasized that people should not revolt until injustices become deeply felt. The Declaration of Independence accented the same point, declaring that "governments long established should not be changed for light and transient causes." But when matters went beyond "patient sufferance," severing these ties was not only inevitable but also necessary.

JEFFERSON'S HANDIWORK: THE AMERICAN CREED

There are some remarkable parallels between Locke's thought and Jefferson's language in the Declaration of Independence (see Table 2.1). Jefferson, like Locke, finessed his way past the issue of how the rebels knew men had rights. Jefferson simply declared that it was "self-evident" that men were equally "endowed by their Creator with certain unalienable rights," including "life, liberty, and the pursuit of happiness." Because it was the purpose of government to "secure" these rights, the people could form a new government if it failed to do so.[4]

natural rights
Rights inherent in human beings, not dependent on governments, which include life, liberty, and property. The concept of natural rights was central to English philosopher John Locke's theories about government and was widely accepted among America's Founders.

consent of the governed
The idea that government derives its authority by sanction of the people.

limited government
The idea that certain restrictions should be placed on government to protect the **natural rights** of citizens.

TABLE 2.1

Locke and the Declaration of Independence: Some Parallels

LOCKE	DECLARATION OF INDEPENDENCE
Natural Rights	
"The state of nature has a law to govern it" "life, liberty, and property"	"Laws of Nature and Nature's God" "life, liberty, and the pursuit of happiness."
Purpose of Government	
"to preserve himself, his liberty, and property"	"to secure these rights."
Equality	
"men being by nature all free, equal and independent"	"all men are created equal"
Consent of the Governed	
"for when any number of men have, by the consent of every individual, made a community, with a power to act as one body, which is only by the will and determination of the majority"	"Governments are instituted among men, deriving their just powers from the consent of the governed."
Limited Government	
"Absolute arbitrary power, or governing without settled laws, can neither of them consist with the ends of society and government." "As usurpation is the exercise of power which another has a right to, so tyranny is the exercise of power beyond right, which nobody can have a right to."	"The history of the present King of Great Britain is a history of repeated injuries and usurpations."
Right to Revolt	
"The people shall be the judge.... Oppression raises ferments and makes men struggle to cast off an uneasy and tyrannical yoke."	"Prudence, indeed, will dictate that Governments long established should not be changed for light and transient causes.... But when a long train of abuses and usurpations, pursuing invariably the same Object evinces a design to reduce them under absolute Despotism, it is their right, it is their duty, to throw off such Government."

IN CONGRESS. July 4. 1776.

The unanimous Declaration of the thirteen united States of America.

Locke represented only one element of revolutionary thought from which Jefferson borrowed. In the English countryside, there was also a well-established tradition of opposition to the executive power of the Crown and support for recovering the rights of the people. An indigenous American republicanism—stressing moral virtue, patriotism, relations based on merit, and the equality of independent citizens—intensified the radicalism of this "country" ideology and linked it with older currents of European thought stretching back to antiquity.

It was in the American colonies that the powerful ideas of European political thinkers took root and grew into what Seymour Martin Lipset has termed the "first new nation."[5] With these revolutionary ideas in mind, Jefferson claimed in the Declaration of Independence that people should have primacy over governments, that they should rule instead of be ruled. Moreover, each person was important as an individual, "created equal" and endowed with "unalienable rights." Consent of the governed, not divine rights or tradition, made the exercise of political power legitimate.

No government had ever been based on these principles. Ever since 1776, Americans have been concerned about fulfilling the high aspirations of the Declaration of Independence.

WINNING INDEPENDENCE

The pen may be mightier than the sword, but declaring independence did not win the Revolution—it merely announced its beginning. John Adams wrote to his wife Abigail, "You will think me transported with enthusiasm, but I am not. I am well aware of the toil, blood, and treasure that it will cost us to maintain this Declaration, and support and defend these states." Adams was right. The colonists seemed little match for the finest army in the world, whose size was nearly quadrupled by hired guns from the German state of Hesse and elsewhere. In 1775, the British had 8,500 men stationed in the colonies and had hired nearly 30,000 mercenaries. Initially, the colonists had only 5,000 men in uniform, and their number waxed and waned as the war progressed. Nevertheless, in 1783, the American colonies won their war of independence. How they eventually won is a story best left to history books. However, in the following sections we will explore how they formed a new government.

THE "CONSERVATIVE" REVOLUTION

Revolutions such as the 1789 French Revolution, the 1917 Russian Revolution, and the 1978–1979 Iranian Revolution produced great societal change—as well as plenty of bloodshed. The American Revolution was different. Although many people lost their lives during the Revolutionary War, the Revolution itself was essentially a conservative movement that did not drastically alter the colonists' way of life. Its primary goal was to restore rights the colonists felt were already theirs as British subjects.

American colonists did not feel the need for great social, economic, or political upheavals. They "were not oppressed people; they had no crushing imperial shackles to throw off."[6] As a result, the Revolution did not create class conflicts that would split society for generations to come. The colonial leaders' belief that they needed the consent of the governed blessed the new nation with a crucial element of stability—a stability the nation would need.

THE GOVERNMENT THAT FAILED: 1776–1787

The Continental Congress that adopted the Declaration of Independence was only a voluntary association of the states. In 1776, the Congress appointed a committee to draw up a plan for a permanent union of the states. That plan, our first constitution, was the **Articles of Confederation**.[7]

Articles of Confederation
The first constitution of the United States, adopted by Congress in 1777 and enacted in 1781. The Articles established a national legislature, the Continental Congress, but most authority rested with the state legislatures.

THE ARTICLES OF CONFEDERATION

The Articles established a government dominated by the states. The United States, according to the Articles, was a confederation, a "league of friendship and perpetual union" among 13 states. The Articles established a national legislature with one house; states could send as many as seven delegates or as few as two, but each state had only one vote. There was no president and no national court, and the powers of the national legislature were strictly limited. Most authority rested with the state legislatures because the new nation's leaders feared that a strong central government would become as tyrannical as British rule.

Because unanimous consent of the states was needed to put the Articles into operation, the Articles adopted by the Continental Congress in 1777 did not go into effect until 1781, when laggard Maryland finally ratified them. In the meantime, the Continental Congress barely survived, lurching from crisis to crisis. At one point during the war, some of Washington's troops threatened to create a monarchy with him as king unless Congress paid their overdue wages.

Even after the states ratified the Articles of Confederation, many logistical and political problems plagued the Congress. State delegations attended haphazardly. The Congress had few powers outside maintaining an army and navy—and little money to do even that. It had to request money from the states because it had no power to tax. If states refused to send money (which they often did), Congress did without. In desperation, Congress sold off western lands (land east of the Mississippi and west of the states) to speculators, issued securities that sold for less than their face value, or used its own presses to print money that was virtually worthless. Congress also voted to disband the army despite continued threats from Britain and Spain.

Congress lacked the power to regulate commerce, which inhibited foreign trade and the development of a strong national economy. It did, however, manage to develop sound policies for the management of the western frontiers, passing the Northwest Ordinance of 1787 that encouraged the development of the Great Lakes region.

In general, the weak and ineffective national government could take little independent action. All government power rested in the states. The national government could not compel the states to do anything, and it had no power to deal directly with individual citizens. The weakness of the national government prevented it from dealing with the hard times that faced the new nation. There was one benefit of the Articles, however: When the nation's leaders began to write a new Constitution, they could look at the provisions of the Articles of Confederation and know some of the things they should avoid.

CHANGES IN THE STATES

What was happening in the states was more important than what was happening in the Congress. The most important change was a dramatic increase in democracy and liberty, at least for White males. Many states adopted bills of rights to protect freedoms, abolished religious qualifications for holding office, and liberalized requirements for voting. Expanded political participation brought a new middle class to power.

This middle class included farmers who owned small homesteads rather than manorial landholders and artisans instead of lawyers. Before the Revolution, almost all members of New York's assembly were either urban merchants or wealthy landowners. In the 1769 assembly, for example, 25 percent of the legislators were farmers even though nearly 95 percent of New Yorkers were farmers. But after the Revolution, a major power shift occurred. With expanded voting privileges, farmers and craftworkers became a decisive majority, and the old elite

? Why It Matters
A Strong National Government

One of the most important features of the Constitution is the creation of a strong national government. If the Framers had retained a weak national government, as under the Articles of Confederation, Congress could not create a great national economic market through regulating interstate commerce, the president could not conduct a vigorous foreign policy, federal courts could not issue orders to protect civil rights, and the federal government could not raise the funds to pay for Social Security benefits or grants and loans for college students.

of professionals, wealthy merchants, and large landholders saw its power shrink. The same change happened in other states as power shifted from a handful of wealthy individuals to a more broad-based group (see Figure 2.2). Democracy was taking hold everywhere.

The structure of government in the states also became more responsive to the people. State constitutions concentrated power in the legislatures because most people considered legislators to be closer to the voters than governors or judges. Legislatures often selected the governors and kept them on a short leash, with brief tenures and limited veto and appointment powers. Legislatures also overruled court decisions and criticized judges for unpopular decisions.

The idea of equality, at least among white males, was driving change throughout the nation. Although the Revolutionary War itself did not transform American society, it unleashed the republican tendencies in American life. Americans were in the process of becoming "the most liberal, the most democratic, the most commercially minded, and the most modern people in the world."[8] Members of the old colonial elite found this turn of affairs quite troublesome because it challenged their hold on power.

FIGURE 2.2

Power Shift: Economic Status of State Legislators Before and After the Revolutionary War

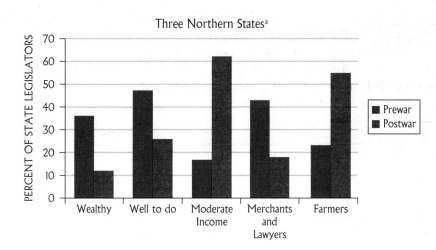

Three Northern States[a]

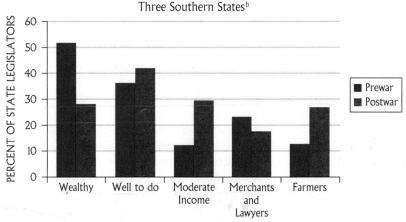

Three Southern States[b]

[a]New York, New Jersey, New Hampshire
[b]Maryland, South Carolina, Virginia

After the Revolution, power in the state legislatures shifted from the hands of the wealthy to those with more moderate incomes and from merchants and lawyers to farmers. This trend was especially evident in the northern states.

ECONOMIC TURMOIL

After the Revolution, James Madison observed that "the most common and durable source of factions [special interests] has been the various and unequal division of property."[9] The post-Revolutionary legislatures epitomized Madison's argument that economic inequality played an important role in shaping public policy.

Economic issues were at the top of the political agenda. A postwar depression had left many small farmers unable to pay their debts and threatened them with mortgage foreclosures. Now under control of people more sympathetic to debtors, the state legislatures listened to the demands of small farmers. A few states, notably Rhode Island, demonstrated their support of debtors, passing policies favoring them over creditors. Some printed tons of paper money and passed "force acts" requiring reluctant creditors to accept the almost worthless money. Debtors could thus pay big debts with cheap currency.

Shays' Rebellion, in which farmers physically prevented judges from foreclosing on farms, helped spur the birth of the Constitution. News of the small rebellion spread quickly around the country, and some of the Philadelphia delegates thought a full-fledged revolution would result. The event reaffirmed the Framers' belief that the new federal government needed to be a strong one.

SHAYS' REBELLION

Policies favoring debtors over creditors did not please the economic elite who had once controlled nearly all the state legislatures. They were further shaken when, in 1786, a small band of farmers in western Massachusetts rebelled at losing their land to creditors. Led by Revolutionary War Captain Daniel Shays, this rebellion, called **Shays' Rebellion**, was a series of armed attacks on courthouses to prevent judges from foreclosing on farms. Farmers in other states—though never in large numbers—were also unruly. Jefferson was not distressed at this behavior, calling the attack a "little rebellion," but it remained on the minds of the economic elite. They were scared at the thought that people had taken the law into their own hands and violated the property rights of others. Neither Congress nor the state was able to raise a militia to stop Shays and his followers, and elites assembled a privately paid force to do the job, which further fueled dissatisfaction with the weakness of the Articles of Confederation system.

Shays' Rebellion

A series of attacks on courthouses by a small band of farmers led by Revolutionary War Captain Daniel Shays to block foreclosure proceedings.

THE ABORTED ANNAPOLIS MEETING

In September 1786, a handful of leaders assembled at Annapolis, Maryland, to discuss problems with the Articles of Confederation and suggest solutions. The assembly was an abortive attempt at reform. Only five states—New York, New Jersey, Delaware, Pennsylvania, and Virginia—were represented at the meeting; the 12 delegates were few enough in number to meet around a dinner table. Called to consider commercial conflicts that had arisen among the states under the Articles of Confederation, the Annapolis delegates decided that a larger meeting and a broader proposal were needed to organize the states. Holding most of their meetings at a local tavern, this small and unofficial band of reformers issued a call for a full-scale meeting of the states in Philadelphia the following May—in retrospect, a rather bold move by so small a group. The Continental Congress granted their request, however, and called for a meeting of all the states. In May 1787, what we now call the Constitutional Convention got down to business in Philadelphia.

MAKING A CONSTITUTION: THE PHILADELPHIA CONVENTION

Representatives from 12 states came to Philadelphia to heed the Continental Congress's call to "take into consideration the situation in the United States." Only Rhode Island, a stronghold of paper-money interests and thus skeptical of reforms favoring creditors, refused to send delegates. Virginia's Patrick Henry (the colonial firebrand who had declared, "Give me liberty or give me death!"), fearing a centralization of power, also did not attend.

The delegates were ordered to meet "for the sole and express purpose of revising the Articles of Confederation." The Philadelphia delegates did not pay much attention to this order, however, because amending the Articles required the unanimous consent of the states, which they knew would be impossible. Thus, the 55 delegates ignored their instructions and began writing what was to become the **U.S. Constitution**.

> **U.S. Constitution**
> The document written in 1787 and ratified in 1788 that sets forth the institutional structure of U.S. government and the tasks these institutions perform. It replaced the Articles of Confederation.

GENTLEMEN IN PHILADELPHIA

Who were these 55 men? They may not have been "demigods," as Jefferson, perhaps sarcastically, called them, but they were certainly an elite group of economic and political notables. They were mostly wealthy planters, successful (or once successful) lawyers and merchants, and men of independent wealth. Many were college graduates, and most had practical political experience. Most were coastal residents rather than residents of the expanding western frontiers, and a significant number were urbanites rather than part of the primarily rural American population.

PHILOSOPHY INTO ACTION

The delegates in Philadelphia were an uncommon combination of philosophers and shrewd political architects. The debates moved from high principles on the big issues to self-interest on the small ones.[10] The delegates devoted the first two weeks mainly to general debates about the nature of republican government (government in which ultimate power rests with the voters). After that, practical and divisive issues sometimes threatened to dissolve the meeting.

Obviously, these 55 men did not share the same political philosophy. Democratic Benjamin Franklin held very different views from a number of delegates who were wary of democracy. Yet at the core of their ideas existed a common center. The group agreed on questions of (1) human nature, (2) the causes of political conflict, (3) the objects of government, and (4) the nature of a republican government.

Alexander Hamilton, a New York delegate to the Convention, favored a strong central government. Hamilton was less influential at the Convention than he would be later as an architect of the nation's economic policy.

Human Nature In his famous work titled *Leviathan* written in 1651, Thomas Hobbes argued that man's natural state was war and that a strong absolute ruler was necessary to restrain man's bestial tendencies. Without a strong government, Hobbes wrote, life would be "solitary, poor, nasty, brutish, and short." The delegates opposed Hobbes' powerful monarch, however, siding with Locke's argument that government should be limited.

Nevertheless, the delegates held a cynical view of human nature. People, they thought, were self-interested. Franklin and Hamilton, poles apart philosophically, both voiced this sentiment.

Said Franklin, "There are two passions which have a powerful influence on the affairs of men: the love of power and the love of money." Hamilton agreed in his characteristically straightforward manner: "Men love power." The men at Philadelphia believed that government should play a key role in containing the natural self-interest of people.[11]

Political Conflict   Of all the words written by and about the delegates, none have been more widely quoted than these by James Madison: "The most common and durable source of factions has been the various and unequal distribution of property." In other words, *the distribution of wealth* (land was the main form of wealth in those days) *is the source of political conflict*. "Those who hold and those who are without property," Madison went on, "have ever formed distinct interests in society." Other sources of conflict included religion, views of governing, and attachment to various leaders.[12]

Arising from these sources of conflict are **factions**, which we might call parties or interest groups. A majority faction might well be composed of the many who have little or no property; the minority faction, of those with property. If unchecked, the delegates thought, one of these factions would eventually tyrannize the other. The majority would try to seize the government to reduce the wealth of the minority; the minority would try to seize the government to secure its own gains. Governments run by factions, the Founders believed, are prone to instability, tyranny, and even violence. The Founders intended to check the effects of factions.

factions

Interest groups arising from the unequal distribution of property or wealth that James Madison attacked in *Federalist Paper No. 10*. Today's parties or interest groups are what Madison had in mind when he warned of the instability in government caused by factions.

Objects of Government   To Gouverneur Morris of Pennsylvania, the preservation of property was the "principal object of government." Morris was outspoken and plainly overlooked some other objects of government, including security from invasion, domestic tranquility, and promotion of the general welfare. However, Morris's remark typifies the philosophy of many of the delegates. John Locke (who was, remember, the intellectual patron saint of many of the delegates) had said a century before that "The preservation of property is the end of government." Few of these men would have disagreed. As property holders themselves, these delegates could not imagine a government that did not make its principal objective an economic one: the preservation of individual rights to acquire and hold wealth. A few (like Morris) were intent on shutting out the propertyless altogether. "Give the votes to people who have no property," Morris claimed, "and they will sell them to the rich who will be able to buy them."

Pennsylvania delegate Gouverneur Morris was a man of considerable means and was concerned primarily with protecting property holders. He was responsible for the style and wording of the Constitution.

Nature of Government   Given their beliefs about human nature, the causes of political conflict, the need to protect property, and the threat of tyranny by a faction, what sort of government did the delegates believe would work? They answered in different ways, but the message was always the same. Power should be set against power so that no one faction would overwhelm the others. The secret of good government is "balanced" government. They were influenced in their thinking by writings of a French aristocrat, Baron Montesquieu, who advocated separate branches of government with distinct powers and the ability to check the other branches. The Founders agreed, concluding that a limited government would have to contain checks on its own power. So long as no faction could seize the whole of government at once, tyranny could be avoided. A balanced government required a complex network of checks, balances, and separation of powers.

THE AGENDA IN PHILADELPHIA

The delegates in Philadelphia could not merely construct a government from ideas. They wanted to design a government that was consistent with their political philosophy, but they also had to confront some of the thorniest issues facing the fledgling nation at the time—issues of equality, the economy, and individual rights.

THE EQUALITY ISSUES

The Declaration of Independence states that all men are created equal; the Constitution, however, is silent on equality. Nevertheless, some of the most important issues on the policy agenda in Philadelphia concerned equality. Three issues occupied more attention than almost any others: whether the states were to be equally represented, what to do about slavery, and whether to ensure equality in voting.

Equality and Representation of the States   One crucial policy issue was how to constitute the new Congress. The **New Jersey Plan**, proposed by William Paterson of New Jersey, called for each state to be equally represented in the new Congress. The opposing strategy, suggested by Edmund Randolph of Virginia, is usually called the **Virginia Plan**. It called for giving each state representation in Congress based on the state's share of the American population.

The delegates resolved this conflict with a compromise devised by Roger Sherman and William Johnson of Connecticut. The solution proposed by this **Connecticut Compromise** was to create two houses in Congress. One body, the Senate, would have two members from each state (the New Jersey Plan), and the second body, the House of Representatives, would have representation based on population (the Virginia Plan). The U.S. Congress is still organized in exactly the same way. Each state has two senators, and the state's population determines its representation in the House.

Although the Connecticut Compromise was intended to maximize equality among the states, it actually gives more power to people who live in states with small populations than to those who live in more heavily populated states. Every state has two senators and at least one member of the House, no matter how small its population. To take the most extreme case, Wyoming and California have the same number of votes in the Senate (two), although Wyoming has less than 2 percent of California's population. Thus, a citizen of Wyoming has more than *50 times* the representation in the Senate as does a citizen of California.[13]

Because it is the Senate, not the House, that ratifies treaties, confirms presidential nominations, and hears trials of impeachment, citizens in less populated states have a greater say in these key tasks. In addition, the electoral college (the body that actually elects the president and is discussed in Chapter 10) gives small states greater weight. If no presidential candidate receives a majority in the electoral college, the House of Representatives makes the final decision—with each state having one vote. In such a case (which has not occurred since 1824), the votes of citizens of Wyoming would again carry over 50 times as much weight as those of Californians.

Whether representation in the Senate is "fair" is a matter of debate. What is not open to question is that the delegates to the 1787 convention had to accommodate various interests and viewpoints in order to convince all the states to join an untested union.

Slavery   The second equality issue was slavery. The contradictions between slavery and the sentiments of the Declaration of Independence are obvious, but in 1787 slavery was legal in every state except Massachusetts. It was concentrated in the South, however, where slave labor was commonplace in agriculture. Some delegates, like Gouverneur Morris, denounced slavery in no uncertain terms. But the Convention could not accept Morris's position in the face of powerful Southern opposition

Why It Matters
Representation in the Senate
The Senate both creates a check on the House and overrepresents states with small populations. If there were only one house of Congress, governance would be more efficient. If representation were based solely on population, interests centered in states with small populations would lose an advantage. At the same time, there would be one less important check on government action and perhaps a closer correspondence between public opinion and public policy. Which do you prefer?

New Jersey Plan
The proposal at the Constitutional Convention that called for equal **representation** of each state in Congress regardless of the state's population.

Virginia Plan
The proposal at the Constitutional Convention that called for **representation** of each state in Congress in proportion to that state's share of the U.S. population.

Connecticut Compromise
The compromise reached at the Constitutional Convention that established two houses of Congress: the House of Representatives, in which **representation** is based on a state's share of the U.S. population, and the Senate, in which each state has two representatives.

DOONESBURY   Garry Trudeau

led by Charles C. Pinckney of South Carolina. The delegates did agree that Congress could limit *future importing* of slaves (they allowed it to be outlawed after 1808), but they did not forbid slavery itself. The Constitution, in fact, inclines toward recognizing slavery; it states that persons legally "held to service or labour" (referring to slaves) who escaped to free states had to be returned to their owners.

Another difficult question about slavery arose at the Convention. How should slaves be counted in determining representation in Congress? Southerners were happy to see slaves counted toward determining their representation in the House of Representatives (though reluctant to count them for apportionment of taxation). Here the result was the famous *three-fifths compromise.* Representation and taxation were to be based on the "number of free persons," plus three-fifths of the number of "all other persons." Everyone, of course, knew who those other persons were.

Equality in Voting   The delegates dodged one other issue on equality. A handful of delegates, led by Franklin, suggested that national elections should require universal manhood suffrage (that is, a vote for all free adult males). This still would have left a majority of the population disenfranchised, but for those still smarting from Shays' Rebellion and the fear of mob rule, the suggestion was too democratic. Many delegates wanted to put property qualifications on the right to vote. Ultimately, as the debate wound down, they decided to leave the issue to the states. People qualified to vote in state elections could also vote in national elections. Table 2.2 summarizes how the Founders dealt with the three issues of equality.

THE ECONOMIC ISSUES

The Philadelphia delegates were deeply concerned about the state of the American economy. Economic issues were high on the Constitution writers' policy agenda. People disagreed (in fact, historians still disagree) as to whether the postcolonial economy was in a shambles. Advocates of the Constitution, called Federalists, stressed the economy's "weaknesses, especially in the commercial sector, and Anti-Federalists (those opposed to a strong national government, and thus opposed to a new constitution) countered with charges of exaggeration."[14] The writers of the Constitution, already committed to a strong national government, charged that the economy was indeed in disarray and that they need to address the following problems:

TABLE 2.2

How the Constitution Resolved Three Issues of Equality

PROBLEM	SOLUTION
Equality of the States	
Should states be represented equally (the New Jersey Plan) or in proportion to their population (the Virginia Plan)?	Both, according to the Connecticut Compromise. have equal representation in the Senate, but representation in the House is proportionate to population.
Slavery	
What should be done about slavery?	Although Congress was permitted to stop the importing of slaves after 1808 and states were required to return runaway slaves from other states, the Constitution is mostly silent on the issue of slavery.
How should slaves be counted for representation in the House of Representatives?	Give states credit for three-fifths of slaves in determining population for representation.
Equality in Voting	
Should the right to vote be based on universal manhood suffrage, or should it be very restricted?	Finesse the issue. Let the states decide qualifications for voting.

- The states had erected tariffs against products from other states.
- Paper money was virtually worthless in some states, but many state governments, which were controlled by debtor classes, forced it on creditors anyway.
- The Congress was having trouble raising money because the economy was in a recession.

Understanding something about the delegates and their economic interests gives us insight into their views on political economy. They were, by all accounts, the nation's postcolonial economic elite. Some were budding capitalists. Others were creditors whose loans were being wiped out by cheap paper money. Many were merchants who could not even carry on trade with a neighboring state. Virtually all of them thought a strong national government was needed to bring economic stability to the chaotic union of states that existed under the Articles of Confederation.[15]

It is not surprising, then, that the Framers of the Constitution would seek to strengthen the economic powers (and thus the scope) of the new national government. One famous historian, Charles A. Beard, claimed that their principal motivation for doing so was to increase their personal wealth. The Framers, he said, not only were propertied, upper-class men protecting their interests, but also held bonds and investments whose value would increase if the Constitution were adopted. The best evidence, however, indicates that although they were concerned about protecting

When the Constitution was written, many northern and southern delegates assumed that slavery, being relatively unprofitable, would soon die out. A single invention—Eli Whitney's cotton gin—made it profitable again. Although Congress did act to control the growth of slavery, the slave economy became entrenched in the South. Could the Founders have prohibited slavery in the new nation?

property rights, the Founders' motivations were in the broad sense of building a strong economy rather than in the narrow sense of increasing their personal wealth.[16]

The delegates made sure that the Constitution clearly spelled out the economic powers of Congress (see Table 2.3). Consistent with the general allocation of power in the Constitution, Congress was to be the chief economic policymaker. It could obtain revenues through taxing and borrowing. These tools, along with the power to appropriate funds, became crucial instruments for influencing the economy (as we will see in Chapter 17). By maintaining sound money and guaranteeing payment for the national debt, Congress was to encourage economic enterprise and investment in the United States. The Constitution also allocates to Congress power to build the nation's infrastructure by constructing post offices and roads and to establish standard weights and measures. To protect property rights, Congress was charged with punishing counterfeiters and pirates, ensuring patents and copyrights, and legislating rules for bankruptcy. Equally important (and now a key congressional power, with a wide range of implications for the economy) was Congress's new ability to regulate interstate and foreign commerce. In sum, the Constitution granted Congress the power to create the conditions within which markets could flourish.

In addition, the Framers prohibited practices in the states that they viewed as inhibiting economic development, such as maintaining individual state monetary systems, placing duties on imports from other states, and interfering with lawfully contracted debts. Moreover, the states were to respect civil judgments and contracts

TABLE 2.3
Economics in the Constitution

Powers of Congress

1. Levy taxes.	7. Punish piracy.
2. Pay debts.	8. Punish counterfeiting.
3. Borrow money.	9. Create standard weights and measures.
4. Coin money and regulate its value.	10. Establish post offices and post roads.
5. Regulate interstate and foreign commerce.	11. Protect copyrights and patents.
6. Establish uniform laws of bankruptcy.	

Prohibitions on the States

1. States cannot pass laws impairing the obligations of contract.	4. States cannot tax imports or exports from abroad or from other states.
2. States cannot coin money or issue paper money.	5. States cannot free runaway slaves from other states (now defunct).
3. States cannot require payment of debts in paper money.	

Other Key Provisions

1. The new government assumes the national debt contracted under the Articles of Confederation.	3. The states must respect civil court judgments and contracts made in other states.
2. The Constitution guarantees a republican form of government.	

made in other states, and they were to return runaway slaves to their owners. (This last protection of "property" rights is now, of course, defunct as a result of the Thirteenth Amendment, which outlawed slavery.) To help the states, the national government guaranteed them "a republican form of government" to prevent a recurrence of Shays' Rebellion, in which some people used violence, instead of legislation and the courts, to resolve commercial disputes.

The Constitution also obligated the new government to repay all the public debts incurred under the Continental Congress and the Articles of Confederation—debts that totaled $54 million. Although this requirement may seem odd, there was sound economic reason for it. Paying off the debts would ensure from the outset that money would flow into the American economy and would also restore the confidence of investors in the young nation. Even today, people trade in government debt (in the form of bonds) just as they do in the stocks of corporations. Thus, the Constitution helped to spur a capitalist economy.

THE INDIVIDUAL RIGHTS ISSUES

Another major item on the Constitutional Convention agenda for the delegates was designing a system that would preserve individual rights. There was no dispute about the importance of safeguarding individualism, and the Founders believed that this would be relatively easy. After all, they were constructing a limited government that, by design, could not threaten personal freedoms. In addition, they dispersed power among the branches of the national government and between the national and state governments so that each branch or level could restrain the other. Also, most of the delegates believed that the various states were already doing a sufficient job of protecting individual rights.

As a result, the Constitution says little about personal freedoms. The protections it does offer are the following:

- It prohibits suspension of the **writ of habeas corpus** (except during invasion or rebellion). Such a court order enables persons detained by authorities to secure an immediate inquiry into the causes of their detention. If no proper explanation is offered, a judge may order their release. (Article I, Section 9)
- It prohibits Congress or the states from passing bills of attainder (which punish people without a judicial trial). (Article I, Section 9)
- It prohibits Congress or the states from passing *ex post facto* laws (which punish people or increase the penalties for acts that were not illegal or not as punishable when the act was committed). (Article I, Section 9)
- It prohibits the imposition of religious qualifications for holding office in the national government. (Article VI)
- It narrowly defines and outlines strict rules of evidence for conviction of treason. To be convicted, a person must levy war against the United States or adhere to and aid its enemies during war. Conviction requires confession in open court or the testimony of *two* witnesses to the *same* overt act. The Framers of the Constitution would have been executed as traitors if the Revolution had failed, and they were therefore sensitive to treason laws. (Article III, Section 3)
- It upholds the right to trial by jury in criminal cases. (Article III, Section 2)

The delegates were content with their document. When it came time to ratify the Constitution, however, there was widespread criticism of the absence of specific protections of individual rights, such as free expression and the rights of the accused.

writ of habeas corpus
A court order requiring jailers to explain to a judge why they are holding a prisoner in custody.

THE MADISONIAN MODEL

The Framers believed that human nature was self-interested and that inequalities of wealth were the principal source of political conflict. Regardless, they had no desire to remove the divisions in society by converting private property to common ownership; they also believed that protecting private property was a key purpose of government. Their experience with state governments under the Articles of Confederation reinforced their view that democracy was a threat to property. Many of them felt that the nonwealthy majority—an unruly mob—would tyrannize the wealthy minority if given political power. Thus, the delegates to the Constitutional Convention faced the dilemma of reconciling economic inequality with political freedom.

THWARTING TYRANNY OF THE MAJORITY

James Madison was neither wealthy nor a great orator. He was, however, a careful student of politics and government and became the principal architect of the government's final structure.[17] He and his colleagues feared both majority and minority factions. Either could take control of the government and use it to their own advantage. Factions of the minority, however, were easy to handle; the majority could simply outvote them. Factions of the majority were harder to handle. If the majority united around some policy issue, such as the redistribution of wealth, they could oppress the minority, violating the latter's basic rights.[18]

As Madison would later explain:

Ambition must be made to counteract ambition. . . . If men were angels, no government would be necessary. If angels were to govern men, neither external nor internal controls would be necessary. In framing a government which is to be administered by men over men, the great difficulty lies in this: you must first enable the government to control the governed; and then in the next place oblige it to control itself.[19]

To prevent the possibility of a tyranny of the majority, Madison proposed the following:

1. Place as much of the government as possible beyond the direct control of the majority.
2. Separate the powers of different institutions.
3. Construct a system of checks and balances.

The American System of Checks and Balances

Limiting Majority Control Madison believed that to thwart tyranny by the majority, it was essential to keep most of the government beyond their power. His plan placed only one element of government, the House of Representatives, within direct control of the votes of the majority. In contrast, state legislatures were to elect senators, and special electors were to select the president; in other words, government officials would be elected by a small minority, not by the people themselves. The president was to nominate judges (see Figure 2.3). Even if the majority seized control of the House of Representatives, they still could not enact policies without the agreement of the Senate and the president. To further insulate governmental officials from public opinion, the Constitution gave judges lifetime tenure and senators terms of six years, with only one-third elected every

FIGURE 2.3

The Constitution and the Electoral Process: The Original Plan

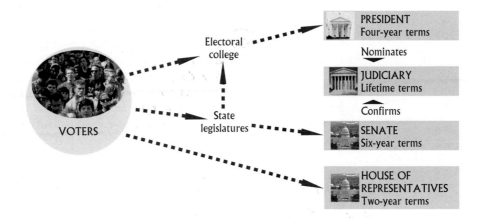

Under Madison's plan, which was incorporated in the Constitution, voters' electoral influence was limited. Voters directly elected only the House of Representatives. Senators and presidents were indirectly elected, and the president nominated judges. Over the years, Madison's original model has been substantially democratized. The Seventeenth Amendment (1913) established direct election of senators by popular majorities. Today, the electoral college has become largely a rubber stamp, voting the way the popular majority in each state votes.

two years, compared with the two-year election intervals of all members of the House of Representatives.

Separating Powers   The Madisonian scheme also provided for a **separation of powers**. Each of the three branches of government—executive (the president), legislative (Congress), and judicial (the courts)—would be relatively independent of one another so that no single branch could control the others. The Founders gave the president, Congress, and the courts independent elements of power. The Constitution does not divide power absolutely, however; rather, it *shares* it among the three institutions.

Creating Checks and Balances   Because powers were not completely separate, each branch required the consent of the others for many of its actions. This created a system of **checks and balances** that reflected Madison's goal of setting power against power to constrain government actions. He reasoned that if a faction seized one institution, it still could not damage the whole system. The system of checks and balances was an elaborate and delicate creation. The president checks Congress by holding veto power; Congress holds the purse strings of government and must approve presidential appointments.

The courts also figured into the system of checks and balances. Presidents could nominate judges, but their confirmation by the Senate was required. The Supreme Court itself, in *Marbury v. Madison* (1803), asserted its power to check the other branches through judicial review: the right to hold actions of the other two branches unconstitutional. This right, which is not specifically outlined in the Constitution, considerably strengthened the Court's ability to restrain the other branches of government. For a summary of separation of powers and the checks and balances system, see Figure 2.4.

separation of powers
A feature of the Constitution that requires each of the three branches of government—executive, legislative, and judicial—to be relatively independent of the others so that one cannot control the others. Power is shared among these three institutions.

checks and balances
Features of the Constitution that limit government's power by requiring that power be balanced among the different governmental institutions. These institutions continually constrain one another's activities.

FIGURE 2.4

Separation of Powers and Checks and Balances in the Constitution

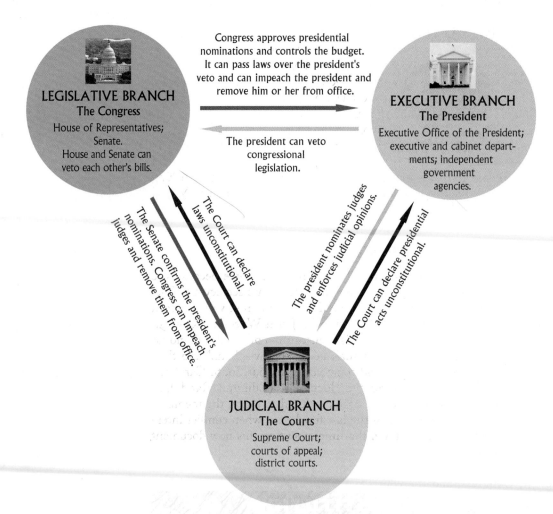

LEGISLATIVE BRANCH
The Congress
House of Representatives;
Senate.
House and Senate can
veto each other's bills.

Congress approves presidential
nominations and controls the budget.
It can pass laws over the president's
veto and can impeach the president and
remove him or her from office.

EXECUTIVE BRANCH
The President
Executive Office of the President;
executive and cabinet departments; independent
government
agencies.

The president can veto
congressional
legislation.

The Court can declare
laws unconstitutional.

The Senate confirms the president's
nominations. Congress can impeach
judges and remove them from office.

The president nominates judges
and enforces judicial opinions.

The Court can declare presidential
acts unconstitutional.

JUDICIAL BRANCH
The Courts
Supreme Court;
courts of appeal;
district courts.

The doctrine of separation of powers allows the three institutions of government to check and balance one another. Judicial review—the power of courts to hold executive and congressional policies unconstitutional—was not explicit in the Constitution but was asserted by the Supreme Court in *Marbury v. Madison*.

? Why It Matters
Checks and Balances
People often complain about gridlock in government, but that is a product of checks and balances. Making it difficult for either a minority or a majority to dominate easily also makes it difficult to pass legislation over which there is disagreement.

Establishing a Federal System   As we will discuss in detail in Chapter 3, the Founders also established a federal system of government that divided the power of government between a national government and the individual states. Most government activity at the time occurred in the states. The Framers of the Constitution anticipated that this would be an additional check on the national government.

THE CONSTITUTIONAL REPUBLIC

When asked what kind of government the delegates had produced, Benjamin Franklin is said to have replied, "A republic . . . if you can keep it." Because the Founders did not wish to have the people directly make all decisions (as in a town meeting where everyone has one vote), and because even then the country was far too large for such a proposal to be feasible, they did not choose to create a direct democracy. Their solution was to establish a **republic**: a system based on the consent of the governed in which representatives of the public exercise power. This deliberative democracy required and encouraged reflection and refinement of the public's views through an elaborate decision-making process.

> **republic**
> A form of government in which the people select representatives to govern them and make laws.

The system of checks and balances and separation of powers favors the status quo. People who desire change must usually have a sizable majority, not just a simple majority of 51 percent. Those opposed to change need only win at one point in the policymaking process—say in obtaining a presidential veto—whereas those who favor change must win *every* battle along the way. Change usually comes slowly, if at all. As a result, the Madisonian system encourages moderation and compromise and slows change. It is difficult for either a minority or a majority to tyrannize, and both property rights and personal freedoms (with only occasional lapses) have survived.

Franklin was correct that such a system is not easy to maintain. It requires careful nurturing and balancing of diverse interests. Some critics argue that the policymaking process lacks efficiency, preventing effective responses to pressing matters. We will examine this issue closely throughout *Government in America*.

THE END OF THE BEGINNING

On the 109th day of the meetings, in stifling heat made worse because the windows of the Pennsylvania statehouse were closed to ensure secrecy, the final version of the Constitution was read aloud. Then Dr. Franklin rose with a speech he had written but was so enfeebled that he had to ask James Wilson to deliver it. Franklin noted, "There are several parts of this Constitution of which I do not at present approve, but I am not sure that I shall never approve them," and then asked for a vote. Ten states voted yes, and none voted no, but South Carolina's delegates were divided. After signing the document (Edmund Randolph, Elbridge Gerry, and George Mason of Virginia refused to sign), the members adjourned to a tavern. The experience of the last few hours, when conflict intermingled with consensus, reminded them that implementing this new document would be no small feat.

RATIFYING THE CONSTITUTION

The Constitution did not go into effect once the Constitutional Convention in Philadelphia was over. It had to be ratified by the states. Our awe of the Founders sometimes blinds us to the bitter politics of the day. There is no way of determining the public's feelings about the new document, but as John Marshall (who later became chief justice) suggested, "It is scarcely to be doubted that *in some of the adopting states, a majority of the people were in opposition*" (emphasis added).[20] The Constitution itself required that only 9 of the 13 states approve the document before it could be implemented, ignoring the requirement that the Articles of Confederation be amended only by unanimous consent.

> **Federalists**
> Supporters of the U.S. Constitution at the time the states were contemplating its adoption.

FEDERALISTS AND ANTI-FEDERALISTS

Throughout the states, a fierce battle erupted between the **Federalists**, who supported the Constitution, and the **Anti-Federalists**, who opposed it. Newspapers were filled with letters and articles, many written under pseudonyms, praising or condemning the document. In praise of the Constitution, three men—James Madison, Alexander Hamilton, and John Jay—wrote a series of articles under the name

> **Anti-Federalists**
> Opponents of the American Constitution at the time when the states were contemplating its adoption.

George Washington presides over the signing of the Constitution. "The business being closed," he wrote, "the members adjourned to the City Tavern, dined together and took cordial leave of each other."

Federalist Papers

A collection of 85 articles written by Alexander Hamilton, John Jay, and James Madison under the name "Publius" to defend the Constitution in detail.

Publius. These articles, known as the **Federalist Papers**, are second only to the Constitution itself in reflecting the thinking of the Framers.

Beginning on October 27, 1787, barely a month after the Convention ended, the *Federalist Papers* began to appear in New York newspapers as part of the ratification debate in New York. Eighty-five were eventually published. They not only defended the Constitution detail by detail but also represented an important statement of political philosophy. (The essays influenced few of the New York delegates, however, who voted to ratify the Constitution only after New York City threatened to secede from the state if they did not.)

Far from being unpatriotic or un-American, the Anti-Federalists sincerely believed that the new government was an enemy of freedom, the very freedom they had just fought a war to ensure. Adopting names like Aggrippa, Cornelius, and Monteczuma, the Anti-Federalists launched bitter, biting, even brilliant attacks on the Philadelphia document. They frankly questioned the motives of the Constitution writers.

One objection was central to the Anti-Federalists' attacks: The new Constitution was a class-based document, intended to ensure that a particular economic elite controlled the public policies of the national government. The following quotations are from Anti-Federalist critics of the Constitution:

> Thus, I conceive, a foundation is laid for throwing the whole power of the federal government into the hands of those who are in the mercantile interest; and for the landed, which is the great interest of this country to lie unrepresented, forlorn and without hope.
>
> —"Cornelius"

> These lawyers, men of learning, and moneyed men . . . expect to get into Congress themselves . . . so they can get all the power and all the money into their own hands.[21]
>
> —Amos Singletary of Massachusetts

Remember that these charges of conspiracy and elitism were being hurled at the likes of Washington, Madison, Franklin, and Hamilton.

The Anti-Federalists had other fears. Not only would the new government be run by a few, but it would also erode fundamental liberties. In the South Carolina ratifying convention, James Lincoln declared that he "would be glad to know why, in this Constitution, there is a total silence with regard to the liberty of the press. Was it forgotten? Impossible! Then it must have been purposely omitted; and with what design, good or bad, I leave the world to judge." You can compare the views of the Federalists and Anti-Federalists in Table 2.4.

These arguments about the lack of protections of individual rights were persuasive. To allay fears that the Constitution would restrict personal freedoms, the Federalists promised to add amendments to the document specifically protecting individual liberties. They kept their word; James Madison introduced 12 constitutional amendments during the First Congress in 1789. Ten were ratified by the states and took effect in 1791. These first 10 amendments to the Constitution, which restrain the national government from limiting personal freedoms, have come to be known as the **Bill of Rights** (see Table 2.5). Another of Madison's original 12 amendments, one dealing with congressional salaries, was ratified 201 years later as the Twenty-seventh Amendment (see the Appendix in this book).

As an explanation and defense of the Constitution, the *Federalist Papers* were often discussed at dinner parties and debated in public places. Today, the U.S. has higher literacy rates than in the 1780s. Do you think that a similar set of documents, so rich in political philosophy, would be so widely read in modern America?

Bill of Rights

The first 10 amendments to the **U.S. Constitution,** drafted in response to some of the **Anti-Federalist** concerns. These amendments define such basic liberties as freedom of religion, speech, and press and guarantee defendants' rights.

Opponents also feared that the Constitution would weaken the power of the states (which it did). Patrick Henry railed against strengthening the federal government at the expense of the states. "We are come hither," he told his fellow delegates to the Virginia ratifying convention, "to preserve the poor commonwealth of Virginia."[22] Many state political leaders feared that the Constitution would diminish their own power as well.

TABLE 2.4

Federalists and Anti-Federalists Compared

ANTI-FEDERALISTS	FEDERALISTS
Backgrounds	
Small farmers, shopkeepers, laborers	Large landowners, wealthy merchants, professionals
Government Preferred	
Strong state government	Weaker state governments
Weak national government	Strong national government
Direct election of officials	Indirect election of officials
Shorter terms	Longer terms
Rule by the common man	Government by the elite
Strengthened protections for individual liberties	Expected few violations of individual liberties

TABLE 2.5

The Bill of Rights (Arranged by Function)

Protection of Free Expression Amendment 1:	Freedom of speech, press, and assembly Freedom to petition government
Protection of Personal Beliefs Amendment 1:	No government establishment of religion Freedom to exercise religion
Protection of Privacy Amendment 3: Amendment 4:	No forced quartering of troops in homes during peacetime No unreasonable searches and seizures
Protection of Defendants' Rights Amendment 5: Amendment 6: Amendment 7: Amendment 8:	Grand jury indictment required for prosecution of serious crime No second prosecution for the same offense No compulsion to testify against oneself No loss of life, liberty, or property without due process of law Right to a speedy and public trial by a local, impartial jury Right to be informed of charges against oneself Right to legal counsel Right to compel the attendance of favorable witnesses Right to cross-examine witnesses Right to jury trial in civil suit where the value of controversy exceeds $20 No excessive bail or fines No cruel and unusual punishments
Protection of Other Rights Amendment 2: Amendment 5: Amendment 9: Amendment 10:	Right to bear arms No taking of private property for public use without just compensation Unlisted rights are not necessarily denied Powers not delegated to the national government or denied to the states are reserved for the states or the people

You Are James Madison

Finally, not everyone wanted the economy placed on a more sound foundation. Creditors opposed the issuance of paper money because it would produce inflation and make the money they received as payment on their loans decline in value. Debtors favored paper money, however. Their debts (such as the mortgages on their farms) would remain constant, but if money became more plentiful, it would be easier for them to pay off their debts.

RATIFICATION

Federalists may not have had the support of the majority, but they made up for it in shrewd politicking. They knew that many members of the legislatures of some states were skeptical of the Constitution and that state legislatures were populated with political leaders who would lose power under the Constitution. Thus, the Federalists specified that the Constitution be ratified by special conventions in each of the states—not by state legislatures.

Delaware was the first to approve, on December 7, 1787. Only six months passed before New Hampshire's approval (the ninth) made the Constitution official. Virginia and New York then voted to join the new union. Two states were holdouts: North Carolina and Rhode Island made the promise of the Bill of Rights their price for joining the other states.

With the Constitution ratified, it was time to select officeholders. The Framers of the Constitution assumed that George Washington would be elected the first president of the new government—even giving him the Convention's papers for safekeeping—and they were right. The general was the unanimous choice of the electoral college for president. He took office on April 30, 1789, in New York City, the first national capital. New Englander John Adams became "His Superfluous Excellence," as Franklin called the vice president.

CONSTITUTIONAL CHANGE

"The Constitution," said Jefferson, "belongs to the living and not to the dead." The U.S. Constitution is frequently—and rightly—referred to as a living document. It is constantly being tested and altered.

Generally, constitutional changes are made either by formal amendments or by a number of informal processes. Formal amendments change the letter of the Constitution. There is also an unwritten body of tradition, practice, and procedure that, when altered, may change the spirit of the Constitution. In fact, not all nations, even those such as Britain that we call democratic, have written constitutions.

THE FORMAL AMENDING PROCESS

The most explicit means of changing the Constitution is through the formal process of amendment. Article V of the Constitution outlines procedures for formal amendment. There are two stages to the amendment process—proposal and ratification—and each stage has two possible avenues (see Figure 2.5). An amendment may be proposed either by a two-thirds vote in each house of Congress or by a

SIMULATION

You Are Proposing a Constitutional Amendment

FIGURE 2.5

How the Constitution Can Be Amended

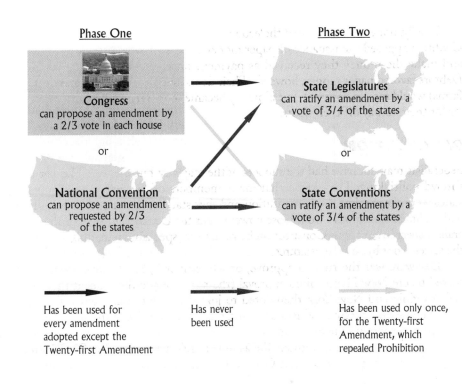

The Constitution sets up two alternative routes for proposing amendments and two for ratifying them. One of the four combinations has been used in every case but one.

Phase One

Congress
can propose an amendment by a 2/3 vote in each house

or

National Convention
can propose an amendment requested by 2/3 of the states

Phase Two

State Legislatures
can ratify an amendment by a vote of 3/4 of the states

or

State Conventions
can ratify an amendment by a vote of 3/4 of the states

Has been used for every amendment adopted except the Twenty-first Amendment

Has never been used

Has been used only once, for the Twenty-first Amendment, which repealed Prohibition

AMERICA IN PERSPECTIVE

The Unusual Rigidity of **the U.S. Constitution**

In the *Federalist #43*, James Madison wrote that the Founders designed a process for adopting amendments to the U.S. Constitution that "guards equally against that extreme facility, which would render the Constitution too mutable; and that extreme difficulty, which might perpetuate its discovered faults." In other words, Madison felt that the American Constitution was rigid enough to provide stability in government, yet also flexible enough to allow adaptation over time.

Most other democracies have a procedure for adopting constitutional amendments, but few of the world's established democracies have made it as difficult as it is in the United States. In *Patterns of Democracy*, Arend Lijphart developed a measure of constitutional rigidity based on the percentage vote required at the most demanding stage of the amending process. In the U.S., this would be 75 percent because at least three-quarters of the state legislatures or of conventions in three-quarters of the states must approve constitutional amendments. As you can see in the table below, only 4 of the other 22 established democracies require a majority of greater than two-thirds to amend their national constitution. In this regard, then, the U.S. Constitution is unusually rigid.

Requirements for Constitutional Amendments in Developed Democracies

SIMPLE MAJORITY (50% PLUS 1)	BETWEEN A SIMPLE MAJORITY AND TWO-THIRDS	TWO-THIRDS MAJORITY	SUPERMAJORITY (GREATER THAN TWO-THIRDS)
Great Britain	Denmark	Austria	Australia
Iceland	France	Belgium	Canada
Israel	Greece	Finland	Japan
New Zealand	Ireland	Germany	Switzerland
	Italy	Netherlands	U.S.
	Sweden	Norway	
		Portugal	
		Spain	

Source: Arend Lijphart, *Patterns of Democracy* (New Haven, CT: Yale University Press, 1999), p 220.

QUESTIONS FOR DISCUSSION

▶ What are the advantages of having a constitution that is very difficult to change, as in the United States?

▶ Most established democracies have decided to make their constitutions more flexible than the American Constitution. What are the advantages of greater flexibility in a constitution? Do you think these advantages outweigh the advantages of a more rigid constitution? Why or why not?

The History of Constitutional Amendments

national convention called by Congress at the request of two-thirds of the state legislatures. An amendment may be ratified either by the legislatures of three-fourths of the states or by special state conventions called in three-fourths of the states. The president has no formal role in amending the Constitution, although the chief executive may influence the success of proposed amendments. In general, it is difficult to formally amend the Constitution (see "America in Perspective: The Unusual Rigidity of the U.S. Constitution").

All but one of the successful amendments to the Constitution have been proposed by Congress and ratified by the state legislatures. The exception was the Twenty-first Amendment, which repealed the short-lived Eighteenth Amendment—the prohibition amendment that outlawed the sale and consumption of alcohol. The amendment was ratified by special state conventions rather than by state legislatures. Because proponents of repeal doubted that they could win in conservative legislatures, they persuaded Congress to require that state conventions be called.

Unquestionably, formal amendments have made the Constitution more egalitarian and democratic. Amendments that emphasize equality and increase the ability of a popular majority to affect government now provide a balance to the emphasis on economic issues in the original document. The Bill of Rights, which Chapter 4 will discuss in detail, head the amendments (see Table 2.5). Later amendments, including the Thirteenth Amendment abolishing slavery, forbid various political and social inequalities based on race, gender, and age (Chapter 5 discusses these amendments). Other amendments, discussed later in this chapter, have democratized the political system, making it easier for voters to influence the government. Only one existing amendment specifically addresses the economy—the Sixteenth, or "income tax," Amendment. Overall, it is clear that the most important effect of these constitutional amendments has been to expand liberty and equality in the United States.

Some amendments have been proposed but not ratified. The best known of these in recent years is the **Equal Rights Amendment (ERA)**. First introduced in Congress in 1923 by the nephew of suffragist Susan B. Anthony, the ERA had to wait 49 years—until 1972—before Congress passed it and sent it to the states for ratification. The ERA stated simply, "Equality of rights under the law shall not be denied or abridged by the United States or by any State on account of sex."

Nevertheless, the ERA was not ratified. It failed, in part, because of the system of checks and balances. Three-fourths of the states, not simply a national majority, had to approve the ERA for it to become part of the Constitution. Many conservative Southern states opposed it, thus exercising their veto power despite approval by a majority of Americans.

Of course, supporters of the ERA can propose it again, and proponents of other constitutional amendments have been active in recent years. You can consider the issue of frequently amending the Constitution in "You Are the Policymaker: How Frequently Should We Amend the Constitution?"

Amending the Constitution to give women the right to vote was an important step in the women's rights movement.

Equal Rights Amendment
A constitutional amendment passed by Congress in 1972 stating that "equality of rights under the law shall not be denied or abridged by the United States or by any state on account of sex." The amendment failed to acquire the necessary support from three-fourths of the state legislatures.

THE INFORMAL PROCESS OF CONSTITUTIONAL CHANGE

Think for a moment about all the changes in American government that have taken place without altering a word or a letter of the written document. In fact, there is not a word in the Constitution that would lead us to suspect any of the following developments:

- The United States has the world's oldest two-party system, wherein almost every member of Congress and every president since Washington has declared, "I am a Democrat (or Republican, or Federalist, or Whig, or whatever)."
- Abortions through the second trimester of pregnancy (when the fetus cannot live outside the mother's womb) are legal in the United States.
- Members of the electoral college consider themselves honor bound (and in some places even legally bound) to follow the preference of their state's electorate.

- Proceedings of both the Senate and the House are on television, and television influences our political agenda and guides our assessments of candidates and issues.
- Government now taxes and spends about one-third of our gross domestic product, an amount the Convention delegates might have found gargantuan.

None of these things is "unconstitutional." The parties emerged, first technology and then the law permitted abortions, television came to prominence in American life—all without having to tinker with the Founders' handiwork. These developments could occur because the Constitution changes *informally* as well as formally. There are several ways in which the Constitution changes informally: through judicial interpretation, through political practice, and as a result of changes in technology and changes in the demands on policymakers.

Judicial Interpretation   Disputes often arise about the meaning of the Constitution. If it is the "supreme law of the land," then someone has to decide how to interpret the Constitution when disputes arise. In 1803, in the famous case of *Marbury v. Madison*, the Supreme Court decided it would be the one to resolve differences of opinion (Chapter 16 discusses this case in detail). It claimed for itself the power of **judicial review**. Implied but never explicitly stated in the Constitution,[23] this power gives courts the right to decide whether the actions of the legislative and executive branches of state and national governments are in accord with the Constitution.

Judicial interpretation can profoundly affect how the Constitution is understood because the Constitution usually means what the Supreme Court says it

---

Marbury v. Madison

The 1803 case in which Chief Justice John Marshall and his associates first asserted the right of the **Supreme Court** to determine the meaning of the **U.S. Constitution**. The decision established the Court's power of judicial review over acts of Congress, in this case the Judiciary Act of 1789.

---

judicial review

The power of the courts to determine whether acts of Congress and, by implication, the executive are in accord with the **U.S. Constitution**. Judicial review was established by John Marshall and his associates in *Marbury v. Madison.*

YOU ARE THE POLICYMAKER

How Frequently Should We Amend the Constitution?

Since the ratification of the Bill of Rights in 1791, there have been only 17 amendments to the Constitution—an average of one amendment every 13 years. It is now common, however, for political activists—and even political party platforms—to call for amendments. Some recent examples include prohibiting gay marriage, the burning of the American flag, and abortion; permitting prayer in public schools; requiring a balanced national budget; limiting the length of congressional terms; guaranteeing women's rights (the ERA); and protecting victims' rights.

Conservatives have been in the forefront of most recent calls for amendments (the ERA being an exception); many of the proposals for constitutional change are designed to overcome liberal Supreme Court decisions. Liberals, quite naturally, have opposed these amendments. There is a larger question here than just the particular changes that advocates of amending the Constitution support, however. The big question is, how frequently should we change the fundamental law of the land?

Those who support amending the Constitution argue that it should reflect the will of the people. If the overwhelming majority of the public wants to prohibit burning the American flag, for example, why shouldn't the Constitution reflect its preference? There is little

possibility that a minority or even a narrow majority will be able to impose its will on the people, they argue, because the Constitution requires an extraordinary majority to ratify an amendment. So why should we be reluctant to test the waters of change?

Opponents of changing the Constitution frequently have their own arguments. It is ironic, they say, that conservatives, who typically wish to preserve the status quo, should be in the forefront of fundamental change. They argue that the Constitution has served the United States very well for more than two centuries with few changes. Why should we risk altering the fundamentals of the political system? And if we do, will we be setting a dangerous precedent that will encourage yet more change in the future? Will such changes undermine the very nature of a constitution that is designed to set the basic rules of the game and be above the political fray?

What do *you* think? Are the arguments simply a reflection of ideologies? Should the Constitution reflect the current sentiment of the public and be changed whenever that opinion changes? Or should we show more caution in amending the Constitution no matter how we feel about a specific amendment?

means. For example, in 1896 the Supreme Court decided that the Constitution allowed racial discrimination despite the presence of the Fourteenth Amendment. Fifty-eight years later, it overruled itself and concluded that segregation by law violated the Constitution. In 1973, the Supreme Court decided that the Constitution protected a woman's right to an abortion during the first two trimesters of pregnancy when the fetus is not viable outside the womb—an issue the Founders never imagined. (We discuss these cases in Chapters 4 and 5.)

Changing Political Practice   Current political practices also change the Constitution—stretching it, shaping it, and giving it new meaning. Probably no changes are more important to American politics than those related to parties and presidential elections.

Political parties as we know them did not exist when the Constitution was written. In fact, its authors would have disliked the idea of parties, which encourage factions. Regardless, by 1800 a party system had developed, and it plays a key role in making policy today. American government would be radically different if there were no political parties, even though the Constitution is silent about them.

Changing political practice has also altered the role of the electoral college, which has now been reduced to a clerical one in selecting the president. The writers of the Constitution, eager to avoid giving too much power to the uneducated majority, intended that there be no popular vote for the president; instead, state legislatures or the voters (depending on the state) would select wise electors who would then choose a "distinguished character of continental reputation" (as the *Federalist Papers* put it) to be president. These electors formed the electoral college. Each state would have the same number of electors to vote for the president as it had senators and representatives in Congress.

In 1796, the first election in which George Washington was not a candidate, electors scattered their votes among 13 candidates. By the election of 1800, domestic and foreign policy issues had divided the country into two political parties. To avoid dissipating their support, the parties required electors to pledge in advance to vote for the candidate who won their state's popular vote, leaving electors with a largely clerical function.

Although electors are now rubber stamps for the popular vote, nothing in the Constitution prohibits an elector from voting for any candidate. Every so often, electors have decided to cast votes for their own favorites; some state laws require electors to vote for the candidate chosen by a plurality of their state's citizens, but such laws have never been enforced. The idea that the electoral college would exercise wisdom independent of the majority of people is now a constitutional anachronism, changed not by formal amendment but by political practice.

Technology   Technology has also greatly changed the Constitution. The media have always played an important role in politics—questioning governmental policies, supporting candidates, and helping shape citizens' opinions. Modern technology, however, has spurred the development of a *mass* media that can rapidly reach huge audiences, something unimaginable in the eighteenth century. The bureaucracy has grown in importance with the development of computers, which create new potential for bureaucrats to serve the public (such as writing over 40 million Social Security checks each month)—and, at times, create mischief. Electronic communications and the development of atomic weapons have given the president's role as commander in chief added significance, increasing the power of the president in the constitutional system. More recently, the Internet has fundamentally changed the way we select elected officials.

Increasing Demands on Policymakers   The significance of the presidency has also grown as a result of increased demands for new policies. The evolution of the United States in the realm of international affairs—from an insignificant country that kept to itself to a superpower with an extraordinary range of international obligations—has concentrated additional power in the hands of the chief executive, whom the Constitutions designates to take the lead in foreign affairs. Similarly, the increased demands of domestic policy have positioned the president in a more prominent role in preparing the federal budget and a legislative program.

All wars increase presidential power because they place additional demands on the commander in chief. Congress of necessity delegates to the president the authority to prosecute a war, which involves a multitude of decisions, ranging from military strategy to logistics. The war on terrorism has taken delegation of authority one step further, however. Because the enemy may not be a country but rather an amorphous group of people who employ the weapons of terrorism as political instruments, it is more difficult for Congress to specify the president's authority. Thus, a few days following the terrorist attacks of September 11, 2001, Congress passed a broad resolution authorizing the president to use force against those nations, organizations, or persons that he alone determined were involved in the attacks. Thus, Congress asked the president to determine the identity of the enemy. This resolution served as the legal basis for the war in Afghanistan in 2002.

In October 2002, Congress passed another resolution authorizing the president to use "all means necessary and appropriate," which included the use of military force, to defend the United States against Iraq and enforce UN resolutions regarding Iraq. Congress delegated to the president the right to determine if and when the United States would go to war. This broad grant of power provided the authority to invade Iraq in March 2003. The president also interpreted this resolution as authorizing him to order the National Security Agency to secretly monitor the international telephone calls and e-mail messages of people inside the United States who might be communicating with terrorists abroad.

In addition to fighting terrorists abroad, securing the homeland also became a highly salient issue. Only six weeks after the terrorist attacks, Congress passed the USA Patriot Act. This law gave the executive branch broad new powers for the wiretapping, surveillance, and investigation of terrorism suspects. The act gave the federal government the power to examine a suspect's records held by third parties such as doctors, libraries, bookstores, universities, and Internet service providers. It also allowed searches of private property without probable cause and without prior notice to the owner, limiting a person's opportunities to challenge a search.

Thus, the war on terrorism has resulted in substantially increased demands on the president and a notable increase in authority to meet those demands. Some also see it as resulting in the loosening of protections of personal privacy. Whether Congress or the courts will reassert their own authority is an open question. In the meantime, the war on terrorism has altered the balance of power in our constitutional system.

THE IMPORTANCE OF FLEXIBILITY

The Constitution, even with all 27 amendments, is a short document containing fewer than 8,000 words. It does not prescribe in detail the structure and functioning of the national government. Regarding the judiciary, the Constitution simply tells Congress to create a court system as it sees fit. The Supreme Court is the only court required by the Constitution, and even here the Constitution leaves the number of justices and their qualifications up to Congress. Similarly, many of the governing units we have today—such as the executive departments, the various offices in the White House, the independent regulatory commissions, and the committees of Congress, to name only a few examples—are not mentioned at all in the Constitution.

It is easy to see that the document the Framers produced over 200 years ago was not meant to be static, written in stone. Instead, the Constitution's authors created a

MyState | The Length of State Constitutions

In contrast to the U.S. Constitution, state constitutions tend to be long and very detailed, with numerous amendments. They average about four times the length of the U.S. Constitution. In addition, the average state constitution has been amended approximately 100 times. Only 6 of the 50 state constitutions have fewer than the 27 amendments to the U.S. Constitution. Greater length usually means greater specificity of detail about how a government must work and what it can do, which in turn reduces its flexibility.

The adjacent map classifies the constitutions of the 50 states according to their length in terms of number of words. The word count includes amendments to each constitution.

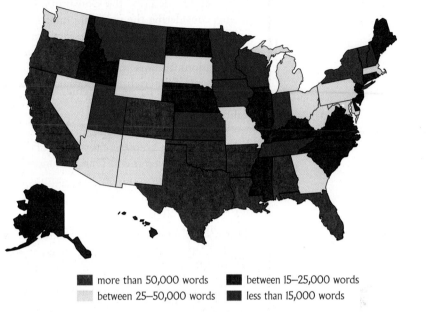

more than 50,000 words   between 15–25,000 words

between 25–50,000 words   less than 15,000 words

Source: Adapted from Harold W. Stanley and Richard G. Niami, *Vital Statistics on American Politics, 2007–2008* (Washington, DC: CQ Press, 2008), pp. 308-310.

QUESTIONS FOR DISCUSSION

▷ How does your state rank in terms of the length of its constitution?

▷ Do you think it would best for your state if it were longer and more specific, shorter and less specific, or is its current length about right? Why?

flexible system of government, one that could adapt to the needs of the times without sacrificing personal freedom. The Framers allowed future generations to determine their own needs. (The constitutions of the various states tend to be much longer and much more detailed, as you can see in "My State: The Length of State Constitutions.") As muscle grows on the constitutional skeleton, it inevitably gives new shape and purpose to the government. This flexibility has helped ensure the Constitution's—and the nation's—survival. Although the United States is young compared to other Western nations, it has the oldest functioning Constitution. France, which experienced a revolution in 1789, the same year the Constitution took effect, has had 12 constitutions over the past two centuries. Despite the great diversity of the American population, the enormous size of the country, and the extraordinary changes that have taken place over the nation's history, the U.S. Constitution is still going strong.

UNDERSTANDING THE CONSTITUTION

The Constitution sets the broad rules of the game of politics in America, allowing certain types of competition among certain players. *These rules are never neutral,* however. Instead, they give some participants and some policy options advantages over others in the policymaking process.

THE CONSTITUTION AND DEMOCRACY

Comparing Constitutions

Although the United States is often said to be one of the most democratic societies in the world, few describe the Constitution as democratic. This paradox is hardly surprising, considering the political philosophies of the men who wrote it. Members of eighteenth-century upper-class society generally despised democratic government. If democracy was a way of permitting the majority's preference to become policy, the Constitution's authors wanted no part of it. The American government was to be a government of the "rich, well-born, and able," as Hamilton said, a government where John Jay's wish that "the people who own the country ought to govern it" would be a reality. Few people today would consider these thoughts democratic.

The Constitution did not, however, create a monarchy or a feudal aristocracy. It created a republic, a representative form of democracy modeled after the Lockean tradition of limited government. Thus, the undemocratic—even antidemocratic—Constitution established a government that permitted substantial movement toward democracy.

One of the central themes of American history is the gradual democratization of the Constitution. What began as a document characterized by numerous restrictions on direct voter participation has slowly become much more democratic. Today, few people share the Founders' fear of democracy. The expansion of voting rights has moved the American political system away from the elitist model of democracy and toward the pluralist model.

The Constitution itself offered no guidelines on voter eligibility, leaving it to each state to decide. As a result, only a small percentage of adults could vote; states excluded women and slaves entirely. Of the 17 constitutional amendments passed since the Bill of Rights, five have focused on the expansion of the electorate. The Fifteenth Amendment (1870) prohibited discrimination on the basis of race in determining voter eligibility (although it took the Voting Rights Act of 1965, discussed in Chapter 5, to make the amendment effective). The Nineteenth Amendment (1920) gave women the right to vote (although some states had already done so). The Twenty-third Amendment (1961) accorded the residents of Washington, D.C., the right to vote in presidential elections. Three years later, the Twenty-fourth Amendment prohibited poll taxes (which discriminated against the poor). Finally, the Twenty-sixth Amendment (1971) lowered the voter eligibility age to 18 (see "Young People and Politics: Lowering the Voting Age").

Not only are more people eligible to vote, but voters now have more officials to elect. The Seventeenth Amendment (1913) provided for direct election of senators. The development of political parties has fundamentally altered presidential elections. By placing the same candidate on the ballot in all the states and requiring members of the electoral college to support the candidate who receives the most votes, parties have increased the probability that the candidate for whom most Americans vote will also receive a majority of the electoral college vote. (For more on the electoral college, see Chapter 10.) Nevertheless, it is possible for the candidate who receives the most popular votes to lose the election, as occurred in 1824, 1876, 1888, and 2000.

Mike Luckovich
Times-Picayune

Takes a licking and keeps on ticking.

200 yrs.

We the People

Philadelphia

MIKE LUCKOVICH
Courtesy Times-Picayune (New Orleans)

YOUNG PEOPLE AND POLITICS

Lowering **the Voting Age**

The 1960s was a tumultuous era, and massive protests by students and other young people regarding the war in Vietnam were common in the last half of the decade. Many young people felt that protesting was the best they could do because the voting age was 21 in most states—even though 18-year-olds were old enough to marry, work, and pay taxes as others adults did. In the Vietnam War, the average age of U.S. soldiers was 19, and young citizens often asserted, "If we're old enough to fight, we're old enough to vote." (Imagine the response today if soldiers fighting in Afghanistan and Iraq could not vote.)

Majorities in both houses of Congress agreed that the voting age was unfair and passed the Voting Rights Act of 1970, lowering the voting age to 18 in both federal and state elections. The Supreme Court, however, held that Congress had exceeded its authority and only could set voting ages in national elections.

In 1971, Senator Jennings Randolph, a Democrat from West Virginia, proposed a constitutional amendment to lower the voting age to 18 years: "The right of citizens of the United States, who are eighteen years of age or older, to vote shall not be denied or abridged by the United States or by any State on account of age." Randolph was a warrior for peace and had great faith in young people, arguing, "They possess a great social con-science, are perplexed by the injustices in the world, and are anxious to rectify those ills."

Randolph had introduced legislation lowering the voting age 11 times, beginning in 1942. This time, aided by appreciation of the sacrifices of young soldiers in Vietnam, he was successful. The amendment passed the Senate unanimously, and it passed the House of Representatives by a vote of 400 to 19. It was then sent to the states to be ratified. No state wanted to maintain two sets of voter registration books and go to the expense of running separate election systems for federal elections and for all other elections. Thus, the states were receptive to the proposed amendment, and in just 100 days three-fourths of the states ratified it.

On July 5, the Twenty-sixth Amendment was formally adopted into the Constitution, adding 11 million potential voters to the electorate. Half of these young voters cast their ballots in the 1972 presidential election.

QUESTIONS FOR DISCUSSION

➤ There are proposals in some states to lower the voting age below 18. What is the appropriate age for voting?

➤ Would it be appropriate for different states to have different ages for voting?

Technology has also diminished the separation of the people from those who exercise power. Officeholders communicate directly with the public through television, radio, and targeted mailings. Air travel makes it easy for members of Congress to commute regularly between Washington and their districts. Similarly, public opinion polls, the telephone, e-mail, and the Internet enable officials to stay apprised of citizens' opinions on important issues. Even though the American population has grown from fewer than 4 million to more than 300 million people since the first census was taken in 1790, the national government has never been closer to those it serves.

THE CONSTITUTION AND THE SCOPE OF GOVERNMENT

The Constitution created political institutions and the rules for politics and policymaking. Many of these rules limit government action. This limiting function is what the Bill of Rights and related provisions in the Constitution are all about. No matter how large the majority, for example, it is unconstitutional to establish a state-supported church.

The goal of most of these limitations is primarily to protect liberty and to open the system to a broad range of participants. The potential range of action for the government is actually quite wide. Thus, it is constitutionally permissible, although highly unlikely, for the national government either to abolish Social Security payments to the elderly or to take over ownership of the oil industry or the nation's airlines.

The appropriate scope of government, such as government support for the social welfare efforts of religious organizations, is one of the most important—and most difficult—constitutional issues. Here President George W. Bush visits a Washington, DC charity, SOME that feeds the needy and the homeless.

Yet the system of government created by the Constitution has profound implications for what the government does. On one hand, the system reinforces individualism at every turn. The separation of powers and the checks and balances established by the Constitution allow almost all groups some place in the political system where their demands for public policy can be heard. Because many institutions share power, groups can usually find at least one sympathetic ear in government. Even if the president opposes the policies a particular group favors, Congress, the courts, or some other institution can help the group achieve its policy goals. In the early days of the civil rights movement, for example, African Americans found Congress and the president unsympathetic, so they turned to the Supreme Court. Getting their interests on the political agenda would have been much more difficult if the Court had not had important constitutional power.

On the other hand, the Constitution encourages stalemate. By providing effective access for so many interests, the Founders created a system of policymaking in which it is difficult for the government to act. The separation of powers and the system of checks and balances promote the politics of bargaining, compromise, and playing one institution against another. The system of checks and balances implies that one institution is checking another. *Thwarting*, *blocking*, and *impeding* are synonyms for *checking*. But if I block you, and you block someone else, and that person blocks me, none of us is going to accomplish anything, and we have gridlock.

Some scholars suggest that so much checking was built into the American political system that effective government is almost impossible. The historian and political scientist James MacGregor Burns has argued,

> We have been too much entranced by the Madisonian model of government. . . . The system of checks and balances and interlocked gears of government . . . requires the consensus of many groups and leaders before the nation can act; . . . we underestimate the extent to which our system was designed for deadlock and inaction.[24]

If the president, Congress, and the courts all pull in different directions on policy, the result may be either no policy at all (gridlock) or an inadequate, makeshift policy. The outcome may be nondecisions when the country requires that difficult decisions be made. If government cannot respond effectively because its policymaking processes are too fragmented, then its performance will be inadequate. Perhaps the Madisonian model has reduced the ability of government to reach effective policy decisions. Certainly, radical departures from the status quo are atypical in American politics.

SUMMARY

The year 1787 was crucial in building the American system of government. The 55 men who met in Philadelphia created a policymaking system that responded to a complex policy agenda. Critical conflicts over equality led to key compromises in the New Jersey and Virginia Plans, the three-fifths compromise on slavery, and the decision to leave the issue of voting rights to the states. There was more consensus, however, about the economy. These merchants, lawyers, and large landowners believed that the American economy was in a shambles, and they intended to make the national government an economic stabilizer. The specificity of the powers assigned to Congress left no doubt that Congress was to forge national economic policy. The delegates knew, too, that the global posture of the fledgling nation was pitifully weak. A strong national government would be better able to ensure its own security and that of the nation.

Madison and his colleagues were less clear about the protection of individual rights. Because they believed that the limited government they had constructed would protect freedom, they said little about individual rights in the Constitution. However, the ratification struggle revealed that protection of personal freedoms was much on the public's mind. As a result, the Bill of Rights was proposed. These first 10 amendments to the Constitution, along with the Thirteenth and Fourteenth Amendments, provide Americans with protection from governmental restraints on individual freedoms.

It is important to remember that 1787 was not the only year of nation building. The nation's colonial and revolutionary heritage shaped the meetings in Philadelphia. Budding industrialism in a basically agrarian nation put economic issues on the Philadelphia agenda. What Madison was to call an "unequal division of property" made equality an issue, particularly after Shays' Rebellion. The greatest inequality of all, that between slavery and freedom, was so contentious an issue that the Founders simply avoided addressing it in the Constitution.

Nor did ratification of the Constitution end the nation-building process. Constitutional change—both formal and informal—continues to shape and alter the letter and the spirit of the Madisonian system.

Because that system includes separate institutions sharing power, it results in many checks and balances. Today, some Americans complain that this system has created a government too responsive to too many interests and too fragmented to act. Others praise the way it protects minority views. In Chapter 3, we will look at yet another way in which the Constitution divides governmental power: between the national and the state governments.

Chapter Test

Multiple Choice Questions

1. Gregory Lee Johnson won his case at the U.S. Supreme Court because of:
   a. His ability to speak well and his knowledge of law
   b. His ability to afford excellent lawyers
   c. The nature of the U.S. Constitution
   d. The nature of the U.S. legal system
   e. The nature of the U.S. Supreme Court

2. Which of the following is NOT true for a nation's constitution?
   a. It creates political institutions
   b. It represents an unwritten accumulation of tradition and precedents
   c. It provides guarantees to citizens
   d. It centralizes power
   e. It represents a nation's basic law

3. Which of the following was NOT one of the foundations of John Locke's philosophy that Thomas Jefferson was heavily influenced by?
   a. Sanctity of property rights
   b. Natural rights
   c. Consent of the governed
   d. Limited government
   e. He was influenced by all of the above

4. The so-called "force acts" passed by a few state legislatures after the Revolution...
   a. Abolished religious qualifications for holding office
   b. Forced creditors to accept almost worthless currency from debtors
   c. Redistributed material wealth and property
   d. Overruled court decisions and criticized judges
   e. Allowed states to print tons of paper money

5. According to James Madison, which of the following is the primary source of political conflict?
   a. Differing political ideologies
   b. Different religious views
   c. The distribution of wealth
   d. Self-interested human nature
   e. The lack of education

6. All but which of the following arguably influenced the delegates in Philadelphia when they decided the nature of American government?
   a. Their beliefs about human nature
   b. Their beliefs about the causes of political conflict
   c. Their belief in the protection of property
   d. Their concern about the effects of factions
   e. Their belief in the need of a strong, centralized government

7. The system of governance set up in the Constitutional Republic tends to:
   a. Favor the status quo as opposed to political change
   b. Be rather efficient in producing political results
   c. Encourage direct democracy
   d. Centralize power
   e. All of the above

8. The original document of the U.S. Constitution can be said to emphasize:
   a. Economic issues over issues of equality
   b. Issues of equality over economic issues
   c. Both economic and equality issues to a large degree
   d. Both economic and equality issues are only mentioned in passing
   e. Neither economic nor equality issues are mentioned

True/False

9. According to the textbook, the Revolutionary War fundamentally transformed American society.
   True_____   False_____

10. The delegates at the Philadelphia Convention held a primarily cynical view of human nature.
    True_____   False_____

11. On the question of equality and representation, the Virginia Plan called for each state to be equally represented in the new Congress.
    True_____   False_____

12. The Constitution is silent on the matter of equality.
    True_____   False_____

13. In its original form, the U.S. Constitution was rather antidemocratic.
    True_____   False_____

14. On average, state constitutions are harder to amend than the U.S. Constitution.
    True_____   False_____

Short Answer

15. Please explain the post-Revolutionary context of Shays' Rebellion.

16. Despite differences in their political views, the 55 delegates at the Philadelphia Convention agreed on a core of ideas. Please summarize three of the four ideas outlined in the textbook.

17. How does the U.S. Constitution compare to other countries' constitutions in terms of its rigidity?

18. The textbook states that the American Revolution was "conservative" compared to revolutions in other countries. Please explain this notion as well as the social implications for future generations of Americans.

19. Please explain the power shift that occurred in America's society after the Revolution. Which groups gained power, which groups lost power? What were the consequences of this power shift?

20. Briefly explain three of the issues the Federalists and Anti-Federalists disagreed on.

21. Please outline the opinions the Founding Fathers held about the notion of democracy.

Short Answer/Essay Questions

22. Please outline how technological developments have informally changed the Constitution up until now. In the future, what further changes do you anticipate and why?

23. What do you think would be the consequences for future elections in this country, if the voting age were lowered to 16?

24. Historian and political scientists James McGregor Burns has argued that the extensive system of checks and balances in the U.S. Constitution has made effective government almost impossible. Do you agree or disagree with him, and why? Please use concrete examples to support your opinion.

25. How could the beliefs of the Founding Fathers regarding human nature, political conflict, and objects/nature of government explain the rigidity of the U.S. Constitution?

26. According to the textbook, the Constitution was never meant to be static, but rather a "living thing." Please write an essay that outlines some of the major changes to the Constitution over time and what produced these changes. What do you think are the pros and cons of having such a flexible system of government? In your answer, please refer to specific concepts and examples from the textbook as often as possible.

27. The textbook addresses the question of lowering the voting age below 18. How useful do you believe such a measure would, especially given the fact that currently, 18- to 24-year-olds are the least likely age group to vote?

Answer Key

1. C   2. D   3. A   4. B   5. C   6. E   7. A   8. A   9. False   10. True   11. False   12. True   13. True   14. False

Key Terms

constitution (32)
Declaration of Independence (34)
natural rights (35)
consent of the governed (35)
limited government (35)
Articles of Confederation (37)
Shays' Rebellion (40)
U.S. Constitution (41)

factions (42)
New Jersey Plan (43)
Virginia Plan (43)
Connecticut Compromise (43)
writ of habeas corpus (47)
separation of powers (48)
checks and balances (49)
republic (51)

Federalists (51)
Anti-Federalists (51)
Federalist Papers (52)
Bill of Rights (53)
Equal Rights Amendment (57)
Marbury v. Madison (58)
judicial review (58)

Internet Resources

http://www.foundingfathers.info/
Federalist Papers in support of the ratification of the Constitution.

http://www.wepin.com/articles/afp/index.htm
Anti-Federalist writings opposing the ratification of the Constitution.

www.law.emory.edu/erd/docs/usconst.html
The Constitution.

http://www.colonialhall.com/biography.php
Biographies of the Founders.

www.earlyamerica.com/earlyamerica/milestones/articles/text.html
The Articles of Confederation. Also provides access to a wide range of documents from the founding period.

GetConnected

Constitutional Change

The Founders did not intend for the Constitution, the rules of our political system, to be static. Instead, they designed the Constitution specifically so that it could be changed—added to or subtracted from—as needed. Figure 2.5 illustrates the ways the Constitution can be formally amended. Although proposed constitutional changes can originate from national and state conventions, all constitutional changes to date have originated in Congress. So far there have been 27 amendments, but there have been many more proposed changes. Even now, there are several proposed changes to the Constitution being debated in the chambers of Congress and in the media. One of the most recent controversial amendment debates defined marriage and reads:

> *Marriage in the United States shall consist only of the union of a man and a woman. Neither this Constitution nor the constitution of any State, nor state or federal law, shall be construed to require that marital status or the legal incidents thereof be conferred upon unmarried couples or groups.*

The proposed amendment failed to pass Congress in the fall of 2004.

Search the Web

Go to the Web sites of a number of groups and people who are on opposite sides of the marriage constitutional amendment debate, including the Alliance for Marriage, *www.allianceformarriage.org/site/PageServer*; the American Civil Liberties Union, *www.aclu.org/marriageamendment*; Focus on the Family, *http://family.org/socialissues/A000000627.cfm*; the Human Rights Campaign, *www.hrc.org/marriage*; and the Log Cabin Republicans, *www.logcabin.org/logcabin/defendconstitution.html*. Review their positions on the proposed constitutional amendment defining marriage. For additional information, review the Guidelines for Constitutional

Amendments developed by Citizens for the Constitution, *www.constitutionproject.org/pdf/guidelines.pdf* (the guidelines are listed on page 7 of the publication, which requires a PDF reader to view).

Questions to Ask

- Why was the idea of amending a definition of marriage into the U.S. Constitution controversial?
- Which of these groups favored the proposed amendment, and what are their reasons for supporting it?
- Which of these groups opposed the amendment, and why?
- What is your position on the proposed amendment, and why did you reach that conclusion?
- Did the proposed marriage amendment violate the spirit of the separation of church and state found in the First Amendment?

Why It Matters

Some say the process of amending the Constitution is too difficult and prevents necessary constitutional change. Other observers argue that the obstacles to amending the Constitution are good because they keep proposals like the gay marriage amendment, on which opinion may change in the next decade, from becoming part of the document. Would our nation be improved if the Constitution were more easily amended? Should constitutional amendments only change governmental structures, or should they deal with social issues such as marriage?

Get Involved

The definition of marriage amendment is just one of the many proposals introduced in Congress to amend the Constitution. Can you think of amendments you would like to see added to the Constitution? Make a list of your proposed amendments and compare your list with those of other students in class. For more exercises, go to *www.longmanamericangovernment.com*.

For Further Reading

Bailyn, Bernard. *The Ideological Origins of the American Revolution.* Cambridge, MA: Harvard University Press, 1967. A leading work on the ideas that spawned the American Revolution.

Becker, Carl L. *The Declaration of Independence: A Study in the History of Political Ideas.* New York: Random House, 1942. Classic work on the meaning of the Declaration.

Dahl, Robert A. *How Democratic Is the American Constitution?* 2nd ed. New Haven, CT: Yale University Press, 2003. Questions the extent to which the Constitution furthers democratic goals.

Hamilton, Alexander, James Madison, and John Jay. *The Federalist Papers.* 2nd ed. Edited by Roy P. Fairfield. Baltimore: Johns Hopkins University Press, 1981. Key tracts in the campaign for the Constitution and cornerstones of American political thought.

Higginbotham, A. Leon, Jr. *In the Matter of Color: Race and the American Legal Process, the Colonial Period.* New York: Oxford University Press, 1978. Chronicles how colonial governments established the legal foundations for the enslavement of African Americans.

Jensen, Merrill. *The Articles of Confederation.* Madison: University of Wisconsin Press, 1940. Definitive and balanced treatment of the Articles.

Jillson, Calvin C. *Constitution Making: Conflict and Consensus in the Federal Convention of 1787.* New York: Agathon, 1988. Sophisticated analysis of the drafting of the Constitution.

Lipset, Seymour Martin. *The First New Nation.* New York: Basic Books, 1963. Political sociologist Lipset sees the early American experience as one of nation building.

Maier, Pauline. *American Scripture.* New York: Knopf, 1997. Argues that the Declaration was the embodiment of the American mind and historical experience.

McDonald, Forrest B. *Novus Ordo Seclorum: The Intellectual Origins of the Constitution.* Lawrence: University Press of Kansas, 1986. Discusses the ideas behind the Constitution.

Morris, Richard B. *The Forging of the Union, 1781–1789.* New York: Harper & Row, 1987. Written to coincide with the bicentennial of the Constitution, this is an excellent history of the document's making.

Norton, Mary Beth. *Liberty's Daughters.* Boston: Little, Brown, 1980. Examines the role of women during the era of the Revolution and concludes that the Revolution transformed gender roles, setting women on the course to equality.

Rossiter, Clinton. *1787: The Grand Convention.* New York: Macmillan, 1966. A well-written study of the making of the Constitution.

Storing, Herbert J. *What the Anti-Federalists Were For.* Chicago: University of Chicago Press, 1981. Analysis of the political views of those opposed to ratification of the Constitution.

Wood, Gordon S. *The Creation of the American Republic.* Chapel Hill: University of North Carolina Press, 1969. In-depth study of American political thought prior to the Constitutional Convention.

Wood, Gordon S. *The Radicalism of the American Revolution.* New York: Vintage, 1993. Shows how American society and politics were thoroughly transformed in the decades following the Revolution.

FEDERALISM

POLITICS IN ACTION:
AIDING DISASTER VICTIMS

On August 29, 2005, Hurricane Katrina, a category 5 storm, swept across the Mississippi Gulf Coast, devastating New Orleans and parts of Mississippi and Alabama. Levees that had protected New Orleans for generations gave way to the force of the storm, stranding thousands of citizens without electricity, food, water, health care, communications, or police protection.

State and local governments are the first responders to natural disasters, but the breadth of the disaster quickly overwhelmed most of the local infrastructure. The national government is supposed to supplement state and local efforts; instead, a virtual standoff between hesitant federal officials and besieged authorities in Louisiana deepened the crisis in New Orleans.

Chaos reigned as the fractured division of responsibility meant no one person or agency was in charge. Federal and state officials clashed over the issue of "federalizing" the Louisiana National Guard, which the governor was reluctant to do because she feared losing authority over it and lacked confidence in the national government.

State and local officials assumed that Washington would provide rapid and substantial aid, but leaders in Louisiana and New Orleans were not always sure what they needed. Thus, desperate state and local officials made open-ended pleas for help, which federal officials found difficult to interpret. Rather than initiate relief efforts—such as providing buses, food and water, troops, diesel fuel, and rescue boats—federal officials waited for specific requests and, weighing legalities and logistics, proceeded at a deliberate pace.

As a result, Americans watched in horror as their favorite news anchors reported from New Orleans standing beside suffering victims while federal officials were still unable to move the necessary personnel (including members of the world's mightiest military force) and supplies to aid those stricken by the storm.

Aid did arrive eventually, but it was followed very closely by a public relations battle to assign blame for what everyone agreed was a wholly inadequate response at all levels.

The issue was not whether to aid disaster victims. Everyone agreed with that. Instead, the issue was determining the appropriate federal and state powers and responsibilities. The issue of federalism and the delegation of responsibility to different levels of government is a crucial political

battleground—policymakers' answers to the questions of how we should be governed (in this case, by the states or by the federal government) and what should be the scope of the national government in shaping public policies.

The complications surrounding the government response to Hurricane Katrina illustrate the importance of understanding American federalism, the complex relationships between different levels of government in the United States. In exploring American federalism, we will be especially attentive to our themes of democracy and the scope of government. Does federalism, the vertical division of power, enhance democracy in the United States? Does the additional layer of policymakers at the state level make government more responsive to public opinion or merely more complicated? Does it enhance the prospects that a national majority of Americans will have their way in public policy? And what are the implications of federalism for the scope of the national government's activities? Why has the national government grown so much in relation to state governments, and has this growth been at the expense of the states?

The relationships between governments at the local, state, and national levels often confuse Americans. Locally elected school boards run neighborhood schools, but the schools also receive state and national funds, and with those funds come state and national rules and regulations. Local airports, sewage systems, pollution control systems, and police departments also receive a mix of local, state, and national funds, so they operate under a complex web of rules and regulations imposed by each level of government.

DEFINING FEDERALISM

Federalism is a rather unusual system for governing, with particular consequences for those who live within it. This section explains the federal system and how it affects Americans living in such a system.

WHAT IS FEDERALISM?

federalism
A way of organizing a nation so that two or more levels of government have formal authority over the same land and people. It is a system of shared power between units of government.

Federalism is a way of organizing a nation so that two or more levels of government have formal authority over the same area and people. It is a system of shared power between units of government. For example, the state of California has formal authority over its inhabitants, but the national government can also pass laws and establish policies that affect Californians. We are subject to the formal authority of both state and national governments.

Although federalism is not unique to the United States, it is not a common method of governing. Only 11 of the 190 or so nations of the world have federal systems, and these countries, which include Germany, Mexico, Argentina, Canada, Australia, India, and the United States, share little else as a group (see "America in Perspective: Why Federalism?").

unitary governments
A way of organizing a nation so that all power resides in the central government. Most national governments today are unitary governments.

Most governments in the world today are not federal but **unitary governments**, in which all power resides in the central government. If the French Assembly, for instance, wants to redraw the boundaries of local governments or change their forms of government, it can (and has). However, if the U.S. Congress wants to abolish Alabama or Oregon, it cannot.

American states are unitary governments with respect to their local governments. Local governments receive their authority from the states, which can create or abolish local governments and make rules for the local governments within their boundaries. They can tell them what their speed limits will be, the way in which they will be organized, how they can tax people, on what they can spend money, and so forth. States, however, receive their authority not from the national government but *directly* from the Constitution.

Comparing Federal and Unitary Systems

TABLE 3.1

Authority Relations in Three Systems of Government

	UNITARY	CONFEDERATE	FEDERAL
Central government	Holds primary authority Regulates activities of states	Limited powers to coordinate state activities	Shares power with states
State government	Few or no powers Duties regulated by central government	Sovereign Allocates some duties to central government	Shares power with central government
Citizens	Vote for central government officials	Vote for state government officials	Vote for both state and central government officials

There is a third form of governmental structure, a *confederation*. The United States began as a confederation under the Articles of Confederation. In a confederation, the national government is weak, and most or all power is in the hands of the country's components—for example, the individual states. Today, confederations are rare except in international organizations such as the United Nations (see Chapter 20). Table 3.1 provides a summary of the authority relations in the three systems of government.

AMERICA IN PERSPECTIVE

Why **Federalism?**

Only 11 countries have federal systems. Trying to determine why these particular nations chose a federal system is an interesting but difficult task. All three North American nations have federal systems, but the trend does not continue in South America, where only two nations have federal systems. Countries large in size—such as Canada and Australia—or large in both size and population—such as India, the United States, Brazil, and Mexico—tend to have federal systems, which decentralize the administration of governmental services. Nevertheless, China and Indonesia—two large and heavily populated countries—have unitary governments, and tiny Malaysia and Switzerland have federal systems.

A nation's diversity may also play a role in the development of a federal system. Brazil, Canada, India, Malaysia, Switzerland, and the United States have large minority ethnic groups that often speak different languages and practice different religions. Many nations with unitary systems, however, ranging from Belgium to most African countries, are also replete with ethnic diversity.

Most federal systems are democracies, although most democracies are not federal systems. Authoritarian regimes generally do not wish to disperse power away from the central government. Both the former Soviet Union and the former Yugoslavia, perhaps reflecting the extraordinary diversity of their populations, had federal systems—of a sort. In both countries, the central government, until recently, retained ultimate power. As democracy swept through these countries, their national governments dissolved, and several smaller nations were formed.

NATION	POPULATION	AREA (THOUSANDS SQUARE MILES)	DIVERSITY (ETHNIC, LINGUISTIC, AND RELIGIOUS)
Argentina	40,301,927	1,068	Low
Australia	20,434,176	2,968	Low
Austria	8,199,783	32	Low
Brazil	190,010,647	3,286	Medium
Canada	33,390,141	3,852	High
Germany	82,400,996	138	Low
India	1,129,866,154	1,269	High
Malaysia	24,821,286	127	High
Mexico	108,700,891	762	Low
Switzerland	7,554,661	16	Medium
United States	301,139,947	3,718	Medium

Source: Central Intelligence Agency, *The World Factbook, 2007.*

intergovernmental relations
The workings of the federal system—the entire set of interactions among national, state, and local governments.

The workings of the federal system are sometimes called **intergovernmental relations**. This term refers to the entire set of interactions among national, state, and local governments.

WHY IS FEDERALISM SO IMPORTANT?

The federal system in America *decentralizes our politics*. Voters elect senators as representatives of individual states, not of the entire nation. On Election Day in November, there are actually 51 presidential elections, one in each state and one in Washington, D.C. (see Chapter 10). It is even possible—as happened in 2000—for a candidate who receives the most popular votes in the country to lose the election because of the way the Constitution distributes electoral votes by state.

The federal system decentralizes our politics in more fundamental ways than our electoral system. With more layers of government, more opportunities exist for political participation. With more people wielding power, there are more points of access in government and more opportunities for government to satisfy the demands of interests for public policies. With states making more decisions, there are fewer sources of conflict at the national level.

As we will see, federalism also enhances judicial power. Dividing government power and responsibilities necessitates umpires to resolve disputes between the two levels of government. In the American system, judges serve as the umpires. Thus, when the national government places prohibitions or requirements on the states, inevitably issues arise for the courts to decide.

The federal system not only decentralizes our politics but also *decentralizes our policies*. The history of the federal system demonstrates the tension between the states and the national government about policy: who controls it and what it should be. In the past, people debated whether the states or the national government should regulate the railroads, pass child labor laws, or adopt minimum-wage legislation. Today, people debate whether the states or the national government should regulate abortions, set standards for public schools, determine speed limits on highways, protect the environment, provide health care for the poor, or tell 18-year-olds they cannot drink alcohol.[1]

Policies about healthcare, the economy, the environment, and other matters are subject to both the centralizing force of the national government and the dispersing force of the states. The overlapping powers of the two levels of government mean that most of our public policy debates are also debates about federalism.

States are responsible for most public policies dealing with social, family, and moral issues. The Constitution does not give the national government the power to pass laws that *directly* regulate drinking ages, marriage and divorce, or speed limits. These policy prerogatives belong to the states. They become national issues, however, when aggrieved or angry groups take their cases to Congress or the federal courts

National campaigns for the presidency actually take place in the states. Candidates must win states rather than the national vote, and they focus their energies on politically competitive states. Here, Barack Obama campaigns before the 2008 presidential election.

in an attempt to use the power of the national government to *influence* states or to convince federal courts to find a state's policy unconstitutional.

A good example of this process is the federal requirement that states raise their drinking age to 21 in order to receive highway funds. Candy Lightner, a California real estate broker grieving over the death of her 13-year-old daughter at the hands of a drunk driver, formed Mothers Against Drunk Driving (MADD). MADD lobbied Congress to pass a law withholding federal highway funds from any state that did not raise its drinking age. Today, every state has a legal drinking age of 21.

The American states have always been policy innovators.[2] The states overflow with reforms, new ideas, and new policies. From clean-air legislation to welfare reform, the states constitute a national laboratory to develop and test public policies and share the results with other states and the national government. Almost every policy the national government has adopted had its beginnings in the states. One or more states pioneered child labor laws, minimum-wage legislation, unemployment compensation, antipollution legislation, civil rights protections, and the income tax. More recently, states have been active in reforming health care, education, and welfare—and the national government is paying close attention to their efforts.

THE CONSTITUTIONAL BASIS OF FEDERALISM

The word *federalism* is absent from the Constitution, and not much was said about it at the Constitutional Convention. Eighteenth-century Americans had little experience in thinking of themselves as Americans first and state citizens second. In fact, loyalty to state governments was so strong that the Constitution would have been resoundingly defeated had it tried to abolish them. In addition, a central government, working alone, would have had difficulty trying to govern eighteenth-century Americans. The people were too widely dispersed and the country's transportation and communication systems too primitive to allow governing from a central location. There was no other practical choice in 1787 but to create a federal system of government.

THE DIVISION OF POWER

The Constitution's writers carefully defined the powers of state and national governments (see Table 3.2). Although they favored a stronger national government, the Framers still made states vital components in the machinery of government. The Constitution guaranteed states equal representation in the Senate (and even made this provision unamendable in Article V). It also made states responsible for both state and national elections—an important power. Further, the Constitution virtually guaranteed the continuation of each state; Congress is forbidden to create new states by chopping up old ones, unless a state's legislature approves (an unlikely event).

The Constitution also created obligations of the national government toward the states; it is to protect states against violence and invasion, for example. At times, however, the states find the national government deficient in meeting its obligations, as we will discuss later in this chapter.

In Article VI of the Constitution, the Framers dealt with what remains a touchy question: In a dispute between the states and the national government, which prevails?

TABLE 3.2

The Constitution's Distribution of Powers

TO THE NATIONAL GOVERNMENT	TO BOTH THE NATIONAL AND STATE GOVERNMENT	TO THE STATE GOVERNMENTS
SOME POWERS GRANTED BY THE CONSTITUTION		
Coin money Conduct foreign relations Regulate commerce with foreign nations and among states Provide an army and a navy Declare war Establish courts inferior to the Supreme Court Establish post offices Make laws necessary and proper to carry out the foregoing powers	Tax Borrow money Establish courts Make and enforce laws Charter banks and corporations Spend money for the general welfare Take private property for public purposes, with just compensation	Establish local governments Regulate commerce within a state Conduct elections Ratify amendments to the federal Constitution Take measures for public health, safety, and morals Exert powers the Constitution does not delegate to the national government or prohibit the states from using
SOME POWERS DENIED BY THE CONSTITUTION		
Tax articles exported from one state to another Violate the Bill of Rights Change state boundaries	Grant titles of nobility Permit slavery (Thirteenth Amendment) Deny citizens the right to vote because of race, color, or previous servitude (Fifteenth Amendment) Deny citizens the right to vote because of gender (Nineteenth Amendment)	Tax imports or exports Coin money Enter into treaties Impair obligations of contracts Abridge the privileges or immunities of citizens or deny due process and equal protection of the law (Fourteenth Amendment)

supremacy clause

Article VI of the Constitution, which makes the Constitution, national laws, and treaties supreme over state laws when the national government is acting within its constitutional limits.

Tenth Amendment

The constitutional amendment stating, "The powers not delegated to the United States by the Constitution, nor prohibited by it to the states, are reserved to the states respectively, or to the people."

The answer that the delegates provided, often referred to as the **supremacy clause,** is reasonably clear. They stated that the following three items were the supreme law of the land:

1. The Constitution
2. Laws of the national government (when consistent with the Constitution)
3. Treaties (which can be made only by the national government)

Judges in every state were specifically directed to obey the Constitution, even if their state constitutions or state laws directly contradicted it. Today, all state executives, legislators, and judges are bound by oath to support the Constitution.

The national government, however, can operate only within its appropriate sphere. It cannot usurp the states' powers. But what are the boundaries of the national government's powers? According to some commentators, the **Tenth Amendment** provides part of the answer. It states that the "powers not delegated to the United States by the Constitution, nor prohibited by it to the states, are reserved to the states respectively, or to the people." To those advocating states' rights, the amendment clearly means that the national government has only those powers the Constitution specifically assigned to it. The states or people have supreme power over any activity not mentioned there. Despite this interpretation, in 1941 the Supreme Court (in *United States v. Darby*) called the Tenth Amendment a constitutional truism, a mere assertion that the states have independent powers of their own—not a declaration that state powers are superior to those of the national government.

The Court seemed to backtrack on this ruling in favor of national government supremacy in a 1976 case, *National League of Cities v. Usery,* in which it held that extending national minimum-wage and maximum-hours standards to employees of state and local governments was an unconstitutional intrusion of the national government into the domain of the states. In 1985, however (in *Garcia v. San Antonio Metro*), the Court overturned the *National League of Cities* decision. The Court held, in essence, that it was up to Congress, not the courts, to decide which actions of the states should be regulated by the national government. Once again, the Court ruled that the Tenth Amendment did not give states power superior to that of the national government for activities not mentioned in the Constitution.

Occasionally, issues arise in which states challenge the authority of the national government. In the late 1980s, the governors of several states refused to allow their state National Guards to engage in training exercises in Central America. National Guards are state militias, but the Constitution provides that the president can nationalize them. In 1990, the Supreme Court reiterated the power of the national government by siding with the president. Similarly, South Dakota sued the federal government over its efforts to raise states' drinking-age laws and over its efforts to mandate a 55-mile-per-hour speed limit on highways. The state lost both cases. (In 1995, however, Congress changed the law on speed limits, deciding to leave it up to the states.) Several states are in the process of challenging federal education regulations resulting from the No Child Left Behind Act.

Federal courts can order states to obey the Constitution or federal laws and treaties. However, in deference to the states the *Eleventh Amendment* prohibits individual damage suits against state officials (such as a suit against a police officer for violating one's rights) and protects state governments from being sued against their consent by private parties in federal courts or in state courts[3] or before federal administrative agencies.[4] In 2001, the Court voided the application of the Americans with Disabilities Act to the states, finding it a violation of the Eleventh Amendment (*Board of Trustees of University of Alabama, et al. v. Garrett, et al.*). Cases arising under the Fourteenth Amendment (usually cases regarding racial discrimination) are an exception.[5] The federal government may also bring suits against states in federal courts, as may individuals seeking to prohibit future illegal actions of state officials.

Recently the Supreme Court has made it easier for citizens to control the behavior of local officials. The Court ruled that a federal law passed in 1871 to protect newly freed slaves permits individuals to sue local governments for damages or seek injunctions against any local official acting in an official capacity who they believe has deprived them of any right secured by the Constitution or by federal law.[6] Such suits are now common in the federal courts.

ESTABLISHING NATIONAL SUPREMACY

Why is it that the federal government has gained power relative to the states? Four key events have largely settled the issue of how national and state powers are related: (1) the elaboration of the doctrine of implied powers, (2) the definition of the commerce clause, (3) the Civil War, and (4) the long struggle for racial equality.

Implied Powers As early as 1819, the issue of state versus national power came before the Supreme Court in the case of ***McCulloch v. Maryland***. The new American government had moved quickly on many economic policies. In 1791, it created a national bank, a government agency empowered to print money, make loans, and engage in many other banking tasks. A darling of Alexander Hamilton and his allies, those opposed to strengthening the national government's control of the economy hated the bank. Opponents—including Thomas Jefferson, farmers, and state legislatures—saw the bank as an instrument of the elite. Congress allowed the First Bank of the United States to expire but created the Second Bank during James Madison's presidency, fueling a great national debate.

SIMULATION

You Are a Federal Judge

McCulloch v. Maryland
An 1819 Supreme Court decision that established the supremacy of the national government over state governments. In deciding this case, Chief Justice John Marshall and his colleagues held that Congress had certain **implied powers** in addition to the **enumerated powers** found in the Constitution.

Railing against the "Monster Bank," the state of Maryland passed a law in 1818 taxing the national bank's Baltimore branch $15,000 a year. The Baltimore branch refused to pay, whereupon the state of Maryland sued the cashier, James McCulloch, for payment. When the state courts upheld Maryland's law and its tax, the bank appealed to the U.S. Supreme Court. John Marshall was chief justice when two of the country's most capable lawyers argued the case before the Court.

Daniel Webster, widely regarded as one of the greatest senators in U.S. history, argued for the national bank, and Luther Martin, a delegate to the Constitutional Convention, argued for Maryland. Martin maintained that the Constitution was very clear about the powers of Congress (as outlined in Article I). The power to create a national bank was not among them. Thus, Martin concluded, Congress had exceeded its powers, and Maryland had a right to tax the bank. On behalf of the bank, Webster argued for a broader interpretation of the powers of the national government. The Constitution was not meant to stifle congressional powers, he said, but rather to permit Congress to use all means "necessary and proper" to fulfill its responsibilities.

Marshall, never one to sidestep a big decision, wrote his ruling in favor of the bank before the arguments ended. He and his colleagues set forth two great constitutional principles in their decision. The first was the *supremacy of the national government over the states.* Marshall wrote, "If any one proposition could command the universal assent of mankind, we might expect it to be this—that the government of the United States, though limited in its power, is supreme within its sphere of action." As long as the national government behaved in accordance with the Constitution, said the Court, its policies took precedence over state policies. Accordingly, federal laws or regulations, such as many civil rights acts and rules regulating hazardous substances, water quality, and clean-air standards, *preempt* state or local laws or regulations and thus preclude their enforcement.

The other key principle of *McCulloch* was that *the national government has certain implied powers that go beyond its enumerated powers.* The Court held that Congress was behaving consistently with the Constitution when it created the national bank. It was true, Marshall admitted, that Congress had certain **enumerated powers,** powers *specifically* listed in Article I, Section 8, of the Constitution. Congress could coin money, regulate its value, impose taxes, and so forth. The Constitution did not enumerate creating a bank, but it added that Congress has the power to "make all laws necessary and proper for carrying into execution the foregoing powers." That, said Marshall, gave Congress certain **implied powers**. It could make economic policy consistent with the Constitution in a number of ways.

Today, the notion of implied powers has become like a rubber band that can be stretched without breaking; commentators often refer to the "necessary and proper" clause of the Constitution as the **elastic clause.** Hundreds of congressional policies involve powers not specifically mentioned in the Constitution, especially in the domain of economic policy. Federal policies to regulate food and drugs, build interstate highways, protect consumers, clean up dirty air and water, and do many other things are all justified as implied powers of Congress.

Commerce Power   The Constitution gives Congress the power to regulate interstate and international commerce. American courts have spent many years trying to define commerce. In 1824, the Supreme Court, in deciding the case of ***Gibbons v. Ogden,*** defined commerce very broadly to encompass virtually every form of commercial activity. Today, commerce covers not only the movement of goods, but also radio signals, electricity, telephone messages, the Internet, insurance transactions, and much more.

The Supreme Court's decisions establishing the national government's implied powers (*McCulloch v. Maryland*) and a broad definition of interstate

TIMELINE

Federalism and the Supreme Court

enumerated powers
Powers of the federal government that are specifically addressed in the Constitution; for Congress, these powers are listed in Article I, Section 8, and include the power to coin money, regulate its value, and impose taxes.

implied powers
Powers of the federal government that go beyond those enumerated in the Constitution. The Constitution states that Congress has the power to "make all laws necessary and proper for carrying into execution" the powers enumerated in Article I.

elastic clause
The final paragraph of Article I, Section 8, of the Constitution, which authorizes Congress to pass all laws "necessary and proper" to carry out the enumerated powers.

Gibbons v. Ogden
A landmark case decided in 1824 in which the Supreme Court interpreted very broadly the clause in Article I, Section 8, of the Constitution giving Congress the power to regulate interstate commerce, encompassing virtually every form of commercial activity.

commerce (*Gibbons v. Ogden*) created a source of national power as long as Congress employed its power for economic development through subsidies and services for business interests. In the latter part of the nineteenth century, however, Congress sought to use these same powers to regulate the economy rather than to promote it. The Court then interpreted the interstate commerce power as giving Congress no constitutional right to regulate local commercial activities such as establishing safe working conditions for laborers or protecting children from working long hours.

The Great Depression placed new demands on the national government. Beginning in 1933, the New Deal of President Franklin D. Roosevelt produced an avalanche of regulatory and social welfare legislation, much of which was voided by the Supreme Court (see Chapter 16). After 1937, however, the Court eased up on restricting the efforts of the national government to regulate commerce at any level. In 1964, Congress prohibited racial discrimination in places of public accommodation such as restaurants, hotels, and movie theaters on the basis of its power to regulate interstate commerce. Thus, regulating commerce is one of the national government's most important sources of power.

In recent years the Supreme Court has scrutinized the use of the commerce power with a skeptical eye, however. In 1995 the Court held in *United States v. Lopez* that the federal Gun-Free School Zones Act of 1990, which forbade the possession of firearms in public schools, exceeded Congress's constitutional authority to regulate commerce. Guns in a school zone, the majority said, have nothing to do with commerce. Similarly, in 2000 the Court ruled in *United States v. Morrison* that the power to regulate interstate commerce did not provide Congress with authority to enact the 1994 Violence Against Women Act, which provided a federal civil remedy for the victims of gender-motivated violence. Gender-motivated crimes of violence are not, the Court said, in any sense economic activity.

The Supreme Court announced another limitation on the commerce power in 1996. In *Seminole Tribe of Florida v. Florida*, the Court dealt with the case of a right Congress had given Indian tribes to sue state officials to force good-faith negotiations (in this case over a license to run a casino). Contrary to previous decisions, the Court declared that the Eleventh Amendment prohibits Congress from using the interstate commerce power to revoke states' immunity from such lawsuits by private parties. The principal effect of the decision is to limit suits seeking to enforce rights granted by Congress within its authority under the Commerce Clause (which encompasses much of modern federal regulation).

Several other recent cases have had important implications for federalism. In *Printz v. United States* (1997) and *Mack v. United States* (1997), the Supreme Court voided the congressional mandate in the Brady Handgun Violence Prevention Act that the chief law enforcement officer in each local community conduct background checks on prospective gun purchasers. According to the Court, "The federal government may neither issue directives requiring the states to address particular problems, nor commend the states' officers, or those of their political subdivision, to administer or enforce a federal regulatory program."

The Civil War   What *McCulloch* pronounced constitutionally the Civil War (1861–1865) settled militarily. We typically think of the Civil War as mainly a struggle over slavery; but it was also, and perhaps more importantly, a struggle between states and the national government. In fact, Abraham Lincoln announced in his 1861 inaugural address that he would willingly support a constitutional amendment guaranteeing slavery if it would save the Union. Instead, it took a bloody civil war for the national government to assert its power over the Southern states' claim of sovereignty.

In 1963, Alabama Governor George Wallace made a dramatic stand at the University of Alabama to resist integration of the all-White school. Federal marshals won this confrontation, and since then the federal government in general has been able to impose national standards of equal opportunity on the states.

The Struggle for Racial Equality A century later, conflict between the states and the national government again erupted over states' rights and national power. In 1954, in *Brown v. Board of Education,* the Supreme Court held that school segregation was unconstitutional. Southern politicians responded with what they called "massive resistance" to the decision. When a federal judge ordered the admission of two African American students to the University of Alabama in 1963, Governor George Wallace literally blocked the school entrance to prevent federal marshals and the students from entering the admissions office. Despite Wallace's efforts, the students were admitted, and throughout the 1960s the federal government enacted laws and policies to end segregation in schools, housing, public accommodations, voting, and jobs. In 1979 (after African Americans began voting in large numbers in Alabama), George Wallace himself said of his stand in the schoolhouse door: "I was wrong. Those days are over and they ought to be over." The conflict between states and the national government over equality issues was decided in favor of the national government. National standards of racial equality prevailed.

The national government is supreme within its sphere, but the sphere for the states remains a large and important one.

STATES' OBLIGATIONS TO EACH OTHER

Federalism involves more than relationships between the national government and state and local governments. The states must deal with each other as well, and the Constitution outlines certain obligations that each state has to every other state.

Full Faith and Credit Suppose that, like millions of other Americans, a person divorces and then remarries. For each marriage this person purchases a marriage license, which registers the marriage with a state. On the honeymoon for the second marriage, the person travels across the country. Is this person married in each state passed through, even though the marriage license is with only one state? Can the person be arrested for bigamy because the divorce occurred in only one state?

The answer, of course, is that a marriage license and a divorce, like a driver's license and a birth certificate, are valid in all states. Article IV of the Constitution requires that states give **full faith and credit** to the public acts, records, and civil judicial proceedings of every other state. This reciprocity is essential to the functioning of society and the economy. Without the full faith and credit clause, people could avoid their obligations, say, to make payments on automobile loans simply by crossing a state boundary. In addition, because courts can enforce contracts between business firms across state boundaries, firms incorporated in one state can do business in another.

Usually, the full faith and credit provision in the Constitution poses little controversy. An exception occurred in 1996 when courts in Hawaii recognized

full faith and credit
A clause in Article IV, Section 1, of the Constitution requiring each state to recognize the official documents and civil judgments rendered by the courts of other states.

same-gender marriages. What would happen in other states that did not recognize Hawaiian marriages between same-gender partners? Congress answered with the Defense of Marriage Act, which permits states to disregard gay marriages, even if they are legal elsewhere in the United States. Hawaii has since overturned recognition of gay marriage, but in 2000 Vermont accorded legal status to gay civil unions. In 2003 the Massachusetts supreme court held that the state constitution guaranteed full marriage rights for gay couples. California followed suit in 2008. It remains to be seen whether courts will uphold Congress's power to make exceptions to the full faith and credit clause, but opponents of gay marriage have focused on amending the Constitution to allow states not to recognize same-gender marriages.

Extradition   What about criminal penalties? Almost all criminal law is state law. If someone robs a store, steals a car, or commits a murder, the chances are that this person is breaking a state, not a federal, law. The Constitution says that states are required to return a person charged with a crime in another state to that state for trial or imprisonment, a practice called **extradition**. Although there is no way to force states to comply, they usually are happy to do so, not wishing to harbor criminals and hoping that other states will reciprocate. Thus, a lawbreaker cannot avoid punishment by simply escaping to another state.

extradition
A legal process whereby an alleged criminal offender is surrendered by the officials of one state to officials of the state in which the crime is alleged to have been committed.

Privileges and Immunities   The most complicated obligation among the states is the requirement that citizens of each state receive all the **privileges and immunities** of any other state in which they happen to be. The goal of this constitutional provision is to prohibit states from discriminating against citizens of other states. If, for example, a Texan visits California, the Texan will pay the same sales tax and receive the same police protection as residents of California.

privileges and immunities
A clause in Article IV, Section 2, of the Constitution according citizens of each state most of the privileges of citizens of other states.

There are many exceptions to the privileges and immunities clause, however. Many of you attend public universities. If you reside in the same state as your university, you generally pay a tuition substantially lower than that paid by your fellow students from out of state. Similarly, only residents of a state can vote in state elections. States often attempt to pass the burdens of financing the state government to those outside the state, such as through taxes on minerals mined in the state but consumed elsewhere or special taxes on hotel rooms rented by tourists.

The Supreme Court has never clarified just which privileges a state must make available to all Americans and which privileges can be limited to its own citizens. In general, the more fundamental the rights—such as owning property or receiving police protection—the less likely it is that a state can discriminate against citizens of another state. In 1999, the Supreme Court held in *Saenz v. Roe* that California could not require a new resident to wait a year before becoming eligible for welfare benefits that exceeded those available in the state from which the new resident came.

Because of the full faith and credit clause of the Constitution, marriage certificates issued by one state are valid in every state. People are also entitled to most of the benefits—and subject to most of the obligations—of citizenship in any state they visit, thanks to the privileges and immunities clause. Gay marriage is straining these principles, however, as most states refuse to recognize marriages between same-gender partners.

INTERGOVERNMENTAL RELATIONS TODAY

The past two centuries have seen dramatic changes in American federalism. These changes are apparent in two main areas. First, there has been a gradual shift from a dual federalism to a cooperative federalism, which emphasizes power sharing between two levels of government.[7] The second major change has been the rise of fiscal federalism, the elaborate assortment of federal grants-in-aid to the states and localities.

FROM DUAL TO COOPERATIVE FEDERALISM

dual federalism
A system of government in which both the states and the national government remain supreme within their own spheres, each responsible for some policies.

One way to understand the changes in American federalism over the past 200 years is to contrast two types of federalism. The first type is called **dual federalism**, in which both the national government and the states remain supreme within their own spheres. The states are responsible for some policies, the national government for others. For example, the national government has exclusive control over foreign and military policy, the postal system, and monetary policy. States are exclusively responsible for schools, law enforcement, and road building. In dual federalism, the powers and policy assignments of the layers of government are distinct, as in a layer cake, and proponents of dual federalism believe that the powers of the national government should be interpreted narrowly.

Most politicians and political scientists today argue that dual federalism is outdated. They are more likely to describe the current American federal system as one of **cooperative federalism**, where states and the national government share powers and policy assignments.[8] Instead of a layer cake, they see American federalism as more like a marble cake, with mingled responsibilities and blurred distinctions between the levels of government. After the terrorist attacks on September 11, 2001, the national government asked state and local governments to investigate suspected terrorists, and both national and state public health officials dealt with the threat caused by anthrax in the mail in Florida, New York, and Washington, D.C.

cooperative federalism
A system of government in which powers and policy assignments are shared between states and the national government. They may also share costs, administration, and even blame for programs that work poorly.

Before the national government began to assert its dominance over state governments, the American federal system leaned toward dual federalism. The American system, however, was never neatly separated into purely state and purely national responsibilities. For example, education was usually thought of as being mainly a state and local responsibility, yet even under the Articles of Confederation, Congress set aside land in the Northwest Territory to be used for schools. During the Civil War, the national government adopted a policy to create land grant colleges. Important American universities such as Wisconsin, Texas A&M, Illinois, Ohio State, North Carolina State, and Iowa State owe their origins to this national policy. (To learn more about how federalism affects college education, see "Young People and Politics: Federal Support for Colleges and Universities.")

In the 1950s and 1960s, the national government began supporting public elementary and secondary education. In 1958 Congress passed the National Defense Education Act, largely in response to Soviet success in the space race. The act provided federal grants and loans for college students and financial support for elementary and secondary education in science and foreign languages. In 1965, Congress passed the Elementary and Secondary Education Act, which provided federal aid to numerous schools. Although these policies expanded the national government's role in education, they were not a sharp break with the past.

Today, the federal government's presence is felt in every schoolhouse. Almost all school districts receive some federal assistance. To do so, they must comply with federal rules and regulations. They must, for example, maintain desegregated and nondiscriminatory programs. In 2002, George W. Bush signed the No Child Left

Behind Act, establishing standards of performance and sanctions, including loss of federal aid, for failuring to meet them. In addition, as we will see in Chapters 4 and 5, federal courts have ordered local schools to implement elaborate desegregation plans and have placed constraints on school prayers.

Highways are another example of the movement toward cooperative federalism. In an earlier era, states and cities were largely responsible for building roads, although the Constitution does authorize Congress to construct "post roads." In 1956, Congress passed an act creating an interstate highway system. Hundreds of red, white, and blue signs were planted at the beginnings of interstate construction projects. The signs announced that the interstate highway program was a joint federal–state project and specified the cost and sharing of funds. In this and many other areas, the federal system has promoted a partnership between the national and state governments.

Cooperative federalism today rests on several standard operating procedures. For hundreds of programs, cooperative federalism involves the following:

- *Shared costs*. Cities and states can receive federal money for airport construction, sewage treatment plants, youth programs, and many other programs, but only if they pay part of the bill.
- *Federal guidelines*. Most federal grants to states and cities come with strings attached. Congress spends billions of dollars to support state highway construction, for example, but to get their share, states must adopt and enforce limits on the legal drinking age.
- *Shared administration*. State and local officials implement federal policies, but they have administrative powers of their own. The U.S. Department of Labor, for example, gives billions of dollars to states for job training, but states have considerable latitude in spending the money.

The cooperation between the national government and state governments is such an established feature of American federalism that it persists even when the two

VISUAL LITERACY

Federalism and Regulations

YOUNG PEOPLE AND POLITICS
Federal **Support for Colleges and Universities**

Because most colleges and universities are public institutions created by state and local governments, federalism has direct consequences for the students who attend them. State and local governments provide most of the funding for public colleges and universities, but almost everyone agrees that this funding is inadequate. In response to this problem, the national government has stepped in to support postsecondary education programs.

One could argue that the federal government makes it possible for many students to attend college at all because it is the primary source of financial aid. The federal government provides more than $82 billion in financial assistance (including grants, loans, and work-study assistance) to about 23 million postsecondary students each year. Nearly two-thirds of all full-time undergraduates receive some form of financial aid from the federal government.

The federal government also provides several billion dollars of direct grants to colleges and universities across the nation. Billions more in federal funds support research and training in certain areas, especially science and engineering—which receive about $30 billion a year. The library, laboratories, and the buildings in most colleges and universities have received funds from the federal government.

Each year the federal government provides about 13 percent of the revenue for public colleges and universities (14 percent for private, not-for-profit schools). Few colleges and universities could withstand a 13 or 14 percent budget cut and the loss of most of the financial assistance for its students. Federalism, then, matters quite a lot to college students.

QUESTIONS FOR DISCUSSION

▶ Why do state institutions of higher education require aid from the federal government? Why don't the states provide adequate funds to run their own colleges and universities?

▶ Federal aid comes with strings attached. Would it be better to rely completely on state support?

Source: U.S. Department of Education, National Center for Education Statistics, *Digest of Education Statistics*, 2007, Tables 320, 338, 340, 371; U.S. Department of Commerce, *Statistical Abstract of the United States*, 2008 (Washington, DC: U.S. Government Printing Office, 2008), Table 284.

levels of government are in conflict on certain matters. For example, in the 1950s and 1960s, Southern states cooperated well with Washington in building the interstate highway system while they clashed with the national government over racial integration.

DEVOLUTION?

For most of the twentieth century, Democrats supported increasing the power of the federal government in order to advance policies ranging from child labor laws and education to Social Security and health care. Republicans, on the other hand, generally opposed these policies and favored states taking responsibility for these issues. They often articulated their opposition to increased federal power in terms of a defense of state authority in a federal system.

In his first inaugural address, Ronald Reagan articulated a traditional conservative view when he argued that the states had primary responsibility for governing in most policy areas, and he promised to "restore the balance between levels of government." Few officials at either the state or the national level agreed with Reagan about ending the national government's role in domestic programs. Nevertheless, Reagan's opposition to the national government's spending on domestic policies and the huge federal deficits of the 1980s forced a reduction in federal funds for state and local governments and shifted some responsibility for policy back to the states.

When the Republicans captured Congress in the 1994 elections, the first time they had majorities in both houses in 40 years, they often referred to a "revolution" in public policy, one aimed primarily at restricting the scope of the national government and returning responsibility for policies to the states. **Devolution**, transferring responsibility for policies from the federal government to state and local governments, was at the center of their rhetoric. They followed this rhetoric with action as they repealed federal speed limits, allowed states more latitude in dealing with welfare policy, and made it more difficult for state prisoners to seek relief in federal courts.

Since the mid-1990s, however, Republicans have been less concerned with abstract principles and more with adopting a pragmatic approach to federalism to accomplish their goals. They found turning to the federal government—and *restricting* state power—the most effective way to achieve many of their policy objectives, including loosening economic and environmental regulations, controlling immigration, setting health insurance standards, restricting the expansion of government health care coverage, stiffening penalties for criminals, extending federal criminal penalties, and tracking child-support violators. During the presidency of George W. Bush, Republicans passed a law removing most class-action lawsuits from state courts. Most significantly, they passed the No Child Left Behind Act, the largest expansion of the federal role in education since Lyndon Johnson's Great Society and one of the most intrusive policies into traditional federal relations in U.S. history. Many states have complained loudly about the problems and the cost of implementing the legislation.

Today, most Americans embrace a pragmatic view of governmental responsibilities, seeing the national government as more capable of—and thus responsible for—handling some issues (such as managing the economy, ensuring access to health care and that food and medicines are safe, preserving the environment, and providing income security for the elderly), while they view state and local governments as better at managing others (such as crime, welfare, and education).[9]

FISCAL FEDERALISM

The cornerstone of the national government's relations with state and local governments is **fiscal federalism**: the pattern of spending, taxing, and providing grants in the federal system. Subnational governments can influence the

devolution
Transferring responsibility for policies from the federal government to state and local governments.

fiscal federalism
The pattern of spending, taxing, and providing grants in the federal system; it is the cornerstone of the national government's relations with state and local governments.

national government through local elections for national officials, but the national government has a powerful source of influence over the states—money. Grants-in-aid, federal funds appropriated by Congress for distribution to state and local governments, are the main instrument the national government uses for both aiding and influencing states and localities.

Federal aid (including loan subsidies) amounted to about $484 billion in 2010. Figure 3.1 illustrates the growth in the amount of money spent on federal grants. Federal aid, covering a wide range of policy areas (see "A Generation of Change: Functions of Federal Grants"), accounts for about 21 percent of all the funds spent by state and local governments and for about 16 percent of all federal government expenditures.[10]

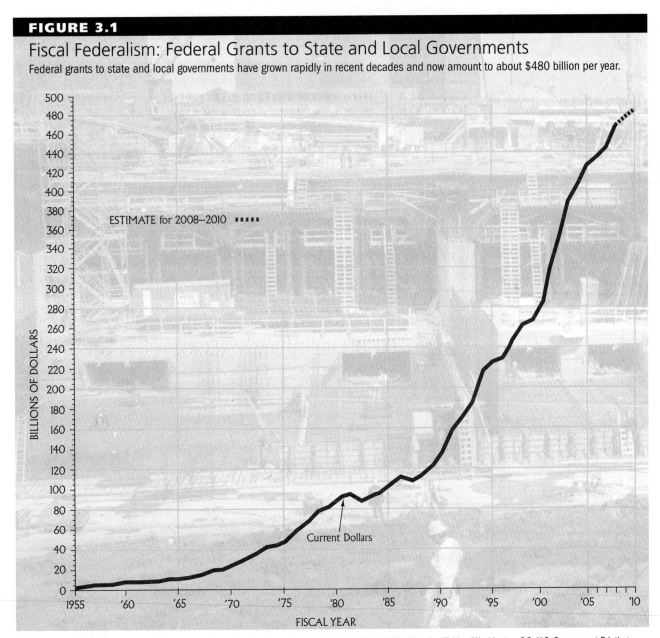

FIGURE 3.1

Fiscal Federalism: Federal Grants to State and Local Governments

Federal grants to state and local governments have grown rapidly in recent decades and now amount to about $480 billion per year.

ESTIMATE for 2008–2010

Current Dollars

BILLIONS OF DOLLARS

FISCAL YEAR

Source: Office of Management and Budget, *Budget of the United States Government, Fiscal Year 2009: Historical Tables* (Washington, DC: U.S. Government Printing Office, 2008), Table 12.1.

Cooperative federalism began during the Great Depression of the 1930s and continues into the twenty-first century. This photo shows the Big Dig in Boston, the largest and most complex highway and tunnel project in the nation's history. The federal government provided about half of the funds for this extraordinarily expensive public work.

categorical grants

Federal grants that can be used only for specific purposes, or "categories," of state and local spending. They come with strings attached, such as nondiscrimination provisions. Compare **block grants**.

Why It Matters

Grants-in-Aid

The federal system of grants-in-aid sends revenues from federal taxes to state and local governments. This transfers the burden of paying for services from those who pay state and local taxes, such as taxes on sales and property, to those who pay national taxes, especially the federal income tax.

The Grant System: Distributing the Federal Pie   The national government regularly publishes the *Catalogue of Federal Domestic Assistance,* a massive volume listing the federal aid programs available to states, cities, and other local governments. The book lists federal programs that support energy assistance for the elderly poor, housing allowances for the poor, drug abuse services, urban rat control efforts, community arts programs, state disaster preparedness programs, and many more.

There are two major types of federal aid for states and localities: categorical grants and block grants. **Categorical grants** are the main source of federal aid to state and local governments. These grants can be used only for one of several hundred specific purposes, or categories, of state and local spending.

Because direct orders from the federal government to the states are rare (an exception is the Equal Opportunity Act of 1982, which bars job discrimination by state and local governments), most federal regulation is accomplished in a more indirect manner. Instead of issuing edicts that tell citizens or states what they can and cannot do, Congress attaches conditions to the grants that states receive. The federal government has been especially active in appending restrictions to grants since the 1970s.

One string commonly attached to categorical and other federal grants is a nondiscrimination provision, stating that aid may not be used for purposes that discriminate against minorities, women, or other groups. Another string, a favorite of labor unions, is that federal funds may not support construction projects that pay below the local union wage. Other restrictions may require an environmental impact statement for a federally supported construction project or provisions for community involvement in the planning of the project.

The federal government may also employ *crossover sanctions*—using federal dollars in one program to influence state and local policy in another, such as when funds are withheld for highway construction unless states raise the drinking age to 21 or establish highway beautification programs.

Crosscutting requirements occur when a condition on one federal grant is extended to all activities supported by federal funds, regardless of their source. The grandfather of these requirements is Title VI of the 1964 Civil Rights Act (see Chapter 5), which bars discrimination in the use of federal funds because of race, color, national origin, gender, or physical disability. For example, if a university discriminates illegally in one program—such as athletics—it may lose the federal aid it receives for all its programs. There are also crosscutting requirements dealing with environmental protection, historic preservation, contract wage rates, access to government information, the care of experimental animals, the treatment of human subjects in research projects, and a host of other policies.

A GENERATION OF CHANGE

Functions of **Federal Grants**

Federal grants support many policies, and the distribution of grants is not static. The priorities of federal grants have changed over the past generation. The percentage of grants devoted to health care, especially Medicaid, has increased substantially, mostly at the expense of income security and education and training programs.

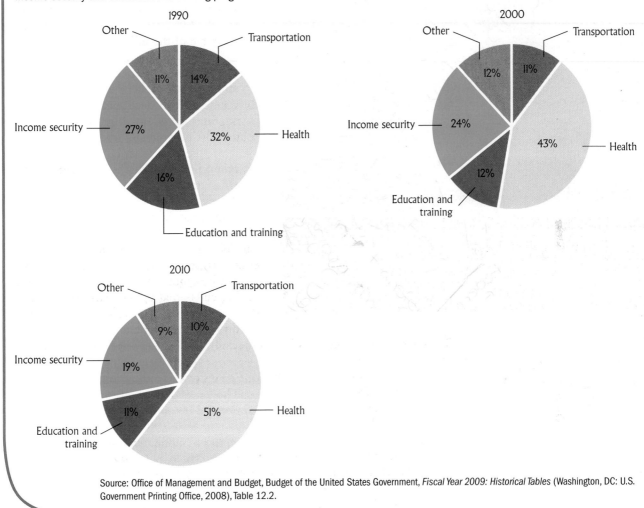

Source: Office of Management and Budget, Budget of the United States Government, *Fiscal Year 2009: Historical Tables* (Washington, DC: U.S. Government Printing Office, 2008), Table 12.2.

There are two types of categorical grants. The most common type is a **project grant**. A project grant is awarded on the basis of competitive applications. National Science Foundation grants obtained by university professors are examples of project grants.

As their name implies, **formula grants** are distributed according to a formula. These formulas vary from grant to grant and may be computed on the basis of population, per capita income, percentage of rural population, or some other factor. A state or local government does not apply for a formula grant; a grant's formula determines how much money the particular government will receive. As a result, Congress is the site of vigorous political battles over the formulas themselves. The most common formula grants are those for Medicaid,

project grants
Federal **categorical grants** given for specific purposes and awarded on the basis of the merits of applications.

formula grants
Federal **categorical grants** distributed according to a formula specified in legislation or in administrative regulations.

The federal government often uses grants-in-aid as a carrot and stick for the states. For example, aid has been withheld from some cities until police departments have been racially and sexually integrated.

child nutrition programs, sewage treatment plant construction, public housing, community development programs, and training and employment programs.

Applications for categorical grants typically arrive in Washington in boxes, not envelopes. Complaints about the cumbersome paperwork and the many strings attached to categorical grants led to the adoption of the other major type of federal aid, **block grants**. These grants are given more or less automatically to states or communities, which then have discretion within broad areas in deciding how to spend the money. First adopted in 1966, block grants support programs in areas like community development and social services. The percentage of federal aid to state and local governments in the form of block grants began increasing in 1995 as the new Republican majority in Congress passed more federal aid in the form of block grants, including grants for welfare programs.

block grants

Federal grants given more or less automatically to states or communities to support broad programs in areas such as community development and social services.

The Scramble for Federal Dollars   With more than $480 billion in federal grants at stake, most states and many cities have established full-time staffs in Washington.[11] Their task is to keep track of what money is available and to help their state or city get some of it. There are many Washington organizations of governments—the U.S. Conference of Mayors and the National League of Cities, for example—that act like other interest groups in lobbying Congress. Senators and representatives regularly go to the voters with stories of their influence in securing federal funds for their constituencies. They need continued support at the polls, they say, so that they will rise in seniority and get key posts to help "bring home the bacon."

There are some variations in the amount of money that states give to, and get back from, the national government. On the whole, however, federal grant distribution follows the principle of *universalism*: something for everybody. The vigilance of senators and representatives keeps federal aid reasonably well spread among the states. Indeed, federal aid to states and cities is more equitably distributed than most other things in America, including income, access to education, and taxes.

This equality makes good politics, but it also may undermine public policy. Chapter I of the 1965 Elementary and Secondary Education Act is the federal government's principal endeavor to assist public schools. The primary intent of Chapter I was to give extra help to poor children. Yet the funds are allocated to 95 percent of all the school districts in the country. President Clinton's proposal to concentrate Chapter I funds on the poorest students failed when it ran into predictable opposition in Congress.

The Mandate Blues   States and localities are usually pleased to receive aid from the national government, but there are times when they would just as soon not have it. For example, say Congress decides to extend a program administered by the states and funded, in part, by the national government. It passes a law requiring the states to extend the program if they want to keep receiving aid, which most states do. Requirements that direct states or local governments to comply with federal rules under threat of penalties or as a condition of receipt of a federal grant are called *mandates*. Congress usually (though not always) appropriates some funds to help pay for the new policy, but either way, the states suddenly have to budget more funds for the project just to receive federal grant money.

Medicaid, which provides health care for poor people, is a prime example of a federal grant program that puts states in a difficult situation. Administered by the states, Medicaid receives wide support from both political parties. The national government pays the majority of the bill, and the states pick up the rest. In the past two decades, Congress has moved aggressively to expand Medicaid to specific populations, requiring the states to extend coverage to certain children, pregnant women, and elderly poor. Congress has also increased its funding for the program, but new requirements have meant huge new demands on state budgets as well. In effect, Congress has set priorities for the states.

A related problem arises when Congress passes a law creating financial obligations for the states but provides no funds to meet these obligations. For example, in 1990 Congress passed the Americans with Disabilities Act, requiring states to make facilities, such as state colleges and universities, accessible to individuals with disabilities. Congress allocated no funds to implement this policy, however. Similarly, the Clean Air Act of 1970 established national air quality standards but requires states to administer them and to appropriate funds for their implementation.

In 1995, the newly elected Republican majorities in Congress made limiting unfunded and underfunded mandates on state and local governments a high priority. Congress passed, and President Clinton signed, a law that requires both chambers to take a separate, majority vote in order to pass any bill that would impose unfunded mandates of more than $50 million on state and local governments. The law also requires the Congressional Budget Office to estimate the costs of all bills that impose such mandates. All antidiscrimination legislation and most legislation requiring state and local governments to take various actions in exchange for continued federal funding (such as grants for transportation) are exempt from this procedure.

State and local governments are the first responders in most emergencies, as we have seen in the case with Hurricane Katrina. Their police forces provide most of the nation's internal security, they maintain most of the country's transportation infrastructure (such as highways, mass transit, port facilities, and airports), and they are responsible for protecting the public's health and providing emergency health care. The heightened concern for homeland security since September 11, 2001, has led Congress to impose sizable new mandates on the states to increase their ability to deal with acts of terrorism, but it has not provided all the resources necessary to increase state and local capabilities. Similarly, the No Child Left Behind Act, passed in 2002, threatens school systems with the loss of federal funds if their schools do not

Policies of the federal government may have major impacts on core policies of state and local governments like elementary and secondary education and determine how much is spent on these policies. Here, President George W. Bush speaks about his No Child Left Behind education policy in Nashville, Tennessee.

improve student performance. Such improvements cost money, however, and the federal government has provided only a modest increase in funding.

Federal courts also create unfunded mandates for the states. In recent years, federal judges have issued states orders in areas such as prison construction and management, school desegregation, and facilities in mental health hospitals, sometimes even temporarily taking them over. These court orders often require states to spend funds to meet standards imposed by the judge.

A combination of federal regulations and inadequate resources may also put the states in a bind. The national government requires that a local housing authority build or acquire a new low-income housing facility for each one it demolishes. But for years Congress has provided little money for the construction of public housing. As a result, a provision intended to help the poor by ensuring a stable supply of housing actually hurts them because it discourages local governments from demolishing unsafe and inadequate housing.

The federal government may also unintentionally create financial obligations for the states. In 1994, California, New York, Texas, Florida, and other states sued the federal government for reimbursement for the cost of health care, education, prisons, and other public services that the states provide to illegal residents. The states charged that the federal government's failure to control its borders was the source of huge new demands on their treasuries and that Washington, not the states, should pay for the problem. Although the states did not win their cases, their point is a valid one.

UNDERSTANDING FEDERALISM

The federal system is central to politics, government, and policy in America. The division of powers and responsibilities among different levels of government has implications for both the themes of democracy and the scope of government.

FEDERALISM AND DEMOCRACY

Federalism

One of the reasons the Founders established a federal system was to allay the fears of those who believed that a powerful and distant central government would tyrannize the states and limit their voice in government. By decentralizing the political system, federalism was designed to contribute to democracy—or at least to the limited form of democracy supported by the Founders. Has it done so?

The more levels of government, the more opportunities there are for participation in politics. State governments provide thousands of elected offices for which citizens may vote and/or run.

Additional levels of government also contribute to democracy by increasing access to government. Because different citizens and interest groups will have better access to either state-level governments or the national government, the two levels increase the opportunities for government to be responsive to demands for policies. For example, in the 1950s and 1960s when advocates of civil rights found themselves stymied in Southern states, they turned to the national level for help in achieving racial equality. Business interests, on the other hand, have traditionally found state governments to be more responsive to their demands. Organized labor is not well established in some states, but it can usually depend on some sympathetic officials at the national level who will champion its proposals.

Different economic interests are concentrated in different states: energy in Texas, citrus growing in Florida and California, and copper mining in Montana, for example. The federal system allows an interest concentrated in a state to exercise substantial influence in the election of that state's officials, both local and national. In turn, these officials promote policies advantageous to the interest in both Washington and the state capital. This is a pluralism of interests that James Madison, among others, valued within a large republic.

State and local bases have another advantage. Even if a party loses at the national level, it can rebuild in its areas of strength and develop leaders under its banner at the state and local levels. As a result, losing an election becomes more acceptable, and the peaceful transfer of power is more probable. This was especially important in the early years of the nation before our political norms had become firmly established.

Because the federal system assigns states important responsibilities for public policies, it is possible for the diversity of opinion within the country to be reflected in different public policies among the states. If the citizens of Texas wish to have a death penalty, for example, they can vote for politicians who support it, whereas those in Wisconsin can vote to abolish the death penalty altogether (see "You Are the Policymaker: Should *Whether* You Live Depend on *Where* You Live?").

States may also take initiatives on what most people view as national policies when the federal government acts contrary to the views of people within those states. Many states raised the minimum wage when Congress did not. Some states funded stem cell research after George W. Bush severely restricted it on the federal

YOU ARE THE **Policymaker**

Should *Whether* You Live Depend on *Where* You Live?

Because the federal system allocates major responsibilities for public policy to the states, policies often vary with the different views of the population in different locations. The differences among public policies are especially dramatic in the criminal justice system.

A conviction for first-degree murder in 36 states may well mean the death penalty for the convicted murderer. In 14 other states and the District of Columbia, first-degree murderers are subject only to a maximum penalty of life behind bars.

Some people see diversity in public policy as one of the advantages of federalism. Others may argue that citizens of the same country ought to be subject to uniform penalties. What do *you* think? Should *whether* you live depend on *where* you live?

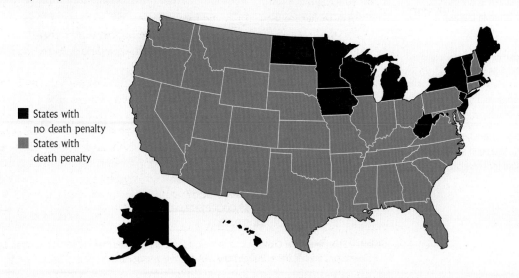

■ States with no death penalty
■ States with death penalty

level. Similarly, many states have taken the lead in raising the standards for environmental protection after they concluded the national government was too lenient.

By handling most disputes over policy at the state and local levels, federalism also reduces decision making and conflict at the national level. If every issue had to be resolved in Washington, the national government would be overwhelmed.

Despite its advantages for democracy, relying on states to supply public services has some drawbacks. States differ in the resources they can devote to services like public education. Thus, the quality of education a child receives is heavily dependent on the state in which the child's parents happen to reside. In 2005, the District of Columbia and New Jersey spent $16,550 and $13,740 per student, respectively, while Utah spent only $5,574 (see "My State: State and Local Spending on Public Education).

Diversity in policy can also discourage states from providing services that would otherwise be available. Political scientists have found that generous welfare benefits can strain a state's treasury by attracting poor people from states with lower benefits. As a result, states may be deterred from providing generous benefits to those in need. A national program with uniform welfare benefits would provide no incentive for welfare recipients to move to another state in search of higher benefits.[12]

Federalism may also have a negative effect on democracy insofar as local interests are able to thwart national majority support of certain policies. As we discussed earlier in this chapter, in the 1960s the states—especially those in the South— became battlegrounds when the national government tried to enforce national civil

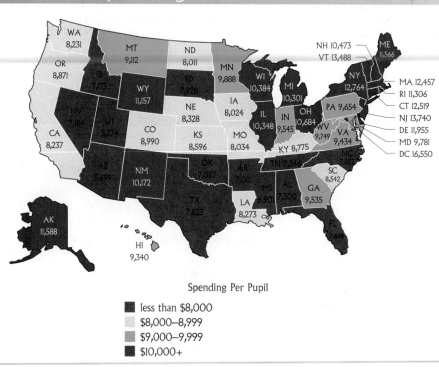

MyState | State and Local Spending on Public Education

The downside of the public policy diversity fostered by federalism is that states are largely dependent on their own resources for providing public services; these resources vary widely from state to state. This map shows the great variation among the states in the money spent on children in the public schools.

QUESTIONS FOR DISCUSSION

▶ How does your state rank in terms of education spending?

▶ Would you have been better off if there had been a national standard for spending?

Spending Per Pupil

■ less than $8,000
▨ $8,000–8,999
▨ $9,000–9,999
■ $10,000+

Source: U.S. Department of Commerce, *Statistical Abstract of the United States*, 2008 (Washington, DC: U.S. Government Printing Office, 2008), Table 249. The data are for 2005.

rights laws and court decisions. Federalism complicated and delayed efforts to end racial discrimination because state and local governments were responsible for public education and voting eligibility, for example, and because they had passed most of the laws supporting racial segregation.

Finally, the sheer number of governments in the United States is, at times, as much a burden as a boon to democracy. Program vendors at baseball games say, "You can't tell the players without a scorecard"; unfortunately, scorecards are not available for local governments, where the players are numerous and sometimes seem to be involved in different games. The U.S. Bureau of the Census counts not only people but also governments. Its latest count revealed an astonishing 87,576 American governments (see Table 3.3).

Certainly, 87,000 governments ought to be enough for any country. Are there too many? Americans speak eloquently about their state and local governments as grassroots governments, close to the people. Yet having so many governments makes it difficult to know which governments are doing what. Exercising democratic control over them is even more difficult; voter turnout in local elections is often less than 20 percent.

FEDERALISM AND THE SCOPE OF THE NATIONAL GOVERNMENT

One of the most persistent questions in American politics has been the scope of the national government relative to that of the states. To understand the relative roles of the two levels of government, we must first understand why the national government grew and then ask whether this growth was at the expense of the states or whether it occurred because of the unique capabilities and responsibilities of the national government.

President Ronald Reagan negotiated quotas on imports of Japanese cars in order to give advantages to the American auto industry, raising the price of all automobiles in the process. At the behest of steel companies, President George H. W. Bush exercised his authority to continue Reagan's quotas on the amount of steel that could be

---

TABLE 3.3

The Number of Governments in America

GOVERNMENT LEVEL	NUMBER OF GOVERNMENTS
U.S. government	1
States	50
Counties	3,034
Municipalities	19,429
Townships or towns	16,504
School districts	13,506
Special districts	35,052
Total	87,576

Source: U.S. Department of Commerce, *Statistical Abstract of the United States, 2008* (Washington, DC: U.S. Government Printing Office, 2008), Table 414.

imported (thereby making steel products more expensive). In addition, the first major piece of legislation the Bush administration sent to Congress in 1989 was a bailout plan for the savings and loan industry, which had gotten into financial trouble through a combination of imprudent loans, declining property values, deregulation of banking, incompetence, and corruption. President Clinton proposed that the Pentagon spend nearly $600 million to fund the development of a U.S. industry in "flat-panel displays" used for laptop computers, video games, and advanced instruments. In 2002, President George W. Bush raised tariffs on imported steel—contrary to his position in favor of the open marketplace. He also signed bills providing tax breaks and loan guarantees to oil and pipeline companies.

In each of these cases and dozens of others, the national government has involved itself (some might say interfered) in the economic marketplace with quotas and subsidies intended to help American businesses. As Chapter 2 explained, the national government took a direct interest in economic affairs from the very founding of the republic. As the United States changed from an agricultural to an industrial nation, new problems arose and with them new demands for governmental action. The national government responded with a national banking system, subsidies for railroads and airlines, and a host of other policies that dramatically increased its role in the economy.

The industrialization of the country raised other issues as well. With the formation of large corporations in the late nineteenth century—Cornelius Vanderbilt's New York Central Railroad and John D. Rockefeller's Standard Oil Company, for example—came the potential for such abuses as monopoly pricing. If there is only one railroad in town, it can charge farmers inflated prices to ship their grain to market. If a single company distributes most of the gasoline in the country, it can set the price at which gasoline sells. Thus, many interests asked the national government to restrain monopolies and to encourage open competition.

There were additional demands on the national government for new public policies. Farmers sought services such as agricultural research, rural electrification, and price supports. Unions wanted the national government to protect their rights to organize and bargain collectively and to help provide safer working conditions, a minimum wage, and pension protection. Along with other groups, labor unions supported a wide range of social welfare policies, from education to health care, that would benefit the average worker. As the country became more urbanized, new problems arose in the areas of housing, welfare, the environment, and transportation. In each case, the relevant interest turned to the national government for help.

Why not turn to the state governments instead? In most cases, the answer is simple: A problem or policy requires the authority and resources of the national government. The Constitution forbids states from having independent defense policies. And even if it did not, how many states would want to take on a responsibility that represents more than half the federal workforce and about one-fifth of federal expenditures?

It is constitutionally permissible but not sensible for the states to handle a wide range of other issues. It makes little sense for Louisiana to pass strict controls on polluting the Mississippi River if most of the river's pollution occurs upstream, where Louisiana has no jurisdiction. Rhode Island has no incentive to create an energy policy because no natural energy reserves are located in the state. Similarly, how effectively can a state regulate an international conglomerate such as General Motors? How can each state, acting individually, manage the nation's money supply?

Each state could have its own space program, but it is much more efficient if the states combine their efforts in one national program. The largest category of federal expenditures is that for economic security, including the Social Security program. Although each state could have its own retirement program, how could state governments determine which state should pay for retirees who move to

FIGURE 3.2

Fiscal Federalism: The Public Sector and the Federal System

The federal government's spending increased rapidly during the Great Depression and World War II. In recent years, the role of both federal and state governments has increased slightly.

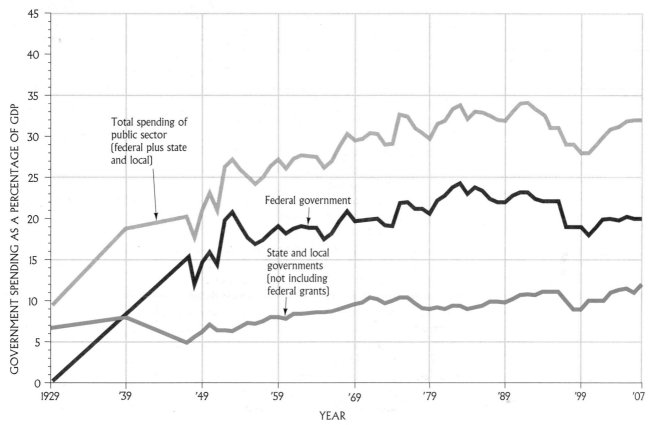

Source: Office of Management and Budget, *Budget of the United States Government, Fiscal Year 2009: Historical Tables* (Washington, DC: U.S. Government Printing Office, 2008), Table 15.3.

Florida or Arizona? A national program is the only feasible method of ensuring the incomes of the mobile elderly of today's society.

Figure 3.2 shows that the national government's share of American governmental expenditures has grown rapidly since 1929; most of this growth occurred during the Great Depression. At that time, the national government spent an amount equal to only 2.5 percent of the size of the economy, the gross domestic product (GDP); today, it spends about 20 percent of our GDP (this includes grants to states and localities). The proportion of our GDP spent by state and local governments has grown less rapidly than the national government's share. States and localities spent 7.4 percent of our GDP in 1929; they spend about 12 percent today (not including federal grants).[13]

Figure 3.2 demonstrates that the states have not been supplanted by the national government; indeed, they carry out virtually all the functions they always have. Instead, with the support of the American people, the national government has taken on new responsibilities. In addition, the national government has added programs to help the states meet their own responsibilities.

SUMMARY

Federalism is a governmental system in which power is shared between a central government and other governments. Federalism is much less common than are the unitary governments typical of most parliamentary democracies. American federalism consists of 50 state governments joined in an "indestructible union" (as the Supreme Court once called it) under one national government. Today, federal power over the states is indisputable; the Supreme Court cases *McCulloch v. Maryland* and *Gibbons v. Ogden,* the Civil War, and the struggle for racial equality all helped to determine national supremacy. The federal government often uses its fiscal leverage to influence state and local policies.

The United States has moved from a system of dual federalism to one of cooperative federalism, in which the national and state governments share responsibility for public policies. Fiscal federalism is of great help to states. The federal government distributes about $480 billion in federal funds to states and cities each year.

The Founders instituted federalism largely to enhance democracy in America, and it strengthens democratic government in many ways. At the same time, diverse state policies and the sheer number of local governments cause problems as well. Demands for new policies and the necessity for national policy on certain issues have contributed to the growth of national government relative to state governments. Yet the state governments continue to play a central role in governing the lives of Americans.

Although American federalism concerns state power and national power, it is not a concept removed from most Americans' lives. Federalism affects a vast range of social and economic policies. Slavery, school desegregation, abortion, and teenage drinking have all been debated in terms of federalism.

Chapter Test

Multiple Choice

1. Governments in which all power resides in the central government are called:
   a. Federal governments
   b. Confederate governments
   c. Unitary governments
   d. Pluralist governments
   e. National governments

2. How common is a federal governmental structure around the world?
   a. Fewer than 1 in 10 nations have them
   b. Only about one-third of nations have them
   c. Roughly half of nations have them
   d. More than three-quarters of nations have them
   e. All nations have some form of federalism

3. Which of the following is NOT considered part of the supreme law of the land, according to the supremacy clause?
   a. The Constitution
   b. Laws of the national government
   c. Treaties
   d. Executive orders
   e. All of the above are considered part of the supreme law of the land

4. The Eleventh Amendment protects states from:
   a. Individual damage suits against state officials
   b. Being sued against their consent by private parties in federal courts
   c. Being sued against their consent by private parties in state courts

   d. Being sued against their consent by private parties before federal administrative agencies
   e. All of the above

5. The term "devolution" refers to the transfer of responsibility for policies:
   a. From the local to the state level
   b. From the local to the national level
   c. From the state to the national level
   d. From one state to another
   e. From the national to the state or local level

6. In the past, there have been debates among some groups about adding Puerto Rico as the United States' 51st state. Based on the division of power in the U.S. federalist system, at what

level would this decision need to be made?
a. In the U.S. Senate only
b. In the House of Representatives only
c. In Congress, with presidential approval
d. In Congress, with state legislatures' approval
e. In state legislatures only

7. The "full faith and credit" clause in Article IV of the Constitution is primarily design to ensure the principle of _____ between states.
a. Communication
b. Reciprocity
c. Honesty
d. Commerce
e. Goodwill

8. According the regulation of privileges and immunities between states, a tourist from Michigan buying a product in California:
a. Pays the Michigan sales tax
b. Pays the California sales tax
c. Pays both the California and the Michigan sales tax
d. Can choose whether s/he wants to pay the California or Michigan sales tax
e. Pays the California sales tax, but can ask to be reimbursed when returning to Michigan

9. Which of the following is NOT an example of cooperative federalism?
a. No Child Left Behind
b. The National Defense Education Act

c. The Elementary and Secondary Education Act
e. The U.S. Postal Service Act

10. If the federal government tells a state that in order to receive federal funds to fight drug abuse the state has to agree to restrict access of teenagers to cigarettes, this is an example of:
a. Categorical grants
b. Block grants
c. Formula grants
d. Crossover sanctions
e. Crosscutting requirements

True/False

11. Federalism is a governmental system in which three or more levels of government (local, state, federal) have formal authority over the same area and people.
True_____   False_____

12. In the United States, the national government has the power to pass laws that directly regulate drinking ages, marriage and divorce, or speed limits.
True_____   False_____

13. It is possible to force states to extradite a criminal to the state in which the crime was committed.
True_____   False_____

14. Over the past generation, the percentage of federal grants devoted to education and training programs has decreased in favor of grants devoted to health care.
True_____   False_____

Short Answer

15. Please explain in your own words how the aid efforts following Hurricane Katrina illustrate the complex relationship between local, state, and federal levels of government.

16. Please name and briefly explain the four key events that have largely settled the issue of how national and state powers are related.

17. Please explain the difference between dual federalism and cooperative federalism, using examples to illustrate your answer.

18. Explain at least two possible factors that might prompt a nation to adopt a federal system, and why they do so.

19. Please address the debate surrounding the Tenth Amendment and the state power vis-à-vis the national government's power. In your answer, outline the different interpretations of the Tenth Amendment with regard to this question, as well as the important Supreme Court decisions that contributed to the debate over time.

Short Answer/Essay Questions

20. Imagine that you are a state official in charge of creating a new program designed to reduce high school dropout rates. Also assume that you want to be able to have as much freedom in the process as possible. In order to finance your program, however, you require assistance through federal grants. Using your knowledge of the different types of grants available from the federal government (e.g., categorical vs. block grant, project vs. formula grant, etc.), which type would you prefer to receive for your program, and why?

21. Look at the MyState map on page 92. How does your state compare to other states in terms of its state and local spending? If you were in a position of power, how would

you redistribute your state's spending, and why would you do so? (If you would leave the spending the same, please explain why you feel there is no need for change.)

22. What are the pros and cons of decentralized politics and policies? Please name and explain at least two each.

23. The textbook illustrates the gradual shift from a dual federalism to a cooperative federalism in the United States over time. In your opinion, what are some of the factors that might explain such a shift? In addition, what are the possible advantages and disadvantages that have resulted from this development? Please use concrete examples to illustrate your arguments.

24. Explain in what ways the process of devolution is related to the concept of balance of power between the different levels of government.

25. Please compare and contrast the distribution of power between central government, state government, and citizens in a confederate as opposed to a federal system of government. In your opinion, which is the more democratic system, and why?

26. Based on what you know about the phenomenon of globalization and advances in transportation and communication technology, in what ways could you see these developments affecting the debate surrounding the "commerce powers" of Congress? Specifically, do you believe the changing nature of commerce should warrant a reinterpretation of these power, and if so, why?

27. The textbook raises the question of whether or not diversity in public policy—such as different penalties for convicted murderers—from state to state can be considered an advantage or a disadvantage. In your opinion, is such diversity democratic? Why or why not?

Answer Key

1. C   2. A   3. D   4. E   5. E   6. D   7. B   8. B   9. E   10. D   11. False   12. False   13. False   14. True

Key Terms

federalism (72)

unitary governments (72)

intergovernmental relations (74)

supremacy clause (76)

Tenth Amendment (76)

McCulloch v. Maryland (77)

enumerated powers (78)

implied powers (78)

elastic clause (78)

Gibbons v. Ogden (78)

full faith and credit (80)

extradition (81)

privileges and immunities (81)

dual federalism (82)

cooperative federalism (82)

devolution (84)

fiscal federalism (84)

categorical grants (86)

project grants (86)

formula grants (88)

block grants (88)

Internet Resources

www.cfda.gov
Allows you to search through hundreds of federal grants.

www.ncsl.org/statefed/statefed.htm
Information and discussion of issues on federal–state relations.

www.census.gov/compendia/statab/
The *Statistical Abstract of the United States* Contains a wealth of data on state public policies.

www.csg.org/CSG/default.aspx
Council of State Governments Web site with information on states and state public policies.

GetConnected

Intergovernmental Relations

Even though education, like public safety and public health, is the responsibility of the states, the national government still finds ways to shape education policy. In January 2002, President George W. Bush signed the No Child Left Behind Act into law. This act sets federal standards for education and then makes federal grants available to states that agree to achieve these new national standards. Let us take a closer look at this federal law to determine its impact on federalism.

Search the Web

Reviewing a federal law can be challenging. This review will not be that difficult, however. First, review the Statement of Purposes (just review sec. 1001) of the No Child Left Behind Act, *www.ed.gov/policy/elsec/leg/esea02/pg1. html#sec1001*, so you can gain a basic understanding of the intent of the legislation. Now review the part of the bill that says what the federal government will do for the states (just review secs. 6111 and 6112), *www.ed.gov/policy/elsec/ leg/esea02/pg87.html#sec6111*. Finally, read what the states must do in order to receive federal money (sec. 1111), *www.ed.gov/policy/elsec/leg/esea02/pg2.html#sec1111*. The National Education Association, *www.nea.org/esea/ index.html*, is a critic of No Child Left Behind. The C-SPAN Web site, *www.c-span.org/guide/congress/ glossary/unfunded.htm*, has a definition of "unfunded mandate."

Questions to Ask

- What do states get from the federal government under this act?
- What are some of the things states have to do in order to get the federal money?
- On what does the National Education Association base its criticism of the No Child Left Behind Act?
- Is the No Child Left Behind Act an unfunded mandate?

Why It Matters

Even though the United States is a federal system of governance, increasingly the national government establishes national standards and then encourages states to comply with those standards through a system of spending, taxing, and providing grants—all of which can have a direct effect on you.

Get Involved

Talk to an elementary or high school teacher or a school board member in your community about the No Child Left Behind Act. How does it affect them? How do they think this act will affect the quality of education in the community? *For more exercises, go to www. longmanamericangovernment.com.*

For Further Reading

Beer, Samuel H. *To Make a Nation: The Rediscovery of American Federalism.* Cambridge, MA: Harvard University Press, 1993. An excellent study of the philosophical bases of American federalism.

Conlan, Timothy J. *From New Federalism to Devolution: Twenty-Five Years of Intergovernmental Reform.* Washington, DC: Brookings Institution, 1998. An analysis of the efforts to restructure intergovernmental relations since the late 1960s.

Elazar, Daniel J. *American Federalism: A View from the States,* 3rd ed. New York: Harper&Row, 1984. A well-known work surveying federalism from the standpoint of state governments.

Gerston, Larry N. *American Federalism.* New York: M.E. Sharpe, 2007. A concise introduction to federalism.

O'Toole, Laurence. *American Intergovernmental Relations,* 4th ed. Washington, DC: CQ Press, 2006. Essays on many aspects of federalism.

Peterson, Paul E. *The Price of Federalism.* Washington, DC: Brookings Institution, 1995. A good assessment of the costs and benefits of federalism.

Posner, Paul L, and Timothy J. Conlan. *Intergovernmental Management for the 21st Century.* Washington, DC: Brookings Institution, 2007. Assesses the state of intergovernmental relations in the U.S. and an agenda for improving them.

Walker, David B. *The Rebirth of Federalism.* 2nd ed. Chatham, NJ: Chatham House, 2000. A history of American federalism and an analysis of its current condition.

Bishop Byrne
Middle & High School
PRO-LIFE
Memphis, Tennessee
FACE IT
Abortion Kills!
AMERICAN LIFE LEAGUE www.all.org

CIVIL LIBERTIES AND PUBLIC POLICY

POLITICS IN ACTION:
FREE SPEECH ON CAMPUS

The Board of Regents of the University of Wisconsin System requires students at the university's Madison campus to pay an activity fee that supports various campus services and extracurricular student activities. In the university's view, such fees enhance students' educational experiences by promoting extracurricular activities, stimulating advocacy and debate on diverse points of view, enabling participation in campus administrative activity, and providing opportunities to develop social skills, all consistent with the university's broad educational mission. Registered student organizations (RSOs) engaging in a number of diverse expressive activities are eligible to receive a portion of the fees, which are administered by the student government subject to the university's approval.

There has been broad agreement that the process for reviewing and approving RSO applications for funding is administered in a viewpoint-neutral fashion. RSOs may also obtain funding through a student referendum. Some students, however, sued the university, alleging that the activity fee violated their First Amendment rights and that the university must grant them the choice not to fund RSOs that engage in political and ideological expression offensive to their personal beliefs.

In 2000, the Supreme Court held in a unanimous decision in *Board of Regents of University of Wisconsin System v. Southworth* that if a university determines that its mission is

Issues of civil liberties present many vexing problems for the courts to resolve. For example, is a display of the Ten Commandments on a government site simply a recognition of their historic importance to the development of law or an impermissible use of government power to establish religion?

well served if students have the means to engage in dynamic discussion on a broad range of issues, it may impose a mandatory fee to sustain such dialogue. The Court recognized that it was all but inevitable that the fees will subsidize speech that some students find objectionable or offensive. Thus, the Court required that a university provide some protection to its students' First Amendment interests by requiring viewpoint neutrality in the allocation of funding support.

The University of Wisconsin case is the sort of complex controversy that shapes American civil liberties. Debates about the right to abortion, the right to bear arms, the separation of church and state, and similar issues are constantly in the news. Some of these issues arise from conflicting interests. The need to protect society against crime often conflicts with society's need to protect the rights of people accused of crime. Other conflicts derive from strong differences of opinion about what is ethical, moral, or right. To some Americans, abortion is murder, the taking of a human life. To others, a woman's choice whether to bear a child, free of governmental intrusion, is a fundamental right. Everyone, however, is affected by the extent of our civil liberties.

Deciding complex questions about civil liberties requires balancing competing values, such as maintaining an open system of expression while protecting individuals from the excesses such a system may produce. As we learned in Chapter 1, civil liberties are essential to democracy. How could we have free elections without free speech, for example? But does it follow that critics of officials should be able to say whatever they want, no matter how untrue? And who should decide the extent of our liberty? Should it be a representative institution such as Congress or a judicial elite such as the Supreme Court?

The role of the government in resolving civil liberties controversies is also the subject of much debate. Conservatives usually advocate narrowing the scope of government, yet many strongly support government-imposed limits on abortion and government-sanctioned prayers in public schools. They also want government to be less hindered by concern for defendants' rights. Liberals, who typically support a broader scope of government, usually want to limit government's role in prohibiting abortion and encouraging religious activities and to place greater constraints on government's freedom of action in the criminal justice system.

Civil liberties are individual legal and constitutional protections against the government. Americans' civil liberties are set down in the **Bill of Rights**, the first 10 amendments to the Constitution. At first glance, many questions about civil liberties look easy to resolve. The Bill of Rights' guarantee of a free press seems straightforward; either Americans can write what they choose, or they cannot. In the real world of American law, however, these issues are subtle and complex.

Disputes about civil liberties often end up in court. The Supreme Court of the United States is the final interpreter of the content and scope of our liberties; this ultimate power to interpret the Constitution accounts for the ferocious debate over presidential appointments to the Supreme Court.

Throughout this chapter you will find special features titled "You Are the Judge." Each feature describes an actual case brought before the courts and asks you to apply your sense of fairness and your standards to arrive at a judgment.

To understand the specifics of American civil liberties, we must first understand the Bill of Rights.

Civil liberties

The legal constitutional protections against government. Although our civil liberties are formally set down in the **Bill of Rights**, the courts, police, and legislatures define their meaning.

Bill of Rights

The first 10 amendments to the **U.S. Constitution**, which define such basic liberties as freedom of religion, speech, and press and guarantee defendants' rights.

THE BILL OF RIGHTS—THEN AND NOW

By 1787, all state constitutions had bills of rights, some of which survive, intact, to this day. Although the new U.S. Constitution had no bill of rights, the state ratifying conventions made its inclusion a condition of ratification. The First Congress passed the Bill of Rights in 1789 and sent it to the states for ratification. In 1791, these amendments became part of the Constitution.

The Bill of Rights ensures Americans' basic liberties, such as freedom of speech and religion, and protection against arbitrary searches and being held for long periods without trial (see Table 4.1). The Bill of Rights was ratified when British abuses of the colonists' civil liberties were still a fresh and bitter memory. Colonial officials had jailed newspaper editors; arrested citizens without cause; and detained people and forced them to confess at gunpoint or worse. Thus, the first 10 amendments enjoyed great popular support.

Political scientists have discovered that people are devotees of rights in theory but that their support wavers when it comes time to put those rights into practice.[1] For example, Americans in general believe in freedom of speech, but many citizens would not let the Ku Klux Klan speak in their neighborhood or allow their public schools to teach about atheism or homosexuality. In addition, Americans seem willing to trade off civil liberties for security when they feel that the nation is threatened, as in the case of terrorism.[2] Few rights are absolute; we cannot avoid the difficult questions of balancing civil liberties and other individual and societal values.

THE BILL OF RIGHTS AND THE STATES

Take another look at the **First Amendment**. Note the first words: "Congress shall make no law. . . ." The Founders wrote the Bill of Rights to restrict the powers of the new national government. In 1791, Americans were comfortable with their state governments; after all, every state constitution had its own bill of rights. Thus, a literal reading of the First Amendment suggests that it does not prohibit a state government from passing a law prohibiting the free exercise of religion, free speech, or freedom of the press.

What happens, however, if a state passes a law violating one of the rights protected by the federal Bill of Rights and the state's constitution does not prohibit this abridgment of freedom? In 1833, the answer to that question was "nothing." The Bill of Rights, said the Court in **Barron v. Baltimore**, restrained only the national government, not states and cities.

Almost a century later, however, the Court ruled that a state government must respect some First Amendment rights. The 1925 ruling in **Gitlow v. New York** relied not on the First Amendment but on the Fourteenth—the second of three "Civil War Amendments" that ended slavery, gave former slaves legal protection, and ensured their voting rights. Ratified in 1868, the **Fourteenth Amendment** declared,

> No state shall make or enforce any law which shall abridge the privileges or immunities of citizens of the United States nor shall any state deprive any person of life, liberty, or property, without due process of law; nor deny to any person within its jurisdiction the equal protection of the laws.

In *Gitlow*, the Court announced that freedoms of speech and press "were fundamental personal rights and liberties protected by the **due process clause** of the Fourteenth Amendment from impairment by the states." In effect, the Court interpreted the Fourteenth Amendment to say that states could not abridge the freedoms of expression protected by the First Amendment. This decision began the development

First Amendment
The constitutional amendment that establishes the four great liberties: freedom of the press, of speech, of religion, and of assembly.

Barron v. Baltimore
The 1833 Supreme Court decision holding that the **Bill of Rights** restrained only the national government, not the states and cities.

Gitlow v. New York
The 1925 Supreme Court decision holding that freedoms of press and speech are "fundamental personal rights and liberties protected by the **due process clause** of the **Fourteenth Amendment** from impairment by the states" as well as by the federal government. Compare **Barron v. Baltimore**.

Fourteenth Amendment
The constitutional amendment adopted after the Civil War that states, "No State shall make or enforce any law which shall abridge the privileges or immunities of citizens of the United States; nor shall any state deprive any person of life, liberty, or property, without due process of law; nor deny to any person within its jurisdiction the **equal protection of the laws**." See also **due process clause**.

due process clause
Part of the Fourteenth Amendment guaranteeing that persons cannot be deprived of life, liberty, or property by the United States or state governments without due process of law. See also **Gitlow v. New York**.

TABLE 4.1

The Bill of Rights

These amendments were passed by Congress on September 25, 1789, and ratified by the states on December 15, 1791.

Amendment I—Religion, Speech, Assembly, Petition

Congress shall make no law respecting an establishment of religion, or prohibiting the free exercise thereof; or abridging the freedom of speech, or of the press; or the right of the people peaceably to assemble, and to petition the Government for a redress of grievances.

Amendment II—Right to Bear Arms

A well-regulated militia, being necessary to the security of a free State, the right of the people to keep and bear arms, shall not be infringed.

Amendment III—Quartering of Soldiers

No Soldier shall, in time of peace be quartered in any house, without the consent of the owner, nor in time of war, but in a manner to be prescribed by law.

Amendment IV—Searches and Seizures

The right of the people to be secure in their persons, houses, papers, and effects, against unreasonable searches and seizures, shall not be violated, and no warrants shall issue, but upon probable cause, supported by oath or affirmation, and particularly describing the place to be searched, and persons or things to be seized.

Amendment V—Grand Juries, Double Jeopardy, Self-Incrimination, Due Process, Eminent Domain

No person shall be held to answer to a capital, or otherwise infamous crime, unless on a presentment or indictment of a Grand Jury, except in cases arising in the land or naval forces, or in the militia, when in actual service in time of war or public danger: nor shall any person be subject for the same offense to be twice put in jeopardy of life or limb; nor shall be compelled in any criminal case to be a witness against himself, nor be deprived of life, liberty, or property, without due process of law; nor shall private property be taken for public use, without just compensation.

Amendment VI—Criminal Court Procedures

In all criminal prosecutions, the accused shall enjoy the right to a speedy and public trial, by an impartial jury of the State and district wherein the crime shall have been committed, which district shall have been previously ascertained by law, and to be informed of the nature and cause of the accusation; to be confronted with the witnesses against him; to have compulsory process for obtaining witnesses in his favor, and to have the assistance of counsel for his defense.

Amendment VII—Trial by Jury in Common-Law Cases

In Suits at common law, where the value in controversy shall exceed twenty dollars, the right of trial by jury shall be preserved, and no fact tried by a jury, shall be otherwise re-examined in any Court of the United States.

Amendment VIII—Bails, Fines, and Punishment

Excessive bail shall not be required, nor excessive fines imposed, nor cruel and unusual punishments inflicted.

Amendment IX—Rights Retained by the People

The enumeration in the Constitution, of certain rights, shall not be construed to deny or disparage others retained by the people.

Amendment X—Rights Reserved to the States

The powers not delegated to the United States by the Constitution, nor prohibited by it to the States, are reserved to the States respectively, or to the people.

incorporation doctrine
The legal concept under which the **Supreme Court** has nationalized the **Bill of Rights** by making most of its provisions applicable to the states through the **Fourteenth Amendment**.

of the **incorporation doctrine**, the legal concept under which the Supreme Court has nationalized the Bill of Rights by making most of its provisions applicable to the states through the Fourteenth Amendment. However, not everyone agreed that the Fourteenth Amendment incorporated parts of the Bill of Rights into state laws. For example, Edwin Meese, who served as attorney general under Ronald Reagan, strongly criticized *Gitlow* and called for "disincorporation" of the Bill of Rights.

Initially, the Supreme Court held only parts of the First Amendment to be binding on the states as a result of *Gitlow*. Gradually, especially during the 1960s when Earl Warren was chief justice, the Court applied most of the Bill of Rights to the states (see Table 4.2). Many of the judicial decisions that empowered the Bill of Rights were controversial, but today the Bill of Rights guarantees individual freedoms against infringement by state and local governments as well as by the national government. Only the Third and Seventh Amendments, the grand jury requirement of the Fifth Amendment, and the prohibition against excessive fines and bail in the Eighth Amendment have not been applied specifically to the states.

TABLE 4.2

The Nationalization of the Bill of Rights

DATE	AMENDMENT	RIGHT	CASE
1925	First	Freedom of speech	Gitlow v. New York
1931	First	Freedom of the press	Near v. Minnesota
1937	First	Freedom of assembly	De Jonge v. Oregon
1940	First	Free exercise of religion	Cantwell v. Connecticut
1947	First	Establishment of religion	Everson v. Board of Education
1958	First	Freedom of association	NAACP v. Alabama
1963	First	Right to petition government	NAACP v. Button
2008	Second	Right to bear arms	District of Columbia v. Heller
	Third	No quartering of soldiers	Not incorporated[a]
1949	Fourth	No unreasonable searches and seizures	Wolf v. Colorado
1961	Fourth	Exclusionary rule	Mapp v. Ohio
1897	Fifth	Guarantee of just compensation	Chicago, Burlington, and Quincy RR v. Chicago
1964	Fifth	Immunity from self-incrimination	Mallory v. Hogan
1969	Fifth	Immunity from double jeopardy	Benton v. Maryland
	Fifth	Right to grand jury indictment	Not incorporated
1932	Sixth	Right to counsel in capital cases	Powell v. Alabama
1948	Sixth	Right to public trial	In re Oliver
1963	Sixth	Right to counsel in felony cases	Gideon v. Wainwright
1965	Sixth	Right to confrontation of witnesses	Pointer v. Texas
1966	Sixth	Right to impartial jury	Parker v. Gladden
1967	Sixth	Right to speedy trial	Klopfer v. North Carolina
1967	Sixth	Right to compulsory process for obtaining witnesses	Washington v. Texas
1968	Sixth	Right to jury trial for serious crimes	Duncan v. Louisiana
1972	Sixth	Right to counsel for all crimes involving jail terms	Argersinger v. Hamlin
	Seventh	Right to jury trial in civil cases	Not incorporated
1962	Eighth	Freedom from cruel and unusual punishment	Robinson v. California
	Eighth	Freedom from excessive fines or bail	Not incorporated
1965	Ninth	Right of privacy	Griswold v. Connecticut

[a] The quartering of soldiers has not occurred under the Constitution.

FREEDOM OF RELIGION

The First Amendment contains two elements regarding religion and government. These elements are commonly referred to as the establishment clause and the free exercise clause. The **establishment clause** states that "Congress shall make no law respecting an establishment of religion." The **free exercise clause** prohibits the abridgment of citizens' freedom to worship or not to worship as they please. Sometimes these freedoms conflict. The government's practice of providing chaplains on military bases is one example of this conflict; some accuse the government of establishing religion in order to ensure that members of the armed forces can freely practice their religion. Usually, however, establishment clause and free exercise clause cases raise different kinds of conflicts.

establishment clause
Part of the **First Amendment** stating that "Congress shall make no law respecting an establishment of religion."

free exercise clause
A **First Amendment** provision that prohibits government from interfering with the practice of religion.

THE ESTABLISHMENT CLAUSE

Some nations, such as Great Britain, have an established church that is officially supported by the government and recognized as a national institution. A few American colonies had official churches, but the religious persecutions that incited many colonists to move to America discouraged any desire the First Congress might have had to establish a national church in the United States. Thus, the First Amendment prohibits an established national religion.

It is much less clear, however, what else the first Congress intended to be included in the establishment clause. Some people argued that it meant only that the government could not favor one religion over another. In contrast, Thomas Jefferson argued that the First Amendment created a "wall of separation" between church and state, forbidding not just favoritism but also any support for religion at all. These interpretations continue to provoke argument, especially when religion is mixed with education.

Debate is especially intense over aid to church-related schools and prayers in public schools. Proponents of such aid argue that it does not favor any specific religion. Opponents claim that the Roman Catholic Church has by far the largest religious school system in the country and gets most of the aid. It was Protestant Lyndon Baines Johnson who obtained the passage of the first substantial aid to parochial elementary and secondary schools in 1965. He argued that aid went to students, not schools, and thus should go wherever the students were, including church-related schools.

In *Lemon v. Kurtzman* (1971), the Supreme Court declared that aid to church-related schools must do the following:

1. Have a secular legislative purpose
2. Have a primary effect that neither advances nor inhibits religion
3. Not foster an excessive government "entanglement" with religion

Since that time the Court has had to draw a fine line between aid that is permissible and aid that is not. For instance, the Court has allowed religiously affiliated colleges and universities to use public funds to construct buildings. Tax funds may also be used to provide students in parochial schools with textbooks, computers and other instructional equipment, lunches, and transportation to and from school and to administer standardized testing services. However, schools may not use public funds to pay teacher salaries or to provide transportation for students on field trips. The theory underlying these decisions is that it is possible to determine that buildings, textbooks, lunches, school buses, and national tests are not used to support sectarian education. However, determining how teachers handle a subject in class or focus a field trip may require complex and constitutionally impermissible regulation of religion.

In an important loosening of its constraints on aid to parochial schools, the Supreme Court decided in 1997 in *Agostini v. Felton* that public school systems could send teachers into parochial schools to teach remedial and supplemental classes to needy children. In a landmark decision in 2002, the Court in *Zelman v. Simmons-Harris* upheld a program that provided some families in Cleveland, Ohio, vouchers that could be used to pay tuition at religious schools.

Controversy over aid to schools is not limited to Roman Catholic schools or any other single religion. In 1994, the Supreme Court ruled in *Kiryas Joel v. Grumet* that New York state had gone too far in favoring religion when it created a public school district for the benefit of a village of Hasidic Jews.

At the same time, the Supreme Court has been opening public schools to religious activities. The Court decided that public universities that permit student groups to use their facilities must allow student religious groups on campus to use the facilities for religious worship.[3] In the 1984 Equal Access Act, Congress made it unlawful for any public high school receiving federal funds (almost all of them do) to keep student groups from using school facilities for religious worship if the school opens its facilities for other student meetings.[4] In 2001, the Supreme Court extended this

---

Lemon v. Kurtzman

The 1971 Supreme Court decision that established that aid to church-related schools must (1) have a secular legislative purpose; (2) have a primary effect that neither advances nor inhibits religion; and (3) not foster excessive government entanglement with religion.

Zelman v. Simmons-Harris

The 2002 Supreme Court decision that upheld a state providing families with vouchers that could be used to pay for tuition at religious schools.

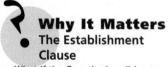

Why It Matters

The Establishment Clause

What if the Constitution did not prohibit the establishment of religion? If a dominant religion received public funds and was in a position to control health care, public education, and other important aspects of public policy, these policies might be quite different from what they are today. In addition, the potential for conflict between followers of the established religion and adherents to other religions would be substantial.

principle to public elementary schools.[5] Similarly, in 1993 the Court required public schools that rent facilities to organizations to do the same for religious groups.[6]

In 1995, the Court held that the University of Virginia was constitutionally required to subsidize a student religious magazine on the same basis as other student publications.[7] However, in 2004 the Court held that the state of Washington was within its rights when it excluded students pursuing a devotional theology degree from its general scholarship program.[8]

The threshold of constitutional acceptability becomes higher when public funds are used in a more direct way to support education. Thus, school authorities may not permit religious instructors to come into public school buildings during the school day to provide religious education,[9] although they may release students from part of the compulsory school day to receive religious instruction elsewhere.[10] In 1980, the Court also prohibited the posting of the Ten Commandments on the walls of public classrooms.[11]

School prayer is perhaps the most controversial religious issue. In 1962 and 1963, the Court aroused the wrath of many Americans by ruling that voluntary recitations of prayers or Bible passages, when done as part of classroom exercises in public schools, violated the establishment clause. In *Engel v. Vitale* and *School District of Abington Township, Pennsylvania v. Schempp* the justices observed that "the place of religion in our society is an exalted one . . . [but] in the relationship between man and religion, the State is firmly committed to a position of neutrality."

It is *not* unconstitutional, of course, to pray in public schools. Students may pray silently as much as they wish. What the Constitution forbids is the sponsorship or encouragement of prayer, directly or indirectly, by public school authorities. Thus, in 1992 the Court ruled that a school-sponsored prayer at a public school graduation violated the constitutional separation of church and state.[12] In 2000, the Court held that student-led prayer at football games was also unconstitutional.[13] Three Alabama laws authorized schools to hold one-minute periods of silence for "meditation or voluntary prayer," but the Court rejected this approach because the state made it clear that the purpose of the statute was to return prayer to the schools. The Court did indicate, however, that a less clumsy approach would pass its scrutiny.[14]

Political scientist Kenneth D. Wald observes that a great ferment in the relationship between religion and American political life has marked recent years. Religious issues and controversies have assumed much greater importance in political debate than they commanded before.[15] Much of this new importance is due to fundamentalist religious groups that have spurred their members to political action. Many school districts have simply ignored the Supreme Court's ban on school prayer and continue to allow prayers in their classrooms. Some religious groups and many members of Congress, especially conservative Republicans, have pushed for a constitutional amendment permitting prayer in school. A majority of the public consistently supports school prayer.[16]

Fundamentalist Christian groups have pressed some state legislatures to mandate the teaching of "creation science"—their alternative to Darwinian theories of evolution—in public schools. Louisiana, for example, passed a law requiring schools that taught Darwinian

Engel v. Vitale
The 1962 Supreme Court decision holding that state officials violated the **First Amendment** when they wrote a prayer to be recited by New York's schoolchildren.

School District of Abington Township, Pennsylvania v. Schempp
A 1963 Supreme Court decision holding that a Pennsylvania law requiring Bible reading in schools violated the **establishment clause** of the **First Amendment**.

One of the most controversial issues regarding the First Amendment's prohibition of the establishment of religion is prayer in public schools. Although students may pray on their own, school authorities may not sponsor or encourage prayer. Some schools violate the law, however. What was your experience with prayer in school?

theory to teach creation science, too. Regardless, the Supreme Court ruled in 1987 that this law violated the establishment clause.[17] The Court had already held in a 1968 case that states cannot prohibit Darwin's theory of evolution from being taught in the public schools.[18] More recently, some groups have advocated "intelligent design," the view that living things are too complicated to have resulted from natural selection and thus must be the result of an intelligent cause, as an alternative to evolution. Although they claim that their belief has no religious implications, lower courts have begun to rule that requiring teachers to present intelligent design as an alternative to evolution is a constitutionally unacceptable promotion of religion in the classroom.

The Supreme Court's struggle to interpret the establishment clause is also evident in areas other than education. In 2005, the Supreme Court found that two Kentucky counties violated the establishment clause value of official religious neutrality when they posted large, readily visible copies of the Ten Commandments in their court-houses. The Court concluded that the counties' ostensible and predominant purpose was to advance religion.[19] However, the Court did not hold that a governmental body can never integrate a sacred text constitutionally into a governmental display on law or history. Thus, in 2005 the Court also upheld the inclusion of a monolith inscribed with the Ten Commandments among the 21 historical markers and 17 monuments surrounding the Texas State Capitol. The Court argued that simply having religious content or promoting a message consistent with a religious doctrine does not run afoul of the establishment clause. Texas's placement of the Commandments monument on its capitol grounds was a far more passive use of those texts than where they confront elementary school students every day and also served a legitimate historical purpose.[20]

Displays of religious symbols during the holidays have prompted considerable controversy. In 1984, the Court found that Pawtucket, Rhode Island, could set up a Christmas nativity scene on public property—along with Santa's house and sleigh, Christmas trees, and other symbols of the Christmas season.[21] Five years later, the Court extended the principle to a Hanukkah menorah placed next to a Christmas tree. The Court concluded that these displays had a secular purpose and provided little or no benefit to religion. At the same time, the Court invalidated the display of the nativity scene without secular symbols in a courthouse because, in this con-text, the county gave the impression of endorsing the display's religious message.[22]

In this case, the Court said the Constitution does not require complete separa-tion of church and state; it mandates accommodation of all religions and forbids hostility toward any. At the same time, the Constitution forbids government endorsement of religious beliefs. Drawing the line between neutrality toward religion and promotion of it is not easy; this dilemma ensures that cases involving the establishment of religion will continue to come before the Court.

THE FREE EXERCISE CLAUSE

The First Amendment also guarantees the free exercise of religion. This guarantee seems simple enough. Whether people hold no religious beliefs, practice voodoo, or go to church, temple, or mosque, they should have the right to practice religion as they choose. In general, Americans are tolerant of those with religious views outside the mainstream, as you can see in "America in Perspective: Tolerance for the Free Speech Rights of Religious Extremists."

The matter is, of course, more complicated. Religions sometimes forbid actions that society thinks are necessary; or, conversely, religions may require actions that society finds unacceptable. For example, what if a religion justifies multiple marriages or the use of illegal drugs? Muhammad Ali, the boxing champion, refused induction into the armed services during the Vietnam War because, he said, military service would violate his Muslim faith. Amish parents often refuse to send their children to public schools. Jehovah's Witnesses and

AMERICA IN PERSPECTIVE

Tolerance for **the Free Speech Rights of Religious Extremists**

Despite 9/11, Americans are more tolerant of the free speech rights of religious extremists than are people in other democracies with developed economies. Why do you think Americans are so tolerant?

Question: Should religious extremists be allowed to hold public meetings?

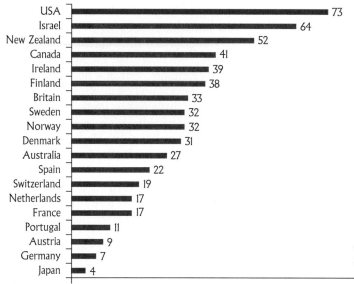

USA	73
Israel	64
New Zealand	52
Canada	41
Ireland	39
Finland	38
Britain	33
Sweden	32
Norway	32
Denmark	31
Australia	27
Spain	22
Switzerland	19
Netherlands	17
France	17
Portugal	11
Austria	9
Germany	7
Japan	4

Percent for allowing meetings of religious extremists

Source: Authors' analysis of 2004 International Social Survey Program data.

Christian Scientists may refuse to accept blood transfusions and certain other kinds of medical treatment for themselves or their children.

Consistently maintaining that people have an inviolable right to *believe* what they want, the courts have been more cautious about the right to *practice* a belief. What if, the Supreme Court once asked, a person "believed that human sacrifices were a necessary part of religious worship?" In *Employment Division v. Smith* (1988), the Court discarded its previous requirement for a *compelling interest* before a government could even indirectly limit or prohibit religious practices. In *Smith*, the Court decided that state laws interfering with religious practices but not specifically aimed at religion are constitutional. As long as a law does not single out and ban religious practices because they are engaged in for religious reasons or only because of the religious belief they display, a general law may be applied to conduct even if the conduct is religiously inspired (denying people unemployment compensation is an exception). In *Smith*, the state of Oregon was allowed to prosecute persons who used the drug peyote as part of their religious rituals.

Cassius Clay was the world heavyweight boxing champion before he converted to Islam, changed his name to Muhammad Ali, and was drafted during the war in Vietnam. Arguing that he opposed war on religious grounds, he refused to join the army. The federal government prosecuted him for draft dodging, and he was stripped of his title. In 1971, the Supreme Court overturned his conviction for draft evasion. He is pictured here at the Houston induction center in 1967.

Even before this decision, the Supreme Court had never permitted religious freedom to be an excuse for any and all behaviors. The Court had upheld laws and regulations forbidding polygamy, outlawing business activities on Sunday as applied to Orthodox Jews, denying tax exemptions to religious schools that discriminate on the basis of race,[23] approving building a road through ground sacred to some Native Americans, and even prohibiting a Jewish air force captain from wearing his yarmulke (Congress later intervened to permit military personnel to wear yarmulkes).

Congress and the Supreme Court have granted protection to other religiously motivated practices under the free exercise clause. The Court allowed Amish parents to take their children out of school after the eighth grade. Reasoning that the Amish community was well established and that its children would not burden the state, the Court held that religious freedom took precedence over compulsory education laws.[24] More broadly, although a state can compel parents to send their children to an accredited school, parents have a right to choose religious schools rather than public schools for their children's education. A state may not require Jehovah's Witnesses or members of other religions to participate in public school flag-saluting ceremonies. Congress has also ruled—and the courts have upheld—that people can become conscientious objectors to war on religious grounds. You can examine another free exercise case in "You Are the Judge: The Case of Animal Sacrifices."

In the Religious Freedom Restoration Act of 1993, Congress attempted to overturn the principle the Court articulated in *Smith*. This act conferred on all persons the right to perform their religious rituals unless the government can show that the law or regulation in question is narrowly tailored and in pursuit of a "compelling interest." In 1997, however, the Supreme Court declared this act an unconstitutional intrusion by Congress into the states' prerogatives for regulating the health and welfare of citizens.[25] In 2000, Congress passed narrower legislation that made it more difficult for local governments to enforce zoning or other regulations against religious groups and required governments to allow those institutionalized in state facilities (such as prisons) to practice their faith according to the "compelling interest" standard. The Supreme Court upheld this law in 2005.[26] The Religious Freedom Restoration Act applies to the federal government, however, and in 2006 the Court allowed a small religious sect to use a hallucinogenic tea in its rituals.[27]

YOU ARE THE Judge

The Case of Animal Sacrifices

The church of Lukumi Babalu Aye, in Hialeah, Florida, practiced Santeria, a Caribbean-based mix of African ritual, voodoo, and Catholicism. Central to Santeria is the ritual sacrifice of animals—at birth, marriage, and death rites as well as at ceremonies to cure the sick and initiate new members.

Offended by these rituals, the city of Hialeah passed ordinances prohibiting animal sacrifices in religious ceremonies. The church challenged the constitutionality of these laws, claiming they violated the free exercise clause of the First Amendment because the ordinances essentially barred the practice of Santeria. The city, the Santerians claimed, was discriminating against a religious minority. Besides, many other forms of killing animals were legal, including fishing, using animals in medical research, selling lobsters to be boiled alive, and feeding live rats to snakes.

You Be the Judge: Do the Santerians have a constitutional right to sacrifice animals in their religious rituals? Does the city's interest in protecting animals outweigh the Santerians' requirement for animal sacrifice?

Decision: In 1993, the Court overturned the Hialeah ordinances that prohibited the use of animal sacrifice in religious ritual. In *Church of the Lukumi Babalu Aye, Inc. v. City of Hialeah*, the justices concluded that governments that permit other forms of killing animals may not then ban sacrifices or ritual killings. In this instance, the Court found no compelling state interest that justified the abridgment of the freedom of religion.

FREEDOM OF EXPRESSION

A democracy depends on the free expression of ideas. Thoughts that are muffled, speech that is forbidden, and meetings that cannot be held are the enemies of the democratic process. Totalitarian governments know this, which is why they go to enormous trouble to limit expression.

Americans pride themselves on their free and open society. Freedom of conscience is absolute; Americans can *believe* whatever they want. The First Amendment plainly forbids the national government from limiting freedom of *expression*—that is, the right to say or publish what one believes. Is freedom of expression, then, like freedom of conscience, also *absolute?* Supreme Court Justice Hugo Black thought so; he was fond of pointing out that the First Amendment said Congress shall make *no* law. "I read no law abridging to mean no law abridging." In contrast, Justice Oliver Wendell Holmes offered a classic example of impermissible speech in 1919: "The most stringent protection of free speech would not protect a man in falsely shouting 'fire' in a theater and causing a panic."

The courts have been called on to decide where to draw the line separating permissible from impermissible speech. In doing so, judges have had to balance freedom of expression against competing values like public order, national security, and the right to a fair trial. One controversial freedom of expression issue involves so-called hate speech. Advocates of regulating hate speech forcefully argue that racial insults, like fighting words, are "undeserving of First Amendment protection because the perpetrator's intent is not to discover the truth or invite dialogue, but to injure the victim."[28] In contrast, critics of hate speech policy argue that "sacrificing free speech rights is too high a price to pay to advance the cause of equality."[29] In 1992, the Supreme Court ruled that legislatures and universities may not single out racial, religious, or sexual insults or threats for prosecution as "hate speech" or "bias crimes."[30]

The courts have also had to decide what kinds of activities do and do not constitute *speech* (or press) within the meaning of the First Amendment. Holding a political rally to attack an opposing candidate's stand on important issues gets First Amendment protection. Obscenity and libel, which are also expressions, do not. To make things more complicated, certain forms of nonverbal speech, such as picketing, are considered symbolic speech and receive First Amendment protection. The courts consider other forms of expression, such as fraud and incitement to violence, to be action rather than speech. Government can limit action more easily than it can limit expression.

The one thing all freedom-of-expression cases have in common is the question of whether a certain expression receives the protection of the Constitution.

PRIOR RESTRAINT

One principle stands out clearly in the complicated history of freedom of expression laws: Time and time again, the Supreme Court has struck down prior restraint on speech and the press. **Prior restraint** refers to a government's actions that prevent material from being published; in a word, prior restraint is censorship. In the United States, the First Amendment ensures that even if the government frowns on some material, a person's right to publish it is all but inviolable. A landmark case involving prior restraint is ***Near v. Minnesota*** (1931). A blunt newspaper editor called local officials a string of names including "grafters" and "Jewish gangsters." The state closed down his business, but the Supreme Court ordered the paper reopened.[31] Of course, the newspaper editor—or anyone else—could later be punished for violating a law or someone's rights *after* publication.

You Are a Supreme Court Justice Deciding a Free Speech Case

Prior restraint
A government preventing material from being published. This is a common method of limiting the press in some nations, but it is usually unconstitutional in the United States, according to the **First Amendment** and as confirmed in the 1931 Supreme Court case of ***Near v. Minnesota***.

Near v. Minnesota
The 1931 Supreme Court decision holding that the **First Amendment** protects newspapers from **prior restraint**.

Civil Liberties and National Security

What Speech is Protected
by the Constitution?

The extent of an individual's or group's freedom from prior restraint does depend in part, however, on who that individual or group is. Expressions of students in public school may be limited more than those of adults in other settings. In 1988, the Supreme Court ruled that a high school newspaper was not a public forum and could be regulated in "any reasonable manner" by school officials.[32] In 2007, the Court held that the special characteristics of the school environment and the governmental interest in stopping student drug abuse allow schools to restrict student expressions that they reasonably regard as promoting such abuse.[33]

The Supreme Court has also upheld restrictions on the right to publish in the name of national security. Wartime often brings censorship to protect classified information. These restrictions often have public support; few would find it unconstitutional if a newspaper, for example, were hauled into court for publishing troop movement plans during a war. Critics of the press during the Persian Gulf War complained that press reporting might have helped to pinpoint locations of SCUD missile attacks, knowledge of which would help the enemy aim future missiles more precisely. Defenders of the freedom of the press complained that never before had the press been as "managed" as in that conflict: Reporters could get to the field only in the company of official Pentagon press representatives—and some who tried other ways of getting in the field were captured by the Iraqis.

The national government demanded and received prior restraint of a different sort for books written by former CIA agents Victor Marchetti and Frank Snepp. The government sued Snepp for failing to submit his book about Vietnam, *A Decent Interval*, to the agency for censorship, even though the book revealed no classified information.[34] When they joined the CIA, both men had signed agreements allowing the agency to clear their future writings.

Nevertheless, the courts are reluctant to issue injunctions prohibiting the publication of material even in the area of national security. The most famous case regarding prior restraint and national security involved the publication of stolen Pentagon papers. You can examine this case in "You Are the Judge: The Case of the Purloined Pentagon Papers."

FREE SPEECH AND PUBLIC ORDER

Not surprisingly, government has sometimes been a zealous opponent of speech that opposes government policies. In wartime and peacetime, the biggest conflict between press and government has been about the connection between a free press and the need for public order. During World War I, Charles T. Schenck, the secretary of the American Socialist Party, distributed thousands of leaflets urging young men to resist the draft. Schenck was charged with impeding the war effort. The Supreme Court upheld his conviction in 1919 (*Schenck v. United States*). Justice Holmes declared that government could limit speech if it provokes a clear and present danger of substantive evils. Only when such danger exists can government restrain speech. It is difficult to say, of course, when speech becomes dangerous rather than simply inconvenient for the government.

The courts confronted the issue of free speech and public order during the 1950s. In the late 1940s and early 1950s there was widespread fear that communists had infiltrated the government. American anticommunism was a powerful force, and the national government was determined to jail the leaders of the Communist Party. Senator Joseph McCarthy and others in Congress persecuted people they thought subversive, based on the Smith Act of 1940, which forbade advocating the violent overthrow of the American government. In *Dennis v. United States* (1951), the Supreme Court upheld prison sentences for several Communist Party leaders for conspiring to advocate the violent overthrow of the government—even in the absence of evidence that they actually urged people to commit specific acts of

Schenck v. United States

A 1919 decision upholding the conviction of a socialist who had urged young men to resist the draft during World War I. Justice Holmes declared that government can limit speech if the speech provokes a "clear and present danger" of substantive evils.

violence. Although the activities of this tiny, unpopular group resembled yelling "Fire!" in an empty theater rather than a crowded one, the Court ruled that a Communist takeover was so grave a danger that government could squelch their threat. Free-speech advocates were unable to stem the relentless persecution of the 1950s; the Supreme Court, as in the *Dennis* case, concluded that protecting national security out weighed First Amendment rights.

Soon the political climate changed, however, and the Court narrowed the interpretation of the Smith Act, making it more difficult to prosecute dissenters. In later years, the Court has found that it is permissible to advocate the violent overthrow of the government in the abstract but not actually to incite anyone to imminent lawless action (*Yates v. United States* [1957]; *Brandenburg v. Ohio* [1969]).

The 1960s brought waves of protest that strained and expanded the constitutional meaning of free speech. Among the unrest over political, economic, racial, and social issues, the Vietnam War was the source of the most bitter controversy. Many people saw military service as a duty and war as an issue that government should decide. Others felt that citizens should not be asked to die or pay for conflicts that they felt were unjust. Organized protests on college and university campuses became common. People burned draft cards, seized university buildings, marched, and demonstrated against the Southeast Asian conflict.

Americans today live in relatively less turbulent times, yet many people still engage in public demonstrations, such as those opposing the war in Iraq. Courts

The prevailing political climate often determines what limits the government will place on free speech. During the early 1950s, Senator Joseph McCarthy's persuasive—if unproven—accusations that many public officials were communists created an atmosphere in which the courts placed restrictions on freedom of expression—restrictions that would be unacceptable today.

Comparing Civil Rights

YOU ARE THE **Judge**

The Case of the Purloined Pentagon Papers

During the Johnson administration, the Department of Defense amassed an elaborate secret history of American involvement in the Vietnam War that included hundreds of documents, many of them secret cables, memos, and war plans. Many documented American ineptitude and South Vietnamese duplicity. One former Pentagon official, Daniel Ellsberg, who had become disillusioned with the Vietnam War, managed to retain access to a copy of these Pentagon papers. Hoping that revelations of the Vietnam quagmire would help end American involvement, he decided to leak the Pentagon papers to the *New York Times*.

The Nixon administration pulled out all the stops in its effort to embarrass Ellsberg and prevent publication of the Pentagon papers. Nixon's chief domestic affairs adviser, John Ehrlichman, approved a burglary of Ellsberg's psychiatrist's office, hoping to find damaging information on Ellsberg. (The burglary was bungled, and it eventually led to Ehrlichman's conviction and imprisonment.)

In the courts, Nixon administration lawyers sought an injunction against the *Times* that would have ordered it to cease publication of the secret documents. Government lawyers argued that national security was being breached and that Ellsberg had stolen the documents from the government. The *Times* argued that its freedom to publish would be violated if an injunction were granted. In 1971 the case of *New York Times v. United States* was decided by the Supreme Court.

You Be the Judge: Did the *Times* have a right to publish secret, stolen Department of Defense documents?

Decision: In a 6-to-3 decision, a majority of the justices agreed that the "no prior restraint" rule prohibited prosecution before the papers were published. The justices also made it clear that if the government brought prosecution for theft, the Court might be sympathetic. No such charges were filed.

Free speech sometimes conflicts with public order. The Constitution protects the rights of protestors, such as those pictured here opposing the war with Iraq, to have their say.

Comparing Civil Liberties

Balancing Liberty and Security in a Time of War

have been quite supportive of the right to protest, pass out leaflets, or gather signatures on petitions—as long as it is done in public places. People may even distribute campaign literature anonymously.[35] Constitutional protections diminish once a person steps on private property, such as most shopping centers. The Supreme Court has held that federal free-speech guarantees did not apply when a person was on private property.[36] However, it upheld a state's power to include politicking in shopping centers within its own free-speech guarantee,[37] and in 1994, the Supreme Court ruled that cities cannot bar residents from posting signs on their own property.[38]

FREE PRESS AND FAIR TRIALS

The Bill of Rights is an inexhaustible source of potential conflicts among different types of freedoms. One is the conflict between the right of the press to print what it wants and the right to a fair trial. The quantity of press coverage given the 1995 trial (and pretrial hearings) of football star O. J. Simpson, accused of murdering his wife and her friend, surpassed that given the Super Bowl, and little of it was sympathetic to Simpson. The press has also devoted extraordinary coverage to the legal issues of other celebrities such as Britney Spears, Kobe Bryant, and Martha Stewart. Does such extensive media coverage compromise the fairness of the trial? Defense attorneys argue that such publicity can inflame the community—and potential jurors—against defendants. It may very well. The trouble is that the Constitution's guarantee of freedom of the press entitles journalists to cover every trial.

In addition to arguing that the public has a "right to know," some journalists hope to capitalize on their coverage of lurid crime stories to sell newspapers, gain ratings, or attract advertisers. Those motivations have prompted newspapers to challenge courts' restrictions on media coverage of trials. When a Nebraska judge issued a gag order forbidding the press to report any details of a particularly gory murder (or even to report the gag order itself), the outraged Nebraska Press Association took the case to the Supreme Court. The Court sided with the editors and revoked the gag order.[39] In 1980, the Court reversed a Virginia judge's order to close a murder trial to the public and the press. "The trial of a criminal case," said the Court, "must be open to the public."[40] A pretrial hearing, though, is a different matter. In a 1979 case, the Supreme Court permitted a closed hearing on the grounds that pretrial publicity might compromise the defendant's right to fairness.

Although reporters always want access to trials, they do not always want the courts to have access to their files. Occasionally a reporter withholds some critical evidence that either the prosecution or the defense wants in a criminal case. Reporters argue that "protecting their sources" should exempt them from revealing notes from confidential informants. More than one reporter has gone to jail for this principle, arguing that they had no obligation to produce evidence that might bear on the guilt or innocence of a defendant. *New York Times* reporter Judith Miller spent several months in jail in 2005 for refusing to turn over her notes relevant to the investigation of a leak that revealed the identity of CIA operative Valerie Plame.

Some states have passed *shield laws* to protect reporters in these situations. In most states, however, reporters have no more rights than other citizens once a case has come to trial. The Supreme Court ruled in *Branzburg v. Hayes* (1972) that in the absence of shield laws, the right of a fair trial preempts the reporter's right to protect sources. This issue came to a head in one celebrated case involving the student newspaper at Stanford University. After a violent confrontation with student protestors, the police got a search warrant and marched off to the *Stanford Daily*, which they believed to have pictures of the scene—from which they could make arrests. The paper argued that its files were protected by the First Amendment, but the decision in ***Zurcher v. Stanford Daily*** (1978) sided with the police, not the paper.

It is one thing to attempt to obtain the press's cooperation in trials and quite another to limit the press's coverage of judicial proceedings. The balance between a free press and a fair trial is not an even one. The Court has *never* upheld a restriction on the press in the interest of a fair trial. Ultimately, the only feasible measure the judicial system can take against the influence of publicity in high-profile cases is to sequester the jury, thereby isolating it from the media and public opinion.

Fundamental rights are sometimes in conflict. Press coverage of the murder trial of O. J. Simpson, pictured here with one of his lawyers, made it very difficult to impanel a jury whose members had not reached conclusions about his guilt before the trial began.

Zurcher v. Stanford Daily

A 1978 Supreme Court decision holding that a proper **search warrant** could be applied to a newspaper as well as to anyone else without necessarily violating the **First Amendment** rights to freedom of the press.

OBSCENITY

In *The Brethren*, a gossipy portrayal of the Supreme Court, Bob Woodward and Scott Armstrong recount the tale of Justice Thurgood Marshall's lunch with some law clerks. Glancing at his watch at about 1:50 P.M., the story goes, Marshall exclaimed, "My God, I almost forgot. It's movie day, we've got to get back."[41] Movie day at the Court was an annual event when movies brought before the Court on obscenity charges were shown in a basement storeroom.

Several justices boycotted these showings, arguing that obscenity should never be banned and so how "dirty" a movie is has no relevance. In 1957, however, the majority held that "obscenity is not within the area of constitutionally protected speech or press" (***Roth v. United States***). The doctrine set forth in this case still prevails. Deciding what is obscene, however, has never been an easy matter. In a line that would haunt him for the rest of his life, Justice Potter Stewart once remarked that although he could not define obscenity, "I know it when I see it." During the Supreme Court's movie day, law clerks echoed Stewart's line, punctuating particularly racy scenes with cries of "That's it! That's it! I know it when I see it."

Efforts to define obscenity have perplexed the courts for years. Obviously, public standards vary from time to time, place to place, and person to person. Much of today's MTV would have been banned a decade or two ago. What might be acceptable in Manhattan's Greenwich Village would shock residents of some other areas of the country. Works that some people call obscene might be good entertainment

Roth v. United States

A 1957 Supreme Court decision ruling that "obscenity is not within the area of constitutionally protected speech or press."

or even great art to others. At one time or another, the works of Aristophanes, those of Mark Twain, and even the "Tarzan" stories by Edgar Rice Burroughs were banned. The state of Georgia banned the acclaimed film *Carnal Knowledge*—a ban the Supreme Court struck down in 1974.[42]

The Court tried to clarify its doctrine by spelling out what could be classified as obscene and thus outside First Amendment protection in the 1973 case of ***Miller v. California***. Then Chief Justice Warren Burger wrote that materials were obscene under the following circumstances:

> **Miller v. California**
> A 1973 Supreme Court decision that avoided defining obscenity by holding that community standards be used to determine whether material is obscene in terms of appealing to a "prurient interest" and being "patently offensive" and lacking in value.

1. The work, taken as a whole, appealed "to a prurient interest in sex."
2. The work showed "patently offensive" sexual conduct that was specifically defined by an obscenity law.
3. The work, taken as a whole, lacked "serious literary, artistic, political, or scientific value."

Decisions regarding whether material was obscene, said the Court, should be based on average people (in other words, juries) applying the contemporary standards of local—not national—communities.

The Court did provide "a few plain examples" of what sort of material might fall within this definition of obscenity. Among these examples were "patently offensive representations of ultimate sexual acts . . . actual or simulated," "patently offensive representations of masturbation or excretory functions," or "lewd exhibition of the genitals." Cities throughout the country duplicated the language of *Miller* in their obscenity ordinances. The difficulty remains in determining what is *lewd* or *offensive*. Laws must satisfy these qualifying adjectives to prevent communities from banning anatomy texts, for example, as obscene.

Another reason why obscenity convictions can be difficult to obtain is that no nationwide consensus exists that offensive material should be banned—at least not when it is restricted to adults. In many communities the laws are lenient regarding pornography, and prosecutors know that they may not get a jury to convict, even when the disputed material is obscene as defined by *Miller*. Thus, obscene material is widely available in adult bookstores, video stores, and movie theaters.

Regulations aimed at keeping obscene material away from the young, who are considered more vulnerable to its harmful influences, are more popular, and courts have consistently ruled that states may protect children from obscenity. The rating scheme of the Motion Picture Association of America is one example, as is the more recent TV ratings system. Equally popular are laws designed to protect the young against pornographic exploitation. It is a violation of federal law to receive sexually explicit photographs of children through the mail or over the Internet, and in 1990 the Supreme Court upheld Ohio's law forbidding the possession of child pornography.[43]

Advances in technology have created a new wrinkle in the obscenity issue. The Internet and the World Wide Web make it easier to distribute obscene material rapidly, and a number of online information services have taken advantage of this opportunity. Congress, especially concerned with protecting minors from exposure to pornography, has recently decided that the Internet is not the electronic equivalent of the printing press and thus does not deserve the free-speech protection of the First Amendment. Instead, it regards the Internet as a broadcast medium, subject to government regulation (discussed later in this chapter).

In 1996, Congress passed the Communications Decency Act, banning obscene material and criminalizing the transmission of indecent speech or images to anyone under 18 years of age. The new law made no exception for material that has serious literary, artistic, political, or scientific merit as outlined in *Miller v. California*. In 1997, the Supreme Court overturned this law as being overly broad and vague and a violation of free speech.[44] In 2002, the Court overturned a law banning virtual child pornography on similar grounds.[45] Apparently the Supreme Court views the Internet similarly to print media, with similar protections against government regulation. In 1999, however, the Court upheld prohibitions on obscene e-mail and faxes.

Despite the Court's best efforts to define obscenity and determine when it can be banned, state and local governments continue to struggle with the application of these rulings. In one famous case, a small New Jersey town tried to get rid of a nude dancing parlor by using its zoning power to ban all live entertainment. The Court held that the measure was too broad and thus unlawful.[46] However, the Court has upheld laws banning nude dancing when their effect on overall expression was minimal.[47] Jacksonville, Florida, tried to ban drive-in movies containing nudity. You can examine the Court's reaction in "You Are the Judge: The Case of the Drive-in Theater."

Legal scholar Catherine MacKinnon claims that pornography degrades and dehumanizes women and is an "industry of rape and battery and sexual harassment."[48] Some cities, at the urging of an unusual alliance of conservative Christians and feminists, have passed antipornography ordinances on the grounds that pornography harms women. So far, however, courts have struck these ordinances down on First Amendment grounds. No such case has reached the Supreme Court—yet.

LIBEL AND SLANDER

Another type of expression not protected by the First Amendment is **libel**: the publication of false statements that are malicious and damage a person's reputation. *Slander* refers to spoken defamation, whereas libel refers to written defamation. Of course, if politicians could collect damages for every untrue thing said about them, the right to criticize the government—which the Supreme Court termed "the central meaning of the First Amendment"—would be stifled. No one would dare be critical for fear of making a factual error.

To encourage public debate, the Supreme Court has held in cases such as *New York Times v. Sullivan* (1964) that statements about public figures are libelous only if made with malice and reckless disregard for the truth. Public figures have to prove to a jury, in effect, that whoever wrote or said untrue statements about them knew that the statements were untrue and intended to harm them. This standard makes libel cases difficult for public figures to win because it is difficult to prove that a publication was intentionally malicious.[49]

Private individuals have a lower standard to meet for winning libel lawsuits. They need show only that statements made about them were defamatory falsehoods and that the author was negligent. Nevertheless, it is unusual for someone to win a libel case; most people do not wish to draw attention to critical statements about themselves.

Libel cases must balance freedom of expression with respect for individual reputations. If public debate is not free, there can be no democracy. On the other hand, some reputations will be damaged (or at least bruised) in the process. In one widely publicized case, General William Westmoreland, once the commander of American troops in South Vietnam, sued CBS over a documentary it broadcast called "The Uncounted Enemy." It claimed that American military leaders in Vietnam, including Westmoreland, systematically lied to Washington about their success there to make it appear that the United States was winning the war. All the evidence, including CBS's own internal memoranda, showed that the documentary made errors of fact. Westmoreland sued CBS for libel. Ultimately, the power of the press—in this case, a sloppy, arrogant press—prevailed. Fearing defeat at the trial, Westmoreland settled for a mild apology.[50]

libel
The publication of false or malicious statements that damage someone's reputation.

New York Times v. Sullivan
Decided in 1964, this case established the guidelines for determining whether public officials and public figures could win damage suits for libel. To do so, individuals must prove that the defamatory statements were made with "actual malice" and reckless disregard for the truth.

? Why It Matters
Libel Law
It is difficult for public figures to win libel cases. Public figures will likely lose even if they can show that the defendant made defamatory falsehoods about them. This may not be fair, but it is essential for people to feel free to criticize public officials. Fear of losing a lawsuit would have a chilling effect on democratic dialogue.

YOU ARE THE Judge

The Case of the Drive-in Theater

Almost everyone concedes that *sometimes* obscenity should be banned by public authorities. One instance might be when a person's right to show pornographic movies clashes with another's right to privacy. Presumably, no one wants hard-core pornography shown in public places where schoolchildren might see it. Showing dirty movies in an enclosed theater or in the privacy of your own living room is one thing. Showing them in public is something else. Or is it?

The city of Jacksonville, Florida, wanted to limit the showing of certain kinds of movies at drive-in theaters. Its city council reasoned that drive-ins were public places and that drivers passing by would be involuntarily exposed to movies they might prefer not to see. Some members of the council argued that drivers distracted by steamy scenes might even cause accidents. So the council passed a local ordinance forbidding movies showing nudity (defined in the ordinance as "bare buttocks . . . female bare breasts, or human bare pubic areas") at drive-in theaters.

Arrested for violating the ordinance, a Mr. Erznoznik challenged the constitutionality of the ordinance. He claimed that the law was overly broad and banned nudity, not obscenity. The lawyers for the city insisted that the law was acceptable under the First Amendment. The government, they claimed, had a responsibility to forbid a "public nuisance," especially one that might cause a traffic hazard.

You Be the Judge: Did Jacksonville's ban on nudity in movies at drive-ins go too far, or was it a constitutional limit on free speech?

Decision: In *Erznoznik v. Jacksonville* (1975), the Supreme Court held that Jacksonville's ordinance was unconstitutionally broad. The city council had gone too far; it could end up banning movies that might not be obscene. The ordinance would, said the Court, ban a film "containing a picture of a baby's buttocks, the nude body of a war victim or scenes from a culture where nudity is indigenous." Said Justice Powell for the Court, "Clearly, all nudity cannot be deemed obscene."

An unusual case that explored the line between parody and libel came before the Supreme Court in 1988, when Reverend Jerry Falwell sued *Hustler* magazine. *Hustler* editor Larry Flynt had printed a parody of a Campari Liquor ad about various celebrities called "First Time" (in which celebrities related the first time they drank Campari, but with an intentional double meaning). When *Hustler* depicted the Reverend Jerry Falwell having had his "first time" in an outhouse with his mother, Falwell sued. He alleged that the ad subjected him to great emotional distress and mental anguish. The case tested the limits to which a publication could go to parody or lampoon a public figure. The Supreme Court ruled that they can go pretty far—all nine justices ruled in favor of the magazine.

SYMBOLIC SPEECH

Freedom of speech, more broadly interpreted, is a guarantee of freedom of expression. In 1965, school authorities in Des Moines, Iowa, suspended Mary Beth Tinker and her brother John when they wore black armbands to protest the Vietnam War. The Supreme Court held that the suspension violated the Tinkers' First Amendment rights. The right to freedom of speech, said the Court, went beyond the spoken word.[51]

When Gregory Johnson set a flag on fire at the 1984 Republican National Convention in Dallas to protest nuclear arms buildup, the Supreme Court decided that the state law prohibiting flag desecration violated the First Amendment (*Texas v. Johnson* [1989]). Burning the flag, the Court said, constituted speech and not just dramatic action.[52] When Massachusetts courts ordered the organizers of the annual St. Patrick's Day parade to include the Irish-American Gay, Lesbian, and Bisexual Group of Boston, the Supreme Court declared that a parade is a form of protected speech and thus that the organizers are free to include or exclude whomever they want.

Texas v. Johnson

A 1989 case in which the Supreme Court struck down a law banning the burning of the American flag on the grounds that such action was **symbolic speech** protected by the **First Amendment**.

Wearing an armband, burning a flag, and marching in a parade are examples of **symbolic speech**: actions that do not consist of speaking or writing but that express an opinion. Court decisions have classified these activities somewhere between pure speech and pure action. The doctrine of symbolic speech is not precise; for example, although burning a flag is protected speech, burning a draft card is not.[53] In 2003, the Court held that states may make it a crime to burn a cross with a purpose to intimidate, as long as the law clearly gives prosecutors the burden of proving that the act was intended as a threat and not as a form of symbolic expression.[54] The relevant cases make it clear, however, that First Amendment rights are not limited by a rigid definition of what constitutes speech.

symbolic speech

Nonverbal communication, such as burning a flag or wearing an armband. The Supreme Court has accorded some symbolic speech protection under the **First Amendment**.

COMMERCIAL SPEECH

Not all forms of communication receive the full protection of the First Amendment. Laws restrict **commercial speech**, such as advertising, far more extensively than expressions of opinion on religious, political, or other matters. The Federal Trade Commission (FTC) decides what kinds of goods may be advertised on radio and television and regulates the content of such advertising. These regulations have responded to changes in social mores and priorities. Thirty years ago, for example, tampons could not be advertised on TV, whereas cigarette commercials were everywhere. Today the situation is just the reverse.

The FTC attempts to ensure that advertisers do not make false claims for their products, but "truth" in advertising does not prevent misleading promises. For example, when ads imply that the right mouthwash or deodorant will improve one's love life, that dubious message is perfectly legal.

Nevertheless, laws may regulate commercial speech on the airwaves in ways that would clearly be impossible in the political or religious realm—even to the point of forcing a manufacturer to say certain words. For example, the makers of Excedrin pain reliever were forced to add the words "on pain other than headache" in their commercials describing tests that supposedly supported the product's claims of superior effectiveness. (The test results were based on the pain women experienced after giving birth.)

Although commercial speech is regulated more rigidly than other types of speech, the courts have been broadening its protection under the Constitution. For years, many states had laws that prohibited advertising for professional services—such as legal and engineering services—and for certain products ranging from eyeglasses and prescription drugs to condoms and abortions. Advocates of these laws claimed that they were designed to protect consumers against misleading claims, while critics charged that the laws prevented price competition. In recent years, the courts have struck down many such restrictions as violations of freedom of speech. In 1999 the Supreme Court overturned restrictions on advertising casino gambling in states where such gambling is legal.[55] In general, the Supreme Court has allowed the regulation of commercial speech when the speech concerns unlawful activity or is misleading, but otherwise regulations must advance a substantial government interest and be no more extensive than necessary to serve that interest.[56]

commercial speech

Communication in the form of advertising. It can be restricted more than many other types of speech but has been receiving increased protection from the Supreme Court.

REGULATION OF THE PUBLIC AIRWAVES

The Federal Communications Commission (FCC) regulates the content, nature, and very existence of radio and television broadcasting. Although newspapers do not need licenses, radio and television stations do. A licensed station must comply with regulations, including the requirement that they devote a certain percentage

Although the Supreme Court ruled in *Roth v. United States* that obscenity is not protected by the First Amendment, determining just what is obscene has proven difficult. Popular radio personality Howard Stern pressed the limits of obscenity rules when he worked for radio stations using the public airwaves. Ultimately, he moved to satellite radio, where the rules are much less restrictive.

Miami Herald Publishing Company v. Tornillo

A 1974 case in which the Supreme Court held that a state could not force a newspaper to print replies from candidates it had criticized, illustrating the limited power of government to restrict the **print media**.

Red Lion Broadcasting Company v. Federal Communications Commission

A 1969 case in which the Supreme Court upheld restrictions on radio and television broadcasting. These restrictions on the **broadcast media** are much tighter than those on the **print media** because there are only a limited number of broadcasting frequencies available.

of broadcast time to public service, news, children's programming, political candidates, or views other than those its owners support. The rules are more relaxed for cable channels, which can specialize in a particular type of broadcasting because consumers pay for, and thus have more choice about, the service.

This sort of governmental interference would clearly violate the First Amendment if it were imposed on the print media. For example, the state of Florida passed a law requiring newspapers in the state to provide space for political candidates to reply to newspaper criticisms. The Supreme Court, without hesitation, voided this law (***Miami Herald Publishing Company v. Tornillo*** [1974]). Earlier, in ***Red Lion Broadcasting Company v. Federal Communications Commission*** (1969), the Court upheld similar restrictions on radio and television stations, reasoning that such laws were justified because only a limited number of broadcast frequencies were available.

One FCC rule regulating the content of programs restricts the use of obscene words. Comedian George Carlin had a famous routine called "Filthy Words" that could never be said over the airwaves. A New York City radio station tested Carlin's assertion by airing his routine. The ensuing events proved Carlin right. In 1978, the Supreme Court upheld the commission's policy of barring these words from radio or television when children might hear them.[57]

Similarly, the FCC has twice fined New York disc jockey Howard Stern $600,000 for indecency. It is especially interesting that if Stern's commentaries had been carried by cable or satellite instead of the airwaves, he could have expressed himself with impunity. (In 2006, he made the move to satellite transmission.) Technological change has blurred the line between broadcasting and private communications between individuals. With cable television now in most American homes, the Supreme Court is now faced with ruling on the application of free-speech guidelines to cable broadcasting.

Section 505 of the Telecommunications Act of 1996 requires cable television operators providing channels "primarily dedicated to sexually-oriented programming" either to "fully scramble or otherwise fully block" those channels or to limit their transmission to hours when children are unlikely to be viewing, set by administrative regulation as between 10:00 P.M. and 6:00 A.M. The Playboy Entertainment Group pointed out that banning transmission restricts sexually oriented programming even to households without children. It challenged the law as an unconstitutional violation of the First Amendment free-speech guarantee, arguing that Congress had less restrictive ways to accomplish its goals.

In 2000 in *United States v. Playboy Entertainment Group*, the Supreme Court agreed. It held that although government had a legitimate right to regulate sexually oriented programming, any such regulation must be narrowly tailored to promote a compelling government interest. If a less restrictive alternative would serve the government's purpose, Congress must use that alternative. The Court concluded that targeted blocking, in which subscribers can ask their cable companies to block a signal to their homes, is less restrictive than banning and is a feasible and effective means of furthering its compelling interests. Thus, the more restrictive option of banning a signal for most of the day cannot be justified.

FREEDOM OF ASSEMBLY

The last of the great rights guaranteed by the First Amendment is the freedom to "peaceably assemble." Commentators often neglect this freedom in favor of the more trumpeted freedoms of speech, press, and religion, yet it is the basis for forming interest groups, political parties, and professional associations as well as for picketing and protesting.

RIGHT TO ASSEMBLE

There are two facets of the freedom of assembly. First is the literal right to assemble—that is, to gather together in order to make a statement. This freedom can conflict with other societal values when it disrupts public order, traffic flow, peace and quiet, or bystanders' freedom to go about their business without interference. Within reasonable limits, called *time, place,* and *manner restrictions,* freedom of assembly includes the rights to parade, picket, and protest. Whatever a group's cause, it has the right to demonstrate, but no group can simply hold a spontaneous demonstration anytime, anywhere, and anyway it chooses. Usually, a group must apply to the local city government for a permit and post a bond of a few hundred dollars—a little like making a security deposit on an apartment. The governing body must grant a permit as long as the group pledges to hold its demonstration at a time and place that allows the police to prevent major disruptions. There are virtually no limitations on the content of a group's message. In one important case, the American Nazi Party applied to the local government to march in the streets of Skokie, Illinois, a Chicago suburb with a sizable Jewish population, including many survivors of Hitler's death camps. You can examine the Court's response in "You Are the Judge: The Case of the Nazis' March in Skokie."

Protest that verges on harassment tests the balance between freedom and order. Protestors lined up outside abortion clinics have been a common sight. Members of groups such as "Operation Rescue" try to shame clients into staying away and may harass them if they do visit a clinic. Rights are in conflict in such cases: A woman seeking to terminate her pregnancy has the right to obtain an abortion; the demonstrators have the right to protest the very existence of the clinic. The courts have acted to restrain these protestors, setting limits on how close they may come to the clinics and upholding damage claims of clients against the protestors. In one case, pro-life demonstrators in a Milwaukee, Wisconsin, suburb paraded outside the home of a physician who was reported to perform abortions. The town board forbade future picketing in residential neighborhoods. In 1988, the Supreme Court agreed that the right of residential privacy was a legitimate local concern and upheld the ordinance.[58] In 1994, Congress passed a law enacting broad new penalties against abortion protestors.

White supremacists and anti–White supremacists square off. The Supreme Court has generally upheld the right of any group, no matter how controversial or offensive, to peaceably assemble, as long as the group's demonstrations remain on public property.

YOU ARE THE Judge

The Case of the Nazis' March in Skokie

Hitler's Nazis slaughtered 6 million Jews in death camps like Bergen-Belsen, Auschwitz, and Dachau. Many of the survivors migrated to the United States, and many settled in Skokie, Illinois. Skokie, with 80,000 people, is a suburb just north of Chicago. In its heavily Jewish population are thousands of survivors of German concentration camps.

The American Nazi Party in the Skokie area was a ragtag group of perhaps 25 to 30 members. Their headquarters was a storefront building on the West Side of Chicago, near an area of an expanding African American population. After Chicago denied them a permit to march in an African American neighborhood, the American Nazis announced their intention to march in Skokie. Skokie's city government required that they post a $300,000 bond to obtain a parade permit. The Nazis claimed that the high bond was set in order to prevent their march and that it infringed on their freedoms of speech and assembly. The American

Civil Liberties Union (ACLU), despite its loathing of the Nazis, defended the Nazis' claim and their right to march. The ACLU lost half its Illinois membership because it took this position.

You Be the Judge: Do Nazis have the right to parade, preach anti-Jewish propaganda, and perhaps provoke violence in a community peopled with survivors of the Holocaust? What rights or obligations does a community have to maintain order?

Decision: A federal district court ruled that Skokie's ordinance did restrict freedom of assembly and association. No community could use its power to grant parade permits to stifle free expression. In *Collins v. Smith* (Collins was the Nazi leader, and Smith was the mayor of Skokie), the Supreme Court let this lower-court decision stand. In fact, the Nazis did not march in Skokie, settling instead for some poorly attended demonstrations in Chicago.

RIGHT TO ASSOCIATE

The second facet of freedom of assembly is the right to associate with people who share a common interest, including an interest in political change. In a famous case at the height of the civil rights movement, Alabama tried to harass the state chapter of the National Association for the Advancement of Colored People (NAACP) by requiring it to turn over its membership list. The Court found this demand an unconstitutional restriction on freedom of association (***NAACP v. Alabama*** [1958]).

In 2006, some law schools argued that Congress's insistence that law schools grant military recruiters access to their students violated the schools' freedoms of speech and association. The Supreme Court concluded that the law regulates conduct, not speech. In addition, nothing about recruiting suggests that law schools agree with any speech by recruiters, and nothing in the law restricts what they may say about the military's policies. Nor does the law force a law school to accept members it does not desire and students and faculty are free to voice their disapproval of the military's message.[59]

NAACP v. Alabama

The Supreme Court protected the right to assemble peaceably in this 1958 case when it decided the NAACP did not have to reveal its membership list and thus subject its members to harassment.

RIGHT TO BEAR ARMS

Few issues generate as much controversy as gun control. In an attempt to control gun violence, many communities have passed restrictions on owning and carrying handguns. National and state and local laws have also mandated background checks for gun buyers and limited the sale of certain types of weapons altogether. Yet other laws have required that guns be stored in a fashion to prevent their theft or children from accessing and firing them. Some groups, most notably the National Rifle Association, have invested millions of dollars to fight almost all gun control efforts, arguing that they violated the Second Amendment's guarantee of a right to bear arms. Many advocates of gun control argued that the Second Amendment applied only to the right of states to create militias. Surprisingly, the Supreme Court has rarely dealt with gun control.

In 2008, however, the Supreme Court directly faced the issue. The District of Columbia passed a law banning handgun possession by making it a crime to carry an unregistered firearm and prohibiting the registration of handguns. No person could carry an unlicensed handgun, but the law authorized the police chief to issue 1-year licenses. The law also required residents to keep lawfully owned firearms unloaded and dissembled or bound by a trigger lock or similar device. The Supreme Court in *District of Columbia v. Heller* (2008) held that the Second Amendment protects an individual right to possess a firearm unconnected with service in a militia, and to use that arm for traditionally lawful purposes, such as self-defense within the home. Similarly, the requirement that any lawful firearm in the home be disassembled or bound by a trigger lock is unconstitutional because it makes it impossible for citizens to use arms for the core lawful purpose of self-defense.

Nevertheless, like most rights, the Second Amendment right is not unlimited. It is not a right to keep and carry any weapon whatsoever in any manner whatsoever and for whatever purpose. For example, prohibitions on concealed weapons are permissible, as are limits on the possession of firearms by felons and the mentally ill, laws forbidding the carrying of firearms in sensitive places such as schools and government buildings, laws imposing conditions and qualifications on the commercial sale of arms, and laws restricting "dangerous and unusual weapons" that are not typically used for self-defense or recreation.

The four freedoms guaranteed by the First Amendment—religion, speech, press, and assembly—are one key part of Americans' civil liberties, and so is the right to bear arms. When people confront the American legal system as suspected or convicted criminals, they also have certain rights under the Constitution. These rights regulate how the government can investigate, interrogate, try, and punish them.

DEFENDANTS' RIGHTS

The Bill of Rights contains only 45 words that guarantee the freedoms of religion, speech, press, and assembly. Most of the remaining words concern the rights of people accused of crimes. The Founders intended these rights to protect the accused in *political* arrests and trials; British abuse of colonial political leaders was still fresh in the memory of American citizens. Today the courts apply the protections in the Fourth, Fifth, Sixth, Seventh, and Eighth Amendments mostly in criminal justice cases.

It is useful to think of the stages of the criminal justice system as a series of funnels decreasing in size. Generally speaking, a *crime* is (sometimes) followed by an *arrest*, which is (sometimes) followed by a *prosecution*, which is (sometimes) followed by a *trial*, which (usually) results in a *verdict* of innocence or guilt. The funnels get smaller and smaller, each dripping into the next. Many more crimes occur than are reported, many more crimes are reported than arrests are made (the ratio is about five to one), many more arrests are made than prosecutors prosecute, and many more prosecutions occur than jury trials. At each stage of the criminal justice system, the Constitution protects the rights of the accused (see Table 4.3).

INTERPRETING DEFENDANTS' RIGHTS

The Bill of Rights sets out civil liberties that American citizens have if they are arrested or brought to court. At every stage of the criminal justice system, police, prosecutors, and judges must behave in accordance with the Bill of Rights. Any misstep may invalidate a conviction.

The language of the Bill of Rights comes from the late 1700s and is often vague. For example, just how speedy is a "speedy trial"? How "cruel and unusual"

TABLE 4.3

The Constitution and the Stages of the Criminal Justice System

Although our criminal justice system is complex, it can be broken down into stages. The Constitution protects the rights of the accused at every stage.

STAGE	PROTECTIONS
1. Evidence gathered	"Unreasonable search and seizure" forbidden (Fourth Amendment)
2. Suspicion cast	Guarantee that "writ of habeas corpus" will not be suspended, forbidding imprisonment without evidence (Article I, Section 9)
3. Arrest made	Right to have the "assistance of counsel" (Sixth Amendment)
4. Interrogation held	Forced self-incrimination forbidden (Fifth Amendment) "Excessive bail" forbidden (Eighth Amendment)
5. Trial held	"Speedy and public trial" by an impartial jury required (Sixth Amendment) "Double jeopardy" (being tried twice for the same crime) forbidden (Fifth Amendment) Trial by jury required (Article III, Section 2) Right to confront witnesses (Sixth Amendment)
6. Punishment imposed	"Cruel and unusual punishment" forbidden (Eighth Amendment)

Muahh

does a punishment have to be in order to violate the Eighth Amendment? The courts continually must rule on the constitutionality of actions by police, prosecutors, judges, and legislatures—actions that a citizen or group could claim violate certain rights. Defendants' rights, just like those rights protected by the First Amendment, are not clearly defined in the Bill of Rights.

One thing is clear, however. The Supreme Court's decisions have extended specific provisions of the Bill of Rights—one by one—to the states as part of the general process of incorporation we discussed earlier. Virtually all the rights we discuss in the following sections affect the actions of both national and state authorities.

SEARCHES AND SEIZURES

Police cannot arrest a citizen without reason. They need evidence to arrest, and courts need evidence to convict. Before making an arrest, police need what the courts call **probable cause**, reasonable grounds to believe that someone is guilty of a crime. Often police need to get physical evidence—a car thief's fingerprints, a snatched purse—to use in court. The Fourth Amendment is quite specific in forbidding **unreasonable searches and seizures**. To prevent abuse of police power, the Constitution requires that no court may issue a **search warrant** unless probable cause exists to believe that a crime has occurred or is about to occur. These written warrants must specify the area to be searched and the material sought in the police search.

A warrant is not a constitutional requirement for a reasonable police search, however. Most searches in this country take place without warrants. Such searches are valid if probable cause of a crime exists, if the search is necessary to protect an officer's safety, or if the search is limited to material relevant to the suspected crime or within the suspect's immediate control. The Supreme Court has also held that police may enter a home without a warrant when they have an objectively reasonable basis for believing that an occupant is seriously injured or imminently threatened with such injury.[60]

Normally, if police find anything in a search, they find what they have probable cause to believe is there. In two cases involving Fourth Amendment issues, authorities used aerial searches to secure the evidence they needed. The first case

probable cause

The situation occurring when the police have reason to believe that a person should be arrested. In making the arrest, police are allowed legally to search for and seize incriminating evidence.

unreasonable searches and seizures

Obtaining evidence in a haphazard or random manner, a practice prohibited by the Fourth Amendment. **Probable cause** and/or a **search warrant** are required for a legal and proper search for and seizure of incriminating evidence.

search warrant

A written authorization from a court specifying the area to be searched and what the police are searching for.

involved a marijuana grower named Ciraolo. When police, responding to a tip, went to look at his place, it was surrounded by a 10-foot fence. The police then rented a private plane, took pictures of the crop, and secured a conviction. Environmental Protection Agency officials took a similar aerial photo of Dow Chemical's Midland, Michigan, plant and located environmental violations. Both Ciraolo and Dow sued, claiming they were the victims of unconstitutional search and seizure. Both lost, however, when their cases came before the Supreme Court. Since then, the Court has also upheld roadside checkpoints in which police randomly examine drivers for signs of intoxication,[61] the use of narcotics-detecting dogs at a routine stop for speeding,[62] and the search of a passenger and car following a routine check of the car's registration.[63] The Court also has approved warrantless "hot pursuit" of criminal suspects; warrantless car stops and "stop-and-frisk" encounters with pedestrians based on reasonable suspicion (not probable cause) of criminal activity; and mandatory drug testing of transportation workers and high school athletes with no individualized suspicion at all.

One of the most important principles of constitutional law is that defendants in criminal cases have rights. Probable cause and/or a search warrant are required for a legal search for and seizure of incriminating evidence. Here police officers read the suspect his rights based on the Supreme Court's decision in *Miranda v. Arizona*.

Ever since 1914, the Supreme Court has used an **exclusionary rule** to weigh evidence in criminal cases. This rule prevents prosecutores from introducing illegally seized evidence in court, but until 1961 the rule applied only to the federal government. The Supreme Court broadened the application in the case of a Cleveland woman named Dollree Mapp, who was under suspicion for illegal gambling activities. The police broke into her home looking for a fugitive, and while there, they searched the house and found a cache of obscene materials. Mapp was convicted of possessing them. She appealed her case to the federal courts, claiming that the exclusionary rule should be made a part of the Fourth Amendment. Since the local police had no probable cause to search for obscene materials—only for materials related to gambling—she argued, the evidence should not be used against her. In an important decision (*Mapp v. Ohio* [1961]), the Supreme Court ruled that the evidence had been seized illegally, and the Court reversed Mapp's conviction. Since then, the exclusionary rule has been part of the Fourth Amendment and has been incorporated within the rights that restrict the states, as well as the federal government.

Critics of the exclusionary rule, including some Supreme Court justices, argue that its strict application may permit guilty persons to go free because of police carelessness or innocent errors. The guilty, they say, should not go free because of a "technicality." Supporters of the exclusionary rule respond that the Constitution is not a technicality and that—because everyone is presumed innocent until proven guilty—defendants' rights protect the *accused*, not the guilty. You can examine one contemporary search-and-seizure case in "You Are the Judge: The Case of Ms. Montoya."

An increasingly conservative Court made some exceptions to the exclusionary rule beginning in the 1980s. The Court allowed the use of illegally obtained evidence when this evidence led police to a discovery that they eventually would have made without it.[64] The justices also decided to establish the good-faith exception to the rule; evidence can be used if the police who seized it mistakenly thought they were operating under a constitutionally valid warrant.[65] In 1995, the Court held that the exclusionary rule does not bar evidence obtained illegally as the result of clerical errors.[66] In 2006, it held that a police violation of the knock-and-announce

exclusionary rule
The rule that evidence, no matter how incriminating, cannot be introduced into a trial if it was not constitutionally obtained. The rule prohibits use of evidence obtained through **unreasonable search and seizure**.

Mapp v. Ohio
The 1961 Supreme Court decision ruling that the Fourth Amendment's protection against **unreasonable searches and seizures** must be extended to the states as well as to the federal government.

? Why It Matters
The Exclusionary Rule
The exclusionary rule, in which courts disregard evidence obtained illegally, has been controversial. Although critics view the rule as a technicality that helps criminals to avoid justice, this rule protects defendants (who have not been proven guilty) from abuses of police power.

YOU ARE THE **Judge**

The Case of Ms. Montoya

Rose Elviro Montoya de Hernandez arrived at the Los Angeles International Airport on Avianca Flight 080 from Bogotá, Colombia. Her first official encounter was with U.S. Customs inspector Talamantes, who noticed that she spoke no English. Interestingly, Montoya's passport indicated eight recent quick trips from Bogotá to Los Angeles. She had $5,000 in cash but no pocketbook or credit cards.

Talamantes and his fellow customs officers were suspicious. Stationed in Los Angeles, they were hardly unaware of the fact that Colombia was a major drug supplier. They questioned Montoya, who explained that her husband had a store in Bogotá and that she planned to spend the $5,000 at Kmart and JC Penney, stocking up on items for the store.

The inspector, somewhat wary, handed Montoya over to female customs inspectors for a search. These agents noticed what the Supreme Court later referred to delicately as a "firm fullness" in Montoya's abdomen. Suspicions, already high, increased. The agents applied for a court order to conduct pregnancy tests, X-rays, and other examinations, and eventually

they found 88 balloons containing 80 percent pure cocaine in Montoya's alimentary canal.

Montoya's lawyer argued that this constituted unreasonable search and seizure and that her arrest and conviction should be set aside. There was, he said, no direct evidence that would have led the officials to suspect cocaine smuggling. The government argued that the arrest had followed from a set of odd facts leading to reasonable suspicion that something was amiss.

You Be the Judge: Was Montoya's arrest based on a search-and-seizure incident that violated the Fourth Amendment?

Decision: The Supreme Court held that U.S. Customs agents were well within their constitutional authority to search Montoya. Even though collection of evidence took the better part of two days, Justice Rehnquist, the opinion's author, remarked wryly that "the rudimentary knowledge of the human body which judges possess in common with the rest of mankind tells us that alimentary canal smuggling cannot be detected in the amount of time in which other illegal activities may be investigated through brief . . . stops."

rule was not a justification for suppressing the evidence they found upon entry with a warrant.[67] The Court even allowed evidence illegally obtained from a banker to be used to convict one of his customers.[68]

However, some decisions offer more protection against searches. An Iowa police officer stopped Patrick Knowles for speeding and issued him a citation. The officer then conducted a full search of the car without either Knowles's consent or probable cause, found marijuana and a "pot pipe," and arrested Knowles. The Supreme Court held that the search of Knowles's car violated the Fourth Amendment. The Court said that although officers may order a driver and passengers out of a car while issuing a traffic citation and may search for weapons to protect themselves from danger, Knowles presented no threat to the officer's safety and thus provided no justification for the intrusion of a search of his car.[69] Similarly, the Supreme Court prohibited highway checkpoints designed to detect ordinary criminal wrongdoing, such as possessing illegal drugs,[70] and it ruled that an anonymous tip that a person is carrying a gun is not sufficient justification for a police officer to stop and frisk that person.[71] In addition, the Court found that police use of a thermal imaging device to detect abnormal heat (needed for growing marijuana) in a home violated the Fourth Amendment.[72]

The *USA Patriot Act*, passed just six weeks after the September 11, 2001, terrorist attacks, gave the government broad new powers for the wiretapping, surveillance, and investigation of terrorism suspects. Attorney General John Ashcroft also eased restrictions on domestic spying in counterterrorism operations, allowing agents to monitor political or religious groups without any connection to a criminal investigation. The Patriot Act gave the federal government the power to examine a terrorist suspect's records held by third parties such as doctors, libraries, bookstores, universities, and Internet service providers. It also allowed searches of private property without probable cause and without notice to the owner until after the search has

DEBATE

Privacy and Government Surveillance Powers

been executed, limiting a person's opportunities to challenge a search. Congress reauthorized the law in 2006 with few changes.

In December 2005, reports revealed that the president had ordered the National Security Agency, without the court-approved warrants ordinarily required for domestic spying, to monitor the international telephone calls and e-mail messages of people inside the United States. In 2008, Congress overhauled the nation's surveillance law, the Foreign Intelligence Surveillance Act, allowing officials to use broad warrants to eavesdrop on large groups of foreign targets at once rather than requiring individual warrants for wiretapping purely foreign communications, like phone calls and e-mail messages that pass through American telecommunications switches. In targeting and wiretapping Americans, however, officials must obtain individual court orders from the special intelligence court, although in "exigent" or emergency circumstances they can wiretap for at least seven days without a court order if it they assert that "intelligence important to the national security of the United States may be lost."

SELF-INCRIMINATION

Suppose that evidence has been gathered and suspicion directed toward a particular person, and the police are ready to make an arrest. In the American system, the burden of proof rests on the police and the prosecutors. Suspects cannot be forced to help with their own conviction by, say, blurting out a confession in the stationhouse. The **Fifth Amendment** forbids forced **self-incrimination**, stating that no person "shall be compelled to be a witness against himself." Whether in a congressional hearing, a courtroom, or a police station, suspects need not provide evidence that can later be used against them. However, the government may guarantee suspects *immunity*—exemption from prosecution in exchange for suspects' testimony regarding their own and others' misdeeds.

You have probably seen television shows in which an arrest is made and the arresting officers recite, often from memory, a set of rights to the arrestee. These rights are authentic and originated from a famous court decision—perhaps the most important modern decision in criminal law—involving an Arizona man named Ernesto Miranda.[73]

Miranda was picked up as a prime suspect in the rape and kidnapping of an 18-year-old girl. Identified by the girl from a police lineup, police questioned Miranda for two hours. During this time, they did not tell him of either his constitutional right against self-incrimination or his right to counsel. In fact, it is unlikely that Miranda had even heard of the Fifth Amendment. He said enough to lead eventually to a conviction. The Supreme Court reversed his conviction on appeal, however. In *Miranda v. Arizona* (1966), the Court established guidelines for police questioning. Suspects must be told that:

- They have a constitutional right to remain silent and may stop answering questions at any time
- What they say can be used against them in a court of law
- They have a right to have a lawyer present during questioning and that the court will provide an attorney if they cannot afford their own lawyer

Police departments throughout the country were originally disgruntled by *Miranda*. Officers felt that interrogation was crucial to any investigation. Warning suspects of their rights and letting them call a lawyer were almost certain to silence them. Most departments today, however, seem to take *Miranda* seriously and usually read a *Miranda* card advising suspects of their rights. Ironically, when Ernesto Miranda himself was murdered, police read the suspect his rights from a *Miranda* card.

In the decades since the *Miranda* decision, the Supreme Court has made a number of exceptions to its requirements. In 1991, for example, the Court held that

Fifth Amendment
A constitutional amendment designed to protect the rights of persons accused of crimes, including protection against double jeopardy, **self-incrimination**, and punishment without due process of law.

self-incrimination
The situation occurring when an individual accused of a crime is compelled to be a witness against himself or herself in court. The **Fifth Amendment** forbids self-incrimination.

Miranda v. Arizona
The 1966 Supreme Court decision that sets guidelines for police questioning of accused persons to protect them against **self-incrimination** and to protect their right to counsel.

You Are a Police Officer

THE WIZARD OF ID

a coerced confession introduced in a trial does not automatically taint a conviction. If other evidence is enough for a conviction, then the coerced confession is a "harmless error" that does not necessitate a new trial.[74] Nevertheless, in 2000 in *Dickerson v. U.S.*, the Court made it clear that it supported the *Miranda* decision and that Congress was not empowered to change it.

The Fifth Amendment prohibits not only coerced confessions but also coerced crimes. The courts have overturned convictions based on *entrapment*—when law enforcement officials encourage persons to commit crimes (such as accepting bribes or purchasing illicit drugs) that they otherwise would not commit. "You Are the Judge: The Case of the Enticed Farmer" addresses this issue.

THE RIGHT TO COUNSEL

One of the most important of the *Miranda* rights is the right to secure counsel. Even lawyers who are taken to court hire another lawyer to represent them. (There is an old saying in the legal profession that a lawyer who defends himself has a fool for a client.) Although the **Sixth Amendment** has always ensured the right to counsel in federal courts, this right was not extended to people tried in state courts until the 1960s. Winning this right for poor defendants was a long fight. Until the 1930s, individuals were tried and sometimes convicted for capital offenses (those in

> **Sixth Amendment**
> A constitutional amendment designed to protect individuals accused of crimes. It includes the right to counsel, the right to confront witnesses, and the right to a speedy and public trial.

YOU ARE THE Judge

The Case of the Enticed Farmer

In 1984, Keith Jacobson, a 56-year-old farmer who supported his elderly father in Nebraska, ordered two magazines and a brochure from a California adult bookstore. He expected nude photographs of adult males but instead found photographs of nude boys. He ordered no other magazines.

Three months later, Congress changed federal law to make the receipt of such materials illegal. Finding his name on the mailing list of the California bookstore, two government agencies repeatedly enticed Jacobson through five fictitious organizations and a bogus pen pal with solicitations for sexually explicit photographs of children. After 26 months of enticement, Jacobson finally ordered a magazine and was arrested for violating the Child Protection Act.

He was convicted of receiving child pornography through the mail, which he undoubtedly did. Jacobson claimed, however, that he had been entrapped into committing the crime.

You Be the Judge: Was Jacobson an innocent victim of police entrapment, or was he truly seeking child pornography?

Decision: The Court agreed with Jacobson. In *Jacobson v. United States* (1992), it ruled that the government had overstepped the line between setting a trap for the "unwary innocent" and the "unwary criminal" and failed to establish that Jacobson was independently predisposed to commit the crime for which he was arrested. Jacobson's conviction was overturned.

which the death penalty could be imposed) without a lawyer. In 1932, the Supreme Court ordered the states to provide an attorney for indigent (poor) defendants accused of a capital crime (*Powell v. Alabama*).

Most crimes are not capital crimes, however, and most crimes are tried in state courts. It was not until 1963, in **Gideon v. Wainwright,**[75] that the Supreme Court extended the right to an attorney for everyone accused of a felony in a state court. Subsequently, the Court went a step further than *Gideon* and held that whenever imprisonment could be imposed, a lawyer must be provided for the accused (*Argersinger v. Hamlin* [1972]). In addition, the Supreme Court found that a trial court's erroneous deprivation of a criminal defendant's *choice* of counsel entitles him to reversal of his conviction.[76]

TRIALS

Television's portrayal of courts and trials is almost as dramatic as its portrayal of detectives and police officers—both often vary from reality. Highly publicized trials are dramatic but rare. The murder trial of O. J. Simpson made headlines for months. Cable News Network even carried much of the pretrial and trial live. But in reality, most cases, even ones in which the evidence is solid, do not go to trial.

If you visit a typical American criminal courtroom, you will rarely see a trial complete with judge and jury. In American courts, 90 percent of all cases begin and end with a guilty plea. Most cases are settled through a process called **plea bargaining**. A plea bargain results from a bargain struck between a defendant's lawyer and a prosecutor to the effect that a defendant will plead guilty to a lesser crime (or fewer crimes) in exchange for a state not prosecuting that defendant for a more serious (or additional) crime.

Critics of the plea-bargaining system believe that it permits many criminals to avoid the full punishment they deserve. The process, however, works to the advantage of both sides; it saves the state the time and money that would otherwise be spent on a trial, and it permits defendants who think they might be convicted of a serious charge to plead guilty to a lesser one.

Whether plea bargaining serves the ends of justice is much debated. To its critics, plea bargaining benefits defendants. A study of sentencing patterns in three California counties discovered that a larger proportion of defendants who went to trial (rather than plea bargained) ended up going to prison compared with those who pleaded guilty and had no trial. In answer to their question "Does it pay to plead guilty?" the researchers gave a qualified yes.[77] Good or bad, plea bargaining is a practical necessity. Only a vast increase in resources would allow the court system cope with a trial for every defendant.

The defendants in the 300,000 cases per year that actually go to trial are entitled to many rights, including the Sixth Amendment's provision for a speedy trial by an impartial jury. An impartial jury includes one that is not racially biased.[78] These days, defendants (those who can afford it, at least) do not leave jury selection to chance. A sophisticated technology of jury selection has developed. Jury consultants—often psychologists or other social scientists—develop profiles of jurors likely to be sympathetic or hostile to a defendant. Lawyers for both sides spend hours questioning prospective jurors in a major case.

The Constitution does not specify the size of a jury; in principle, it could be anywhere from one to 100 people. Tradition in England and America has set jury size at 12, although in petty cases six jurors are sometimes used. Whereas traditionally a jury had to be unanimous in order to convict, the Supreme Court eroded those traditions, permitting states to use fewer than 12 jurors and to convict with a less-than-unanimous vote. Federal courts still employ juries of 12 persons and require unanimous votes for a criminal conviction.

Gideon v. Wainwright
The 1963 Supreme Court decision holding that anyone accused of a felony where imprisonment may be imposed, however poor he or she might be, has a right to a lawyer. See also **Sixth Amendment**.

plea bargaining
A bargain struck between the defendant's lawyer and the prosecutor to the effect that the defendant will plead guilty to a lesser crime (or fewer crimes) in exchange for the state's promise not to prosecute the defendant for a more serious (or additional) crime.

In recent years the Supreme Court has aggressively defended the jury's role in the criminal justice process—and limited the discretion of judges in sentencing. In several cases the Court has held that other than a previous conviction, any fact that increases the penalty for a crime beyond the prescribed statutory maximum or even the ordinary range must be submitted to a jury and proved beyond a reasonable doubt.[79] These decisions ensure that the judge's authority to sentence derives wholly from the jury's verdict.

The Sixth Amendment (and the protection against the suspension of the writ of *habeas corpus*) also guarantees that persons who are arrested have a right to be brought before a judge. This occurs at two stages of the judicial process. First, those detained have a right to be informed of the accusations against them. Second, they have a right to a *speedy and public trial*. Normally, these guarantees present few issues. However, in the aftermath of the September 11, 2001, terrorist attacks, the FBI detained more than 1,200 persons as possible dangers to national security. Of these persons, 762 were illegal aliens (mostly Arabs and Muslims), and many of them languished in jail for months until cleared by the FBI.

For the first time in U.S. history, the federal government withheld the names of detainees, reducing their opportunities to exercise their rights for access to the courts and to counsel. The government argued that releasing the names and details of those arrested would give terrorists a window on the terror investigation. In 2004, the Supreme Court refused to consider whether the government properly withheld names and other details about these prisoners. However, in other cases the Court found that detainees held both in the United States and at the naval base at Guantánamo Bay, Cuba, had the right to challenge their detention before a judge or other neutral decision maker (*Hamdi v. Rumsfeld* and *Rasul v. Bush* [2004]).

Prisoners held at the U.S. naval base at Guantánamo Bay, Cuba, present difficult issues of prisoners' rights.

In an historic decision in 2006 (*Hamdan v. Rumsfeld*), the Supreme Court held that the procedures President Bush had approved for trying prisoners at Guanatánamo Bay lacked congressional authorization and violated both the Uniform Code of Military Justice and the Geneva Conventions. The flaws the Court cited were the failure to guarantee defendants the right to attend their trail and the prosecution's ability under the rules to introduce hearsay evidence, unsworn testimony, and evidence obtained through coercion. Equally important, the Constitution did not empower the president to establish judicial procedures on his own.

Later that year, Congress passed the Military Commissions Act (MCA), which specifically authorized military commissions to try alien unlawful enemy combatants and denied access to the courts for any alien detained by the United States government who was determined to be an enemy combatant, or who was awaiting determination regarding enemy combatant status. This allowed the United States government to detain such aliens indefinitely without prosecuting them in any manner. However, in June 2008, the Supreme Court held in *Boumediene v. Bush* that foreign terrorism suspects held at Guantánamo Bay have constitutional rights to challenge their detention in U.S. courts. "The laws and Constitution are designed to survive, and remain in force, in extraordinary times," the Court proclaimed as it declared unconstitutional the provision of the MCA that stripped the federal courts of jurisdiction to hear habeas corpus petitions from detainees seeking to challenge their designation as enemy combatants. The Court also found that the truncated review procedure provided by the Detainee Treatment Act of 2005 fell short of being a constitutionally adequate substitute because it failed to offer the fundamental procedural protections of habeas corpus.

In addition, defendants have the right to confront the witnesses against them. The Supreme Court has held that prosecutors cannot introduce testimony into a trial unless the accused can cross-examine the witness (*Crawford v. Washington* [2004]).

CRUEL AND UNUSUAL PUNISHMENT

Citizens convicted of a crime can expect punishment ranging from mild to severe, the mildest being some form of probation and the most severe, of course, being the death penalty. The **Eighth Amendment** forbids **cruel and unusual punishment**, although it does not define the phrase. Through the Fourteenth Amendment, this provision of the Bill of Rights applies to the states.

Almost the entire constitutional debate over cruel and unusual punishment has centered on the death penalty (an exception can be found in "You Are the Judge: The Case of the First Offender"). More than 3,300 people are currently on death row, nearly half of them in California, Texas, and Florida. In 1968, the Court overturned a death sentence because opponents of the death penalty had been excluded from the jury at sentencing (*Witherspoon v. Illinois*), a factor that stacked the cards, said the Court, in favor of the extreme penalty.

The Court first confronted the question of whether the death penalty is inherently cruel and unusual punishment in *Furman v. Georgia* (1972), when it overturned Georgia's death penalty law because the state imposed the penalty in a "freakish" and "random" manner. In response to this decision, 35 states passed new laws permitting the death penalty. Some states, to prevent arbitrariness in punishment, mandated death penalties for some crimes. In *Woodson v. North Carolina* (1976), the Supreme Court ruled against mandatory death penalties.

Since then the Court has come down more clearly on the side of the death penalty. In ***Gregg v. Georgia*** (1976), the Court upheld capital punishment, concluding

Eighth Amendment
The constitutional amendment that forbids **cruel and unusual punishment**, although it does not define this phrase. Through the **Fourteenth Amendment**, this **Bill of Rights** provision applies to the states.

cruel and unusual punishment
Court sentences prohibited by the **Eighth Amendment**. Although the Supreme Court has ruled that mandatory death sentences for certain offenses are unconstitutional, it has not held that the death penalty itself constitutes cruel and unusual punishment.

Gregg v. Georgia
The 1976 Supreme Court decision that upheld the constitutionality of the death penalty, stating, "It is an extreme sanction, suitable to the most extreme of crimes." The Court did not, therefore, believe that the death sentence constitutes **cruel and unusual punishment**.

YOU ARE THE Judge

The Case of the First Offender

Ronald Harmelin of Detroit was convicted of possessing 672 grams of cocaine (a gram is about one-thirtieth of an ounce). Michigan's mandatory sentencing law required the trial judge to sentence Harmelin, a first-time offender, to life imprisonment without possibility of parole. Harmelin argued that this was cruel and unusual punishment because it was "significantly disproportionate," meaning that, as we might say, the punishment did not fit the crime. Harmelin's lawyers argued that many other crimes more serious than cocaine possession would net similar sentences.

You Be the Judge: Was Harmelin's sentence cruel and unusual punishment?

Decision: The Court upheld Harmelin's conviction in *Harmelin v. Michigan* (1991), spending many pages to explain that severe punishments were quite commonplace, especially when the Bill of Rights was written. Severity alone does not qualify a punishment as "cruel and unusual." The severity of punishment was up to the legislature of Michigan, which, the justices observed, knew better than they the conditions on the streets of Detroit. Later, Michigan reduced the penalty for possession of smalll amounts of cocaine and released Harmelin from jail.

that it was "an expression of society's outrage at particularly offensive conduct. . . . It is an extreme sanction, suitable to the most extreme of crimes."

Shortly before retiring from the bench in 1994, Supreme Court Justice Harry Blackmun declared that the administration of the death penalty "fails to deliver the fair, consistent and reliable sentences of death required by the Constitution" (*Callins v. Callins* [1994]). Social scientists have shown that minority defendants and murderers whose victims were White are more likely to receive death sentences than are White murderers or those whose victims were not White. For example, about 80 percent of the murder victims in cases resulting in an execution were White, even though only 50 percent of murder victims generally are White. Nevertheless, in *McCleskey v. Kemp* (1987), the Supreme Court concluded that the death penalty did not violate the equal protection of the law guaranteed by the Fourteenth Amendment. The Court insisted that the unequal distribution of death penalty sentences was constitutionally acceptable because there was no evidence that juries intended to discriminate on the basis of race.

McCleskey v. Kemp
The 1987 Supreme Court decision that upheld the constitutionality of the death penalty against charges that it violated the **Fourteenth Amendment** because minority defendants were more likely to receive the death penalty than were White defendants.

Today, the death penalty is a part of the American criminal justice system, and about 1,100 persons have been executed since the Court's decision in *Gregg*. The Court has also made it more difficult for death row prisoners to file petitions that would force legal delays and appeals to stave off their appointed executions; it has made it easier for prosecutors to exclude jurors opposed to the death penalty (*Wainwright v. Witt*, 1985); and it has allowed "victim impact" statements detailing the character of murder victims and their families' suffering to be used against a defendant. Most Americans support the death penalty, although there is evidence that racism plays a role in the support of Whites.[80] It is interesting to note that the European Union prohibits the death penalty in member countries.

In recent years, however, evidence that courts have sentenced innocent people to be executed has reinvigorated the debate over the death penalty. Attorneys have employed the new technology of DNA evidence in a number of states to obtain the release of dozens of death row prisoners. Governor George Ryan of Illinois declared a moratorium on executions in his state after researchers proved that 13 people on death row were innocent. Later, he commuted the death sentences of all prisoners in the state. In general, there has been a decline in executions, as you can see in "A Generation of Change: The Decline in Executions."

In addition, the Supreme Court has placed constraints on the application of the death penalty, holding that the Constitution barred the execution of the mentally ill (*Ford v. Wainwright*, 1986); mentally retarded persons (*Atkins v. Virginia*, 2002); those under the age of 18 when they committed their crimes (*Roper v. Simmons*, 2005); and those convicted of raping adult women (*Coker v. Georgia*, 1977) and children (*Kennedy v. Louisiana*, 2008) where the crime did not result and was not intended to result, in the victim's death. In *Kennedy*, the Court went beyond the question in the case to rule out the death penalty for any individual crime—as opposed to offenses against the state, like treason or espionage—where the victim's life was not taken. In addition, the Court has required that a jury, not just a judge, find an aggravating circumstance necessary for imposition of the death penalty (*Ring v. Arizona*). The Court also required lawyers for defendants in death penalty cases to make reasonable efforts to fight for their clients at a trial's sentencing phase (*Rompilla v. Beard* [2005]).

Debate over the death penalty continues. In 2008, the Supreme Court upheld the use of lethal injection, concluding that challengers to this method of execution must show not only that a state's method "creates a demonstrated risk of severe pain," but also that there were alternatives that were "feasible" and "readily implemented" that would "significantly" reduce that risk.[81] You can see what some students are doing about the injustices they perceive in the death penalty system in "Young People and Politics: College Students Help Prevent Wrongful Deaths."

A GENERATION OF CHANGE

The Decline of **Executions**

Supreme Court decisions, new DNA technology, and perhaps a growing public concern about the fairness of the death penalty have resulted in the number of death sentences dropping dramatically—from 98 in 1998 to 42 in 2007. Although the number of executions in Texas been relatively constant, the state's share of total executions nationwide has steadily increased: from 32 percent in 2005 to 45 percent in 2006 to 62 percent in 2007. Texas prosecutors and juries are no more apt to seek and impose death sentences than those in the rest of the country. However, once a death sentence is imposed there, prosecutors, the courts, the pardon board, and the governor are united in moving the process along.

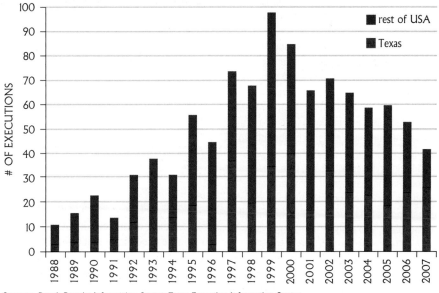

Sources: Death Penalty Information Center; Texas Execution Information Center.

THE RIGHT TO PRIVACY

The members of the First Congress who drafted the Bill of Rights and enshrined American civil liberties would never have imagined that Americans would go to court to argue about wiretapping, surrogate motherhood, abortion, or pornography. New technologies have raised ethical issues unimaginable in the eighteenth century. Today, one of the greatest debates concerning Americans' civil liberties lies in the emerging area of privacy rights.

IS THERE A RIGHT TO PRIVACY?

Nowhere does the Bill of Rights say that Americans have a **right to privacy**. Clearly, however, the First Congress had the concept of privacy in mind when it crafted the first 10 amendments. Freedom of religion implies the right to exercise private beliefs; the Third Amendment's prohibition against the government forcing citizens to quarter soldiers in their homes during times of peace; protections against "unreasonable searches and seizures" make persons secure in their homes; and private property cannot be seized without "due process of law." In 1928, Justice Brandeis hailed privacy as "the right to be left alone—the most comprehensive of the rights and the most valued by civilized men."

right to privacy
The right to a private personal life free from the intrusion of government.

College **Students Help Prevent Wrongful Deaths**

The Center on Wrongful Convictions at Northwestern University investigates possible wrongful convictions and represents imprisoned clients with claims of actual innocence. The young staff, including faculty, cooperating outside attorneys, and Northwestern University law students, pioneered the investigation and litigation of wrongful convictions—including the cases of nine innocent men sentenced to death in Illinois.

Undergraduates as well as law students have been involved in establishing the innocence of men who had been condemned to die. One instance involved the case of a man with an IQ of 51. The Illinois Supreme Court stayed his execution, just 48 hours before it was due to be carried out, because of questions about his mental fitness. This stay provided a professor and students from a Northwestern University investigative journalism class an opportunity to investigate the man's guilt.

They tracked down and reinterviewed witnesses. One eyewitness recanted his testimony, saying that investigators had pressured him into implicating the man. The students found a woman who pointed to her ex-husband as the killer. Then a private investigator interviewed the ex-husband, who made a videotaped statement claiming he killed in self-defense. The students literally helped to save the life of an innocent man.

On January 11, 2003, Governor George H. Ryan of Illinois chose Lincoln Hall at Northwestern University's School of Law to make an historic announcement. He commuted the death sentences of all 167 death row prisoners in Illinois (he also pardoned four others based on innocence the previous day). The governor felt it was fitting to make the announcement there before "the students, teachers, lawyers, and investigators who first shed light on the sorrowful conditions of Illinois' death penalty system."

In addition to saving the lives of wrongfully convicted individuals in Illinois, the Northwestern investigations have also helped trigger a nationwide reexamination of the capital punishment system. To learn more about the Center on Wrongful Convictions, visit its Web site at http://www.law.northwestern.edu/wrongfulconvictions/.

QUESTIONS FOR DISCUSSION

▶ Why do you think college students and others were able to determine the truth about the innocence of condemned men better than the police and prosecutors at the original trials?

▶ Are there other areas of public life in which students can make important contributions through their investigations?

The idea that the Constitution guarantees a right to privacy was first enunciated in a 1965 case involving a Connecticut law forbidding the use of contraceptives. It was a little-used law, but a doctor and a family planning specialist were arrested for disseminating birth control devices. The state reluctantly brought them to court, and they were convicted. The Supreme Court, in the case of *Griswold v. Connecticut*, wrestled with the privacy issue. Seven justices finally decided that various portions of the Bill of Rights cast "penumbras" (or shadows)—unstated liberties implied by the explicitly stated rights—protecting a right to privacy, including a right to family planning between husband and wife. Supporters of privacy rights argued that this ruling was reasonable enough, for what could be the purpose of the Fourth Amendment, for example, if not to protect privacy? Critics of the ruling—and there were many of them—claimed that the Supreme Court was inventing protections not specified by the Constitution.

There are other areas of privacy rights, including the sexual behavior of gays and lesbians, which we discuss in the next chapter. The most important application of privacy rights, however, came in the area of abortion. The Supreme Court unleashed a constitutional firestorm in 1973 that has not yet abated.

CONTROVERSY OVER ABORTION

In the summer of 1972, Supreme Court Justice Harry Blackmun returned to Minnesota's famous Mayo Clinic, where he had once served as general counsel. The clinic lent him a tiny desk in the corner of a librarian's office, where he worked quietly for two weeks. His research during this short summer vacation focused on the medical aspects of abortion. The Court had assigned Blackmun the task of writing the majority opinion in one of the most controversial cases ever to come before the Court. Under the pseudonym of "Jane Roe," a Texas woman named Norma McCorvey sought an abortion. She argued that the state law allowing the procedure only to save the life of a mother was unconstitutional. Texas argued that states had the power to regulate moral behavior, including abortions.

The opinion in **Roe v. Wade** (1973) followed medical authorities in dividing pregnancy into three equal trimesters. *Roe* forbade any state control of abortions during the first trimester; it permitted states to regulate abortion procedures, but only in a way that protected the mother's health, in the second trimester; and it allowed the states to ban abortion during the third trimester, except when the mother's life or health was in danger. This decision unleashed a storm of protest. The Court's staff needed extra mailboxes to handle the correspondence, some of which contained death threats.[82]

Since *Roe v. Wade*, women have received about 1.5 million legal abortions annually, 1.2 million in 2007. Abortion is a common experience: at current rates, about one in three American women will have had an abortion by the time she reaches age 45. Moreover, a broad cross section of U.S. women have abortions. Fifty-six percent of women having abortions are in their twenties; 61 percent have one or more children; 67 percent have never married; 57 percent are economically disadvantaged; and 78 percent report a religious affiliation. No racial or ethnic group makes up a majority: 41 percent of women obtaining abortions are white non-Hispanic, 32 percent are black non-Hispanic, 20 percent are Hispanic and 7 percent are of other racial backgrounds.[83]

Yet the furor has never subsided. Congress has passed numerous statutes forbidding the use of federal funds for abortions. Many states have passed similar restrictions. Missouri went as far as any other state, forbidding the use of state funds or state employees to perform abortions. A clinic in St. Louis challenged the law as unconstitutional, but in *Webster v. Reproductive Health Services* (1989), the Court upheld the law. It has also upheld laws requiring minors to notify one or both parents or a judge before obtaining an abortion.

In 1991, the conservative Court went even further in upholding restrictions on abortions. In *Rust v. Sullivan*, the Court found that a Department of Health and Human Services ruling—specifying that family planning services receiving federal funds could not provide women any counseling regarding abortion—was constitutional. This decision was greeted by a public outcry that the rule would deny many poor women abortion counseling and limit the First Amendment right of a medical practitioner to counsel a client. On his third day in office, President Clinton lifted the ban on abortion counseling.

In 1992, in **Planned Parenthood v. Casey**, the Court changed its standard for evaluating restrictions on abortion from one of "strict scrutiny" of any restraints on a "fundamental right" to one of "undue burden" that permits considerably more regulation. The Court upheld a 24-hour waiting period, a parental or judicial consent requirement for minors (you can see variations among the states on this restriction in "My State: Laws on Abortions for Minors"), and a requirement that doctors present women with information on the risks of the operation. The Court struck down a provision requiring a married woman to tell her husband of her intent to have an abortion. At the same time, the majority also affirmed their commitment to the basic right of a woman to obtain an abortion.

In 2000, the Court held in *Sternberg v. Carhart* that Nebraska's prohibition of "partial birth" abortions was unconstitutional because it placed an undue burden on women seeking an abortion by limiting their options to less safe

Roe v. Wade
The 1973 Supreme Court decision holding that a state ban on all abortions was unconstitutional. The decision forbade state control over abortions during the first trimester of pregnancy, permitted states to limit abortions to protect the mother's health in the second trimester, and permitted states to protect the fetus during the third trimester.

Planned Parenthood v. Casey
A 1992 case in which the Supreme Court loosened its standard for evaluating restrictions on abortion from one of "strict scrutiny" of any restraints on a "fundamental right" to one of "undue burden" that permits considerably more regulation.

MyState | Laws on Abortions for Minors

Abortions are legal in the United States. However, for teenagers under the age of 18, the laws on abortions differ from state to state. In some states, parental permission is required before a girl under age 18 can have an abortion. Some states allow a judge to bypass this rule.

This map shows which states require parental consent before a minor can obtain an abortion.

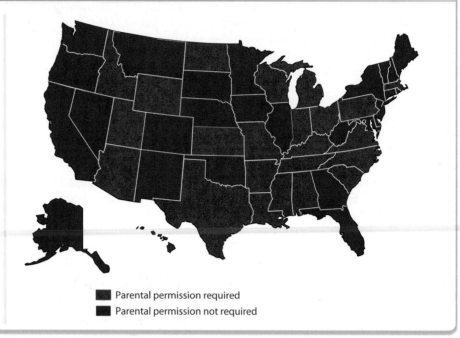

Source: Guttmacher Institute, 2008.

■ Parental permission required
■ Parental permission not required

procedures, because the law provided no exception for cases where the health of the mother was at risk, and because the law did not clearly specify prohibited behavior. In 2003, Congress passed a law banning partial birth abortions, providing an exception to the ban in order to save the life of a mother but no exception to preserve a mother's health, as it found that the procedure was never necessary for a woman's health. In *Gonzales v. Carhart* (2007), the Supreme Court upheld the law, finding it was specific and did not subject women to significant health risks or impose an undue burden on a woman's right to an abortion. The court also took pains to point out that the law would not affect most abortions, which are performed early in a pregnancy, and that safe alternatives to the prohibited procedure are available.

Americans are deeply divided on the issue of abortion (see Figure 4.1). Proponents of choice believe that access to abortion is essential if women are to be fully

FIGURE 4.1

The Abortion Debate

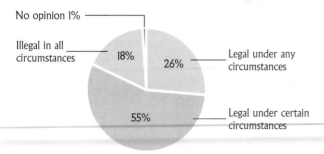

No opinion 1%

Illegal in all circumstances 18%

Legal under any circumstances 26%

Legal under certain circumstances 55%

Source: Gallup Poll, May 10–13, 2007.

In few areas of public opinion research do scholars find more divided opinion than on abortion. Some people feel very strongly about the matter, enough so that they are "single-issue voters" unwilling to support any candidate who disagrees with them on abortion. Most take a middle position, one that supports the principle of abortion but that also accepts restrictions on access to abortions.

Question: Now, on the issue of abortion: Do you think abortions should be legal under any circumstances, legal only under certain circumstances, or illegal in all circumstances?

autonomous human beings. Opponents call themselves pro-life because they believe that the fetus is fully human; therefore, an abortion deprives a fetus of the right to life. These positions are irreconcilable, making abortion a politician's nightmare. Wherever a politician stands on this divisive issue, a large number of voters will be enraged.

Because passions run so strongly on the issue, advocates may take extreme action. In the last two decades abortion opponents have bombed a number of abortion clinics, and they murdered two physicians who performed abortions in Pensacola, Florida.

Efforts to protect women's access to clinics sometimes clash with protesters' rights to free speech and assembly. In 1994, the Court consolidated the right to abortion established in *Roe* with the protection of a woman's right to enter an abortion clinic to exercise that right. Citing the government's interest in preserving order and maintaining women's access to pregnancy services, the Court upheld a state court's order of a 36-foot buffer zone around a

Passions sometimes rule in the debate over abortion. Paul Hill went so far as to murder a physician who performed abortions, arguing that he had a right to do so to save the lives of the unborn. The jury did not agree, and Hill was sentenced to death.

clinic in Melbourne, Florida.[84] That same year Congress passed the Freedom of Access to Clinic Entrances Act, which makes it a federal crime to intimidate abortion providers or women seeking abortions. In 2000, it upheld a 100 foot restriction on approaching close to someone at a health care facility to discourage abortions.[85] In another case, the Court decided that abortion clinics could invoke the federal racketeering law to sue violent antiabortion protest groups for damages.[86]

UNDERSTANDING CIVIL LIBERTIES

American government is both democratic and constitutional. America is democratic because it is governed by officials who are elected by the people and, as such, are accountable for their actions. The American government is constitutional because it has a fundamental organic law, the Constitution, that limits the things government may do. By restricting the government, the Constitution limits what the people can empower the government to do. The democratic and constitutional components of government can produce conflicts, but they also reinforce one another.

CIVIL LIBERTIES AND DEMOCRACY

The rights ensured by the First Amendment—the freedoms of speech, press, and assembly—are essential to a democracy. If people are to govern themselves, they need access to all available information and opinions in order to make intelligent, responsible, and accountable decisions. If the right to participate in public life is to be open to all, then Americans—in all their diversity—must have the right to express their opinions.

Individual participation and the expression of ideas are crucial components of democracy, but so is majority rule, which can conflict with individual rights. The majority does not have the freedom to decide that there are some ideas it would rather not hear, although at times the majority tries to enforce its will on the minority. The conflict is even sharper in relation to the rights guaranteed by the Fourth, Fifth, Sixth, Seventh, and Eighth Amendments. These rights protect all Americans, but they also make it more difficult to punish criminals. It is easy—although misleading—for the majority to view these guarantees as benefits for criminals at the expense of society.

With some notable exceptions, the United States has done a good job in protecting the rights of diverse interests to express themselves. There is little danger that a political or economic elite will muffle dissent. Similarly, the history of the past four decades is one of increased protections for defendants' rights, and defendants are typically not among the elite. Ultimately, the courts have decided what constitutional guarantees mean in practice. Although federal judges, appointed for life, are not directly accountable to popular will,[87] "elitist" courts have often protected civil liberties from the excesses of majority rule.

CIVIL LIBERTIES AND THE SCOPE OF GOVERNMENT

Civil liberties in America are both the foundation for and a reflection of our emphasis on individualism. When there is a conflict between an individual or a group attempting to express themselves or worship as they please and an effort by a government to constrain them in some fashion, the individual or group usually wins. If protecting the freedom of an individual or group to express themselves results in inconvenience or even injustice for the public officials they criticize or the populace they wish to reach, so be it. Every nation must choose where to draw the line between freedom and order. In the United States, we generally choose liberty.

Today's government is huge and commands vast, powerful technologies. Americans' Social Security numbers, credit cards, driver's licenses, and school records are all on giant computers to which the government has immediate access. It is virtually impossible to hide from the police, the FBI, the Internal Revenue Service, or any governmental agency. Because Americans can no longer avoid the attention of government, strict limitations on governmental power are essential. The Bill of Rights provides these vital limitations.

Thus, in general, civil liberties limit the scope of government. Yet substantial government efforts are often required to protect the expansion of rights that we have witnessed thus far. Those seeking abortions may need help reaching a clinic, defendants may demand that lawyers be provided them at public expense, advocates of unpopular causes may require police protection, and litigants in complex lawsuits over matters of birth or death may rely on judges to resolve their conflicts. It is ironic—but true—that an expansion of freedom may require a simultaneous expansion of government.

SUMMARY

Civil liberties are an individual's protection against the government. The Bill of Rights makes it clear that American government is a constitutional democracy in which individual rights limit government. Disputes about civil liberties are frequent because the issues involved are complex and divisive. Legislatures and courts are constantly defining in practice what the Bill of Rights guarantees in theory.

In a way, the notion that government can protect people from government is contradictory. Thomas Jefferson wrote in the Declaration of Independence that all people "are endowed by their creator with certain unalienable rights." Jefferson's next "self-evident truth" was that "to secure these rights, governments are instituted." People, said Jefferson, do not get their rights from government. Instead, rights precede government, which then gets its power to rule from the people. The Bill of Rights does not give Americans freedom of religion or the right to a fair trial; these amendments merely recognize that these rights exist. People often speak, however, as though rights are things that government gives them.

The First Amendment guarantees freedoms of religion, expression, and assembly. The Bill of Rights also contains protections that are especially important to those accused or convicted of crimes. Together, these rights provide Americans with more liberty than that enjoyed by most other people on Earth.

One task that government must perform is to resolve conflicts between rights. Often, First Amendment rights and rights at the bar of justice exist in uneasy tension; a newspaper's right to inform its readers may conflict with a person's right to a fair trial. Today, the Supreme Court has extended to the states most of the rights enjoyed under the U.S. Constitution.

Today's technologies raise key questions about ethics and the Constitution. Although the Constitution does not specifically mention a right to privacy, the Supreme Court found this right implied by several guarantees in the Bill of Rights. The most controversial application of privacy rights has been in abortion cases.

Chapter Test

Multiple Choice

1. Which of the following is NOT addressed in the Bill of Rights?
   a. The right to bear arms
   b. The quartering of soldiers
   c. Criminal court procedures
   d. Rights reserved to the states
   e. Right to an education

2. The legal concept under which the Supreme Court has nationalized the Bill of Rights is the:
   a. Incorporation Doctrine
   b. Disincorporation Doctrine
   c. Inclusion Doctrine
   d. Privileges and Immunities Clause
   e. Due Process Clause

3. According to the ruling of the Supreme Court, what right does the government have regarding the regulation of religion?
   a. It can prohibit religious beliefs and practices it considers inappropriate
   b. It can prohibit religious beliefs and practices, if it has a compelling interest
   c. It can prohibit religious practices, but not religious beliefs
   d. It can neither prohibit religious beliefs nor religious practices
   e. It depends on the religion

4. In all but which of the following situations can officials potentially exercise prior restraint?
   a. If obscenity and libel are involved
   b. In the name of national security
   c. Under certain circumstances in the school environment
   d. In cases of religious insults
   e. In cases of incitement to violence

5. What measures can the judicial system take in order to guarantee the right to a fair trial?
   a. It can limit journalists' access to particularly sensitive trials
   b. It can exercise prior constraint against the publication of information that might influence the jury
   c. It can force journalists to hold back sensitive information until after the trial has ended
   d. It cannot stop journalists from printing sensitive information, but it can punish them for doing so after the fact
   e. It can only attempt to keep the jury away from media influence

6. Which of the following allows the federal government to monitor communications that begin or end in a foreign country without a warrant?
   a. The USA Patriot Act
   b. The Protect America Act
   c. The International Wiretap Act
   d. The Anti-Terrorism Act
   e. The Surveillance Act

7. The USA Patriot Act allows searches of private property:
   a. Of any and all individuals in the United States
   b. Only if there is probable cause
   c. Without probable cause, if the owner is notified prior to the search
   d. Without probable cause and without notification of the owner
   e. Only with a court order

8. Imagine that you are an administrator at a public university. The Political Science Club and the Christian Fellowship have petitioned you for use of university facilities. According to Supreme Court decisions on the matter of religion and public schools, you:
   a. Must allow the political science club the use of the university facilities, but can deny the Christian Fellowship that use
   b. Must allow both groups the same use of the facilities
   c. Must allow the Christian Fellowship the use of the facilities, as long as it is not for worship
   d. Must put the question to a vote of your student body.
   e. The Supreme Court has never addressed this issue

9. If a newspaper prints an article in which the author is knowingly spreading false information about a private person, this is considered an example of:
   a. Slander
   b. Libel
   c. Obscenity
   d. Free speech
   e. Hate speech

10. Court decisions concerning the freedom of expression of so-called "symbolic speech":
   a. Have clearly defined symbolic speech and what type of symbolic speech is protected
   b. Have clearly defined symbolic speech, but have ruled that it is never protected
   c. Have clearly defined symbolic speech, but have decided that some forms are protected while others are not
   d. Have not yet clearly defined symbolic speech
   e. Have not addressed the matter of symbolic speech

11. According to the Federal Communications Commission (FCC), which of the following does NOT need a license?
   a. The Los Angeles Times
   b. Fox News
   c. Cable Network News (CNN)
   d. National Public Radio (NPR)
   e. All of the above need a license.

12. The largest portion of the Bill of Rights addresses issues of:
   a. Religion
   b. Expression
   c. Assembly
   d. Criminal justice
   e. Public order

True/False

13. The Supreme Court has ruled that high school newspapers are a public forum and cannot be regulated in "any reasonable manner" by school officials.
   True——————   False——————

14. The right to freedom of speech applies to both public and private property equally.
   True——————   False——————

15. Congress has recently decided that, unlike material published by means of the printing press, material on the Internet is not protected by the First Amendment.
   True——————   False——————

Short Answer

16. Briefly outline the general positions of conservatives and liberals in the debate about the role of the government with regard to civil liberties.

17. What difference does current legislation make between public and private individuals with regard to libel cases?

18. What are the three types of restrictions to the First Amendment right to "peaceably assemble," and what is an example of each?

19. What are three necessary conditions for a police search without a warrant?

20. Assume that Joe S. has been convicted of a crime in a court of law. One of the pieces of evidence brought against him in the case was his own confession. After the trial is over, it is revealed that the confession was coerced. Under what circumstances is Joe S. entitled to a new trial, and under what circumstances does the conviction stand?

Short Answer/Essay Questions

21. Looking at the A Generation of Change feature on p. 133, how would you interpret the statistics on the number of executions in the United States? First, describe the data presented. Second, explain what factors may have produced this trend. Third, address what possible consequences this trend might bring with it for the future.

22. Based on the information provided in the America in Perspective feature on p. 109, how does the United States compare to other democracies in terms of tolerance of the free speech of religious extremists? What do you think explains this fact?

23. Using concrete arguments/evidence, what are the pros and cons of plea bargaining? Do you personally agree or disagree with the practice, and why?

24. When thinking about citizens' rights, one can distinguish between the rights of an individual citizen and the rights of society as a whole. Based on what you have learned in Chapter 4 of the textbook, under what circumstances are the courts and the government more likely to give preference to individual rights over the rights of society? By the same token, under what circumstances are concerns for society as a whole likely to override individual rights?

25. In your opinion, in what situations—if any—should the government be able to exercise prior restraint, and why?

26. Imagine that a group of students at your university is operating a Web site that allows students to rate their professors and post comments about them. Imagine also that it has come to a professor's attention that a comment made about her is untrue and, she suspects, has been posted with the intent to harm her reputation. What would be the professor's rights in this situation, if she were considered a private individual? What if she were considered a public figure? In your personal opinion, would you consider professors to be private or public figures, and why?

Answer Key

1. E   2. A   3. C   4. D   5. E   6. B   7. D   8. B   9. B   10. C   11. A   12. D   13. False   14. False   15. True

Key Terms

civil liberties (102)
Bill of Rights (102)
First Amendment (103)
Fourteenth Amendment (103)
due process clause (103)
incorporation doctrine (104)
establishment clause (105)
free exercise clause (105)
prior restraint (111)

libel (117)
symbolic speech (119)
commercial speech (119)
probable cause (124)
unreasonable searches and seizures (124)
search warrant (124)
exclusionary rule (125)

Fifth Amendment (127)
self-incrimination (127)
Sixth Amendment (128)
plea bargaining (129)
Eighth Amendment (131)
cruel and unusual punishment (131)
right to privacy (133)

Key Cases

Barron v. Baltimore (1833)
Gitlow v. New York (1925)
Lemon v. Kurtzman (1971)
Zelman v. Simmons-Harris (2002)
Engel v. Vitale (1962)
School District of Abington Township, Pennsylvania v. Schempp (1963)
Near v. Minnesota (1931)
Schenck v. United States (1919)

Zurcher v. Stanford Daily (1978)
Roth v. United States (1957)
Miller v. California (1973)
New York Times v. Sullivan (1964)
Texas v. Johnson (1989)
Miami Herald Publishing Company v. Tornillo (1974)
Red Lion Broadcasting Company v. Federal Communications Commission (1969)

NAACP v. Alabama (1958)
Mapp v. Ohio (1961)
Miranda v. Arizona (1966)
Gideon v. Wainwright (1963)
Gregg v. Georgia (1976)
McCleskey v. Kemp (1987)
Roe v. Wade (1973)
Planned Parenthood v. Casey (1992)

Internet Resources

www.freedomforum.org
Background information and recent news on First Amendment issues.

www.eff.org
Web site concerned with protecting online civil liberties.

www.aclu.org
Home page of the American Civil Liberties Union offering links to many other sites concerned with civil liberties.

www.firstamendmentcenter.org/rel_liberty/overview.aspx
Overview of freedom of religion in the United States.

www.law.cornell.edu/wex/index.php/Criminal_law
The text of the landmark cases on criminal justice and background material.

www.law.cornell.edu/wex/index.First_amentment
The text of the landmark cases on freedom of religion, speech, press, and assembly and background material.

www.cc.org/
Christian Coalition home page containing background information and discussion of current events.

www.guttmacher.org/
The Guttmacher Institute, a nonpartisan source of information on all aspects of abortion.

GetConnected

The Bill of Rights and the Pledge of Allegiance

The U.S. Constitution did not originally include basic civil liberties such as those found in the Bill of Rights. In fact, as the text notes, the states made inclusion of the Bill of Rights a condition for ratification of the Constitution. The United States was the first nation to guarantee these basic rights to its citizens. The First Amendment provides that "Congress shall make no law respecting an establishment of religion, or prohibiting the free exercise thereof. . . ." In its 2003–2004 term, the U.S. Supreme Court was asked to decide a case, *Elk Grove v. Newdow*, in which a man challenged the inclusion of the words "under God" in the Pledge of Allegiance. The Court ultimately held that the man bringing the case, Dr. Newdow, did not have legal standing to sue, but a similar case is likely in the near future.

Search the Web

After reviewing the U.S. Bill of Rights in the Appendix, visit the Pledge of Allegiance Resource page at the Pew Forum on Religion and Public Life *http://pewforum.org/religion-schools/pledge/*. Read the summary of the case's progress through the federal judicial system, then scroll down to the list of *amicus* briefs. Click on several of the *amicus* briefs in support of the petitioner and several in support of the respondent. The briefs' arguments usually are summarized in the "Interest of Amicus" section near the beginning of each document.

Questions to Ask

- In your opinion, should people, especially children, be forced to repeat a pledge that violates their beliefs? What if the pledge violates their parents' beliefs—or one of their parent's beliefs?
- After reading several of the *amicus* briefs, why did some of the people and groups think "under God" should be removed from the Pledge?
- Why did other groups think "under God" should stay in the Pledge of Allegiance?
- Do the words "under God" in the Pledge of Allegiance violate the First Amendment? Why or why not?

Why It Matters

Any survey of the world shows that religion is a source of intense conflict, often within a single nation. The Bill of Rights guarantees American citizens certain protections from government, including against the establishment of religion. The question is how to prevent the establishment of religion without restricting the free exercise of religion. It is important—but often difficult—to draw the line properly between government neutrality toward religion on the one hand and government support of it on the other.

Get Involved

Examine some of the other religious liberty cases identified on the Pew Forum's Religion and Public Schools Issues page to compare the Pledge case with previous cases. For more exercises, go to *www.longmanamericangovernment.com*.

For Further Reading

Adler, Renata. *Reckless Disregard*. New York: Knopf, 1986. The story of two monumental conflicts between free press and individual reputations.

Baker, Liva. *Miranda: The Crime, the Law, the Politics*. New York: Atheneum, 1983. An excellent book-length treatment of one of the major criminal cases of our time.

Garrow, David J. *Liberty and Sexuality*. New York: Macmillan, 1994. The most thorough treatment of the development of the law on the right to privacy and abortion.

Heymann, Philip B. *Terrorism, Freedom, and Security*. Cambridge, MA: MIT Press, 2004. Thoughtfully balances concerns for freedom with those of safety from terrorism.

Irons, Peter. *The Courage of Their Convictions: Sixteen Americans Who Fought Their Way to the Supreme Court*. New York: Penguin Books, 1990. Accounts of 16 Americans over a period of 50 years who took their cases to the Supreme Court in defense of civil liberties.

Levy, Leonard W. *The Emergence of a Free Press*. New York: Oxford University Press, 1985. A major work on the Framers' intentions regarding freedom of expression.

Levy, Leonard W. *The Establishment Clause: Religion and the First Amendment*. New York: Macmillan, 1986. The author argues that it is unconstitutional for government to provide aid to any religion.

Lewis, Anthony. *Make No Law: The Sullivan Case and the First Amendment*. New York: Random House, 1991. A well-written story of the key case regarding American libel law and an excellent case study of a Supreme Court case.

Rose, Melody. *Safe, Legal, and Unavailable: Abortion Politics in the United States*. Washington, DC: CQ Press, 2007. Explores how many women do not have the ability to exercise their constitutional right to an abortion.

Rosenblatt, Roger. *Life Itself: Abortion in the American Mind*. New York: Random House, 1992. The author seeks to reconcile the clash of absolutes in the abortion controversy with scholarly analysis and interview data.

CIVIL RIGHTS AND PUBLIC POLICY

POLITICS IN ACTION:
LAUNCHING THE CIVIL RIGHTS MOVEMENT

A 42-year-old seamstress named Rosa Parks was riding in the "colored" section of a Montgomery, Alabama, city bus on December 1, 1955. A White man got on the bus and found that all the seats in the front, which were reserved for Whites, were taken. He moved on to the equally crowded colored section. J. F. Blake, the bus driver, then ordered all four passengers in the first row of the colored section to surrender their seats because the law prohibited Whites and African Americans from sitting next to or even across from one another.

Three of the African Americans hesitated and then complied with the driver's order. But Rosa Parks, a politically active member of the National Association for the Advancement of Colored People, said no. The driver threatened to have her arrested, but she refused to move. He then called the police, and a few minutes later two officers boarded the bus and arrested her.

At that moment the civil rights movement was born. There had been substantial efforts—and some important successes—to use the courts to end racial segregation, but Rosa Parks's refusal to give up her seat led to extensive mobilization of African Americans. Protestors employed a wide range of methods to end segregation, including nonviolent resistance. A new preacher in town, Martin Luther King Jr. of Atlanta, organized a boycott of the city buses. He was jailed, his house was bombed, and his wife and infant daughter were almost killed, but neither he nor the African American community wavered. Although they were harassed by the police and went without motor transportation by walking or even riding mules, they persisted in boycotting the buses.

It eventually took the U. S. Supreme Court to end the boycott. On November 13, 1956, the Court declared that Alabama's state and local laws requiring segregation on buses were illegal. On December 20, federal injunctions were served on the city and bus company officials, forcing them to follow the Supreme Court's ruling.

On December 21, 1956, Rosa Parks boarded a Montgomery city bus for the first time in over a year. She could sit wherever she liked and chose a seat near the front.

Americans have never fully come to terms with equality. Most Americans favor equality in the abstract—a politician who advocated inequality would not attract many votes—yet the concrete struggle for equal rights under the Constitution has been our nation's most bitter battle. It pits person against person, as in the case of Rosa Parks and the nameless White passenger, and group against group. Those people who enjoy privileged positions in American society have been reluctant to give them up.

Individual liberty is central to democracy. So is a broad notion of equality, such as that implied by the concept of "one person, one vote." Sometimes these values conflict, as when individuals or a majority of the people want to act in a discriminatory fashion. How should we resolve such conflicts between liberty and equality? Can we have a democracy if some citizens do not enjoy basic rights to political participation or suffer discrimination in employment? Can we or should we try to remedy past discrimination against minorities and women?

In addition, many people have called on government to protect the rights of minorities and women, increasing the scope and power of government in the process. Ironically, this increase in government power is often used to *check* government, as when the federal courts restrict the actions of state legislatures. It is equally ironic that society's collective efforts to use government to protect civil rights are designed not to limit individualism but to enhance it, freeing people from suffering and from prejudice. But how far should government go in these efforts? Is an increase in the scope of government to protect some people's rights an unacceptable threat to the rights of other citizens?

The phrase "all men are created equal" is at the heart of American political culture; yet implementing this principle has proved to be one of our nation's most enduring struggles. Throughout our history, issues involving African Americans, women, Hispanic Americans, and other minorities have raised constitutional questions about slavery, segregation, equal pay, and a host of other issues. Their rallying cry has been **civil rights**, which are policies designed to protect people against arbitrary or discriminatory treatment by government officials or individuals.

civil rights
Policies designed to protect people against arbitrary or discriminatory treatment by government officials or individuals.

The resulting controversies have been fought in the courts, Congress, and the bureaucracy, but the meaning of *equality* remains as elusive as it is divisive. Today's equality debates center on these key types of inequality in America:

- *Racial discrimination.* Two centuries of discrimination against racial minorities have produced historic Supreme Court and congressional policies that seek to eliminate racial discrimination from the constitutional fabric. Americans have yet to resolve issues such as the appropriate role of affirmative action programs, however.

- *Gender discrimination.* The role of women in American society has changed substantially since the 1700s. However, equal rights for women have yet to be constitutionally guaranteed. The Equal Rights Amendment was not ratified, and women continue to press for equality and to seek protection from sexual harassment.

- *Discrimination based on age, disability, sexual orientation, and other factors.* As America is "graying," older Americans are demanding a place under the civil rights umbrella. People with disabilities are among the newest claimants for civil rights. Also seeking constitutional protections against discrimination are groups such as gays and lesbians, people with acquired immuno deficiency syndrome (AIDS), and the homeless.

RACIAL EQUALITY: TWO CENTURIES OF STRUGGLE

The struggle for equality has been a persistent theme in our nation's history. Slaves sought freedom, free African Americans fought for the right to vote and to be treated as equals, women pursued equal participation in society, and the economically disadvantaged called for better treatment and economic opportunities. This fight for equality affects all Americans. Philosophically, the struggle involves defining the term *equality*. Constitutionally, it involves interpreting laws. Politically, it often involves power.

CONCEPTIONS OF EQUALITY

What does *equality* mean? Jefferson's statement in the Declaration of Independence that "all men are created equal" did not mean that he believed everybody was exactly alike or that there were no differences among human beings. Jefferson insisted throughout his long life that African Americans were genetically inferior to Whites. The Declaration went on to speak, however, of "inalienable rights" to which all are equally entitled. A belief in *equal rights* has often led to a belief in *equality of opportunity*; in other words, everyone should have the same chance. What individuals make of that equal chance depends on their abilities and efforts.

American society does not emphasize *equal results* or *equal rewards*; few Americans argue that everyone should earn the same salary or have the same amount of property. In some other countries, including Scandinavian nations, the government uses its taxing power to distribute resources much more equally than in the United States. These countries thus have much less poverty. On the other hand, critics of these more egalitarian countries often complain that emphasis on the equal distribution of resources stifles initiative and limits opportunity.

THE CONSTITUTION AND INEQUALITY

In 1789, the year in which the Constitution took effect, the French began their revolution with cries of "liberty, equality, fraternity." Whereas in France the king lost his head in the name of equality, in America the king lost his colonies in the name of independence. It is perhaps not surprising, then, that the word *equality* does not appear in the original Constitution. In addition, America in 1787 was a place far different from contemporary America, with far different values.

The delegates to the Constitutional Convention did their best to avoid facing the tension between slavery and the principles of the Declaration of Independence. Women's rights got even less attention than slavery at the Convention. John Adams, for instance, was uncharacteristically hostile to his wife Abigail's feminist opinions. Abigail's claim that "if particular care and attention is not paid to the ladies, we are determined to foment a rebellion" prompted her husband to reply, "I cannot but laugh."[1] The privileged delegates would have been baffled, if not appalled, at discussions of equal rights for 12-year-old children, deaf students, gay soldiers, or female road dispatchers. The delegates created a plan for government, not guarantees of individual rights.

Not even the Bill of Rights mentions equality. It does, however, have implications for equality in that it does not limit the scope of its guarantees to specified groups within society. It does not say, for example, that only Whites have freedom from compulsory self-incrimination or that only men are entitled to freedom of speech. The First Amendment guarantees of freedom of expression, in particular, are important because they allow those who are discriminated against to work toward achieving equality. This kind of political activism, for instance, led to the constitutional amendment that enacted a guarantee of equality, the Fourteenth Amendment.

The first and only place in which the idea of equality appears in the Constitution is in the **Fourteenth Amendment**, one of the three amendments passed after the Civil War. (The Thirteenth abolishes slavery, and the Fifteenth extends the right to vote to African Americans.) The Fourteenth Amendment forbids the states from denying to anyone "equal protection of the laws." Those five words represent the only reference to the idea of equality in the entire Constitution, yet within them was enough force to begin ensuring equal rights for all Americans. The full force of the amendment was not felt for nearly 100 years, for it was not until the mid-twentieth century that the Fourteenth Amendment was used as an instrument for unshackling disadvantaged groups. Once dismissed as "the traditional last resort of constitutional arguments," the equal protection clause now has few rivals in generating legal business for the Supreme Court.

But what does **equal protection of the laws** mean? The Fourteenth Amendment does not say that "the states must treat everybody exactly alike" or that "every state must promote equality among all its people." Presumably, it means, as one member of Congress said during the debate on the amendment, "equal protection of life, liberty, and property" for all. Thus, for example, a state cannot confiscate an African American's property under the law while letting Whites keep theirs or otherwise give Whites privileges denied to African Americans. Some members of Congress interpreted the clause to be a much more lavish protection of rights than this interpretation. But shortly after the states ratified the amendment in 1868, the narrow interpretation won out in the courts. In *Strauder v. West Virginia* (1880), the Supreme Court invalidated a law barring African Americans from jury service, but the Court refused to extend the amendment to remedy more subtle kinds of discrimination.

Over the past 100 years, however, the equal protection clause has become the vehicle for more expansive constitutional interpretations. In order to determine whether a particular form of discrimination is permissible, the Supreme Court developed three levels of scrutiny, or analysis, called standards of review (see Table 5.1). The Court has ruled that most classifications that are *reasonable*—that bear a rational relationship to some legitimate governmental purpose—are constitutional. The person who challenges these classifications has the burden of proving that they are arbitrary. Thus, for example, the states can restrict the right to vote to people over the age of 18; age is a reasonable classification and hence a permissible basis for determining who

Fourteenth Amendment

The constitutional amendment adopted after the Civil War that states, "No State shall make or enforce any law which shall abridge the privileges or immunities of citizens of the United States; nor shall any state deprive any person of life, liberty, or property, without due process of law; nor deny to any person within its jurisdiction the **equal protection of the laws.**" See also **due process clause.**

equal protection of the laws

Part of the **Fourteenth Amendment** emphasizing that the laws must provide equivalent "protection" to all people.

The African American struggle for equality paved the way for civil rights movements by women and other minorities. Here, civil rights leaders Roy Wilkins, James Farmer, Martin Luther King Jr., and Whitney Young meet with President Lyndon B. Johnson.

TABLE 5.1

Supreme Court's Standards for Classifications Under the Equal Protection Clause of the Fourteenth Amendment

BASIS OF CLASSIFICATION	STANDARD OF REVIEW	APPLYING THE TEST
Race	Inherently suspect (difficult to meet)	Is the classification necessary to accomplish a compelling governmental purpose and the least restrictive way to reach the goal?
Gender	Intermediate standard (moderately difficult to meet)	Does the classification bear a substantial relationship to an important governmental goal?
Other (age, wealth, etc.)	Reasonableness (easy to meet)	Does the classification have a rational relationship to a legitimate governmental goal?

may vote. A classification that is arbitrary—a law singling out, say, people with red hair or blue eyes for inferior treatment—is invalid.

The Court has also ruled that racial and ethnic classifications are *inherently suspect*. Courts presume these classifications to be invalid and uphold them only if they serve a "compelling public interest" and there is no other way to accomplish the purpose of the law. In the case of such classifications, the burden of proof is on the government to prove that they will serve a compelling public interest. Classifications by race and ethnicity, such as for college admissions, may be acceptable if they are made in laws seeking to remedy previous discrimination. However, as we will see in our discussion of affirmative action, the future of such laws is in doubt.

Classifications based on gender fit *somewhere between* these two extremes; the courts presume them to be neither constitutional nor unconstitutional. A law that discriminates on the basis of gender must bear a substantial relationship to an important legislative purpose. If these three levels of judicial scrutiny (reasonable, inherently suspect, and somewhere in between) appear confusing, indeed they are— even judges and legal scholars struggle to interpret these standards.

Today courts interpret the equal protection clause broadly enough to forbid racial government-sponsored segregation in public schools, prohibit job discrimination, reapportion state legislatures, and permit court-ordered busing and affirmative action. Conditions for women and minorities would be radically different if it were not for the "equal protection" clause.[2] The next three sections show how equal protection litigation has worked to the advantage of minorities, women, and other groups seeking protection under the civil rights umbrella.

TIMELINE

The Struggle for Equal Protection

RACE, THE CONSTITUTION, AND PUBLIC POLICY

Throughout American history, African Americans have been the most visible minority group in the United States. These individuals have blazed the constitutional trail for securing equal rights for all Americans. Three eras delineate African Americans' struggle for equality in America: (1) the era of slavery, from the beginnings of colonization until the end of the Civil War in 1865; (2) the era of reconstruction and resegregation, from roughly the end of the Civil War until 1953; and (3) the era of civil rights, roughly from 1954 to the present.

TABLE 5.2

Toward Racial Equality: Milestones in the Era of Slavery

1600–1865

Slavery took hold in the South, came to characterize almost all relations between African Americans and Whites, was constitutionally justified, and was finally abolished.

1619	Slaves from Africa are brought to Jamestown and sold to planters.
1776	The Continental army enlists African Americans to fight the British after the British offer freedom to slaves who would fight on their side.
1787	The Constitution provides for a slave to be counted as three-fifths of a person in representation and taxation and permits Congress to forbid the importation of new slaves after 1808.
1808	Congress prohibits importation of slaves.
1857	The *Scott v. Sandford* decision holds that slaves may not gain freedom by escaping to a free state or territory; it upholds the constitutionality of the slave system.
1862	President Lincoln issues the Emancipation Proclamation.
1865	The Thirteenth Amendment abolishes slavery and involuntary servitude.

THE ERA OF SLAVERY

The first African immigrants to America were kidnapped from their home countries. Most African Americans lived in slavery for the first 250 years of American settlement. Slaves were the property of their masters. They could be bought and sold, and they could neither vote nor own property. The Southern states, whose plantations required large numbers of unpaid workers, were the primary market for slave labor.

During the slavery era, any public policy of the slave states or the federal government had to accommodate the property interests of slave owners, who were often wealthy and enjoyed substantial political influence. The Supreme Court got into the act, too, along with the legislative and executive branches (see Table 5.2). The boldest decision supporting slavery was *Scott v. Sandford* (1857), wherein Chief Justice Taney bluntly announced that a Black man, slave or free, was "chattel" and had no rights under a White man's government and that Congress had no power to ban slavery in the western territories. This decision invalidated the hard-won Missouri Compromise, which allowed Missouri to become a slave state on the condition that northern territories would remain free of slavery. As a result, the *Scott* decision was an important milestone on the road to the Civil War.

The Union victory in the Civil War and the ratification of the **Thirteenth Amendment** ended slavery. The promises implicit in this amendment and the other two Civil War amendments introduced the era of reconstruction and resegregation in which these promises were first honored and then broken.

Scott v. Sandford

The 1857 Supreme Court decision ruling that a slave who had escaped to a free state enjoyed no rights as a citizen and that Congress had no authority to ban slavery in the territories.

Thirteenth Amendment

The constitutional amendment ratified after the Civil War that forbade slavery and involuntary servitude.

THE ERA OF RECONSTRUCTION AND RESEGREGATION

After the Civil War ended, Congress imposed strict conditions on the former confederate states before it would seat their representatives and senators. No one who had served in secessionist state governments or in the Confederate army could hold state office, the legislatures had to ratify the new amendments, and the military would govern the states like "conquered provinces" until they complied with the tough federal plans for reconstruction. Many African American men held state and federal offices during the 10 years following the war. Some government agencies, such as the Freedmen's Bureau, provided assistance to former slaves who were making the difficult transition to independence.

To ensure his election in 1876, Rutherford Hayes promised to pull the troops out of the South and let the old slave states resume business as usual. This done, Southerners lost little time reclaiming power and imposing a code of *Jim Crow laws*, or segregational laws, on African Americans. ("Jim Crow" was the name of a stereo-typical African American in a nineteenth-century minstrel song.) These laws relegated African Americans to separate public facilities, separate school systems, and even separate restrooms. Most Whites lost interest in helping former slaves. And what the Jim Crow laws mandated in the South was also common practice in the North. Indeed, the national government practiced segregation in the armed forces, employment, housing programs, and prisons.[3] In this era, racial segregation affected every part of life, from the cradle to the grave. African Americans were delivered by African American physicians or midwives and buried in African American cemeteries. Groups such as the Ku Klux Klan terrorized African Americans who violated the norms of segregation, lynching hundreds of them during this era.

The Supreme Court provided a constitutional justification for segregation in the 1896 case of ***Plessy v. Ferguson***. The Louisiana legislature required "equal but separate accommodations for the White and colored races" in railroad transportation. Although Homer Plessy was seven-eighths White, he had been arrested for refusing to leave a railway car reserved for Whites. The Court upheld the law, saying that segregation in public facilities was not unconstitutional as long as the separate facilities were substantially equal. In subsequent decisions, the Court paid more attention to the "separate" than to the "equal" part of this principle. For example, it allowed Southern states to maintain high schools and professional schools for Whites even when there were no such schools for African Americans. A measure of segregation in both the South and the North existed as late as the 1960s; nearly all the African American physicians in the United States were graduates of two medical schools, Howard University in Washington, D.C., and Meharry Medical College in Tennessee.

Nevertheless, some progress on the long road to racial equality was made in the first half of the twentieth century. The Supreme Court and the president began to prohibit a few of the most egregious practices of segregation (see Table 5.3), paving the way for a new era of civil rights.

THE ERA OF CIVIL RIGHTS

After searching carefully for the perfect case to challenge legal school segregation, the Legal Defense Fund of the National Association for the Advancement of Colored People (NAACP) selected the case of Linda Brown. Brown was an African American student in Topeka, Kansas, required by Kansas law to attend a segregated school. In Topeka, the visible signs of education—teacher quality, facilities, and so on—were equal between African American and White schools. Thus, the NAACP chose the case in order to test the *Plessy v. Ferguson* doctrine of "separate but equal." It wanted to force the Court to rule directly on whether school segregation was inherently unequal and thereby violated the Fourteenth Amendment's requirement that states guarantee "equal protection of the laws."

President Eisenhower had just appointed Chief Justice Earl Warren. So important was the case that the Court heard two rounds of arguments, one before Warren joined the Court. The justices, after hearing the oral arguments, met in the Supreme Court's conference room. Believing that a unanimous decision would have the most impact, the justices negotiated a broad agreement and then determined that Warren himself should write the opinion.

In ***Brown v. Board of Education*** (1954), the Supreme Court set aside its precedent in *Plessy* and held that school segregation was inherently unconstitutional

Plessy v. Ferguson
An 1896 Supreme Court decision that provided a constitutional justification for segregation by ruling that a Louisiana law requiring "equal but separate accommodations for the White and colored races" was constitutional.

TIMELINE

The Civil Rights Movement

Brown v. Board of Education
The 1954 Supreme Court decision holding that school segregation was inherently unconstitutional because it violated the **Fourteenth Amendment's** guar-antee of **equal protection**. This case marked the end of legal segregation in the United States.

TABLE 5.3

Toward Racial Equality: Milestones in the Era of Reconstruction and Resegregation

1866–1953
Segregation was legally required in the South and sanctioned in the North, lynchings of African Americans occurred in the South, and civil rights policy began to appear.

1868	The Fourteenth Amendment makes African Americans U.S. citizens and guarantees "equal protection of the law." This guarantee is widely ignored for nearly a century.
1870	The Fifteenth Amendment forbids racial discrimination in voting, although many states find ways to prevent or discourage African Americans from voting.
1877	End of Reconstruction. African American gains made in the South (such as antidiscrimination laws) are reversed as former Confederates return to power. Jim Crow laws flourish, making segregation legal.
1883	In the *Civil Rights Cases*, the Supreme Court rules that the Fourteenth Amendment does not prohibit discrimination by private businesses and individuals.
1896	The *Plessy v. Ferguson* decision permits "separate but equal" public facilities, providing a constitutional justification for segregation.
1909	The National Association for the Advancement of Colored People (NAACP) is founded by African Americans and Whites.
1915	*Guinn v. United States* bans the grandfather clause that had been used to prevent African Americans from voting.
1941	Executive order forbids racial discrimination in defense industries.
1944	The *Smith v. Allwright* decision bans all-White primaries.
1948	President Truman orders the armed forces desegregated.
1950	*Sweatt v. Painter* finds the "separate but equal" formula generally unacceptable in professional schools.

Why It Matters

Brown v. Board of Education

In *Brown v. Board of Education*, the Supreme Court overturned its decision in *Plessy v. Ferguson*. This decision was a major step in changing the face of America. Just imagine what the United States would be like today if we still had segregated public facilities and services like universities and restaurants.

because it violated the Fourteenth Amendment's guarantee of equal protection. Legal segregation had come to an end.

A year after its decision in *Brown*, the Court ordered lower courts to proceed with "all deliberate speed" to desegregate public schools. Desegregation proceeded slowly in the South, however. A few counties threatened to close their public schools; enrollment in private schools by Whites soared. In 1957, President Eisenhower had to send troops to desegregate Central High School in Little Rock, Arkansas. In 1969, 15 years after its first ruling that school segregation was unconstitutional and in the face of continued massive resistance, the Supreme Court withdrew its earlier grant of time to school authorities and declared, "Delays in desegregating school systems are no longer tolerable" (*Alexander v. Holmes County Board of Education*). In 1964, under the Civil Rights Act, Congress prohibited federal aid to schools that remained segregated. Thus, after nearly a generation of modest progress, Southern schools were suddenly integrated (see Figure 5.1).

The Court found that if schools were legally segregated before, authorities had an obligation to overcome past discrimination. This could include the distribution of students and pupils on a racial basis. Some federal judges ordered the busing of students to achieve racially balanced schools, a practice upheld (but not required) by the Supreme Court in *Swann v. Charlotte-Mecklenberg County Schools* (1971).

Not all racial segregation is what is called *de jure* ("by law") segregation. *De facto* ("in reality") segregation results, for example, when children are assigned to schools near their homes and those homes are in neighborhoods that are racially segregated for social and economic reasons. Sometimes the distinction between *de jure* and *de facto* segregation has been blurred by past official practices. Because minority groups and

FIGURE 5.1

Percentage of Black Students Attending School with Any Whites in Southern States

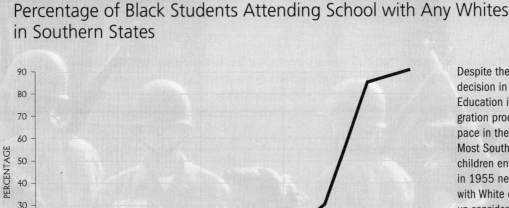

Despite the Supreme Court's decision in Brown v. Board of Education in 1954, school integration proceeded at a snail's pace in the South for a decade. Most Southern African American children entering the first grade in 1955 never attended school with White children. Things picked up considerably in the late 1960s, however, when the Supreme Court insisted that obstruction of implementation of its decision in Brown must come to an end.

These table entries are based on elementary and secondary students in 11 Southern states, including: Virginia, North Carolina, South Carolina, Georgia, Alabama, Mississippi, Louisiana, Texas, Arkansas, Tennessee, and Florida.

Source: Lawrence Baum, *The Supreme Court*, 8th ed. (Washington, DC: CQ Press, 2004), 199.

federal lawyers demonstrated that Northern schools, too, had purposely drawn district lines to promote segregation, school busing came to the North as well. Denver, Boston, and other cities instituted busing for racial balance, just as Southern cities did.

Majorities of both Whites and African Americans have opposed busing, which is one of the least popular remedies for discrimination. In recent years, it has become less prominent as a judicial instrument.

Courts do not have the power to order busing between school districts; thus, school districts that are composed largely of minorities must rely on other means to integrate. Kansas City, Missouri, spent years and $1.5 billion under federal court orders to attract White students from the city's suburbs, but with limited success. In 1995, in *Missouri v. Jenkins*, the Supreme Court indicated that it would not look favorably on continued federal control of the district.

The civil rights movement organized both African Americans and Whites to end the policies and practices of segregation. Sit-ins, marches, and civil disobedience were key strategies of the civil rights movement, which sought to establish equal opportunities in the political and economic sectors and to end policies that put up barriers between people because of race (see "Young People and Politics: Freedom Riders"). The movement's trail was long and sometimes bloody. Police turned their dogs on nonviolent marchers in Birmingham, Alabama. Racists murdered other activists in Meridian, Mississippi, and Selma, Alabama. Fortunately, the goals of the civil rights movement appealed to the national conscience. By the 1970s, overwhelming majorities of White Americans supported racial integration.[4] Today, the principles established in *Brown* have near-universal support.

It was the courts as much as the national conscience that put civil rights goals on the nation's policy agenda. *Brown v. Board of Education* was only the beginning of a string of Supreme Court decisions holding various forms of discrimination unconstitutional. *Brown* and these other cases gave the civil rights movement momentum that would grow in the years that followed (see Table 5.4).

Race and the Death Penalty

TABLE 5.4

Toward Racial Equality: Milestones in the Era of Civil Rights

1954–2009

Integration became a widely accepted goal; the civil rights movement grew, followed by urban racial disorders in the 1960s; African American voting increased; and attention shifted to equal results and affirmative action.

1954	*Brown v. Board of Education* holds that segregated schools are inherently unequal and violate the Fourteenth Amendment's equal protection clause.
	Hernandez v. Texas extends protection against discrimination to Hispanics.
1955	Martin Luther King Jr. leads a bus boycott in Montgomery, Alabama.
1957	Federal troops enforce desegregation of a Little Rock, Arkansas, high school.
1963	Civil rights demonstrators numbering 250,000 march on Washington, D.C. Martin Luther King Jr. delivers "I have a dream" speech.
1964	The Civil Rights Act forbids discrimination in public accommodations and employment.
	The Twenty-fourth Amendment ends the poll tax in federal elections.
1965	The Voting Rights Act sends federal registrars to Southern states and counties to protect African Americans' right to vote and gives registrars the power to impound ballots to enforce the act.
	Executive order requires companies with federal contracts to take affirmative action to ensure equal opportunity.
	Riots occur in Watts, California, and other cities and reappear every summer in various cities for the next five years.
1966	*Harper v. Virginia* holds that the Fourteenth Amendment forbids making payment of a tax a condition of voting in any election.
1967	Cleveland becomes the first major city to elect an African American mayor (Carl Stokes).
	Loving v. Virginia ends prohibition of mixed-race marriages.
1968	The *Jones v. Mayer* decision and the Civil Rights Act of 1968 make all racial discrimination in the sale or rental of housing illegal.
	Martin Luther King Jr. is assassinated.
1971	*Swann v. Charlotte-Mecklenberg County Schools* approves busing as a means of combating state-enforced segregation.
1978	*California Board of Regents v. Bakke* forbids rigid racial quotas for medical school admissions but does not forbid considering race as a factor when deciding admissions.
1979	*United Steelworkers of America v. Weber* permits an affirmative action program to favor African Americans if the program is designed to remedy past discrimination.
	Dayton Board of Education v. Brinkman upholds school busing to remedy Northern school segregation.
1984	Jesse Jackson becomes the first African American candidate for president to receive substantial support in the primaries.
	Grove City College v. Bell forbids the federal government from withholding all federal funds from a college that refuses to file forms saying that it does not discriminate. (Only a specific program risked its federal funds.)
1988	Congress rewrites the Civil Rights Act to "overturn" the implications of *Grove City College.*
1991	After three years of conflict, Congress enacts the Civil Rights and Women's Equity in Employment Act, which counters the effects of several Supreme Court decisions making it more difficult for workers to bring and win job discrimination suits.
1995	*Adarand Constructors v. Pena* holds that affirmative action programs must undergo strict scrutiny to determine that they are narrowly tailored to serve a compelling governmental interest.
2003	*Grutter v. Bollinger* approves use of race as one factor in college admissions.
2007	*Parents Involved in Community Schools v. Seattle School District No. 1* declares the use of race in voluntary integration plans violates the equal protection clause.
2008	Barack Obama elected president.

YOUNG PEOPLE AND POLITICS

Freedom Riders

Most political activity is quite safe. There have been occasions, however, when young adults have risked bodily harm and even death to fight for their beliefs. Years after *Brown v. Board of Education* (1954), segregated transportation continued in some parts of the Deep South. To change this system, the Congress of Racial Equality (CORE) organized freedom rides in 1961. Young Black and White volunteers in their teens and early twenties traveled on buses through the Deep South. In Anniston, Alabama, segregationists destroyed one bus, and men armed with clubs, bricks, iron pipes, and knives attcked riders on another. In Birmingham, the passengers were greeted by members of the Ku Klux Klan with further acts of violence. At Montgomery, the state capital, a White mob beat the riders with chains and ax handles.

The Ku Klux Klan hoped that this violent treatment would stop other young people from taking part in freedom rides. It did not. Over the next six months, more than a thousand people took part in freedom rides. A young White man from Madison, Wisconsin, James Zwerg, was badly injured by a mob and left in the road for over an hour. White-run ambulances refused to take him to the hospital. In an interview afterward, he reflected the grim determination of the freedom riders: "Segregation must be stopped. It must be broken down. Those of us on the Freedom Ride will continue. No matter what happens we are dedicated to this. We will take the beatings. We are willing to accept death."

As with the Montgomery bus boycott and the conflict at Little Rock, the freedom riders gave worldwide publicity to the racial discrimination suffered by African Americans, and in doing so they helped to bring about change. Attorney General Robert Kennedy petitioned the Interstate Commerce Commission (ICC) to draft regulations to end racial segregation in bus terminals. The ICC was reluctant, but in September 1961 it issued the necessary orders.

The freedom riders did not limit themselves to desegregating buses. During the summer of 1961, they also sat together in segregated restaurants, lunch counters, and hotels. Typically they were refused service, and they were often threatened and sometimes attacked. The sit-in tactic was especially effective when it focused on large companies that feared boycotts in the North and that began to desegregate their businesses.

In the end, the courage of young people committed to racial equality prevailed. They helped to change the face of America.

QUESTIONS FOR DISCUSSION

➤ What are young adults doing to fight racism today?

➤ Does civil disobedience have a role in contemporary America?

As a result of national conscience, the courts, the civil rights movement, and the increased importance of African American voters, the 1950s and 1960s saw a marked increase in public policies seeking to foster racial equality. These innovations included policies to promote voting rights, access to public accommodations, open housing, and nondiscrimination in many other areas of social and economic life. The **Civil Rights Act of 1964** did the following:

- Made racial discrimination illegal in hotels, motels, restaurants, and other places of public accommodation
- Forbade discrimination in employment on the basis of race, color, national origin, religion, or gender[5]
- Created the Equal Employment Opportunity Commission (EEOC) to monitor and enforce protections against job discrimination
- Provided for withholding federal grants from state and local governments and other institutions that practiced racial discrimination
- Strengthened voting rights legislation
- Authorized the U.S. Justice Department to initiate lawsuits to desegregate public schools and facilities

The Voting Rights Act of 1965 (discussed next) was the most extensive federal effort to crack century-old barriers to African American voting in the South. The *Open Housing Act of 1968* took steps to forbid discrimination in the sale or rental of housing.

Congressional and judicial policies attacked virtually every type of segregation after 1954. By the 1980s, there were few, if any, forms of racial discrimination left to legislate against. Efforts for legislation were successful, in part, because by the

Civil Rights Act of 1964
The law that made racial discrimination against any group in hotels, motels, and restaurants illegal and forbade many forms of job discrimination.

mid-1960s federal laws effectively protected the right to vote, in fact as well as on paper. Members of minority groups thus had some power to hold their legislators accountable.

GETTING AND USING THE RIGHT TO VOTE

When the Constitution was written, no one thought about extending the right to vote to African Americans (most of whom were slaves) or to women. The early Republic limited **suffrage**, the legal right to vote, to a handful of the population—mostly property-holding White males. Only after the Civil War was the right to vote extended, slowly and painfully, to African American males and then to other minority groups.

The **Fifteenth Amendment**, adopted in 1870, guaranteed African Americans the right to vote—at least in principle. It said, "The right of citizens to vote shall not be abridged by the United States or by any state on account of race, color, or previous condition of servitude." The gap between these words and their implementation, however, remained wide for a full century. States seemed to outdo one another in developing ingenious methods of circumventing the Fifteenth Amendment.

Many states required potential voters to complete literacy tests before registering to vote. These tests typically required prospective voters to read, write, and understand their state constitution or the U.S. Constitution. In practice, however, registrars rarely administered the literacy tests to Whites, while the standard of literacy they required of Blacks was so high that few were ever able to pass the test. In addition, Oklahoma and other Southern states used a *grandfather clause* that exempted persons whose grandfathers were eligible to vote in 1860 from taking these tests. This exemption did not apply, of course, to the grandchildren of slaves but did allow illiterate Whites to vote. The law was blatantly unfair; it was also unconstitutional, said the Supreme Court in the 1915 decision *Guinn v. United States.*

To exclude African Americans from registering to vote, most Southern states also relied on **poll taxes**, which were small taxes levied on the right to vote that often fell due at a time of year when poor sharecroppers had the least cash on hand. To render African American votes ineffective, most Southern states also used the **White primary**, a device that permitted political parties in the heavily Democratic South to exclude African Americans from voting in primary elections, thus depriving them of a voice in the most important contests and letting them vote only when it mattered least. The Supreme Court declared White primaries unconstitutional in 1944 in *Smith v. Allwright.*

The civil rights movement put suffrage high on its political agenda; one by one, the barriers to African American voting fell during the 1960s. The **Twenty-fourth Amendment**, which was ratified in 1964, prohibited poll taxes in federal elections. Two years later, the Supreme Court voided poll taxes in state elections in *Harper v. Virginia State Board of Elections.*

To combat the use of discriminatory voter registration tests—requiring literacy or an understanding of the Constitution, for example—the **Voting Rights Act of 1965** prohibited any government from using voting procedures that denied a person the vote on the basis of race or color and abolished the use of literacy requirements for anyone who had completed the sixth grade. The federal government sent election registrars to areas with long histories of discrimination, and these same areas had to submit all proposed changes in their voting laws or practices to a federal official for approval. As a result of these provisions, hundreds of thousands of African Americans registered to vote in Southern states.

The effects of these efforts were swift and certain, as the civil rights movement turned from protest to politics.[6] When the Voting Rights Act passed in 1965, only 70 African Americans held public office in the 11 Southern states. By the early

---

suffrage

The legal right to vote, extended to African Americans by the **Fifteenth Amendment,** to women by the **Nineteenth Amendment,** and to people over the age of 18 by the **Twenty-sixth Amendment.**

Fifteenth Amendment

The constitutional amendment adopted in 1870 to extend **suffrage** to African Americans.

poll taxes

Small taxes levied on the right to vote that often fell due at a time of year when poor African American sharecroppers had the least cash on hand. This method was used by most Southern states to exclude African Americans from voting. Poll taxes were declared void by the **Twenty-fourth Amendment** in 1964.

White primary

One of the means used to discourage African American voting that permitted political parties in the heavily Democratic South to exclude African Americans from primary elections, thus depriving them of a voice in the real contests. The Supreme Court declared White primaries unconstitutional in 1944.

Twenty-fourth Amendment

The constitutional amendment passed in 1964 that declared **poll taxes** void in federal elections.

Voting Rights Act of 1965

A law designed to help end formal and informal barriers to African American **suffrage.** Under the law, hundreds of thousands of African Americans were registered, and the number of African American elected officials increased dramatically.

1980s, more than 2,500 African Americans held elected offices in those states, and the number has continued to grow. There are currently more than 9,400 African American elected officials in the United States.[7]

The Voting Rights Act of 1965 not only secured the right to vote for African Americans but also attempted to ensure that their votes would not be diluted through racial gerrymandering (drawing district boundaries to advantage a specific group). For example, White-majority districts frequently elected members of a city council in at-large seats (in which council members were elected from the entire city) and prevented a geographically concentrated minority from electing a minority council member. When Congress amended the Voting Rights Act in 1982, it further insisted that minorities be able to "elect representatives of their choice" when their numbers and configuration permitted. Thus, redrawing district boundaries was to avoid discriminatory *results* and not just discriminatory *intent*. In 1986, the Supreme Court upheld this principle in *Thornburg v. Gingles*.

Officials in the Justice Department, which was responsible for enforcing the Voting Rights Act, and state legislatures that drew new district lines interpreted these actions as a mandate to create minority-majority districts. Consequently, when congressional district boundaries were redrawn following the 1990 census, several states, including Florida, North Carolina, Texas, Illinois, New York, and Louisiana, created odd-shaped districts that were designed to give minority-group voters a numerical majority. Fourteen new U.S. House districts were drawn specifically to help elect African Americans to Congress, and six districts were drawn to elect new Hispanic members (these efforts worked, as we will see in Chapter 12).

The Voting Rights Act of 1965 produced a major increase in the number of African Americans registered to vote in Southern states. Voting also translated into increased political clout for African Americans. President Lyndon Johnson is shown here signing the bill.

However, in 1993, the Supreme Court heard a challenge to a North Carolina congressional district that in some places was cut no wider than a superhighway to create an African American majority winding snakelike for 160 miles. In its decision in *Shaw v. Reno*, the Court decried the creation of districts based solely on racial composition, as well as the district drawers' abandonment of traditional redistricting standards such as compactness and contiguity. Thus, the Court gave legal standing to challenges to any congressional map with an oddly shaped minority-majority district that may not be defensible on grounds other than race (such as shared community interest or geographical compactness). The next year, in *Johnson v. DeGrandy*, the Court ruled that a state legislative redistricting plan does not violate the Voting Rights Act if it does not create the greatest possible number of districts in which minority-group votes would make up a majority.

In 1995, in *Miller v. Johnson*, the Court rejected the efforts of the Justice Department to achieve the maximum possible number of minority districts. It held that the use of race as a "predominant factor" in drawing district lines should be presumed to be unconstitutional. The next year, in *Bush v. Vera* and *Shaw v. Hunt*, the Supreme Court voided three convoluted districts in Texas and one in North Carolina on the grounds that race had been the primary reason for abandoning compact district lines and that the state legislatures had crossed the line into unconstitutional racial gerrymandering.

In yet another turn, in 1999 the Court declared in *Hunt v. Cromartie* that conscious consideration of race is not automatically unconstitutional if the state's primary motivation was potentially political rather than racial. We can expect continued litigation concerning this question, especially since the Court has decided that state legislatures may redraw district boundaries at any time and not only after a census.[8]

Why It Matters

The Voting Rights Act

In passing the Voting Rights Act of 1965, Congress enacted an extraordinarily strong law to protect the rights of minorities to vote. There is little question that officials pay more attention to minorities when they can vote. And many more members of minority groups are now elected to high public office.

OTHER MINORITY GROUPS

As we discuss in Chapter 6, America is heading toward a *minority majority*: a situation in which minority groups will outnumber Caucasians of European descent (see "My State: A Nation of Minorities"). African Americans are not the only racial group that has suffered legally imposed discrimination, and Hispanic Americans are now the largest minority group in the United States. Even before the civil rights struggle, Native Americans, Hispanics, and Asians learned how powerless they could become in a society dominated by Whites. The civil rights laws for which African Americans fought have benefited members of these groups as well. In addition, social movements tend to beget new social movements; thus, the African American civil rights movement of the 1960s spurred other minorities to mobilize to protect their rights.

Native Americans The earliest inhabitants of the continent, the American Indians, are, of course, the oldest minority group. About 4.5 million people identify themselves as at least party Native American or Native Alaskan, and they comprise 11 percent of Oklahomans and New Mexicans and 18 percent of Alaskans. The history of poverty, discrimination, and exploitation experienced by American Indians is a long one. For generations, U.S. policy promoted westward expansion at the expense of Native Americans' lands. The government first isolated Native Americans on reservations, where they lost their lands and their rights in the process. The Dawes Act of 1887 switched the federal government's strategy and focused on assimilating Native Americans into mainstream American life. The government

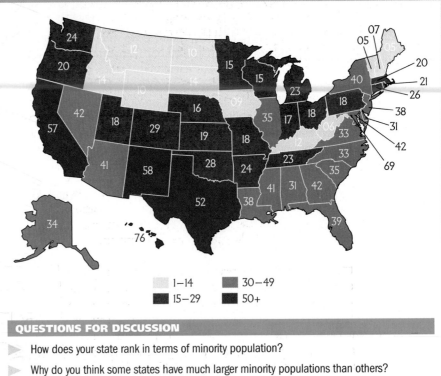

MyState | A Nation of Minorities

The country's minority population has now reached over 100 million, including about 45 million Hispanic Americans and 40 million African Americans. Minorities comprise approximately a third of all Americans.

This map shows the percent of non-Whites in each state. Hawaii has the largest minority population at 75 percent, followed by the District of Columbia (68 percent), New Mexico (57 percent), California (57 percent), and Texas (52 percent).

Source: U.S. Census Bureau, News Release, May 17, 2007.

1–14   30–49
15–29   50+

QUESTIONS FOR DISCUSSION

▶ How does your state rank in terms of minority population?

▶ Why do you think some states have much larger minority populations than others?

▶ How have these groups impacted the nature of politics in your state?

sent children to boarding schools off the reservations, often against the will of their families, and banned tribal rituals and languages.

Finally, in 1924 Congress made American Indians citizens of the United States and gave them the right to vote, a status that African Americans had achieved a half century before. Not until 1946 did Congress establish the Indian Claims Act to settle financial disputes arising from lands taken from the American Indians.[9] Today, most Native Americans still live in poverty and ill health, almost half on or near a reservation. American Indians know, perhaps better than any other group, the significance of the gap between public policy and private realization regarding discrimination.

But progress is being made. The civil rights movement of the 1960s created a more favorable climate for Native Americans to secure guaranteed access to the polls, to housing, and to jobs and to reassert their treaty rights. The Indian Bill of Rights was adopted as Title II of the Civil Rights Act of 1968, applying most of the provisions of the Constitution's Bill of Rights to tribal governments. In *Santa Clara Pueblo v. Martinez* (1978), the Supreme Court strengthened the tribal power of individual tribe members and furthered self-government by Indian tribes.

American Indian activists such as Dennis Means of the American Indian Movement (AIM), Vine Deloria, and Dee Brown drew attention to the plight of American Indian tribes. Several Native Americans seized Alcatraz Island in San Francisco Bay in 1969 to protest the loss of Indian lands. In 1973, armed members of AIM seized 11 hostages at Wounded Knee, South Dakota—the site of an 1890 massacre of 200 Sioux (Lakota) by U.S. cavalry—and remained there for 71 days until the federal government agreed to examine Indian treaty rights. Ben Nighthorse Campbell won election as a U.S. senator from Colorado in 1992, the first Native American elected to Congress in more than 20 years.

Equally important, Indians began to use the courts to protect their rights. The Native American Rights Fund (NARF), founded in 1970, has won important victories concerning hunting, fishing, and land rights. Native Americans are also retaining access to their sacred places and have had some success in stopping the building of roads and buildings on ancient burial grounds or other sacred spots. Several tribes have won court cases protecting them from taxation of tribal profits.

As in other areas of civil rights, the preservation of Native American culture and the exercise of Native American rights sometimes conflict with the interests of the majority. For example, there is conflict over special rights that some tribes have to fish and even hunt whales. Anglers concerned with the depletion of fishing stock and environmentalists worried about loss of the whale population have voiced protests. Similarly, Native American rights to run businesses denied to others by state law and to avoid taxation on tribal lands have made running gambling casinos a lucrative option for Indians. This has irritated both those who oppose gambling and those who are offended by the tax-free competition.

Hispanic Americans Hispanic Americans (or Latinos, as some prefer to be called)—chiefly from Mexico, Puerto Rico, and Cuba but also from El Salvador, Honduras, and other countries in Central America—have displaced African Americans as the largest minority group. Today they number more than 45 million and comprise about 15 percent of the U.S. population. In New Mexico, Hispanics make up 44 percent of the population of New Mexico and 36 percent of both California and Texas.

In Texas and throughout much of the Southwestern United States in the first half of the twentieth century, people of Mexican origin were subjected to discrimination and worse. They were forced to use segregated public restrooms and attend segregated schools. Hundreds of them were

Their growing numbers have made Hispanic Americans the largest minority group in the United States. Their political power is reflected in the two dozen members of the U.S. House of Representatives, such as Loretta and Linda Sanchez of California, the first set of sisters to serve simultaneously in Congress.

killed in lynchings. Approximately 500,000 Latinos served in the U.S. armed forces in World War II, but many of these veterans faced discrimination upon their return. Dr. Hector P. Garcia founded the American GI Forum, the country's first Latino veterans' advocacy group, in 1948 after he saw the Naval Station at Corpus Christi refusing to treat sick Latino veterans. Garcia's organization received national attention when the remains of Felix Longoria, a Mexican American soldier killed while on a mission in the Pacific, were returned to his relatives in Three Rivers, Texas, for final burial. The only funeral parlor in his hometown would not allow Longoria's family to hold services for Longoria because of his Mexican heritage. Soon the incident became subject of outrage across the country. With the help of the Forum and the sponsorship of then Senator Lyndon B. Johnson, Longoria was buried in Arlington National Cemetery.

In Jackson County, Texas, where Mexican Americans made up 14 percent of the population by the early 1950s, not a single person with a Spanish surname had been allowed to serve on a jury in 25 years. Some 70 Texas counties had similar records of exclusion. When an all-Anglo jury convicted Pete Hernandez, a migrant cotton picker, of murder in Jackson County, a team of Hispanic civil rights lawyers from the American G.I. Forum and the League of United Latin American Citizens (LULAC) filed suit, arguing that the jury that convicted him of murder could not be impartial because of the exclusion of members of other races were from the jury. This case eventually reached the Supreme Court, the first time Hispanic lawyers had argued before the Court. The Supreme Court unanimously ruled in Hernandez's favor in ***Hernandez v. Texas* (1954)**, holding that in excluding Hispanics from jury duty, Texas had unreasonably singled out a class of people for different treatment. The defendant had been deprived of the equal protection guaranteed by the Fourteenth Amendment, a guarantee "not directed solely against discrimination between whites and Negroes." This landmark decision, which protected Hispanics and the right to fair trials, helped widen the definition of discrimination beyond race.

Hernandez v. Texas
A 1954 Supreme Court decision that extended protection against discrimination to Hispanics.

The Mexican-American Civil Rights Movement

Hispanic leaders drew from the tactics of the African American civil rights movement and used sit-ins, boycotts, marches, and related activities to draw attention to their cause. Inspired by the NAACP's Legal Defense Fund, they also created the Mexican American Legal Defense and Education Fund (MALDEF) in 1968 to help argue their cause in court. In the 1970s, MALDEF established the Chicana Rights Project to challenge sex-discrimination against Mexican American women. In addition, Hispanic groups began mobilizing in other ways to protect their interests. An early prominent example was the United Farm Workers, led by César Chávez, who in the 1960s publicized the plight of migrant workers, a large proportion of whom are Hispanic.

The rights of illegal immigrants has been a matter of controversy for decades. In 1975, Texas revised its education laws to withhold state funds for educating children who had not been legally admitted to the United States and authorized local school districts to deny enrollment to such students. In *Plyler v. Doe* (1982), the Supreme Court struck down the law as a violation of the Fourteenth Amendment because illegal immigrant children are people and therefore had protection from discrimination unless a substantial state interest could be shown to justify it. The Court found no substantial state interest that would be served by denying students (who had no control over being brought to the U.S.) an education, and observed that denying them a proper education would likely contribute to "the creation and perpetuation of a subclass of illiterates within our boundaries, surely adding to the problems and costs of unemployment, welfare, and crime."

A major concern of Latinos has been discrimination in employment hiring and promotion. Using the leverage of discrimination suits, MALDEF has won a number of consent decrees with employers to increase the opportunities for employment for Latinos.

Like Native Americans, Hispanic Americans benefit from the nondiscrimination policies originally passed to protect African Americans. Provisions of the

Voting Rights Act of 1965 covered San Antonio, Texas, and thereby permitted Hispanic voters to lend weight to the election of Mayor Henry Cisneros. There are now more than 4,900 elected Hispanic officials in the United States,[10] and Hispanic Americans play a prominent role in the politics of such major cities as Houston, Miami, Los Angeles, and San Diego. In 1973, Hispanics won a victory when the Supreme Court found that multimember electoral districts (in which more than one person represents a single district) in Texas discriminated against minority groups because they decreased the probability of a minority being elected.[11] Nevertheless, poverty, discrimination, and language barriers continue to depress Hispanic voter registration and turnout.

Asian Americans   Asian Americans are the fastest-growing minority group and the 15 million persons who are at least part Asian comprise about 5 percent of the population. They suffered discrimination in education, jobs, and housing as well as restrictions on immigration and naturalization for more than a hundred years prior to the civil rights acts of the 1960s. Discrimination was especially egregious during World War II when the U.S. government, beset by fears of a Japanese invasion of the Pacific Coast, rounded up more than 100,000 Americans

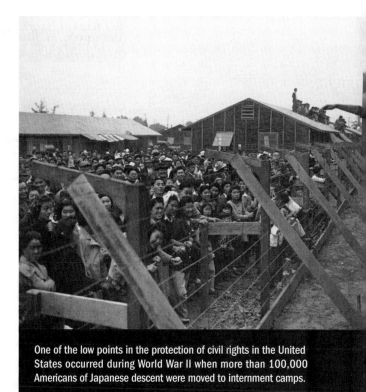

One of the low points in the protection of civil rights in the United States occurred during World War II when more than 100,000 Americans of Japanese descent were moved to internment camps.

of Japanese descent and herded them into encampments. These internment camps were, critics claimed, America's concentration camps. The Supreme Court, however, in *Korematsu v. United States* (1944), upheld the internment as constitutional. Congress has since authorized benefits to the former internees. Today, Americans of Chinese, Japanese, Korean, Vietnamese, and other Asian cultures have assumed prominent positions in U.S. society.

Korematsu v. United States

A 1944 Supreme Court decision that upheld as constitutional the internment of more than 100,000 Americans of Japanese descent in encampments during World War II.

Arab Americans and Muslims   There are more than 1.2 million persons of Arab ancestry in the United States. Since the terrorist attacks of September 11, 2001, Arab, Muslim, Sikh, and South Asian Americans and those perceived to be members of these groups have been the victims of increased numbers of bias-related assaults, threats, vandalism, and arson. The incidents have consisted of telephone, Internet, mail, and face-to-face threats; minor assaults as well as assaults with dangerous weapons and assaults resulting in serious injury and death; and vandalism, shootings, arson, and bombings directed at homes, businesses, and places of worship. Members of these groups have also experienced discrimination in employment, housing, education, and access to public accommodations and facilities.

As we saw in Chapter 4, in the wake of the September 11, 2001, terrorist attacks, the FBI detained more than 1,200 persons as possible threats to national security. About two-thirds of these persons were illegal aliens—mostly Arabs and Muslims—and many of them languished in jail for months until cleared by the FBI. This process seemed to violate the right of detainees to be informed of accusations against them found in the Sixth Amendment and the protection against the suspension of the writ of habeas corpus. As we have seen, in 2004 the Supreme Court declared that detainees had the right to challenge their detention before a judge or other neutral decision maker.

The struggle for equal rights has not been limited to racial minorities, however. Political activity on behalf of women has been so energetic and so far-reaching that a separate section is needed to examine this struggle for equality.

WOMEN, THE CONSTITUTION, AND PUBLIC POLICY

Abigail Adams may have been unusual in her feminist views in the 1770s, but the next century brought significant feminist activity. The first women's rights activists were products of the abolitionist movement, where they often encountered sexist opposition. Noting that the status of women shared much in common with that of slaves, some leaders resolved to fight for women's rights.

Two of these women, Lucretia Mott and Elizabeth Cady Stanton, organized a meeting at Seneca Falls in upstate New York. They had much to discuss. Not only were women denied the vote, but they were also subjected to patriarchal (male-dominated) family law and denied educational and career opportunities. The legal doctrine known as *coverture* deprived married women of any identity separate from that of their husbands; wives could not sign contracts or dispose of property. Divorce law was heavily biased in favor of husbands. Even abused women found it almost impossible to end their marriages, and men had the legal advantage in securing custody of the children.

THE BATTLE FOR THE VOTE

On July 19, 1848, 100 men and women signed the Seneca Falls Declaration of Sentiments and Resolutions. Patterned after the Declaration of Independence, it proclaimed, "The history of mankind is a history of repeated injuries and usurpations on the part of man toward woman, having in direct object the establishment of an absolute tyranny over her." Thus began the movement that would culminate in the ratification of the **Nineteenth Amendment** 72 years later, giving women the vote. Charlotte Woodward, 19 years old in 1848, was the only signer of the Seneca Falls Declaration who lived to vote for the president in 1920.

Nineteenth Amendment
The constitutional amendment adopted in 1920 that guarantees women the right to vote. See also **suffrage**.

Advocates of women's suffrage hoped that women would be included in the Fifteenth Amendment but were disappointed when they were excluded from protections accorded to newly freed slaves. Thus, the battle for women's suffrage was fought mostly in the late nineteenth and early twentieth centuries. Leaders like Stanton and Susan B. Anthony were prominent in the cause, which emphasized the vote but also addressed women's other grievances. The suffragists had considerable success in the states, especially in the West. Several states allowed women to vote before the constitutional amendment passed. The feminists lobbied, marched, protested, and even engaged in civil disobedience.[12]

THE "DOLDRUMS": 1920–1960

Winning the right to vote did not automatically win equal status for women. In fact, the feminist movement seemed to lose rather than gain momentum after winning the vote, perhaps because the vote was about the only goal on which all feminists agreed. There was considerable division within the movement on other priorities.

Many suffragists accepted the traditional model of the family. Fathers were breadwinners, mothers bread bakers. Although most suffragists thought that women should have the opportunity to pursue any occupation they chose, many also believed that women's primary obligations revolved around the roles of wife and mother. Many suffragists had defended the vote as basically an extension of the maternal role into public life, arguing that a new era of public morality would emerge when women could vote. These *social feminists* were in tune with prevailing attitudes.

Public policy toward women continued to be dominated by protectionism rather than by the principle of equality. Laws protected working women from the burdens of overtime work, long hours on the job, and heavy lifting. The fact that these laws also protected male workers from female competition received little attention. State laws tended to reflect—and reinforce—traditional family roles. These laws concentrated on limiting women's work opportunities outside the home so they could concentrate on their duties within it. The laws in most states required husbands to support their families (even after a divorce) and to pay child support, though divorced fathers did not always pay. When a marriage ended, mothers almost always got custody of the children, although husbands had the legal advantage in custody battles. Public policy was designed to preserve traditional motherhood and hence, supporters claimed, to protect the family and the country's moral fabric.[13]

Only a minority of feminists challenged these assumptions. Alice Paul, the author of the original **Equal Rights Amendment** (ERA), was one activist who claimed that the real result of protectionist law was to perpetuate gender inequality. Simply worded, the ERA reads, "Equality of rights under the law shall not be denied or abridged by the United States or by any state on account of sex." Most people saw the ERA as a threat to the family when it was introduced in Congress in 1923. It gained little support. In fact, women were less likely to support the amendment than men were.

THE SECOND FEMINIST WAVE

The civil rights movement of the 1950s and 1960s attracted many female activists, some of whom also joined student and antiwar movements. These women often met with the same prejudices as had women abolitionists. Betty Friedan's book *The Feminine Mystique*, published in 1963, encouraged women to question traditional assumptions and to assert their own rights. Groups such as the National Organization for Women (NOW) and the National Women's Political Caucus were organized in the 1960s and 1970s.

Before the advent of the contemporary feminist movement, the Supreme Court upheld virtually any instance of gender-based discrimination. The state and federal governments could discriminate against women—and, indeed, men—as they chose. In the 1970s, the Court began to take a closer look at gender discrimination. In *Reed v. Reed* (1971), the Court ruled that any "arbitrary" gender-based classification violated the equal protection clause of the Fourteenth Amendment. This was the first time the Court declared any law unconstitutional on the basis of gender discrimination. Five years later, *Craig v. Boren* established a "medium scrutiny" standard: The Court would not presume gender discrimination to be either valid or invalid. The courts were to show less deference to gender classifications than to more routine classifications but more deference than to racial classifications. Nevertheless, the Court has repeatedly said that there must be an "exceedingly persuasive justification" for any government to classify people by gender. Table 5.5 lists important policy milestones on gender equality.

The Supreme Court has struck down many laws and rules for discriminating on the basis of gender. For example, the Court voided laws giving husbands exclusive control over family property.[14] The Court also voided employers' rules that denied women equal monthly retirement benefits because they live longer than men.[15]

Men have not always prevailed in their efforts for equal treatment, however. The Court upheld a statutory rape law applying only to men[16] and the male-only draft, which we will discuss shortly. The Court also allowed a Florida law giving property tax exemptions only to widows, not to widowers.[17]

Equal Rights Amendment
A constitutional amendment originally introduced in Congress in 1923 and passed by Congress in 1972, stating that "equality of rights under the law shall not be denied or abridged by the United States or by any state on account of sex." Despite public support, the amendment failed to acquire the necessary support from three-fourths of the state legislatures.

Reed v. Reed
The landmark case in 1971 in which the Supreme Court for the first time upheld a claim of gender discrimination.

Craig v. Boren
In this 1976 ruling, the Supreme Court established the "medium scrutiny" standard for determining gender discrimination.

TABLE 5.5

Toward Gender Equality: Public Policy Milestones

1969	Executive order declares that offering equal opportunities for women at every level of federal service is to be national policy and establishes a program for implementing the policy.
1971	In *Reed v. Reed,* the Supreme Court invalidates a state law preferring men to women in court selection of an estate's administrator.
1972	Provisions of Title VII of the Civil Rights Act of 1964 are extended to cover the faculty and professional staffs of colleges and universities.
	The Education Act forbids gender discrimination in public schools (with some exceptions for historically single-gender schools).
	The ERA is proposed by Congress and sent to the states for ratification.
1974	A woman—Ella Grasso of Connecticut—is elected governor for the first time without succeeding her husband to the office.
1975	Congress opens armed services academies to women.
1976	Courts strike down an Oklahoma law setting different legal drinking ages for men and women.
1977	Supreme Court voids arbitrary height and weight requirements for employees in *Dothard v. Rawlinson.*
1978	The deadline for ratification of the ERA is extended.
	Congress passes the Pregnancy Discrimination Act.
1981	The Supreme Court rules that male-only military draft registration is constitutional.
	Sandra Day O'Connor becomes the first woman Supreme Court justice.
1982	The ERA ratification deadline passes without ratification of the amendment.
1984	Geraldine Ferraro is nominated as the first woman vice-presidential candidate of a major party.
1988	The Supreme Court unanimously upholds a 1984 New York City law aimed primarily at requiring the admission of women to large, private clubs that play an important role in professional life.
1991	After three years of conflict, Congress enacts the Civil Rights and Women's Equity in Employment Act, which counters the effects of several Supreme Court decisions making it more difficult for workers to bring and win job discrimination suits.
1992	California becomes the first state to be represented by two female U.S. senators.
1993	Supreme Court in *Harris v. Forklift Systems* lowers the threshold for proving sexual harassment in the workplace.
1994	Forty-eight women elected to U.S. House and eight to the Senate, the most in history.
1996	In *United States v. Virginia et al.,* the Supreme Court declares categorical exclusion of women from state-funded colleges unconstitutional.
1997	Madeline Albright appointed secretary of state, the first woman to serve in that role.
2001	Condoleezza Rice appointed national security adviser, the first woman to hold that post.
2002	Representative Nancy Pelosi is elected by her colleagues as House Democratic leader, becoming the first woman to head her party in Congress.
2007	Nancy Pelosi is elected speaker of the House of Representatives.

TIMELINE

Women's Struggle for Equality

Contemporary feminists have suffered defeats as well as victories. The ERA was revived when Congress passed it in 1972 and extended the deadline for ratification until 1982. Nevertheless, the ERA was three states short of ratification when time ran out. Paradoxically, the defeat of the ERA had just the opposite effect of that which the 1920 suffrage victory had on feminism. Far from weakening the movement, losing the ERA battle stimulated vigorous feminist activity. Proponents have vowed to keep reintroducing the amendment in Congress and continue to press hard for state and federal action on women's rights.

WOMEN IN THE WORKPLACE

One reason why feminist activism persists has nothing to do with ideology or other social movements. The family pattern that traditionalists sought to preserve—father at work, mother at home—is becoming a thing of the past. There are more than 70 million women in the civilian labor force (compared to 81 million males), representing 59 percent of adult women. Fifty-one percent of these women are married and living with their spouse. There are also 34 million female-headed households (8 million of which include children), and about two-thirds of American mothers who have children below school age are in the labor force.[18] As conditions have changed, public opinion and public policy demands have changed, too. Protectionism is not dead. In general, women still assume more duties inside the home than men do, and debates over policies like the "mommy track" (reduced work responsibilities for women workers with children) parental leaves to women reflect this social phenomenon. Demands for equality, however, keep nudging protectionism into the background.

In recent years women have entered many traditionally male-dominated occupations. Here astronauts Peggy Wilson and Pam Melroy meet in the International Space Station.

Congress has made some important progress, especially in the area of employment. The Civil Rights Act of 1964 banned gender discrimination in employment. The protection of this law has been expanded several times. For example, in 1972, Congress gave the EEOC the power to sue employers suspected of illegal discrimination. The Pregnancy Discrimination Act of 1978 made it illegal for employers to exclude pregnancy and childbirth from their sick leave and health benefits plans. The Civil Rights and Women's Equity in Employment Act of 1991 shifted the burden of proof in justifying hiring and promotion practices to employers, who must show that employment practices regarding gender are related to job performance and that they are consistent with "business necessity" (an ambiguous term, however).

The Supreme Court also weighed in against gender discrimination in employment and business activity. In 1977, it voided laws and rules barring women from jobs through arbitrary height and weight requirements (*Dothard v. Rawlinson*). Any such prerequisites must be directly related to the duties required in a particular position. Women have also been protected from being required to take mandatory pregnancy leaves from their jobs[19] and from being denied a job because of an employer's concern for harming a developing fetus.[20] Many commercial contacts are made in private business and service clubs, which often have excluded women from membership. The Court has upheld state and city laws that prohibit such discrimination.[21]

Education is closely related to employment. Title IX of the Education Act of 1972 forbids gender discrimination in federally subsidized education programs (which include almost all colleges and universities), including athletics. But what about single-gender schooling? In 1996, the Supreme Court declared that Virginia's categorical exclusion of women from education opportunities at the state-funded Virginia Military Institute (VMI) violated women's rights to equal protection of the law.[22] A few days later, The Citadel, the nation's only other state-supported all-male college, announced that it would also admit women.

Women have made substantial progress in their quest for equality, but debate continues as Congress considers new laws. Three of the most controversial issues that legislators will continue to face are wage discrimination, the role of women in the military, and sexual harassment.

WAGE DISCRIMINATION AND COMPARABLE WORTH

Traditional women's jobs often pay much less than men's jobs that demand comparable skill; a female secretary often earns far less than a male accounts clerk with the same qualifications. Median weekly earnings for full-time women workers are only 81 percent as much as the wages of men.[23] In other words, women earn $0.81 for every $1.00 men make. You can see the trend in wage ratios in "A Generation of Change: The Shrinking Gap between Men's and Women's Wages."

In 1983, the Washington State Supreme Court ruled that its state government had discriminated against women for years by denying them equal pay for jobs of **comparable worth**. The U.S. Supreme Court has remained silent so far on the merits of this issue. The executive branch under Ronald Reagan consistently opposed the idea of comparable worth. The late Clarence Pendleton, Ronald Reagan's appointee as head of the U.S. Civil Rights Commission, argued that lawsuits based on comparable worth would interfere with the free market for wages by reducing incentives for women to seek higher-paying, traditionally male jobs. Pendleton called comparable worth "the craziest idea since Looney Tunes." Ridicule has not made this serious dispute go away, however.

WOMEN IN THE MILITARY

Military service is another controversial aspect of gender equality. Women have served in every branch of the armed services since World War II. Originally, they served in separate units such as the WACS (Women's Army Corps), the WAVES

comparable worth
The issue raised when women who hold traditionally female jobs are paid less than men for working at jobs requiring comparable skill.

Why It Matters
Changes in the Workplace
Laws and Supreme Court decisions striking down barriers to employment for women are not just ornaments. Instead, they have important consequences for employment opportunities for millions of women and have helped them make substantial gains in entering careers formerly occupied almost entirely by men.

A GENERATION OF CHANGE

The Shrinking Gap Between Men's and Women's Wages

Over the past generation, the gender gap between the earnings of a typical American woman and that a typical American man has narrowed. In 1985, women's median weekly earnings were 68 percent of that of men. As you can see in the graph below, the most recent data show that this disparity is no longer as great, with women now earning about 81 percent of what men earn.

QUESTIONS FOR DISCUSSION

▷ Do you think the gender gap in earnings will continue to shrink as your generation moves into the work force? Why or why not?

▷ Some people think that the government should take steps to promote pay equity between men and women. For some proposals along these lines, see *http://www.pay-equity.org/cando.html*. What do you think? Is this the sort of area where the government should take action, or is this a matter best left to private enterprise?

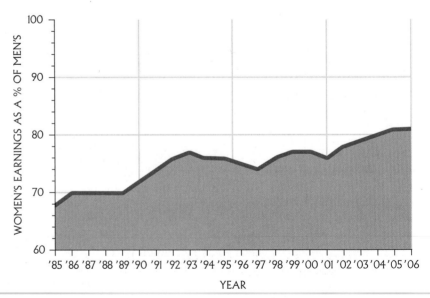

Source: U.S. Department of Labor, Bureau of Labor Statistics, *Women in the Labor Force: A Databook* (2007 edition), Table 16.

(Women Accepted for Volunteer Emergency Service in the navy), and the Nurse Corps. The military had a 2 percent quota for women (which was never filled) until the 1970s. Now women are part of the regular service. They make up 14 percent of the armed forces (19 percent of the air force),[24] and compete directly with men for promotions. Congress opened all the service academies to women in 1975. Women have done well, including graduating first at the U.S. Naval Academy in Annapolis and serving as first captain of the Corps of Cadets at West Point.

Two important differences between the treatment of men and that of women persist in military service. First, only men must register for the draft when they turn 18 (see "You Are the Judge: Is Male-Only Draft Registration Gender Discrimination?"). Second, statutes and regulations also prohibit women from serving in combat. A breach exists between policy and practice, however, as the Persian Gulf War and the war in Iraq showed. Women piloted helicopters at the front and helped to operate antimissile systems; some were taken as prisoners of war. Women are now permitted to serve as combat pilots in the navy and air force and to serve on navy warships. However, they are still not permitted to serve in ground combat units in the army or marines.

These actions have reopened the debate over whether women should serve in combat. Some experts insist that because women, on average, have less upper-body strength than men, they are less suited for combat. Others argue that men will not be able to fight effectively beside wounded or dying women. Critics of these views point out that some women surpass some men in upper-body strength and that we do not know how well men and women will fight together. This debate is not only a controversy about ability; it also touches on the question of whether engaging in combat is a burden or a privilege. Clearly some women—and some who would deny them combat duty—take the latter view.

SEXUAL HARASSMENT

Whether in the military, on the assembly line, or in the office, women for years have voiced concern about sexual harassment, which, of course, does not affect only women. The U.S. Equal Employment Opportunity Commission defines sexual harassment as "unwelcome sexual advances, requests for sexual favors, and

YOU ARE THE Judge

Is Male-Only Draft Registration Gender Discrimination?

There is no military conscription at present (the United States has had a volunteer force since 1973), but President Jimmy Carter asked Congress to require both men and women to register for the draft after the Soviet Union invaded Afghanistan in 1979. Registration was designed to facilitate any eventual conscription. In 1980, Congress reinstated registration for men only, a policy that was not universally popular. Federal courts ordered registration suspended while several young men filed a suit. These men argued that the registration requirement was gender-based discrimination that violated the due process clause of the Fifth Amendment.

You Be the Judge: Does requiring only males to register for the draft unconstitutionally discriminate against them?

Decision: The Supreme Court displayed its typical deference to the elected branches in the area of national security when it ruled in 1981 in *Rostker v. Goldberg* that male-only registration did not violate the Fifth Amendment. The Court found that male-only registration bore a substantial relationship to Congress's goal of ensuring combat readiness and that Congress acted well within its constitutional authority to raise and regulate armies and navies when it authorized the registration of men and not women. Congress, the Court said, was allowed to focus on the question of military need rather than "equity."

other verbal or physical conduct of a sexual nature . . . when this conduct explicitly or implicitly affects an individual's employment, unreasonably interferes with an individual's work performance, or creates an intimidating, hostile, or offensive work environment."[25]

In 1986, the Supreme Court articulated this broad principle: Sexual harassment that is so pervasive as to create a hostile or abusive work environment is a form of gender discrimination, which is forbidden by the 1964 Civil Rights Act.[26] In 1993, in *Harris v. Forklift Systems*, the Court reinforced its decision. No single factor, the Court said, is required to win a sexual harassment case under Title VII of the 1964 Civil Rights Act. The law is violated when the workplace environment "would reasonably be perceived, and is perceived, as hostile or abusive." Thus, workers are not required to prove that the workplace environment is so hostile as to cause them "severe psychological injury" or that they are unable to perform their jobs. The protection of federal law comes into play before the harassing conduct leads to psychological difficulty.

In 1998 the Supreme Court again spoke expansively about sexual harassment in the workplace. In *Faragher v. City of Boca Raton*, the Court made it clear that employers are responsible for preventing and eliminating harassment at work. They can be held liable for even those harassing acts of supervisory employees that violate clear policies and of which top management has no knowledge. In 2004 in *Pennsylvania State Police v. Suders*, the Court held that if harassment culminates in a tangible action such as a discharge or demotion, an employer is strictly liable if there is no legal defense such as one showing that the employer had set up a system for reporting and correcting sexual harassment but that the employee had unreasonably failed to use that system.

In *Burlington Industries, Inc. v. Ellerth*, the Court found that an employee could sue for sexual harassment even without being able to show job-related harm. Victims must have availed themselves of effective complaint policies and other protection offered by the company first, however. The Court has also held that the 1964 Civil Rights Act's prohibition against employer retaliation against someone filing a complaint about sexual harassment extends beyond being fired or demoted to include a change in work assignments.[27] The Court also made it clear that the law also prevents sexual harassment by people of the same gender (*Oncale v. Sundower Offshore Services*).

In 1999, the Court turned its attention to sexual harassment in public schools. It held that school districts can be held liable for sexual harassment in cases of student-on-student harassment where the school district has knowledge of the harassment or is deliberately indifferent to it. The harassment must be so severe, pervasive, and objectively offensive that it can be said to deprive the victims of access to the educational opportunities or benefits provided by the school (*Davis v. Monroe County Board of Education*).

Sexual harassment can occur anywhere but may be especially prevalent in male-dominated occupations such as the military. A 1991 convention of the Tailhook Association, an organization of naval aviators, made the news after reports surfaced of drunken sailors jamming a hotel hallway and sexually assaulting female guests,

Comparing Civil Rights

Hillary Clinton, shown here speaking to supporters during her 2008 run for the Democratic presidential nomination, is symbolic of the increasing prominence of women in American Society.

including naval officers, as they stepped off the elevator. After the much-criticized initial failure of the navy to identify the officers responsible for the assault, heads rolled, including those of several admirals and the secretary of the navy. In 1996 and 1997, a number of army officers and noncommissioned officers were discharged—and some went to prison—for sexual harassment of female soldiers in training situations. Behavior that was once viewed as simply male high jinks is now recognized as intolerable. The Pentagon removed top officials at the Air Force Academy in 2003 following charges that female cadets were frequently raped by male cadets.

NEWLY ACTIVE GROUPS UNDER THE CIVIL RIGHTS UMBRELLA

Racial and ethnic minorities and women are not the only Americans who can claim civil rights; policies enacted to protect one or two groups can be applied to others. Three recent entrants into the civil rights arena are aging Americans, people with disabilities, and homosexuals. All these groups claim equal rights, as racial minorities and women do, but represent different challenges to mainstream America.

CIVIL RIGHTS AND THE GRAYING OF AMERICA

America is aging rapidly. People in their eighties make up the fastest-growing age group in this country. There were 37.3 million people 65 and older in 2006, accounting for 12 percent of the total population. The number of people 85 and older reached 5.3 million.

When the Social Security program began in the 1930s, 65 was the retirement age. Although this age was apparently chosen arbitrarily, it soon became the mandatory retirement age for many workers. Although many workers might prefer to retire while they are still healthy and active enough to enjoy leisure, not everyone wants or can afford to do so. Social Security is not—and was never meant to be—an adequate income, and not all workers have good pension plans or retirement savings plans. Nevertheless, employers routinely refused to hire people over a certain age. Graduate and professional schools often rejected applicants in their thirties on the grounds that their professions would get fewer years—and thus less return—out of them. This policy had a severe impact on housewives and veterans who wanted to return to school.

As early as 1967, Congress banned some kinds of age discrimination. In 1975, civil rights law denied federal funds to any institution discriminating against people over the age of 40 because of their age. Congress amended the Age Discrimination in Employment Act in 1978 to raise the general compulsory retirement age to 70. Now compulsory retirement has been phased out altogether. No one knows what other directions the *gray liberation movement* may take as its members approach the status of a minority majority. In 1976 the Supreme Court, however, declared that it would not place age in the suspect classification category when it upheld a state law requiring police officers to retire at the age of 50. Age classifications would fall under the rational basis test.[28]

Job bias is often hidden, and proving it depends on inference and circumstantial evidence. The Supreme Court made it easier to win cases of job bias in 2000 when it held in *Reeves v. Sanderson* that a plaintiff's evidence of an employer's bias, combined with sufficient evidence to find that the employer's asserted justification is false, may permit juries and judges to conclude that an employer unlawfully discriminated. Five years later the Court found that employers can be held liable for discrimination even if they never intended any harm. Older employees need only show an employer's policies disproportionately harmed them—and that there was no reasonable basis for the employer's policy.[29] Thus, employees can win lawsuits without direct evidence of an employer's illegal intent. In 2008, the Supreme Court ruled that it is up to the employer to show that action against a worker stems form reasonable factors other than age (*Meacham v. Knolls Atomic Power Laboratory*). The impact of these decisions is likely to extend beyond questions of age discrimination to the litigation of race and gender discrimination cases brought under Title VII of the Civil Rights Act of 1964 as well as cases brought under the Americans with Disabilities Act.

CIVIL RIGHTS AND PEOPLE WITH DISABILITIES

Americans with disabilities have suffered from both direct and indirect discrimination. Governments and employers have often denied them rehabilitation services (a kind of affirmative action), education, and jobs. Many people with disabilities have been excluded from the workforce and isolated without overt discrimination. Throughout most of American history, public and private buildings have been hostile to the blind, deaf, and mobility impaired. Stairs, buses, telephones, and other necessities of modern life have been designed in ways that keep these individuals out of offices, stores, and restaurants. As one slogan said, "Once, blacks had to ride at the back of the bus. We can't even get on the bus."

The first rehabilitation laws were passed in the late 1920s, mostly to help veterans of World War I. Accessibility laws had to wait another 50 years. The Rehabilitation Act of 1973 (twice vetoed by Richard Nixon as "too costly") added people with disabilities to the list of Americans protected from discrimination. Because the law defines an inaccessible environment as a form of discrimination, wheelchair ramps, grab bars on toilets, and Braille signs have become common features of American life. The Education of All Handicapped Children Act of 1975 entitled all children to a free public education appropriate to their needs. The **Americans with Disabilities Act of 1990** (ADA) strengthened these protections, requiring employers and administrators of public facilities to make "reasonable accommodations" and prohibiting employment discrimination against people with disabilities.

Determining who is "disabled" has generated controversy. Are people with AIDS entitled to protections? In 1998 the Supreme Court answered yes. It ruled that the ADA offered protection against discrimination to people with AIDS.[30] What about people with bad eyesight or high blood pressure? In 1999 the Supreme Court ruled that people with physical impairments who can function normally when they wear glasses or take their medicine cannot be considered disabled and thus do not fall under the ADA's protection against employment discrimination.[31]

Nobody wants to oppose policies beneficial to people with disabilities. After all, people like Helen Keller and Franklin Roosevelt are popular American heroes. Nevertheless, civil rights laws designed to protect the rights of these individuals have met with vehement opposition and, once passed, with sluggish enforcement. The source of this

---

Americans with Disabilities Act of 1990

A law passed in 1990 that requires employers and public facilities to make "reasonable accommodations" for people with disabilities and prohibits discrimination against these individuals in employment.

New Americans with disabilities are among the successors to the 1960s civil rights activists. Recently, they have been active in demanding government benefits.

resistance is the same concern that troubled Nixon: cost. Budgeting for such programs is often shortsighted, however. People often forget that changes allowing people with disabilities to become wage earners, spenders, and taxpayers are a gain rather than drain on the economy.

You Are the Mayor and Need to Make Civil Rights Decisions

GAY AND LESBIAN RIGHTS

Gay and lesbian activists may face the toughest battle for equality. *Homophobia*—fear and hatred of homosexuals—has many causes; some are very powerful. Some religious groups, for instance, condemn homosexuality, which is unlikely to encourage tolerance. Homophobia appeared to be the motive for the brutal 1998 killing of Matthew Shepard, a 21-year-old political science freshman at the University of Wyoming. Students attacked Shepard after he attended a meeting for Gay Awareness Week events on campus. He was found tied to a fence, where his assailants had hit him in the head with a pistol 18 times and repeatedly kicked him in the groin.

Even by conservative estimates, several million Americans are homosexual, representing every social stratum and ethnic group. Gays and lesbians often face discrimination in hiring, education, access to public accommodations, and housing. Of particular concern to the gay community is the AIDS virus, which had an especially devastating effect on male homosexuals when the epidemic struck in the early 1980s.

A notorious incident in a New York City bar in 1969 stimulated the growth of the gay rights movement. Police raided the Stonewall bar, frequented by gay men. Unwarranted violence, arrests, and injury to persons and property resulted. Both gay men and lesbians organized throughout the 1970s and 1980s in an effort to protect their civil rights. During this time, they developed political skills and formed significant interest groups.

The record of gay rights is mixed. In 1986 the Supreme Court, in *Bowers v. Hardwick*, allowed states to ban homosexual relations. In 2000 the Supreme Court held that the Boy Scouts could exclude a gay man from being an adult member because homosexuality violates the organization's principles.[32]

Attitudes are changing, however. Few Americans oppose equal employment opportunities for homosexuals, and majorities support the legality of homosexual relations and the acceptability of homosexuality as a lifestyle. Nearly half the public views homosexual relations as morally acceptable and supports making same-sex marriages legal.[33]

In the summer of 1993, after months of negotiation with the Pentagon and an avalanche of criticism, President Clinton announced a new policy that barred the Pentagon from asking military recruits or service personnel to disclose their sexual orientation. Popularly known as the "don't ask, don't tell" policy, it also reaffirmed the Defense Department's strict prohibition against homosexual conduct. Service members who declare their homosexuality face discharge unless they can prove they will remain celibate, and they are barred from even disclosing to a friend in private conversation that they are gay or bisexual. The policy also requires commanders to have "credible information" that the policy is being violated before launching an investigation.

Gay activists have also won important victories. Several states, including California, and more than 100 communities have passed laws protecting homosexuals against some forms of discrimination.[34] Most colleges and universities now have gay rights organizations on campus. In 1996, in *Romer v. Evans*, the Supreme Court voided a state constitutional amendment approved by the voters of Colorado that denied homosexuals protection against discrimination. The Court found that the Colorado amendment violated the U.S. Constitution's guarantee of equal protection of the law. In 2003, in *Lawrence v. Texas*, the Supreme Court overturned *Bowers v. Hardwick* when it voided a Texas antisodomy law on the grounds that

When the Massachusetts Supreme Court held that the state's constitution required recognition of gay marriage, the issue became a factor in the 2004 presidential election. Here, supporters and opponents of gay marriage protest outside the Massachusetts State House as the legislators considered amending the Massachusetts constitution to overturn the court's decision.

DEBATE

Civil Rights and Gay Adoption

such laws were unconstitutional intrusions of the right to privacy.

The newest issue concerning gay rights is same-sex marriage. Most states have laws banning such marriages and the recognition of same-sex marriages that occur in other states. In 1996, Congress passed the Defense of Marriage Act, which permits states to disregard same-gender marriages, even if they are legal elsewhere in the United States. However, the states of Vermont, Connecticut, New Jersey, and New Hampshire recognize same-sex "civil unions," and several states, including California, Hawaii, Maine, Washington, and Oregon provide domestic partnership benefits to same-sex couples. In November 2003, the Massachusetts Supreme Court declared that the state's constitution guaranteed same-sex couples the right to marry (California's Supreme Court followed suit in 2008). From San Francisco to Boston, gays rushed to the altar, provoking a strong backlash from social conservatives. President Bush called for a constitutional amendment to ban same-sex marriage, but Congress did not support such an amendment.

Amending the Constitution is difficult, and both the public and elected officials are divided on the wisdom of doing so. In the meantime, gays push for benefits associated with marriage, including health insurance, taxes, Social Security payments, hospital visitation rights, and many other aspects of life that most people take for granted.

AFFIRMATIVE ACTION

Some people argue that groups that have suffered invidious discrimination require special efforts to provide them access to education and jobs. In 1965, President Lyndon Johnson signed Executive Order 11246, prohibiting federal contractors and federally assisted construction contractors and subcontractors from discriminating in employment decisions on the basis of race, color, religion, sex, or national origin. The order also required contractors to take "affirmative action" to ensure against employment discrimination, including the implementation of plans to increase the participation of minorities and women in the workplace.

affirmative action
A policy designed to give special attention to or compensatory treatment for members of some previously disadvantaged group.

Affirmative action involves efforts to bring about increased employment, promotion, or admission for members of groups who have suffered from discrimination. The goal is to move beyond *equal opportunity* (in which everyone has the same chance of obtaining good jobs, for example) toward *equal results* (in which different groups have the same percentage of success in obtaining those jobs). This goal might be accomplished through special rules in the public and private sectors that recruit or otherwise give preferential treatment to previously disadvantaged groups. Numerical quotas that ensure that a portion of government contracts, law school admissions, or police department promotions go to minorities and women are the strongest and most controversial form of affirmative action.

The constitutional status of affirmative action is not clear. Some state and federal laws have discriminated *in favor of* previously disadvantaged groups, and some state governments adopted affirmative action programs to increase minority enrollment, job holding, or promotion. At one point, the federal government mandated that all state and local governments, as well as each institution receiving aid from or contracting with the federal government, adopt an affirmative action program.

The University of California at Davis (UC–Davis) introduced one such program. Eager to produce more minority physicians in California, the medical school set aside 16 of 100 places in the entering class for "disadvantaged groups." One White applicant who did not make the freshman class was Allan Bakke. After receiving his rejection letter from Davis for two straight years, Bakke learned that the mean scores on the Medical College Admissions Test of students admitted under the university's program were the 46th percentile on verbal tests and the 35th on science tests. Bakke's scores on the same tests were at the 96th and 97th percentiles, respectively. He sued UC–Davis, claiming that it had denied him equal protection of the laws by discriminating against him because of his race.

The result was an important Supreme Court decision in Bakke's favor, *Regents of the University of California v. Bakke* (1978).[35] The Court ordered Bakke admitted, holding that the UC–Davis Special Admissions Program did discriminate against him because of his race. Yet the Court refused to order UC–Davis never to use race as a criterion for admission. A university could, said the Court, adopt an "admissions program where race or ethnic background is simply one element—to be weighed fairly against other elements—in the selection process." It could *not*, as the UC–Davis Special Admissions Program did, set aside a quota of spots for particular groups.

Although Bakke ended up in medical school, Brian Weber did not get into an apprenticeship program he wanted to enter in Louisiana. In *United Steelworkers of America, AFL-CIO v. Weber* (1979), the Court found that the Kaiser Aluminum Company intended its special training program, which employed a quota for minorities, to rectify years of past employment discrimination at Kaiser. Thus, said the Court, a voluntary union- and management-sponsored program to take more African Americans than Whites did *not* discriminate against Weber.

Until 1995, the Court was more deferential to Congress than to local government in upholding affirmative action programs. In 1989, the Court found a Richmond, Virginia, plan that reserved 30 percent of city subcontracts for minority firms to be unconstitutional.[36] In 1980, on the other hand, the Court upheld a federal rule setting aside 10 percent of all federal construction contracts for minority-owned firms.[37] In 1990, the Court agreed that Congress may require preferential treatment for minorities to increase their ownership of broadcast licenses.[38] This event marked the first time the Supreme Court upheld a specific affirmative action program that was not devised to remedy past discrimination.

Things changed in 1995, however. In *Adarand Constructors v. Pena*, the Court overturned the decision regarding broadcast licenses and cast grave doubt on its holding regarding contracts set aside for minority-owned firms. It held that federal programs that classify people by race, even for an ostensibly benign purpose such as expanding opportunities for members of minorities, should be presumed to be unconstitutional. Such programs must be subject to the most searching judicial inquiry and can survive only if they are "narrowly tailored" to accomplish a "compelling governmental interest." In other words, the Court applied criteria for evaluating affirmative action programs similar to those it applies to other racial classifications, the less benign suspect classifications we discussed earlier in the chapter. These are also the same criteria the Court has applied to state affirmative action programs since 1989. Although *Adarand Constructors v. Pena* did not void federal affirmative action programs in general, it certainly limits their potential impact.

Regents of the University of California v. Bakke

A 1978 Supreme Court decision holding that a state university could not admit less qualified individuals solely because of their race.

Adarand Constructors v. Pena

A 1995 Supreme Court decision holding that federal programs that classify people by race, even for an ostensibly benign purpose such as expanding opportunities for minorities, should be presumed to be unconstitutional.

On other matters, the Court has approved preferential treatment of minorities in promotions;[39] and it has also ordered quotas for minority union memberships.[40] We examine a case of a public employer using affirmative action promotions to counter underrepresentation of women and minorities in the workplace in "You Are the Judge: The Case of the Santa Clara Dispatcher."

On the other hand, the Court has ruled that affirmative action does not exempt recently hired minorities from traditional work rules specifying the "last hired, first fired" order of layoffs.[41] In 1986, the Court found unconstitutional an effort to give preference to African American teachers in layoffs because this policy punished innocent White teachers and the African American teachers had not been the actual victims of past discrimination.[42]

Not everyone agrees that affirmative action is a wise or fair policy. There is little support from the general public for programs such as those that set aside jobs or employ quotas for members of minority groups. Opposition is especially strong when people view affirmative action as *reverse discrimination*—as in the case of individuals like Allan Bakke who are themselves blameless—and less qualified individuals are hired or admitted to educational or training programs because of their minority status.

Critics of reverse discrimination argue that any race or gender discrimination is wrong, even when its purpose is to rectify past injustices rather than to reinforce them. After all, Bakke and Johnson could no more help being White and male than Diane Joyce could help being a woman. Opponents of affirmative action believe that merit is the only fair basis for distributing benefits. Bakke and Johnson found that the rules by which institutions operated had suddenly changed—and they suffered as a result. It is easy to sympathize with them.

In 1996, California voters passed Proposition 209, which banned state affirmative action programs based on race, ethnicity, or gender in public hiring, contracting, and educational admissions (Washington State passed a similar ban in 1998). Opponents immediately filed a lawsuit in federal court to block enforcement of the law, claiming that it violated the Fourteenth Amendment, but courts upheld the

YOU ARE THE Judge

The Case of the Santa Clara Dispatcher

For four years, Diane Joyce patched asphalt with a Santa Clara county road crew around San Jose, California, and its suburbs. She applied for a promotion, hoping to work in the less strenuous and better-paid position of dispatcher. Another applicant for the job was Paul Johnson, a White male who had worked for the agency for 13 years.

Like Diane, Paul did well on the exam given to all applicants; in fact, the two scored among the top six applicants, Diane with a score of 73 and Paul with 75. Knowing that Paul's score was a shade better and his work experience longer, the supervisor decided to hire him. The county's affirmative action officers overruled the supervisor, however, and Diane got the job. Paul decided to get a lawyer.

Paul's lawyer argued that Diane's promotion violated Title VII of the Civil Rights Act of 1964. This law, originally passed to guarantee minority access to jobs and promotions, makes it unlawful for an employer to deprive any individual of employment opportunities because of his or her race, color, religion, gender, or national origin.

You Be the Judge: Should Diane Joyce have been promoted?

Decision: In *Johnson v. Transportation Agency, Santa Clara County* (1987), the Supreme Court held that public employers may use carefully constructed affirmative action promotion plans, designed to remedy specific past discriminations, to counter women's and minorities' underrepresentation in the workplace. Thus, Diane Joyce kept her job. In a stinging dissent, Justice Scalia complained that the Court was "converting [the law] from a guarantee that race or sex will not be a basis for employment determinations, to a guarantee that it often will."

law. There is little question that support for Proposition 209 represents a widespread skepticism about affirmative action programs.

In 2003, the Supreme Court made two important decisions on affirmative action in college admissions. First, the Court agreed that there was a compelling interest in promoting racial diversity on campus. The Court upheld the University of Michigan law school's use of race as one of many factors in admission in *Grutter v. Bollinger* (2003). The Court found that the law school's use of race as a plus in the admissions process was narrowly tailored and that it made individualistic, holistic reviews of applicants in a nonmechanical fashion. In response, in 2006 Michigan voters passed a ballot initiative banning affirmative action in college admissions and government hiring.

In *Gratz v. Bollinger* (2003), however, the Court struck down the University of Michigan's system of undergraduate admissions in which every applicant from an underrepresented racial or ethnic minority group was automatically awarded 20 points of the 100 needed to guarantee admission. The Court said that the system was tantamount to using a quota, which it outlawed in *Bakke*, because it made the factor of race decisive for virtually every minimally qualified underrepresented minority applicant. The 20 points awarded to minorities were more than the school awarded for some measures of academic excellence, writing ability, or leadership skills.

In 2007, the Supreme Court addressed racially balancing in the public schools. The Seattle, Washington, school district, which had never operated legally segregated schools or been subject to court-ordered desegregation, classified children as White or non-White, and used the racial classifications as a "tie-breaker" to allocate slots in particular high schools. The Jefferson County, Kentucky, district was subject to a desegregation decree until 2000, which the district court dissolved after finding that the school district had eliminated the vestiges of prior segregation to the greatest extent practicable. In 2001, the district adopted a plan classifying students by race to make certain elementary school assignments and to rule on transfer requests. Some parents filed law suits contending that allocating children to different public schools based solely on their race violated the Fourteenth Amendment's equal protection guarantee.

In *Parents Involved in Community Schools v. Seattle School District No. 1* (2007), the Supreme Court held that the school districts' use of race in their voluntary integration plans, even for the purpose of preventing resegregation, violated the 14th Amendment's guarantee of equal protection and therefore was unconstitutional. Using the strict scrutiny standard for evaluating racial classifications, the Court found that the school districts lacked the compelling interest of remedying the effects of past intentional discrimination and concluded that racial balancing by itself was not a compelling state interest. The Court did indicate that school authorities might use a "race conscious" means to achieve diversity but that the school districts must be sensitive to other aspects of diversity besides race and narrowly tailor their programs to achieve diversity.

Whatever the Court may rule, it is not difficult to understand why many support affirmative action policies. Proponents of them argue that what constitutes merit is highly subjective and can embody prejudices of which the decision maker may be quite unaware. Experts suggest that a man can "look more like" a road dispatcher and thus get a higher rating from interviewers than a woman might. Affirmative action advocates believe that increasing the number of women and minorities in desirable jobs is such an important social goal that it should be considered when determining an individual's qualifications. They claim that what White males lose from affirmative action programs are privileges to which they were never entitled in the first place; after all, nobody has the right to be a doctor or a road dispatcher. Research has found that affirmative action offers significant benefits for women and minorities with relatively small costs for White males.[43]

UNDERSTANDING CIVIL RIGHTS AND PUBLIC POLICY

The original Constitution is silent on the issue of equality. The only direct reference is in the Fourteenth Amendment, which forbids the states to deny "equal protection of the laws." Those five words have been the basis for major civil rights statutes and scores of judicial rulings protecting the rights of minorities and women. These laws and decisions, granting people new rights, have empowered groups to seek and gain still more victories. The implications of their success for democracy and the scope of government are substantial.

CIVIL RIGHTS AND DEMOCRACY

Equality is a basic principle of democracy. Every citizen has one vote because democratic government presumes that each person's needs, interests, and preferences are neither any more nor any less important than the needs, interests, and preferences of every other person. Individual liberty is an equally important democratic principle, one that can conflict with equality.

Equality tends to favor majority rule. Because under simple majority rule everyone's wishes rank equally, the policy outcome that most people prefer seems to be the fairest choice in cases of conflict. What happens, however, if the majority wants to deprive the minority of certain rights? In situations like these, equality threatens individual liberty. Thus, the principle of equality can invite the denial of minority rights, whereas the principle of liberty condemns such action.[44] In general, Americans today strongly believe in protecting minority rights, as you can see in "America in Perspective: Respect for Minority Rights."

AMERICA IN PERSPECTIVE

Respect for **Minority Rights**

Americans rate the importance of protection of minority rights relatively highly compared to other democracies. Why do you think that is?

Question: There are different opinions about people's rights in a democracy. On a scale of 1 to 10, where 1 is not at all important and 7 is very important, how important is it that government authorities respect and protect rights of minorities?

% shown responding 7 shown in graph

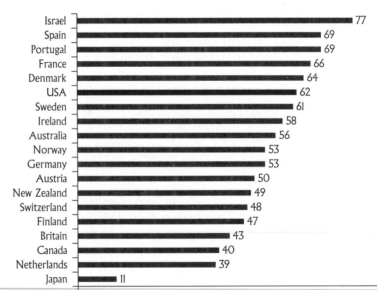

Percent rating respect for minority rights as very important

Israel	77
Spain	69
Portugal	69
France	66
Denmark	64
USA	62
Sweden	61
Ireland	58
Australia	56
Norway	53
Germany	53
Austria	50
New Zealand	49
Switzerland	48
Finland	47
Britain	43
Canada	40
Netherlands	39
Japan	11

Source: Authors' analysis of 2004 International Society Survey Program data.

Majority rule is not the only threat to liberty. Politically and socially powerful minorities have suppressed majorities as well as other minorities. Women have long outnumbered men in America, about 53 percent to 47 percent. In the era of segregation, African Americans outnumbered Whites in many Southern states. Inequality persisted, however, because customs that reinforced it were entrenched within the society and because inequality often served the interests of the dominant groups. When slavery and segregation existed in an agrarian economy, Whites could get cheap agricultural labor. When men were breadwinners and women were homemakers, married men had a source of cheap domestic labor.

Both African Americans and women made many gains even when they lacked one essential component of democratic power: the vote. They used other rights—such as their First Amendment freedoms—to fight for equality. When Congress protected the right of African Americans to vote in the 1960s, the nature of Southern politics changed dramatically. The democratic process is a powerful vehicle for disadvantaged groups to press their claims.

CIVIL RIGHTS AND THE SCOPE OF GOVERNMENT

Civil rights laws increase the scope and power of government. These laws regulate the behavior of individuals and institutions. Restaurant owners must serve all patrons regardless of race. Professional schools must admit women. Employers must accommodate people with disabilities and make an effort to find minority workers, whether they want to or not. Those who want to reduce the scope of government are uneasy with these laws, if not downright hostile to them.

The Founders might be greatly perturbed if they knew about all the civil rights laws the government has enacted; these policies do not conform to the eighteenth-century idea of limited government. But the Founders would expect the national government to do whatever is necessary to hold the nation together. The Civil War showed that the original Constitution did not adequately deal with issues like slavery that could destroy the society the Constitution's writers had struggled to secure.

However, civil rights, like civil liberties, is an area in which increased government activity in protecting basic rights can lead to greater checks on government by those who benefit from such protections. Remember that much of segregation was *de jure*, established by governments. Moreover, we can view government action in the area of civil rights as the protection of individualism. Basic to the notion of civil rights is that individuals are not to be judged according to characteristics they share with a group. Thus, civil rights protect the individual against collective discrimination.

The question of where to draw the line in the government's efforts to protect civil rights has received different answers at different points in American history, but few Americans want to turn back the clock to the days of *Plessy v. Ferguson* and Jim Crow laws or to the exclusion of women from the workplace.

SUMMARY

Racial minorities have struggled for equality since the very beginning of the republic. In the era of slavery, the Supreme Court upheld the practice and denied slaves any rights. After the Civil War and Reconstruction ended, governments at all levels established legal segregation. For a time, the Supreme Court sanctioned Jim Crow laws, but in 1954, the *Brown v. Board of Education* case held that *de jure* racial segregation violated equal protection of the laws, which was guaranteed by the Fourteenth Amendment. This event marked the beginning of the era of civil rights. *Brown* inaugurated a movement that succeeded in ending virtually every form of legal discrimination against minorities.

Although feminists have not ignored the courts, the struggle for women's equality has emphasized legislation over litigation. Women won the right to vote in 1920, but the states failed to ratify the Equal Rights Amendment. This defeat did not kill the feminist movement, however. Comparable worth, women's role in the military, sexual harassment, and the balance between work and family are among the many controversial women's issues society is still debating.

The interests of women and minorities have converged on the issue of affirmative action—that is, policies requiring special efforts on behalf of disadvantaged groups. In the *Bakke* case and in decisions like *Johnson v. Santa Clara*, the Court ruled that affirmative action plans were constitutional. However, there is substantial opposition to what many see as reverse discrimination, and the Court has raised new obstacles to affirmative action.

The civil rights umbrella is a large one. Increasing numbers of groups seek protection for their rights. Older and younger Americans, people with disabilities, and homosexuals have used the laws to ensure their equality. People with AIDS and other chronically ill people are mounting battles in the political arena. It is difficult to predict what controversies the next decades will bring, when minority groups will outnumber the current majority.

Chapter Test
Multiple Choice

1. Which of the following is the only place in which the idea of equality directly appears in the U.S. Constitution?
   a. The First Amendment
   b. The Fourth Amendment
   c. The Sixth Amendment
   d. The Thirteenth Amendment
   e. The Fourteenth Amendment

2. Courts presume classifications based on gender to be:
   a. Constitutional
   b. Unconstitutional
   c. Neither constitutional nor unconstitutional
   d. Reasonable
   e. Inherently suspect

3. Slavery in the United States was ended by the:
   a. First Amendment
   b. Ninth Amendment
   c. Thirteenth Amendment
   d. Fourteenth Amendment
   e. Fifteenth Amendment

4. Which of the following did the Civil Rights Act of 1964 NOT accomplish?
   a. It strengthened voting rights legislation
   b. It took forbade discrimination in the sale or rental of housing
   c. It created the Equal Employment Opportunity Commission (EEOC)
   d. It forbade discrimination in employment on the basis of race, color, national origin, religion, or gender
   e. It did all of the above

5. The legal doctrine known as used to give men the legal advantage in securing custody of their children in case of a divorce.
   a. Convention
   b. Custom
   c. Coverture
   d. Patronage
   e. Paternalism

6. Most of the United States' provisions on equality are:
   a. Directly outlined in the Constitution
   b. Directly outlined in the Declaration of Independence
   c. Implied in the Constitution
   d. Implied in the Declaration of Independence
   e. The result of legal interpretation over the years

7. Assume that 12-year-old Mike R. lives in a predominantly minority neighborhood in a major U.S. city. He is required by law to attend the school closest to his home, making his school also predominantly attended by minorities. This could be seen as an example of:
   a. De jure segregation
   b. De facto segregation
   c. De jure racism
   d. De facto racism
   e. None of the above

True/False

8. According to the textbook, courts can uphold racial and ethical classifications if they serve a compelling public interest.
   True_____   False_____

9. Many African American men held state and federal offices during the 10 years following the Civil War.
   True_____   False_____

Short Answer

10. Name and briefly explain what characterized the three eras that delineate African Americans' struggle for equality in America.

11. What were at least three different ways in which many states tried to make it more difficult— if not impossible— for African Americans to vote?

12. In what ways does majority rule pose a threat to liberty?

13. What are some of the arguments for and against affirmative action? In your answer, consider both the historical and the current context of affirmative action.

14. How would the Founding Fathers view the historical development of civil rights laws?

Short Answer/Essay Questions

15. Looking at the A Generation of Change feature on p. 166, please interpret the numbers illustrating the pay gap between American men and women. In your opinion, what are at least three factors that explain the existence of such a gap? By the same token, what are at least three factors that have contributed (and will continue to contribute) to shrinking the gap?

16. The textbook points out that America is heading toward a minority majority. In your opinion, in what ways might this development affect future political, social, and other dynamics in this country?

17. Using your knowledge of the history of civil rights in the United States, what similarities and what differences do you see in the experiences of the different minority groups discussed in the textbook? What might explain these? Finally, what is your assessment of the current status of civil rights? What, if any, improvements do you believe are necessary?

18. Please address the question of whether or not women should serve in combat. What are arguments for and against opening up combat branches of the military to women (social, political, practical, and otherwise)? In what ways—if any—do you believe advances in technology have affected this debate?

Answer Key

1. E   2. C   3. C   4. B   5. C   6. E   7. B   8. True   9. True

Key Terms

civil rights (146)
Fourteenth Amendment (148)
equal protection of the laws (148)
Thirteenth Amendment (150)
Civil Rights Act of 1964 (155)
suffrage (156)

Fifteenth Amendment (156)
poll taxes (156)
White primary (156)
Twenty-fourth Amendment (156)
Voting Rights Act of 1965 (156)
Nineteenth Amendment (162)

Equal Rights Amendment (163)
comparable worth (166)
Americans with Disabilities Act of 1990 (170)
affirmative action (172)

Key Cases

Scott v. Sandford (1857)
Plessy v. Ferguson (1896)
Brown v. Board of Education (1954)

Hernandez v. Texas (1954)
Korematsu v. United States (1944)
Reed v. Reed (1971)

Craig v. Boren (1976)
Regents of the University of California v. Bakke (1978)
Adarand Constructors v. Pena (1995)

Internet Resources

www.law.cornell.edu/wex/index.php/Equal_protection
The background material and text of the landmark cases on equal protection.

www.usdoj.gov/crt/
Home page of the Civil Rights Division of the U.S. Department of Justice containing background information and discussion of current events.

www.usdoj.gov/crt/ada/adahom1.htm
Home page of the Americans with Disabilities Act of the U.S. Department of Justice containing background information and discussion of current events.

www.naacp.org
Home page of the NAACP containing background information and discussion of current events.

http://www.lulac.org/
League of United Latin American Citizens home page, with information on Latino rights and policy goals.

http://www.civilrightsproject.ucla.edu/aboutus.php
Home page of the Civil Rights Project at UCLA, with background information and other resources on civil rights.

http://www.now.org/
Home page of the National Organization of Women containing material on issues dealing with women's rights.

www.hrc.org/
Human Rights Campaign home page, with information on lesbian, gay, bisexual, and transgender rights.

www.usccr.gov/
U.S. Commission on Civil Rights home page, with news of civil rights issues around the country.

GetConnected

Race, Affirmative Action, and Equal Opportunity

Race is an enduring issue in American politics. Historically, the debate has focused on relations between Blacks and Whites, but demographic trends and immigration is changing the debate. The Hispanic population in the United States is growing, adding to the complexity of race relations. Decision makers have been asked to develop ways to provide for equal opportunities for all races without creating a system of race-based quotas. Let us compare several strategies for implementing affirmative action and/or equal opportunity.

Search the Web

Go to the Civil Rights.org Web page on affirmative action, *www.civilrights.org/issues/affirmative/*. You may want to read the information on affirmative action in university admissions decisions more closely. Also visit the Center for Equal Opportunity's Web site, *www.ceousa.org/*. You will find some information on affirmative action in university admissions as well.

Questions to Ask

- What is affirmative action? Do the two groups define affirmative action differently?
- What evidence does Civil Rights.org use to defend affirmative action? What evidence does the Center for Equal Opportunity use to oppose affirmative action?
- What do the two groups think should be done to increase access to higher education for all people regardless of race?

Why It Matters

Equality is central to our political culture. One of the most difficult tasks of policymakers is bridging the gap between equality of opportunity and equality of results. It is critical that they integrate all citizens fully into American life, but they must do so in a manner that most citizens perceive to be fair to those who have not suffered from past discrimination.

Get Involved

Look at the other students in the class. How many are of a race different than yours? How many are of the opposite gender? Ask several of those students about racial preferences in college admissions decisions. Are the other students' views about racial preferences different from your own? For more exercises, go to *www.longmanamericangovernment.com*.

For Further Reading

Anderson, Terry H. *The Pursuit of Fairness.* New York: Oxford University Press, 2005. A History of Affirmative Action.

Arsenault, Raymond. *Freedom Riders: 1961 and the Struggle for Racial Justice.* New York: Oxford University Press, 2006. The story of the freedom riders' efforts to desegregate the South.

Baer, Judith A. *Women in American Law: The Struggle Toward Equality from the New Deal to the Present* 3rd rev. ed. New York: Holmes and Meier, 2003. An excellent analysis of women's changing legal status.

Berger, Raoul. *Government by Judiciary: The Transformation of the Fourteenth Amendment.* Cambridge, MA: Harvard University Press, 1977. Berger is not one who favors use of the Fourteenth Amendment to expand equality.

Bergman, Barbara R. *In Defense of Affirmative Action.* New York: Basic Books, 1996. An argument on behalf of affirmative action policies.

Bowen, William G., and Derek Bok. *The Shape of the River: The Long-Term Consequences of Considering Race in College and University Admissions.* Princeton, NJ: Princeton University Press, 1998. Former presidents of Harvard and Princeton discuss affirmative action in higher education.

García, John A. *Latino Politics in America: Community, Culture, and Interests.* Lanham, MD: Rowman & Littlefield, 2003. An insightful view of Latino politics.

Mansbridge, Jane. *Why We Lost the ERA.* Chicago: University of Chicago Press, 1986. The politics of women's rights.

McClain, Paula D., and Joseph Stewart. *"Can't We All Get Along?"* 5th ed. Boulder, CO: Westview, 2009. Racial and ethnic minorities in American politics.

McGlen, Nancy, Karen O'Connor, Laura Van Assendelft, and Wendy Gunther. *Women, Politics, and American Society*, 4th ed. New York: Longman, 2004. Explores the efforts, achievements, and setbacks in the movement toward equality for women.

Nakanishi, Don T., and James S. Lai, eds. *Asian American Politics: Law, Participation, and Policy.* Lanham, MD: Rowman&Littlefield, 2003. Essays focusing on Asian American politics.

Perry, Barbara A. *The Michigan Affirmative Action Cases.* Lawrence, KS: University Press of Kansas, 2007. Behind the scenes story of the politics and law of attempting to overturn affirmative action programs in higher education.

Pinello, Daniel R. *America's Struggle for Same-Sex Marriage.* New York: Cambridge University Press, 2006. The social movement for same-sex marriage and the political controversies surrounding it.

Rimmerman, Craig A. *The Lesbian and Gay Movements.* Boulder, CO: Westview, 2008. Examines the strategies and issues of gay and lesbian politics.

Urofsky, Melvin I. *A Conflict of Rights: The Supreme Court and Affirmative Action.* New York: Scribner's, 1991. A case study of the issues, people, and events surrounding the case of *Joyce v. Johnson.*

Wilkins, David E. *American Indian Politics and the American Political System*, rev. ed. Lanham, MD: Rowman & Littlefield, 2003. Excellent treatment of Native American issues and politics.

Woodward, C. Vann. *The Strange Career of Jim Crow.* 2nd ed. New York: Oxford University Press, 1966. Examines the evolution of Jim Crow laws in the South.

CHAPTER 6

PUBLIC OPINION AND POLITICAL ACTION

POLITICS IN ACTION:
A RARE MOMENT OF CONSENSUS
IN PUBLIC OPINION

American public opinion about the events of September 11, 2001, and the subsequent war in Afghanistan reflected a unanimity that is rarely seen. Normally, analysts find a great diversity of views among the American public, and public opinion surveys usually reveal many conflicting attitudes that frequently reflect ambivalence. But such was not the case in this instance. Hundreds of millions of Americans responded with remarkably near-unanimous opinions. Most everyone agreed that this was an act of war that demanded an immediate response by force. Partisan differences, racial differences, and regional differences mattered little in understanding attitudes about the events of September 11 and the war against terrorism.

A CNN/*USA Today* poll conducted on September 11, 2001, found that 86 percent felt that the attacks that day had been an act of war. A *Washington Post* /ABC poll conducted on September 13 found 93 percent favored military action when asked, "If the United States can identify the groups or nations responsible for the attacks, would you support or oppose taking military action against them?" The same poll found that 85 percent favored striking at Afghanistan if Osama bin Laden was found to be culpable and Afghanistan refused to turn him over. Support for military action dropped a bit when people were asked if it meant innocent civilians might be hurt or killed

and a bit more when posed with the scenario of a long war with large numbers of U.S. troops killed or injured. But 69 percent of the population nevertheless supported the use of force even under the conditions of Afghan civilian casualties and high military costs to the United States.

Not only did the vast majority of the American public immediately give their support for military action, but they continued to support such action once hostilities commenced in Afghanistan. At *www.pollingreport.com*, there were reports of 18 different public opinion polls in the two months following 9/11 that asked people whether they approved or disapproved of U.S. military action being taken in response to the terrorist attacks. The level of support was consistently high, ranging from 86 to 92 percent. Such support levels exceeded public support levels for the Persian Gulf War in 1991, which is typically thought of as an overwhelmingly supported military operation.

The case of September 11 is clearly an exception to the rule regarding public opinion. Usually, public opinion polls are taken to find out the level of disagreement in the country and what sorts of people favor which actions. As will be seen in this chapter, the degree of unanimity apparent in public opinion immediately after the terrorist attacks is most unusual.

Politicians and columnists commonly intone the words "the American people" and then claim their view as that of the citizenry. Yet it would be hard to find a statement about the American people—who they are and what they believe—that is either 100 percent right or 100 percent wrong. The American people are wondrously diverse. There are over 300 million Americans, forming a mosaic of racial, ethnic, and cultural groups. America was founded on the principle of tolerating diversity and individualism, and it remains one of the most diverse countries in the world today. Most Americans view this diversity as one of the most appealing aspects of their society.

public opinion

The distribution of the population's beliefs about politics and policy issues.

The study of American **public opinion** aims to understand the distribution of the population's belief about politics and policy issues. Because there are many groups with a great variety of opinions in the United States, this is an especially complex task. This is not to say that public opinion would be easy to study even if America were a more homogeneous society; as you will see, measuring public opinion involves painstaking interviewing procedures and careful wording of questions. Further complicating the task is the fact that people are often not well informed about the issues. The least informed are also the least likely to participate in the political process, a phenomenon that creates imbalances in who takes part in political action.

For American government to work efficiently and effectively, the diversity of the American public and its opinions must be faithfully channeled through the political process. This chapter reveals just how difficult this task is.

THE AMERICAN PEOPLE

demography

The science of population changes.

One way of looking at the American public is through **demography**—the science of human populations. The most valuable tool for understanding demographic changes in America is the **census**. The U.S. Constitution requires that the government conduct an "actual enumeration" of the population every 10 years. The first census was conducted in 1790; the most recent census was done in 2000.

census

A valuable tool for understanding demographic changes. The U.S. Constitution requires that the government conduct an "actual enumeration" of the population every 10 years.

The Census Bureau tries to conduct the most accurate count of the population humanly feasible. It isn't an easy job, even with the allocation of billions of federal dollars to the task. After the 1990 census was completed, the census Bureau estimated that 4.7 million people were not counted. Furthermore, they found that members of minority groups were disproportionately undercounted, as they were apparently more suspicious of government and thus less willing to cooperate with census workers. In order to correct for such an undercount in 2000, the Clinton administration approved a plan to scientifically estimate the characteristics of those people who failed to respond to the census forms and follow-up visits from census workers and then to incorporate this information into the official count. Conservatives maintained that such a procedure would be subject to manipulation, less accurate than a traditional head count, and unconstitutional. In the 1999 case of *Department of Commerce v. U.S. House of Representatives,* the Supreme Court ruled that sampling could not be used to determine the number of congressional districts each state is entitled to. However, the Court left the door open for the use of sampling procedures to adjust the count for other purposes, such as the allocation of federal grants to states. In the end, the Bush administration decided not to use the sampling option.

Changes in the U.S. population, as reflected in census figures, impact our culture and political system in numerous ways, which will be examined in the next few sections.

THE IMMIGRANT SOCIETY

The United States has always been a nation of immigrants. As John F. Kennedy said, America is "not merely a nation but a nation of nations."[1] All Americans except Native Americans are either descended from immigrants or are immigrants themselves. Today, federal law allows up to 800,000 new immigrants to be legally admitted to the country every year. This is equivalent to adding a city with the population of Indianapolis every year. And in recent years, illegal immigrants have outnumbered legal immigrants.

There have been three great waves of immigration to the United States:

Responding to criticisms that many minority groups had been undercounted in the previous census, the Census Bureau launched special advertising campaigns to improve cooperation rates in these communities in 2000. Here you can see a poster in Detroit targeted at the large number of Iraqi immigrants in the city.

*   Prior to the late nineteenth century, northwestern Europeans (English, Irish, Germans, and Scandinavians) constituted the first wave of immigration.
*   During the late nineteenth and early twentieth centuries, southern and eastern Europeans (Italians, Jews, Poles, Russians, and others) made up much of the second wave. Most of these passed through Ellis Island in New York (now a popular museum) as their first stop in the new world.
*   In recent decades, a third wave of immigrants has consisted of Hispanics (from Cuba, Central America, and Mexico) and Asians (from Vietnam, Korea, the Philippines, and elsewhere). The 1980s saw the second-largest number of immigrants of any decade in American history, and this high level of immigration has remained fairly constant to this day.[2]

Immigrants bring with them their aspirations as well as their own political beliefs. For example, Cubans in Miami, who nearly constitute a majority of the city's population, first came to America to escape Fidel Castro's Marxist regime and have brought their anticommunist sentiments with them. Similarly, the Vietnamese came to America after a communist takeover there. Cubans and Vietnamese are just two recent examples of the many types of immigrants who have come to America over the years to flee an oppressive government. Other examples from previous periods of heavy immigration include the Irish in the first wave and the Russians in the second. Throughout American history, such groups have fostered a great appreciation for individualism in American public policy by their wish to be free of oppressive governmental control.

MyState | Immigrants as a Percentage of State Populations

The adjacent map classifies the 50 states according to the percentage of their population who were born in another country as of the 2000 Census.

QUESTIONS FOR DISCUSSION

▶ How does your state rank in terms of immigrants in its population? Why do you think your state ranks as it does in terms of attractiveness to immigrants?

▶ What ethnic groups are prominent among immigrants to America living in your state? Have these groups impacted the nature of politics in your state? If so, how?

▶ Do you think people in your state would generally welcome more immigrants over the next decade? Why or why not?

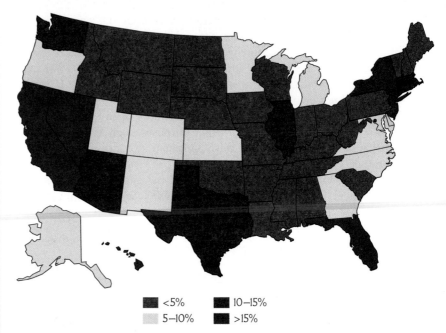

■ <5% ■ 10–15%
□ 5–10% ■ >15%

Source: "The Foreign-Born Population: 2000." Washington, D.C.: U.S. Census Bureau, December 2003.

In 2000, the census found that 11 percent of the nation's population were immigrants, of which 42 percent had already become United States citizens. States vary substantially in terms of the percentage of residents who are foreign born, ranging from a high of 26 percent in California to a low of 1 percent in West Virginia. You can get a sense of how your state ranks in this respect in "My State: Immigrants as a Percentage of State Populations."

THE AMERICAN MELTING POT

melting pot

The mixing of cultures, ideas, and peoples that has changed the American nation. The United States, with its history of immigration, has often been called a melting pot.

minority majority

The emergence of a non-Caucasian majority, as compared with a White, generally Anglo-Saxon majority. It is predicted that by about 2045, Hispanic Americans, African Americans, and Asian Americans together will outnumber White Americans.

With its long history of immigration, the United States has often been called a **melting pot**. This phrase refers to a mixture of cultures, ideas, and peoples. As the third wave of immigration continues, policy makers have begun to speak of a new **minority majority**, meaning that America will eventually cease to have a White, generally Anglo-Saxon majority. The 2000 census data found an all-time low in the percentage of non-Hispanic White Americans—just over 69 percent of the population. African Americans made up 12 percent of the population, Hispanics 13 percent, Asians 4 percent, and Native Americans slightly less than 1 percent. In recent years, minority populations have been growing at a much faster rate than the White population. As you can see in Figure 6.1, the Census Bureau estimates that by the middle of the twenty-first century Whites will represent only 48 percent of the population.

Until recently, the largest minority group in the country has been the African American population. One in eight Americans is a descendant of these reluctant immigrants: Africans who were brought to America by force as slaves. As discussed in Chapter 5, a legacy of racism and discrimination has left a higher proportion of the African American population economically and politically disadvantaged than

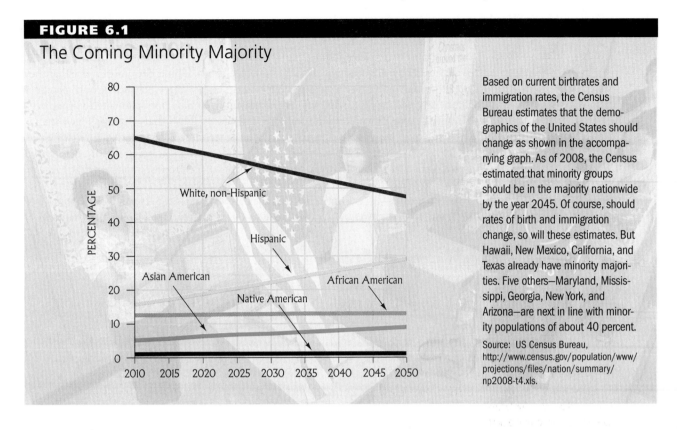

FIGURE 6.1

The Coming Minority Majority

Based on current birthrates and immigration rates, the Census Bureau estimates that the demographics of the United States should change as shown in the accompanying graph. As of 2008, the Census estimated that minority groups should be in the majority nationwide by the year 2045. Of course, should rates of birth and immigration change, so will these estimates. But Hawaii, New Mexico, California, and Texas already have minority majorities. Five others—Maryland, Mississippi, Georgia, New York, and Arizona—are next in line with minority populations of about 40 percent.

Source: US Census Bureau, http://www.census.gov/population/www/projections/files/nation/summary/np2008-t4.xls.

the White population. In 2006, the Census Bureau found that 24 percent of African Americans lived below the poverty line compared to 10 percent of Whites.

Despite this economic disadvantage, African Americans have recently been exercising a good deal of political power. The number of African American elected officials has increased by over 600 percent since 1970.[3] African Americans have been elected as mayors of many of the country's biggest cities, including Los Angeles, New York, and Chicago. In 2001, Colin Powell became the first African American secretary of state, and Condoleezza Rice became the nation's first African American to serve as the president's national security advisor. (Rice later succeeded Powell as secretary of state.) And the biggest African-American political breakthrough of all occurred when Barack Obama won the Democratic Party's nomination for president in 2008.

The familiar problems of African Americans sometimes obscure the problems of other minority groups, such as Hispanics (composed largely of Mexicans, Cubans, and Puerto Ricans). The 2000 census reported that for the first time the Hispanic population outnumbered the African American population. Like African Americans, Hispanics are concentrated in cities. Hispanics are rapidly gaining power in the Southwest, and cities such as San Antonio and Los Angeles have elected mayors of Hispanic heritage. As of 2007, the state legislatures of New Mexico, Texas, Arizona, Florida, and California had at least 10 percent Hispanic representation.[4]

Immigration reform has been a hotly contested issue in American politics in recent years. Hispanic groups often argue that illegal immigrants from Latin America have made substantial contributions to American society and have called for legislation to pave the way for them to become citizens.

An issue of particular concern to the Hispanic community is what to do about the problem of illegal immigration. The Simpson-Mazzoli Act, named after its congressional sponsors, requires that employers document the citizenship of their employees. Whether people are born in Canton, Ohio, or Canton, China, they must prove that they are either U.S. citizens or legal immigrants in order to work. Civil and criminal penalties can be assessed against employers who knowingly employ undocumented immigrants. However, it has proved difficult for authorities to establish that employers have knowingly accepted false social security cards and other forged identity documents. Hence, the Simpson-Mazzoli Act has proved to be inadequate in stopping illegal immigration from Mexico and other Latin American countries. One proposed solution that has been very controversial in recent years involves denying all benefits from government programs to people who cannot prove that they are legal residents of the United States (see "You Are the Policymaker: Do We Need to Get Tougher with Illegal Immigrants?").

YOU ARE THE Policymaker

Do We Need to Get Tougher with Illegal Immigrants?

Americans have traditionally welcomed immigrants with open arms. However, some immigrants have recently become less welcome: those who are in the country illegally. In states such as Texas and California, where many illegal immigrants from south of the border live, there is concern that providing public services to these people is seriously draining state resources. This became the topic of heated debate when Californians voted on Proposition 187 in 1994. Labeled by its proponents as the "Save Our State Initiative," this measure sought to cut illegal immigrants off from public services, such as education and medical assistance. According to its advocates, not only would Proposition 187 save the state treasury, but it would also cut down on the number of illegal immigrants—many of whom, they argued, had come mostly to take advantage of the free goods offered in America.

Opponents replied that although illegal immigration is surely a problem, the idea of cutting off public services could easily do more harm than good. They pointed out the public-health risks of denying illegal immigrants basic health care, such as immunizations that help control communicable diseases. And by denying an education to the children of illegal immigrants, many, with nothing to do all day, they argued, would inevitably turn to crime. Besides, though they may be here illegally, these immigrants pay sales taxes and rent—a portion of which indirectly goes to the state when their landlords pay their property taxes. Given that they contribute to the tax base that pays for public services, opponents of Proposition 187 argued that they should in all fairness be entitled to make use of them.

The proponents of Proposition 187 won at the ballot box. However, they lost in their attempts to get the measure enforced. The courts ruled that the proposition violated the rights of illegal immigrants, as well as national laws concerning eligibility for federally funded benefits. Overall, the proposition was held to be an unconstitutional state scheme to regulate immigration.

California's experience with Proposition 187 has not stopped other states from trying to follow a similar course. In 2007, Oklahoma Governor Brad Henry signed into law the "Taxpayer and Citizen Protection Act," which many advocates of cracking down on illegal immigration praised as the most meaningful piece of immigration reform in the country. Like California's Proposition 187, this act was designed to deny illegal immigrants any right to receive welfare benefits, scholarships, and all but emergency medical care. The act also made it a crime to transport or house illegal immigrants in the state of Oklahoma. As with California's law in the 1990s, the Oklahoma law was immediately challenged in court by Hispanic groups on the grounds that the federal government is responsible for enforcing immigration laws, not the states.

Until the federal government comes up with a comprehensive immigration reform package, it is likely that states will continue to experiment with ways to deal with undocumented immigrants. In 2008, the parties offered widely different approaches to this policy issue. The Republican Party platform emphasized tighter border security, and advocated "smarter enforcement at the workplace, against illegal workers and lawbreaking employers alike, along with those who traffic in fraudulent documents." In contrast, the Democratic Party platform proposed "a system that requires undocumented immigrants who are in good standing to pay a fine, pay taxes, learn English, and go to the back of the line for the opportunity to become citizens." The Republican platform called such a proposal "amnesty" and argued that "the rule of law suffers if government policies reward illegal activity."

What do you think? Do you think a tough approach is the way to go, or do you favor incorporating into American society illegal immigrants who prove themselves worthy? What are the advantages and disadvantages of each approach?

Unlike Hispanics who have come to America to escape poverty, the recent influx of Asians has been driven by a new class of professional workers looking for greater opportunity. Asians who have come to America since the 1965 Immigration Act[5] opened the nation's doors to them make up the most highly skilled immigrant group in American history.[6] Indeed, Asian Americans have often been called the super-achievers of the minority majority. This is especially true in the case of educational attainment—49 percent of Asian Americans over the age of 25 hold a college degree, almost twice the national average. As a result, their median family income has already surpassed that of non-Hispanic Whites. Although still a very small minority group, Asian Americans have had some notable political successes. In 1996, Gary Locke (a Chinese American) was elected governor of Washington, in 2001 Norman Mineta (a Japanese American) was appointed to be secretary of transportation, and in 2007 Bobby Jindal (an Indian American) was elected governor of Louisiana.

By the time this little girl (born in China but now an American citizen) is eligible to vote, Asian-Americans will represent 7 percent of the U.S. population. As the most highly educated segment of the coming "minority majority," it is likely that they will be exercising a good deal of political power by then.

Whereas Asian Americans are the best off of America's minority groups, by far the worst off is the one indigenous minority known today as Native Americans. Before Europeans arrived in America, 12 million to 15 million Native Americans lived here. War and disease reduced their numbers to a mere 210,000 by 1910. About 4 million Americans currently list themselves as being of Native American heritage. Statistics show that they are the least healthy, the poorest, and the least educated group in the American melting pot. Only a handful of Native Americans have found wealth; even fewer have found power. Some tribes have discovered oil or other minerals on their land and have used these resources successfully. Other tribes have opened profitable casinos on their native lands. Many Native Americans, though, remain economically and politically disadvantaged in American society. In the Dakotas, site of the largest Sioux reservations, census data show that roughly half the Native Americans live below the poverty line.

Americans live in an increasingly multicultural and multilingual society. Yet, regardless of ethnic background, most Americans share a common **political culture**—an overall set of values widely shared within a society. For example, there is much agreement among ethnic groups about many basic American values, such as the principle of treating all equally. Yet not all observers view this most recent wave of immigration without concern. Ellis Cose, a prominent journalist, has written that "racial animosity has proven to be both an enduring American phenomenon and an invaluable political tool." Because America has entered a period of rapid ethnic change, Cose predicts immigration "will be a magnet for conflict and hostility."[7]

political culture
An overall set of values widely shared within a society.

The emergence of the minority majority is just one of several major demographic changes that have altered the face of American politics. In addition, the population has been moving and aging.

THE REGIONAL SHIFT

For most of American history, the most populous states were concentrated in the states north of the Mason–Dixon Line and east of the Mississippi River. As you can see in Figure 6.2, though, since World War II much of America's population growth has been centered in the West and South. In particular, the populations of Florida, California, and Texas have grown rapidly as people moved to the Sun

Belt. From 1990 to 2000, the rate of population growth was 24 percent in Florida, 14 percent in California, and 23 percent in Texas. In contrast, population growth in the Northeast was a scant 5 percent.

Demographic changes are associated with political changes. States gain or lose congressional representation as their population changes, and thus power shifts as well. This **reapportionment** process occurs once a decade, after every census. After each census, the 435 seats in the House of Representatives are reallocated to the states on the basis of population changes. Thus, as California grew in population size, its representation in the House increased from just 23 in 1950 to 53 after the 2000 census. New York, on the other hand, lost about one-third of its delegation during the same period.

reapportionment

The process of reallocating seats in the House of Representatives every 10 years on the basis of the results of the census.

FIGURE 6.2

Shifting Population

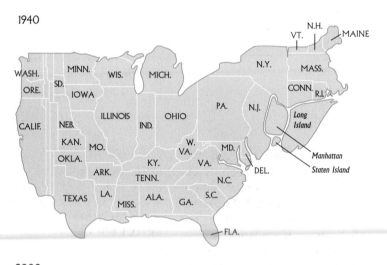

These maps paint a population portrait of the United States over the past six decades. The states are drawn to scale on the basis of population. In 1940, the most populous states were concentrated east of the Mississippi River. New York, Pennsylvania, and Illinois stand out. By 2000 the national population picture—and the map—had changed considerably. Today, the country's 300 million citizens are scattered more widely, and although large concentrations of population still dominate the East, there has been huge growth on the West Coast, in Texas, and in Florida.

Source: The 1940 map was the work of the National Opinion Research Center, University of Denver, as printed in John Gunther's 1946 book *Inside U.S.A.*

THE GRAYING OF AMERICA

Florida, currently the nation's fourth most populous state, has grown in large part as a result of its attractiveness to senior citizens. Nationwide, the fastest-growing age-group in America is composed of citizens over 65. Not only are people living longer as a result of medical advances, but in addition the fertility rate has dropped substantially. In 1960, the typical American woman bore 3.6 children; today it is about 2.1.

Social Security is structured as a pay-as-you-go system. That means today's workers pay the benefits for today's retirees. In 1940, there were 42 workers per retiree; today there are three. By 2040 there will be only two, which will put tremendous pressure on the Social Security system. Begun under the New Deal, Social Security is exceeded only by national defense as America's most costly public policy. The current group of older Americans and those soon to follow can lay claim to trillions of dollars guaranteed by Social Security. People who have been promised benefits naturally expect to collect them, especially benefits for which they have made monthly contributions. Thus, both political parties have long treated Social Security benefits as sacrosanct. For example, whenever President George W. Bush spoke on behalf of his proposal to allow younger workers to put part of their Social Security payroll taxes into personal retirement accounts, he carefully stated his view that Social Security should remain unchanged for anyone born before 1950.

HOW AMERICANS LEARN ABOUT POLITICS: POLITICAL SOCIALIZATION

As the most experienced segment of the population, the elderly have undergone the most **political socialization.** Political socialization is "the process through which an individual acquires his or her particular political orientations—his or her knowledge, feelings, and evaluations regarding his or her political world."[8] As people become more socialized with age, their political orientations grow firmer. It should not be surprising that governments aim their socialization efforts largely at the young, not the elderly. Authoritarian regimes are particularly concerned with indoctrinating their citizens at an early age. For example, youth groups in the former Soviet Union were organized into the Komsomols, the Young Communist League. Membership in these groups was helpful in gaining admission to college and entering certain occupations. In the Komsomols, Soviet youth were taught their government's view of the advantages of communism (though apparently not well enough to keep the system going). In contrast, socialization is a much more subtle process in the United States.

political socialization
The process through which a young person acquires political orientations as they grow up, based on inputs from parents, teachers, the media, and friends.

THE PROCESS OF POLITICAL SOCIALIZATION

Only a small portion of Americans' political learning is formal. Civics or government classes in high school teach citizens some of the nuts and bolts of government—how many senators each state has, what presidents do, and so on. But such formal socialization is only the tip of the iceberg. Americans do most of their political learning without teachers or classes.

Informal learning is really much more important than formal, in-class learning about politics. Most informal socialization is almost accidental. Few parents sit down with their children and say, "Johnny, let us tell you why we're Republicans." Words like *pick up, absorb,* and *acquire* perhaps best describe the informal side of socialization. The family, the media, and the schools all serve as important agents of socialization.

The Family   The family's role in socialization is central because of its monopoly on two crucial resources in the early years: time and emotional commitment. The powerful influence of the family is not easily undermined. Most students in an American government class like to think of themselves as independent thinkers, especially when it comes to politics. Yet one can predict how the majority of young people will vote simply by knowing the political leanings of their parents.[9]

As children approach adult status, though, some degree of adolescent rebellion against parents and their beliefs often takes place. Witnessing the outpouring of youthful rebellion in the late 1960s and early 1970s, many people thought a generation gap was opening up. Radical youth supposedly condemned their backward-thinking parents. Although such a gap did exist in a few families, the overall evidence for it was slim. Eight years after Jennings and Niemi first interviewed a sample of high school seniors and their parents in the mid-1960s, they still found far more agreement than disagreement across the generational divide.[10] Recent research has demonstrated that one of the reasons for the long-lasting impact of parental influence on political attitudes is simply genetics, as shown by the data presented in Table 6.1.

The Mass Media   The mass media are "the new parent," according to many observers. Average grade-school youngsters spend more time each week watching television than they spend at school. And television now displaces parents as the chief source of information as children get older.

Unfortunately, today's generation of young adults is significantly less likely to watch television news and read newspapers than their elders. Many studies have attributed the relative lack of political knowledge of today's youth to their media consumption or, more appropriately, to their lack of it.[11] In 1965, Gallup found virtually no difference between age categories in frequency of following politics through the media. In recent years, however, a considerable age gap has opened up, with older people paying the most attention to the news and young adults the least. The median age of viewers of the CBS, ABC, and NBC News in 2006 was 60 years of age—18 years older than the audience for a typical prime-time program.[12] If you have ever turned on the TV news and wondered why so many of the commercials seem to be for various prescription drugs, now you know why.

School   Political socialization is as important to a government as it is to an individual. This is one reason why governments (including America's) often use schools to promote national loyalty and support for its basic values. In most American schools, the day begins with the Pledge of Allegiance. During the 1988 presidential campaign, George Bush argued that teachers should be required to lead students in the Pledge. His opponent, Michael Dukakis, had vetoed a bill to require this in Massachusetts, claiming that it was unconstitutional. Underlying Bush's argument was the assumption that proper socialization in the schools was crucial to the American political system—a position Dukakis disagreed with more in terms of means than in ends.

Governments throughout the world use schools to attempt to raise children committed to the basic values of the system. For years, American children have been successfully educated about the virtues of capitalism and democracy. In the hands of an unscrupulous government, though, educational socialization can sometimes be a dangerous tool. For example, in Nazi Germany, textbooks were used to justify murderous policies. Consider the following example from a Nazi-era math book:

> If a mental patient costs 4 Reichsmarks a day in maintenance, a cripple 5.50, and a criminal 3.50, and about 50,000 of these people are in our institutions, how much does it cost our state at a daily rate of 4 Reichsmarks—and how many marriage loans of 1,000 Reichsmarks per couple could have been given out instead?[13]

TABLE 6.1

The Role of Genetics in Transmitting Political Attitudes

In an article published in 2005, Alford, Funk, and Hibbing demonstrate the impact of genetics on political values by comparing identical and nonidentical twins. If the political similarity between parents and their offspring is completely due to environmental factors, then the correspondence between the beliefs of identical and nonidentical twins ought to be about equal because both types of twins share the same home environment. However, if genetics are an important factor, then identical twins should be found to agree with one another more often than nonidentical twins, as they share the same genes. In the world of genetics research, comparing different kinds of twins has become known as the "gold test," as it enables scholars to control for environmental factors while varying genetic factors.

In the data that Alford, Funk, and Hibbing analyzed there was a Wilson-Patterson Attitude Inventory. This involved presenting respondents with items like "the death penalty" and asking them whether they agreed or disagreed with this or were uncertain. In the following table, the correlations between twins are shown on a variety of items that relate to political issues. The higher the correlation, the more similarity there was in the attitudes of the twins. As you can see, in every case there was substantially more agreement among the identical twins—clearly demonstrating that genetics play an important role in shaping political attitudes.

	IDENTICAL TWINS	NONIDENTICAL TWINS
School prayer	.66	.46
The draft	.41	.21
Pacifism	.34	.15
Unions	.44	.26
Socialism	.43	.25
Foreign aid	.41	.23
Immigration	.45	.29
Women's liberation	.46	.30
The death penalty	.56	.40
Gay rights	.60	.46
Nuclear power	.42	.29
Abortion	.64	.52

Source: John R. Alford, Carolyn L. Funk, and John R. Hibbing, "Are Political Orientations Genetically Transmitted?", *American Political Science Review*, May 2005, 153–67.

One can only imagine how students' constant exposure to this kind of thinking warped the minds of some young people growing up in Nazi Germany.

Both authoritarian and democratic governments care that students learn the positive features of their political system because it helps ensure that youth will grow up to be supportive citizens. David Easton and Jack Dennis have argued that "those children who begin to develop positive feelings toward the political authorities will grow into adults who will be less easily disenchanted with the system than those children who early acquire negative, hostile sentiments."[14] Of course, this is not always the case. Well-socialized youths of the 1960s led the opposition to the American regime and the war in Vietnam. It could be argued, however, that even these protestors had been positively shaped by the socialization process, for the goal of most activists was to make the system more democratically responsive rather than to change American government radically.

Today, education is often the issue that people cite as the most important to them, and there is no doubt that educational policy matters a great deal. Most

American schools are public schools, financed by the government. Their textbooks are often chosen by the local and state boards, and teachers are certified by the state government. Schooling is perhaps the most obvious intrusion of the government into Americans' socialization. Education exerts a profound influence on a variety of political attitudes and behavior. Better-educated citizens are more likely to vote in elections, they exhibit more knowledge about politics and public policy, and they are more tolerant of opposing (even radical) opinions.

The payoffs of schooling extend beyond better jobs and better pay. Educated citizens also more closely approximate the model of a democratic citizen. A formal civics course may not make much difference, but the whole context of education does. As Albert Einstein once said, "Schools need not preach political doctrine to defend democracy. If they shape men and women capable of critical thought and trained in social attitudes, that is all that is necessary."

POLITICAL LEARNING OVER A LIFETIME

Political learning does not, of course, end when one reaches 18 or even when one graduates from college. Politics is a lifelong activity. Because America is an aging society, it is important to consider the effects of growing older on political learning and behavior.

Aging increases political participation as well as strength of party attachment. Young adults (those 18 through 25) lack experience with politics. Because political behavior is to some degree learned behavior, there is some learning yet to do. Political participation rises steadily with age until the infirmities of old age make it harder to participate, as can be seen in the data presented in Figure 6.3. Similarly, strength of party identification also increases as one grows older and often develops a pattern for usually voting for one party or another.

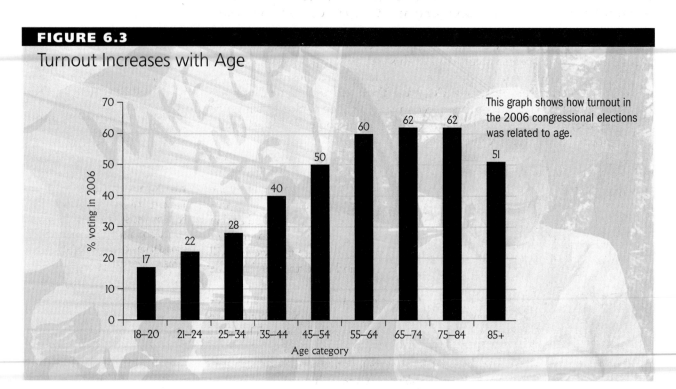

FIGURE 6.3
Turnout Increases with Age

This graph shows how turnout in the 2006 congressional elections was related to age.

Source: Authors' analysis of 2006 Census Bureau data via Data Ferret.

Politics, like most other things, is thus a learned behavior. Americans learn to vote, to pick a political party, and to evaluate political events in the world around them. One of the products of all this learning is what is known as public opinion.

MEASURING PUBLIC OPINION AND POLITICAL INFORMATION

Before examining the role that public opinion plays in American politics, it is essential to learn about the science of public opinion measurement. How do we really know the approximate answers to questions such as what percentage of young people favor abortion rights, how many Hispanics supported Barack Obama's 2008 campaign, or what percentage of the public continues to believe that Iraq had weapons of mass destruction before the U.S. invasion? Polls provide these answers, but there is much skepticism about polls. Many people wonder how accurately public opinion can be measured by interviewing only 1,000 or 1,500 people around the country. This section provides an explanation of how polling works; it is hoped that this will enable you to become a well-informed consumer of polls.

HOW POLLS ARE CONDUCTED

Public opinion polling is a relatively new science. It was first developed by a young man named George Gallup, who initially did some polling for his mother-in-law, a long-shot candidate for secretary of state in Iowa in 1932. With the Democratic landslide of that year, she won a stunning victory, thereby further stimulating Gallup's interest in politics. From that little acorn the mighty oak of public opinion polling has grown. The firm that Gallup founded spread throughout the democratic world, and in some languages *Gallup* is actually the word used for an opinion poll.[15]

It would be prohibitively expensive and time consuming to ask every citizen his or her opinion on a whole range of issues. Instead, polls rely on a **sample** of the population—a relatively small proportion of people who are chosen to represent the whole. Herbert Asher draws an analogy to a blood test to illustrate the principle of sampling.[16] Your doctor does not need to drain a gallon of blood from you to determine whether you have mononucleosis, AIDS, or any other disease. Rather, a small sample of blood will reveal its properties.

In public opinion polling, a sample of about 1,000 to 1,500 people can accurately represent the "universe" of potential voters. The key to the accuracy of opinion polls is the technique of **random sampling**, which operates on the principle that everyone should have an equal probability of being selected as part of the sample. Your chance of being asked to be in the poll should therefore be as good as that of anyone else—rich or poor, African American or White, young or old, male or female. If the sample is randomly drawn, about 12 percent of those interviewed will be African American, slightly over 50 percent female, and so forth, matching the population as a whole.

Remember that the science of polling involves estimation; a sample can represent the population with only a certain degree of confidence. The level of confidence is known as the **sampling error**, which depends on the size of the sample. The more people interviewed in a poll, the more confident one can be of the results. A typical poll of about 1,500 to 2,000 respondents has a sampling error of ±3 percent. What this means is that 95 percent of the time the poll results are within 3 percent of what the entire population thinks. If 60 percent of the sample say they approve of the job

sample
A relatively small proportion of people who are chosen in a survey so as to be representative of the whole.

random sampling
The key technique employed by sophisticated survey researchers, which operates on the principle that everyone should have an equal probability of being selected for the sample.

sampling error
The level of confidence in the findings of a public opinion poll. The more people interviewed, the more confident one can be of the results.

You Are a Polling Consultant

the president is doing, one can be pretty certain that the true figure is between 57 and 63 percent.

In order to obtain results that will usually be within sampling error, researchers must follow proper sampling techniques. In perhaps the most infamous survey ever, a 1936 *Literary Digest* poll underestimated the vote for President Franklin Roosevelt by 19 percent, erroneously predicting a big victory for Republican Alf Landon. The well-established magazine suddenly became a laughingstock and soon went out of business. Although the number of responses the magazine obtained for its poll was a staggering 2,376,000, its polling methods were badly flawed. Trying to reach as many people as possible, the magazine drew names from the biggest lists they could find: telephone books and motor vehicle records. In the midst of the Great Depression, the people on these lists were above the average income level (only 40 percent of the public had telephones then; fewer still owned cars) and were more likely to vote Republican. The moral of the story is this: Accurate representation, not the number of responses, is the most important feature of a public opinion survey. Indeed, as polling techniques have advanced over the past 70 years, typical sample sizes have been getting smaller, not larger.

The newest computer and telephone technology has made surveying less expensive and more commonplace. In the early days of polling, pollsters needed a national network of interviewers to traipse door-to-door in their localities with a clipboard of questions. Now most polling is done on the telephone with samples selected through **random-digit dialing**. Calls are placed to phone numbers within randomly chosen exchanges (for example, 512-471-XXXX) around the country. In this manner, both listed and unlisted numbers are reached at a cost of about one-fifth that of person-to-person interviewing. There are a couple of disadvantages, however. About 7 percent of the population does not have a phone, and people are somewhat less willing to participate over the telephone than in person—it is easier to hang up than to slam the door in someone's face. These are small trade-offs for political candidates running for minor offices, for whom telephone polls are the only affordable method of gauging public opinion. However, in this era of cell phones, many pollsters are starting to worry whether this methodology will continue to work much longer.

random-digit dialing
A technique used by pollsters to place telephone calls randomly to both listed and unlisted numbers when conducting a survey.

From its modest beginning with George Gallup's 1932 polls for his mother-in-law in Iowa, polling has become a big business. Public opinion polling is one of those American innovations, like soft drinks and fast-food restaurants, that has spread throughout the world. From Manhattan to Moscow, from Tulsa to Tokyo, people want to know what other people think.

Public opinion polls these days are done mostly over the telephone. Interviewers, most of whom are young people (and frequently college students), sit in front of computer terminals and read the questions that appear on the screen to randomly chosen individuals they have reached on the phone. They then enter the appropriate coded responses directly into the computer database. Such efficient procedures make it possible for analysts to get survey results very quickly.

THE ROLE OF POLLS IN AMERICAN DEMOCRACY

Polls help political candidates detect public preferences. Supporters of polling insist that it is a tool for democracy. With it, they say, policymakers can keep in touch with changing opinions on the issues. No longer do politicians have to wait until the next election to see whether the public approves or disapproves of the government's course. If the poll results suddenly turn, then government officials can make corresponding midcourse corrections. Indeed, it was George Gallup's fondest hope that polling could contribute to the democratic process by providing a way for public desires to be heard at times other than elections.

Critics of polling, by contrast, say it makes politicians more concerned with following than leading. Polls might have told the constitutional convention delegates that the Constitution was unpopular or might have told President Thomas Jefferson that people did not want the Louisiana Purchase. Certainly they would have told William Seward not to buy Alaska, a transaction known widely at the time as "Seward's Folly." Polls may thus discourage bold leadership, like that of Winston Churchill, who once said,

> Nothing is more dangerous than to live in the temperamental atmosphere of a Gallup poll, always taking one's pulse and taking one's temperature. . . . There is only one duty, only one safe course, and that is to try to be right and not to fear to do or say what you believe.[17]

Recent research by Jacobs and Shapiro argues that the common perception of politicians pandering to the results of public opinion polls may be mistaken. Their examination of major policy debates in the 1990s finds that political leaders "track public opinion not to make policy but rather to determine how to craft their public presentations and win public support for the policies they and their supporters favor."[18] Staff members in both the White House and Congress repeatedly remarked that their purpose in conducting polls was not to set policies but rather to find the key words and phrases with which to promote policies already in place. Thus, rather than using polls to identify centrist approaches that will have the broadest popular appeal, Jacobs and Shapiro argue that elites use them to formulate strategies that enable them to avoid compromising on what they want to do.

Polls can also weaken democracy by distorting the election process. They are often accused of creating a *bandwagon effect*. The wagon carrying the band was the centerpiece of nineteenth-century political parades, and enthusiastic supporters would literally jump on it. Today, the term refers to voters who support a candidate merely because they see that others are doing so. Although only 2 percent of people in a recent CBS/*New York Times* poll said that poll results had influenced them, 26 percent said they thought others had been influenced (showing that Americans feel that "it's the other person who's susceptible"). Beyond this, polls play to the media's interest in who's ahead in the race. The issues of recent presidential campaigns have sometimes been drowned out by a steady flood of poll results.

Probably the most widely criticized type of poll is the Election Day **exit poll**. For this type of poll, voting places are randomly selected around the country. Workers are then sent to these places and told to ask every tenth person how they voted. The results are accumulated toward the end of the day, enabling the television networks to project the outcomes of all but very close races before the polls even close. In the presidential elections of 1980, 1984, 1988, and 1996, the networks declared a national winner while millions on the West Coast still had hours to vote. Critics have charged that this practice discourages many people from voting and thereby affects the outcome of some state and local races.

In 2000, the exit polls received much of the blame for the media's inaccurate calls of the Florida result on election night. The fact that the Florida exit poll showed a small advantage for Gore contributed to their inaccurate projection of a Gore victory. Then, in 2004, the leaking of incomplete exit poll data via the Internet led to the dissemination of stories leading people to expect a Kerry victory as the votes were being counted. This time, however, the television networks were much more cautious in interpreting exit poll results, having learned their lesson from 2000 that a winner shouldn't be declared until a candidate clearly establishes an insurmountable margin of votes over the other.

exit poll
Public opinion surveys used by major media pollsters to predict electoral winners with speed and precision.

War, Peace, and Public Opinion

Perhaps the most pervasive criticism of polling is that by altering the wording of a question, pollsters can usually get the results they want. Sometimes subtle changes in question wording can produce dramatic differences. For example, in August 2005 the percentage of the public who thought the U.S. should withdraw its troops from Iraq was 15 points higher in the Harris poll than in the ABC/*Washington Post* poll. The Harris poll asked the following question: "Do you favor keeping a large number of U.S. troops in Iraq until there is a stable government there or bringing most of our troops home in the next year?" The ABC/*Washington Post* poll posed the question somewhat differently: "Do you think the United States should keep its military forces in Iraq until civil order is restored there, even if that means continued U.S. military casualties, or, do you think the United States should withdraw its military forces from Iraq in order to avoid further military casualties, even if it means civil order is not restored there?"[19] Apparently, the wording in the ABC/*Washington Post* poll made people think more about the possible negative consequences of withdrawing from Iraq, which in turn made them less likely to favor this option. This example illustrates why it is crucial to carefully evaluate how questions are posed when reading public opinion data. Fortunately, as the Internet has progressed, most newspapers and polling organizations have come to routinely post their questionnaires online, thereby making it much easier than ever before for everyone to scrutinize their work.

Polling sounds scientific with its talk of random samples and sampling error; it is easy to take results for solid fact. But being an informed consumer of polls requires more than just a nuts-and-bolts knowledge of how they are conducted. You should think about whether the questions are fair and unbiased before making too much of the results. The good—or the harm—that polls do depends on how well the data are collected and how thoughtfully the data are interpreted.

WHAT POLLS REVEAL ABOUT AMERICANS' POLITICAL INFORMATION

Abraham Lincoln spoke stirringly of the inherent wisdom of the American people: "It is true that you may fool all of the people some of the time; and you can even fool some of the people all of the time; but you can't fool all of the people all the time." Obviously, Lincoln recognized the complexity of public opinion.

Thomas Jefferson and Alexander Hamilton had very different views about the wisdom of common people. Jefferson trusted people's good sense and believed that education would enable them to take the tasks of citizenship ever more seriously. Toward that end, he founded the University of Virginia. Hamilton held a contrasting view. His infamous words "Your people, sir, are a great beast" do not reflect confidence in people's capacity for self-government.

If there had been polling data in the early days of the American republic, Hamilton would probably have delighted in throwing some of the results in Jefferson's face. If public opinion analysts agree about anything, it is that the level of public knowledge about politics is dismally low. As discussed in Chapter 1, this is particularly true for young people, but the overall levels of political knowledge are not particularly encouraging either. For example, in October 2008 the National Annenberg Election Survey asked a set of factual questions about some prominent policy stands taken by Obama and McCain during the campaign. The results were as follows:

- 63 percent knew that Obama would provide more middle class tax cuts
- 47 percent knew McCain favored overturning Roe v. Wade
- 30 percent knew McCain was more likely to support free trade agreements
- 8 percent knew that both candidates supported stem cell research funding

If so many voters did not know these hotly debated issues, then there is little doubt that most were also unaware of the detailed policy platforms the candidates were running on.

Why It Matters
Political Knowledge of the Electorate

The average American clearly has less political information than most analysts consider to be desirable. While this level of information is surely adequate to maintain our democracy, survey data plainly show that citizens with above-average levels of political knowledge are more likely to vote and to have stable and consistent opinions on policy issues. If political knowledge were to increase overall, it would in all likelihood be good for American democracy.

No amount of Jeffersonian faith in the wisdom of the common people can erase the fact that Americans are not well informed about politics. Polls have regularly found that less than half the public can name their representative in the House, and much less say how he or she generally votes. Asking most people to explain their opinion on whether trade policy toward China should be liberalized, or the proposed "Star Wars" missile defense system, or whether the strategic oil reserve should be tapped when gasoline prices skyrocket often elicits blank looks. When trouble flares in a far-off country, polls regularly find that people have no idea where that country is. In fact, surveys show that citizens around the globe lack a basic awareness of the world around them (see "America in Perspective: Citizens Show Little Knowledge of Geography").

AMERICA IN PERSPECTIVE

Citizens Show Little Knowledge of Geography

In 2002, a major cross-national study sponsored by *National Geographic* interviewed representative samples of 18- to 24-year-olds to assess their knowledge of world geography. As this test shows, the results were discouraging—particularly with regard to American youth, who came in last in terms of placing countries accurately on the map. The average young person in the United States got less than half the questions right. Believe it or not, 11 percent of young Americans could not even find their own country on the map. Despite the American military campaign in Afghanistan after September 11, only 17 percent could correctly place this country on the map. Such lack of basic geographic knowledge is fairly common throughout the world. Here is the average score for each of the 9 countries in which the test was administered:

COUNTRY	AVERAGE % CORRECT
Sweden	79
Germany	77
Italy	75
France	71
Japan	62
Canada	56
United Kingdom	54
Mexico	49
United States	**46**

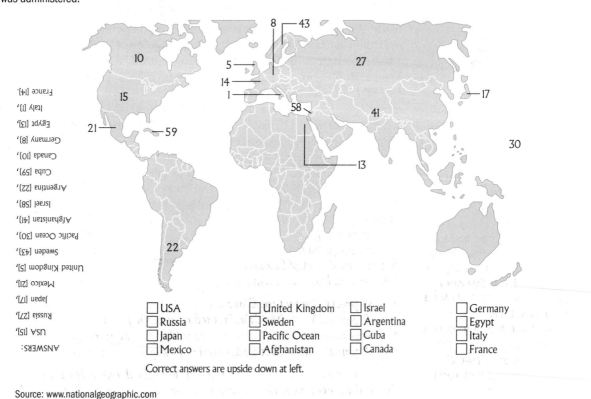

ANSWERS:
USA [15], Russia [27], Japan [17], Mexico [21], United Kingdom [5], Sweden [43], Pacific Ocean [30], Afghanistan [41], Israel [58], Argentina [22], Cuba [59], Canada [10], Germany [8], Egypt [13], Italy [1], France [14].

Correct answers are upside down at left.

☐ USA ☐ United Kingdom ☐ Israel ☐ Germany
☐ Russia ☐ Sweden ☐ Argentina ☐ Egypt
☐ Japan ☐ Pacific Ocean ☐ Cuba ☐ Italy
☐ Mexico ☐ Afghanistan ☐ Canada ☐ France

Source: www.nationalgeographic.com

As Lance Bennett points out, these findings provide "a source of almost bitter humor in light of what the polls tell us about public information on other subjects."[20] He notes that more people know their astrological sign (76 percent) than know the name of their representative in the House. Slogans from TV commercials are better recognized than famous political figures. A Zogby national poll in August 2006 found that 74 percent of respondents were able to name each of the "Three Stooges"—Larry, Curly and Moe—whereas just 42 percent could name each of the three branches of the U.S. government—judicial, executive and legislative.

How can Americans, who live in the most information-rich society in the world, be so ill informed about politics? Some blame the schools. E. D. Hirsch Jr. criticizes schools for a failure to teach "cultural literacy."[21] People, he says, often lack the basic contextual knowledge—for example, where Afghanistan is, what the Vietnam War was about, and so forth—necessary to understand and use the information they receive from the news media or from listening to political candidates. Indeed, it has been found that increased levels of education over the past five decades have scarcely raised public knowledge about politics.[22] Despite the apparent glut of information provided by the media, Americans do not remember much about what they are exposed to through the media. (Of course, there are many critics who say that the media fail to provide much meaningful information, a topic that will be discussed in Chapter 7.)

The "paradox of mass politics," says Russell Neuman, is that the American political system works as well as it does given the discomforting lack of public knowledge about politics.[23] Part of the reason for this phenomenon is that people may not know the ins and outs of policy questions or the actors on the political stage, but they know what basic values they want upheld.

THE DECLINE OF TRUST IN GOVERNMENT

Sadly, the American public has become increasingly dissatisfied with government over the past four decades, as shown in Figure 6.4. In the late 1950s and early 1960s, about three-quarters of Americans said that they trusted the government in Washington to do the right thing always or mostly. Following the 1964 election, however, researchers started to see a precipitous drop in public trust in government. First Vietnam and then Watergate shook the people's confidence in the federal government. The economic troubles of the Carter years and the Iran hostage crisis helped continue the slide; by 1980, only one-quarter of the public thought the government could be trusted most of the time or always. During the Reagan years, public cynicism abated a bit, but by 1994, trust in government had plummeted again to another all-time low. Since 1994, trust in government has improved somewhat, but it seems unlikely that we will see a long-lasting return to the optimistic levels of trust in government of the early 1960s. For a brief time after September 11, 2001, media polls showed that trust in government had risen to nearly this level, but by 2006, trust levels had fallen back to below where they were before the events of September 11th.

Some analysts have noted that a healthy dose of public cynicism helps to keep politicians on their toes. Others, however, note that a democracy is based on the consent of the governed and that a lack of public trust in the government is a reflection of their belief that the system is not serving them well. These more pessimistic analysts have frequently wondered whether such a cynical population would unite behind their government in a national emergency. Although the short-lived decrease in political cynicism after September 11 was not too great, the fact that it

FIGURE 6.4

The Decline of Trust in Government, 1958–2006

This graph shows how people have responded over time to the following question: How much of the time do you think you can trust the government in Washington to do what is right—just about always, most of the time, or only some of the time?

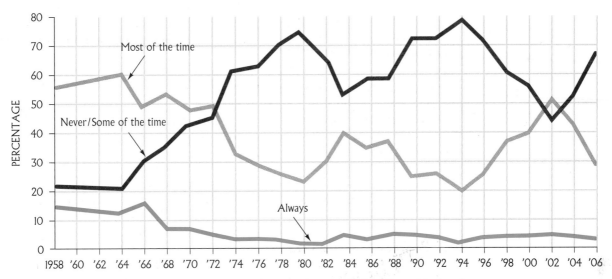

Sources: Authors' analysis of 1958–2004 American National Election Study data; December 2006 Pew Research Center poll.

occurred at all indicates that cynicism will not stop Americans from rallying behind their government in times of national crisis. Widespread political cynicism about government apparently applies only to "normal" times; it has not eroded Americans' fundamental faith in our democracy.

Perhaps the largest impact of declining trust in government since the 1960s has been the way it has drained public support for policies that address the problems of poverty and racial inequality. Mark Hetherington argues, "People need to trust the government when they pay the costs but do not receive the benefits, which is exactly what antipoverty and race-targeted programs require of most Americans. When government programs require people to make sacrifices, they need to trust that the result will be a better future for everyone."[24] Hetherington's careful data analysis shows that declining trust in government has caused many Americans to believe that "big government" solutions to social problems are wasteful and impractical, thereby draining public support from them.

WHAT AMERICANS VALUE: POLITICAL IDEOLOGIES

A coherent set of values and beliefs about public policy is a **political ideology**. Liberal ideology, for example, supports a wide scope for the central government, often involving policies that aim to promote equality. Conservative ideology, in contrast, supports a less active scope of government that gives freer reign to the private sector. Table 6.2 attempts to summarize some of the key differences between liberals and conservatives.

political ideology

A coherent set of beliefs about politics, public policy, and public purpose. It helps give meaning to political events, personalities, and policies.

TABLE 6.2

How to Tell a Liberal from a Conservative

Liberal and *conservative*—these labels are thrown around in American politics as though everyone knows what they mean. Here are some of the political beliefs likely to be preferred by liberals and conservatives. This table, to be sure, is oversimplified.

	LIBERALS	CONSERVATIVES
Foreign Policy		
Military spending	Believe we should spend less	Believe we should maintain peace through strength
Use of force	Less willing to commit troops to action, such as in Iraq War	More likely to support military intervention around the world
Social Policy		
Abortion	Support "freedom of choice"	Support "right to life"
Prayer in schools	Are opposed	Are supportive
Affirmative action	Favor	Oppose
Economic Policy		
Scope of government	View government as a regulator in the public interest	Favor free-market solutions
Taxes	Want to tax the rich more	Want to keep taxes low
Spending	Want to spend more on the poor	Want to keep spending low
Crime		
How to cut crime	Believe we should solve the problems that cause crime	Believe we should stop "coddling criminals"
Defendants' rights	Believe we should guard them carefully	Believe we should stop letting criminals hide behind laws

WHO ARE THE LIBERALS AND CONSERVATIVES?

Who Are Liberals and Conservatives? What's the Difference?

Overall, more Americans consistently choose the ideological label of conservative over liberal. The 2006 General Social Survey found that of those who labeled themselves, 37 percent were conservatives, 38 percent were moderates, and just 25 percent were liberals. The predominance of conservative thinking in America is one of the most important reasons for the relatively restrained scope of government activities compared to most European nations.

Yet there are some groups that are more liberal than others and thus would generally like to see the government do more. Among people under the age of 30, there are just as many liberals as conservatives, as shown in "Young People and Politics: How Younger and Older Americans Compare on the Issues." The younger the individual, the less likely that person is to be a conservative. The fact that younger people are also less likely to vote means that conservatives are overrepresented at the polls.

In general, groups with political clout tend to be more conservative than groups whose members have often been shut out from the halls of political power. This is because excluded groups have often looked to the government to rectify the inequalities they have faced. For example, African Americans benefited from government activism in the form of the major civil rights bills of the 1960s to bring them into the mainstream of American life. Many African American leaders currently place a high priority on retaining social welfare and affirmative action programs in order to assist their progress. It should come as little surprise then that African Americans are more liberal than the national average. Similarly, Hispanics

How Younger and Older Americans Compare on the Issues

The following table compares young adults and senior citizens on a variety of issues. Because younger citizens are much less likely to vote than older people, the differences between the two groups give us some indication of how public opinion is not accurately reflected at the polls. As you can see, younger people are substantially more likely to call themselves liberal than senior citizens. Befitting their liberalism, they are more supportive of government policies to reduce income differences. And their spending priorities are more on the liberal side as well: They are more in favor of spending on education and environmental protection and less inclined than seniors to spend more on defense. Younger voters are also more supportive of gay rights.

However, younger people are not always more likely to take the liberal side of an issue. Younger people are more supportive of investing Social Security funds in the stock market and more in favor of school vouchers to help parents send their children to private schools. Both of these reform proposals have been primarily championed by conservative politicians such as George W. Bush. The fact that young adults are the most likely to support them suggests that the nation's youth are most open to new ideas, be they liberal or conservative.

QUESTIONS FOR DISCUSSION

➤ Only a few issues could be covered in this table because of space limitations. Are there other issues on which you think there are likely to be differences of opinion between young and old people?

➤ Do you think the differences shown in the table are important? If so, what difference might it make to the American political agenda if young people were to vote at the same rate as the elderly?

	18–29 YEARS OLD	65 AND OLDER
Very liberal	7	2
Liberal	25	14
Moderate	39	39
Conservative	24	38
Very conservative	5	7
Favor investing Social Security funds in the stock market	71	45
Oppose investing Social Security funds in the stock market	29	55
Favor school vouchers	44	30
Oppose school vouchers	56	70
Spending on education should be increased	81	53
Spending on education is about right	16	34
Spending on education should be reduced	3	13
Military spending should be increased	35	65
Military spending is about right	49	30
Military spending should be reduced	16	5
Favor gays in the military	64	53
Oppose gays in the military	36	47
Favor government policies to reduce income differences	61	42
Oppose government policies to reduce income differences	39	58
Spending to protect the environment should be increased	77	59
Spending to protect the environment is about right	18	28
Spending to protect the environment should be decreased	5	13

Source: Authors' analysis of the 2000 National Annenberg Election Study.

also are less conservative than Whites, and if this pattern continues, the influx of many more Hispanics into the electorate will move the country in a slightly more liberal direction.

Women are not a minority group, making up about 54 percent of the population, but they have nevertheless been politically and economically disadvantaged. Compared to men, women are more likely to support spending on social services and to oppose the higher levels of military spending, which conservatives typically advocate. These issues concerning the priorities of government rather than the issue of abortion—on which men and women actually differ very little—lead women to be significantly less conservative than men. This ideological difference between men and women has led to the **gender gap**, which refers to the regular pattern by which women are more likely to support Democratic candidates. Bill Clinton carried the women's vote while Bob Dole was preferred among men in 1996, making Clinton the first president who can be said to be elected via the support of only one gender. In 2008, exit polls showed that women were about 7 percent more likely to support Barack Obama than men.

The gender gap is a relatively new predictor of ideological positions, dating back only to 1980, when Ronald Reagan was first elected. A much more traditional source of division between liberals and conservatives has been financial status, or what is often known as social class. But in actuality, the relationship between family income and ideology is now relatively weak. As a result, social class has become much less predictive of political behavior than it used to be.[25]

The role of religion in influencing political ideology has also changed greatly in recent years. Catholics and Jews, as minority groups who struggled for equality, have long been more liberal than Protestants. Today, Jews remain by far the most liberal demographic group in the country.[26] However, the ideological gap between Catholics and Protestants is now smaller than the gender gap. Ideology is now determined more by religiosity—that is, the degree to which religion is important in one's life—than by religious denomination. What is known as the new Christian Right consists of Catholics and Protestants who consider themselves fundamentalists or "born again." The influx of new policy issues dealing with matters of morality and traditional family values has recently tied this aspect of religious beliefs to political ideology. Those who identify themselves as born-again Christians are currently the most conservative demographic group. On the other hand, people who say they have no religious affiliation (roughly one-tenth of the population) are more liberal than conservative.

Just as some people are very much guided by their religious beliefs whereas others are not, the same is true for political ideology. It would probably be a mistake to assume that when conservative candidates do better than they have in the past, this necessarily means people want more conservative policies, for not everyone thinks in ideological terms.

DO PEOPLE THINK IN IDEOLOGICAL TERMS?

The authors of the classic study *The American Voter* first examined how much people rely on ideology to guide their political thinking.[27] They divided the public into four groups, according to ideological sophistication. Their portrait of the American electorate was not flattering. Only 12 percent of the people showed evidence of thinking in ideological terms and thus were classified as *ideologues*. These people could connect their opinions and beliefs with broad policy positions taken by parties or candidates. They might say, for example, that they liked the Democrats because they were more liberal or the Republicans because they favored a smaller government. Forty-two percent of Americans were classified as *group*

gender gap

A term that refers to the regular pattern by which women are more likely to support Democratic candidates. Women tend to be significantly less conservative than men and are more likely to support spending on social services and to oppose higher levels of military spending.

Are You a Liberal or a Conservative?

benefits voters. These people thought of politics mainly in terms of the groups they liked or disliked; for example, "Republicans support small business owners like me" or "Democrats are the party of the working person." Twenty-four percent of the population were *nature of the times* voters. Their handle on politics was limited to whether the times seemed good or bad to them; they might vaguely link the party in power with the country's fortune or misfortune. Finally, 22 percent of the voters were devoid of any ideological or issue content in their political evaluations. They were called the *no issue content* group. Most of them simply voted routinely for a party or judged the candidates solely by their personalities. Overall, at least during the 1950s, Americans seemed to care little about the differences between liberal and conservative politics.

There has been much debate about whether this portrayal accurately characterizes the public today. Nie, Verba, and Petrocik took a look at the changing American voter, arguing that voters were more sophisticated in the 1970s than in the 1950s.[28] Others, though, have concluded that people seemed more informed and ideological only because the wording of the questions had changed.[29] Recently, the authors of *The American Voter Revisited* updated the analysis of *The American Voter* using survey data from the 2000 election. They found that just 20 percent of the population met the criteria for being classified as an ideologue in 2000, as compared to 12 percent in 1956. Echoing the analysts of the 1950s, they conclude that "It is problematic to attribute ideological meaning to aggregate voting patterns when most of the individuals making their decisions about the candidates are not motivated by ideological concepts."[30]

These findings do not mean that the vast majority of the population does not have a political ideology. Rather, for most people the terms *liberal* and *conservative* are just not as important as they are for the political elite such as politicians, activists, journalists, and the like. Relatively few people have ideologies that organize their political beliefs as clearly as shown in Table 6.2. Thus, the authors of *The American Voter* concluded that to speak of election results as indicating a movement of the public either left (to more liberal policies) or right (to more conservative policies) is not justified because most voters do not think in such terms. Furthermore, those who do are actually the least likely to shift from one election to the next. The relatively small percentage of voters who made up their minds in the last couple days of the Bush–Gore campaign in 2000 were more concerned with integrity and competence than ideology.

Morris Fiorina makes a similar argument with regard to the question of whether America is in the midst of a political culture war. In the media these days, one frequently hears claims that Americans are deeply divided on fundamental political issues, making it seem like there are two different nations—the liberal blue states versus the conservative red states. After a thorough examination of public opinion data, Fiorina concludes that "the views of the American citizenry look moderate, centrist, nuanced, ambivalent—choose your term—rather than extreme, polarized, unconditional, dogmatic."[31] He argues that the small groups of liberal and conservative activists who act as if they are at war with one another have left most Americans in a position analogous to "unfortunate citizens of some third-world countries who try to stay out of the crossfire while Maoist guerrillas and right-wing death squads shoot at each other."[32]

One of the topics that many commentators believe have led to a political culture war is that of gay rights. However, as shown in "A Generation of Change: Attitudes Toward Gays and Lesbians," the survey data over the past two decades show a growing acceptance of homosexuals among liberals, moderates, and conservatives alike. Rather than an ideological culture war, this example shows how all ideological groups have changed with the changing social mores of the times.

Attitudes Toward Gays and Lesbians

It is often said that public opinion surveys are merely "snapshots in time." What this means is that public opinion can change from one time point to the next, as people's attitudes are subject to change. Furthermore, generational replacement can often produce substantial changes in public opinion over an extended period of time, as the attitudes of new entrants into the electorate are sometimes quite different from generations that are dying out. Such is the case with attitudes toward gays and lesbians over the past five presidential elections.

The American National Election Studies have regularly asked respondents to rate gays and lesbians on a "feeling thermometer" scale ranging from 0 to 100. They are told that 0 represents very cool feelings, whereas 100 represents very warm feelings, with 50 being the neutral point. The following graph displays the average ratings that liberals, moderates, and conservatives gave gays and lesbians from 1988 to 2004. It is interesting to note that as recently as 1988, all three ideological groups expressed more negative than positive feelings toward gays and lesbians, giving them an average rating well below 50 degrees. If reports of a culture war were correct, then we would have seen liberals become more positive toward homosexuals and conservatives turn even more negative. This has certainly not been the case. By 2004, the average rating given to gays and lesbians had risen by 21 points among liberals and 18 points among moderates and conservatives. Thus, societal attitudes have changed across the political spectrum. A key reason for this change is that young people have expressed more favorable ratings toward gays and lesbians within each ideological group. This is clearly a case of a generation of change being driven by a new generation of voters.

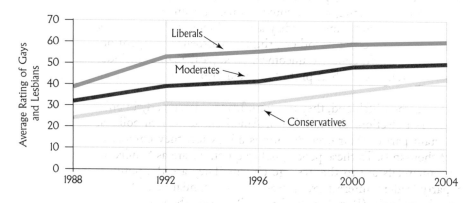

Source: Authors' analysis of American National Election Studies data.

HOW AMERICANS PARTICIPATE IN POLITICS

In politics, as in many other aspects of life, the squeaky wheel gets the grease. The way citizens "squeak" in politics is to participate. Americans have many avenues of political participation open to them:

- Mrs. Jones of Iowa City goes to a neighbor's living room to attend her local precinct's presidential caucus.
- Demonstrators against abortion protest at the Supreme Court on the anniversary of the *Roe v. Wade* decision.
- Parents in Alabama file a lawsuit to oppose textbooks that, in their opinion, promote "secular humanism."
- Mr. Smith, a Social Security recipient, writes to his senator to express his concern about a possible cut in his cost-of-living benefits.
- Over 120 million people vote in a presidential election.

All these activities are types of **political participation**, which encompasses the many activities in which citizens engage to influence the selection of political leaders

political participation
All the activities used by citizens to influence the selection of political leaders or the policies they pursue. The most common but not the only means of political participation in a democracy is voting. Other means include **protest** and **civil disobedience**.

or the policies they pursue.[33] Participation can be overt or subtle. The mass protests against communist rule throughout Eastern Europe in the fall of 1989 represented an avalanche of political participation, yet quietly writing a letter to your congressperson also represents political participation. Political participation can be violent or peaceful, organized or individual, casual or consuming.

Generally, the United States has a culture that values political participation. Americans express very high levels of pride in their democracy: the 2004 General Social Survey found that 84 percent said they were proud of how democracy works in the United States. Nevertheless, just 60 percent of adult American citizens voted in the presidential election of 2004, and only 40 percent turned out for the 2006 midterm elections. At the local level, the situation is even worse, with elections for city council and school board often drawing less than 10 percent of the eligible voters. (For more on voter turnout and why it is so low, see Chapter 10.)

CONVENTIONAL PARTICIPATION

Although the line is hard to draw, political scientists generally distinguish between two broad types of participation: conventional and unconventional. Conventional participation includes many widely accepted modes of influencing government—voting, trying to persuade others, ringing doorbells for a petition, running for office, and so on. In contrast, unconventional participation includes activities that are often dramatic, such as protesting, civil disobedience, and even violence.

For a few, politics is their lifeblood; they run for office, work regularly in politics, and live for the next election. The number of Americans for whom political activity is an important part of their everyday life is minuscule; they number at most in the tens of thousands. To these people, policy questions are as familiar as slogans on TV commercials are to the average citizen. They are the political elites—activists, party leaders, interest group leaders, judges, members of Congress, and other public officials. (Part 3 of this book will discuss the political elite in detail.)

Millions take part in political activities beyond simply voting. In two comprehensive studies of American political participation conducted by Sidney Verba and his colleagues, samples of Americans were asked in 1967 and 1987 about their role in various kinds of political activities, such as voting, working in campaigns, contacting government officials, signing petitions, working on local community issues, and participating in political protests.[34] Recently, Russell Dalton has extended the time series for some of these dimensions of political participation into the twenty-first century.[35] All told, voting is the only aspect of political participation that a majority of the population reported engaging in but also the only political activity for which there is evidence of a decline in participation in recent years. Substantial increases in participation have been found on the dimensions of giving money to candidates and contacting public officials, and small increases are evident for all the other activities. Thus, although the decline of voter turnout is a development Americans should rightly be concerned about (see Chapter 10), a broader look at political participation reveals some positive developments for participatory democracy.

The right of political protest is constitutionally protected as an integral part of freedom of speech in the United States. Although the Iraq War has not engendered the kind of mass protests seen during the Vietnam War, there have nevertheless been some major anti-war demonstrations, such as this one in Washington during 2007.

PROTEST AS PARTICIPATION

protest

A form of **political participation** designed to achieve policy change through dramatic and unconventional tactics.

From the Boston Tea Party to burning draft cards to demonstrating against abortion, Americans have engaged in countless political protests. **Protest** is a form of political participation designed to achieve policy change through dramatic and unconventional tactics. The media's willingness to cover the unusual can make protests worthwhile, drawing attention to a point of view that many Americans might otherwise never encounter. For example, when an 89-year-old woman walked across the country to draw attention to the need for campaign finance reform, she put this issue onto the front page of newspapers most everywhere she traveled. Using much more flamboyant means, the AIDS activist group appropriately called "ACT-UP" interrupts political gatherings to draw attention to the need for AIDS research. In fact, protests today are often orchestrated to provide television cameras with vivid images. Demonstration coordinators steer participants to prearranged staging areas and provide facilities for press coverage.

civil disobedience

A form of **political participation** that reflects a conscious decision to break a law believed to be immoral and to suffer the consequences.

Throughout American history, individuals and groups have sometimes used **civil disobedience** as a form of protest; that is, they have consciously broken a law that they thought was unjust. In the 1840s, Henry David Thoreau refused to pay his taxes as a protest against the Mexican War and went to jail; he stayed only overnight because his friend Ralph Waldo Emerson paid the taxes. Influenced by India's Mahatma Gandhi, the Reverend Martin Luther King Jr. won a Nobel Peace Prize for his civil disobedience against segregationist laws in the 1950s and 1960s. His "Letter from a Birmingham Jail" is a classic defense of civil disobedience.[36]

Sometimes political participation can be violent. The history of violence in American politics is a long one—not surprising, perhaps, for a nation born in rebellion. The turbulent 1960s included many outbreaks of violence. African American neighborhoods in American cities were torn by riots. College campuses were sometimes turned into battle zones as protestors against the Vietnam War fought police and National Guard units. At a number of campuses, demonstrations turned violent; students were killed at Kent State and Jackson State in 1970. Although supported by few people, violence has been a means of pressuring the government to change its policies throughout American history.

Nonviolent civil disobedience was one of the most effective techniques of the civil rights movement in the American South. Young African Americans sat at "Whites only" lunch counters to protest segregation. Photos such as this drew national attention to the injustice of racial discrimination.

CLASS, INEQUALITY, AND PARTICIPATION

Rates of political participation are unequal among Americans. Virtually every study of political participation has come to the conclusion that "citizens of higher social economic status participate more in politics. This generalization . . . holds true whether one uses level of education, income, or occupation as the measure of social status."[37] Figure 6.5 presents recent evidence on this score. Note that people with higher incomes are more likely not only to donate money to campaigns but also to participate in other ways that do not require financial resources, such as signing petitions. Theorists who believe that America is ruled by a small, wealthy elite make much of this fact to support their view.

The scenes of despair among poor African Americans in New Orleans during the aftermath of Hurricane Katrina have refocused attention on racial inequalities in the United States. Some commentators have speculated that one of the reasons that the federal government was so slow in coming to the aid of African Americans in New Orleans is that they are less likely to vote. But in actuality, the difference in turnout rates between Whites and African Americans has been relatively small in Louisiana in recent years. In 2004, for example, 60 percent of Louisiana Whites over the age of 18 turned out to vote compared to 54 percent of African Americans in the state.[38] (Notably, in the area that encompasses the poverty-stricken lower Ninth Ward, the turnout rate of African Americans was exactly the same as it was statewide).

One reason for this relatively small participation gap is that minorities have a group consciousness that gives them an extra incentive to vote. In fact, when African Americans and Whites of equal income and education are compared, the former actually participate more in politics.[39] In other words, a poor African American is more likely to participate than a poor White person. In general, lower rates of political participation among African Americans are linked with lower socioeconomic status.

People who believe in the promise of democracy should definitely be concerned with the inequalities of political participation in America. Those who participate are easy to listen to; nonparticipants are easy to ignore. Just as the makers of denture

Perhaps the best-known image of American political violence from the late 1960s to early 1970s: A student lies dead on the Kent State campus, one of four killed when members of the Ohio National Guard opened fire on anti–Vietnam War demonstrators.

FIGURE 6.5

Political Participation by Family Income

The following graph shows, by their income status, the percentage of the adult population who said they participated in various forms of political activity during the past year.

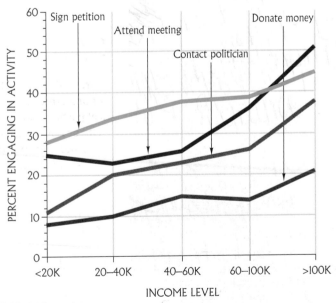

Source: Authors' analysis of 2004 General Social Survey data.

cream do not worry too much about people with healthy teeth, many politicians don't concern themselves much with the views of groups with low participation rates, such as the young and people with low incomes. Who gets what in politics therefore depends in part on who participates.

UNDERSTANDING PUBLIC OPINION AND POLITICAL ACTION

Comparing Governments and Public Opinion

In many third-world countries, there have been calls for more democracy in recent years. One often hears that citizens of developing nations want their political system to be like America's in the sense that ordinary people's opinions determine how the government is run. However, as this chapter has shown, there are many limits on the role public opinion plays in the American political system. The average person is not very well informed about political issues, including the crucial issue of the scope of government.

PUBLIC ATTITUDES TOWARD THE SCOPE OF GOVERNMENT

? Why it Matters

Political Participation

Inequality in political participation is a problem in a representative democracy. Public policy debates and outcomes would probably be substantially different if people of all age groups and income groups participated equally. If young adults participated more, politicians would be more inclined to work on ways by which the government could help young people get the training necessary to get good jobs. And if the poor participated at higher levels, government programs to alleviate poverty would likely be higher on the political agenda than they are today.

Central to the ideology of the Republican Party is the belief that the scope of American government has become too wide ranging. According to Ronald Reagan, probably the most admired Republican in recent history, government was not the solution to society's problems—it was the problem. He called for the government to "get off the backs of the American people."

Reagan's rhetoric about an overly intrusive government was reminiscent of the 1964 presidential campaign rhetoric of Barry Goldwater, who lost to Lyndon Johnson in a landslide. Indeed, Reagan first made his mark in politics by giving a televised speech on behalf of the embattled Goldwater campaign. Although the rhetoric was much the same when Ronald Reagan was first elected president in 1980, public opinion about the scope of government had changed dramatically. In 1964, only 30 percent of the population thought the government was getting too powerful; by 1980, this figure had risen to 50 percent.

For much of the population, however, questions about the scope of government have consistently elicited no opinion at all. Indeed, when this question was last asked in the 2000 National Election Study, 42 percent of those interviewed said they had not thought about the question (among those under 25 years of age, this figure was 60 percent). The question of government power is a complex one, but as *Government in America* will continue to emphasize, it is one of the key controversies in American politics today. Once again, it seems that the public is not nearly so concerned with political issues as would be ideal in a democratic society.

Nor does public opinion on different aspects of the same issue exhibit much consistency. Thus, although more people today think that overall the government is too big, a plurality has consistently called for more spending on such programs as education, health care, aid to cities, protecting the environment, and fighting crime. Many political scientists have looked at these contradictory findings and concluded that Americans are ideological conservatives but operational liberals—meaning that they oppose the idea of big government in principle but favor it in practice. The fact that public opinion is often contradictory in this respect sometimes leads to policy gridlock because it is hard for politicians to know which aspect of the public's attitudes to respond to.

DEMOCRACY, PUBLIC OPINION, AND POLITICAL ACTION

Remember, though, that American democracy is representative rather than direct. As *The American Voter* stated many years ago, "The public's explicit task is to decide not what government shall do but rather who shall decide what government shall do."[40] When individuals under communist rule protested for democracy, what they wanted most was the right to have a say in choosing their leaders. Americans can—and often do—take for granted the opportunity to replace their leaders at the next election. Protest is thus directed at making the government listen to specific demands, not overthrowing it. In this sense, it can be said that American citizens have become well socialized to democracy.

If the public's task in democracy is to choose who is to lead, we must still ask whether it can do so wisely. If people know little about where candidates stand on issues, how can they make rational choices? Most choose performance criteria over policy criteria. As Morris Fiorina has written, citizens typically have one hard bit of data to go on: "They know what life has been like during the incumbent's administration. They need not know the precise economic or foreign policies of the incumbent administration in order to see or feel the results of those policies."[41] Thus, even if they are voting only according to the nature of the times, their voices are clearly being heard—holding public officials accountable for their actions.

SUMMARY

American society is amazingly varied. The ethnic makeup of America is changing to a minority majority. Americans are moving toward warmer parts of the country and growing older as a society. All these changes have policy consequences. One way of understanding the American people is through demography—the science of population changes. Demography, it is often said, is destiny.

Another way to understand the American people is through examination of public opinion in the United States. What Americans believe—and what they believe they know—is public opinion, the distribution of people's beliefs about politics and policy issues. Polling is one important way of studying public opinion; polls give us a fairly accurate gauge of public opinion on issues, products, and personalities. On the positive side for democracy, polls help keep political leaders in touch with the feelings of their constituents. On the negative side, polls may lead politicians to "play to the crowds" instead of providing leadership.

Polls have revealed again and again that the average American has a low level of political knowledge. For example, only about forty percent of the population can name the three branches of government, and far more Americans can name the judges on *American Idol* than the justices on the Supreme Court. Ideological thinking is not widespread in the American public, nor are people necessarily consistent in their attitudes. Often they are conservative in principle but liberal in practice; that is, they are against big government but favor more spending on a wide variety of programs.

Acting on one's opinions is political participation. Although Americans live in a participatory culture, their actual level of participation is less than spectacular. In this country, participation is a class-biased activity; certain groups participate more than others. Those who suffer the most inequality sometimes resort to protest as a form of participation. Perhaps the best indicator of how well socialized Americans are to democracy is that protest typically is aimed at getting the attention of the government, not overthrowing it.

Chapter Test

Multiple Choice

1. Which of the following groups tends to be undercounted in the national census?
   a. Senior citizens
   b. College students
   c. Women
   d. Minorities
   e. Working adults

2. The second great wave of immigration, during the late nineteenth and early twentieth century, was primarily characterized by an influx of immigrants from all but which of the following countries?
   a. Italy
   b. Poland
   c. Russia
   d. Eastern Europe
   e. Scandinavia

3. In 2000, the census found that roughly how many people living in America at the time were born in a foreign country?
   a. One in ten
   b. Two in ten
   c. Three in ten
   d. Four in ten
   e. Five in ten

4. The Simpson-Mazzoli Act requires that employers:
   a. Hire a certain quota of minorities
   b. Hire a certain quota of non-citizens
   c. Document the citizenship of their employees
   d. Give preference to qualified minorities when hiring and promoting employees
   e. Cannot employ non-citizens.

5. What happened to California's Proposition 187, which called for illegal immigrants to be denied access to public services?
   a. It won at the ballot box and has been implemented since then
   b. It won at the ballot box, but there have been practical obstacles to its implementation
   c. It won at the ballot box, but there have been legal obstacles to its implementation
   d. It did not win at the ballot box
   e. It has not been voted on yet

6. Which of the following is not generally true of women's political beliefs compared to men's?
   a. They tend to be more likely to support spending on social services
   b. They tend to oppose higher levels of military spending
   c. They are more likely to be pro-choice
   d. They tend to be more likely to support Democratic candidates
   e. All of the above are true

7. Based on what we know about processes of political socialization, a young adult in America is most likely to be influenced by:
   a. What he or she picked up while watching TV
   b. His or her high school civics and government classes
   c. His or her college courses
   d. His or her parents' political views
   e. The political opinions of her friends

8. All else being equal, the chance of a sampling error is the highest in a poll that questioned:
   a. 500 people
   b. 800 people
   c. 1,000 people
   d. 1,500 people
   e. 2,000 people

9. Assume that Gallup conducted an opinion poll in which 2,000 randomly selected individuals were asked whether they approved or disapproved of the Congress. The results show that 58 percent of respondents approved. Knowing what you know about the science of polling, you now know with 95 percent certainty that the percentage for the American population is:
   a. Between 53 percent and 65 percent
   b. Between 55 percent and 61 percent
   c. Between 55 percent and 61 percent
   d. Exactly 58 percent
   e. Uncertain, because you can't know about the total population, only your sample

10. A person who votes for the Democratic Party because he or she thinks, "I am a minority and Democrats support minorities" is considered to be a(n):
    a. Ideologue
    b. Group benefits voter
    c. Nature of the times voter
    d. No issue content voter
    e. None of the above

True/False

11. The increase in the number of cell phones in America has made it easier for pollsters to reach people for survey research purposes.
    True _____ False _____

12. According to a 2006 poll, almost twice as many respondents were able to name the Three Stooges as were able to name the three branches of government.
    True _____ False _____

13. America is characterized by the predominance of conservative political thought.
    True _____ False _____

14. Most American voters think in terms of "liberal" or "conservative" ideology when they go to the polls.
    True _____ False _____

Short Answer

15. Please outline the positions of the Democratic and the Republican parties on the issue of illegal immigration.

16. Explain the so-called "bandwagon effect" of public opinion polls.

17. Summarize at least three main differences in the political ideologies of liberals and conservatives.

18. Please explain the relationship between a person's level of education and level of political participation (in its various forms) and his or her level of openness and tolerance. In your opinion, what accounts for this relationship?

19. What are three possible obstacles to conducting a reliable public opinion poll, and how can you overcome them?

20. What is the so-called "paradox of mass politics"? Do you agree with this assessment?

Short Answer/Essay Questions

21. Using your knowledge about the science of polling and the potential biases that can result from the way a question is worded, how would you analyze the following questions in terms of their likelihood to produce reliable results without influencing the respondents' answers? Explain how and why respondents might react differently to each of the questions below.
    a. Do you agree that the government should help those in need?
    b. Do you agree that the government should help those on welfare?
    c. Do you agree that the government should help the needy, even if it means raising taxes for new programs?

22. Analyzing the data presented in Figure 6.5, please give at least three explanations for why increasing income seems to also produce an increase in political participation. Applying what you know about the democratic process and the ideal of democracy, how would you evaluate these numbers?

23. In your opinion, what are some of the possible consequences (political, social, economic) that might result once the United States reaches a so-called "minority majority"? Support your arguments logically.

24. What do you believe are at least three reasons younger people are less likely to vote than older people? How would you remedy the problem of such low voter turnout among your peers?

25. Why are older people more likely to be conservative than younger people? Give at least three possible explanations.

26. Looking at the data presented in Figure 6.4, please explain the trends you recognize in the levels of trust Americans have for their government. What are at least three factors that might explain the ebb and flow of trust in addition to the factors mentioned in this textbook? What possible connection do you see between the data in Figure 6.4 and this textbook's discussion of levels of political knowledge and political participation?

27. This textbook addresses the role of public opinion polls in American democracy. Please summarize the different views on opinion polls presented here. In your own opinion, what is the connection between opinion polls and policymakers in Washington, D.C., and elsewhere? How likely do you believe politicians are to respond to public preferences, and under what circumstances? Should they be more responsive or less, and why?

28. This textbook quotes *The American Voter* as stating many years ago, "The public's explicit task is to decide not what government shall do but rather who shall decide what government shall do." Please evaluate this statement.

Answer Key

1. D   2. E   3. A   4. C   5. C   6. D   7. A   8. C   9. B   10. B   11. False   12. True   13. True   14. False

Key Terms

public opinion (184)
demography (184)
census (184)
melting pot (186)
minority majority (186)
political culture (189)

reapportionment (190)
political socialization (191)
sample (195)
random sampling (195)
sampling error (195)
random-digit dialing (196)

exit poll (197)
political ideology (201)
gender gap (204)
political participation (206)
protest (207)
civil disobedience (208)

Internet Resources

www.census.gov
The census is the best source of information on America's demography. Go to the list of topics to find out the range of materials that are available.

www.gallup.com
The Gallup poll regularly posts reports about their political surveys at this site.

www.census.gov/compendia/statab/
The *Statistical Abstract of the United States* contains a wealth of demographic and political information and is available in Adobe Acrobat format off the Internet.

www.pollster.com
A good source of information about current polls and the polling business.

GetConnected

Public Opinion and SLOPs

Public opinion polls play an important role in American politics and government. Some observers even argue that policymakers keep an eye on polls when trying to develop policy, a practice that may be to the detriment of our system of government. Some polls are conducted scientifically and provide useful information about what Americans are thinking. There are other polls called self-selected opinion polls, or SLOPs, that may provide biased or misleading information. You may have seen SLOPs on an interest group's Web site or even on the local news. How are scientific polls conducted, and how do they differ from SLOPs?

Search the Web

The Gallup Organization is one of the oldest public opinion polling firms in the country. Go to the "How Polls are Conducted" page at the Gallup Web site, *http://media.gallup .com/PDF/FAQ/HowArePolls.pdf.* Now review the National Council on Public Polls' "Statement About Internet Polls," *www.ncpp.org/?q=node/3.1* While the National Council on Public Polls' statement is about Internet polls, this type of public opinion poll could have the same shortcomings as the self-selected opinion poll you might see on television or find on an interest group's Web site.

Questions to Ask

- What are the important characteristics about Gallup's polling methods that allow people to have confidence in the findings revealed by the organization's polls?

- Why does the National Council on Public Polls think it is important to know if people were able to participate in the poll more than once?
- What are the shortcomings of any public opinion poll?

Why It Matters

The people are able to voice their opinions through public opinion polls, but polls may cause problems for our political system if they are not conducted correctly. It is important for the consumers of public opinion polls, including policymakers and voters, to have confidence in the information such polls present.

Get Involved

Find the results of an Internet poll at the CNN Web site, *www.cnn.com;* Fox News Channel's Web site, *www.foxnews.com;* or in your local media. Evaluate the poll using the National Council on Public Polls' "Statement About Internet Polls." Contact the person or group who published the poll and ask them to answer the questions on the statement if the poll doesn't provide the answers directly. Consult this issue brief from the Pew Research Center for the People and the Press, *http://people-press.org/commentary/display.php3? AnalysisID=20,* to offer suggestions on how to improve the poll. For more exercises, go to *www.longmanamericangovernment.com.*

For Further Reading

Asher, Herbert. *Polling and the Public: What Every Citizen Should Know.* 7th ed. Washington, DC: Congressional Quarterly Press, 2007. A highly readable introduction to the perils and possibilities of polling and surveys.

Bean, Frank D. and Gillian Stevens, *America's Newcomers and the Dynamics of Diversity.* New York: Russell Sage Foundation, 2003. A balanced examination of the positive and negative consequences of immigration to the United States.

Bryan, Frank M. *Real Democracy: The New England Town Meeting and How It Works.* Chicago: University of Chicago Press, 2004. This book reviews data collected by undergraduates at roughly 1,500 Vermont town meetings in order to test numerous theories of political participation at the local level.

Campbell, Andrea Louise. *How Policies Make Citizens: Senior Political Activism and the American Welfare Sate.* Princeton, NJ: Princeton University Press, 2003. Senior citizens have bucked the trend of declining political participation in recent years; Campbell explains why.

Campbell, Angus, et al. *The American Voter.* New York: Wiley, 1960. The classic study of the American voter, based on data from the 1950s.

Conway, M. Margaret. *Political Participation,* 3rd ed. Washington, DC: Congressional Quarterly Press, 2000. A good review of the literature on political participation.

Delli Carpini, Michael X., and Scott Keeter. *What Americans Know About Politics and Why It Matters.* New Haven, CT: Yale University Press, 1996. The best study of the state of political knowledge in the electorate.

DeSipio, Louis. *Counting on the Latino Vote: Latinos as a New Electorate.* Charlottesville: University Press of Virginia, 1998. An examination of the current state of Latino public opinion and how more Latinos could be politically mobilized in the future.

Fiorina, Morris P. *Culture War? The Myth of a Polarized America.* 2nd ed. New York: Longman, 2006. This book argues that the so-called culture war between the red and blue states is highly exaggerated, as most Americanspossess relatively moderate and nuanced opinions on political issues.

Hetherington, Marc J. *Why Trust Matters.* Princeton, NJ: Princeton University Press, 2005. The author argues that the decline of trust in government in recent decades has weakened support for progressive policies to address problems of poverty and racial inequality.

Jacobs, Lawrence R., and Robert Y. Shapiro. *Politicians Don't Pander.* Chicago: University of Chicago Press, 2000. Contrary to popular notions that politicians hold their fingers to the wind and try to follow the polls, Jacobs and Shapiro argue that politicians use polls to figure out how to best persuade the public to support their preferred policies.

Jennings, M. Kent, and Richard G. Niemi. *Generations and Politics: A Panel Study of Young Adults and Their Parents.* Princeton, NJ: Princeton University Press, 1981. A highly influential study of the class of 1965, their parents, and how both generations changed over the course of eight years.

Lewis-Beck, Michael S., et al. *The American Voter Revisited.* Ann Arbor, MI: University of Michigan Press, 2008. A replication of the classic analysis in *The American Voter* employing data from the 2000 and 2004 National Election Studies.

Nie, Norman H., Jane Junn, and Kenneth Stehlik-Barry. *Education and Democratic Citizenship in America.* Chicago: University of Chicago Press, 1996. An in-depth investigation of the role of education in fostering political tolerance and participation.

Tate, Katherine. *From Protest to Politics: The New Black Voters in American Elections.* Enlarged ed. Cambridge, MA: Harvard University Press, 1998. An excellent examination of public opinion and participation among the African American community.

Verba, Sidney, and Norman H. Nie. *Participation in America.* New York: Harper & Row, 1972. A landmark study of American political participation.

Verba, Sidney, Kay Lehman Schlozman, and Henry E. Brady. *Voice and Equality: Civic Voluntarism in American Politics.* Cambridge, MA: Harvard University Press, 1995. A worthy update and extension to *Participation in America.*

THE
MASS MEDIA
AND THE
POLITICAL
AGENDA

POLITICS IN ACTION:
HOW TELEVISION HAS BROUGHT A SENSE OF IMMEDIACY TO GOVERNING

In Washington's Smithsonian Museum, the television console used by President Lyndon Johnson in the mid-1960s can be seen on permanent display. Not wanting to miss anything on TV, Johnson asked for three screens to be installed in one console so he could monitor CBS, NBC, and ABC all at the same time. White House technicians rigged up a special remote control for the president, enabling him to switch the audio easily from one network to another. According to many observers, whenever he saw his picture appear, he immediately turned on the audio from that screen to hear what was being said about him.

As a piece of genuine Americana, LBJ's triple TV set symbolizes the tremendous importance television had assumed in U.S. politics by the mid-1960s. By bringing major events live into people's living rooms, television would sometimes set the stage for leaders to take quick action affecting the scope of government. The case of protests for minority voting rights in the South provides one such example. Lyndon Johnson was watching his triple-screen TV set when NBC interrupted its airing of *Judgment at Nuremberg* to show film that had just become available of civil rights demonstrators being brutally attacked by police in Selma, Alabama. Sensing the public outrage at this violence and injustice, Johnson soon proposed and pushed through the historic Voting Rights Act of 1965 (see Chapters 5).

Today, anytime a president takes strong action on some important policy problem, television sets the stage by focusing attention on the issue and putting it high on the policy agenda. This process was clearly evident in the immediate aftermath of the catastrophic flooding of New Orleans caused by Hurricane Katrina. When TV reporters broadcast images of poor people stranded and desperately calling out for help, many Americans felt that the federal government should take quick action to deal with the situation. According to *Newsweek,* Dan Bartlett, counselor to the president, compiled a DVD of these reports to impress on President Bush the urgency of the problem. Soon after seeing these televised images, the president accelerated the military's response to the situation and started to develop a major reconstruction package of aid for the city.

The rise of television has had a profound impact on the two central questions we emphasize in this text—How should we govern? and What should government do? Television has brought an immediacy to how we govern, removing the filter of time from events. Whatever the problem or event, it is happening now—live on the TV screen. People thus have more reason than ever to expect immediate governmental responses. However, the Founding Fathers designed a very deliberative governing process in which problems would be considered by multiple centers of political power and acted on only after lengthy give-and-take. Given the difficulties of getting quick action through the American political system, it is no wonder the public has come to be generally more dissatisfied with our government in the television age.

The American political system has entered a new period of **high-tech politics**—a politics in which the behavior of citizens and policymakers, as well as the political agenda itself, is increasingly shaped by technology. The **mass media** are a key part of this technology. Television, radio, newspapers, magazines, the Internet, and other means of popular communication are called *mass media* because they reach and profoundly influence not only the elites but also the masses. This chapter examines media politics, focusing on the following:

- The rise of modern media in America's advanced technological society
- The making of the news and its presentation through the media
- The biases in the news
- The impact of the media on policymakers and the public

This chapter also reintroduces the concept of the policy agenda, in which the media play an important role.

THE MASS MEDIA TODAY

Whether promoting a candidate, drawing attention to a social issue, or generating a government program, effectively communicating a message is critical to political success. The key is gaining control over the political agenda, which involves getting one's priorities presented at the top of the daily news. Politicians have learned that one way to guide the media's focus successfully is to limit what they can report on to carefully scripted events. A **media event** is staged primarily for the purpose of being covered. If the media were not there, the event would probably not happen or would have little significance. For example, one day while campaigning for the presidency in Iowa, Barack Obama went door-to-door in a middle-class neighborhood with TV crews in tow. The few dozen people he met could scarcely have made a difference, but Obama was not really there to win votes by personal contact. Rather, the point was to get television coverage of him

---

high-tech politics

A politics in which the behavior of citizens and policymakers and the political agenda itself are increasingly shaped by technology.

mass media

Television, radio, newspapers, magazines, the Internet, and other means of popular communication.

media events

Events purposely staged for the media that nonetheless look spontaneous. In keeping with politics as theater, media events can be staged by individuals, groups, and government officials, especially presidents.

reaching out to ordinary people. Getting the right image on the TV news for just 30 seconds can have a much greater payoff than a whole day's worth of handshaking. Whereas once a candidate's G.O.T.V. program stood for "Get Out the Vote," today it is more likely to mean "Get on TV."

In addition, a large part of today's so-called 30-second presidency is the slickly produced TV commercial. Approximately 60 percent of presidential campaign spending is now devoted to TV ads. In recent presidential elections, about two-thirds of the prominently aired ads were negative commercials.[1] Many people are worried that the tirade of accusations, innuendoes, and countercharges in political advertising is poisoning the American political process and possibly even contributing to declining turnout.[2] Other democracies typically allocate free airtime to parties for longer ads that go into more depth than is possible than with the American-style 30-second ad.

Image making does not stop with the campaign; it is also a critical element in day-to-day governing. Politicians' images in the press are seen as good indicators of their clout. Image is especially important for presidents, who in recent years have devoted much attention to maintaining a well-honed public image, as shown in the following internal White House memo written by President Nixon:

> When I think of the millions of dollars that go into one lousy 30-second television spot advertising a deodorant, it seems to me unbelievable that we don't do a better job in seeing that presidential appearances always have the very best professional advice whenever they are to be covered on TV. . . . The President should never be without the very best professional advice for making a television appearance.[3]

Few, if any, administrations devoted so much effort and energy to the president's media appearance as did Ronald Reagan's. It has often been said that Reagan played to the media as he had played to the cameras in Hollywood. According to journalist Mark Hertsgaard, news management in the Reagan White House operated on the following seven principles: (1) plan ahead, (2) stay on the offensive, (3) control the flow of information, (4) limit reporters' access to the president, (5) talk about the issues you want to talk about, (6) speak in one voice, and (7) repeat the same message many times.[4]

To Ronald Reagan, the presidency was often a performance, and his aides helped to choreograph his public appearances. Like many recent presidents, Reagan realized that for a president to ignore the power of image and the media would be perilous. In today's high-tech age, presidents can hardly lead the country if they cannot communicate effectively with it. President Clinton once reflected on the unexpected dimensions of his job on *Larry King Live*: "The thing that has surprised me most is how difficult it is . . . to really keep communicating what you're about to the American people. That to me has been the most frustrating thing." According to journalist Bob Woodward, Clinton confided to a friend that "I did not realize the importance of communications and the overriding importance of what is on the evening television news. If I am not on, or there with a message, someone else is, with their message."[5]

Politicians often stage activities primarily for the benefit of TV cameras. For example, the sight of a major national candidate going door-to-door asking ordinary people for their support is something that the media finds difficult to pass up. In this swing through an Iowa neighborhood, Barack Obama met perhaps 30 of the 90,000 people that voted for him in the Iowa caucuses. But the number of people who saw pictures like this in their newspaper or viewed the video footage on TV was far, far greater.

THE DEVELOPMENT OF MEDIA POLITICS

There was virtually no daily press when the U.S. Constitution was written. The daily newspaper is largely a product of the mid-nineteenth century; radio and television have been around only since the first half of the twentieth century. As recently as the presidency of Herbert Hoover (1929–1933), reporters submitted their questions to the president in writing, and he responded in writing—if at all. As Hoover put it, "The President of the United States will not stand and be questioned like a chicken thief by men whose names he does not even know."[6]

Hoover's successor, Franklin D. Roosevelt (1933–1945), practically invented media politics. To Roosevelt, the media were a potential ally. Roosevelt promised reporters two **press conferences**—presidential meetings with reporters—a week, resulting in about 1,000 press conferences during his 12 years in the White House. FDR was also the first president to use radio, broadcasting a series of reassuring "fireside chats" to the Depression-ridden nation. Roosevelt's crafty use of radio helped him win four presidential elections. Another of Roosevelt's talents was knowing how to feed the right story to the right reporter. He used presidential wrath to warn reporters off material he did not want covered, and he chastised news reports he deemed inaccurate. His wrath was rarely invoked, however, and the press revered him, never even reporting to the American public that the president was confined to a wheelchair. The idea that a political leader's health status might be public business was alien to journalists in FDR's day.

This relatively cozy relationship between politicians and the press lasted through the early 1960s. ABC's Sam Donaldson said that when he first came to Washington in 1961, "many reporters saw themselves as an extension of the government, accepting, with very little skepticism, what government officials told them."[7] And coverage of a politician's personal life was generally off limits. For example, as a young reporter R. W. Apple Jr. of the *New York Times* once observed a beautiful woman being escorted to President Kennedy's suite. Thinking he had a major scoop, he rushed to tell his editor. But he was quickly told, "Apple, you're supposed to report on political and diplomatic policies, not girlfriends. No story."[8]

The events of the Vietnam War and the Watergate scandal, though, soured the press on government. Today's newspeople work in an environment of cynicism. To them, politicians rarely tell the whole story; the press sees ferreting out the truth as their job. As Sam Donaldson of ABC News wrote in his book, *Hold On, Mr. President!*,

If you send me to cover a pie-baking contest on Mother's Day, I'm going to ask dear old Mom whether she used artificial sweetener in violation of the rules, and while she's at it, could I see the receipt for the apples to prove she didn't steal them.

press conferences
Meetings of public officials with reporters.

When someone becomes an instant political celebrity, it takes a police escort to get them through the hordes of cameras and reporters. Here, Monica Lewinsky leaves a federal courthouse amid much commotion after providing evidence for the special prosecutor's investigation into charges of wrongdoing by President Clinton.

I maintain that if Mom has nothing to hide, no harm will have been done. But the questions should be asked.[9]

When the Clinton–Lewinsky scandal broke, the entire press corps reacted in this fashion. So strong was the desire to find out what the president had to hide in his personal life that 75 percent of the questions asked during the daily White House press briefing concerned this scandal in the first week after the story broke.[10]

Carefully scrutinizing claims made by government officials is one of the most important things that reporters consider they do, as demonstrated by the results from a national survey of journalists displayed in Figure 7.1. Yet, many political scientists are critical of such **investigative journalism**—the use of detective-like reporting methods to check up on the statements of governmental officials. This adversarial role of the media often pits reporters against political leaders. There is evidence that TV's fondness for investigative journalism has contributed to greater public cynicism and negativity about politics.[11]

In his analysis of media coverage of presidential campaigns since 1960, Thomas Patterson found that news coverage of presidential candidates has become increasingly less favorable. His tally of *Time* and *Newsweek* stories about the campaigns reveals that favorable references about Kennedy and Nixon outnumbered unfavorable ones by a 3-to-1 margin. In contrast, in 1992 there were three negative references regarding Clinton and Bush for every two favorable references. Patterson's careful analysis uncovers several aspects of the trend toward more negative media coverage of presidential candidates. First, he finds that the emphasis of campaign reporting has changed dramatically from "what" to "why." Patterson's content analysis of front-page *New York Times* stories revealed that in 1960 over 90 percent of news stories employed a descriptive framework, whereas by 1992 less than 20 percent did so. Second, the type of interpretative story that

investigative journalism

The use of in-depth reporting to unearth scandals, scams, and schemes, at times putting reporters in adversarial relationships with political leaders.

FIGURE 7.1

The Importance Journalists Assign to Various Roles of the Mass Media

A recent national survey of journalists in America asked them to rate the importance of "a number of things that the news media do or try to do today." Below are the percentages of journalists who ranked each of these media roles as "extremely important."

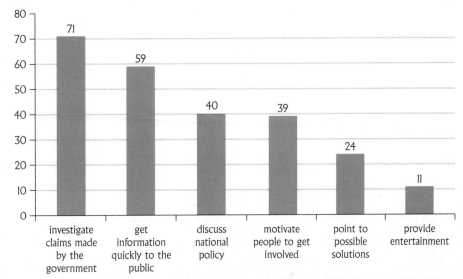

Source: Adapted from David. H. Weaver et al. *The American Journalist in the 21st Century.* (Mahwah, NJ: Lawrence Erlbaum, 2007), p. 140.

has become more prominent is hard-biting analysis of political maneuvering and the horse race.

Such reporting tends toward unfavorable impressions of the candidates because the unstated assumption behind much of today's coverage of the issues has shifted from policy statements to campaign controversies. Coverage of such issues as whether George W. Bush fulfilled his military obligations or John F. Kerry lied about his experiences in Vietnam are not likely to draw favorable references. Those who run campaigns naturally complain about such coverage. As Karl Rove, one of George W. Bush's top political advisers, said after the 2000 election was over,

> The general nature of the tone of the coverage was very much in keeping with what Patterson suggests, that it is process oriented, highly cynical, negative, dismissive of issue positions, focused on the internals of the campaign and not on the big messages and really serves to trivialize the whole contest.[12]

The White House press room is often the scene of much activity, with daily briefings on the president's activities each day the president is in residence. Contrary to the image that is often presented on television, reporters work in a cramped environment at the White House.

print media
Newspapers and magazines, as compared with broadcast media.

broadcast media
Television, radio, and the Internet, as compared with print media.

TIMELINE

Three Hundred Years of American Mass Media

Whether or not such media coverage is ultimately in the public's best interest is much debated. The press maintains that the public is now able to get a complete, accurate, and unvarnished look at the candidates. Critics of the media charge that they overemphasize the controversial aspects of the campaign at the expense of an examination of the major issues.

Scholars distinguish between two kinds of media: the **print media**, which include newspapers and magazines, and the **broadcast media**, which include radio, television, and the Internet. Each has reshaped political communication at different points in American history. It is difficult to assess the likely impact of the Internet at this point, but there is at least some reason to believe that political communication is being reshaped once again.

The first American daily newspaper was printed in Philadelphia in 1783, but such papers did not proliferate until the technological advances of the mid-nineteenth century. The ratification of the First Amendment in 1791, guaranteeing freedom of speech, gave even the earliest American newspapers freedom to print whatever they saw fit. This has given the media a unique ability to display the government's dirty linen, a propensity that continues to distinguish the American press today.

At the turn of the twentieth century, newspaper magnates William Randolph Hearst and Joseph Pulitzer ushered in the era of "yellow journalism." This sensational style of reporting focused on violence, corruption, wars, and gossip, often with a less-than-scrupulous regard for the truth. On a visit to the United States at that time, young Winston Churchill said that "the essence of American journalism is vulgarity divested of truth."[13] In the midst of the Spanish–American conflict over Cuba, Hearst once boasted of his power over public opinion by telling a news artist, "You furnish the pictures and I'll furnish the war."

Among the press there is a pecking order. Almost from the beginning, the *New York Times* was a cut above most newspapers in its influence and impact; it is the nation's "newspaper of record" and can be found online at *www.nytimes.com*. Its clearest rival in government circles is the *Washington Post* (*www.washingtonpost. com*), offering perhaps the best coverage inside Washington and a sprightlier alternative to the *Times*. Papers such as the *Chicago Tribune* (*www.chicagotribune.com*) and the *Los Angeles Times* (*www.latimes.com*), as well as those in Atlanta, Boston, and other big cities, are also major national institutions. For most newspapers in medium-sized and small towns, though, the main source of national and world news is the Associated Press wire service, whose stories are reprinted in small newspapers across the country. With 2,700 reporters, photographers, and editors scattered around every major location in the United States, the Associated Press has more news-gathering ability than any other news organization.

Ever since the rise of TV news, however, newspaper circulation rates have been declining. Whereas one newspaper was sold for every two adults in 1960, by 2008 one paper was sold for every five adults. Most political scientists who have studied the role of media in politics believe this is an unfortunate trend, as studies invariably find that regular newspaper readers are better informed and more likely to vote.[14] This should hardly be surprising given the greater degree of information available in a newspaper compared to TV. A major metropolitan newspaper averages roughly 100,000 words daily, whereas a typical broadcast of the nightly news on TV will amount to only about 3,600 words.[15] It remains to be seen whether the availability of most newspapers on the Web will lead more people to look at newspapers in the future or rather will prove to be a desperate gasp for a fading business.

You Are the News Editor

Magazines, the other component of the print media, are also struggling in the Internet age, especially when it comes to the few that are heavily concerned with political events. The so-called newsweeklies—mainly *Time, Newsweek*, and *U.S. News and World Report*—rank well behind such popular favorites as *Reader's Digest, TV Guide*, and *National Geographic*. Although *Time*'s circulation is a bit better than that of the *National Enquirer, Playboy* and *People* edge out *Newsweek* in sales competition. Serious magazines of political news and opinion tend to be read by the educated elite; magazines such as the *New Republic, National Review*, and the *Atlantic Monthly* are outsold by magazines such as *Hot Rod, Weightwatchers Magazine*, and *Organic Gardening*.

THE BROADCAST MEDIA

Gradually, the broadcast media have displaced the print media as Americans' principal source of news and information. By the middle of the 1930s, radio ownership had become almost universal in America, and during World War II, radio went into the news business in earnest. The 1950s and early 1960s were the adolescent years for American television. During those years, the political career of Richard Nixon was made and unmade by television. In 1952, while running as Dwight Eisenhower's vice-presidential candidate, Nixon made a famous speech denying that he took gifts and payments under the table. He did admit accepting one gift—his dog, Checkers. Noting that his daughters loved the dog, Nixon said that regardless of his political future, they would keep it. His homey appeal brought a flood of sympathetic telegrams to the Republican National Committee, and party leaders had little choice but to leave him on the ticket.

In 1960, Nixon was again on television's center stage, this time in the first televised presidential debate against Senator John F. Kennedy. Nixon blamed his poor appearance in the first of the four debates for his narrow defeat in the election. Haggard from a week in the hospital and with his five-o'clock shadow and perspiration clearly visible, Nixon looked awful compared to the crisp, clean, attractive Kennedy. The poll results from this debate illustrate the visual power of television in American politics; people listening on the radio gave the edge to Nixon, but those who saw the debate on television thought Kennedy won. Russell Baker, who covered the event for the *New York Times,* writes in his memoirs that "television replaced newspapers as the most important communications medium in American politics" that very night.[16]

Just as radio had taken the nation to the war in Europe and the Pacific during the 1940s, television took the nation to the war in Vietnam during the 1960s. TV exposed governmental naïveté (some said it was outright lying) about the progress of the war. Every night, in living color, Americans watched the horrors of war on television. President Johnson soon had two wars on his hands, one in faraway Vietnam and the other at home with antiwar protesters—both covered in detail by the media. In 1968, CBS anchor Walter Cronkite journeyed to Vietnam for a firsthand look at the state of the war. In an extraordinary TV special, Cronkite reported that the war was not being won, nor was it likely to be. Watching from the White House, Johnson sadly remarked that if he had lost Cronkite, he had lost the support of the American people.[17]

The days of network anchors like Walter Cronkite being highly trusted and influential are clearly coming to an end, as cable news and the Internet have supplanted the nightly news shows. As *New York Times* media critic Frank Rich recently wrote, "The No. 1 cliché among media critics is that we're watching the 'last hurrah' of network news anchors as we have known them for nearly half a century."[18] You can see the evidence for this recent trend in "A Generation of Change: How Network News Broadcasts Are Going the Way of the Dinosaurs."

GOVERNMENT REGULATION OF THE BROADCAST MEDIA

When broadcast media first appeared with the invention of radio, a number of problems that the government could help with (such as overlapping use of the same frequency) soon became apparent. In 1934, Congress created the Federal Communications Commission (FCC) to regulate the use of airwaves. Today, the FCC regulates communications via radio, television, telephone, cable, and satellite. The FCC is an independent regulatory body, but in practice it is subject to many political pressures. Congress uses its control over the purse strings of the agency to influence the commission, and presidential appointments to it are naturally made with political considerations in mind.

The FCC has regulated the airwaves in three important ways. First, to prevent near monopolies of control over a broadcast market, it has instituted rules to limit the number of stations owned or controlled by one company. This once involved a variety of limitations but since 1996 has been simplified to simply state that no single owner can control more than 35 percent of the broadcast market. Second, the FCC conducts periodic examinations of the goals and performance of stations as part of its licensing authority. Congress long ago stipulated that in order to receive a broadcasting license, a station must serve the public interest. The FCC has on only rare occasions withdrawn licenses for failing to do so, such as when a Chicago station lost its license for neglecting informational programs and for presenting obscene movies. Third, the FCC has issued a number of fair treatment rules concerning access to the airwaves for political candidates and officeholders. The equal time rule stipulates that if a station sells advertising time to one candidate, it must be willing to sell equal time to other candidates for the same office. And the right-of-reply rule states if a person is attacked on a broadcast other than the news, then that person has a right to reply via the same station. For many years, the fairness doctrine was in place, which required broadcasters to give time to opposing views if they broadcast a program slanted to one side of a controversial issue. But with the development of so many TV channels via cable, this was seen as an unnecessary rule by the late 1980s, when it was abolished.

A GENERATION OF CHANGE

How Network News Broadcasts Are Going the Way of the Dinosaurs

Over the past quarter century, the NBC, ABC, and CBS nightly news broadcasts have gone from being instrumental in setting the nation's agenda to the TV equivalent of dinosaurs on their last legs. By 1981, one could make a legitimate argument that network newscasts had played a significant role in the political downfall of Presidents Johnson, Nixon, and Carter because of the way they drew attention to these presidents' shortcomings. As the media historian Barbara Matusow wrote about the stars of the evening news in 1983, "They have taken their place beside presidents, congressmen, labor leaders, industrialists, and others who shape public policy and private attitudes."*

Between 1983 and 2004, Tom Brokaw, Peter Jennings, and Dan Rather anchored the nightly news at NBC, ABC, and CBS, respectively. Throughout this period, these anchors saw their Nielsen ratings slip lower and lower, as shown in this graph. Usually, TV stars do not find that they have a job for very long once their shows start to sink in the Nielsen ratings. When Tom Brokaw was asked near the end of his career as anchor of the NBC Evening News what he perceived his mission to be, he simply responded "to survive." Because of the loyal viewership each of these three longtime anchors had built up, they were able to keep their news shows going. Whether their successors, whose ratings continue to set new all-time lows, can do the same for another generation remains to be seen.

In its heyday, network TV news broadcasts put afternoon newspapers out of business. Too few people felt they needed an afternoon paper once the nightly news was available every evening on television. Today, turning on the television to get the news at a set time early in the evening seems like a quaint remnant of the past in this era of 24-hour cable news channels and the Internet.

*Barbara Matusow, *The Evening Stars: The Making of the Network News Anchor* (Boston: Houghton Mifflin, 1983), 1.

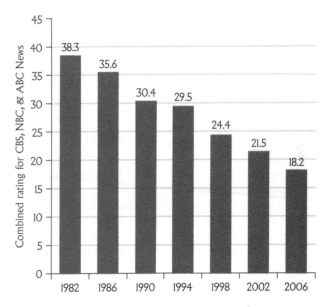

Source: *State of the News Media, 2007,* http://www.stateofthenewsmedia.org/2007/index.asp. Ratings are for November of each year.

FROM BROADCASTING TO NARROWCASTING: THE RISE OF CABLE NEWS CHANNELS

The first major networks—ABC, NBC, and CBS—adopted the term "broadcasting" in the names of their companies because their signal was being sent out to a broad audience. As long as these networks dominated the industry, each would have to deal with general topics that the public as a whole was concerned with, such as politics and government. But with the development of cable TV, market segmentation has taken hold. Sports buffs can watch ESPN all day, music buffs can tune in to MTV or VH1, history buffs can stay glued to the History Channel, and so forth. If you are interested in politics, you can switch between C-SPAN, C-SPAN2, CNN, MSNBC, Fox News Channel, and others. Rather than appealing to a general audience, channels such as ESPN, MTV, and C-SPAN focus on a narrow particular interest. Hence, their mission can be termed "**narrowcasting**," rather than traditional broadcasting. An analysis of media usage patterns by age shows that young adults are the least likely to be using newspapers and broadcast media, having grown up with the more recently established narrowcasting alternatives. (See "Young People and Politics: How the Under-30 Crowd Learns from Different Media Sources Compared to Older Americans.")

narrowcasting
Media programming on cable TV or the Internet that is focused on one topic and aimed at a particular audience. Examples include MTV, ESPN, and C-SPAN.

YOUNG PEOPLE AND POLITICS

How the Under-30 Crowd Learns from Different
Media Sources Compared to Older Americans

In December of 2007, the Pew Research Center asked a representative sample whether they regularly learned about the presidential campaign from a variety of media sources. This table shows the results, broken down by age. Notice that young people are substantially more likely to learn from the Internet and comedy TV shows. In contrast, older people are more likely to learn from the traditional sources of newspapers and network TV news (NBC, CBS, and ABC). Because so many young people are bypassing these sources, both newspapers and network news are facing the likely prospect of declining audiences for some time to come.

Cable TV news—CNN, MSNBC, and the Fox News Channel—have seen their audiences expand in recent years, as Americans of all ages have come to rely on them fairly heavily. However, given how little time most people stay tuned to these channels, one has to be skeptical that people are getting much more than basic headlines from them. In theory, the Internet offers all the details about public policy and government that anyone could want. Whether people who learn about politics via the Internet take advantage of the opportunities offered there remains to be seen. Comedy shows, on the other hand, offer very limited chances for learning about politics. Commenting on this survey finding, Jon Stewart of *The Daily Show* at first dismissed out of hand any notion that young people were turning to his comedy show to learn about political events. Subsequently, his show has adopted the slogan of "Keeping America Informed—Unintentionally."

% SAYING THEY REGULARLY LEARN SOMETHING ABOUT THE PRESIDENTIAL CAMPAIGN FROM:	AGE 18–29	AGE 30–49	AGE 50+
Cable news networks	35	36	41
Nightly network news	24	28	40
Daily newspaper	25	26	38
Comedy TV shows	12	7	6
Internet	42	25	15

Source: December 2007 survey by the Pew Research Center for the People and the Press, *http://people-press.org/reports/questionnaires/384.pdf*.

QUESTIONS FOR DISCUSSION

▷ How much do you think can really be learned about politics from the comedy shows that one out of eight young people say they learn from?

▷ Why do you think young people are so much less likely to learn from the traditional major news sources—TV network news and newspapers?

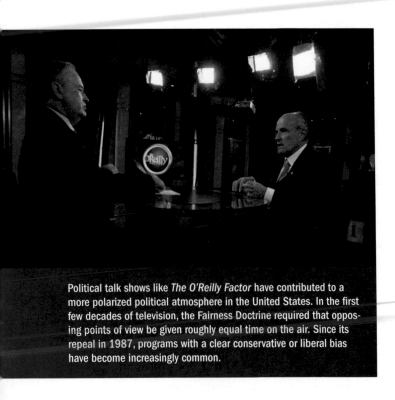

Political talk shows like *The O'Reilly Factor* have contributed to a more polarized political atmosphere in the United States. In the first few decades of television, the Fairness Doctrine required that opposing points of view be given roughly equal time on the air. Since its repeal in 1987, programs with a clear conservative or liberal bias have become increasingly common.

With the growth of cable TV news channels, television has recently entered a new era of bringing the news to people—and to political leaders—as it happens. Michael Bohn, a former high ranking government intelligence officer, writes that cable news has become a valuable source of breaking information in the White House Situation Room.[19] President Bush and his aides regularly turned to cable news stations when a major terrorist incident grabbed worldwide attention. A frequent response from U.S. officials to reporters' questions during the war against terrorism has been something along the lines of "I don't know any more than what you saw on CNN."

The future of political communication seems destined to bring more and more choices regarding what we can see about our government. About two-thirds of the American public currently subscribes to cable television, thereby giving them access to dozens of channels. Sometime in the not-too-distant future it is expected that most cable systems will offer 500 channels. As the number of channels increases, it is clear that anyone who is really interested in politics will find more political information readily available than ever before.

Yet it is important to note that the potential of cable news is often not realized in practice. Although these channels have seemingly unlimited opportunities to cover political events and issues, their resources are far from up to the task. Political scientist William Taubman experienced the constraints of cable news firsthand when he served as CNN's expert analyst during the Reagan–Gorbachev summit in 1988. Taubman "thought of the all-news network as having twenty-four hours a day to play with" and proposed numerous interviews with Soviets about their country's struggle to transform itself. However, he soon found that CNN thought of itself as having "forty-eight half-hour segments, each of which had to cover the world and pay for that coverage with regularly scheduled features."[20] Of the numerous interviews he recommended, only a few were done, lasting just a couple minutes each. And when Taubman was on the air, it usually wasn't long before he heard the dreaded words of "wrap it up and head for commercial" in his earpiece.

William Taubman's experience is instructive as to the shortcomings of cable news. A recent content analysis of CNN, Fox News, and MSNBC programming confirms just how little substantive information is usually conveyed via cable news channels. Columbia University's Project for Excellence in Journalism analyzed 240 hours of cable news programming during 2003. Their report on this content analysis provides a telling indictment of the medium. Among their many findings were that (1) only 11 percent of the time was taken up with written and edited stories; (2) the role of the reporter was primarily to talk extemporaneously; (3) stories were repeated frequently, usually without any important new information; and (4) coverage of the news was spotty, ignoring many important topics. All in all, this comprehensive study paints a very unflattering portrait of what is shown on cable news networks, labeling much of it as simply "talk radio on television."[21]

Many scholars of the media feel that the transition from network news to cable news has reduced the overall quality of political journalism. As media critic Thomas Rosensteil writes, "Network journalism originally was designed not to make a profit but to create prestige. Cable is all about profit and keeping costs low. What is disappearing is an idealism about the potential of TV as a medium to better our politics and society."[22]

THE IMPACT OF THE INTERNET

Some scholars have expressed quite optimistic predictions that the development of the Internet will be a boon for American democracy. As any college student knows, the Internet is the ultimate research tool. Want to know something specific? The answer can usually be found by searching the Internet using a few key words. If you want to know how the presidential candidates stand on federal support for higher education, an Internet search should quickly reveal the answers. Or if you want to know how your two U.S. senators voted recently on Medicaid appropriations, the records of the Senate roll calls can be found on the Internet. In short, for anyone with basic computing skills, the ability to become well informed about political issues is now easier than ever before.

Yet simply because so much political information is at one's fingertips via the Internet doesn't necessarily mean that many people will take advantage of these unprecedented opportunities to become well informed. One of the things that makes the Internet different from TV is that is purposive—that is, what people see is the product of their own intentional choices. Politics is only one of a myriad of subjects that one can find out about on the Internet. As we saw in the previous chapter on public opinion, most Americans' interest in politics is fairly limited. Most people with limited political interest will probably not be motivated to use the Internet to look up detailed information about politics very often. Indeed, the data on Lycos searches displayed in Table 7.1 indicate that even during the week of the

Why It Matters
The Increasing Speed of News Dissemination
When Samuel Morse sent the first telegraph message from the U.S. Capitol building, he tapped out a question, "What hath God wrought?" The answer back was, "What is the news from Washington?" Ever since then, the transmission of news via electronic means has become faster and faster. As a result, over time there has been less and less time for deliberative action to provide for the future, and the political agenda has come to focus more on the here and now.

TABLE 7.1

The Top 25 Lycos Searches for the Week of the First 2008 Presidential Debate

Every week, the search engine Lycos lists the search terms that its users have most frequently used to seek information on the Internet. Here you can find the top 25 searches for the week ending September 30, 2008—the week of the first Obama–McCain presidential debate. As you can see, only 2 of the top 25 search items reflect an interest in the election or news events. More people used the Internet to get information about pop culture figures such as Clay Aiken and Paris Hilton than to learn about the stunning news of Lehman Brothers going bankrupt or about the presidential candidates.

The rankings reflect what Internet users are most interested in. Political scientists have long argued that politics are only a peripheral part of most people's lives, and these rankings clearly reflect that fact.

RANK	SEARCH TERM	RANK	SEARCH TERM
1.	Clay Aiken	14.	Naruto
2.	Paris Hilton	15.	WWE
3.	YOUTUBE	16.	Kanye West
4.	Travis Barker	17.	Lance Armstrong
5.	Pamela Anderson	18.	Biggest Loser
6.	Kim Kardashian	19.	Bristol Palin
7.	Facebook	20.	Lehman Brothers Bankruptcy
8.	DJ AM	21.	RUNESCAPE
9.	Britney Spears	22.	Kendra Wilkinson
10.	Dragonball	23.	Carmen Electra
11.	Lindsay Lohan	24.	Jennifer Hudson
12.	Sarah Palin	25.	Eva Mendes
13.	Megan Fox		

Source: http://50.lycos.com/.

first 2008 presidential election debate Americans were more likely to be looking for information on pop culture than politics.

The impact of the Internet on politics has thus far been more subtle than revolutionary. The major changes stem from the fact that the Internet facilitates more communication in every conceivable direction. Journalists, politicians, and interest group organizers can communicate more readily with the public at large, and ordinary citizens can now respond more easily and more frequently than ever before. As a result of the new lines of communication opened up by the Internet, there have been some important changes in the nature of journalism and campaigning.

Journalists who were once constrained by the amount of space in their newspaper or time on their TV show now have the ability to post additional information regarding their stories on the Internet. Perhaps more important, readers and viewers now have a way of challenging and supplementing media stories by posting their own material via blogs. For example, when Dan Rather and CBS News ran a story in 2004 about documents that allegedly showed that George W. Bush had shirked his duties with the National Guard in the 1970s, a number of bloggers quickly raised questions concerning their authenticity. The bloggers were ultimately proven right, and CBS News apologized for running the story.

For campaigns, the ability to post more information and communicate with supporters via the Internet has helped somewhat in terms of political mobilization. Bruce Bimber and Richard Davis's study of campaigning online found that "campaign web sites attract supporters of the candidates who display them, and the messages of these sites have a modest tendency to strengthen and reinforce voters' predispositions."[23] As these authors point out, with the decline of traditional neighborhood-based party organizations, the Internet is providing a much-needed means to bring activists together, employing such vehicles as meetup.com.

PRIVATE CONTROL OF THE MEDIA

As we have seen, America has a rich diversity of media sources. One of the main reasons that this has long been the case is that journalism has long been big business in the United States, with control of virtually all media outlets being in private hands. Only a relatively small number of TV stations are publicly owned in America, and these PBS stations play a minimal role in the news business, attracting low ratings. In contrast, in many other countries major TV networks are owned by the government. In Canada the most prominent stations are part of the state-run Canadian Broadcasting Company, and most anywhere in Europe the major networks are government owned. In these established democracies, government ownership is not supposed to inhibit journalists from criticizing the government because the journalists are assured autonomy. In underdeveloped countries like China, where democracy has yet to take root, it is a different story: Both television and newspapers are typically government enterprises and have to carefully avoid any criticism of their country's government. Private ownership of the media as well as the First Amendment right to free speech has long meant that American journalists have an unfettered capacity to criticize government leaders and policies. As you can see in "America in Perspective: Press Freedom Around the World," the United States rates pretty well in terms of freedom of the press.

Although the American media is independent when it comes to journalistic content, they are totally dependent on advertising revenues to keep their businesses going. Public ownership means that the media can serve the public interest without worrying about the size of their audience; private ownership means that getting the biggest audience is the primary—indeed, sometimes the only—objective. The major media in America are big business today and potentially the source of great profits. In recent years, the major television networks have been bought out by giant corporations. The Disney Corporation bought ABC, General Electric acquired NBC, Viacom (a conglomerate that owns many entertainment companies, including Blockbuster, Paramount Pictures, MTV, and Simon & Schuster) took over CBS, and CNN became part of Time Warner. Major metropolitan newspapers are owned mostly by **chains**, such as Gannett, Knight-Ridder, and Newhouse. Today's massive media conglomerates control newspapers with over 80 percent of the nation's daily circulation.[24] Thus, four out of five newspaper subscribers now read a newspaper owned not by a fearless local editor but by a corporation headquartered elsewhere. Often these chains control television and radio stations as well.

With corporate business managers increasingly calling the shots, American journalism has definitely been affected. For example, the major television networks once had bureaus all over the world and felt a responsibility to report on world affairs. Such foreign bureaus became an easy target for cost-cutting business executives, as they were expensive to operate and survey data showed that the public

Comparing News Media

chains
Newspapers published by massive media conglomerates that account for over four-fifths of the nation's daily newspaper circulation. Often these chains control broadcast media as well.

AMERICA IN PERSPECTIVE

Press Freedom Around the World

Freedom of the press varies substantially around the world. In general, the United States and other well-established democracies value freedom of the press, allowing journalists to openly criticize their government without fear of physical threats or censorship.

Journalists in some other countries are not so fortunate. They sometimes work directly for the state and dare not think of contradicting government policy or criticizing their country's leaders. In countries where freedom of the press is restricted, journalists often work in fear of physical threats, imprisonment, and even being murdered. They find that their offices can be searched at any time or their work confiscated and that only stories that are cleared by government censors ever make it into print.

On the basis of these criteria for freedom of the press, in 2007 the international organization known as Reporters Without Borders produced an index of press freedom for 167 countries. The graph below shows the scores for 20 selected countries. A low score indicates unfettered freedom of the press, whereas a high score indicates many restrictions on journalists.

Compared to other established democracies, the United States ranked among the worst in terms of press freedom in 2007. The reason for this relatively poor rating was the Justice Department's attempts to force reporters to disclose their confidential sources in cases of leaks of classified information (which even led to the imprisonment of Judith Miller of the *New York Times* for 85 days). Yet these incidents pale in comparison to the restrictions on freedom of the press in countries like Cuba, Iran, and North Korea—all of which had extremely high scores on the index.

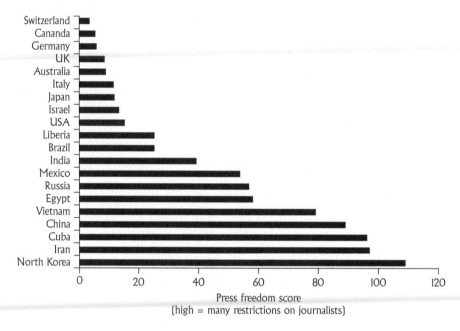

Press freedom score
(high = many restrictions on journalists)

Source: Reporters Without Borders, "Worldwide Press Freedom Index," 2007, www.rsf.org/article.php3?id_article=24025.

was not much interested in news from overseas. A study of network news broadcasts found that ABC, NBC, and CBS broadcast just 1,382 minutes of foreign news in 2000 compared to 4,032 minutes in 1989.[25] Consequently, by September 11, 2001, the American public was largely unfamiliar with overseas news, and the TV networks had to scramble to establish an ability to cover it. As we shall see in the following section, striving for profits greatly shapes how the news is reported in America.

REPORTING THE NEWS

As journalism students will quickly tell you, news is what is timely and different. It is a man biting a dog, not a dog biting a man. An often-repeated speech on foreign policy or a well-worn statement on fighting drug abuse is less newsworthy than an odd episode. The public rarely hears about the routine ceremonies at state dinners, but when President George Bush threw up all over the Japanese prime minister in

1992, the world's media jumped on the story. Similarly, when Howard Dean screamed to a crowd of supporters after the 2004 Iowa caucuses, the major networks and cable news channels played the clip over 600 times in the following four days, virtually obliterating any serious discussion of the issues. In its search for the unusual, the news media can give its audience a peculiar view of events and policymakers.

Millions of new and different events happen every day; journalists must decide which of them are newsworthy. A classic look into how the news is produced can be found in Edward J. Epstein's *News from Nowhere*,[26] which summarizes his observations from a year of observing NBC's news department from inside the organization. Epstein found that in their pursuit of high ratings, news shows are tailored to a fairly low level of audience sophistication. To a large extent, TV networks define news as what is entertaining to the average viewer. A dull and complicated story would have to be of enormous importance to get on the air; in contrast, relatively trivial stories can make the cut if they are interesting enough. Leonard Downie Jr. and Robert Kaiser of the *Washington Post* argue that entertainment has increasingly pushed out information in the TV news business. They write that the history of TV news can be summarized in a couple sentences:

> As audiences declined, network executives decreed that news had to become more profitable. So news divisions sharply reduced their costs, and tried to raise the entertainment value of their broadcasts.[27]

Regardless of the medium, it cannot be emphasized enough that news reporting is a business in America. The quest for profits shapes how journalists define what is newsworthy, where they get their information, and how they present it. Because some types of news stories attract more viewers or readers than others, certain biases are inherent in what the American public sees and reads.

FINDING THE NEWS

Americans' popular image of correspondents or reporters somehow uncovering the news is accurate in some cases, yet most news stories come from well-established sources. Major news organizations assign their best reporters to particular **beats**— specific locations from which news often emanates, such as Congress. For example, during the 1991 Gulf War, more than 50 percent of the lead stories on TV newscasts came from the White House, Pentagon, and State Department beats.[28] Numerous studies of both the electronic and the print media show that journalists rely almost exclusively on such established sources to get their information.[29]

Those who make the news depend on the media to spread certain information and ideas to the general public. Sometimes they feed stories to reporters in the form of **trial balloons**: information leaked to see what the political reaction will be. For example, a few days prior to President Clinton's admission that he had an "inappropriate relationship" with Monica Lewinsky, top aides to the president leaked the story to Richard Berke of the *New York Times*. The timing of the leak was obvious; the story appeared just before Clinton had to decide how to testify before Kenneth Starr's grand jury. When the public reacted that it was about time he admitted this relationship, it was probably easier for him to do so—at least politically.

Reporters and their official sources have a symbiotic relationship. News makers rely on journalists to get their message out at the same time that reporters rely on public officials to keep them in the know. When reporters feel that their access to information is being impeded, complaints of censorship become widespread. During the 1991 Gulf War, reporters' freedom of movement and observation was severely restricted. After the fighting was over, 15 influential news organizations sent a letter to the secretary of defense complaining that the rules for reporting the war were designed more to control the news than to facilitate it.[30] In response to complaints about the lack of

beats
Specific locations from which news frequently emanates, such as Congress or the White House. Most top reporters work a particular beat, thereby becoming specialists in what goes on at that location.

trial balloons
An intentional news leak for the purpose of assessing the political reaction.

access for reporters in the first Gulf War, the Pentagon embedded about 500 reporters with coalition fighting forces during the 2003 military campaign to oust Saddam Hussein from power, thus enabling them to report on combat activity as it happened. The result was an increased ability to transmit combat footage. A content analysis by Farnsworth and Lichter found that 35 percent of major TV network stories contained combat scenes compared to just 20 percent in 1991.[31] The public response to this new form of war reporting was largely positive.[32]

Although journalists are typically dependent on familiar sources, an enterprising reporter occasionally has an opportunity to live up to the image of the crusading truth seeker. Local reporters Carl Bernstein and Bob Woodward of the *Washington Post* uncovered important evidence in the Watergate case in the early 1970s. Ever since the Watergate scandal, news organizations have regularly sent reporters on beats to expose the uglier side of government corruption and inefficiency. Such reporting is highly valued among the media elite.

There are many cases of good investigative reporting making a difference in politics and government. For example, in 1997 the *New York Times* won a Pulitzer prize for its in-depth reports on how a proposed gold-mining operation threatened the environment of part of Yellowstone National Park. When President Clinton vacationed at nearby Jackson Hole, he decided to go up and see the mine because he had been reading about it in the *New York Times*. Soon afterward, the project was stopped, and the government gave the owners of the property a financial settlement. In 1999, the *Chicago Tribune* documented the experiences of numerous Illinois men sentenced to death who had been convicted on questionable evidence or coerced into confessing. Soon after the series was published, the governor of Illinois suspended all executions in the state. And in 2006 four reporters from the *Washington Post* were awarded a Pulitzer Prize for their probe into the dealings of the infamous Washington lobbyist Jack Abramoff that exposed congressional corruption and led to lobbying reform.

PRESENTING THE NEWS

Once the news has been "found," it has to be neatly compressed into a 30-second news segment or fit in among the advertisements in a newspaper. If you had to pick a single word to describe news coverage by the print and broadcast media, it would be *superficial*. "The name of the game," says former White House Press Secretary Jody Powell, "is skimming off the cream, seizing on the most interesting, controversial, and unusual aspects of an issue."[33] Editors do not want to bore or confuse their audience. TV news, in particular, is little more than a headline service. According to former CBS anchor Dan Rather, "You simply cannot be a well-informed citizen by just watching the news on television."[34]

Except for the little-watched but highly regarded *NewsHour* on PBS and ABC's late-night *Nightline,* analysis of news events rarely lasts more than a minute. Patterson's study of campaign coverage (see Chapter 9) found that only skimpy attention was given to the issues during a presidential campaign. Clearly, if coverage of political events during the height of an election campaign is thin, coverage of day-to-day policy questions is even thinner. Issues such as reforming the Medicare system, adjusting how the consumer price index is calculated, and deregulating the communications industry are highly complex and difficult to treat in a short news clip. A careful study of media coverage of Bill and Hillary Clinton's comprehensive health care proposal in 1993–94 found that the media focused much more on strategy and who was winning the political game than on the specific policy issues involved.[35]

Strangely enough, as technology has enabled the media to pass along information with greater speed, news coverage has become less thorough.[36] Modern high-tech communications equipment has helped reporters do their job faster but not necessarily better. Newspapers once routinely reprinted the entire text of important political speeches; now the *New York Times* is virtually the only paper that does so— and even the *Times* has cut back sharply on this practice. In place of speeches, Americans now hear **sound bites** of 10 seconds or less on TV. As you can see in Figure 7.2, the average length of time that a presidential candidate has been given to talk uninterrupted on the TV news has declined precipitously since the late 1960s. Responding to criticism of sound-bite journalism, in 1992 CBS News briefly vowed that it would let a candidate speak for at least 30 seconds at a time. However, CBS found this to be unworkable and soon dropped the threshold to 20 seconds, noting that even this was flexible.[37] In 2004, the average sound bite of a candidate shown talking on the nightly news was just 7.8 seconds.

Even successful politicians sometimes feel frustrated by sound-bite journalism. A year after his election to the presidency, Jimmy Carter told a reporter that

> it's a strange thing that you can go through your campaign for president, and you have a basic theme that you express in a 15- or 20-minute standard speech . . . but the traveling press—sometimes exceeding 100 people—will never report that speech to the public. The peripheral aspects become the headlines, but the basic essence of what you stand for and what you hope to accomplish is never reported.[38]

Rather than presenting their audience with the whole chicken, the media typically give just a McNugget. Why should politicians work to build a carefully crafted case for their point of view when a catchy line will do just as well? As former

sound bites
Short video clips of approximately 10 seconds. Typically, they are all that is shown from a politician's speech on the nightly television news.

FIGURE 7.2

The Incredible Shrinking Sound Bite

Following is the average length of time a presidential candidate was shown speaking without interruptions on the evening network news from 1968 to 2004.

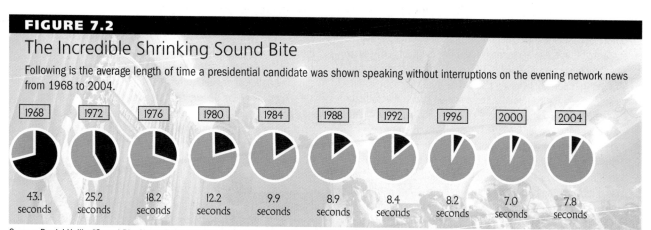

1968	1972	1976	1980	1984	1988	1992	1996	2000	2004
43.1 seconds	25.2 seconds	18.2 seconds	12.2 seconds	9.9 seconds	8.9 seconds	8.4 seconds	8.2 seconds	7.0 seconds	7.8 seconds

Source: Daniel Hallin, "Sound Bite News: Television Coverage of Elections," *Journal of Communications,* Spring 1992; 1992–2004 data from studies by the Center for Media and Public Affairs.

CBS anchor Walter Cronkite writes, "Naturally, nothing of any significance is going to be said in seven seconds, but this seems to work to the advantage of many politicians. They are not required to say anything of significance, and issues can be avoided rather than confronted."[39] Cronkite and others have proposed that in order to force candidates to go beyond sound bites, they should be given blocks of free airtime for a series of nights to discuss their opposing views (see "You Are the Policymaker: Should the Networks Have to Provide Free Air Time to Presidential Candidates?").

Over the past decade, politicians have found it increasingly difficult to get their message covered on the major networks, as ratings pressures have led to a decrease in political coverage, leaving the field to the much less watched channels like CNN and MSNBC. The three major networks *together* devoted an average of 12.6 minutes per night to the exceedingly close 2000 presidential election campaign; just half the 24.6 minutes they devoted to the 1992 campaign.[40] Indeed, in the presidential election of 2000, voters had to bypass network television newscasts and watch TV talk shows to hear candidates deliver their messages. George Bush was on-screen for a total of 13 minutes during his appearance on *Late Night with David Letterman* on October 19, which exceeded his entire speaking time on all three network news shows during that month. Similarly, Al Gore received more speaking time on his September 14 *Letterman* appearance than he did during the entire month of September on the network evening newscasts.[41]

During the Cold War, presidents could routinely obtain coverage for their speeches on the three major networks anytime they requested it. Now, with the networks able to shunt the coverage to CNN and other cable news outlets, it is easy for

YOU ARE THE Policymaker

Should the Networks Have to Provide Free Air Time to Presidential Candidates?

In 1996, a group of prominent political and media figures proposed the idea of a series of free prime-time television appearances for presidential candidates to address the issues. The Coalition for Free Air Time called on the networks to turn over two to five minutes a night to the candidates in the month before the presidential election. Furthermore, the coalition suggested that these segments should be "roadblocked"—shown simultaneously on all networks, PBS, and interested cable stations so that people watching prime-time entertainment would be sure to see the candidates. The coalition hoped this format would promote a nightly dialogue on the issues, with candidates making news with their replies to each other's previous segments. The only requirement would be that the candidates look straight into the camera and talk. There would be no manipulation of images or unseen narrators—just candidates making their case directly to the biggest potential audience every night.

Most of the networks did eventually grant the candidates some free time in 1996, but the approach was a scattershot

one. The segments varied from one to two and a half minutes, and each network chose a different time to broadcast them. A survey done by the Annenberg School of Communication immediately after the election found that only 22 percent of registered voters even knew that the free-time effort existed. Virtually everyone involved was disappointed with the results. The results from the 2000 and 2004 elections were similarly disheartening, as the networks adopted different approaches and the audiences tended to be relatively small.

Many observers believe that the experience of the recent presidential elections has demonstrated the necessity of adopting a common format and time for all networks; some even advocate using the government's regulatory powers to force the networks to adopt this approach. Others point to the poor ratings of the televised debates as an example of the ineffectiveness of roadblocking political dialogue when the public just isn't interested. You be the policymaker. Is this an experiment that the government should mandate in future presidential elections?

them to say "no" to even the president. In May 2000, for example, Bill Clinton was rebuffed when he asked for time on ABC, NBC, and CBS to address U.S.–China relations. "Are you crazy? It's sweeps month!" was one of the responses.[42]

Until September 11, the Bush White House found it harder to get media attention than any administration in a long time. A study of the first 60 days of coverage of the presidencies of Bill Clinton and George W. Bush on ABC, NBC, CBS, and PBS, and on the section fronts and opinion pages of the *Washington Post,* the *New York Times,* and *Newsweek* found that there were about 40 percent fewer stories on Bush than on Clinton.[43] The prominence of the president increased briefly after the September 11 terrorist attacks, but Farnsworth and Lichter's study concluded that, "even the deadliest terrorist attack in our history, and the subsequent military intervention in Afghanistan, could not reverse the trend of decreasing coverage of the executive branch."[44]

BIAS IN THE NEWS

Many people believe that the news is biased in favor of one point of view. In recent years, Republicans have often charged that the press was against them. The charge that the media have a liberal bias has become a familiar one in American politics, and there is some limited evidence to support it. David Weaver et al. have conducted four comprehensive surveys of American journalists between 1971 and 2002 and consistently found that reporters were more likely to classify themselves as liberal than the general public. In 2002, 40 percent of journalists surveyed said they leaned to the left compared to only 25 percent who leaned to the right.[45]

However, the vast majority of social science studies have found that reporting is not systematically biased toward a particular ideology or party. Most stories are presented in a "point/counterpoint" format in which two opposing points of view (such as liberal versus conservative) are presented, and the audience is left to draw its own conclusions. Two factors explain why the news is typically characterized by such political neutrality. Most reporters strongly believe in journalistic objectivity, and those who practice it best are usually rewarded by their editors. In addition, media outlets have a direct financial stake in attracting viewers and subscribers and do not want to lose their audience by appearing biased—especially when multiple versions of the same story are readily available. It seems paradoxical to say that competition produces uniformity, but this often happens in the news business.

To conclude that the news contains little explicit partisan bias is not to argue that it does not distort reality in its coverage. Former CBS News reporter Bernard Goldberg spoke for many observers when he wrote in his recent bestselling book *Bias* that "real media bias comes not so much from what party they attack. Liberal bias is the result of how they see the world."[46] Goldberg argues on social issues like feminism, gay rights, and welfare

Why It Matters
Media as a Business
In his classic book *Understanding Media,* Marshall McLuhan coined the famous phrase, "The medium is the message." By this, McLuhan meant that the way we communicate information can be more influential than the information itself. In the United States, news is a commodity controlled by the media, not a public service. Therefore, the news media have far more incentive to make their reports interesting than informative about policy issues. The public would probably be exposed to more policy information were it not for this incentive system.

Media Bias

LIVE

DAVID BLOOM
WITH THE THIRD INFANTRY DIVISION
IN IRAQ

In 2003, during the Iraq War, a number of journalists were embedded with fighting units, meaning that they traveled along with them day after day and literally became part of the unit. Being right in with the action enabled an immediacy of reporting that was never possible before. One much-praised example of embedded reporting was that of NBC's David Bloom, who sent back stunningly clear pictures of what it was like to move through the desert with an infantry division. Sadly, Bloom was one of a number of journalists who died during the conflict with Iraq. He suffered a pulmonary embolism, a condition that may have been brought on by long hours confined to a very small space inside an armored tank.

talking head

A shot of a person's face talking directly to the camera. Because this is visually unappealing, the major commercial networks rarely show a politician talking one-on-one for very long.

that the nightly news clearly leans to the left, shaped by the cosmopolitan big-city environment in which network reporters live. He asks a telling question when he writes, "Do we really think that if the media elites worked out of Nebraska instead of New York; and if they were overwhelmingly social conservatives instead of liberals . . . do we really think that would make no difference?"[47]

Ideally, the news should mirror reality; in practice there are far too many possible stories for this to be the case. Journalists must choose which stories to cover and to what degree. The overriding bias is toward stories that will draw the largest audience. As Bernard Goldberg writes, "In the United States of Entertainment there is no greater sin than to bore the audience. A TV reporter could get it wrong from time to time. He could be snippy and snooty. But he could not be boring."[48] Surveys show that people are most fascinated by stories with conflict, violence, disaster, or scandal, as can be seen in Table 7.2. Good news is unexciting; bad news has the drama that brings in big audiences.

Television is particularly biased toward stories that generate good pictures. Seeing a **talking head** (a shot of a person's face talking directly to the camera) is boring; viewers will switch channels in search of more interesting visual stimulation. For example, during an unusually contentious and lengthy interview of George Bush by Dan Rather concerning the Iran-Contra scandal in the 1980s, CBS's ratings actually went down as people tired of watching two talking heads argue for an extended period of time.[49] A shot of ambassadors squaring off in a fistfight at the United Nations, on the other hand, will increase the ratings. Such a scene was shown three times in one day on CBS. Not once, though, was the cause of the fight discussed.[50] Network practices like these have led observers such as Lance Bennett to write that "the public is exposed to a world driven into chaos by seemingly arbitrary and mysterious forces."[51]

THE NEWS AND PUBLIC OPINION

How does the threatening, hostile, and corrupt world often depicted by the news media shape what people believe about the American political system? This question is difficult to answer. Studying the effects of the news media on people's opinions and behaviors is a difficult task. One reason is that it is hard to separate the media from other influences. When presidents, legislators, and interest groups—as well as news organizations—are all discussing an issue, it is not easy to isolate the opinion changes that come from political leadership from those that come from the news. Moreover, the effect of one news story on public opinion may be trivial; the cumulative effect of dozens of news stories may be important.

For many years, students of the subject tended to doubt that the media had more than a marginal effect on public opinion. The "minimal effects hypothesis" stemmed from the fact that early scholars were looking for direct impacts—for

VISUAL LITERACY

Use of the Media by the American Public

TABLE 7.2

Stories Citizens Have Tuned In and Tuned Out

Since 1986, the monthly survey of the Pew Research Center for the People and the Press has asked Americans how closely they have followed major news stories. As one would expect, stories involving disaster or human drama have drawn more attention than complicated issues of public policy. A representative selection of their findings is presented here. The percentage in each case is the proportion who reported following the story "very closely."

Story	Percent
The explosion of the space shuttle *Challenger* in 1986	80%
Terrorist attacks on the World Trade Center and Pentagon	74%
Impacts of hurricanes Katrina and Rita	73%
Los Angeles riots	70%
Rescue of baby Jessica McClure from a well	69%
School shootings at Columbine High School in Colorado	68%
Iraq's invasion of Kuwait in 1990	66%
Start of hostilities against Iraq in 2003	57%
Supreme Court decision on flag burning	51%
Opening of the Berlin Wall	50%
Arrest of O. J. Simpson	48%
Nuclear accident at Chernobyl	46%
Capture of Saddam Hussein	44%
Controversy over whether Elián González should have to return to Cuba	39%
2000 presidential election outcome	38%
Impeachment trial of President Clinton in the Senate	31%
Confirmation of John Roberts as Chief Justice	28%
Prescription drug benefit added to the Medicare program	25%
2004 Republican National Convention	22%
Release of President Bush's education plan in 2002	21%
Congressional debate about NAFTA	21%
Jack Abramoff's admission that he bribed members of Congress	18%
Ethnic violence in the Darfur region of Sudan	16%
Passage of the Communications Deregulation Bill	12%
Violent protests in Tibet against the Chinese government in 2008	12%
2003 Supreme Court decision upholding campaign finance reform	8%

Source: Pew Research Center for the People and the Press.

example, whether the media affected how people voted.[52] When the focus turned to how the media affect *what Americans think about,* more positive results were uncovered. In a series of controlled laboratory experiments, Shanto Iyengar and Donald Kinder subtly manipulated the stories participants saw on the TV news.[53] They found that they could significantly affect the importance people attached to a given problem by splicing a few stories about it into the news over the course of a week. Iyengar and Kinder do not maintain that the networks can make something out of nothing or conceal problems that actually exist. But they do conclude that "what television news does, instead, is alter the priorities Americans attach to a circumscribed set of problems, all of which are plausible contenders for public concern."[54] Subsequent research by Miller and Krosnick has revealed that agenda-setting effects are particularly strong among politically knowledgeable citizens who trust the media. Thus, rather than the media manipulating the public, they argue that agenda setting reflects a deliberate and thoughtful process on the part of sophisticated

Conservative Republicans often criticize the media for being biased against them. Studies have indeed shown that TV and newspaper reporters are more likely to be liberals than conservatives. However, there is little evidence that the personal views of reporters influence their coverage.

citizens who rely on what they consider to be a credible institutional source of information.[55]

This effect has far-reaching consequences. By increasing public attention to specific problems, the media influence the criteria by which the public evaluates political leaders. When unemployment goes up but inflation goes down, does public support for the president increase or decrease? The answer could depend in large part on which story the media emphasized. The fact that the media emphasized the country's slow economic growth in 1992 rather than the good news of low inflation and interest rates was clearly instrumental in setting the stage for Bill Clinton ousting the incumbent president (George H. W. Bush) in that year. Similarly, the emphasis on candidate character in 2000 as opposed to the excellent economic performance under the Clinton–Gore administration clearly helped the candidacy of George W. Bush.

The media can even have a dramatic effect on how the public evaluates specific events by emphasizing one particular news aspect over all others. When the press gave substantial coverage to President Ford's misstatement about Soviet domination of Eastern Europe, this coverage had an impact on the public. Polls showed that most people did not realize the president had made an error until the press told them so. Afterward, pro-Ford evaluations of the debate declined noticeably as voters' concerns for competence in foreign policymaking became salient.[56] Similarly, the media's focus on Al Gore's misstatements during the first presidential debate of 2000 had an impact on public opinion. In the days immediately following this debate, the percentage who thought that Gore had beaten Bush declined markedly.[57]

Much remains unknown about the effects of the media and the news on American political behavior. Enough is known, however, to conclude that the media make up a key political institution. The media control much of the technology that in turn controls much of what Americans believe about politics and government. For this reason, it is important to look at the American policy agenda and the media's role in shaping it.

THE MEDIA'S AGENDA-SETTING FUNCTION

policy agenda
The issues that attract the serious attention of public officials and other people actively involved in politics at the time.

Someone who asks you "What's your agenda?" wants to know something about your priorities. As discussed in Chapter 1, governments also have agendas. John Kingdon defines **policy agenda** as "the list of subjects or problems to which government officials, and people outside of government closely associated with those officials, are paying some serious attention at any given time."[58] Interest groups, political parties, individual politicians, public relations firms, bureaucratic agencies—and, of course, the president and Congress—are all pushing for their priorities to take precedence over others. Health care, education, unemployment, and welfare reform—these and scores of other issues compete for attention from the government.

Political activists depend heavily on the media to get their ideas placed high on the governmental agenda. Political activists are often called **policy entrepreneurs**—people who invest their political "capital" in an issue (as an economic entrepreneur invests capital in an idea for making money). Kingdon says that policy entrepreneurs can "be in or out of government, in elected or appointed positions, in interest groups or research organizations."[59] Policy entrepreneurs' arsenal of weapons includes press releases, press conferences, and letter writing; convincing reporters and columnists to tell their side; trading on personal contacts; and, in cases of desperation, resorting to staging dramatic events.

The Internet site YouTube.com has had an immediate impact on politics. By enabling users to share videos and access them widely, the site has given otherwise obscure home videos national attention. One of the most widely viewed political videos on YouTube in 2008 was "I Got a Crush on Obama" by Obama Girl. As of election day, it had been viewed over 10 million times.

The media are not always monopolized by political elites; the poor and downtrodden have access to them too. Civil rights groups in the 1960s relied heavily on the media to tell their stories of unjust treatment. Many believe that the introduction of television helped to accelerate the movement by showing Americans—in the North and South alike—just what the situation was.[60] Protest groups have learned that if they can stage an interesting event that attracts the media's attention, at least their point of view will be heard. Radical activist Saul Alinsky once dramatized the plight of one neighborhood by having its residents collect rats and dump them on the mayor's front lawn. The story was one that local reporters could hardly resist. In 2002, graduate students at the University of California, Irvine, camped out in tents in the campus park to protest the lack of investment in on-campus housing. The prime organizer, a teaching assistant for an introduction to American government course, issued press releases and made calls to news directors urging them to come down and take a look. Soon after several stations put the sorry scene on TV, the university administration gave in to the graduate students' demands.

Conveying a long-term, positive image via the media is more important than a few dramatic events. Policy entrepreneurs—individuals or groups, in or out of government—depend on goodwill and good images. Sometimes it helps to hire a public relations firm that specializes in getting a specific message across. Groups, individuals, and even countries have hired public relations firms to improve their image and their ability to peddle their issue positions.[61]

policy entrepreneurs
People who invest their political "capital" in an issue. According to John Kingdon, a policy entrepreneur "could be in or out of government, in elected or appointed positions, in interest groups or research organizations."

UNDERSTANDING THE MASS MEDIA

The media act as key linkage institutions between the people and the policymakers and have a profound impact on the political policy agenda. Bernard Cohen goes so far as to say, "No major act of the American Congress, no foreign adventure, no act of diplomacy, no great social reform can succeed unless the press prepares the public mind."[62] If Cohen is right, then the growth of government in America would have been impossible without the need for it being established through the media.

THE MEDIA AND THE SCOPE OF GOVERNMENT

The media's watchdog function helps to keep politicians in check. Notably, this is one aspect of the media's job performance that Americans consistently evaluate positively. For over two decades, the Pew Research Center for People and the Press has consistently found that a clear majority of the public has said that press criticism of political leaders does more good than harm. In 2007, a Pew Research Center poll found that 58 percent said that press criticism of political leaders is worth it because keeps leaders from doing things that should not be done, while 27 percent believed criticism keeps political leaders from doing their jobs.[63]

To many reporters, exposing officeholders is an essential role of the press in a free society, as demonstrated in Figure 7.1. They often hold disparaging views of public officials, believing that they are self-serving, hypocritical, lacking in integrity, and preoccupied with reelection. Thus, it is not surprising that journalists frequently see a need to debunk public officials and their policy proposals.

INDIVIDUALISM AND THE MEDIA

More than any other development in the past century, the rise of television broadcasting has reinforced and furthered individualism in the American political process. Candidates are now much more capable of running for office on their own by appealing to people directly through television. Individual voters can see the candidates "up close and personal" for themselves, and they have much less need for political parties or social groups to help them make their decisions.

Television finds it easier to focus on individuals than on groups. As a result, parties have declined, and candidate personality is more important than ever. Congress is difficult to cover on television because there are 535 members, but there is only one president. Doris Graber's recent study of nightly news broadcasts found that 60 percent of the coverage devoted to the three branches of government was devoted to the president as compared to 31 percent for the Congress. The Supreme Court, which does not allow TV cameras to cover its proceedings and whose members rarely give interviews, is almost invisible on TV newscasts, receiving only a mere 9 percent of the coverage.[64]

DEMOCRACY AND THE MEDIA

As Ronald Berkman and Laura Kitch remark, "Information is the fuel of democracy."[65] Widespread access to information could be the greatest boon to democracy since the secret ballot, yet most observers think it has fallen far short of this potential. Noting the vast increase in information available through the news media, Berkman and Kitch state, "If the sheer quantity of news produced greater competency in the citizenry, then we would have a society of political masters. Yet, just the opposite is happening."[66] The rise of the "information society" has not brought about the rise of the "informed society."

Whenever the media are criticized for being superficial, their defense is to say that this is what people want. Network executives remark that if people suddenly started to watch in-depth shows such as PBS's *NewsHour*, then they would gladly imitate them. If the American people wanted serious coverage of the issues, networks would be happy to give it to them. Network executives claim they are in business to make a profit and that, to do so, they must appeal to the maximum number of people. As Matthew Kerbel observes, "The people who bring you the evening news would like it to be informative *and* entertaining, but when these two values collide, the shared orientations of the television news world push the product inexorably toward the latter."[67] It is not their fault if the resulting news coverage is superficial, network executives argue; blame capitalism or the people—most of whom like news to be more entertaining than educational. Thus, if people are not better informed in the high-tech age, it is largely because they do not care to hear about complicated political issues. In this sense, one can say that the people really do rule through the media.

SUMMARY

Plenty of evidence points to the power of the media in American politics. The media are ubiquitous. There is evidence that the news and its presentation are an important—perhaps the most important—shaper of public opinion on political issues. The media are an important ingredient in shaping the policy agenda, and political entrepreneurs carefully use the media for this purpose.

Gradually, the broadcast media have replaced the print media as the principal source of news. Recently, the development of cable TV channels and Web sites has led to narrowcasting—appealing to specific segments of the mass public rather than to the entire population. The media define "news" largely as people and events out of the ordinary. Because of economic pressures, the media are biased in favor of stories with high drama that will attract people's interest instead of extended analyses of complex issues. With the media's superficial treatment of important policy issues, it should be no surprise that the incredible amount of information available to Americans today has not visibly increased their political awareness or participation.

Chapter Test
Multiple Choice

1. A "media event" is:
   a. Any event that is covered by the media
   b. Only events that are covered by the national media
   c. Only a really important event, such as a party's national convention or the presidential election
   d. A banquet for reporters and television executives
   e. An event that is staged primarily for the media

2. On average, how much of a presidential candidate's campaign budget is spent on TV ads?
   a. 80 percent
   b. 60 percent
   c. 40 percent
   d. 20 percent
   e. Less than 10 percent

3. Which president was arguably the most influential when it comes to conception of "media politics"?
   a. Herbert Hoover
   b. Franklin D. Roosevelt
   c. Richard Nixon
   d. Ronald Reagan
   e. Bill Clinton

4. The media generally became more cynical in its coverage of politicians after:
   a. The Great Depression
   b. World War II
   c. The Korean War
   d. Vietnam and Watergate
   e. The Lewinsky scandal

5. Which of the following is NOT one of the responsibilities of the Federal Communications Commission (FCC)?
   a. To prevent near monopolies of control over a broadcast market
   b. To conduct periodic examinations of the goals and performance of stations
   c. To ensure that licensed stations serve the public interest
   d. To uphold fair treatment rules concerning access to airwaves for political candidates and officeholders
   e. To ensure the quality and reliability of information that is broadcast.

6. Which of the following can be said to be the best example of "yellow journalism"?
   a. A story on the election of Hamas in the Palestinian territories in 2006
   b. The coverage of the Pope's visit to the White House in 2008
   c. The in-depth coverage of the Vietnam War in the 1960s and 1970s
   d. A story on the voting record of a member of Congress
   e. The coverage of the Monica Lewinsky affair

7. If ABC sells a 30-second time slot for a campaign commercial to Barack Obama:
   a. It must sell a 60-second time slot to John McCain, but not Hillary Clinton
   b. It must sell a 60-second time slot both to John McCain and Hillary Clinton
   c. It must sell at least a 30-second time slot to either of the other candidates
   d. It must give McCain and Clinton a 60-second time slot so they can respond
   e. It can sell time slots to whomever it wants, but cannot be forced to do so

8. According to Epstein's account in *News from Nowhere,* stories were deemed newsworthy based primarily on factors:
   a. Authenticity
   b. Timeliness
   c. Importance
   d. Entertainment
   e. All of the above

True/False

9. In recent presidential elections, the large majority of the prominently aired TV ads of candidates were negative commercials.
   True_____ False_____

10. Over time, media coverage of presidential campaigns has become increasingly negative.
    True_____ False_____

11. Studies have found that people who watch the news on TV on a regular basis are more likely to vote than people who rely on print media.
    True_____ False_____

12. According to social science studies, there is a "liberal bias" among reporters that is echoed in their coverage of political issues.
    True_____ False_____

13. If Barack Obama verbally attacks Hillary Clinton during an NBC program that is not the news, Clinton has the right-of-reply on the same station, according to FCC rules.
    True_____ False_____

14. The impact of the Internet on politics has been revolutionary.
    True_____ False_____

Short Answer

15. In what ways has the rise of television impacted citizens' levels of satisfaction with government, and why?

16. Explain the concept of so-called "trial balloons" in the context of media coverage, and provide an example.

17. In your own words, explain the difference between "broadcasting" and "narrowcasting."

18. This textbook differentiates between publicly and privately owned media. What impact does the type of ownership have on the quality and nature of media broadcasting?

19. Please explain the agenda-setting role of the media, and particularly the role of so-called "policy entrepreneurs."

Short Answer/Essay Questions

20. Take a look at Figure 7.1, which shows the levels of importance journalists assign to various roles of the mass media. Based on what you have read about the media in this textbook, to what degree have journalists succeeded in fulfilling these roles? In other words, how well does the data presented match up with reality? Please be specific in your assessment and provide examples to support your arguments.

21. This textbook quotes President Richard Nixon as having said: "When I think of the millions of dollars that go into one lousy 30-second television spot advertising a deodorant, it seems to me unbelievable that we don't do a better job in seeing that presidential appearances always have the very best professional advice whenever they are to be covered on TV." How would you assess this statement today, 40 years later? How, and how much, has the situation changed? Is this change for the better or worse? And why?

22. What are the pros and cons of the intense scrutiny presidential candidates and presidents undergo in the mass media?

23. According to studies, the quality of political journalism has declined since the advent of cable television. In what ways has the quality suffered? What do you believe accounts for this trend? What are the possible implications of this?

24. Looking at Figure 7.2, describe how the average length of time that a presidential candidate is given to talk has changed over time. What would you say are at least three factors that might explain this development? In addition, what are three possible consequences of this?

25. When looking at Table 7.2, what can you say about the types of stories that hold America's interest? In other words, how would you categorize the kinds of stories that are more likely to be followed than others, and why do you suppose that is?

26. In your opinion, what are the consequences of the vast amounts of money presidential candidates spend on TV commercials, both for the electoral process and for democracy in general? Support your arguments.

27. Based on everything you have read in Chapter 7, how would you evaluate the relationship between the media and politicians. (provide 3-4 arguments) In particular, which of the two is more likely to influence the other, and how/why?

Answer Key

1. E   2. B   3. B   4. D   5. E   6. E   7. B   8. D   9. True   10. True   11. False   12. False   13. False   14. False

Key Terms

high-tech politics (218)
mass media (218)
media event (218)
press conferences (220)
investigative journalism (221)

print media (222)
broadcast media (222)
narrowcasting (225)
chains (229)
beats (231)

trial balloons (231)
sound bites (233)
talking head (236)
policy agenda (238)
policy entrepreneurs (239)

Internet Resources

www.people-press.org
The Pew Center for the People and the Press regularly surveys people regarding their attitudes toward the media's coverage of politics and measures which news events people follow most closely.

www.appcpenn.org
The Annenberg Public Policy Center conducts studies that analyze the content of TV coverage of politics, which they post at this site.

www.usnpl.com
Listings for newspapers all over the country, including Web links where available.

www.cmpa.com
The Center for Media and Public Affairs posts its studies of the content of media coverage of politics at this site.

www.livingroomcandidate.movingimage.us/
A great collection of classic and recent political commercials from 1952 through 2008.

GetConnected

Campaign Advertising

Today's political campaigns rely heavily on campaign advertising to reach voters. Television stations also appear to rely on political campaigns to produce revenue for the station. The Alliance for Better Campaigns found that local television stations increased the prices of candidate ads in the two months before the 2002 elections. How much did candidates in your state spend on political advertising?

Search the Web

Go to the "In Your State" page at the Alliance for Better Campaigns' Web site. Look at how much the TV stations you watch earned from political advertising. Compare that amount with the amounts in neighboring states.

Questions to Ask

- How much money did your local television stations earn from campaign advertising?
- How does this compare to the amount of money stations in neighboring states earned? What might explain the differences you find?
- The Alliance for Better Campaigns advocates providing free airtime for candidates. You can read about this proposal on the organization's Web page. Does it sound like a good idea to provide free airtime to candidates?

Why It Matters

In order for voters to make informed decisions in a world with increasingly complicated issues, more detailed information is necessary. Often sound bites don't provide enough information or the right kind of information. The costs of television advertising sometimes cause candidates to end their campaigns, and some candidates can't afford to advertise on television. If television is the primary way that most voters get political information, it is possible that some candidates' messages may not be heard.

Get Involved

Do you agree or disagree with the Alliance for Better Campaigns' goals? Send them an e-mail to let them know. The Alliance lists its state partner organizations on its Web page. Contact these state organizations to find out what they are doing in your state. For more exercises, go to *www.longmanamericangovernment.com.*

For Further Reading

Baum, Matthew A. *Soft News Goes to War: Public Opinion and American Foreign Policy in the New Media Age.* Princeton, NJ: Princeton University Press, 2003. A path-breaking examination of how people learn about major foreign policy events from entertainment news shows like *Oprah* and *Dateline.*

Downie, Leonard, Jr., and Robert G. Kaiser. *The News About the News: American Journalism in Peril.* New York: Alfred A. Knopf, 2002. A good look at how the changing economics of the news profession is altering media values and practices.

Epstein, Edward J. *News from Nowhere: Television and the News.* New York: Random House, 1973. A classic analysis of how financial considerations shape what is presented on TV news broadcasts.

Farnsworth, Stephen J., and S. Robert Lichter. *The Mediated Presidency: Television News and Presidential Governance.* Lanham, MD: Rowman & Littlefield, 2006. An in-depth content analysis of how the news media covered the administrations of Ronald Reagan, Bill Clinton, and George W. Bush.

Goldberg, Bernard. *Bias: A CBS Insider Exposes How the Media Distort the News.* Washington, DC: Regnery, 2002. A best-selling account of the network news that argues there is a liberal bias on many issues, especially social policies.

Graber, Doris A. *Mass Media and American Politics.* 7th ed. Washington, DC: Congressional Quarterly Press, 2006. The standard textbook on the subject.

Hamilton, James T. *All the News That's Fit to Sell.* Princeton, NJ: Princeton University Press, 2004. An examination of how marketing considerations shape what does and does not make the news.

Iyengar, Shanto, and Donald R. Kinder. *News That Matters.* Chicago: University of Chicago Press, 1987. Two political psychologists show how the media can affect the public agenda.

Kalb, Marvin. *One Scandalous Story: Clinton, Lewinsky, and Thirteen Days That Tarnished American Journalism.* New York: Free Press, 2001. An indictment of how journalistic standards have been compromised in recent years, as illustrated by the media's coverage of the Lewinsky scandal.

Kingdon, John W. *Agendas, Alternatives, and Public Policy.* 2nd ed. New York: HarperCollins, 1995. The best overall study of the formation of policy agendas.

Mindich, David T. Z. *Tuned Out: Why Americans Under 40 Don't Follow the News.* New York: Oxford University Press, 2005. An interesting examination of why today's young people are not following political news nearly as closely as older people.

Patterson, Thomas E. *Out of Order.* New York: Knopf, 1993. A highly critical and well-documented examination of how the media cover election campaigns.

Prior, Markus. *Post-Broadcast Democracy: How Media Choice Increases Inequality in Political Involvement and Polarizes Elections.* New York: Cambridge University Press, 2007. The best book so far on how the transition from broadcasting to narrowcasting has impacted American politics.

Weaver, David H. et al. *The American Journalist in the 21st Century.* Mahwah, NJ: Lawrence Erlbaum, 2007. A thorough examination of journalists in America—who they are, what they believe about politics, and how their professional values and practices have evolved over the past three decades.

West, Darrell M. *Air Wars: Television Advertising in Election Campaigns, 1952–2004.* Washington, DC: Congressional Quarterly Press, 2005. An analysis of how TV campaign ads have evolved over the past four decades and what impact they have had on elections.

CHAPTER 8

POLITICAL PARTIES

POLITICS IN ACTION:
HOW POLITICAL PARTIES CAN MAKE ELECTIONS USER FRIENDLY FOR VOTERS

In the 2006 midterm elections, the Democrats won control of the House of Representatives after being in the minority for the previous 12 years. They did so largely on the basis of public discontent with the Iraq War. By casting ballots for the opposition party, voters were able to send a message of dissatisfaction even though the Democrats had not made it clear how they would deal with the war differently.

The story of the 2006 midterms contrasts greatly from that of 1994, when the Republicans took control of the House of Representatives after 40 years of Democratic control. In that year, 367 House Republican candidates stood on the steps of the U.S. Capitol in late September of 1994 to sign a document they titled "Contract with America." This document outlined reforms the Republicans promised to pass on the first day of the new Congress as well as 10 bills they agreed would be brought to the floor for a vote within the first 100 days of the new Republican-controlled House of Representatives. The contract was the brainchild of Newt Gingrich and Richard Armey, both of whom were college professors before they were elected to Congress. Gingrich and Armey thought the Republicans needed a stronger message in 1994 than simply saying they opposed President Clinton's policies. The contract was an attempt to offer voters a positive program for reshaping American public policy and reforming how Congress works. Without actually knowing much about the individual candidates themselves, voters would know what to expect of the signers of the contract and would be able to hold them accountable for these promises in the future. In this sense, the contract endeavored to make politics user friendly for the voters.

America's Founding Fathers were more concerned with their fear that political parties could be forums for corruption and national divisiveness than they were with the role that parties could play in making politics user friendly for ordinary

voters. Thomas Jefferson spoke for many when he said, "If I could not go to heaven but with a party, I would not go there at all." In his farewell address, George Washington also warned of the dangers of parties.

Today, most observers would agree that political parties have contributed greatly to American democracy. In one of the most frequently—and rightly—quoted observations about American politics, E. E. Schattschneider said that "political parties created democracy . . . and democracy is unthinkable save in terms of the parties."[1] Political scientists and politicians alike believe that a strong party system is desirable.

The strength of the parties has an impact not only on how we are governed but also on what government does. Major expansions or contractions of the scope of government have generally been accomplished through the implementation of one party's platform. Currently, the Democrats and Republicans differ greatly on the issue of the scope of government. Which party controls the presidency and whether the same party also controls the Congress makes a big difference.

party competition

The battle of the parties for control of public offices. Ups and downs of the two major parties are one of the most important elements in American politics.

The alternating of power and influence between the two major parties is one of the most important elements in American politics. **Party competition** is the battle between Democrats and Republicans for the control of public offices. Without this competition there would be no choice, and without choice there would be no democracy. Americans have had a choice between two major political parties since the early 1800s, and this two-party system remains intact more than two centuries later.

THE MEANING OF PARTY

Almost all definitions of political parties have one thing in common: Parties try to win elections. This is their core function and the key to their definition. By contrast, interest groups do not nominate candidates for office, though they may try to influence elections. For example, no one has ever been elected to Congress as the nominee of the National Rifle Association, though many nominees have received the NRA's endorsement. Thus, Anthony Downs defined a **political party** as a "team of men [and women] seeking to control the governing apparatus by gaining office in a duly constituted election."[2]

political party

According to Anthony Downs, a "team of men [and women] seeking to control the governing apparatus by gaining office in a duly constituted election."

The word *team* is the slippery part of this definition. Party teams may not be so well disciplined and single-minded as teams fielded by top football coaches. Party teams often run every which way and are difficult to lead. Party leaders often disagree about policy, and between elections the party organizations seem to all but disappear. So who are the members of these teams? A widely adopted way of thinking about parties in political science is as "three-headed political giants." The three heads are (1) the party in the electorate, (2) the party as an organization, and (3) the party in government.[3]

The *party in the electorate* is by far the largest component of an American political party. Unlike many European political parties, American parties do not require dues or membership cards to distinguish members from nonmembers. Americans may register as Democrats, Republicans, Libertarians, or whatever, but registration is not legally binding and is easily changed. To be a member of a party, you need only claim to be a member. If you call yourself a Democrat, you are one—even if you never talk to a party official, never work in a campaign, and often vote for Republicans.

The *party as an organization* has a national office, a full-time staff, rules and bylaws, and budgets. In addition to its national office, each party maintains state and local headquarters. The party organization includes precinct leaders, county chairpersons, state chairpersons, state delegates to the national committee, and officials in the party's Washington office. These are the people who keep the party running between elections and make its rules. From the party's national chairperson to its local precinct captain, the party organization pursues electoral victory.

The *party in government* consists of elected officials who call themselves members of the party. Although presidents, members of Congress, governors, and lesser officeholders may share a common party label, they do not always agree on policy. Presidents and governors may have to wheedle and cajole their own party members into voting for their policies. In the United States, it is not uncommon to put personal principle—or ambition—above loyalty to the party's leaders. These leaders are the main spokespersons for the party, however. Their words and actions personify the party to millions of Americans. If the party is to translate its promises into policy, the job must be done by the party in government.

Political parties are everywhere in American politics—present in the electorate's mind, as an organization, and in government offices—and one of their major tasks is to link the people of the United States to their government and its policies.

TASKS OF THE PARTIES

The road from public opinion to public policy is long and winding. Millions of Americans cannot raise their voices to the government and indicate their policy preferences in unison. In a large democracy, **linkage institutions** translate inputs from the public into outputs from the policymakers. Linkage institutions sift through all the issues, identify the most pressing concerns, and put these onto the governmental agenda. In other words, linkage institutions help ensure that public preferences are heard loud and clear. In the United States, there are four main linkage institutions: parties, elections, interest groups, and the media.

Kay Lawson writes that "parties are seen, both by the members and by others, as agencies for forging links between citizens and policymakers."[4] Here is a checklist of the tasks that parties perform—or should perform—if they are to serve as effective linkage institutions:

linkage institutions
The channels through which people's concerns become political issues on the government's policy agenda. In the United States, linkage institutions include elections, political parties, interest groups, and the media.

Parties Pick Candidates   Almost no one above the local level (and often not even there) gets elected to a public office without winning a party's endorsement.[5] A party's endorsement is called a *nomination*. Up until the early twentieth century, American parties chose their candidates with little or no input from voters. Progressive reformers led the charge for primary elections, in which citizens would have the power to choose nominees for office. The innovation of primary elections spread rapidly, transferring the nominating function from the party organization to the party identifiers.

Parties Run Campaigns   Through their national, state, and local organizations, parties coordinate political campaigns. However, television has made it easier for candidates to campaign on their own, without the help of the party organization. For example, Ross Perot received 18.9 percent of the presidential vote in 1992 and 8.5 percent in 1996 with hardly any organizational support at all.

Parties Give Cues to Voters   Just knowing whether a candidate is a Democrat or a Republican provides crucial information to many voters. Voters can reasonably assume that if a candidate is a Republican, chances are good he or she favors conservative principles and supported President George W. Bush's policies. On the other side of the coin, it can be reasonably assumed that any Democrat has opposed many of President Bush's controversial stands in the past. A voter therefore need not do extensive research on the individual candidates but rather can rely on the informational shortcut provided by their party affiliations.

? Why It Matters
Political Parties

Parties perform many important tasks in American politics. Among the most important are: generating symbols of identification and loyalty, mobilizing majorities in the electorate and in government, recruiting political leaders, implementing policies, and fostering stability in government. Hence, it has often been argued that the party system has to work well for the government to work well.

Parties Articulate Policies   Within the electorate and within the government, each political party advocates specific policy alternatives. For example, the Democratic Party platform has for many years advocated support for a woman's right to an abortion, whereas the Republican Party platform has repeatedly called for restrictions on abortion.

Parties Coordinate Policymaking   In America's fragmented government, parties are essential for coordination among the branches of government. Virtually all major public officials are also members of a party. When they need support to get something done, the first place they look is to their fellow partisans.

The importance of these tasks makes it easy to see why most political scientists accept Schattschneider's famous assertion that modern democracy is unthinkable without competition between political parties.

PARTIES, VOTERS, AND POLICY: THE DOWNS MODEL

rational-choice theory

A popular theory in political science to explain the actions of voters as well as politicians. It assumes that individuals act in their own best interest, carefully weighing the costs and benefits of possible alternatives.

The parties compete, at least in theory, as in a marketplace. A party is in the market for voters; its products are its candidates and policies. Anthony Downs has provided a working model of the relationship among citizens, parties, and policy, employing a rational-choice perspective.[6] **Rational-choice theory** "seeks to explain political processes and outcomes as consequences of purposive behavior. Political actors are assumed to have goals and to pursue those goals sensibly and efficiently."[7] Downs argues that (1) voters want to maximize the chance that policies they favor will be adopted by government and that (2) parties want to win office. Thus, in order to win office, the wise party selects policies that are widely favored. Parties and candidates may do all sorts of things to win—kiss babies, call opponents ugly names, even lie and cheat—but in a democracy they will use primarily their accomplishments and policy positions to attract votes. If Party A figures out what the voters want more accurately than does Party B, then Party A should be more successful.

The long history of the American party system has shown that successful parties rarely stray far from the midpoint of public opinion. In the American electorate, a few voters are extremely liberal and a few extremely conservative, but the majority are in the middle (see Figure 8.1). If Downs is right, then centrist parties will win, and extremist parties will be condemned to footnotes in the history books. Indeed, occasionally a party may misperceive voters' desires or take a risky stand on a principle—hoping to persuade voters during the campaign—but in order to survive in a system where the majority opinion is middle of the road, parties must stay fairly near the center.

We frequently hear criticism that there is not much difference between the Democrats and the Republicans. Given the nature of the American political market, however, these two parties have little choice. We would not expect two competing department stores to locate at opposite ends of town when most people live on Main Street. Downs also notes, though, that from a rational-choice perspective, one should expect the parties to differentiate themselves at least somewhat. Just as Chrysler tries to offer something different from and better than General Motors in order to build buyer loyalty, so Democrats and Republicans have to forge different identities to build voter loyalty. In recent years, the American National Election Study has found that two-thirds of the population

One's party affiliation is an important part of one's political identity. Although clubs of college Republicans and college Democrats are common on campuses around the country, roughly half of college-age Americans do not have a party affiliation, preferring to call themselves Independents.

FIGURE 8.1

The Downs Model: How Rational Parties Match Voters' Policy Preferences

In 2004, the National Election Study asked a sample of the American electorate to classify themselves on a 7-point scale from extremely liberal to extremely conservative. The graph shows how the people located themselves in terms of ideology and how they perceived the ideology of the parties.

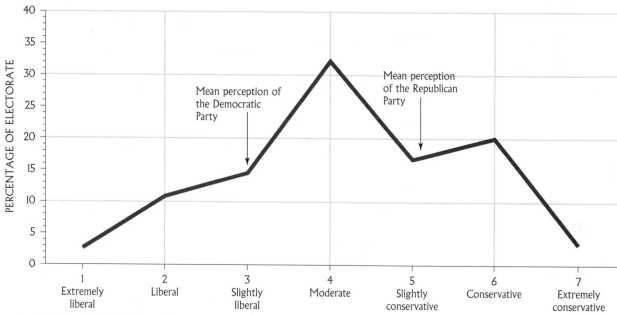

Source: From the National Election Studies conducted by the University of Michigan, Center for Political Studies, 2004.

believes that important differences exist between the parties. When asked what those differences are, respondents most frequently comment that the Republicans favor lower taxes and less domestic spending, whereas Democrats favor more government programs to help working-class and less advantaged Americans.

THE PARTY IN THE ELECTORATE

In most European nations, being a party member means formally joining a political party. You get a membership card to carry around, you pay dues, and you vote to pick your local party leaders. In America, being a party member takes far less work. There is no formal "membership" in the parties at all. If you believe you are a Democrat or a Republican, then you are a Democrat or a Republican. Thus, the party in the electorate consists largely of symbolic images and ideas. For most people the party is a psychological label. Most voters have a **party image** of each party; that is, they know (or think they know) what the Republicans and Democrats stand for. Liberal or conservative, pro-business or pro-labor, pro-choice or pro-life—these are some of the elements of each party's images.

Party images help shape people's **party identification**, the self-proclaimed preference for one party or the other. Because many people routinely vote for the party they identify with (all else being equal), even a shift of a few percentage points in the distribution of party identification is important. Since 1952, the

party image

The voter's perception of what the Republicans or Democrats stand for, such as conservatism or liberalism.

party identification

A citizen's self-proclaimed preference for one party or the other.

National Election Study surveys have asked a sample of citizens, "Generally speaking, do you usually think of yourself as a Republican, a Democrat, or an Independent?" Repeatedly asking this question permits political scientists to trace party identification over time (see Figure 8.2). In recent presidential elections, two clear patterns have been evident. First, unlike earlier periods when Democrats greatly outnumbered Republicans, the Democratic Party's edge in terms of identifiers in the electorate has lately been quite modest. In 1964 there were more than twice as many Democrats as Republicans, whereas by 2008 Republicans trailed Democrats by a mere 9 percentage points. Second, in most recent elections the most frequent response to the party identification question has been the Independent option. In 2008, 37 percent of the population called themselves Independents. As you can see in "Young People and Politics: The Parties Face an Independent Youth," survey data demonstrate that the younger one is, the more likely he or she is to be a political independent.

People who call themselves Independents are the most likely voters to engage in the practice of **ticket splitting**—voting with one party for one office and the other party for another office. For example, the 2004 National Exit Poll found that 25 percent of Independents who voted for Bush did not support a Republican for the House of Representatives, compared to just 7 percent among Republican identifiers who voted for Bush. The result of many voters being open to splitting their tickets is that even when one party has a big edge in a state, the other party always has a decent shot at winning at least some important offices. In other words, regardless of media labels of red and blue states, the practice of ticket splitting means that no state is ever completely safe for a given party. Thus, California, Hawaii, and Vermont lean heavily toward the Democrats in national elections, but as of 2009 all the governors of these states were Republicans. On the other side of the coin, Democrats were serving as governors in heavily Republican states like Kansas, Arizona, and Oklahoma.

ticket splitting

Voting with one party for one office and with another party for other offices. It has become the norm in American voting behavior.

FIGURE 8.2

Party Identification in the United States, 1952–2008[a]

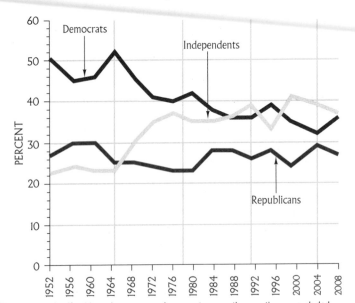

[a]In percentage of people; the small percentage who identify with a minor party or who cannot answer the question are excluded.

Sources: 1952–2004—American National Election Studies; 2008—nine CBS/*New York Times* and ABC/*Washington Post* polls conducted in Sept/Oct 2008.

YOUNG PEOPLE AND POLITICS
The Parties Face an Independent Youth

Younger people have always had a tendency to be more independent of the major political parties than older people. But this has rarely been as evident in survey data as it is now. As you can see from the 2006 national survey data displayed here, 52 percent of people between the ages of 18 and 24 said they were political independents. In contrast, only 32 percent of people over 65 called themselves independents. As one looks down the age groups in the table, it is clear that what varies by age is not the ratio of Democrats to Republicans but rather the likelihood of someone being an independent. Data over time indicate that as people get older, they become more likely to identify with one of the major parties. But whether this will be true for the current generation of youth remains to be seen.

QUESTIONS FOR DISCUSSION

▷ Do you think that as the current generation of young people ages they will become more likely to identify with the major political parties?

▷ Because younger people are so likely to be independent, does this mean many young voters are particularly open to persuasion during campaigns? If so, why don't the Democrats and Republicans pay special attention to getting them on their side?

▷ In some states, such as New York and Florida, only voters who are registered with a party can participate in that party's primary. Given that younger people are less likely to identify with a party, does this mean that their influence in primary elections is diminished in such states?

AGE	DEMOCRAT	INDEPENDENT	REPUBLICAN
18–24	27	52	21
25–34	28	50	22
35–44	27	45	28
45–54	31	43	26
55–64	34	38	27
65+	36	32	32

Source: Authors' analysis of the 2006 General Social Survey.

THE PARTY ORGANIZATIONS: FROM THE GRASS ROOTS TO WASHINGTON

An organizational chart is usually shaped like a pyramid, with those who give orders at the top and those who carry them out at the bottom. In drawing an organizational chart of an American political party, you could put the national committee and national convention of the party at the apex of the pyramid, the state party organizations in the middle, and the thousands of local party organizations at the bottom. Such a chart, however, would provide a misleading depiction of an American political party. The president of General Motors is at the top of GM in fact as well as on paper. By contrast, the chairperson of the Democratic or Republican national committee is on top on paper but not in fact.

As organizations, American political parties are decentralized and fragmented. One can imagine a system in which the national office of a party resolves conflicts among its state and local branches, states the party's position on the issues, and then passes orders down through the hierarchy. One can even imagine a system in which the party leaders have the power to enforce their decisions by offering greater influence and resources to officeholders who follow the party line and by punishing those who do not. Many European parties work just that way, but in America the formal party organizations have little such power. Candidates in the United States can get elected on their own. They do not need the help of the party most of the time, and hence the party organization is relegated to a comparatively limited role.

LOCAL PARTIES

The urban political party was once the main political party organization in America. From the late nineteenth century through the New Deal of the 1930s, scores of cities were dominated by **party machines**. A machine is a kind of party organization, very different from the typical fragmented and disorganized political party in America today. It can be defined as a party organization that depends on rewarding its members in some material fashion.

Patronage is one of the key inducements used by party machines. A patronage job is one that is awarded for political reasons rather than for merit or competence alone. In the late nineteenth century, political parties routinely sold some patronage jobs to the highest bidder. Party leaders made no secret of their corruption, openly selling government positions to raise money for the party. Some of this money was used to buy votes, but a good deal went to line the pockets of the politicians themselves. The most notable case was that of Boss Tweed of New York, whose ring reportedly made between $40 million and $200 million from tax receipts, payoffs, and kickbacks.

At one time, urban machines in Albany, Chicago, Philadelphia, Kansas City, and elsewhere depended heavily on ethnic group support. Some of the most fabled machine leaders were Irish politicians, including New York's George Washington Plunkett, Boston's James Michael Curley, and Chicago's Richard J. Daley. Daley's Chicago machine was the last survivor, steamrolling its opposition amid charges of racism and corruption. Even today there are remnants of the Chicago machine, particularly in White and ethnic neighborhoods. The survival of machine politics in Chicago can be traced to its ability to limit the scope of reform legislation. A large proportion of city jobs were classified as "temporary" even though they had been held by the same person for decades, and these positions were exempted from the merit system of hiring. At its height, the Daley machine in Chicago dispensed 40,000 patronage jobs, the recipients of which were expected to deliver at least 10 votes each on Election Day and to kick back 5 percent of their salary in the form of a donation to the local Democratic Party.[8]

Urban party organizations are also no longer very active as a rule. Progressive reforms that placed jobs under the merit system rather than at the machine's discretion weakened the machines' power. Regulations concerning fair bidding on government contracts also took away much of their ability to reward the party faithful. As ethnic integration occurred in big cities, the group loyalties that the machines often relied on no longer seemed very relevant to many people.

Partly filling in the void created by the decline of the inner-city machines has been a revitalization of party organization at the county level—particularly in affluent suburbs. These county organizations distribute yard signs and campaign literature, get out the vote on Election Day, and help state and local candidates any way they can. Traditionally, local organizations relied on personal knowledge of individuals in the neighborhood who could be persuaded to support the party. Today, these organizations have access to computerized lists with all sorts of details about registered voters that they use to try to tailor their appeals to each individual.

party machines
A type of political party organization that relies heavily on material inducements, such as patronage, to win votes and to govern.

patronage
One of the key inducements used by party machines. A patronage job, promotion, or contract is one that is given for political reasons rather than for merit or competence alone.

Mayor Richard J. Daley ruled the city of Chicago from 1955 until his death in 1976. His Cook County Democratic Party organization was highly organized at the precinct level. Members of the organization kept people in their neighborhoods happy by providing for their local needs, such as street maintenance, new stoplights, no-parking zones, and so on, and the people reciprocated on Election Day by supporting the organization's candidates.

THE 50 STATE PARTY SYSTEMS

American national parties are a loose aggregation of state parties, which are themselves a fluid association of individuals, groups, and local organizations. There are 50 state party systems, and no two are exactly alike. In a few states, the parties are well organized, have sizable staffs, and spend a lot of money. Pennsylvania is one such state. In other states, however, parties are weak. California, says Kay Lawson, "has political parties so weak as to be almost nonexistent; it is the birthplace of campaigning by 'hired guns' and it has been run by special interests for so long that Californians have forgotten what is special about that."[9]

The states are allowed wide discretion in the regulation of party activities, and how they choose to organize elections influences the strength of the parties profoundly. Some states give parties greater power than others to limit who can participate in their nomination contests. In **closed primaries** only people who have registered in advance with the party can vote in its primary, thus encouraging greater party loyalty. In contrast, **open primaries** allow voters to decide on Election Day whether they want to participate in the Democratic or Republican contests. And most antiparty of all are **blanket primaries**, which present voters with a list of candidates from all the parties and allow them to pick some Democrats and some Republicans if they like. (See "You Are the Policymaker: Was the Blanket Primary a Good Idea?")

When it comes to the general election, some states promote voting according to party by listing the candidates of each party down a single column, whereas others place the names in random order. About a third of the states currently have a provision on their ballots that enables a voter to cast a vote for all of one party's candidates with a single act. This option clearly encourages straight-ticket voting and makes the support of the party organization more important to candidates in these states.

Organizationally, state parties are on the upswing throughout the country. As recently as the early 1960s, half the state party organizations did not even maintain a permanent headquarters; when the state party elected a new chairperson, the party organization simply shifted its office to his or her hometown.[10] In contrast, almost all state parties today have a permanent physical headquarters, typically in the capital city or the largest city. State party budgets have also increased greatly, as parties have acquired professional staffs and high-tech equipment. As of 1999, the typical state party budget for an election year was more than eight times greater than it was 20 years earlier.[11]

In terms of headquarters and budgets, state parties are better organized than they used to be. Nevertheless, as John Bibby points out, they mostly serve to supplement the candidates' own personal campaign organizations; thus, state party organizations rarely manage campaigns. The job of the state party, writes Bibby, is merely "to provide technical services" within the context of a candidate-centered campaign.[12]

THE NATIONAL PARTY ORGANIZATIONS

The supreme power within each of the parties is its **national convention**. The convention meets every four years, and its main task is to write the party's platform and then nominate its candidates for president and vice president. (Chapter 9 will discuss conventions in detail.) Keeping the party operating between conventions is the job of the **national committee**, composed of representatives from the states and territories. Typically, each state has a national committeeman and a national committeewoman as delegates to the party's national committee. The Democratic

You Are Redrawing the Districts in Your State

closed primaries
Elections to select party nominees in which only people who have registered in advance with the party can vote for that party's candidates, thus encouraging greater party loyalty.

open primaries
Elections to select party nominees in which voters can decide on Election Day whether they want to participate in the Democratic or Republican contests.

State Control and National Platforms

blanket primaries
Elections to select party nominees in which voters are presented with a list of candidates from all the parties. Voters can then select some Democrats and some Republicans if they like.

national convention
The meeting of party delegates every four years to choose a presidential ticket and write the party's platform.

national committee
One of the institutions that keeps the party operating between conventions. The national committee is composed of representatives from the states and territories.

YOU ARE THE **Policymaker**

Was the Blanket Primary a Good Idea?

In the 1996 California primary, voters were presented with an initiative to change the state's closed primary process to a blanket primary. Proponents of this initiative argued that a closed primary system favors the election of party hard-liners, contributes to legislative gridlock, and stacks the deck against moderate problem solvers. By opening up the primary process to allow voters to vote for any set of candidates they like regardless of partisanship, advocates of the blanket primary argued that politicians would be encouraged to focus on the median voter rather than a narrow group of partisans. They also noted that participation in primary elections would increase by allowing Independents a chance to take part and by giving minority party voters in noncompetitive districts a real say in selecting their representatives.

Both the Democratic and Republican state parties of California came out strongly against this initiative. They argued that the blanket primary would be an invitation to political mischief, with political consultants and special interests manipulating the system to help the candidate they'd most like to face in November get the other party's nomination. A frequently used analogy during the campaign was that allowing members of one party a large voice in choosing another party's nominee was like letting UCLA's football team choose USC's head coach. Rather than seeing this reform as giving voters more choice, opponents argued that it would diminish choice in the long run by muddling the differences between major parties.

In the end, the voters approved the blanket primary by a margin of 60 to 40. The exit polls showed that the initiative was supported by Democrats and Republicans alike. However, the party organizations immediately took the case to federal court,

arguing that the blanket primary infringed on their constitutional rights of freedom of association by giving nonmembers a say in their activities. U.S. District Judge David Levy listened to a variety of testimony from political consultants, party leaders, and political scientists (including one of the coauthors of this book). In *Democratic Party et al. v. Jones*, he ruled that although the blanket primary weakened the parties, it was what the voters wanted and shouldn't be overruled by the courts. Subsequently, the Ninth Circuit Court of Appeals upheld the ruling. But the Supreme Court had the final word in June 2000, ruling that the blanket primary violated the parties' right to freedom of association. Writing for the majority, Justice Antonin Scalia stated that the blanket primary forces the parties "to adulterate their candidate-selection process—the basic function of a political party—by opening it up to persons wholly unaffiliated with the party."

On hearing of the Supreme Court decision, California's Democratic governor and Republican secretary of state both pledged to try to retain a blanket primary system by making primary elections nonpartisan, as currently practiced in Louisiana. In his opinion, Justice Scalia indicated that such a system is constitutional because party nominees are not chosen through such a process; indeed, sometimes this system leads to a general election between two members of the same party. It would be ironic if the parties' court victory led them to be excluded from the primary process in some states altogether.

You Be the Policymaker: Should the Supreme Court have outlawed California's blanket primary? Is the nonpartisan blanket primary an idea that should now be tried in a number of states?

---

committee also includes assorted governors, members of Congress, and other party officials.

Day-to-day activities of the national party are the responsibility of the party's **national chairperson**. The national party chairperson hires the staff, raises the money, pays the bills, and attends to the daily duties of the party. When asked what their biggest organizational challenge was at a 1998 joint appearance, the chairs of the Democratic and Republican parties both promptly responded "money."[13]

The chairperson of the party that controls the White House is normally selected by the president himself (subject to routine ratification by the national committee). In the early 1970s, two of the people who served for a while as chair of the Republican Party at the request of President Nixon were Bob Dole and George Bush, both of whom used this position as a means of political advancement. These days party chairs are typically career staffers who have worked their way up through a series of behind-the-scenes jobs to the role of a visible spokesperson for the party. A recent exception to this general pattern is former presidential candidate Howard Dean, who sought after and won the job of chair of the Democratic Party after the 2004 election.

national chairperson

The national chairperson is responsible for the day-to-day activities of the party and is usually handpicked by the presidential nominee.

THE PARTY IN GOVERNMENT: PROMISES AND POLICY

Which party controls each of America's many elected offices matters because both parties and the elected officials who represent them usually try to turn campaign promises into action. As a result, the party that has control over the most government offices will have the most influence in determining who gets what, where, when, and how.

Voters are attracted to a party in government by its performance and policies. What a party has done in office—and what it promises to do—greatly influences who will join its **coalition**—a set of individuals and groups supporting it. Sometimes voters suspect that political promises are made to be broken. To be sure, there are notable instances in which politicians have turned—sometimes 180 degrees—from their policy promises. Lyndon Johnson repeatedly promised in the 1964 presidential campaign that he would not "send American boys to do an Asian boy's job" and involve the United States in the Vietnam War, but he did.

coalition
A group of individuals with a common interest on which every political party depends.

In the 1980 campaign, Ronald Reagan asserted that he would balance the budget by 1984, yet his administration quickly ran up the largest deficit in American history. Throughout the 1988 campaign George Bush proclaimed, "Read my lips—no new taxes," but he reluctantly changed course two years later when pressured on the issue by the Democratic majority in Congress. Bill Clinton promised a tax cut for the middle class during the 1992 campaign, but after he was elected, he backed off, saying that first the deficit would have to be substantially reduced.

It is all too easy to forget how often parties and presidents do exactly what they say they will do. For every broken promise, many more are kept. Ronald Reagan promised to step up defense spending and cut back on social welfare expenditures, and his administration quickly delivered on these pledges. Bill Clinton promised to support bills providing for family leave, easing voting registration procedures, and tightening gun control that had been vetoed by his predecessor. He lobbied hard to get these measures through Congress again and proudly signed them into law once they arrived on his desk. George W. Bush promised a major tax cut for every taxpayer in America, and he delivered just that in 2001. In sum, the impression that politicians and parties never produce policy out of promises is off the mark.

In fact, the parties have done a fairly good job over the years of translating their platform promises into public policy. Gerald Pomper has shown that party platforms are excellent predictors of a party's actual policy performance in office. He tabulated specific pledges in the major parties' platforms over a number of years on 3,194 policy pronouncements. Pomper then looked to see whether the party that won the presidency actually fulfilled its promises. Nearly three-fourths of all promises resulted in policy actions. Others were tried but floundered for one reason or another. Only 10 percent were ignored altogether.[14]

If parties generally do what they say they will, then the party platforms adopted at the national conventions represent blueprints, however vague, for action. Consider what the two major parties promised the voters in 2008 (see Table 8.1). There is little doubt that the choice between Democratic and Republican policies in 2008 was clear on many important issues facing the country.

PARTY ERAS IN AMERICAN HISTORY

While studying political parties, remember the following: *America is a two-party system and always has been.* Of course, there are many minor parties around—Libertarians, Socialists, Reform, Greens—but they rarely have a chance of winning a major office. In contrast, most democratic nations have more than two parties represented in their national legislature. Throughout American history, one party has been the dominant majority party for long periods of time. A majority of voters identify with the party in power; thus, this party tends to win a majority of the elections. Political scientists call these periods **party eras**.

Punctuating each party era is a **critical election**.[15] A critical election is an electoral earthquake: Fissures appear in each party's coalition, which begins to fracture; new issues appear, dividing the electorate. Each party forms a new coalition—one that endures for years. A critical election period may require more than one election before change is apparent, but in the end, the party system will be transformed.

This process is called **party realignment**—a rare event in American political life that is akin to a political revolution. Realignments are typically associated with a major crisis or trauma in the nation's history. One of the major realignments, when the Republican Party emerged, was connected to the Civil War. Another was linked to the Great Depression of the 1930s, when the majority Republicans were displaced by the Democrats. The following sections look more closely at the various party eras in American history.

1796–1824: THE FIRST PARTY SYSTEM

In the *Federalist Papers*, James Madison warned strongly against the dangers of "factions," or parties. But Alexander Hamilton, one of the coauthors of the *Federalist Papers*, did as much as anyone to inaugurate our party system.[16] Hamilton was the nation's first secretary of the treasury, for which service his picture appears on today's $10 bill. To garner congressional support for his pet policies, particularly a national bank, he needed votes. From this politicking and coalition building came the rudiments of the Federalist Party, America's first political party. The Federalists were also America's shortest-lived major party. After Federalist candidate John Adams was defeated in his reelection bid in 1800, the party quickly faded. The Federalists were poorly organized, and by 1820 they no longer bothered to offer up a candidate for president. In this early period of American history, most party leaders did not regard themselves as professional politicians. Those who lost often withdrew completely from the political arena. The ideas of a loyal opposition and rotation of power in government had not yet taken hold.[17] Each party wanted to destroy the other party, not just defeat it—and such was the fate of the Federalists.

The party that crushed the Federalists was led by Virginians Jefferson, Madison, and Monroe, each of whom was elected president for two terms in succession. They were known as the Democratic-Republicans, or sometimes as the Jeffersonians. The

party eras
Historical periods in which a majority of voters cling to the party in power, which tends to win a majority of the elections.

critical election
An electoral "earthquake" where new issues emerge, new coalitions replace old ones, and the majority party is often displaced by the minority party. Critical election periods are sometimes marked by a national crisis and may require more than one election to bring about a new party era.

party realignment
The displacement of the majority party by the minority party, usually during a **critical election** period.

TABLE 8.1

Party Platforms, 2008

Although few people actually read party platforms, they are one of the best written sources for what the parties believe in. A brief summary of some of the contrasting positions in the Democratic and Republican platforms of 2008 illustrates major differences in beliefs between the two parties.

REPUBLICANS	DEMOCRATS
The War in Iraq	**The War in Iraq**
To those who have sacrificed so much, we owe the commitment that American forces will leave that country in victory and with honor. That outcome is too critical to our own national security to be jeopardized by artificial or politically inspired timetables that ignore the advice of our on-the-ground commanders.	We will give our military a new mission: ending this war and giving Iraq back to it its people. We will be as careful getting out of Iraq as we were careless getting in. We can remove our combat brigades at the pace of one to two per month and expect to complete redeployment within 16 months.
Energy Independence	**Energy Independence**
We simply must draw more American oil from American soil if we are to have the resources we need to achieve energy independence. We support accelerated exploration and drilling of American sources, from oilfields off the nation's coasts to proven fields... Confident in the promise offered by science and technology, Republicans will pursue dramatic increases in the use of safe, affordable, reliable—and clean—nuclear power.	We know we can't drill our way to energy independence and so we must summon all of our ingenuity and legendary hard work and we must invest in research, development, and deployment of forms of new energy—solar, wind, as well as technologies to store energy through advanced batteries and clean up our coal plants. ... We are committed to getting at least 25% of our electricity from renewable sources by 2025.
Abortion	**Abortion**
We assert the inherent dignity and sanctity of all human life and affirm that the unborn child has a fundamental individual right to life which cannot be infringed.	The Democratic Party strongly and unequivocally supports *Roe v. Wade*, and a woman's right to choose a safe and legal abortion, regardless of ability to pay.
Gay Marriage	**Gay Marriage**
A Republican Congress enacted the Defense of Marriage Act, affirming the right of states not to recognize same-sex marriages licensed in other states. ... We urge renewed use of that Article III power to prevent activist federal judges from imposing upon the rest of the nation the judicial activism in Massachusetts and California.	We oppose the Defense of Marriage Act and all attempts to use this issue to divide us.
Health Care	**Health Care**
The American people rejected Democrats' attempted government takeover of health care in 1993, and they remain skeptical of politicians who would send us down that road. Republicans pledge that as we reform our health care system we *will not* put the system on a path that empowers Washington bureaucrats at the expense of patients.	We believe that quality and affordable health care is a basic right. ... Health care should be a shared responsibility between employers, workers, insurers, providers and government. All Americans should have coverage they can afford; employers should have incentives to provide coverage to their workers; insurers and providers should ensure high quality affordable care; and the government should ensure that health insurance is affordable and provides meaningful coverage.
Taxes	**Taxes**
The last thing Americans need right now is tax hikes. ... Along with making the 2001 and 2003 tax cuts permanent so American families will not face a large tax hike, Republicans will advance tax policies to support American families, promote savings and innovation, and put us on a path to fundamental tax reform.	We will shut down the corporate loopholes and tax havens and use the money so that we can provide an immediate middle-class tax cut that will offer relief to workers and their families. ... For families making more than $250,000 we'll ask them to give back a portion of the Bush tax cuts to invest in health care and other key priorities.
Education	**Education**
To get our schools back to the basics of learning, we support initiatives to block-grant more Department of Education funding to the states, with requirements for state-level standards, assessments, and public reporting to ensure transparency. Local educators must be free to end ineffective programs and reallocate resources where they are most needed.	We will make an unprecedented national investment to provide teachers with better pay and better support to improve their skills, and their students' learning. We'll reward effective teachers who teach in underserved areas, take on added responsibilities like mentoring new teachers, or consistently excel in the classroom.

Source: Excerpts from party platforms as posted on the Web sites of each organization.

Democratic-Republican Party derived its coalition from agrarian interests rather than from the growing number of capitalists who supported the Federalists. This made the party particularly popular in the largely rural South. As the Federalists disappeared, however, the old Jeffersonian coalition was torn apart by factionalism as it tried to be all things to all people.

1828–1856: JACKSON AND THE DEMOCRATS VERSUS THE WHIGS

More than anyone else, General Andrew Jackson founded the modern American political party. In the election of 1828, he forged a new coalition that included Westerners as well as Southerners, new immigrants as well as settled Americans. Like most successful politicians of his day, Jackson was initially a Democratic-Republican, but soon after his ascension to the presidency his party became known as simply the Democratic Party, which continues to this day. The "Democratic" label was particularly appropriate for Jackson's supporters because their cause was to broaden political opportunity by eliminating many vestiges of elitism and mobilizing the masses.

The Evolution of Political Parties in the United States

Whereas Jackson was the charismatic leader, the Democrats' behind-the-scenes architect was Martin Van Buren, who succeeded Jackson as president. Van Buren's one term in office was relatively undistinguished, but his view of party competition left a lasting mark. He "sought to make Democrats see that their only hope for maintaining the purity of their own principles was to admit the existence of an opposing party."[18] A realist, Van Buren argued that a party could not aspire to pleasing all the people all the time. He argued that a governing party needed a loyal opposition to represent parts of society that it could not. This opposition was provided by the Whigs. The Whig Party included such notable statesmen as Henry Clay and Daniel Webster, but it was able to win the presidency only when it nominated aging but popular military heroes such as William Henry Harrison (1840) and Zachary Taylor (1848). The Whigs had two distinct wings—Northern industrialists and Southern planters—who were brought together more by the Democratic policies they opposed than by the issues on which they agreed.

1860–1928: THE TWO REPUBLICAN ERAS

In the 1850s, the issue of slavery dominated American politics and split both the Whigs and the Democrats. Slavery, said Senator Charles Sumner, an ardent abolitionist, "is the only subject within the field of national politics which excites any real interest."[19] Congress battled over the extension of slavery to the new states and territories. In *Dred Scott v. Sandford*, the Supreme Court of 1857 held that slaves could not be citizens and that former slaves could not be protected by the Constitution. This decision further sharpened the divisions in public opinion, making civil war increasingly likely.

The Republicans rose in the late 1850s as the antislavery party. Folding in the remnants of several minor parties, in 1860 the Republicans forged a coalition strong enough to elect Abraham Lincoln president and to ignite the Civil War. The "War Between the States" was one of those political earthquakes that realigned the parties. After the war, the Republican Party thrived for more than 60 years. The Democrats controlled the South, though, and the Republican label remained a dirty word in the old Confederacy.

A second Republican era was initiated with the watershed election of 1896, perhaps the most bitter battle in American electoral history. The Democrats nominated William Jennings Bryan, populist proponent of "free silver" (linking money with silver, which was more plentiful than gold, and thus devaluing money to help debtors). The Republican

Party made clear its positions in favor of the gold standard, industrialization, the banks, high tariffs, and the industrial working classes as well as its positions against the "radical" Western farmers and "silverites." "Bryan and his program were greeted by the country's conservatives with something akin to terror."[20] The *New York Tribune* howled that Bryan's Democrats were "in league with the Devil." On the other side, novelist Frank Baum lampooned the Republicans in his classic novel *The Wizard of Oz*. Dorothy follows the yellow brick road (symbolizing the gold standard) to the Emerald City (representing Washington), only to find that the Wizard (whose figure resembles McKinley) is powerless. But by clicking on her *silver* slippers (the color was changed to ruby for Technicolor effect in the movie), she finds that she can return home.

The election of 1860 proved to be a realigning election. Having only been formed six years earlier in 1854, the Republican Party suddenly became the nation's majority party with the victory of the Lincoln-Hamlin ticket.

Political scientists call the 1896 election a realigning one because it shifted the party coalitions and entrenched the Republicans for another generation. (For more on the election of 1896, see Chapter 10.) For the next three decades the Republicans continued as the nation's majority party, until the stock market crashed in 1929. The ensuing Great Depression brought about another fissure in the crust of the American party system.

1932–1964: THE NEW DEAL COALITION

President Herbert Hoover's handling of the Depression turned out to be disastrous for the Republicans. He solemnly pronounced that economic depression could not be cured by legislative action. Americans, however, obviously disagreed and voted for Franklin D. Roosevelt, who promised the country a *New Deal*. In his first 100 days as president, Roosevelt prodded Congress into passing scores of anti-Depression measures. Party realignment began in earnest after the Roosevelt administration got the country moving again. First-time voters flocked to the polls, pumping new blood into the Democratic ranks and providing much of the margin for Roosevelt's four presidential victories. Immigrant groups in Boston and other cities had been initially attracted to the Democrats by the 1928 campaign of Al Smith, the first Catholic to be nominated by a major party for the presidency.[21] Roosevelt reinforced the partisanship of these groups, and the Democrats forged the **New Deal coalition**.

The basic elements of the New Deal coalition were the following:

- *Urban dwellers.* Big cities such as Chicago and Philadelphia were staunchly Republican before the New Deal realignment; afterward, they were Democratic bastions.

New Deal coalition
A coalition forged by the Democrats, who dominated American politics from the 1930s to the 1960s. Its basic elements were the urban working class, ethnic groups, Catholics and Jews, the poor, Southerners, African Americans, and intellectuals.

- *Labor unions.* FDR became the first president to support unions enthusiastically, and they returned the favor.
- *Catholics and Jews.* During and after the Roosevelt period, Catholics and Jews were strongly Democratic.
- *The poor.* Although the poor had low turnout rates, their votes went overwhelmingly to the party of Roosevelt and his successors.
- *Southerners.* Ever since pre–Civil War days, White Southerners had been Democratic loyalists. This alignment continued unabated during the New Deal. For example, Mississippi voted over 90 percent Democratic in each of FDR's four presidential election victories.
- *African Americans.* The Republicans freed the slaves, but under FDR the Democrats attracted the majority of African Americans.

As you can see in Figure 8.3, many of the same groups that supported FDR's New Deal continue to shape the party coalitions today.

FIGURE 8.3

Party Coalitions Today

The two parties continue to draw support from very different social groups, many of which have existed since the New Deal era. This figure shows the percentage identifying as Democrats and Republicans for various groups in 2008.

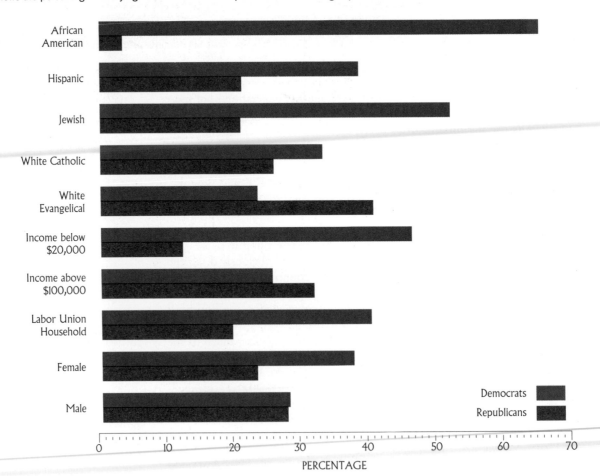

Source: Authors' analysis of Pew Research Center polls conducted in January and February 2008.

The New Deal coalition made the Democratic Party the clear majority party for decades. Harry S Truman, who succeeded Roosevelt in 1945, promised a Fair Deal. World War II hero and Republican Dwight D. Eisenhower broke the Democrats' grip on power by being elected president twice during the 1950s, but the Democrats regained the presidency in 1960 with the election of John F. Kennedy. His New Frontier was in the New Deal tradition, with platforms and policies designed to help labor, the working classes, and minorities. Lyndon B. Johnson, picked as Kennedy's vice president because he could help win Southern votes, became president on Kennedy's assassination and was overwhelmingly elected to a term of his own in 1964. Johnson's Great Society programs included a major expansion of government programs to help the poor, the homeless, and minorities. His War on Poverty was reminiscent of Roosevelt's activism in dealing with the Depression. Johnson's Vietnam War policies, however, tore the Democratic Party apart in 1968, leaving the door to the presidency wide open for Republican candidate Richard M. Nixon.

1968–PRESENT: SOUTHERN REALIGNMENT AND THE ERA OF DIVIDED PARTY GOVERNMENT

When Richard Nixon was first elected to the presidency in 1968, he formulated what became widely known as his "Southern strategy." Emphasizing his support for states' rights, law and order, and a strong military posture, Nixon hoped to win over Southern conservatives to the Republican Party, thereby breaking the Democratic Party's long dominance in the former confederacy. Party realignment in the South did not happen as quickly as Nixon would have liked, but it has taken place gradually over in the four decades since 1968.[22] As you can see in "A Generation of Change: Realignment in the South," the South was still a Democratic congressional stronghold as of the late-1980s, but now it clearly leans in the Republican direction.

Another noteworthy aspect of Nixon's 1968 election was that for the first time in the twentieth century, a newly elected president moved into the White House without having his party in control of both houses of Congress. Prior to 1968, most newly elected presidents had swept a wave of their fellow partisans into office with them. For example, the Democrats gained 62 seats in the House when Woodrow Wilson was elected in 1912 and 97 when FDR was elected in 1932. Nixon's inability to bring in congressional majorities with him was not to be an exception, however, but rather the beginning of a new pattern—repeated in the presidential elections won by Ronald Reagan and George Bush. For a time, it seemed that the normal state of affairs in Washington was for American government to be divided with a Republican president and a Democratic Congress.

Bill Clinton's election in 1992 briefly restored united party government until the Republicans won both houses of Congress in the 1994 elections. After the 1994 elections, Republican leaders were optimistic that they were at

Franklin Roosevelt reshaped the Democratic Party, bringing together a diverse array of groups that had long been marginalized in American political life. Many of the key features of the Democratic Party today, such as support from labor unions, can be traced to the FDR era.

A GENERATION OF CHANGE

Realignment in the South

One of the most significant political changes over the past generation has been the partisan realignment in the Southern states that has transformed this region from one where Democrats occupied the majority of congressional seats to a crucial bastion of Republican support. In 1987, none of the Southern delegations to the House of Representatives had a Republican majority, and the GOP controlled only 6 of the region's 22 Senate seats. A generation later, the Republicans hold the majority of Southern House and Senate seats. The South is now the only region of the country where Republicans outnumber Democrats in Congress.

Without strong Southern support for the Republicans in recent elections, it is doubtful that the GOP would have been able to attain majority party status in the Congress for most of the period from 1995 to 2006. The crucial role of the South in Republican politics has lately been reflected in the makeup of the GOP congressional leadership. Trent Lott of Mississippi and Bill Frist of Tennessee have served as the Republicans' majority leader in the Senate. Georgia's Newt Gingrich served as Speaker of the House for three terms, and Texans Richard Armey and Tom DeLay have recently held the position of Republican House majority leader.

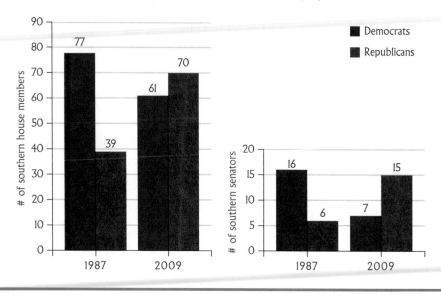

Why It Matters
Divided Party Government

When one party controls the White House and the other party controls one or both houses of Congress, divided party government exists. Given that one party can check the other's agenda, it is virtually impossible for a party to say what it is going to do and then actually put these policies into effect. This situation is bad if you want clear lines of accountability on policy, but it is good if you prefer that the two parties be forced to work out compromises.

last on the verge of a new Republican era in which they would control both the presidency and Congress simultaneously. On the other side, Democratic leaders were hopeful that voters would not like the actions of the new Republican Congress and would restore unified Democratic control of the government. In the end, the ambitions of both sides were frustrated as voters opted to continue divided party government in 1996. The election of George W. Bush in 2000 led to a very brief period of united Republican control of the White House in Congress. But four months after Bush took the inaugural oath, Senator James Jeffords of Vermont defected from the GOP, thereby giving the Democrats the majority in the upper chamber. In 2002, the GOP regained control of the Senate, and in 2004 unified Republican control of the Congress and the presidency was ratified. But voters opted for divided government once again in 2006 by giving the Democrats majorities in both congressional chambers. By electing Barack Obama to the presidency in 2008 along with a Democratic Congress, voters restored unified party government for at least the next two years.

With only about 60 percent of the electorate currently identifying with the Democrats or Republicans, it may well be difficult for either one to gain a strong enough foothold to maintain simultaneous control of both sides of Pennsylvania Avenue for very long—even with the GOP's dominance in the South. All told, both houses of Congress and the presidency have been simultaneously controlled by the same party for just 12.3 of the 42 years from 1969 to 2010.[23] The discrepancy between the patterns of presidential and congressional voting during this era of divided party government is unprecedented in American history.

Divided party government is frequently seen not only at the federal level but at the state level as well. As Morris Fiorina shows, the percentage of states that have unified party control of the governorship and the state legislature has declined substantially over the past sixty years.[24] Whereas 85 percent of state governments had one party controlling both houses of the legislature and the governorship in 1946, by 2009 this was the case in only 50 percent of the states (see "My State: Partisan Control of State Governments, 2009"). Divided government, once an occasional oddity in state capitols, is now commonplace.

The recent pattern of divided government has caused many political scientists to believe that the party system has dealigned rather than realigned. Whereas realignment involves people changing from one party to another, **party dealignment** means that many people are gradually moving away from both parties. When your car is realigned, it is adjusted in one direction or another to improve its steering. Imagine if your mechanic were to remove

party dealignment
The gradual disengagement of people and politicians from the parties, as seen in part by shrinking party identification.

MyState | Partisan Control of State Governments, 2009

This map shows which states as of 2009 were totally under Democratic or Republican control—that is, had one party controlling both houses of the legislature as well as the governorship. Divided party control means that either one or both houses of the legislature are controlled by a party different than the governor. Nebraska has a nonpartisan legislature and hence cannot be classified.

QUESTIONS FOR DISCUSSION

➤ Why do think your state has a divided government, a Republican-controlled government, or a Democratic-controlled government? Does this reflect how your state usually votes in presidential elections? Why or why not?

➤ When was the last time there was a change in the partisan control of your state government? What precipitated this change, and what difference did it make in terms of the policy direction of your state's government?

➤ What do you think would be best for your state in the near future—a divided party control of the state government, or having either the Democrats or Republicans in control of both the legislature and the governorship? Why?

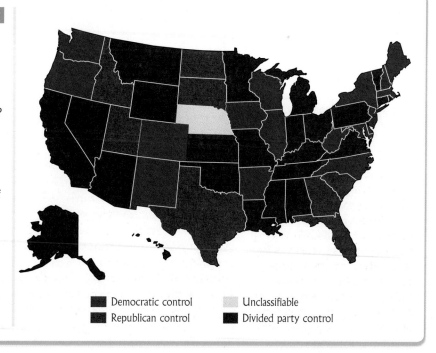

Democratic control   Unclassifiable
Republican control   Divided party control

the steering mechanism instead of adjusting it—your car would be useless and ineffective. This is what many scholars fear has been happening to the parties.

THIRD PARTIES: THEIR IMPACT ON AMERICAN POLITICS

third parties
Electoral contenders other than the two major parties. American third parties are not unusual, but they rarely win elections.

winner-take-all system
An electoral system in which legislative seats are awarded only to the candidates who come in first in their constituencies. In American presidential elections, the system in which the winner of the popular vote in a state receives all the electoral votes of that state.

The story of American party struggle is primarily the story of two major parties, but **third parties** are a regular feature of American politics and occasionally attract the public's attention. Third parties in the United States come in three basic varieties. First are parties that promote certain causes—either a controversial single issue (prohibition of alcoholic beverages, for example) or an extreme ideological position such as socialism or libertarianism. Second are splinter parties, which are offshoots of a major party. Teddy Roosevelt's Progressives in 1912, Strom Thurmond's States' Righters in 1948, and George Wallace's American Independents in 1968 all claimed they did not get a fair hearing from Republicans or Democrats and thus formed their own new parties. Finally, some third parties are merely an extension of a popular individual with presidential aspirations. Both John Anderson in 1980 and Ross Perot in 1992 and 1996 offered voters who were dissatisfied with the Democratic and Republican nominees another option.

Although third-party candidates almost never win office in the United States, scholars believe they are often quite important.[25] They have brought new groups into the electorate and have served as "safety valves" for popular discontent. The Free Soilers of the 1850s were the first true antislavery party; the Progressives and the Populists put many social reforms on the political agenda. George Wallace told his supporters in 1968 they had the chance to "send a message" to Washington—a message of support for tougher law and order measures, which is still being felt to this day. Ross Perot used his saturation of the TV airwaves in 1992 to ensure that the issue of the federal deficit was not ignored in the campaign. In 1998, a former professional wrestler stunned the political world when he won the governorship of Minnesota as a third-party candidate. And in 2000, Green Party candidate Ralph Nader forced more attention on environmental issues and ultimately cost Gore the presidency by drawing away a small percentage of liberal votes.

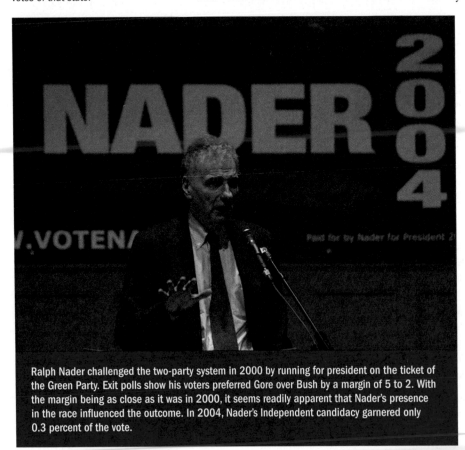

Ralph Nader challenged the two-party system in 2000 by running for president on the ticket of the Green Party. Exit polls show his voters preferred Gore over Bush by a margin of 5 to 2. With the margin being as close as it was in 2000, it seems readily apparent that Nader's presence in the race influenced the outcome. In 2004, Nader's Independent candidacy garnered only 0.3 percent of the vote.

Despite the regular appearance of third parties, the two-party system is firmly entrenched in American politics. Would it make a difference if America had a multiparty system, as so many European countries have? The answer is clearly yes. The most obvious consequence of two-party governance is the moderation of political conflict. If America had many parties, each would have to make a special appeal in order to stand out from the crowd. It is not hard to imagine what a multiparty system might look like in the United States. Quite possibly, African American groups would form their own party, pressing vigorously for racial equality. Environmentalists could constitute another party, vowing to clean up the rivers, oppose nuclear power, and save the wilderness. America could have religious parties, union-based parties, farmers' parties, and all sorts of others. As in some European countries, there could be half a dozen or more parties represented in Congress (see "America in Perspective: Multiparty Systems in Other Countries").

proportional representation

An electoral system used throughout most of Europe that awards legislative seats to political parties in proportion to the number of votes won in an election.

coalition government

When two or more parties join together to form a majority in a national legislature. This form of government is quite common in the multiparty systems of Europe.

AMERICA IN PERSPECTIVE

Multiparty Systems in Other Countries

One of the major reasons why the United States has only two parties represented in government is structural. America has a **winner-take-all system**, in which whoever gets the most votes wins the election. There are no prizes awarded for second or third place. Suppose there are three parties; one receives 45 percent of the vote, another 40 percent, and the third 15 percent. Although it got less than a majority, the party that finished first is declared the winner. The others are left out in the cold. In this way, the American system discourages small parties. Unless a party wins, there is no reward for the votes it gets. Thus, it makes more sense for a small party to form an alliance with one of the major parties than to struggle on its own with little hope. In this example, the second- and third-place parties might merge (if they can reach an agreement on policy) to challenge the governing party in the next election.

In a system that employs **proportional representation**, however, such a merger would not be necessary. Under this system, which is used in most European countries, legislative seats are allocated according to each party's percentage of the nationwide vote. If a party wins 15 percent of the vote, then it receives 15 percent of the seats. Even a small party can use its voice in Parliament to be a thorn in the side of the government, standing up strongly for its principles. Such has often been the role of the Greens in Germany, who are ardent environmentalists. After the 2002 German election they formed a **coalition government** along with Germany's Social Democratic Party. Together the coalition controlled over half the seats in the German parliament for three years. Coalition governments are common in Europe. Italy has regularly been ruled by a coalition since the end of World War II, for example.

Even with proportional representation, not every party gets represented in the legislature. To be awarded seats, a party must always achieve a certain percentage of votes, which varies from country to country. Israel has one of the lowest thresholds at 1.5 percent. This explains why there are always so many parties represented in the Israeli Knesset. The founders of Israel's system wanted to make sure that all points of view were represented, but sometimes this has turned into a nightmare, with small extremist parties holding the balance of power.

Parties have to develop their own unique identities to appeal to voters in a multiparty system. This requires strong stands on the issues, but after the election compromises must be made to form a coalition government. If an agreement cannot be reached on the major issues, the coalition is in trouble. Sometimes a new coalition can be formed; other times the result is the calling of a new election. In either case, it is clear that proportional representation systems are more fluid than the two-party system in the United States.

QUESTIONS FOR DISCUSSION

▶ If the United States adopted a form of proportional representation guaranteeing that any party would get seats in the House of Representatives if it won at least 5 percent of the national vote, how many political parties do you think would obtain seats? What new parties do you think would be formed and would become important players in a proportional representation system?

▶ Do you think your political views would end up being better represented if we had proportional representation and there were more viable parties to choose from on Election Day? If so, how?

▶ Do you think the United States ought to consider using proportional representation to determine how many members of each party get elected to Congress? Why or why not?

Third Parties in American History

The American two-party system contributes to political ambiguity. Why should parties risk taking a strong stand on a controversial policy if doing so will only antagonize many voters? Ambiguity is a safe strategy,[26] as extremist candidates Barry Goldwater in 1964 and George McGovern in 1972 found out the hard way. The two-party system thus throttles extreme or unconventional views.

UNDERSTANDING POLITICAL PARTIES

Political parties are considered essential elements of democratic government. Indeed, one of the first steps taken toward democracy in formerly communist Eastern European countries was the formation of competing political parties to contest elections. After years of one-party totalitarian rule, Eastern Europeans were ecstatic to be able to adopt a multiparty system like those that had proved successful in the West. In contrast, the founding of the world's first party system in the United States was seen as a risky adventure in the then uncharted waters of democracy. Wary of having parties at all, the Founders designed a system that has greatly restrained their political role to this day. Whether American parties should continue to be so loosely organized is at the heart of today's debate about their role in American democracy.

DEMOCRACY AND RESPONSIBLE PARTY GOVERNMENT: HOW SHOULD WE GOVERN?

Ideally, in a democracy candidates should say what they mean to do if elected and, once they are elected, should be able to do what they promised. Critics of the American party system lament that this is all too often not the case and have called for a "more responsible two-party system."[27] Advocates of the **responsible party model** believe the parties should meet the following conditions:

responsible party model
A view favored by some political scientists about how parties should work. According to the model, parties should offer clear choices to the voters, who can then use those choices as cues to their own preferences of candidates. Once in office, parties would carry out their campaign promises.

1. Parties must present distinct, comprehensive programs for governing the nation.
2. Each party's candidates must be committed to its program and have the internal cohesion and discipline to carry out its program.
3. The majority party must implement its programs, and the minority party must state what it would do if it were in power.
4. The majority party must accept responsibility for the performance of the government.

A two-party system operating under these conditions would make it easier to convert party promises into governmental policy. A party's officeholders would have firm control of the government, so they would be collectively rather than individually responsible for their actions. Voters would therefore know whom to blame for what the government does and does not accomplish.

As this chapter has shown, American political parties fall short of these conditions. They are too decentralized to take a single national position and then enforce it. Most candidates are self-selected, gaining their nomination by their own efforts rather than the party's. Virtually anyone can vote in party primaries; thus, parties do not have control over those who run under their labels. In 1991, for example, a former grand wizard of the Ku Klux Klan, David Duke, became the Republican nominee for governor of Louisiana despite denunciations from

Comparing Political Parties

President Bush, who ultimately said he preferred the Democratic nominee. Had Duke won the election, the Republican Party would have been powerless to control his actions in office.

In America's loosely organized party system, there simply is no mechanism for a party to discipline officeholders and thereby ensure cohesion in policymaking. Party leaders can help a candidate raise money, get on to the prestigious committees, and sometimes provide support in their efforts to get special benefits for their constituency. But what they cannot do is even more telling: They cannot deny them the party's nomination at the next election or take away their congressional staff support. Thus, as David Mayhew writes, "Unlike most politicians elsewhere, American ones at both legislative and executive levels have managed to navigate the last two centuries of history without becoming minions of party leaders."[28] American officeholders try to go along with their parties' platform whenever they can. But when the party line conflicts with their own personal opinion and/or the clear desires of their constituents, then they feel perfectly comfortable in voting against their party's leaders. As you can see in Table 8.2, even on the key issues that the

TABLE 8.2

Partisan Divisions on Key House Roll Call Votes in 2004

At the end of every year, *Congressional Quarterly* selects a series of key votes for both the House and Senate on major issues of the year. These votes are chosen based on the extent to which they represent (1) a matter of major controversy; (2) a subject of presidential or political power, and (3) an issue of potentially great national impact. In the following table, you can see how Republicans and Democrats voted on the 10 key roll call votes that *Congressional Quarterly* selected for the House of Representatives in 2004.

There are a number of interesting patterns to note in these roll-call votes. First, contrary to any notions that the majority party always wins, an examination of these 10 votes finds that on half of them the minority Democrats actually contributed more votes to the winning side. In particular, measures extending unemployment benefits and providing identification cards to Mexican citizens working in the United States were passed over the objections of most Republicans. Second, only 4 of the 10 votes fit the very loose American criteria for a party-line vote: a vote in which over 50 percent of the majority party votes differently than over 50 percent of the minority party. In most European democracies a party-line vote is defined as being a vote where every member of the majority coalition votes one way and every member of the opposition votes the other way. None of the key votes in the House in 2004 met this criteria.

Key Vote	REPUBLICANS		DEMOCRATS	
	Yes	No	Yes	No
Extension of unemployment benefits	39	179	187	0
Resolution praising the Iraq War	222	2	105	90
Transportation spending	162	59	194	6
Limiting discretionary federal spending	146	72	0	195
Limits on federal search powers	18	206	192	4
Identification cards for Mexican workers	49	161	172	16
Extending tax cuts	213	0	125	65
Gay marriage prohibition	191	27	36	158
Corporate tax overhaul	207	16	73	124
Intelligence gathering overhaul	152	67	183	8

Note: Votes in BLUE are ones where the minority party contributed more votes to the winning side than the party that then had the majority (the Republicans).

House of Representatives voted on in 2004, there were numerous disagreements among members of the same party.

Not everyone thinks that America's decentralized parties are a problem, however. Critics of the responsible party model argue that the complexity and diversity of American society are too great to be captured by such a simple model of party politics. Local differences need an outlet for expression, they say. One cannot expect Texas Democrats always to want to vote in line with New York Democrats. In the view of those opposed to the responsible party model, America's decentralized parties are appropriate for the type of limited government the Founders sought to create and most Americans wish to maintain.[29]

The Founding Fathers were very concerned that political parties would trample on the rights of individuals. They wanted to preserve individual freedom of action by various elected officials. With America's weak party system, this has certainly been the case. Individual members of Congress and other elected officials have great freedom to act as they see fit rather than toeing the party line.

AMERICAN POLITICAL PARTIES AND THE SCOPE OF GOVERNMENT

The lack of disciplined and cohesive European-style parties in America goes a long way to explain why the scope of governmental activity in the United States is not as broad as it is in other established democracies. The absence of a national health care system in America provides a perfect example. In Britain, the Labour Party had long proposed such a system, and after it won the 1945 election, all its members of Parliament voted to enact national health care into law. On the other side of the Atlantic, President Truman also proposed a national health care bill in the first presidential election after World War II. But even though he won the election and had majorities of his own party in both houses of Congress, his proposal never got very far. The weak party structure in the United States allowed many congressional Democrats to oppose Truman's health care proposal. Over four decades later, President Clinton again proposed a system of universal health care and had a Democratic-controlled Congress to work with. To emphasize the importance he placed on this bill, Bill Clinton placed his wife Hillary in charge of the efforts to draft a proposal and shepherd it into law. The Clintons' experience in 1994 was much the same as Truman's: The Clinton health care bill never even came up for a vote in Congress because of the president's inability to get enough members of his own party to go along with the plan. Substantially increasing the scope of government in America is not something that can be accomplished through the disciplined actions of one party's members, as is the case in other democracies.

On the other hand, because it is rarely the case that one single party can ever be said to have firm control over American government, the hard choices necessary to cut back on existing government spending are rarely addressed. A disciplined and cohesive governing party might have the power to say no to various demands on the government. In contrast, America's loose party structure makes it possible for many individual politicians—Democrats and Republicans alike—to focus their efforts on getting more from the government for their own constituents.

IS THE PARTY OVER?

The key problem for American political parties is that they are no longer the main source of political information, attention, and affection. The party of today has rivals that appeal to voters and politicians alike, the biggest of which is the media. With the advent of television, voters no longer need the party to find out what the candidates are like and what they stand for. The interest group is another party rival. As Chapter 11 will discuss, the power of interest groups has grown enormously in recent years. Interest groups, not the parties, pioneered much of the technology of modern politics, including mass mailings and sophisticated fund-raising.

The parties have clearly been having a tough time lately, but there are indications that they are beginning to adapt to the high-tech age. Although the old city machines are largely extinct, state and national party organizations have become more visible and active than ever. Two out of every five Americans call themselves Independents, but the majority still identify with a party, and this percentage seems to have stabilized.

For a time, some political scientists were concerned that parties were on the verge of disappearing from the political scene. A more realistic view is that parties will continue to play an important but significantly diminished role in American politics. Leon Epstein sees the situation as one in which the parties have become "frayed." He concludes that the parties will "survive and even moderately prosper in a society evidently unreceptive to strong parties and yet unready, and probably unable, to abandon parties altogether."[30]

SUMMARY

Even though political parties are one of Americans' least beloved institutions, political scientists see them as a key linkage between policymakers and the people. Parties are pervasive in politics; for each party there is a *party in the electorate*, a *party organization*, and a *party in government*. Political parties affect policy through their platforms. Despite much cynicism about party platforms, they serve as important roadmaps for elected officials once they come into office.

America has a two-party system. This fact is of fundamental importance in understanding American politics. The ups and downs of the two parties constitute party competition. In the past, one party or the other has dominated the government for long periods of time. These periods were punctuated by critical elections in which party coalitions underwent realignment. Since 1968, the South has realigned from a solidly Democratic region into an area of strength for the Republicans. Overall, however, American government has experienced a unique period of party dealignment, with the result that partisan control of the presidency and Congress has frequently been divided.

Even when partisan control is united, the decentralized nature of American politics makes it difficult for them to carry out ambitious plans for major changes, such as Bill and Hillary Clinton's health care reform plan or George W. Bush's plan to revamp Social Security. Some political observers would have them be far more centralized and cohesive, following the responsible party model. The loose structure of American parties allows politicians to avoid collective responsibility but also promotes individualism that many Americans value.

Chapter Test

Multiple Choice

1. The Founding Fathers believed that political parties:
   a. Would contribute an important checks-and-balances function to American politics
   b. Would provide a means for representation for the American population
   c. Had some flaws, but were ultimately necessary for the good of America
   d. Could become dangerous, if led by the wrong people
   e. Would become a source of division and friction

2. According to the textbook's definition of rational-choice theory, which of the following is *not* part of rational behavior?
   a. It is purposive
   b. It is efficient
   c. It is sensible
   d. It is correct
   e. All of the above are

3. The internal organization of political parties in the United States is best characterized by:
   a. Hierarchy
   b. Fragmentation
   c. Centralization
   d. Lack of leadership
   e. Strong leadership

4. In a closed primary system:
   a. Only party officials may vote to select the party's candidates
   b. Only certain states' voters participate
   c. Only members of a party may vote to select that party's candidates
   d. The vote for a party's candidates is conducted by secret ballot
   e. The vote for a party's candidates is kept secret until the general election

5. Which of the following allows voters to pick some Democrats and some Republicans on the primary, if they like?
   a. Closed primaries
   b. Open primaries
   c. Blanket primaries
   d. Free primaries
   e. All primaries

6. The task of writing a party's political platform is left to:
   a. The national convention
   b. The national committee
   c. The national chairperson
   d. The national party platform committee
   e. Each state party writes its own

7. Which of the following were *not* elements of the New Deal Coalition?
   a. African Americans
   b. Southerners
   c. Urban dwellers
   d. Catholics and Jews
   e. Hispanics

8. The term "party dealignment" refers to:
   a. The fragmentation of a political party into splinter parties
   b. The loss of party members as more people identify as independents
   c. The loss of party members to the other party
   d. The realignment of party coalitions
   e. The reformulation of a party's platform

9. The term "linkage institution" refers to:
   a. The ways in which citizens' policy preferences are converted into policy initiatives
   b. The linkage between different political institutions
   c. The linkage between interest groups and political parties
   d. The linkage between different policy areas
   e. The ways in which policymakers link issues in order to convince voters (i.e., "security" and "immigration")

10. Which of the following is *not* an example of a linkage institution?
    a. Political parties
    b. Elections
    c. Interest groups
    d. The media
    e. The White House

True/False

11. American political parties, unlike European ones, require membership dues and pass out membership cards.
    True_____   False_____

12. Successful parties in the United States remain as close to the center of public opinion as possible.
    True_____   False_____

13. Young people under the age of 24 are most likely to identify themselves as Democrats.
    True_____   False_____

14. By and large, American parties have kept most of their platform promises and translated them into public policy.
    True_____   False_____

15. The national committee of a political party can prevent an unwelcome local candidate from running under their party label.
    True_____   False_____

16. European parties tend to be more disciplined and structured than American parties.
    True_____   False_____

17. In a "winner-take-all" electoral system, a candidate can win without winning greater than 50 percent of the vote.
    True_____   False_____

18. The two American political parties offer clear choices for voters in their party platforms.
    True_____   False_____

Short Answer

19. Please explain three of the five ways in which parties perform their role as a linkage institution.

20. Briefly describe President Nixon's so-called "Southern strategy" and its impact.

21. What are at least two pros and two cons associated with so-called "blanket primaries"? Do you think such a system would be a good idea for your state?

22. Explain what the terms "party era," "critical election," and "party realignment" mean and how they are connected to each other.

23. If third parties almost never win office in the United States, why are they nonetheless important? Provide concrete examples to illustrate your answer.

Short Answer/Essay Questions

24. The textbook addresses the difficulty of bringing about major reforms, such as public health care, in a two-party system. Based on what you know about American politics and society, to what degree is it the party system that accounts for this and to what degree could this be attributed to other factors (e.g., social, psychological, economic, etc.)? In your opinion, what would it take for America to see government-regulated public health care?

25. The textbook mentioned the "three heads" of political parties, each of which comes with its own unique characteristics and responsibilities. Please outline these three aspects of parties, then address how they relate to each other. In particular, can you imagine a situation in which the goals of one "head" might interfere with that of the others?

26. Figure 8.2 shows that over the last several elections, more people have said they were Independents than either Democrats or Republicans. Why do you think so many people decline to identify with the two major parties?

27. What factors might explain why voters engage in so-called "ticket splitting"? What message should political parties

take away from this increasing trend? And what do you think such behavior means for the state of democracy?

28. Do you believe a system of proportional representation would work in the United States? In your answer, refer to specific political, social, economic, and ideological divisions among the American population that might lead to the creation of multiple parties which would then participate in elections. What do you believe the pros and cons of this would be?

29. In your opinion, what are the strengths and weaknesses of the American two-party system in terms of efficiency in policymaking, democratic representation, and any other category you might think of? How does this system compare to a system of proportional representation? Which system do you believe is "better" (use the above categories as a basis for your evaluation), and why?

30. In your opinion, are third parties in the United States weak because Americans do not vote for them, or do Americans not vote for third parties because they know they cannot win?

Answer Key

1. E 2. D 3. B 4. C 5. C 6. B 7. E 8. B 9. A 10. E 11. False 12. True 13. False 14. True 15. False 16. True 17. True 18. False

Key Terms

party competition (248)	**closed primaries** (255)	**party realignment** (259)
political party (248)	**open primaries** (255)	**New Deal coalition** (261)
linkage institutions (249)	**blanket primaries** (255)	**party dealignment** (265)
rational-choice theory (250)	**national convention** (255)	**third parties** (266)
party image (251)	**national committee** (255)	**winner-take-all system** (266)
party identification (251)	**national chairperson** (256)	**proportional representation** (267)
ticket splitting (252)	**coalition** (257)	**coalition government** (267)
party machines (254)	**party eras** (259)	**responsible party model** (268)
patronage (254)	**critical election** (259)	

Internet Resources

www.rnc.org
The official site of the Republican National Committee.

www.democrats.org
The Democratic Party online.

www.lp.org
Although Libertarians rarely get more than a few percent of the vote, they consistently get many of their candidates on the ballot for many offices. You can learn more about their beliefs at this official site.

www.gp.org
The official Web site for the Green Party, which emphasizes environmental protection over corporate profits.

GetConnected

Third Parties

Most people have heard of the Democratic and Republican parties, but many people would be surprised to learn that there are many other parties besides these in the United States. The text notes that these other parties, called "minor parties" or "third parties," come in three basic varieties: those that promote certain causes, those that are offshoots of the major parties, and those organized around popular individuals. What do these third parties stand for? Should you identify with one of the third parties?

Search the Web

Go to the Party Matchmaking Service, www.3pc.net/matchmaker/, and take the quiz. Think about the questions carefully and try to answer honestly.

Questions to Ask

- According to the quiz, with which party do you have the highest compatibility? Do you already identify with this party?
- Were you surprised by the results? Why?
- Find out whether this party has had a candidate for federal office on the ballot in your state in recent elections.

(You can check your state's secretary of state or election board Web pages or search with Google.) If so, did the candidate win?

Why It Matters

Despite the fact that their candidates are rarely elected, third parties exist because of the diversity of ideas in America, and they play an important role in our system of government. Third parties propose policies that are often adopted by the two major parties and sometimes are enacted into law. Third parties also allow voters a "protest" vote when they don't like the Democratic or Republican candidate. In some parts of the country, third-party candidates are the only opponents faced by Democratic or Republican candidates.

Get Involved

You can find the contact information and Web page addresses of political parties at the Politics1.com Web site, *www. politics1.com/parties.htm*. Research the party with which you are most compatible according to the quiz results. Are you interested in associating with this party? If so, find out how you can become an active member. For more exercises, go to *www.longmanamericangovernment.com*.

For Further Reading

Black, Earl, and Merle Black. *The Rise of Southern Republicanism*. Cambridge, MA: Harvard University Press, 2002. An excellent examination of the transformation of party politics in the South.

Burden, Barry C., and David C. Kimball. *Why Americans Split Their Tickets: Campaigns, Competition and Divided Government*. Ann Arbor: University of Michigan Press, 2002. A good analysis of who splits their ticket and under what conditions they are most likely to do so.

Downs, Anthony. *An Economic Theory of Democracy*. New York: Harper&Row, 1957. An extremely influential theoretical work that applies rational-choice theory to party politics.

Epstein, Leon. *Political Parties in the American Mold*. Madison: University of Wisconsin Press, 1986. Epstein demonstrates the remarkable persistence of both parties during a century of profound social change.

Green, John C., and Daniel M. Shea. *The State of the Parties*. 5th ed. Lanham, MD: Rowman & Littlefield, 2007. A diverse set of articles on numerous aspects of party politics, with an emphasis on how well the party system is working.

Hershey, Marjorie Randon. *Party Politics in America*. 13th ed. New York: Longman, 2009. The standard textbook on political parties.

Maisel, L. Sandy, ed. *The Parties Respond: Changes in the American Parties and Campaigns*. 4th ed. Boulder, CO: Westview, 2002. A good collection of readings on how parties have adapted to changes in the political system.

Mayhew, David R. *Electoral Realignments: A Critique of an American Genre*. New Haven, CT: Yale University Press, 2002. A critical look at the historical evidence concerning realignment theory.

Rosenstone, Steven, Roy Behr, and Edward Lazarus. *Third Parties in America*. 2nd ed. Princeton, NJ: Princeton University Press, 1996. An analytical study of why third parties appear, when they do, and what effect they have.

Sundquist, James L. *Dynamics of the Party System*. Rev. ed. Washington, DC: Brookings Institution, 1983. One of the best books ever written on the major realignments in American history.

Wattenberg, Martin P. *The Decline of American Political Parties, 1952–1996*. Cambridge, MA: Harvard University Press, 1998. An account of the decline of parties in the electorate.

NOMINATIONS
AND
CAMPAIGNS

POLITICS IN ACTION:
HOW RUNNING FOR OFFICE CAN BE MORE DEMANDING THAN GOVERNING

Campaigning for any major office has become a massive undertaking in today's political world. Consider Barack Obama's grueling schedule for March 21, 2008, a relatively low-key period of the presidential campaign:

- The senator arrives at the Benson Hotel in Portland, Oregon, after midnight, following a 2,550 mile plane ride from Charleston, West Virginia, where he had spent the previous day campaigning.
- At 7:00 A.M., Obama leaves his hotel for a jog around downtown Portland.
- After returning to the hotel for a change of clothes, Obama meets privately with Governor Bill Richardson of New Mexico, who has just decided to endorse him. The pair then proceed to a scheduled rally at the Portland Memorial Coliseum, where the endorsement is publicly announced to an enthusiastic crowd of 12,800 people.
- Following the morning rally Obama holds a press conference, taking questions from the corps of reporters traveling with him as well as members of the Oregon media.
- Obama then hops on his campaign bus for an hour's drive down to Oregon's capital city of Salem, where he responds to questions from ordinary Oregonians at a town-hall meeting attended by about 3,000 people.
- While in Salem, Obama manages to do six separate interviews with Oregon news organizations before getting back on the campaign bus.
- After another hour on the road, the bus pulls up in front of American Dream Pizza in Corvallis, where the candidate pops in for a slice of pizza and an impromptu chat with some pleasantly surprised fellow diners (as pictured in the photo at left).
- Obama then re-boards his bus for another hour's ride to Eugene to address a crowd of 10,000 people at the University of Oregon's basketball arena.

• Following this evening rally, the candidate goes to the Eugene airport to board his campaign plane for a 200 mile flight to Medford, Oregon. Just after 1:00 A.M., Obama walks into his hotel for the night, knowing that he has another day like this to look forward to tomorrow.

It is often said that the presidency is the most difficult job in the world, but getting elected to the position may well be tougher. It is arguable that the long campaign for the presidency puts candidates under more continuous stress than they could ever face in the White House. As Karl Rove, George W. Bush's veteran political adviser, wrote just before the first primary votes were cast in 2008, "There are few more demanding physical activities than running for president, other than military training or athletics at a very high level."[1] When asked if he was exhausted by the demands of campaigning in 2008, Barack Obama simply answered, "Sometimes, yes, of course."

The current American style of long and arduous campaigns has evolved from the belief of reformers that the cure for the problems of democracy is more democracy. Whether this approach is helpful or harmful to democracy is a question that arouses much debate with respect to American political campaigns. Some scholars believe it is important that presidential candidates go through a long and difficult trial by fire. Others, however, worry that the system makes it difficult for politicians with other responsibilities—such as incumbent governors and senior senators—to take a run at the White House.

The consequences for the scope of government are also debatable. Anthony King argues that American politicians do too little governing because they are always "running scared," in today's perpetual campaign.[2] From King's perspective, the campaign process does not allow politicians the luxury of trying out solutions to policy problems that might be initially unpopular but would work well in the long run. The scope of government thus stays pretty much as is, given that politicians are usually too concerned with the next election to risk fundamental change. Of course, many analysts would argue that having officeholders constantly worrying about public opinion is good for democracy and that changes in the scope of government shouldn't be undertaken without extensive public consultation.

As you read this chapter, consider whether today's nomination and campaign process provides *too much* opportunity for interaction between the public and candidates for office. Also, consider whether the entire process takes too much time and costs too much money—two very important topics of debate in American politics today.

With about half a million elected officials in this country, there is always someone somewhere running for office. This chapter will focus mainly on the campaign for the world's most powerful office: the presidency of the United States. On some topics that are broadly generalizable, such as money and campaigning, we will include examples from congressional races as well. Chapter 12 will specifically discuss the congressional election process.

Campaigns in American politics can be divided into two stages: first, nominations, and, second, campaigns between the two nominees. The prize for a nomination campaign is garnering a party's nod as its candidate; the prize for an election campaign is winning an office. This chapter discusses what happens up to Election Day. Chapter 10 explores how people decide whether to vote and whom to vote for.

nomination
The official endorsement of a candidate for office by a **political party**. Generally, success in the nomination game requires momentum, money, and media attention.

THE NOMINATION GAME

A **nomination** is a party's official endorsement of a candidate for office. Anyone can play the nomination game, but few have any serious chance of victory. Generally, success in the nomination game requires money, media attention, and momentum.

Campaign strategy is the way in which candidates attempt to manipulate each of these elements to achieve the nomination.

DECIDING TO RUN

Believe it or not, not every politician wants to run for president. One reason why is that campaigns have become more physically and emotionally taxing than ever. As former Speaker of the House Thomas Foley once said, "I know of any number of people who I think would make good presidents, even great presidents, who are deterred from running by the torture candidates are obliged to put themselves through."[3] Running for president is an around-the-clock endurance test for over a year: sleep deprivation and strange hotel beds, countless plane rides, junk food eaten on the run, a lack of regular exercise, and copious amounts of stress. As 1984 Democratic nominee Walter Mondale once said, "For four years, that's all I did. I mean, all I did. That's all you think about. That's all you talk about. . . . That's your leisure. That's your luxury . . . I told someone, 'The question is not whether I can get elected. The question is whether I can be elected and not be nuts when I get there.' "[4]

In most advanced industrialized countries, campaigns last no more than two months according to either custom and/or law. In contrast, American campaigns seem endless; a presidential candidacy needs to be either announced or an open secret for at least a year before the election. Virtually all of the major candidates for president in 2008 had declared their candidacy and started to run at full steam ahead by the winter of 2007.

The road to the convention is long and full of stumbling blocks. From the convention, held in the summer of election years, only one candidate emerges as each party's nominee.

COMPETING FOR DELEGATES

In some ways, the nomination game is tougher than the general election game; it whittles a large number of players down to two. The goal of the nomination game is to win the majority of delegates' support at the **national party convention**—the supreme power within each of the parties, which functions to select presidential and vice presidential candidates and to write a party platform.

There are 50 different roads to the national convention, one through each state. From February through June of the election year, the individual state parties busily choose their delegates to the national convention via either caucuses or primaries. Candidates try to ensure that delegates committed to them are chosen.

The Caucus Road   Before primaries existed, all state parties selected their delegates to the national convention in a meeting of state party leaders called a **caucus**. Sometimes one or two party "bosses" ran the caucus show, such as Mayor Daley of Chicago or Governor Connally of Texas. Such state party leaders could control who went to the convention and how the state's delegates voted once they got there. They were the kingmakers of presidential politics who met in smoke-filled rooms at the convention to cut deals and form coalitions.

Today's caucuses are different from those of the past. In the dozen states that still have them, caucuses are now open to all voters who are registered with the party. Caucuses are usually organized like a pyramid. Small, neighborhood, precinct-level caucuses are held initially—often meeting in a church, an American Legion hall, or even someone's home. At this level, delegates are chosen, on the basis of their preference for a certain candidate, to attend county caucuses and then congressional district caucuses, where delegates are again chosen to go to a higher level—a state convention. At the state convention, which usually occurs months after the precinct caucuses, delegates are finally chosen to go to the national convention.

campaign strategy
The master game plan candidates lay out to guide their electoral campaign.

national party convention
The supreme power within each of the parties. The convention meets every four years to nominate the party's presidential and vice-presidential candidates and to write the party's platform.

caucus
A meeting of all state party leaders for selecting delegates to the **national party convention**. Caucuses are usually organized as a pyramid.

Iowa Caucuses

Since 1972, the state of Iowa has held the nation's first caucuses. Because the Iowa caucuses are the first test of the candidates' vote-getting ability, they usually become a full-blown media extravaganza.[5] Well-known candidates like Dick Gephardt in 2004 and John Glenn in 1984 have seen their campaigns virtually fall apart as a result of poor showings in Iowa. Most important, some candidates have received tremendous boosts from unexpected strong showings in Iowa. An obscure former Georgia governor named Jimmy Carter took his first big presidential step by winning there in 1976. Four years later, George Bush also made his first big step into the national scene with an upset victory over Ronald Reagan in Iowa. In 2008, Barack Obama's victory over Hillary Clinton shocked the political world and landed him on the covers of the major weekly magazines, *Time* and *Newsweek*. Because of the impact that Iowa's first-in-the-nation caucus can have, candidates spend far more time during the nomination season there than they do in the big states like California, Texas, and Florida. As David Yepsen, Iowa's top political reporter, wrote in the *Des Moines Register* the day before the 2008 Iowa caucus, "For more than a year, Iowans have been carpet-bombed by record numbers of candidate visits, interest groups, commercials, mail, phone calls and people knocking on doors. Millions of dollars have been spent here and hundreds of staffers deployed, using the most advanced political tactics and technologies. Day in and day out, we have been told how important we are and how so much is at stake."[6] Like most years, the results from the 2008 the Iowa caucus winnowed down the number of viable candidates for the primaries to come.

presidential primaries
Elections in which voters in a state vote for a candidate (or delegates pledged to him or her). Most delegates to the **national party conventions** are chosen this way.

The Primary Road Today, most of the delegates to the Democratic and Republican national conventions are selected in **presidential primaries**, in which voters in a state go to the polls and vote for a candidate or delegates pledged to that candidate. The presidential primary was promoted around the turn of the century by reformers who wanted to take nominations out of the hands of the party bosses. The reformers wanted to let the people vote for the candidate of their choice and then bind the delegates to vote for that candidate at the national convention.

The increase in the number of presidential primaries occurred after the Democratic Party's disastrous 1968 national convention led many to rethink the delegate selection procedures then in place. As the war in Southeast Asia raged, another war of sorts took place in the streets of Chicago during the Democratic convention. Demonstrators against the war battled Mayor Richard Daley's Chicago police in what an official report later called a "police riot." Beaten up in the streets and defeated in the convention hall, the antiwar faction won one concession from the party regulars: a special committee to review the party's structure and delegate selection procedures, which they felt had discriminated against them. Minorities, women, youth, and other groups that had been poorly represented in the party leadership also demanded a more open process of convention delegate selection. The result was a committee of inquiry, which was chaired

Televised debates are a regular feature of the presidential nomination process. These debates involve face-offs between members of the same party, as the candidates battle to control the direction of their party. Here, Republicans Mike Huckabee, Ron Paul, John McCain, and Mitt Romney face off at the Reagan Library prior to the 2008 California primary. (In the background, the actual plane that President Reagan used as Air Force One can be seen).

first by Senator George McGovern and later by Representative Donald Fraser, who took over when McGovern left the committee to run for president.

The **McGovern-Fraser Commission** had a mandate to try to make Democratic Party conventions more representative. As a result of their decisions, party leaders could no longer handpick the convention delegates virtually in secret. All delegate selection procedures were required to be open, so that party leaders had no more clout than college students or anyone else who wanted to participate. One of the unforeseen results of these new rules was that many states decided that the easiest way to comply was simply to hold primary elections to select convention delegates.[7] Because state laws instituting primaries typically apply to both parties' selection of delegates, the Republican Party's nomination process was similarly transformed.

Few developments have changed American politics as much as the proliferation of presidential primaries. Presidential election watcher Theodore White calls the primaries the "classic example of the triumph of goodwill over common sense." Says White,

Riots at the 1968 Democratic national convention led to the creation of the McGovern-Fraser Commission, which established open procedures and affirmative action guidelines for delegate selection. These reforms have made party conventions more representative than they once were.

> Delegates, who were supposed to be free to vote by their own common sense and conscience, have become for the most part anonymous faces, collected as background for the television cameras, sacks of potatoes packaged in primaries, divorced from party roots, and from the officials who rule states and nation.[8]

Whereas once many of the delegates were experienced politicians who knew the candidates, today they are typically people who have worked on a candidate's campaign and who owe their position as a delegate strictly to that candidate's ability to pull in primary votes.

The Democratic Party became so concerned about the lack of a role for party leaders at their conventions that starting in 1984 they automatically set aside about 20 percent of their delegate slots for Democratic office holders (governors, senators, and members of the House of Representatives) as well as members of the Democratic National Committee. These politicians, who are awarded convention seats on the basis of their position, are known as **superdelegates**. The addition of these delegates to the Democratic national convention was designed to restore an element of "peer review" to the process, ensuring that the people most familiar with the candidates and with a long-term stake in the party's success get to participate. The 2008 convention marked the first time that the nomination race was so close that the superdelegates played a pivotal role, with the majority of these party leaders opting to support Barack Obama at the convention.

The primary season begins during the winter in New Hampshire. Like the Iowa caucuses, the importance of New Hampshire is not the number of delegates or how representative the state is but rather that it is traditionally the first primary.[9] At this early stage, the campaign is not for delegates but for images—candidates want the rest of the country to see them as front-runners. The frenzy of political activity in this small state is given lavish attention in the national press. During the week of

McGovern-Fraser Commission

A commission formed at the 1968 Democratic convention in response to demands for reform by minority groups and others who sought better representation.

superdelegates

National party leaders who automatically get a delegate slot at the Democratic **national party convention**.

the primary, half the portable satellite dishes in the country can be found in Manchester, New Hampshire, and the networks move their anchors and top reporters to the scene to broadcast the nightly news. In recent years, over a fifth of TV coverage of the nomination races has been devoted to the New Hampshire primary.[10]

With so much attention being paid to the early contests, more states have moved their primaries up in the calendar to capitalize on the media attention. This **frontloading** of the process resulted in about two-thirds of both Democratic and Republican delegates being chosen within six weeks of the Iowa caucus in 2008. At one time, it was considered advantageous for a state to choose its delegates late in the primary season so that it could play a decisive role. However, in recent years, states that have held late primaries have frequently proved to be irrelevant given that one candidate had already secured the nomination by the time their primaries were held. The very close race between Obama and Clinton for the Democratic nomination in 2008 is the one recent exception to this rule.

State laws determine how delegates are allocated, operating within the general guidelines set by the parties. Some are limited to only people who are registered with the party, whereas others are open. The Democrats require all states to use some form of proportional representation in which a candidate who gets 15 percent or more of a state's vote is awarded a roughly proportional share of the delegates. Republicans believe in less regulation, and consequently give states a large degree of discretion. Some states like Florida allocate all Republican delegates to whoever wins the most votes, others like California award delegates according to who wins each congressional district, and yet others employ some form of proportional representation.

Week after week, the primaries serve as elimination contests, as the media continually monitor the count of delegates won. The politicians, the press, and the public all love a winner. Candidates who fail to score early wins get labeled as losers and typically drop out of the race. Usually they have little choice since losing quickly inhibits a candidate's ability to raise the money necessary to win in other states. As one veteran fund-raiser put it, "People don't lose campaigns. They run out of money and can't get their planes in the air. That's the reality."[11]

In the 1980 delegate chase, a commonly used football term became established in the language of American politics. After George Bush scored a surprise victory over Ronald Reagan in Iowa, he proudly claimed to possess "the big mo"—momentum. Actually, Bush had only a little "mo" and quickly fell victim to a decisive Reagan victory in New Hampshire. But the term neatly describes what candidates for the nomination are after. Primaries and caucuses are more than an endurance contest, though they are certainly that; they are also proving grounds. Week after week, the challenge is to do better than expected. Learning from his father's experience, George W. Bush jokingly told the reporters on his 2000 campaign plane, "Please stow your expectations securely in your overhead bins, as they may shift during the trip and can fall and hurt someone—especially me."[12]

frontloading
The recent tendency of states to hold primaries early in the calendar in order to capitalize on media attention.

The Electoral College: Campaign Consequences and Mapping the Results

For a number of months, Howard Dean's formidable fund-raising and high poll standing made him the front-runner in the race for the 2004 Democratic presidential nomination. But when he repeatedly screamed during a concession speech after the first delegate contest in Iowa, his reputation took a drastic hit from which his campaign never recovered.

To get "mo" going, candidates have to beat people they were not expected to beat, collect margins above predictions, and—above all else—never lose to people they were expected to trounce. Momentum is good to have, but it is no guarantee of victory because candidates with a strong base sometimes bounce back. Political scientist Larry Bartels found that "substantive political appeal may overwhelm the impact of momentum."[13] Indeed, after being soundly trounced by John McCain in New Hampshire in 2000, George W. Bush quickly bounced back to win the big states necessary to get the Republican nomination. Eight years later it was John McCain who bounced back to win after Mike Huckabee scored a victory in the first 2008 Republican contest in Iowa.

Evaluating the Primary and Caucus System The primaries and the caucuses are here to stay. That reality does not mean, however, that political scientists or commentators are particularly happy with the system. Criticisms of this marathon campaign are numerous; here are a few of the most important:

- *Disproportionate attention goes to the early caucuses and primaries.* Take a look at "My State: How Obama and Clinton Visited Some States Far More Than Others During the 2008 Nomination Campaign," which shows that the focus of the major candidates was amazingly concentrated on the early contests for delegates in 2008. In particular, the first caucus in Iowa and the first primary in New Hampshire received far more attention than later contests in some of the most heavily populated states. Although Iowa and New Hampshire are not always "make or break" contests, they play a key—and a disproportionate—role in building momentum, generating money and media attention.
- *Prominent politicians find it difficult to take time out from their duties to run.* Running for the presidency has become a full-time job. It is hard to balance the demands of serving in high public office with running a presidential campaign. Of the six U.S. Senators who were candidates for the presidency in 2008, the average voting participation rate in 2007 was a mere 63 percent—far below the average senatorial attendance rate of about 95 percent.[14]
- *Money plays too big a role in the caucuses and primaries.* Momentum means money—getting more of it than your opponents do. Many people think that money plays too large a role in American presidential elections. (This topic will be discussed in detail shortly.) Candidates who drop out early in the process often lament that their inability to raise money left them without a chance to compete.
- *Participation in primaries and caucuses is low and unrepresentative.* Although about 60 percent of adult citizens vote in the November presidential election, only about 25 percent casts ballots in presidential primaries. Participation in caucus states is much smaller because a person must usually devote several hours to attending a caucus. Except for Iowa, where the extraordinary media attention usually boosts the participation, only about 5 percent of registered voters typically show up for caucuses. Moreover, voters in primaries and caucuses are hardly representative of voters at large; they tend to be older and more affluent than the typical citizen.
- *The system gives too much power to the media.* Critics contend that the media have replaced the party bosses as the new kingmakers. Deciding who has momentum at any given moment, the press readily labels candidates as winners and losers.

Is this the best way to pick a president? Critics think not and have come up with a number of reform proposals (see "You Are the Policymaker: National and Regional Presidential Primary Proposals").

Why It Matters
Early Delegate Contests
In baseball, no one would declare a team out of the pennant race after it lost the first two games of the season. But in the race for the presidential nomination, the results of the Iowa caucus and the New Hampshire primary frequently end the campaigns of many candidates after only a handful of national delegates have been selected. These contests are important not because of the number of delegates that are chosen but rather because they are the first indicators of public support. If a candidate does not do well in these first two contests, money and media attention dry up quickly.

TIMELINE

Nominating Process

MyState | How Obama and Clinton Visited Some States Far More Than Others During the 2008 Nomination Campaign

For the first time in recent years, the 2008 contest for the Democratic nomination turned into a 50 state contest, with Obama and Clinton battling in a close race for every delegate. Yet, as usual, the first caucus in Iowa and the first primary in New Hampshire still received far more attention from the candidates than their number of delegates would warrant. Together, these two states selected just 2 percent of the delegates to the 2008 Democratic National Convention. Yet, 29 percent of the public events held by Obama and Clinton during the campaign took place in these two small states. Here, you can see a map of the 50 states drawn to scale in terms of the number of events the two major Democratic candidates held in them; note how blown out of proportion Iowa and New Hampshire are on the map.

QUESTIONS FOR DISCUSSION

▶ Do you think your state got the attention it deserved from Obama and Clinton during the Democratic nomination campaign in 2008?

▶ Examine where in the calendar year your state had its Democratic primary or caucus by going to: http://politics.nytimes.com/election-guide/2008/primaries/democraticprimaries/index.html. How do you think the timing of your state's delegate selection contest influenced the amount of attention it received from the major Democratic candidates?

▶ Do you think your state should change its position in the primary calendar for 2012 so as to attract more attention from the candidates? If so, where in the calendar do you think it should move to?

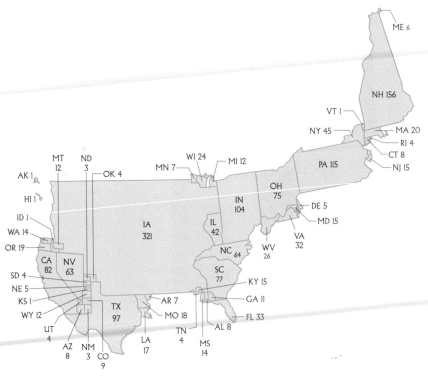

Source: Washington Post campaign tracker data for Jan 2007 through May 20, 2008
http://projects.washingtonpost.com/2008-presidential-candidates/tracker/.

Barring some major reform, states will continue to select delegates in primaries and caucuses who will attend the national conventions, where the nominees are formally chosen.

THE CONVENTION SEND-OFF

At one time party conventions provided great drama. Great speeches were given, dark-horse candidates suddenly appeared, and numerous ballots were held as candidates jockeyed to be the first to obtain the support of a majority of the delegates. With delegates having the chance to vote again every time there was no clear winner, candidate support could change dramatically from ballot to ballot, thereby adding to the excitement of this political spectacle. Multi-ballot conventions died out after 1952, however, with the advent of television.

YOU ARE THE **Policymaker**

National and Regional Presidential Primary Proposals

The idea of holding a **national primary** to select party nominees has been discussed virtually ever since state primaries were introduced. In 1913, President Woodrow Wilson proposed it in his first message to Congress. Since then, over 250 proposals for a national presidential primary have been introduced in Congress. These proposals do not lack public support; opinion polls have consistently shown that a substantial majority of Democrats, Republicans, and Independents alike favor such reform.

According to its proponents, a national primary would bring directness and simplicity to the process for the voters as well as the candidates. The length of the campaign would be shortened, and no longer would votes in one state have more political impact than votes in another. The concentration of media coverage on this one event, say its advocates, would increase not only political interest in the nomination decision but also public understanding of the issues involved.

A national primary would not be so simple, respond the critics. Because Americans would not want a candidate nominated with 25 percent of the vote from among a field of six candidates, in most primaries a runoff election between the top two finishers in each party would have to be held. So much for making the campaign simpler, national primary critics note. Each voter would have to vote three times for president—twice in the primaries and once in November.

Another common criticism of a national primary is that only well-established politicians would have a shot at breaking through in such a system. Big money and big attention from the national media would become more crucial than ever. Talented politicians who operate in relative national obscurity because of the small size of their state would never have a chance. Do Americans, however, really want politicians without an established reputation to become president?

Perhaps more feasible than a national primary is holding a series of **regional primaries** in which, say, states in the eastern time zone would vote one week, those in the central time zone the next, and so on. This would impose a more rational structure and cut down on candidate travel. A regional primary system would also put an end to the jockeying between states for an advantageous position in the primary season. In the fall of 2005, a bipartisan commission on electoral reform led by former President Jimmy Carter and former Secretary of State James Baker endorsed a plan to establish regional primaries (see www.american.edu/ia/cfer/).

The major problem with the regional primary proposal, however, is the advantage gained by whichever region goes first. For example, if the Western states were the first to vote, any candidate from California would have a clear edge in building momentum. Although most of the proposed plans call for the order of the regions to be determined by lottery, this would not erase the fact that regional advantages would surely be created from year to year.

Another prominent proposal is to have states vote in four stages according to their population size, with the least populous states leading off and the big states like California and Texas voting last. Such a proposal received serious consideration from the Republican National Committee in 2000 and was about to be voted on at the convention until George W. Bush let it be known that he did not favor it. Bush expressed concern that the plan would be unworkable because candidates would be asked to campaign all over the country in each stage.

Put yourself in the role of policymaker. Do the advantages of the reform proposals outweigh the disadvantages? Would any of them represent an improvement over the current system? Keep in mind that there are almost always unintended consequences associated with reforms.

Today, the drama has largely been drained from the conventions because the winner is a foregone conclusion. No longer can a powerful governor shift a whole block of votes at the last minute. Delegates selected in primaries and open caucuses have known preferences. The last time there was any doubt about who would win at the convention was in 1976, when Gerald Ford barely edged out Ronald Reagan for the Republican nomination.

Without such drama, the networks have substantially scaled back the number of hours of coverage in recent years, as you can see in Figure 9.1. Even with the condensed TV coverage, the Nielsen ratings have fallen to abysmal levels.[15] About 38 million people watched Barack Obama's speech to the 2008 Democratic convention, which was covered by all the major broadcast networks as well as the cable news channels. By contrast, over 97 million people tuned in to see the Giants defeat the Patriots in the 2008 Super Bowl, which was broadcast on only one network.

Although conventions are no longer very interesting, they are a significant rallying point for the parties. As George W. Bush said prior to the Republican

national primary

A proposal by critics of the **caucuses** and **presidential primaries**, which would replace these electoral methods with a nationwide **primary** held early in the election year.

regional primaries

A proposal by critics of the **caucuses** and **presidential primaries** to replace these electoral methods with a series of primaries held in each geographic region.

FIGURE 9.1

The Declining Coverage of Conventions on Network TV

Believe it or not, Democratic and Republican conventions once got far more coverage on the major networks (CBS, NBC, and ABC) than the Summer Olympics. As the number of presidential primaries has increased, however, nominations have come to be decided in these contests. Thus, by the time the conventions are held, there is little element of political suspense. Hence, the networks have drastically cut back on their coverage of these events, as you can see in the data displayed here.

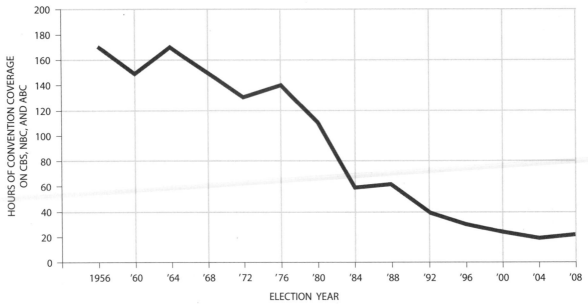

Source: For 1956-1984, calculated from data reported in Byron E. Schafer, *Bifurcated Politics: Evolution and Reform in the National Party Convention* (Cambridge, MA: Harvard University Press, 1988), 274; updated by the authors for 1988 through 2008.

convention in 2000, "The convention system provides a system of rewards for hardworking, grass-roots people who end up being delegates. I view it as an opportunity for these people to go back home, energized to help me get elected."[16] Modern conventions are carefully scripted to present the party in its best light. As Barack Obama wrote in his 2006 book, *The Audacity of Hope*, the party convention "serves as a weeklong infomercial for the party and its nominee."[17] Delegates are no longer there to argue for their causes but merely to support their candidate. The parties carefully orchestrate a massive send-off for the presidential and vice-presidential candidates. The party's leaders are there in force, as are many of its most important followers—people whose input will be critical during the general election campaign.

The conventions are also important in developing the party's policy positions and in promoting political representation. In the past, conventions were essentially an assembly of party leaders, gathered together to bargain over the selection of the party's ticket. Almost all delegates were White, male, and over 40. Lately, party reformers, especially among the Democrats, have worked hard to make the conventions far more demographically representative. Meeting in an oversized, overstuffed convention hall in a major city, a national convention is a short-lived affair. The highlight of the first day is usually the keynote speech, in which a dynamic speaker recalls party heroes, condemns the opposition party, and touts the nominee apparent.

The second day centers on the **party platform**—the party's statement of its goals and policies for the next four years. The platform is drafted prior to the

party platform

A political party's statement of its goals and policies for the next four years. The platform is drafted prior to the party convention by a committee whose members are chosen in rough proportion to each candidate's strength. It is the best formal statement of a party's beliefs.

convention by a committee whose members are chosen in rough proportion to each candidate's strength. Any time over 20 percent of the delegates to the platform committee disagree with the majority, they can bring an alternative minority plank to the convention floor for debate. In former times, contests over the platform were key tests of candidates' strength before the actual nomination. When a peace plank failed to be adopted by the 1968 Democratic national convention, it was clear that Vice President Hubert Humphrey would defeat antiwar candidate Eugene McCarthy. In contrast, recent contests over the platform have served mostly as a way for the minority factions in the party to make sure that their voices are heard. Since 1992, pro-choice Republicans have often tried in vain to force a vote on the solidly antiabortion plank in the GOP platform. Fearing the negative publicity the party would incur by showing open disagreement on this emotionally charged issue, pro-choice Republican leaders have dissuaded delegates from forcing such a confrontation.

The third day of the convention is devoted to formally nominating a candidate for president. One of each candidate's eminent supporters gives a speech extolling the candidate's virtues; a string of seconding speeches then follow. Toward the end of the evening, balloting begins as states announce their votes. After all the votes are counted, the long-anticipated nomination becomes official.

The vice-presidential nominee is chosen by roll-call vote on the convention's final day, though custom dictates that delegates simply vote for whomever the presidential nominee recommends. The vice-presidential candidate then comes to the podium to make a brief acceptance speech. This speech is followed by the grand finale—the presidential candidate's acceptance speech, in which the battle lines for the coming campaign are drawn. Afterward, all the party leaders come out to congratulate the party's ticket, raise their hands, and bid the delegates farewell.

THE CAMPAIGN GAME

Once nominated, candidates concentrate on campaigning for the general election. These days, the word *campaign* is part of the American political vocabulary, but it was not always so. The term was originally a military one: Generals mounted campaigns, using their limited resources to achieve strategic objectives. Political campaigns proceed in a similar fashion, with candidates allocating their scarce resources of time, money, and energy to achieve their political objectives.

Campaigns involve more than organization and leadership. Artistry also enters the picture, for campaigns deal in images. The campaign is the canvas on which political strategists try to paint portraits of leadership, competence, caring, and other images Americans value in presidents. Campaigning today is an art and a science, heavily dependent—like much else in American politics—on technology.

In writing a party platform, disagreements between various factions of the party often become evident. In recent years, Ann Stone has led a movement of Republican women in favor of a pro-choice plank on abortion. Although Ann Stone's efforts have received a fair amount of media attention, she has been unsuccessful in getting the Republican convention to consider changing its pro-life platform.

THE HIGH-TECH MEDIA CAMPAIGN

The new machines of politics have changed the way campaigns are run. During the first half of the twentieth century, candidates and their entourage piled onto a campaign train and tried to speak to as many people as time, energy, and money

TIMELINE

Television and Presidential Campaigns

would allow. Voters journeyed from miles around to see a presidential whistle-stop tour go by and to hear a few words in person from the candidate. Today, television is the most prevalent means used by candidates to reach voters. Thomas Patterson stresses that "today's presidential campaign is essentially a mass media campaign. . . . It is no exaggeration to say that, for the majority of voters, the campaign has little reality apart from its media version."[18] Barack Obama puts this into a candidate's perspective when he writes that, "I—like every politician at the federal level—am almost entirely dependent on the media to reach my constituents. It is the filter through which my votes are interpreted, my statements analyzed, my beliefs examined. For the broad public at least, I am who the media says I am."[19]

The computer revolution has also now overtaken political campaigns. At the end of the first presidential debate in 1996, Bob Dole encouraged viewers to go to his Web site for more information on his issue stands. So many people immediately tried to check it out that the server soon crashed. Today, one of the first things a presidential candidate does is establish a Web site with detailed information about their issue stands and background, videos of his or her key speeches, a schedule of upcoming events, and a form enabling people to donate to the campaign online. A May 2008 survey by the Pew Internet and American Life Project found that 29 percent of Americans had gone online to read or watch campaign material posted on a candidate's Web site. The same study also found that 23 percent said they regularly receive emails with political content and that 10 percent had used sites like Facebook or MySpace for some kind of political activity.[20]

Nowhere has the impact of the internet been greater than on political fundraising. The Pew study found that 6 percent of American adults had donated to a candidate online in the first 5 months of 2008. Six percent may not sound like a big slice of the American adult population, but it amounts to about 14 million people. If the average online donor contributed just $75, that would translate into over a billion dollars in political contributions. The most prominent receipient of this flood of online donations in 2008 was the Obama campaign, which received contributions from over a million people via the internet. But there is reason to suspect that the internet may soon revolutionize fundraising for less prominent candidates as well.

One of the most important uses of computer technology in campaigns has long been the use of targeted mailings to prospective supporters. The technique of **direct mail** involves locating potential supporters by sending information and a request for money to huge lists of people who have supported candidates of similar views in the past. Conservative fund-raiser Richard Viguerie pioneered the mass mailing list, including in his computerized list the names and addresses of hundreds of thousands of individuals who contributed to conservative causes. The accumulation of mailing lists enables candidates to pick almost any issue, be it helping the homeless, opposing abortion, aiding Israel, or anything else, and write to a list of people concerned about that issue. Direct mail induces millions of people each year to contribute over $1 billion to various candidates and political causes.[21] The high-tech campaign is no longer a luxury. Candidates *must* use the media and computer technology just to stay competitive.

direct mail

A high-tech method of raising money for a political cause or candidate. It involves sending information and requests for money to people whose names appear on lists of those who have supported similar views or candidates in the past.

Technology has changed the way campaigns are run and the way candidates attempt to reach the people. Most serious candidates for a major office these days have their own official Web site. This provides an effective way to make their policy positions available for anyone interested. Here you can see the front page of Ashwin Madia's 2008 congressional campaign web site.

The most important goal of any media campaign is simply to get attention. Media coverage is determined by two factors: (1) how candidates use their advertising budget and (2) the "free" attention they get as news makers. The first, obviously, is relatively easy to control; the second is more difficult but not impossible. Almost every logistical decision in a campaign—where to eat breakfast, whom to include on stage, when to announce a major policy proposal—is calculated according to its intended media impact. In the first half of the twentieth century, the biggest item in a campaign budget might have been renting a railroad train. Today, the major item is unquestionably television advertising. At least half the total budget for a presidential or U.S. Senate campaign will be used for campaign commercials.

You Are a Media Consultant to a Political Candidate

Many observers worry that we have entered a new era of politics in which the slick slogan and the image salesperson dominates—an era when Madison Avenue is more influential than Main Street. Most political scientists, however, are concluding that such fears are overblown. Research has shown that campaign advertising can be a source of information about issues as well as about images. Thomas Patterson and Robert McClure examined the information contained in TV advertising and found that viewers learned more about candidates' stands on the issues from watching their ads than from watching TV news shows. Most news coverage stresses where the candidates went, how big their crowds were, and other campaign details. The networks only occasionally delve into where the candidates stand on the issues. In contrast, political ads typically address issues; a study of 230,000 candidate ads that ran in 1998 found that spots that emphasized policy outnumbered those that stressed personal image by a 6-to-1 ratio.[22] Most candidates apparently believe that their policy positions are a crucial part of their campaign, and they are willing to pay substantial sums to communicate them to voters.

Candidates have much less control over the other aspect of the media, news coverage. To be sure, most campaigns have press aides who feed "canned" news releases to reporters. Still, the media largely determine for themselves what is happening in a campaign. Campaign coverage seems to be a constant interplay between hard news about what candidates say and do and the human interest angle, which most journalists think sells newspapers or interests television viewers.

Apparently, news organizations believe that policy issues are of less interest to voters than the campaign itself. The result is that news coverage is disproportionately devoted to campaign strategies, speculation about what will happen next, poll results, and other aspects of the campaign game. Once a candidate has taken a policy position and it has been reported, it becomes old news. The latest poll showing Smith ahead of Jones is thus more newsworthy in the eyes of the media. Roger Ailes, the president of Fox News, calls this his "orchestra pit" theory of American politics: "If you have two guys on stage and one guy says, 'I have a solution to the Middle East problem,' and the other guy falls in the orchestra pit, who do you think is going to be on the evening news"?[23]

A study of the first five months of media coverage of the 2008 nomination campaign by the Project for Excellence in Journalism found that that 63 percent of the stories dealt with the horse race and strategies whereas only 32 percent dealt with the substance of the campaign—issues, policies, and the backgrounds of the candidates.[24] Figure 9.2 shows that in recent years, the major TV networks have usually focused more on the horse race than policy issues. Interestingly, the 2004 election was an exception to this general rule. Even with the race between Bush and Kerry being very close, there was just as much focus on policy matters as to who was winning and losing. The media's greater focus on policies in 2004 probably reflects the fact that the issues of the year stirred great passions and an unusual degree of viewer interest. It remains to be seen whether such public interest in candidates' policy stands can be maintained in future campaigns.

FIGURE 9.2

Horse Race Versus Policy Coverage on the Network News, 1988–2004

Since 1988, the Center for Media and Public Affairs has been analyzing the content of ABC, CBS, and NBC nightly news during the fall of presidential election campaigns. For every story that has been broadcast, they have examined the content to see if it focused on the horse race and/or policy issues. The results can be seen below. Keep in mind that the numbers do not add up to 100 percent because some stories focused on both aspects, and some focused on neither.

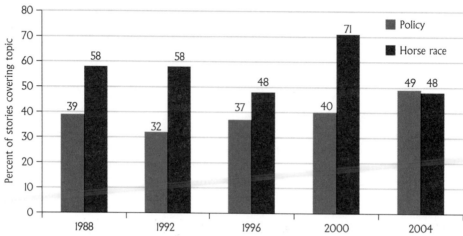

Source: Stephen J. Farnsworth and S. Robert Lichter, "The *Nightly News Nightmare* Revisited: Network Television's Coverage of the 2004 Presidential Election" (paper presented at the 2005 annual meeting of the American Political Science Association), 31.

ORGANIZING THE CAMPAIGN

In every campaign, there is too much to do and too little time to do it. Every candidate must prepare for nightly banquets and endless handshaking. More important, to organize their campaigns effectively, candidates must do the following:

You Are a Campaign Manager: McCain and the Swingers: Help McCain Win Swing States and Swing Voters

- *Get a campaign manager.* Some candidates try to run their own campaign, but they usually end up regretting it. A professional campaign manager can keep the candidate from getting bogged down in organizational details. This person also bears the day-to-day responsibility for keeping the campaign square on its message and setting its tone.
- *Get a fund-raiser.* Money, as this chapter will soon discuss in detail, is an important key to election victory.
- *Get a campaign counsel.* With all the current federal regulation of campaign financing, legal assistance is essential to ensure compliance with the laws.
- *Hire media and campaign consultants.* Candidates have more important things to do with their time than plan ad campaigns, contract for buttons and bumper stickers, and buy TV time and newspaper space. Professionals can get them the most exposure for their money.
- *Assemble a campaign staff.* It is desirable to hire as many professionals as the campaign budget allows, but it is also important to get a coordinator of volunteers to ensure that envelopes are licked, doorbells rung, and other small but vital tasks addressed. Many campaign volunteers are typically young people, who are the most likely to have the energy and freedom from commitments required for this sort of intensive work. However, in recent years high school seniors have expressed less and less interest in participating in campaigns (see "Young People and Politics: Declining Interest in Working in Campaigns").
- *Plan the logistics.* A modern presidential campaign involves jetting around the country at an incredible pace. Aides known as "advance workers" handle the complicated details of candidate scheduling and see to it that events are well publicized and well attended.

- *Get a research staff and policy advisers.* Candidates have little time to master the complex issues reporters will ask about. Policy advisers—often distinguished academics—feed them the information they need to keep up with events.
- *Hire a pollster.* Dozens of professional polling firms conduct opinion research to tell candidates how the voters view them and what is on the voters' minds.
- *Get a good press secretary.* Candidates running for major office have reporters dogging them every step of the way. The reporters need news, and a good press secretary can help them make their deadlines with stories that the campaign would like to see reported.
- *Establish a Web site.* A Web site is a relatively inexpensive way of getting a candidate's message out.

You Are a Campaign Manager: Voter Mobilization and Suppression: Political Dirty Tricks or Fair Games?

Most of these tasks cost money. Campaigns are not cheap, and the role of money in campaigns is a controversial one.

YOUNG PEOPLE AND POLITICS

Declining Interest in Working in Campaigns

Walk into any campaign headquarters and chances are good that you'll find a lot of young people at work. Many of our nation's leaders got their political start working in a campaign when they were young. If you want to get involved in politics as a possible career, this is where you begin. The work is often tedious, the hours are long, and the financial rewards are usually minimal. Hence, full-time campaign work is not really suitable for someone with an active career or for a retired person. Campaign jobs have been and likely will continue to be filled primarily by young people.

Nevertheless, as you can see in this figure, there has been a decline in interest in working on campaigns among high school seniors over the past quarter century. Whereas between 15 and 20 percent of those interviewed in the late 1970s and early 1980s said they planned to work on a campaign or had already done so, in recent years only about 10 percent have expressed an interest in campaign work.

QUESTIONS FOR DISCUSSION

▷ At the same time that young people have been expressing less interest in working on political campaigns, they have been volunteering for community organizations at record rates. Might the decline in interest in campaign work simply be because today's young people are focusing on nonpolitical forms of community action?

▷ Do you think that one reason young people may not be very interested in working in campaigns may be that the issues discussed in recent campaigns aren't of much interest to them? If so, what sort of issues might stimulate more young people to sign up for campaign work?

▷ If more young people were to volunteer for work in campaigns, what difference might it make? Do you think the tenor of recent campaigns would have been changed if more young people had been involved?

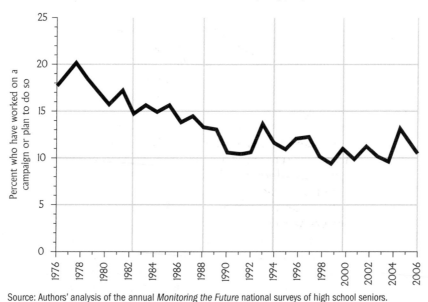

Source: Authors' analysis of the annual *Monitoring the Future* national surveys of high school seniors.

MONEY AND CAMPAIGNING

There is no doubt that campaigns are expensive and, in America's high-tech political arena, growing more so. Candidates need money to build a campaign organization and to get their message out. Many people and groups who want certain things from the government are all too willing to give it; thus, there is the common perception that money buys votes and influence. The following sections examine the role of money in campaigns.

THE MAZE OF CAMPAIGN FINANCE REFORMS

As the costs of campaigning skyrocketed with the growth of television and as the Watergate scandal exposed large, illegal campaign contributions, momentum developed for campaign finance reform in the early 1970s. Several public interest lobbies (see Chapter 11), notably Common Cause and the National Committee for an Effective Congress, led the drive. In 1974, Congress passed the **Federal Election Campaign Act**. It had two main goals: tightening reporting requirements for contributions and limiting overall expenditures. The 1974 act and its subsequent amendments did the following:

- *Created the **Federal Election Commission**.* A bipartisan body, the six-member Federal Election Commission (FEC) administers campaign finance laws and enforces compliance with their requirements.
- *Created the **Presidential Election Campaign Fund**.* The FEC is in charge of doling out money from this fund to qualified presidential candidates. Money for this fund is raised via a $3 voluntary check-off box on income tax returns, which currently only about 10 percent of taxpayers do.
- *Provided partial public financing for presidential primaries.* Presidential candidates who raise $5,000 in at least 20 states can get individual contributions of up to $250 matched by the federal treasury. Money received at this stage of the campaign is commonly known as **matching funds**. If presidential candidates accept federal support, they agree to limit their campaign expenditures to an amount prescribed by federal law. From the inception of the matching fund program in 1976 through 1996, every Democratic and Republican nominee relied on matching funds to partially fund their campaigns in the primaries. George W. Bush became the first to break from this pattern in 2000, and since then most major candidates have followed this course during the nomination process. As you can see in "A Generation of Change: The Incredible Increase in Fund-Raising for Presidential Nomination Campaigns," by forgoing matching funds and therefore not subjecting themselves to overall spending limits, the party nominees in 2008 spent an incredible amount compared to the party nominees just a generation ago.
- *Provided full public financing for major party candidates in the general election.* For the general election, each major party nominee is eligible to receive a fixed amount of money to cover his or her total campaign expenses. For 2008 this amounted to $85 million. Unlike in the primaries, federal funds come in the form of a grant, thereby making the offer much more attractive. From the inception of this system in 1976 through 2004, every Democratic and Republican nominee accepted the grant. In 2008, Barack Obama became the first major party nominee to turn it down, opting instead to raise as much money as he could in increments of $2300 or less. This ultimately gave him a substantial edge in campaign funds over John McCain, who opted to just take the $85 million from the Federal Election Commission.

Federal Election Campaign Act

A law passed in 1974 for reforming campaign finances. The act created the **Federal Election Commission**, provided public financing for presidential primaries and general elections, limited presidential campaign spending, required disclosure, and attempted to limit contributions.

Federal Election Commission

A six-member bipartisan agency created by the **Federal Election Campaign Act** of 1974. The Federal Election Commission administers and enforces campaign finance laws.

Presidential Election Campaign Fund

Money from the $3 federal income tax check-off goes into this fund, which is then distributed to qualified candidates to subsidize their presidential campaigns.

matching funds

Contributions of up to $250 are matched from the Presidential Election Campaign Fund to candidates for the presidential nomination who qualify and agree to meet various conditions, such as limiting their overall spending.

A GENERATION OF CHANGE

The Incredible Increase in Fund-Raising for Presidential Nomination Campaigns

A generation ago, fund-raising for presidential nomination campaigns was rather limited compared to the vast sums of money that are raised by the parties' presidential nominees today. As you can see in the adjacent graph, the 1988 nomination campaigns of George Bush and Michael Dukakis cost a total of $60.3 million. About 29 percent of this amount came from federal matching funds, which were designed to supplement small contributions from individuals. Acceptance of these matching funds requires candidates to limit the total amount they raise. In 1988, both Bush and Dukakis ended up spending close to the legal limit of $32 million for that year. By 2008, the cap on nomination expenditures had risen to about $57 million as the result of inflation over the years. For both the Obama and McCain campaigns this seemed too constraining in light of what they thought they could raise on their own without matching funds. All told, the two campaigns raised a stunning $408 million just to fund their activities up to the end of the primary season in early June. Even taking inflation into account, this is about four times what the party nominees raised a generation ago.

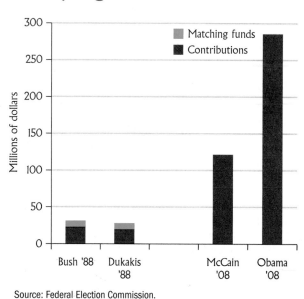

Source: Federal Election Commission.

- *Required full disclosure.* Regardless of whether they accept any federal funding, all candidates for federal office must file periodic reports with the FEC, listing who contributed and how the money was spent.
- *Limited contributions.* Scandalized to find out that some wealthy individuals had contributed $1 million to the 1972 Nixon campaign, Congress limited individual contributions to presidential and congressional candidates to $1,000. The McCain-Feingold Act increased this limit to $2,000 as of 2004 and provided for it to be indexed to rise along with inflation in the future; hence, the limit for 2008 was $2,300.

You Are a Campaign Manager: McCain Navigates Campaign Financing: Rules and Trends Regarding the "Mother's Milk" of Politics

Although the 1974 campaign reforms were generally welcomed by both parties, the constitutionality of the Federal Election Campaign Act was challenged in the 1976 case of *Buckley v. Valeo*. In this case the Supreme Court struck down, as a violation of free speech, the portion of the act that had limited the amount individuals could contribute to their own campaigns. This aspect of the Court ruling made it possible for Ross Perot to spend over $60 million of his own fortune on his independent presidential candidacy in 1992 and for Mitt Romney to spend $44 million out of his own pocket in pursuit of the Republican presidential nomination in 2008.

Another loophole was opened in 1979 with an amendment to the original act that made it easier for political parties to raise money for voter registration drives and the distribution of campaign material at the grass-roots level or for generic party advertising. Money raised for such purposes was known as **soft money** and for over two decades was not subject to any contribution limits. In 2000, nearly half a billion dollars was raised by the two parties via soft money contributions, with many of the contributions coming in increments of hundreds of thousands of dollars. AT&T alone gave over $3 million in soft money, as did the American Federation of State, County, and Municipal Employees.

soft money
Political contributions earmarked for party-building expenses at the grass-roots level or for generic party advertising. Unlike money that goes to the campaign of a particular candidate, such party donations are not subject to contribution limits. For a time, such contributions were unlimited, until they were banned by the McCain-Feingold Act.

Senators John McCain (R-Ariz.) and Russell Feingold (D-Wis.) crusaded for years to remove the taint of large soft money campaign contributions from the political system. Their efforts finally came to fruition in 2002 when their bill was passed by the Congress and signed into law by President George W. Bush. The major provision of the McCain-Feingold Act was to ban soft money contributions. In addition, it also prohibited corporations and unions from using their general treasury funds to pay for electioneering communications in the last 60 days of federal campaigns. However, in 2007 the Supreme Court ruled that this was an unconstitutional restriction on free speech unless the advertisements were explicit appeals for or against candidates.[25]

No sooner had the soft money loophole been closed than another loophole for big contributors opened up. Some scholars call this the "hydraulic theory of money and politics," noting that money, like water, inevitably finds its way around any obstacle. Wealthy individuals on both sides of the political spectrum found that they could make unlimited contributions to what is known as **527 groups**, which are named after the section of the federal tax code that governs these political groups. In a controversial ruling, the FEC in 2004 declined to subject 527 groups to contribution restrictions as long as their political messages did not make explicit endorsements of candidates by using phrases like "Vote for" and "Vote against." The result was that many people who had in the past given big soft money contributions to the parties decided instead to give big donations to a 527 group, such as the anti-Kerry group Swift Boat Veterans for Truth or the anti-Bush group MoveOn.org. Fifty-two individuals gave over $1 million each to a 527 group, and another 213 individuals gave over $100,000. All told, 527 groups spent about $424 million on political messages in 2004.[26]

Even with the loopholes that have developed in campaign finance law, there is little doubt that efforts to regulate campaign contributions since 1974 have made this aspect of American politics more open and honest. All contribution and expenditure records are now open for all to examine. As Frank Sorauf writes, detailed reports of American campaign contributions and expenditures have "become a wonder of the

527 groups
Independent groups that seek to influence the political process but are not subject to contribution restrictions because they do not directly seek the election of particular candidates. Their name comes from Section 527 of the federal tax code, under which they are governed.

democratic political world. Nowhere else do scholars and journalists find so much information about the funding of campaigns, and the openness of Americans about the flow of money stuns many other nationals accustomed to silence and secrecy about such traditionally private matters."[27]

THE PROLIFERATION OF PACs

The campaign reforms of the 1970s also encouraged the spread of **political action committees**, generally known as PACs. Before the 1974 reforms, corporations were technically forbidden to donate money to political campaigns, but many wrote big checks anyway. Unions could make indirect contributions, although limits were set on how they could aid candidates and political parties. The 1974 reforms created a new, more open way for interest groups such as business and labor to contribute to campaigns. Any interest group, large or small, can now get into the act by forming its own PAC to directly channel contributions of up to $5,000 per candidate in both the primary and the general election.

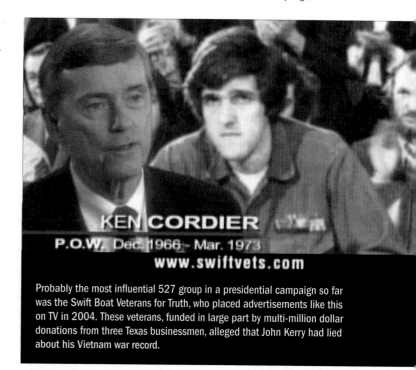

Probably the most influential 527 group in a presidential campaign so far was the Swift Boat Veterans for Truth, who placed advertisements like this on TV in 2004. These veterans, funded in large part by multi-million dollar donations from three Texas businessmen, alleged that John Kerry had lied about his Vietnam war record.

In 2006, the FEC reported that there were 4,217 PACs, which contributed $372.1 million to House and Senate candidates. A PAC is formed when a business association or some other interest group decides to contribute to candidates whom it believes will support legislation it favors. The group registers as a PAC with the FEC and then puts money into the PAC coffers. The PAC can collect money from stockholders, members, and other interested parties. It then donates the money to candidates, often after careful research on their issue stands and past voting records. One very important ground rule prevails: All expenditures must be meticulously reported to the FEC. If PACs are corrupting democracy, as many believe, at least they are doing so openly.

Candidates need PACs because high-tech campaigning is expensive. Tightly contested races for the House of Representatives now frequently cost over $1 million; Senate races can easily cost $1 million for television alone. PACs play a major role in paying for expensive campaigns. Thus, there emerges a symbiotic relationship between the PACs and the candidates: Candidates need money, which they insist can be used without compromising their integrity; PACs want access to officeholders, which they insist can be gained without buying votes. Most any lobbyist will tell their clients that politicians will listen to any important interest group but that with a sizable PAC donation they'll listen better.

There is an abundance of PACs willing to help out candidates. There are big PACs, such as the Realtors Political Action Committee and the American Medical Association Political Action Committee. There are little ones, too, representing smaller industries or business associations: EggPAC, FishPAC, FurPAC, LardPAC, and, for the beer distributors, SixPAC.[28] Table 9.1 lists the business, labor, and ideological PACs that gave the most money to congressional candidates in 2004 and shows which party each favored.

Critics of the PAC system worry that all this money leads to PAC control over what the winners do once in office. Archibald Cox and Fred Wertheimer write that the role of PACs in campaign finance "is robbing our nation of its democratic ideals and giving us a government of leaders beholden to the monied interests who make their election possible."[29] On some issues, it seems clear that PAC money has made a difference. The Federal Trade Commission (FTC), for example, once passed a

political action committees

Funding vehicles created by the 1974 campaign finance reforms. A corporation, union, or some other interest group can create a political action committee (PAC) and register it with the **Federal Election Commission**, which will meticulously monitor the PAC's expenditures.

TIMELINE

Interest Groups and Campaign Finance

TABLE 9.1

The Big-Spending PACs

According to an analysis of Federal Election Commission data by the Center for Responsive Politics, here are the largest business, labor, and ideological/single-issue PAC contributors to congressional candidates for the 2004 election cycle and the percentage that they gave to Republicans.

BUSINESS	AMOUNT CONTRIBUTED	PERCENTAGE GIVEN TO REPUBLICANS
National Association of Realtors	$3,787,083	52
National Auto Dealers	2,603,300	73
National Beer Wholesalers	2,314,000	76
National Association of Home Builders	2,201,500	67
Association of Trial Lawyers	2,181,499	6
United Parcel Service	2,142,679	72
American Medical Association	2,092,425	79
American Bankers Association	1,978,013	64
SBC Communications	1,955,116	65
Wal-Mart Stores	1,677,000	78
LABOR		
Laborers Union	2,684,250	14
International Brotherhood of Electrical Workers	2,369,500	4
United Auto Workers	2,075,700	1
Carpenters & Joiners Union	2,074,560	26
Service Employees International Union	1,985,000	15
Machinists/Aerospace Workers Union	1,942,250	1
Teamsters Union	1,917,413	11
American Federation of Teachers	1,717,372	3
IDEOLOGICAL/SINGLE-ISSUE		
Human Rights Campaign	1,165,138	9
National Rifle Association	1,026,649	85
Planned Parenthood	483,614	5
Sierra Club	388,960	6
National Pro-Life Alliance	209,600	100

Source: Center for Responsive Politics.

regulation requiring that car dealers list known mechanical defects on the window stickers of used cars. The National Association of Automobile Dealers quickly became one of the largest donors to congressional incumbents. Soon afterward, 216 representatives cosponsored a House resolution nullifying the FTC regulation. Of these House members, 186 had been aided by the auto dealers' PAC.[30]

It is questionable, however, whether such examples are the exception or the rule. Most PACs give money to candidates who agree with them in the first place. For instance, labor PACs will not waste their money trying to influence members of Congress who have consistently opposed raising the minimum wage. Frank Sorauf's careful review of the subject concludes that "there simply are no data in the systematic studies that would support the popular assertions about the 'buying' of the Congress or about any other massive influence of money on the legislative process."[31]

The impact of PAC money on presidents is even more doubtful. Presidential campaigns, of course, are partly subsidized by the public and so are less dependent on PACs. Moreover, presidents have well-articulated positions on most important issues. A small contribution from any one PAC is not likely to turn a presidential candidate's head.

Money matters in campaigns and sometimes also during legislative votes. Although the influence of PACs may be exaggerated, the high cost of running for office ensures their continuing major role in the campaign process.

ARE CAMPAIGNS TOO EXPENSIVE?

Every four years, Americans spend over $2 billion on national, state, and local elections. This seems like a tremendous amount of money. Yet American elections cost, per person, about as much as a DVD movie. Bradley Smith, who formerly served as a commissioner on the FEC, writes that the proportion of the nation's gross domestic product spent on political activity is a mere .05 percent.[32] What bothers politicians most about the rising costs of high-tech campaigning is that fund-raising takes up so much of their time. Many American officeholders feel that the need for continuous fund-raising distracts them from their jobs as legislators. They look with envy at how politicians in other countries can win major office without worrying about raising huge sums of money (see "America in Perspective: Arlene McCarthy's Election to the European Parliament").

Public financing of congressional campaigns would take care of this problem. Some lawmakers support some sort of public financing reform; however, it will be very difficult to get Congress to consent to equal financing for the people who will challenge them for their seats. Incumbents will not readily give up the advantage they have in raising money.

DEBATE

Campaign Finance Regulations

AMERICA IN PERSPECTIVE

Arlene McCarthy's Election to the European Parliament

Arlene McCarthy is one of Europe's up-and-coming young politicians. She was first elected to represent England in the European Parliament at the age of 33, and since then she has twice been easily reelected. When asked if she could have won a similar election in the United States, she responds with a firm "No—I would never have been able to raise enough money."

A substantial bankroll, however, was not required for Ms. McCarthy to get her start in European politics. All told, she estimates that she spent about $1,600 to get the Labour Party's nomination in her district. Of this, roughly half was spent on new clothes, with the rest going for traveling costs, such as hotels, gasoline, and food. No one contributed any money to support her campaign for the nomination, and she never felt this was necessary. The party took charge of sending out information about her to the voters who would decide the nomination, and all candidates were forbidden from sending out anything else. Only 4,500 dues-paying members of the party could participate in the nomination process, thus making it possible for Ms. McCarthy to speak personally with many of the activists who ultimately gave her a start in politics. Her major appeal was that she had gained much knowledge about how the European Parliament worked during her service as a staff member there and that she could effectively represent the interests of people back home in England.

About 1,800 voters returned their mail ballot, and Arlene McCarthy finished first among five candidates. The general election loomed only six weeks away when she became the Labour Party's nominee, but the party took charge of her campaign from this point on. The party provided her with about $40,000 in campaign funds, as well as staff and campaign literature. When Labour won a smashing victory across the country, Ms. McCarthy was swept into office and had suddenly gone from being a young staff member to a member of the European Parliament.

The nomination and general election campaign of Arlene McCarthy illustrates several differences between European campaigns and those of the United States. Had she run a similar campaign in the United States, she would have had to raise far more money, appeal to far more people to get her party's nomination, and run a much longer campaign.

QUESTIONS FOR DISCUSSION

▶ Which type of nomination campaign do you think is best—the wide-open American style, or the more limited type of European campaign that Arlene McCarthy had to run?

▶ Do you think the European-style campaign makes it easier, compared to the U.S., for young people and women like Arlene McCarthy to get started in politics? Why, or why not?

Source: Personal interview with Arlene McCarthy, December 12, 1998.

Perhaps the most basic complaint about money and politics is that there may be a direct link between dollars spent and votes received. Few have done more to dispel this charge than political scientist Gary Jacobson. His research has shown that "the more incumbents spend, the worse they do."[33] This fact is not as odd as it sounds. It simply means that incumbents who face a tough opponent must raise more money to meet the challenge. When a challenger is not a serious threat, as they all too often are not, incumbents can afford to campaign cheaply.

More important than having "more" money is having "enough" money. Herbert Alexander calls this "the doctrine of sufficiency." As he writes, "Enough money must be spent to get a message across to compete effectively but outspending one's opponent is not always necessary—even an incumbent with a massive ratio of higher spending."[34] One case in point is that of the late Paul Wellstone, a previously obscure political science professor who beat an incumbent senator in 1990 despite being outspent by 5 to 1.[35] In 2004, Howard Dean was crowned by the media as the early front-runner for the Democratic presidential nomination as a result of his fundraising prowess, but John Kerry proved to be a much better vote getter.

THE IMPACT OF CAMPAIGNS

Almost all politicians presume that a good campaign is the key to victory. Many political scientists, however, question the importance of campaigns. Reviewing the evidence, Dan Nimmo concluded, "Political campaigns are less crucial in elections than most politicians believe."[36] For years, researchers studying campaigns have stressed that campaigns have three effects on voters: reinforcement, activation, and conversion. Campaigns can reinforce voters' preferences for candidates; they can activate voters, getting them to contribute money or ring doorbells as opposed to merely voting; and they can convert, changing voters' minds.

Over half a century of research on political campaigns leads to a single message: Campaigns mostly reinforce and activate; only rarely do they convert. The evidence on the impact of campaigns points clearly to the conclusion that the best-laid plans of campaign managers change very few votes. Given the billions of dollars spent on political campaigns, it may be surprising to find that they do not have a great effect. Several factors tend to weaken campaigns' impact on voters:

selective perception
The phenomenon that people often pay the most attention to things they already agree with and interpret them according to their own predispositions.

- Most people pay relatively little attention to campaigns in the first place. People have a remarkable capacity for **selective perception**—paying most attention to things they already agree with and interpreting events according to their own predispositions.
- Factors such as party identification—though less important than they used to be—still influence voting behavior regardless of what happens in the campaign.
- Incumbents start with a substantial advantage in terms of name recognition and an established track record.

Such findings do not mean, of course, that campaigns never change voters' minds or that converting a small percentage is unimportant. In tight races, a good campaign can make the difference between winning and losing.

UNDERSTANDING NOMINATIONS AND CAMPAIGNS

Throughout the history of American politics, election campaigns have become longer and longer as the system has become increasingly open to public participation. Reformers in the nineteenth and twentieth centuries held that the solution to democratic problems was more democracy—or as John Lennon sang, "Power to the people." In principle, more democracy always sounds better than less, but it is not such a simple issue in practice.

ARE NOMINATIONS AND CAMPAIGNS TOO DEMOCRATIC?

Comparing Political Campaigns

If American campaigns are judged solely by how open they are, then certainly the American system must be viewed favorably. In other countries, the process of leadership nomination occurs within a relatively small circle of party elites. Thus, politicians must work their way up through an apprenticeship system. In contrast, America has an entrepreneurial system in which the people play a crucial role at every stage from nomination to election. In this way, party outsiders can get elected in a way virtually unknown outside the United States. By appealing directly to the people, a candidate can emerge from obscurity to win the White House. For example, former one-term Governor Jimmy Carter was scarcely known outside of his home state a year before his election to the presidency. After serving a dozen years as governor of Arkansas, Bill Clinton was only in a slightly better position than Carter in terms of name recognition when he announced his first campaign for the presidency in 1991. In this sense, the chance to win high office is open to almost any highly skilled politician with even a small electoral base.

There is a price to be paid for all this openness, however. The process of selecting American leaders is a long and convoluted one that has little downtime before it revs up all over again. George W. Bush had scarcely been reelected when potential candidates for 2008 started to schedule visits to Iowa and New Hampshire. Some analysts have even called the American electoral process "the permanent campaign."[37] Many wonder whether people would pay more attention to politics if it did not ask so much of them. Given so much democratic opportunity, many citizens are simply overwhelmed by the process and stay on the sidelines. Similarly, the burdens of the modern campaign can discourage good candidates from throwing their hats into the ring. One of the most worrisome burdens that candidates face is amassing a sufficient campaign treasury. The system may be open, but it requires a lot of fund-raising to be able to take one's case to the people.

Today's campaigns clearly promote individualism in American politics. The current system of running for office has been labeled by Wattenberg the "candidate-centered age."[38] It allows for politicians to decide on their own to run, to raise their own campaign funds, to build their own personal organizations, and to make promises about how they specifically will act in office. The American campaign game is one of individual candidates, by individual candidates, and for individual candidates.

Television has been the primary way that candidates for national office have gotten out their message since about 1960. As the number of channels has proliferated in recent years, candidates have appeared on a wide variety of news, talk, and even comedy shows. Here, John McCain is shown appearing on the Ellen show, where he engaged in a good-natured debate about the issue of gay marriage.

DO BIG CAMPAIGNS LEAD TO AN INCREASED SCOPE OF GOVERNMENT?

Today's big campaigns involve much more communication between candidates and voters than America's Founders ever could have imagined. In their view, the presidency was to be an office responsible for seeing to the public interest as a whole. They wished to avoid "a contest in which the candidates would have to pose as 'friends' of the people or make specific policy commitments."[39] Thus, the Founders would probably be horrified by the modern practice in which candidates make numerous promises during nomination and election campaigns.

States are the key battlegrounds of presidential campaigns, and candidates must tailor their appeals to the particular interests of each major state. When in Iowa, for instance, candidates typically promise to keep agricultural subsidies high and support the ethanol program; in New York, to help big cities with federal programs; and in Texas, to help the oil and gas industry. To secure votes from each region of the country, candidates end up supporting a variety of local interests. Promises mount as the campaign goes on, and these promises usually add up to new government programs and money. The way modern campaigns are conducted is thus one of many reasons why politicians usually find it easier to promise, at least, that government will do more. Furthermore, with their finger constantly to the wind assessing all the different political crosscurrents, it is hard for politicians to promise that the scope of government will be limited through specific cuts.

SUMMARY

In this age of high-tech politics, campaigns have become more media oriented and far more expensive. There are really two campaigns of importance in presidential (and other) contests: the campaign for nomination and the campaign for election.

There are two ways by which delegates are selected to the national party conventions: state caucuses and primaries. The first caucus is traditionally held in Iowa, the first primary in New Hampshire. These two small, atypical American states have disproportionate power in determining who will be nominated and thus become president. This influence stems from the massive media attention devoted to these early contests and the momentum generated by winning them.

Money matters in political campaigns. As the costs of campaigning have increased, it has become more essential to amass large campaign war chests. Although federal campaign finance reform in the 1970s lessened the impact of big contributors, it also allowed the proliferation of PACs. Some observers believe that PACs have created a system of legal graft in campaigning; others say that the evidence for this view is relatively weak.

In general, politicians tend to overestimate the impact of campaigns; political scientists have found that campaigning serves primarily to reinforce citizens' views rather than to convert them. American election campaigns are easily the most open and democratic in the world—some say too open. They are also extraordinarily long, leading politicians to make many promises that contribute to big government.

Chapter Test

Multiple-Choice Questions

1. Which state has the first-in-the-nation caucus?
   a. Indiana
   b. California
   c. Texas
   d. Iowa
   e. Delaware

2. The term "frontloading" specifically refers to:

   a. States holding their primaries earlier and earlier in the primary season
   b. Candidates campaigning hard to win the early primaries
   c. The bundling of primaries, such as on "Super Tuesday"
   d. The fact that candidates are more likely to make vast campaign promises early in the primary season

   e. Candidates spending most of their campaign money during the first few months

3. Which of the following is *not* a criticism of the primary and caucus system?
   a. The early primaries and caucuses receive disproportionate attention

b. Campaign success depends too much on the ability to raise enough money

c. Participation in the primaries and caucuses is unrepresentative

d. The system gives too much power to the media

e. Candidates with lots of political experience have a disproportionate chance of winning

4. Which of the following tends to receive less attention in television campaign coverage than the candidates would like?
a. Campaign strategies
b. Human interest stories
c. Poll results
d. Issues and policies
e. Speculation

5. Approximately how many states still have caucuses today?
a. All of them do
b. About three in four
c. About half
d. About one in four
e. About one in ten

6. The reformers who promoted the presidential primaries at the turn of the century wanted to:
a. Reduce the power of the party bosses over presidential nominations
b. Enable citizens to play a more direct role in choosing their president
c. Bind the votes of delegates at the national convention
d. Improve the democratic process
e. All of the above

7. The so-called "superdelegates" are the result of:
a. A concern about the lack of a role for party leaders at conventions
b. A desire to restore an element of peer review to the process
c. A "reward" for people with a long-term stake in the party's success
d. A desire to have delegates who are familiar with the candidates.
e. All of the above

8. With regard to the regulation of the allocation of delegates:
a. There are clear, national laws that determine the process
b. Each state is able to allocate delegates at its own discretion
c. Only citizens who are registered are allowed to participate in the primaries
d. States allocate all delegates to the candidate who wins
e. There is no consistent rule

9. Research on the effects of political campaigns on voters shows that they:
a. Reinforce preferences, activate voters, and convert voters
b. Reinforce preferences, but rarely activate or convert voters
c. Reinforce preferences and activate voters, but rarely convert voters
d. Convert voters, but rarely reinforce preferences or activate voters
e. Activate voters, but rarely reinforce preferences or convert voters

True/False

10. According to opinion polls, a majority of Americans across party lines favors a national primary.
True_____ False_____

11. Currently, so-called 527 Groups are subject to campaign contribution restrictions.
True_____ False_____

12. The Presidential Election Campaign Fund currently matches campaign contributions of up to $250 unconditionally, and contributions beyond $250 only if the candidate promises to abide by an overall spending limit.
True_____ False_____

13. Superdelegates have traditionally played an important role in the presidential nomination process.
True_____ False_____

14. The New Hampshire primary is especially important because it serves as an indicator for how the rest of the country is likely to vote.
True_____ False_____

Short Answer

15. When thinking about reforming the primary and caucuses, what are the pros and cons of regional primaries as opposed to a national primary?

16. What is so-called "soft money"?

17. Please explain the importance of the events of 1968 for the role of presidential primaries in the United States.

What role in particular did the McGovern-Fraser Commission play?

18. Sidney Blumenthal has called the American electoral process "the permanent campaign." In your own words, please explain what he means by this.

Short Answer/Essay Questions

19. According to the Founding Fathers, the office of president was designed to care for the public interest as a whole. Given what you have learned about the nomination and campaign process, campaign financing, and campaign strategies, what is your assessment of how well the original intention of the Founding Fathers has been met?

20. Take a look at the data that is represented in Figure 9.2 about the proportion of TV campaign coverage devoted to policy issues. The results for the presidential campaigns of 2000 and 2004 represent the two extreme ends of the spectrum. Based on your knowledge of these two events, what are some of the factors that explain each?

21. Table 9.1 gives an overview of the largest PAC contributors and what percentage was donated to the Republican Party. What patterns are you able to discern in the spending habits, i.e., which types of groups are more likely to support the Republican Party and which are less likely to do so? Why do you believe that is?

22. If you had the power to do so, which aspect of campaign finance would you change, how would you change it, and why? Which aspect would you keep the same, and why?

23. Why does presidential election watcher Theodore White call the primaries the "classic example of the triumph of goodwill over common sense"? Do you agree or disagree with his observations? Please substantiate your answer.

24. The graph on p. 291 illustrates the declining rate of high school seniors who have worked on a political campaign or plan to do so. In your opinion, what are at least three different factors that have contributed to this decline? What are the possible consequences of this apparent lack of interest among young people? What would be the pros and cons of formally integrating some form of campaign work into the high school curriculum, i.e., in the form of internships?

Answer Key

1. D   2. A   3. E   4. D   5. D   6. E   7. E   8. E   9. C   10. True   11. False   12. False   13. False   14. False

Key Terms

nomination (278)
campaign strategy (279)
national party convention (279)
caucus (279)
presidential primaries (280)
McGovern-Fraser Commission (281)
superdelegates (281)

frontloading (282)
national primary (285)
regional primaries (285)
party platform (287)
direct mail (288)
Federal Election Campaign Act (292)
Federal Election Commission (292)

Presidential Election Campaign Fund (292)
matching funds (292)
soft money (293)
527 groups (294)
political action committees (295)
selective perception (298)

Internet Resources

www.fec.gov
The Federal Election Commission's reports on campaign spending can be found at this site.

www.fundrace.org
This site allows one to look up donations from particular individuals and to map contribution patterns for particular areas.

www.opensecrets.org
The Center for Responsive Politics posts a wealth of analysis about PAC contributions at its site.

www.campaignline.com
Campaigns and Elections magazine posts some of its articles here.

GetConnected

The Delegate Selection Process and Presidential Nominations

Running for president is a very demanding job. It begins years before the election. An important part of the process for each candidate involves getting delegates pledged to him or her at the national party conventions. The nomination process involves a complex procedure that is neatly outlined on a Web page called "The Green Papers."

Search the Web

Go to the Green Papers page on the nomination process for 2004, *www.thegreenpapers.com/P04/*. Find your state and examine the number of delegates that were selected for the Democratic and Republican national conventions in 2004. Also, look at neighboring states and then find when your state selected the delegates.

Questions to Ask

- How many delegates did your state send to the Democratic and Republican national conventions in 2004? Were they selected through a primary or a caucus or some combination of methods?

- How does your state compare with neighboring states? How about states with more or less population than yours?
- Considering your state's vote for president in 2004, will your state have more or fewer delegates to the national conventions in 2008?

Why It Matters

Presidential candidates spend much time, energy, and money trying to accumulate delegates pledged to their candidacy who will attend the national convention. The media also focus on "delegate count" as an important measure to determine which candidate is leading the presidential race. It is important for you to understand how the delegate selection process works.

Get Involved

As we get closer to the 2008 presidential election, find out how you can become a delegate from your state to your party's national convention. The political parties are particularly interested in getting younger people involved. *For more exercises, go to www.longmanamericangovernment.com.*

For Further Reading

Bartels, Larry M. *Presidential Primaries and the Dynamics of Public Choice.* Princeton, NJ: Princeton University Press, 1988. An excellent analysis of voters' decision-making process in the nominating season.

Bimber, Bruce, and Richard Davis. *Campaigning Online: The Internet in U.S. Elections.* New York: Oxford University Press, 2003. An interesting study of how candidates use Web sites and how voters react to them.

Farnsworth, Stephen J., and S. Robert Lichter. *The Nightly News Nightmare: Network Television's Coverage of U.S. Presidential Elections, 1988–2000.* Lanham, MD: Rowman & Littlefield, 2003. An interesting study of the content of TV news coverage of four recent presidential election campaigns.

Franz, Michael M., et al. *Campaign Advertising and American Democracy.* Philadelphia: Temple University Press, 2008. A thorough examination of the role of campaign ads in recent elections, arguing that political ads are beneficial to the working of democracy in America.

Hull, Christopher C. *Grassroots Rules: How the Iowa Caucus Helps Elect American Presidents.* Stanford, CA: Stanford University Press, 2008. A detailed study of the impact of the Iowa caucus from 1976 to 2004.

Institute of Politics, ed. *Campaign for President: The Managers Look at 2004.* Lanham, MD: Rowman & Littlefield, 2006. The campaign managers for all the 2004 presidential

candidates gathered at Harvard to discuss their experiences in the primaries and the general election.

King, Anthony. *Running Scared.* New York: Free Press, 1997. King argues that American politicians campaign too much and govern too little.

Malbin, Michael J., ed. *The Election After Reform: Money, Politics, and the Bipartisan Campaign Reform Act.* Lanham, MD: Rowman & Littlefield, 2006. A comprehensive set of readings that covers many aspects of how the McCain-Feingold Act worked in practice.

Mayer, William G., ed. *The Making of the Presidential Candidates 2004.* Lanham, MD: Rowman & Littlefield, 2004. A good set of current readings on the presidential nomination process.

Patterson, Thomas E. *Out of Order.* New York: Knopf, 1993. A good review of the role of the media in elections.

Semiatin, Richard J. *Campaigns on the Cutting Edge.* Washington, DC: Congressional Quarterly Press, 2008. A provocative set of articles on how campaigns are taking advantage of innovative new technologies.

Smith, Bradley A. *Unfree Speech: The Folly of Campaign Finance Reform.* Princeton, NJ: Princeton University Press, 2001. A provocative book that argues that most regulations concerning donations to political campaigns should be eliminated.

ELECTIONS AND VOTING BEHAVIOR

POLITICS IN ACTION:
THE CHALLENGE OF FIGURING OUT THE MEANING OF A VOTE

One of the most memorable images of the 2000 presidential election was the regularly repeated scene of Florida election officials holding up a ballot to the light to try to determine whether a punch was present. When Joseph Harris, professor of political science at the University of California at Berkeley, invented the first punch-card voting system in the early 1960s, it was hailed as a great technological innovation, enabling unprecedented speed in vote counting. But although also reputed to be more accurate than previous methods of voting, by 2000 the punch cards had become antiquated technology compared to modern Scantron and touch-screen methods. Embarrassed election officials were quick to admit that they had long been aware of the problems with punch-card voting systems. Such systems theoretically worked fine as long as people followed the directions—placing the cards in the machines properly and punching the chads through the card completely. But as we saw in Florida in 2000, many people did not follow the instructions. With the election coming down to just hundreds of votes, the question became whether election officials could accurately and fairly ascertain the intent of voters whose ballots had not been properly punched. Should a vote be counted if one, two, or three of the four corners of the chad had been perforated? How about if only a dimple was visible on the chad, indicating that the voter had at least touched the stylus to the ballot at that point? Election officials struggled to do the best they could by holding them up to the light and examining them carefully. Some applauded the process as a valiant attempt to make sure every vote was counted, whereas others criticized officials for trying to "divine the intent of the voter."

Scholars who analyze elections have a seemingly easier job—figuring out the meaning of the vote totals once they have been counted. But as Walter Lippmann, one of the most astute observers of American politics, once remarked,

> We call an election an expression of the popular will. But is it? We go into a polling booth and mark a cross on a piece of paper for one of two, or perhaps three or four names. Have we expressed our thoughts on the public policy of the United States? Presumably we have a number of thoughts on this and that with many buts and ifs and ors. Surely the cross on a piece of paper does not express them.[1]

This chapter will discuss why it is difficult for elections to be a faithful mechanism for expressing the public's desires concerning what government should do. The fact that only about 60 percent of citizens of voting age participate is one such factor. And those who do go to the polls often have to choose from candidates who obscure the issues. Even on an issue as fundamental as the scope of government, candidates are not always crystal clear about what they would do if elected. As you read this chapter, the crucial question to consider is: Are the people represented by elections in America?

Elections serve a critical function in American society. They *institutionalize* political activity, making it possible for most political participation to be channeled through the electoral process rather than bubbling up through demonstrations, riots, or revolutions. Elections provide *regular access to political power*, so that leaders can be replaced without being overthrown. This is possible because elections have **legitimacy** in the eyes of the American people; that is, they are almost universally accepted as a fair and free method of selecting political leaders. Furthermore, by choosing who is to lead the country, the people—if they make their choices carefully—can also guide the policy direction of the government.

This chapter will give you a perspective on how elections function in the American system as well as how voters generally behave—both in terms of their decisions on whether to vote and how those who do vote make their choices. The focus here is primarily on presidential elections; Chapter 12 on Congress will examine congressional elections in detail.

legitimacy

A characterization of elections by political scientists meaning that they are almost universally accepted as a fair and free method of selecting political leaders. When legitimacy is high, as in the United States, even the losers accept the results peacefully.

HOW AMERICAN ELECTIONS WORK

The United States has three general kinds of elections: primary elections in which voters select party nominees, general elections that are contested between the nominees of the parties, and elections on specific policy questions in which voters engage in making or ratifying legislation. Primary elections were covered in the previous chapter, and general elections will be the main topic of this chapter. But before turning to this subject, we briefly examine elections that decide policy questions because such contests are becoming increasingly important in many states.

At present, there is no constitutional provision for specific policy questions to be decided by a nationwide vote. It is certainly conceivable that this may come to pass sometime in the twenty-first century,[2] as a number of European democracies have recently started to put questions of great importance—such as joining the European Monetary Union—to a national vote. Procedures allowing the public to pass legislation directly have been in effect for quite some time in many American states. There are two methods for getting items on a state ballot. The first is via a **referendum**, whereby voters are given the chance to approve or disapprove some legislative act, bond issue, or constitutional amendment proposed by the legislature. The second method is through an **initiative petition**, which typically requires gaining signatures on a proposed law equal to 10 percent of the number of voters in the previous election.

referendum

A state-level method of direct legislation that gives voters a chance to approve or disapprove proposed legislation or a proposed constitutional amendment.

initiative petition

A process permitted in some states whereby voters may put proposed changes in the state constitution to a vote if sufficient signatures are obtained on petitions calling for such a referendum.

Initiative petitions are often portrayed as lawmaking from the ground up, with the people taking charge of the political agenda. In this way, citizens can force a decision on an issue on which state legislatures have failed to act. Twenty-four states, mostly in the West, currently enable voters to propose and decide legislation through the route of an initiative petition. The most famous example is California's Proposition 13, which in 1978 put a limit on the rise in property taxes in California. Eighteen years and 196 propositions later, California voters passed Proposition 209, a measure intended to end affirmative action programs in the state. In 2008, many initiatives were voted on around the country. Voters in California, Florida, and Arizona passed measures to ban same sex marriages. In Arkansas, voters approved a ballot measure forbidding unmarried couples from adopting or serving as foster parents. Measures that would have severely restricted a woman's ability to obtain an abortion were defeated in South Dakota and Colorado. Michigan joined 12 other states by voting to allow the use of marijuana for medical purposes. Washington state voters opted to legalize assisted suicide for terminally ill people. And in Massachusetts animal rights activists succeeded in banning dog racing.

Although such initiatives require the support of a majority of voters, Daniel Smith argues that they often stem from the actions of a dedicated political entrepreneur more than anything.[3] For example, he writes that Barbara Anderson—a housewife without any previous political experience—spearheaded a Massachusetts initiative that is considered one of the most significant tax-cutting measures enacted in any state. Smith's examples of policy entrepreneurs who successfully used the initiative process all lacked public notoriety and personal wealth. These case studies of people who have spearheaded major initiative campaigns demonstrate how ordinary individuals can sometimes change the course of public policy.

One of the most controversial propositions on any state ballot in 2008 was California's Proposition 8 regarding the state's definition of marriage. Over $75 million was spent by the two sides of the issue. In the end, the effort to outlaw gay marriage passed by a narrow margin.

A TALE OF THREE ELECTIONS

Times change, and so do elections. Modern campaigns are slick, high-tech affairs. A glance at three American elections—1800, 1896, and 2008—should give you a good idea of how elections have changed over nearly two centuries.

1800: THE FIRST ELECTORAL TRANSITION OF POWER

By current standards, the 1800 election was not much of an election at all. There were no primaries, no nominating conventions, no candidate speeches, and no entourage of reporters. Both incumbent President John Adams and challenger Thomas Jefferson were nominated by their parties' elected representatives in Congress—Federalists for Adams and Democratic-Republicans for Jefferson. Once nominated, the candidates sat back and let their state and local organizations promote their cause. Communication and travel were too slow for candidates to get their message across themselves. Besides, campaigning was considered below the dignity of the presidential office.

At that time, however, newspapers were little concerned with dignity—or honesty for that matter. Most were rabidly partisan and did all they could to run down the opposition's candidate. Jefferson was regularly denounced as a Bible-burning atheist, the father of mulatto children (much later shown to be probably true based on DNA tests), and a mad scientist. Adams, on the other hand, was said to be a monarchist "whose grand object was to destroy every man who differed from his opinions."[4]

The focus of the campaign was not on voters but rather on the state legislatures, which had the responsibility for choosing members of the electoral college. When the dust settled, the Jeffersonians had won a slim victory in terms of electoral votes; however, they had also committed a troubling error. In the original constitutional system, each elector cast two ballots, and the top vote getter was named president, and the runner-up became vice president.[5] In 1796, Jefferson had become Adams's vice president by virtue of finishing second. Not wanting Adams to be his vice president, Jefferson made sure that all his electors also voted for his vice-presidential choice—Aaron Burr of New York. The problem was that when each and every one of them did so, Jefferson and Burr ended up tied for first. This meant that the Federalist-controlled House of Representatives would have to decide between the two Democratic-Republican candidates. Burr saw the chance to steal the presidency from Jefferson by cutting a deal with the Federalists, but his efforts failed. After 35 indecisive ballots in the House, the Federalists finally threw their support to Jefferson. On March 4, 1801, the transition from Adams to Jefferson marked the first peaceful transfer of power between parties via the electoral process in world history.

1896: A BITTER FIGHT OVER ECONOMIC INTERESTS

Nearly a century later the election of 1896 was largely fought over economics. By then national nominating conventions had become well established, and Republicans, meeting in St. Louis for their convention, nominated former Congressman William McKinley. The Republicans' major issues were support for the gold standard and high tariffs. The gold standard linked money to this scarce precious metal so that debtors never got a break from inflation. Tariffs protected capitalists and their workers from foreign competition.

The Democrats met in Chicago's sticky July heat. They had an issue—unlimited coinage of silver—but no clear front-runner. The high point of the Chicago convention was a speech by 36-year-old William Jennings Bryan of Nebraska, who proclaimed the virtues of the silver rather than the gold standard. Bryan went on to win the nomination on the fifth ballot and to become the youngest nominee of a major party in American history.

The flamboyant Bryan broke with tradition and took to the stump in person. He gave 600 speeches as his campaign train traveled through 26 states, logging 18,000 miles. Debtors and

William Jennings Bryan was the Democratic Party's standard bearer at the turn of the century. Eastern industrialists, fearing Bryan's powerful speeches and populist politics, used their financial clout to help William McKinley defeat "The Boy Orator of the Platte" (thus named after a river in his native Nebraska) in the 1896 and 1900 presidential elections.

silver miners were especially attracted to Bryan's pitch for cheap silver money. In contrast, the serene McKinley was advised to sit home in Ohio and run a front-porch campaign. He did, and he managed to label the Democrats as the party of depression ("In God We Trust, with Bryan We Bust").

Bryan won the oratory, but McKinley won the election. Eastern manufacturers contributed a small fortune to the Republicans. Only White Southerners, Westerners in the silver-producing states, and rural debtors lined up behind the Democrats. The Republicans won overwhelmingly in the industrial Northeast and Midwest and became firmly entrenched as the nation's majority party for the next several decades. McKinley triumphed by a margin of 271 to 176 in the electoral college. Nearly 80 percent of the eligible electorate voted in one of the highest turnouts ever.

2008: AN ELECTION ABOUT CHANGE

Late in the 2008 presidential campaign, Barack Obama told a crowd of supporters in Detroit that, "You couldn't have written a novel with all the crazy stuff that has happened in this election." Indeed, Obama's rise from an obscure Illinois state senator in 2004 to the nation's first successful African-American candidate for president in 2008 was truly incredible.

Like the great 19th century orator, William Jennings Bryan, Barack Obama was catapulted to national prominence as the result of a debut speech that electrified the Democratic Convention. Most notable in Obama's nationally televised address in 2004 was when he said:

> There is not a liberal America and a conservative America—there
> is the United States of America. There is not a Black America and a
> White America and Latino America and Asian America – there is the
> United States of America. The pundits like to slice-and-dice our
> country into Red States and Blue States; Red States for Republicans,
> Blue States for Democrats. But I've got news for them, too. We worship
> an "awesome God" in the Blue States, and we don't like federal agents
> poking around in our libraries in the Red States. We coach Little League
> in the Blue States and yes, we've got some gay friends in the Red States.
> There are patriots who opposed the war in Iraq and there are patriots
> who supported the war in Iraq. We are one people, all of us pledging
> allegiance to the stars and stripes, all of us defending the United States
> of America.

With this message of unity and multi-culturalism, Obama was viewed as a rising star and potential presidential candidate from his first day as a U.S. Senator in 2005. Within two years he had two books on the best-seller list—an autobiography entitled *Dreams From My Father* and a collection of policy proposals entitled *The Audacity of Hope*.

By the time Obama declared his presidential candidacy in February 2007, he had built a national constituency and established himself as the primary alternative to the front-runner, Senator Hillary Clinton. On a cold day in Springfield, Illinois, he proclaimed that, "I recognize there is a certain presumptuousness—a certain audacity—to this announcement. I know I haven't spent a lot of time learning the ways of Washington. But I've been there long enough to know that the ways of Washington must change." Indeed, his call for change resonated slightly more effectively than Clinton's emphasis on experience in the Democratic primaries. With strong support from young people, the highly educated, and African-Americans, Obama ekked out one of the closest nomination victories ever, as he and Senator Clinton contested all 50 states from January to June.

Newsstands from New York to Seattle quickly sold out of newspapers declaring Barack Obama the nation's first African-American president, as some jubilant customers picked up multiple copies as keepsakes. The *New York Times* and the *Chicago Tribune* in Obama's hometown were among papers that restarted their printing presses to produce additional copies across the country.

You Are a Campaign Manager: Navigating Negativity: Help Obama Handle Negative Attacks

You Are a Campaign Manager: Seven Days to Victory: Obama's Last Minute Choices in the Election's Final Week

In contrast, the Republican presidential nomination was wrapped up faster and more decisively by Senator John McCain. Nevertheless, he too seemed to be an improbable nominee, having long been viewed with suspicion by the party's conservative base. But in 2008, when even many Republicans wanted change, his reputation as a maverick (someone who thinks independently and doesn't always toe the party line) had special appeal. And when he surprised everyone with his historic choice of the first Republican woman to be nominated for vice president—Alaska's little-known Governor Sarah Palin—he energized the party's base and took a short-lived lead in the polls.

As the Fall campaign began, the race seemed to be shaping up as a close battle between Obama's perceived advantages on economic issues and personal intelligence versus McCain's perceived advantages on foreign policy issues and political experience. But then the nation's agenda changed dramatically as a credit crisis rocked the financial markets in late September. McCain took an aggressive approach, even suspending his campaign in order to try to stitch together a congressional coalition to address the crisis. Obama on the other hand, approached the situation coolly, noting that the campaign should go on as presidents have to work on multiple things all the time. When McCain's fellow Republicans in the House of Representatives voted against the financial bailout bill that both candidates had endorsed, his leadership image clearly suffered. Furthermore, the intense focus on the economy for the rest of the campaign provided Obama with opportunities to emphasize his popular plans for a middle-class tax cut, extension of health care coverage, and programs to support education.

Obama also gained ground on McCain as voters compared the choices for vice president. Although Sarah Palin proved to be an effective stump speaker, her one-on-one interviews with the anchors of ABC and CBS News revealed apparent gaps in her knowledge of policies in the view of many observers. By election day, exit polls found that just 38 percent of voters thought she was qualified to assume the presidency compared to 66 percent for Democratic vice presidential nominee Joe Biden.

Most importantly, Obama was able to inextricably link McCain to President George W. Bush, whose 70 percent disapproval approval rating was the worst ever recorded. In their final televised debate, McCain looked right at Obama and said, "I'm not George Bush. If you wanted to run against President Bush, you should have run four years ago." In turn, the Obama campaign responded with a powerful ad that tied the two together by showing a clip in which McCain acknowledged he had voted with President Bush 90 percent of the time.

The people's verdict in 2008, just as in 1800 and 1896, was that it was time for a change in Washington. Obama carried 53 percent of the popular vote compared to 46 percent for McCain and 1 percent for third party candidates. As shown in Figure 10.1, this translated into a 365-173 margin in the electoral college, with the Democrats winning 9 states they had lost in 2004 – Florida, Ohio, Indiana, Iowa, New Mexico, Colorado, Nevada, North Carolina, and Virginia.

In 2008, as in all election years, voters faced two key choices: whether to vote and, if they chose to do so, how to vote. The following sections will investigate how voters make these choices.

FIGURE 10.1

The Electoral College Results for 2004 and 2008

2008

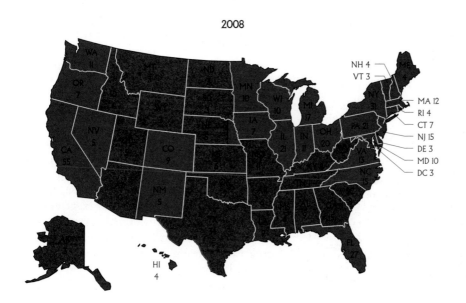

These two maps show the number of votes each state had in the electoral college in 2004 and 2008 and which states were carried by the Democrats (BLUE) and Republicans (RED).

2004

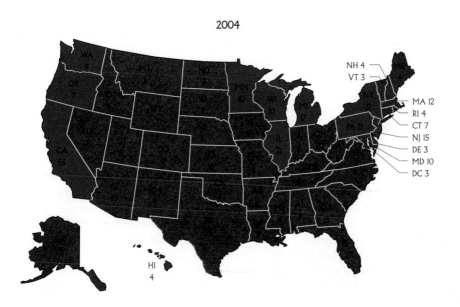

WHETHER TO VOTE: A CITIZEN'S FIRST CHOICE

suffrage
The legal right to vote, extended to African Americans by the **Fifteenth Amendment**, to women by the **Nineteenth Amendment**, and to people over the age of 18 by the **Twenty-sixth Amendment**.

Over two centuries of American electoral history, federal laws have greatly expanded **suffrage**—the right to vote. In the election of 1800, only property-owning White males over the age of 21 were typically allowed to vote. Now virtually everyone over the age of 18—male or female, White or non-White, rich or poor—has the right to vote. (For these developments, particularly as they affect women and minorities, see Chapter 5.) The two major exceptions concern noncitizens and convicted criminals. No state currently permits residents who are not citizens to vote. Some immigrant groups feel that this ought to at least be changed at the local level. State law varies widely when it comes to crime and voting: Virtually all states deny prisoners the right to vote, about half extend the ban to people on parole, and 10 states impose a lifetime ban on convicted felons.

Interestingly, as the right to vote has been extended, proportionately fewer of those eligible have chosen to exercise that right. In the past 120 years, the 80 percent turnout in the 1896 election was the high point of electoral participation. In 2008, 61 percent of adult citizens voted in the presidential election.

DECIDING WHETHER TO VOTE

Realistically, when over 125 million people vote in a presidential election, as they did in 2008, the chance of one vote affecting the outcome is very, very slight. Once in a while, of course, an election is decided by a small number of votes, as occurred in Florida in 2000. It is more likely, however, that you will be struck by lightning during your lifetime than participate in an election decided by a single vote.

Not only does your vote probably not make much difference to the outcome, but voting is somewhat costly. You have to spend some of your valuable time becoming informed, making up your mind, and getting to the polls. If you carefully calculate your time and energy, you might rationally decide that the costs of voting outweigh the benefits. Indeed, the most frequent response given by nonvoters in the 2004 Census Bureau survey on turnout was that they could not take time off from work or school that day.[6] Some scholars have therefore proposed that one of the easiest ways to increase American turnout levels would be to move Election Day to Saturday or make it a holiday, as practiced in many other countries.[7]

Economist Anthony Downs, in his model of democracy, tries to explain why a rational person would ever bother to vote. He argues that rational people vote if they believe that the policies of one party will bring more benefits

"You mean, like, wow, we can actually get rid of, you know, incumbents with this whatchamacallit?"

than the policies of the other party.[8] Thus, people who see policy differences between the parties are more likely to join the ranks of voters. If you are an environmentalist and you expect the Democrats to pass more environmental legislation than the Republicans, then you have an additional incentive to go to the polls. On the other hand, if you are truly indifferent—that is, if you see no difference whatsoever between the two parties—you may rationally decide to abstain.

Another reason why many people vote is that they have a high sense of **political efficacy**—the belief that ordinary people can influence the government. Efficacy is measured by asking people to agree or disagree with statements such as "I don't think public officials care much what people like me think." Those who lack strong feelings of efficacy are being quite rational in staying home on Election Day because they don't think they can make a difference. Yet even some of these people will vote anyway, simply to support democratic government. In this case, people are impelled to vote by a sense of civic duty. The benefit from doing one's **civic duty** is the long-term contribution made toward preserving democracy.

REGISTERING TO VOTE

A century ago politicians used to say, "Vote early and often." Cases such as West Virginia's 159,000 votes being cast by 147,000 eligible voters in 1888 were not that unusual. Largely to prevent corruption associated with stuffing ballot boxes, states adopted **voter registration** laws around the turn of the century, which require individuals to first place their name on an electoral roll in order to be allowed to vote. Although these laws have made it more difficult to vote more than once, they have also discouraged some people from voting at all. Voter registration requirements in the United States are, in part, to blame for why Americans are significantly less likely to go to the polls than citizens of other democratic nations (see "America in Perspective: Why Turnout in the United States Is So Low Compared to Other Countries").

Registration procedures currently differ from state to state. In sparsely populated North Dakota, there is no registration at all, and in Minnesota, Wisconsin, Iowa, Wyoming, Idaho, New Hampshire, and Maine voters can register on Election Day. Advocates of this user-friendly procedure are quick to point out that these states all ranked near the top in voter turnout in 2004, as you can see in "My State: Turnout of Adult Citizens in 2004." For many years, some states—particularly in the South—had burdensome registration procedures, such as requiring people to make a trip to their county courthouse during normal business hours. As a result of the 1993 **Motor Voter Act**, this is no longer the case. The Motor Voter Act made voter registration easier by requiring states to allow eligible voters to register by simply checking a box on their driver's license application or renewal form. Nevertheless, its impact on turnout has thus far been largely disappointing. Turnout for the presidential election of 2008 was virtually the same as it was in 1992 before the Motor Voter Act was passed.

Future reform designed to increase turnout may well focus on conducting elections through e-mail (see "You Are the Policymaker: Registering and Voting by E-Mail?") on p. 316.

WHO VOTES?

When just over half the population votes, the necessity of studying nonvoters takes on added importance. Table 10.1 displays data regarding the turnout rates of various

political efficacy
The belief that one's **political participation** really matters—that one's vote can actually make a difference.

civic duty
The belief that in order to support democratic government, a citizen should always vote.

voter registration
A system adopted by the states that requires voters to register well in advance of Election Day. A few states permit Election Day registration.

Motor Voter Act
Passed in 1993, this act went into effect for the 1996 election. It requires states to permit people to register to vote at the same time they apply for their driver's license.

Voting Turnout: Who Votes in The United States?

Why Turnout in the United States Is So Low Compared to Other Countries

Despite living in a culture that encourages participation, Americans have a woefully low turnout rate compared to other democracies. The figure below displays the most recent election turnout rates in the United States and a variety of other nations.

There are several reasons given for Americans' abysmally low turnout rate. Probably the reason most often cited is the American requirement of voter registration. The governments of many (but not all) other democracies take the responsibility of seeing to it that all their eligible citizens are on the voting lists. In America, the responsibility for registration lies solely with the individual. If we were like the Scandinavian countries, where the government registers every eligible citizen, no doubt our turnout rate would be higher.

A second difference between the United States and other countries is that the American government asks citizens to vote far more often. Whereas the typical European voter may cast two or three ballots in a four-year period, many Americans are faced with a dozen or more separate elections in the space of four years. Furthermore, Americans are expected to vote for a much wider range of political offices. With one elected official for every 442 citizens and elections held somewhere virtually every week, it is no wonder that it is so difficult to get Americans to the polls. It is probably no coincidence that the one European country that has a lower turnout rate—Switzerland—has also overwhelmed its citizens with voting opportunities, typically asking people to vote three times every year.

Third, the stimulus to vote is low in the United States because the choices offered Americans are not as starkly different as in other countries. The United States is quite unusual in that it has always lacked a major left-wing socialist party. When European voters go to the polls, they are deciding on whether their country will be run by parties with socialist goals or by conservative (and in some cases religious) parties. The consequences of their vote for redistribution of income and the scope of government are far greater than the ordinary American voter can imagine.

Finally, the United States is one of the few democracies that still vote mid-week, when most people are working. Article I, Section III of the U.S. Constitution allows Congress to determine the timing of federal elections. In the 1840s, Congress established the first Tuesday after the first Monday in November as the date for presidential elections. Americans have become quite accustomed to Tuesday elections, just as they are used to other outdated practices such as the nonmetric system for weights and measures. States continue to set primary election dates on Tuesday, even though they are perfectly free to pick any day of the week for these contests. Comparative research has shown that countries that hold elections on the weekend have higher turnout, but so far there has been no groundswell to change the American practice of holding elections on Tuesday.

QUESTIONS FOR DISCUSSION

▶ Some people would like the United States to emulate other countries and have the government register everyone who is eligible to vote. Others oppose this European-style system, believing that this would lead to an intrusive big government that would require everyone to have a national identity card. What do you think?

▶ Do you think American turnout rates would be better if we followed the lead of most other democracies and held elections on the weekend? Do you think young Americans, in particular, would be more likely to vote if elections were held on the weekend? Why or why not?

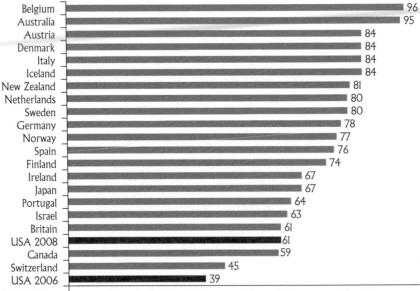

Percent of citizens (USA) or registered (other countries) voting

Sources: Official reports of the percentage of registered voters participating in all countries other than the United States. For the U.S., the percentage of citizens participating was calculated based on Census Bureau reports of the number of citizens of voting age and reports from the states regarding how many people voted.

MyState | Turnout of Adult Citizens in 2004

This map enables you to see whether the turnout rate of adult citizens in your state in 2004 was far above average, above average, below average, or far below average.

QUESTIONS FOR DISCUSSION

▷ How did your state rank in turnout in 2004, both in terms of the nation and within its own region of the country?

▷ Two of the most important factors which influence state turnout rates are the ease of registration procedures and how close the race for president is in each state. (You can find this information on the Web site of your state's secretary of state or Elections Bureau.) Do these two factors help explain why your state had either high or low turnout in 2004?

▷ What steps, if any, do you think your particular state could take to increase turnout in future elections?

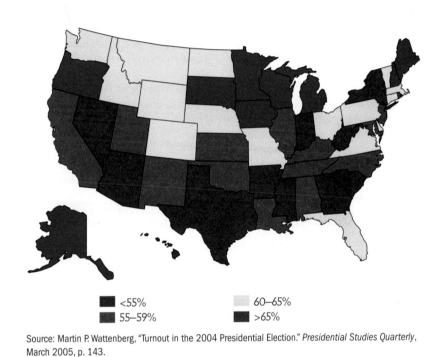

■ <55%   ▨ 60–65%
■ 55–59%   ■ >65%

Source: Martin P. Wattenberg, "Turnout in the 2004 Presidential Election." *Presidential Studies Quarterly*, March 2005, p. 143.

---

groups in the 2004 presidential election. This information reveals numerous demographic factors that are related to turnout:

- *Education.* People with higher-than-average educational levels have a higher rate of voting than people with less education. Highly educated people are more capable of discerning the major differences between the candidates. In addition, their educational training comes in handy in clearing the bureaucratic hurdles imposed by registration requirements.
- *Age.* Older people are far more likely to vote than younger people. Younger citizens are less likely to be registered, but even just analyzing turnout patterns among registered voters yields wide differences by age. For example, Iowa's secretary of state reported that of those on the registration rolls under 25 years of age, only 22 percent voted in 2006 as compared to 72 percent among those over 65 years of age.[9]
- *Race.* African Americans and Hispanics are underrepresented among voters relative to their share of the citizenry. This finding can largely be explained by

Registering and Voting by E-Mail?

Although modern technology is widely available, Americans have not harnessed much of it to improve democracy. Although many precincts now use computer touch screens to record votes, the high-tech age has not yet made much of an impact on the voting process. There is good reason to expect that this will change in the twenty-first century.

The development of the personal computer and the World Wide Web are likely to facilitate the process of voter registration. Already, one can go to the Web site of the Election Assistance Commission (*http://www.eac.gov/index_html1*) and download the "National Mail Voter Registration Form." Twenty-two states currently accept copies of this application printed from the computer image, signed by the applicant, and mailed in the old-fashioned way. As e-mail becomes ever more popular and "snail mail" fades into a method reserved mostly for packages, the entire voter registration process may someday be conducted mostly through electronic means. In an age where personal computers in the home are nearly as common as television sets are today, this technology would clearly make registering to vote more user friendly.

If people can register by computer, the next step is voting by e-mail. A growing trend in the Pacific Coast states has been voting by mail. In 1998, Oregon voters approved a referendum to eliminate traditional polling places and conduct all future elections by mail. In California, approximately 35 percent of the votes cast currently come in via the post office. Again, as e-mail takes the place of regular mail, why not have people cast their votes through cyberspace?

Voting through the Internet would be less costly for the state as well as easier for the average citizen—assuming that computer literacy reaches near-universal proportions sometime in the future. The major concerns, of course, would be ensuring that no one votes more than once and preserving the confidentiality of the vote. These security concerns are currently being addressed by some of the world's top computer programmers, as commercial enterprises look toward using the Internet to conduct business. If the technology can be perfected to allow trillions of dollars of business to be conducted via the Internet, then it seems reasonable that similar problems can be overcome with regard to the voting process.

Whether these possible developments will improve democracy in America is debatable. Making voting more user friendly should encourage turnout, but people will still have to be interested enough in the elections of the future to send in their e-mail ballots. If old-style polling places are relegated to the history books and everyone votes electronically in the convenience of their own homes, the sense of community on Election Day may be lost. This loss could lead to even lower turnout. You be the policymaker: Do the benefits of voting by e-mail outweigh the potential costs?

Why It Matters
Youth Turnout

Voter turnout rates in the United States have been declining for quite some time. The very low participation rate of young people has been one of the biggest reasons for this decline. Who votes matters not only because these individuals decide who wins elections but also because politicians pay attention primarily to voters. The fact that so few young people vote means that politicians are not likely to pay too much attention to their opinions or to promote policies that will particularly help them.

TABLE 10.1

Reported Turnout Rate in 2004

SOCIAL GROUPS	PERCENT
18–20	41
21–24	42
25–44	52
45–64	67
65 and over	69
No high school diploma	30
High school	52
Some college	66
College	74
White	66
African American	56
Hispanic citizens	47
Asian American citizens	44
Men	56
Women	60
Married	65
Single	47
Government workers	75
Self-employed	64
Work in private industry	57
Unemployed	46

Source: Authors' analysis of 2004 U.S. Census Bureau survey.

their below-average levels of education. African Americans and Hispanics with high levels of education actually have a higher turnout rate than Whites with comparable educational achievement.

- *Gender.* In an earlier period many women were discouraged from voting, but today women actually participate in elections at a slightly higher rate than men.
- *Marital status.* People who are married are more likely to vote than those who are not. This pattern is true among all age categories and generally reflects the fact that married people are more tied into their community.
- *Government employment.* Having something at stake (their jobs and the future of the programs they work on) and being in a position to know more about government impels government workers to high levels of participation.

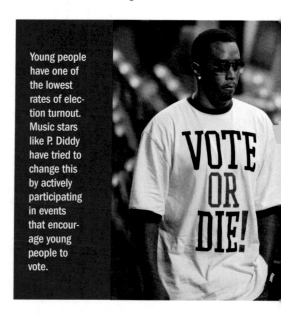

Young people have one of the lowest rates of election turnout. Music stars like P. Diddy have tried to change this by actively participating in events that encourage young people to vote.

These differences in turnout rates are cumulative. Possessing several of these traits (say, being elderly, well educated, and married) adds significantly to one's likelihood of voting. Conversely, being young, poorly educated, and single is likely to add up to a very low probability of voting. If you possess many of the demographic traits of nonvoters, then the interests of people like you are probably not drawing a great deal of attention from politicians—regardless of whether you personally vote or not. Politicians listen far more carefully to groups with high turnout rates, as they know their fate may well be in their hands. Who votes does matter.

HOW AMERICANS VOTE: EXPLAINING CITIZENS' DECISIONS

A common explanation of how Americans vote—one favored by journalists and politicians—is that people vote because they agree more with the policy views of Candidate A than with those of Candidate B. Of course, the candidates have invested a lot of time and money to get those views implanted in the public mind. Because citizens vote for the candidate whose policy promises they favor, many journalists and politicians say that the election winner has a mandate from the people to carry out the promised policies. This idea is sometimes called the **mandate theory of elections.**

Politicians, of course, are attracted to the mandate theory. It lets them justify what they want to do by claiming public support for their policies. As President Clinton said during the final presidential debate in 1992, "That's why I am trying to be so specific in this campaign—to have a mandate, if elected, so Congress will know what the American people have voted for." Immediately after declaring victory in the 2004 presidential election, President Bush forcefully asserted that he had a mandate to enact his proposed policies over the next four years. As Bush stated, "When you win there is a feeling that the people have spoken and embraced your point of view, and that's what I intend to tell Congress."

Political scientists, however, think little of the mandate theory of elections.[10] Whereas victorious politicians are eager to interpret even a slim victory as indicating public support for their platform, political scientists know that the people rarely vote a certain way for the same reasons. Instead, political scientists focus on three major elements of voters' decisions: (1) voters' party identification, (2) voters' evaluation of the candidates, and (3) the match between voters' policy positions and those of the candidates and parties—a factor termed "**policy voting.**"

mandate theory of elections
The idea that the winning candidate has a mandate from the people to carry out his or her platforms and politics. Politicians like the theory better than political scientists do.

policy voting
Electoral choices that are made on the basis of the voters' policy preferences and on the basis of where the candidates stand on policy issues.

PARTY IDENTIFICATION

Party identifications are crucial for many voters because they provide a regular perspective through which voters can view the political world. "Presumably," say Niemi and Weisberg, "people choose to identify with a party with which they generally agree.... As a result they need not concern themselves with every issue that comes along, but can generally rely on their party identification to guide them."[11] Parties tend to rely on groups that lean heavily in their favor to form their basic coalition. Even before an election campaign begins, Republicans usually assume they will not receive much support from African Americans and Jews. Democrats have an uphill struggle attracting groups that are staunchly Republican in their leanings, such as conservative evangelical Christians or upper-income voters. As you can see in Table 10.2, there have been substantial

TABLE 10.2

Changing Patterns in Voting Behavior: 1960 and 2008 Compared

The demographic correlates of presidential voting behavior have changed in a number of important ways since 1960. When Kennedy was elected in 1960, Protestants and Catholics voted very differently, as Kennedy's Catholicism was a major issue during the campaign. By 2008, Catholics were only slightly more likely to support the Democratic nominee than Protestants. Today, the major difference along religious lines involves how often one attends religious services, with those who attend regularly being substantially more likely to support Republican presidential candidates. The least likely group to support Republicans these days is African Americans. As you can see in data here, Obama clearly drew more support from African Americans than did Kennedy. Another advantage that Democrats now enjoy is with female voters, who preferred Obama by 7 percent more than men. Interestingly, women were actually slightly less likely than men to have supported the handsome JFK in 1960. Finally, the rapidly expanding Hispanic population in the U.S. has reshaped the electoral scene with their tendency to support Democratic candidates. Hispanics numbered only about 1 percent of voters in 1960—too small to be captured accurately in any survey—but by 2008 they accounted for 9 percent of Americans who voted for president.

	KENNEDY	NIXON	OBAMA	McCAIN
Protestant	36	63	45	54
Catholic	83	17	54	45
Jewish	89	11	78	21
Regularly attend religious services	49	50	43	55
Often attend religious services	36	64	53	46
Seldom attend religious services	55	44	59	39
Never attend religious services	51	49	67	30
White	48	52	43	56
African American	71	29	95	4
Hispanic	NA	NA	67	31
Male	52	48	49	48
Female	47	53	56	43
18–29	53	47	66	32
30–44	51	49	52	46
45–64	50	50	50	49
65+	39	61	45	53
No high school diploma	55	45	63	35
High school diploma	52	48	52	46
Some college	33	67	51	47
College degree	38	62	53	45

Source: 1960 National Election Study and 2008 National Voter Exit Poll.

changes in how various groups have voted for president since the days of Kennedy versus Nixon in 1960.

With the emergence of television and candidate-centered politics, the parties' hold on voters eroded substantially during the 1960s and 1970s and then stabilized at a new and lower level.[12] In the 1950s, scholars singled out party affiliation as the best single predictor of a voter's decision. For example, it was said that many Southern Democrats would vote for a yellow dog if their party nominated one. "My party—right or wrong" was the motto that typified strong party identifiers. Today, many voters agree with the statement that "I choose the best person for the office, regardless of party," as modern technology makes it possible for them to evaluate and make their own decisions about the candidates. For these voters, election choices have become largely a matter of individual choice, and their support is up for grabs in each election (the so-called floating voters). Young people are particularly likely to be up for grabs and open to the possibility of voting for candidates who are neither Democrats nor Republicans, as you can read about in "Young People and Politics: How Young Voters Have Consistently Been More Supportive of Third-Party Candidates."

CANDIDATE EVALUATIONS: HOW AMERICANS SEE THE CANDIDATES

All candidates try to present a favorable personal image. Using laboratory experiments, political psychologists Shawn Rosenberg and Patrick McCafferty showed that it is possible to manipulate a candidate's appearance in a way that affects voters' choices. Holding a candidate's policy views and party identification constant, they

YOUNG PEOPLE AND POLITICS

How Young Voters Have Consistently Been More Supportive of Third-Party Candidates

Over the past four decades, there have been a number of important third-party or independent candidates for the presidency. These candidates differed a great deal according to political ideology. George Wallace ran in 1968 as a conservative, Ross Perot offered voters a centrist choice in the 1992 and 1996 elections, and John Anderson in 1980 and Ralph Nader in 2000 were liberals. Yet all of these candidates had one thing in common in terms of their supporters—they all drew a higher percentage of the votes of young adults than any other age group, as you can see in the national survey findings displayed here.

The reason young voters have been consistently more supportive of third-party or independent candidates is that they are more likely to be political independents, without habitual ties to Democrats or Republicans. As we saw in Chapter 8, young people are more likely to be political independents, and independents are more open to alternatives outside the two-party system. Thus, when a conservative third-party candidate is on the ballot, young conservatives are more likely to vote for him than older conservatives, and when a liberal third-party candidate runs, young liberals are more likely to support him than older liberals. Should a third-

party candidate ever win nationwide, it is likely that young voters will be in forefront of his or her political supporters.

QUESTIONS FOR DISCUSSION

▷ Are young people sending a message to the two major parties by supporting alternative candidates?

▷ If America were like most European countries in using proportional representation in its elections, would young people be the supporters of new parties that might have a big impact?

% OF AGE GROUP VOTING FOR:	GEORGE WALLACE, 1968	JOHN ANDERSON, 1980	ROSS PEROT, 1992	ROSS PEROT, 1996	RALPH NADER, 2000
18–29	15	16	28	14	5
30–44	11	11	19	11	2
45–64	12	8	17	7	2
65+	8	3	12	5	2

Sources: 1968, 1980, 1992, and 1996 National Election Studies; 2000 National Voter Exit Poll.

found that when good pictures are substituted for bad ones, a candidate's vote-getting ability is significantly increased. Although a laboratory setting may not be representative of the real world, Rosenberg and McCafferty conclude that "with appropriate pretesting and adequate control over a candidate's public appearance, a campaign consultant should be able to significantly manipulate the image projected to the voting public."[13]

To do so, a consultant would need to know what sort of candidate qualities voters are most attuned to. Research by Miller, Wattenberg, and Malanchuk shows that the three most important dimensions of candidate image are integrity, reliability, and competence.[14] In 2000, one of the key factors that helped George W. Bush was that he was rated fairly positively on integrity, whereas Al Gore scored rather poorly on this dimension. In addition to honesty and integrity, a good candidate should also be seen as dependable and decisive—traits that Miller, Wattenberg, and Malanchuk label as "reliability." When the Bush campaign repeatedly labeled John Kerry a "flip-flopper" during the 2004 campaign, his image of reliability clearly suffered. The personal traits most often mentioned by voters, though, involve competence. Incumbent presidents typically score much higher on competence, as they have proven experience in dealing with national and international crises. This is one of the biggest reasons why it is so difficult to defeat a sitting president who is running for a second term.

Such evaluations of candidate personality are sometimes seen as superficial and irrational judgments. Miller and his colleagues disagree with this interpretation, arguing that voters rely on their assessments of candidates' personalities to predict how they would perform in office. If a candidate is too incompetent to carry out policy promises, or too dishonest for those promises to be trusted, it makes perfect sense for a voter to pay more attention to personality than policies. Interestingly, Miller and his colleagues find that college-educated voters are actually the most likely to view the candidates in terms of their personal attributes. They argue that better-educated voters are able to make important issue-oriented inferences from these attributes (for example, that a candidate who is unreliable may not be the right person to be the commander in chief of the armed forces).

POLICY VOTING

Policy voting occurs when people base their choices in an election on their own issue preferences. True policy voting can only take place when four conditions are met. First, voters must have a clear sense of their own policy positions. Second, voters must know where the candidates stand on policy issues. Third, they must see differences between the candidates on these issues. And finally, they must actually cast a vote for the candidate whose policy positions coincide with their own.

Given these conditions, policy voting is not always easy—even for the educated voter. Abramson, Aldrich, and Rohde analyzed responses to nine questions about policy issues in the 2004 National Election Study. They found that on the average issue 62 percent of the respondents met the first three informational criteria for policy voting. If someone knew the candidates' stances and saw differences between them, they voted for the candidate closest to their own position about 75 percent of the time.[15] Of course, we should never expect all votes to be consistent with policy views, as many people will prefer one candidate on some policies and another candidate on other policies.

One regular obstacle to policy voting is that candidates often decide that the best way to handle a controversial issue is to cloud their positions in rhetoric. For example, in 1968 both major party candidates—Nixon and Humphrey—were deliberately ambiguous about what they would do to end the Vietnam War. This made it extremely difficult for voters to cast their ballots according to how they felt about the war. The media may not be much help, either, as they typically focus more on the "horse race" aspects of the campaign than on the policy stands of the candidates, as discussed in Chapter 7. Voters thus often have to work fairly hard just to be well informed enough to potentially engage in policy voting.

In today's political world, it is easier for voters to vote according to policies than it was in the 1960s. The key difference is that candidates are now regularly forced to take clear stands to appeal to their own party's primary voters. As late as 1968, it was still possible to win a nomination by dealing with the party bosses; today's candidates must appeal first to the issue-oriented activists in the primaries. Whatever the major issues are in the next presidential election, it is quite likely that the major contenders for the Democratic and Republican nominations will be taking stands on them in order to gain the support of these activists. Thus, what has changed is not the voters but the electoral process, which now provides much more incentive for candidates to draw clear policy distinctions between one another. In particular, George W. Bush took particularly strong and clear policy stances on tax cuts, the war on terror, appointing conservative judges, and many other areas. Many scholars feel that as a result he became a particularly polarizing figure whom voters either love or hate.[16] Rather than clouding his rhetoric in ambiguity like most of his successors, George W. Bush took pride in being straightforward and plainspoken. Part of what made Bush such a polarizing figure may have been stylistic, but we suspect that at least some of the difference is due to a change in the tenor of the times, with more divisive issues facing the country than was the case a generation ago.

Party voting, candidate evaluation, and policy voting all play a role in elections. Their impact is not equal from one election to another, but they are the main factors affecting voter decisions. Once voters make their decisions in presidential elections, it is not just a simple matter of counting the ballots to see who has won the most support nationwide. Rather, the complicated process of determining **electoral college** votes begins.

Why It Matters
Mandate Theory of Elections
The mandate theory of elections asserts that voters send a policy message when they elect one candidate over another. Ideally, American democracy would work this way. The fact that it often does not indicates that leaders may be claiming more support from the people for their policies than is really justified.

electoral college
A unique American institution, created by the Constitution, providing for the selection of the president by electors chosen by the state parties. Although the electoral college vote usually reflects a popular majority, the winner-take-all rule gives clout to big states.

"It's a good speech—just a couple of points that need obfuscation."

THE LAST BATTLE: THE ELECTORAL COLLEGE

It is the members of the electoral college, not the people at large, who actually cast the determining votes for president and vice president of the United States. The electoral college is a unique American institution, created by the Constitution. The American Bar Association once called it "archaic, undemocratic, complex, ambiguous, indirect, and dangerous."[17] Many, but certainly not all, political scientists oppose its continued use, as do most voters.

The Founders wanted the president to be selected by the nation's elite, not directly by the people. They created the electoral college for this purpose and left the decision as to how the electors are chosen to each state. Since 1828, though, political practice has been for electors to vote for the candidate who won their state's popular vote. This is how the electoral college system works today:

You Are a Campaign Manager: Lead Obama to Battleground State Victory

- Each state, according to the Constitution, has as many electoral votes as it has U.S. senators and representatives.[18] The state parties select slates of electors, positions they use as a reward for faithful service to the party.
- Aside from Maine and Nebraska, each state has a winner-take-all system.[19] Electors vote as a bloc for the winner, whether the winner got 35 percent or 75 percent of the popular vote in their state.
- Electors meet in their states in December, following the November election, and then mail their votes to the vice president (who is also president of the Senate). The vote is counted when the new congressional session opens in January and is reported by the vice president. Thus, Dick Cheney had the duty of announcing the election of Barack Obama in January 2009.
- If no candidate receives an electoral college majority, then the election is thrown into the House of Representatives, which must choose from among the

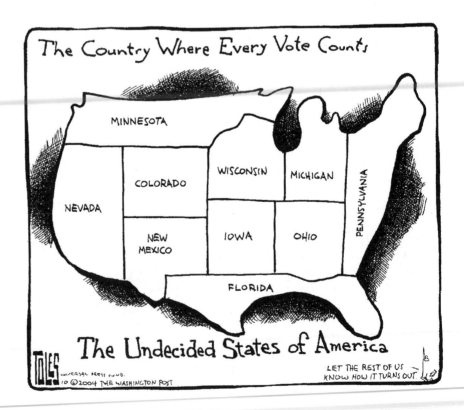

TABLE 10.3

Presidential Vote in 2000 by State Representation in the Electoral College (in percents)

States with less than seven electoral votes are overrepresented in the electoral college. Therefore, the fact that George W. Bush did especially well in these states in 2000, as shown in this table, helped him to win the presidency without winning the popular vote—the first time a candidate accomplished this feat since 1888.

	BUSH	GORE	NADER	OTHERS
Electoral votes <7	52.5	42.3	3.7	1.5
7–18	48.9	47.6	2.5	1.0
>18	45.7	50.7	2.7	0.9

Source: Calculated by the authors from official election returns.

top three electoral vote winners. A significant aspect of the balloting in the House is that each state delegation has one vote, thus giving the one representative from Wyoming an equal say with the 53 representatives from California. Though the Founders envisioned that the House would often have to vote to choose the president, this has not occurred since 1824.

The electoral college is important to the presidential election for two reasons. First, it introduces a bias into the campaign and electoral process. Because each state gets two electors for its senators regardless of population, the less populated states are overrepresented. One of the key reasons that George W. Bush won the electoral college vote in 2000 without winning the popular vote was that he did better in the less-populated states, as shown in Table 10.3. Second, the winner-take-all rule means that candidates will necessarily focus on winning the states where the polls show that there appears to be a close contest. Thus, Obama and McCain paid a great deal of attention to Ohio and Florida during the last month of the 2008 campaign but spent little time or money on states where the outcome seemed to be a foregone conclusion, such as New York and Texas.

Electoral College

UNDERSTANDING ELECTIONS AND VOTING BEHAVIOR

Elections accomplish two tasks according to democratic theory. First, and most obviously, they *select the policymakers*. Second, elections are supposed to help *shape public policy*. Whether elections in fact make the government pay attention to what the people think is at the center of debate concerning how well democracy works in America. In the hypothetical world of rational choice theory and the Downs model (see Chapter 8), elections do in fact guide public policy; however, over a generation of social science research on this question has produced mixed findings. It is more accurate to describe the connection between elections and public policy as a two-way street: Elections, to some degree, affect public policy, and public policy decisions partly affect electoral outcomes.

DEMOCRACY AND ELECTIONS

There will probably never be a definitive answer to the question of how much elections affect public policy—for it is a somewhat subjective matter. The broad contours of the answer, however, seem reasonably clear: *The greater the policy differences between the candidates, the more likely voters will be able to steer government policies by their choices.*

Of course, the candidates do not always help to clarify the issues. One result is that the policy stands are often shaped by what Benjamin Page once called "the art of ambiguity," in which "presidential candidates are skilled at appearing to say much while actually saying little."[20] Learning how to side-step controversial questions and hedge answers is indeed part of becoming a professional politician, as you can observe at almost every presidential press conference.

retrospective voting
A theory of voting in which voters essentially ask this simple question: "What have you done for me lately?"

When individual candidates do offer a plain choice to the voters (what 1964 Republican nominee Barry Goldwater once called "a choice, not an echo"), voters are better able to guide the government's policy direction. Ronald Reagan followed in Goldwater's footsteps in the 1980s by making clear his intention to cut the growth of domestic spending, reduce taxes, and build up American military capability. Once elected, he proceeded to do much of what he said he would—demonstrating that elections can sometimes dramatically affect public policy.

If elections affect policies, then policies can also affect elections. Most policies have consequences for the well-being of certain groups or the society as a whole. Those who feel better off as a result of certain policies are likely to support candidates who pledge to continue those policies, whereas those who feel worse off are inclined to support opposition candidates. This is known as the theory of **retrospective voting**,[21] in which voters essentially ask the simple question, "What have you done for me lately?" Incumbents who provide desired results are rewarded; those who fail to do so are not reelected.

Nothing makes incumbent politicians more nervous than the state of the economy. When the economy takes a downturn, the call to "throw the rascals out" usually sweeps the nation. In presidential elections, people unhappy with the state of the economy tend to blame the incumbent. Republican Herbert Hoover was in office when the stock market crash of 1929 sparked the Great Depression. Hoover and his fellow Republicans were crushed by Franklin Roosevelt in the 1932 elections. In 2008, Democrats were still hitting the Republicans with the memory of Hoover—calling George W. Bush a modern-day Hoover whose administration had presided over the worst annual job creation record of any president since the Great Depression.

Economic conditions can have a profound effect on election outcomes. In 1932, voters expressed their despair over the Great Depression by electing Franklin Roosevelt in a landslide over Herbert Hoover. Here, an unemployed man sells "Hoover apples" in front of the U.S. Capitol.

Clearly, elections affect policy, and public policy—especially the perception of economic policy impacts—can affect elections. Once in office, politicians use fiscal policy to keep the American economy running on an even keel. (How they try to do this is considered in Chapter 17.) If economic troubles mount, voters point their fingers at incumbent policymakers, and those fingers are more likely to pull the lever for the challengers on Election Day. In recent elections people who felt the national economy had improved voted strongly for the incumbent, whereas those who thought the economy had gotten worse strongly favored the major challenger. As V. O. Key once wrote, "The only really effective weapon of popular control in a democratic regime is the capacity of the electorate to throw a party from power."[22]

ELECTIONS AND THE SCOPE OF GOVERNMENT

While the threat of electoral punishment constrains policymakers, it also helps to increase generalized support for government and its powers. Voters know that the government can be replaced at the next election, so they are much more likely to feel that it will be responsive to their needs. Furthermore, when people have the power to dole out electoral reward and punishment, they are more likely to see government as their servant instead of their master. As Benjamin Ginsberg writes, "Democratic elections help to persuade citizens that expansion of the state's powers represents an increase in the state's capacity to serve them."[23]

Comparing Voting and Elections

Therefore, rather than wishing to be protected from the state, citizens in a democracy often seek to benefit from it. It is no coincidence that "individuals who believe they can influence the government's actions are also more likely to believe, in turn, that the government should have more power."[24] Voters like to feel that they are sending a message to the government to accomplish something. It should thus be no surprise that as democracy has spread, government has come to do more and more, and its scope has grown.

SUMMARY

This chapter has examined the final act in the electoral drama. Once the parties have made their nominations and the campaign has concluded, voters take center stage. Elections have changed dramatically since 1800 when Adams ran against Jefferson. By 1896, it was acceptable for candidates to campaign in person, and William Jennings Bryan did so with a vengeance. At that time suffrage—the right to vote—was still limited mostly to White males. Now the democratization of elections has made suffrage available to virtually all American citizens over the age of 18.

Voters make two basic decisions at election time. The first is whether to vote. Americans' right to vote is well established, but in order to do so citizens must go through the registration process. Although registration reform has been touted as the answer to America's low turnout problems, the Motor Voter Act of 1993 has yet to produce the benefit of greater voter participation that most people hoped for. Turnout in 2008 was still relatively low, virtually identical to what it was in 1992. Second, those who choose to vote must decide for whom to cast their ballots. Over a generation of research on voting behavior has helped political scientists understand the dominant role played by three factors in voters' choices: party identification, candidate evaluations, and policy positions.

Elections are the centerpiece of democracy. Few questions are more important in understanding American government than this: Do elections matter? Under the right conditions, elections can influence public policy, and policy outcomes can influence elections. Elections also legitimize the power of the state, thereby making it easier to expand the scope of the government.

Chapter Test

Multiple Choice

1. An initiative petition is:
   a. When a member of the legislature proposes a bill
   b. When the governor proposes a bill
   c. When citizens put a proposed law on the ballot
   d. When a congressional committee proposes a bill
   e. When the courts strike down a law as unconstitutional

2. In order to qualify for the ballot, an initiative usually requires signatures equal to:
   a. 10 percent of the total population
   b. 10 percent of the registered voters
   c. 10 percent of the eligible voters
   d. 10 percent of the number of voters in the previous election
   e. The minimum is always 500 signatures.

3. A referendum is defined as:
   a. Voters gathering in town-hall-style meetings to discuss new laws they would like to see enacted
   b. Voters nullifying a law passed by the legislature
   c. Voters proposing a law to the legislature
   d. The governor asking voters to pass a law that the legislature refuses to act on
   e. The legislature overriding the president's veto on a law

4. The term "political efficacy" is defined as a person's:
   a. Sense of civic duty
   b. Level of political knowledge
   c. Political ideology
   d. Eligibility to vote in elections
   e. Belief in the ability to influence politics

5. Which of the following is *not* a reason why voter turnout in European countries is so much higher than in the United States?
   a. European electoral campaigns are more effective
   b. Europeans have fewer elections to vote in
   c. European governments take care of voter registration for their citizens
   d. European political parties are more diverse
   e. European elections usually take place on weekends

6. Approximately what percentage of states currently allows voters to influence legislation through initiatives?
   a. Fewer than 15 percent
   b. About 25 percent
   c. About 50 percent
   d. More than 75 percent
   e. All of them do

7. Initiatives can be considered _____ lawmaking.
   a. Top down
   b. Bottom up
   c. Vertical
   d. Lateral
   e. Upright

8. Which of the following is *not* true about Americans' voting behavior, according to the data presented in Table 10.1 of this textbook?
   a. Level of education positively impacts voter turnout
   b. Single people are more likely to vote than married people
   c. Women are more likely to vote than men
   d. People with public jobs are more likely to vote than people in the private industry
   e. Asian American citizens are less likely to vote than Hispanic citizens

9. Which of the following is *most* likely to hinder an incumbent president's chances of reelection?
   a. The incumbent has admitted to past use of marijuana
   b. Spending on education has been cut
   c. Unemployment rates have gone up drastically during the last year
   d. The incumbent has opposed an important environmental treaty
   e. The incumbent has gone against his party platform on occasion.

True/False

10. Federal law requires that once people serve their time for a felony conviction their right to vote is automatically restored.
    True_____   False_____

11. Voter registration was introduced in the United States to avoid people "stuffing ballot boxes."
    True_____   False_____

12. All U.S. states currently require some form of voter registration, but they differ in the specific procedures.
    True_____   False_____

13. The Motor Voter Act of 1993 has had a very positive impact on voter turnout.
    True_____   False_____

14. According to studies cited in this textbook, college educated voters are the most likely to be influenced by personality attributes of presidential candidates.
    True_____   False_____

Short Answer

15. Please name and briefly explain the three most important dimensions of political candidates' images. What other dimension would you add?

16. What happens, if no presidential candidate receives a majority of the votes from the Electoral College?

17. Please define "retrospective voting."

18. In your own words, explain the three major elements that influence voters' decisions during an election.

19. Please explain the term "political efficacy." What are at least three factors that are likely to influence a person's level of political efficacy?

20. Based on what you know about elections and voting behavior, what do you believe are the two greatest strengths and weaknesses of the U.S. electoral system? Be specific in your answer and provide examples.

Short Answer/Essay Questions

21. Of all the liberal democracies around the world, Switzerland is generally considered the country whose political system is closest to a so-called "direct democracy." This means that in Switzerland, virtually every important decision is put to the vote by the people in the form of a referendum. In your opinion, what are at least two pros and two cons of having people vote on every major political decision?

22. In your opinion, what are at least two arguments in favor and two arguments against voting by e-mail? Generally speaking, do you believe that allowing e-mail voting would improve or harm democracy in this country, and why?

23. Imagine that you were put in charge of addressing the low voter turnout rates in American elections. As part of your job, please compose a brief report that outlines the potential causes for the low turnout and offers a number of possible solutions. In your report, you should specifically address the differences—both in causes and solutions—among the younger, middle-aged, and older age groups.

24. Several countries around the world have made voting in national elections mandatory for their citizens. As a result of compulsory voting, a country like Australia boasts voter turnout rates of well over 90 percent in all its elections. In your opinion, is compulsory voting a good idea? Do you believe it improves the quality of democracy? Why, or why not? Please be specific in your explanations and address several aspects of the issue.

25. Do you agree or disagree with the "mandate theory of elections"? Specifically, do you believe that voters truly send candidates a "policy message" through their votes? And do policymakers heed that message once they are in office? Please provide concrete arguments and support your answer with examples.

Answer

1. C   2. D   3. B   4. E   5. A   6. C   7. B   8. B   9. C   10. False   11. True   12. False   13. False   14. True

Key Terms

legitimacy (306)
referendum (306)
initiative petition (306)
suffrage (312)

political efficacy (313)
civic duty (313)
voter registration (313)
Motor Voter Act (313)

mandate theory of elections (317)
policy voting (317)
electoral college (321)
retrospective voting (324)

Internet Resources

www.electionstudies.org/
The American National Election Studies are a standard source of survey data about voting behavior. This site offers information about these studies, as well as some of their results.

www.annenbergpublicpolicycenter.org/ProjectDetails.aspx?myId=1
A good source of information on public views during the 2008 presidential campaign.

www.census.gov/population/www/socdemo/voting.html
The Census Bureau's studies of registration and turnout can be found at this address.

GetConnected

The Help America Vote Act

On October 29, 2002, President Bush signed HR 3295, the Help America Vote Act (HAVA). This federal legislation created many new mandates for state and local government. The new law was enacted to improve voting system technology and election administration procedures. It was a result of the problems that occurred during the 2000 presidential election, especially the problems with outdated punch-card voting technology.

Search the Web

Go to the National Association of Secretaries of State Web page on HAVA to find out how your state is implementing the federal law. Take a look at the League of Women Voters' page on HAVA, *www.lwv. org/AM/Template.cfm?Section=Election_Reform*, and read about the group's suggestions for implementing HAVA and some of the issues related to electronic voting technology.

Questions to Ask

- What actions are election officials in your state taking to implement HAVA?

- What are some of the issues raised by election officials in your state in implementing HAVA?
- Are there any problems with electronic voting technology? What are those problems?

Why It Matters

Voting is an integral part of the American form of government. It is through voting that people can voice their concerns and choose people to represent them. If the voting technology does not adequately record votes, then voters will lose confidence in their ability to change government through their vote. We certainly do not want a repeat of the public problems that plagued voting in the 2000 presidential elections.

Get Involved

Find out what voting technology is used in your local area. Working with your local election officials, prepare a guidebook to help voters better understand that technology so they are less likely to be intimidated by the technology when they enter the polling place. *For more exercises, go to www.longmanamericangovernment.com.*

For Further Reading

Abramson, Paul R., John H. Aldrich, and David W. Rohde. *Change and Continuity in the 2004 Elections.* Washington, DC: Congressional Quarterly Press, 2006. A good overview of voting behavior in the 2004 elections, which also focuses on recent historical trends.

Campbell, Angus, et al. *The American Voter.* New York: Wiley, 1960. The classic study of the American electorate in the 1950s, which has shaped scholarly approaches to the subject ever since.

Institute of Politics, ed. *Campaign for President: The Managers Look at 2004.* Lanham, MD: Rowman & Littlefield, 2006. The campaign managers for all the 2004 presidential candidates gathered at Harvard to discuss their experiences in the primaries and the general election.

Kelley, Stanley G., Jr. *Interpreting Elections.* Princeton, NJ: Princeton University Press, 1983. Presents a theory of "the simple act of voting."

Lewis-Beck, Michael S., et al. *The American Voter Revisited.* Ann Arbor, MI: University of Michigan Press, 2008. A replication of the classic analysis in *The American Voter* employing data from the 2000 and 2004 National Election Studies.

Martin, Fenton S., and Robert U. Goehlert. *How to Research Elections.* Washington, DC: Congressional Quarterly Press, 2001. A very useful guide to many sources of information about elections.

Nie, Norman H., Sidney Verba, and John R. Petrocik. *The Changing American Voter.* Cambridge, MA: Harvard University Press, 1976. Challenges some of the assumptions of Campbell et al.'s *The American Voter.*

Niemi, Richard G., and Herbert F. Weisberg, eds. *Controversies in Voting Behavior.* 4th ed. Washington, DC: Congressional Quarterly Press, 2001. An excellent set of readings on some of the most hotly debated facets of voting.

Polsby, Nelson W., and Aaron Wildavsky. *Presidential Elections.* 11th ed. Lanham, MD: Rowman & Littlefield, 2004. A classic text on the subject.

Smith, Daniel A. *Tax Crusaders and the Politics of Direct Democracy.* New York: Routledge, 1998. A collection of interesting essays about activists who have made a difference through their advocacy of tax cut initiatives.

Wattenberg, Martin P. *Where Have All the Voters Gone?* Cambridge, MA: Harvard University Press, 2002. A review of the reasons for declining voter turnout, both in the United States and in other advanced industrialized countries.

Wolfinger, Raymond E., and Steven J. Rosenstone. *Who Votes?* New Haven, CT: Yale University Press, 1980. A classic quantitative study of who turns out and why.

INTEREST GROUPS

POLITICS IN ACTION:
HOW INTEREST GROUP LOBBYISTS WORK ON SMALL DETAILS WITH BIG PAYOFFS

Just before Christmas of 2002, a very unusual quarter-page advertisement appeared in the *New York Times* and other major papers around the country. It was placed by the public interest journal titled *TomPaine.commonsense* (*www.tompaine.com*). The bold headline read, "Reward $10,000: For Information Leading to the Identification of the Eli Lilly Bandit." The story they told was one of corporate lobbyists using their influence to get a special provision written into law at the last minute with no one watching. As a public interest journal, *TomPaine.commonsense* strives to insure open and accountable government. They regularly seek to expose cases of corporations getting sweet deals from government policymakers. Eli Lilly & Company, a giant drug manufacturer, had gotten such a deal, and *TomPaine.commonsense* sought to at least publicize this fact, if not get to the bottom of how their lobbyists accomplished the feat.

The mystery is one worthy of Sherlock Holmes. In November 2002, Congress passed a 475-page bill creating the new Department of Homeland Security. Somehow or other, a little provision was slipped into this bill that seemingly had nothing to do with the topic of homeland security. This provision gave Eli Lilly & Company something it badly wanted—a shield from multi-million-dollar lawsuits. Lilly was facing numerous lawsuits from parents who claimed that their children's autism was linked to Thimerosal, a mercury-based preservative made by Lilly that is a common ingredient in childhood vaccines. The provision diverted those suits from state courts to a federal vaccine court, where damages are capped at $250,000. How did such a measure end up in a bill dealing with homeland security? It was slipped in during the conference committee negotiations, which are held behind closed doors. But who slipped it in? That's what *TomPaine.commonsense* offered $10,000 to find out.

Strangely, in a city where knowledge is power and where people are usually eager to take credit for any political accomplishment, no one in Washington was willing to take

credit for the passage of the measure helping Eli Lilly. The company's lobbyists claimed ignorance. Of course they had long wanted to get something like this passed, but they claimed they had never thought of getting it into the Homeland Security Act. And Office of Management and Budget Director Mitch Daniels, a former company executive at Eli Lilly, went to considerable lengths to deny any knowledge of the matter. As of this writing, the mystery still remains, and the $10,000 reward money remains unclaimed.

The worst and oldest stereotype of a lobbyist is of someone who bribes a lawmaker to get a favorable policy decision. In contrast, whoever the "Eli Lilly Bandit" was, he or she used leverage with members of Congress that was probably obtained by open and legal means. The fact that Eli Lilly & Company had donated $1.6 million to the national parties and to federal candidates in the preceding two years likely had something to do with what happened. Note that such donations were perfectly legal and a matter of public record.

Because the American political system is so openly democratic, an incredible array of interests can make their voices heard loud and clear in Washington. Some critics believe that too many interest groups make demands on the government; others say the real problem is that the moneyed interests get a disproportionate share of access and influence. Those who are concerned the system is too democratic often argue that the result is the frustration of any proposals for changing the existing scope of government. For those most concerned with the domination of well-off interest groups, the scope of government that results is inevitably seen as helping the rich get richer. Nevertheless, there are scholars who believe the interest group system is working pretty much as the Founders intended. James Madison argued in *Federalist Paper No. 10* that the sphere of influence must be extended in order to prevent any one group from having too much power. Whether we are far along in reaching this goal is a crucial question for you to consider when reading this chapter.

Our nation's capital has become a hub of interest group activity. On any given day, it is possible to observe pressure groups in action in many forums. In the morning, you could attend congressional hearings in which you are sure to see interest groups testifying for and against proposed legislation. At the Supreme Court, you might stop in to watch a public interest lawyer arguing for strict enforcement of environmental regulations. Take a break for lunch at a nice Washington restaurant, and you may see a lobbyist entertaining a member of Congress.

You could spend the afternoon in any department of the executive branch (such as commerce, labor, or the interior), where you might catch bureaucrats working out rules and regulations with friendly—or sometimes unfriendly—representatives of the interests they are charged with overseeing. You could stroll past the impressive headquarters of the National Rifle Association, the AFL-CIO, or the American Association of Retired Persons to get a sense of the size of some of the major lobbying organizations. To see some lobbying done on college students' behalf, you might drop by One Dupont Circle, where many of the higher education groups have their offices. These groups lobby for student loans and scholarships, as well as for aid to educational institutions. At dinnertime, if you are able to finagle an invitation to a Georgetown cocktail party, you may see lobbyists trying to get the ear of government officials—both elected and unelected.

All this lobbying activity poses an interesting paradox: Although turnout in elections has declined since 1960, participation in interest groups has mushroomed. As Kay Schlozman and John Tierney write, "Recent decades have witnessed an expansion of astonishing proportions in the involvement of private organizations in Washington politics."[1] This chapter will explore the factors behind the interest group explosion, how these groups enter the policymaking process, and what they get out of it.

THE ROLE OF INTEREST GROUPS

All Americans have some interests they want represented. Organizing to promote these interests is an essential part of democracy. The right to organize groups is protected by the Constitution, which guarantees people the right "peaceably to assemble, and to petition the Government for a redress of grievances." This important First Amendment right has been carefully defended by the Supreme Court. The freedom to organize is as fundamental to democratic government as freedom of speech and freedom of the press.

The term *interest group* seems simple enough to define. Interest refers to a policy goal; a group is a combination of people. An **interest group**, therefore, is an organization of people with similar policy goals who enter the political process to try to achieve those aims. Whatever their goals—outlawing abortion or ensuring the right to one or regulating tax loopholes or creating new ones—interest groups pursue them in many arenas. Every branch of government is fair game; every level of government, local to federal, is a possible target. A policy battle lost in Congress may be turned around when it comes to bureaucratic implementation or to the judicial process.

This multiplicity of policy arenas helps distinguish interest groups from political parties. Parties fight their battles through the electoral process; they run candidates for public office. Interest groups may support candidates for office, but American interest groups do not run their own slate of candidates, as in some other countries. In other words, no serious candidate is ever listed on the ballot as a candidate of the National Rifle Association or Common Cause. It may be well known that a candidate is actively supported by a particular group, but that candidate faces the voters as a Democrat, a Republican, or a third-party candidate.

Another key difference between parties and interest groups is that interest groups are often policy specialists, whereas parties are policy generalists. Most interest groups have a handful of key policies to push: A farm group cares little about the status of urban transit; an environmental group has its hands full bringing polluters into court without worrying about the minimum wage. Unlike political parties, these groups need not limit themselves by trying to appeal to everyone.

interest group
An organization of people with shared policy goals entering the policy process at several points to try to achieve those goals. Interest groups pursue their goals in many arenas.

THEORIES OF INTEREST GROUP POLITICS

Understanding the debate over whether honest lobbying—and interest groups in general—create problems for government in America requires an examination of three important theories, which were introduced in Chapter 1. **Pluralist theory** argues that interest group activity brings representation to all. According to pluralists, groups compete and counterbalance one another in the political marketplace. In contrast, **elite theory** argues that a few groups (primarily the wealthy) have most of the power. Finally, **hyperpluralist theory** asserts that too many groups are getting too much of what they want, resulting in government policy that is often contradictory and lacking in direction. The following sections will examine each of these three theories with respect to interest groups.

PLURALISM AND GROUP THEORY

Pluralist theory rests its case on the many centers of power in the American political system. Pluralists consider the extensive organization of competing groups evidence that influence is widely dispersed among them. They believe

pluralist theory
A theory of government and politics emphasizing that politics is mainly a competition among groups, each one pressing for its own preferred policies.

elite theory
A theory of government and politics contending that societies are divided along class lines and that an upper-class elite will rule, regardless of the formal niceties of governmental organization.

hyperpluralist theory
A theory of government and politics contending that groups are so strong that government is weakened. Hyperpluralism is an extreme, exaggerated, or perverted form of **pluralism**.

"YOU'LL LIKE THEM ... THEIR SPECIAL INTEREST IS GIVING AWAY MORE MONEY THAN OTHER SPECIAL INTEREST GROUPS!"

that groups win some and lose some but that no group wins or loses all the time. Pluralist theorists offer a *group theory of politics*, which consists of several essential arguments.[2]

- *Groups provide a key link between people and government.* All legitimate interests in the political system can get a hearing from government once they are organized.
- *Groups compete.* Labor, business, farmers, consumers, environmentalists, and other interests constantly make competing claims on the government.
- *No one group is likely to become too dominant.* When one group throws its weight around too much, its opponents are likely to intensify their organization and thus restore balance to the system. For every action, there is a reaction.
- *Groups usually play by the "rules of the game."* In the United States, group politics is a fair fight, with few groups lying, cheating, stealing, or engaging in violence to get their way.
- *Groups weak in one resource can use another.* Big business may have money on its side, but labor has numbers. All legitimate groups are able to affect public policy by one means or another.

Pluralists would never deny that some groups are stronger than others or that competing interests do not always get an equal hearing. Still, they can point to many cases in which a potential group organized itself and, once organized, affected policy decisions. African Americans, women, and consumers are all groups who were long ignored by government officials but who, once organized, redirected the course of public policy. In sum, pluralists argue that lobbying is open to all and is therefore not to be regarded as a problem.

ELITES AND THE DENIAL OF PLURALISM

Whereas pluralists are impressed by the vast number of organized interests, elitists are impressed by how insignificant most of them are. Real power, elitists say, is held by relatively few people, key groups, and institutions. They maintain that the government is run by a few big interests looking out for themselves—a view that the majority of the public has usually agreed with in recent decades, as you can see in Figure 11.1

Elitists critique pluralist theory by pointing to the concentration of power in a few hands. Where pluralists find dispersion of power, elitists find interlocking and concentrated power centers. About one-third of top institutional positions—corporate boards, foundation boards, university trusteeships, and so on—are occupied by people who hold more than one such position.[3] Elitists see the rise of mighty multinational corporations as further tightening the control of corporate elites. A prime example is America's giant oil companies. Robert Engler has tried to show that government has always bent over backward to maintain high profits for the oil industry.[4] When they come up against the power of these multinational corporations, consumer interests are readily pushed aside, according to elitists.

In sum, the elitist view of the interest group system makes the following assertions:

- The fact that there are numerous groups proves nothing because groups are extremely unequal in power.
- Awesome power is held by the largest corporations.
- The power of a few is fortified by an extensive system of interlocking directorates.

FIGURE 11.1

Perceptions of the Dominance of Big Interests

Question Wording: Would you say the government is pretty much run by a few big interests looking out for themselves or that it is run for the benefit of all the people?

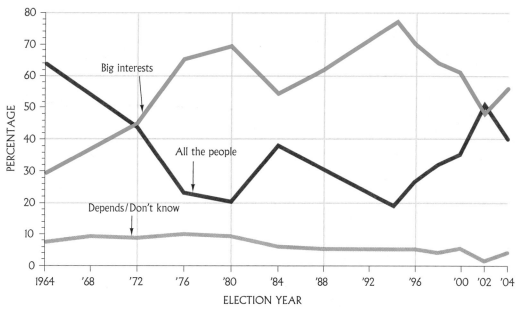

Source: Authors' analysis of 1964–2004 American National Election Study data.

- Other groups may win many minor policy battles, but corporate elites prevail when it comes to the big decisions.

Thus, even honest lobbying is a problem, say elite theorists, because it benefits few at the expense of many.

HYPERPLURALISM AND INTEREST GROUP LIBERALISM

Hyperpluralists, also critical of pluralism, argue that the pluralist system is out of control. Theodore Lowi coined the phrase *interest group liberalism* to refer to the government's excessive deference to groups. Interest group liberalism holds that virtually all pressure group demands are legitimate and that the job of the government is to advance them all.[5]

In an effort to please and appease every interest, agencies proliferate, conflicting regulations expand, programs multiply, and, of course, the budget skyrockets. If environmentalists want clean air, government imposes clean-air rules; if businesses complain that cleaning up pollution is expensive, government gives them a tax write-off for pollution control equipment. If the direct-mail industry wants cheap rates, government gives it to them; if people complain about junk mail, the Postal Service gives them a way to take their names off mailing lists. If cancer researchers convince the government to launch an antismoking campaign, tobacco sales may drop; if they do, government will subsidize tobacco farmers to ease their loss.[6]

All candidates for public office seek to obtain the votes of various interest groups. In their interactions with organized groups, candidates usually offer assurances that they care about people like them and share common interests. Here, John McCain—a prominent veteran himself—addresses the annual convention of the Veterans of Foreign Wars.

subgovernments

A network of groups within the American political system that exercise a great deal of control over specific policy areas. Also known as iron triangles, subgovernments are composed of interest group leaders interested in a particular policy, the government agency in charge of administering that policy, and the members of congressional committees and subcommittees handling that policy.

Why It Matters
Theories of Interest Group Politics

Suppose James Madison's descendants were studying American government in order to assess how well the system he devised controls the power of special interests. They would definitely draw different conclusions depending on whether they assessed the current system using pluralist, elitist, or hyperpluralist interpretations. A pluralist interpretation could be seen as evidence that Madison's system has worked as intended. An elitist interpretation would hold that the wealthy in particular hold too much power, whereas a hyperpluralist interpretation would indicate that too many groups have too much power.

Interest group liberalism is promoted by the network of **subgovernments** in the American political system that exercise a great deal of control over specific policy areas. These subgovernments, which are also known as iron triangles, are composed of key interest group leaders interested in policy X, the government agency in charge of administering policy X, and the members of congressional committees and subcommittees handling policy X.

All the elements composing subgovernments have the same goal: protecting their self-interest. The network of subgovernments in the agricultural policy area of tobacco is an excellent example. Tobacco interest groups include the Tobacco Institute, the Retail Tobacco Distributors of America, and the tobacco growers. Various agencies in the Department of Agriculture administer tobacco programs, and they depend on the tobacco industry's clout in Congress to help keep their agency budgets safe from cuts. Finally, most of the members of the House Tobacco Subcommittee are from tobacco-growing regions. All these elements want to protect the interests of tobacco farmers. Similar subgovernments of group-agency-committee ties exist in scores of other policy areas.

Hyperpluralists' major criticism of the interest group system is that relations between groups and the government have become too cozy. Hard choices about national policy are rarely made. Instead of making choices between X and Y, the government pretends there is no need to choose and instead tries to favor both policies. It is a perfect script for policy gridlock. In short, the hyperpluralist position on group politics is characterized as follows:

- Groups have become too powerful in the political process as government tries to appease every conceivable interest.
- Interest group liberalism is aggravated by numerous subgovernments—comfortable relationships among a government agency, the interest group it deals with, and congressional subcommittees.
- Trying to please every group results in contradictory and confusing policy.

Ironically, the recent interest group explosion is seen by some scholars as weakening the power of subgovernments. As Morris Fiorina writes, "A world of active public interest groups, jealous business competitors, and packs of budding investigative reporters is less hospitable to subgovernment politics than a world lacking in them."[7] With so many more interest groups to satisfy, and with many of them competing against one another, a cozy relationship between groups and the government is plainly more difficult to sustain.

WHAT MAKES AN INTEREST GROUP SUCCESSFUL?

In recent years, *Fortune* magazine has issued a yearly list of the 25 most powerful interest groups in politics. Table 11.1 displays one of their lists and a quick look will probably reveal some surprises. Some of these powerful lobbying groups are relatively unknown.

Many factors affect the success of an interest group, as indicated by the diversity of groups in *Fortune's* "Power 25." Among these factors are the size of the group, its intensity, and its financial resources. While greater intensity and more financial resources work to a group's advantage, surprisingly, smaller groups are more likely to achieve their goals than larger groups.

TABLE 11.1

The Power 25

Fortune magazine has long been famous for its lists of the richest companies and individuals in the country. Lately, editors have expanded their analysis to ranking the most powerful lobbying associations. Members of Congress, prominent congressional staffers, senior White House aides, and top-ranking officers of the largest lobbying groups in Washington were asked to assess, on a scale of 0 to 100, the political clout of 87 major trade associations, labor unions, and interest groups. Here is the list of the groups that finished in the top 25 in terms of political clout in 2001.

1.	National Rifle Association	14.	National Education Association
2.	American Association of Retired Persons	15.	American Farm Bureau Federation
3.	National Federation of Independent Business	16.	Motion Picture Association of America
4.	American Israel Public Affairs Committee	17.	National Association of Broadcasters
5.	Association of Trial Lawyers of America	18.	National Right to Life Committee
6.	AFL-CIO	19.	Health Insurance Association of America
7.	Chamber of Commerce	20.	National Restaurant Association
8.	National Beer Wholesalers Association	21.	National Governors' Association
9.	National Association of Realtors	22.	Recording Industry
10.	National Association of Manufacturers	23.	American Bankers Association
11.	National Association of Homebuilders	24.	Pharmaceutical Research and Manufacturers of America
12.	American Medical Association		
13.	American Hospital Association	25.	International Brotherhood of Teamsters

Source: *Fortune* magazine.

THE SURPRISING INEFFECTIVENESS OF LARGE GROUPS

In one of the most often quoted statements concerning interest groups, E. E. Schattschneider wrote that "pressure politics is essentially the politics of small groups. . . . Pressure tactics are not remarkably successful in mobilizing general interests."[8] There are perfectly good reasons why consumer groups are less effective than producer groups, patients are less effective than doctors, and energy conservationists are less effective than oil companies: Small groups have organizational advantages over large groups.

To shed light on this point, it is important to distinguish between a potential and an actual group. A **potential group** is composed of all people who might be group members because they share some common interest.[9] In contrast, an **actual group** is composed of those in the potential group who choose to join. Groups vary enormously in the degree to which they enroll their potential membership. Consumer organizations are minuscule when compared with the total number of consumers, which is almost every American. Some organizations, however, do very well in organizing virtually all their potential members. The National Beer Wholesalers Association (ranked number 8 in Table 11.1), the Tobacco Institute, and the Air Transport Association include a good portion of their potential members. Compared with consumers, these groups are tightly organized.

potential group

All the people who might be **interest group** members because they share some common interest. A potential group is almost always larger than an actual group.

actual group

That part of the **potential group** consisting of members who actually join.

collective good

Something of value (money, a tax write-off, prestige, clean air, and so on) that cannot be withheld from a group member.

free-rider problem

The problem faced by unions and other groups when people do not join because they can benefit from the group's activities without officially joining. The bigger the group, the more serious the problem.

Olson's law of large groups

Advanced by Mancur Olson, a principle stating that "the larger the group, the further it will fall short of providing an optimal amount of a collective good."

selective benefits

Goods (such as information publications, travel discounts, and group insurance rates) that a group can restrict to those who pay their annual dues.

Economist Mancur Olson explains this phenomenon in *The Logic of Collective Action*.[10] Olson points out that all groups, unlike individuals, are in the business of providing collective goods. A **collective good** is something of value, such as clean air, that cannot be withheld from a potential group member. When the AFL-CIO wins a higher minimum wage, all low-paid workers benefit, regardless of whether they are members of the union. In other words, members of the potential group share in benefits that members of the actual group work to secure. If this is the case, an obvious and difficult problem results: Why should potential members work for something if they can get it free? Why join the group, pay dues, and work hard for a goal when a person can benefit from the group's activity without doing anything at all? A perfectly rational response is thus to sit back and let other people do the work. This is commonly known as the **free-rider problem**.

The bigger the group, the more serious the free-rider problem. That is the gist of **Olson's law of large groups**: "The larger the group, the further it will fall short of providing an optimal amount of a collective good."[11] Small groups thus have an organizational advantage over large ones. In a small group, members' shares of the collective good may be great enough that they will try to secure it. The old saying that "everyone can make a difference" is much more credible in the case of a relatively small group. In the largest groups, however, each member can expect to get only a tiny share of the policy gains. Weighing the costs of participation against the relatively small benefits, the temptation is always to "let somebody else do it." Therefore, as Olson argues, the larger the potential group, the less likely potential members are to contribute.

This distinct advantage of small groups helps explain why consumer groups have a hard time making ends meet. Such groups claim to seek "public interest" goals, but the gains they win are usually spread thin over millions of people. In contrast, the lobbying costs and benefits for business are concentrated. Suppose, for example, that consumer advocates take the airlines to court over charges of price fixing and force the airlines to return $10 million to consumers in the form of lower prices. This $10 million settlement is spread over 300 million Americans—about 4 cents per person (actually, the benefit is a little higher if one divides only by the number of people who use airlines). The $10 million airline loss is shared by 60 carriers at over $165,000 apiece. One can quickly see which side will be better organized in such a struggle.

In sum, Olson's law of large groups explains why interest groups with relatively few members are often so effective. The power of business in the American political system is thus due to more than just money as proponents of elite theory would have us believe. Besides their financial strength, wealthy corporations also enjoy an inherent size advantage. Because there are a limited number of multinational corporations, these businesses have an easier time organizing themselves for political action than larger potential groups, such as consumers. Once well organized, large groups may be very effective, but it is much harder for them to get together in the first place.

The primary way for large potential groups to overcome Olson's law is to provide attractive benefits for only those who join the organization. **Selective benefits** are goods that a group can restrict to those who pay their yearly dues, such as information publications, travel discounts, and group insurance rates. The number 2 rated group in Fortune's "Power 25"—the American Association of Retired Persons—has built up a membership list of 35 million senior citizens by offering a variety of selective benefits (see Figure 11.2). Similarly, Consumers Union gains most of its members not because of its efforts on behalf of product safety but by offering the selective benefit of receiving *Consumer Reports*, a monthly magazine that rates the reliability, safety, and cost effectiveness of products.

FIGURE 11.2

The Benefits of Membership in the American Association of Retired Persons

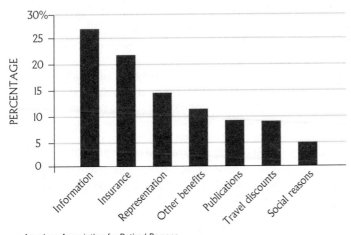

This chart illustrates the answers given by a sample of members of the American Association of Retired Persons when they were asked why they had joined the organization.

Source: American Association for Retired Persons.

INTENSITY

Another way a large potential group may be mobilized is through an issue that people feel intensely about. Intensity is a psychological advantage that can be enjoyed by small and large groups alike. When a group shows that it cares deeply about an issue, politicians are more likely to listen; many votes may be won or lost on a single issue. The rise of single-issue groups (discussed in Chapter 1) has been one of the most dramatic political developments in recent years. Even college students have gotten into the act, forming groups to lobby against tuition increases in recent years, as you can read about in "Young People and Politics: The Virginia 21 Coalition."

A **single-issue group** can be defined as a group that has a narrow interest, dislikes compromise, and single-mindedly pursues its goal. Anti–Vietnam War activists may have formed the first modern single-issue group. Opponents of nuclear power plants, gun control (ranked number 1 in "The Power 25"), and

single-issue groups
Groups that have a narrow interest, tend to dislike compromise, and often draw membership from people new to politics. These features distinguish them from traditional **interest groups**.

LITMUS TEST

YOUNG PEOPLE AND POLITICS

The Virginia 21 Coalition

As budget crunches have hit most states in recent years, many state legislatures have cut back on funding for higher education and approved sharp increases in tuition at public colleges and universities. In response, college students in some states have started to form interest groups to fight for more state subsidies for higher education and for limiting tuition increases. In Virginia, a group called the "21st Century Virginia Coalition," or simply "Virginia 21" for short, has recently had some success in getting the state's politicians to listen to the opinions of college students regarding funding for higher education.

Virginia 21 first entered the political scene with a campaign to garner support for a bond referendum on the 2002 Virginia ballot to provide over $900 million to state universities for capital improvements. The group raised over $17,000 to support the campaign, made roughly 20,000 telephone calls to round up votes for it, and aired a student-written and student-produced radio commercial on behalf of the referendum, which passed with overwhelming support.

One of the organization's priorities was to push for a 1 cent increase in the state's sales tax that would be dedicated to increasing funds available for education. The organization collected over 10,000 signatures for a petition titled "Fund Virginia's Future" and presented them to the state legislature. But they grabbed more attention when they dropped off over 200,000 pennies at the office of the state treasurer in support of the proposed 1 cent increase in the sales tax. The pennies weighed approximately three-quarters of a ton, and the gesture was designed to show that college students care "a ton" about the funding of higher education. The local media could hardly ignore such a gripping visual image.

In 2006, Virginia 21 successfully lobbied the state legislature to pass a bill designed to cut the costs of textbooks for students in Virginia colleges. The measure required public universities to come up with guidelines mandating that professors acknowledge that they are aware of the exact costs of the books they assign, and to specify whether supplements sold with these books are actually required.

Virginia 21 is committed to lobbying the state legislature to substantially increase funds for higher education. It may or may not succeed in this goal, but it does seem destined to at least make sure that the views of college students are heard by policymakers. As of 2006, the Coalition had 22,000 members.

QUESTIONS FOR DISCUSSION

▶ Would you give money and/or volunteer for a group in your state like Virginia 21? Why or why not?

▶ Which of the strategies of interest group lobbying discussed in this chapter do you think would be most effective for a group like Virginia 21?

Source: www.virginia21.org.

abortion are some of the many such groups that exist today. All these groups deal with issues that evoke the strong emotions characteristic of single-interest groups.

Perhaps the most emotional issue of recent times has been that of abortion. As befits the intensity of the issue, activities have not been limited to conventional means of political participation. Protesting—often in the form of blocking entrances to abortion clinics—has now become a common practice for antiabortion activists. Pro-choice activists have organized as well, especially in the wake of the 1989 *Webster v. Reproductive Health Services* case, which allowed states greater freedom to restrict abortions. Both groups' positions are clear, not subject to compromise, and influence their vote. Regardless of which side candidates for political office are on, they will be taking heat on the abortion issue for years to come.

FINANCIAL RESOURCES

One of the major indictments of the American interest group system is that it is biased toward the wealthy. When he was the majority leader in the Senate, Bob Dole once remarked that he had never been approached by a Poor People's political action committee. There is no doubt that money talks in the American political system, and those who have it get heard. All groups listed in Table 11.1 spend over a million dollars a year on lobbying and campaign contributions. A big campaign contribution may ensure a phone call, a meeting, or even a favorable vote or action on a particular policy. When Lincoln Savings and Loan Chair Charles Keating was asked whether the $1.3 million he had funneled into the campaigns of five U.S.

senators had anything to do with these senators later meeting with federal regulators on his behalf, he candidly responded, "I certainly hope so."

It is important to emphasize, however, that even on some of the most important issues, the big interests do not always win. An excellent example of this is the historic Tax Reform Act of 1986. In *Showdown at Gucci Gulch,* two reporters from the *Wall Street Journal* chronicle the improbable victory of sweeping tax reform.[12] In this case, a large group of well-organized, highly paid (and Gucci-clad) lobbyists were unable to preserve many of their most prized tax loopholes. One of the heroes of the book, former Senator Robert Packwood of Oregon, was Congress's top political action committee recipient during the tax reform struggle; he had raked in $992,000 for his reelection campaign. As chair of the Senate Finance Committee, however, Packwood ultimately turned against the hordes of lobbyists trying to get his ear on behalf of various loopholes. The only way to deal with the tax loophole problem, he concluded, was to go virtually cold turkey by eliminating all but a very few. "There is special interest after special interest that is hit in this bill," Packwood gloated, pointing out that many of them contributed to his campaign. In the end, passage of the reform bill offered "encouraging proof that moneyed interests could not always buy their way to success in Congress."[13]

THE INTEREST GROUP EXPLOSION

The number of interest groups in the United States has been increasing rapidly over the past several decades. Although no one has ever compiled a *Who's Who* of interest groups, the closest thing is the annual *Encyclopedia of Associations.*[14] Between 1959 and 2007, the number of groups listed in the *Encyclopedia* skyrocketed from about 6,000 to 22,000.[15] As you can see in Figure 11.3, the increase in the number

FIGURE 11.3

Associations by Type

The following two pie charts illustrate how the interest group world has become more diverse since the late 1950s.

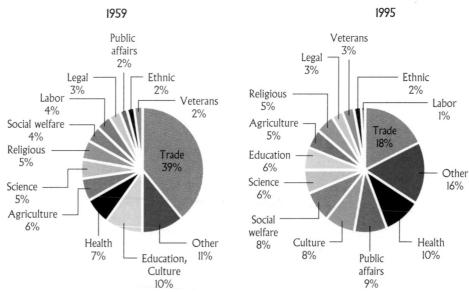

Source: Data from Frank R. Baumgartner and Beth L. Leech, *Basic Interests: The Importance of Groups in Politics and in Political Science* (Princeton, NJ: Princeton University Press, 1998), 109.

of groups reflects a growing diversity in the interest group universe. Whereas trade groups clearly dominated the picture in 1959, this is no longer the case.

It seems that there is now an organized group for every conceivable interest. Jack Walker studied 564 groups listed in the *Washington Information Directory* and tried to trace their origins and expansion.[16] He found that 80 percent of the groups originated from occupational, industrial, or professional memberships. Interestingly, half the groups he studied were established after World War II. Walker also found a gravitation of groups to Washington, D.C. In 1960, only 66 percent of the groups in his study were headquartered in the nation's capital; today, over 90 percent are located there. Very few occupations or industries now go without an organized group to represent them in Washington. Even lobbyists themselves now have lobbies to represent their profession, such as the American League of Lobbyists.

There are many reasons for this explosion in the number of interest groups. Certainly one of the major factors has been the development of sophisticated technology. Andrew McFarland observes,

> Technological innovations have made the coordination of constituents' activities and efforts of lobbyists much easier. Many lobbyists, for example, have available computerized lists of names and phone numbers of group members that can be easily arranged by congressional district or state. Address labels can be printed automatically or members can be called by WATS line from a group's headquarters.[17]

Technology has also made it easier for groups back on Main Street to make their voices immediately heard in Washington. A well-organized interest group can deluge members of Congress with tens of thousands of faxes and e-mail messages in a matter of hours. Technology did not create interest group politics, but it has surely made the process much easier.

HOW GROUPS TRY TO SHAPE POLICY

No interest group has enough staff, money, or time to do everything possible to achieve its policy goals. Interest groups must therefore choose from a variety of tactics. The four basic strategies are lobbying, electioneering, litigation, and appealing to the public.

LOBBYING

lobbying
According to Lester Milbrath, a "communication, by someone other than a citizen acting on his own behalf, directed to a governmental decision maker with the hope of influencing his decision."

The term **lobbying** comes from the place where petitioners used to collar legislators. In the early years of politics in Washington, members of Congress had no offices and typically stayed in boardinghouses or hotels while Congress was in session. A person could not call them up on the phone or make an appointment with their secretary; the only sure way of getting in touch with a member of Congress was to wait in the lobby where he was staying to catch him either coming in or going out. These people were dubbed *lobbyists* because they spent so much of their time waiting in lobbies.

Of course, merely loitering in a lobby does not make one a lobbyist; there must be a particular reason for such action. Lester Milbrath has offered a more precise definition of the practice. He writes that lobbying is a "communication, by someone other than a citizen acting on his or her own behalf, directed to a governmental decision maker with the hope of influencing his or her decision."[18] Lobbyists, in other words, are political persuaders who represent organized groups. They usually work in Washington, handling groups' legislative business. They are often former legislators themselves. Over 40 percent of members of Congress who retired between 1998 and

2004 registered as lobbyists, according to a study by Public Citizen's Congress Watch—many of them earning sums they only could have dreamed of as lawmakers.[19]

There are two basic types of lobbyists. Members of the first type are regular, paid employees of a corporation, union, or association. They may hold a title such as vice president for government relations, but everyone knows that their office is in Washington for a reason, even if the company headquarters is in Houston. Members of the second type are available for hire on a temporary basis. One group may be too small to afford a full-time lobbyist; another may have a unique, but temporary, need for access to Congress or the executive branch.

The Lobbying Disclosure Act of 1995 established criteria for determining whether an organization or firm should register their employees as lobbyists. Those who fit the criteria must register with the Secretary of the U.S. Senate and file a report regarding each of their clients and how much they were paid by them for lobbying services. This information is made public by the Senate's Office of Public Records, and combing through about 20,000 disclosure forms per year has become a substantial business in itself. The 2008 edition of *Washington Representatives,* a $400 reference book on participants in the federal lobbying process, advertised that it provided "detailed access to over 18,000 government relations professionals, 7,500 firms, and their 12,000 clients."[20] Since 1998, The Center for Responsive Politics has been categorizing lobbying expenses according to the type of industry. In Figure 11.4, you can see the enormous amounts that the top spenders doled out for lobbying over the course of a decade.

Although lobbyists are primarily out to influence members of Congress, it is important to remember that they can be of help to them as well. Ornstein and Elder list four important ways in which lobbyists can help a member of Congress.[21]

* *They are an important source of information.* Members of Congress have to concern themselves with many policy areas; lobbyists can confine themselves to only one area and can thus provide specialized expertise. If information is power, then lobbyists can often be potent allies.

You Are a Lobbyist

FIGURE 11.4

The Big Spenders on Lobbying, 1998–2007

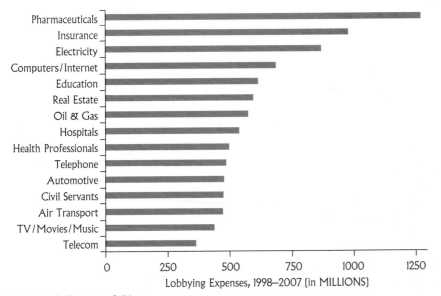

Lobbying Expenses, 1998–2007 (in MILLIONS)

This graph presents the total amount spent on lobbying by these industries from 1998 to 2007. Keep in mind that the data are presented in terms of the number of millions spent. The fact that the pharmaceutical industry spent over $1,000 million on lobbying therefore means that they spent over a billion dollars. All told, just these 15 industries spent $9.4 billion on lobbying during these 10 years.

Source: Center for Responsive Politics.

- *They can help politicians with political strategy for getting legislation through.* Lobbyists are politically savvy people, and they can be useful consultants. When Leon Panetta served as White House chief of staff in the Clinton administration, he regularly convened a small group of Washington lobbyists to discuss how the administration should present its proposals.[22]

- *They can help formulate campaign strategy and get the group's members behind a politician's reelection campaign.* Labor union leaders, for example, often provide help in how to appeal to typical working people, and they often provide volunteers to help out in campaigns as well.

- *They are a source of ideas and innovations.* Lobbyists cannot introduce bills, but they can peddle their ideas to politicians eager to attach their name to an idea that will bring them political credit.

Like anything else, lobbying can be done crudely or gracefully. Lobbyists can sometimes be heavy-handed. They can threaten or cajole a legislator, implying that electoral defeat is a certain result of not "going along." They can even make it clear that money flows to the reelection coffers of those who cooperate. It is often difficult to tell the difference between lobbying as a shady business and lobbying as a strictly professional representation of legitimate interests.

Gun Rights and Gun Control

High-priced lobbyists are often compared to the airline mechanic who is called in to fix the plane, turns just one screw and submits a bill for a thousand dollars. Asked to justify such a huge fee for such a little bit of work, the mechanic says, "Well it's $10 for turning the screw, and $990 for knowing which screw to turn." Similarly, the skilled lobbyist is paid for knowing who to contact and with what information. A recent in-depth study of lobbyists and their work by Rogan Kersh concludes that their success depends largely on their ability to deploy information strategically on behalf of their clients. As Kersh writes, "Searching for, analyzing, and presenting information compose the central activity in most lobbyists' daily work."[23] As Richard Hall and Alan Deardorff have recently argued, lobbying can often be viewed as a form of "legislative subsidy," which they define as a "matching grant of costly policy information, political intelligence, and labor to the enterprises of strategically selected legislators."[24] They argue that the purpose of such a strategy is not to change anyone's mind but rather to help one's political allies.

Other evidence, however, suggests that sometimes lobbying can persuade legislators to support a certain policy.[25] The National Rifle Association, which for years kept major gun control policies off the congressional agenda, has long been one of Washington's most effective lobbying groups.[26] In a more specific example, intensive lobbying by the nation's most wealthy senior citizens—enraged by the tax burden imposed on them by the Catastrophic Health Care Act—led Congress to repeal the act only a year after it was passed in the late 1980s.

Nailing down the specific effects of lobbying is difficult, partly because it is difficult to isolate its effects from other influences. Lobbying clearly works best on people already committed to the lobbyist's policy position. Thus, like campaigning, lobbying is directed toward primarily activating and reinforcing supporters. For example, antiabortion lobbyists would not think of approaching California's

For years, the National Rifle Association has successfully lobbied against gun control measures, arguing that the Second Amendment to the Constitution guarantees all citizens the right to bear arms. The late Charlton Heston was a prominent member of the group and served for a time as its president.

Barbara Boxer to attempt to convert her to their position, because Boxer clearly supports the pro-choice movement. If Senator Boxer is lobbied by anyone on the abortion issue, it will be by the pro-choice faction, urging her not to compromise with the opposition.

ELECTIONEERING

Because lobbying works best with those already on the same side, getting the right people into office and keeping them there is also a key strategy of interest groups. Many groups therefore get involved in **electioneering**—aiding candidates financially and getting group members out to support them. Pressure group involvement in campaigns is nothing new. In the election of 1896 (see Chapter 10), silver-mining interests poured millions into the losing presidential campaign of William Jennings Bryan, who advocated unlimited coinage of silver.

Political action committees (PACs) provide a means for groups to participate in electioneering. The number of PACs has exploded from 608 in 1974 to 4,210 in 2006, according to the Federal Election Commission. No major interest group seeking to exert influence on the political process these days can pass up the opportunity to funnel money honestly and openly into the campaign coffers of its supporters. For example, Major League Baseball's PAC gave $178,000 to congressional candidates and the major parties during the 2006 election cycle,[27] mostly to members of congressional committees who were considering legislation that might impact the business of baseball. As economist Roger Noll of Stanford University remarked about the activity of baseball's PAC, "Any industry that has any kind of dependence on government is pretty much forced to do what they're doing," he said. "Unfortunately, this has become the cost of doing business."[28]

As campaign costs have risen, PACs have come along to help pay the bill. In recent years, nearly half the candidates running for reelection to the House of Representatives have received the majority of their campaign funds from PACs. Furthermore, their challengers did not enjoy this advantage. PACs gave a whopping $279 million to House incumbents during the 2006 election cycle, compared to a mere $36 million to the challengers.[29] Why does PAC money go so overwhelmingly

electioneering
Direct group involvement in the electoral process. Groups can help fund campaigns, provide testimony, and get members to work for candidates, and some form **political action committees.**

political action committees (PACs)
Political funding vehicles created by the 1974 campaign finance reforms. A corporation, union, or some other interest group can create a political action committee (PAC) and register it with the **Federal Election Commission,** which will meticulously monitor the PAC's expenditures.

? Why It Matters
PACs

The great increase in the number of PACs over the past several decades has enabled far more groups to become involved in electioneering. If more participation is always desirable, then the increase of PACs has to be considered a positive development. But given that only groups that can successfully organize and raise substantial sums of money can take advantage of the PAC system, some obvious biases have been introduced to the electoral process because of the increased importance of PACs.

to incumbents? The answer is that PAC contributions are basically investments for the future, and incumbents are the most likely to return the investment. When R. Kenneth Godwin and Barry J. Seldon asked a sample of PAC directors to explain why their PACs gave money to certain candidates, the top five answers were that these candidates were (1) on committees that are important to their interests, (2) very supportive of issues important to them, (3) from a district or state where they had facilities, (4) helping them with executive and regulatory agencies, and (5) in leadership positions that enabled them to influence issues that affect the PAC.[30]

Only a handful of serious congressional candidates have resisted the lure of PAC money in recent years. One candidate described his experiences trying to get on the PAC bandwagon. When Democrat Steve Sovern ran for the House from Iowa's Second District, he made the now common pilgrimage to Washington to meet with potential contributors. "I found myself in line with candidates from all over," he reported. Each PAC had eager candidates fill out a multiple-choice questionnaire on issues important to the PAC. Candidates who shared the same concerns and views and who looked like winners got the money. Sovern later reported that "the process made me sick." After his defeat, he organized his own PAC called LASTPAC (for Let the American System Triumph), which urged candidates to shun PAC campaign contributions.[31] There have been serious calls to do away with PACs altogether, as discussed in "You Are the Policymaker: Should PACs Be Eliminated?"

YOU ARE THE Policymaker

Should PACs Be Eliminated?

The effect of PAC campaign contributions on congressional votes has become a perennial issue in American politics. Critics of PACs are convinced that they are distorting the democratic process and corrupting our political system in favor of those who can raise the most money. Many politicians freely admit—once they are out of office—that it is a myth to think that the PACs don't want something in return. They may only want to be remembered on one or two crucial votes or with an occasional intervention with government agencies, but multiply this by the thousands of special interests that are organized today and the worst fears of the hyperpluralists could be realized—a government that constantly yields to every special interest.

Common Cause (www.commoncause.org) has made it its primary mission to expose what it sees as the evils of the PAC system. It argues that the influence of corporate PACs on Capitol Hill has led to "corporate welfare" and costs taxpayers billions of dollars. For example, Common Cause asserts that $5 million in PAC contributions from the broadcast industry led to a massive government giveaway of free digital TV licenses worth as much as $70 billion. Similarly, it maintains that the Bush administration's decision to eliminate the roadless rule, which protected 1.9 million acres of federal forests in Oregon from logging, was a clear payback for PAC contributions by the timber industry. And Common Cause and others have attributed the failure of Congress to further regulate tobacco and cigarette advertising to the more than $35 million of PAC contributions from tobacco companies over the past decade.

However, others argue that connection is not causation. They believe that most members of Congress are not affected by PAC contributions, which come largely from groups they already agree with anyway. Defenders of the PAC system also point out that the PAC system further increases participation in the political process. As opposed to individual donations, PACs—which represent groups of people—allow better representation of occupational groups. The PAC system allows people with common professional interests, such as farmers, lawyers, dentists, and college professors, to express their support of candidates jointly through political contributions.

Similarly, corporation PACs represent the interests of many stockholders and employees with common political interests. If James Madison's notion that the key to controlling the power of interest groups is to expand their sphere of participation, then PACs certainly do this according to their defenders. Beyond this, the money for today's expensive media campaigns has to come from somewhere. Those who wish to maintain the PAC system typically argue that the alternative of the government providing campaign funds is impractical given that only about one in ten taxpayers participates in the $3 voluntary income tax check-off system for financing federal campaigns (see Chapter 9).

You Be the Policymaker: What would you do? Would you consider eliminating PACs? Or, as a middle course, would you favor further limits on the amount of money they can donate? Or, would you prefer just to leave things as they are at present?

In addition to their role in financing campaigns, interest groups also participate in elections in numerous other ways. Among these are recruiting interest groups members to run as candidates for office, issuing official group endorsements, providing volunteer labor to participate in campaign work, and sending delegates to state and national party conventions to try to influence party platforms.

LITIGATION

If interest groups fail in Congress or get only a vague piece of legislation, the next step is to go to court in the hope of getting specific rulings. Karen Orren has linked much of the success of environmental interest groups to their use of lawsuits. "Frustrated in Congress," she wrote, "they have made an end run to the courts, where they have skillfully exploited and magnified limited legislative gains."[32]

Environmental legislation, such as the Clean Air Act, typically includes written provisions allowing ordinary citizens to sue for enforcement. As a result, every federal agency involved in environmental regulation now has hundreds of suits pending against it at any given time. These suits may not halt environmentally troublesome practices, but the constant threat of a lawsuit increases the likelihood that businesses will consider the environmental impact of what they do.

Perhaps the most famous interest group victories in court were by civil rights groups in the 1950s. While civil rights bills remained stalled in Congress, these groups won major victories in court cases concerning school desegregation, equal housing, and labor market equality. More recently, consumer groups have used suits against businesses and federal agencies as a means of enforcing consumer regulations. As long as law schools keep producing lawyers, groups will fight for their interests in court.

One tactic that lawyers employ to make the views of interest groups heard by the judiciary is the filing of **amicus curiae briefs** ("friend of the court" briefs). *Amicus* briefs consist of written arguments submitted to the courts in support of one side of a case. Through these written depositions, a group states its collective position as well as how its own welfare will be affected by the outcome of the case. Numerous groups may file *amicus* briefs in highly publicized and emotionally charged cases. For example, in the case of *Regents of the University of California v. Bakke* (see Chapter 5), which challenged affirmative action programs as reverse discrimination, over 100 different groups filed *amicus* briefs. A study of participation in *amicus* briefs by Caldeira and Wright found that the Supreme Court has been accessible to a wide array of organized interests, in terms of deciding both which cases to hear and how to rule.[33]

A more direct judicial strategy employed by interest groups is the filing of **class action lawsuits**, which enable a group of people in a similar situation to combine their common grievances into a single suit. For instance, in 1977 flight attendants won a class action suit against the airline industry's regulation that all stewardesses be unmarried. As one lawyer who specializes in such cases states, "The class action is the greatest, most effective legal engine to remedy mass wrongs."[34]

GOING PUBLIC

Groups are also interested in the opinions of the public. Because public opinion ultimately makes its way to policymakers, interest groups carefully cultivate their public image and use public opinion to their advantage when they can. As Ken Kollman finds, even the wealthiest and most powerful groups in America appeal to public opinion to help their cause. For example, when the government instituted a requirement for tax-withholding on savings accounts, the American Bankers Association appealed to their customers to protest this to their congressional representatives. After 22 million postcards flooded into Congress, lawmakers quickly reversed the policy.[35]

Interest groups market not only their stand on issues but also their reputations. Business interests want people to see them as "what made America great," not as

Federal Election Rules, PACs, and the Money Trail

amicus curiae briefs
Legal briefs submitted by a "friend of the court" for the purpose of raising additional points of view and presenting information not contained in the briefs of the formal parties. These briefs attempt to influence a court's decision.

class action suits
Lawsuits permitting a small number of people to sue on behalf of all other people similarly situated.

Paid for by the Coalition to Scare Your Pants Off

Interest groups spent over $100 million appealing to public opinion during the debate over health care in 1994. In a counter-ad produced by the Democratic National Committee, the argument was made that opponents of the Clinton health care plan were using scare tactics. You can see the tag end of the ad in this photo.

wealthy Americans trying to ensure large profits. The Teamsters Union likes to be known as a united organization of hardworking men and women, not as an organization that has in the past been influenced by organized crime. Farmers promote the image of a sturdy family working to put bread on the table, not the huge agribusinesses that have largely replaced family farms. In this way, many groups try to create a reservoir of goodwill with the public.

Interest groups' appeals to the public for support have a long tradition in American politics. In 1908, AT&T launched a major magazine advertising campaign to convince people of the need for a telephone monopoly. Similarly, after President Truman proposed a system of national health insurance in 1948, the American Medical Association spent millions of dollars on ads attacking "socialized medicine." In 1994, the Health Insurance Association of America ran a $15 million nationally televised ad campaign criticizing President Clinton's health care package that many analysts believe lessened public support for the reform bill. So many groups placed advertisements regarding the Clinton health care reform package and so much money was spent (over $100 million) that many observers compared this activity to a national electoral campaign.

Lately, more and more organizations have undertaken expensive public relations (PR) efforts. After September 11, the media was full of ads from various groups expressing their sympathy for the victims. Some other recent examples include Phillip Morris running ads countering the arguments of antitobacco legislation, Microsoft condemning its prosecution by the Justice Department for alleged monopolistic practices, and Ford and Bridgestone defending themselves against charges of negligence regarding defective tires. Mobil Oil has long run a visible corporate PR effort to influence the public with its regular editorial-style ads in the *New York Times* and other major publications. These ads typically address issues that affect the oil industry and big business in general. Once Mobil even ran an ad titled "Why Do We Buy This Space?" It answered "that business needs voices in the media, the same way labor unions, consumers, and other groups in our society do."[36] No one knows just how effective these image-molding efforts are, but many groups seem to believe firmly that advertising pays off.

TYPES OF INTEREST GROUPS

You Are the Leader of Concerned Citizens for World Justice

Whether they are lobbying, electioneering, litigating, or appealing to the public, interest groups are omnipresent in the American political system. As with other aspects of American politics and policymaking, political scientists loosely categorize interest groups into clusters. Among the most important clusters are those that deal with (1) economic issues, (2) environmental concerns, (3) equality issues, and (4) the interests of all consumers. An examination of these four distinct types of interest groups will give you a good picture of much of the American interest group system.

ECONOMIC INTERESTS

All economic interests are ultimately concerned with wages, prices, and profits. In the American economy, government does not determine these directly. Only on rare occasions has the government imposed wage and price controls. This has usually been during wartime, although the Nixon administration briefly used wage and price controls to combat inflation. More commonly, public policy in America has economic effects through regulations, tax advantages, subsidies and contracts, and international trade policy.

Business, labor, and farmers all fret over the impact of government regulations. Even a minor change in government regulatory policy can cost industries a great deal or bring increased profits. Tax policies also affect the livelihood of individuals and firms. How the tax code is written determines whether people and producers pay a lot or a little of their incomes to the government. Because government often provides subsidies to farmers, small businesses, railroads, minority businesses, and others, every economic group wants to get its share of direct aid and government contracts. In this era of economic global interdependence, all groups worry about import quotas, tariffs (fees imposed on imports), and the soundness of the American dollar. In short, business executives, factory workers, and farmers seek to influence government because regulations, taxes, subsidies, and international economic policy all affect their economic livelihoods. The following sections discuss some of the major organized interests and their impact on economic policy.

Labor   Labor has more affiliated members than any other interest group except the American Association for Retired Persons. About 10 million workers are members of unions belonging to the AFL-CIO—itself a union of unions. Millions of other workers belong to unions, such as the National Education Association, the Teamsters, and the Service Employees International Union, that are not affiliated with the AFL-CIO but share common interests with them.

The major aim of American union organizations, like labor unions everywhere, is to press for policies to ensure better working conditions and higher wages. Recognizing that many workers would like to enjoy union benefits without actually joining a union and paying dues, unions have fought hard to establish the **union shop**, which requires new employees to join the union representing them. In contrast, business groups have supported **right-to-work laws**, which outlaw union membership as a condition of employment. They argue that such laws deny a basic freedom—namely, the right not to belong to a group. In 1947, the biggest blow ever to the American labor movement occurred when Congress passed the Taft-Hartley Act, permitting states to adopt right-to-work laws (known as "slave labor laws" within the AFL-CIO). Most of the states that have right-to-work laws are in the South, which traditionally has had the lowest percentage of unionized workers, as you can see in "My State: Labor Union Membership as a Percentage of State Workforces."

The American labor movement reached its peak in 1956, when 33 percent of the nonagricultural workforce belonged to a union; since then, the percentage has declined to about 13 percent. One factor behind this decline is that low wages in other countries have diminished the American job market in a number of key manufacturing areas. Steel, an industry once dominated by U.S. manufacturers, now has to compete with imports from foreign producers based in Brazil, Korea, and other fast-developing economies. The United Auto Workers has found its clout greatly reduced as Detroit has faced heavy competition from Japanese automakers. Some political scientists, however, believe labor's problems result from more than the

union shop

A provision found in some collective bargaining agreements requiring all employees of a business to join the union within a short period, usually 30 days, and to remain members as a condition of employment.

right-to-work laws

A state law forbidding requirements that workers must join a union to hold their jobs. State right-to-work laws were specifically permitted by the Taft-Hartley Act of 1947.

Strikes are among labor unions' most powerful weapons. This strike by the Writers Guild of America attracted a great deal of public attention and shut down the production of many TV shows for months. The new contract the writers agreed to gave them residual payments for shows streamed over the Internet, and secured the union's jurisdiction for programming created for the Web.

MyState | Labor Union Membership as a Percentage of State Workforces

The map below classifies the 50 states according to the percentage of their non-agricultural workers who were members of a labor union in 2006.

QUESTIONS FOR DISCUSSION

▷ How does your state rank in terms of the prevalence of labor union membership in its workforce? Why does your state rank as it does in terms of joining labor unions?

▷ What types of labor unions, if any, are particularly prominent in your state? Have these labor unions influenced the nature of politics in your state? If so, how?

▷ Do you think it would best for your state if labor union membership were increased, stayed about the same, or decreased over the next decade? Why?

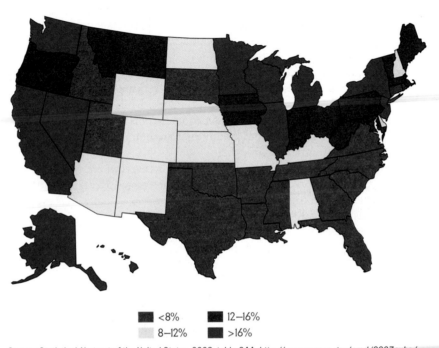

■ <8%   ■ 12–16%
░ 8–12%   ■ >16%

Source: *Statistical Abstract of the United States, 2008*, table 644, *http://www.census.gov/prod/2007pubs/ 08abstract/labor.pdf.*

decline of blue-collar industries. Paul Johnson argues that the biggest factor causing the decline in union membership is the problems unions have had in convincing today's workers that they will benefit from unionization. In particular, Johnson argues that this task has become more difficult in recent years because of employers' efforts to make nonunion jobs satisfying.[37]

Whatever the reason, it is clear that labor unions' ability to shape public policy has decreased. Labor is still a major Democratic constituency, and it surely preferred Bill Clinton to George W. Bush on many issues, such as raising the minimum wage. But the Clinton agenda and labor's agenda were hardly one and the same. Organized labor could not expect to be protected from policies that may have cost their members jobs when the Democrats were in office. In particular, labor found themselves battling in vain to stop trade agreements negotiated by Bill Clinton.

Business   If the elite theorists are correct, however, and there is an American power elite, it certainly must be dominated by leaders of the biggest banks, insurance companies, and multinational corporations. Elitists' views may or may not be

A GENERATION OF CHANGE

How Non-Labor PACs Shifted to the GOP

Despite the tax-cutting and deregulatory agenda advocated by Ronald Reagan and the Republican Party in the 1980s, throughout this era business and trade association PACs gave slightly more campaign contributions to Democratic than Republican candidates for the House of Representatives. The major reason for this pattern was that the Democrats had long held the majority in the House and therefore held the balance of power on the committees through which any pro-business legislation would have to pass. Many political analysts at the time argued that business groups gave money to the Republicans because they wanted to and the Democrats because they had to (in order to curry favor with the party in power).

This situation changed markedly when the Republicans became the majority party in both the House and Senate, starting in 1995. The Republican leadership in Congress started to actively encourage business interest groups and PACs to hire Republicans as part of what has become known as the "K Street Project." The idea behind this was that if the big lobbying associations on K Street in Washington, D.C., were being run by Republicans, then the contributions would naturally go the GOP's way. As you can see in the adjacent graph, this strategy proved to be a successful one for the Republicans. During the 1996 through 2006 election-year cycles, when the Republicans held the majority in the House, they consistently received roughly two out of every three PAC dollars donated to House campaigns by corporate, trade, and non-connected PACs. Only Labor PACs stuck with the Democrats during this period.

Despite the Republicans' advantage in PAC donations, the Democrats regained control of both Houses of Congress in the 2006 elections. It will be interesting to see if the Republicans can maintain their advantage in PAC donations now that they are again in the minority in Congress. If the "K Street Project" has been truly successful in putting committed Republicans in charge of big lobbying associations, then PAC contributions should continue to be tilted toward the Republicans (though probably by not quite as much as when they were the majority party in Congress).

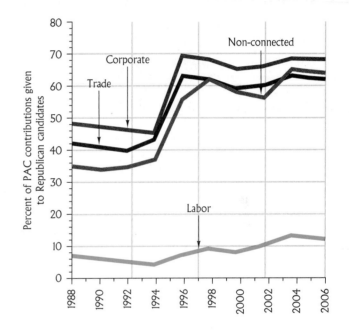

Source: Federal Election Commission.

exaggerated, but business is certainly well organized for political action. Most large corporations now have offices in Washington that monitor legislative activity. And the Chamber of Commerce has become an imposing lobbying force, spending roughly $20 million a year lobbying on behalf of its mission to fulfill "the unified interests of American business." Business PACs have increased more dramatically than any other category of PACs over the past several decades. Furthermore, corporate and trade PAC contributions have shifted dramatically in favor of the Republican Party and its tax-cutting and deregulatory agenda, as you can see in "A Generation of Change: How Non-Labor PACs Shifted to the GOP."

Different business interests compete on many specific issues, however. Both Microsoft and Google have their lobbyists on Capitol Hill pressing their competing interests. Trucking and construction companies want more highways, but railroads do not. An increase in international trade will help some businesses expand their markets, but others may be hurt by foreign competition. Business interests are generally unified when it comes to promoting greater profits but are often fragmented when policy choices have to be made.

Hundreds of trade and product associations fight regulations that would reduce their profits and seek preferential tax treatment as well as government subsidies and

Environmental lobbies have been successful in preventing the building of any new nuclear power plants for the last 30 years. Some of the older nuclear plants are now being destroyed, as you can see in this photo.

contracts. America's complex schedules of tariffs are monuments to the activities of the trade associations. Although they are the least visible of Washington lobbies, their successes are measured in amendments won, regulations rewritten, and exceptions made. It is not only American trade associations that are concerned with these policies, but foreign corporations and governments as well. The practice of foreign economic interests hiring influential former governmental officials to lobby on their behalf has recently led to a number of reform proposals.[38]

ENVIRONMENTAL INTERESTS

Among the newest political interest groups are the environmentalists. A handful, such as the Sierra Club and the Audubon Society, have been around since the nineteenth century, but many others trace their origins to the first Earth Day, April 22, 1970. On that day, ecology-minded people marched on Washington and other places to symbolize their support for environmental protection. Just two decades later, one estimate pegged the number of environmental groups at over 10,000 and their combined revenues at $2.9 billion—demonstrating "how widely and deeply green values had permeated the society."[39] As you can see in

AMERICA IN PERSPECTIVE

Membership in Environmental Groups

Question wording: Are you a member of any group whose main aim is to preserve or protect the environment?

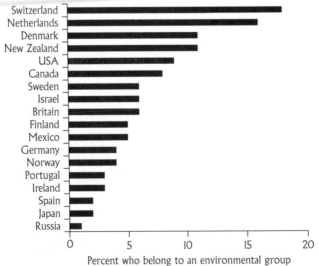

Percent who belong to an environmental group

Source: Authors' analysis of the 2000 International Social Survey Program surveys.

"America in Perspective: Membership in Environmental Groups," the United States ranks very high compared to other democracies in terms of the percentage of the adult population that belongs to a group whose main aim is to protect the environment. Among the environmental groups that can boast of at least a million members in the United States are the World Wildlife Fund, the Nature Conservancy, and the National Wildlife Federation.

Environmental groups have promoted pollution-control policies, wilderness protection, animal rights, and population control. Perhaps more significant, however, is what they have opposed. Their hit list has included oil drilling in Alaska's Arctic National Wildlife Refuge, strip mining, supersonic aircraft, and nuclear power plants. On these and other issues, environmentalists have exerted a great deal of influence on Congress and state legislatures. In particular, the arguments of environmentalists about radiation risks have had a profound impact on public policy. No new nuclear power plants have been approved since 1977, and many that had been in the works were canceled.[40]

A few interest groups use unconventional methods to get attention for their views and demands. The environmental activist group Greenpeace is well known for coming up with activities the media can hardly ignore. Here, group members can be seen protesting the Bush administration's policies by placing a huge banner in front of the main entrance of the Department of the Interior early in the morning.

EQUALITY INTERESTS

The Fourteenth Amendment guarantees equal protection under the law. American history, though, shows that this is easier said than done. Two sets of interest groups, representing minorities and women, have made equal rights their main policy goal. Chapter 5 reviewed the long history of the civil rights movement; this section is concerned with its policy goals and organizational base.

Equality at the polls, in housing, on the job, in education, and in all other facets of American life has long been the dominant goal of African American groups. The oldest and largest of these groups is the National Association for the Advancement of Colored People (NAACP). It argued and won the monumental *Brown v. Board of Education* case in 1954, in which the Supreme Court held that segregated schools were unconstitutional. Although the NAACP has won many victories in principle, equality in practice has been much slower in coming. Today, civil rights groups continue to push for more effective affirmative action programs to ensure that minority groups are given educational and employment opportunities. In recent years, the NAACP's main vehicle has been the Fair Share program, which negotiates agreements with national and regional businesses to increase minority hiring and the use of minority contractors.[41] As an issue, affirmative action is not as emotionally charged as was desegregation, but it too has been controversial.

Although the work of civil rights interest groups in fighting segregation and discrimination is well known, Dona and Charles Hamilton argue that "much less is known about the 'social welfare agenda,'—the fight for social welfare policies to help the poor."[42] They argue that since the 1930s, civil rights groups have been concerned with larger and more universal economic problems in American society.

Like other public interest groups, the Children's Defense Fund faces the challenge of overcoming Olson's law of large group—that it is easier to organize a small group with clear economic goals than it is to organize a large group with broader goals. Therefore, it helps that celebrities like Jennifer Garner (shown here) are willing to publicize their support.

When the NAACP was just beginning, suffragists were in the streets and legislative lobbies were demanding women's right to vote. The Nineteenth Amendment, ratified in 1920, guaranteed women the vote, but other guarantees of equal protection remained absent from the Constitution. More recently, women's rights groups, such as the National Organization for Women (NOW), have lobbied for an end to gender discrimination. Their primary goal has been the passage of the Equal Rights Amendment (ERA), which states that "equality of rights under the law shall not be abridged on account of sex."

In the first month after the ERA was approved by Congress in 1972, it was overwhelmingly ratified by 15 states. Even Texas and Kansas, fairly conservative states, voted decisively for the ERA in the first year. The quiet consensual politics of the ERA ratification process soon came to a boisterous end, however, when Phyllis Schlafly, a conservative activist from Alton, Illinois, began a highly visible STOP ERA movement. She and her followers argued the ERA would destroy the integrity of the family, require communal bathrooms, lead to women in combat, and eliminate legal protections that women already had. Their emotional appeal was just enough to stop the ERA three states short of the 38 necessary for ratification.

Although the ERA seems dead for the moment, NOW remains committed to enacting the protection that the amendment would have constitutionally guaranteed by advocating the enactment of many individual statutes. As is often the case with interest group politics, issues are rarely settled once and for all; rather, they shift to different policy arenas.

CONSUMERS AND PUBLIC INTEREST LOBBIES

Pluralist theory holds that for virtually every interest in society, there is an organized group. But what about the interests of all of us—the buying public? Today thousands of organized groups are championing various causes or ideas "in the public interest." These **public interest lobbies** are organizations that seek "a collective good, the achievement of which will not selectively and materially benefit the membership or activists of the organization."[43] If products are made safer by the lobbying of consumer protection groups, it is not the members of such groups alone that benefit. Rather, everyone should be better off, regardless of whether they joined in the lobbying.

If ever a lobbying effort was spurred by a single person, it was the consumer movement. At first, Ralph Nader took on American business almost single-handedly in the name of consumerism. He was propelled to national prominence by his book *Unsafe at Any Speed*, which attacked General Motors' Corvair as a mechanically deficient and dangerous automobile. General Motors made the mistake of hiring a private detective to dig into Nader's background and follow him around, hoping that there might be some dirt they could uncover that would discredit him. Nader eventually learned about the investigation, sued General Motors

public interest lobbies
According to Jeffrey Berry, organizations that seek "a collective good, the achievement of which will not selectively and materially benefit the membership or activities of the organization."

for invasion of privacy, and won a hefty damage settlement in court. He used the proceeds to launch the first major consumer group in Washington.

Consumer groups have won many legislative victories. In 1973, Congress responded to consumer advocacy by creating the Consumer Product Safety Commission. Congress authorized it to regulate all consumer products and even gave it the power to ban particularly dangerous ones, bearing in mind that household products are responsible for 30,000 deaths annually. Among the products the commission has investigated are children's sleepwear (some of which contained a carcinogen), hot tubs, and lawn mowers.

Consumer groups are not the only ones that claim to be public interest groups. Groups speaking for those who cannot speak for themselves seek to protect children, animals, and the mentally ill; good-government groups such as Common Cause push for openness and fairness in government; and religious groups like the Christian Coalition crusade for what they consider to be the protection of ethical and moral standards in American society.

UNDERSTANDING INTEREST GROUPS

The problem of interest groups in America today remains much the same as James Madison defined it over 200 years ago. A free society must allow for the representation of all groups that seek to influence political decision making. Yet groups are usually more concerned with their own self-interest than with the needs of society as a whole, and for democracy to work well, it is important that they not be allowed to assume a dominant position.

INTEREST GROUPS AND DEMOCRACY

Madison's solution to the problems posed by interest groups was to create a wide-open system in which many groups would be able to participate. In such an extended sphere of influence, according to Madison, groups with opposing interests would counterbalance one another. Pluralist theorists believe that a rough approximation of the public interest emerges from this competition.

With the tremendous growth of interest group politics in recent years, some observers say that Madison may at last have gotten his wish. For every group with an interest, there now seems to be a competing group to watch over it—not to mention public interest lobbies to watch over them all. Robert Salisbury argues that "the growth in the number, variety, and sophistication of interest groups represented in Washington" has transformed policymaking such that it "is not dominated so often by a relatively small number of powerful interest groups as it may once have been."[44] Paradoxically, Salisbury concludes that the increase in lobbying activity has resulted in less clout overall for interest groups—and better democracy.

Elite theorists clearly disagree with this conclusion and point to the proliferation of business PACs as evidence of more interest group corruption in American politics than ever. A democratic process requires a free and open exchange of ideas in which candidates and voters should be able to hear one another out, but PACs—the source of so much money in elections—distort the process. Elite theorists particularly note that wealthier interests are greatly advantaged by the PAC system. It is true that there are over four thousand PACs, but the relatively few big-spending ones dominate the fundraising game. In 2004, a quarter of all PAC contributions came from just 48 PACs, each of which gave over a million dollars. In contrast, the 2,180 smallest PACs (in terms of donations made) accounted for just 10 percent of all PAC contributions.[45]

PACs can sometimes link money to politics at the highest levels. The old party machines may have bought votes in the voting booth; the new PACs are accused of buying votes in legislatures. Technology, especially television, makes American elections expensive; candidates need money to pay for high-tech campaigns, and PACs are able to supply that money. In return, they ask only to be remembered when their interests are clearly at stake.

Hyperpluralist theorists maintain that whenever a major interest group objects strongly to proposed legislation, policymakers will bend over backward to try to accommodate it. With the formation of so many groups in recent years and with so many of them having influence in Washington, hyperpluralists argue that it has been increasingly difficult to accomplish major policy change in Washington. Thus hyperpluralist theory offers a powerful explanation for the policy gridlock often evident in American politics today.

INTEREST GROUPS AND THE SCOPE OF GOVERNMENT

Although individualistic, Americans are also very associational. As Alexis de Tocqueville wrote in the 1830s, "Americans of all ages, all conditions, and all dispositions constantly form associations."[46] This is not at all contradictory. By joining a number of political associations, Americans are able to politicize a variety of aspects of their own individualism. The multiplicity of the American interest group structure and the openness of American politics to inputs from interest groups allow individuals many channels for political participation and thus facilitate representation of individual interests.

Although individualism is most often treated in this book as being responsible for the relatively small scope of American government, when it works its way through interest group politics, the result is just the opposite. Individual interest groups fight to sustain government programs that are important to them, thereby making it hard for politicians ever to reduce the scope of government. Both President Carter and President Reagan remarked at the end of their time in office that their attempts to cut waste in federal spending had been frustrated by interest groups. In his farewell address, Carter "suggested that the reason he had so much difficulty in dealing with Congress was the fragmentation of power and decision making that was exploited by interest groups."[47] Similarly, Reagan remarked a month before leaving office that "special interest groups, bolstered by campaign contributions, pressure lawmakers into creating and defending spending programs."[48] Above all, most special interest groups strive to maintain established programs that benefit them.

Comparing Interest Groups

However, one can also argue that the growth in the scope of government in recent decades accounts for a good portion of the proliferation of interest groups. The more areas in which the federal government has become involved, the more interest groups have developed to attempt to influence policy. As William Lunch notes, "A great part of the increase was occasioned by the new government responsibility for civil rights, environmental protection, and greater public health and safety."[49] For example, once the government got actively involved in protecting the environment, many groups sprung up to lobby for strong standards and enforcement. Given the tremendous effects of environmental regulations on many industries, it should come as no surprise that these industries also organized to ensure that their interests were taken into account. As Salisbury writes, many groups have "come to Washington out of need and dependence rather than because they have influence."[50] He argues that interest groups spend much of their time merely monitoring policy developments in order to alert their membership and develop reactive strategies.

SUMMARY

This chapter discusses the vast array of interest groups in American politics—all vying for policies they prefer. Pluralists see groups as the most important way people can have their policy preferences represented in government. Hyperpluralists, though, fear that too many groups are getting too much of what they want, skillfully working the many subgovernments in the American system. Elitist theorists believe that a few wealthy individuals and multinational corporations exert control over the major decisions regarding distribution of goods and services.

A number of factors influence a group's success in achieving its policy goals. Most surprising is that small groups have an organizational advantage over large groups. Large groups often fall victim to the free-rider problem, which is explained by Olson's law of large groups. Both large and small groups can benefit from the intensity of their members' beliefs. Money always helps lubricate the wheels of power, though it is hardly a surefire guarantee of success.

Interest groups use four basic strategies to maximize their effectiveness. Lobbying is one well-known group strategy. Although the evidence on its influence is mixed, it is clear that lobbyists are most effective with those legislators already sympathetic to their side. Thus, electioneering becomes critical because it helps put supportive people in office. Often today, groups operate in the judicial as well as the legislative process, using litigation in the courts when lobbying fails or is not enough. Many also find it important to project a good image, employing public relations techniques to present themselves in the most favorable light.

This chapter also examined some of the major kinds of interest groups, particularly those concerned with economic, environmental, and equality policy. Public interest lobbies claim to be different from other interest groups, representing, they say, an important aspect of the public interest. Recently there has been a rapid growth of single-interest groups, which focus narrowly on one issue and are not inclined to compromise.

The issue of controlling interest groups remains as crucial to democracy today as it was in Madison's time. Some scholars believe that the growth of interest groups has worked to divide political influence just as Madison hoped it would. Other scholars point to the PAC system as the new way in which special interests corrupt American democracy.

Chapter Test

Multiple Choice

1. All but which of the following are elements of the pluralist *group theory of politics*?
   a. Groups provide a link between people and government
   b. Groups usually follow the rules of the game
   c. Groups compete with each other
   d. Groups can balance each other's strengths and weaknesses
   e. Groups can occasionally become too dominant

2. Which of the following is *not* true of the success of interest groups?
   a. The more intense the group, the more successful it is
   b. Greater financial resources contribute to a group's success
   c. The better-known groups are more successful
   d. The smaller a group, the more successful it tends to be
   e. All of the above are true

3. Political Action Committees (PACs):
   a. Contribute much more money to the campaigns of challengers than to incumbents
   b. Contribute much more money to the campaigns of incumbents than to challengers
   c. Contribute equally to the campaigns of incumbents and challengers
   d. Contribute no money to political campaigns
   e. Receive money from political candidates

4. Which of the following is *not* a tactic interest groups use?
   a. Lobbying
   b. Campaign contributions
   c. Running for office
   d. Litigation
   e. Volunteer campaign labor

5. Which of the following is *not* true about interest groups' targets?
   a. They target local, state, and national government
   b. They groups frequently target the judiciary
   c. They target only elected officials
   d. They target the legislative as well as the executive branch
   e. All of the above are true

6. According to elitist group theory, which of the following is most likely to impact policy decisions by the government?
   a. ExxonMobil
   b. Israel Policy Forum
   c. Greenpeace
   d. American Educational Research Association
   e. American Federation of Labor

7. In his systematic study of more than 500 interest groups, Jack Walker found all but which of the following to be true?
   a. The large majority of interest groups originated from occupational, industrial, or professional memberships

b. About 9 out of 10 groups are headquartered in Washington, D.C.
c. Approximately half of all groups have been around for more than 60 years
d. Most occupations and industries now have their own interest group
e. All of the above are true

8. According to a study by Public Citizen's Congress Watch, approximately how many former members of Congress who retired between 1998 and 2004 became lobbyists?
   a. None of them did
   b. 1 in 10
   c. 2 in 10
   d. 4 in 10
   e. 6 in 10

True/False

9. As voter turnout has decreased over time, interest group activity has also declined.
   True_____ False_____

10. Interest groups occasionally try to run a candidate for public office.
    True_____ False_____

11. Interest groups are often policy specialists, whereas political parties are policy generalists.
    True_____ False_____

12. The so-called "right-to-work laws" have positively impacted union membership in those states who adopted them.
    True_____ False_____

13. Prior to the 1990s, business and trade PACs donated more money to Democratic campaigns than to Republican campaigns.
    True_____ False_____

Short Answer

14. Briefly explain the position of "interest group liberalism" with regard to the role of interest groups in American politics.

15. What is the hyperpluralists' criticism of the so-called "iron triangles"?

16. In what ways have advances in technology impacted interest groups?

17. What functions can lobbyists have in addition to trying to influence policy? Please name and briefly explain at least three.

18. Please compare and contrast the main arguments pluralists make about groups as opposed to elitists. Which one do you agree with the most, and why?

19. What is the definition of a "collective good" and what is the main problem generally associated with such goods? Provide and briefly explain an example other than the one given in this textbook.

20. Explain the two judicial strategies interest groups employ in order to achieve their goals.

Short Answer/Essay

21. In what ways do interest groups and lobbyists positively influence American politics and democracy? In what ways do they hinder or even harm them? Are there any aspects of interest groups and lobbying you would change, and how would you do so? If you wouldn't change anything, please explain why not.

22. What are the main arguments brought forth by advocates and critics of Political Action Committees (PACs)? Which side do you agree with more, and why? Would you favor the abolition of PACs? Why, or why not?

23. How would you reconcile the data summarized in the graph on p. 352 with the fact that, as of 2007, the United States is the only developed country—and one of fewer than 20 worldwide—that has not yet ratified the Kyoto Protocol, which is aimed at combating global warming? What role might interest groups and lobbyists play in this?

24. The so-called "free-rider problem" is a well-documented aspect of unions' and other groups' failure to attract membership. In addition to Olson's suggestion of selective benefits, what other approaches would you recommend in order to deal with this problem?

25. This textbook mentions that one of the services lobbyists can provide is using their political knowledge to help candidates formulate campaign strategies. How do you feel about the idea of lobbyists helping candidates get elected?

26. Do you believe we need more or less regulation of interest groups? If more, what do you think would be a necessary regulation? If less, what would you get rid of? If you think the current level of regulation is fine, why do you believe so?

Answer Key

1. E   2. D   3. B   4. C   5. C   6. A   7. E   8. D   9. False   10. False   11. True   12. False   13. True

Key Terms

interest group (333)
pluralist theory (333)
elite theory (333)
hyperpluralist theory (333)
subgovernments (336)
potential group (337)
actual group (337)

collective good (338)
free-rider problem (338)
Olson's law of large groups (338)
selective benefits (338)
single-issue group (339)
lobbying (342)
electioneering (345)

political action committees (345)
amicus curiae briefs (347)
class action lawsuits (347)
union shop (349)
right-to-work laws (349)
public interest lobbies (354)

Internet Resources

www.aarp.org
The official site of the American Association of Retired Persons.

www.aflcio.org
The nation's largest labor association, the AFL-CIO, posts material at this site.

www.nea.org
The site of the National Education Association.

www.greenpeaceusa.org
The place to go to learn more about the activities of this environmental protection group.

www.commoncause.org
The official site of Common Cause, one of the nation's oldest and largest public affairs interest groups.

www.freespeech.org
A site for an interest group that represents young people, particularly on Social Security issues.

GetConnected

Interest Groups and PACs

Many interest groups try to influence government by getting the right people into office and helping them stay there. In this process, called electioneering, interest groups aid candidates financially and get members of the interest group out to vote for them. In order to contribute to campaigns, interest groups create political action committees, or PACs. The costs of campaigns have risen over the past few decades, and PACs have stepped in to help with the costs. PACs typically give to incumbent candidates, especially those who serve on committees important to the group. From what interests do the U.S. senators from your state receive campaign contributions?

Search the Web

Go to the U.S. Senate Web site, *www.senate.gov*, and find the senators from your state. Also find the committees on which they serve. Develop a hypothesis about the groups that might contribute to the senators based on their committee membership. Then go to the Web site of the Center for Responsive Politics, *www.opensecrets.org*. Look at the most recent filings for the senators. You also may want to look at the records for the senators' opponents, if they had opponents in their most recent election.

Questions to Ask

• Which interest groups contributed the most to each senator?

• Was your hypothesis supported? Did the senators receive support from groups with an interest in the senators' committees?
• Did different interest groups contribute to each of the senators? Does it appear that political party makes a difference? How about seniority or leadership position in the Senate?
• Have you heard of any of the interest groups that contributed to your senators?

Why It Matters

As the size of government has grown, so has the number of interest groups. These groups participate in politics in part by contributing money to political campaigns. Some people complain that the amount of money is hurting politics and government in the United States. You should try to learn about the interest groups that contribute to the elected public officials who represent you. It is possible that one or more of the groups advocate a position similar to your feelings on an issue.

Get Involved

Find our more about the groups that contribute to your senators by sending one or more of them an e-mail request for information. You may want to consider joining an interest group as well. For see more exercises, go to *www.longmanamericangovernment.com*.

For Further Reading

Baumgartner, Frank R., and Beth L. Leech. *Basic Interests: The Importance of Groups in Politics and in Political Science.* Princeton, NJ: Princeton University Press, 1998. An excellent review and analysis of the academic literature on interest groups.

Berry, Jeffrey M. *The New Liberalism: The Rising Power of Citizen Groups.* Washington, DC: Brookings Institution, 1999. Berry argues that citizen groups have been strikingly successful in influencing the policy agenda in recent decades.

Berry, Jeffrey M., and Clyde Wilcox, *The Interest Group Society,* 5th ed. New York: Longman, 2008. One of the best contemporary textbooks on interest groups in American politics.

Cigler, Allan J., and Burdett A. Loomis, eds. *Interest Group Politics.* 7th ed. Washington, DC: Congressional Quarterly Press, 2007. An excellent collection of original articles on the modern interest group system.

CQ Press Editors. *Public Interest Group Profiles, 2006–7.* Washington, DC: Congressional Quarterly Press, 2006. A comprehensive reference book about interest groups that provides information about internship and employment opportunities with many groups.

Dye, Thomas R. *Who's Running America?* 7th ed. Englewood Cliffs, NJ: Prentice Hall, 2002. A good summary of the elitist view of interest groups.

Herrnson, Paul S., Ronald G. Shaiko, and Clyde Wilcox, eds. *The Interest Group Connection.* 2nd ed. Washington, DC:

Congressional Quarterly Press, 2005. A collection of essays on how interest groups attempt to influence elections and the three branches of government.

Kollman, Ken. *Outside Lobbying: Public Opinion and Interest Group Strategies.* Princeton, NJ: Princeton University Press, 1998. An insightful study of how many interest groups use public opinion in the lobbying process.

Lowi, Theodore J. *The End of Liberalism.* 2nd ed. New York: Norton, 1979. A critique of the role of subgovernments and the excessive deference to interest groups in the American political system.

Olson, Mancur. *The Logic of Collective Action.* Cambridge, MA: Harvard University Press, 1965. Develops an economic theory of groups, showing how the cards are stacked against larger groups.

Rauch, Jonathan. *Demosclerosis: The Silent Killer of American Government.* New York: Random House, 1994. A good treatment of hyperpluralism in American politics.

Rozell, Mark J., Clyde Wilcox, and David Madland. *Interest Groups in American Campaigns.* 2nd ed. Washington, DC: Congressional Quarterly Press, 2006. A good review of how interest groups are playing an increasingly important role in electioneering.

CONGRESS

POLITICS IN ACTION: GOVERNING IN CONGRESS

As Nancy Pelosi gaveled the U.S. House of Representatives into session in January 2009, she may have wondered why she wanted the job at all. Yes, she was Speaker of the House, the highest level congressional official—and the first women to hold that post. And, yes, she had effectively maintained a high level of unity among her Democratic colleagues for most of the past two years. Yet during those years she had experienced a lifetime of frustration.

The Framers of the Constitution conceived of the legislature as the center of policymaking in America. Their plan was for the great disputes over public policy to be resolved in Congress, not in the White House or the Supreme Court. Although the prominence of Congress has ebbed and flowed over the course of American history, as often as not, Congress is the true center of power in Washington.

Yet it is difficult to get anything done. The movement of legislation through the congressional labyrinth is complicated and slow, and there are many checks on policymaking. Power is fragmented within Congress, and representatives and senators are typically fiercely independent. Former Senate Majority Leader Howard Baker declared that moving the Senate is like "trying to push a wet noodle." Often, then, when Congress faces the great issues of the day it cannot arrive at any decision at all.

And then there is the president. It is common that the majority in Congress and the chief executive are of different political parties. In such cases, the president leads his party in opposing the majority. If Congress succeeds in passing a bill, it may be vetoed at the White House. Even when the president's party has majorities in both houses of Congress, disagreements within the party may hinder policymaking. President George W. Bush experienced his own frustration when he found limited support for his Social Security and immigration reform proposals among members of his party. At the same time, members of Congress often feel the president exceeds his constitutional authority.

To many Americans, being a member of Congress may seem like a glamorous job. What citizens do not see are the 14-hour days spent dashing from one meeting to the next, the continuous travel between Washington and constituencies, the lack of time for reflection or exchange of ideas, the constant fund-raising, the partisan rancor that permeates Congress, and—perhaps most important of all—the feeling that Congress is making little

headway in solving the country's problems. It is ironic that such frustrations exist in an organization whose members put so much blood, sweat, and tears into joining.

Congress is not only our central policymaking branch but also our principal *representative* branch. As such, it lies at the heart of American democracy. How does Congress combine its roles of representing constituents *and* making effective public policy? Not very well, according to many critics. Some argue that Congress is too responsive to constituents and, especially, to organized interests and is thus unable to make difficult choices regarding public policy. Conversely, others argue that Congress is too insulated from ordinary citizens and makes policy to suit the few rather than the many. In both cases, detractors argue that Congress is incapable of making decisions that will serve the long-run interests of the average person.

Other critics focus on Congress as the source of government expansion. Does Congress' responsiveness predispose the legislature to increase the size of government to please those in the public wishing more or larger government programs? Does providing constituents with pork barrel spending and casework services provide an incentive for members of Congress to expand government programs so there are more potential ways members can help their constituencies?

Congress's tasks become more difficult each year. On any day a representative or senator can be required to make a sensible judgment about missiles, nuclear waste dumps, abortion, trade competition with China, income tax rates, the soaring costs of Social Security and Medicare, and countless other issues. President Clinton's 1993 health care reform proposal was 1,342 pages long and weighed six pounds. Just finding time to think about these issues—much less debate them—has become increasingly difficult.

Despite the many demands of the job, there is no shortage of men and women running for congressional office. The following sections will introduce you to these people.

THE REPRESENTATIVES AND SENATORS

Being a member of Congress is a difficult and unusual job. A person must be willing to spend considerable time, trouble, and money to obtain a crowded office on Capitol Hill. To nineteenth-century humorist Artemus Ward, such a quest was inexplicable: "It's easy to see why a man goes to the poorhouse or the penitentiary. It's because he can't help it. But why he should voluntarily go live in Washington is beyond my comprehension."

THE JOB

Hard work is perhaps the most prominent characteristic of a congressperson's job. The typical representative is a member of about six committees and subcommittees; a senator is a member of about 10. Members are often scheduled to be in two places at the same time.[1]

There are attractions to the job, however. First and foremost is power. Members of Congress make key decisions about important matters of public policy. In addition, the salary and the perks that go with the job help make it tolerable. Members of Congress receive the following:

- A salary of $169,300 in 2008, about three times the income of the typical American family but well below that of hundreds of corporate presidents who earn several times as much

- Generous retirement benefits
- Office space in Washington and in their constituencies
- A substantial congressional staff who serve individual members, committees, and party leaders
- Handsome travel allowances to see their constituents each year, plus opportunities to travel at low fares or even free to foreign nations on congressional inquiries (what critics call "junkets")
- Franking privileges—the free use of the mail system to communicate with constituents and machines that duplicate a member's signature in real ink
- Plenty of small privileges, such as free flowers from the National Botanical Gardens, research services from the Library of Congress, and access to exercise rooms and pools

THE MEMBERS

There are 535 members of Congress. An even hundred, two from each state, are members of the Senate. The other 435 are members of the House of Representatives. The Constitution specifies only that members of the House must be at least 25 years old and American citizens for seven years; senators must be at least 30 and American citizens for nine years. In addition, all members of Congress must be residents of the states from which they are elected.

Members of Congress are not typical or average Americans, however, as the figures in Table 12.1 reveal. Those who argue the country is run by a power elite are quick to point out that members come largely from occupations with high status and usually have substantial incomes. Although calling the Senate a "millionaires' club" is an exaggeration, the proportion of millionaires and near millionaires is much higher in Congress than in an average crowd of 535 people. Business and law are the dominant prior occupations; other elite occupations such as academia are also well represented.

Law especially attracts persons interested in politics and provides the flexibility (and often the financial support of a law firm) to wage election campaigns. In addition, many government positions in which aspiring members of Congress can make their marks, such as district attorney, are reserved for lawyers.

Less than 10 percent of the members of the House are African American (compared with about 13 percent of the total population), and most (but not all) of these representatives have been elected from overwhelmingly African American constituencies. No state is predominantly African American, and there is only one African American in the Senate. There are 24 Hispanics in the House and three in the Senate. Asian and Native Americans are also underrepresented. In terms of numbers, however, women are the most underrepresented group; more than half the population is female, but only 17 senators and 72 voting representatives are female (the representative from Washington, D.C., does not vote).

How important are the personal characteristics of members of Congress? Can a group of predominantly White, upper-middle-class, middle-aged Protestant

Despite their gains in recent congressional elections, women are the most underrepresented demographic group in Congress. Here women senators and representatives meet to raise awareness of domestic violence.

TABLE 12.1

A Portrait of the 111th Congress: Some Statistics

CHARACTERISTIC	HOUSE (435 TOTAL)	SENATE (100 TOTAL)
Party		
Democrat	257	56
Republican	178	42
Independent	–	2
Gender		
Men	363	83
Women	72	17
Race		
Asian	4	2
African American	40	1
Hispanic	24	3
White and other	367	94
Religion[+]		
Protestant	260	63
Roman Catholic	128	25
Jewish	30	13
Other and unspecified	14	1
Prior occupation[*][+]		
Law	161	61
Business	168	27
Education	87	14
Public service/politics	172	31
Agriculture	23	6
Journalism	7	7
Real estate	36	3
Medicine	13	3
Other	61	9

[+]Data for 110th Congress.

[*]Some members specify more than one occupation.

Source: *Congressional Quarterly*

males adequately represent a much more diverse population? Would a group of more typical citizens be more effective in making major policy decisions? Because power in Congress is highly decentralized, the backgrounds of representatives and senators can be important if they influence how issues are prioritized and how officials vote on these issues. There is evidence that African American members are more active than White members in serving African American constituents,[2] and they appear to increase African American constituents' contact with and knowledge about Congress.[3] Similarly, on the average, women legislators seem to be more active than men in pursuing the interests of women.[4]

Obviously, members of Congress cannot claim *descriptive* representation—that is, representing constituents by mirroring their personal, politically relevant characteristics. They may, however, engage in *substantive* representation—representing the interests of groups.[5] For example, members of Congress with a background of wealth and privilege, such as Senator Edward Kennedy, can be champions for the interests of the poor. Moreover, most members of Congress have lived in the constituencies they represent for many years and share the beliefs and attitudes of at least a large proportion of their constituents. If they do not share such perspectives, they may find it difficult to keep their seats come election time. At the same time, women and African Americans in Congress are achieving important positions on committees, increasing the chances of making descriptive representation effective.[6]

WHY AREN'T THERE MORE WOMEN IN CONGRESS?

Sarah Fulton, a scholar of women in politics, found that in the 2006 midterm elections, women won 52 percent of the House races, and 67 percent of the Senate races in which they competed.[7] Yet, despite this winning record, we have seen that women in the 111th Congress (2009–2010) occupied just 17 percent of both U.S. House and Senate seats. If women have proven themselves as capable of competing with and winning against men, then why aren't there more women in Congress?

Part of the reason for women's under-representation is that fewer women than men become major party nominees for office. For example, a female major-party nominee contested only 31 percent of the 435 House races in 2006. In a recent article, Fulton and her coauthors report that women are significantly less ambitious to run for office than their

Members of Congress who do not share their constituents' economic and social backgrounds can nonetheless represent their concerns. Senator Edward Kennedy, for example, born into one of America's wealthiest families, has championed the poor and underprivileged throughout his career. Here, Kennedy speaks to workers concerned over proposed cuts in their pay and benefits.

male counterparts, largely because they have greater childcare responsibilities. Interestingly, there is no gender disparity in ambition among men and women without children. The authors also suggest that women's decisions to run are more sensitive than men's to their perceptions of the odds of winning—women are less likely than men to run when they perceive their chances of winning to be poor; however, they are more likely than men to run when they detect a political opportunity.[8]

It appears that women's under-representation will persist until childcare responsibilities are more evenly distributed among spouses. Also, if women can overcome their reluctance to run when they perceive their electoral prospects to be less than stellar, they may encounter some unexpected electoral success.

CONGRESSIONAL ELECTIONS

Congressional elections are demanding, expensive,[9] and, as you will see, generally foregone conclusions—yet the role of politician is the most universal one in Congress. Men and women may run for Congress to forge new policy initiatives, but they also enjoy politics and consider a position in Congress near the top of their chosen profession. Even if they dislike politics, without reelection they will not be around long enough to shape policy.

WHO WINS ELECTIONS?

Everyone in Congress is a politician, and politicians continually have their eyes on the next election. The players in the congressional election game are the incumbents and the challengers.

Incumbents are individuals who already hold office. Sometime during each term, the incumbent must decide whether to run again or to retire voluntarily. Most decide to run for reelection. They enter their party's primary, almost always emerge victorious, and typically win in the November general election, too. Indeed, the most important fact about congressional elections is this: *Incumbents usually win.*

Thus, the key to ensuring an opponent's defeat is not having more money than the opponent, although that helps. It is not being more photogenic, although that helps, too. The best thing a candidate can have going for him or her is simply to be the incumbent (see Figure 12.1). Even in a year of great political upheaval such as 1994, in which the Republicans gained eight seats in the Senate and 53 seats in the House, 92 percent of incumbent senators and 89 percent of incumbent representatives won their bids for reelection.

Not only do more than 90 percent of incumbents seeking reelection win, but most of them win with more than 60 percent of the vote. Perhaps most astonishing is the fact that even when challengers' positions on the issues are closer to the voters' positions, incumbents still tend to win.[10]

The picture for the Senate is a little different. Even though senators still have a good chance of beating back a challenge, the odds of reelection are often not as handsome as for House incumbents; senators typically win by narrower margins.

One reason for the greater competition in the Senate is that an entire state is almost always more diverse than a congressional district and thus provides a larger base for opposition to an incumbent. At the same time, senators have less personal contact with their constituencies, which on average are about 10 times larger than those of members of the House of Representatives. Senators also receive more coverage in the media than representatives do and are more likely to be held accountable on controversial issues. Moreover, senators tend to draw more visible challengers, such as governors or members of the House, whom voters already know and who have substantial financial backing—a factor that lessens the advantages of incumbency. Many of these challengers know that the Senate is a stepping-stone to national prominence and sometimes even the presidency.

Despite their success at reelection, incumbents often feel quite vulnerable. As Thomas Mann put it, members of Congress perceive themselves as "unsafe at any

FIGURE 12.1

The Incumbency Factor in Congressional Elections

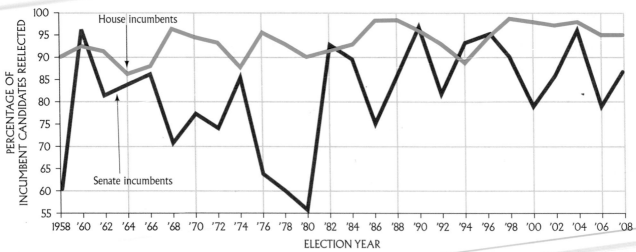

Source: Norman J. Ornstein, Thomas E. Mann, and Michael J. Malbin, *Vital Statistics on Congress, 1997–1998* (Washington, DC: Congressional Quarterly Press, 1998). Data for 1998–2008 compiled by the authors. Figures reflect incumbents running in both primary and general elections.

margin."[11] Thus, they have been raising and spending more campaign funds, sending more mail to their constituents, visiting their states and districts more often, and staffing more local offices than ever before.[12]

THE ADVANTAGES OF INCUMBENCY

There are several possible explanations for the success of incumbents. One is that voters know how their elected representatives vote on important policy issues and agree with their stands, sending them back to Washington to keep up the good work. This, however, is usually not the case. In fact, voters are rather oblivious to how their senators and representatives actually vote. One study found that only about one-fifth of Americans can make an accurate guess about how their representatives have voted on any issue in Congress.[13] As one expert put it, "Mass public knowledge of congressional candidates declines precipitously once we move beyond simple recognition, generalized feelings, and incumbent job ratings."[14]

Another possibility is that voter assessments of presidential candidates influence their voting for Congress. Most stories of presidential "coattails" (when voters support congressional candidates because of their support for the president), however, seem to be just stories.[15] Bill Clinton and George W. Bush won four presidential elections between them. Yet they received a *smaller* percentage of the vote than did almost every winning member of their party in Congress in each election. They had little in the way of coattails.

Journalists often claim that voters are motivated primarily by their pocketbooks. Yet members of Congress do not gain or lose many votes as a result of the ups and downs of the economy.[16]

What accounts for the success of congressional incumbents? Members of Congress engage in three primary activities that increase the probability of their reelection: advertising, credit claiming, and position taking.[17] In addition, the lack of strong opponents further ensures their success.

TIMELINE

Critical Congressional (Mid-Term) Elections

Advertising   For members of Congress, advertising means much more than placing ads in the newspapers and on television. Most congressional advertising takes place between elections in the form of contact with constituents. The goal is *visibility*.

Members of Congress work hard to get themselves known in their constituencies, and they usually succeed. Not surprisingly, members concentrate on staying visible and make frequent trips home. In a typical week, members spend some time in their home districts,[18] even though their districts may be hundreds of miles from Washington. Similarly, members use the franking privilege to mail newsletters to every household in their constituency.

More recently, members of Congress have employed technology to bring franking into the digital age. Congressional staffers track the interests of individual voters, file the information in a database, and then use e-mails or phone calls to engage directly with voters on issues they know they care about. Using taxpayers' money, legislators employ a new technology that allows them to call thousands of households simultaneously with a recorded message, asking people in their districts to join in on a conference call with their representative. With the push of a button, the constituent is on the line with the House member—and often 1,000 or more fellow constituents. Equally important, the lawmaker knows from the phone numbers where the respondents live and, from what they say on the call, what issues interest them. Information gathered from these events, as well as e-mails and phone calls from constituents, gets plugged into a database, giving the incumbent something a challenger could only dream of: a detailed list of the specific interests of thousands of would-be voters. E-mail then allows for personal interaction—and a free reminder of why the incumbent should be reelected.

Credit Claiming   Congresspersons also engage in credit claiming, which involves enhancing their standing with constituents through service to individuals and the district. One member told Richard Fenno about the image he tried to cultivate in his constituency:

> [I have] a very high recognition factor. And of all the things said about me, none of them said, "He's a conservative or a liberal," or "He votes this way on such and such an issue." None of that at all. There were two things said. One, "He works hard." Two, "He works for us." Nothing more than that. So we made it our theme, "O'Connor gets things done"; and we emphasized the dams, the highways, the buildings, the casework.[19]

Morris Fiorina has emphasized this close link between service and success.[20] Members of Congress, he says, *can* go to the voters and stress their policymaking record and their stands on new policy issues on the agenda. The problem with facing the voters on one's record—past, present, and future—is that policy positions make enemies as well as friends. A member of Congress's vote for reducing government spending may win some friends, but it will make enemies of voters who happen to link that vote with service cutbacks. Besides, a congressperson can almost never show that he or she alone was responsible for a major policy. Being only one of 435 members of the House or one of 100 senators, a person can hardly promise to end inflation, cut taxes, or achieve equal rights for women single-handedly.

One thing, however, always wins friends and almost never makes enemies: *servicing the constituency.* There are two ways in which members of Congress can do so: through casework and through the pork barrel. **Casework** is helping constituents as individuals—cutting through some bureaucratic red tape to give people what they think they have a right to get. Do you have trouble getting your check from the Social Security Administration on time? Call your congressperson; he or she can cut red tape. Does your town have trouble getting federal bureaucrats to respond to its request for federal construction money? Call your congressperson. Representatives and senators can single-handedly take credit for each of these favors. Fiorina puts it like this:

> Even committee chairmen have a difficult time claiming credit for a piece of major legislation, let alone a rank-and-file congressman. Ah, but casework, and the pork barrel. In dealing with the bureaucracy, the congressman is not merely 1 vote in 435. Rather he is a nonpartisan power, someone whose phone calls snap an office to attention. He is not kept on hold. The constituent who receives aid believes that his congressman and his congressman alone got results. Similarly, congressmen find it easy to claim credit for federal projects awarded in their districts. The congressman may have instigated the project in the first place, issued regular progress reports, and ultimately announced the award through his office. Maybe he can't claim credit for the 1965 Voting Rights Act, but he can take credit for Littletown's spanking new sewage treatment plant.[21]

Getting things done for the folks back home often gets an incumbent the chance to serve them again.

The **pork barrel** is the mighty list of federal projects, grants, and contracts available to cities, businesses, colleges, and institutions. In the past, Congress tended to appropriate funds for grants and let institutions—such as universities—compete for funding for specific projects. In recent years, however, members of Congress have grown increasingly aggressive in "earmarking" funds that must be spent for particular projects in specific districts. The Office of Management and

casework
Activities of members of Congress that help constituents as individuals; cutting through bureaucratic red tape to get people what they think they have a right to get.

pork barrel
The mighty list of federal projects, grants, and contracts available to cities, businesses, colleges, and institutions available in a congressional district.

Budget reported that there were nearly 12,000 such earmarks in 2007, costing about $17 billion.

As a result of the advantages of incumbency in advertising and credit claiming, incumbents, especially in the House, are usually much better known and have a more favorable public image than do their opponents.[22] Shrewd use of the resources available to incumbents may give them an advantage, but by themselves, casework and pork barrel do not determine congressional elections.[23]

Position Taking   Members of Congress must also engage in position-taking on issues when they vote and when they respond to constituents' questions. In establishing their public images, members of Congress emphasize their personal qualities as experienced, hardworking, trustworthy representatives who have served their constituencies—an image often devoid of partisan or programmatic content. Nevertheless, all members must take policy stands, and the positions they take may affect the outcome of an election, especially if the issues are on matters salient to voters and the candidates' stands differ from those of a majority of their constituents. This is especially true in elections for the Senate, in which issues are likely to play a greater role than in House elections.

Because credit claiming is so important to reelection, members of Congress rarely pass up the opportunity to increase federal spending in their state or district. The early 2000s witnessed a surge in earmarks of expenditures of specific projects. One of the most notorious was the down payment of $223 million for the "Bridge to Nowhere," proposed to replace the ferry connecting Ketchikan, Alaska (population of about 9,000), to the Ketchikan International Airport on Gravina Island (population of about 50). After widespread criticism, Alaska canceled the project.

Weak Opponents   Another advantage for incumbents is that they are likely to face weak opponents. Confronted with the advantages of incumbency, potentially effective opponents are often unlikely to risk challenging members of the House.[24] Those individuals who do run are usually not well known or well qualified and lack experience and organizational and financial backing.[25] The lack of adequate campaign funds is a special burden because challengers need money to compensate for the "free" recognition incumbents receive from their advertising and credit claiming.[26]

Campaign Spending   It costs a great deal of money to elect a Congress. The Federal Election Commission reports that in the 2005–2006 election cycle, congressional candidates and supporting party committees spent more than $2 billion to contest 435 House and 33 Senate seats. Challengers have to raise large sums if they hope to defeat an incumbent, and the more they spend, the more votes they receive. Money buys them name recognition and a chance to be heard. Incumbents, by contrast, already have high levels of recognition among their constituents and benefit less (but still benefit) from campaign spending; what matters most is how much their opponents spend. (In contests for open seats, the candidate who spends the most usually wins.[27]) In the end, however, challengers are usually substantially outspent by incumbents. In the House races in 2006, the typical incumbent outspent the typical challenger by a ratio of more than 2 to 1.[28]

Where do campaign funds come from? And, more important, what do they buy? Although most of the money spent in congressional elections comes from individuals, about one-fourth of the funds raised by candidates for Congress comes from political action committees (PACs) (see Chapters 9 and 11). Critics of PACs offer plenty of complaints about the present system of campaign finance. Why, they ask, is money spent to pay the campaign costs of a candidate who is already heavily favored to win? Even more interesting is that PACs often make contributions *after* the election.

There is a continuous debate on whether PACs "buy" votes in Congress (see "You Are the Policymaker: Should PACs be Eliminated?" in Chapter 11). Although this question remains unresolved, everyone agrees that at the very least, PACs seek *access* to policymakers. Thus, they give most of their money to incumbents, who are likely to win anyway. When they support someone who loses, they often quickly make amends and contribute to the winner. PACs want to keep the lines of communication open and create a receptive atmosphere in which to be heard. Because each PAC is limited to an expenditure of $5,000 per candidate in both the primary and the general election, a single PAC can at most account for only a small percentage of a winner's total spending. If one PAC does not contribute to a candidate, there are always other PACs from which to seek funds.

Aside from the question of whether money buys influence, what does it buy the candidates who spend it? In 2000, Jon Corzine of New Jersey spent more than $60 million to win a Senate seat. However, in 2006, Rick Santorum of Pennsylvania spent $28 million, James Talent of Missouri spent $24 million, and Ned Lamont of Connecticut spent $21 million—and all lost. Obviously, prolific spending in a campaign is no guarantee of success.

THE ROLE OF PARTY IDENTIFICATION

At the base of every electoral coalition are the members of the candidate's party in the constituency. Most members of Congress represent constituencies in which their party is in the clear majority, and most people who identify with a party reliably vote for its candidates. Indeed, about 90 percent of voters who identify with a party vote for the House candidates of their party. State legislatures have eagerly employed advances in technology to draw the boundaries of House districts so that there is a safe majority for one party, and both demographic trends and ideological realignment in the electorate have made the constituencies of both senators and representatives less competitive.

DEFEATING INCUMBENTS

In light of the advantages of incumbents, it is reasonable to ask why anyone challenges them at all. One of the main reasons is simply that challengers are often naive about their chances of winning. Because few have money for expensive polls, they rely on friends and local party leaders, who often tell them what they want to hear. Sometimes they do get some unexpected help; incumbents almost have to beat themselves, and some do.

An incumbent tarnished by scandal or corruption becomes instantly vulnerable. Clearly, voters do take out their anger at the polls. For example, representatives who bounced large numbers of checks at the House bank were much more likely to lose their seats in the 1992 elections than their more fiscally responsible colleagues.[29] In a close election, negative publicity can turn victory into defeat.[30]

Incumbents may also lose many of their supporters if the boundaries of their districts change. After each federal census, Congress reapportions its membership. States that have gained significantly in population will be given more House seats; states that have lost substantial population will lose one or more of their seats. The state legislatures must then redraw their states' district lines; one incumbent may be moved into another's district, where the two must battle for one seat.[31] A state party majority is more likely to move two of the opposition party's representatives into a single district than two of its own. Or an incumbent of the minority party might find his or her district split up to make it more competitive. In 2004, Republicans in

Texas redrew the state's congressional boundaries for the second time since 2000, removing many Democratic constituents from the districts of Democratic representatives. In the end, the Republicans gained four seats in the state's delegation in the U.S. House of Representatives.

Finally, major political tidal waves occasionally roll across the country, leaving defeated incumbents in their wake. One such wave occurred in 1994, when the public mood turned especially sour and voters took out their frustration on Democratic incumbents, defeating 34 in the House and two in the Senate. In 2006, the tide reversed as six Republican senators and 23 Republican representatives lost their seats.

OPEN SEATS

When an incumbent is not running for reelection and the seat is open, there is greater likelihood of competition. If the party balance in a constituency is such that either party has a chance of winning, each side may offer a strong candidate—each with enough money to establish name recognition among the voters. Most of the turnover in the membership of Congress results from vacated seats.

STABILITY AND CHANGE

Because incumbents usually win reelection, there is some stability in the membership of Congress. This stability allows representatives and senators to gain some expertise in dealing with complex questions of public policy. At the same time, it also may insulate them from the winds of political change. Safe seats make it more difficult for citizens to "send a message to Washington" with their votes. Particularly in the House, it takes a large shift in votes to affect the outcomes of most elections. To increase turnover in the membership of Congress, some reformers have proposed *term limitations* for representatives and senators[32] (see "You Are the Policymaker: Should We Impose Term Limits on Members of Congress?").

YOU ARE THE **Policymaker**

Should We Impose Term Limits on Members of Congress?

In the late 1980s, many reformers were concerned that the incumbency advantage enjoyed by legislators created, in effect, lifetime tenure, which served as a roadblock to change and encouraged ethics abuses. To increase turnover among legislators, these reformers proposed term limitations, generally restricting representatives to 6 or 12 consecutive years in office.

The movement to limit the terms of legislators spread rapidly across the country. Within a few years, 23 states enacted term limitations for members of their state legislatures. The House Republicans made terms limits for Congress part of their Contract with America in the 1994 election. Yet changing the terms of members of Congress requires changing the Constitution, which is difficult to do, and many members of Congress have fought term limitations fiercely.

Opponents of term limitations object to the loss of experienced legislators and of the American people's ability to vote for whomever they please. In addition, they add, there is plenty of new blood in the legislature: At the beginning of the 110th Congress

(in 2007), most members of the House and Senate had served fewer than 10 years in Congress. Moreover, recent research indicates that the movement of party fortunes in the House follows the movement of citizen preferences for public policy.*

Proponents of term limits suffered two setbacks in 1995 when Congress failed to pass a constitutional amendment on term limitations (it also failed in 1997) and when the Supreme Court, in *U.S. Term Limits, Inc. et al. v. Thornton et al.*, decided that state-imposed term limits on members of Congress were unconstitutional. In the meantime, most people seem comfortable with their own representatives and senators and appear content to reelect them again and again.

Nevertheless, many Americans support a constitutional amendment to impose term limitations on members of Congress. You be the policymaker: What would *you* do?

*Suzanna De Boef and James A. Stimson, "The Dynamic Structure of Congressional Elections," *Journal of Politics* 57 (August 1995): 630–48.

HOW CONGRESS IS ORGANIZED TO MAKE POLICY

Of all the senators' and representatives' roles, making policy is the toughest. Congress is a collection of generalists trying to make policy on specialized topics. Members are short on time and specific expertise. As generalists on most subjects, they are surrounded by people who know (or claim to know) more than they do—lobbyists, agency administrators, even their own staffs. Even if they had time to study all the issues thoroughly, making wise national policy would be difficult. If economists disagree about policies to fight unemployment, how are legislators to know which policies may work better than others?

When ringing bells announce a roll-call vote, representatives or senators rush into the chamber from their offices or from a hearing—often unsure of what is being voted on. Frequently, "uncertain of their position, members of Congress will seek out one or two people who serve on the committee which considered and reported the bill, in whose judgment they have confidence."[33]

SIMULATION

How a Bill Becomes a Law

The Founders gave Congress's organization just a hint of specialization when they split it into the House and the Senate. The complexity of today's issues, however, requires much more specialization. Congress tries to cope with policymaking demands through its elaborate committee system.

bicameral legislature
A legislature divided into two houses. The U.S. Congress and every American state legislature except Nebraska's are bicameral.

AMERICAN BICAMERALISM

A **bicameral legislature** is a legislature divided into two houses. The U.S. Congress is bicameral, as is every American state legislature except Nebraska's, which has one house (unicameral). As we learned in Chapter 2, the Connecticut Compromise at the Constitutional Convention created a bicameral Congress. Each state is guaranteed two senators, and its number of representatives is determined by the population of the state (California has 53 representatives; Alaska, Delaware, Montana, North Dakota, South Dakota, Vermont, and Wyoming have just one each). By creating a bicameral Congress, the Constitution set up yet another check and balance. No bill can be passed unless both House and Senate agree on it; each body can thus veto the policies of the other. Table 12.2 shows some of the basic differences between the two houses.

The House More than four times larger than the Senate, the House is also more institutionalized—that is, more centralized, more hierarchical, and less anarchic.[34] Party loyalty to leadership and party-line voting are more common in the House than in the Senate. Partly because there are more members, leaders in the House do more leading than do leaders in the Senate. First-term House members are more likely to be seen and not heard, and they have less power than senior representatives.[35]

Both the House and the Senate set their own agendas. Both use committees, which we will examine shortly, to winnow down the thousands of bills introduced. One institution unique to the House, however, plays a key role in agenda setting: the **House Rules Committee**. This committee reviews most bills coming from a House committee before they go to the full House. Performing a traffic cop function, the Rules Committee gives each bill a "rule," which schedules the bill on the calendar, allots time for debate, and sometimes even specifies what kind of amendments may be offered. Today, the committee usually brings legislation to the floor under rules that limit or prohibit amendments and thus the opportunities for the minority to propose changes. The Rules Committee is generally responsive to the House leadership, in part because the Speaker of the House now appoints the committee's members.

House Rules Committee
An institution unique to the House of Representatives that reviews all **bills** (except revenue, budget, and appropriations bills) coming from a House committee before they go to the full House.

TABLE 12.2

House Versus Senate: Some Key Differences

CHARACTERISTIC	HOUSE OF REPRESENTATIVES	SENATE
Constitutional powers	Must initiate all revenue bills; must pass all articles of impeachment	Must give "advice and consent" to many presidential nominations; must approve treaties; tries impeached officials
Membership	435 members	100 members
Term of office	2 years	6 years
Constituencies	Usually smaller	Usually larger
Centralization of power	More centralized; stronger leadership	Less centralized; weaker leadership
Political prestige	Less prestige	More prestige
Role in policymaking	More influential on budget; more specialized	More influential on foreign affairs; less specialized
Turnover	Small	Moderate
Role of seniority	More important in determining power	Less important in determining power
Procedures	Limited debate; limits on floor amendments allowed	Unlimited debate

The Senate The Constitution's framers thought the Senate would protect elite interests to counteract the tendencies of the House to protect the masses. They gave the House power to initiate all revenue bills and to impeach officials; they gave the Senate the responsibility to ratify all treaties, to confirm important presidential nominations (including nominations to the Supreme Court), and to try impeached officials. History shows that when the same party controls each chamber, the Senate is just as liberal as—and perhaps more liberal than—the House.[36] The real differences between the bodies lie in the Senate's organization and decentralized power.

Smaller than the House, the Senate is also less disciplined and less centralized. Today's senators are more nearly equal in power than representatives are. They are also more nearly equal in power than senators have been in the past. Even incoming senators sometimes get top committee assignments; they may even become chairs of key subcommittees.

Committees and party leadership are important in determining the Senate's legislative agenda, just as they are in the House. Party leaders do for Senate scheduling what the Rules Committee does in the House.

One activity unique to the Senate is the **filibuster**. This is a tactic by which opponents of a bill use their right to unlimited debate as a way to prevent the Senate from ever voting on a bill. Unlike their fellow legislators in the House, once senators have the floor in a debate, tradition holds that they can talk as long as they wish. Strom Thurmond of South Carolina once held forth for 24 hours and 18 minutes opposing a civil rights bill in 1957. Working together, then, like-minded senators can practically debate forever, tying up the legislative agenda until the proponents of a bill finally give up their battle. In essence, they literally talk the bill to death.

The power of the filibuster is not absolute, however. Sixty members present and voting can halt a filibuster by voting for *cloture* on debate, but many senators are reluctant to vote for cloture for fear of setting a precedent to be used against them when *they* want to filibuster.

At its core the filibuster raises profound questions about American democracy because it is used by a minority, sometimes a minority of one, to defeat a majority. Southern senators once used filibusters to prevent civil rights legislation.[37] More recently, the opponents of all types of legislation have used them. Indeed, during Bill Clinton's presidency, filibusters became the weapon of first resort for even the most trivial matters. Each senator knows that he or she has at least six opportunities to filibuster a single bill and that these opportunities can be used one after another. In addition, the tactical uses of a filibuster have expanded. A senator might threaten to filibuster an unrelated measure in order to gain concessions on a bill he or she opposes.

If the minority is blocking the majority, why doesn't the majority change the rules to prevent filibuster? The answer is twofold. First, changing the rules requires 67 votes. It is always difficult to obtain the agreement of two-thirds of the Senate on a controversial matter. Second, every senator knows that he or she might be in the minority on an issue at some time. A filibuster gives senators who are in the minority a powerful weapon for defending their (or their constituents') interests.

In the meantime, Americans complain about gridlock in Congress. Nevertheless, senators have decided that they are more concerned with allowing senators to block legislation they oppose than with expediting the passage of legislation a majority favors.

CONGRESSIONAL LEADERSHIP

Leading 100 senators or 435 representatives in Congress—each jealous of his or her own power and responsible to no higher power than the constituency—is no easy task. "Few members of the House, fewer still in the Senate," Robert Peabody once

filibuster
A strategy unique to the Senate whereby opponents of a piece of legislation try to talk it to death, based on the tradition of unlimited debate. Today, 60 members present and voting can halt a filibuster.

wrote, "consider themselves followers."[38] Chapter 8 discussed the party in government. Much of the leadership in Congress is really party leadership. There are a few formal posts whose occupants are chosen by nonparty procedures, but those who have the real power in the congressional hierarchy are those whose party put them there.

The House   Chief among leadership positions in the House of Representatives is the **Speaker of the House**. This is the only legislative office mandated by the Constitution. In practice, the majority party selects the Speaker. Before each Congress begins, the majority party presents its candidate for Speaker, who—because this person attracts the unanimous support of the majority party—turns out to be a shoo-in. Typically, the Speaker is a senior member of the party. Nancy Pelosi of California, who has served in Congress since 1987, was elected Speaker in 2007, the first women to serve in that post. The Speaker is also two heartbeats away from the presidency, being second in line (after the vice president) to succeed a president who resigns, dies in office, or is convicted after impeachment.

Years ago, the Speaker was king of the congressional mountain. Autocrats such as "Uncle Joe Cannon" and "Czar Reed" ran the House like a fiefdom. A great revolt in 1910 whittled down the Speaker's powers and gave some of them to committees, but six decades later, members of the House restored some of the Speaker's powers. Today the Speaker does the following:

- Presides over the House when it is in session
- Plays a major role in making committee assignments, which are coveted by all members to ensure their electoral advantage
- Appoints or plays a key role in appointing the party's legislative leaders and the party leadership staff
- Exercises substantial control over which bills get assigned to which committees

In addition to these formal powers, the Speaker has a great deal of informal clout inside and outside Congress. When the Speaker's party differs from the president's party, as it frequently does, the Speaker is often a national spokesperson for the party. The bank of microphones in front of the Speaker of the House is a commonplace feature of the evening news. A good Speaker also knows the members well—including their past improprieties, the ambitions they harbor, and the pressures they feel.

Leadership in the House, however, is not a one-person show. The Speaker's principal partisan ally is the **majority leader**—a job that has been the main

Speaker of the House
An office mandated by the Constitution. The Speaker is chosen in practice by the majority party, has both formal and informal powers, and is second in line to succeed to the presidency should that office become vacant.

TIMELINE

The Power of the Speaker of the House

majority leader
The principal partisan ally of the Speaker of the House or the party's manager in the Senate. The majority leader is responsible for scheduling **bills**, influencing committee assignments, and rounding up votes in behalf of the party's legislative positions.

Nancy Pelosi of California was elected Speaker of the House in 2007, the first woman to serve in that post. Majority Leader Harry Reid of Nevada leads the Democrats in the Senate, which makes him the most powerful member of that body. Nevertheless, in the decentralized power structure in the upper chamber, even he must work for support and negotiate with Minority Leader Mitch McConnell of Kentucky.

whips

Party leaders who work with the majority leader or minority leader to count votes beforehand and lean on waverers whose votes are crucial to a bill favored by the party.

minority leader

The principal leader of the minority party in the House of Representatives or in the Senate.

stepping-stone to the Speaker's role. The majority leader is responsible for scheduling bills in the House. More important, the majority leader is responsible for rounding up votes on behalf of the party's position on legislation. Working with the majority leader are the party's **whips**, who carry the word to party troops, counting votes before they are cast and leaning on waverers whose votes are crucial to a bill. Party whips also report the views and complaints of the party rank and file back to the leadership. The current majority leader is Steny Hoyer of Maryland.

The minority party is also organized, poised to take over the Speakership and other key posts if it should win a majority in the House. The Republicans had been the minority party in the House for 40 years before 1995, although they had a president to look to for leadership for much of that period. After 12 years in the majority, Republicans again are experiencing minority status, led by the **minority leader**, John Boehner of Ohio.

The Senate   The Constitution makes the vice president of the United States the president of the Senate; this is the vice president's only constitutionally defined job. However, even the mighty Lyndon Johnson, who had been the Senate majority leader before becoming vice president, found himself an outsider when he returned as the Senate's president. Vice presidents usually slight their senatorial chores, leaving power in the Senate to party leaders. Senators typically return the favor, ignoring vice presidents except in the rare case when their vote can break a tie.

Thus, the Senate majority leader (currently Harry Reid of Nevada)—aided by the majority whips—is a party's workhorse, corralling votes, scheduling floor action, and influencing committee assignments. The majority leader's counterpart in the opposition, the minority leader (currently Mitch McConnell of Kentucky), has similar responsibilities. Power is widely dispersed in the contemporary Senate; it no longer lies in the hands of a few key members of Congress who are insulated from the public. Therefore, party leaders must appeal broadly for support, often speaking to the country directly or indirectly over television.

Congressional Leadership in Perspective   Despite their stature and power, congressional leaders cannot always move their troops. Power in both houses of Congress, but especially the Senate, is decentralized. Leaders are elected by their party members and must remain responsive to them. Except in the most egregious cases (which rarely arise), leaders cannot administer severe punishments to those who do not support the party's stand, and no one expects members to vote against their constituents' interests. Senator Robert Dole nicely summed up the leader's situation when he once dubbed himself the "Majority Pleader."

Nevertheless, party leadership, at least in the House, has been more effective in recent years. As the party contingents have become more homogeneous, there has been more policy agreement within the parties and thus more party unity in voting on the floor. Increased agreement has made it easier for the Speaker to exercise his prerogatives regarding the assignment of bills and members to committees, the rules under which the House considers legislation on the floor, and the use of an expanded whip system—all developments that have enabled the parties to advance an agenda that reflects party preferences.[39]

THE COMMITTEES AND SUBCOMMITTEES

Will Rogers, the famous Oklahoman humorist, once remarked that "outside of traffic, there is nothing that has held this country back as much as committees." Members of the Senate and the House would apparently disagree. Most of the real work of Congress goes on in committees, and committees dominate congressional policymaking in all its stages.

Committees regularly hold hearings to investigate problems and possible wrongdoing and to oversee the executive branch. Most of all, *they control the*

? Why It Matters
Weak Parties
Parties organize Congress, but historically they have been relatively weak. If parties are strong, they can enforce strict party loyalty and thus are better able to keep their promises to voters. At the same time, strict party loyalty makes it more difficult for members of Congress to break from the party line to represent their constituents' special needs and interests.

congressional agenda and guide legislation from its introduction to its send-off to the president for his signature. We can group committees into four types, the first of which is by far the most important.

1. **Standing committees** handle bills in different policy areas (see Table 12.3). Each house of Congress has its own standing committees; members do not belong to a committee in the other house. In the 110th Congress, the typical representative served on two committees and four subcommittees; senators averaged three committees and seven subcommittees each. Subcommittees are smaller units of a committee created out of the committee membership.
2. **Joint committees** exist in a few policy areas, such as the economy and taxation, and draw their membership from both the Senate and the House.
3. **Conference committees** are formed when the Senate and the House pass different versions of the same bill (which they typically do). Appointed by the party leadership, a conference committee consists of members of each house chosen to iron out Senate and House differences and to report back a compromise bill.
4. **Select committees** may be temporary or permanent and usually have a focused responsibility. The House and Senate each have a select committee on intelligence, for example.

standing committees
Separate subject-matter committees in each house of Congress that handle **bills** in different policy areas.

joint committees
Congressional committees on a few subject-matter areas with membership drawn from both houses.

conference committees
Congressional committees formed when the Senate and the House pass a particular **bill** in different forms. Party leadership appoints members from each house to iron out the differences and bring back a single bill.

select committees
Congressional committees appointed for a specific purpose, such as the Watergate investigation.

TABLE 12.3

Standing Committees in the Senate and in the House

SENATE COMMITTEES	HOUSE COMMITTEES
Agriculture, Nutrition, and Forestry	Agriculture
Appropriations	Appropriations
Armed Services	Armed Services
Banking, Housing, and Urban Affairs	Budget
Budget	Education and Labor
Commerce, Science, and Transportation	Energy and Commerce
Energy and Natural Resources	Financial Services
Environment and Public Works	Foreign Affairs
Finance	Homeland Security
Foreign Relations	House Administration
Health, Education, Labor, and Pensions	Judiciary
Homeland Security and Governmental Affairs	Natural Resources
Judiciary	Oversight and Government Reform
Rules and Administration	Rules
Small Business and Entrepreneurship	Science and Technology
Veterans' Affairs	Small Business
	Standards of Official Conduct
	Transportation and Infrastructure
	Veterans' Affairs
	Ways and Means

The Committees at Work: Legislation and Oversight With more than 9,000 bills submitted by members every two years, some winnowing is essential. Every bill goes to a committee, which has virtually the power of life and death over it. The whole House or Senate usually considers only bills that obtain a favorable committee report.

A new bill that the Speaker sends to a committee typically goes directly to a subcommittee, which can hold hearings on the bill. Sizable committee and subcommittee staffs conduct research, line up witnesses for hearings, and write and rewrite bills. Committees and their subcommittees produce reports on proposed legislation. A committee's most important output, however, is the "marked-up" (rewritten) bill itself, which it submits to the full House or Senate for debate and voting.

The work of committees does not stop when the bill leaves the committee room. Members of the committee usually serve as "floor managers" of the bill, helping party leaders hustle votes for it. They are also the "cue givers" to whom other members turn for advice. When the Senate and House pass different versions of the same bill, some committee members serve on the conference committee.

The committees and subcommittees do not leave the scene even after legislation passes. They stay busy in **legislative oversight**, the process of monitoring the bureaucracy and its administration of policy. Committees handle oversight mainly through hearings. When an agency wants a bigger budget, the relevant committee reviews its current budget. Even if no budgetary issues are involved, members of committees constantly monitor how the bureaucracy is implementing a law. Agency heads and even cabinet secretaries testify, bringing graphs, charts, and data on the progress they have made and the problems they face. Committee staffs and committee members grill agency heads about particular problems. For example, a member may ask a Small Business Administration official why constituents who are applying for loans get the runaround. On another committee, officials charged with listing endangered species might defend the gray wolf against a member of Congress whose sheep-ranching constituents are not fond of wolves.

Oversight, one of the checks Congress can exercise on the executive branch, gives Congress the power to pressure agencies and, in extreme cases, cut their budgets in order to secure compliance with congressional wishes and even congressional whims.[40] Oversight also provides an opportunity to refine existing policies or respond to new problems.

Occasionally, congressional oversight rivets the nation's attention. In 1973 the Senate established the Select Committee on Presidential Campaign Activities to investigate the misdeeds and duplicity of the 1972 presidential campaign, otherwise known as the Watergate scandal. The House Judiciary Committee conducted hearings the next year on the impeachment of President Nixon for his conduct in attempting to cover up the scandal. Shortly after the Judiciary Committee recommended three articles of impeachment, the president resigned.

In 1987, Congress established a special joint committee to investigate what became known as the Iran-Contra affair, a term that refers to the secret sale of arms to Iran (for which President Reagan hoped to obtain the release of American hostages held in the Middle East) and the diversion of some of the funds from these sales to the Contras fighting the Sandinista government in Nicaragua (in the face of congressional prohibition of such aid). Many people thought the hearings,

legislative oversight
Congress's monitoring of the bureaucracy and its administration of policy, performed mainly through hearings.

Most of Congress's work takes place—and most of its members' power is wielded—in the standing committees and their numerous subcommittees. Here, the Senate Foreign Relations Committee hears from General David Petraeus on the situation in Iraq.

especially the testimony of Lieutenant Colonel Oliver North, made for great spy novel entertainment but did little to illuminate the issues involved in the matter.

Congress keeps tabs on more routine activities of the executive branch through its committee staff members. These members have specialized expertise in the fields and agencies that their committees oversee and maintain an extensive network of formal and informal contacts with the bureaucracy. By reading the voluminous reports that Congress requires of the executive and by receiving information from numerous sources—agencies, complaining citizens, members of Congress and their personal staff, state and local officials, interest groups, and professional organizations—staff members can keep track of the implementation of public policy.[41]

As the size and complexity of the national government grew in the 1960s and after numerous charges that the executive branch had become too powerful (especially in response to the widespread belief that Presidents Johnson and Nixon had abused their power), Congress responded with more oversight. The tight budgets of recent years have provided additional incentives for oversight, as members of Congress have sought to protect programs they favor from budget cuts and to get more value for the tax dollars spent on them. As the publicity value of receiving credit for controlling governmental spending has increased, so has the number of representatives and senators interested in oversight.[42]

Nevertheless, members of Congress have many competing responsibilities, and there are few political payoffs for carefully watching a government agency to see whether it is implementing policy properly. It is difficult to go to voters and say, "Vote for me. I oversaw the routine handling of road building." Because of this lack of incentives, problems may be overlooked until it is too late to do much about them. A major scandal involving the Department of Housing and Urban Development's administration of housing programs during the Reagan presidency was not uncovered until 1989, after Reagan had left office. Similarly, taxpayers could have saved well over $100 billion if Congress had insisted that the agencies regulating the savings and loan industry enforce their regulations more rigorously. More recently, there was clear evidence of fundamental problems in the operations and management of the Federal Emergency Management Agency in its response to the four hurricanes that hit Florida in 2004. Nevertheless, when hurricanes Katrina and Rita hit the next year, Congress had still not held oversight hearings.

In addition, the majority party largely determines if and when a committee will hold hearings. When the president's party has a majority in a house of Congress, that chamber is generally not aggressive in overseeing the administration because it does not wish to embarrass the president. Democrats were critical of what they regarded as timid Republican oversight of the nation's intelligence establishment and President Bush's planning and implementation of the aftermath of the war in Iraq, including the treatment of prisoners. Nevertheless, the president's partisans resisted holding the White House accountable, fearing that the Democrats would use hearings to discredit Bush. Similarly, critics charge that the failure to discern and make explicit the true costs of policy initiatives—from tax cuts to Medicare prescription drugs to the war in Iraq—made it impossible for a realistic cost-benefit analysis to enter the calculus before Congress approved the policies.[43] Once the Democrats gained majorities in Congress in the 2006 elections, the number of oversight hearings increased substantially.

Getting on a Committee One of the first worries for an incoming member of Congress (after paying off campaign debts) is getting on the right committee. Although it is not always easy to figure out what the right committee is, it is fairly easy to recognize some wrong committees. The Iowa newcomer does not want to get stuck on the Financial Services Committee; the Brooklyn freshman would like to avoid Agriculture. Members seek committees that will help them achieve three goals: reelection, influence in Congress, and the opportunity to make policy in areas they think are important.[44]

Just after their election, new members communicate their committee preferences to their party's congressional leaders and members of their state delegation. Every committee includes members from both parties, but a majority of each committee's members, as well as its chair, come from the majority party in the chamber. Each party in each house has a slightly different way of picking its committee members. Party leaders almost always play a key role.

Those who have supported the leadership are favored in the committee selection process, but generally the parties try to grant members' requests for committee assignments whenever possible. They want their members to please their constituents (being on the right committee should help them represent their constituency more effectively and reinforce their ability to engage in credit claiming) and to develop expertise in an area of policy. The parties also try to apportion the influence that comes with committee membership among the state delegations in order to accord representation to diverse components of the party.[45]

Getting Ahead on the Committee: Chairs and the Seniority System

If committees are the most important influencers of the congressional agenda, **committee chairs** are the most important influencers of the committee agenda. Committee chairs play dominant roles in scheduling hearings, hiring staff, appointing subcommittees, and managing committee bills when they are brought before the full house.

Until the 1970s, there was a simple way of picking committee chairs: the **seniority system**. If committee members had served on their committee longest and their party controlled the chamber, they got to be chairs—regardless of their party loyalty, mental state, or competence.

Woodrow Wilson, a political scientist before he became a politician, once said that the government of the United States was really government by the chairs of the standing committees of Congress. The chairs were so powerful for most of the twentieth century that they could bully members or bottle up legislation at any time—and with almost certain knowledge that they would be chairs for the rest of their electoral life. Richard Fenno, a veteran congressional observer, once remarked that the "performance of Congress as an institution is very largely the performance of its committees" but that the committee system is the "epitome of fragmentation and decentralization."[46] The more that congressional power is dispersed to committee chairs, the more difficult it is to make coherent policy.

In the 1970s, younger members of Congress revolted. Both parties in both branches permitted members to vote on committee chairs; in 1975, the House Democrats dumped four chairs with 154 years of seniority among them. The Democrats also increased the independence of subcommittees, which limited the chairs' power and widened the distribution of authority, visibility, and resources in both chambers.[47] Today seniority remains the *general rule* for selecting chairs, especially in the Senate, but there are plenty of exceptions. House Republicans skipped over several senior representatives when they named committee chairs in 1995 and continued to do so in subsequent Congresses. House Democrats also did not strictly adhere to seniority when they regained the majority in 2007.

Partially in response to the problems of decentralized power in the House, the Republicans passed other prominent committee reforms when they took control in 1995. The new rules eliminated some subcommittees and allowed committee chairs to choose the chairs of subcommittees on their committees and to hire all the committee and subcommittee staff. These changes centralized more power in the committee chairs. At the same time, the rules limited both committee and subcommittee chairs to three consecutive two-year terms as chair (Senate Republicans also adopted this rule, as did House Democrats in 2007), and committee chairs lost the power to cast proxy votes for those committee members not in attendance. The Speaker also

committee chairs

The most important influencers of the congressional agenda. They play dominant roles in scheduling hearings, hiring staff, appointing subcommittees, and managing committee **bills** when they are brought before the full house.

seniority system

A simple rule for picking **committee chairs**, in effect until the 1970s. The member who had served on the committee the longest and whose party controlled the chamber became chair, regardless of party loyalty, mental state, or competence.

put the committees on short leashes, giving them instructions regarding the legislation they were to report and a timetable for reporting it. In a few instances, the leadership bypassed committees by setting up separate task forces to prepare legislation.

By 1997, however, the leadership backed off and gave committee chairs greater leeway to set their committee's agenda and promised to allow committees to have the first chance to fashion legislation. The fact remains, however, that committee chairs are not as powerful as they were before the reform era, and the party leadership in the House has much more control over legislation. When the Democrats regained power in 2007, the House leadership also bypassed committees for its priority legislation.

CAUCUSES: THE INFORMAL ORGANIZATION OF CONGRESS

Although the formal organization of Congress consists of its party leadership and its committee structures, the informal organization of the House and Senate is also important. The informal networks of trust and mutual interest can spring from numerous sources. Friendship, ideology, and geography are long-standing sources of informal organization.

Lately, these traditional informal groupings have been dominated by a growing number of caucuses. In this context, a **caucus** is a group of members of Congress who share some interest or characteristic. There are about 300 of these caucuses, most of them containing members from both parties and some containing members from both the House and the Senate. The goal of all caucuses is to promote the interests around which they are formed. Within Congress they press for committees to hold hearings, they push particular legislation, and they pull together votes on bills they favor. They are somewhat like interest groups but with a difference: Their members are members of Congress, not petitioners to Congress on the outside looking in. Thus caucuses—interest groups within Congress—are nicely situated to pack more punch than interest groups outside Congress.[48]

This explosion of informal groups in Congress has made the representation of interests in Congress a more direct process. Some, such as the Black Caucus, the Caucus for Women's Issues, and the Hispanic Caucus, focus on advancing the interests of demographic groups. Others, such as the Sunbelt Caucus, are based on regional groupings. Still others, such as the Republican Study Committee, are ideological groupings. Many other caucuses are based on economic interests (ranging from Small Brewers to Tourism and Travel), health issues, or foreign policy matters dealing with specific countries—and all are interests important to at least some constituencies.

CONGRESSIONAL STAFF

As we discussed earlier, members of Congress are overwhelmed with responsibilities. It is virtually impossible to master the details of the hundreds of bills on which they must make decisions each year or to prepare their own legislation. They need help to meet their obligations, so they turn to their staff.

Personal Staff Most staff members work in the personal offices of individual members of Congress. The average representative has 17 assistants and the average senator has 40. In total, more than 11,000 individuals serve on the personal staffs of members of Congress. (Another 400 serve the congressional leaders.) In the summer, about 4,000 interns also work in members' offices on Capitol Hill (see "Young People and Politics: Are Opportunities to Intern Biased in Favor of the Wealthy?").

Why It Matters
The Committee System
The committee system in Congress is highly decentralized. As a result, it is open to the appeals of a wide range of "special" interests, especially those represented by highly paid lobbyists. If Congress were more *centralized* and only those interests cleared by the elected leadership received a hearing, special interests might be constrained. However, there is also a danger that only the interests reflecting the views of the leadership would be heard.

caucus (congressional)
A group of members of Congress sharing some interest or characteristic. Most are composed of members from both parties and from both houses.

The proliferation of congressional caucuses gives members of Congress an informal yet powerful means of shaping the policy agenda. Composed of legislative insiders who share similar concerns, the caucuses—such as the Hispanic Caucus pictured here with Barack Obama—exert a much greater influence on policymaking than most citizen-based interest groups can.

YOUNG PEOPLE AND POLITICS

Are Opportunities to Intern Biased in Favor of the Wealthy?

Many college students spend their summers working to pay for their studies during the rest of the year. Others, in contrast, serve as interns. Many of the interns have parents who support them financially during the summer. According to some experts, the focus on internships as a tool for professional success has never been greater, and about 80 percent of graduating college seniors have done a paid or unpaid internship. To some, an internship is an essential stepping-stone to career success.

Because Washington internships are in high demand, in most cases they do not pay, or they pay very little. The White House does not pay the interns who work there during the summer, in most cases the Supreme Court does not pay its undergraduate interns, and a vast majority of congressional offices do not pay the 4,000 summer interns who work on Capitol Hill, though a few, mostly on the Senate side, provide a limited stipend. To make matters worse, Washington is an expensive place to live, widening the gap between the haves and have-nots in the opportunities to gain experience as an intern. In some cases, universities or other programs provide some financial help, but most interns are on their own.

As internships rise in importance as critical milestones along the path to success, some people question whether they are creating a class system that discriminates against students from less affluent families who must turn down unpaid internships to earn money for college expenses. To the extent that Washington internships serve as a pipeline for people to become policymakers in the nation's capital, critics fear that over time internships, like the rising costs of college tuition, will squeeze voices from the working class and even the middle class out of high-level policy debates.

QUESTIONS FOR DISCUSSION

▷ Is the internship system in Washington likely to bias policymaking in the future?

▷ Should Congress appropriate funds so internships are more available to students from less wealthy backgrounds?

Source: Jennifer Lee, "Crucial Unpaid Internships Increasingly Separate the Haves from the Have-Nots," *New York Times*, August 10, 2004.

Members of Congress depend heavily on their staffs for everything from information and advice to scheduling and negotiating with other members of Congress. Here, Senator Joe Biden of Delaware confers with a staffer regarding policy in Iraq.

Most of these staffers spend their time on casework, providing services to constituents. They answer mail, communicate the member's views to voters, and help constituents solve problems. Nearly one-half of these House staffers and nearly one-third of the Senate personal staff work in members' offices in their constituencies, not in Washington. This makes it easier for people to make contact with the staff. Other personal staff help members of Congress with legislative functions, including drafting legislation, meeting with lobbyists and administrators, negotiating agreements on behalf of their bosses, writing questions to ask witnesses at committee hearings, summarizing bills, and briefing legislators. Senators, who must cover a wider range of committee assignments than members of the House, are especially dependent on staff. Indeed, members of both houses are now more likely to deal with each other through staff intermediaries than through personal interactions.

Committee Staff The committees of the House and Senate employ another 2,000 or so staff members. These staff members organize hearings, research legislative options, draft committee reports on bills, write legislation, and, as we have seen, keep tabs on the activities of the executive branch. Committee staff members often possess high levels of expertise and can become very influential in policymaking. As a result, lobbyists spend a lot of time cultivating these staffers both to obtain information about likely legislative actions and to plant ideas for legislation.

Staff Agencies   Finally, Congress has three important staff agencies that aid it in its work. The first is the *Congressional Research Service (CRS)*, administered by the Library of Congress and composed of researchers, many with advanced degrees and highly developed expertise. Each year it responds to more than 250,000 congressional requests for information and provides members with nonpartisan studies. CRS also tracks the progress of major bills, prepares summaries of bills, and makes this information available electronically.

The *Government Accountability Office (GAO)*, with more than 3,200 employees, helps Congress perform its oversight functions by reviewing the activities of the executive branch to see if it is following the congressional intent of laws and by investigating the efficiency and effectiveness of policy implementation. The GAO also sets government standards for accounting, provides legal opinions, and settles claims against the government.

The *Congressional Budget Office (CBO)* (discussed in more detail in Chapter 14) focuses on analyzing the president's budget and making economic projections about the performance of the economy, the costs of proposed policies, and the economic effects of taxing and spending alternatives.

Committees, caucuses, and individual legislators follow bills from their introduction to their approval. The next sections will discuss this process, which is often termed "labyrinthine" to reflect the fact that getting a bill through Congress is very much like navigating a difficult, intricate maze.

THE CONGRESSIONAL PROCESS

Congress's agenda is, of course, a crowded one—members introduce about 9,000 bills in each Congress. A **bill** is a proposed law, drafted in precise, legal language. Anyone can draft a bill. The White House and interest groups are common sources of polished bills. However, only members of the House or the Senate can formally submit a bill for consideration. The traditional route for a bill as it works its way through the legislative labyrinth is depicted in Figure 12.2. Most bills are quietly killed off early in the process. Some are introduced mostly as a favor to a group or a constituent; others are private bills, granting citizenship to a constituent or paying a settlement to a person whose car was demolished by a postal service truck. Still other bills may alter the course of the nation.

Congress is typically a reactive and cumbersome decision-making body. Rules are piled on rules and procedures on procedures.[49] Moreover, reforms in the 1970s decentralized the internal distribution of power in Congress, making legislating more difficult. The polarized political climate of the 1980s also exacerbated the problems of legislating. Party leaders sought ways to cope with these problems, and what Barbara Sinclair has termed *unorthodox lawmaking* has become common in the congressional process, especially for the most significant legislation.[50]

In both chambers party leaders involve themselves in the legislative process on major legislation earlier and more deeply, using special procedures to aid the passage of legislation. Leaders in the House often refer bills to several committees at the same time, bringing more interests to bear on an issue but complicating the process of passing legislation. Since committee leaders cannot always negotiate compromises *among* committees, party leaders have accepted this responsibility, often negotiating compromises and making adjustments to bills after a committee or committees report legislation. On the other hand, party leaders often bypass committees for high-priority legislation.

In the House, special rules from the Rules Committee have become powerful tools for controlling floor consideration of bills and sometimes for shaping the

bill
A proposed law, drafted in legal language. Anyone can draft a bill, but only a member of the House of Representatives or the Senate can formally submit a bill for consideration.

SIMULATION
You Are a Member of Congress

FIGURE 12.2

How a Bill Becomes a Law

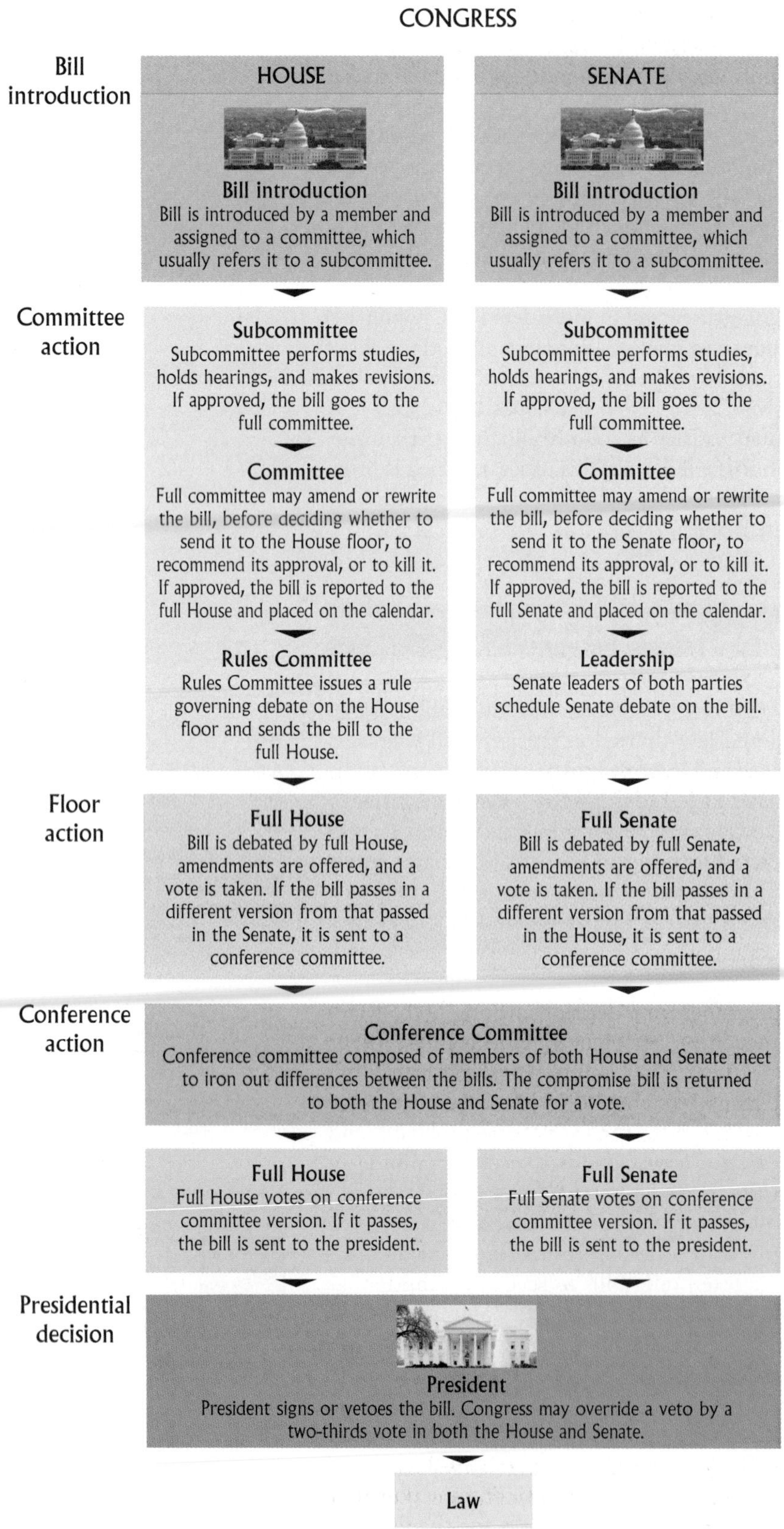

CONGRESS

Many bills travel full circle, coming first from the White House as part of the presidential agenda, then returning to the president at the end of the process. In the interim, there are two parallel processes in the Senate and House, starting with committee action. If a committee gives a bill a favorable report, the whole chamber considers it. When the two chambers pass different versions of it, a conference committee drafts a single compromise bill.

Bill introduction

HOUSE

Bill introduction
Bill is introduced by a member and assigned to a committee, which usually refers it to a subcommittee.

SENATE

Bill introduction
Bill is introduced by a member and assigned to a committee, which usually refers it to a subcommittee.

Committee action

Subcommittee
Subcommittee performs studies, holds hearings, and makes revisions. If approved, the bill goes to the full committee.

Subcommittee
Subcommittee performs studies, holds hearings, and makes revisions. If approved, the bill goes to the full committee.

Committee
Full committee may amend or rewrite the bill, before deciding whether to send it to the House floor, to recommend its approval, or to kill it. If approved, the bill is reported to the full House and placed on the calendar.

Committee
Full committee may amend or rewrite the bill, before deciding whether to send it to the Senate floor, to recommend its approval, or to kill it. If approved, the bill is reported to the full Senate and placed on the calendar.

Rules Committee
Rules Committee issues a rule governing debate on the House floor and sends the bill to the full House.

Leadership
Senate leaders of both parties schedule Senate debate on the bill.

Floor action

Full House
Bill is debated by full House, amendments are offered, and a vote is taken. If the bill passes in a different version from that passed in the Senate, it is sent to a conference committee.

Full Senate
Bill is debated by full Senate, amendments are offered, and a vote is taken. If the bill passes in a different version from that passed in the House, it is sent to a conference committee.

Conference action

Conference Committee
Conference committee composed of members of both House and Senate meet to iron out differences between the bills. The compromise bill is returned to both the House and Senate for a vote.

Full House
Full House votes on conference committee version. If it passes, the bill is sent to the president.

Full Senate
Full Senate votes on conference committee version. If it passes, the bill is sent to the president.

Presidential decision

President
President signs or vetoes the bill. Congress may override a veto by a two-thirds vote in both the House and Senate.

Law

outcomes of votes. Often party leaders from each chamber negotiate among themselves instead of creating conference committees. Party leaders also use *omnibus* legislation that addresses numerous and perhaps unrelated subjects, issues, and programs to create winning coalitions, forcing members to support the entire bill to obtain the individual parts.

These new procedures are generally under the control of party leaders in the House, but in the Senate, leaders have less leverage, and *individual* senators have retained substantial opportunities for influence (such as using the filibuster). As a result, it is often more difficult to pass legislation in the Senate.

There are, of course, countless influences on this legislative process. Presidents, parties, constituents, interest groups, the congressional and committee leadership structure—these and other influences offer members cues for their decision making.

PRESIDENTS AND CONGRESS: PARTNERS AND PROTAGONISTS

Political scientists sometimes call the president the *chief legislator*, a phrase that might have appalled the Constitution writers, with their insistence on separation of powers. Presidents do, however, help create the congressional agenda. They are also their own best lobbyists.

Presidents have their own legislative agenda, based in part on their party's platform and their electoral coalition. Their task is to persuade Congress that their agenda should also be Congress's agenda, and they have a good chance that Congress will at least give their proposals a hearing.[51]

Presidents have many resources with which to influence Congress. (The next chapter will examine presidential leadership.) They may try to influence members directly—calling up wavering members and telling them that the country's future hinges on their votes, for example—but they do not do this often. If presidents were to pick just one key bill and spend 10 minutes on the telephone with each of the 535 members of Congress, they would spend 89 hours chatting with them. Instead, presidents wisely leave most White House lobbying to staff members and administration officials and work closely with the party's leaders in the House and Senate.

It seems a wonder that presidents, even with all their power and prestige, can push and wheedle anything through the labyrinthine congressional process. The president must usually win at least 10 times to hope for final passage:

1. In one House subcommittee
2. In the full House committee
3. In the House Rules Committee to move to the floor
4. On the House floor
5. In one Senate subcommittee
6. In the full Senate committee
7. On the Senate floor
8. In the House–Senate conference committee to work out the differences between the two bills
9. On the House floor for final passage
10. On the Senate floor for final passage

As one scholar put it, presidential leadership of Congress is *at the margins.*[52] In general, successful presidential leadership of Congress has not been the result of the dominant chief executive of political folklore who reshapes the contours of the political landscape to pave the way for change. Rather than creating the conditions for important shifts in public policy, the effective American leader is the less heroic *facilitator* who works at the margins of coalition building to recognize and exploit opportunities presented by a favorable configuration of political forces. Of course, presidents can exercise their veto to *stop* legislation they oppose.

Presidents are only one of many claimants for the attention of Congress, especially on domestic policy. As we will show in the next chapter, popular presidents and presidents with a large majority of their party in each house of Congress have a good chance of getting their way. Yet presidents often lose. Ronald Reagan was considered a strong chief executive, and budgeting was one of his principal tools for affecting public policy. Yet commentators typically pronounced the budgets he proposed to Congress DOA, dead on arrival. Members of Congress truly compose an independent branch.

PARTY, CONSTITUENCY, AND IDEOLOGY

Presidents come and go; the parties endure. Presidents do not determine a congressional member's electoral fortunes; constituents do. Where presidents are less influential, on domestic policies especially, party, personal ideology, and constituency are more important.

Party Influence   On some issues, members of the parties stick together like a marching band. They are most cohesive when Congress is electing its official leaders. A vote for Speaker of the House is a straight party-line vote, with every Democrat on one side and every Republican on the other. On other issues, however, the party coalition may come unglued. In the past, votes on civil rights policies, for example, revealed deep divisions within each party.

Differences between the parties are sharpest on questions of social welfare and economic policy.[53] When voting on labor issues, Democrats traditionally cling together, leaning toward the side of the unions, whereas Republicans almost always vote with business. On social welfare issues—for example, the minimum wage, aid to the poor, unemployed, or uninsured, and grants for education—Democrats are more supportive of government action than are Republicans. This split between the parties should not be too surprising if you recall the party coalitions described in Chapter 8. Once in office, party members favor their electoral coalitions. Because the constituencies of House members are now more solidly Republican or Democrat, the differences between party members in the House have increased, as we discuss below.

Party leaders in Congress help "whip" their members into line. Their power to do so is limited, of course. They cannot drum a recalcitrant member out of the party. Leaders have plenty of influence, however, including making committee assignments, boosting a member's pet projects, and the subtle but significant influence of providing critical information to a member.

The congressional parties can also impact who sits in Congress. The congressional campaign committees have energized both parties, helping to recruit candidates, running seminars in campaign skills, and conducting polls. They are also a source of funding, as are PACs headed by members of the party leadership.

Polarized Politics   In the 1970s, it was not unusual to find political analysts commenting on how Americans were growing less partisan and less ideological in their politics. Over the past three decades, however, it is clear that the distance between the congressional parties has been growing steadily, as you can see in the figure in this box. As the parties pulled apart ideologically, they also became more homogeneous internally. In other words, Republicans in Congress became more consistently conservative, Democrats became more consistently liberal, and the distance between the center of each party increased.

By the time George W. Bush took office in 2001, the typical views of members of the parties in both chambers had moved further apart than they had been at any time since before World War I, and they separated even further during his tenure as president (see "A Generation of Change: Polarization in Congress"). As a result of these ideological differences between the parties in Congress, it has been more difficult to reach a compromise.

Polarization in Congress

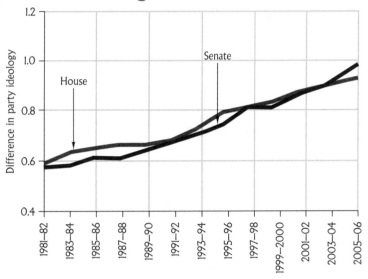

Differences between Democrats and Republicans in Congress have grown considerably since 1980.

Source: Authors' calculation of data from Keith Poole, posted at *http://www.voteview.com/dwnl.htm.*

It has been especially difficult for the president because the opposition party is generally not a fertile ground for obtaining policy support. Because of the polarized partisan divide—and thus a dwindling number of moderate-to-conservative Democrats—there have been few Democrats who were potential supporters of the Republican president in the White House.

Why did this change happen? At the core of the increased ideological distance between the parties have been increasingly divergent electoral coalitions. One important factor is that state legislatures drew the boundaries of House districts so that the partisan divisions in the constituencies of representatives became more one-sided. Most House members no longer had to worry about pleasing the center of the electorate because their own districts were either clearly conservative or liberal.

In addition, liberal and conservative voters sorted themselves into the Democratic and Republican parties, respectively. There are many fewer liberal Republicans or conservative Democrats than there were a generation ago. Thus, conservatives have been more likely to support the more conservative party and liberals the more liberal party. As supporters of each party have matched their partisan and ideological views, they have made the differences between the parties more distinctive. Moreover, party loyalty among voters in congressional elections also increased, so the relationship between ideology and voting became notably stronger.

The changes in the preferences, behavior, and distribution of congressional voters gave the congressional parties more internally homogeneous, divergent, and polarized electoral constituencies. These constituencies in turn elected more ideologically polarized representatives in Congress.

Congressional Redistricting

Constituency Versus Ideology   Members of Congress are representatives; their constituents expect them to represent their interests in Washington. In 1714, Anthony Henry, a member of the British Parliament, received a letter from some of his constituents asking him to vote against an excise tax. He is reputed to have replied in part,

Gentlemen: I have received your letter about the excise, and I am surprised at your insolence in writing to me at all . . . may God's curse light upon you all, and may it make your homes as open and as free to the excise officers as your wives and daughters have always been to me while I have represented your rascally constituency.[54]

Needless to say, notions of representation have changed since Henry's time.

Sometimes representation requires a balancing act. If some representatives favor more defense spending but suspect that their constituents do not, what are they to do? The English politician and philosopher Edmund Burke favored the concept of legislators as *trustees*, using their best judgment to make policy in the interests of the people. Others prefer the concept of representatives as *instructed delegates*, mirroring the preferences of their constituents. Actually, members of Congress are *politicos*, adopting both trustee and instructed delegate roles as they strive to be both representatives and policymakers.[55]

The best way constituents can influence congressional voting is also simple: elect a representative or senator who agrees with their views. Congressional candidates tend to take policy positions different from their opponent's. Moreover, the winners generally vote on roll calls as they said they would during their campaigns.[56] If voters use their good sense to elect candidates who share their policy positions, then constituents *can* influence congressional policy.

If voters miss their chance and elect someone out of step with their thinking, it may be difficult to influence that person's votes. It is a challenge for even well-intentioned legislators to know what people want. Some legislators pay careful attention to their mail, but the mail is a notoriously unreliable indicator of people's thinking; individuals with extreme opinions on an issue are more likely to write than those with moderate views. Some members send questionnaires to constituents, but the answers they receive are unreliable because few people respond. Some try public opinion polling, but it is expensive if professionally done and unreliable if not.

Defeating an incumbent is no easy task. Even legislators whose votes conflict with the views of their constituents tend to be reelected. Most citizens have trouble recalling the names of their congressional representatives (one study found that only 28 percent of the public could name their representatives in the House),[57] let alone keeping up with their representatives' voting records. According to one expert, "Probably less than a third of all constituents can recognize who their representatives are and what policy positions they have generally taken—and even that third tends not to evaluate incumbents on the basis of policy."[58] A National Election Study found that only 11 percent of the people even claimed to remember how their congressperson voted on a particular issue.

On some controversial issues, however, legislators ignore constituent opinion at great peril. For years, Southern members of Congress would not have dared to vote for a civil rights law. Lately, representatives and senators have been concerned about the many new single-issue groups. Such groups care little about a member's overall record; to them, a vote on one issue—gun control, abortion, gay marriage—is all that counts. Ready to pounce on one wrong vote and pour money into an opponent's campaign, these new forces in constituency politics make every legislator nervous. When issues are visible and salient to voters and easy for them to understand, their representatives are likely to be quite responsive to constituency opinion.[59]

Nevertheless, many issues are complex, obscure, and not salient to voters. On such issues legislators can safely ignore constituency opinion. On a typical issue, the prime determinant of a congressional member's vote is personal ideology. On issues where ideological divisions are sharp and constituency preferences and knowledge are likely to be weak, such as defense and foreign policy, ideology is virtually the only determinant of voting.[60] As ideological divisions weaken and constituency preferences strengthen, members are more likely to deviate from their own position and adopt those of their constituencies.[61] Thus, when they have differences of opinion with their constituencies, members of Congress consider constituency preferences but are not controlled by them.[62]

LOBBYISTS AND INTEREST GROUPS

The nation's capital is crawling with lawyers, lobbyists, registered foreign agents, public relations consultants, and others—there are about 35,000 registered lobbyists representing 12,000 organizations—all seeking to influence Congress.[63] Lobbyists spend nearly $3 billion on lobbying federal officials—plus millions more in campaign contributions and attempts to try to persuade members' constituents to send messages to Washington.[64]

We saw in the last chapter that lobbyists, some of them former members of Congress, can provide legislators with crucial policy information, political intelligence, and often with assurances of financial aid in the next campaign—making those legislators with whom they agree more effective in the legislative process.[65] They often coordinate their efforts at influencing members with party leaders who share their views. Grass-roots lobbying—such as computerized mailings to encourage citizens to pressure their representatives on an issue—is a common activity. Interest groups also distribute scorecards of how members of Congress voted on issues important to the groups, threatening members with electoral retaliation if they do not support the groups' stands. Of course, lobbyists usually make little headway with their opponents: The lobbyist for General Motors arguing against automobile pollution controls will not have much influence with a legislator concerned about air pollution.

Lobbyists have never been held in high esteem by the public, and they have come under especially harsh criticism in recent years. Nevertheless, lobbyists play an important role in the legislative process. Here, lobbyists line up to attend a session of the Senate Finance Committee focusing on a tax cut for U.S. manufacturers.

Concerned about inappropriate influence from lobbyists, Congress passed a law in 1995 requiring anyone hired to lobby members of Congress, congressional staff members, White House officials, and federal agencies to report what issues they were seeking to influence, how much they were spending on the effort, and the identities of their clients. Congress also placed severe restrictions on the gifts, meals, and expense-paid travel that public officials may accept from lobbyists. In theory, these reporting requirements and restrictions would not only prevent shady deals between lobbyists and members of Congress but also curb the influence of special interests. Nevertheless, slippage occurred. In 2005 and 2006, the country saw some members caught up in bribery scandals. The nation also learned of lobbyist Jack Abramoff's success in charging six Indian tribes more than $80 million for his lobbying services in less than a decade—and his extraordinary contributions to and expenditures on some representatives and senators. In response, Congress in 2007 passed a new law and the House revised its ethics rules. Together, they strengthened public disclosure requirements concerning lobbying activity and funding, placed more restrictions on gifts and travel for members of Congress and their staff, provided for mandatory disclosure of earmarks in expenditure bills, and slowed the revolving door between Congress and the lobbying world. We will have to wait to see if lobbyists and their lawyers find loopholes in the law.

There are many forces that affect senators and representatives as they decide how to vote on a bill. After his exhaustive study of influences on congressional decision making, John Kingdon concluded that none was important enough to suggest that members of Congress vote as they do because of one influence.[66] The process is as complex for individual legislators as it is for those who want to influence their votes.

UNDERSTANDING CONGRESS

Congress is a complex institution. Its members want to make sound national policy, but they also want to return to Washington after the next election. How do these sometimes conflicting desires affect American democracy and the scope of American government?

CONGRESS AND DEMOCRACY

Comparing Legislatures

In a large nation, the success of democratic government depends on the quality of representation. Americans could hardly hold a national referendum on every policy issue on the government agenda; instead, they delegate decision-making power to representatives. If Congress is a successful democratic institution, it must be a successful representative institution.

Certainly, some aspects of Congress make it very *un*representative. Its members are an American elite. Its leadership is chosen by its own members, not by any vote of the American people. Voters have little direct influence over the individuals who chair key committees or lead congressional parties. In addition, the Senate is apportioned to represent states, not population. As we learned in Chapter 2, this distribution of power accords citizens in less populated states have a greater say in key decisions. As you can see in "America in Perspective: Malapportionment in the Upper House," malapportionment is high in the U.S.

Nevertheless, the evidence in this chapter demonstrates that Congress *does* try to listen to the American people. Whom voters elect makes a difference in how congressional votes turn out; which party is in power affects policies. Perhaps Congress could do a better job at representation than it does, but there are many obstacles to improved representation. Legislators find it hard to know what constituents want. Groups may keep important issues off the legislative agenda. Members may

AMERICA IN PERSPECTIVE

Malapportionment in the Upper House

In a perfectly apportioned system, no citizen's vote weighs more than another's. In a malapportioned system, by contrast, the votes of some citizens weigh more than the votes of others. A number of democracies in developed countries have upper Houses with significant powers. The U.S. Senate is the most malapportioned among them.

How content are you with the malapportionment of power in the Senate?

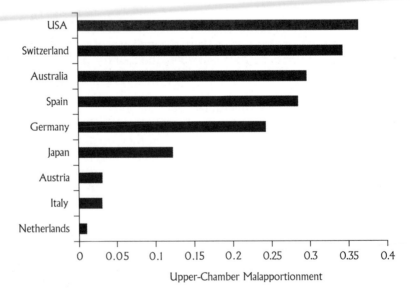

Source: David Samuels and Richard Snyder, "The Value of a Vote: Malapportionment in Comparative Perpective," *British Journal of Political Science* 31 (October 2001), p. 662.

spend so much time servicing their constituencies that they have little time left to represent those constituencies in the policymaking process.

Members of Congress are responsive to the people, if the people make clear what they want. For example, in response to popular demands, Congress established a program in 1988 to shield the elderly against the catastrophic costs associated with acute illness. In 1989, in response to complaints from the elderly about higher Medicare premiums, Congress abolished most of what it had created the previous year.

Representativeness Versus Effectiveness   The central legislative dilemma for Congress is combining the faithful representation of constituents with making effective public policy. Supporters see Congress as a forum in which many interests compete for a spot on the policy agenda and over the form of a particular policy— which is just as the Founders intended it to be.

Critics charge that Congress is too representative—so much so that it is incapable of taking decisive action to deal with difficult problems. The agricultural committees busily tend to the interests of farmers, while committees focusing on foreign trade worry about cutting agricultural subsidies. One committee wrestles with domestic unemployment, while another makes tax policy that encourages businesses to open new plants out of the country. One reason why government spends too much, critics say, is that Congress is protecting the interests of too many people. As long as each interest tries to preserve the status quo, Congress cannot enact bold reforms.

On the other hand, defenders of Congress point out that, thanks to its being decentralized, there is no oligarchy in control to prevent the legislature from taking comprehensive action. In fact, Congress has enacted the huge tax cuts of 1981 and 2001, the comprehensive (and complicated) tax reform of 1986, and various bills structuring the budgetary process designed to balance the budget.[67] In recent years, Congress has also passed important trade bills, a prescription drug addition to Medicare, and a major program for elementary and secondary education.

There is no simple solution to Congress's dilemma. It tries to be both a representative and an objective policymaking institution. As long as this is true, it is unlikely that Congress will please all its critics.

Cable television's live coverage of Congress has further democratized the legislative process by letting Americans see their representatives at work. Here, the U.S. House of Representatives concludes a vote on education policy.

CONGRESS AND THE SCOPE OF GOVERNMENT

Congress is responsive to a multitude of interests many of which desire government policies. Does this responsiveness predispose the legislature to increase the size of government to please the public? Does providing constituents with pork barrel spending and casework services provide an incentive for members of Congress to expand government programs so there are more potential ways members can help their constituencies? One can argue that big government helps members of Congress get reelected and even gives them good reason to support making it bigger.

Members of Congress vigorously protect the interests of their constituents. At the same time, there are many members who agree with the conservative argument that government is not the answer to problems but rather *is* the problem. These individuals make careers out of fighting against government programs (although these same senators and representatives typically support programs aimed at aiding *their* constituents).

Americans have contradictory preferences regarding public policy. As we have noted in previous chapters, they want to balance the budget and pay low taxes, but majorities also support most government programs. Congress does not impose programs on a reluctant public; instead, it responds to the public's demands for them.

SUMMARY

According to the Constitution, members of Congress are the government's policymakers, but legislative policymaker is only one of the roles of members of Congress. They are also politicians, and politicians always keep one eye on the next election. Success in congressional elections may be determined as much by constituency service—casework and the pork barrel—as by policymaking. Senators and representatives have become so secure in their constituencies that incumbents have a big edge over challengers, making it more difficult to bring about major changes in the makeup, and thus the policies, of Congress.

The structure of Congress is so complex that it seems remarkable that legislation gets passed at all. Its bicameral division means that bills have two sets of committee hurdles to clear. Because power is often decentralized, especially in the Senate, the job of leading Congress is more difficult than ever.

Presidents try hard to influence Congress, and parties and elections can also shape legislators' choices. The impact of these factors clearly differs from one policy area to another. Party impacts are clearest on issues for which the party's coalitions are clearest, especially social welfare and economic issues. Constituencies influence policy mostly by the initial choice of a representative. Members of Congress do pay attention to voters, particularly on visible issues, but most issues do not interest voters. On these less visible issues, other factors, such as lobbyists and members' individual ideologies, influence policy decisions.

Congress clearly has some undemocratic and unrepresentative features. Its members are hardly average Americans. Even so, members usually pay attention to popular preferences, when they can determine what they are. People inside and outside the institution, however, think that Congress is ineffective. Its objective policymaking decisions and representative functions sometimes conflict, yet from time to time Congress does show that it can deal with major issues in a comprehensive fashion. Many members of Congress have incentives to increase the scope of the federal government, but the people who put those representatives in office provide these incentives.

Chapter Test

Multiple Choice

1. In terms of numbers, which of the following is the most underrepresented group in Congress?
   a. African Americans
   b. Asian Americans
   c. Hispanics
   d. Native Americans
   e. Women

2. All but which of the following are true of incumbents in Congress?
   a. Most of them decide to run for reelection
   b. Their views on policy are well known to their constituents
   c. Most of them win with more than 60 percent of the vote
   d. Most of them have more financial support than their opponents
   e. Most of them are better known than their opponents

3. Which of the following make reelection in the Senate more

difficult than in the House of Representatives?

a. Senators represent an entire, often diverse state
b. Senators have less personal contact with voters
c. Senators are challenged by more powerful opponents
d. Senators are more likely to be held accountable for issues
e. All of the above

4. The only state in America with a unicameral legislature is:

a. Nebraska
b. North Dakota
c. Alaska
d. Montana
e. Delaware

5. When a senator engages in unlimited debate in order to prevent a bill from being voted on, this is called:

a. Cloture
b. Log rolling
c. Filibuster
d. Investiture
e. Rhetoric

6. Which of the following is the only legislative office mandated by the Constitution?

a. The Senate majority leader
b. The Speaker of the House
c. The Office of Legislative Management
d. The party whips
e. The majority leader

7. The president of the Senate is:

a. Elected by the Senate as a whole
b. Elected by the majority party in the Senate
c. The most senior member of the Senate
d. Appointed by the U.S. president
e. The vice-president of the United States

8. Which committee is charged with reconciling different versions of a bill passed by the House and the Senate?

a. Standing committee
b. Joint committee
c. Conference committee
d. Select committee
e. Reconciliation committee

9. Which of the following is NOT a recent reason for women's underrepresentation in Congress?

a. Women are less likely to run for office, if they feel their chances of winning are poor
b. Women are less likely to become major party nominees
c. Women are less likely to win races they enter
d. Women are less likely to run for office because of childcare responsibilities
e. All of the above

10. What contributes to the success of incumbents in elections?

a. Voters are familiar with the incumbents' voting patterns
b. Incumbents face weaker opponents
c. Incumbents frequently "ride the coattails" of presidential candidates
d. Voters are motivated by their pocketbooks
e. All of the above

True/False

11. Congressional elections are generally foregone conclusions.
    True_____   False_____

12. The vast majority of people are more likely to vote based on party identification than the specific candidate's characteristics and/or platform.
    True_____   False_____

13. The president of the Senate usually plays an active role in daily Senate activities.
    True_____   False_____

14. Only a member of the House or Senate can officially propose a bill to Congress.
    True_____   False_____

Short Answer

15. Given the overwhelming tendency of incumbents to win elections, what are three possible reasons why an incumbent loses?

16. Name and briefly explain the four formal powers of the Speaker of the House.

17. Explain why the president has sometimes been called the "chief legislator." In what concrete ways can the president try to influence the legislative process?

18. What is the difference between descriptive and substantive representation? In your opinion, can Congress as a whole claim either? Why, or why not?

19. Please explain the key differences between the Senate and the House of Representatives with regard to the following characteristics: 1) Constitutional powers; 2) centralization of power; 3) role in policymaking; and 4) procedures.

20. Describe the function of committees and subcommittees that summarized under the term "legislative oversight."

21. What have been at least two causes and two consequences of the increased polarization of parties in Congress over the last few decades?

Short Answer/Essay Questions

22. Senator Robert Dole once said that the position of Majority leader is more akin to that of "Majority Pleader." Drawing on what you have learned about the position of leaders in Congress, what speaks for this assessment, and what speaks against it? How important do you feel strong leadership is in the House and in the Senate? Which aspects of leaders' powers would you change, and why? If you would not change anything, explain why not.

23. Based on what you have learned about the formal and the informal organization of Congress, which do you believe has a greater influence over the legislative process? Provide specific details of the role of committees, subcommittees, and congressional caucuses in your answer, as well as examples to support your arguments.

24. In your opinion, what are two pros and two cons of introducing term limits for members of Congress? What would you consider a reasonable amount of time for such term limits, and why? Why have term limits been successfully introduced for many state legislatures, but not for Congress?

25. First and foremost, members of Congress serve as representatives of their constituents. However, there appears to be some debate about whether we should think of legislators as *trustees*, *instructed delegates*, or *politicos*. Which concept do you believe best describes the role of members of Congress, and why? Support your argument.

Answer Key

1. E   2. B   3. E   4. A   5. C   6. B   7. E   8. C   9. C   10. B   11. True   12. True   13. False   14. True

Key Terms

incumbents (368)
casework (370)
pork barrel (370)
bicameral legislature (374)
House Rules Committee (375)
filibuster (376)
Speaker of the House (377)

majority leader (377)
whips (378)
minority leader (378)
standing committees (379)
joint committees (379)
conference committees (379)
select committees (379)

legislative oversight (380)
committee chairs (382)
seniority system (382)
caucus (383)
bill (385)

Internet Resources

www.house.gov/
The official House Web site contains information on the organization, operations, schedule, and activities of the House and its committees. The site also contains links to the offices of members and committees and enables you to contact your representative directly.

www.senate.gov/
The official Senate Web site contains information and links similar to those for the House.

Thomas.loc.gov/
Information on the activities of Congress, the status and text of legislation, the *Congressional Record*, committee reports, and historical documents.

www.rollcall.com/
Roll Call, the online version of the Capitol Hill newspaper.

www.fec.gov/
Federal Election Commission data on campaign expenditures.

www.opensecrets.org
The Center for Responsive Politics Web site with data on the role of money in politics.

www.c-span.org
Video coverage of Congress in action.

http://www.cawp.rutgers.edu/
The Center for American Women and Politics Web site, with information on women in politics at all levels of government.

GetConnected

The Organization of Congress

Both the Senate and the House are organized into committees, where much of the real work takes place. As the text notes, senators and representatives seek membership on committees that have something to do with their home state or district. They seek membership on the right committees because good work on the right committees will help them get reelected, make good policy, and gain influence in Congress. See whether you can pick the committees on which your local representative serves.

First, make a list of the important characteristics of your district, such as whether it is urban or rural, whether it has a lot of farming or industry, whether it has a large international airport or sits next to the ocean, or whether there is a lot of military in the district. Your list should have five or six items on it. Next, go to the House of Representatives Web site and look at the jurisdictional duties of each standing House committee. Based on your list, pick the committees on which you think your representative might serve. Once you have done that, go to your representative's Web site to see how accurate you are.

Search the Web

Go to *www.house.gov/rules/comm_jurisdiction.htm* to review the jurisdiction of the standing committees. Go to *www.house.gov/* to find your representative's Web site to check the accuracy of your picks.

Questions to Ask

- Does your representative appear to be on the kinds of committees that will allow him or her to best represent your district?
- If you could place your representative on another committee, one that might be more important to the district, which would it be? Why?

- Not all committees are focused on district-level interests. Some deal with broader issues such as foreign affairs, national defense, and tax policy. Is your representative on a committee on which he or she can influence policies critical to the nation as a whole?

Why It Matters

One job of congressional representatives is to represent the issues and concerns of their constituents. Because committees are where most work gets done in Congress, it is important for representatives to be on a committee that will allow them to best represent their districts. Constituents also have broader interests, however, and the committees on which their representatives serve are an opportunity to influence important policies.

Get Involved

Send your representative an e-mail asking why he or she serves on certain committees. Ask why he or she serves on a committee that does not seem to fit the district and not on a committee that seems important for the district. Ask also whether the representative has any plans to change committee assignments in the future. For more exercises, go to *www.longmanamericangovernment.com*.

For Further Reading

Aberbach, Joel D. *Keeping a Watchful Eye: The Politics of Congressional Oversight.* Washington, DC: Brookings Institution, 1990. A thorough study of congressional oversight of the executive branch.

Bernstein, Robert A. *Elections, Representation, and Congressional Voting Behavior.* Englewood Cliffs, NJ: Prentice Hall, 1989. Examines the issue of constituency control over members of Congress.

Binder, Sarah A. *Stalemate.* Washington, DC: Brookings Institution, 2003. Discusses the causes and consequences of legislative gridlock.

Deering, Christopher J., and Steven S. Smith. *Committees in Congress.* 3rd ed. Washington, DC: Congressional Quarterly Press, 1997. A thorough overview of the complex committee structure in the House and Senate.

Dodd, Lawrence C., and Bruce I. Oppenheimer. *Congress Reconsidered.* 8th ed. Washington, DC: Congressional Quarterly, 2005. Excellent essays covering many aspects of Congress.

Fenno, Richard F., Jr. *Home Style.* Boston: Little, Brown, 1978. How members of Congress mend fences and stay in political touch with the folks back home.

Fiorina, Morris P. *Congress: Keystone of the Washington Establishment.* 2nd ed. New Haven, CT: Yale University Press, 1989. Argues that members of Congress are self-serving in representing their constituents, ensuring their reelection but harming the national interest.

Jacobson, Gary C. *The Politics of Congressional Elections.* 7th ed. New York: Addison-Wesley Longman, 2007. An excellent review of congressional elections.

Kingdon, John W. *Congressmen's Voting Decisions.* 3rd ed. Ann Arbor: University of Michigan Press, 1989. A thorough and insightful study of congressional voting decisions.

Lee, Frances E., and Bruce I. Oppenheimer. *Sizing Up the Senate: The Unequal Consequences of Equal Representation.* Chicago: University of Chicago Press, 1999. How representation in the Senate affects how people are represented, the distribution of government benefits, and the nature of election campaigns.

Mann, Thomas E., and Norman J. Ornstein. *The Broken Branch.* New York: Oxford University Press, 2006. How Congress is failing America and how to get it back on track.

Mayhew, David R. *Congress: The Electoral Connection.* 2nd ed. New Haven, CT: Yale University Press, 2005. An analysis of Congress based on the premise that the principal motivation of congressional behavior is reelection.

Sinclair, Barbara. *Party Wars.* Norman, OK: University of Oklahoma Press, 2006. The impact of partisan polarization on congressional policy making.

Sinclair, Barbara. *Unorthodox Lawmaking.* 3rd ed. Washington, DC: Congressional Quarterly Press, 2007. Explains how Congress tries to cope with decentralization and polarization.

THE
PRESIDENCY

POLITICS IN ACTION:
PRESIDENTIAL POWER

As George W. Bush sat on the inaugural platform in January 2009, waiting for his successor to take the oath of office, he could reflect on his tenure as president. It had certainly been eventful. Elected in 2000 without even a plurality of the vote and after a protracted battle in the courts, he had to create a new administration under the difficult circumstances of a substantially shortened transition period. Once in office, he had led the successful fight on his highest priority—a major tax cut. Soon, however, his approval ratings dropped, and the Democratic opposition gained control of the Senate.

Shortly afterward, terrorists launched a devastating attack on the United States, and the focus of his administration abruptly changed to a war on terrorism. His approval ratings rocketed to the highest on record, and his party won majorities in Congress in the midterm elections. Nevertheless, Congress was often resistant to his proposals, and members of both Congress and the press raised disturbing questions about the bureaucracy's performance regarding homeland security.

After winning reelection, he launched a campaign to reform the massive Social Security program. His efforts came to nothing. The same thing happened with his proposals for immigration reform. Even more frustrating were the difficulties he faced in pacifying and democratizing Iraq, and throughout his second term most Americans disapproved of his performance in office.

Powerful, strong, leader of the free world, commander in chief—these are common images of the American president. The only place in the world where television networks assign permanent camera crews is the White House. The presidency is power—at least according to popular myth. Problems are brought to their desk, they decide on the right courses of action, they issue orders, and an army of aides and bureaucrats carry out their commands.

As George W. Bush and all other presidents soon discover, nothing could be further from the truth. The main reason why presidents have trouble getting things done is that other policymakers with whom they deal have their own agendas, their own interests, and their own sources of power. Presidents operate in an environment filled with checks and balances and competing centers of power. As one presidential aide put it, "Every time you turn around people resist you."[1] Congress is beholden not to the president but to the individual constituencies of its members. Cabinet members often push their departmental interests and their constituencies (the Department of Agriculture has farmers as its constituency, for example). Rarely can presidents rely on unwavering support from their party, the public, or even their own appointees.

As the pivotal leader in American politics, the president is the subject of unending political analysis and speculation. A perennial question focuses on presidential power. World history is replete with examples of leaders who have exceeded the prescribed boundaries of their power. Can the presidency become too powerful and thus pose a threat to democracy? Or is the Madisonian system strong enough to check any such tendencies? On the other hand, is the president *strong enough* to stand up to the diverse interests in the United States? Does the president have enough power to govern on behalf of the majority?

A second fundamental question regarding democratic leaders is the nature of their relationship with the public and its consequences for public policy. The president and vice president are the only officials elected by the entire nation. In their efforts to obtain public support from the broad spectrum of interests in the public, are presidents natural advocates of an expansion of government? Do they promise more than they should in order to please the voters? As they face the frustrations of governing, do presidents seek to centralize authority in the federal government, where they have greater influence, while reducing that of the states? Does the chief executive seek more power through increasing the role of government?

Because not everyone bends easily to even the most persuasive president, the president must be a *leader*. As Richard Neustadt has argued, presidential power is the power to *persuade*.[2] To accomplish policy goals, the president must get other people—important people—to do things they otherwise would not do. To be effective, the president must have highly developed *political skills* to mobilize influence, manage conflict, negotiate, and fashion compromises. Presidential leadership has varied over the years, depending in large part on the individual who holds our nation's highest office.

THE PRESIDENTS

The presidency is an institution composed of the roles presidents must play, the powers at their disposal, and the large bureaucracy at their command. It is also a highly personal office. The personality of the individual serving as president makes a difference.

GREAT EXPECTATIONS

When a new president takes the oath of office, he faces many daunting tasks. Perhaps the most difficult is living up to the expectations of the American people. Americans expect the chief executive to ensure peace, prosperity, and security.[3] As President Carter remarked, "The President . . . is held to be responsible for the state of the economy . . . and for the inconveniences, or disappointments, or the concerns of the American people."[4] Americans want a good life, and they look to the president to provide it.

Americans are of two minds about the presidency. On the one hand, they want to believe in a powerful president, one who can do good. They look back longingly on the great presidents of the first American century—Washington, Jefferson, Lincoln—and some in the second century as well, especially Franklin D. Roosevelt.

On the other hand, Americans dislike a concentration of power. Although presidential responsibilities have increased substantially since the Great Depression and World War II, there has not been a corresponding increase in presidential authority or administrative resources to meet these new expectations. Americans are basically individualistic and skeptical of authority. According to Samuel Huntington, "The distinctive aspect of the American Creed is its antigovernment character. Opposition to power, and suspicion of government as the most dangerous embodiment of power, are the central themes of American political thought."[5] The American political culture's tenets of limited government, liberty, individualism, equality, and democracy generate a distrust of strong leadership, authority, and the public sector in general.

Because Americans' expectations of the presidency are so high, who serves as president is especially important. Just who are the people who have occupied the Oval Office?

WHO THEY ARE

When Warren G. Harding, one of the least illustrious American presidents, was in office, attorney Clarence Darrow remarked, "When I was a boy, I was told that anybody could become president. Now I'm beginning to believe it." The Constitution simply states that the president must be a natural-born citizen at least 35 years old and must have resided in the United States for at least 14 years. Until 2009, all American presidents have been White, male, and (except for John Kennedy) Protestant. In other ways, however, the recent collection of presidents suggests considerable variety. Since World War II, the White House has been home to a Missouri haberdasher, a war hero, a Boston-Irish politician, a small-town Texas boy who grew up to become the biggest wheeler-dealer in the Senate, a California lawyer described by his enemies as "Tricky Dick" and by his friends as a misunderstood master of national leadership, a former Rose Bowl player who had spent his entire political career in the House of Representatives, a former governor who had been a Georgia peanut wholesaler, an actor who was also a former governor of California, a CIA chief and ambassador who was the son of a U.S. senator, an ambitious governor from a small state, and a former managing director of a major league baseball team who won his first election only six years before becoming president (see Table 13.1).

So far, no woman has served as president (Barack Obama is the first member of an ethnic minority group to do so). As social prejudices diminish and more women are elected to positions that serve as stepping stones to the presidency, it is likely that this situation will change.

All manner of men have occupied the Oval Office. Thomas Jefferson was a scientist and scholar who assembled dinosaur bones when presidential business was slack. Woodrow Wilson, the only political scientist ever to become president, combined a Presbyterian moral fervor and righteousness with a professor's intimidating style of leadership and speech making. His successor, Warren G. Harding, became president because Republican leaders thought he looked like one. Poker was his pastime. Out of his element in the job, Harding is almost everyone's choice as the worst American president. His speech making, said opponent William G. McAdoo, sounded "like an army of pompous phrases marching across the landscape in search of an idea." Harding's friends stole the government blind, prompting his brief assessment of the presidency: "God, what a job!"

HOW THEY GOT THERE

No one is born to be the future president of the United States solely because of royal lineage like the kings or queens of England. Regardless of their background or character, all presidents must come to the job through one of two basic routes.

TABLE 13.1

Recent Presidents

PRESIDENT	TERM	PARTY	BACKGROUND	SIGNIFICANT EVENTS
Dwight D. Eisenhower	1953–1961	Republican	• Commander of Allied forces in Europe in World War II • Never voted until he ran for president	• Presided over relatively tranquil 1950s • Conservative domestic policies • Cool crisis management • Enjoyed strong public approval
John F. Kennedy	1961–1963	Democrat	• U.S. senator from Massachusetts • From very wealthy family • War hero	• Known for personal style • Presided over Cuban missile crisis • Ushered in era of liberal domestic policies • Assassinated in 1963
Lyndon B. Johnson	1963–1969	Democrat	• Senate majority leader • Chosen as Kennedy's running mate; succeeded him after the assassination	• Skilled legislative leader with a coarse public image • Launched the Great Society • Won passage of major civil rights laws • Escalated the Vietnam War • War policies proved unpopular; did not seek reelection
Richard M. Nixon	1969–1974	Republican	• U.S. senator from California • Served two terms as Eisenhower's vice president • Lost presidential election of 1960 to John F. Kennedy	• Presided over period of domestic policy innovation • Reopened relations with China • Ended Vietnam War • Resigned as result of Watergate scandal
Gerald R. Ford	1974–1977	Republican	• House minority leader • First person ever nominated as vice president under Twenty-fifth Amendment	• Pardoned Richard Nixon • Helped heal the nation's wounds • Lost election in 1976 to Jimmy Carter
Jimmy Carter	1977–1981	Democrat	• Governor of Georgia • Peanut farmer	• Viewed as honest but politically unskilled • Managed Iranian hostage crisis • Lost bid for reelection in 1980 • Brokered peace between Egypt and Israel
Ronald W. Reagan	1981–1989	Republican	• Governor of California • Well-known actor	• Won a substantial tax cut • Led fight for a large increase in defense spending • Hurt by Iran-Contra scandal • Known as the Great Communicator
George Bush	1989–1993	Republican	• U.S. representative from Texas • Director of CIA • Ambassador to UN • Served two terms as Reagan's vice president	• Led international coalition to victory in Gulf War • Presided over end of Cold War • Popular until economy stagnated • Lost reelection bid in 1992
William J. Clinton	1993–2001	Democrat	• Governor of Arkansas • Rhodes Scholar	• Moved Democrats to center • Presided over balanced budget • Benefited from strong economy • Tenure marred by Monica Lewinsky scandal • Impeached but not convicted

| George W. Bush | 2001–2009 | Republican | • Governor of Texas
• Son of President George Bush
• Elected without plurality of the vote | • Launched war on terrorism
• Won large tax cut
• Established Department of Homeland Security
• Began war with Iraq |
| Barack Obama | 2009– | Democrat | • Senator from Illinois
• First African American elected as president | • Dealt with financial crisis
• Continued war on Terrorism |

Elections: The Typical Road to the White House Most presidents take a familiar journey to 1600 Pennsylvania Avenue: They run for president through the electoral process, which we describe in Chapters 9 and 10. The Constitution guarantees a four-year term once in office (unless the president is convicted in an impeachment trial), but the **Twenty-second Amendment**, ratified in 1951, limits presidents to being elected to only two terms.

Only 13 of the 43 presidents have actually served two or more full terms in the White House: Washington, Jefferson, Madison, Monroe, Jackson, Grant, Cleveland (whose terms were not consecutive), Wilson, Franklin Roosevelt, Eisenhower, Reagan, Clinton, and George W. Bush. A few decided against a second term ("Silent Cal" Coolidge said simply, "I do not choose to run"). Five other presidents (Polk, Pierce, Buchanan, Hayes, and Lyndon Johnson) also threw in the towel at the end of one full term. Seven others (both the Adamses, Van Buren, Taft, Hoover, Carter, and George Bush) thought they had earned a second term, but the voters disagreed.

Succession and Impeachment For more than 10 percent of American history, the presidency has actually been occupied by an individual who was not elected to the office. About one in five presidents got the job because they were vice president when the incumbent president either died or (in Nixon's case) resigned (see Table 13.2). In the twentieth century, almost one-third (five of 18) of

Twenty-second Amendment

Passed in 1951, the amendment that limits presidents to two terms of office.

? Why It Matters
Standards of Impeachment

It is not easy to impeach a president; the threshold for an impeachable offense is a high one. This standard makes it very difficult to remove a president Congress feels is performing poorly *between* elections. A lower threshold for impeachment would have the potential to turn the United States into a parliamentary system in which the legislature could change the chief executive at any time.

'Okay, bring in the new guy . . .'

TABLE 13.2

Incomplete Presidential Terms

PRESIDENT	TERM	SUCCEEDED BY
William Henry Harrison	March 4, 1841–April 4, 1841	John Tyler
Zachary Taylor	March 4, 1849–July 9, 1850	Millard Fillmore
Abraham Lincoln	March 4, 1865–April 15, 1865[a]	Andrew Johnson
James A. Garfield	March 4, 1881–September 19, 1881	Chester A. Arthur
William McKinley	March 4, 1901–September 14, 1901[a]	Theodore Roosevelt
Warren G. Harding	March 4, 1921–August 2, 1923	Calvin Coolidge
Franklin D. Roosevelt	January 20, 1945–April 12, 1945[b]	Harry S. Truman
John F. Kennedy	January 20, 1961–November 22, 1963	Lyndon B. Johnson
Richard M. Nixon	January 20, 1973–August 9, 1974[a]	Gerald R. Ford

[a]Second term.
[b]Fourth term.

impeachment

The political equivalent of an indictment in criminal law, prescribed by the Constitution. The House of Representatives may impeach the president by a majority vote for "Treason, Bribery, or other high Crimes and Misdemeanors."

Watergate

The events and scandal surrounding a break-in at the Democratic National Committee headquarters in 1972 and the subsequent cover-up of White House involvement, leading to the eventual resignation of President Nixon under the threat of **impeachment**.

Twenty-fifth Amendment

Passed in 1967, this amendment permits the vice president to become acting president if both the vice president and the president's cabinet determine that the president is disabled. The amendment also outlines how a recuperated president can reclaim the job.

those who occupied the office were "accidental presidents." The most accidental of all was Gerald Ford, who did not run for either the vice presidency or the presidency before taking office. President Nixon nominated Ford as vice president when Vice President Spiro Agnew resigned; Ford then assumed the presidency when Nixon himself resigned.

Removing a discredited president before the end of a term is not easy. The Constitution prescribes the process of **impeachment**, which is roughly the political equivalent of an indictment in criminal law. The House of Representatives may, by majority vote, impeach the president for "Treason, Bribery, or other high Crimes and Misdemeanors." Once the House votes for impeachment, the case goes to the Senate, which tries the accused president, with the chief justice of the Supreme Court presiding. By a two-thirds vote, the Senate may convict and remove the president from office.

The House has impeached only two presidents. It impeached Andrew Johnson, Lincoln's successor, in 1868 on charges stemming from his disagreement with radical Republicans. He narrowly escaped conviction. On July 31, 1974, the House Judiciary Committee voted to recommend that the full House impeach Richard Nixon as a result of the **Watergate** scandal. Nixon escaped a certain vote for impeachment by resigning. In 1998, the House voted two articles of impeachment against President Bill Clinton on party-line votes. The public clearly opposed the idea, however, and the Senate voted to acquit the president on both counts in 1999. In both cases, the question of what constituted an impeachable offense was hotly debated, as you can read in, "You Are the Policymaker: What Should Be the Criteria for Impeaching the President?"

Constitutional amendments cover one other important problem concerning the presidential term: presidential disability and succession. Several times a president has become disabled, incapable of carrying out the job for weeks or even months at a time. After Woodrow Wilson suffered a stroke, his wife, Edith Wilson, became virtual acting president. The **Twenty-fifth Amendment**

Richard Nixon was the only American president ever to resign his office. Nixon decided to resign rather than face impeachment for his role in the Watergate scandal, a series of illegal wiretaps, break-ins, and cover-ups.

YOU ARE THE Policymaker

What Should Be the Criteria for Impeaching the President?

When the Monica Lewinsky story first broke in January 1998, astute political observers immediately perceived that this was more than a lurid sex scandal involving the president. For although the sex angle attracted the most attention, there were also allegations of President Clinton committing perjury when questioned about the affair and obstructing justice by urging Lewinsky to lie under oath. These charges would clearly put any private citizen in danger of being indicted in a criminal court. For a president, who cannot be indicted while in office, it meant possible impeachment by the House of Representatives followed by a Senate trial.

After months of investigation into the allegations, Independent Counsel Kenneth Starr issued a report to Congress accusing President Clinton of 11 counts of possible impeachable offenses, including perjury, obstruction of justice, witness tampering, and abuse of power. The president's detractors used the report as a basis for charging that he had broken the law, failed in his primary constitutional duty to take care that the laws be faithfully executed, betrayed the public's trust, and dishonored the nation's highest office. As a result, they argued the president should be removed from office through the process of impeachment.

The White House fought back. First, the president apologized to the nation, and engaged in a round of expressions of remorse before a variety of audiences. At the same time, the White House accused Starr of an intrusive investigation motivated by a political vendetta against the president. The White House argued that the president made a mistake in his private behavior, apologized for it, and should continue to do the job he was elected to do. Impeachment, the president's defenders said, was grossly disproportionate to the president's offense.

The Constitution provides only the most general guidelines as to the grounds for impeachment. Article II, Section 4, says, "The President, Vice President and all civil Officers of the United States, shall be removed from Office on Impeachment for, and Conviction of, Treason, Bribery, or other high Crimes and Misdemeanors."

There is agreement on at least four points regarding impeachable offenses.

1. Impeachable behavior does not have to be a crime. If the president refused to work or chose to invade a country solely to increase his public support, his actions could be grounds for impeachment, even though they would not violate the law.

2. The offense should be grave for it to be impeachable. A poker game in the White House, even though it may violate the law, would not constitute an impeachable offense.

3. A matter of policy disagreement is not grounds for impeachment. The only president who had been impeached before Clinton was Andrew Johnson, who was tried in 1868. He survived by one vote. The real issue was disagreement between the president and Congress over the policy of Reconstruction following the Civil War. Johnson's impeachment and trial are widely viewed as an abuse of impeachment power.

4. Impeachment is an inherently political process. The grounds for impeachment are ultimately whatever Congress decides they are because the Constitution assigns these calibrations to members' political judgment.

Beyond these points of agreement, we enter speculative territory. In 1974, the House Judiciary Committee passed three articles of impeachment against President Richard Nixon, but the president resigned before the House took up the charges. The three articles charged that Nixon had (1) obstructed justice, (2) abused his power, and (3) failed to comply with congressional subpoenas. The Democrats on the Judiciary Committee unanimously supported all three articles. In contrast, 10 of the 17 Republicans opposed impeachment, arguing that there needed to be a "smoking gun," demonstrating the president's guilt beyond a doubt. Soon thereafter, the release of another Nixon tape provided enough evidence that even Nixon's defenders on the committee felt was sufficiently convincing, and President Nixon resigned the presidency rather than face a trial in the Senate.

In 1998 and 1999, the tables were turned, as the Republicans supported a lower threshold for an impeachable offense while the Democrats argued for a higher one. In December 1998, the House voted two articles of impeachment against President Clinton on nearly straight party-line votes. The articles charged him with lying to a grand jury and obstructing justice. In the Senate trial that followed, the standards for removing a president from office were hotly debated. Ultimately, neither article received support from even a bare majority of senators, much less the two-thirds threshold necessary to convict him of high crimes and misdemeanors.

If you were a member of the Senate, would *you* have voted to convict the president?

(1967) clarifies some of the Constitution's vagueness about disability. The amendment permits the vice president to become acting president if the vice president and the president's cabinet determine that the president is disabled or if the president declares his own disability, and it outlines how a recuperated president can reclaim the Oval Office. Other laws specify the order of presidential succession—from the vice president, to the Speaker of the House, to the president pro tempore of the Senate and down through the cabinet members.

The Twenty-fifth Amendment also created a means for selecting a new vice president when the office becomes vacant. The president nominates a new vice president, who assumes the office when both houses of Congress approve the nomination by majority vote.

PRESIDENTIAL POWERS

The contemporary presidency hardly resembles the one the Constitution Framers designed in 1787. The executive office they conceived had more limited authority, fewer responsibilities, and much less organizational structure than today's presidency. The Founders feared both anarchy and monarchy. They wanted an independent executive but disagreed about both the form the office should take and the powers it should exercise. In the end, they created an executive unlike any the world had ever seen[6] (see "America in Perspective: President or Prime Minister?").

CONSTITUTIONAL POWERS

The Constitution says remarkably little about presidential power. The discussion of the presidency begins with these general words: "The executive power shall be vested in a president of the United States of America." It goes on to list just a few powers (see Table 13.3). The Framers' invention fit nicely within the Madisonian system of shared power and checks and balances, forcing the president to persuade officials in the other branches of government.

TABLE 13.3

Constitutional Powers of the President

NATIONAL SECURITY POWERS

Serve as commander in chief of the armed forces
Make treaties with other nations, subject to the agreement of two-thirds of the Senate
Nominate ambassadors, with the agreement of a majority of the Senate
Receive ambassadors of other nations, thereby conferring diplomatic recognition on other governments

LEGISLATIVE POWERS

Present information on the state of the union to Congress
Recommend legislation to Congress
Convene both houses of Congress on extraordinary occasions
Adjourn Congress if the House and Senate cannot agree on adjournment
Veto legislation (Congress may overrule with two-thirds vote of each house)

ADMINISTRATIVE POWERS

"Take care that the laws be faithfully executed"
Nominate officials as provided for by Congress and with the agreement of a majority of the Senate
Request written opinions of administrative officials
Fill administrative vacancies during congressional recesses

JUDICIAL POWERS

Grant reprieves and pardons for federal offenses (except impeachment)
Nominate federal judges, who are confirmed by a majority of the Senate

Institutional balance was essential to the convention delegates, who had in mind the abuses of past executives (including both the king and colonial governors) combined with the excesses of state legislatures (discussed in Chapter 2). The problem was how to preserve the balance without jeopardizing the independence of the separate branches or impeding the lawful exercise of their authority. The Framers resolved this problem by checking those powers they believed to be most dangerous, the ones that historically had been subject to the greatest abuse (for example, they gave Congress the power to declare war and the Senate the power to approve treaties and presidential appointments), while protecting the general spheres of authority from encroachment (the executive, for instance, was given a qualified veto).

Provisions for reelection and a short term of office also encouraged presidential responsibility. For those executives who flagrantly abused their authority, impeachment was the ultimate recourse.

THE EXPANSION OF POWER

Today there is more to presidential power than the Constitution alone suggests, and that power is derived from many sources. The role of the president has changed as America has increased in prominence on the world stage; technology has also reshaped the presidency. George Washington's ragtag militias (mostly disbanded by the time the first commander in chief took command) were much different from the mighty nuclear arsenal that today's president commands.

Presidential Leadership: Which Hat Do You Wear?

Presidents themselves have taken the initiative to develop new roles for the office. In fact, many presidents have enlarged the power of the presidency by expanding the president's responsibilities and political resources. Thomas Jefferson was the first leader of a mass political party. Andrew Jackson presented himself as the direct representative of the people. Abraham Lincoln mobilized the country for war. Theodore Roosevelt mobilized the public behind his policies. He and Woodrow Wilson set precedents for presidents to serve as world leaders; Wilson and Franklin D. Roosevelt developed the role of the president as manager of the economy.

AMERICA IN PERSPECTIVE

President **or Prime Minister?**

The Founders selected a presidential system of government for the United States. Most democracies in developed countries, however, have chosen a parliamentary system. In such a system the chief executive, the prime minister, is selected by the legislature, not the voters. The prime minister is a member of the legislature, elected from one district as a member of parliament. The majority party, or the largest bloc of votes in the legislature if there is no majority party, votes its party leader to be prime minister. The prime minister may remain in power for a long time—as long as his or her party or coalition has a majority of the seats and supports the leader.

Presidents and prime ministers govern quite differently. Prime ministers never face divided government, for example. Since they represent the majority party or coalition, they can almost always depend on winning votes. In addition, party discipline is better in parliamentary systems than in the United States. Parties know that if the prime minister should lose on an important vote, the government might have to call elections under circumstances unfavorable

to the majority. As a result, members of parliament almost always support their leaders.

Prime ministers generally differ in background from presidents as well. They must be party leaders, as we have seen, and they are usually very effective communicators, with skills honed in the rough-and-tumble of parliamentary debate. In addition, they have had substantial experience dealing with national issues, unlike American governors who may move directly into the presidency. Cabinet members, who are usually senior members of parliament, have similar advantages.

So why does the United States maintain a presidential system? The Founders were concerned about the concentration of power, such as that found in the prime minister. Instead, they wanted to separate power so that the different branches could check each other. More concerned with the abuse of power than its effective use, they chose a presidential system—the first the world had ever known.

PERSPECTIVES ON PRESIDENTIAL POWER

During the 1950s and 1960s it was fashionable for political scientists, historians, and commentators to favor a powerful presidency. Historians rated presidents from strong to weak—and there was no question that "strong" meant good and "weak" meant bad. Political scientists waxed eloquent about the presidency as the epitome of democratic governments.[7] By the 1970s, many felt differently. Lyndon Johnson and the unpopular Vietnam war made people reassess the role of presidential power, and Richard Nixon and the Watergate scandal heightened public distrust. The *Pentagon Papers*, a secret history of the Vietnam War, revealed presidential duplicity. Nixon's "enemies list" and his avowed goal to "screw our enemies" by illegally auditing their taxes, tapping their phones, and using "surreptitious entry" (a euphemism for burglary) asserted that the president was above the law, possessing "inherent powers" that permitted presidents to order acts that otherwise would be illegal.

Early defenders of a strong presidency made sharp turnabouts in their position. In his book *The Imperial Presidency*, historian Arthur Schlesinger argued that the presidency had become too powerful for the nation's own good.[8] (Critics pointed out that Schlesinger did not seem to feel that way when he worked in the Kennedy White House.) Whereas an older generation of scholars had written glowing accounts of the presidency, a newer generation wrote about "The Swelling of the Presidency" and "Making the Presidency Safe for Democracy."[9]

The Nixon era was followed by the presidencies of Gerald Ford and Jimmy Carter, whom many critics saw as weak leaders and failures. Ford himself spoke out in 1980, claiming that Carter's weakness had created an "imperiled" presidency. In the 1980s, Ronald Reagan experienced short periods of great influence and longer periods of frustration as the American political system settled back into its characteristic mode of stalemate and incremental policymaking. The Iran-Contra affair kept concern about a tyrannical presidency alive, while, in most instances, Reagan's inability to sway Congress evoked a desire on the part of some (mostly conservatives) for a stronger presidency. Reagan's immediate successors, George Bush and Bill Clinton, often found it difficult to get things done.

The presidency of George W. Bush raised anew the issue of presidential power. He asserted an expansive view of the president's constitutional powers, including withholding information from Congress under the doctrine of executive privilege, issuing signing statements asserting the right to disregard certain provisions of new laws, ordering without warrents electronic surveillance of individuals, and holding prisoners without trial for an indefinite period. Once again, critics charged that presidential power threatened the constitutional balance of powers.

The following sections explore the relationship between the president's responsibilities and resources by examining how contemporary presidents try to lead the nation.

The Executive Order Over Time

RUNNING THE GOVERNMENT: THE CHIEF EXECUTIVE

Comparing Chief Executives

Although we often refer to the president as the "chief executive," it is easy to forget that one of the president's most important roles is presiding over the administration of government. This role does not receive the same publicity as other functions do, such as appealing to the public for support of policy initiatives, dealing with Congress, or negotiating with foreign powers, but it is of great importance nevertheless.

The Constitution exhorts the president to "take care that the laws be faithfully executed." In the early days of the republic, this clerical-sounding function was fairly easy. Today, the sprawling federal bureaucracy spends more than $3 trillion a year and numbers more than 4 million civilian and military employees. Running such a large organization would be a full-time job for even the most talented of executives, yet it is only one of the president's many jobs.

One of the resources for controlling this bureaucracy is the presidential power to appoint top-level administrators. New presidents have about 500 high-level positions available for appointment—cabinet and subcabinet jobs, agency heads, and other noncivil service posts—plus 2,500 lesser jobs. Since passage of the Budgeting and Accounting Act of 1921, presidents have had one other important executive tool: the power to recommend agency budgets to Congress.

The vastness of the executive branch, the complexity of public policy, and the desire to accomplish their policy goals have led presidents in recent years to pay even closer attention to appointing officials who will be responsive to the president's policies. Presidents have also taken more interest in the regulations issued by agencies. This trend toward centralizing decision making in the White House pleases those who think the bureaucracy should be more responsive to elected officials. On the other hand, it dismays those who believe that increased presidential involvement in policymaking will undermine the "neutral competence" of professional bureaucrats by encouraging them to follow the president's policy preferences rather than the intent of laws as passed by Congress.

Chapter 15 on the bureaucracy explores the president's role as chief executive further. This chapter focuses on how presidents go about organizing and using the parts of the executive branch most under their control—the vice president, the cabinet, the Executive Office of the President, and the White House staff.

Comparing Executive Branches

THE VICE PRESIDENT

Neither politicians nor political scientists have paid much attention to the vice presidency. Once the choice of a party's "second team" was an afterthought; it has also often been an effort to placate some important symbolic constituency. Southerner Jimmy Carter selected a well-known liberal, Walter Mondale, as his running mate, and Ronald Reagan chose his chief rival, George Bush, in part to please Republican moderates.[10]

Vice presidents have rarely enjoyed the job. John Nance Garner of Texas, one of Franklin Roosevelt's vice presidents, declared that the job was "not worth a pitcher of warm spit." Some have performed so poorly that they were deemed an embarrassment to the president. After Woodrow Wilson's debilitating stroke, almost everyone agreed that Vice President Thomas Marshall—a man who shirked all responsibility, including cabinet meetings—would be a disaster as acting president. Spiro Agnew, Richard Nixon's first vice president, had to resign and was convicted of evading taxes (on bribes he had accepted).

Before the mid-1970s, vice presidents usually found that their main job was waiting. The Constitution assigns them the minor tasks of presiding over the Senate and voting in case of a tie among the senators. As George Bush put it when he was vice president, "The buck doesn't stop here." Recent presidents, however, have taken their vice presidents more seriously, involving them in policy discussions and important diplomacy.[11]

Jimmy Carter, a Washington outsider, chose Walter Mondale, an experienced senator, as his vice president. Their relationship marked a watershed in the vice presidency, as Mondale became an close advisor to the president. Ronald Reagan also chose a vice president with extensive Washington experience, George Bush. To become intimates of the president, both had to be completely loyal, losing their political independence in the process. Vice President Bush, for example, was accused of knowing more about the Iran-Contra affair than he admitted, but he steadfastly refused to reveal his discussions with President Reagan on the matter.

When his turn came to choose a vice president, Bush selected Senator Dan Quayle of Indiana, considered by many a political lightweight. Albert Gore, Bill Clinton's vice president, was a Washington insider and played a prominent role in the administration. He met regularly with the president, represented him in discussions with the leaders of numerous countries, and chaired a prominent effort to "reinvent" government.

George W. Bush chose Richard Cheney, who had extensive experience in high-level positions in the national government—including service as White House chief of staff, secretary of defense, and House minority whip—as his vice president and assigned him a central role in his administration. Cheney advised the president on a wide range of issues and chaired task forces dealing with major policy issues. He also was the focus of criticism, especially from those opposed to his support for the aggressive use of military power and an expansive view of presidential power.

Barack Obama chose Senator Joseph Biden of Delaware as his vice president. Biden had substantial experience in government and became a close adviser to the president, especially on foreign policy.

You Are the President and Need to Appoint a Supreme Court Justice

cabinet

A group of presidential advisers not mentioned in the Constitution, although every president has had one. Today the cabinet is composed of 14 secretaries, the attorney general, and others designated by the president.

THE CABINET

Although the Constitution does not mention the group of presidential advisers known as the **cabinet**, every president has had one. The cabinet is too large and too diverse, and its members are too concerned with representing the interests of their departments for it to serve as a collective board of directors, however. The major decisions remain in the president's hands. Legend has it that Abraham Lincoln asked his cabinet to vote on an issue, and the result was unanimity in opposition to his view. He announced the decision as "seven nays and one aye, the ayes have it."

George Washington's cabinet was small, consisting of just three secretaries (state, treasury, and war) and the attorney general. Presidents since Washington have increased the size of the cabinet by requesting that new executive departments be established. These requests must be approved by Congress, which creates the departments. Today 14 secretaries and the attorney general head executive departments and constitute the cabinet (see Table 13.4). In addition, presidents may designate other officials (the ambassador to the United Nations is a common choice) as cabinet members.[12]

Even in making his highest-level appointments, the president is subject to the constitutional system of checks and balances. President George Bush met resistance when he nominated John Tower, a former senator, to be secretary of defense. After a bitter debate (which focused on the nominee's use of alcohol and relations with women), the Senate handed the president a serious defeat by rejecting Tower. President Clinton's first nominee to serve as attorney general, Zoe Baird, withdrew from consideration after she came under fire from senators of both parties for hiring an undocumented alien as her babysitter and for failing to pay Social Security taxes for her employee.

Members of the president's cabinet are important for both the power they exercise and the status they symbolize. President George W. Bush formed a cabinet that was representative of America's demographic diversity. Pictured here is President Bush with Attorney General Alberto Gonzales, a Hispanic, who also served as White House counsel.

TABLE 13.4

The Cabinet Departments

DEPARTMENT	YEAR CREATED	FUNCTION
State	1789	Makes foreign policy, including treaty negotiations
Treasury	1789	Serves as the government's banker
Defense	1947	Formed by the consolidation of the former Departments of War and the Navy
Justice	1870	Serves as the government's attorney; headed by the attorney general
Interior	1849	Manages the nation's natural resources, including wildlife and public lands
Agriculture	1862	Administers farm and food stamp programs and aids farmers
Commerce	1903	Aids businesses and conducts the U.S. census
Labor	1913	Formed through separation from the Department of Commerce; runs programs and aids labor in various ways
Health and Human Services	1953	Originally created as the Department of Health, Education, and Welfare, it lost its education function in 1979 and Social Security in 1995
Housing and Urban Development	1966	Responsible for housing and urban programs
Transportation	1966	Responsible for mass transportation and highway programs
Energy	1977	Responsible for energy policy and research, including atomic energy
Education	1979	Responsible for the federal government's education programs
Veterans Affairs	1988	Responsible for programs aiding veterans
Homeland Security	2002	Responsible for protecting against terrorism and responding to natural disasters

THE EXECUTIVE OFFICE

Next to the White House sits an ornate building called the EEOB, or Eisenhower Executive Office Building. It houses a collection of offices and organizations loosely grouped into the Executive Office of the President.[13] Congress has created some of these offices by legislation, and the president has simply organized the rest. The Executive Office started small in 1939 when President Roosevelt established it, but has grown with the rest of government. Three major policymaking bodies are housed in the Executive Office—the National Security Council, the Council of Economic Advisers, and Office of Management and Budget—along with several other units that serve the president (see Figure 13.1).

The **National Security Council** (NSC) is the committee that links the president's key foreign and military policy advisers. Its formal members include the president, vice president, and secretaries of state and defense, but its informal membership is broader. The president's special assistant for national security affairs plays a major role in the NSC. The occupant of this post has responsibility for running the council's staff; together they provide the president with information and policy recommendations on national security, aid the president in national security crisis management, coordinate agency and departmental activities bearing on national security, and monitor the implementation of national security policy.

The **Council of Economic Advisers** (CEA) has three members, each appointed by the president, who advise him on economic policy. They prepare the annual *Economic Report of the President*, which includes data and analysis on the current state and future trends of the economy, and help the president make policy on inflation, unemployment, and other economic matters.

The **Office of Management and Budget** (OMB) grew out of the Bureau of the Budget (BOB) created in 1921. The OMB is composed of a handful of political appointees and more than 600 career officials, many of whom are highly skilled professionals. Its major responsibility is to prepare the president's budget (discussed

National Security Council

An office created in 1947 to coordinate the president's foreign and military policy advisers. Its formal members are the president, vice president, **secretary of state**, and **secretary of defense**, and it is managed by the president's national security assistant.

Council of Economic Advisers

A three-member body appointed by the president to advise the president on economic policy.

Office of Management and Budget

An office that grew out of the Bureau of the Budget, created in 1921, consisting of a handful of political appointees and hundreds of skilled professionals. The Office of Management and Budget performs both managerial and budgetary functions.

FIGURE 13.1

Executive Office of the President

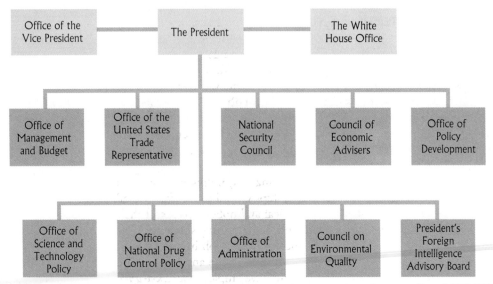

Source: White House (*www.whitehouse.gov/government/eop.html*); Office of the Federal Register, *The United States Government Manual, 2007/2008* (Washington, DC: U.S. Government Printing Office, 2008), 87–101.

in Chapter 14). President Nixon revamped the BOB in 1970 in an attempt to make it a managerial as well as a budgetary agency, changing its name in the process to stress its managerial functions.

Because each presidential appointee and department has their own agenda, presidents need a clearinghouse—the OMB. Presidents use the OMB to review legislative proposals from the cabinet and other executive agencies so that they can determine whether they want an agency to propose these initiatives to Congress. The OMB assesses the proposals' budgetary implications and advises presidents on the proposals' consistency with their overall program. The OMB also plays an important role in reviewing regulations proposed by departments and agencies.

Although presidents find that the Executive Office is smaller and more manageable than the cabinet departments, it is still filled with people who often are performing jobs required by law. There is, however, one part of the presidential system that presidents can truly call their own: the White House staff.

THE WHITE HOUSE STAFF

Before Franklin D. Roosevelt, the president's personal staff resources were minimal. Only one messenger and one secretary served Thomas Jefferson. One hundred years later the president's staff had grown only to 13, including clerks and secretaries. Woodrow Wilson was in the habit of typing his own letters. As recently as the 1920s, the entire budget for the White House staff was no more than $80,000 per year.

At the top of the White House staff are the key aides the president sees daily: the chief of staff, congressional liaison people, a press secretary, a national security assistant, and a few other administrative and political assistants. Today, there are about 600 people at work on the White House staff—many of whom the president rarely sees—who provide the chief executive with a wide variety of services ranging from making advance travel preparations to answering the avalanche of letters received each year (see Figure 13.2).

The top aides in the White House hierarchy are people who are completely loyal to the president, and the president turns to them for advice on the most serious or mundane matters of governance. Good staff people are self-effacing, working only for the boss and shunning the limelight. The 1939 report of the Brownlow Committee, which served as the basis for the development of the modern White House staff, argued that presidential assistants should have a "passion for anonymity." So important are their roles, though, that the names of top White House aides quickly become well known. Woodrow Wilson's Colonel Edward M. House, Franklin D. Roosevelt's Harry Hopkins, and Richard Nixon's Henry Kissinger, for example, did much to shape domestic and global policy.

Presidents rely heavily on their staffs for information, policy options, and analysis. Different presidents have different relationships with their staffs. They all organize the White House to serve their own political and policy needs and their own decision-making style. Most presidents end up choosing some form of *hierarchical* organization with a chief of staff at the top, whose job it is to see that everyone else is doing his or her job and that the president's time and interests are protected. A few presidents, such as John F. Kennedy, have employed a *wheel-and-spokes* system of White House management in which many aides have equal status and are balanced against one another in the process of decision making.[14] Whatever

FIGURE 13.2

Principal Offices in the White House

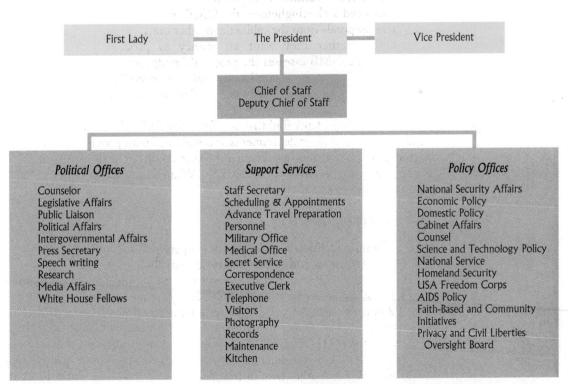

Source: Adapted from George C. Edwards III and Stephen J. Wayne, *Presidential Leadership,* 7th ed. (New York: St. Martin's Press, 2005), Figure 6.2.

the system, White House aides are central in the policymaking process—fashioning options, negotiating agreements, writing presidential statements, controlling paperwork, molding legislative details, and generally giving the president their opinions on most matters.

No presidential management styles contrasted more sharply than those of Presidents Carter and Reagan. Carter was a detail man, pouring endlessly over memoranda and facts. President Reagan was the consummate delegator. George Bush's operating style fell between the extremes of his two immediate predecessors. He consulted widely both within and outside of government, and he insisted on letting others' views reach him unfiltered by his staff. He was considerably more accessible than Reagan and devoted more energy to decision making. At the same time, he liked to delegate responsibility to his subordinates and took little initiative in domestic policy.

President Clinton, like Carter, immersed himself in the details of policy. He ran an open White House, dealing directly with a large number of aides and reading countless policy memoranda. His emphasis on deliberation and his fluid staffing system generated criticism that his White House was "indecisive" and "chaotic." George W. Bush took pride in being decisive, and was more likely to delegate responsibility than was Clinton. Bush, however, was less likely to persist in asking probing questions. Although the Bush White House was an orderly one, investigations into the decision making regarding the war in Iraq have found that the president's aides sometimes failed to properly vet information and follow other appropriate procedures.

Despite presidents' reliance on their staffs, it is the president who sets the tone for the White House. Although it is common to blame presidential advisers for mistakes made in the White House, it is the president's responsibility to demand that staff members analyze a full range of options and their probable consequences before they offer the president their advice. If the chief executive does not demand quality staff work, then the work is less likely to be done, and disaster or embarrassment may follow.

THE FIRST LADY

The First Lady has no official government position, yet she is often at the center of national attention. The media chronicles every word she speaks and every hairstyle she adopts. Although many people think of First Ladies as well-dressed homemakers presiding over White House dinners, there is much more to the job.

Abigail Adams (an early feminist) and Dolley Madison counseled and lobbied their husbands. Edith Galt Wilson was the most powerful First Lady, virtually running the government when her husband, Woodrow, suffered a paralyzing stroke in 1919. Eleanor Roosevelt wrote a nationally syndicated newspaper column and tirelessly traveled and advocated New Deal policies. She became her crippled husband's eyes and ears around the country and urged him to adopt liberal social welfare policies. Lady Bird Johnson chose to focus on one issue, beautification, and most of her successors followed this single-issue pattern. Rosalyn Carter chose mental health, Nancy Reagan selected drug abuse prevention, and Barbara Bush advocated literacy, as did Laura Bush, a former librarian.

Although the First Lady has no official government position, she is often at the center of national attention. In recent years, First Ladies have taken active roles in promoting policies ranging from highway beautification and mental health to literacy and health care. Here First Lady Laura Bush reads to Washington-area students. How would things change if a woman were elected president and her spouse were the First Man?

In what was perhaps a natural evolution in a society where women have moved into positions formerly held only by males, Hillary Rodham Clinton attained the most responsible and visible leadership position ever held by a First Lady. She was an influential adviser to the president, playing an active role in the selection of nominees for cabinet and judicial posts, for example. Most publicly, she headed the planning for the president's massive health care reform plan in 1993 and became, along with her husband, its primary advocate.

Although many have hailed her as a model for our times, successfully combining career and family, others have criticized her as a political liability. The health plan failed to pass Congress, and many observers viewed it as a leading cause of the Democrats' crushing defeat in the 1994 congressional elections. As a result, she retreated to a more traditional role, focusing on representing the United States abroad and on advocating policies to help children and women in developing countries. In 2000 and 2006, however, the voters of New York elected her to the U.S. Senate. In 2008, she campaigned for the Democratic nomination for president, winning more primaries and delegates than any other woman in U.S. history.

Presidents not only have responsibility for running the executive branch; they must also deal intensively with the legislative branch. This relationship is the topic of the following section.

PRESIDENTIAL LEADERSHIP OF CONGRESS: THE POLITICS OF SHARED POWERS

Near the top of any presidential job description would be "working with Congress." The American system of separation of powers is actually one of *shared* powers, so if presidents are to succeed in leaving their stamp on public policy, much of their time in office must be devoted to leading the legislature to support presidential initiatives.

CHIEF LEGISLATOR

Nowhere does the Constitution use the phrase *chief legislator;* it is strictly a phrase invented to emphasize the executive's importance in the legislative process. The Constitution does require that the president give a State of the Union address to Congress and instructs the president to bring other matters to Congress' attention "from time to time." In fact, as noted in Chapter 12, the president plays a major role in shaping the congressional agenda.

The Constitution also gives the president power to **veto** congressional legislation. Once Congress passes a bill, the president may (1) sign it, making it law; (2) veto it, sending it back to Congress with the reasons for rejecting it; or (3) let it become law after 10 working days by not doing anything. Congress can pass a vetoed law, however, if two-thirds of each house vote to override the president. At one point in the lawmaking process the president has the last word, however: If Congress adjourns within 10 days after submitting a bill, the president can simply let it die by neither signing nor vetoing it. This process is called a **pocket veto**. Table 13.5 shows how frequently recent presidents have used the veto.

The presidential veto is usually effective; Congress has overridden only about 4 percent of all vetoed bills since the nation's founding. Thus, even the threat of a presidential veto can be an effective tool for persuading Congress to give more weight to the president's views. On the other hand, the veto is a blunt instrument. Presidents must accept or reject bills in their entirety; they cannot veto only the parts they do

Why It Matters
The President's Veto
Unlike most governors, the president does not have the power to veto parts of a bill. As a result, he cannot choose to delete what he views as wasteful items from the budget. At the same time, the lack of a line-item veto helps to maintain the delicate balance of separate institutions sharing powers.

veto
The constitutional power of the president to send a bill back to Congress with reasons for rejecting it. A two-thirds vote in each house can override a veto.

pocket veto
A veto taking place when Congress adjourns within 10 days of submitting a bill to the president, who simply lets it die by neither signing nor vetoing it.

TABLE 13.5

Presidential Vetoes

PRESIDENT	REGULAR VETOES	VETOES OVERRIDDEN	PERCENTAGE OF VETOES OVERRIDDEN	POCKET VETOES	TOTAL VETOES
Eisenhower	73	2	3	108	181
Kennedy	12	0	0	9	21
Johnson	16	0	0	14	30
Nixon	26	7	27	17	43
Ford	48	12	25	18	66
Carter	13	2	15	18	31
Reagan	39	9	23	39	78
G. Bush	29	1	3	15	44
Clinton	37	2	5	1	38
G. W. Bush	12	4	33	0	12

not like (in contrast, most governors have a *line-item veto* that allows them to veto particular portions of a bill). As a result, the White House often must accept provisions of a bill it opposes in order to obtain provisions that it desires. For example, in 1987, Congress passed the entire discretionary budget of the federal government in one bill (called an "omnibus" bill). President Reagan had to accept the whole package or lose appropriations for the entire government. In recent years, presidents have issued signing statements that interpret legislation and often in effect veto part of a bill.

In 1996, Congress passed a law granting the president authority to propose rescinding funds in appropriations bills and tax provisions that apply to only a few people. Opponents of the law immediately challenged it in the courts as being an unconstitutional grant of power to the president. In 1998 the Supreme Court agreed, voiding the law in *Clinton v. City of New York*.

There are some bills, such as those appropriating funds for national defense, that *must* be passed. Knowing this, the president may veto a version containing provisions he opposes on the theory that Congress does not want to be held responsible for failing to defend the nation. Nevertheless, the presidential veto is an inherently negative resource. It is most useful for preventing legislation. Much of the time, however, presidents are more interested in passing their own legislation. To do so, they must marshal their political resources to obtain positive support for their programs. Presidents' three most useful resources are their party leadership, public support, and their own legislative skills.

PARTY LEADERSHIP

No matter what other resources presidents may have at their disposal, they remain highly dependent on their party to move their legislative programs. Representatives and senators of the president's party usually form the nucleus of coalitions supporting presidential proposals and provide considerably more support than do members of the opposition party. Thus, party leadership in Congress is every president's principal task when countering the natural tendency toward conflict between the executive and legislative branches that is inherent in the government's system of checks and balances.[15]

The Bonds of Party   For most senators and representatives, being in the same political party as the president creates a psychological bond. Personal loyalties or emotional commitments to their party and their party leader, a desire to avoid embarrassing "their" administration and thus hurting their chances for reelection, and a basic distrust of the opposition party are inclinations that produce support for the White House. Members of the same party also agree on many matters of public policy, and they are often supported by similar electoral coalitions, reinforcing the pull of party ties.

If presidents could rely on their party members to vote for whatever the White House sent up to Capitol Hill, presidential leadership of Congress would be rather easy. All presidents would have to do is make sure members of their party showed up to vote. If their party had the majority, presidents would always win. If their party was in the minority, presidents would only have to concentrate on converting a few members of the other party.

Slippage in Party Support   Things are not so simple, however. Despite the pull of party ties, all presidents experience at least some slippage in the support of their party in Congress. Because presidents cannot always count on their own party members for support, even on key votes, they must be active party leaders and devote their efforts to conversion as much as to mobilization of members of their party.

The primary obstacle to party unity is the lack of consensus on policies among party members, especially in the Democratic Party. Jimmy Carter, a Democrat, remarked, "I learned the hard way that there was no party loyalty or discipline when a complicated or controversial issue was at stake—none."[16]

This diversity of views often reflects the diversity of constituencies represented by party members. For many years the frequent defection of Southern Democrats from Democratic presidents (such defectors were called "boll weevils") was one of the most prominent features of American politics. When constituency opinion and the president's proposals conflict, members of Congress are more likely to vote with their constituents, whom they rely on for reelection. If the president is not popular with their constituencies, congressional party members may avoid identifying too closely with the White House.

Leading the Party   The president has some assets as party leader, including congressional party leaders, services and amenities for party members, and campaign aid. Each resource is of limited utility, however.

The president's relationship with party leaders in Congress is a delicate one. Although the leaders are predisposed to support presidential policies and typically work closely with the White House, they are free to oppose the president or lend only symbolic support; some party leaders may be ineffective themselves. Moreover, party leaders, especially in the Senate, are not in strong positions to reward or discipline members of Congress on the basis of presidential support.

To create goodwill with congressional party members, the White House provides them with many amenities, ranging from photographs with the president to rides on Air Force One. Although this arrangement is to the president's advantage and may earn the benefit of the doubt on some policy initiatives, party members consider it their right to receive benefits from the White House and as a result are unlikely to be especially responsive to the president's largesse.

Just as the president can offer a carrot, so too can the president wield a stick in the form of withholding favors, although this is rarely done. Despite the resources available to the president, if party members wish to oppose the White House, the president can do

Presidents depend heavily on their parties' leaders in Congress to pass their initiatives. They also must frequently seek support from the opposition party. Here President George W. Bush meets with Republican and Democratic leaders of the House and Senate.

little to stop them. The parties are highly decentralized, as we saw in Chapter 8. National party leaders do not control those aspects of politics that are of vital concern to members of Congress—nominations and elections. Members of Congress are largely self-recruited, gain their party's nomination by their own efforts and not the party's, and provide most of the money and organizational support needed for their elections. Presidents can do little to influence the results of these activities.

One way for the president to improve the chances of obtaining support in Congress is to increase the number of fellow party members in the legislature. The phenomenon of **presidential coattails** occurs when voters cast their ballots for congressional candidates of the president's party because those candidates support the president. Most recent studies show a diminishing connection between presidential and congressional voting, however, and few races are determined by presidential coattails.[17] The change in party balance that usually emerges when the electoral dust has settled is strikingly small. In the 15 presidential elections between 1952 and 2008, the party of the winning presidential candidate gained an average of eight seats (out of 435) per election in the House. In the Senate the opposition party actually gained seats in seven of the elections (1956, 1960, 1972, 1984, 1988, 1996, and 2000), and there was no change in 1976 and 1992. The net gain for the president's party in the Senate averaged only one seat per election (see Table 13.6).

What about midterm elections—those held between presidential elections? Can the president depend on increasing the number of fellow party members in Congress then? Actually, the picture is even bleaker than during presidential elections. As you can see in Table 13.7, the president's party typically *loses* seats in these elections. In

presidential coattails

These occur when voters cast their ballots for congressional candidates of the president's party because they support the president. Recent studies show that few races are won this way.

TABLE 13.6

Congressional Gains or Losses for the President's Party in Presidential Election Years

Presidents cannot rely on their coattails to carry their party's legislators into office to help pass White House legislative programs. The president's party typically gains few, if any, seats when the president wins election. For instance, the Republicans lost seats in both houses when President George W. Bush was elected in 2000.

YEAR	PRESIDENT	HOUSE	SENATE
1952	Eisenhower (R)	+22	+1
1956	Eisenhower (R)	−2	−1
1960	Kennedy (D)	−22	−2
1964	Johnson (D)	+37	+1
1968	Nixon (R)	+5	+6
1972	Nixon (R)	+12	−2
1976	Carter (D)	+1	0
1980	Reagan (R)	+34	+12
1984	Reagan (R)	+14	−2
1988	G. Bush (R)	−3	−1
1992	Clinton (D)	−10	0
1996	Clinton (D)	+9	−2
2000	G. W. Bush (R)	−2	−4
2004	G. W. Bush (R)	+3	+4
2008	Obama	+21	+7
	Average	+7.9	+1.1

TABLE 13.7

Congressional Gains or Losses for the President's Party in Midterm Election Years

For decades the president's party typically lost seats in midterm elections. Thus, presidents could not be certain of helping to elect members of their party once in office. The elections of 1998 and 2002 deviated from this pattern, and the president's party gained a few seats.

YEAR	PRESIDENT	HOUSE	SENATE
1954	Eisenhower (R)	−18	−1
1958	Eisenhower (R)	−47	−13
1962	Kennedy (D)	−4	+3
1966	Johnson (D)	−47	−4
1970	Nixon (R)	−12	+2
1974	Ford (R)	−47	−5
1978	Carter (D)	−15	−3
1982	Reagan (R)	−26	0
1986	Reagan (R)	−5	−8
1990	G. Bush (R)	−9	−1
1994	Clinton (D)	−52	−8
1998	Clinton (D)	+5	0
2002	G. W. Bush (R)	+6	+2
2006	G. W. Bush (R)	−30	−6
	Average	−22	−3

1986, the Republicans lost eight seats in the Senate, depriving President Reagan of a majority. In 1994, the Democrats lost eight Senate seats and 52 House seats, losing control of both houses in the process.[18] Recently, there have been exceptions. In 1998, the Democrats gained five seats in the House, and in 2002, Republicans made small gains in both houses. In 2006, however, George W. Bush's Republicans lost majorities in both houses of Congress.

To add to these party leadership burdens, the president's party often lacks a majority in one or both houses of Congress. Since 1953 there have been 30 years in which Republican presidents faced a Democratic House of Representatives and 22 years in which they encountered a Democratic Senate. Democrat Bill Clinton faced both a House and a Senate with Republican majorities from 1995 through 2000. Republican George W. Bush faced a Democratic Senate from May 2001 through December 2002 and 2007 through 2008.

As a result of election returns and the lack of dependable party support, the president usually has to solicit help from the opposition party. This is often a futile endeavor, however, since the opposition is generally not fertile ground for seeking support. Nevertheless, even a few votes may be enough to give the president the required majority.

PUBLIC SUPPORT

One of the president's most important resources for leading Congress is public support. Presidents who enjoy the backing of the public have an easier time influencing Congress. Said one top aide to Ronald Reagan, "Everything here is built on the idea that the president's success depends on grassroots support."[19] Presidents with low approval ratings in the polls find it difficult to influence Congress. As one of President Carter's aides put it when the president was low in the polls, "No president whose popularity is as low as this president's has much clout on the Hill."[20] Members of Congress and others in Washington closely watch two indicators of public support for the president: approval in the polls and mandates in presidential elections.

Presidential Success in Polls and Congress

Public Approval   Members of Congress anticipate the public's reactions to their support for or opposition to presidents and their policies. They may choose to be close to or independent of the White House—depending on the president's standing with the public—to increase their chances for reelection. Representatives and senators may also use the president's standing in the polls as an indicator of presidential ability to mobilize public opinion against presidential opponents.

Public approval also makes other leadership resources more efficacious. If the president is high in the public's esteem, the president's party is more likely to be responsive, the public is more easily moved, and legislative skills become more effective. Thus public approval is the political resource that has the most potential to turn a stalemate between the president and Congress into a situation supportive of the president's legislative proposals.

Public approval operates mostly in the background and sets the limits of what Congress will do for or to the president. Widespread support gives the president leeway and weakens resistance to presidential policies. It provides a cover for members of Congress to cast votes to which their constituents might otherwise object. They can defend their votes as support for the president rather than support for a certain policy alone.

Lack of public support strengthens the resolve of the president's opponents and narrows the range in which presidential policies receive the benefit of the doubt. In addition, low ratings in the polls may create incentives to attack the president, further eroding an already weakened position. For example, after the U.S. occupation of Iraq turned sour and the country rejected his proposal to reform Social Security, it became more acceptable in Congress and in the press to raise questions about George W. Bush's capacities as president. Disillusionment is a difficult force for the White House to combat.

The impact of public approval or disapproval on the support the president receives in Congress is important, but it occurs at the margins of the effort to build coalitions behind proposed policies. No matter how low presidential standing dips, the president still receives support from a substantial number of senators and representatives. Similarly, no matter how high approval levels climb, a significant portion of Congress will still oppose certain presidential policies. Members of Congress are unlikely to vote against the clear interests of their constituencies or the firm tenets of their ideology out of deference to a widely supported chief executive, as George W. Bush learned following the terrorist attacks on September 11, 2001. Public approval gives the president leverage, not command.[21]

In addition, presidents cannot depend on having the approval of the public, and it is not a resource over which they have much control, as we will see later. Once again, it is clear that presidents' leadership resources do not allow them to dominate Congress.

Mandates   The results of presidential elections are another indicator of public opinion regarding presidents. An electoral mandate—the perception that the voters strongly support the president's character and policies—can be a powerful symbol in American politics. It accords added legitimacy and credibility to the newly elected president's proposals. Moreover, concerns for both representation and political survival encourage members of Congress to support new presidents if they feel the people have spoken.[22]

More important, mandates change the premises of decisions. Following Roosevelt's decisive win in the 1932 election, the essential question became *how* government should act to fight the Depression rather than *whether* it should act.

Similarly, following Johnson's overwhelming win in the 1964 election, the dominant question in Congress was not whether to pass new social programs but how many social programs to pass and how much to increase spending. In 1981, the tables were turned; Ronald Reagan's victory placed a stigma on big government and exalted the unregulated marketplace and large defense efforts. Reagan had won a major victory even before the first congressional vote.

Although presidential elections can structure choices for Congress, merely winning an election does not provide presidents with a mandate. Every election produces a winner, but mandates are much less common. Even large electoral victories, such as Richard Nixon's in 1972 and Ronald Reagan's in 1984, carry no guarantee that Congress will interpret the results as mandates from the people to support the president's programs. Perceptions of a mandate are weak if the winning candidate did not stress his policy plans in the campaign or if the voters also elected majorities in Congress from the other party (of course, the winner may *claim* a mandate anyway).[23]

LEGISLATIVE SKILLS

Presidential legislative skills come in a variety of forms, including bargaining, making personal appeals, consulting with Congress, setting priorities, exploiting "honeymoon" periods, and structuring congressional votes. Of these skills, bargaining receives perhaps the most attention from commentators on the presidency, and by examining it, one can learn much about the role that a president's legislative skills play in leading Congress.

Bargains occur in numerous forms. Former budget director David Stockman recalled that "the last 10 or 20 percent of the votes needed for a majority of both houses on the 1981 tax cut had to be bought, period." The concessions for members of Congress included special breaks for oil-lease holders, real estate tax shelters, and generous loopholes that virtually eliminated the corporate income tax. "The hogs were really feeding," declared Stockman. "The greed level, the level of opportunities, just got out of control."[24]

Nevertheless, bargaining, in the form of trading support on two or more policies or providing specific benefits for representatives and senators, occurs less often and plays a less critical role in the creation of presidential coalitions in Congress than one might think. For obvious reasons, the White House does not want to encourage the type of bargaining Stockman describes, and there is a scarcity of resources with which to bargain, especially in an era where balancing the budget is a prominent goal for policymakers (discussed in Chapter 14).

Moreover, the president does not have to bargain with every member of Congress to receive support. On controversial issues on which bargaining may be useful, the president usually starts with a sizable core of party supporters and may add to this group those of the opposition party who provide support on ideological or policy grounds. Others may support the president because of relevant constituency interests or strong public approval. The president needs to bargain only if this coalition does not provide a majority (or two-thirds on treaties and one-third on veto overrides).

Presidents may improve their chances of success in Congress by making certain strategic moves. It is wise, for example, for a new president to be ready to send legislation to the Hill early during the first year in office in order to exploit the "honeymoon" atmosphere that typically characterizes this period. Obviously, this is a one-shot opportunity.

A New Beginning
Welfare to Work

Presidents find the role of legislative leader a challenging one. Often they must compromise with opponents in Congress, as President Bill Clinton did in 1996 when he signed the welfare reform bill.

An important aspect of presidential legislative strategy can be establishing priorities among legislative proposals. The goal of this effort is to set Congress' agenda. If presidents are unable to focus the attention of Congress on their priority programs, these programs may become lost in the complex and overloaded legislative process. Setting priorities is also important because presidents and their staffs can lobby effectively for only a few bills at a time. Moreover, each president's political capital is inevitably limited, and it is sensible to focus on a limited range of personally important issues; otherwise, this precious resource might be wasted.

The president is the nation's key agenda builder; what the administration wants strongly influences the parameters of Washington debate.[25] John Kingdon's careful study of the Washington agenda found that "no other single actor in the political system has quite the capability of the president to set agendas."[26] There are limits to what the president can do, however.

Although the White House can put off dealing with many national issues at the beginning of a new president's term in order to focus on its highest priority legislation, it cannot do so indefinitely. Eventually it must make decisions about a wide range of matters. Soon the legislative agenda is full and more policies are in the pipeline as the administration attempts to satisfy its constituents and responds to unanticipated or simply overlooked problems. Moreover, Congress is quite capable of setting its own agenda, providing competition for the president's proposals.

Presidents influence Congress's agenda, but no matter what a president's skills, Congress often follows its own path. Here George W. Bush delivers his State of the Union address.

In general, presidential legislative skills must compete—as presidential public support does—with other, more stable factors that affect voting in Congress: party, ideology, personal views and commitments on specific policies, constituency interests, and so on. By the time a president tries to exercise influence on a vote, most members of Congress have made up their minds on the basis of these other factors.

After accounting for the status of the president's party in Congress and standing with the public, systematic studies have found that presidents known for their legislative skills (such as Lyndon Johnson) are no more successful in winning votes, even close ones, or obtaining congressional support than those considered less adept at dealing with Congress (such as Jimmy Carter).[27] The president's legislative skills are not at the core of presidential leadership of Congress. Even skilled presidents cannot reshape the contours of the political landscape and *create* opportunities for change. They can, however, recognize favorable configurations of political forces—such as existed in 1933, 1965, and 1981—and effectively exploit them to embark on major shifts in public policy.

Perhaps the most important role of presidents—and their heaviest burden—is their responsibility for national security. Dealing with Congress is only one of the many challenges presidents face in the realm of defense and foreign policy.

THE PRESIDENT AND NATIONAL SECURITY POLICY

Constitutionally, the president has the leading role in American defense and foreign policy (often termed *national security policy*). Such matters, ranging from foreign trade to war and peace, occupy much of the president's time. There are several dimensions to the president's national security responsibilities, including negotiating with other nations, commanding the armed forces, waging war, managing crises, and obtaining the necessary support in Congress.

CHIEF DIPLOMAT

The Constitution allocates certain powers in the realm of national security exclusively to the executive. The president alone extends diplomatic recognition to foreign governments—as Jimmy Carter did on December 14, 1978, when he announced the exchange of ambassadors with the People's Republic of China and the downgrading of the U.S. Embassy in Taiwan. The president can also terminate relations with other nations, as Carter did with Iran after Americans were taken hostage in Tehran.

The president also has the sole power to negotiate treaties with other nations, although the Constitution requires the Senate to approve them by a two-thirds vote. Sometimes presidents win and sometimes they lose when presenting a treaty to the Senate. After extensive lobbying, Jimmy Carter persuaded the Senate to approve a treaty returning the Panama Canal to Panama (over objections such as those of one senator who declared, "We stole it fair and square"). Bill Clinton was not so lucky when he sought ratification of the Comprehensive Nuclear Test Ban Treaty. The Senate rejected it in 1999. At other times senators add "reservations" to the treaties they ratify, altering the treaty in the process.[28]

In addition to treaties, presidents also negotiate *executive agreements* with the heads of foreign governments. However, executive agreements do not require Senate ratification (although the president is supposed to report them to Congress and they may require implementing legislation passed by majorities of each house). Most executive agreements are routine and deal with noncontroversial subjects such as food deliveries or customs enforcement, but some, such as the Vietnam peace agreement and the SALT I agreement limiting offensive nuclear weapons, implement important and controversial policies.

Presidents usually conduct diplomatic relations through envoys, but occasionally they engage in personal diplomacy. Here, President Carter celebrates a peace agreement he brokered between Israeli Prime Minister Menachem Begin and Egyptian President Anwar Sadat.

Occasionally presidential diplomacy involves more than negotiating on behalf of the United States. Theodore Roosevelt won the Nobel Peace Prize for his role in settling the war between Japan and Russia. One of Jimmy Carter's greatest achievements was forging a peace treaty between Egypt and Israel. For 13 days he mediated negotiations between the leaders of both countries at his presidential retreat, Camp David.

As the leader of the Western world, the president must try to lead America's allies on matters of both economics and defense. This is not an easy task, given the natural independence of sovereign nations, the increasing economic might of other countries, and the many competing influences on policymaking in other nations. As in domestic policymaking, the president must rely principally on persuasion to lead.

COMMANDER IN CHIEF

Because the Constitution's framers wanted civilian control of the military, they made the president the commander in chief of the armed forces. President George Washington actually led troops to crush the Whiskey Rebellion in 1794. Today, presidents do not take the task quite so literally, but their military decisions have changed the course of history. Bill Clinton joined the ranks of presidents exerting their prerogatives as commander in chief when he sent American troops to occupy Haiti, keep the peace in Bosnia, restore order in Somalia, prevent an invasion of Kuwait, and bomb Yugoslavia, Iraq, Afghanistan, and Sudan. George W. Bush ordered an attack on the Taliban government in Afghanistan—and on terrorists everywhere.

When the Constitution was written, the United States did not have—nor did anyone expect it to have—a large standing or permanent army. Today the president is commander in chief of about 1.4 million uniformed men and women. In his farewell address, George Washington warned against permanent alliances, but today America has commitments to defend nations across the globe. Even more important, the president commands a vast nuclear arsenal. Never more than a few steps from the president is "the football," a briefcase with the codes needed to unleash nuclear war. The Constitution, of course, states that only Congress has the power to declare war, but it is unreasonable to believe that Congress can convene, debate, and vote on a declaration of war in the case of a nuclear attack. The House and Senate chambers would be gone—*literally* gone—before the conclusion of a debate.

In 1950, President Harry Truman fulfilled his role as commander in chief by pinning a distinguished service medal on the shirt of General Douglas MacArthur, who was commanding American troops in Korea. The following year, Truman exercised his powers by dismissing MacArthur for disobeying orders—an unpopular decision given MacArthur's fame as a World War II hero.

WAR POWERS

Perhaps no issue of executive–legislative relations generates more controversy than the continuing dispute over war powers. Although charged by the Constitution with declaring war and voting on the military budget, Congress long ago accepted that presidents make short-term military commitments of troops or naval vessels. In recent decades, however, presidents have paid even less attention to constitutional details; for example, Congress never declared war during the conflicts in either Korea or Vietnam.

In 1973 Congress passed the **War Powers Resolution** (over President Nixon's veto). As a reaction to disillusionment about American fighting in Vietnam and Cambodia, the law was intended to give Congress a greater voice in the introduction of American troops into hostilities. It required presidents to consult with Congress, whenever possible, before using military force, and it mandated the withdrawal of forces after 60 days unless Congress declared war or granted an extension. Congress could at any time pass a concurrent resolution (which could not be vetoed) ending American participation in hostilities.

Congress cannot regard the War Powers Resolution as a success, however. All presidents serving since 1973 have deemed the law an unconstitutional infringement on their powers, and there is reason to believe the Supreme Court would consider the

War Powers Resolution

A law passed in 1973 in reaction to American fighting in Vietnam and Cambodia that requires presidents to consult with Congress whenever possible prior to using military force and to withdraw forces after 60 days unless Congress declares war or grants an extension. Presidents view the resolution as unconstitutional.

law's use of the **legislative veto** (the ability of Congress to pass a resolution to over-ride a presidential decision) to be a violation of the doctrine of separation of powers. Presidents have largely ignored the law and sent troops into hostilities, sometimes with heavy loss of life, without effectual consultation with Congress. The legislature has found it difficult to challenge the president, especially when American troops were endangered, and the courts have been reluctant to hear a congressional challenge on what would be construed as a political, rather than a legal, issue.[29]

Following numerous precedents, George Bush took an expansive view of his powers as commander in chief. On his own authority, he ordered the invasion of Panama in 1989 and moved half a million troops to Saudi Arabia to liberate Kuwait after its invasion by Iraq in 1990. Matters came to a head in January 1991. President Bush had given President Saddam Hussein of Iraq until January 15 to pull out of Kuwait. At that point, Bush threatened to move the Iraqis out by force. Debate raged over the president's power to act unilaterally to engage in war. A constitutional crisis was averted when Congress passed (on a divided vote) a resolution on January 12 authorizing the president to use force against Iraq.

In a sweeping assertion of presidential authority, Bill Clinton moved toward military intervention in Haiti in 1994 and essentially dared Congress to try to stop him. Congress did nothing but complain to block military action, even though a majority of members of both parties clearly opposed an invasion. In the end, the president avoided an invasion (as opposed to a more peaceful "intervention"), but Congress was unlikely to have cut off funds for such an operation had it occurred. In 1999, the president authorized the United States to take the leading role in a sustained air attack against Serbia, but Congress could not agree on a resolution supporting the use of force.

George W. Bush faced little opposition to responding to the terrorist attacks of September 11, 2001. Congress immediately passed a resolution authorizing the use of force against the perpetrators of the attacks. The next year, Congress passed a resolution authorizing the president to use force against Iraq. However, Congress was less compliant when the press revealed U.S. mistreatment of prisoners of war and the president's authorization (without a judicial warrant) of the National Security Agency to spy on persons residing within the United States.

Analysts continue to raise questions about the relevance of America's 200-year-old constitutional mechanisms for engaging in war. Some observers worry that the rapid response capabilities afforded the president by modern technology allow him to bypass congressional opposition, thus undermining the separation of powers. Others stress the importance of the commander in chief having the flexibility to meet America's global responsibilities and combat international terrorism without the hindrance of congressional checks and balances. All agree that the change in the nature of warfare brought about by nuclear weapons inevitably delegates to the president the ultimate decision to use such weapons.

CRISIS MANAGER

The president's roles as chief diplomat and commander in chief are related to another presidential responsibility: crisis management. A **crisis** is a sudden, unpredictable, and potentially dangerous event. Most crises occur in the realm of foreign policy. They often involve hot tempers and high risks; quick judgments must be made on the basis of sketchy information. Be it American hostages held in Iran or the discovery of Soviet missiles in Cuba, a crisis challenges the president to make difficult decisions. Crises are rarely the president's doing, but handled incorrectly, they can be the president's undoing. On the other hand, handling a crisis well can remake a president's image, as George W. Bush found following the terrorist attacks of September 11, 2001.

Early in American history there were fewer immediate crises. By the time officials were aware of a problem, it often had resolved itself. Communications could

---

legislative veto

The ability of Congress to override a presidential decision. Although the **War Powers Resolution** asserts this authority, there is reason to believe that, if challenged, the Supreme Court would find the legislative veto in violation of the doctrine of separation of powers.

? Why It Matters

War Powers

The U.S. has never fully resolved the question of the president's war powers. The ambiguity about presidents' powers frees them from what some see as excessive constraints on their ability to conduct an effective foreign policy. On the other hand, if the president could only send troops into combat after a congressional resolution authorizing the use of force, it is possible that we would be less likely to go to war.

---

crisis

A sudden, unpredictable, and potentially dangerous event requiring the president to play the role of crisis manager.

You Are a President During a Nuclear Power Plant Meltdown

Crisis management may be the most difficult of the president's many roles. By definition, crises are sudden, unpredictable, and dangerous. Here President George W. Bush stands with firefighters and rescue workers at the World Trade Center site three days after the terrorist attacks on September 11, 2001.

take weeks or even months to reach Washington. Similarly, officials' decisions often took weeks or months to reach those who were to implement them. The most famous land battle of the War of 1812, the Battle of New Orleans, was fought *after* the United States had signed a peace treaty with Great Britain. Word of the treaty did not reach the battlefield; thus, General Andrew Jackson won a victory for the United States that contributed nothing toward ending the war, although it did help put him in the White House as the seventh president.

With modern communications, the president can instantly monitor events almost anywhere. Moreover, because situations develop more rapidly today, there is a premium on rapid action, secrecy, constant management, consistent judgment, and expert advice. Congress usually moves slowly (one might say deliberately), and it is large (making it difficult to keep secrets), decentralized (requiring continual compromising), and composed of generalists. As a result, the president—who can come to quick and consistent decisions, confine information to a small group, carefully oversee developments, and call on experts in the executive branch—has become more prominent in handling crises.

WORKING WITH CONGRESS

As America moves through its third century under the Constitution, presidents might wish the framers had been less concerned with checks and balances in the area of national security. In recent years, Congress has challenged presidents on all fronts, including intelligence operations; the treatment of prisoners of war; foreign aid; arms sales; the development, procurement, and deployment of weapons systems; the negotiation and interpretation of treaties; the selection of diplomats; and the continuation of nuclear testing.

Congress has a central constitutional role in making national security policy, although this role is often misunderstood. The allocation of responsibilities for such matters is based on the Founders' apprehensions about the concentration of power and the subsequent potential for its abuse. They divided the powers of supply and command, for example, in order to thwart adventurism in national security affairs. Congress can thus refuse to provide the necessary authorizations and appropriations for presidential actions, whereas the chief executive can refuse to act (for example, by not sending troops into battle at the behest of the legislature).

Despite the constitutional role of Congress, the president is the driving force behind national security policy, providing energy and direction. Congress is well organized to deliberate openly on the discrete components of policy, but it is not well designed to take the lead on national security matters. Its role has typically been overseeing the executive rather than initiating policy.[30] Congress frequently originates proposals for domestic policy, but it is less involved in national security policy.[31]

The president has a more prominent role in foreign affairs as the country's sole representative in dealing with other nations and as commander in chief of the armed forces (functions that effectively preclude a wide range of congressional diplomatic and military initiatives). In addition, the nature of national security issues may make the failure to integrate the elements of policy more costly than in domestic policy. Thus, members of Congress typically prefer to encourage, criticize, or support the president rather than to initiate their own national security policy. If leadership occurs, it is usually centered in the White House.

Commentators on the presidency often refer to the "two presidencies"—one for domestic policy and the other for national security policy.[32] By this phrase they mean that the president has more success in leading Congress on matters of national security than on matters of domestic policy. The typical member of Congress, however, supports the president on roll-call votes about national security only slightly more than half the time. There is a significant gap between what the president requests and what members of Congress are willing to give. Certainly the legislature does not accord the president automatic support on national security policy.[33] Nevertheless, presidents do end up obtaining much, often most, of what they request from Congress on national security issues. Some of the support they receive is the result of agreement on policy; other support comes from the president's ability to act first, placing Congress in a reactive position and opening it to the charge that it is undermining U.S. foreign policy if it challenges the president's initiatives.

Presidents need resources to influence others to support their policies. One important presidential asset can be the support of the American people. The following sections will take a closer look at how the White House tries to increase and use public support.

POWER FROM THE PEOPLE: THE PUBLIC PRESIDENCY

"Public sentiment is everything. With public sentiment nothing can fail; without it nothing can succeed." These words, spoken by Abraham Lincoln, pose what is perhaps the greatest challenge to any president—to obtain and maintain the public's support. Because presidents are rarely in a position to command others to comply with their wishes, they must rely on persuasion. Public support is perhaps the greatest source of influence a president has, for it is more difficult for other power holders in a democracy to deny the legitimate demands of a president with popular backing.

GOING PUBLIC

Presidents are not passive followers of public opinion. The White House is a virtual whirlwind of public relations activity.[34] John Kennedy, the first "television president," held considerably more public appearances than did his predecessors. Kennedy's successors, with the notable exception of Richard Nixon, have been even more active in making public appearances. Indeed, they have averaged more than one appearance every weekday of the year. Bill Clinton and George W. Bush invested enormous time and energy in attempting to sell their programs to the public.

Often the White House stages the president's appearances purely to get the public's attention. George W. Bush chose to announce the end of major combat in Iraq on board the aircraft carrier the *Abraham Lincoln*. The White House's Office of Communications choreographed every aspect of the event, including positioning the aircraft carrier so the shoreline could not be seen by the camera when the president landed, arraying members of the crew in coordinated shirt colors over Bush's right shoulder, placing a banner reading "Mission Accomplished" to perfectly capture the president and the celebratory two words in a single camera shot, and timing the speech so the sun cast a golden glow on the president. In such a case, the president could have simply made an announcement, but the need for public support drives the White House to employ public relations techniques similar to those used to publicize commercial products.

Presidents often use commercial public relations techniques to win support for their policy initiatives. President George W. Bush, for example, used the backdrop of an aircraft carrier to announce the end of the war in Iraq and obtain support for his stewardship.

In many democracies, different people occupy the jobs of head of state and head of government. For example, the queen is head of state in England, but she holds little power in government and politics. In America, these roles are fused. As head of state, the president is America's ceremonial leader and symbol of government. Trivial but time-consuming activities—tossing out the first baseball of the season, lighting the White House Christmas tree, meeting an extraordinary Boy or Girl Scout—are part of the ceremonial function of the presidency. Meeting foreign heads of state, receiving ambassadors' credentials, and making global goodwill tours represent the international side of this role. Presidents rarely shirk these duties, even when they are not inherently important. Ceremonial activities give them an important symbolic aura and a great deal of favorable press coverage, contributing to their efforts to build public support.

PRESIDENTIAL APPROVAL

Much of the energy the White House devotes to public relations is aimed at increasing the president's public approval. The White House believes that the higher the president stands in the polls, the easier it is to persuade others to support presidential initiatives. Because of the connection between public support and presidential influence, the press, members of Congress, and others in the Washington political community closely monitor the president's standing in the polls. For years, the Gallup Poll has asked Americans, "Do you approve or disapprove of the way [name of president] is handling his job as president?" You can see the results in Figure 13.3.

Presidents frequently do not have widespread public support, often failing to win even majority approval. Figure 13.4 shows the average approval levels of recent presidents. Presidents Nixon, Ford, and Carter did not receive approval from 50 percent of the public on the average. Ronald Reagan had only a 52 percent approval level. For three years, George Bush enjoyed much higher levels of approval on the average than his predecessors did. In his fourth year, however, his ratings dropped below the 40 percent mark. President Clinton struggled to rise above the 50 percent mark in his first term, and George W. Bush was at 51 percent before the September 11, 2001, terrorist attacks. His approval skyrocketed after 9/11 but then steadily diminished and fell well below 50 percent in his second term.

Presidential approval is the product of many factors.[35] At the base of presidential evaluations is the predisposition of many people to support the president. Political party identification provides the basic underpinning of approval or disapproval and mediates the impact of other factors. Historically, those who identify with the president's party give the president approval more than 40 percentage points higher than do those who identify with the opposition party. In the more polarized times under George W. Bush, this difference rose as high as 70 percentage points. Moreover, partisans are not inclined to approve presidents of the other party. Predispositions provide the foundations of presidential approval and furnish it with a basic stability.

Presidents also usually benefit from a "honeymoon" with the American people after taking office. Some observers believe that "honeymoons" are fleeting phenomena in which the public affords new occupants of the White House only a short grace period before they begin their inevitable descent in the polls. You can see in Figure 13.3

FIGURE 13.3

Average Yearly Presidential Approval

For years the Gallup Poll has asked Americans, "Do you approve or disapprove of the way [name of president] is handling his job as president?" Here you can track the percentage approving of presidential performance from Eisenhower to George W. Bush. Notice that most presidents seem to be most popular when they first enter office; later on, their popularity often erodes. Bill Clinton was an exception who enjoyed higher approval in his second term than in his first. George W. Bush had high approval following 9/11, but public support diminished steadily after that.

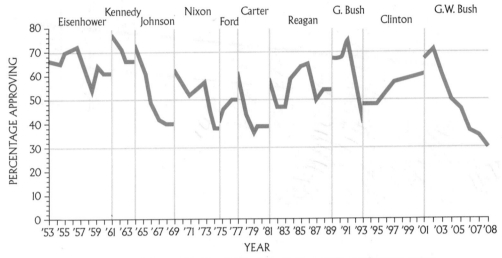

Source: George C. Edwards III, *Presidential Approval* (Baltimore, MD: Johns Hopkins University Press, 1990); updated by the authors.

that declines do take place, but they are neither inevitable nor swift. Throughout his two terms in office, Ronald Reagan experienced considerable volatility in his relations with the public, but his record certainly does not indicate that the loss of public support is inexorable or that support cannot be revived and maintained. George Bush obtained more public support in his third year in office than in his first two years, and Bill Clinton enjoyed more approval in his second term in office than in his first.

Changes in approval levels appear to reflect the public's evaluation of how the president is handling policy areas such as the economy, war, and foreign affairs. Different policies are salient to the public at different times. For example, if international acts of terrorism on American interests are increasing, then foreign policy is likely to dominate the news and to be on the minds of Americans. If the economy turns sour, then people are going to be concerned about unemployment.

Contrary to conventional wisdom, citizens seem to focus on the president's efforts and stands on issues rather than on personality ("popularity") or simply how presidential policies affect them (the "pocketbook"). Job-related personal characteristics of the president, such as integrity and leadership skills, also play an important role in influencing presidential approval.

Sometimes public approval of the president takes sudden jumps. One popular explanation for these surges of support is "rally events," which John Mueller defined as events that are related to international relations, directly involve the United States and particularly the president, and are specific, dramatic, and sharply focused.[36] A classic example is the 18-percentage-point rise in President George Bush's approval ratings immediately after the fighting began in the Gulf War in 1991. George W. Bush's approval shot up 39 percentage points in September 2001. Such occurrences are unusual and isolated events, however; they usually have little enduring impact on a president's public approval. George Bush, for example, dropped precipitously in the polls and lost his bid for reelection in 1992.

The criteria on which the public evaluates presidents—such as the way they are handling the economy, where they stand on complex issues, and whether they are

FIGURE 13.4

Average Presidential Approval for Entire Terms in Office

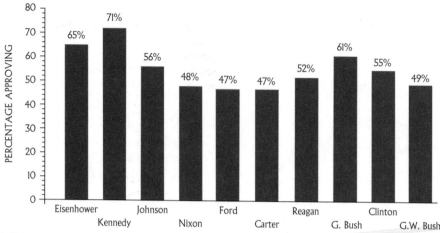

Source: George C. Edwards III, *Presidential Approval* (Baltimore, MD: Johns Hopkins University Press, 1990); updated by the authors.

"strong" leaders—are open to many interpretations. The modern White House makes extraordinary efforts to control the context in which presidents appear in public and the way they are portrayed by the press in order to try to influence how the public views them. The fact that presidents are frequently low in the polls anyway is persuasive testimony to the limits of presidential leadership of the public. As one student of the public presidency put it, "The supply of popular support rests on opinion dynamics over which the president may exert little direct control."[37]

POLICY SUPPORT

Commentators on the presidency often refer to it as a "bully pulpit," implying that presidents can persuade or even mobilize the public to support their policies if they are skilled communicators. Certainly presidents frequently do attempt to obtain public support for their policies with television or radio appearances and speeches to large groups.[38] All presidents since Truman have had media advice from experts on lighting, makeup, stage settings, camera angles, clothing, pacing of delivery, and other facets of making speeches.

Despite this aid and despite politicians' speaking experience, presidential speeches designed to lead public opinion have typically been rather unimpressive. In the modern era only Franklin D. Roosevelt, John Kennedy, Ronald Reagan, and Bill Clinton could be considered especially effective speakers. Partly because of his limitations as a public speaker, George Bush waited until he had been in office for over seven months before making his first nationally televised address in 1989.

Moreover, the public is not always receptive to the president's message. Chapter 6 showed that Americans are not especially interested in politics and government; thus, it is not easy to get their attention (see "Young People and Politics: The Generation Gap in Watching the President"). Citizens also have predispositions about public policy (however ill informed) that act as screens for presidential messages. Evan Parker-Stephen suggests that when people encounter political information, they must balance two conflicting roles: as "updaters" who want to perceive the world objectively and as "biased reasoners" who distort information to make it consistent with their political preferences. The more salient their partisan identities, which are especially heightened during the long campaign periods in the U.S., the more difficult it is for the president to get his message through to the public.[39]

YOUNG PEOPLE AND POLITICS
The Generation Gap in Watching the President

It is difficult for the president to get the public's attention. It is especially challenging to attract young people. The older people are, the more likely they are to tune in to watch a presidential address. As a result, the audience for presidential speeches is now unrepresentative of the general adult public in terms of age.

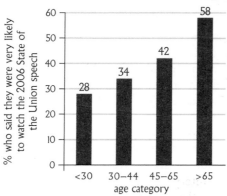

% who said they were very likely to watch the 2006 State of the Union speech

age category	value
<30	28
30–44	34
45–65	42
>65	58

Source: *New York Times*/CBS News Poll, Jan. 20-25, 2006.

Question: President Bush's State of the Union address is scheduled for Tuesday evening, January 31. How likely is it you will watch the President's State of the Union address that night? Is it very likely, somewhat likely, not very likely, or not at all likely?

QUESTIONS FOR DISCUSSION

▶ Will young people be more likely to pay attention to the president as they age?

▶ Do you think presidents can govern effectively if they cannot connect to the people?

The public may even get its basic facts wrong. Before the war with Iraq in 2003, two-thirds of the public expressed the belief that Iraq played an important role in the 9/11 terrorist attacks. After the war, substantial percentages of the public believed that the United States had found clear evidence that Saddam Hussein was working closely with al Qaeda, that the United States had found weapons of mass destruction in Iraq, and that world opinion favored the United States going to war in Iraq.[40] All of these beliefs were inaccurate, as even the White House admitted.

Ronald Reagan, sometimes called the "Great Communicator," was certainly interested in policy change and went to unprecedented lengths to influence public opinion on behalf of such policies as deregulation, decreases in spending on domestic policy, and increases in the defense budget. Bill Clinton was also an extraordinarily able communicator, and he traveled widely and spoke out constantly on behalf of his policies, such as those dealing with the economy, health care reform, and free trade. Nevertheless, both presidents were typically unable to obtain the public's support for their initiatives and generally saw public opinion move against them.[41] Similarly George W. Bush made an extraordinary effort to obtain public backing for his stewardship of the war in Iraq and his major proposal to reform Social Security. In both cases, the public rejected his overtures.[42] In the absence of national crises, most people are unreceptive to political appeals.

John Kennedy was the first president to use public appearances regularly to seek popular backing for his policies. Despite his popularity and skills as a communicator, Kennedy was often frustrated in his attempts to win widespread support for his administration's "New Frontier" policies.

MOBILIZING THE PUBLIC

Sometimes merely changing public opinion is not sufficient, and the president wants the public to communicate its views directly to Congress. Mobilization of the public may be the ultimate weapon in the president's arsenal of resources with which to influence Congress. When the people speak, especially when they speak clearly, Congress listens.

Mobilizing the public involves overcoming formidable barriers and accepting substantial risks. It entails the double burden of obtaining both opinion support and political action from a generally inattentive and apathetic public. If the president tries to mobilize the public and fails, the lack of response speaks clearly to members of Congress.

Perhaps the most notable recent example of the president's mobilization of public opinion to pressure Congress is Ronald Reagan's effort to obtain passage of his tax-cut bill in 1981. Shortly before the crucial vote in the House, the president made a televised plea for support of his tax-cut proposals and asked the people to let their representatives in Congress know how they felt. Evidently Reagan's plea worked; thousands of phone calls, letters, and telegrams poured into congressional offices. The president easily carried the day.

Reagan's success was an anomaly, however. It is rare for a president to mobilize the public. For example, in the remainder of his tenure, Reagan went repeatedly to the people regarding a wide range of policies, including the budget, aid to the Contras in Nicaragua, and defense expenditures. Despite high levels of approval for much of that time, he was never again able to arouse many in his audience to communicate their support of his policies to Congress. Substantial tax cuts hold more appeal to the public than most other issues.

THE PRESIDENT AND THE PRESS

Despite all their efforts to lead public opinion, presidents do not directly reach the American people on a day-to-day basis. The mass media provide people with most of what they know about chief executives and their policies. The media also interpret and analyze presidential activities, even the president's direct appeals to the public. The press is thus the principal intermediary between the president and the public, and relations with the press are an important aspect of the president's efforts to lead public opinion.[43]

No matter who is in the White House or who reports on presidential activities, presidents and the press tend to be in conflict. George Washington complained that the "calumnies" against his administration were "outrages of common decency." Thomas Jefferson once declared that "nothing in a newspaper is to be believed." Presidents are inherently policy advocates. They want to control the amount and timing of information about their administration, whereas the press wants all the information that exists without delay. As long as their goals are different, presidents and the media are likely to be adversaries.

Because of the importance of the press to the president, the White House monitors the media closely. Some presidents have installed special televisions so they can watch the news on all the networks at once; Lyndon Johnson even had news tickers from AP, UPI, and Reuters in the Oval Office. The White House also goes to great lengths to encourage the media to project a positive image of the president's activities and policies. About one-third of the high-level White House staff members are directly involved in media relations and policy of one type or another, and most staff members are involved at some time in trying to influence the media's portrayal of the president.

The person who most often deals directly with the press is the president's *press secretary*, who serves as a conduit of information from the White House to the press. Press secretaries conduct daily press briefings, giving prepared announcements and answering questions. They and their staff also arrange private interviews with White House officials (often done on a background basis, in which the reporter may not attribute remarks to the person being interviewed), photo opportunities, and travel arrangements for reporters when the president leaves Washington.

The best-known direct interaction between the president and the press is the formal presidential press conference. Since the presidency of George Bush, however, prime-time televised press conferences have become rare events. Bill Clinton took office with an antagonistic attitude toward the national media and planned to bypass it rather than use it as part of his political strategy. After a rocky start in his press relations, Clinton made himself somewhat more accessible to the national press. George W. Bush

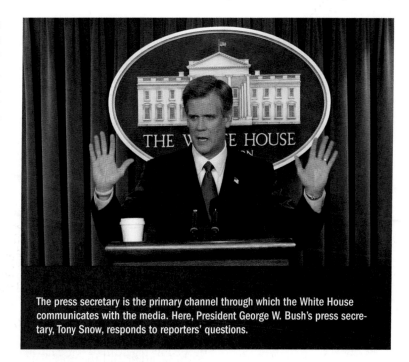

The press secretary is the primary channel through which the White House communicates with the media. Here, President George W. Bush's press secretary, Tony Snow, responds to reporters' questions.

also relied more on travel around the country to gain television time to spread his message than on formal press conferences.

Most of the news coverage of the White House comes under the heading "body watch." In other words, reporters focus on the most visible layer of the president's personal and official activities and provide the public with step-by-step accounts. They are interested in what presidents are going to do, how their actions will affect others, how they view policies and individuals, and how they present themselves rather than in the substance of policies or the fundamental processes operating in the executive branch. Former ABC White House correspondent Sam Donaldson tells of covering a meeting of Western leaders on the island of Guadeloupe. It was a slow news day, so Donaldson did a story on the roasting of the pig the leaders would be eating that night, including "an exclusive look at the oven in which the pig would be roasted."[44] Because there are daily deadlines to meet and television reporters must squeeze their stories into sound bites measured in seconds, not minutes, there is little time for reflection, analysis, or comprehensive coverage.

Bias is the most politically charged issue in relations between the president and the press. A large number of studies have concluded that the news media, including the television networks and major newspapers, are not biased *systematically* toward a particular person, party, or ideology, as measured in the amount or favorability of coverage.[45]

To conclude that the news contains little explicitly partisan or ideological bias is not to argue that the news does not distort reality in its coverage of the president. As the following excerpt from Jimmy Carter's diary regarding a visit to a U.S. Army base in Panama in 1978 illustrates, "objective" reporting can be misleading:

> I told the Army troops that I was in the Navy for 11 years, and they booed. I told them that we depended on the Army to keep the Canal open, and they cheered. Later, the news reports said that there were boos and cheers during my speech.[46]

We learned in Chapter 7 that the news is fundamentally superficial, oversimplified, and often overblown, all of which provides the public with a distorted view of, among other things, presidential activities, statements, policies, and options. We have also seen that the press prefers to frame the news in themes, which both simplifies complex issues and events and provides continuity of persons, institutions, and issues. Once these themes are established, the press tends to maintain them in subsequent stories. Of necessity, themes emphasize some information at the expense of other data, often determining what information is most relevant to news coverage and the context in which it is presented.

Once a stereotype of President Ford as a "bumbler" was established, every stumble was magnified as the press emphasized behavior that fit the mold. He was repeatedly forced to defend his intelligence, and many of his acts and statements were reported as efforts to "act" presidential. Once Ford was typecast, his image was repeatedly reinforced and was very difficult to overcome.[47]

News coverage of the presidency often tends to emphasize the negative (even if the negative stories are presented in a seemingly neutral manner),[48] a trend that has increased over the past 20 years.[49] In the 1980 election campaign, the press portrayed President Carter as mean and Ronald Reagan as imprecise rather than Carter as precise and Reagan as pleasant. The emphasis, in other words, was on the candidates' negative qualities. George Bush received extraordinarily negative press coverage during the 1992 election campaign, and the television networks' portrayal of the economy, for which they held Bush responsible, got worse as the economy actually improved to a robust rate of growth![50]

President Clinton received mostly negative coverage during his tenure in office, with a ratio of negative to positive comments on network television of about 2 to 1.[51] When the story broke regarding his affair with Monica Lewinsky, the press engaged in a feeding frenzy, providing an extraordinary amount of information on both the affair and the president's attempts to cover it up.[52] Little of this coverage was favorable to the president. The trend of negative coverage continued in the George W. Bush presidency.[53]

White House reporters are always looking to expose conflicts of interest and other shady behavior of public officials. In addition, many of their inquiries revolve around the question "Is the president up to the job?" Reporters who are confined in the White House all day may attempt to make up for their lack of investigative reporting with sarcastic and accusatory questioning. Moreover, the desire to keep the public interested and the need for continuous coverage may create in the press a subconscious bias against the presidency that leads to negative stories.

In the past, most editors were reluctant to publish analyses sharply divergent from the president's position without direct confirmation from an authoritative source who would be willing to go on the record in opposition to the White House. This approach restrained media criticism of the president. During the famous investigation of the Watergate scandal, the *Washington Post* verified all information attributed to an unnamed source with at least one other independent source. It also did not print information from other media outlets unless its reporters could independently verify that information.[54] Things have changed, however.

The press relied on analysis, opinion, and speculation as much as on confirmed facts in its coverage of President Clinton's relations with Monica Lewinsky. Even the most prominent news outlets disseminated unsubstantiated reports of charges that those originally carrying the story had not independently verified. If one news outlet carried a charge, the rest, which did not wish to be scooped, soon picked it up. For example, the media widely reported unsubstantiated charges that members of the Secret Service had found the president and Ms. Lewinsky in a compromising position. Such reporting helped sensationalize the story, keeping it alive and undermining the president's efforts to focus the public's attention on matters of public policy.

Similarly, in 2004, the press gave immediate attention to a story on the CBS television program *60 Minutes* that revealed documents regarding President George W. Bush's service in the National Guard. The documents purported to show dissatisfaction with the president's performance—or nonperformance. On closer scrutiny, however, it turned out that the documents were forgeries.

On the other hand, the president has certain advantages in dealing with the press. It typically portrays him with an aura of dignity and treats him with deference.[55] According to Sam Donaldson, who was generally considered an aggressive White House reporter, "For every truly tough question I've put to officials, I've asked a dozen that were about as tough as Grandma's apple dumplings."[56] Thus, when Larry Speakes left after serving as President Reagan's press secretary for six years, he told reporters they had given the Reagan administration "a fair shake."[57]

Remember that the White House can largely control the environment in which the president meets the press—even going so far as to have the Marine helicopters revved as Ronald Reagan approached them so that he could not hear reporters' questions and give unrehearsed responses.

UNDERSTANDING THE AMERICAN PRESIDENCY

Because the presidency is the single most important office in American politics, there has always been concern about whether the president, with all of his power, is a threat to democracy. The importance of the president has raised similar concerns about the scope of government in America.

THE PRESIDENCY AND DEMOCRACY

From the time the Constitution was written, there has been a fear that the presidency would degenerate into a monarchy or a dictatorship. Even America's greatest presidents have heightened these fears at times. Despite George Washington's well-deserved reputation for peacefully relinquishing power, he also had certain regal tendencies that fanned the suspicions of the Jeffersonians. Abraham Lincoln, for all his humility, exercised extraordinary powers at the outbreak of the Civil War. Since that time, political commentators have alternated between extolling and fearing a strong presidency.

Concerns over presidential power are generally closely related to policy views. Those who oppose the president's policies are the most likely to be concerned about *too much* presidential power. As you have seen, however, aside from acting outside the law and the Constitution—an issue that was prominent in the administration of George W. Bush—there is little prospect that the presidency will be a threat to democracy. The Madisonian system of checks and balances remains intact.

This system is especially evident in an era characterized by divided government—government in which the president is of one party and a majority in each house of Congress is of the other party. Some observers are concerned that there is too much checking and balancing and too little capacity to act on pressing national challenges. More potentially important legislation fails to pass under divided government than when one party controls both the presidency and Congress.[58] However, major policy change *is* possible under a divided government. One author found that major change is just as likely to occur when the parties share control as when one party holds both the presidency and a majority in each house of Congress.[59]

THE PRESIDENCY AND THE SCOPE OF GOVERNMENT

Some of the most noteworthy presidents in the twentieth century (including Theodore Roosevelt, Woodrow Wilson, and Franklin Roosevelt) successfully advocated substantial increases in the role of the national government. Supporting an increased role for government is not inherent in the presidency, however; leadership can move in many directions.

The seven presidents following Lyndon Johnson championed constraints on government and limits on spending, especially in domestic policy. It is often said that the American people are ideologically conservative and operationally liberal. For most of the past generation, it has been their will to choose presidents who reflected their ideology and a Congress that represented their appetite for public service. It has been the president more often than Congress who has said "no" to government growth.

SUMMARY

Americans expect a lot from presidents—perhaps too much. The myth of the president as a powerhouse clouds Americans' image of presidential reality. Presidents mainly have the power to persuade, not to impose their will.

Presidents do not work alone. Gone are the days when the presidency meant the president plus a few aides and advisers. The cabinet, the Executive Office of the President, and the White House staff all assist today's presidents. These services come at a price, however, and presidents must organize their subordinates effectively for decision making and policy execution.

Although presidential leadership of Congress is central to all administrations, it often proves frustrating. Presidents rely on their party, the public, and their own legislative skills to persuade Congress to support their policies, but most of the time their efforts are at the margins of coalition building. Rarely are presidents in a position to create—through their own leadership—opportunities for major changes in public policy. They may, however, use their skills to exploit favorable political conditions to bring about policy change.

Some of the president's most important responsibilities fall in the area of national security. As chief diplomat and commander in chief of the armed forces, the president is the country's crisis manager. Still, disputes with Congress over war powers and presidential discretion in foreign affairs demonstrate that even in regard to national security, the president operates within the Madisonian system of checks and balances.

Because presidents are dependent on others to accomplish their goals, their greatest challenge is to obtain support. Public opinion can be an important resource for presidential persuasion, and the White House works hard to influence the public. Public approval of presidents and their policies is often elusive, however; the public does not reliably respond to presidential leadership. The press is the principal intermediary between the president and the public, and relations with the press present yet another challenge to the White House's efforts to lead public opinion.

Chapter Test
Multiple Choice

1. According to Richard Neustadt, presidential power is the power to:
   a. Rule
   b. Coerce
   c. Manipulate
   d. Persuade
   e. Choose

2. The Constitution states that the president of the United States has to be _____ years old and must have resided in the country for at least _____ years.

   a. 25; 10
   b. 40; 10
   c. 35; 14
   d. 30; 14
   e. 45; 10

3. Which Amendment to the Constitution limits the terms a president may serve?
   a. The Fourteenth
   b. The Sixteenth
   c. The Eighteenth
   d. The Twentieth
   e. The Twenty-second

4. The ability to nominate ambassadors, with the agreement of the majority of the Senate, falls into which category of presidential powers?
   a. Administrative powers
   b. Legislative powers
   c. National security powers
   d. Judicial powers
   e. None of the above

5. An organization of the White House staff that emphasizes relatively equal status of staff members and focuses on a "balance of power" is referred to as a:
   a. Hub system
   b. Nuts-and-bolts system
   c. Merry-go-round system
   d. Wheel-and-spokes system
   e. Hierarchical system

6. The Constitution places the power for treaty making in the hands of:
   a. The Senate
   b. The House of Representatives
   c. The president
   d. The State Department
   e. The president and the Senate

7. Executive agreements require:
   a. Ratification by the House of Representatives
   b. Ratification by the Senate
   c. Ratification by all of Congress
   d. The agreement of the vice president
   e. No ratification

8. The War Powers Resolution gives the President _____ days to get consent from Congress after deploying troops.
   a. 100
   b. 80
   c. 60
   d. 40
   e. 20

9. Impeachment of the president requires:
   a. A simple majority in both the House and the Senate
   b. A two-thirds majority in both the House and the Senate
   c. A simple majority in the House and a two-thirds majority in the Senate
   d. A two-thirds majority in the House and a simple majority in the Senate
   e. A two-thirds majority in the Senate only

10. Based on the information presented in Table 13.5, all but which of the following are true?
    a. The total number of presidential vetoes cast has steadily declined since Eisenhower

    b. Eisenhower's presidency can be considered as somewhat of an "outlier"
    c. In general, only a relatively small percentage of presidential vetoes are subsequently overridden
    d. George W. Bush has been one of the presidents least likely to use the presidential veto
    e. The number of pocket vetoes has declined significantly since Reagan

11. Which of the following statements about the data in Table 13.6 is NOT true?
    a. The two most significant Congressional losses in both houses occurred with a Democratic president
    b. Only Republican presidents have experienced Congressional losses in both houses when they were elected
    c. The majority of presidents listed either won seats in both houses or lost seats in both houses
    d. Overall, Ronald Reagan had the most Congressional gains
    e. All of the above are true

True/False

12. According to Samuel Huntington, most Americans typically desire a strong and decisive president.
    True_____   False_____

13. Of all the U.S. presidents throughout history, only one has been Catholic.
    True_____   False_____

14. Most democratic countries around the world have a presidential system.
    True_____   False_____

15. The First Lady fulfills an official government position at the side of her husband.
    True_____   False_____

16. The president does not have the power to line-item veto a bill.
    True_____   False_____

17. Approximately half of the presidents in U.S. history have served two or more terms.
    True_____   False_____

18. In recent years, there has been a trend toward centralizing decision making in the White House.
    True_____   False_____

Short Answer

19. Briefly explain the make-up and functions of the National Security Council, the Council of Economic Advisers, and the Office of Management and Budget.

20. Generally speaking, what has the impact of public approval ratings been on the president's ability to do his job? What role does the perception of an electoral mandate play in this?

21. What is meant by the so-called "honeymoon period" of newly elected presidents?

22. What are at least three different factors that have contributed to the expansion of presidential power over time? In what ways have these factors enabled such an expansion beyond the Founding Fathers' intention? Do you believe these developments are for the better or the worse, and why?

23. Compare and contrast the characteristics of a presidential and a parliamentary political system. What are at least two pros and two cons of each with regard to issues such as effectiveness, representativeness, leadership, and any others your can think of?

24. What are at least three different factors that influence a president's public approval ratings?

Short Answer/Essay Questions

25. Based on what you have learned about the powers of the president, how would you characterize the development of these powers over time? What has necessitated the changes that have come about? Are there any particularly significant events or time periods that have led to either an increase or decrease in presidential power? Support your answer with examples whenever possible.

26. Table 13.7 illustrates that presidents have typically lost seats during midterm elections. The only exceptions are the elections of 1998 and 2002. Based on your knowledge of politics, what factors might explain these exceptions?

27. This textbook outlines the nature of checks and balances in the area of national security, particularly when it comes to war powers. How are these powers currently divided between the president and Congress? How well do you think reality reflects the theory behind such checks and balances? If you could reorganize the responsibilities of Congress and the president, what would you change about the current system, and why? If you couldn't change anything, please explain why the system works as it is.

28. What kind of "quality control" is there for the office of the president? In other words, what are the types of offenses a president can lose his/her job over and what are the general criteria, according to the Constitution? In your opinion, should there be others? If so, what kind? If not, why not? What is the right balance between holding a president accountable enough and holding him/her too accountable? Finally, do you believe there should be the possibility of a public "recall" of the president, in which the voting population—if it changes its mind—can vote the president out of office? Support your arguments.

29. Do you believe that in order to be able to truly fulfill the role of commander in chief, the president needs to have served in the military? In your answer, consider the context of the Constitution and the reasons why the Founding Fathers gave the president this role.

Answer Key

1. D   2. C   3. E   4. C   5. D   6. E   7. E   8. C   9. C   10. A   11. B   12. False   13. True   14. False   15. False   16. True   17. False   18. True

Key Terms

Twenty-second Amendment (403)
impeachment (404)
Watergate (404)
Twenty-fifth Amendment (404)
cabinet (410)

National Security Council (411)
Council of Economic Advisers (411)
Office of Management and Budget (411)
veto (415)

pocket veto (415)
presidential coattails (418)
War Powers Resolution (424)
legislative veto (425)
crisis (425)

Internet Resources

www.whitehouse.gov/
Links to presidential speeches, documents, schedules, radio addresses, federal statistics, and White House press releases and briefings.

www.whitehouse.gov/government/eop.html
Information about the Executive Office of the President.

www.ibiblio.org/lia/president/
Links to presidents and presidential libraries.

www.ipl.org/div/potus
Background on presidents and their administrations.

www.lib.umich.edu/govdocs/fedprs.html
Wide range of documents regarding the president's activities.

www.presidency.ucsb.edu/
Presidential papers, documents, and data.

www.archives.gov/federal-register/publications/weekly-compilation.html
The *Weekly Compilation of Presidential Documents*, the official publication of presidential statements, messages, remarks, and other materials released by the White House Press Secretary.

GetConnected

Approving of the President

The White House invests a great deal of time and energy in its public relations efforts designed to increase the president's public approval. A president who is popular with the people may find it easier to enact his initiatives. Throughout a president's term in office, approval ratings rise and fall in reaction to current events in the United States and abroad as well as in response to actions taken by the president. Different polling agencies use different questions to gauge presidential approval, but most follow the pattern set by the Gallup Poll: "Do you approve of the way [name of president] is handling his job as president?"

Search the Web

Go to the Polling Report's Politics & Policy page, *www.pollingreport.com/POLPOL.htm,* and click on "White House" to access the president's job approval ratings. Compare the ratings of the president to the historical information on presidential approval ratings presented in this textbook.

Questions to Ask

- When were the president's job approval ratings the highest? The lowest? Are the ratings trending up or down for the president?
- How similar are the ratings of different polling organizations?
- What were the major reasons for changes in the president's approval?

Why It Matters

Presidents believe that public approval is the political resource that has the most potential to turn a stalemate between the president and Congress into a supportive situation for the president's legislative proposals. The White House also believes that lack of public support strengthens the resolve of the president's opponents and narrows the range in which presidential policies receive the benefit of the doubt.

Get Involved

Keep track of how presidential approval is reported in your local newspaper and on the national television networks. Also watch to see whether Congress is more responsive and press coverage is more positive when the president ranks high in the polls. For more exercises, go to *longmanamericangovernment.com.*

For Further Reading

Burke, John P. *The Institutional Presidency.* 2nd ed. Baltimore: Johns Hopkins University Press, 2000. Examines White House organization and presidential advising.

Burke, John P., and Fred I. Greenstein. *How Presidents Test Reality.* New York: Russell Sage Foundation, 1989. Excellent work on presidential decision making.

Cohen, Jeffrey E. *The Presidency in the Era of 24-Hour News.* Princeton, NJ: Princeton University Press, 2008. Explores how changes in the news media have affected the relationship between the president and the press.

Cooper, Phillip J. *By Order of the President.* Lawrence: University Press of Kansas, 2002. The use and abuse of executive direct action.

Edwards, George C., III. *At the Margins: Presidential Leadership of Congress.* New Haven, CT: Yale University Press, 1989. Examines the presidents' efforts to lead Congress and explains their limitations.

Edwards, George C., III. *On Deaf Ears: The Limits of the Bully Pulpit.* New Haven, CT: Yale University Press, 2003. The effect of presidents' efforts to change public opinion in the White House's pursuit of popular support.

Edwards, George C., III. *The Strategic President: Persuasion and Opportunity in Presidential Leadership.* Princeton, NJ: Princeton University Press, 2009. Argues that presidential power is not the power to persuade.

Fisher, Louis. *Constitutional Conflicts Between Congress and the President.* 4th ed. rev. Lawrence: University Press of Kansas, 1997. Presents the constitutional dimensions of the separation of powers.

Greenstein, Fred. *The Presidential Difference.* 2nd ed. New York: Free Press, 2005. Leadership styles of modern presidents.

Howell, William G. *Power Without Persuasion.* Princeton, NJ: Princeton University Press, 2003. Focuses on the use of the president's discretionary power.

Howell, William G., and Jon C. Pevehouse, *While Dangers Gather* (Princeton, NJ: Princeton University Press, 2007). Congressional checks on presidential war powers.

Jacobson, Gary C. *A Divider, Not a Uniter: George W. Bush and the American Public,* 2nd ed. New York: Longman, 2007. Examines the polarization of public opinion in the Bush presidency.

Kumar, Martha. *Managing the President's Message: The White House Communications Operation.* Baltimore, MD: Johns Hopkins University Press, 2007. Explains White House communications and media operations.

Neustadt, Richard E. *Presidential Power and the Modern Presidents.* New York: Free Press, 1990. The most influential book on the American presidency; argues that presidential power is the power to persuade.

Rudalevige, Andrew. *The New Imperial Presidency: Renewing Presidential Power After Watergate.* Ann Arbor: University of Michigan Press, 2005. The expansion of presidential power in recent decades.

CHAPTER 14

THE
CONGRESS,
THE
PRESIDENT,
AND THE
BUDGET

THE POLITICS OF
TAXING AND SPENDING

POLITICS IN ACTION:
THE POLITICS OF BUDGETING

In 1776, the cry of "no taxation without representation" was enough to spark a revolution. Today issues of taxes and budgetary measures continue to dominate national public policy: How much should we spend for homeland security, health care for the elderly, subsidized student loans, or cleaning up the environment? And how should we pay for these programs?

Politicians who attempt to make tough decisions about the budget risk incurring voters' wrath. In 1985, Republican senators took the lead with a reform that was designed to balance the budget. In the 1986 congressional elections, Republicans lost control of the Senate. In 1990, President George Bush bit the bullet and reversed his pledge not to raise taxes. He agreed to a budget deal with the congressional Democrats that succeeded in reducing the deficit and limiting spending. In 1992, he lost his bid for reelection. In 1993, President Clinton followed Bush's precedent and reversed his promise to lower taxes with a program of higher taxes and spending constraints. In the 1994 elections, Republicans won majorities in both houses of Congress for the first time since 1952.

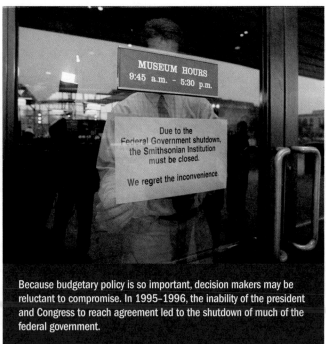

Because budgetary policy is so important, decision makers may be reluctant to compromise. In 1995–1996, the inability of the president and Congress to reach agreement led to the shutdown of much of the federal government.

And so it goes. In the presidential election of 2008, John McCain argued that we should make the large temporary tax cuts passed during the presidency of George W. Bush cuts permanent and that we should decrease the size of the federal government. Barack Obama, on the other hand, proposed increasing taxes on the wealthiest Americans and adding to the services government provides. It is not surprising that the battle of the budget remains at the center of American politics.

Two questions are central to public policy: *Who bears the burdens of paying for government?* and *Who receives the benefits?* Some observers are concerned that democracy poses a danger to budgeting. Do politicians seek to "buy" votes by spending public funds on things voters will like—and will remember on Election Day? Or is spending the result of demands made on government services by the many segments of American society? In addition, does the public choose to "soak the rich" with taxes that redistribute income?

Budgets are central to our theme of the scope of government. Indeed, for many programs, budgeting *is* policy. The amount of money spent on a program determines how many people are served, how well they are served, or how much of something (weapons, vaccines, and so on) the government can purchase. The bigger the budget, the bigger the government. But is the growth of the government's budget inevitable? Or are the battles over the allocation of scarce public resources actually a *constraint* on government?

The Constitution allocates various tasks to both the president and Congress, but it generally leaves to each branch the decision of whether to exercise its power to perform a certain task. There is an exception, however. Every year the president and Congress must appropriate funds. If they fail to do so, the government will come to a standstill. The army will be idled, Social Security offices will close, and food stamps will not be distributed to the poor.

Everyone has a basic understanding of budgeting. Public budgets are superficially like personal budgets. Aaron Wildavsky remarked that a budget is a document that "contains words and figures that propose expenditures for certain objects and purposes." There is more to public budgets than bookkeeping, however, because such a **budget** is a policy document allocating burdens (taxes) and benefits (expenditures). Thus, "budgeting is concerned with translating financial resources into human purposes. A budget therefore may also be characterized as a series of goals with price tags attached."[1]

Over the past 30 years, the national government has run up large annual budget deficits. A budget **deficit** occurs when **expenditures** exceed **revenues** in a fiscal year. In other words, the national government spends more money than it receives in taxes. As a result, the total national debt rose sharply during the 1980s, increasing from less than $1 trillion to about $11 trillion by 2010. About 9 percent of all current budget expenditures go to paying just the *interest* on this debt.[2]

The president and Congress have often been caught in a budgetary squeeze: Americans want them to balance the budget, maintain or increase the level of government spending on most policies, and keep taxes low. As a result, the president and Congress are preoccupied with budgeting, trying to cope with these contradictory demands.

budget

A policy document allocating burdens (taxes) and benefits (expenditures).

deficit

An excess of federal **expenditures** over federal **revenues**.

expenditures

Government spending of **revenues**. Major areas of federal spending are social services and national defense.

revenues

The financial resources of the government. The individual income tax and Social Security tax are two major sources of the federal government's revenue.

In this chapter you will learn how the president and Congress produce a budget, making decisions on both taxes and expenditures. In short, you will look at how government manages its money—which is, of course, really *your* money.

SOURCES OF FEDERAL REVENUE

"Taxes," said the late Supreme Court Justice Oliver Wendell Holmes Jr., "are what we pay for civilization." Despite his assertion that "I like to pay taxes," most taxpayers throughout history do not agree. The art of taxation, said Jean-Baptiste Colbert, Louis XIV's finance minister, is in "so plucking the goose as to procure the largest quantity of feathers with the least possible amount of hissing."[3] In Figure 14.1, you can see where the federal government has been getting its feathers. Only a small share comes from excise taxes (a tax levied on the manufacture, transportation, sale, or consumption of a good—for example, those on gasoline) and other sources; the three major sources of federal revenues are the personal and corporate income tax, social insurance taxes, and borrowing.

FIGURE 14.1

Federal Revenues

Individual income taxes make the largest contribution to federal revenues, but more than a third comes from social insurance taxes. This is a stacked graph in which the *difference* between the lines indicates the revenues raised by each tax.

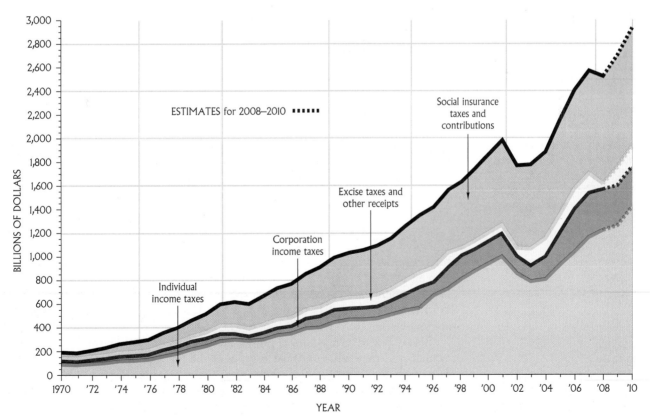

Source: *Budget of the United States Government, Fiscal Year 2009: Historical Tables* (Washington, DC: U.S. Government Printing Office, 2008), Table 2.1.

INCOME TAX

Millions of bleary-eyed American taxpayers struggle to the post office before midnight every April 15 to mail their income tax forms. Most individuals are required to pay the government a portion of the money they earn; this portion is an **income tax**. In the early years of the nation, long before the days of a large national defense, Social Security, and the like, fees collected on imported goods financed most of the federal government. Congress briefly adopted an income tax to pay for the Civil War, but the first peacetime income tax was enacted in 1894. Even though the tax was only 2 percent of income earned beyond the then magnificent sum of $4,000, a lawyer opposing it called the tax the first step of a "communist march." The Supreme Court wasted little time in declaring the tax unconstitutional in *Pollock v. Farmer's Loan and Trust Co.* (1895).

In 1913, the **Sixteenth Amendment** was added to the Constitution, explicitly permitting Congress to levy an income tax. Congress was already receiving income tax revenue before the amendment was ratified, however, and the Internal Revenue Service (IRS) was established to collect it. Today the IRS receives more than 132 million individual tax returns each year. People or computers scrutinize each return. In addition, the IRS audits more than a million returns in greater detail, investigates thousands of suspected criminal violations of the tax laws, and annually prosecutes and secures the conviction of thousands of errant taxpayers or nonpayers.[4] Never a popular agency, in recent years the IRS has received substantial criticism for abusing taxpayers with its aggressive efforts to enforce the tax code. In 1998 Congress passed a law designed to rein in the IRS and make it a more consumer-oriented agency.

Corporations, like individuals, pay income taxes. Although corporate taxes once yielded more revenues than individual income taxes, this is no longer true. In 2008, corporate taxes yielded about 13 cents of every federal revenue dollar, compared with 48 cents from individual income taxes.

The income tax is generally *progressive*, meaning that those with more taxable income not only pay more taxes but also pay higher *rates* of tax on that income. As a result, the 10 percent of taxpayers with the highest taxable incomes pay about two-thirds of all the federal income taxes in the country, while those in the bottom 50 percent of taxable income pay about 3 percent of all federal income taxes.[5] Some people feel that a progressive tax is the fairest type of taxation because those who have the most pay higher rates. Others see things differently and propose a "flat" tax, with everyone taxed at the same rate. Still others suggest that we abandon the income tax altogether and rely on a national sales tax, much like the sales taxes in most states. As you can see, it is easy to criticize the income tax but difficult to obtain agreement on a replacement.

SOCIAL INSURANCE TAXES

Both employers and employees pay Social Security taxes. Money is deducted from employees' paychecks and matched by their employers. Unlike other taxes, these payments are earmarked for a specific purpose: the Social Security Trust Fund that pays benefits to the elderly, the disabled, the widowed, and the unemployed.

Social Security taxes have grown faster than any other source of federal revenue, and they will continue to grow as the population ages. In 1957, these taxes made up a mere 12 percent of federal revenues; today they account for about 36 percent. In 2008, employees and employers each paid a Social Security tax equal to 6.2 percent of the first $102,000 of earnings, and for Medicare they paid another 1.45 percent on all earnings.

BORROWING

Like families and firms, the federal government may borrow money to make ends meet. When families and firms need money, they go to their neighborhood bank, savings and loan association, or moneylender. When the federal government wants to borrow money, the Treasury Department sells bonds, guaranteeing to pay interest to bondholders. Citizens, corporations, mutual funds, other financial institutions, and even foreign governments may purchase these bonds; there is always a lively market for government bonds. In addition, the federal government has "intragovernmental" debt on its books. This debt is what the Treasury owes various Social Security and other trust funds because the government has been using for its general purposes payroll taxes and other taxes designated to fund specific programs.

Most government borrowing is not for its capital needs (such as buildings and machinery) but for its day-to-day expenses. Most families wisely do not borrow money for their food and clothing, yet the government has largely borrowed money for its farm subsidies, its military pensions, and its aid to states and cities.

Today the **federal debt**—all the money borrowed over the years that is still outstanding—is nearing *$11 trillion* (see Figure 14.2). Nine percent of all federal expenditures go to paying interest on this debt rather than paying for current

federal debt
All the money borrowed by the federal government over the years and still outstanding. Today the federal debt is more than $9 trillion.

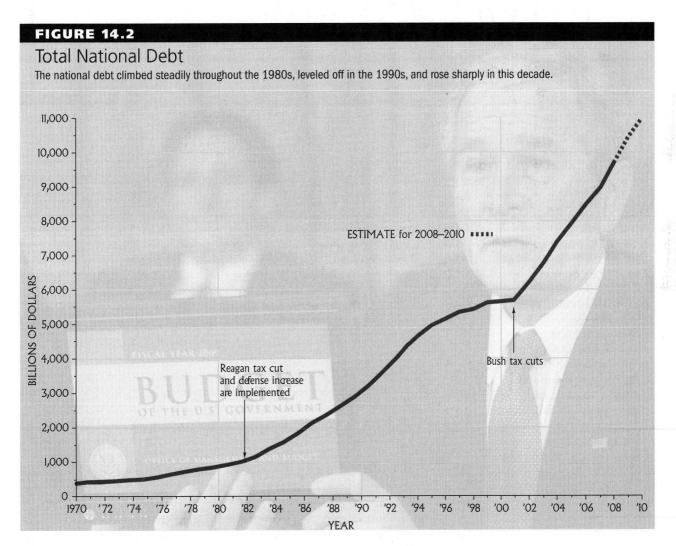

FIGURE 14.2

Total National Debt
The national debt climbed steadily throughout the 1980s, leveled off in the 1990s, and rose sharply in this decade.

Source: *Budget of the United States Government, Fiscal Year 2009: Historical Tables* (Washington, DC: U.S. Government Printing Office, 2008), table 7.1.

policies. Yesterday's consumption of public policies is at the expense of tomorrow's taxpayers because borrowing money shifts the burden of repayment to future taxpayers who will have to service the debt and pay the principal. Every dollar that the government borrows today will cost taxpayers many more dollars in interest over the next 30 years. These dollars cannot be spent on health care, education, or lower taxes. Paying the interest on the debt is not optional.

Many economists and policymakers are concerned about the national debt.[6] Some believe that government borrowing may crowd out private borrowers, both individuals and businesses, from the loan marketplace. For instance, your local bank may know that you are a low-risk borrower, but it thinks the federal government is an even lower risk. Over the past 70 years a substantial percentage of all the net private savings in the country have gone to the federal government. Most economists believe that under some conditions this competition to borrow money increases interest rates and makes it more difficult for businesses to invest in capital expenditures (such as new plants and equipment) that produce economic growth. Higher interest rates also raise the costs to individuals of financing homes or credit card purchases.

Large deficits also make the American government dependent on foreign investors, including other governments, to fund its debt—not a favorable position for a superpower. Foreign investors currently hold a majority of the federal government's public debt. If they stop lending us money, perhaps to gain leverage in foreign policy, interest rates would rise and the economy would be depressed.

Others say such fears are overblown and that the national debt has relatively little to do with the overall health of the U.S. economy. Our national debt, they argue, is no larger a percentage of our economy and of the total amount of money available for borrowing than in many past years. For decades a defining principle of the Republican Party was to curtail federal spending to reduce the federal deficit. In recent years, however, this philosophy has changed, and Republicans now support cutting taxes (and thus decreasing revenues), hopefully to stimulate the economy so that it produces more tax revenue in the long run. George W. Bush based his tax-cut proposals on this principle.

Critics see the issue differently, arguing that such tax cuts never replace all the lost revenue and leave the country with an ever-increasing debt to service in the future. They also dispute a prominent conservative claim that cutting taxes is a useful way to limit government expansion is to "starve the beast" by cutting taxes. In reality, government often *grows* more rapidly following substantial tax cuts.[7]

Sometimes politicians complain that because families and businesses and even state and local governments balance their budgets, the federal government ought to be able to do the same. Such statements reflect a fundamental misunderstanding of budgeting, however. Most families do *not* balance their budgets. They use credit cards to give themselves instant loans, and they go to the bank to borrow money to purchase automobiles, boats, and, most important, homes. The mortgages on their homes are debts they owe for most of their lives.

Unlike state and local governments and private businesses, the federal government does not have a *capital budget*, a budget for expenditures on items that will serve for the long term, such as equipment, roads, and buildings. Thus, for example, when airlines purchase new airplanes or when school districts build new schools, they do not pay for them out of current income. Instead, they borrow money, often through issuing bonds. These debts do not count against the operating budget. When the federal government purchases new jets for the air force or new buildings for medical research, however, these purchases are counted as current expenditures and run up the deficit.

Despite its borrowing habits, most of the government's income still comes from taxes. Few government policies provoke more heated discussion than taxation.

Why It Matters
Deficit Spending
The federal government can run a deficit and borrow money to pay its current expenses. States and cities can only borrow (by issuing bonds) for long-term capital expenses such as roads and schools. If the Constitution required a balanced budget, the federal government could not borrow money to provide increased services during an economic downturn, nor could it cut taxes to stimulate the economy in such a situation.

TAXES AND PUBLIC POLICY

No government policy affects as many Americans as tax policy. In addition to raising revenues to finance its services, the government can use taxes to make citizens' incomes more nearly or less nearly equal, to encourage or discourage growth in the economy, and to promote specific interests. Whereas Chapters 17 and 18 discuss how taxes affect economic and equality issues, the following sections focus on how tax policies can promote the interests of particular groups or encourage specific activities.

Tax Expenditures   The 1974 Budget Act defines **tax expenditures** as "revenue losses attributable to provisions of the federal tax laws which allow a special exemption, exclusion, or deduction." These expenditures represent the difference between what the government actually collects in taxes and what it would have collected without special exemptions. Thus, tax expenditures amount to subsidies for different activities. Here are some examples:

tax expenditures
Revenue losses that result from special exemptions, exclusions, or deductions on federal tax law.

- The government *could* send checks for billions of dollars to charities. Instead, it permits taxpayers to deduct their contributions to charities from their income. Thus, the government encourages charitable contributions.
- The government *could* give cash to families with the desire and financial means to buy a home. Instead, it permits home owners to deduct from their income the billions of dollars they collectively pay each year in mortgage interest.
- The government *could* write a check to all businesses that invest in new plants and equipment. Instead, it allows such businesses to deduct these expenses from their taxes at a more rapid rate than they deduct other expenses. In effect, the owners of these businesses, including stockholders, get a subsidy that is unavailable to owners of other businesses.

Tax expenditures are among the most obscure aspects of a generally obscure budgetary process, partly because they receive no regular review by Congress—a great advantage for those who benefit from a tax expenditure. Few ordinary citizens seem to realize their scope; you can see the magnitude of tax expenditures in Table 14.1.

Jimmy Carter, campaigning for the presidency, called the American tax system a "national disgrace" because of its special treatment of favored taxpayers. Businesspeople, he complained, could deduct costly "three-martini lunches" as business expenses, whereas ordinary workers, carrying coffee in a Thermos and a sandwich to work, could not write off their lunch expenses. On the whole, tax expenditures benefit middle- and upper-income taxpayers and corporations. Poorer people, who tend not to own homes, can take little advantage of provisions that permit home owners to deduct mortgage interest payments. Likewise, poorer people in general can take less advantage of the exclusion of taxes on contributions to individual retirement accounts or interest on state and local bonds. Students, however, are an exception to this generalization (see "Young People and Politics: Education and the Federal Tax Code" on page 449).

To some, tax expenditures such as business-related deductions, tuition tax credits, and capital gains tax rates are "loopholes." To others, they are public policy choices that support a social activity worth subsidizing. Either way, they amount to the same thing: revenues that the government loses because certain items are exempted from normal taxation or are taxed at lower rates. The Office of Management and Budget estimates that the total tax expenditures equal more than a third of the federal government's total receipts.

TABLE 14.1

Tax Expenditures: The Money Government Does Not Collect

Tax expenditures are essentially money that government could collect but does not because they are exempted from taxation. The Office of Management and Budget estimated that the total tax expenditures in 2009 would be about $925 billion—an amount equal to more than a third of the total federal receipts. Individuals receive most of the tax expenditures, and corporations get the rest. Here are some of the largest tax expenditures and their cost to the treasury:

TAX EXPENDITURE	MAIN BENEFICIARY	COST
Exclusion of employer contributions to health care and insurance	Families	$168 billion
Deduction of mortgage interest on owner-occupied houses	Families	$101 billion
Exclusion of IRA and 401(k) retirement account contributions and earnings	Families	$64 billion
Deductions for charitable contributions	Families and businesses	$58 billion
Capital gains (nonhome)	Families	$56 billion
Deductions for state and local taxes	Families	$50 billion
Exclusion of company contributions to pension funds	Families	$46 billion
Accelerated depreciation of machinery and equipment	Businesses	$44 billion
Capital gains at death	Families	$37 billion
Exclusion of capital gains on home sales	Families	$35 billion
Child credit	Families	$30 billion
Exclusion for interest earned on state and local government bonds	Families	$26 billion
Exclusion of interest on life insurance savings	Families	$24 billion
Exclusion of Social Security benefits	Families	$19 billion

Government could lower overall tax rates by taxing things it does not currently tax, such as Social Security benefits, pension fund contributions, charitable contributions, and the like. You can easily figure out, though, that these are not popular items to tax, and doing so would evoke strong opposition from powerful interest groups.

Source: *Budget of the United States Government, Fiscal Year 2009: Analytical Perspectives* (Washington, DC: U.S. Government Printing Office, 2008), Tables 19.1 and 19.3.

Tax Reduction   The annual rite of spring—the preparation of individual tax returns—is invariably accompanied by calls for tax reform and, frequently, tax reduction. Early in his administration, President Reagan proposed a massive tax-cut bill. Standing in the way of tax cuts is never popular, and in July 1981, Congress passed Reagan's tax-cutting proposal. Over a three-year period, the federal tax bills of Americans were reduced 25 percent, corporate income taxes were also reduced, new tax incentives were provided for personal savings and corporate investment, and taxes were *indexed* to the cost of living. Indexing taxes meant that beginning in 1985, government no longer received a larger share of income when inflation pushed incomes into higher brackets while the tax rates stayed the same. (This point is important because people with high incomes also pay a higher *percentage* of their incomes in taxes.)

Families with high incomes saved many thousands of dollars on taxes, but those at the lower end of the income ladder saw little change in their tax burden because social insurance and excise taxes (which fall disproportionately on these people) rose during the same period. Many blamed the massive deficits of the 1980s and 1990s at least partially on the 1981 tax cuts, as government continued to spend but at the same time reduced its revenues.

To deal with these deficits, in 1993 President Clinton persuaded Congress to raise the income tax rate on those in the top 2 percent of income and the top corporate income tax rate. Congress also increased a small energy tax that would be paid by all but those with low incomes.

When budget surpluses materialized (briefly) in the late 1990s, cutting taxes was once again a popular rallying cry for some politicians, including George W. Bush. In 2001, Congress enacted a tax cut that gradually lowered tax rates over the next 10 years, and in 2003 it reduced the tax rates on capital gains and dividends. When deficits reappeared, critics charged that the president was fiscally irresponsible. The appropriate level of taxation remains one of the most vexing problems in American politics.

You Are the President and Need to Get a Tax Cut Passed

Tax Reform   Gripes about taxes in America are at least as old as the Boston Tea Party. When President Reagan first revealed his massive tax simplification plan in 1985—with its proposals to eliminate many tax deductions and tax expenditures—it was met with howls of protest. The insurance industry, for example, launched a $6 million advertising campaign to save the tax deductions for fringe benefits (much of which are in the form of life and health insurance) that employers set aside for employees. A pitched battle raged between tax reformers and interest groups determined to hold on to their tax benefits.

For once, however, a tax reform plan was not derailed. Democrats, including the powerful House Ways and Means Committee chair, Dan Rostenkowski, were

YOUNG PEOPLE AND POLITICS
Education and the Federal Tax Code

If you think that the federal income tax is something that does not affect you much as a student, you are wrong. If you are footing the costs of higher education for yourself or your family, education tax credits can help offset these costs. On the other hand, if you think the rules for obtaining a tax credit are simple, you are also wrong.

First, there is the Hope Credit, which applies only for the first two years of postsecondary education, such as college or vocational school. It can be worth up to $1,650 per eligible student, per year to a family (100 percent of the first $1,100 of qualified tuition and related fees paid during the tax year, plus 50 percent of the next $1,100). It does not apply to graduate and professional-level programs, however, and you must be enrolled at least half time to receive the credit.

The Lifetime Learning Credit applies to undergraduate, graduate, and professional degree courses, including instruction to acquire or improve your job skills. If you qualify, your credit equals 20 percent of the first $10,000 of postsecondary tuition and fees you pay during the year for all eligible students in a family, for a maximum credit of $2,000 per tax return.

The Hope Credit and the Lifetime Learning Credit are education credits you can subtract in full from your federal income tax, not just deduct from your taxable income.

Naturally, there are restrictions on claiming these credits. To qualify for either credit, you must pay postsecondary tuition and fees for yourself, your spouse, or your dependent. The credit may be claimed by the parent or the student but not by both. However, if the student was claimed as a dependent, the student cannot claim the credit. Moreover, you cannot claim both the Hope and the Lifetime Learning Credits for the same student (such as

yourself) in the same year. Parents with children or attending school themselves can claim more than one Hope credit but only one Lifetime Learning Credit.

These credits are not for everyone. They are gradually reduced for those with modified adjusted gross income (MAGI) between $47,000 and $57,000 ($94,000 and $114,000 for married filing jointly) and eliminated completely for MAGI of $57,000 or more ($114,000 for married filing jointly). If a taxpayer is married, the credit may be claimed only on a joint return. In addition, the Hope Credit is not allowed for a student convicted of a felony drug offense while in school.

A taxpayer may also take a deduction for up to $4,000 of higher-education expenses, but only when opting not to use the education credits. A different deduction lets taxpayers recoup some of the cost of student loan interests. It and other deductions and credits also begin to diminish as taxpayers earn more.

Welcome to the federal tax code. As you can see, Congress has chosen to give students benefits in the tax code, but it has also been concerned that people do not abuse these benefits. Thus, even students have to face the intricacies of the federal tax code and work out the myriad tax credits and deductions that help defray the costs of a college education. In the end, however, most people agree that it is worth the effort.

QUESTIONS FOR DISCUSSION

▶ Why doesn't Congress simply appropriate money for students and send them a check instead of relying on the tax code?

▶ What are the obstacles to simplifying the tax code?

President Reagan signs the Tax Reform Act of 1986, passed with the backing of congressional leaders and administration officials. The legislation—the most wide-ranging reform of federal tax policy since the Sixteenth Amendment legalized income taxes in 1913—was implemented despite protests from numerous interest groups that did not want to lose their tax deductions.

enthusiastic about tax reform. They also did not want the Republicans to get all the credit for it. In fact, the president actually had more problems obtaining the support of those in his own party and had to make an unusual trip to Capitol Hill to plead with House Republicans to support the tax bill after its initial defeat when it came to the floor.

The Senate posed an even bigger problem because the bill was loaded with special tax treatments for a wide variety of groups. While the president was on a trip abroad, the Finance Committee met behind closed doors and emerged with a bill similar in spirit to the bill supported by the president and the House. The *Tax Reform Act of 1986* was one of the most sweeping alterations in federal tax policy history. It eliminated or reduced the value of many tax deductions, removed several million low-income individuals from the tax rolls, and greatly reduced the number of tax brackets (categories of income that are taxed at different rates).

FEDERAL EXPENDITURES

In 1932, when President Franklin D. Roosevelt took office in the midst of the Great Depression, the federal government was spending just over $3 billion a year. Today, the federal government spends that much in a single morning. Program costs once measured in the millions are now measured in billions. Comparisons over time are a little misleading, of course, because they do not account for changes in the value of the dollar. You can see in Figure 14.3 how the federal budget has grown in actual dollars.

Figure 14.3 makes two interesting points. First, the policies and programs on which the government spends money change over time. Second, expenditures keep rising. The following sections explore three important questions: Why are government budgets so big? Where does the money go? Why is it difficult to control federal expenditures?

BIG GOVERNMENTS, BIG BUDGETS

One answer to the question of why budgets are so large is simple: Big budgets are necessary to pay for big governments. Among the most important changes of the twentieth century is the rise of large governments.[8] Actually, as you can see in "America in Perspective: How Big is the Public Sector?," among Western nations, America has one of the *smallest* public sectors relative to the size of the economy, which is measured as the gross domestic product (GDP). Nevertheless, it is difficult to characterize the national government, with a budget of about $3 trillion per year, as anything but large—some critics would say enormous.

As with other Western nations, the growth of government in the United States has been dramatic. Political scientist E. E. Schattschneider described the small beginnings of American government:

President Washington made his budget on a single sheet of paper. Jefferson ran his Department of Foreign Affairs with a staff of six writing clerks.... As late as 1822 the government spent $1,000 for the improvement of rivers and

FIGURE 14.3

Federal Expenditures

The biggest category of federal expenditures is payments to individuals, composing about 60 percent of the budget. National defense accounts for about one-fifth of the budget. This is a stacked graph in which the *difference* between the lines indicates the amount spent on each category.

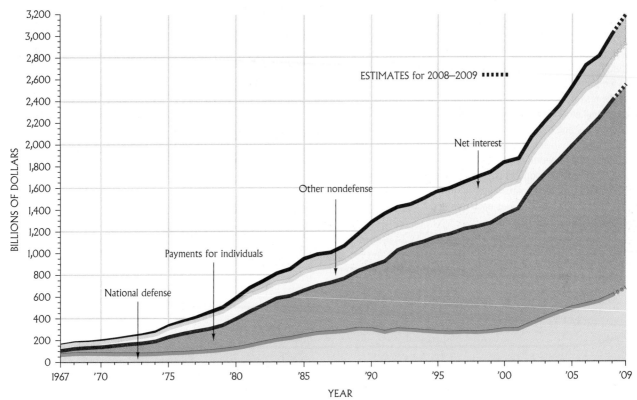

Source: *Budget of the United States Government, Fiscal Year 2009: Historical Tables* (Washington, DC: U.S. Government Printing Office, 2008), Table 6.1.

harbors and President Monroe vetoed a $9,000 appropriation for the repair of the Cumberland Road.[9]

This relatively tiny government was, said Schattschneider, the "grain of mustard seed" from which today's huge government has grown. American governments—national, state, and local—spend an amount equal to one-third of the GDP. The national government's expenditures alone equal about one fifth of the GDP.

Of course, no one knows for sure exactly why government has grown so rapidly in all the Western democracies. William Berry and David Lowery found that the public sector expands principally in response to the public's preferences and changes in economic and social conditions that affect the public's level of demand for government activity.[10] This is why the rise of big government has been strongly resistant to reversal: Citizens like government services. Even Ronald Reagan, a strong leader with an antigovernment orientation, succeeded only in slowing the growth of government, not in actually trimming its size. When he left office, the federal government employed more people and spent more money than when he was inaugurated.

Two conditions associated with government growth in America are the rise of the national security state and the rise of the social service state.

AMERICA IN PERSPECTIVE

How Big Is the Public Sector?

It is common for Americans to complain that taxes are too high, and it is equally common to think of "big government" with federal budgets that run into the trillions and budget deficits that may exceed $400 billion in a single year. The figures in the accompanying graph show that the national, state, and local governments in the United States tax a smaller percentage of the resources of the country than do those in almost all other democracies with developed economies, and that they spend less as well. Compared with these countries, the United States has a rather modest public sector. The Scandinavian countries of Sweden and Denmark, in contrast, take about half the wealth of the country in taxes each year and spend even more.

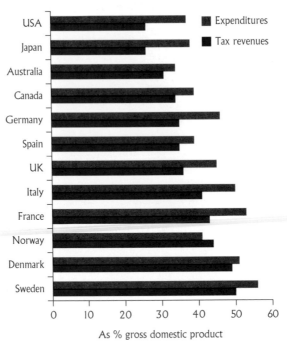

As % gross domestic product

Source: Organization for Economic Cooperation and Development, 2008.

THE RISE AND DECLINE OF THE NATIONAL SECURITY STATE

Growth of the Budget and Federal Spending

Forty years ago, the most expensive part of the federal budget was not its social services but its military budget. Until World War II, the United States customarily disbanded a large part of its military forces at the end of a war. After World War II, however, the Cold War with the Soviet Union resulted in a permanent military establishment and expensive military technology. Fueling the military machine greatly increased the cost of government. It was President Eisenhower—a five-star general—who coined the phrase *military industrial complex* to characterize the close relationship between the military hierarchy and the defense industry that supplies its hardware needs.

In the 1950s and early 1960s, spending for past and present wars amounted to more than half the federal budget. The Department of Defense received the majority of federal dollars. Liberals complained that government was shortchanging the poor while lining the pockets of defense contractors. Things soon changed, however. Over 15 years, from the mid-1960s to the early 1980s, defense expenditures crept downward in real dollars while social welfare expenditures more than doubled.

Although President Reagan proposed eliminating scores of domestic programs in his annual budget requests, he also urged Congress to increase the defense budget substantially. Throughout his entire second term, Congress balked, however, and in the 1990s defense expenditures decreased in response to the lessening tensions in Europe (discussed in Chapter 20). Defense expenditures increased again following the terrorist attacks of September 11, 2001, and especially with the war in Iraq. Nevertheless, the budget of the Department of Defense, once the driving force in the expansion of the federal budget, now constitutes only about one-fifth of all federal expenditures (see Figure 14.4).

Payrolls and pensions for the more than 7 million persons who work for the Pentagon, serve in the reserves, or receive military retirement pay, veterans pensions, or disability compensation constitute a large component of the defense budget. So do the research, development, and *procurement* (purchasing) of military hardware. The costs of procurement are high, and advanced technology makes any weapon, fighter plane, or component more expensive than its predecessors. Moreover, cost overruns are common. The American fleet of Stealth Bombers cost several times the original estimate—over $2 *billion* each.

The U.S. Air Force unveiled its new Stealth Bomber in 1989. The plane's unusual shape allows it to fly undetected by enemy radar, but such technology costs money—over $2 billion per plane. These huge expenditures contributed to substantial increases in the defense budget in the 1980s.

FIGURE 14.4

Trends in National Defense Spending

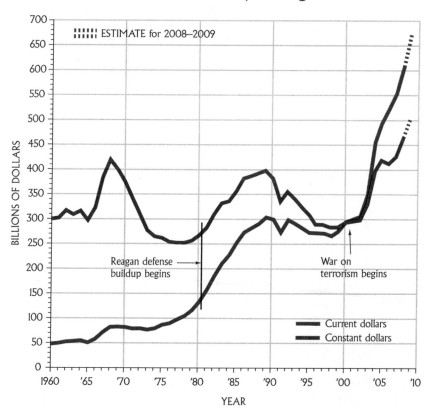

Defense expenditures increased rapidly during the Reagan administration, but they declined with the end of the Cold War. They increased again after the September 11, 2001, terrorist attacks and the invasion of Iraq in 2003.

Source: *Budget of the United States Government, Fiscal Year 2009: Historical Tables* (Washington, DC: U.S. Government Printing Office, 2008), Table 6.1.

THE RISE OF THE SOCIAL SERVICE STATE

The biggest slice of the budget pie, once reserved for defense, now belongs to *income security* expenditures, a bundle of policies extending direct and indirect aid to the elderly, the poor, and the needy. In 1935, during the Great Depression and the administration of President Franklin D. Roosevelt, Congress passed the **Social Security Act**. The act was intended to provide a minimal level of sustenance to older Americans, saving them from poverty.

In January 1940, the treasurer of the United States sent the nation's first Social Security check to Ida Fuller of Brattleboro, Vermont, in the amount of $22.54. An early entrant into the fledgling Social Security program, Fuller had contributed less than the amount of her first check to the system. By the time she died in December 1974 at the age of 100, she had collected $22,888.92 from the Social Security Administration. The typical retired worker received about $1,100 a month in 2008.

In the 1950s, disability insurance became a part of the Social Security program; thus, workers who had not retired but who were disabled could also collect benefits. In 1965, Congress added **Medicare**, which provides both hospital and physician coverage to the elderly, to the system. Congress added an expensive prescription drug benefit to Medicare in 2003. Today, about 55 million Americans receive payments from the Social Security system each month.

Social Security is less an insurance program than a kind of intergenerational contract. As Chapter 18 explains, essentially, money is taken from the working members of the population and spent on the retired members. Today, however, demographic and economic realities threaten to dilute this intergenerational relationship. In 1940, the entire Social Security system was financed with a 3 percent tax on payrolls; by 1990, the tax exceeded 15 percent. In 1945, 50 workers paid taxes to support each Social Security beneficiary. In 1990, about three workers supported each beneficiary. By the year 2055, when today's college students will be getting their Social Security checks, only about two workers will be supporting each beneficiary.

Not surprisingly, by the early 1980s the Social Security program faced a problem. As Paul Light candidly described it, "It was going broke fast."[11] And that was only the short-term problem. The aging population has added more people to the Social Security rolls annually; once there, people tend to stay on the rolls because life expectancies are increasing. Congress responded by increasing social insurance taxes so that more was coming into the Social Security Trust Fund than was being spent. The goal was to create a surplus to help finance payments when the baby boomers retire.

In 1999, President Clinton proposed allocating much of the new budget surplus to Social Security and investing some of it in the stock market. Everyone agreed that saving Social Security was a high priority, but not everyone agreed with the president's solutions. As a result, no major changes occurred. George W. Bush faced similar resistance to his proposals for investing part of individuals' tax payments in the stock market. Nevertheless, the fiscal clock keeps ticking, and it will not be long before Social Security's costs will begin to exceed its income from tax collections. Medicare is in even greater fiscal jeopardy, as its expenditures will exceed its income in about 2011

Social Security Act

A 1935 law passed during the Great Depression that was intended to provide a minimal level of sustenance to older Americans and thus save them from poverty.

Medicare

A program added to the Social Security system in 1965 that provides hospitalization insurance for the elderly and permits older Americans to purchase inexpensive coverage for doctor fees and other health expenses.

Evaluating Federal Spending and Economic Policy

President Harry S. Truman proposed national healthcare for senior citizens in 1949. Here President Lyndon B. Johnson signs the Medicare bill in Truman's presence in 1965.

and the trust fund for the hospital insurance part of Medicare will be depleted by the end of the next decade. Financing Social Security and Medicare will be one of the greatest challenges for the next president and Congress.

Social Security is the largest social policy of the federal government (Social Security and Medicare account for more than one-third of the federal budget).[12] However, other social service expenditures have paralleled the upward growth of income security. In health, education, job training, and many other areas, the rise of the social service state has also contributed to America's growing budget. No brief list can do justice to the range of government social programs, which provide funds for the elderly, businesses run by minority entrepreneurs, consumer education, drug rehabilitation, environmental education, food subsidies for the poor, guaranteed loans to college students, housing allowances for the poor, inspections of hospitals, and so on. Liberals often favor these programs to assist individuals and groups in society; conservatives see them as a drain on the federal treasury. In any event, they cost money—a lot of it (see Figure 14.5).

The rise of the social service state and the national security state are linked with much of American governmental growth since the end of World War II. Although

FIGURE 14.5

Trends in Social Service Spending

Social Service spending has increased rapidly since the 1960s and now makes up about two-thirds of the budget.

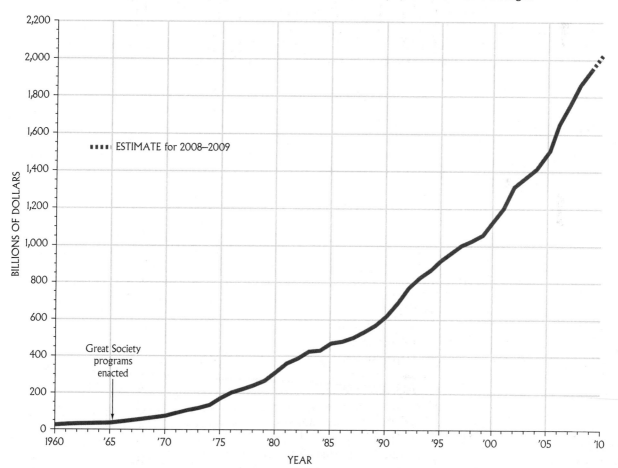

Source: *Budget of the United States Government, Fiscal Year 2009: Historical Tables* (Washington, DC: U.S. Government Printing Office, 2008), table 3.1.

American social services expanded less than similar services in Western European nations, for most of the postwar period American military expenditures expanded more rapidly. Together, these factors help explain why the budget is the center of attention in American government today. Why is it so difficult to bring this increasing federal budget under control?

INCREMENTALISM

incrementalism

A description of the budget process where the best predictor of this year's **budget** is last year's budget, plus a little bit more (an increment). According to Aaron Wildavsky, "Most of the budget is a product of previous decisions."

Sometimes political scientists use the term *incrementalism* to describe the spending and appropriations process. **Incrementalism** means simply that the best predictor of this year's budget is last year's budget plus a little bit more (an increment). According to Wildavsky and Caiden, "The largest determining factor of the size and content of this year's budget is last year's. Most of each budget is a product of previous decisions."[13] Incremental budgeting has several features:

- Policymakers focus little attention on the budgetary base—the amounts agencies have had over the previous years.
- Usually, agencies can safely assume they will get at least the budget they had the previous year.
- Most of the debate and most of the attention of the budgetary process focus on the proposed increment.
- The budget for any given agency tends to grow by a little bit every year.

This picture of the federal budget is one of constant growth. Expenditures mandated by an existing law or obligation (such as Social Security) are particularly likely to follow a neat pattern of increase.[14] There are exceptions, however. Paul Schulman observed that budgets for the National Aeronautics and Space Administration (NASA) were hardly incremental; they initially rose as fast as a NASA rocket but later plummeted to a fraction of their former size.[15] Incrementalism may be a general tendency of the budget, but it does not fully describe all budgetary politics.[16]

Because so much of the budgetary process looks incremental, there is a never-ending call for budgetary reform. The idea is always to make it easier to compare programs so that the "most deserving" ones can be supported and the "wasteful" ones cut. Nevertheless, the budgetary process, like all aspects of government, is affected by groups with interests in taxes and expenditures. These interests make it difficult to pare the budget. In addition, the budget is too big to review from scratch each year, even for the most systematic and conscientious members of Congress. The federal budget is a massive document, detailing annual outlays larger than the entire economies of individual countries except those of the United States, Japan, and Russia. Although efforts to check incrementalism have failed, so have attempts to reduce more rapidly rising expenses. Much of the federal budget has become "uncontrollable."

"UNCONTROLLABLE" EXPENDITURES

At first glance, it is hard to see how one could call the federal budget uncontrollable. After all, Congress has the constitutional authority to budget—to add or subtract money from an agency. Indeed, all recent presidents have proposed and Congress has adopted some proposals to cut the growth of government spending. How, then, can one speak of an uncontrollable budget?

Consider for a moment what we might call the "allowance theory" of the budget. Using this theory, a government budget works like an allowance. Mom and Dad hand over to Mary Jean and Tommy a monthly allowance, say $10 each, with the stern admonition, "Make that last to the end of the month because that's all we're giving you until then." In the allowance model of the budget, Congress plays this parental role; the agencies play the roles of Mary Jean and Tommy. Congress thus allocates a lump sum—say, $5.2 billion—and instructs agencies to meet their payrolls and other expenses throughout the fiscal year. When most Americans think of the government's budget, they envision the budget as a kind of allowance to the agencies.

About two-thirds of the government's budget, however, does not work this way at all. **Uncontrollable expenditures** result from policies that make some group automatically eligible for some benefit or by previous obligations of the government, such as pensions and interest on the national debt. The government does not decide each year, for example, whether it will pay the interest on the federal debt or that it will chop the pensions earned by former military personnel in half.

Many expenditures are uncontrollable because Congress has in effect obligated itself to pay X level of benefits to Y number of recipients. Congress writes the eligibility rules; the number of people eligible and their level of guaranteed benefits determine how much Congress must spend. Such policies are called **entitlements**, and they range from agricultural subsidies to veterans' aid. Each year, Congress's bill is a straightforward function of the X level of benefits times the Y beneficiaries. The biggest uncontrollable expenditure of all is the Social Security system, including Medicare, which costs about $1.1 *trillion* dollars per year in 2009. The Social Security Administration does not merely provide benefits on a first-come, first-served basis until the money runs out. Instead, eligible individuals automatically receive Social Security payments. Of course, Congress can, if it desires, cut the benefits or tighten eligibility restrictions. Doing so, however, would provoke a monumental outcry from millions of elderly voters.

uncontrollable expenditures
Expenditures that are determined not by a fixed amount of money appropriated by Congress but by how many eligible beneficiaries there are for a program or by previous obligations of the government.

entitlements
Policies for which Congress has obligated itself to pay X level of benefits to Y number of recipients. Social Security benefits are an example.

THE BUDGETARY PROCESS

Budgets are produced through a long and complex process that starts and ends with the president and has the Congress squarely in the middle. Because budgets are so important to almost all other policies, the budgetary process is the center of political battles in Washington and involves nearly everyone in government. The distribution of the government's budget is the outcome of a very complex budgetary process. Nestled inside the tax and expenditures figures are thousands of policy choices, each prompting plenty of politics.

BUDGETARY POLITICS

Public budgets are the supreme example of Harold Lasswell's definition of politics as "who gets what, when, and how." Budget battles are fought over contending interests, ideologies, programs, and agencies.

Stakes and Strategies Every political actor has a stake in the budget. Mayors want to keep federal grants-in-aid flowing in, defense contractors like a big defense budget, and scientists push for a large budget for the National Science Foundation. Agencies within the government also work to protect their interests. Individual members of Congress act as policy entrepreneurs for new ideas and support constituent benefits, both of which cost money. Presidents try to use budgets to manage the economy and leave their imprint on Congress's policy agenda.

Think of budgetary politics as resembling a game in which players choose among strategies.[17] Agencies pushing their budgetary needs to the president and Congress,

Why It Matters
"Uncontrollable" Spending
Much of the federal budget is "uncontrollable" in the sense that it does not come up for reauthorization on a regular basis. If entitlement programs were subject to the same annual authorizations that most other programs receive, they would probably have less secure funding. We might spend less money on them and more on other services. This flexibility might please some people, especially those not receiving entitlement benefits, but those receiving Social Security and Medicare payments, for example, prefer more reliable funding.

for instance, try to link the benefits of their program to a senator's or representative's electoral needs.[18] Often, agencies pad their requests a bit, hoping that the almost inevitable cuts will be bearable. President John Adams justified this now common budgetary gambit by saying to his cabinet, "If some superfluity not be given Congress to lop off, they will cut into the very flesh of the public necessities." Interest groups try to identify their favorite programs with the national interest. Mayors tell Congress not how much they like to receive federal aid but how crucial cities are to national survival. Farmers stress not that they like federal aid but that feeding a hungry nation and world is the main task of American agriculture. In the game of budgetary politics, there are plenty of players, all with their own strategies.

The Players   Deciding how to carve up one-fifth of the GDP is a process likely to attract plenty of interest—from those formally required to participate in the budgeting process as well as those whose stakes are too big to ignore it. Here are the main actors in the budgetary process:

- *Interest groups.* No lobbyist worth his or her pay would ignore the budget. Lobbying for a group's needs takes place in the agencies, with presidents (if the lobbyist has access to them), and before congressional committees. A smart agency head will be sure to involve interest groups in defending the agency's budget request.
- *Agencies.* Convinced of the importance of their mission, the heads of agencies almost always push for higher budget requests. They send their requests to the Office of Management and Budget and later get a chance to present themselves before congressional committees as well.[19]
- *The Office of Management and Budget (OMB).* The OMB is responsible to the president, its boss, but no president has the time to understand and make decisions about the billions of dollars in the budget—parceled out to hundreds of agencies, some of which the chief executive knows little or nothing about. The director and staff of the OMB have considerable independence from the president, which makes them major actors in the annual budget process.
- *The president.* The president makes final decisions on what to propose to Congress. In early February, the president unveils the proposed budget; the president then spends many a day trying to ensure that Congress will stick close to the recommendations.
- *Tax Committees in Congress.* The government cannot spend money it does not have (or cannot borrow). The **House Ways and Means Committee** and the **Senate Finance Committee** write the tax codes, subject to the approval of Congress as a whole.
- *Budget Committees and the Congressional Budget Office (CBO).* The CBO—which is the congressional equivalent of the OMB—and its parent committees, the Senate and House Budget Committees, set the parameters of the congressional budget process through examining revenues and expenditures in the aggregate and proposing resolutions to bind Congress within certain limits.
- *Subject-matter committees.* Committees of Congress, ranging from Agriculture to Veterans' Affairs, write new laws, which require new expenditures. Committee members may use hearings either to publicize the accomplishments of their pet agencies, thus supporting larger budgets for them, or to question agency heads about waste or overspending.
- *Appropriations Committees and their subcommittees.* The Appropriations Committee in each house decides who gets what. These committees take new or old policies coming from the subject-matter committees and decide how much to spend. Appropriations subcommittees hold hearings on specific agency requests.

House Ways and Means Committee
The House of Representatives committee that, along with the **Senate Finance Committee**, writes the tax codes, subject to the approval of Congress as a whole.

Senate Finance Committee
The Senate committee that, along with the **House Ways and Means Committee**, writes the tax codes, subject to the approval of Congress as a whole.

- *Congress as a whole*. The Constitution requires that Congress as a whole approve taxes and appropriations, and senators and representatives alike have a strong interest in delivering federal dollars to their constituents. A dam here, a military base there, and a job-training program somewhere else—these are items that members look for in the budget.
- *The Government Accountability Office (GAO)*. Congress's role does not end when it has passed the budget. The GAO works as Congress's eyes and ears, auditing, monitoring, and evaluating what agencies are doing with their budgets.

Budgeting involves a cast of thousands. However, their roles are carefully scripted, and their time on stage is limited because budget making is both repetitive (the same things must be done each year) and sequential (actions must occur in the proper order and more or less on time). The budget cycle begins in the executive branch a full 19 months before the fiscal year begins.

Both the president and Congress are centrally involved in budgeting. Here House Budget Committee Chairman John Spratt examines a chart regarding the president's budget proposal.

THE PRESIDENT'S BUDGET

Until 1921, the various agencies of the executive branch sent their budget requests to the secretary of the treasury, who in turn forwarded them to the Congress. Presidents played a limited role in proposing the budget; sometimes they played no role at all. Agencies basically peddled their own budget requests to Congress. In 1921 Congress, concerned about retiring the debt the country had accumulated during World War I, passed the Budget and Accounting Act, which required presidents to propose an executive budget to Congress, and created the Bureau of the Budget to help them. In the 1970s, President Nixon reorganized the Bureau of the Budget and gave it a new name, the Office of Management and Budget (OMB). The OMB, whose director is a presidential appointee requiring Senate approval, now supervises preparation of the federal budget and advises the president on budgetary matters.

It takes a long time to prepare a presidential budget.[20] By law, the president must submit a budget by the first Monday in February. The process begins almost a year before (see Table 14.2), when the OMB communicates with each agency, sounding out its requests and tentatively issuing guidelines. By the summer, the president has decided on overall policies and priorities and has established general targets for the budget. These are then communicated to the agencies.

The budget makers now get down to details. During the fall, the agencies submit formal, detailed estimates for their budgets, zealously pushing their needs to the OMB. Budget analysts at the OMB pare, investigate, weigh, and meet on agency requests. Typically, the agency heads ask for hefty increases; sometimes they threaten to go directly to the president if their priorities are not met by the OMB. As the Washington winter sets in, the budget document is readied for final presidential approval. There is usually some last-minute juggling—agencies may be asked to change their estimates to conform with the president's decisions, or cabinet members may make a last-ditch effort to bypass the OMB and convince the president to increase their funds. With only days—or hours—left before the submission deadline, the budget document is rushed to the printers. Then the president sends it to Capitol Hill. The next steps are up to Congress.

TABLE 14.2

The President's Budget: An Approximate Schedule

SPRING	
Budget policy developed	The OMB presents the president with an analysis of the economic situation, and they discuss the budgetary outlook and policies. The OMB then gives guidelines to the agencies, which in turn review current programs and submit to the OMB their projections of budgetary needs for the coming year. The OMB reviews these projections and prepares recommendations to the president on final policy, programs, and budget levels. The president establishes guidelines and targets.
SUMMER	
Agency estimates submitted	The OMB conveys the president's decisions to the agencies and advises and assists them in preparing their budgets.
FALL	
Estimates reviewed	The agencies submit to the OMB formal budget estimates for the coming fiscal year, along with projections for future years. The OMB holds hearings, reviews its assessment of the economy, and prepares budget recommendations for the president. The president reviews these recommendations and decides on the agencies' budgets and overall budgetary policy. The OMB advises the agencies of these decisions.
WINTER	
President's budget determined and submitted	The agencies revise their estimates to conform with the president's submitted decisions. The OMB once again reviews the economy and then drafts the president's budget message and prepares the budget document. The president revises and approves the budget message and transmits the budget document to Congress.

CONGRESS AND THE BUDGET

According to the Constitution, Congress must authorize all federal appropriations. Thus, Congress always holds one extremely powerful trump card in national policy-making: the power of the purse.[21] This year Congress will decide how to spend nearly $3 trillion.

Reforming the Process   For years Congress budgeted in a piecemeal fashion. A subcommittee of the House and Senate Appropriations Committees handled each agency request; then all these appropriations were added to produce a total budget. People never quite knew what the budget's bottom line would be until all the individual bills were totaled up. What Congress spent had little to do with any overall judgment of how much it should spend.

The **Congressional Budget and Impoundment Control Act of 1974** was designed to reform the congressional budgetary process. Its supporters hoped that it would also make Congress less dependent on the president's budget and more able to set and meet its own budgetary goals. The act established the following:

- *A fixed budget calendar.* Each step in the budgetary process has an established completion date. In the past, Congress sometimes failed to appropriate money to agencies until after the fiscal year was over, leaving agencies drifting for months with no firm budget. Now there is a timetable mandated by law, which has been amended several times (see Table 14.3).
- *A budget committee in each house.* These two committees are supposed to recommend target figures to Congress for the total budget size by April 1 of each year. By April 15, Congress is to agree on the *total* size of the budget,

Congressional Budget and Impoundment Control Act of 1974

An act designed to reform the congressional budgetary process. Its supporters hoped that it would also make Congress less dependent on the president's budget and better able to set and meet its own budgetary goals.

TABLE 14.3

The Congressional Budget Process: Targets and Timetables

DATE	ACTION TO BE COMPLETED
First Monday in February	Congress receives the president's budget.
February 15	The CBO submits a budget report to the House and Senate Budget Committees, including an analysis of the president's budget.
February 25	Other committees submit reports on outlays and revenues to Budget Committees in each house.
April 1	Budget Committees report concurrent resolution on the budget, which sets a total for budget outlays, an estimate of expenditures for major budget categories, and the recommended level of revenues. This resolution acts as an agenda for the remainder of the budgetary process.
April 15	Congress completes action on concurrent resolution on the budget.
May 15	Annual appropriations bills may be considered in the House.
June 10	House Appropriations Committee reports last annual appropriations bill.
June 15	Congress completes action on reconciliation legislation, bringing budget totals into conformity with established ceilings.
June 30	House completes action on annual appropriation bills.
October 1	The new fiscal year begins.

which guides the Appropriations Committee to juggling figures for individual agencies.

- *A Congressional Budget Office.* The **Congressional Budget Office** (CBO) advises Congress on the probable consequences of its budget decisions, forecasts revenues, and is a counterweight to the president's OMB.

One purpose of the new budgeting system was to force Congress to consider the budget (both projected expenditures and projected revenues) as a whole rather than in bits and pieces as it had done before. An important part of the process of establishing a budget is to set limits on expenditures on the basis of revenue projections—a step that is supposed to be done through a **budget resolution**. Thus, in April of each year, both houses are expected to agree on a budget resolution—thereby binding Congress to a total expenditure level that should form the bottom line of all federal spending for all programs. Only then is Congress supposed to begin acting on the individual appropriations.

In terms of a family budget, Family A might decide to budget by adding up all its needs and wants and calling that its budget. Such a strategy almost guarantees overspending the family income. Family B, though, might begin by looking first at its revenue and then trying to bring its total expenditures into line with its revenue before dealing with its individual expenditure decisions. With its 1974 reforms, Congress was trying to force itself to behave more like Family B than Family A.

Like the president's budget proposal, the congressional budget resolution often requests that certain changes be made in law, primarily to achieve savings incorporated into the spending totals and thus meet the budget resolution. These changes are legislated in two separate ways.

Congressional Budget Office

Advises Congress on the probable consequences of its decisions, forecasts revenues, and is a counterweight to the president's Office of Management and Budget.

budget resolution

A resolution binding Congress to a total expenditure level, supposedly the bottom line of all federal spending for all programs.

reconciliation

A congressional process through which program authorizations are revised to achieve required savings. It usually also includes tax or other revenue adjustments.

authorization bill

An act of Congress that establishes, continues, or changes a discretionary government program or an entitlement. It specifies program goals and maximum expenditures for discretionary programs.

appropriations bill

An act of Congress that actually funds programs within limits established by authorization bills. Appropriations usually cover one year.

continuing resolutions

When Congress cannot reach agreement and pass appropriations bills, these resolutions allow agencies to spend at the level of the previous year.

First is budget **reconciliation**, a process by which program authorizations are revised to achieve required savings; it frequently also includes tax or other revenue adjustments. Usually reconciliation comes near the end of the budgetary process. However, in an attempt to strike while his political standing was high and to overcome the opposition of special interests and the parochialism and power of congressional committees, President Reagan in 1981 successfully proposed using an extremely complex reconciliation bill to reduce the budget by approximately $40 billion. Reagan thought that he could obtain substantial cuts only if he lumped them all together in one bill in which everyone lost something. The preparation of the bill was so hurried that few members of Congress could give it serious consideration.

The second way that laws are changed to meet the budget resolution (or to create or change programs for other reasons) involves more narrowly drawn legislation. An **authorization bill** is an act of Congress that establishes a discretionary government program or an entitlement or that continues or changes such programs. Authorizations specify program goals and, for discretionary programs, set the maximum amount that they may spend. For entitlement programs, an authorization sets or changes eligibility standards and benefits that must be provided by the program. Authorizations may be for one year, or they may run for a specified or indefinite number of years.

Congress must pass an additional measure, termed an **appropriations bill**, to fund programs established by authorization bills. For example, if Congress authorizes expenditures on building highways, Congress must pass another bill to appropriate the funds to build them. Appropriations bills usually fund programs for one year and cannot exceed the amount of money authorized for a program; in fact, they may appropriate *less* than was authorized.

Evaluating the 1974 Reforms   Have these reforms worked? If *worked* means that Congress has brought its spending into line with its revenues, then the reforms have been almost a total failure. Congressional budgets were in the red every year between the 1974 amendments and 1998. In fact, the red ink grew from a puddle to an ocean (see "A Generation of Change: Fluctuating Deficits"). Presidents made matters worse, submitting budget proposals that contained large deficits.

In addition, Congress has often failed to meet its own budgetary timetable. There has been too much conflict over the budget for the system to work according to design. Moreover, in many instances Congress has not been able to reach agreement and pass appropriations bills at all and has instead resorted to **continuing resolutions**—laws that allow agencies to spend at the previous year's level. Sometimes, as in 1986 and 1987, and 2007, appropriations bills have been lumped together in one enormous and complex bill (rather than in the 13 separate appropriations bills that are supposed to pass), precluding adequate review by individual members of Congress and forcing the president either to accept unwanted provisions or to veto the funding for the entire government. These omnibus bills may also become magnets for unrelated and controversial pieces of legislation that could not pass on their own.

On the other hand, the 1974 reforms have helped Congress view the entire budget early in the process; now Congress can at least see the forest as well as the trees. The problem is not so much the procedure as disagreement over how scarce resources should be spent—or whether they should be spent at all.

More Reforms   By 1985, Congress was desperate. President Reagan refused to consider tax increases to pay for federal spending and continued to submit budgets that contained huge deficits. In response to growing frustration at its inability to reduce annual budget deficits substantially, Congress enacted the Balanced Budget and Emergency Deficit Control Act, better known as Gramm-Rudman-Hollings

Fluctuating Deficits

Annual federal deficits mushroomed during the Reagan administration (1981–1988), despite the president's oft-repeated commitment to a balanced budget. The deficit disappeared during the Clinton administration, and the nation began running a surplus in fiscal year 1998. By 2002, however, the United States was back in the red.

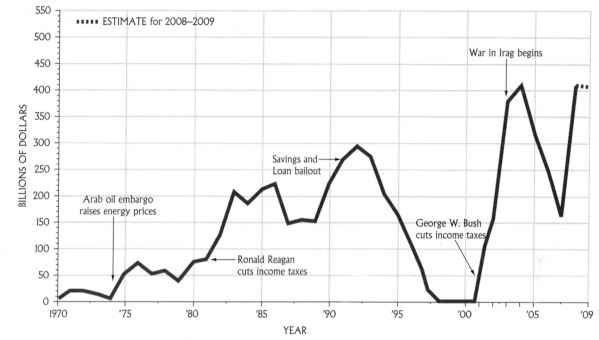

Source: *Budget of the United States Government, Fiscal Year 2009: Historical Tables* (Washington, DC: U.S. Government Printing Office, 2008), table 1.1.

after its cosponsors, Senators Phil Gramm (R) of Texas, Warren Rudman (R) of New Hampshire, and Ernest Hollings (D) of South Carolina.

This legislation, as it was amended in 1987, mandated maximum allowable deficit levels for each year until 1993, when the budget was supposed to be in balance. If Congress failed to meet the deficit goals, automatic across-the-board spending cuts, called *sequestrations*, were to be ordered by the president (a number of programs, including Social Security and interest on the national debt, were exempt from this process).

Gramm-Rudman-Hollings was clearly an indelicate, unthinking approach to budgeting; no one liked the arbitrary nature of the automatic budget cuts, half of which were to come from defense and half from domestic programs. Even Senator Rudman described it as "a bad idea whose time has come." In the absence of consensus on spending priorities, Congress believed it had no other way to force itself to reduce the deficit. Success was elusive, however.

Near the end of 1990, Congress abandoned Gramm-Rudman-Hollings and approved a major change in budgeting policy, deciding to shift its focus from controlling the size of the deficit to controlling increases in spending. It divided discretionary spending into three categories: domestic, defense, and international. Any new spending in any of these categories had to be offset by decreases elsewhere within the category. Violations of these strictures would lead to across-the-board sequestration within the affected category. Spending for entitlement programs such as Medicare was placed on a "pay-as-you-go" basis, requiring that any expansion be

YOU ARE THE **Policymaker**

Balancing the Budget

You have seen that the national government is running large budget deficits and that the national debt continues to grow. Here is the situation you would face as a budget decision maker: According to the OMB, in fiscal year 2009 the national government will have revenues (including Social Security taxes) of about $2,700 billion. Mandatory expenditures for domestic policy (entitlements such as Social Security and other prior obligations) total about $1,636 billion. Nondiscretionary payments on the national debt will cost another $260 billion. National defense will cost an additional $675 billion. That leaves you with just $129 billion to spend and still balance the budget. The president's proposals for discretionary domestic policy programs will take $541 billion, however. If you spend this amount, you will

run a deficit of $412 billion—and you will not even have had a chance to fund any significant new programs. Moreover, you are likely to have to ask Congress for additional funds to pay for the occupation of Iraq.

What would you do? Would you drastically reduce defense expenditures? Or would you leave them alone and close down substantial portions of the rest of the government, such as programs for space and science, transportation and public works, economic subsidies and development, education and social services, health research and services, or law enforcement and other core functions of government—programs that also have broad public support? Perhaps you would show great political courage and seek a tax increase to pay for these programs.

paid for by a corresponding entitlement cut or revenue increase. Similarly, any tax cut was to be paid for by a compensating tax increase or entitlement cut.

President Clinton presented his first budget to Congress in 1993. After the dust cleared following a highly partisan legislative battle in which Republicans gave him no support at all, the president and Congress had made a significant decrease in the deficit. There was a single cap for all discretionary spending (rather than one for each of the three components), imposing a hard freeze on appropriations, yet there was little prospect of balancing the budget in the foreseeable future.

The results of the 1994 congressional elections once again altered the budgetary game. In 1995, the new Republican majorities in each house, determined to balance the budget within seven years, argued for substantial cuts in the rate of growth of popular entitlement programs such as Medicaid and for the outright elimination of many other programs. Most Democrats strongly opposed these proposals. The president agreed with the goal of balancing the budget—but on his terms—and took his case to the voters in 1996. The outcome was divided government.

In 1997, the president and Congress agreed to a budget that was to be in balance—by 2002. Each political party claimed victory, but the path to a balanced budget was eased by the booming economy, which produced more tax revenues than either side had anticipated. Indeed, the economy was so strong that the government began running surpluses. However, decreased tax revenues resulting from the economic downturn in 2000–2001 and the income tax cut of 2001 sent the budget into deficit again. Even with economic recovery, deficits persisted, partially as a result of decreased tax revenues and partially the result of increased spending, including spending for the war on terrorism and the occupation of Iraq. In the meantime, the budget deficit continues to be a source of conflict (see "You Are the Policymaker: Balancing the Budget").

SIMULATION

You Are an Informed Voter Helping Your Classmates Decide How to Vote

UNDERSTANDING BUDGETING

Citizens and politicians alike fret about whether government is too big. In 1988, President George Bush won the presidency, arguing that government had too many hands in Americans' pockets. He promised not to raise taxes to pay for more government spending. Of course, not everyone agrees that the national government is too large—even Bush backtracked on his "no new taxes" pledge by 1990 and was defeated by the more activist Bill Clinton in 1992. There is agreement on the centrality of budgeting to modern government and politics, however.

DEMOCRACY AND BUDGETING

Almost all democracies have seen a substantial growth in government in the twentieth century. One explanation for this growth is that politicians spend money to "buy" votes. They do not buy votes in the sense that a corrupt political machine pays voters to vote for its candidates; rather, policymakers spend public money on things that are important to voters—and that voters will remember on Election Day. As you saw in Chapter 12, members of Congress have incentives to make government grow; they use both constituency services and pork-barrel policies to deliver benefits to the folks back home, and government grows as a result.

Economists Allan Meltzer and Scott Richard have argued that government grows in a democracy because of the equality of suffrage. They maintain that in the private sector, people's incomes are unequal, whereas in the political arena, power is much more equally distributed. Each voter has one vote, so those with less income have considerable clout. Parties must appeal to a majority of the voters. Hence, claim Meltzer and Richard, poorer voters will always use their votes to support public policies that redistribute benefits from the rich to the poor. Even if such voters cannot win in the marketplace, they can use the electoral process to their advantage.[22] Many politicians willingly cooperate with the desire of the working-class voters to expand their benefits because voters return the favor at election time. Not surprisingly, the most rapidly growing areas of expenditures are Social Security, Medicaid, Medicare, and social welfare programs, which benefit the poor more than the rich.

Public opinion is a key element in the budgeting process. Occasionally, the public has a direct role in budget making, as when the citizens of California voted on Proposition 13, a referendum proposing strict limits to local property taxes. Despite protests against the proposed legislation—many citizens argued that tax limits would restrict many government services—the proposition was passed.

Many believe that elites, particularly corporate elites, oppose big government. However, Lockheed, United Airlines, and Chrysler Corporation appealed to the government for large bailouts when times got rough. Corporations support a big government that offers them contracts, subsidies, and other benefits. A $185 billion procurement and research-and-development budget at the Department of Defense[23] benefits defense contractors, their workers, and their shareholders.

Low-income and wealthy voters alike have voted for parties and politicians who promised them benefits. When the air is foul, Americans expect government to help clean it up. When Americans get old, they expect a Social Security check. In a democracy, what people want affects what government does. Citizens are not helpless victims of big government and its big taxes; they are at least coconspirators.

Government also grows by responding to groups and their demands. The parade of political action committees is one example of groups asking government for assistance. From agricultural lobbies supporting loans to zoologists pressing for aid from the National Science Foundation, groups seek to expand their favorite part of the budget. They are aided by committees and government agencies that work to fund projects favored by supportive groups (see the discussion on iron triangles in Chapter 15).

You have also seen, however, that some politicians compete for votes by promising not to spend money. After all, Ronald Reagan and George W. Bush did not each win election to the presidency twice by promising to raise taxes and provide more services, nor did the Republicans who took control of Congress in 1995. No country has a more open political system than the United States, but as the "America in Perspective" feature in this chapter demonstrates, Americans have chosen to tax less and spend less on public services than almost all other democracies with developed economies. The size of government budgets varies widely among democratic nations. Democracy may encourage government spending, but it does not compel it.

One of the most common criticisms of government is its failure to balance the budget. Public officials are often criticized for lacking the will to deal with the problem, yet it is not lack of resolve that prevents a solution to enormous budget deficits. Instead, it is a lack of consensus on policy. Americans want to spend but not pay taxes, and, being a democracy, this is exactly what the government does. The inevitable result is red ink.

THE BUDGET AND THE SCOPE OF GOVERNMENT

Issues regarding the scope of government have pervaded this chapter. The reason is obvious—in many ways, the budget *is* the scope of government. The bigger the budget, the bigger the government. When the country sees a need, whether to defend itself or to provide for the elderly, it has found a way to pay for it. Some presidents, such as Ronald Reagan and George W. Bush, have led the fight to cut taxes. They also wanted to subtantially expand at least part of the government. It may seem, then, that there is no limit to budgetary growth.

The budgetary process can also limit government, however. One could accurately characterize policymaking in the American government since 1980 as the "politics of scarcity"—scarcity of funds, that is. Thus, the budget can be a force for reining in the government as well as for expanding its role.[24] For example, President Bill Clinton came into office hoping to make new investments in education, worker training, and the country's physical infrastructure, such as roads and bridges, and to expand health care coverage. He soon found, however, that there was no money to fund new programs. Instead, he had to emphasize cutting the budget deficit.

America's large budget deficits have been as much a constraint on government as they have been evidence of a burgeoning public sector.

SUMMARY

When the federal government's budget consumes one-fifth of America's gross domestic product, it demands close attention. The government's biggest revenue source remains the income tax, but the Social Security tax is becoming increasingly important. Lately, much of the government's budget has been financed through borrowing. Annual deficits sometimes exceeding $400 billion have boosted the federal debt to about $11 trillion by 2010.

In all Western democracies, government budgets grew during the twentieth century. In the United States, government spending also experienced significant change. Defense spending dominated the 1950s; social services spending dominated the 1990s. President Reagan, for one, wanted to reverse this trend by increasing military expenditures and cutting domestic ones. Nonetheless, much of the American budget consists of "uncontrollable" expenditures that are extremely difficult to pare. Many of these expenditures are associated with Social Security and Medicare payments and with grants-in-aid.

Budget making is complex, with many actors playing many roles. The president sets the budgetary agenda, whereas Congress and its committees approve the budget itself.

Some critics believe that democracy turns politics into a bidding war for votes, increasing the size of the budget in the process. In the United States, however, many candidates campaign on *not* spending money or increasing taxes. Although larger budgets mean larger government, the budget, at least in times of substantial deficits such as those the United States experienced in the previous decade, may also serve as a constraint on further government growth.

Chapter Test

Multiple Choice

1. Which Amendment explicitly author-izes Congress to collect an income tax?
   a. The Twelfth
   b. The Fourteenth
   c. The Sixteenth
   d. The Eighteenth
   e. The Twentieth

2. Which taxes have grown faster than any other source of federal revenue?
   a. Social security taxes
   b. Personal income taxes
   c. Corporate income taxes
   d. Sales taxes
   e. All of the above have grown equally

3. Tax expenditures are:
   a. The amount of money a person or family spends on taxes
   b. Exemptions, exclusions, or deductions people can claim
   c. Reduced government revenues due to unpaid taxes
   d. Things the government spends collected taxes on
   e. None of the above

4. Which of the following writes the tax code?
   a. The House Ways and Means Committee and the Senate Finance Committee
   b. The Office of Management and Budget
   c. The Congressional Budget Office
   d. The Tax Code Committee
   e. Congress as a whole

5. How long before the fiscal year begins does the budget cycle begin in the executive branch?
   a. Two months
   b. Nine months
   c. Twelve months
   d. Fifteen months
   e. Nineteen months

6. Since the 1980s, the total nation debt of the United States has increased approximately _____.
   a. Twofold
   b. Threefold
   c. Fourfold
   d. Sixfold
   e. Tenfold

7. Approximately how much of the fed-eral expenditure goes to paying taxes on the federal debt?
   a. 25 cents of every ten dollars
   b. 50 cents of every ten dollars
   c. One of every ten dollars
   d. One dollar and fifty cents of every ten dollars
   e. Two of every ten dollars

8. Which of the following is an example of a "progressive income tax"?
   a. Person A earned $9,000 and paid $900 in taxes, while Person B earned $18,000 and paid $1,800
   b. Person A earned $25,000 and paid $3,750, while Person B earned $50,000 and paid $7,500
   c. Person A earned $30,000 and paid $6,000, while Person B earned $60,000 and paid $9,000
   d. All of the above are examples of a progressive income tax
   e. None of the above; a progressive income tax merely means that tax rates have increased over time

True/False

9. Compared to other Western nations, the United States' public service sector is relatively large.

   True_____   False_____

10. A so-called "budget resolution" is drafted each April and binds Congress to a total expenditure level before it embarks on making the actual budget.

    True_____   False_____

11. The peacetime income tax wasn't enacted until the 20th century.

    True_____   False_____

12. The 1974 budget reforms have been largely successful in accomplishing their declared goals.

    True_____   False_____

13. Veterans' benefits can be considered part of the government's uncontrollable expenditures while Medicare cannot.

    True_____   False_____

Short Answer

14. Describe the two conditions that, according to this textbook, have primarily contributed to the growth of government in America.

15. How did Congress decide the budget before the reform of 1974? What are the three aspects that the Congressional Budget and Impoundment Control Act of 1974 changed?

16. Explain in what ways Social Security is an "intergenerational contract." What obstacles is this program facing given the demographic trends in this country?

17. What are the names and roles of at least three different "players" in the national budgetary process? In your opinion, which of them is the most influential, and why?

18. Explain in your own words the concept of an authorization bill and the concept of an appropriations bill.

Short Answer/Essay Questions

19. Based on what you know, to what degree is "incrementalism" a necessary evil of budgeting, and to what degree is it more of an "institutional habit"? Do you believe incremental budgeting is always necessary? Why, or why not?

20. When the first peacetime income tax was enacted, a lawyer back then called it the first step of a "communist march." Please explain briefly what he meant by that. What is your personal assessment of his attitude?

21. This textbook raises the question of why the government allows people tax breaks in the tax code, as opposed to simply giving them the money or lowering taxes. What do you think?

22. Many of the social democracies of Europe tax their citizens at very high rates, but subsequently use that money to pay for free public health care, free public education—including higher education—and various other programs. In the United States, citizens are taxed at a much lower rate, but then frequently have to spend their own money on securing health care and paying for college tuition. In your opinion, what explains this difference in attitude? Why do you think so many Americans are opposed to public health care, if it means higher taxes, but then pay out of their own pocket for these very services?

Answer Key

1. C   2. A   3. B   4. A   5. E   6. E   7. C   8. C   9. False   10. True   11. False   12. False   13. False

Key Terms

budget (442)
deficit (442)
expenditures (442)
revenues (442)
income tax (444)
Sixteenth Amendment (444)
federal debt (445)
tax expenditures (447)
Social Security Act (454)

Medicare (454)
incrementalism (456)
uncontrollable expenditures (457)
entitlements (457)
House Ways and Means Committee (458)
Senate Finance Committee (458)
Congressional Budget and Impoundment Control Act of 1974 (460)

Congressional Budget Office (461)
budget resolution (461)
reconciliation (462)
authorization bill (462)
appropriations bill (462)
continuing resolutions (462)

Internet Resources

www.gpoaccess.gov/eop/
The *Economic Report of the President* and the budget for the federal government.

www.irs.ustreas.gov
The Internal Revenue Service home page, containing a wealth of information about taxes.

www.whitehouse.gov/omb
The Office of Management and Budget home page. Clicking on the current year's budget takes you to all the current budget documents.

www.cbo.gov/
Congressional Budget Office home page, containing budgetary analyses and data.

www.taxpolicycenter.org
A joint venture of the Urban Institute and the Brookings Institution, containing many studies of budgets and taxes.

www.taxfoundation.org/
The Tax Foundation site with a wealth of tax information.

www.concordcoalition.org/
The nonpartisan Concord Coalition provides studies of budgetary issues.

GetConnected

The Budgetary Process

The process of making the federal budget is long and cumbersome. Although the Constitution gives the legislative branch the responsibility to tax and spend, the president is heavily invested in the budget process. Indeed, Congress requires the president to recommend what the federal budget should be. Its thinking was that since the executive branch was responsible for spending most of the money Congress allocated, it only made sense to ask the president to recommend a budget each year. Recommending a budget is not an easy job. Economists say that running a large deficit is bad for the economy, and so is running a large surplus. Usually, the government should spend about what it collects in taxes each year. Try putting together a budget on your own. Go to the National Budget Simulation and create a budget that reflects your values.

Search the Web

Go to the National Budget Simulation (Short Version), *www.nathannewman.org/nbs/shortbudget06.html,* and create your budget. Once you have made your choices, see how well you did.

Questions to Ask

- Did your budget balance, or did you have a large surplus or deficit?
- How did you make your decisions on what to change in making your budget?
- Do you think your decisions expressed conservative, liberal, or centrist values?

Why It Matters

The federal budget is more than $2.75 *trillion* (that is $2,750,000,000,000), and it is supposed to reflect the values of the nation. Because presidents recommend the annual budget to Congress, their values have a large influence on the budget.

Get Involved

How do you feel about the current federal budget? Do you think the president is recommending the right kind of budget? What would you change? For more exercises, go to *www.longmanamericangovernment.com.*

For Further Reading

Bennett, Linda L. M., and Stephen Earl Bennett. *Living with Leviathan*. Lawrence: University Press of Kansas, 1990. Examines Americans' coming to terms with big government and their expectations of government largesse.

Berry, William D., and David Lowery. *Understanding United States Government Growth*. New York: Praeger, 1987. An empirical analysis of the causes of the growth of government in the period since World War II.

Jones, Bryan D., and Walter Williams. *The Politics of Bad Ideas*. New York: Pearson Longman, 2007. Shows that there are many bad ideas regarding budgetary policy and explains why they persist.

King, Ronald F. *Money, Taxes, and Politics*. New Haven, CT: Yale University Press, 1993. Explains why democratically elected officials approve tax policies that make rich people richer.

Rubin, Irene S. *The Politics of Public Budgeting: Getting and Spending, Borrowing and Balancing*. Washington, DC: Congressional Quarterly Press, 2006. Emphasizes how politics pervades budgetary decisions at every stage.

Schick, Allen. *The Federal Budget*. Rev. ed. Washington, DC: Brookings Institution, 2000. A useful "hands-on" view of federal budgeting.

Wildavsky, Aaron, and Naomi Caiden. *The New Politics of the Budgetary Process*. 6th ed. New York: Longman, 2007. The standard work on the budgetary process.

CHAPTER 15

THE
FEDERAL
BUREAUCRACY

POLITICS IN ACTION:
REGULATING FOOD

Americans do not want to worry about the safety of the food we eat. Indeed, food safety is something we take for granted. But who assures this safety? Bureaucrats. It is their job to keep our food safe from contamination. Although we rarely think about food inspections, they represent one of the most important regulatory functions of government. The fact that we rarely think about food safety is testimony to the success of bureaucrats in carrying out their tasks.[1]

Policing the food supply is not a straightforward task, however. It involves a complex web of federal agencies with overlapping jurisdictions. At least twelve agencies and 35 statutes regulate food safety. Eggs in the shell fall under the purview of the Food and Drug Administration (FDA), but once cracked and processed, they come under the jurisdiction of the U.S. Department of Agriculture (USDA). The USDA is responsible for regulating meat and poultry, while the FDA handles most other food products, including seafood and produce. Cheese pizzas are the FDA's responsibility, but if they have pepperoni on top, Agriculture inspectors step in.

Other parts of the government also play a prominent role in enforcing food safety laws. For example, the Environmental Protection Agency oversees pesticides applied to crops, the Centers for Disease Control and Prevention track food-related illnesses, and the Department of Homeland Security coordinates agencies' safety and security activities.

Is this complex system the result of bureaucratic maneuvering? No, Congress created the system layer on top of layer, with little regard to how it should work as a whole. Critics argue that the system is outdated and that it would be better to create a single food safety agency that could target inspections, streamline safety programs, and use resources more efficiently. Such proposals have generated little enthusiasm in Congress, however, where committees are sensitive about losing jurisdiction over agencies. For example, in the House the Energy and Commerce Committee has oversight over the FDA, while the Agriculture Committee has responsibility for the USDA.

Growers and manufacturers fear a single agency would impose onerous new regulations, product recalls, and fines and could be used by empire-building bureaucrats to expand their budget and regulatory authority. So little change occurs.

Bureaucrats face other challenges in insuring safe food. The FDA is so short of staff that it can inspect the average U.S. food company just once every 10 years. Even worse, it can inspect less than 1 percent of all food imports—despite repeated problems with contaminated products. Indeed, only 20 percent of food imports appear in its computer system for review by the field inspection force.

Bureaucrats are central to our lives. They provide essential public services. They possess crucial information and expertise that make them partners with the president and Congress in decision making about public policy. Who knows more than bureaucrats about Social Security recipients or the military capabilities of China? Bureaucrats are also central to politics. They do much more than simply follow orders. Because of their expertise, bureaucrats inevitably have discretion in carrying out policy decisions, which is why congressional committees and interest groups take so much interest in what they do.

Bureaucratic power extends to every corner of American economic and social life, yet bureaucracies are scarcely hinted at in the Constitution. Congress creates each bureaucratic agency, sets its budget, and writes the policies it administers. Most agencies are responsible to the president, whose constitutional responsibility to "take care that the laws shall be faithfully executed" sheds only a dim light on the problems of managing so large a government. How to manage and control bureaucracies is a central problem of democratic government.

Reining in the power of bureaucracies is also a common theme in debates over the scope of government in America. Some political commentators see the bureaucracy as the prime example of a federal government growing out of control. They view the bureaucracy as acquisitive, constantly seeking to expand its size, budgets, and authority while being entwined in red tape and spewing forth senseless regulations. Others see the bureaucracy as laboring valiantly against great odds to fulfill the missions elected officials have assigned it. Where does the truth lie? The answer is less obvious than you may think. Clearly, bureaucracies require closer examination.

The German sociologist Max Weber advanced his classic conception of bureaucracy, stressing that the bureaucracy was a "rational" way for a modern society to conduct its business.[2] According to Weber, a **bureaucracy** depends on certain elements: It has a *hierarchical authority structure*, in which power flows from the top down and responsibility flows from the bottom up; it uses *task specialization* so that experts instead of amateurs perform technical jobs; and it develops extensive *rules*, which may seem extreme at times, but which allow similar cases to be handled similarly instead of capriciously.

Bureaucracies operate on the *merit principle*, in which entrance and promotion are awarded on the basis of demonstrated abilities rather than on "who you know." Bureaucracies behave with *impersonality* so that they treat all their clients impartially. Weber's classic prototype of the bureaucratic organization depicts the bureaucracy as a well-organized machine with plenty of working, but hierarchical, parts.

bureaucracy

According to Max Weber, a hierarchical authority structure that uses task specialization, operates on the merit principle, and behaves with impersonality. Bureaucracies govern modern states.

THE BUREAUCRATS

Bureaucrats are typically much less visible than the president or members of Congress. As a result, Americans usually know little about them. This section examines some myths about bureaucrats and explains who they are and how they got their jobs.

SOME BUREAUCRATIC MYTHS AND REALITIES

Bureaucrat baiting is a popular American pastime. George Wallace, former Alabama governor and frequent presidential hopeful, warmed up his crowds with a line about "pointy-headed Washington bureaucrats who can't even park their bicycles straight." Even successful presidential candidates have climbed aboard the antibureaucracy bandwagon. Jimmy Carter complained about America's "complicated and confused and overlapping and wasteful" bureaucracies, Gerald Ford complained about the "dead weight" of bureaucracies, and Ronald Reagan insisted that bureaucrats "over-regulated" the American economy, causing a decline in productivity.

Any object of such unpopularity will spawn plenty of myths. The following are some of the most prevalent myths about bureaucracy:

- *Americans dislike bureaucrats.* Despite the rhetoric about bureaucracies, Americans are generally satisfied with bureaucrats and the treatment they get from them. Americans may dislike bureaucracies, but they like individual bureaucrats. Surveys have found that two-thirds or more of those who have had encounters with a bureaucrat evaluate these encounters positively. In most instances, people describe bureaucrats as helpful, efficient, fair, courteous, and working to serve their clients' interests.[3]
- *Bureaucracies are growing bigger each year.* This myth is half true and half false. The number of government employees has been expanding but not the number of *federal* employees. Almost all the growth in the number of public employees has occurred in state and local governments. The 19.5 million state and local public employees far outnumber the approximately 2.7 million civilian and 1.4 million military federal government employees (see Figure 15.1). As a percentage of

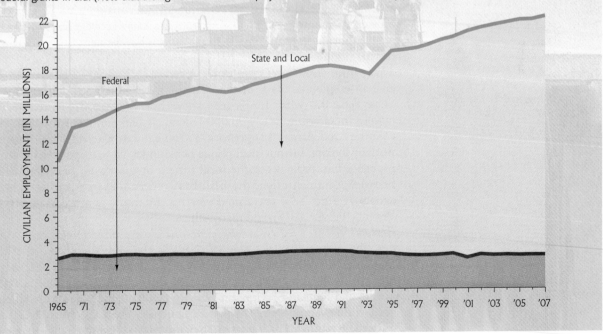

FIGURE 15.1

Growth in Civilian Government Employees

The number of government employees has grown since 1965. The real growth, however, has been in the state and local sector, with its millions of teachers, police officers, and other service deliverers. Many state and local employees and programs, though, are supported by federal grants-in-aid. (Note that the figures for federal employment do not include military personnel.)

Source: *Budget of the United States Government, Fiscal Year 2009: Historical Tables* (Washington, DC: U.S. Government Printing Office, 2008), table 17.5.

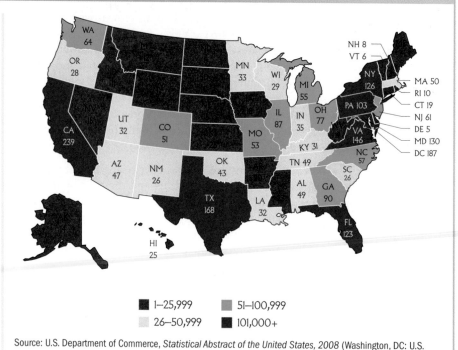

MyState | Federal Civilian Employees

Federal employees are distributed throughout the country. California leads the nation with 239,000 federal civilian employees. Texas has 168,000 and New York 126,000.

QUESTIONS FOR DISCUSSION

▶ How does your state rank in terms of federal employment?

▶ Why do you think some states have more federal employees than others? Are the differences only the result of differences in population?

▶ Is it important for a state to have a substantial number of federal employees?

Legend: 1–25,999; 26–50,999; 51–100,999; 101,000+

Source: U.S. Department of Commerce, *Statistical Abstract of the United States, 2008* (Washington, DC: U.S. Government Printing Office, 2008), Table 484.

America's total workforce, *federal* government employment has been shrinking, not growing; it now accounts for about 3 percent of all civilian jobs.

Of course, many state and local employees work on programs that are federally funded, and the federal government hires many private contractors to provide goods and services ranging from hot meals to weapons systems.[4] Such people provide services directly to the federal government or to citizens on its behalf.

- *Most federal bureaucrats work in Washington, D.C.* Only 12 percent of federal civilian employees work in the Washington, D.C. metropolitan area. "My State: Federal Civilian Employees" shows how they are distributed within the nation. In addition, nearly 90,000 federal civilian employees work in foreign countries and American territories.[5] You can see where federal bureaucrats work by looking in your local phone book under "U.S. Government." You will probably find listings for the local offices of the Postal Service, the Social Security Administration, the FBI, the Department of Agriculture's county agents, recruiters for the armed services, air traffic controllers, the Internal Revenue Service (IRS), and many others.

- *Bureaucracies are ineffective, inefficient, and always mired in red tape.* No words describing bureaucratic behavior are better known than "red tape."[6] Bureaucracy, however, is simply a way of organizing people to perform work. General Motors, a college or university, the U.S. Army, the Department of Health and Human Services, and the Roman Catholic Church are all bureaucracies. Bureaucracies are a little like referees: When they work well, no one gives them much credit, but when they work poorly, everyone calls them unfair, incompetent, or inefficient. Bureaucracies may be inefficient at times, but no one has found a substitute for them, and no one has yet demonstrated that government bureaucracies are more or less inefficient, ineffective, or mired in red tape than private bureaucracies.[7]

Anyone who looks with disdain on American bureaucracies should contemplate life without them. Despite all the complaining about bureaucracies, the vast majority of tasks carried out by governments at all levels are noncontroversial. Bureaucrats deliver mail, test milk, issue Social Security and student loan checks, run national parks, and perform other routine governmental tasks in a perfectly acceptable manner. Most of the people who work for cities, states, and the national government are typical Americans, the type who are likely to be your neighbors.

Most federal civilian employees work for just a few of the agencies (see Table 15.1). The Department of Defense (DOD) employs about 25 percent of federal *civilian* workers in addition to the more than 1.4 million men and women in uniform. Altogether, the DOD makes up more than half the federal

TABLE 15.1

Federal Civilian Employment

EXECUTIVE DEPARTMENTS	NUMBER OF EMPLOYEES[a]
Defense (military functions)	677,200
Veterans Affairs	253,400
Homeland Security	166,200
Justice	115,800
Treasury	109,600
Agriculture	91,100
Interior	68,600
Health and Human Services	60,800
Transportation	55,500
Commerce	53,900
State	32,200
Labor	16,800
Energy	16,100
Housing and Urban Development	9,500
Education	4,200
Larger Noncabinet Agencies	
U.S. Postal Service	762,305
Social Security Administration	69,800
Corps of Engineers	17,000
National Aeronautics and Space Administration	18,100
Environmental Protection Agency	17,100
Tennessee Valley Authority	11,500
General Services Administration	12,000

[a]Figures are for 2009.

Source: *Budget of the United States Government, Fiscal Year 2009: Analytical Perspectives* (Washington, DC: U.S. Government Printing Office, 2009), Tables 24.1 and 24.2.

bureaucracy. The Postal Service accounts for an additional 28 percent of the federal civilian employees, and the Department of Veterans Affairs, clearly related to national defense, has nearly 253,000 employees. All other functions of government, including homeland security, are handled by the remaining quarter of federal employees.

WHO THEY ARE AND HOW THEY GOT THERE

Because there are about 2.7 million civilian bureaucrats, it is hard to imagine a statistically typical bureaucrat. Bureaucrats are male and female, all races and religions, well paid and not so well paid. Like other institutions, the federal government has sought to expand its hiring of women and minorities. Congress has ordered federal agencies to make special efforts to recruit and promote previously disadvantaged groups, but women and non-Whites still cluster at the lower ranks. As a whole, however, the permanent bureaucracy is more broadly representative of the American people than are legislators, judges, or presidential appointees in the executive branch[8] (see Figure 15.2).

The diversity of bureaucratic jobs mirrors the diversity of private-sector jobs, including occupations literally ranging from A to Z. Accountants, bakers, census analysts, defense procurement specialists, electricians, foreign service officers, guards in federal prisons, home economists, Indian Affairs agents, judges, kitchen workers, lawyers, missile technologists, narcotics agents, ophthalmologists, postal carriers, quarantine specialists, radiologists, stenographers, truck drivers, underwater demolition experts, virologists, wardens, X-ray technicians, youth counselors, and zoologists all work for the government.

Civil Service: From Patronage to Protection. Until roughly a hundred years ago, a person got a job with the government through the patronage system. **Patronage** is a hiring and promotion system based on political reasons rather than on merit or competence. Working in a congressional campaign, making large donations, and having the right connections helped people secure jobs with the government.

You Are Deputy Director of the Census Bureau

patronage

One of the key inducements used by political machines. A patronage job, promotion, or contract is one that is given for political reasons rather than for merit or competence alone. Compare **civil service** and the **merit principle**.

FIGURE 15.2

Characteristics of Federal Non-Postal Civilian Employees

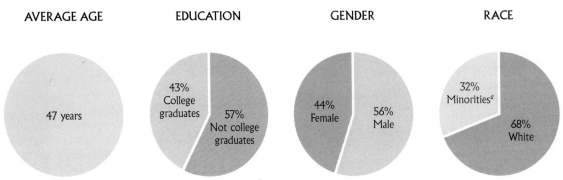

AVERAGE AGE — 47 years

EDUCATION — 43% College graduates; 57% Not college graduates

GENDER — 44% Female; 56% Male

RACE — 32% Minorities[a]; 68% White

[a]Includes African Americans, Asian Americans, Native Americans, and Hispanics.

Source: United States Office of Personnel Management, *Profile of Federal Civilian Non-Postal Employees, September 30, 2006.*

Nineteenth-century presidents staffed the government with their friends and allies, following the view of Andrew Jackson that "to the victors belong the spoils." Scores of office seekers would swarm the White House after Inauguration Day. It is said that during a bout with malaria, Lincoln told an aide to "send in the office seekers" because he finally had something to give them.

A disappointed office seeker named Charles Guiteau helped end this "spoils system" of federal appointments in 1881. Frustrated because President James A. Garfield would not give him a job, Guiteau shot and killed Garfield. The so-called Prince of Patronage himself, Vice President Chester A. Arthur, then became president. Arthur, who had been collector of the customs for New York—a patronage-rich post—surprised his critics by encouraging passage of the **Pendleton Civil Service Act** (1883), which created the federal civil service. Today, most federal agencies are covered by some sort of civil service system.

All **civil service** systems are designed to hire and promote members of the bureaucracy on the basis of merit and to create a nonpartisan government service. The **merit principle**—using entrance exams and promotion ratings to reward qualified individuals—is intended to produce an administration of people with talent and skill. Creating a nonpartisan civil service means insulating government workers from the risk of being fired when a new party comes to power. At the same time, the **Hatch Act**, originally passed in 1939 and amended most recently in 1993, prohibits civil service employees from actively participating in partisan politics while on duty. While off duty they may engage in political activities, but they cannot run for partisan elective offices or solicit contributions from the public. Employees with sensitive positions, such as those in the national security area, may not engage in political activities even while off duty.

The **Office of Personnel Management** (OPM) is in charge of hiring for most federal agencies. The president appoints its director, who is confirmed by the Senate. The OPM has elaborate rules about hiring, promotion, working conditions, and firing. To get a civil service job, usually candidates must first take a test. If they pass, their names are sent to agencies when jobs requiring their particular skills become available. For each position open, the OPM will send three names to the agency. Except under unusual circumstances, the agency must hire one of these three individuals. Each job is assigned a **GS (General Schedule) rating** ranging from GS 1 to GS 18. Salaries are keyed to rating and experience.

At the very top of the civil service system (GS 16–18) are about 9,000 members of the **Senior Executive Service**, the "cream of the crop" of the federal employees. These executives earn high salaries, and the president may move them from one agency to another as leadership needs change.

Once hired, and after a probationary period, the civil service system protects civil servants—overprotects them, critics claim. Ensuring a nonpartisan civil service requires that workers have protection from dismissals that are politically motivated. Protecting all workers against political firings may also protect a few from dismissal for good cause. Firing incompetents is hard work and is unusual. According to civil service regulations, employees must exhaust their right of appeal before the government can stop their paychecks. Appeals can consume weeks, months, or even years. More than one agency has decided to tolerate incompetents, assigning them trivial or no duties, rather than invest its resources in the nearly hopeless task of discharging them. Firing incompetent female, minority, or older workers may be even more difficult than dislodging incompetent young or middle-aged White males. These groups not only have the usual civil service protections but also can resort to antidiscrimination statutes to appeal their dismissals. After a protracted battle, Congress agreed to President George W. Bush's proposal to limit job protection for employees in the Department of Homeland Security.

Pendleton Civil Service Act

Passed in 1883, an Act that created a federal **civil service** so that hiring and promotion would be based on merit rather than **patronage**.

civil service

A system of hiring and promotion based on the **merit principle** and the desire to create a nonpartisan government service.

merit principle

The idea that hiring should be based on entrance exams and promotion ratings to produce administration by people with talent and skill.

Hatch Act

A federal law prohibiting government employees from active participation in partisan politics.

Office of Personnel Management

The office in charge of hiring for most agencies of the federal government, using elaborate rules in the process.

GS (General Schedule) rating

A schedule for federal employees, ranging from GS 1 to GS 18, by which salaries can be keyed to rating and experience.

Senior Executive Service

An elite cadre of about 9,000 federal government managers, established by the Civil Service Reform Act of 1978, who are mostly career officials but include some political appointees who do not require Senate confirmation.

THE OTHER ROUTE TO FEDERAL JOBS: RECRUITING FROM THE PLUM BOOK

As an incoming administration celebrates its victory and prepares to take control of the government, Congress publishes the *plum book*, which lists top federal jobs (that is, "plums") available for direct presidential appointment, often with Senate confirmation. There are about 500 of these top policymaking posts (mostly cabinet secretaries, undersecretaries, assistant secretaries, and bureau chiefs) and about 2,500 lesser positions.

All incoming presidents launch a nationwide talent search for qualified personnel. Presidents seek individuals who combine executive talent, political skills, and sympathy for policy positions similar to those of the administration. Often, the president tries to include men and women, Whites and non-Whites, people from different regions, and party members who represent different interests. Some positions, especially ambassadorships, go to large campaign contributors. A few of these appointees will be civil servants, temporarily elevated to a "political" status; most, however will be political appointees, "in-and-outers" who stay for a while and then leave.[9]

Once in office, these administrative policymakers constitute what Hugh Heclo has called a "government of strangers." Their most important trait is their transience. The average assistant secretary or undersecretary lasts less than two years.[10] Few top officials stay long enough to know their own subordinates well, much less people in other agencies. Administrative routines, budget cycles, and legal complexities are often new to them. To these new political executives, the possibilities of power may seem endless. Nevertheless, although plum book appointees may have the outward signs of power, many of them find it challenging to exercise real control over much of what their subordinates do and have difficulty leaving their mark on policy. They soon learn that they are dependent on senior civil servants who know more, have been there longer, and will outlast them.

Although analytical intelligence, substantive expertise, and managerial skills may be crucial to implementing policies effectively, the president usually places a premium on personal loyalty and commitment to his programs when evaluating candidates for positions in the bureaucracy. The White House wants bureaucratic responsiveness to its policies. Interestingly, the best evidence is that bureaucratic resistance to change does not pose a substantial obstacle to the president achieving his goals and that career civil servants are more effective than political appointees at managing agencies.[11]

In addition, the president faces a need to reward individuals, constituencies, and contributors who helped him win office and the demands of high-level appointees to name some of their own subordinates. These demands can be harmful, however. George W. Bush's nomination of the former president of the Arabian Horse Association to head the Federal Emergency Management Agency came back to haunt him in the wake of the agency's performance in dealing with the destruction caused by Hurricane Katrina.

You Are the Head of FEMA

HOW BUREAUCRACIES ARE ORGANIZED

A complete organizational chart of the American federal government would be big enough to occupy a large wall. You could pore over this chart, trace the lines of responsibility and authority, and see how government is organized—at least on paper. A very simplified organizational chart of the executive branch appears in Figure 15.3. A much easier way to look at how the federal executive branch is organized is to group agencies into four basic types: cabinet departments, independent regulatory commissions, government corporations, and independent executive agencies.

CABINET DEPARTMENTS

Each of the 15 cabinet departments is headed by a secretary (except the Department of Justice, which is headed by the attorney general), chosen by the president, and approved by the Senate. Undersecretaries, deputy undersecretaries, and assistant secretaries report to the secretary. Each department manages specific policy areas (see the list in Table 13.4, page 411), and each has its own budget and its own staff.

Each department has a unique mission and is organized somewhat differently. The Department of the Interior, charged with overseeing the nation's natural resources and administering policies that affect Native Americans, is an example of a well-established and traditional department (see Figure 15.4). The real work of a department is done in the bureaus, which divide the work into more specialized areas (a bureau is sometimes called a *service*, *office*, *administration*, or other name).

Until the 1970s, the largest cabinet department was the Department of Defense. From then until 1995, the Department of Health and Human Services (HHS) was the largest federal department in dollars spent (although the Department of Defense still had more employees). The Social Security Administration split from HHS and became an independent agency in 1995, spending one-third of the federal budget on the massive programs of Social Security and Medicare.

Sometimes status as a cabinet department can be controversial. For several years, Republicans tried to disband the Departments of Education, Energy, and Commerce, arguing that they wasted tax dollars and implemented policies that should be terminated.

INDEPENDENT REGULATORY COMMISSIONS

Each **independent regulatory commission** has responsibility for some sector of the economy, making and enforcing rules designed to protect the public interest. The independent regulatory commissions also judge disputes over these rules.[12] Some

independent regulatory commission

A government agency responsible for some sector of the economy, making and enforcing rules to protect the public interest. It also judges disputes over these rules.

FIGURE 15.3

Organization of the Executive Branch

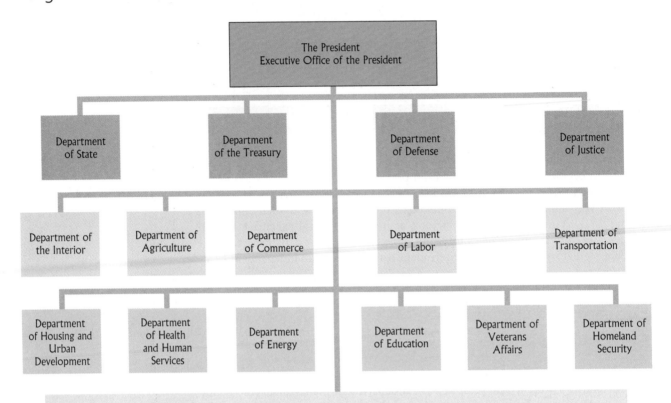

INDEPENDENT ESTABLISHMENTS AND GOVERNMENT CORPORATIONS

African Development Foundation
Broadcasting Board of Governors
Central Intelligence Agency
Commodity Futures Trading Commission
Consumer Product Safety Commission
Corporation for National and
    Community Service
Defense Nuclear Facilities Safety Board
Environmental Protection Agency
Equal Employment Opportunity
    Commission
Export-Import Bank of the United States
Farm Credit Administration
Federal Communications Commission
Federal Deposit Insurance Corporation
Federal Election Commission
Federal Housing Finance Board
Federal Labor Relations Authority
Federal Maritime Commission
Federal Mediation and Conciliation Service
Federal Mine Safety and Health Review
    Commission

Federal Reserve System
Federal Retirement Thrift Investment Board
Federal Trade Commission
General Services Administration
Inter-American Foundation
Merit Systems Protection Board
National Aeronautics and Space
    Administration
National Archives and Records
    Administration
National Capital Planning Commission
National Credit Union Administration
National Foundation on the Arts and
    Humanities
National Labor Relations Board
National Mediation Board
National Railroad Passenger Corporation
    (Amtrak)
National Science Foundation
National Transportation Safety Board
Nuclear Regulatory Commission
Occupational Safety and Health Review
    Commission

Office of the Director of
    National Intelligence
Office of Government Ethics
Office of Personnel Management
Office of Special Counsel
Overseas Private Investment
    Corporation
Peace Corps
Pension Benefit Guaranty Corporation
Postal Rate Commission
Railroad Retirement Board
Securities and Exchange Commission
Selective Service System
Small Business Administration
Social Security Administration
Tennessee Valley Authority
Trade and Development Agency
U.S. Agency for International
    Development
U.S. Commission on Civil Rights
U.S. International Trade Commission
U.S. Postal Service

Source: Office of the Federal Register, *United States Government Manual 2008–2009* (Washington, DC: U.S. Government Printing Office, 2008), 21.

FIGURE 15.4

Organization of the Department of the Interior

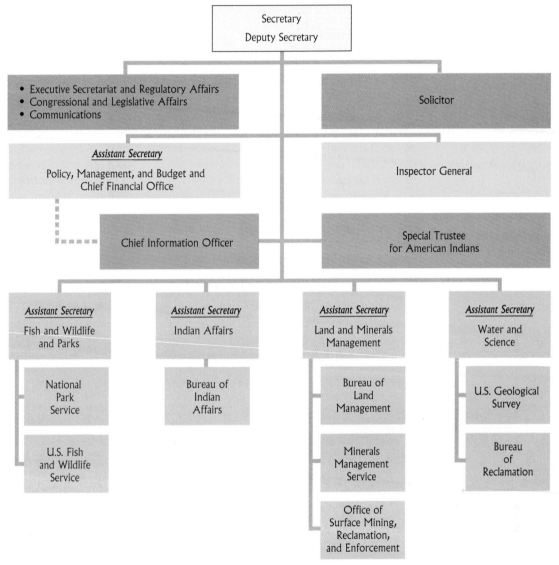

Source: Office of the Federal Register, *United States Government Manual 2008–2009* (Washington, DC: U.S. Government Printing Office, 2008), 247.

also call them the alphabet soup of American government because most such agencies are known in Washington by their initials. Some examples follow:

- *FRB (the Federal Reserve Board)*, charged with governing banks and, even more important, regulating the supply of money and thus interest rates
- *NLRB (the National Labor Relations Board)*, created to regulate labor–management relations
- *FCC (the Federal Communications Commission)*, charged with licensing radio and TV stations and regulating their programming in the public interest as well as with regulating interstate long-distance telephone rates, cable television, and the Internet

government corporation
A government organization that, like business corporations, provides a service that could be provided by the private sector and typically charges for its services. The U.S. Postal Service is an example. Compare **independent regulatory agency** and **independent executive agency**.

- *FTC (the Federal Trade Commission)*, responsible for regulating business practices and controlling monopolistic behavior, and now involved in policing the accuracy of advertising
- *SEC (the Securities and Exchange Commission)*, created to police the stock market

Each of these independent regulatory commissions is governed by a small commission, usually with 5 to 10 members appointed by the president and confirmed by the Senate for fixed terms. The president cannot fire regulatory commission members as easily as he can cabinet officers and members of the White House staff. The Supreme Court determined this rule after President Franklin Roosevelt fired a man named Humphrey from the FTC. Humphrey took the matter to court but died shortly afterward. The angry executors of his estate sued for back pay, and the Court held that presidents could not fire members of regulatory agencies without just cause (*Humphrey's Executor v. United States*, 1935). "Just cause" has never been defined clearly, and no member of a regulatory commission has been fired since.

Interest groups consider the rule making by independent regulatory commissions (and, of course, their membership) very important. The FCC can deny a multi-million-dollar TV station a license renewal—a power that certainly sparks the interest of the National Association of Broadcasters. The FTC regulates business practices—a power that prompts both business and consumers to pay careful attention to its activities and membership.

Interest groups are so concerned with these regulatory bodies that some critics point to the "capture" of the regulators by the regulatees.[13] It is common for members of commissions to be recruited from the ranks of the regulated. Sometimes, too, members of commissions or staffs of these agencies move on to jobs in the very industries they were regulating. Some lawyers among them use contacts and information gleaned at the commission when they represent clients before their former employers at the commission. A later section of this chapter discusses the bureaucracy's relationship with interest groups.

GOVERNMENT CORPORATIONS

The federal government also has a handful of **government corporations**. These are not exactly like private corporations in which you can buy stock and collect dividends, but they *are* like private corporations—and different from other parts of the government—in two ways. First, they provide a service that *could be* handled by the private sector. Second, they typically charge for their services, though often at rates cheaper than those the consumer would pay to a private-sector producer.

The granddaddy of the government corporations is the Tennessee Valley Authority (TVA). Established in 1933 as part of the New Deal, it has controlled floods, improved navigation, protected the soil against erosion, and provided inexpensive electricity to millions of Americans in Tennessee, Kentucky, Alabama, and neighboring states. The post office, one of the original cabinet departments (first headed by Benjamin Franklin), has become the government's largest corporation: the U.S. Postal Service.

In an effort to make the agency financially independent as well as more responsive to consumers, in 1970, Congress transformed the Post Office Department into the U.S. Postal Service, the government's largest corporation. The agency has improved its fiscal performance (partly as a result of increased postal rates), although it is now subject to direct competition from private businesses that offer parcel and overnight mail services.

Occasionally the government has taken over a "sick industry" and turned it into a government corporation. Amtrak, the railroad passenger service, is one example. Congress grumbles about Amtrak's multi-billion-dollar subsidy (although some critics point out that billions of dollars in federal highway funds also constitute something of a subsidy for the auto industry), but members of Congress have only reluctantly agreed to let Amtrak shed its most unprofitable runs.

THE INDEPENDENT EXECUTIVE AGENCIES

The **independent executive agencies** are essentially all the rest of the government—not cabinet departments, not regulatory commissions, and not government corporations. Their administrators typically are appointed by the president and serve at his will. The 45 to 50 of such bureaus are listed in the current issue of the *United States Government Manual*. A few of the biggest independent executive agencies (in size of budget) are the following:

*   *General Services Administration (GSA)*, the government's landlord, which handles buildings, supplies, and purchasing
*   *National Science Foundation (NSF)*, the agency supporting scientific research
*   *National Aeronautics and Space Administration (NASA)*, the agency that takes Americans to the moon and points beyond

The Environmental Protection Agency (EPA) is an important independent agency, overseeing the administration of all environmental legislation. Here, EPA workers clean up hazardous waste.

BUREAUCRACIES AS IMPLEMENTORS

Bureaucracies are essentially *implementors* of policy. They take congressional, presidential, and sometimes even judicial pronouncements and develop procedures and rules for implementing policy goals. They also manage the routines of government, from delivering mail to collecting taxes to training troops.

WHAT IMPLEMENTATION MEANS

Public policies are rarely self-executing. Congress typically announces the goals of a policy in broad terms, sets up an administrative apparatus, and leaves the bureaucracy the task of working out the details of the program. In other words, the bureaucracy is left to implement the program. **Policy implementation** is the stage of policymaking between the establishment of a policy (such as the passage of a legislative act, the issuing of an executive order, the handing down of a judicial decision, or the promulgation of a regulatory rule) and the results of the policy for individuals.[14] In other words, implementation is a critical aspect of policymaking. At a minimum, implementation includes three elements:

1. Creation of a new agency or assignment of a new responsibility to an old agency
2. Translation of policy goals into operational rules and development of guidelines for the program
3. Coordination of resources and personnel to achieve the intended goals[15]

independent executive agency

The government not accounted for by cabinet departments, independent regulatory commissions, and government corporations. Its administrators are typically appointed by the president and serve at the president's pleasure. NASA is an example.

policy implementation

The stage of policymaking between the establishment of a policy and the consequences of the policy for the people whom it affects. Implementation involves translating the goals and objectives of a policy into an operating, ongoing program.

WHY THE BEST-LAID PLANS SOMETIMES FLUNK THE IMPLEMENTATION TEST

The Scottish poet Robert Burns once wrote, "The best laid schemes o'mice and men/Gang aft a-gley [often go awry]." So, too, with the best intended public policies. Policies that people expect to work often fail. In 1996, Congress overwhelmingly passed a bill to guarantee health insurance to millions of Americans when they change or lose their jobs or lose coverage. Yet the law has been ineffective because insurance companies often charge these individuals premiums far higher than standard rates.[16] High expectations followed by dashed hopes are the frequent fate of well-intended public policies.

Program Design   Implementation can break down for several reasons. One is faulty program design. "It is impossible," said Eugene Bardach, "to implement well a policy or program that is defective in its basic theoretical conception." Consider, he suggested, the following hypothetical example:

> If Congress were to establish an agency charged with squaring the circle with compass and straight edge—a task mathematicians have long ago shown is impossible—we could envision an agency coming into being, hiring a vast number of consultants, commissioning studies, reporting that progress was being made, while at the same time urging in their appropriations request for the coming year that the Congress augment the agency's budget.

And the circle would remain round.[17]

Lack of Clarity   Congress is fond of stating a broad policy goal in legislation and then leaving implementation up to the bureaucracies. Members of Congress can thus escape messy details, and place blame for the implementation decisions elsewhere (see "Young People and Politics: Drug Offenses and Financial Aid").

Such was the case with the controversial Title IX of the Education Act of 1972,[18] which said, "No person in the United States shall, on the basis of sex, be excluded from participation in, be denied the benefits of, or be subjected to discrimination under any education program or activity receiving federal financial assistance." Because almost every college and university receives some federal financial assistance, almost all were thereby forbidden to discriminate on the basis of gender. Interest groups supporting women's athletics convinced Congress to include a provision about college athletics as well. Thus, Section 844 reads,

> The Secretary of [Health, Education, and Welfare (HEW) then, today of Education] shall prepare and publish . . . proposed regulations implementing the provisions of Title IX . . . relating to prohibition of sex discrimination in Federally assisted education programs which shall include with respect to intercollegiate athletic activities reasonable provisions considering the nature of the particular sports.

Just what does this section mean? Proponents of women's athletics thought it meant that discrimination against women's sports was also prohibited. Some, with good reason, looked forward to seeing women's sports on an equal footing with men's. One member of the House-Senate Conference Committee proposed language specifically exempting "revenue-producing athletics" (meaning men's football and basketball) from the prohibition. The committee rejected this suggestion, but to colleges and universities with big-time athletic programs and to some alumni, the vague Section 844 called for equality in golf and swimming, not men's football and basketball programs, which could continue to have the lion's share of athletic budgets.

Joseph Califano, President Carter's secretary of HEW, was the man in the middle on this tricky problem. His staff developed a "policy interpretation" of the

Drug Offenses and Financial Aid

In 1998, Congress wrote a provision into the law governing financial aid for college students that prohibited students convicted of drug offenses from receiving grants and loans from the federal government. It did not matter whether the offense was relatively minor or whether the conviction happened years ago—a student convicted of a drug offense as an adult could be denied financial aid from one year to life, depending on the number of offenses and severity of conviction. Not surprisingly, the law has been a matter of contention.

The law itself might seem a bit severe, but there is more. Someone convicted of armed robbery, rape, or even murder would not have been in the same predicament. Once out of prison, such a person was entitled to government grants and loans with no questions asked. But under the law, tens of thousands of would-be college students were denied financial aid because of drug offenses, even though the crimes may have been committed long ago and the sentences already served.

Members of Congress accused the Clinton and Bush administrations of distorting the law's intent. They argued that the Department of Education, which administers financial aid programs, should not be strict in its interpretation of the law. The department responded that Congress wrote a vague law—one that refers to "a student who has been convicted," and that it was faithfully implementing the letter of the law. In effect, the department argued that it had no discretion in the matter and could not act on its own to make financial aid policy more just.

The George W. Bush administration suggested ending the prohibition on aid for those who violated drug laws before entering college. However, it wanted to continue the aid ban for those who commit such crimes while enrolled in college. Its goal, the administration said, was to discourage students from using drugs. The problem, as others saw it, was that such a rule would still impose stiffer penalties for drug use than for any other crime. It would also have the effect of barring some first-time, minor offenders from getting financial aid while restoring it for more serious drug lawbreakers.

Eight years after passing the original ban on financial aid for drug use, Congress revised the law. The new statute allowed students with past drug convictions to receive student aid, but current students who are convicted of drug offenses will still lose their federal aid for a year for a first offense, two years for a second offense, and indefinitely for a third offense.

Anticipating implementation problems is difficult. Putting together coalitions within Congress is also difficult. One consequence of these difficulties is that laws are often vague—and often have unintended consequences as well.

QUESTIONS FOR DISCUSSION

➤ How much discretion should a bureaucratic unit have to correct injustices in laws?

➤ Why is it so difficult for Congress to anticipate problems implementing laws?

---

legislation that he announced in December 1978. HEW's interpretation of the 100 or so words of Section 844 of Title IX numbered 30 pages. The interpretation recognized that football was "unique" among college sports. If football was unique, then the interpretation implied (but did not directly say) that male-dominated football programs could continue to outspend women's athletic programs.

Supporters of equal budgets for male and female athletics were outraged. Charlotte West of the Association for Intercollegiate Athletics for Women called HEW's interpretation "a multitude of imprecise and confusing explanations, exceptions, and caveats." Even the football-oriented National Collegiate Athletic Association was wary of the interpretation. One of its lawyers allowed, "They are trying to be fair. The question is how successful they are." A 100-word section in a congressional statute, which prompted a 30-page interpretation by the bureaucracy, in turn prompted scores of court cases. The courts have had to rule on such matters as whether Title IX requires that exactly equivalent dollar amounts be spent on women's and men's athletics. Litigation continues to this day.

The complex case of implementing Title IX for intercollegiate athletics contains an important lesson: Policy problems that Congress cannot resolve are not likely to be easily resolved by bureaucracies.

Bureaucrats receive not only unclear orders but also contradictory ones. James Q. Wilson points out that the Immigration and Naturalization Service (INS) was supposed to keep out illegal immigrants but let in necessary agricultural workers, to carefully screen foreigners seeking to enter the country but facilitate the entry of

Bureaucracies are often asked to implement unclear laws. When Congress decided to prohibit gender discrimination in college athletics, for example, it left bureaucrats the task of creating guidelines that would end discrimination while addressing the diverse needs of different sports. It took years—and several lawsuits—to establish the law's meaning.

foreign tourists, and to find and expel undocumented aliens but not break up families, impose hardships, violate civil rights, or deprive employers of low-paid workers. "No organization can accomplish all of these goals well, especially when advocates of each have the power to mount newspaper and congressional investigations of the agency's 'failures.'"[19] Similarly, Congress has ordered the National Park Service to preserve the environmental quality of national parks; it has also obliged it to keep the parks accessible to tourists at the same time. The Forest Service is supposed to help timber companies exploit the lumber potential in the national forests *and* preserve the natural environment.

Lack of Resources   As noted earlier, we often hear the charge that bureaucracies are bloated. The important issue, however, is not the size of the bureaucracy in the abstract but whether it is the appropriate size to do the job it has been assigned to do. As big as a bureaucracy may seem in the aggregate, it frequently lacks the staff—along with the necessary training, funding, supplies, and equipment—to carry out the tasks it has been assigned. Recently, for example, the news has been filled with complaints such as the following:

- U.S. troops in Iraq had insufficient numbers of body armor and armored Humvees and trucks to protect them against roadside bombs.
- Although 80 percent of the nation's drug supply and a large percentage of its medical devices and food is now imported, the Federal Drug Administration lacks the personnel and computer systems to identify, much less inspect, the plants producing these items. At its current pace, the agency will need at least 27 years to inspect every foreign medical device plant that exports to the United States, 13 years to check every foreign drug plant, and 1,900 years to examine every foreign food plant.
- Because of lack of funding, the popular Head Start program serves only about half the children who are theoretically eligible to participate.
- Because of lack of personnel, it takes the Social Security Administration well over a year to process claims for Disability Insurance.
- The U.S. Immigration and Customs Enforcement (ICE) lacks the personnel to track most of the aliens who overstay their visas or who engage in suspicious activities. The ICE also lacks the resources even to identify, much less deport, more than 10 percent of the 200,000 convicted criminal aliens in the United States.
- In their inspections of facilities handling and storing hazardous wastes, inadequately trained inspectors for the Environmental Protection Agency (EPA) overlooked more than half the serious violations. The computer system the EPA uses to track and control water pollution is obsolete, full of faulty data, and does not take into account thousands of significant pollution sources.
- The FBI lacks computers at its headquarters that allow it to search its own databases for multiple terms such as "aviation" and "schools." Only about 50 agents can converse in Arabic, and the agency has a serious shortage of translators for intercepted communications.
- National Guard Units have only a third of the equipment they need to respond to domestic disasters and terrorist attacks.

- The Federal Aviation Administration (FAA) lacks the proper personnel and equipment to direct the nation's air traffic safely.
- The lack of financing to maintain national parks may lead to permanent deterioration of such treasured American vacation spots as Yosemite and Yellowstone.
- The IRS lacks the appropriate computer systems to integrate the dozens of databases that contain the information necessary to collect the more than $2 trillion in taxes that finance the federal government.
- There is a shortage of epidemiologists who are trained to recognize and investigate the outbreak of infectious disease.

Why does Congress not simply give the bureaucracy more resources? Some well-organized interests fight against adding resources to certain agencies because they do not wish to be inspected or regulated and prefer an ineffective bureaucracy. Equally important is the battle over scarce budgetary resources. Pressures to allocate personnel to direct services, such as the provision of agricultural expertise to farmers, keep the staff available to implement other policies small. In addition, the irresistible urges of policy makers to provide public services (at least in form), helps to ensure that the bureaucracy will lack the resources to adequately implement the programs. Finally, in an age when "big government" is under attack, there are strong political incentives to downsize the bureaucracy.

Agencies may also lack the *authority* necessary to meet their responsibilities. For example, many observers believe that the FDA lacks adequate powers to protect the public from dangerous drugs such as the sleeping pill Halcion and the sedative Versed. The FDA does no testing of its own and must rely entirely on the test results submitted by manufacturers. Yet it lacks the subpoena power to obtain documents when it suspects that drug companies are withholding data about adverse drug reactions or misrepresenting test results. It often lacks access to potentially damaging company documents that have been involved in private product-liability cases. Similarly, the Department of Agriculture lacks authority to close meat processing plants—even ones with serious violations of food safety standards.

As we saw in Chapter 3, many policies are implemented by state and local governments. The federal government may try to influence elementary and secondary education, for example, but it is the state and local governments that provide the actual services. Federal influence over these governments is indirect, at best. Other policies, ranging from safety in the workplace to pollution control, are implemented by thousands of private individuals, groups, and businesses.[20] With such implementers, bureaucrats are more likely to request, educate, and negotiate than to issue orders and institute legal proceedings.

Administrative Routine   For most bureaucrats, administration is a routine matter most of the time. They follow **standard operating procedures**, better known as SOPs, to help them make numerous everyday decisions. Standard rules save time. If a Social Security caseworker had to invent a new rule for every potential client and then have it cleared at higher levels, few clients would be served. Thus, agencies write detailed manuals to cover as many particular situations as officials can anticipate. The regulations elaborating the Internal Revenue Code compose an IRS agent's bible. Similarly, a customs agent has binders filled with rules and regulations about what can and cannot be brought into the United States duty free.

SOPs also bring uniformity to complex organizations. Justice is better served when officials apply rules uniformly, as in the implementation of welfare policies that distribute benefits to the needy or in the levying of fines for underpayment of taxes. Uniformity also makes personnel interchangeable. The army, for example, can transfer soldiers to any spot in the world, and they can find out how to do their job by referring to the appropriate manual.

standard operating procedures

Better known as SOPs, these procedures are used by bureaucrats to bring uniformity to complex organizations. Uniformity improves fairness and makes personnel interchangeable. See also **administrative discretion**.

Routines are essential to bureaucracy. Yet they sometimes become frustrating to citizens, who term them "red tape" when they do not seem appropriate to a situation. SOPs then become obstacles to action. An October 1983 terrorist attack on their barracks outside Beirut, Lebanon, killed 241 Marines while they slept. A presidential commission appointed to examine the causes of the tragedy concluded that, among other factors contributing to the disaster, the Marines in the peacekeeping force were "not trained, organized, staffed, or supported to deal effectively with the terrorist threat."[21] In other words, they had not altered their SOPs regarding security, which is basic to any military unit, to meet the unique challenges of a terrorist attack.

The FAA's protocols (routines) for hijackings assumed that the pilot of a hijacked aircraft would notify an air traffic controller that there had been a hijacking, that the FAA could identify the plane, that there would be time for the FAA and NORAD to address the issue, and that the hijacking would not be a suicide mission. As the 9/11 Commission put it, these SOPs were "unsuited in every respect" for the 9/11 terrorist hijackings.[22]

Sometimes an agency simply fails to establish routines that are necessary to complete its tasks. For example, in late 1997, the General Accounting Office found that the FAA failed to determine whether the violations its inspectors uncovered at aircraft repair stations were ever corrected. The FAA did not keep the proper paperwork for adequate follow-up activities.

Problems with SOPs are nothing new. They certainly frustrated Franklin D. Roosevelt:

> The Treasury is so . . . ingrained in its practices that I find it impossible to get the action and results I want. . . . But the Treasury is not to be compared with the State Department. You should go through the experience of trying to get any changes in the thinking, policy, and action of the career diplomats. . . . But both put together are nothing as compared to the Na-a-vy. . . . To change anything in the Na-a-a-vy is like punching a feather bed. You punch it with your right and you punch it with your left until you are finally exhausted, and then you find the damn bed just as it was before you started punching.[23]

Administrators' Dispositions Paradoxically, bureaucrats operate not only within the confines of routines, but often with considerable discretion to behave independently. **Administrative discretion** is the authority of administrative actors to select among various responses to a given problem.[24] Discretion is greatest when rules do not fit a particular case, and this is often the case—even in agencies with elaborate rules and regulations.

Some administrators exercise more discretion than others. Michael Lipsky coined the phrase **street-level bureaucrats** to refer to those bureaucrats who are in constant contact with the public (often a hostile one) and have considerable discretion; they include police officers, welfare workers, and lower-court judges.[25] No amount of rules, not even the thousands of pages of IRS rules, will eliminate the need for bureaucratic discretion on some policies. It is up to the highway patrol officer who stops you to choose whether to issue you a warning or a ticket.

administrative discretion

The authority of administrative actors to select among various responses to a given problem. Discretion is greatest when routines, or **standard operating procedures**, do not fit a case.

street-level bureaucrats

A phrase coined by Michael Lipsky, referring to those bureaucrats who are in constant contact with the public and have considerable **administrative discretion**.

Bureaucrats typically apply thousands of pages of rules in the performance of routine tasks, but many bureaucrats—especially street-level bureaucrats—must use administrative discretion as well. These border patrol officers, shown arresting undocumented immigrants on the U.S.-Mexican border, must decide whom they will search carefully and whom they will let pass with a quick check.

Because bureaucrats will inevitably exercise discretion, it is important to understand how they use it. Ultimately, how they use discretion depends on their dispositions about the policies and rules they administer. Although bureaucrats may be indifferent to the implementation of many policies, other policies may conflict with their views or their personal or organizational interests. When people are asked to execute orders with which they do not agree, slippage is likely to occur between policy decisions and performance. A great deal of mischief may occur as well.

On one occasion, President Nixon ordered Secretary of Defense Melvin Laird to bomb a Palestine Liberation Organization hideaway, a move Laird opposed. According to the secretary, "We had bad weather for forty-eight hours. The Secretary of Defense can always find a reason not to do something."[26] The president's order was stalled for days and eventually rescinded.

Controlling the exercise of discretion is a difficult task. It is not easy to fire bureaucrats in the civil service, and removing appointed officials may be politically embarrassing to the president, especially if those officials have strong support in Congress and among interest groups. In the private sector, leaders of organizations provide incentives such as pay raises to encourage employees to perform their tasks in a certain way. In the public sector, however, special bonuses are rare, and pay raises tend to be small and across the board. Moreover, there is not necessarily room at the top for qualified bureaucrats. Unlike a typical private business, a government agency cannot expand just because it is performing a service effectively and efficiently.

In the absence of positive and negative incentives, the government relies heavily on rules to limit the discretion of implementors. As former Vice President Al Gore put it in a report issued by the National Performance Review,

> Because we don't want politicians' families, friends, and supporters placed in "no-show" jobs, we have more than 100,000 pages of personnel rules and regulations defining in exquisite detail how to hire, promote, or fire federal employees. Because we don't want employees or private companies profiteering from federal contracts, we create procurement processes that require endless signatures and long months to buy almost anything. Because we don't want agencies using tax dollars for any unapproved purpose, we dictate precisely how much they can spend on everything from telephones to travel.[27]

Often these rules end up creating new obstacles to effective and efficient governing, however. As U.S. forces were streaming toward the Persian Gulf in the fall of 1990 to liberate Kuwait from Iraq, the air force placed an emergency order for 6,000 Motorola commercial radio receivers. But Motorola refused to do business with the air force because of a government requirement that the company set up separate accounting and cost-control systems to fill the order. The only way the U.S. Air Force could acquire the much-needed receivers was for Japan to buy them and donate them to the United States!

Fragmentation   Sometimes responsibility for a policy is dispersed among several units within the bureaucracy. The federal government has had as many as 96 agencies involved with the issue of nuclear proliferation. Similarly, in the field of welfare, 10 different departments and agencies administer more than 100 federal human services programs. The Department of Health and Human Services has responsibility for basic welfare grants to the states to aid families, the Department of Housing and Urban Development provides housing assistance for the poor, the Department of Agriculture runs the food stamp program, and the Department of Labor administers training programs and provides assistance in obtaining employment.

The resources and authority necessary for the president to attack a problem comprehensively are often distributed among many bureaucratic units. President

George W. Bush's creation of the Office of Homeland Security in 2001 dramatically illustrates the challenge of diffusion of responsibility. The president ordered the office to coordinate the implementation of a comprehensive national strategy to protect the United States from terrorist threats or attacks. This involved directing the counterterrorism efforts of 46 federal agencies, encompassing much of the federal government. Of course, each of these agencies also reported to other officials for other purposes.

One piece of the puzzle of homeland security is securing our borders. Table 15.2 lists the agencies with responsibilities for border control in 2002, prior to the establish of the Department of Homeland Security. As you can see, at least 33 departments and agencies had responsibility for protecting America's borders, focusing on threats ranging from illegal immigrants and chemical toxins to missiles and electronic sabotage. It is difficult to coordinate so many different agencies, especially when they lack a history of trust and cooperation. Moreover, there are often physical obstacles to cooperation, such as the largely incompatible computer systems of the INS and the Coast Guard. Once the borders have been breached and an attack has occurred, many other offices get involved in homeland security, including hundreds of state and local agencies.

If fragmentation is a problem, why not reorganize the government? The answer lies in hyperpluralism and the decentralization of power. Congressional committees recognize that they would lose jurisdiction over agencies if these agencies were merged with others. Interest groups (such as the nuclear power industry) do not want to give up the close relationships they have developed with "their" agencies.

TABLE 15.2

Departments and Agencies with Responsibility for Border Security in 2002

DEPARTMENT OF AGRICULTURE
Animal and Plant Health Inspection Service

CENTRAL INTELLIGENCE AGENCY

DEPARTMENT OF COMMERCE
Critical Infrastructure Assurance Office National Oceanic and Atmospheric Administration

DEPARTMENT OF DEFENSE
Defense Intelligence Agency
Inspector General
National Guard
National Reconnaissance Office
National Security Agency
North American Aerospace Defense Command

DEPARTMENT OF ENERGY
Office of Science and Technology Policy

ENVIRONMENTAL PROTECTION AGENCY
Office of International Activities

DEPARTMENT OF JUSTICE
Bureau of Alcohol, Tobacco, and Firearms
Drug Enforcement Administration
Federal Bureau of Investigation

Immigration and Naturalization Service
Marshals Service
Office of Special Investigations

DEPARTMENT OF STATE
Bureau of Consular Affairs
Bureau of Intelligence and Research
Bureau of Population, Refugees, and Migration
Bureau for International Narcotics and Law Enforcement
   Agencies
Passport Office

POSTAL SERVICE

DEPARTMENT OF TREASURY
Customs Service
Financial Crimes Enforcement Network
Internal Revenue Service
Office of the Inspector General
Secret Service

DEPARTMENT OF TRANSPORTATION
Coast Guard
Federal Aviation Administration
Federal Motor Carrier Administration
Maritime Administration

Agencies themselves do not want to be submerged within a broader bureaucratic unit. All these forces fight reorganization, and they usually win.[28] President Clinton's proposal to merge the Drug Enforcement Administration and the Customs Service met with immediate opposition from the agencies and their congressional allies. Pursuing the merger became too costly for the president, who had to focus on higher-priority issues.

Nevertheless, under the right conditions, reorganization is possible. In 2001, congressional Democrats proposed a new Department of Homeland Security. In the summer of 2002, President George W. Bush concluded that the only way to overcome the fragmentation of agencies involved in providing homeland security was to create a new department, one that combined many of the agencies listed in Table 15.2. Congress created the new department at the end of 2002, the largest reorganization of the federal government in half a century.

Fragmentation also allows some agencies to work at cross-purposes. For years, one agency supported tobacco farmers while another discouraged smoking. One agency encouraged the redevelopment of inner cities while another helped build highways making it easier for people to live in the suburbs. One agency helped farmers grow crops more efficiently while another paid them to produce less. As long as Congress refuses to make clear decisions about priorities, bureaucrats will implement contradictory policies.

A CASE STUDY: THE VOTING RIGHTS ACT OF 1965

Even when a policy is controversial, implementation can be effective if goals are clear and there are adequate means to achieve them. In 1965, Congress, responding to generations of discrimination against prospective African American voters in the South, passed the Voting Rights Act. The act singled out six states in the Deep South in which the number of registered African American voters was minuscule. Congress ordered the Justice Department to send federal registrars to each county in those states to register qualified voters. Congress outlawed literacy tests and other tests previously used to discriminate against African American registrants. The government promised stiff penalties for those who interfered with the work of federal registrars.

Congress charged the attorney general with implementing the Voting Rights Act. He acted quickly and dispatched hundreds of registrars—some protected by U.S. marshals—to Southern counties. Within seven and a half months after the act's passage, more than 300,000 new African American voters were on the rolls. The proportion of the Southern African American population registered to vote increased from 43 percent in 1964 to 66 percent in 1970, partly (though not entirely) because of the Voting Rights Act.[29]

The Voting Rights Act was a successful case of implementation by any standard, but not because it was popular with everyone. Southern representatives and senators were outraged by it, and a filibuster delayed its passage in the Senate. It was successful because its goal was clear (to register large numbers of African American voters), its implementation was straightforward

The Voting Rights Act of 1965 was successfully implemented because its goal was clear: to register African Americans to vote in Southern counties where their voting rights had been denied for years. In addition, implementators had the authority to do the job. This federal registrar, like hundreds of others working for the Department of Justice, helped bring the vote to some 300,000 African Americans in less than a year.

(sending out people to register them), and the authority of the implementors was clear (they had the support of the attorney general and even U.S. marshals) and concentrated in the Justice Department, which was disposed to implementing the law vigorously.

PRIVATIZATION

A movement to "reinvent government" started in the 1980s. At the heart of this endeavor were efforts to decentralize authority and provide performance incentives through market competition and competitive public-versus-private bidding on government services. Since that time private contractors have become a virtual fourth branch of the national government, spending about $400 billion a year. The war in Iraq, domestic security, and Hurricane Katrina gave this trend a further impetus.

Everyone seems to agree that the government cannot operate without contractors, which provide the surge capacity to handle crises without expanding the permanent bureaucracy. Moreover, contractors may provide specialized skills the government lacks. Some government executives favor contractors because they find the federal bureaucracy slow, inflexible or incompetent. Using contractors also allows officials to brag about cutting the federal work force while actually expanding the number of people working for the government.[30]

The theory behind contracting for services is that competition in the private sector will result in better service at lower costs than that provided by public bureaucracies, who have traditionally had a monopoly on providing services. Although there is evidence that some local governments have saved money on services such as garbage collection, there is no evidence that private contactors have provided services more efficiently at the federal level. Moreover, competition is not always present. One study found that fewer than half of the new contracts and payments against existing contracts are now subject to full and open competition.[31] For example, the government has spent billions of dollars in no-bid contracts for companies such as Halliburton to rebuild Iraq.

Contracting also almost always leads to less public scrutiny, as government programs are hidden behind closed corporate doors. Companies, unlike agencies, are not subject to the Freedom of Information Act. Members of Congress have sought unsuccessfully for years to get the Army to explain the contracts for Blackwater USA security officers in Iraq, which involve several costly layers of subcontractors. Partly because of the relative lack of openness, efforts to privatize public services have been marked by extensive corruption and sometimes by extensive cost overruns.

BUREAUCRACIES AS REGULATORS

regulation

The use of governmental authority to control or change some practice in the private sector. Regulations pervade the daily lives of people and institutions.

Government **regulation** is the use of governmental authority to control or change some practice in the private sector. Regulations by government pervade Americans' everyday lives and the lives of businesses, universities, hospitals, and other institutions, filling hundreds of volumes. (You can see the trend in the volume of regulations in "A Generation of Change: Trends in Regulation.") Regulation is the most controversial role of the bureaucracies, yet Congress gives bureaucrats broad mandates to regulate activities as diverse as interest rates, the location of nuclear power plants, and food additives.

A GENERATION OF CHANGE

Trends in Regulation

Some people call the Federal Register the bureaucracy's bulletin board because it is where new regulations are posted. You can see that the number of pages of regulations fell sharply in 1981 at the beginning of the Reagan administration and then gradually increased with each new president.

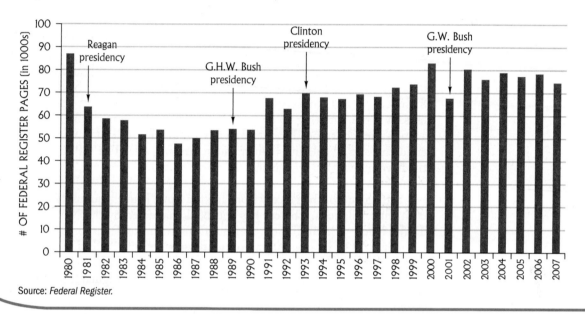

Source: *Federal Register.*

REGULATION IN THE ECONOMY AND IN EVERYDAY LIFE

The notion that the American economy is largely a "free enterprise" system, unfettered by government intervention, is about as up to date as a Model T Ford. You can begin to understand the sweeping scope of governmental regulation by examining how the automobile industry is regulated:

- The Securities and Exchange Commission regulates buying and selling stock in an automobile corporation.
- Relations between the workers and managers of the company come under the scrutiny of the National Labor Relations Board.
- The Department of Labor and the Equal Employment Opportunity Commission mandate affirmative action in hiring workers in automobile production plants because automakers are major government contractors.
- The EPA, the National Highway Traffic Safety Administration, and the Department of Transportation require that cars include pollution-control, energy-saving, and safety devices.
- Unfair advertising and deceptive consumer practices in marketing cars come under the watchful eye of the FTC.

A Full Day of Regulation   Everyday life itself is the subject of bureaucratic regulation. Almost all bureaucratic agencies—not merely the ones called independent regulatory commissions—are in the regulatory business. Consider a typical factory worker (we'll name him John Smith) who works in the city of Chicago and lives with his wife, Joan Smith, and their three young children in suburban Mount

You Are a Federal Administrator

Prospect, Illinois. Both at work and at home, federal regulations affect John's life. At 5:30 A.M. he is awakened by his clock radio, which is set to a country music station licensed to operate by the FCC. For breakfast he has cereal, which has passed inspection by the FDA, as has the lunch Joan packs for him. The processed meat in his sandwich is packed under the supervision of the Food Safety and Quality Service of the U.S. Department of Agriculture.

John takes the train to work and buys a quick cup of coffee before the journey. The FDA has warned that the caffeine in his coffee has caused birth defects in laboratory animals, and there is discussion in Washington about regulating it. After paying his fare (regulated by the state government), he hops aboard and shortly arrives at work, a small firm that makes equipment for the food industry.

At home, Joan Smith is preparing breakfast for the children. The price of the milk she serves is affected by the dairy price supports regulated by the Agricultural Stabilization and Conservation Service. As the children play, she evaluates the toys they use, wanting to avoid any that could be dangerous. A Washington agency, the Consumer Product Safety Commission (CPSC), also takes note of children's toys, regulating their manufacture and sale. The CPSC also regulates the lawn mower, the appliances, the microwave oven, and numerous other items around the Smith house.

Setting out for the grocery store and the bank, Joan encounters even more government regulations. The car has seat belts mandated by the National Highway Traffic Safety Administration, and the Department of Transportation certifies its gas mileage. The car's pollution-control devices are now in need of service because they do not meet the requirements of the EPA. The bank where Joan deposits money and writes a check is among the most heavily regulated institutions she encounters in her daily life. Her passbook savings rate is regulated by the Depository Institutions Deregulation Committee, and her account is insured by the Federal Deposit Insurance Commission.

Meanwhile, John Smith is at work assembling food-processing machinery. He and the other workers are members of the International Association of Machinists. Their negotiations with the firm are held under rules laid down by the National Labor Relations Board. Not long ago, the firm was visited by inspectors from the Occupational Safety and Health Administration (OSHA), a federal agency charged with ensuring worker safety. OSHA inspectors noted several violations and forwarded a letter recommending safety changes to the head of the firm.

Back at home, John has a beer before dinner. It was made in a brewery carefully supervised by the Bureau of Alcohol, Tobacco, and Firearms, and federal and state taxes were collected when it was sold. After dinner (almost all the food served has been transported by the regulated trucking industry), the children are sent to bed. An hour or so of television, broadcast on regulated airwaves, is followed by bedtime. A switch will turn off the electric lights, whose rates are regulated by the Illinois Commerce Commission and the Federal Energy Regulatory Commission.[32]

REGULATION: HOW IT GREW, HOW IT WORKS

The Evolution of the Federal Bureaucracy

From the beginnings of the American republic until 1887, the federal government made almost no regulatory policies; the little regulation produced was handled by state and local authorities. Opponents disputed even the minimal regulatory powers of state and local governments. In 1877, the Supreme Court upheld the right of government to regulate the business operations of a firm. The case, *Munn v. Illinois*, involved the right of the state of Illinois to regulate the charges and services of a Chicago warehouse. During this time, farmers were seething about alleged overcharging by railroads, grain elevator companies, and other business firms. In 1887—a decade after *Munn*—Congress created the first regulatory agency, the Interstate Commerce Commission (ICC), and charged it with regulating the railroads, their prices, and their services to farmers; the ICC thus set the precedent for regulatory policymaking.

As regulators, bureaucratic agencies typically operate with a large grant of power from Congress, which may detail goals to be achieved but may also permit the agencies to sketch out the regulatory means. In 1935, for example, Congress created the National Labor Relations Board to control "unfair labor practices," but the NLRB had to play a major role in defining "fair" and "unfair." Most agencies charged with regulation must first develop a set of rules, often called *guidelines*. The appropriate agency may specify how much food coloring it will permit in a hot dog, how many contaminants it will allow an industry to dump into a stream, how much radiation from a nuclear reactor is too much, and so forth. Guidelines are developed in consultation with—and sometimes with the agreement of—the people or industries being regulated.

Next, the agency must apply and enforce its rules and guidelines, either in court or through its own administrative procedures. Sometimes it waits for complaints to come to it, as the Equal Employment Opportunity Commission does; sometimes it sends inspectors into the field, as OSHA does; and sometimes it requires application for a permit or license to demonstrate performance consistent with congressional goals and agency rules, as the FCC does. Often government agencies take violators to court, hoping to secure a judgment and fine against an offender (see "You Are the Policymaker: How Should We Regulate?"). Whatever strategy Congress permits a regulating agency to use, all regulation contains these elements: (1) *a grant of power and set of directions from Congress*, (2) *a set of rules and guidelines* by the regulatory agency itself, and (3) *some means of enforcing compliance* with congressional goals and agency regulations.

Government regulation of the American economy and society has grown in recent decades. The budgets of regulatory agencies, their level of employment, and the number of rules they issue are all increasing—and did so even during conservative administrations. As we have seen, few niches in American society are *not* affected by regulation. Not surprisingly, this situation has led to charges that government is overdoing it.

TOWARD DEREGULATION

Deregulation—the lifting of government restrictions on business, industry, and professional activities—is currently a fashionable term.[33] The idea behind deregulation is that the number and complexity of regulatory policies have made regulation too complicated and burdensome. To critics, the problem with regulation is that it raises prices, distorts market forces, and—worst of all—does not work. They claim that the regulatory system does the following:

deregulation
The lifting of restrictions on business, industry, and professional activities for which government rules had been established and that bureaucracies had been created to administer.

- *Raises prices.* If the producer is faced with expensive regulations, the cost will inevitably be passed on to the consumer in the form of higher prices.
- *Hurts America's competitive position abroad.* Other nations may have fewer regulations on pollution, worker safety, and other business practices than the United States. Thus, American products may cost more in the international marketplace, undermining sales in other countries.
- *Does not always work well.* Tales of failed regulatory policies are numerous. Regulations may be difficult or cumbersome to enforce. Critics charge that regulations sometimes do not achieve the results that Congress intended and maintain that they simply create massive regulatory bureaucracies.

YOU ARE THE Policymaker

How Should We Regulate?

Almost every regulatory policy was created to achieve some desirable social goal. When more than 6,000 people are killed annually in industrial accidents, who would disagree with the goal of a safer workplace? Who would dissent from greater highway safety, when more than 40,000 die each year in automobile accidents? Who would disagree with policies to promote equality in hiring when the history of opportunities for women and minorities is one of discrimination? Who would disagree with policies to reduce industrial pollution, when pollution threatens health and lives? However, there may be more than one way to achieve these—and many other—desirable social goals.

Charles L. Schultze, former chair of President Carter's Council of Economic Advisors, is—like Murray L. Weidenbaum, who held the same position under President Reagan—a critic of the current state of federal regulation. Schultze reviewed the regulatory activities of the EPA and OSHA. Neither agency's policies, he concluded, had worked very well. He described the existing system as **command-and-control policy**: The government tells business how to reach certain goals, checks that these commands are followed, and punishes offenders.

Schultze advocates an **incentive system**. He argues that instead of telling construction businesses how their ladders must be constructed, measuring the ladders, and charging a small fine for violators, it would be more efficient and effective to levy a high tax on firms with excessive worker injuries. Instead of trying to develop standards for about 100,000

pollution sources, as the EPA now does, it would be easier and more effective to levy a high tax on those who cause pollution. The government could even provide incentives in the form of rewards for such socially valuable behavior as developing technology to reduce pollution. Incentives, Schultze argues, use marketlike strategies to regulate industry. They are, he claims, more effective and efficient than command-and-control regulation.

Not everyone is as keen on the use of incentives as Schultze. Defenders of the command-and-control system of regulation compare the present system to preventive medicine—it is designed to minimize pollution or workplace accidents before they become too severe. Defenders of the system argue, too, that penalties for excessive pollution or excessive workplace accidents would be imposed only after substantial damage had been done. They also add that if taxes on pollution or unsafe work environments were merely externalized (that is, passed along to the consumer as higher prices), they would not be much of a deterrent. Moreover, it would take a large bureaucracy to carefully monitor the level of pollution discharged, and it would require a complex calculation to determine the level of tax necessary to encourage businesses not to pollute.

The issue of the manner of regulation is a complex one. What would *you* do?

Source: Charles L. Schultze, *The Public Use of the Private Interest* (Washington, DC: Brookings Institution, 1977); Steven Kelman, *What Price Incentives? Economists and the Environment* (Boston: Auburn House, 1981).

---

command-and-control policy

The typical system of **regulation** whereby government tells business how to reach certain goals, checks that these commands are followed, and punishes offenders. Compare **incentive system**.

incentive system

According to Charles Schultze, a more effective and efficient policy than **command-and-control**; in the incentive system, marketlike strategies are used to manage public policy.

In the 1970s, sentiment favoring deregulation was building in the Washington community. Even liberals sometimes joined the antiregulation chorus; for example, Senator Edward Kennedy of Massachusetts pushed for airline deregulation. The airline industry also pressed for deregulation, and in 1978 the Civil Aeronautics Board (CAB) began to deregulate airline prices and airline routes. In 1984, the CAB formally disbanded; it even brought in a military bugler to play taps at its last meeting.

Not everyone, however, believes that deregulation is in the nation's best interest.[34] For example, critics point to severe environmental damage resulting from lax enforcement of environmental protection standards during the Reagan administration. Similarly, many observers attribute at least a substantial portion of the blame for the enormously expensive bailout of the savings and loan industry to deregulation in the 1980s. Californians found that deregulation led to severe power shortages in 2001. The burst of the real estate bubble in 2007 and 2008 led to demands for increased regulation of mortgage lenders.

In addition, many regulations have proved beneficial to Americans. As a result of government regulations, we breathe cleaner air,[35] we have lower levels of lead in our blood, miners are safer at work,[36] seacoasts have been preserved,[37] and children are more likely to survive infancy.[38]

UNDERSTANDING BUREAUCRACIES

As both implementors and regulators, bureaucracies are making public policy, not just administering someone else's decisions. The fact that bureaucrats, who are not elected, compose most of the government raises fundamental issues about who controls governing and what the bureaucracy's role should be.

BUREAUCRACY AND DEMOCRACY

Bureaucracies constitute one of America's two unelected policymaking institutions (courts are the other). In democratic theory, popular control of government depends on elections, but we could not possibly elect the more than 4 million federal civilian and military employees, or even the few thousand top men and women, though they spend more than $3 trillion of the American gross domestic product. Furthermore, the fact that voters do not elect civil servants does not mean that bureaucracies cannot respond to and represent the public's interests. When we compare the backgrounds of bureaucrats with those of members of Congress or presidents, we find that bureaucrats are more representative than elected officials. Much depends on whether bureaucracies are effectively controlled by the policymakers citizens do elect—the president and Congress.[39]

The Changing Face of the Federal Bureaucracy

Presidents Try to Control the Bureaucracy Chapter 13 looked at some of the frustrations presidents endure in trying to control the government they are elected to run. Presidents try hard—not always with success—to impose their policy preferences on agencies (see "America in Perspective: Influencing Independent Agencies"). Following are some presidential methods of exercising control over bureaucracies:

- *Appoint the right people to head the agency.* Normally, presidents control the appointments of agency heads and subheads. Putting their people in charge is one good way for presidents to influence agency policy,[40] yet even this has its problems. President Reagan's efforts to whittle the powers of the EPA led to his appointment of controversial Anne Gorsuch to head the agency. Gorsuch had previously supported policies contrary to the goals of the EPA. When she attempted to implement her policies, legal squabbles with Congress and political controversy ensued, ultimately leading to her resignation. To patch up the damage Gorsuch had done to his reputation, Reagan named a moderate and seasoned administrator, William Ruckelshaus, to run the agency. Ironically, Ruckelshaus demanded—and got—more freedom from the White House than Gorsuch had sought. President Clinton

J. Edgar Hoover headed the FBI from its founding in 1924 until his death in 1972. Partly because they were afraid of what he might have in his files, elected officials were unwilling to control him. More recently, Louis Freeh, (pictured here) director from 1993–2001, had a poisonous relationship with President Bill Clinton, who viewed him as insubordinate and not competent. The president was unable to fire Freeh, however, because of the FBI's investigations of the White House and Freeh's powerful Republican allies.

executive orders

Regulations originating from the executive branch. Executive orders are one method presidents can use to control the bureaucracy.

had no use for FBI Director Louis Freeh, who would barely talk to the president. Yet Clinton felt he could not fire him because he feared unleashing denunciations from those claiming he was purging an enemy.

- *Issue orders.* Presidents can issue **executive orders** to agencies. These orders carry the force of law and are used to implement statutes, treaties, and provisions of the Constitution.[41] Sometimes presidential aides simply pass the word that the president wants something done. These messages usually suffice, although agency heads are reluctant to run afoul of Congress or the press on the basis of a broad presidential hint. The president's rhetoric in speeches outside the bureaucracy may also influence the priorities of bureaucrats.[42]

- *Alter an agency's budget.* The Office of Management and Budget (OMB) is the president's own final authority on any agency's budget. The OMB's threats to cut here or add there will usually get an agency's attention. Each agency, however, has its constituents within and outside of Congress, and Congress, not the president, does the appropriating.

- *Reorganize an agency.* Although President Reagan promised, proposed, and pressured to abolish the Department of Energy and the Department of Education, he never succeeded—largely because each department was in the hands of an entrenched bureaucracy backed by elements in Congress and strong constituent groups. Reorganizing an agency is hard to do if it is a large and strong agency, and reorganizing a small and weak agency is often not worth the trouble. A massive reorganization occurred in 2002 with the creation of the Department of Homeland Security. It is not clear, however, that it has improved the implementation of policy.

AMERICA IN PERSPECTIVE

Influencing Independent Agencies

We often think of the president as head of the executive branch, but there are agencies, such as the Federal Reserve Board, that are very powerful and are generally free from the chief executive's direction. This often leaves presidents frustrated, as when they wish the Federal Reserve Board to lower interest rates to stimulate the economy. There are even more autonomous agencies in Latin America, however—agencies removed from the direct control of the president and the legislature.

Why would Latin American governments create agencies they cannot control? The primary reason is to protect a new agency providing a new service from changes in policy made by future decision makers. Those who create an agency fear that its policies will be undone by a new administration or legislature, so they make it autonomous.

These agencies often have their own sources of revenue and thus can increase their budgets without going through the public and controversial process of government budget debates. They are also freer from legislative oversight and formal presidential

controls than are regular agencies, and conflict over their programs is less visible. Until recently, expenditures for autonomous agencies also allowed the government to engage in creative financing because when these agencies contracted debt, it did not count against the central government's debt (which is substantial in Latin America).

Autonomy is decidedly a mixed blessing, however. Creative financing is not necessarily good for a nation, nor is the difficulty policymakers have in consolidating bureaucracies and increasing their efficiency. The lack of traditional means of influence also makes it difficult to alter the priorities of agencies, such as shifting the emphasis from building roads to building apartments.

Sources: Michelle M. Taylor, "When Are Juridicially Autonomous Agencies Responsive to Elected Officials? A Simulation Based on the Costa Rican Case," *Journal of Politics* 57 (November 1995): 1070–92; Bruce M. Wilson, Juan Carlos Rodríguez Cordero, and Roger Handberg, "The Best Laid Schemes . . . Gang Aft A-gley: Judicial Reform in Latin America—Evidence from Costa Rica," *Journal of Latin American Studies* 36 (August 2004).

Congress Tries to Control the Bureaucracy   Congress exhibits a paradoxical relationship with the bureaucracies. On the one hand (as we have seen), members of Congress may find a big bureaucracy congenial.[43] Big government provides services to constituents, who may show their appreciation at the polls. Moreover, when Congress lacks the answers to policy problems, it hopes the bureaucracies will find them. Unable itself, for example, to resolve the touchy issue of equality in intercollegiate athletics, Congress passed the ball to the Department of Health, Education, and Welfare. Unable to decide how to make workplaces safer, Congress produced OSHA. As you saw in Chapter 12, Congress is increasingly the problem-identifying branch of government, setting the bureaucratic agenda but letting the agencies decide how to implement the goals it sets.

On the other hand, Congress has found it hard to control the government it helped create. There are several measures Congress can take to oversee the bureaucracy:

- *Influence the appointment of agency heads.* Even when the law does not require senatorial approval of a presidential appointment, members of Congress are not shy in offering their opinions about who should and should not be running the agencies. When congressional approval is required, members are doubly influential. Committee hearings on proposed appointments are almost guaranteed to produce lively debates if some members find the nominee's probable orientations objectionable.

- *Alter an agency's budget.* With the congressional power of the purse comes a mighty weapon for controlling bureaucratic behavior. At the same time, Congress knows that many agencies perform services that its constituents demand. Too much budget cutting may make an agency more responsive—at the price of losing an interest group's support for a reelection campaign.

- *Hold hearings.* Committees and subcommittees can hold periodic hearings as part of their oversight responsibilities. They may parade flagrant agency abuses of congressional intent in front of the press, but the very committee that created a program usually has responsibility for oversight of it and thus has some stake in showing the agency in a favorable light. We also learned in Chapter 12 that members of Congress have other disincentives for vigorous oversight, including a desire not to embarrass the chief executive.

- *Rewrite the legislation or make it more detailed.* Every statute is filled with instructions to its administrators. To limit bureaucratic discretion and make its instructions clearer, Congress can write new or more detailed legislation. Still, even voluminous detail (as in the case of the IRS) can never eliminate discretion.

Through these and other devices, Congress tries to keep bureaucracies under its control. Never entirely successful, Congress faces a constant battle to limit and channel the vast powers that it delegated to the bureaucracy in the first place.

Sometimes these efforts are detrimental to bureaucratic performance. In 2006, at least 60 House and Senate committees and subcommittees claimed jurisdiction over a portion of homeland security issues. Officials in the Department of Homeland Security have to spend a large percentage of their time testifying to these committees, and the balkanized jurisdiction has undermined the ability of Congress to perform comprehensive oversight. Moreover, different committees may send different signals to the same agency. One may press for stricter enforcement of regulations, for example, while another seeks for more exemptions.

Iron Triangles and Issue Networks Agencies' strong ties to interest groups on the one hand and to congressional committees and subcommittees on the other further complicate efforts to control the bureaucracy. Chapter 11 illustrated that bureaucracies often enjoy cozy relationships with interest groups and with committees or subcommittees of Congress. When agencies, groups, and committees all depend on one another and are in close, frequent contact, they form what are sometimes called **iron triangles** or *subgovernments*. These triads have advantages on all sides (see Figure 15.5).

There are plenty of examples of subgovernments at work. A subcommittee on aging, senior citizens' interest groups, and the Social Security Administration are likely to agree on the need for more Social Security benefits. Richard Rettig has

iron triangles

A mutually dependent relationship between bureaucratic agencies, interest groups, and congressional committees or subcommittees. Iron triangles dominate some areas of domestic policymaking.

FIGURE 15.5

Iron Triangles: One Example

Iron triangles—composed of bureaucratic agencies, interest groups, and congressional committees or subcommittees—have dominated some areas of domestic policymaking by combining internal consensus with a virtual monopoly on information in their area. The tobacco triangle is one example; there are dozens more. Iron triangles are characterized by mutual dependency in which each element provides key services, information, or policy for the others. The arrows indicate some of these mutually helpful relationships. In recent years, a number of well-established iron triangles, including the tobacco triangle, have been broken up.

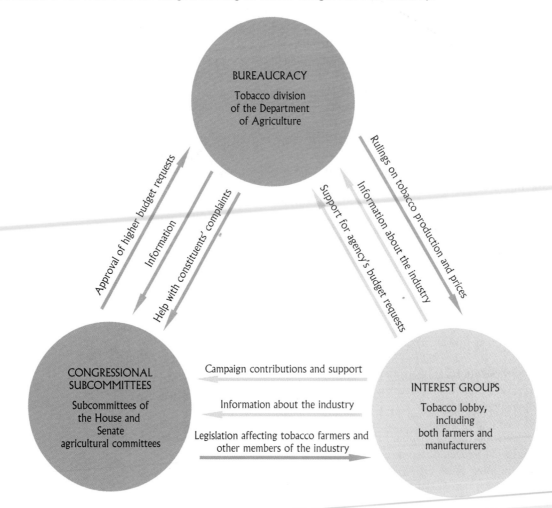

recounted how an alliance slowly jelled around the issue of fighting cancer. It rested on three pillars: cancer researchers, agencies within the National Institutes of Health, and members of congressional health subcommittees.[44]

When these iron triangles shape policies for senior citizens, cancer, tobacco, or any other interest, officials make each policy independently of the others, sometimes even in contradiction to other policies. For example, for years the government supported tobacco farmers in one way or another while encouraging people not to smoke. Moreover, the iron triangles' decisions tend to bind larger institutions, such as Congress and the White House. Congress often defers to the decisions of committees and subcommittees, especially on less visible issues. The White House may be too busy wrestling with global concerns to fret over agricultural issues or cancer. Emboldened by this lack of involvement, subgovernments flourish and add a strong decentralizing and fragmenting element to the policymaking process.

There is often a cozy relationship between the components of three sides of a subgovernment. For example, in 2003, Congress added a massive prescription drug benefit under Medicare. Representative Billy Tauzin shepherded the drug bill through the House as chair of the Energy and Commerce Committee. He then retired from Congress to head the Pharmaceutical Research and Manufacturers of America, a powerful industry lobby group, for an estimated $2 million a year. Thomas Scully, the Medicare administrator and lead negotiator for the administration, resigned his position within weeks after the passage of the bill to join a lobbying firm that represented several health care industry companies significantly affected by the new law. He also announced he would be working part time for an investment firm with interests in several more companies affected by the new law.

The system of subgovernments is now overlaid with an amorphous system of *issue networks*. There is more widespread participation in bureaucratic policymaking, and many of the participants have technical policy expertise and are drawn to issues because of intellectual or emotional commitments rather than material interests. Those concerned with environmental protection, for example, have challenged formerly closed subgovernments on numerous fronts (see Chapter 19). This opening of the policymaking process complicates the calculations and decreases the predictability of those involved in the stable and relatively narrow relationships of subgovernments.[45]

Although subgovernments are often able to dominate policymaking for decades, they are not indestructible.[46] For example, the subgovernment pictured in Figure 15.5 long dominated smoking and tobacco policy, focusing on crop subsidies to tobacco farmers. But increasingly, these policies came under fire from health authorities, who were not involved in tobacco policymaking in earlier years. Similarly, Congress no longer considers pesticide policy, once dominated by chemical companies and agricultural interests, separately from environmental and health concerns.

An especially vivid example of the death of an iron triangle is the case of nuclear power.[47] During the 1940s and 1950s, Americans were convinced that the technology that had ended World War II could also serve peaceful purposes. Nuclear scientists spoke enthusiastically about harnessing the atom to achieve all sorts of goals, eventually making electricity so inexpensive that it would be "too cheap to meter." Optimism in progress through science was the rule, and the federal government encouraged the development of nuclear power through a powerful iron triangle.

Congress established a special joint committee, the Joint Committee on Atomic Energy, and gave it complete control over questions of nuclear power.

It also created a new executive agency, the Atomic Energy Commission (AEC), and together with the private companies that built the nuclear power plants and the electrical utilities that wanted to operate them, they formed a powerful subgovernment. America built more nuclear power plants than any other country in the world, and American technology was exported overseas to dozens of nations.

Nuclear power today—after the accidents at Three Mile Island and Chernobyl and the various cost overruns associated with the industry—bears almost no resemblance to that of the early 1960s when the iron triangle was at its peak. What happened? The experts lost control. When critics raised questions concerning the safety of the plants and when opponents were able to get local officials to question the policies publicly, the issue grew into a major political debate of the late 1960s, associated with the growth of environmentalism. Opposition to nuclear power destroyed two of the most powerful legs of the iron triangle. Congress disbanded the Joint Committee on Atomic Energy; a variety of congressional committees now claim some jurisdiction over nuclear power questions. Similarly, Congress replaced the AEC with two new agencies: the Nuclear Regulatory Commission and the Department of Energy.

The nuclear power industry has been devastated: No new nuclear power plants have been started in the United States since 1978, and almost all those under construction at that time have been abandoned at huge financial loss. Nuclear power provides only about 12 percent of our total energy production. In sum, the wave of environmental concern that developed in the late 1960s swept away one of the most powerful iron triangles in recent American history.

This is not the end of the story, however. The extraordinarily high price of gasoline and heating fuel since 2005 and concerns over global warming have encouraged a reconsideration of nuclear power. The Gallup Poll has found that a majority of the public supports the use of nuclear energy to produce electricity. President George W. Bush declared on August 8, 2005, "Of all our nation's energy sources, only nuclear power plants can generate massive amounts of electricity without emitting an ounce of air pollution or greenhouse gases. And thanks to the advances in science and technology, nuclear plants are far safer than ever before. . . . We will start building nuclear power plants again by the end of this decade."

If the nuclear power industry should revive, there will be renewed calls for strict regulation—from both the bureaucracy and Congress. Whether an iron triangle reemerges from this change will depend on whether the public is attentive to the issue of nuclear power and whether it allows experts to define safety concerns as technical matters appropriate only for experts to decide.

BUREAUCRACY AND THE SCOPE OF GOVERNMENT

Comparing Bureaucracies

To many, the huge American bureaucracy is the prime example of the federal government growing out of control. As this chapter discussed earlier, some observers view the bureaucracy as acquisitive, constantly seeking to expand its size, budgets, and authority. Much of the political rhetoric against big government also adopts this line of argument, along with complaints about red tape, senseless regulations, and the like. It is easy to take potshots at a faceless bureaucracy that usually cannot respond.

One should keep in mind, however, that the federal bureaucracy has not grown over the past two generations, as Figure 15.1 illustrates. If one considers the fact that the population of the country has grown significantly over this period, then the federal bureaucracy has actually *shrunk* in size relative to the population it serves.

Originally, the federal bureaucracy had the modest role of promoting the economy, defending the country, managing foreign affairs, providing justice, and delivering the mail. Its role gradually expanded to include providing services to farmers, businesses, and workers. The discussion of federalism in Chapter 3 showed that as the economy and the society of the United States changed, a variety of interests placed additional demands on government. We now expect government—and the bureaucracy—to play an active role in dealing with social and economic problems. A good case can be made that the bureaucracy is actually too *small* for many of the tasks currently assigned to it—tasks ranging from the control of illicit drugs to protection of the environment.

In addition, it is important to remember that when the president and Congress have chosen to deregulate certain areas of the economy or cut taxes, the bureaucracy could not and did not prevent them from doing so. The question of what and how much the federal government should do—and thus how big the bureaucracy should be—is answered primarily at the polls and in Congress, the White House, and the courts—not by faceless bureaucrats.

SUMMARY

Americans rarely congratulate someone for being a good bureaucrat. Unsung, taunted by cartoonists, and maligned by columnists, bureaucrats are the scapegoats of American politics. Americans may call presidents great and reelect members of Congress, but almost no one praises bureaucrats. Those who compose the bureaucracy, however, perform most of the vital services the federal government provides.

Although there are many critics of the increasing size of government, the federal bureaucracy has not grown over the past two generations. Instead, it has shrunk, even as the country has grown and the public has made additional demands on government.

Bureaucrats shape policy as administrators, as implementors, and as regulators. In this chapter we examined who bureaucrats are, how they got their positions, and what they do. Today, most bureaucrats working for the federal government get their jobs through the civil service system, although the president appoints a few at the very top.

In general, there are four types of bureaucracies: cabinet departments, independent regulatory commissions, government corporations, and independent executive agencies.

As policymakers, bureaucrats play two key roles. First, they are policy implementors, translating legislative policy goals into programs. Policy implementation does not always work well, and when it does not, bureaucrats usually take the blame, whether they deserve it or not. Much of administration involves a prescribed routine, but nearly all bureaucrats still have some discretion. Second, bureaucrats are regulators. Congress increasingly delegates large amounts of power to bureaucratic agencies and expects them to develop rules and regulations. Scarcely a nook or cranny of American society or the American economy escapes the long reach of bureaucratic regulation.

Although bureaucrats are not elected, bureaucracies are not necessarily undemocratic. Bureaucrats are competent and reasonably representative of Americans. Bureaucracies also may be controlled by elected decision makers, although presidential or congressional control over bureaucracies is difficult. One reason is the strong support many agencies receive from interest groups.

Chapter Test

Multiple Choice

1. Most bureaucratic agencies in the United States are responsible to:
   a. Congress
   b. The Courts
   c. The President
   d. The House of Representatives
   e. The Senate

2. Which of the following is NOT a characteristic of a bureaucracy, according to German sociologist Max Weber?
   a. It has a hierarchical authority structure
   b. It is patrimonial
   c. It uses task specialization
   d. It develops extensive rules
   e. It is rational

3. All but which of the following should be considered myths about the American bureaucracy, according to the textbook?
   a. Americans have mostly negative experiences with bureaucrats
   b. The federal bureaucracy is constantly growing bigger
   c. Most federal bureaucrats work in Washington, D.C.
   d. Bureaucracies are inefficient
   e. Most Americans believe that bureaucrats work to serve their interests

4. The political term for a hiring and promotion system that is based on political reasons rather than on merit or competence is called:
   a. Patronage
   b. Benefaction
   c. Sponsorship
   d. Auspice
   e. Legacy

5. The Pendleton Civil Service Act that established the federal civil service was passed in:
   a. The second half of the 18th century
   b. The first half of the 19th century
   c. The second half of the 19th century
   d. The first half of the 20th century
   e. The second half of the 20th century

6. Civil service employees may:
   a. Not actively participate in partisan politics while on duty
   b. May engage in political activities while not on duty
   c. May not run for partisan elective office
   d. May not solicit contributions from the public
   e. All of the above

7. Which of the following is NOT one of the basic types of agencies in the federal executive branch?
   a. Cabinet departments
   b. Independent regulatory commissions
   c. Government corporations
   d. Independent executive agencies
   e. They all are

8. Which of the following can be considered a virtual fourth branch of the national government?
   a. Private contractors
   b. Government corporations
   c. Interest groups
   d. The media
   e. None of the above

9. Which of the following is NOT a cabinet department?
   a. The Department of the Interior
   b. The Department of Defense
   c. The Federal Communications Commission
   d. The Department of Justice
   e. The Department of Education

10. Which of the following is NOT true for the government's use of private contractors?
    a. It allows officials to claim that they are downsizing the federal work force while actually expanding it
    b. There is evidence that private contractors provide services more efficiently at the federal level
    c. Most contracts for private contractors are not subject to full and open competition
    d. There is less public scrutiny of private contractors
    e. All of the above are true

True/False

11. The Department of Defense makes up more than half of the federal bureaucracy.
    True_____   False_____

12. The permanent bureaucracy is less broadly representative of the American people than are legislators, judges, or presidential appointees.
    True_____   False_____

Short Answer

13. Explain in your own words what the so-called "plum book" is and what it is used for.

14. Explain what "government corporations" are and provide an example.

15. In your own words, explain the policy implementation role of the bureaucracy. In particular, what are the three elements of policy implementation, and what is an example of how the bureaucracy carries out each of them?

16. What are three of the arguments proponents of "deregulation" bring forth to support their claims?

Short Answer/Essay Questions

17. Please compare and contrast the so-called "command-and-control" system of regulation and the "incentive system" and provide an example of each. In your opinion, which is the more efficient approach, and why?

18. One of the roles of the bureaucracy is to regulate activities. Among other areas, the economy is often heavily regulated. Given what you know about the current housing market crisis, the problem of subprime mortgages, and the ripple effects this has had on the economy as a whole, do you believe it is the bureaucracy's responsibility to intervene in and regulate this matter? Explain why you think so. In what ways could this regulation occur?

19. Please address the charge of some against the bureaucracy that it "overprotects" its civil servants. First, in what ways does this overprotection show itself? Second, what are the pros and cons of protecting civil servant employees in such a manner?

20. What are the three of the reasons this textbook gives for the breakdown of policy implementation? What is an example of each? Finally, what other possible reasons—not addressed in this textbook—can you think of to explain such a breakdown? Please explain your

answer carefully and give examples to illustrate your arguments.

21. What are the pros and cons of having standard operations procedures (SOPs) in the American bureaucracy?

22. Max Weber argued that a permanent bureaucracy is an inevitable aspect of a modern society. Based on what you know about bureaucracies and about modernity, what is it about "modern" societies that necessitates a bureaucracy? Address at least three to four different aspects, and support your arguments.

23. Provide two examples from your personal life that illustrate how bureaucracy regulates your daily activities. Do you believe this regulation is fair? That it is effective? Why, or why not?

24. Your textbook gives an overview of federal legislation that potentially bans students who are convicted of drug offenses from receiving federal student aid. In your opinion and based on what you have learned about the penalties for other types of crimes, is this a "fair" policy? Why, or why not? Do you believe this law serves as a deterrent to student drug use? Why, or why not? If you could, how would you change this law to make it more effective?

Answer Key:

1. C   2. B   3. E   4. A   5. C   6. E   7. E   8. A   9. C   10. B   11. True   12. False

Key Terms

bureaucracy (472)
patronage (476)
Pendleton Civil Service Act (477)
civil service (477)
merit principle (477)
Hatch Act (477)
Office of Personnel
  Management (477)
GS (General Schedule) rating (477)

Senior Executive Service (477)
independent regulatory
  commission (479)
government corporations (482)
independent executive
  agency (483)
policy implementation (483)
standard operating procedures
  (487)

administrative discretion (488)
street-level bureaucrats (488)
regulation (492)
deregulation (495)
command-and-control policy (496)
incentive system (496)
executive orders (498)
iron triangles (500)

Internet Resources

www.gpoaccess.gov/gmanual/index.html
U.S. Government Manual that provides information on the organization of the U.S. government.

www.gpoaccess.gov/fr/index.html
The *Federal Register*, which provides information on U.S. laws and regulations.

www.whitehouse.gov/government/cabinet.html
Information on federal cabinet departments.

www.whitehouse.gov/government/independent-agencies.html
Information on federal independent agencies and commissions.

www.opm.gov/feddata/
Federal employment statistics.

www.opm.gov
Office of Personnel Management Web site with information on federal jobs and personnel issues.

www.govexec.com/
The Web site for *Government Executive* magazine.

GetConnected

How Bureaucracies Are Organized

On January 24, 2003, President George W. Bush signed legislation that created a new department and the largest federal bureaucracy since 1947. The new department, called the Department of Homeland Security, was proposed first by Congress in the aftermath of the September 11, 2001, terrorist attacks. The department's mission is to better coordinate the nation's homeland defenses. Do you know how this new bureaucracy is organized? Could you contact the Department of Homeland Security if you needed to? Let us look at this department's Web page to learn more about the agency.

Search the Web

Go to *www.dhs.gov/xcitizens/* and review the information on that page. Then review *America at Risk: A Homeland Security Report Card* published by the Progressive Policy Institute at *www.ppionline.org/documents/HomeSecRptCrd_0703.pdf*.

Questions to Ask

- How many agencies were combined to create the Department of Homeland Security?

- What are some of the challenges the Progressive Policy Institute identifies for the Department of Homeland Security?

Why It Matters

The Department of Homeland Security represents the most dramatic change in the federal bureaucracy in half a century. It is likely that citizens will come into contact with the new agency often, especially as they travel.

Get Involved

Do you have a question about the Department of Homeland Security? If so, go to *www.dhs.gov/xutil/contactus.shtm* and send your question. Discuss the response you get with your class. You also may follow issues related to homeland security by visiting the Web page of the U.S. House of Representatives Select Committee on Homeland Security, *http://hsc.house.gov/*. For more exercises, go to *www.longmanamericangovernment.com*

For Further Reading

Aberbach, Joel D., and Bert A. Rockman. *In the Web of Politics*. Washington, DC: Brookings Institution, 2000. Examines federal executives and the degree to which they are representative of the country and responsive to elected officials.

Arnold, Peri E. *Making the Managerial Presidency*. 2nd ed. Princeton, NJ: Princeton University Press, 1996. A careful examination of efforts to reorganize the federal bureaucracy.

Derthick, Martha, and Paul J. Quirk. *The Politics of Deregulation*. Washington, DC: Brookings Institution, 1985. Explains why advocates of deregulation prevailed over the special interests that benefited from regulation.

Edwards, George C., III. *Implementing Public Policy*. Washington, DC: Congressional Quarterly Press, 1980. A good review of the issues involved in implementation.

Goodsell, Charles T. *The Case for Bureaucracy*. 4th ed. Washington, DC: CQ Press, 2004. A strong case on behalf of the effectiveness of bureaucracy.

Gormley, William T., Jr. *Taming the Bureaucracy*. Princeton, NJ: Princeton University Press, 1989. Examines remedies for controlling bureaucracies.

Gormley, William T., Jr., and Steven J. Balla. *Bureaucracy and Democracy: Accountability and Performance*, 2nd ed. Washington, DC: CQ Press, 2007. Discusses the accountability of unelected bureaucrats in a democracy.

Heclo, Hugh M. *Government of Strangers: Executive Politics in Washington*. Washington, DC: Brookings Institution, 1977. A study of the top executives of the federal government, who constitute (says the author) a "government of strangers."

Kerwin, Cornelius M. *Rulemaking: How Government Agencies Write Law and Make Policy*. 3rd ed. Washington, DC: CQ Press, 2003. Explains how agencies write regulations to implement laws.

Meier, Kenneth J., and Laurence J. O'Toole. *Bureaucracy in a Democratic State*. Baltimore, MD: Johns Hopkins University Press, 2006. Argues that bureaucracy can promote democracy.

Osborne, David, and Peter Plastrik. *Banishing Bureaucracy*, 2nd ed. David Osborne, 2006. Five strategies for reinventing government.

Savas, E. S. *Privatization: The Key to Better Government*. Chatham, NJ: Chatham House, 1987. A conservative economist's argument that many public services performed by bureaucracies would be better handled by the private sector.

Wilson, James Q. *Bureaucracy*. New York: Basic Books, 1989. Presents a "bottom-up" approach to understanding how bureaucrats, managers, and executives decide what to do.

THE
FEDERAL
COURTS

POLITICS IN ACTION:
APPEALING TO THE SUPREME COURT

Say that you are involved in a lawsuit regarding the application of an affirmative action policy in your college or university. A trial is held in a federal district court.

After the trial, a verdict is rendered, and you lose. You are not content to accept this decision, and you appeal to the court of appeals. Once again, you lose. Now you have only two options left: accept the decision or appeal to the U.S. Supreme Court. You decide to appeal, and of the thousands of petitions for hearings presented to the Court each year, yours is one of a few dozen the Court selects.

On the day of the oral argument (there are no trials in the Supreme Court), you walk up the steep steps of the Supreme Court building, the impressive "Marble Palace" with the motto "Equal Justice Under Law" engraved over its imposing columns. The Court's surroundings and procedures suggest the nineteenth century. The justices, clothed in black robes, take their seats at the bench in front of a red velvet curtain. Behind the bench there are still spittoons, one for each justice. (Today, the spittoons are used as wastebaskets.)

Your case, like most of the cases the Court selects for oral arguments, is scheduled for about an hour. Lawyers arguing before the Court often wear formal clothing. They find a goose quill pen on their desk, purchased by the Court from a Virginia supplier. (Lawyers may take the pen with them as a memento of their day in court.) As is the norm, each side is allotted 30 minutes to present its case. The justices may—and do—interrupt the lawyers with questions. When the time is up, a discreet red light goes on at your lawyer's lectern, and he immediately stops talking.

That is the end of the hearing, but not the end of the process. You have asked the Court to overrule a policy established by your

state legislature. As the Court considers doing so, it recognizes that its decision will become precedent for all such policies across the nation. Months will go by, as the justices deliberate and negotiate an opinion, before the Court announces its decision. If you win, it will take many more months for your university, aided by lower courts, to interpret the decision and implement it.

The scope of the Supreme Court's power is great, extending even to overruling the decisions of elected officials. Despite the trappings of tradition and majesty, however, the Court does not reach its decisions in a political vacuum. Instead, it works in a context of political influences and considerations, a circumstance that raises important questions about the role of the judiciary in the U.S. political system.

The federal courts pose a special challenge to American democracy. Although it is common for state judges to be elected in one fashion or another, federal judges are *appointed* to their positions—for life. The Framers of the Constitution purposefully insulated federal judges from the influence of public opinion. How can we reconcile powerful courts populated by unelected judges with American democracy? Do they pose a threat to majority rule? Or do the federal courts actually function to protect the rights of minorities and thus maintain the type of open system necessary for democracy to flourish?

The power of the federal courts also raises the issue of the appropriate scope of judicial power in our society. Federal courts are frequently in the thick of policymaking on issues ranging from affirmative action and abortion to physician-assisted suicide and the financing of public schools. Numerous critics argue that judges should not be actively involved in determining public policy. Instead, the critics say, judges should focus on settlement of routine disputes and leave the determination of policy to elected officials. On the other hand, advocates of a more aggressive role for the courts emphasize that judicial decisions have often met pressing needs—especially needs of those who are politically or economically weak—left unmet by the normal processes of policymaking. For example, we have already seen the leading role that the federal courts played in ending legally supported racial segregation in the United States. To determine the appropriate role of the courts in our democracy, we must first understand the nature of our judicial system.

However impressive the Supreme Court may be, it makes only the tiniest fraction of American judicial policy. To be sure, the Court decides a handful of key issues each year. Some will shape people's lives, perhaps even decide issues of life and death. In addition to the Supreme Court, there are 12 federal courts of appeal, a Court of Appeals for the Federal Circuit, 91 federal district courts, and thousands of state and local courts (we discuss the latter in Chapter 21). Most of America's legal business is transacted in these less august courts. This chapter focuses on federal courts and the judges who serve on them—the men and women in black robes who are important policymakers in the American political system.

THE NATURE OF THE JUDICIAL SYSTEM

The judicial system in the United States is, at least in principle, an adversarial one in which the courts provide an arena for two parties to bring their conflict before an impartial arbiter (a judge). The system is based on the theory that justice will emerge out of the struggle between two contending points of view. The task of the judge is to apply the law to the case, determining which party is legally correct. In reality, most cases never go to trial because they are settled by agreements reached out of court.

There are two basic kinds of cases: criminal law cases and civil law cases. In a *criminal law* case, the government charges an individual with violating specific laws,

such as those prohibiting robbery. The offense may be harmful to an individual or to society as a whole, but in either case it warrants punishment, such as imprisonment or a fine. A *civil law* case involves a dispute between two parties (one of whom may be the government itself) and defines relationships between them. Civil law cases range from divorce proceedings to mergers of multinational companies and violations of civil rights laws. Civil law consists of both statutes (laws passed by legislatures) and common law (the accumulation of judicial decisions).

Just as it is important not to confuse criminal and civil law, it is important not to confuse state and federal courts. The vast majority of all criminal and civil cases involve state law and are tried in state courts. Criminal cases such as burglary and civil cases such as divorce normally begin and end in the state, not the federal, courts.

PARTICIPANTS IN THE JUDICIAL SYSTEM

The serenity and majesty of the U.S. Supreme Court are a far cry from the grimy urban courts where strings of defendants are bused from the local jails for their day—often only a few minutes—in court. Yet every case has certain components in common, including litigants, attorneys, and judges. Sometimes organized groups also become directly involved. Judges are the policymakers of the American judicial system, and we examine them extensively in later sections of this chapter. Here we will discuss the other regular participants in the judicial process.

Litigants   Federal judges are restricted by the Constitution to deciding "cases" or "controversies"—that is, actual disputes rather than hypothetical ones. Judges do not issue advisory opinions on what they think (in the abstract) may be the meaning or constitutionality of a law. The judiciary is essentially passive, dependent on others to take the initiative.

Thus two parties must bring a case to the court before it may be heard. Every case is a dispute between a *plaintiff* and a *defendant* in which the former brings some charge against the latter. Sometimes the plaintiff is the government, which may bring a charge against an individual or a corporation. The government may charge the defendant with the brutal murder of Jones or charge the XYZ Corporation with illegal trade practices. All cases are identified with the name of the plaintiff first and the defendant second, for example, *State v. Smith* or *Anderson v. Baker*. In many (but not all) cases, a *jury*, a group of citizens (usually 12), is responsible for determining the outcome of a lawsuit.

Litigants end up in court for a variety of reasons. Some are reluctant participants—the defendant in a criminal case, for example. Others are eager for their day in court. For some, the courts can be a potent weapon in the search for a preferred policy. For example, in the 1960s, atheist Madalyn Murray O'Hair was an enthusiastic litigant, always ready to take the government to court for promoting religion.

Not everyone can challenge a law, however. Plaintiffs must have what is called **standing to sue**; that is, they must have serious interest in a case, which is typically determined by whether they have sustained or are in immediate danger of sustaining a direct and substantial injury from another party or an action of government. Except in cases pertaining to governmental support for religion, merely being a taxpayer and being opposed to a law do not provide the standing necessary to challenge that law in court. Nevertheless, Congress and the Supreme Court have liberalized the rules for standing, making it somewhat easier for citizens to challenge governmental and corporate actions in court.

The courts have broadened the concept of standing to sue to include **class action suits**, which permit a small number of people to sue on behalf of all other people in similar circumstances. These suits may be useful in cases as varied as civil rights, in which a few persons seek an end to discriminatory practices on behalf of

standing to sue
The requirement that plaintiffs have a serious interest in a case, which depends on whether they have sustained or are likely to sustain a direct and substantial injury from a party or an action of government.

class action suits
Lawsuits permitting a small number of people to sue on behalf of all other people similarly situated.

justiciable disputes
A requirement that to be heard a case must be capable of being settled as a matter of law rather than on other grounds as is commonly the case in legislative bodies.

Linda Brown (left), shown here outside her segregated school, was the plaintiff challenging legal segregation in public education.

amicus curiae briefs
Legal briefs submitted by a "friend of the court" for the purpose of raising additional points of view and presenting information not contained in the briefs of the formal parties. These briefs attempt to influence a court's decision.

School Vouchers

You Are a Young Lawyer

all who might be discriminated against, and environmental protection, in which a few persons may sue a polluting industry on behalf of all who are affected by the air or water the industry pollutes. Following an explosion of such cases, in 1973 the Supreme Court began making it more difficult to file class action suits.

Conflicts must not only arise from actual cases between litigants with standing in court, but they must also be **justiciable disputes**—issues that are capable of being settled by legal methods. One would not go to court to determine whether Congress should fund the Strategic Defense Initiative (SDI), for the matter could not be resolved through legal methods or knowledge.

Groups   Because they recognize the courts' ability to shape policy, interest groups often seek out litigants whose cases seem particularly strong. Few groups have been more successful in finding good cases and good litigants than the National Association for the Advancement of Colored People (NAACP), which selected the school board of Topeka, Kansas, and a young schoolgirl named Linda Brown as the litigants in *Brown v. Board of Education* (1954). NAACP legal counsel Thurgood Marshall believed that Topeka represented a stronger case than other school districts in the United States in the effort to end the policy of "separate but equal"—meaning racially segregated—public education because the city provided segregated facilities that were otherwise genuinely equal. The courts could not resolve the case simply by insisting that expenditures for schools for White and African American children be equalized.

The American Civil Liberties Union (ACLU) is another interest group that is always seeking cases and litigants to support in its defense of civil liberties. One ACLU attorney, stressing that principle took priority over a particular client, even admitted that the ACLU's clients are often "pretty scurvy little creatures. It's the principle that we're going to be able to use these people for that's important."[1] (For an example, review the case in Chapter 4 of the Nazis who tried to march in Skokie, Illinois.)

At other times groups do not directly argue the case for litigants, but support them instead with *amicus curiae* (**"friend of the court") briefs** that attempt to influence the Court's decision, raise additional points of view, and present information not contained in the briefs of the attorneys for the official parties to the case. In controversial cases, groups may submit many such briefs to the Court: They presented 102 in the University of Michigan case on affirmative action in 2003.

Attorneys   Lawyers are indispensable actors in the judicial system. Law is one of the nation's largest professions, with about a million attorneys practicing today.[2] Once primarily available to the rich, today the federally funded Legal Services Corporation employs lawyers to serve the legal needs of the poor and state and local governments provide public defenders for poor people accused of crimes. Some employers and unions now provide legal insurance, which works like medical insurance. Members with legal needs—for a divorce, a consumer complaint, or whatever—can secure legal aid through prepaid plans. As a result, more people than ever before can take their problems to the courts. Equality of access, of course, does not mean equality of representation. The wealthy can afford high-powered attorneys who can invest many hours in their cases and arrange for testimony by expert witnesses. The poor are often served by overworked attorneys with few resources to devote to an individual case.

The audience for the judicial drama is a large and attentive one that includes interest groups, the press (a close observer of the judicial process, especially of its more sensational aspects), and the public, who often have very strong opinions about how the process works. All these participants—plaintiffs, defendants, lawyers, interest groups, and others—play a role in the judicial drama, even though many of their activities take place outside the courtroom. How these participants arrive in the courtroom and which court they go to reflect the structure of the court system.

THE STRUCTURE OF THE FEDERAL JUDICIAL SYSTEM

The Constitution is vague about the structure of the federal court system. Aside from specifying that there will be a Supreme Court, the Constitution left it to Congress's discretion to establish lower federal courts of general jurisdiction. In the Judiciary Act of 1789, Congress created these *constitutional courts*, and although the system has been altered over the years, America has never been without them. The current organization of the federal court system is displayed in Figure 16.1.

Congress has also established *legislative courts* for specialized purposes. These courts include the Court of Military Appeals, the Court of Claims, the Court of International Trade, and the Tax Court. Legislative courts are staffed by judges who have fixed terms of office and who lack the protections against removal or salary reductions that judges on constitutional courts enjoy. The judges apply a body of law within their area of jurisdiction but cannot exercise the power of judicial review. The following sections focus on the courts of general jurisdiction.

First, we must understand another difference among courts. Courts with **original jurisdiction** are those in which a case is heard first, usually in a trial. These are the courts that determine the facts about a case, whether it is a criminal charge or a civil suit. More than 90 percent of court cases begin and end in the court of original jurisdiction.

Lawyers can sometimes appeal an adverse decision to a higher court for another decision. Courts with **appellate jurisdiction** hear cases brought to them on appeal from a lower court. Appellate courts do not review the factual record, only the legal issues involved. At the state level, the appellate process normally ends with the state's highest court of appeal, which is usually called the state supreme court. Appeals from a state high court can be taken only to the U.S. Supreme Court.

original jurisdiction
The jurisdiction of courts that hear a case first, usually in a trial. These are the courts that determine the facts about a case.

appellate jurisdiction
The jurisdiction of courts that hear cases brought to them on appeal from lower courts. These courts do not review the factual record, only the legal issues involved.

FIGURE 16.1

Organization of the Federal Court System

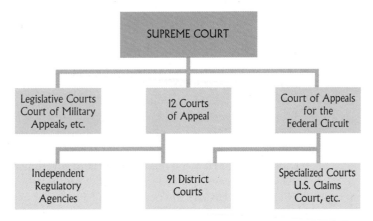

DISTRICT COURTS

The entry point for most litigation in the federal courts is one of the 91 **district courts**, at least one of which is located in each state, in addition to one in Washington, D.C., and one in Puerto Rico (there are also three somewhat different territorial courts for Guam, the Virgin Islands, and the Northern Mariana Islands). The district courts are courts of original jurisdiction; they hear no appeals. They are the only federal courts that hold trials and impanel juries. The 680 district court judges usually preside over cases alone, but certain rare cases require that three judges constitute the court. Each district court has between 2 and 28 judges, depending on the amount of judicial work within its territory.

The jurisdiction of the district courts extends to the following:

- Federal crimes
- Civil suits under federal law
- Civil suits between citizens of different states where the amount in question exceeds $75,000
- Supervision of bankruptcy proceedings
- Review of the actions of some federal administrative agencies
- Admiralty and maritime law cases
- Supervision of the naturalization of aliens

It is important to remember that about 98 percent of all the criminal cases in the United States are heard in state and local court systems, not in the federal courts. Moreover, only a small percentage of the persons convicted of federal crimes in the federal district courts actually have a trial. Most enter guilty pleas as part of a bargain to receive lighter punishment.

State and local courts handle most civil suits in the United States. Litigants settle out of court the vast majority of civil cases that commence in the federal courts. Only about 2 percent of the more than 250,000 civil cases resolved each year are decided by trials.[3]

Diversity of citizenship cases involve civil suits between citizens of different states (such as a citizen of California suing a citizen of Texas) or suits in which one of the parties is a citizen of a foreign nation and the matter in question exceeds $75,000. Congress established this jurisdiction to protect against the possible bias of a state court in favor of a citizen from that state. In these cases, federal judges are to apply the appropriate state laws.

An elaborate supporting cast assists district judges. In addition to clerks, bailiffs, law clerks, stenographers, court reporters, and probation officers, U.S. marshals are assigned to each district to protect the judicial process and to serve the writs that the judges issue. Federal magistrates, appointed to eight-year terms, issue warrants for arrest, determine whether to hold arrested persons for action by a grand jury, and set bail. They also hear motions subject to review by their district judge and, with the consent of both parties in civil cases and of defendants in petty criminal cases, preside over some trials. As the workload for district judges increases (there were more than 347,000 cases commenced in 2006),[4] magistrates are becoming essential components of the federal judicial system.

Another important player at the district court level is the U.S. attorney. Each of the 91 regular districts has a U.S. attorney who is nominated by the president and confirmed by the Senate and who serves at the discretion of the president (U.S. attorneys do not have lifetime appointments). These attorneys and their staffs prosecute violations of federal law and represent the U.S. government in civil cases.

Most of the cases handled in the district courts are routine, and few result in policy innovations. Usually district court judges do not even publish their decisions. Although most federal litigation ends at this level, a large percentage of these cases that district court judges actually decide (as opposed to those settled out of court or by guilty pleas in criminal matters) are appealed by the losers. A distinguishing feature of the American legal system is the relative ease of appeals. U.S. law gives everyone a right to an appeal to a higher court. The loser in a case only has to request an appeal to be granted one. Of course, the loser must pay a substantial legal bill to exercise this right.

COURTS OF APPEAL

Congress has empowered the U.S. **courts of appeal** to review all final decisions of district courts, except in rare instances in which the law provides for direct review by the Supreme Court (injunctive orders of special three-judge district courts and certain decisions holding acts of Congress unconstitutional). Courts of appeal also have authority to review and enforce orders of many federal regulatory agencies, such as the Securities and Exchange Commission and the National Labor Relations Board. About 70 percent of the more than 68,000 cases filed in the courts of appeal each year come from the district courts.[5]

The United States is divided into 12 judicial circuits, including one for the District of Columbia (see "My State: The Federal Judicial Circuits"). Each circuit serves at least two states and has between 6 and 28 permanent circuit judgeships (179 in all), depending on the amount of judicial work in the circuit. Each court of appeal normally hears cases in rotating panels consisting of three judges, but each may sit *en banc* (with all judges present) in particularly important cases. Decisions in either arrangement are made by majority vote of the participating judges.

> **courts of appeal**
> Appellate courts empowered to review all final decisions of district courts, except in rare cases. In addition, they also hear appeals to orders of many federal regulatory agencies. Compare **district courts**.

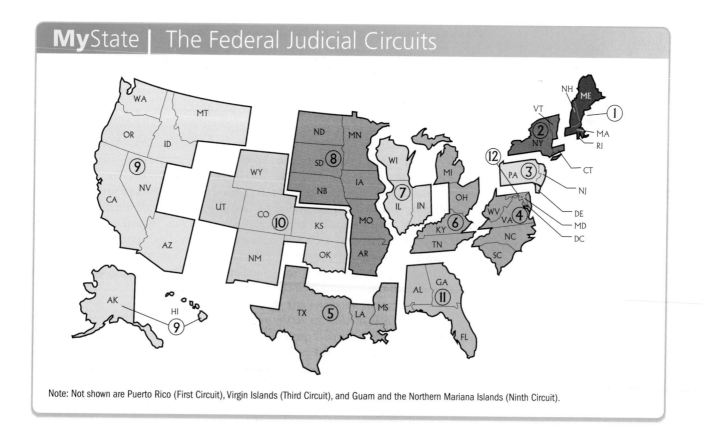

MyState | The Federal Judicial Circuits

Note: Not shown are Puerto Rico (First Circuit), Virgin Islands (Third Circuit), and Guam and the Northern Mariana Islands (Ninth Circuit).

There is also a special appeals court called the U.S. Court of Appeals for the Federal Circuit. Congress established this court, composed of 12 judges, in 1982 to hear appeals in specialized cases, such as those regarding patents, claims against the United States, and international trade.

The courts of appeal focus on correcting errors of procedure and law that occurred in the original proceedings of legal cases, such as when a district court judge gave improper instructions to a jury or misinterpreted the rights provided under a law. These courts are appellate courts and therefore hold no trials and hear no testimony. Their decisions set precedent for all the courts and agencies within their jurisdictions.

THE SUPREME COURT

Supreme Court

The pinnacle of the American judicial system. The Court ensures uniformity in interpreting national laws, resolves conflicts among states, and maintains national supremacy in law. It has both **original jurisdiction** and **appellate jurisdiction**, but unlike other federal courts, it controls its own agenda.

Sitting at the pinnacle of the American judicial system is the U.S. **Supreme Court**. The Court does much more for the American political system than decide individual cases. Among its most important functions are resolving conflicts among the states and maintaining national supremacy in the law. The Supreme Court also plays an important role in ensuring uniformity in the interpretation of national laws. For example, in 1984 Congress created a federal sentencing commission to write guidelines aimed at reducing the wide disparities in punishment for similar crimes tried in federal courts. By 1989, more than 150 federal district judges had declared the law unconstitutional, and another 115 had ruled it valid. Only the Supreme Court could resolve this inconsistency in the administration of justice, which it did when it upheld the law.

There are nine justices on the Supreme Court: eight associates and one chief justice (only members of the Supreme Court are called justices; all others are called judges). The Constitution does not require this number, however, and there have been as few as six justices and as many as 10. Congress altered the size of the Supreme Court many times between 1801 and 1869. In 1866, it reduced the size of the Court from 10 to seven members so that President Andrew Johnson could not nominate new justices to fill two vacancies. When Ulysses S. Grant took office, Congress increased the number of justices to nine because it was confident that he would nominate members to its liking. Since then, the number of justices has remained stable.

All nine justices sit together to hear cases and make decisions. But they must first decide which cases to hear. A familiar battle cry for losers in litigation in lower courts is, "I'll appeal this all the way to the Supreme Court!" In reality, this is unlikely to happen. Unlike other federal courts, the Supreme Court decides which cases it will hear.

You can see in Figure 16.2 that the Court does have an original jurisdiction, yet very few cases arise under it, as Table 16.1 illustrates. Almost all the business of the Court comes from the appellate process, and litigants may appeal cases from both federal and state courts. In the latter instance, however, a "substantial federal question" must be involved. In deference to the states, the Supreme Court hears cases from state courts only if they involve federal law, and then only after the petitioner has exhausted all the potential remedies in the state court system. Losers in a case in a state court cannot appeal to any other federal court.

The Court will not try to settle matters of state law or determine guilt or innocence in state criminal proceedings. To obtain a hearing in the Supreme Court, a defendant convicted in a state court might demonstrate, for example, that the trial was not fair as required by the Bill of Rights, which was extended to cover state court proceedings by the due process clause of the Fourteenth Amendment. The majority of cases heard by the Supreme Court come from the lower federal courts.

TABLE 16.1

Sources of Full Opinions in the Supreme Court, 2007

TYPE OF CASE	NUMBER OF CASES
Original jurisdiction	0
Civil actions from lower federal courts	47
Federal criminal and *habeas corpus* cases	17
Civil actions from state courts	4
State criminal cases	3
Total	**71**

Source: "The Supreme Court, 2006 Term: The Statistics," *Harvard Law Review* 121 (November 2007): 447–449.

The central participants in the judicial system are, of course, the judges. Once on the bench, they must draw on their backgrounds and beliefs to guide their decision-making. Some, for example, will be more supportive of abortion or of prayer in the public schools than others. Because presidents and others involved in the appointment process know perfectly well that judges are not neutral automatons who

FIGURE 16.2

The Organization and Jurisdiction of the Courts

UNITED STATES SUPREME COURT

Original jurisdiction of the Supreme Court	Appellate jurisdiction of the Supreme Court (federal route)	Appellate jurisdiction of the Supreme Court (state route)
Cases involving foreign diplomats **Cases involving a state:** • Between the United States and a state • Between two or more states • Between one state and citizens of another state • Between a state and a foreign country	**U.S. Courts of Appeal** **Court of Appeals for the Federal Circuit** **Legislative Courts**	**State Courts of Last Resort**

methodically and literally interpret the law, they work diligently to place candidates sympathetic to presidential policies on the bench. Who are the men and women who serve as federal judges and justices, and how did they obtain their positions?

THE POLITICS OF JUDICIAL SELECTION

Why It Matters
Senatorial Courtesy
Because of the practice of senatorial courtesy, senators actually end up nominating persons to be district court judges. If the Senate abolished this practice, it would allow the president greater freedom in making nominations and give the White House more opportunity to put its stamp on the judiciary.

Appointing a federal judge or a Supreme Court justice is a president's chance to leave an enduring mark on the American legal system. Guaranteed by the Constitution the right to serve "during good behavior," federal judges and justices enjoy, for all practical purposes, lifetime positions. They may be removed only by conviction of impeachment, which has occurred a mere seven times in two centuries under the Constitution. Congress has never removed a Supreme Court justice from office, although it tried but did not convict Samuel Chase in 1805. Nor can Congress reduce the salaries of judges, a stipulation that further insulates them from political pressures.

Although the president nominates persons to fill judicial slots, the Senate must confirm each nomination by majority vote. Because the judiciary is a coequal branch, the upper house of the legislature sees no reason to be especially deferential to the executive's recommendations. Because of the Senate's role, the president's discretion is actually less important than it appears.

THE LOWER COURTS

senatorial courtesy
An unwritten tradition whereby nominations for state-level federal judicial posts are not confirmed if they are opposed by a senator of the president's party from the state in which the nominee will serve. The tradition also applies to courts of appeal when there is opposition from the nominee's state senator.

The customary manner in which the Senate handles state-level federal judicial nominations is through **senatorial courtesy**. Under this unwritten tradition (which began under George Washington in 1789), the Senate does not confirm nominations for lower-court positions when they are opposed by a senator of the president's party from the state in which the nominee is to serve. In the case of judges for courts of appeal, nominees are not confirmed if opposed by a senator of the president's party from the state of the nominee's residence.

To invoke the right of senatorial courtesy, the relevant senator usually simply states a general reason for opposition. Other senators then honor their colleague's views and oppose the nomination, regardless of their personal evaluations of the candidate's merits.

Because of the strength of this informal practice, presidents usually check carefully with the relevant senator or senators ahead of time to avoid making a nomination that will fail to be confirmed. In many instances, this is tantamount to giving the power of nomination to these senators. Typically, when there is a vacancy for a federal district judgeship, the one or two senators from the state where the judge will serve suggest one or more names to the attorney general and the president. If neither senator is of the president's party, then the party's state congresspersons or other state party leaders may make suggestions. Other interested senators may also try to influence a selection.[6]

Once several names have been submitted to the president, the Department of Justice and the Federal Bureau of Investigation conduct competency and background checks on these persons, and the president usually selects a nominee from those who survive the screening process. It is difficult for the president to reject the recommendation of the party's senator in favor of someone else if the person recommended clears the hurdles of professional standing and integrity. Thus, senatorial courtesy turns the Constitution on its head, and the Senate ends up making nominations, which the president then approves.

Others have input in judicial selection as well. The Department of Justice may ask sitting judges, usually federal judges, to evaluate prospective nominees. Sitting judges may also initiate recommendations to advance or retard someone's chances of being nominated. In addition, candidates for the nomination are often active on their own behalf. They have to alert the relevant parties that they desire the position and may orchestrate a campaign of support. As one appellate judge observed, "People don't just get judgeships without seeking them."[7]

The president usually has more influence in the selection of judges to the federal courts of appeal than to federal district courts. The decisions of appellate courts are generally more significant than those of lower courts, so the president naturally takes a greater interest in appointing people to these courts. At the same time, individual senators are in a weaker position to determine who the nominee will be because the jurisdiction of an appeals court encompasses several states. Although custom and pragmatic politics require that these judgeships be apportioned among the states in a circuit, the president has some discretion in doing this and therefore has a greater role in recruiting appellate judges than in recruiting district court judges. Even here, however, senators of the president's party from the state in which the candidate resides may be able to veto a nomination.

The increasing polarization of partisan politics in recent years has affected courts of appeals nominations. The time for confirmation has increased dramatically,[8] which has decreased the chances of confirmation. Senators of the opposition party have filibustered or otherwise derailed the confirmations of a number of high-profile nominations of Presidents Clinton and George W. Bush. In response, Bush appointed some judges to the courts of appeals as recess appointments. Such appointments are unusual and good only for the remainder of a congressional term. They are also likely to anger opposition senators. After the Republicans nearly voted to end the possibility of filibustering judicial nominations, 14 senators from both parties forged a deal without White House approval that allowed some—but not all—of Bush's stalled judicial nominees to receive floor votes.

THE SUPREME COURT

The president is vitally interested in the Supreme Court because of the importance of its work and is usually intimately involved in recruiting potential justices. Nominations to the Court may be a president's most important legacy to the nation.

A president cannot have much impact on the Court unless there are vacancies to fill. Although on the average there has been an opening on the Supreme Court every two years, there is a substantial variance around this mean.[9] Franklin D. Roosevelt had to wait five years before he could nominate a justice; in the meantime, he was faced with a Court that found much of his New Deal legislation unconstitutional. More recently, Jimmy Carter was never able to nominate a justice. Between 1972 and 1984, there were only two vacancies on the Court. Nevertheless, Richard Nixon was able to nominate four justices in his first three years in office, and Ronald Reagan had the opportunity to add three new members.

When the chief justice's position is vacant, the president may nominate either someone already on the Court or someone from outside to fill the position. Usually presidents choose the latter course to widen their range of options, but if they decide to elevate a sitting associate justice—as President Reagan did with William Rehnquist in 1986—the nominee must go through a new confirmation hearing by the Senate Judiciary Committee.

The president operates under fewer constraints in nominating persons to serve on the Supreme Court than in naming persons to be judges in the lower courts. Although many of the same actors are present in the case of Supreme Court nominations, their influence is typically quite different. The president usually relies on White House aides

? Why It Matters
Judicial Elections
The public directly elects most state and local judges. All federal judges and justices are nominated by the president and confirmed by the Senate for lifetime tenures. If we elected federal judges, their decisions on highly visible issues might be more responsive to the public—but less responsive to the Constitution.

and the attorney general and the Department of Justice to identify and screen candidates for the Court. Sitting justices often try to influence the nominations of their future colleagues, but presidents feel little obligation to follow their advice.

Senators also play a lesser role in the recruitment of Supreme Court justices than in the selection of lower-court judges. No senator can claim that the jurisdiction of the Court falls within the realm of his or her special expertise, interest, or sphere of influence. Thus presidents typically consult with senators from the state of residence of a nominee after they have decided whom to select. At this point, senators are unlikely to oppose a nomination because they like having their state receive the honor and are well aware that the president can simply select someone from another state.

Candidates for nomination usually keep a low profile. They can accomplish little through aggressive politicking, and because of the Court's standing, actively pursuing the position might offend those who play important roles in selecting nominees. The American Bar Association's Standing Committee on the federal judiciary has played a varied but typically modest role at the Supreme Court level. Presidents have not generally been willing to allow the committee to prescreen candidates before their nominations are announced. George W. Bush chose not to seek its advice at all.

Through 2008, there have been 151 nominations to the Supreme Court, and 110 persons have served on the Court. Four people were nominated and confirmed twice, eight declined appointment or died before beginning service on the Court, and 29 failed to secure Senate confirmation. Presidents have failed 20 percent of the time to appoint the nominees of their choice to the Court—a percentage much higher than for any other federal position.

Although home-state senators do not play prominent roles in the selection process for the Court, the Senate as a whole does. Through its Judiciary Committee, it may probe a nominee's judicial philosophy in great detail.

For most of the twentieth century, Supreme Court nominations were routine affairs. Only one nominee failed to win confirmation in the first two-thirds of the century. But the 1960s were tumultuous times and bred ideological conflict. Although John F. Kennedy had no trouble with his two nominations to the Court—Byron White and Arthur Goldberg—his successor, Lyndon Johnson, was not so fortunate. Johnson had to withdraw his nomination of Abe Fortas (already serving on the Court) to serve as chief justice in the face of strong opposition; therefore, the Senate never voted on Homer Thornberry, Johnson's nominee to replace Fortas as an associate justice. Richard Nixon, the next president, had two nominees rejected in a row after bruising battles in the Senate. The next years were even more tumultuous (see Table 16.2).

TABLE 16.2

Unsuccessful Supreme Court Nominees since 1900

NOMINEE	YEAR	PRESIDENT
John J. Parker	1930	Hoover
Abe Fortas[a]	1968	Johnson
Homer Thornberry[b]	1968	Johnson
Clement F. Haynesworth Jr.	1969	Nixon
G. Harrold Carswell	1970	Nixon
Robert H. Bork	1987	Reagan
Douglas H. Ginsburg[a]	1987	Reagan
Harriet Miers[a]	2005	G. W. Bush

[a]Nomination withdrawn. Fortas was serving on the Court as an associate justice and was nominated to be chief justice.

[b]The Senate took no action on Thornberry's nomination.

In 1987, President Reagan nominated Robert H. Bork to fill the vacancy created by the resignation of Justice Lewis Powell. Bork testified before the Senate Judiciary Committee for 23 hours. A wide range of interest groups entered the fray, mostly in opposition to the nominee, whose views they claimed were extremist. In the end, following a bitter floor debate, the Senate rejected the president's nomination by a vote of 42 to 58.

Six days after the Senate vote on Bork, the president nominated Judge Douglas H. Ginsburg to the high court. Just nine days later, however, Ginsburg withdrew his nomination after disclosures that he had used marijuana while a law professor at Harvard.

In June 1991, at the end of the Supreme Court's term, Associate Justice Thurgood Marshall announced his retirement from the Court. Shortly thereafter, President Bush announced his nomination of another African American, federal appeals judge Clarence Thomas, to replace Marshall on the Court. Thomas was a conservative, so this decision was consistent with the Bush administration's emphasis on placing conservative judges on the federal bench.

In 1991, after two weeks of riveting hearings in which Clarence Thomas was charged with sexual harassment, the Senate narrowly confirmed his nomination to the Supreme Court. Historically, about one-fifth of those nominated to the Court have failed to obtain confirmation.

The president claimed that he was not employing quotas when he chose another African American to replace the only African American ever to sit on the Supreme Court. Not everyone believed him, but liberals were placed in a dilemma. On the one hand, they favored a minority group member serving on the nation's highest court. On the other hand, Thomas was unlikely to vote the same way as Thurgood Marshall had voted. Instead, Thomas presented the prospect of strengthening the conservative trend in the Court's decisions. In the end, this ambivalence inhibited spirited opposition to Thomas, who was circumspect about his judicial philosophy in his appearances before the Senate Judiciary Committee. The committee sent his nomination to the Senate floor on a split vote.

Just as the Senate was about to vote on the nomination, however, charges of sexual harassment leveled against Thomas by University of Oklahoma law professor Anita Hill were made public. The Judicial Committee reopened hearings on the charges in response to criticism that the Senate was sexist for not seriously considering them in the first place. For several days, citizens sat transfixed before their television sets as Professor Hill calmly and graphically described her recollections of Thomas's behavior. Thomas then emphatically denied any such behavior and charged the Senate with racism for raising the issue. Ultimately, public opinion polls showed that most people believed Thomas, and he was confirmed in a 52-to-48 vote—the closest vote on a Supreme Court nomination in more than a century.

The Senate's treatment of President Clinton's two nominees harks back to the Kennedy era. Neither Ruth Bader Ginsburg nor Stephen Breyer caused much controversy. Similarly, the Senate easily confirmed George W. Bush's nomination of John Roberts as chief justice. Indeed, he was not an easy target to oppose. His pleasing and professional personal demeanor and his disciplined and skilled testimony before the Senate Judicial Committee gave potential opponents little basis for opposition.

Attention immediately turned to George W. Bush's nomination of White House counsel Harriet Miers in October 2005 to replace Justice O'Connor. Bush apparently thought Miers's lack of a published record would make it easier to push her nomination through. What looked like an adroit political decision soon turned sour, however. Many of the president's most passionate supporters had hoped and expected that he would make an unambiguously conservative choice to fulfill their goal of clearly altering the Court's balance, even at the cost of a bitter confirmation battle. By instead settling on a loyalist with no experience as a judge and little substantive record on abortion, affirmative action, religion, and other socially divisive issues, the president shied away from a direct confrontation with liberals and in effect asked his base on the right to trust him on his nomination. Many conservatives were bitterly disappointed and highly critical of the president. They demanded a known conservative and a top-flight legal figure. The nomination also smacked of cronyism, with the president selecting a friend and a loyalist rather than someone of obvious merit. The comparison with Roberts only emphasized the thinness of Miers's qualifications. In short order, Miers withdrew from consideration, and the president nominated Samuel Alito.

Alito was clearly a traditional conservative and had a less impressive public presence than Roberts. Response to him followed party lines, but the nominee appeared too well qualified and unthreatening in his confirmation hearings to justify a filibuster, and without one, his confirmation was assured. The Senate confirmed Alito by a vote of 58 to 42.

It is difficult to predict the politics surrounding future nominations to the Supreme Court. One prediction seems safe, however: As long as Americans are polarized around social issues and as long as the Court makes critical decisions about these issues, the potential for conflict over the president's nominations is always present.

Nominations are most likely to run into trouble under certain conditions. Presidents whose parties are in the minority in the Senate or who make a nomination at the end of their terms face a greatly increased probability of substantial opposition.[10] Presidents whose views are more distant from the norm in the Senate or who are appointing a person who might alter the balance on the Court are also likely to face additional opposition. Equally important, opponents of a nomination usually must be able to question a nominee's competence or ethics in order to defeat a nomination. Most people do not consider opposition to a nominee's ideology a valid reason to vote against confirmation. For example, liberals disagreed strongly with the views of William Rehnquist, but he was easily confirmed as chief justice. Opponents of a nominee must usually raise questions about their legal competence and ethics in order to attract moderate senators to their side and to make ideological protests seem less partisan.

THE BACKGROUNDS OF JUDGES AND JUSTICES

The Constitution sets no special requirements for judges or justices, but most observers conclude that the federal judiciary is composed of a distinguished group of men and women. Competence and ethical behavior are important to presidents for reasons beyond merely obtaining Senate confirmation of their judicial nominees. Skilled and honorable judges and justices reflect well on the president and are likely to do so for many years. Moreover, these individuals are more effective representatives of the president's views. Although the criteria of competence and character screen out some possible candidates, there is still a wide field from which to choose. Other characteristics then carry considerable weight.

The judges serving on the federal district and circuit courts are not a representative sample of the American people (see Table 16.3). They are all lawyers (although this is not a constitutional requirement), and they are overwhelmingly White males. Jimmy

TABLE 16.3

Backgrounds of Recent Federal District and Appeals Court Judges

CHARACTERISTIC	Appeals Court					District Court				
	G. W. BUSH[a]	CLINTON	BUSH	REAGAN	CARTER	G. W. BUSH[a]	CLINTON	BUSH	REAGAN	CARTER
Total number of nominees	49	61	37	78	56	203	305	148	290	202
Occupation (%)										
Politics/government	22	11	6	5	8	12	11	13	4	8
Judiciary	47	53	60	55	47	47	48	42	37	45
Large law firm	12	18	16	14	11	21	15	26	18	14
Moderate-size firm	6	13	11	9	16	10	13	15	19	19
Solo or small firm	4	2	–	1	5	6	8	5	10	14
Professor of law	4	8	3	13	14	2	2	1	2	3
Other	4	–	–	1	2	2	1	1	1	1
Experience (%)										
Judicial	57	59	62	57	54	52	52	47	46	54
Prosecutorial	35	38	30	44	30	54	41	39	44	38
Neither one	29	30	32	24	39	26	29	28	29	31
Party (%)										
Democrat	6	85	5	7	82	7	88	6	5	91
Republican	92	7	89	85	7	85	6	89	92	5
Independent	2	8	8	8	11	8	6	5	3	5
Past party activism (%)	65	54	70	49	73	51	50	64	60	61
Ethnicity or race (%)										
White	82	74	89	82	79	83	75	89	92	79
African American	12	13	5	7	16	6	17	7	2	14
Hispanic	6	12	5	11	4	11	6	4	5	7
Asian	–	2	–	1	2	1	1	–	1	1
Gender (%)										
Male	78	67	81	74	80	80	72	80	92	86
Female	22	33	19	21	20	20	28	20	8	14
Average age	50	51	49	49	52	50	50	48	49	50

[a]As of January 1, 2007.

Source: Adapted from Sheldon Goldman, Elliot Slotnick, Gerard Gryski, and Sara Schiavoni, "Picking Judges in a Time of Turmoil: W. Bush's Judiciary during the 109th Congress," *Judicature* 90, no. 6 (2007).

Carter appointed 40 women, 37 African Americans, and 16 Hispanics to the federal bench, more than all previous presidents combined. Ronald Reagan did not continue this trend, although he was the first to appoint a woman to the Supreme Court. His administration placed a higher priority on screening candidates on the basis of ideology than on screening them in terms of demographic characteristics. From 1989 to 1992, George Bush continued to place conservatives on the bench, but he was much more likely to appoint women and minorities than was Reagan. Bill Clinton nominated Democrats, who were more liberal than the nominees of Reagan and Bush, and a large percentage of them were women and minorities. George W. Bush's nominees were similar to those of his father.

Federal judges have typically held office as a judge or prosecutor, and often they have been involved in partisan politics. This involvement is generally what brings them to the attention of senators and the Department of Justice when they seek nominees for judgeships. As former U.S. Attorney General and Circuit Court Judge Griffin Bell once remarked, "For me, becoming a federal judge wasn't very difficult. I managed John F. Kennedy's presidential campaign in Georgia. Two of my oldest and closest friends were senators from Georgia. And I was campaign manager and special unpaid counsel for the governor."[11]

The backgrounds of federal judges are not representative of Americans. The Supreme Court had been exclusively male until Sandra Day O'Connor became the first woman to serve on the Court in 1981.

Like their colleagues on the lower federal courts, Supreme Court justices share characteristics that qualify them as an elite group. All have been lawyers, and all but four (Thurgood Marshall, nominated in 1967; Sandra Day O'Connor, nominated in 1981; Clarence Thomas, nominated in 1991; and Ruth Bader Ginsburg, nominated in 1993) have been White males. Most have been in their fifties and sixties when they took office, from the upper-middle or upper class, and Protestants.[12]

Race and gender have become more salient criteria in recent years. In the 1980 presidential campaign, Ronald Reagan promised to appoint a woman to the first vacancy on the Court if he were elected. In 1991, President George Bush chose to replace the first African American justice, Thurgood Marshall, with another African American, Clarence Thomas. Women and minorities may serve on all federal courts more frequently in the future because of increased opportunity for legal education and decreased prejudice against their judicial activity as well as because of their increasing political clout.

Geography was once a prominent criterion for selection to the Court, but it is no longer very important. Presidents do like to spread the slots around, however, as when Richard Nixon decided that he wanted to nominate a Southerner. At various times there have been what some have termed a "Jewish seat" and a "Catholic seat" on the Court, but these guidelines are not binding on the president. For example, after a half century of having a Jewish justice, the Court did not have one from 1969 to 1993.

Typically, justices have held high administrative or judicial positions before moving to the Supreme Court (see Table 16.4). Most have had some experience as a judge, often at the appellate level, and many have worked for the Department of Justice. Some have held elective office, and a few have had no government service but have been distinguished attorneys. The fact that many justices, including some of the most distinguished ones, have not had previous judicial experience may seem surprising, but the unique work of the Court renders this background much less important than it might be for other appellate courts.

TABLE 16.4

Supreme Court Justices, 2009

NAME	YEAR OF BIRTH	PREVIOUS POSITION	NOMINATING PRESIDENT	YEAR OF CONFIRMATION
John G. Roberts Jr.	1955	U.S. Court of Appeals	G. W. Bush	2005
John Paul Stevens	1920	U.S. Court of Appeals	Ford	1975
Antonin Scalia	1936	U.S. Court of Appeals	Reagan	1986
Anthony M. Kennedy	1936	U.S. Court of Appeals	Reagan	1988
David H. Souter	1939	U.S. Court of Appeals	Bush	1990
Clarence Thomas	1948	U.S. Court of Appeals	Bush	1991
Ruth Bader Ginsburg	1933	U.S. Court of Appeals	Clinton	1993
Stephen G. Breyer	1938	U.S. Court of Appeals	Clinton	1994
Samuel A. Alito Jr.	1950	U.S. Court of Appeals	G. W. Bush	2006

Partisanship is another important influence on the selection of judges and justices. Only 13 of 110 members of the Supreme Court have been nominated by presidents of a different party. Moreover, many of the 13 exceptions were actually close to the president in ideology, as was the case in Richard Nixon's appointment of Lewis Powell. Herbert Hoover's nomination of Benjamin Cardozo seems to be one of the few cases in which partisanship was completely dominated by merit as a criterion for selection. Usually more than 90 percent of presidents' judicial nominations are of members of their own parties.

The role of partisanship is really not surprising. Most of a president's acquaintances are made through the party, and there is usually a certain congruity between party and political views. Most judges and justices have at one time been active partisans—an experience that gave them visibility and helped them obtain the positions from which they moved to the courts.

Judgeships are also considered very prestigious patronage plums. Indeed, the decisions of Congress to create new judgeships—and thus new positions for party members—are closely related to whether the majority party in Congress is the same as the party of the president. Members of the majority party in the legislature want to avoid providing an opposition party president with new positions to fill with their opponents.

Ideology is as important as partisanship in the selection of judges and justices. Presidents want to appoint to the federal bench people who share their views. In effect, all presidents try to "pack" the courts. They want more than "justice"; they want policies with which they agree. Presidential aides survey candidates' decisions (if they have served on a lower court),[13] speeches, political stands, writings, and other expressions of opinion. They also glean information from people who know the candidates well. Although it is considered improper to question judicial candidates about upcoming court cases, it is appropriate to discuss broader questions of political and judicial philosophy. The Reagan administration was especially concerned about such matters and had each potential nominee fill out a lengthy questionnaire and be interviewed by a special committee in the Department of Justice. Like its predecessor, the George Bush administration was attentive to appointing conservative judges. Bill Clinton was less concerned with the ideology of his nominees, at least partly to avoid costly confirmation fights. Instead, he focused on identifying persons with strong legal credentials, especially women and minorities. George W. Bush reverted to the Reagan policy of naming clear conservatives to the federal courts.

Members of the federal bench also play the game of politics, of course, and may try to time their retirements so that a president with compatible views will choose their

The U.S. Supreme Court, 2009: Front row, left to right: Anthony M. Kennedy, John Paul Stevens, John G. Roberts, Antonin Scalia, and David H. Souter. Second row, left to right: Stephen G. Breyer, Clarence Thomas, Ruth Bader Ginsburg, and Samuel Alito.

successor. This is one reason why justices remain on the Supreme Court for so long, even when they are clearly infirm. William Howard Taft, a rigid conservative, even feared that a successor would be named by Herbert Hoover, a more moderate conservative.[14]

Presidents are typically pleased with the performance of their nominees to the Supreme Court and through them have slowed or reversed trends in the Court's decisions. Franklin D. Roosevelt's nominees substantially liberalized the Court, whereas Richard Nixon's turned it in a conservative direction.

Nevertheless, it is not always easy to predict the policy inclinations of candidates, and presidents have been disappointed in their nominees about one-fourth of the time. President Eisenhower, for example, was displeased with the liberal decisions of both Earl Warren and William Brennan. Once, when asked whether he had made any mistakes as president, he replied, "Yes, two, and they are both sitting on the Supreme Court."[15] Richard Nixon was certainly disappointed when Warren Burger, whom he had nominated as chief justice, wrote the Court's decision calling for immediate desegregation of the nation's schools shortly after his confirmation. This turn of events did little for the president's "Southern strategy." Burger also wrote the Court's opinion in *United States v. Nixon*, which forced the president to release the Watergate tapes. Nixon's resignation soon followed.

Presidents influence policy through the values of their judicial nominees, but this impact is limited by numerous legal and "extralegal" factors beyond the chief executive's control. As Harry Truman put it, "Packing the Supreme Court can't be done . . . I've tried it and it won't work. . . . Whenever you put a man on the Supreme Court, he ceases to be your friend. I'm sure of that."[16]

There is no doubt that various women's, racial, ethnic, and religious groups desire to have their members appointed to the federal bench. At the very least, judgeships have symbolic importance for them.[17] Presidents face many of the same pressures for representativeness in selecting judges that they experience when they name their cabinet.

What is less clear is what policy differences result when presidents nominate persons with different backgrounds to the bench. The number of female and minority group judges is too few and their service too recent to serve as a sound basis for generalizations about their decisions. Many members of each party have been appointed, of course, and it appears that Republican judges in general are somewhat more conservative than Democratic judges. Former prosecutors serving on the Supreme Court have tended to be less sympathetic toward defendants' rights than other justices. It seems that background does make some difference,[18] yet for reasons that we examine in the following sections, on many issues, party affiliation and other characteristics bring no more predictability to the courts than they do to Congress.

THE COURTS AS POLICYMAKERS

"Judicial decision making," a former Supreme Court law clerk wrote in the *Harvard Law Review*, "involves, at bottom, a choice between competing values by fallible, pragmatic, and at times nonrational men and women in a highly complex process in a very human setting."[19] This is an apt description of policymaking in the Supreme Court and in other courts, too. The next sections look at how courts make policy, paying particular attention to the role of the U.S. Supreme Court. Although it is not the only court involved in policymaking and policy interpretation, its decisions have the widest implications for policy.

ACCEPTING CASES

Deciding what to decide about is the first step in all policymaking. Courts of original jurisdiction cannot very easily refuse to consider a case; appeals courts, including the U.S. Supreme Court, have much more control over their agendas. The approximately 8,000 cases submitted annually to the U.S. Supreme Court must be read, culled, and sifted. Figure 16.3 shows the stages of this process. At least once each week, the nine justices meet in conference. With them in the conference room sit some 25 carts, each wheeled in from the office of one of the nine justices and each filled with petitions, briefs, memoranda, and every item the justices are likely to need during their discussions. These meetings operate under the strictest secrecy; only the justices themselves attend.

At these weekly conferences the justices must hammer out two important matters. First is an agenda: The justices consider the chief justice's "discuss list" and decide which cases they want to discuss. Because few of the justices can take the time to read materials on every case submitted to the Court, most rely heavily on law clerks (each justice has up to four to assist them in considering cases and writing opinions) to screen each case. If four justices agree to grant review of a case (the "rule of four"), it can be scheduled for oral argument or decided on the basis of the written record already on file with the Court.

The most common way for the Court to put a case on its docket is by issuing to a lower federal or state court a *writ of certiorari*, a formal document that calls up a case. Until 1988, some cases—principally those in which federal laws had been found unconstitutional, in which federal courts had concluded that state laws violated the federal Constitution, or in which state laws had been upheld in state courts despite claims that they violated federal law or the Constitution—were technically supposed to be heard by the Court "on appeal." In reality, however, the Court always exercised broad discretion over hearing these and other cases.

Cases that involve major issues—especially civil liberties, conflict between different lower courts on the interpretation of federal law (as when a circuit court of

Case Overload

You Are a Clerk to Supreme Court Justice Judith Gray

FIGURE 16.3

Obtaining Space on the Supreme Court's Docket

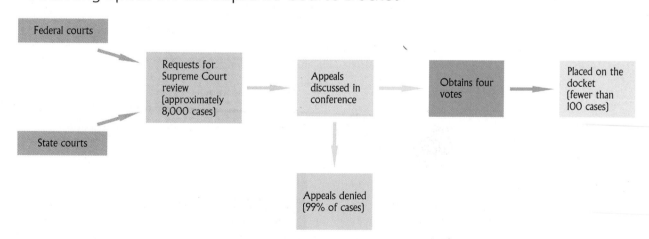

appeals in Texas prohibits the use of affirmative action criteria in college admissions and a court of appeals in Michigan approves them), or disagreement between a majority of the Supreme Court and lower-court decisions—are likely to be selected by the Court.[20]

Because getting into the Supreme Court is half the battle, it is important to remember this chapter's earlier discussion of standing to sue (litigants must have serious interest in a case, having sustained or being in immediate danger of sustaining a direct and substantial injury from another party or an action of government)— a criterion the Court often uses to decide whether to hear a case. In addition, the Court has used other means to avoid deciding cases that are too politically "hot" to handle or that divide the Court too sharply,[21] as we discuss later in this chapter.

Another important influence on the Supreme Court is the **solicitor general**. As a presidential appointee and the third-ranking official in the Department of Justice, the solicitor general is in charge of the appellate court litigation of the federal government. The solicitor general and a staff of about two dozen experienced attorneys have four key functions: (1) to decide whether to appeal cases the government has lost in the lower courts, (2) to review and modify the briefs presented in government appeals, (3) to represent the government before the Supreme Court, and (4) to submit a brief on behalf of a litigant in a case in which the government is not directly involved.[22] Unlike attorneys for private parties, the solicitors general are careful to seek Court review only of important cases. By avoiding frivolous appeals and displaying a high degree of competence, they typically earn the confidence of the Court, which in turn grants review of a large percentage of the cases they submit.[23]

Ultimately, the Supreme Court decides very few cases. In recent years, the Court has made about 80 formal written decisions per year in which their opinions could serve as precedent and thus as the basis of guidance for lower courts. In a few dozen additional cases, the Court reaches a *per curiam decision*—that is, a decision without explanation. Such decisions resolve the immediate case but have no value as precedent because the Court does not offer reasoning that would guide lower courts in future decisions.[24]

solicitor general

A presidential appointee and the third-ranking office in the Department of Justice. The solicitor general is in charge of the appellate court litigation of the federal government.

MAKING DECISIONS

The second task of the justices' weekly conferences is to discuss cases actually accepted and argued before the Court. Beginning the first Monday in October and lasting until June, the Court hears oral arguments in two-week cycles: two weeks of courtroom arguments followed by two weeks of reflecting on cases and writing opinions about them. Figure 16.4 shows the stages in this process.

Before the justices enter the courtroom to hear the lawyers for each side present their arguments, they have received elaborately prepared written briefs from each party involved. They have also probably received several *amicus curiae* briefs from parties (often groups) who are interested in the outcome of the case but who are not formal litigants.

FIGURE 16.4

The Supreme Court's Decision-Making Process

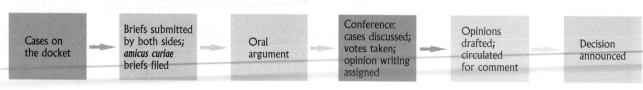

| Cases on the docket | Briefs submitted by both sides; *amicus curiae* briefs filed | Oral argument | Conference: cases discussed; votes taken; opinion writing assigned | Opinions drafted; circulated for comment | Decision announced |

Amicus curiae briefs have another important role: The government, under the direction of the solicitor general, may submit them in cases in which it has an interest. For instance, a case between two parties may involve the question of the constitutionality of a federal law. The federal government naturally wants to have its voice heard on such matters, even if it is not formally a party to the case. These briefs are also a means to urge the Court to change established doctrine. For example, the Reagan administration frequently submitted *amicus curiae* briefs to the Court to try to change the law dealing with defendants' rights.

In most instances, the attorneys for each side have only a half-hour to address the Court. During this time they summarize their briefs, emphasizing their most compelling points.[25] The justices may listen attentively, interrupt with penetrating or helpful questions, request information, talk to one another, read (presumably briefs), or simply gaze at the ceiling. After 25 minutes, a white light comes on at the lectern from which the lawyer is speaking, and five minutes later a red light signals the end of that lawyer's presentation, even if he or she is in midsentence. Oral argument is over.[26]

Back in the conference room, the chief justice, who presides over the Court, raises a particular case and invites discussion, turning first to the senior associate justice. Discussion can range from perfunctory to profound and from courteous to caustic. If the votes are not clear from the individual discussions, the chief justice may ask each justice to vote. Once a tentative vote has been reached, it is necessary to write an **opinion**, a statement of the legal reasoning behind the decision.

Opinion writing is no mere formality. In fact, the content of an opinion may be as important as the decision itself. Broad and bold opinions have far-reaching implications for future cases; narrowly drawn opinions may have little impact beyond the case being decided. Tradition in the Supreme Court requires that the chief justice, if in the majority, write the opinion or assign it to another justice in the majority. The chief justice often writes the opinion in landmark cases, as Earl Warren did in *Brown v. Board of Education* and Warren Burger did in *United States v. Nixon*. If the chief justice is part of the minority, the senior associate justice in the majority assigns the opinion. The person assigned to write an opinion circulates drafts within the Court, justices make suggestions, and they all conduct negotiations among themselves.[27] The content of the opinion can win or lose votes. A justice must redraft an opinion that proves unacceptable to the majority of his or her colleagues on the Court.

Justices are free to write their own opinions, to join in other opinions, or to associate themselves with part of one opinion and part of another. Justices opposed to all or part of the majority's decision write *dissenting opinions*. *Concurring opinions* are those written not only to support a majority decision but also to stress a different constitutional or legal basis for the judgment.

When the justices have written their opinions and taken the final vote, they announce their decision. At least six justices must participate in a case, and decisions are made by majority vote. If there is a tie (because of a vacancy on the Court or because a justice chooses not to participate), the decision of the lower court from which the case came is sustained. Five votes in agreement on the reasoning underlying an opinion are necessary for the logic to serve as precedent for judges of lower courts.

opinion
A statement of legal reasoning behind a judicial decision. The content of an opinion may be as important as the decision itself.

The content of a Supreme Court opinion may be as important as the decision itself, and justices may spend months negotiating a majority opinion. Here, William H. Rehnquist, former chief justice of the Supreme Court, prepares a written opinion.

The vast majority of cases that reach the courts are settled on the principle of **stare decisis** ("let the decision stand"), meaning that an earlier decision should hold for the case being considered. All courts rely heavily on **precedent**—the way similar cases were handled in the past—as a guide to current decisions. Lower courts, of course, are expected to follow the precedents of higher courts in their decision making. If the Supreme Court, for example, rules in favor of the right to abortion under certain conditions, it has established a precedent that lower courts are expected to follow. Lower courts have much less discretion than the Supreme Court.

The Supreme Court is in a position to overrule its own precedents, and it has done so more than 200 times.[28] One of the most famous of such instances occurred with *Brown v. Board of Education* (1954) (see Chapter 5), in which the court overruled *Plessy v. Ferguson* (1896) and found that segregation in the public schools violated the Constitution.

"Call it 'legislating from the bench,' if you will, but on this occasion I should like to repeal the First Amendment."

What happens when precedents are unclear? This is especially a problem for the Supreme Court, which is more likely than other courts to handle cases at the forefront of the law. Precedent is typically less firmly established on these matters. Moreover, the justices are often asked to apply to concrete situations the vague phrases of the Constitution ("due process of law," "equal protection," "unreasonable searches and seizures") or vague statutes passed by Congress. This ambiguity provides leeway for the justices to disagree (only about one-third of the cases in which full opinions are handed down are decided unanimously) and for their values to influence their judgment.

As a result, it is often easy to identify consistent patterns in the decisions of justices. For example, if there is division on the Court (indicating that precedent is not clear) and you can identify a conservative side to the issue at hand, it is likely that Clarence Thomas will be on that side. Ruth Bader Ginsburg may very well be voting on the other side of the issue. Liberalism and conservatism have several dimensions, including freedom, equality, and economic regulation.

The point is that policy preferences do matter in judicial decision making, especially on the nation's highest court[29] (see "You Are the Policymaker: The Debate over Original Intentions").

The Court conveys its decisions to the press as they announce them formally in open court. Media coverage of the Court remains primitive—short and shallow. Doris Graber reports that "much reporting on the courts—even at the Supreme Court level—is imprecise and sometimes even wrong."[30] More important to the legal community, the decisions are bound weekly and made available to every law library and lawyer in the United States. There is, of course, an air of finality to the public announcement of a decision. In fact, however, even Supreme Court decisions are not self-implementing; they are actually "remands" to lower courts, instructing them to act in accordance with the Court's decisions.

IMPLEMENTING COURT DECISIONS

Reacting bitterly to one of Chief Justice Marshall's decisions, President Andrew Jackson is said to have grumbled, "John Marshall has made his decision; now let him enforce it." Court decisions carry legal, even moral, authority, but courts must rely on other units of government to enforce their decisions. **Judicial implementation**

YOU ARE THE Policymaker

The Debate over Original Intentions

The most contentious issue involving the courts is the role of judicial discretion. According to Christopher Wolfe, "The Constitution itself nowhere specifies a particular set of rules by which it is to be interpreted. Where does one go, then, in order to discover the proper way to interpret the Constitution?"

Some have argued for a jurisprudence of **original intent** (sometimes referred to as *strict constructionism*). This view holds that judges and justices should attempt to determine the intent of the Framers of the Constitution regarding a particular matter and decide cases in line with that intent. Such a view is popular with conservatives.

Advocates of strict constructionism view it as a means of constraining the exercise of judicial discretion, which they see as the foundation of the liberal decisions, especially on matters of civil liberties, civil rights, and defendants' rights (discussed in Chapters 4 and 5).

They also see following original intent as the only basis of interpretation consistent with democracy. Judges, they argue, should not dress up constitutional interpretations with *their* views on "contemporary needs," "today's conditions," or "what is right." It is the job of legislators, not judges, to make such judgments.

Other jurists, such as former Justice William Brennan, disagree. They maintain that what appears to be deference to the intentions of the Framers is simply a cover for making conservative decisions. Opponents of original intent assert that the Constitution is subject to multiple meanings by thoughtful people in different ages. Judges will differ in time and place about what they think the Constitution means. Thus, basing decisions on original intent is not likely to have much effect on judicial discretion.

In addition, Brennan and his supporters contend that the Constitution is not like a paint-by-numbers kit. Trying to reconstruct or guess the Framers' intentions is very difficult. Recent key cases before the Supreme Court have concerned issues such as school busing, abortions, the Internet, and wiretapping that the Framers could not have imagined; there were no public schools or buses, no contraceptives or modern abortion techniques, and certainly no computers or electronic surveillance equipment or telephones in 1787.

The Founders embraced general principles, not specific solutions when they wrote the Constitution. They frequently lacked discrete, discoverable intent. Moreover, there is often no record of their intentions, nor is it clear whose intentions should count—those of the writers of the Constitution, those of the more than 1,600 members who attended the ratifying conventions, or those of the voters who sent them there. This problem grows more complex when you consider the amendments to the Constitution, which involve thousands of additional "Framers."

Historian Jack N. Rakove points out that there is little historical evidence that the Framers believed their intentions should guide later interpretations of the Constitution. In fact, there is some evidence for believing that Madison—the key delegate—left the Constitutional Convention bitterly disappointed with the results. What if Madison had one set of intentions but—like anyone working in a committee—got a different set of results?

The lines are drawn. On one side is the argument that any deviation from following the original intentions of the Constitution's Framers is a deviation from principle, leaving unelected judges to impose their views on the American people. If judges do not follow original intentions, then on what do they base their decisions?

On the other side are those who believe that it is often impossible to discern the views of the Framers and that there is no good reason to be constrained by the views of the eighteenth century, which reflect a more limited conception of constitutional rights. In order to cope with current needs, they argue, it is necessary to adapt the principles in the Constitution to the demands of each era.

The choice here is at the very heart of the judicial process. If you were a justice sitting on the Supreme Court and were asked to interpret the meaning of the Constitution, what would *you* do?

Sources: Christopher Wolfe, *The Rise of Modern Judicial Review* (New York: Basic Books, 1986); Raoul Berger, *Government by Judiciary: The Transformation of the Fourteenth Amendment* (Cambridge, MA: Harvard University Press, 1977); Traciel V. Reid, "A Critique of Interpretivism and Its Claimed Influence upon Judicial Decision Making," *American Politics Quarterly* 16 (July 1988): 329–56; Jack N. Rakove, ed., *Interpreting the Constitution* (Boston: Northeastern University Press, 1990); Arthur S. Miller, "In Defense of Judicial Activism," in *Supreme Court Activism and Restraint*, ed. Stephen C. Halpern and Charles M. Lamb (Lexington, MA: D.C. Heath, 1982); Stephen Breyer, *Active Liberty: Interpreting Our Democratic Constitution* (New York: Knopf, 2005); Antonin Scalia, *A Matter of Interpretation: Federal Courts and the Law* (Princeton, NJ: Princeton University Press, 1998).

refers to how and whether court decisions are translated into actual policy, thereby affecting the behavior of others.

Judicial decision is the end of one process—the litigation process—and the beginning of another process—the process of judicial implementation. Sometimes delay and stalling follow even decisive court decisions. There is, for

original intent

A view that the Constitution should be interpreted according to the original intent of the Framers. Many conservatives support this view.

Virgil Hawkins's unsuccessful struggle to attend the all-White University of Florida Law School illustrates how judicial implementation can affect the impact of court decisions. The Supreme Court ordered the school to admit Hawkins in 1956, but the school and state refused to implement the ruling, and continued to appeal the case. Two years later a Florida district court again denied admission to Hawkins, although it did order the school's desegregation.

example, the story of the tortured efforts of a young African American named Virgil Hawkins to get himself admitted to the University of Florida Law School. Hawkins's efforts began in 1949, when he first applied for admission, and ended unsuccessfully in 1958, after a decade of court decisions. Despite a 1956 order from the U.S. Supreme Court to admit Hawkins, continued legal skirmishing produced a 1958 decision by a U.S. district court in Florida ordering the admission of non-Whites but upholding the denial of admission to Hawkins himself. Other courts and other institutions of government can be roadblocks in the way of judicial implementation.

Charles Johnson and Bradley Canon suggest that implementation of court decisions involves several elements.[31] First, there is an *interpreting population*, heavily composed of lawyers and judges. They must correctly understand and reflect the intent of the original decision in their subsequent actions. Usually lower-court judges do follow the Supreme Court, but sometimes they circumvent higher-court decisions to satisfy their own policy interests.[32]

Second, there is an *implementing population*. Suppose the Supreme Court held (as it did) that prayers organized by school officials in the public schools are unconstitutional. The implementing population (school boards and school administrators) must then actually abandon prayers. Police departments, hospitals, corporations, government agencies—all may be part of the implementing population. With so many implementors, many of whom may disagree with a decision, there is plenty of room for "slippage" between what the Supreme Court decides and what actually occurs. Judicial decisions are more likely to be implemented smoothly if implementation is concentrated in the hands of a few highly visible officials, such as the president or state legislators.

Even then, the courts may face difficulties. Responding to the *Brown* decision ending legal segregation in the nation's public schools (see Chapter 4), and abetted by changes in Virginia laws, in 1959 the Board of Supervisors for Prince Edward County refused to appropriate *any* funds for the County School Board at all. This action effectively closed all public schools in the county to avoid integrating them. The schools remained closed for five years until the legal process finally forced them to reopen. Third, every decision involves a *consumer population*. The potential "consumers" of an abortion decision are those who want abortions (and those who oppose them); the consumers of the *Miranda* decision (see Chapter 4) are criminal defendants and their attorneys. The consumer population must be aware of its new-found rights and stand up for them.

Congress and presidents can also help or hinder judicial implementation. The Supreme Court held in 1954 that segregated schools were "inherently unconstitutional" and the next year ordered public schools desegregated "with all deliberate speed." President Eisenhower refused to state clearly that Americans should comply with this famous decision in *Brown v. Board of Education*, which may have encouraged local school boards to resist the decision. Congress was not much help either; only a decade later, in the wake of the civil rights movement discussed in Chapter 5, did it pass legislation denying federal aid to segregated schools. Different presidents have different commitments to a particular judicial policy. After years of court and presidential decisions supporting busing to end racial segregation, in December

Why It Matters
The Lack of a Judicial Bureaucracy
The federal courts lack a bureaucracy to implement their decisions. In fact, some of the Supreme Court's most controversial decisions, such as those dealing with school integration and school prayers, have been implemented only with great difficulty. If the courts had a bureaucracy to enforce their decisions, justice might be better served, but such a bureaucracy would have to be enormous to monitor, for example, every school and police station.

1984 the Reagan administration went before the Supreme Court and argued *against* school busing in a case in Norfolk, Virginia.

THE COURTS AND THE POLICY AGENDA

Even though American courts and judges work largely alone and in isolation from daily contact with other political institutions, they play a key role in shaping the policy agenda. Ultimately, their decisions affect us all (see "Young People and Politics: The Supreme Court Is Closer Than You Think"). Like all policymakers, the courts are choice takers. Confronted with controversial policies, they make controversial decisions that leave some people winners and others losers. The courts have made policy about slavery and segregation, corporate power and capital punishment, and dozens of other controversial matters.

A HISTORICAL REVIEW

Until the Civil War, the dominant questions before the Court concerned the strength and legitimacy of the federal government and slavery. These issues of nation building were resolved in favor of the supremacy of the national government. From the Civil War until 1937, questions of the relationship between the federal

YOUNG PEOPLE AND POLITICS

The Supreme Court Is Closer Than You Think

The Supreme Court of the United States may seem remote and not especially relevant to a college student. Yet a surprising number of its most important decisions have been brought by young adults seeking protection for their civil rights and liberties. For example, we saw in Chapter 5 that in *Rostker v. Goldberg* (1981) several young men filed a suit claiming that the Military Selective Service Act's requirement that only males register for the draft was unconstitutional. Although the Court held that the requirement was constitutional, draft registration was suspended temporarily during the suit.

Students were the center of *Board of Regents of University of Wisconsin System v. Southworth* (2000), in which the Court upheld the University of Wisconsin's requirement of a fee to fund speakers on campus—even if the speakers advocated views that offended some students. The right of the police to search newspaper files was fought over the actions of a campus newspaper in *Zurcher v. Stanford Daily* (1978). In 1992, the Supreme Court ruled that legislatures and universities may not single out racial, religious, or sexual insults or threats for prosecution as "hate speech" or "bias crimes" (*R.A.V. v. St. Paul*). From Gregory Johnson's burning an American flag at the 1984 Republican National Convention to protest nuclear arms buildup (which the Court protected in *Texas v. Johnson* [1989]) to burning a draft card (which the Court did not protect in *United States v. O'Brien*

[1968]), young adults have also been pioneers in the area of symbolic speech.

Issues of religious freedom have also prominently featured college students. In *Widmar v. Vincent* (1981), the Court decided that public universities that permit student groups to use their facilities must allow student religious groups on campus to use the facilities for religious worship. In 1995, the Court held that the University of Virginia was constitutionally required to subsidize a student religious magazine on the same basis as other student publications (*Rosenberger v. University of Virginia*). However, in 2004 the Court held that the state of Washington was within its rights when it excluded students pursuing a devotional theology degree from its general scholarship program (*Locke v. Davey*).

Thus, the Supreme Court has a long history of dealing with issues of importance to young adults. Often it is young adults themselves who initiate the cases—and who take them all the way to the nation's highest court.

QUESTIONS FOR DISCUSSION

▶ Why do you think cases involving young people tend to involve civil liberties issues?

▶ What other issues of particular importance to young people should the Supreme Court decide?

John Marshall, chief justice from 1801 to 1835, established the Supreme Court's power of judicial review in the 1803 case *Marbury v. Madison*. In their ruling on the case, Marshall and his associates declared that the Court has the power to determine the constitutionality of congressional actions.

TIMELINE

Chief Justices of the Supreme Court

Marbury v. Madison
The 1803 case in which Chief Justice John Marshall and his associates first asserted the right of the Supreme Court to determine the meaning of the U.S. Constitution. The decision established the Court's power of judicial review over acts of Congress, in this case the Judiciary Act of 1789.

government and the economy predominated. During this period, the Court restricted the power of the federal government to regulate the economy. From 1938 to the present, the paramount issues before the Court have concerned personal liberty and social and political equality. In this era, the Court has enlarged the scope of personal freedom and civil rights and has removed many of the constitutional restraints on the regulation of the economy.

Few justices played a more important role in making the Court a significant national agenda setter than John Marshall, chief justice from 1801 to 1835. His successors have continued not only to respond to the political agenda but also to shape discussion and debate about it.

John Marshall and the Growth of Judicial Review

Scarcely was the government housed in its new capital when Federalists and Democratic-Republicans clashed over the courts. In the election of 1800, Democratic-Republican Thomas Jefferson beat Federalist incumbent John Adams. Determined to leave at least the judiciary in trusted hands, Adams tried to fill it with Federalists. He is alleged to have stayed at his desk until 9:00 P.M. signing commissions on his last night in the White House (March 3, 1801).

In the midst of this flurry, Adams appointed William Marbury to the minor post of justice of the peace in the District of Columbia. In the rush of last-minute business, however, Secretary of State John Marshall failed to deliver commissions to Marbury and 16 others. He left the commissions to be delivered by the incoming secretary of state, James Madison.

Madison and Jefferson were furious at Adams's actions and refused to deliver the commissions. Marbury and three others in the same situation sued Madison, asking the Supreme Court to order Madison to give them their commissions. They took their case directly to the Supreme Court under the Judiciary Act of 1789, which gave the Court original jurisdiction in such matters.

The new chief justice was none other than Adams's former secretary of state and arch-Federalist John Marshall, himself one of the "midnight appointments" (he took his seat on the Court barely three weeks before Adams's term ended). Marshall and his Federalist colleagues were in a tight spot. Threats of impeachment came from Jeffersonians fearful that the Court would vote for Marbury. Moreover, if the Court ordered Madison to deliver the commissions, he was likely to ignore the order, putting the nation's highest court at risk over a minor issue. Marshall had no means of compelling Madison to act.

The Court could also deny Marbury's claim. Taking that option, however, would concede the issue to the Jeffersonians and give the appearance of retreat in the face of opposition, thereby reducing the power of the Court.

Marshall devised a shrewd solution to the case of **Marbury v. Madison**. In February 1803, he delivered the unanimous opinion of the Court. First, Marshall and his colleagues argued that Madison was wrong to withhold Marbury's commission. The Court also found, however, that the Judiciary Act of 1789, under which Marbury had brought suit, contradicted the plain words of the Constitution about the Court's

original jurisdiction. Thus, Marshall dismissed Marbury's claim, saying that the Court, according to the Constitution, had no power to require that the commission be delivered.

Conceding a small battle over Marbury's commission (he did not get it), Marshall won a much larger war, asserting for the courts the power to determine what is and what is not constitutional. As Marshall wrote, "An act of the legislature repugnant to the Constitution is void," and "it is emphatically the province and duty of the judicial department to say what the law is." The chief justice established the power of **judicial review**, the power of the courts to hold acts of Congress and, by implication, the executive in violation of the Constitution.

Marbury v. Madison was part of a skirmish between the Federalists on the Court and the Democratic-Republican–controlled Congress. Partly to rein in the Supreme Court, for example, the Jeffersonian Congress in 1801 abolished the lower federal appeals courts and made the Supreme Court judges return to the unpleasant task of "riding circuit"—serving as lower-court judges around the country. This was an act of studied harassment of the Court by its enemies.

After *Marbury*, angry members of Congress, together with other Jeffersonians, claimed that Marshall was a "usurper of power," setting himself above Congress and the president. This view, however, was unfair. State courts, before and after the Constitution, had declared acts of their legislatures unconstitutional. In the *Federalist Papers*, Alexander Hamilton had expressly assumed the power of the federal courts to review legislation, and the federal courts had actually done so. *Marbury* was not even the first case to strike down an act of Congress; a lower federal court had done so in 1792, and the Supreme Court itself had approved a law after a constitutional review in 1796. Marshall was neither inventing nor imagining his right to review laws for their constitutionality.

The case also illustrates that the courts must be politically astute in exercising their power over the other branches. By in effect reducing its *own* power—the authority to hear cases such as Marbury's under its original jurisdiction—the Court was able to assert the right of judicial review in a fashion that the other branches could not easily rebuke.

More than any other power of the courts, judicial review has embroiled them in policy controversy. Before the Civil War, the Supreme Court, headed by Chief Justice Roger Taney, held the Missouri Compromise unconstitutional because it restricted slavery in the territories. The decision was one of many steps along the road to the Civil War. After the Civil War, the Court was again active, this time using judicial review to strike down dozens of state and federal laws curbing the growing might of business corporations.

The "Nine Old Men"

Never was the Court so controversial as during the New Deal. At President Roosevelt's urging, Congress passed dozens of laws designed to end the Depression. However, conservatives (most nominated by Republican presidents), who viewed federal intervention in the economy as unconstitutional and tantamount to socialism, dominated the Court.

The Supreme Court began to dismantle New Deal policies one by one. The National Industrial Recovery Act was one of a string of anti-Depression measures. Although it was never particularly popular, the Court sealed its doom in *Schechter Poultry Corporation v. United States* (1935), declaring the act unconstitutional because it regulated purely local business that did not affect interstate commerce.

Incensed, Roosevelt in 1937 proposed what critics called a "court-packing plan." Noting that the average age of the Court was over 70, Roosevelt railed against those "nine old men." The Constitution gave the justices lifetime jobs (see "America in Perspective: The Tenure of Supreme Court Judges"), but

judicial review
The power of the courts to determine whether acts of Congress and, by implication, the executive are in accord with the U.S. Constitution. Judicial review was established by John Marshall and his associates in *Marbury v. Madison*.

AMERICA IN PERSPECTIVE

The Tenure of Supreme Court Judges

The U.S. Supreme Court plays a crucial role in American government, and federal judges, including Supreme Court justices, have tenure for life. As a result, the average age of U.S. justices is high, and there are typically many justices who are over 75 years old. Life tenure also means that there are fewer changes of justices than there would be in a system with shorter terms.

Interestingly, *every* other established democracy provides for some limits on the tenure of judges on its highest constitutional court. Here are some examples:

Country	Term for Judges on Highest Constitutional Court
France	9-year non-renewable term
Italy	9-year non-renewable term
Portugal	9-year non-renewable term
Spain	9-year non-renewable term
Germany	12-year term, must retire at 68
Japan	10-year term, must retire at 70; voters vote to renew justices every 10 years
India	serve under good behavior up to age 65
Australia	serve under good behavior up to age 70
Canada	serve under good behavior up to age 75

DISCUSSION QUESTIONS:

▶ If a constitutional convention were reconvened today, would we still opt for life tenure?

▶ Do you agree with Alexander Hamilton's argument in Federalist #78 that life tenure was an excellent means of securing "a steady, upright, and impartial administration of the laws"?

Source: Steven G. Calabresi and James Lindgren, "Term Limits for the Supreme Court: Life Tenure Reconsidered," *Harvard Journal of Law and Public Policy* 29 (Summer 2006), pp. 819-822

Congress can determine the number of justices. Thus, FDR proposed that Congress expand the size of the Court, a move that would have allowed him to appoint additional justices sympathetic to the New Deal. Congress objected and never passed the plan. It became irrelevant, however, when two justices, Chief Justice Charles Evans Hughes and Associate Justice Owen Roberts, began switching their votes in favor of New Deal legislation. (One wit called it the "switch in time that saved nine.") Shortly thereafter, Associate Justice William Van Devanter retired, and Roosevelt got to make the first of his many appointments to the Court.

The Warren Court Few eras of the Supreme Court have been as active in shaping public policy as that of the Warren Court (1953–1969), presided over by Chief Justice Earl Warren. Scarcely had President Eisenhower appointed Warren when the Court faced the issue of school segregation. In 1954, it held that laws requiring segregation of the public schools were unconstitutional. Later it expanded the rights of criminal defendants, extending the right to counsel and protections against unreasonable search and seizure and self-incrimination (see Chapter 4). It ordered states to reapportion both their legislatures and their congressional districts according to the principle of one person, one vote, and it prohibited organized prayer in public schools. So active was the Warren Court that right-wing groups, fearing that it was remaking the country, posted billboards all over the United States urging Congress to "Impeach Earl Warren."[33]

The Burger Court Warren's retirement in 1969 gave President Richard Nixon his hoped-for opportunity to appoint a "strict constructionist"—that is, one who interprets the Constitution narrowly—as chief justice. He chose Minnesotan Warren E. Burger, then a conservative judge on the District of Columbia Court of Appeals. As Nixon hoped, the Burger Court turned out to be more conservative than the liberal Warren Court. It narrowed defendants' rights, though it did not overturn the fundamental contours of the *Miranda* decision. The conservative Burger Court, however, also wrote the abortion decision in *Roe v. Wade*, required school busing in certain cases to eliminate historic segregation, and upheld affirmative action programs in the *Weber* case (see Chapter 5). One of the most notable decisions of the Burger Court weighed against Burger's appointer, Richard Nixon. At the height of the Watergate scandal (see Chapter 13), the Supreme Court was called on to decide whether Nixon had to turn his White House tapes over to the courts. It unanimously ordered him to do so in **United States v. Nixon** (1974), thus hastening the president's resignation.

> **United States v. Nixon**
> The 1974 case in which the Supreme Court unanimously held that the doctrine of executive privilege was implicit in the Constitution but could not be extended to protect documents relevant to criminal prosecutions.

The Rehnquist Court   By the late 1990s, the conservative nominees of Republican presidents, led by Chief Justice William Rehnquist, composed a clear Supreme Court majority. Like the Burger Court, it was conservative, and like both the Warren and the Burger Courts, it was neither deferential to Congress nor reluctant to enter the political fray. The Court's decision in *Bush v. Gore* (2000) that decided the 2000 presidential election certainly represents a high point of judicial activism.

However one evaluates the Court's direction, in most cases the Rehnquist Court did not create a revolution in constitutional law. Instead, as discussed in Chapters 4 and 5, it limited rather than reversed rights established by liberal decisions such as those regarding defendants' rights and abortion. Although its protection of the First Amendment rights of free speech and free press remained robust, the Court no longer saw itself as the special protector of individual liberties and civil rights for minorities. In the area of federalism, however, the Court blazed new paths in constraining the federal government's power over the states, as we saw in Chapter 3.

The Supreme Court frequently makes controversial decisions regarding important matters of politics and public policy. Critics often argue that unelected judges are making policy decisions that should be made by elected officials. Here, demonstrators express their opinions about the Supreme Court's abortion decisions.

UNDERSTANDING THE COURTS

Powerful courts are unusual; few nations have them. The power of American judges raises questions about the compatibility of unelected courts with a democracy and about the appropriate role for the judiciary in policymaking.

THE COURTS AND DEMOCRACY

Announcing his retirement in 1981, Justice Potter Stewart made a few remarks to the handful of reporters present. Embedded in his brief statement was this observation: "It seems to me that there's nothing more antithetical to the idea of what a good judge should be than to think it has something to do with representative democracy." He meant that judges should not be subject to the whims of popular majorities. In a nation that insists so strongly that it is democratic, where do the courts fit in?

In some ways, the courts are not a very democratic institution. Federal judges are not elected and are almost impossible to remove. Indeed, their social backgrounds probably make the courts the most elite-dominated policymaking institution. If democracy requires that key policymakers always be elected or be continually responsible to those who are, then the courts diverge sharply from the requirements of democratic government.

Interest groups often use the judicial system to pursue their policy goals, forcing the courts to rule on important social issues. Some Hispanic parents, for example, have successfully sued local school districts to compel them to offer bilingual education.

As you saw in Chapter 2, the Constitution's framers wanted it that way. Chief Justice Rehnquist, a judicial conservative, put the case as follows: "A mere change in public opinion since the adoption of the Constitution, unaccompanied by a constitutional amendment, should not change the meaning of the Constitution. A merely temporary majoritarian groundswell should not abrogate some individual liberty protected by the Constitution."[34]

The courts are not entirely independent of popular preferences, however. Turn-of-the-century Chicago humorist Finley Peter Dunne had his Irish saloonkeeper character "Mr. Dooley" quip that "th' Supreme Court follows th' iliction returns." Many years later, political scientists have found that the Court usually reflects popular majorities.[35] Even when the Court seems out of step with other policymakers, it eventually swings around to join the policy consensus,[36] as it did in the New Deal. A study of the period from 1937 to 1980 found that the Court was clearly out of line with public opinion only on the issue of prayers in public schools.[37]

Despite the fact that the Supreme Court sits in a "marble palace," it is not as insulated from the normal forms of politics as one might think. The two sides in the abortion debate flooded the Court with mail, targeted it with advertisements and protests, and bombarded it with 78 *amicus curiae* briefs in the *Webster v. Reproductive Health Services* (1989) case. Members of the Supreme Court are unlikely to cave in to interest group pressures, but they are aware of the public's concern about issues, and this awareness becomes part of their consciousness as they decide cases. Political scientists have found that the Court is more likely to hear cases for which interest groups have filed *amicus curiae* briefs.[38]

Courts can also promote pluralism. When groups go to court, they use litigation to achieve their policy objectives.[39] Both civil rights groups and environmentalists, for example, have blazed a path to show how interest groups can effectively use the courts to achieve their policy goals. Thurgood Marshall, the legal wizard of the NAACP's litigation strategy, not only won most of his cases but also won for himself a seat on the Supreme Court. Almost every major policy decision these days ends up in court. Chances are good that some judge can be found who will rule in an interest group's favor. On the other hand, agencies and businesses commonly find themselves ordered by different courts to do opposite things. The habit of always turning to the courts as a last resort can add to policy delay, deadlock, and inconsistency.

WHAT COURTS SHOULD DO: THE SCOPE OF JUDICIAL POWER

The courts, Alexander Hamilton wrote in *The Federalist Papers*, "will be least in capacity to annoy or injure" the people and their liberties.[40] Throughout American history, critics of judicial power have disagreed. They see the courts as too powerful for their own—or the nation's—good. Yesterday's critics focused on John Marshall's "usurpations" of power, on the proslavery decision in *Dred Scott*, or on the efforts of the "nine old men" to kill off Franklin D. Roosevelt's New Deal legislation. Today's critics are never short of arguments to show that courts go too far in making policy.[41]

Courts make policy on both large and small issues. In the past few decades, courts have made policies on major issues involving school busing, abortion, affirmative action, nuclear power, legislative redistricting, bilingual education, prison conditions, counting votes in the 2000 presidential election, and many other key issues.[42]

There are strong disagreements about the appropriateness of allowing the courts to have a policymaking role. Many scholars and judges favor a policy of **judicial restraint**, in which judges adhere closely to precedent and play minimal policymaking roles, leaving policy decisions strictly to the legislatures. These observers stress that the federal courts, composed of unelected judges, are the least democratic branch of government and question the qualifications of judges for making policy decisions and balancing interests. Advocates of judicial restraint believe that decisions such as those on abortion and prayer in public schools go well beyond the "referee" role they say is appropriate for courts in a democracy.

On the other side are proponents of **judicial activism**, in which judges make bolder policy decisions, even charting new constitutional ground with a particular decision. Advocates of judicial activism emphasize that the courts may alleviate pressing needs—especially needs of those who are politically or economically weak—left unmet by the majoritarian political process.

It is important not to confuse judicial activism or restraint with liberalism or conservatism. In Table 16.5, you can see the varying levels of the Supreme Court's use of judicial review to void laws passed by Congress in different eras. In the early years of the New Deal, judicial activists were conservatives. During the tenure of Earl Warren as chief justice (1953–1969), activists made liberal decisions. The Courts under Chief Justices Warren Burger (1969–1986) and William Rehnquist (1986–2005), composed of mostly conservative nominees of Republican presidents, marked the most active use of judicial review in the nation's history. In the latter period, conservative justices were the most likely to vote to void congressional legislation.[43]

The problem remains of reconciling the American democratic heritage with an active policymaking role for the judiciary. The federal courts have developed a doctrine of **political questions** as a means to avoid deciding some cases, principally those that involve conflicts between the president and Congress. The courts have shown no willingness, for example, to settle disputes regarding the War Powers Resolution (see Chapter 13).

Similarly, judges typically attempt, whenever possible, to avoid deciding a case on the basis of the Constitution, preferring less contentious "technical" grounds. They also employ issues of jurisdiction, mootness (whether a case presents a real controversy in which a judicial decision can have a practical effect), standing, ripeness (whether the issues of a case are clear enough and evolved enough to serve as the basis of a decision), and other conditions to avoid adjudication of some politically charged cases. The Supreme Court refused to decide, for example, whether it was legal to carry out the war in Vietnam without an explicit declaration of war from Congress.

Comparing Judiciaries

judicial restraint
A judicial philosophy in which judges play minimal policymaking roles, leaving that duty strictly to the legislatures.

judicial activism
A judicial philosophy in which judges make bold policy decisions, even charting new constitutional ground. Advocates of this approach emphasize that the courts can correct pressing needs, especially those unmet by the majoritarian political process.

political questions
A doctrine developed by the federal courts and used as a means to avoid deciding some cases, principally those involving conflicts between the president and Congress.

TABLE 16.5

Supreme Court Rulings in Which Federal Statutes Have Been Found Unconstitutional[a]

Period	Statutes Voided
1798–1864	2
1864–1910	33 (34)[b]
1910–1930	24
1930–1936	14
1936–1953	3
1953–1969	25
1969–1986	35
1986–present	38
Total	**174**

[a]In whole or in part.
[b]An 1883 decision in the *Civil Rights Cases* consolidated five different cases into one opinion declaring one act of Congress void. In 1895, *Pollock v. Farmers Loan and Trust Co.* was heard twice, with the same result both times.

Source: Henry J. Abraham, *The Judicial Process: An Introductory Analysis of the Courts of the United States, England, and France*, 7th ed. (Oxford: Oxford University Press, 1998), 309. Used by permission of Oxford University Press, Inc. Updated by the authors.

As you saw in the discussion of *Marbury v. Madison*, from the earliest days of the Republic, federal judges have been politically astute in their efforts to maintain the legitimacy of the judiciary and to conserve their resources. (Remember that judges are typically recruited from political backgrounds.) They have tried not to take on too many politically controversial issues at one time. They have also been much more likely to find state and local laws unconstitutional (about 1,100) than federal laws (fewer than 200, as shown in Table 16.4).

Another factor that increases the acceptability of activist courts is the ability to overturn their decisions. First, the president and the Senate determine who sits on the federal bench. Second, Congress, with or without the president's urging, can begin the process of amending the Constitution to overcome a constitutional decision of the Supreme Court. Although this process does not occur rapidly, it is a safety valve. The Eleventh Amendment in 1795 reversed the decision in *Chisolm v. Georgia*, which permitted an individual to sue a state in federal court; the Fourteenth Amendment in 1868 reversed the decision in *Scott v. Sandford*, which held African Americans not to be citizens of the United States; the Sixteenth Amendment in 1913 reversed the decision in *Pollock v. Farmer's Loan and Trust Co.*, which prohibited a federal income tax; and the Twenty-sixth Amendment in 1971 reversed part of *Oregon v. Mitchell*, which voided a congressional act according 18- to 20-year-olds the right to vote in state elections.

Even more drastic options are available as well. Just before leaving office in 1801, the Federalists created a tier of circuit courts and populated them with Federalist judges; the Jeffersonian Democrats took over the reins of power and promptly abolished the entire level of courts. In 1869, the Radical Republicans in Congress altered the appellate jurisdiction of the Supreme Court to prevent it from hearing a case (*Ex parte McCardle*) that concerned the Reconstruction Acts. This kind of alteration is rare, but it occurred recently. The George W. Bush administration selected the naval base at Guantánamo as the site for a detention camp for terrorism suspects in the expectation that its actions would not be subject to review by federal courts. In June 2004, however, the Supreme Court ruled that the naval base fell within the jurisdiction of U.S. law and that the habeas corpus statute that allows prisoners to challenge their detentions was applicable. In 2005 and again in 2006, Congress stripped federal courts from hearing habeas corpus petitions from the detainees.

Finally, if the issue is one of **statutory construction**, in which a court interprets an act of Congress, then the legislature routinely passes legislation that clarifies existing laws and, in effect, overturns the courts.[44] In 1984, for example, the Supreme Court ruled in *Grove City College v. Bell* that when an institution receives federal aid, only the program or activity that actually gets the aid, not the entire institution, is covered by four federal civil rights laws. In 1988, Congress passed a law specifying that the entire institution is affected. Congress may also pass laws with detailed language to constrain judicial decisionmaking.[45] The description of the judiciary as the "ultimate arbiter of the Constitution" is hyperbolic; all the branches of government help define and shape the Constitution.

statutory construction
The judicial interpretation of an act of Congress. In some cases where statutory construction is an issue, Congress passes new legislation to clarify existing laws.

SUMMARY

The American judicial system is complex. Sitting at the pinnacle of the judicial system is the Supreme Court, but it is possible to exaggerate its importance. Most judicial policymaking and enforcement of laws take place in the state courts and the lower federal courts.

Throughout American political history, courts have shaped public policy with regard to the economy, liberty, equality, and, most recently, ecology. In the economic arena, until the time of Franklin D. Roosevelt, courts traditionally favored corporations, especially when government tried to regulate them. Since the New Deal, however, the courts have been more tolerant of government regulation of business, shifting much of their policymaking attention to issues of liberty and equality. From *Dred Scott* to *Plessy* to *Brown*, the Supreme Court moved from a role of reinforcing discriminatory policy toward racial minorities to a role of shaping new policies for protecting civil rights. Most recently, environmental groups have used the courts to achieve their policy goals.

A critical view of the courts claims that they are too powerful for the nation's own good and are rather ineffective policymakers besides. Throughout American history, however, judges have been important agenda setters in the political system. Many of the most important political questions make their way into the courts at one time or another. The judiciary is an alternative point of access for those seeking to obtain public policy decisions to their liking, especially those who are not in the majority.

Once in court, litigants face judges whose discretion in decision making is typically limited by precedent. Nevertheless, on questions that raise novel issues (as do many of the most important questions that reach the Supreme Court), the law is less firmly established. Here there is more leeway and judges become more purely political players, balancing different interests and linked to the rest of the political system by their own policy preferences and the politics of their selection.

The unelected and powerful federal courts raise important issues of democracy and the scope of judicial power. Yet court decisions are typically consistent with public opinion, and judges and justices have often used their power to promote democracy. Reconciling the American democratic heritage with an active policy-making role for the judiciary remains a matter of debate. The courts have been sensitive to the issue of their power and often avoid the most controversial issues, at least for a time. It has also been easier for opponents of court decisions to accept judicial power because it is possible to overturn judicial decisions.

Chapter Test
Multiple Choice

1. Laws passed by legislatures are referred to as _____, whereas the accumulation of judicial decisions is called _____.
   a. Common law; statues
   b. Statues; common law
   c. Criminal law; civil law
   d. Civil law; criminal law
   e. Laws; litigation

2. In a court case, the plaintiff is the:
   a. Person who is accused of a charge
   b. Person who charges someone else
   c. Lawyer of the accuser
   d. Lawyer of the accused
   e. Person who reads the charges in court

3. Who can challenge a law in an American court?
   a. Any citizen can challenge any law
   b. Any tax-paying citizen can challenge any law
   c. Only a person who has a serious interest in a case can challenge a law
   d. Only a person who is included in a class action suit can challenge a law
   e. Only a lawyer can challenge a law

4. Who can challenge a law pertaining to governmental support for religion?
   a. Any citizen can challenge such as law
   b. Any tax-paying citizen can challenge such a law
   c. Only a person with standing can challenge such a law
   d. Only a person who is directly affected by the law
   e. Only a lawyer can challenge such a law

5. Which of the following was actually specified in the U.S. Constitution?
   a. Constitutional courts
   b. Legislative courts
   c. The Court of Military Appeals
   d. The Tax Court
   e. None of the above

6. Legislative courts:
   a. Are staffed by judges with fixed terms
   b. Cannot exercise judicial review
   c. Are staffed by judges who lack protection against removal
   d. Have been established for specialized purposes
   e. All of the above

7. Approximately what percentage of court cases begin and end in the court of original jurisdiction?
   a. More than 90 percent
   b. 75–90 percent
   c. 60–75 percent
   d. 45–60 percent
   e. Less than 45 percent

8. All but which of the following are true for district courts?
   a. At least one is located in each state
   b. They are courts of original jurisdiction
   c. They are the only federal courts that hold trials and impanel juries
   d. A district court judge always presides over cases alone
   e. All of the above are true

9. The United States is divided into _____ judicial circuits.
   a. 4

   b. 8
   c. 12
   d. 26
   e. 51

10. The formal document the Supreme Court issues to a lower court in order to call up a case is called:
    a. *Amicus curiae*
    b. *Writ of certiorari*
    c. *Habeas corpus*
    d. *Acceptus litigoris*
    e. A judiciary request

11. Which of the following is NOT a civil law case?
    a. A company's CEO is charged with embezzlement of funds
    b. An employee of a business is bringing discrimination charges against his superior
    c. A wife is suing her husband for child support
    d. A merger of two firms is investigated for its legality
    e. All of the above are civil law cases

12. Which of the following is NOT a "diversity of citizenship" case?
    a. A woman from Alaska is suing a man from California for $30,000
    b. A man from Texas is suing a man from Ohio
    c. A man from the United States is suing a man from Brazil for $76,000
    d. A woman from Maryland is suing a man from Maryland
    e. A man from Brazil is suing a woman from the United States for $120,000

13. Assume that there is a dispute concerning the import of European computer equipment into the United States. In which court would this case be heard in the United States?
    a. The Supreme Court
    b. The U.S. Court of Appeals for the Federal Circuit
    c. A district court in the state in which the plaintiff resides
    d. A legislative court
    e. Neither; such a case could only be heard at the WTO

14. All but which of the following is true, based on the data presented in Table 16.3?
    a. Generally speaking, nominees tend to be more likely to come from larger law firms as opposed to smaller firms
    b. It is not unusual for nominees to not have neither judicial nor prosecutorial experience
    c. Presidents largely choose nominees from within their own party
    d. George W. Bush has been the most likely president to choose nominees for appeals courts from within political professions
    e. All of the above are true

True/False

15. Most legal cases are settled by agreements reached out of court.
    True_____   False_____

16. The courts in America hear actual as well as hypothetical cases.
    True_____   False_____

17. Only a small percentage of people convicted of federal crimes in the federal district courts actually have a trial.
    True_____   False_____

18. The Constitution requires that there be nine justices making up the U.S. Supreme Court.
    True_____   False_____

19. The Constitution requires that federal judges and justices have a law degree.
    True_____   False_____

20. If four Supreme Court justices agree to grant review of a case, it can be scheduled for oral argument.
    True_____   False_____

21. Most cases reaching appellate courts are settled on the principle of *stare decisis*.
    True_____   False_____

22. Once nominated for a position at the Supreme Court, candidates often actively lobby for political support.
    True_____   False_____

23. The approval of Supreme Court nominees is based strictly on the candidates' professional accomplishments.
    True_____   False_____

Short Answer Questions

24. Briefly explain the term *amicus curiae* and provide an example.

25. Name and briefly explain three different types of cases the jurisdiction of district courts extends to.

26. Explain the four key functions of the solicitor general and his/her staff.

27. Explain the concept of judicial review, including how and when it was first established.

28. Explain in your own words the term "senatorial courtesy" as it applies to the nomination of judges.

Do you approve of this practice? Why, or why not?

29. Explain in what way selecting which cases to hear is part of the Supreme Court's "policymaking" role.

30. What is the difference between the "implementing population," the "interpreting population," and the "consumer population" when it comes to judicial implementation? What is the potential of each for hindering the successful implementation of a decision?

Short Answer/Essay Questions

31. The textbook points out that the Supreme Court is in a position to overrule its own precedents and has often done so. Based on what you know about Supreme Court cases, as well as your general knowledge of politics, what are three possible reasons why the Court might decide to overturn a previous decision? Be as specific as possible in

your explanation, giving concrete context information and examples when possible.

32. Summarize the arguments for and against so-called "strict constructionism" when it comes to the issue of judicial discretion. In your own view, what are the strengths and weakness of each side in this debate? Which side do you agree with, and why?

33. Please summarize the different criteria that in the past have been prominent for selection to federal courts. In your opinion, on what basis should federal judges and justices be selected, and why? Furthermore, what are criteria that you absolutely do not agree with as the basis for the selection of judges? Why?

34. Using what you have learned in previous chapters about the role of bureaucracy in the United States, how does the lack of a judicial bureaucracy affect the successful implementation of court decisions? Try to draw specific parallels between the two areas of American government.

35. In your opinion, what are three pros and three cons of federal judges and justices holding what essentially amounts to lifetime positions? Would you change this system? Why, or why not?

36. Based on the information provided in this chapter, how does the tenure of Supreme Court justices compare with other countries' tenure system for their highest constitutional courts? Which do you believe is more effective, and why?

Answer Key

1. B   2. B   3. C   4. A   5. E   6. E   7. A   8. D   9. C   10. B   11. A   12. D   13. B   14. E   15. True   16. False   17. True   18. False   19. False   20. True   21. True   22. False   23. False

Key Terms

standing to sue (511)
class action suits (511)
justiciable disputes (512)
amicus curiae briefs (512)
original jurisdiction (513)
appellate jurisdiction (513)
district courts (514)
courts of appeal (515)

Supreme Court (516)
senatorial courtesy (518)
solicitor general (528)
opinion (529)
stare decisis (530)
precedent (530)
judicial implementation (530)
original intent (531)

Marbury v. Madison (534)
judicial review (535)
United States v. Nixon (537)
judicial restraint (539)
judicial activism (539)
political questions (539)
statutory construction (541)

Internet Resources

www.supremecourtus.gov/
Official site of the U.S. Supreme Court with information about its operations.

http://www.fjc.gov/
Federal Judicial Center web site with information on all federal judgest, landmark legislation, and other judicial matters.

www.oyez.org/oyez/frontpage
Web site that allows you to hear oral arguments before the Supreme Court. Also provides information on the Supreme Court and its docket.

www.cnn.com/CRIME/
Information on recent trials.

www.uscourts.gov/
Explains the organization, operation, and administration of federal courts.

www.usdoj.gov/olp/judicialnominations.htm
Information on current judicial nominations.

GetConnected

The Background of Judges and Justices

As the text notes, the Constitution sets no requirements for judges and historically judges have not represented the cultural diversity of America. For instance, federal judges have been more male and more White than the rest of the population. Advocates of race and gender equality have in recent years increased their call for greater racial and gender diversity on the federal bench. Let us look at the current list of judicial nominations and compare their background characteristics with the background characteristics detailed in Table 16.3 of the text.

Search the Web

Go to *www.usdoj.gov/olp/nominations.htm* and click on the name of the judge to view his or her biography. Do this for all the nominees.

Questions to Ask

- How does the current list of nominees compare with the characteristics outlined in Table 16.3?
- In general, did President George W. Bush nominate judges who will greatly alter the general characteristics of the judiciary or not? If so, how?

Why It Matters

We want the most qualified judges to sit on the bench, and most people also want the judiciary to reflect American cultural diversity. Judges from different backgrounds, such as women and racial and ethnic minorities, may be more sensitive to the implications of issues especially relevant to their experiences.

Get Involved

Find out more about the nominees from your federal district court or federal court of appeals circuit. Contact one or both of your U.S. senators at *www.senate.gov/* to tell him or her your opinions of the nominee. For more exercises, go to *www.longmanamericangovernment.com.*

For Further Reading

Abraham, Henry J. *Justices, Presidents, and Senators: A History of the U.S. Supreme Court Appointments from Washington to Clinton*. Lanham, MD: Rowman & Littlefield, 1999. A readable history of the relationships between presidents and the justices they appointed.

Baum, Lawrence. *The Supreme Court*. 9th ed. Washington, DC: Congressional Quarterly Press, 2007. An excellent work on the operations and impact of the Court.

Breyer, Stephen. *Active Liberty: Interpreting Our Democratic Constitution*. New York: Knopf, 2005. Presents the "contextual" view of how justices should decide cases.

Carp, Robert A., Ronald Stidham, and Kenneth L. Manning. *Judicial Process in America*. 7th ed. Washington, DC: CQ Press, 2007. An overview of federal and state courts.

Ely, John Hart. *Democracy and Distrust*. Cambridge, MA: Harvard University Press, 1980. An appraisal of judicial review and an effort to create a balanced justification for the role of the courts in policymaking.

Epstein, Lee, and Jack Knight. *The Choices Justices Make*. Washington, DC: CQ Press, 1997. A strategic account of Supreme Court decision making.

Epstein, Lee, and Joseph F. Kobylka. *The Supreme Court and Legal Change*. Chapel Hill: University of North Carolina Press, 1992. Examines how interest groups propelled issues regarding abortion and the death penalty to the Supreme Court and how the way they framed their legal arguments affected outcomes on these issues.

Goldman, Sheldon. *Picking Federal Judges*. New Haven, CT: Yale University Press, 1997. The definitive work on backgrounds and the politics of recruiting lower-court judges.

Greenhouse, Linda. *Becoming Justice Blackmun*. New York: Times Books, 2005. Inside story of the career and daily work of a long-serving justice.

Jacob, Herbert. *Law and Politics in the United States*. 2nd ed. Boston: Longman, 1995. An introduction to the American legal system with an emphasis on linkages to the political arena.

Johnson, Charles A., and Bradley C. Canon. *Judicial Policies: Implementation and Impact*. 2nd ed. Washington, DC: CQ Press, 1999. One of the best overviews of judicial policy implementation.

O'Brien, David M. *Storm Center*. 7th ed. New York: Norton, 2005. An overview of the Supreme Court's role in American politics.

Rowland, C. K., and Robert A. Carp. *Politics and Judgment in Federal District Courts*. Lawrence: University Press of Kansas, 1996. An important work on the operations of the federal district courts.

Scalia, Antonin. *A Matter of Interpretation: Federal Courts and the Law*. Princeton, NJ: Princeton University Press, 1998. Presents the "original intentions" view of how justices should decide cases.

Segal, Jeffrey A., and Harold J. Spaeth. *The Supreme Court and the Attitudinal Model*. Cambridge, MA: Cambridge University Press, 1993. Examines how the attitudes and values of justices affect their decisions.

Sunstein, Cass R., David Schkade, Lisa M. Ellman, and Andrews Sawicki. *Are Judges Political?* Washington, DC: Brookings Institution, 2006. An analysis of politics on the federal courts of appeal.

Whittington, Keith E. *Political Foundations of Judicial Supremacy*. Princeton, NJ: Princeton University Press, 2007. Argues that presidents and political leaders have encouraged the Supreme Court to be the ultimate interpreters of the Constitution.

Help-U-Sel

702-647-73

www.SmartBuyLasVeg

EACH OFFICE INDEPENDENTLY OWNED & OPERATED

FORECLOS

ECONOMIC POLICYMAKING

POLITICS IN ACTION: HOW CONGRESS AND THE PRESIDENT TRIED TO STAVE OFF A RECESSION IN 2008

Early in 2008, as the presidential nominating campaigns were heating up, the American economy was cooling down. It was one of those "perfect storms"—one problem piling on to another. Energy prices were battering the economy. The United States imports about 60 percent of its oil. In January 2008 oil topped $100 a barrel. This translated into prices at the pump of $3 or more per gallon. Prices pushing $4 were predicted within a year. The dollar was still weakening against other currencies, too. A weak dollar meant that the United States had to spend even more of its dollars to purchase every barrel of oil (and everything else it purchased from abroad).

A second economic problem was plaguing more and more Americans—paying for their mortgages. Homeownership has long been a part of the American Dream. Over the years, owning one's home was a major, and usually profitable, investment. Then, home prices skyrocketed. Families often took out bigger and bigger loans to pay for mortgages, confident that their home values would go up. Banks also made some shaky loans to help more people afford their mortgage payments. Then it all came tumbling down. Home prices spiraled downward. By the beginning of 2008, more and more homebuyers were stretched beyond their capacity. Nearly 8 percent of all homes were in foreclosure—meaning that the lender was trying to repossess the house—the highest rate in five decades. The Federal Reserve Board reported in March of 2008 that Americans owed more on their homes than all the homes in the country were worth.

Many banks felt the pinch, too. Major U.S. banks sought help from other governments to cover their losses from the mortgage crisis: Abu Dubai, Singapore, and Kuwait were big contributors. Bear, Sterns—the fifth biggest investment bank—collapsed.

Finally, jobs took a hit, too. In February of 2008, employers reduced their payrolls by about 63,000. Workers, nervous about their next paychecks, were heading to the caucuses and primaries to select the party nominees for president.

It was beginning to look a lot like a recession. Not daring to speak its name, politicians sometimes called it "the R word." A recession—often defined as two consecutive quarters of negative economic growth—cannot be proclaimed in advance. A private group of economists called the National Bureau of Economic Research, based in Cambridge, Massachusetts, is the oracle determining what constitutes a recession.

Even so, people expected government to "do something." Doing something may seem preferable to doing nothing, but the U.S. economy pushes a gross domestic product of $14 trillion. It is a private, free market economy. Government has few levers to affect the billions of economic decisions made by consumers and corporations every day. Still, doing nothing is rarely an option for democratically elected governments.

Seeing economic indicators slowing, Congress and President George W. Bush hastily agreed on a $168 billion fix—the government was running a deficit already, and it would have to borrow the money—getting money into people's hands, hoping that they would spend it. The idea of all stimulus packages is simple: give people some money to spend, and more products will be produced, more profits made, and more workers hired. Qualified individuals could expect a $600 check from the IRS; couples could get twice that. (Presidential hopeful Mike Huckabee suspected that the federal government would essentially borrow $168 billion from the Chinese, and get people to spend it to stimulate the economy, probably by buying Chinese products.) The checks began arriving in the summer of 2008.

If George Washington was the father of the country and James Madison the father of the Constitution, then Alexander Hamilton was the father of the American economy. Bright, arrogant, and with a good head for numbers, Hamilton was the first U.S. secretary of the treasury. We may remember Thomas Jefferson better because he became president, but his economic ideas favoring farmers and small towns quickly became outmoded.

The word "capitalism" wasn't even introduced until the middle of the nineteenth century, but Hamilton's economic system laid the basis for it. **Capitalism** is an economic system in which individuals and corporations own the principal means of production, through which they seek to reap profits. The American economic system was never one of pure capitalism by this definition. Hamilton's economic system created a **mixed economy**, in which the government, while not commanding the economy, is deeply involved in economic decisions. Written in an agrarian era, the Constitution still gave large powers over the economy to the new national government. It was Hamilton's job to put them into operation.

Farsighted as he was, though, even Hamilton would not recognize today's interplay between government and the economy, the topic of our chapter. Today we live in a global economy with all its problems and opportunities. Corporations have been getting bigger and bigger. **Multinational corporations**—businesses with vast holdings in many countries such as Disney, Coca-Cola, and Microsoft—dominate the world's economy. There are now about 245,000 people in India answering your phone calls at a service desk, whether you are seeking help for a problem or making a reservation.[1] From your neighborhood Wal-Mart—China's biggest customer—to presidential candidates on the campaign trail arguing about jobs, issues about government and the economy are vital. People expect government to keep the economy moving. Rightly or wrongly, voters often punish politicians when the economy turns sour. Politics and economics are powerful forces, intertwined like the strands of a double helix.

capitalism

An economic system in which individuals and corporations, not the government, own the principal means of production and seek profits.

Making Economic Policy

mixed economy

An economic system in which the government is deeply involved in economic decisions through its role as regulator, consumer, subsidizer, taxer, employer, and borrower.

multinational corporations

Businesses with vast holdings in many countries, some of which have annual budgets exceeding that of many foreign governments.

GOVERNMENT, POLITICS, AND THE ECONOMY

The American economy is made up of the millions or billions of decisions made by corporations, workers, producers, consumers, regulators, and even policymakers. There is an entire academic discipline (called "economics") devoted to understanding it. In one chapter, we could not possibly give you more than a hint about how our economy works. But that is not our goal. We are interested in understanding two things: how government and its policies affect the economy and how economics affect policymakers and politicians.

To do this, we are going to begin with an institution almost all Americans are familiar with: Wal-Mart. A look at Wal-Mart will illustrate two key points. First, the government's long arm of regulation (which we first met in Chapter 15) affects Wal-Mart, as it does the hundreds of thousands of other U.S. companies. Second, Wal-Mart epitomizes the embedding of the U.S. economy in the global economy, a trend that will continue to have an enormous impact on the domestic economy and the politics of economic policy. We will take up the topics of business and economic policy and the impact of globalization again later in this chapter.

ECONOMIC POLICY AT WORK: WAL-MART

It is the store that has saved millions billions. Headquartered in tiny Bentonville, Arkansas, where the fanciest hotel is an Embassy Suites, Wal-Mart, the world's largest company, generated $379 billion with $12.7 billion in profits in 2007 and ranked first on *Fortune* magazine's 500 biggest corporations list.[2] It generated as much revenue as California—the world's sixth-largest economy—collected in taxes. It made Sam Walton's widow and children 5 of the 10 richest people in the United States (they rank sixth to tenth), *each* with assets of $15 billion.[3] Wal-Mart, known for its low prices, is also famous for shaving fractions of pennies from every supplier and every worker. That is why Wal-Mart is partly responsible for the low rate of inflation in the United States. One consulting firm estimated that Wal-Mart was alone responsible for 12 percent of all productivity growth in the United States during the 1990s.[4] Next, we will consider how government economic policy affects such a key player in our economy.

Government Regulation and Business Practices Government regulation affects the way Wal-Mart, like most U.S. companies, does business. The main government regulatory agency responsible for the regulation of business practices is the **Securities and Exchange Commission** (SEC), a federal agency created in 1934 to regulate stock fraud. The SEC regulates stock transactions and the stock market. Wal-Mart is a publicly traded company, listed on the New York Stock Exchange (its "ticker symbol" is WMT), and so its stock trading is

Securities and Exchange Commission

The federal agency created during the New Deal that regulates the stock market.

Wal-Mart's business practices have been amazingly successful, but they have also generated controversy. Here, the group "Jobs With Justice" can be seen expressing their view that Wal-Mart fails to provide adequate healthcare coverage for its employees.

regulated by the SEC. Wal-Mart's officers cannot, for example, enrich themselves by buying and selling Wal-Mart stock on the basis of insider knowledge. Buyers of Wal-Mart stock are entitled to accurate knowledge from the company. The SEC requires that companies hire an auditor and publish an annual review. Crooked accounting led to the demise of one of the nation's hottest and biggest companies, Enron, in 2001. Martha Stewart (her product lines are sold by Wal-Mart's bankrupt rival K-Mart) was convicted of lying about insider information on a stock trade.

Government also affects a company's labor practices. About 1.4 million people work for Wal-Mart—about 1 out of every 100 workers in the United States. Workers there and almost everywhere else are entitled to collect a **minimum wage**, which was set at $6.55 per hour as of 2008. Its workers have a right to join a **labor union**, a workers' organization for bargaining with an employer. Wal-Mart remains fiercely nonunion, however. In the United States, union membership and political power have been declining, partly because of the rise of companies like Wal-Mart and the decline of the manufacturing sector. First guaranteed by law in 1935, labor unions engage in **collective bargaining** about wages and working conditions with their employers under rules controlled by the National Labor Relations Board. When Wal-Mart was ready to expand its grocery operations to southern California, existing grocery chains with unionized workers insisted that workers accept reduced benefits. Only that way, the stores said, could they compete with the coming Wal-Mart onslaught. The chains won a bitter strike, and union workers accepted cuts in wages and health benefits.

Federal law also regulates working conditions and hiring practices. Worker safety is governed by the rules of the Occupational Safety and Health Administration. Like other employers, Wal-Mart is supposed to abide by hiring and employment regulations and laws. American companies cannot employ illegal aliens. In October 2003, federal immigration officers raided 67 Wal-Marts and arrested 250 illegal aliens working on cleaning crews.[5] Wal-Mart, like other companies, cannot discriminate in its hiring, firing, and promotion. It cannot refuse to hire or promote someone because of the person's sex or race. Federal law also protects older workers from job discrimination. Older workers should not have to worry that a company will cut them just before their pensions are available. (Does federal law, though, protect younger workers from age discrimination? See "You Are the Judge: Is It Okay for a Company to Discriminate Against Younger Workers?")

Wal-Mart and the World Economy No institution better epitomizes America's embedding in the world economy than Wal-Mart. Perhaps ironically in retrospect, Wal-Mart founder Sam Walton's autobiography was subtitled "Made in America," the slogan Wal-Mart first used way back in the 1980s. At one point, much of its merchandise was even tagged with a "Made in America" label. Today, the slogan is long gone. Opening one new store a day, Wal-Mart is typical of the globalization of the entire economy. Over the past generation, the proportion of the U.S. gross domestic product (the total value of all the goods and services a nation produces) accounted for by international trade has tripled, to about 30 percent. The elimination of trade barriers among nations has probably added about $2,000 to the annual income of the average U.S. family in the form of cheaper products.[6] The Waltons and the other Wal-Mart stockholders take full advantage of what economists call "comparative advantage." Its $12 billion in imports from China constituted one-tenth of all of China's exports to the United States. The U.S. supplier who cannot provide the retailer with goods cheaply enough can always be replaced with a company elsewhere. So can the Chinese supplier. A company that sells 26 percent of the toothpaste (and about that share of almost every other consumer product) in the United States has real clout. *Business Week* believes that Wal-Mart's "hard line on costs has forced many factories to move overseas."[7]

---

minimum wage
The legal minimum hourly wage for large employers.

labor union
An organization of workers intended to engage in collective bargaining.

collective bargaining
Negotiations between representatives of labor unions and management to determine pay and acceptable working conditions.

? Why It Matters
Employment Discrimination

Employers have a lot of discretion about whom they hire and fire. Federal law, though, prohibits many kinds of job discrimination in hiring, firing, and promoting. Employers cannot use race or gender as a qualification for job decisions. Age, though, is a different matter. Federal law prohibits discrimination in hiring, firing, or promotion if you are over 40 but not if you are younger. Under the law, an employer could legally say to you, "I am not hiring you because you are too young" if you are under the age of 40.

YOU ARE THE Judge

Is It Okay for a Company to Discriminate Against Younger Workers?

Companies face a lot of federal regulations about their workers. For example, companies are required to provide a safe working environment, and they are obligated to follow laws against discrimination. Of course, a company cannot legally say, "We are not going to hire you because you are a woman" or "We do not hire people from your racial group." There is also a federal law against age discrimination. The Age Discrimination in Employment Act of 1967 (ADEA) prohibits discrimination because of an individual's age. Specifically, the law says that a company cannot discriminate against workers over 40. A company could not, for example, conclude that a worker over 40 was too expensive and could be fired so that two cheaper entry-level workers could be hired.

Like many companies, General Dynamics Land Systems Inc. faced rising costs for workers' health plans in 2004. As many companies have done, they decided to continue to offer, under a renegotiated union contract, benefits to workers over 50 but not to younger workers. Instead, younger workers would have to provide their own health benefits. Some workers at General

Dynamics who were 40 but not yet 50 sued, claiming that they were discriminated against because of their age. The law against age discrimination should, they claimed, protect them against discrimination because of their age.

You Be the Judge: Does the ADEA permit a company to provide benefits to older workers but deny the same benefits to younger ones?

Answer: In *General Dynamics Land Systems Inc. v. Cline*, the Supreme Court ruled that Congress intended for the ADEA to protect older workers from age discrimination, not younger ones. The Court could not have been clearer. In its opening paragraph, it said, "The Age Discrimination in Employment Act forbids discriminatory preference for the young over the old. The question in this case is whether it also prohibits favoring the old over the young. We hold that it does not." Younger workers will find it next to impossible to sue when they think a company favors older workers.

Americans often worry—and politicians often stoke these worries during campaigns—that jobs are moving offshore along with production. Senator Sherrod Brown of Ohio is just one of many members of Congress who got there by capitalizing on worker and union worries about job security. Offshore outsourcing is a key concern of the new global economy.

Wal-Mart is more than a microcosm of the American economy. In many ways, it symbolizes the new U.S. economy.[8] Sam Walton may have had as much influence on the American economy as Henry Ford's invention of the assembly line. Wal-Mart is a major player in the globalization of the U.S. economy. Still, as we saw in this illustration, there are lots of government rules and regulations that affect Wal-Mart and other American businesses and consumers. When it comes to the economy, politics and policies matter. Indeed, the economy was one of the major issues in the 2008 presidential election, as it is in nearly every election. Let us see why.

"IT'S THE ECONOMY, STUPID": VOTERS, POLITICIANS, AND ECONOMIC POLICY

It was the most famous sign ever to adorn a campaign headquarters: "It's the economy, stupid." Arkansas Governor William Jefferson Clinton, once the longest of long shots in the 1992 presidential race, was running against an incumbent president, George H. W. Bush ("Bush 41," his son's advisers sometimes called him because he was the forty-first president), whose Gulf War against Iraq had shot his presidential approval into the stratosphere. The economy, though, was weak when the Democrats nominated Bill Clinton in 1992. Clinton hammered home a constant message: The economy under George H. W. Bush was ailing, and Bush didn't understand. Political folklore has it that in the "war room" of the Clinton campaign headquarters in Little Rock, a sign was hung with big letters: "It's the economy, stupid." Presumably this would constantly focus the attention of the campaign staff on the Clinton attack theme.[9] Campaign manager James Carville "drilled [it] into our heads, and every speech, every event, every attack" had to be "on message."[10]

"Bush 41's" son, George W., became president after the bitter 2000 election. As the economy waned in the early years of the younger President Bush's term, White House aides constantly looked over their shoulders at the fate of "41." They knew that voters pay attention to what President Harry S Truman called "the most sensitive part of their anatomies," their pocketbooks. We saw earlier in *Government in America* that economic conditions affect both voting behavior (see Chapter 10) and presidential approval (see Chapter 13). Voters, the parties, and politicians are riveted on economic issues, especially at election time. With all the bad economic news in 2008, the election of that year was no exception to the centrality of economic issues.

Hundreds, if not thousands, of studies by political scientists have reaffirmed the wisdom of Harry S. Truman's observations about voters and their pocketbooks. Summarizing a generation of research, two political scientists put it plainly: "There is little doubt that economic conditions profoundly affect voters' electoral decisions."[11] Economic conditions are the best single predictor of voters' evaluation of how the president is doing his job.[12] Voters may (as we will see) exaggerate the importance of politicians in shaping the economy, but the more sophisticated the voter, the more likely he or she is to engage in "pocketbook voting."[13]

The connection between economic conditions and voting is real but complex. Mary Voter may lose her job, but she does not quickly jump to the conclusion that the current president deserves to be thrown out. Voters in general engage is what political scientists call "sociotropic" voting, assessing the overall rate of employment and unemployment more than their individual circumstances.[14] Two political scientists, Suzanna De Boef and Paul M. Kellstedt, show that the "pictures in their heads" American voters have of the economy are shaped not only by real economic conditions but by politics as well. Presidential approval tracks consumer confidence in the economy; news coverage of the economy is tied to economic perceptions.[15]

Like voters, the parties are economic animals. The two parties have different economic centers of gravity. Traditionally in American politics, Democrats stress the importance of employment. Republicans are worried about inflation. This reflects their constituencies. Democrats appeal to working-class voters, to poorer people, to union members, and to minority groups. Republicans appeal to the "investor class," professionals and business people who can save and invest, and worry that inflation will erode their savings. Presidential and congressional elections usually see "Republicans focusing on the ills of inflation and Democrats on the ills of unemployment."[16] Let us look at the twin economic—and political—quagmires of unemployment and inflation. Too much unemployment and inflation can increase unemployment among politicians.

TWO MAJOR WORRIES: UNEMPLOYMENT AND INFLATION

unemployment rate
As measured by the Bureau of Labor Statistics, the proportion of the labor force actively seeking work but unable to find jobs.

The **unemployment rate** is the percentage of Americans seeking work who are unable to find it. Measuring how many and what types of workers are unemployed is one of the major jobs of the Bureau of Labor Statistics (BLS) in the Department of Labor. To carry out this task, the BLS conducts a huge statistical survey of the population every month. It then announces changes in the "unemployment rate." We have to increase the number of U.S. jobs by about 125,000 every month just to keep up with new entrants (graduates, for example) into the labor force. Of course, the unemployment rate varies from time to time and group to group. Young adults actually face more serious unemployment problems than other sectors of the population. (See "Young People and Politics: Unemployment and Young Workers.") Most people are out of work for only a short time (which is why the connection between the poverty rate and the unemployment rate is weak). Even so, the official unemployment rate underestimates unemployment because it leaves out "discouraged workers," who have given up their job search altogether. "My State: Unemployment Rates by State, 2008" reports on variation in the unemployment rates by states in 2008. You can check out your own state to see where it stands—and learn something about your own chances of getting work. When the unemployment rate increases, public opinion pushes policymakers to "do more" to "expand employment."[17]

The problem of **inflation**—the rise in prices for consumer goods—is the other half of policymakers' regular economic concern. For decades the government has also kept tabs on inflation via the **consumer price index** (CPI), which measures the change in the cost of buying a fixed basket of goods and services. Each month, the BLS's data gatherers fan out over the country looking at the prices of some 80,000 items from eggs to doctor visits. Even so, the CPI is an imperfect index at best (most taxes are excluded, for example). The BLS itself says that "the CPI is frequently

inflation
The rise in prices for consumer goods.

consumer price index
The key measure of inflation that relates the rise in prices over time.

Unemployment and **Young Workers**

The unemployment rate is one of the nation's most important economic indicators and a political issue as well. To measure the rate of unemployment, the Bureau of Labor Statistics (BLS) in the Department of Labor surveys about 60,000 households every month. From this, the BLS produces the familiar "unemployment rate," a number watched carefully by the candidates and policymakers. The higher the unemployment rate, the higher their level of worry.

Sometimes Americans think of unemployment as mainly a problem for middle-aged and older people. Every year, though, the BLS counts the employment rates for young Americans, ages 16 to 24. Young Americans have very high unemployment rates compared to middle-aged and older Americans. Few things plunge a person into unemployment more certainly and more quickly than dropping out of high school. About 500,000 young men and women drop out of high school each year. For 2006, the unemployment rate of recent high school dropouts was a staggering 19.6 percent.

Even recent high school graduates, though, face higher-than-average unemployment. The graph to the right displays unemployment rates for 2006 high school graduates who did not go to college.

Most high school graduates (about 67 percent) go to college. Although college does not come cheap, it pays off economically in the long run. People with a college degree have as much as a million-dollar income advantage in their working lifetimes over those without a degree.

High unemployment rates among the young adult population compete with many other economic issues on the agenda. Partly because young adults are such poor participators in elections, their unemployment rates never seem to rank very high as a

campaign issue. If voter turnout were to improve dramatically among young Americans, however, it is likely that their concerns would capture the attention of more politicians and policymakers.

QUESTIONS FOR DISCUSSION

▷ Which, if any, government policies have an effect on the high youth unemployment rate in the United States?

▷ What accounts for the variations in jobless rates among ethnic and racial groups?

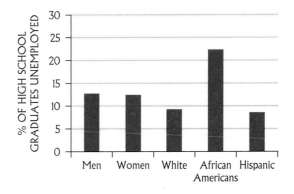

Source: For the unemployment statistics among young adults, see the Bureau of Labor Statistics press release titled "College Enrollment and Work Activity of 2006 High School Graduates," April 26, 2007.

MyState | Unemployment Rates by State, 2008

2.5–3.0 Percent
3.1–4.0 Percent
4.1–5.0 Percent
5.1–6.0 Percent
6.1+ Percent

Source: Bureau of Labor Statistics, March, 2008.

called a cost of living index, but it differs in important ways from a complete cost of living measure."[18] The dawning of 2008 brought a worldwide surge of inflation. A decade before, a barrel of oil cost $10. By the spring of 2008, it was $117. Food, only about 10 percent of the average American's expenditures, began to climb. Corn, milk, rice, bread, and other staples escalated. Part of the reason was greater worldwide demand, particularly from China and India. Americans, Japanese, Chinese, and others used "biofuels" in gasoline, thus raising their costs. Inflation, quiet for two decades, began to bite in the United States.

POLICIES FOR CONTROLLING THE ECONOMY

Farm Subsidies

laissez-faire
The principle that government should not meddle in the economy.

The time when government could ignore economic problems, confidently asserting that the private marketplace could handle them, has long passed, if it ever really existed. Especially since the Great Depression and the New Deal, government has been actively involved in steering the economy. When the stock market crash of 1929 sent unemployment soaring, President Herbert Hoover clung to **laissez-faire**—the principle that government should not meddle with the economy. In the next presidential election, Hoover was handed a crushing defeat by Franklin D. Roosevelt, whose New Deal programs experimented with dozens of new federal policies to put the economy back on track. Since the New Deal, policymakers have regularly sought to control the economy. The American political economy offers two important tools to guide the economy: monetary policy and fiscal policy.

MONETARY POLICY AND THE "FED"

On February 6, 2006, the new chairman took over at the "Fed," making him the most important economist in the world and perhaps the second most powerful individual in the United States. Ben Bernanke's only regret was that his new job, unlike his previous job as chair of the economics department at Princeton, required him to wear a suit and tie to work every day. The chair of the Federal Reserve Board has more power over the U.S. economy than any other person, presidents included. His predecessor, Alan Greenspan, was credited with a steady hand at the helm of the U.S. economy for nearly two decades. What is the Fed, and what does it do?

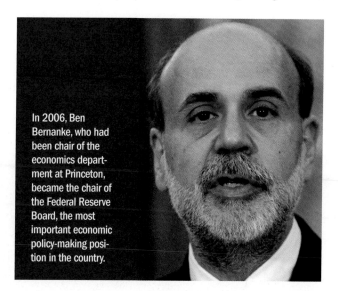

In 2006, Ben Bernanke, who had been chair of the economics department at Princeton, became the chair of the Federal Reserve Board, the most important economic policy-making position in the country.

The most important tool government has to manage the economy is its control over the money supply. Government's main economic policy is **monetary policy**, that is, manipulation of the supply of money and credit in private hands. An economic theory called **monetarism** holds that the supply of money is the key to the nation's economic health. Monetarists believe that having too much cash and credit in circulation generates inflation. Essentially, they advise holding the growth in money supply to the rise in the GDP. Politicians worry constantly about the money supply because it affects the rate of interest their constituents have to pay for home loans, new cars, starting up new businesses, and so on.

The main agency for making monetary policy is the Fed, whose formal title is the Board of Governors of the **Federal Reserve System**. Created by Congress in 1913 to regulate the lending practices of banks and thus the money supply, the Federal Reserve System is intended to be formally beyond the control of the president and Congress. Its seven-member Board of Governors—appointed by the president and confirmed by the Senate—is expected to do its job without regard to partisan politics. Accordingly, members of the Fed's Board of Governors are given 14-year terms designed to insulate them from political pressures.

Here is how the Fed works to affect the supply of money and credit: Its Federal Open Market Committee (FOMC), the policymaking body, meets eight times a year in Washington. Studying carefully a vast amount of economic data, the FOMC sets the "federal funds rate," the interest rate banks can charge each other for overnight loans. The Fed itself purchases or sells government bonds from banks. By buying or selling bonds from banks, the Fed determines whether banks have more or less money to lend out. The more money banks have to lend, the cheaper borrowing is; if banks have less to loan, loans become more expensive, and interest rates rise.

Thus, the amount of money available, interest rates, inflation, and the availability of jobs are all affected either directly or indirectly by the complicated financial dealings of the Fed. The Fed can profoundly influence the state of the economy; no wonder it attracts the attention of politicians. With so much riding on its decisions, presidents quite naturally try to persuade the Fed to pursue policies in line with presidential plans for the country. Longtime Fed Chair Alan Greenspan did indeed lead the Fed to hold the line on interest rates, thus adding more evidence to the general finding that the Fed is responsive to the White House, though not usually to the extent of trying to influence election outcomes.[19]

FISCAL POLICY OF PRESIDENTS AND PARTIES

Presidents don't have as much power over the economy as we think they do, but on matters of economic policy, the president *is* his party. While the Fed is almost entirely responsible for monetary policy, presidents and Congress are responsible for

monetary policy
Based on **monetarism**, monetary policy is the manipulation of the supply of money in private hands by which the government can control the economy.

monetarism
An economic theory holding that the supply of money is the key to a nation's economic health. Monetarists believe that too much cash and credit in circulation produces inflation.

Federal Reserve System
The main instrument for making **monetary policy** in the United States. It was created by Congress in 1913 to regulate the lending practices of banks and thus the money supply.

Why It Matters
Interest Rates
Interest rates are the amount you pay to borrow money for a house or a car, for example. Banks or finance companies charge you these rates, but how high they are—and what you pay—are strongly influenced by decision of the Fed. Even a great credit rating cannot get you a low interest rate if the Federal Reserve Board is keeping the money supply tight.

fiscal policy

The policy that describes the impact of the federal budget—taxes, spending, and borrowing—on the economy. Fiscal policy is almost entirely determined by Congress and the president, who are the budget makers.

fiscal policy, the impact of the federal budget—taxing, spending, and borrowing—on the economy. According to the Constitution, Congress got most of the economic powers (coining money, regulating trade, and so on). As the federal budget grew, its impact on the economy skyrocketed. We saw in Chapter 13, though, that the president has now gained the informal title of "chief economist." Presidents or their parties have to run on their economic record. When the economy sags, they need to change the subject.

Both parties have their presidential icons as economic leaders. If the parties could give out Nobel Prizes for economic leadership, Democrats would honor Franklin D. Roosevelt (1933–1945). The Republicans lionize Ronald Reagan (1981–1989).

Roosevelt, himself a wealthy New Yorker, inherited the Great Depression and created the New Deal. FDR was architect of the Social Security system and federal aid to the poor and also created dozens of regulatory agencies to manage the economy. Conrad Black, his most recent biographer, says that when he left office, "capitalism was no longer a destructive force" and that the United States "enjoyed unexampled prosperity—more than twice as great as when he entered office."[20] Roosevelt was president during the rise of Keynesian economics, named after its founder, English economist John Maynard Keynes. **Keynesian economic theory** emphasized that government could be a positive force in weathering economic ups and downs. Governments should spend more in bad times and contract some in the good times.

More than three decades later, Republicans had a president who crystallized their economic philosophy. For years before he became president, Ronald Reagan gave what his aides called "The Speech." It contained, said Sidney Milkis, "a single, abstract idea, universal in application: the idea that centrally administered government tended to weaken a free people's character."[21] From his inaugural platform in 1981, he argued that "government is not the solution to our problem; government is the problem." He was the anti–New Deal president. Yet, Reagan spoke warmly of Roosevelt. The *New York Times* even called him "Franklin Delano Reagan" after his first nomination.[22] Republicans had their icon.

Ronald Reagan brought the nation—and especially the Republican Party—a new economic philosophy. Reagan proposed a radically different theory based on the premise that the key task for government economic policy is to stimulate the supply of goods, not their demand.[23] This theory has been labeled **supply-side economics**. In economists' language, Keynes focused on the demand side of the economy, while supply-siders focused on the supply side. To supply-siders, big government soaked up too much of the GDP. By taxing too heavily, spending too freely, and regulating too tightly, government actually curtailed economic growth. To supply-siders, "by lowering tax rates, you could increase the motivation to work longer, increase savings and investments, and produce more."[24] Economist Arthur Laffer proposed (legend says he did so on the back of a cocktail napkin) a curve suggesting that the more

Former Federal Reserve Chair Alan Greenspan before the Joint Economic Committee on Capitol Hill. Greenspan made fighting inflation the Federal Reserve's top priority, based on the theory that when inflation is controlled, investors will put their money into enterprises that will produce goods and services, people will be employed, and pensions will be secure.

Keynesian economic theory

The theory emphasizing that government spending and deficits can help the economy weather its normal ups and downs. Proponents of this theory advocate using the power of government to stimulate the economy when it is lagging.

supply-side economics

An economic theory advocated by President Reagan holding that too much income goes to taxes so that too little money is available for purchasing and that the solution is to cut taxes and return purchasing power to consumers.

government taxed, the less people worked and thus the smaller the government's tax revenues. In its most extreme form, this theory held that by taking a smaller percentage of people's income, the government would actually get more total revenue as production increased. Cutting taxes was Job One for the supply-siders. Both Presidents Reagan and George W. Bush were so committed to supply-side economics that they were willing to risk massive budget deficits in its name.

Supply-side economics is far from the mainstream of the discipline of economics, but it seems to be etched into the Republican DNA. President Reagan used it to justify huge tax cuts to Congress. President George W. Bush used supply-side logic to justify his $1.3 trillion, 10-year tax cuts of 2001. His second chair of the Council of Economic Advisers, Gregory Mankiw, had once called it "fad economics" proposed by "charlatans" in his best-selling economics textbook. Far out of the mainstream of modern economics, supply-side economics is popular, though, with many politicians.

WHY IT IS HARD TO CONTROL THE ECONOMY

Managing the economy is a lot harder than many politicians seem to believe. It is harder than most voters think, too. Government can do about as much to control the economy as the average parent can do to control the average teenager. Economist Robert Samuelson doubted that presidents have much impact on the economy. "If presidents could create jobs," he says, "the unemployment rate would rarely exceed 3.5 percent."[25] Even so, some political scientists have tried hard to show that politicians manipulate the economy for short-run advantage to win elections. This was sometimes called a "political business cycle."[26] Presidents, so this argument goes, stimulate the economy just before elections, putting more money (even more government benefits) in voters' hands weeks or months before an election. Presidential power over the economy is—under the best of circumstances—more limited than that.[27] Politicians and presidents may wish they had the kind of power to swing elections. They rarely do—even though voters may blame them for economic woes.

Critics of President Reagan's economic policies called them "Reaganomics" because they cut taxes for well-to-do Americans and tried, not always successfully, to shrink the size of the federal government.

Government makes economic policy very slowly. Most policies must be decided on a year or more before they will have their full impact on the economy. The president's budget, for example, is prepared many months in advance of its enactment into law. The budgetary process, as we saw in Chapter 14, is dominated by "uncontrollable expenditures." These expenditures are mandated by law. In addition, benefits such as Social Security are now indexed. They go up automatically as the cost of living increases. Even conservative Republican presidents see federal expenditures rise on their watch. Given that law already mandates so much spending, it is difficult to make substantial cuts. Keynesianism is thus largely irrelevant in the twenty-first century.

Government in America is big; it is important. Big and important as it is, though, the billions of economic choices made by consumers and businesses are far more important. The American capitalist system itself imposes the biggest restraint on controlling the economy. Because the private sector is much larger than the public sector, it dominates the economy. Big as the federal government is, it still spends less than 20 percent of our GDP. Consumers and businesses still make the vast majority of our economic decisions. This is even truer for the international economy.

POLITICS, POLICY, AND THE INTERNATIONAL ECONOMY

Comparing Economic Policy

Americans live in a global economy. We import more than we export, leading to a gap in our "balance of payments." However, the U.S. economy is so large in the world—about a quarter of its total—that a housing crisis here causes problems everywhere. Still, an economy which purchases most of its oil and consumer goods from elsewhere is no longer master of its own destiny.

If it is difficult for policymakers to control the U.S. economy, it is even more difficult for them to control an increasingly global one.[28] Today's economy is worldwide. A street scene in the Middle East may be played out for television cameras in front of a multinational corporate logo. The U.S. economy depends on international trade for its survival. In the world as a whole, nearly a quarter of world GDP is based on exports. Foreign-owned assets in the United States quadrupled in the 1990s to $8 trillion.[29] "American" cars have U.S. brands on them, but may be made almost entirely abroad; "foreign" cars have a Japanese, German, or Korean brand but may be made mostly in the United States. The distinction between U.S. and other economies has become transparent. "Globalization" has become an issue dividing international institutions and governments on the one hand and protesters on the other. What U.S. policymakers do about the economy can never again be decided in a vacuum. (We will return to these issues again in Chapter 20.)

A big part of today's global economy is that food staples like rice are shipped from one country to another. Here, a worker directs the unloading of rice being imported from Vietnam to the Philippines. A rice shortage in 2008 led some nations to restrict its export and raised the price of rice throughout the world. In Haiti, this even led to deadly riots over rising food prices.

protectionism

Economic policy of shielding an economy from imports.

Most emerging economies want to follow an economic policy of **protectionism**, letting their own fragile economies grow while keeping out products from other countries. Ours was no exception. Alexander Hamilton was our first Secretary of the Treasury and our first protectionist. In the very first Congress he supported a set of tariffs—essentially a tax—on foreign products imported into the new United States. For most of the nineteenth century, the tariff was the major source of federal revenues. For two centuries, economists have been virtually united against tariffs and protectionism. Politicians, though, are another matter. Seeing constituents lose jobs because the products they make will be undersold by another country's products is painful. One country's tariff, though, is likely to provoke retaliation from another country and so on and on. The Smoot-Hawley tariff, a 20 percent hike in U.S. tariffs in 1930, was one of the major causes of the Great Depression.

AMERICA IN PERSPECTIVE

The Roar of the Dragon: China's Economy

China is the world's fasting-growing major economy, roaring along at the astounding growth rate of 10 percent a year. With 1.3 billion people, China has the world's largest population, and is also one of America's biggest trading partners. The Land of the Dragon—the traditional Chinese image of the country—is barreling toward having the largest economy on Earth. China has 100 cities with a million or more people. In 2008, the eyes of the world were on Beijing as it hosted the Olympics. The world debated about human rights in China, but there was no debate about the country's economic surge. Some facts about China's growth:

➤ In 2005 and again in 2006, China added electrical generating capacity equal to the electrical capacity of France.

➤ China uses half the concrete in the world.

➤ One-quarter of the world's construction cranes are in Shanghai.

➤ China adds one new coal-burning power plant every four days—fueling the cities and their sooty air, as observed by the world during the 2008 Olympics.

➤ China is building 96 new airports over the next 12 years (the last major U.S. airport built was in Denver in the 1990s).

➤ The proportion of Chinese who own cars is about the same proportion of Americans who owned cars in 1918. This is a number that is certain to grow—and all of them will need gasoline.

➤ China ranks near the top of all countries holding U.S. government debt.

Over the centuries, Chinese governments have been among the world's most totalitarian. Human rights groups annually document the jailing of union and religious leaders and political dissidents. China's critics claim that its government-owned factories rely on slave labor to keep low labor costs even lower. Congress only reluctantly gave China free trade status with the United States, and China's human rights abuses were the reason for the delay. China shed some of its huge state-owned enterprises for privately owned and more competitive companies. These were not easy transitions. Chinese authorities themselves recorded 50,000 protests a year, signally an edgy population facing political and economic changes.

Americans complained that Chinese products—its toys, drugs, and dog food, for example—were sometimes unsafe. But they bought them by the millions, spending billions of dollars. Many of these products were sold by Wal-Mart, America's largest corporation. China had become the world's factory; Americans were its greatest consumers.

Source: Some of this information was taken from a special report on China's economy. See "A Ravenous Dragon," *The Economist*, March 15, 2008.

After World War II, the world's governments moved slowly but steadily toward free trade and the reductions of tariffs. Two political scientists called this "the growing willingness of national governments to open up their national economy to global market forces."[30] This was harder for Democrats, who depended on labor union votes—worried about job losses to other countries—than for Republicans, whose business supporters wanted new markets. Presidents Bush, Clinton, and Bush pressed Congress hard for more free trade and fewer tariffs. Democratic President Clinton had to overcome the resistance of unions and many Democrats in Congress to pass the World Trade Agreement Treaty, creating an international **World Trade Organization** (WTO). The WTO would become the international organization promoting free trade and punishing protectionist restrictions. Democrats in 2008 railed against their image of a job-draining free trade system.

Unions feared that free trade would essentially promote "a race to the bottom," where massive international corporations would "constantly ransack the globe searching for low costs and high returns."[31] A specter was haunting first the manufacturing worker and later the software engineer: Their jobs were going somewhere else. And, sure enough, that is just the issue that cropped up as the Democrats' "jobs, jobs, jobs" campaign theme in 2008. The virtues of free trade are hard to explain to someone who has just lost his job and sees a similar one crop up in another country.

An often-quoted report by the consulting firm Forrester Research estimated that more than 3 million U.S. jobs would move offshore by 2015. "Not so fast,"

World Trade Organization
International organization that regulates international trade.

said most economists. Even if those estimates were accurate, counting jobs lost to foreign trade is only half the story. Jobs are gained from foreign trade, too. Catherine Mann, an economist with the Institute for International Economics, predicts a new surge of technology employment in the United States because of the explosion of international trade.[32] The distinguished *New York Times* world affairs columnist Thomas Friedman emphasizes that there is an upside to globalization. All those Indian call centers are running Microsoft Windows, their air conditioning units are made by Carrier, and they are drinking Cokes. American exports to India have increased from $2.5 billion in 1990 to $5 billion in 2003.[33] International trade almost certainly creates long-term gain. It may also create short-term pain. And rightly or wrongly, politics is often about the short run.

ARENAS OF ECONOMIC POLICYMAKING

You Are the Director of Economic Development for the City of Los Angeles, California

Economic interests far outnumber any other kind of interest group (see Chapter 11). Liberal or conservative, most interest groups seek benefits, protection from unemployment, tax breaks, or safeguards against some other economic evil (as they see it). Business, consumers, and labor are three of the major actors in and objects of government economic policy. In our Wal-Mart illustration, we looked at some issues relevant to the business and labor arenas. Here, we will look at a few more and will also consider consumers and economic policy.

BUSINESS AND PUBLIC POLICY

President Calvin Coolidge's saying "The business of America is business" rings particularly true when Republican administrations are in office, but some would argue that it applies almost all the time. One of the reasons why Washington, D.C., is so hospitable to business interests is that industry lobbyists in Washington are well organized and well funded (see Chapter 11). Nobody lobbies like business lobbies. Domestic and foreign corporations and their trade associations "account for the preponderance of politically active groups within the United States."[34] On some issues, business sings in a well-tuned chorus, all together. Almost every business wants its Washington representatives to work to keep taxes on business low and regulation sparse. Much business lobbying, though, pits one business interest against another. Cable TV and the broadcast networks, for example, compete for regulatory advantage. And railroads are not interested in government subsidies for the airlines or truckers.

Corporate Corruption and Concentration. The corporation has long stood at the center of the American economy. In the 1990s, the corporations and their chief executive officers were the modern symbols of American success. As the century turned, they seemed to be the symbol of American excess. A go-go time for the stock market turned into a plummeting earnings loss for millions of American investors and retirees. Although there were many culprits in this downturn, corporate corruption also played a part. A string of corporate leaders from Enron, Tyco, HealthSouth, and other companies were charged with fraud and many went to prison. Corporate corruption did not come cheap. Washington's Brookings Institution estimated in 2002 that the first-year fallout of corporate accounting scandals would cost the economy around $35 billion—about what the country was spending on homeland security.[35]

At the turn of the twentieth century, powerful corporate titans took control of entire industries. After they eliminated competitors, they could charge customers essentially whatever they wanted. John D. Rockefeller's control of oil refining and processing was the most famous example. This was the era of the trusts, as monopolies were then called. Government regulation of business is at least as old as the first antitrust act, the Sherman Act of 1890. The purpose of **antitrust policy** is to ensure competition and prevent monopoly (control of a market by one company). Antitrust legislation permits the Justice Department to sue in federal court to break up companies that control too much of the market. The Clinton administration filed a major antitrust lawsuit against Microsoft, which produces the operating system for about 90 percent of the world's computers. Microsoft lost but hardly blinked.

Regulating and Benefiting Business. In our Wal-Mart illustration, we examined the role of the SEC in regulating stock trade. Not surprisingly, the corporate scandals of the early twenty-first century led to a new wave of calls for business regulation. Congress passed a law in 2002 that provided tougher criminal penalties for stock fraud. It created an Accounting Oversight Board within the SEC to regulate accounting industry practices.

Although business owners and managers, especially in small business, often complain about regulation, they should also remember some of the benefits they get from government. One of the oldest protections government gives to business is found in the Constitution: protection for inventions and creative works in the form of patents and copyrights. The Department of Commerce collects data on products and markets through the Census Bureau, helps businesses export their wares, and protects inventions through the Patent Office. The Small Business Administration is the government's counselor, adviser, and loan maker to small businesses. Several agencies fund research that is valued by businesses involved with natural resources, transportation, electronics and computers, and health. In fact, the federal government is the principal source of research and development funding in the United States.

Businesses organized for lobbying have been around for years; consumer groups, by contrast, are a relatively new arrival on the economic policy stage.

CONSUMER POLICY: THE RISE OF THE CONSUMER LOBBY

Years ago, the governing economic principle of consumerism was "let the buyer beware." With a few exceptions, public policy ignored consumers and their interests. The first major consumer protection policy in the United States was the Food and Drug Act of 1906, which prohibited the interstate transportation of dangerous or impure foods and drugs. Today, the **Food and Drug Administration** (FDA) has broad regulatory powers over the manufacturing, contents, marketing, and labeling of food and drugs. It is the FDA's responsibility to ascertain the safety and effectiveness of new drugs before approving them for marketing in the United States.

Consumerism was a sleeping political giant until the 1960s, when self-proclaimed consumer activists such as Ralph Nader awakened it. Uncovering clear cases of unsafe products and false advertising, these activists argued that it was the government's responsibility to be a watchdog on behalf of the consumer. As they garnered broad public support, the 1960s and 1970s saw a flood of consumer protection legislation. Created in 1972 by the Product Safety Act, the Consumer Product Safety Commission (CPSC) has broad powers to ban hazardous products from the market. Today the CPSC regulates the safety of items ranging from toys to lawn mowers.

antitrust policy
A policy designed to ensure competition and prevent monopoly, which is the control of a market by one company.

Food and Drug Administration
The federal agency formed in 1913 and assigned the task of approving all food products and drugs sold in the United States. All drugs, with the exception of tobacco, must have FDA authorization.

The Federal Trade Commission (FTC), traditionally responsible for regulating trade practices, also jumped into the business of consumer protection in the 1960s and 1970s, becoming a defender of consumer interests in truth in advertising. It has made new rules about product labeling, exaggerated product claims, and the use of celebrities in advertising. Congress has also made the FTC the administrator of the new Consumer Credit Protection Act. This act stipulates that whenever you borrow money, even if only by using a credit card, you must receive a form stating the exact amount of interest you must pay. The FTC enforces truth in lending through such forms and other means.

LABOR AND GOVERNMENT

National Labor Relations Act

A 1935 law, also known as the Wagner Act, that guarantees workers the right of **collective bargaining**, sets down rules to protect unions and organizers, and created the National Labor Relations Board to regulate labor-management relations.

Throughout most of the nineteenth century and well into the twentieth, the federal government allied with business elites to squelch labor unions. The courts interpreted the antitrust laws as applying to unions as well as businesses. Until the Clayton Antitrust Act of 1914 exempted unions from antitrust laws, the mighty arm of the federal government was busier busting unions than trusts.

The major turnabout in government policy toward labor took place during the New Deal. In 1935, Congress passed the **National Labor Relations Act**, often called the Wagner Act after its sponsor, Senator Robert Wagner of New York. The Wagner Act guaranteed workers the right of collective bargaining—the right to have labor union representatives negotiate with management to determine working conditions. It also established rules to protect unions and organizers. For example, under the Wagner Act, an employer cannot fire or discriminate against a worker who advocates unionizing.

After World War II, a series of strikes and a new Republican majority in Congress tilted federal policy somewhat back in the direction of management. The Taft-Hartley Act of 1947 continued to guarantee unions the right of collective bargaining, but it prohibited various unfair practices by unions as well. The act also gave the president power to halt major strikes by seeking a court injunction for an 80-day "cooling off" period. Most important, section 14B of the law permitted states to adopt what union opponents call right-to-work laws. Such laws forbid labor contracts from requiring workers to join unions to hold their jobs.

Unions have had some notable successes over the years, which have become staples of the American economy. First, partly as the result of successful union lobbying, the government provides unemployment compensation—paid for by workers and employers—to cushion the blows of unemployment. Second, since the New Deal, the government has guaranteed a minimum wage, setting a floor on the hourly wages earned by employees. As we discussed earlier in the chapter, lately labor unions have fallen on hard times. Membership has dropped, and political power has been declining. Union members themselves no longer vote solidly Democratic as they once did but instead split their votes about evenly.

Andy Stern is president of the Service Employees International Union (SEIU)—a union intent on reversing the decades-long decline in union membership and power. The SEIU is the fastest growing major union in the country, in part because of Stern's focus on organizing via the internet.

UNDERSTANDING ECONOMIC POLICYMAKING

One of the major battles of the twentieth century was the conflict between market-based economic systems and centrally planned ones. The market won. In the communist system envisioned by Karl Marx, all the means of production would be owned by the state—in which each citizen would be an equal shareholder. The communist system in the Soviet Union collapsed in the 1980s. Ever since, Russia has been trying to patch together a market economy and a democratic political system. China's communist system retains much of its harsh political reality, even as it struggles to mix a market economy with a tightly controlled political system.

DEMOCRACY AND ECONOMIC POLICYMAKING

Democratic control means that public policy follows at least in a general way the preference of voters. What voters expect of politicians, though, is not always what politicians can deliver. In the economic arena, voters often expect more of politicians than they can realistically control—at least in a mixed economy. It is even harder in an international economy, where economic decisions are made by corporations and others not easily influenced by U.S. public policy. For the past two generations, U.S. policymakers have followed the near-universal advice of economists ("the theory of comparative advantage") and created international trade agreements. President Clinton had to browbeat his own Democratic Party—traditionally skittish about free trade—to support free trade agreements. Still, it is hard for a party or candidate to tell a voter who lost her job that more free trade is good for her. Sometimes, economic theory and democratic theory may even be at cross-purposes.

Citizens often expect government to solve their economic problems. Sometimes there is short-run pain but long-term gain. People expect politicians to solve their economic problems, and politicians are often only too happy to oblige with campaign promises. Many Americans dislike globalization. In 2008, Democrats railed against free trade. It is a challenge to politicians to carry on serious discussions about economic changes without playing demagogue. Short-run interests and long-run interests may not coincide. Because they have so much at stake, economic policy brings out special interests. In particular, groups that may be adversely affected by an economic policy have many avenues through which they can work to block it. More interest groups are involved in economic issues than any other arena. Groups go to government for special benefits, protections, tax breaks, or regulations. Therefore, one of the consequences of democracy for economic policymaking is that it is difficult to make decisions that hurt particular groups or that involve short-term pain for long-term gain.

ECONOMIC POLICYMAKING AND THE SCOPE OF GOVERNMENT

Liberals and conservatives fundamentally disagree about the scope of government involvement in the economy. Liberals think the economy, especially business, needs a lot of regulating; conservatives don't think so. In general, liberals look to the writings of economists such as John Maynard Keynes, whose works offer justification for an expanded role of government in stimulating the economy during times of recession. Today, government is a major regulator of the economy. Government policy toward the market is central to conflict between the parties today. Republicans favor a light touch, Democrats a heavier hand. Republicans have become the "supply-side party," which makes tax cuts their favored solution to almost every economic problem. The parties' different positions on the economy and the scope of government are deeply rooted in their constituencies. Whereas liberals focus on the imperfections of the market and what government can do about them, conservatives focus on the imperfections of government.

SUMMARY

In the United States, the political and economic sectors are closely intermingled. Our tour of Wal-Mart showed the role of regulation and the growth of the international economy. The 2008 elections told us that the economy is almost always on voters' minds. Voters expect a lot from politicians, probably more than they can deliver on the economy. Voters want unemployment kept low and inflation in check. Although politicians have strong feelings about the economy and pay close attention to it, only scattered evidence indicates that they can successfully manipulate the economic situation at election time, even though voters think they can work wonders with economic policy. The two parties do have different economic policies, particularly with respect to unemployment and inflation: Democrats try to curb unemployment more than Republicans, though they risk inflation in so doing, and Republicans are generally more concerned with controlling inflation. Two major instruments are available to government for managing the economy: monetary policy and fiscal policy. Republicans have become the party of supply-side economics, believing that tax cuts will lead to economic growth and jobs. Democrats disagree.

Chapter Test
Multiple Choice

1. The term "sociotropic" voting refers to the fact that voters tend to:
   a. Assess the overall rate of employment and unemployment more than their individual circumstances
   b. Base their vote on their personal economic circumstances
   c. Be influenced by their social backgrounds
   d. Vote for the candidate whom they perceive to best represent them
   e. None of the above

2. Traditionally, Democrats have stressed the importance of _____, while Republicans have been more worried about _____.
   a. Inflation; employment
   b. Employment; inflation
   c. Trade; business practices

   d. Business practices; trade
   e. Investment; subsidies

3. Which of the following age groups tends to have higher rates of unemployment?
   a. Ages 16–24
   b. Ages 25–34
   c. Ages 36–44
   d. Ages 45–54
   e. Age 55 and above

4. The most important tool the government has for controlling the economy is:
   a. Trade policy
   b. Government subsidies
   c. Labor laws
   d. Money supply
   e. Investment

5. Franklin D. Roosevelt favored _____, whereas Ronald Reagan preferred _____.
   a. Lower taxes; higher tariffs
   b. Higher tariffs; lower taxes
   c. Supply-side economics; Keynesian economics
   d. Keynesian economics; supply-side economics
   e. None of the above

6. The "balance of payments" refers to:
   a. The balance of supply and demand
   b. The ratio of national income vs. national debts
   c. The ratio of imports vs. exports
   d. The balance of public vs. private spending
   e. The balance of U.S. debt vs. interest on that debt

7. The first antitrust act was the:
   a. Sherman Act of 1890
   b. Celler-Kefauver Act of 1950
   c. Hart-Scott-Rodino Act of 1976
   d. Robinson-Patman Act in 1936
   e. Smoot-Hawley Act of 1930

8. A proponent of the principle of laissez-faire is most likely to:
   a. Favor price controls
   b. Advocate wage controls
   c. Push for minimum wage laws
   d. Approve of government subsidies
   e. Believe that market forces should determine prices and wages

9. The "New Deal" that President Roosevelt proposed in the 1930s best illustrates the belief that:
   a. Businesses thrive when the government does not interfere
   b. Economic policy should become more decentralized
   c. The government should take an active role in managing the economy.
   d. Labor unions cripple the American economy
   e. Trade barriers are essential to the economy

10. Antitrust legislation is intended to limit the:
    a. Power of business lobbyists in Washington
    b. Unethical behavior of business elites
    c. Nationalization of industries
    d. Monopolization of industries
    e. Insider trading

True/False

11. Legally, a company can discriminate against younger workers, but not against older workers over 40.
    True_____   False_____

12. Less sophisticated voters are more likely to base their vote on the state of the economy than more sophisticated voters.
    True_____   False_____

13. The United States usually has a gap in its "balance of payments."
    True_____   False_____

14. Labor unions fall under the government's antitrust legislation.
    True_____   False_____

Short Answer

15. Briefly explain three different ways in which the government affects and regulates business practices in the United States.

16. Describe the characteristics and the role of the "Fed." What are the main ways in which the Fed influences the American economy?

17. Please define "monetary policy" and "fiscal policy." Who is in charge of each?

18. When and to what purpose was the Securities and Exchange Commission (SEC) created?

19. What is the consumer price index designed to measure, and how does it do this?

20. What is the role of the WTO?

21. What is the rationale behind supply-side economics, and what are the measures supporters of this approach propose?

22. Explain what the term "political business cycle" refers to.

23. In your own words, outline two of the major successes labor unions have had over the years.

Essay

24. Based on what you know, what are two positive and two negative aspects of economic globalization? If you were an economic adviser, what would you recommend the U.S. government's response to increasing globalization should be?

25. The rate of unemployment in a country is considered to be one of the best indicators of the state of its economy. How is unemployment measured in the United States? What potential problems do you see with this measurement? How good of an indicator do you believe unemployment rates are for the overall health of the economy, and why? What possible alternative factors would you pay attention to, if you wanted to know how well the economy is doing, and why?

26. Take a look at the statistics presented in the "MyState" graph on page 554. Do you detect any patterns among the states that have noticeably larger and smaller unemployment rates than the average? Choose one of the states with a relatively small unemployment rate and one with a relatively high one and explain what might explain these figures for that specific state.

27. Given what you know about the American economy during the first half of the twentieth century, what were some of the major events, developments, and conditions—economic, social, and political—that likely prompted Franklin D. Roosevelt to propose the New Deal? What is the theoretical rationale of the New Deal? In what ways was it supposed to address the problems of that time?

28. Thomas Friedman once referred to globalization as a "golden straightjacket." Based on what you have learned in this chapter, please explain what Friedman might have meant by this. Give concrete examples to illustrate your arguments. In your opinion, who gains the most from globalization, and who loses? What should (or can) the government do to protect domestic business and American workers?

Answer Key

1. A 2. B 3. A 4. D 5. D 6. C 7. A 8. E 9. C 10. D 11. True 12. False 13. True 14. False

Key Terms

capitalism (548)
mixed economy (548)
multinational corporations (548)
Securities and Exchange
  Commission (549)
minimum wage (550)
labor union (550)
collective bargaining (550)

unemployment rate (552)
inflation (553)
consumer price index (553)
laissez-faire (554)
monetary policy (555)
monetarism (555)
Federal Reserve System (555)
fiscal policy (556)

Keynesian economic theory (556)
supply-side economics (556)
protectionism (558)
World Trade Organization (559)
antitrust policy (561)
Food and Drug Administration
  (561)
National Labor Relations Act (562)

Internet Resources

www.whitehouse.gov/cea
Reports of the President's Council of Economic Advisers, such as the annual Economic Report of the President.

www.federalreserve.gov
Information about the activities of the Federal Reserve Board.

www.cbpp.org
The Council on Budget and Policy Priorities presents information and research on economics and the budget from a liberal perspective.

www.cato.org
The Cato Institute is a conservative organization with plenty of papers and data on the economy.

Get Connected

Do Something About the Economy!

Congratulations! You have been elected to Congress. As you prepare to head to Washington for orientation and to complete all the tasks that face a new member of the House of Representatives, you remember that you promised to do something about the economy. In fact, exit polls show that a majority of the people who voted for you wanted you to do something about the economy.

Search the Web

Go to Public Agenda's issues page on the economy, *www.publicagenda.org/citizen/issueguides/economy*, and read the detailed perspectives and the section on how the perspectives differ. As a member of Congress, think about which perspective would help your constituents back in the district as well as the entire United States. It is possible that one perspective might not fit your constituency, and you may need to combine ideas presented in each of the perspectives. You also may find that none of the perspectives fits your district terribly well. What potential solutions can you recommend? Remember that it will be difficult to satisfy all the people all the time.

Questions to Ask

- How would you defend your choice of strategies against other members of Congress who may support another strategy?
- What characteristics of your district (the type of industries, the age of the people, and so on) did you consider in evaluating the perspectives?
- If you did not think any of the perspectives would work to help your district, what was missing from the perspectives?

Why It Matters

Economic policy is important to most Americans, even when they do not think about it or even understand how economic policy is made. High levels of inflation make goods and services less affordable to many Americans. Too much government regulation may also increase the prices of goods and services. High levels of unemployment also negatively impact Americans' "pursuit of happiness."

Get Involved

Talk with your parents or older relatives or friends about life in the United States during some of the recessions of recent decades, especially the 1970s, late 1980s, and early 1990s. Did the recession affect their lives in any way? For more exercises, go to *www.longmanamericangovernment.com*.

For Further Reading

Barber, Benjamin. *Jihad vs. McWorld*. New York: Ballentine Books, 1996. A very readable account of globalization and its consequences.

Friedman, Thomas, L. *The World Is Flat: A Brief History of the Twenty-First Century*. New York: Farrar, Straus, and Giroux, 2005. The *New York Times* global affairs columnist takes a look at the plusses and minuses of globalization.

Gilder, George. *Wealth and Poverty*. New York: Basic Books, 1981. A supply-sider's bible.

Gosling, James J. *Politics and the American Economy, 2000*. New York: Longman, 2002. A brief introduction to the politics of economic policy.

Greider, William. *Secrets of the Temple: How the Federal Reserve Runs the Country*. New York: Simon and Schuster, 1987. A book that demystifies the Fed.

Sloan, John. *The Reagan Effect*. Lawrence: University Press of Kansas, 1999. The enduring effect of Ronald Reagan's supply-side economics on the economy and political system.

Yergin, Daniel, and Joseph Stanislaw. *The Commanding Heights: The Battle for the World Economy*. New York: Touchstone, 2002. A good exposition of the new global economy.

BUILDING TRUST
IN SOCIAL SECURITY

Iowa.BarackObama.com

SOCIAL WELFARE POLICYMAKING

POLITICS IN ACTION:
THE FAMILY AND SOCIAL POLICY

Social policy—the topic of this chapter—is about many things. For one thing, it is about money. Our social policies represent far and away the most expensive things government funds in the United States. But social policy is also about families. Everyone knows what a family is. Or do they?

Some people connect the word "family" only or mainly with marriage or with married couples with children. "Married with children" was once the norm and not just the name of a TV show (which aired in the 1980s–1990s). In fact, today only about 5 percent of all Americans live in the very traditional family in which dad works and mom stays home with the kids. Only 50 percent of all adults are married, and 40 percent of all mothers today have never been married. Singles will outnumber marrieds by the next census in 2010.

Yet even as the traditional family has waned, it crowds its way onto center stage of the political agenda. Politicians sometimes peddle "family values." The Republican convention that renominated President George Bush in 1992 made "family values" its theme. Later, his son President George W. Bush wanted to push marriage and spend federal funds to do so. And Americans were sharply divided about the wisdom of permitting same-sex couples to marry. People in traditional families are more likely to vote Republican; singles lean more toward Democrats.

Traditionally, families have also been among our most important economic institutions. Long before there were government programs, families had the economic responsibility for people too young or too old to work. Debates about social policy are often debates about social responsibility for dependent populations. With the rapid growth of an aged population—80-to 90-year-old Americans are the fastest-growing age-group—few families would be able to pick up financial support for their elderly relatives today. That is one reason why Social Security—a major topic of this chapter—has become the most expensive public policy in the history of the world.

How much government should benefit immigrants, though, is another matter. In this chapter, we will meet one of the oldest and newest social policy debates, the immigration battle. We are simultaneously "a nation of immigrants" and also one deeply suspicious of more immigration. Immigration issues can also become family issues: several states have passed laws giving in-state tuition to the children of immigrants even if they were here illegally. In 2006, President Bush and many congressional leaders—including Senators John McCain and Ted Kennedy—proposed a major immigration reform. It generated a firestorm of opposition.

Social welfare policies involve the vast range of public policies that support individuals and families. The parties differ sharply on the desirable size and scope of such policies. In this chapter, we will see what the debate is about.

Americans believe strongly that people should take personal responsibility for themselves. Many are suspicious of government programs in general. Congress hammered out a major reform of public welfare in 1996 to "end welfare as we know it," in President Clinton's words. The new law was called the *Personal Responsibility and Work Opportunity Reconciliation Act* (PRWORA). While skeptical of a government "handout," Americans also believe in a "hand up." The late President Reagan, one of the most conservative of recent presidents, still favored a "safety net" of social programs, partly to signal his sympathy with poor people. President George W. Bush had a slogan about "compassionate conservatism." Even in these days of terrorism and costly wars, federal spending on social programs (close to $2 trillion) dwarfs federal spending on the Iraq War (about $150 billion) and homeland security (about $40 billion).

Debates about social policy are debates about social responsibility. Americans believe the people are—or should be—masters of their own fate. Social policies are often called "social insurance," however, because they are intended to "insure" people against life's crises and catastrophes—serious sickness, disability, the ravages of aging, or job loss.[1] You (or you and your employer) have paid into a benefit program designed to ease the burden of aging or job loss. Social Security and unemployment compensation are social insurance programs. Social insurance, though, has waned in the United States, according to political scientist Jacob Hacker.[2] Employers are doing less for workers. Fewer are providing pension funds or health care plans. Governments, too, have cut back on welfare benefits (as we shall see) and struggle to hold the line on soaring health care and social security benefits. As consumer debt has soared, families have resorted to credit cards, says Hacker, those "plastic safety nets" we carry around.[3]

WHAT IS SOCIAL WELFARE, AND WHY IS IT SO CONTROVERSIAL?

social welfare policies
Policies that provide benefits to individuals, either through entitlements or means testing.

Social welfare policies are the government policies which most directly affect individuals. In our federal system, both the national government and the states have policies affecting the daily lives of nearly every American—who can marry and when, who can obtain government assistance and how much, and who can become a citizen and how. Government's economic policies affect all Americans, but individuals feel their effects only indirectly. Social policies affect people very directly.

They are also expensive. They include the hundreds of programs through which government provides support and assistance to specific groups of people. The Social Security check for the retired grandmother, the food stamp coupon for the poor family, the school buildings and programs, and the Medicare reimbursement for a hip replacement are but a few examples. Altogether, social programs dwarf what government spends on anything else, including national defense and security.

No public policy stimulates more argument and causes more confusion than social welfare. Here is one major confusion: Many Americans equate social welfare exclusively with government moneys given to the poor. Yet the government gives far more money to the nonpoor than to people below the poverty line. Political scientist Martin Gilens says that while "the welfare state is often associated with aid to the poor," in fact about five-sixths of all money for social programs goes to universally available benefit programs (Social Security and Medicare being the biggest examples) available to middle class and well-off Americans; only 17 percent of social spending goes to the poor. Few Americans have the slightest qualms about assisting older Americans with government programs (even though most retirees will get back in benefits many times what they put in). Handing out money to the poor may be another matter. As two political scientists put it, Americans may be humanitarians, but they are not egalitarians.[4]

Social welfare policies consist of two kinds of programs. First are the **entitlement programs** (see Chapter 14). An entitlement is any benefit provided by law and regardless of need. Entitlement programs are sometimes called "social insurance" programs because people typically pay into them and later get money back. The two biggest entitlement programs are Social Security and Medicare. You don't have to be poor to get an entitlement, nor does being rich disqualify you. Most "entitlement" programs are really social insurance—programs you (or you and your employer) contributed to in the first place. So large are federal entitlements that they cost $3 billion a day and leave just one-sixth of the federal budget for everything else the federal government does—fight a war in Iraq, protect the nation's borders, issue passports, aid cancer research, and so forth. While we tend to sneer at "pork-barrel" projects from members of Congress, they total by one estimate only $27.3 billion. Eliminating every one of them would save 1/100 of the federal budget dollar. The 2006 *increase* in entitlement spending was almost $100 billion.[5]

Means-tested programs, on the other hand, provide benefits selectively only to people with specific needs. To be eligible for means-tested programs, people have to prove that they qualify for them. Entitlement programs are rarely controversial in America. They are often overwhelmingly popular (perhaps because everyone is *entitled* to them). Means-tested programs, though, generate powerful political controversy. Much of that conflict has to do with how people see the poor and the causes of poverty. People who see the poor as mostly shiftless and irresponsible are hostile to what they see as "government handouts" to the poor. If people see poverty as largely beyond people's control, they are much more sympathetic to governmental assistance. Thus Americans

entitlement programs
Government benefits that certain qualified individuals are entitled to by law, regardless of need.

means-tested programs
Government programs available only to individuals who qualify for them based on specific needs.

People who receive food stamps and use them for buying groceries, as shown here, must pass a means test in order to receive this government benefit.

have often distinguished between the "deserving poor" and the "undeserving poor." The deserving poor are victims of things they are not responsible for: the loss of the breadwinner, disabilities, or poor economic opportunities. The undeserving poor have presumably created their own problems and do not warrant government's help. With respect to helping the poor, "throughout the twentieth century, U.S. welfare policy was caught between two competing values: the desire to help those who could not help themselves, and the concern that charity would create dependency."[6]

Let's look, therefore, at who's rich, who's poor, who's in between—and what public policy has to do with income.

INCOME, POVERTY, AND PUBLIC POLICY

Americans are a rich people. Only a handful of nations have higher per capita incomes than the United States, but most other countries have—by our standards—staggering costs of living and staggering tax rates, too. When we factor in purchasing power, only tiny Luxembourg ranks ahead of the United States. The Census Bureau reported that in 2006 the median American household income was $48,201—that is, half of American households made more, and half made less than this amount. However, no industrialized country has wider extremes of income than the United States. Timothy Smeeding, the dean of American poverty researchers, says that "over the last four decades, the United States has seen large increases in income inequality. In this, it is not unique; many developed countries have experienced at least modest increases in the inequality of . . . income, but none so sustained as the United States."[7] Income is important to politics, just as it is important to people. McCarty, Poole, and Rosenthal argue that American politics is becoming more polarized and that the main "conflict is basically over income redistribution."[8] Liberals and conservatives are divided about many things, but "who gets what" is a major battleground.

WHO'S GETTING WHAT?

The novelist F. Scott Fitzgerald once wrote to his friend Ernest Hemingway, "The rich are different from you and me." "Yes," replied Hemingway, "they have more money." In fact, the distribution of income across segments of the American population is quite uneven. The concept of **income distribution** describes the share of national income earned by various groups in the United States. You can see in Table 18.1 how income distribution has changed in recent decades. During the 1960s and 1970s, the distribution of income was rather constant. Ever since the 1980s, however, the old adage has proved true: The rich get richer, and the poor get poorer.[9]

Although the words *income* and *wealth* might seem similar, they are not the same thing. **Income** is the amount of money collected between any two points in time; **wealth** is the value of one's assets, including stocks, bonds, bank accounts, cars, houses, and so forth. Studies of wealth show even more inequality than those of income: one-third of America's wealth is held by the wealthiest 1 percent of the population, about one-third is held by the next 9 percent, and about one-third is held by the other 90 percent. For most people in the lower half of the wealth distribution, the value of their house constitutes 60 percent of their wealth.[10]

income distribution

The "shares" of the national income earned by various groups.

income

The amount of funds collected between any two points in time.

wealth

The value of assets owned.

TABLE 18.1

Who Gets What? Income Shares of American Households

The following table demonstrates how much of the nation's income is received by people within each quintile (or fifth) of the population. In other words, the 4.1 percent in 2005 means that people whose income placed them in the lowest 20 percent received just 4.1 percent of the nation's income in that year, while the highest fifth got over half of the nation's income. The rich are getting richer and the poor poorer. What do you think accounts for the growing divide between rich and poor?

INCOME QUINTILE	1960	1970	1980	1990	2005
Lowest fifth	4.9	5.5	5.1	4.6	4.1
Second fifth	11.8	12.0	11.6	10.8	8.9
Third fifth	17.6	17.4	17.5	16.6	13.9
Fourth fifth	23.6	23.5	24.3	23.8	20.4
Highest fifth	42.0	41.6	41.6	44.3	53.5

Source: U.S. Census Bureau, "Current Population Survey, 2004 and 2006 Annual Social and Economic Supplements" and Congressional Budget Office.

WHO'S POOR IN AMERICA?

The searing images of Hurricane Katrina's victims on rooftops reminded Americans of the reality of poverty. Yet it also reinforced some stereotypes of poverty, too. TV images showed African Americans as the biggest poverty class (Whites outnumber Blacks in poverty); TV showed poverty as mostly a big-city problem (our poorest counties are in midwestern rural areas).

To count the poor, the U.S. Bureau of the Census has established the **poverty line**, which takes into account what a family must spend to maintain an "austere" standard of living. This official statistic was designed by Mollie Orshansky during the 1960s. Officially, 36.5 million Americans, about 12.3 percent of the population, were poor in 2006.

The official poverty counts tend to *underestimate* the seriousness of poverty in America because it is a snapshot and not a moving picture. A count of the poor for one year can conceal millions who drop into and out of poverty. Divorce, the loss of a breadwinner, job setbacks, and the addition of a new mouth to feed can precipitate the fall below the poverty line. Economic insecurity—the chance of suddenly falling into a much lower income bracket—is higher in the United States than in most industrialized countries. An impressive 58.5 percent of all Americans between 25 and 75 will spend at least one year in poverty during their lives.[11] Journalist Barbara Ehrenreich chronicled the life of millions of these "near poor" in America.[12] She took a string of low-wage jobs—working at lower-end retail stores and doing janitorial work, for example—and pieced together a meager living. Even during her short stint as a near-poor person, she was lucky: She never got sick or had to work below the minimum wage, and she had no children to feed, house, and clothe. She also had a real life to go back to. Contrary to popular impression, most of the poor work. They often have low-wage jobs, however, which still leave them poor and often without health insurance.[13]

Who's officially poor? Although the poor are a varied group, poverty is more common among some groups—African Americans, Hispanics, unmarried women,

poverty line
A method used to count the number of poor people, it considers what a family must spend for an "austere" standard of living.

Few events in recent American history highlighted the gap between the well-off and the poor more than Hurricane Katrina, which hit New Orleans and its suburbs hard in 2005. Rebuilding in the prosperous suburban areas proceeded quickly, as evidenced by the number of people waiting to tour a model home in the upper picture. But in the poor areas, such as lower 9th Ward, scenes such as the lower picture remained all too common for years after the hurricane.

feminization of poverty

The increasing concentration of poverty among women, especially unmarried women and their children.

progressive tax

A tax by which the government takes a greater share of the **income** of the rich than of the poor—for example, when a rich family pays 50 percent of its income in taxes, and a poor family pays 5 percent.

and inner-city residents—than among others. Race and ethnicity are major factors. African Americans and Hispanic Americans have a little better than a 1-in-5 chance of being in poverty. The group the Census Bureau calls "White non-Hispanic" has a less than 10 percent chance.

We began our discussion of social policy by focusing on the family. Families have a lot to do with poverty. Once poverty claimed the elderly as its main victims. Now it mostly claims women and children. When Social Security was created in 1935, poverty was largely—not entirely—a problem for older Americans. For decades, the constant expansion of the Social Security system and the increase in its benefits have significantly reduced poverty among the elderly. Today, however, unmarried women and their children now greatly outnumber the elderly among the ranks of the poor. Poverty scholar Harrell Rodgers titled his study of contemporary poverty *Poor Women, Poor Children*.[14] Because of the high incidence of poverty among unmarried mothers and their children, experts on poverty often describe the problem today as the **feminization of poverty**. Female-headed families run almost a 30 percent chance of poverty, while families with two parents around have less than a 6 percent poverty rate. Having children out of wedlock, Rodgers says, is the "superhighway to poverty."[15]

Poverty among children varies from state to state, of course. The U.S. Census Bureau tabulates child poverty rates throughout the country, and you can check out your own state in "My State: Percent of Children Living in Poor Families."

WHAT PART DOES GOVERNMENT PLAY?

When government spends a quarter of our gross domestic product, it is bound to have an effect on income. Actually, politicians almost never directly debate about income distribution in America. Income distribution is hiding way off the political agenda. No party platform is likely to proclaim, "If elected, we will make the rich richer and the poor poorer." Nor will one claim, "When we are elected, we will take from the rich in order to end poverty." There are two important ways in which government does indeed affect people's incomes. One is through its taxes; the other is through its expenditures.

Taxation "Nothing," said Benjamin Franklin, "is certain in life but death and taxes." Taxes at least became a little lower in the summer of 2001, when Congress passed President Bush's number one policy proposal, a 10-year, $1.35 trillion (that's trillion with a "t") federal income tax cut. Tax cuts are a mantra of the modern Republican Party.

There are three general types of taxes, and each can affect citizens' incomes in a different way. A **progressive tax** takes a bigger bite from the incomes of the rich than from those of the poor; an example is charging millionaires 50 percent of their

MyState | Percent of Children Living in Poor Families

Poverty is concentrated among children. Older people have a little help from Social Security; working age people usually have jobs. A very large percentage of children, though, live in poor families. You can look at the rate in your own state.

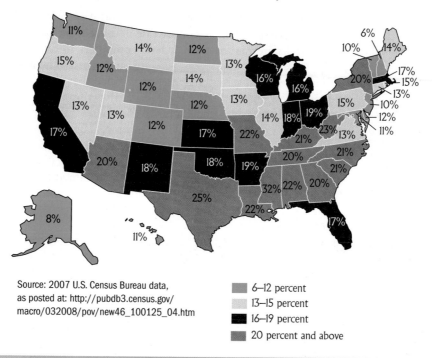

Source: 2007 U.S. Census Bureau data, as posted at: http://pubdb3.census.gov/macro/032008/pov/new46_100125_04.htm

- 6–12 percent
- 13–15 percent
- 16–19 percent
- 20 percent and above

income and the poor 5 percent of theirs. Second, a **proportional tax** takes the same percentage from everyone, rich and poor alike. And finally, a **regressive tax** takes a higher percentage from those at lower income levels than from the well-to-do.

A tax is rarely advocated or defended because it is regressive, but some taxes do take a bigger bite from the poor than they do the rich. Chief among these is the sales tax from which many states derive more than half their revenues. A sales tax looks proportional—6 percent of every purchase, for example, is taxed. However, since poor families spend more of their income on the necessities subject to the tax—food, clothing, and school supplies, for example—they wind up paying a higher percent of their incomes in taxes than do the rich.

In general—and even after the Bush tax cuts—federal taxes are progressive (you only have to look at the rates on your tax forms to see this). The rich send a bigger proportion of their incomes to Washington than the poor. How government helps well-off people—in contrast to poorer people—is through tax expenditures (see Chapter 14). The federal government spends about $18 billion in food stamps for the poor. By contrast, it permits individuals to deduct about $68 billion for employer-sponsored pension plans; another $67 billion is written off as interest on home mortgage interest. Few of the working poor—the folks Barbara Ehrenreich worked with, for example—can take advantage of employer pension plans or home ownership tax breaks, for example. Overall, of the $800 billion in tax breaks, people making less than $50,000 got only 15 percent of them.[16]

In fact, if you are poor enough, you can get money back from the government in lieu of paying income tax. Through the **Earned Income Tax Credit** (EITC), the working poor receive a check from Washington instead of sending one. The EITC

proportional tax

A tax by which the government takes the same share of income from everyone, rich and poor alike—for example, when both a rich family and a poor family pay 20 percent.

regressive tax

A tax in which the burden falls relatively more heavily on low-income groups than on wealthy taxpayers. The opposite of a **progressive tax**, in which tax rates increase as income increases.

Earned Income Tax Credit

A "negative income tax" that provides income to very poor individuals in lieu of charging them federal income taxes.

is a special tax benefit for working people who earn low incomes. In 2005, workers who were raising one child in their home and had family incomes of less than $31,030 could get an EITC of up to $2,700. The Brookings Institution estimates that the EITC puts as much as $20 billion a year into the hands of poor and near-poor families.[17]

Government Expenditures   The second way government can affect personal income is through the expenditure side of the ledger. Each year millions of government checks are mailed from federal computers to Social Security beneficiaries, retired government employees, veterans, and others. The government also provides "in-kind" benefits, something with cash value that is not cash itself, such as food stamps. A low-interest loan for a college education is another in-kind benefit. The federal Children's Health Insurance Program—CHIPs—subsidizes health care insurance for poor families with children. Together these benefits are called **transfer payments**; they transfer money from the federal treasury to individuals.

Table 18.2 summarizes the major government social welfare programs that affect our incomes. Social Security and Medicare are the two major entitlement programs. They are also the most costly social welfare programs. Unemployment

transfer payments

Benefits given by the government directly to individuals. Transfer payments may be either cash transfers, such as Social Security payments and retirement payments to former government employees, or in-kind transfers, such as food stamps and low-interest loans for college education.

You Are the President of MEDICORP

TABLE 18.2

The Major Social Welfare Programs

PROGRAM	DESCRIPTION	BENEFICIARIES	FUNDING
Entitlement Programs—"Social Insurance"			
Social Security	Monthly payments	Retired or disabled people and surviving members of their families	Payroll tax on employees and employers
Medicare (Part A)	Partial payment of cost of hospital care	Retired and disabled people	Payroll taxes on employees and employers
Medicare (Part B)	Voluntary program of medical insurance (pays physicians)	Persons 65 or over and disabled Social Security beneficiaries	Beneficiaries pay premiums
Unemployment Insurance (UI)	Weekly payments; benefits vary by state	Workers who have been laid off and cannot find work	Taxes on employers; states determine benefits
The Means-Tested Programs			
Medicaid	Medical and hospital aid	The very poor	Federal grants to state health programs
Food stamps	Coupons that can be used to buy food	People whose income falls below a certain level	General federal revenues
Temporary Assistance for Needy Families (TANF)	Payment	Families with children, either one-parent families or, in some states, two-parent families where the breadwinner is unemployed	Paid partly by states and partly by the federal government
Supplementary Security Income (SSI)	Cash payments	Elderly, blind, or disabled people whose income is below a certain amount	General federal revenue
Children's Health Insurance Program (CHIPs)	Subsidies for insurance	Poor families with children	Federal and state revenues

payments also count as entitlement programs. Companies and their employees pay into these social insurance programs to provide income in case of job loss. The other programs are means tested and are available only to the poor or the very poor.

HELPING THE POOR? SOCIAL POLICY AND POVERTY

"WELFARE" AS WE KNEW IT

For centuries, societies considered family welfare a private concern. Children were to be nurtured by their parents and, in turn, later nurture them in their old age. When children cast off their parents or when parents let their children go hungry, significant social pressure was often enough to make people accept their proper family responsibilities. Governments took little responsibility for feeding and clothing the poor or anyone else. The life of the poor in America and elsewhere was grim almost beyond our imagining. In England, governments passed Poor Laws intended, historians argue, to make the life of the poor so miserable that people would do almost anything to avoid the specter, disgrace, and agony of poverty.[18] It was scarcely better in the United States.

The **Social Security Act of 1935**—the same one that created our vast entitlement program for the aged—also created a national program to assist the poor—or some of the poor. The program brought together scattered, uneven state programs under a single federal umbrella. It was first called "aid to dependent children," then in 1959 "AFDC," Aid to Families with Dependent Children. The federal government established some uniform standards for the states and subsidized their efforts to help children in families with no breadwinner. However, states were free to give generous or skimpy benefits, and payments ranged widely. For the first quarter century of the program, enrollments remained small. The civil rights movement of the 1960s and the succession of Lyndon Johnson to the presidency in 1963 combined to boost federal and state support for AFDC and other means-tested programs. Johnson declared a national "War on Poverty" in 1964, adding food stamps and other programs to the arsenal of poverty-fighting policies. These programs—collectively called "welfare"—came to bitterly divide Republicans from Democrats and conservatives from liberals.

If Lyndon Johnson had declared war on poverty, the late President Ronald Reagan declared war on antipoverty programs. In 1981, he persuaded Congress to cut welfare benefits, lower the number of Americans on welfare rolls, and cut benefits for many beneficiaries. Conservatives during Reagan's time—and many liberals agreed—convinced many policymakers that welfare was a failure. Conservative economist Charles Murray has offered an influential and provocative argument that the social welfare programs of the Great Society and later administrations not only failed to curb the advance of poverty but also actually made the situation worse.[19] The problem, Murray maintained, was that these public policies discouraged the poor from solving their problems. He contended that the programs made it profitable to be poor and discouraged people from pursuing means by which they could rise out of poverty. For example, Murray pointed out that poor couples could obtain more benefits if they weren't married; thus, most would not marry, a decision that leads to further disintegration of the family. Not all poverty scholars agreed. They mattered little, though, as press and politics came to shape America's condemnation of welfare. No public policy had a worse public perception than welfare. "Deadbeat dads" who ran out on their families, leaving them on welfare, and images of "welfare

Social Security Act of 1935
Created both the Social Security Program and a national assistance program for poor children, usually called AFDC.

TIMELINE

The Evolution of Social Welfare Policy

queens" who collected money they didn't deserve coexisted as media and popular images of a broken system.

No one could be clearer or blunter about why Americans hate welfare than political scientist Martin Gilens.[20] He found that Americans tend to see welfare recipients (wrongly) as overwhelmingly African American. Whites' welfare attitudes were strongly influenced by whether they viewed African Americans as lazy or not.[21] Negative views of African American welfare mothers were more politically potent and generated greater opposition to welfare than comparative views of White welfare mothers. The media was a major culprit here. Gilens counted magazine and newspaper stories about poor people over several decades. About a third of all welfare recipients have been African American, but the media portrayed approximately three-quarters of poor people as African American.[22] Attitudes toward welfare became "race coded." It was not a far jump to the conclusion that lots of the "undeserving poor" were on welfare. The stage for a major welfare reform was set with the 1992 presidential election. Bill Clinton, a centrist Democratic president, and the new Republican congressional majority after 1994 were gunning for the welfare system.

Personal Responsibility and Work Opportunity Reconciliation Act
The official name of the welfare reform law of 1996.

Temporary Assistance for Needy Families
Once called "Aid to Families with Dependent Children," the new name for public assistance to needy families.

ENDING WELFARE AS WE KNEW IT: THE WELFARE REFORMS OF 1996

Bill Clinton was determined to be a "centrist" president, fearing the "tax and spend" label Republicans so eagerly applied to liberal Democrats. In the 1992 presidential election campaign, Clinton promised to "end welfare as we know it" by providing two years of support—training, child care, and health care—in exchange for an agreement to return to work. The congressional Republican Party was even more enthusiastic about welfare reform than the new president. In August 1996 the president and the congressional Republicans completed a welfare reform bill that received almost unanimous backing among congressional Republicans but that was opposed by half of congressional Democrats. The law bore the lofty name of the **Personal Responsibility and Work Opportunity Reconciliation Act** (PRWORA). The major provisions of this bill were that (1) each state would receive a *fixed* amount of money to run its own welfare programs, (2) people on welfare would have to find work within two years or lose all their benefits, and (3) there would be a lifetime maximum of five years for welfare.

Symbolically, the welfare reform policies also changed the name of "welfare" as we knew it. The cash payments to poor families once called AFDC now became known as **Temporary Assistance for Needy Families** (TANF), today's name for the means-tested aid for the poorest of the poor. TANF benefits today are small and declining. The average recipient family collects about $363 monthly in TANF benefits.

President George W. Bush pushed for one other welfare reform: encouraging people to marry. The welfare reform legislation permitted states to use some of their money for programs to promote marriage, and President Bush (and several states)

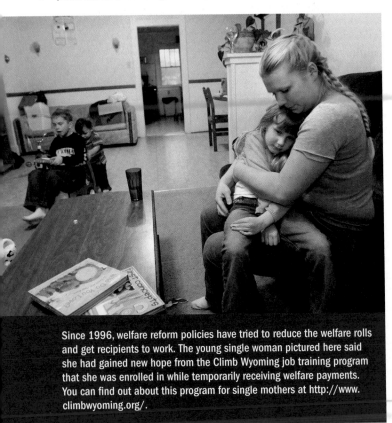

Since 1996, welfare reform policies have tried to reduce the welfare rolls and get recipients to work. The young single woman pictured here said she had gained new hope from the Climb Wyoming job training program that she was enrolled in while temporarily receiving welfare payments. You can find out about this program for single mothers at http://www.climbwyoming.org/.

YOU ARE THE **Policymaker**

Should the Government Promote Marriage?

Fifty years ago, only 4 percent of all babies were born to unmarried women; today about 33 percent are. Marriage rates are on the decline in the United States, partly because people are simply getting married later than they used to. But in the face of such changes, "family values" is a familiar refrain of politicians. The federal government even passed what is called the "Defense of Marriage Act," although it was sponsored by a twice-divorced member of Congress (it was designed to prevent gay marriages by permitting states not to recognize other states' marriages). Social scientists are nearly unanimous in showing that marriage is associated with ("associated with" is not the same thing as "caused by") substantial benefits for the partners as well as the children. Children from two-parent homes have fewer behavior problems, do better in school, and are less likely to be poor. A survey of high school seniors reports that 82 percent of girls and 73 percent of boys think it is "extremely important" to have a good marriage.

But should the government promote marriage? Oklahoma—which, despite its reputation as the "buckle of the Bible Belt," has one of the nation's highest divorce rates—uses some of its Temporary Assistance for Needy Families (TANF) funds to support workshops on marriage. A third of Oklahoma adults are divorced, compared to a fifth of all Americans. West Virginia actually gives its TANF recipients a $100 a month bonus for being married. As a part of the renewal of the welfare reform legislation in 2004, President Bush proposed spending $1.5 billion to promote marriage. Realistically, in a $3 trillion budget, the amount was miniscule. Still, the president argued, we should be willing to spend this for a series of demonstration projects around the country to see what worked to get and keep people married. His critics thought this was little more than a campaign initiative to please religious conservatives. Theodoro Ooms worried that "the conflict mostly isn't about research, however, but about values." She feared that it might stigmatize single parents, "many of whom do a terrific job under difficult circumstances." Unfortunately for the program, too, the Bush administration ended up paying one influential columnist, Maggie Gallaher, a $21,000 consulting fee for touting the program, a fact uncovered only much later.

One of the purposes of government is to support public goals. Liberals and conservatives alike favor government policies to reduce pollution, encourage savings, and even support home ownership. The federal government lets people deduct about $70 billion from their income tax bill for the interest on their mortgage payments. The justification: Home ownership is a valued public goal. What is so different about marriage? Couldn't government spend a bit to see if marriage can be improved? Or should government stay neutral about marriage? Or does the issue carry so much political baggage—gay marriage, for example—that marriage policy is too controversial to consider?

Sources: For information about marriage attitudes, including the survey reported here and other data, see the 2006 *State of Our Unions* report from the Rutgers University National Marriage Project, available at their Web site. See also Linda Waite and Maggie Gallagher, *The Case for Marriage: Why Married People Are Happier, Healthier and Better Off Financially* (New York: Doubleday, 2000). The Ooms quotation is from her article "Marriage Plus," *American Prospect*, April 2002. On the Oklahoma experiment, see Kim Cobb, "Oklahoma Embraces Pro-Marriage Experiment," *Houston Chronicle*, February 22, 2004, A12.

pushed marriage as one solution to the perpetual problem of poverty. (See "You Are the Policymaker: Should the Government Promote Marriage?")

There are many reasons "welfare" is unpopular in the United States. One of them is the emerging suspicion that millions of immigrants are flooding the United States, partly to take advantage of food stamps, health benefits, TANF, and other benefits. There is little truth in the charge—federal law denies nearly all benefits to illegal workers—but it has helped fuel the latest social policy debate: what should we do about immigration?

IMMIGRATION AND SOCIAL POLICY

Immigration policy is one of the most important ways a nation controls its future. Democratic governments don't tell people how many children to have or decide who can have them. They do make decisions about who can join them as citizens. We are, said political scientist Aristide Zolberg, "a nation of immigrants, but not just any immigrants. From the time they managed their own affairs . . . Americans were determined to select who might join them."[23] **Immigration**—the movement

immigration

The movement of people to another country with the intention of remaining there.

of people across national borders with the intent to remain—is even older than the nation itself. A sleeping giant of an issue for decades, immigration has arisen often as a contentious issue in American politics.

There are plenty of American myths and stereotypes about immigrants and immigration: contrary to myth, most immigrants are not here illegally; most are not from Mexico; and most are not consuming federal government benefits without paying taxes (illegal immigrants are actually forbidden to receive most federal benefits—and often pay taxes for them anyway). Most immigrants are not half-hearted Americans, but zealous patriots. Immigrants are hard-working, strong supporters of "American values," especially "family values," and typically eager to learn English as soon as they can.[24]

Americans have almost always been suspicious of immigration. On the one hand, almost all of us (except for a tiny minority of Native Americans) are immigrants or the descendents of immigrants. Historians often describe us as a "nation of immigrants." About 13 percent of us today are first-generation immigrants, a higher number than almost any nation besides Canada. One-seventh of U.S. workers are immigrants. A century ago, immigrants came mostly from Europe; today, they come mostly from Asia and Latin America. About a third of all U.S. immigrants in the past few years have come from Mexico alone. One in eight Californians was born in Mexico. One in nine Mexican nationals lives in the United States. Two-thirds of all immigrants, though, are *not* from Mexico. Some immigrants do work in stereotypical low-paying jobs harvesting fruits and vegetables. But others work in high-tech jobs, often in universities and high-tech corporations. These immigrant workers are often admitted to the United States because of special skills and because they are better educated than native-born Americans. Immigrants from India, for example, average 16 years of education, far more than the average for the non-immigrant U.S. population. Science, technology, medicine, and the arts have attracted countless immigrants to America. The great physicist Albert Einstein, Google co-founder Sergei Brin, thousands of medical and scientific personnel, as well as millions of low-wage laborers in construction, meat-packing, and the restaurant industry, have been immigrants.

Why It Matters
What Jobs Immigrants Do

One of the most popular—and controversial—defenses of immigration is that immigrants supposedly "do jobs that Americans can't (or won't)." People often assume that means picking crops and working construction. Most labor shortages, though, in the United States are in skilled and even highly skilled areas: nurses, physicians, computer engineers, and similar jobs. Cutting back immigration may mean fewer strawberries; more worrisome is that it might mean fewer nurses.

IMMIGRATION POLICY AND POLITICS: OLD AND NEW

Throughout U.S. history, few have supported higher levels of immigration. Benjamin Franklin may have been the most open-minded of our Founding Fathers. Yet even Franklin once said of the German immigrants to his native Pennsylvania that his native state could "become a colony of aliens, who will shortly be so numerous as to Germanize us" and "who will never adopt our language and customs."[25] In Franklin's time and for the next century, pretty much anyone who could afford a trip across the Atlantic could come to American shores. Even after more than two centuries of immigration to the United States, many Americans remain—like Franklin—negative about immigration. Daniel J. Tichenor, in his review of a generation of public opinion surveys about immigration policy, found that only once did support for an "increase" in immigration ever reach double digits (and that was 11 percent).[26] For years, CNN's pinstriped populist, Lou Dobbs, has railed against "broken borders," which, he says, cost Americans jobs and endanger national security. It's time, he says, to take our borders seriously.[27]

The issue of illegal immigration—"illegal aliens," critics call them, "undocumented workers" to their sympathizers—has roared to a central place in American politics in the past decade. For more than a century, though, there was no distinction between illegal and legal immigrants. The issue of "illegal immigrants" is, in fact,

TIMELINE

Immigration.

AMERICA IN PERSPECTIVE

Immigration Policy in Europe

While public pressures in the United States often favor more restrictive policies toward immigration, U.S. policies are far more immigrant-friendly than policies in most other countries. Compared to other countries, the United States is perhaps the most immigrant-friendly country in the world—with the possible exception of Canada.

How do other nations handle immigration? In 2005, one member of Congress wanted to find out. As chairman of the House Judiciary Committee during the bitter immigration debates, Wisconsin Republican James Sensenbrenner was—to pro-immigrant groups—the major villain in the congressional battle over immigration. He railed against illegal immigrants and fought back every effort to open the door to citizenship even a crack. He refused to consider any pathway to citizenship for illegal immigrants until the U.S. border was secure. Needing some ammunition, Sensenbrenner asked the Library of Congress to do a study of immigration policies in six other nations. The study found that in other countries, policies toward illegal immigrants are far harsher than in the United States. Five of the six countries studied have criminal penalties for illegal immigration. (In the United States, deportation is typically the harshest response.)

Europe's experiences integrating immigrants into its political and social fabric has made American immigration look almost easy.

Only Ireland follows the U.S. policy of guaranteeing citizenship to everyone born in the country. The immigrant father of France's President Nicolas Sarkozy advised his son to go the United States, where immigrants have better chances. Many European countries began encouraging immigration of "guest workers" decades ago. Even now, Europe's population is shrinking. In 2006, France's long-standing commitment to creating a culturally integrated nation was put to the test in dozens of heavily Arab suburban neighborhoods. British relations with its Muslim populations are far more difficult than American relations with its Muslim population. France, Britain, and other countries have debated whether schoolgirls can wear headscarves to school. On March 15, 2004, France passed a law forbidding girls from wearing headscarves to public schools. While there were other overt religious symbols also prevented (large crosses worn around the neck, for example), there was little doubt that the law was mostly intended to ban Muslim headscarves. Immigrant groups in most European countries feel a strong backlash against immigration. Nearly every European country has one or more small parties based on nationalist or anti-immigration platforms.

However difficult the American experience with immigration has been, Europe's has often been more contentious. Compared to some European countries, Americans have sent a virtual welcome wagon to immigrants.

---

rather new in American politics. The United States is hardly alone among the world's nations in confronting the issue of immigration, legal and illegal. (See "America in Perspective: Immigration Policy in Europe.")

The immigration issue has been building for years, but the presidential campaign of 2008 was the first in many decades to feature immigration politics as a sharp issue. Candidates and parties walked a fine line between criticizing 12 million illegal immigrants—people who are neither citizens nor visa holders—without offending tens of millions of legal immigrants, who could vote. Republican Senator John McCain began the campaign in hot water with the many conservative members of his party over the immigration issue. He had joined President Bush and Democratic senators, too, in 2006 to sponsor a major immigration reform bill. Critics called it "amnesty" for illegal immigrants, and it got nowhere.

IMMIGRATION AND POLICY: WASHINGTON AND THE STATES

For pretty much the first 100 years of U.S. policy history, there was no immigration policy. Generally, anyone who could afford a boat ticket to the United States simply came. After the Civil War, the Fourteenth Amendment defined

Americans sometimes have stereotypes of immigrants as poor and struggling. Some are, of course. But many immigrants have founded companies, risen to the top of their professions, and are vigorous participators in American politics. This is Jerry Yang, who immigrated from Taiwan to San Jose, California when he was 10. At the age of 27 he founded Yahoo! Inc. and went on to become one of America's great entrepreneurial success stories.

citizenship ("persons born or naturalized in the United States"). It not only defined who could be a citizen, but clearly recognized that immigrants could become citizens, too. Not until the turn of the twentieth century did Congress begin banning or restricting immigration in significant ways (although Congress had specifically excluded Chinese immigration in 1882). Until 1918, the United States did not even require passports. People came, they melted into the economy, and they eventually voted.

In 1924, though, Congress passed a sharply restrictive immigration law that basically set up quotas for immigrants from different countries. The quota system favored newcomers from northwestern Europe, and it discouraged immigrants from eastern Europe, Latin America, Africa, and Asia. The 1924 policy reduced immigration to a fraction of its former levels. After World War II, however, immigration levels began to climb again. Many of these immigrants came from Mexico and Central America, and added to the populations of border states like Texas, California, Arizona, and New Mexico. Cuban refugees, fleeing the Castro regime, went to Florida and other states beginning in the 1960s.

By the 1980s, President Reagan and Congress addressed the rising tide of immigration with a new law called the **Simpson-Mazzoli Act**. The logic of the law, a so-called "grand compromise" between immigration's sympathizers and opponents, was this:

* Immigrants who were in the U.S. when the law was passed were given a "path to citizenship" on a one-time only basis, if they learned English and had no criminal past;
* Border controls would be increased;
* Employers were forbidden to hire illegal immigrants, but they were also forbidden to challenge documentation presented to them, a provision which proved to be loosely enforced.

After Simpson-Mazzoli, more than 3 million immigrants took advantage of the "amnesty" provisions to take up their citizenship. Except for moving the various immigration and border patrol agencies into the Department of Homeland Security, no other major immigration policy has passed since Simpson-Mazzoli. However, Congress did agree to fund hundreds of miles of border fencing (some of which illegal immigrants ended up building).

Meanwhile, as immigration swelled, states and local governments were busy making policy, too. States are typically hit harder than the federal government by the costs of illegal immigrants.[28] In 1994, California voters approved a referendum, Proposition 187, which effectively cut off public services—including schools, social services, and health benefits—to illegal immigrants. Federal courts eventually declared most of its provisions unconstitutional. Other states, and lots of cities, picked up where California started. A few small towns forbade landlords from renting to illegal immigrants. (A few liberal towns, though, declared themselves "sanctuary cities," and promised not to enforce federal immigration laws.) By 2006, most states were sounding tough about illegal immigration. As congressional negotiation about new immigration legislation broke down, states enacted 57 laws about illegal immigration. Oklahoma and Arizona, for example, decided to punish employers who hired illegal immigrant workers, threatening their business licenses. States have also battled over college tuition breaks for the children of illegal immigrants. Texas, California, and New York, for example, give in-state tuition to children of illegal immigrants. Arizona and other states have ordered their universities to review every student's residency status and charge out-of-state rates to children from undocumented families.

Simpson-Mazzoli Act
The Reagan-era law which provided amnesty to many immigrants and toughened border controls.

A Tale of **Two Immigration Reforms**

In 1986, Ronald Reagan was president, and illegal immigration was emerging as a political issue. Congress wanted to stem the further tide of illegal immigration and—at the same time—settle once and for all the question of what to do about millions of illegal immigrants who were already here. The issue was tricky. The final bill was pulled together by Democrat Ron Mazzoli from Kentucky and conservative Republican Senator Alan Simpson from Wyoming. It would be a grand bargain. To supporters of immigration, the bill would offer a one-time-only deal: if you were here legally in 1982, you could get on a pathway to citizenship. (This was an "amnesty" for illegal immigrants and was called that at the time.) More than three million immigrants took advantage of this provision.

But for opponents of illegal immigration, the bill outlawed further hiring of illegal immigrants by requiring employers to check the work status of new hires. This would choke off the incentive to immigrate. Hispanics, though, worried that employers might use this provision to discriminate against Hispanic hiring. They forced an addition to the law, therefore, forbidding employers to challenge the documents they were given. This turned a potentially tough new enforcement provision into a mere formality. Enforcements were a rarity.

Even so, Simpson-Mazzoli was passed by Congress and enthusiastically signed by conservative President Ronald Reagan. It remains our defining immigration law.

It did not, however, stem the tide of new illegal immigrant arrivals, who were coming at the rate of half-a-million or more a year. During the George W. Bush administration, a new coalition for immigration reform took shape. Business groups wanted more workers; farm groups told dire stories about leaving produce unpicked without immigrant workers. Hispanics were a growing voting bloc, one courted by both parties. For three years—2005, 2006, and 2007—various versions of a new reform bill took shape. Once again, it would provide a path to citizenship, crack down on employers, and tighten the border. John McCain of Arizona and Ted Kennedy of Massachusetts co-authored the major bill. Conservative Republicans denounced the bill's new pathways to citizenship as "amnesty." All they wanted was higher fences and tighter borders. Hispanic groups marched against various versions of the bills, turning out hundreds of thousands of people in Dallas, Los Angeles, and elsewhere. In 1986, presidential leadership had pushed Simpson-Mazzoli through; two decades later, presidential leadership by another Republican president wasn't enough.

Immigration has become a social issue that won't go away. By 2050, about one in five Americans will be an immigrant. By then, we will be more a "nation of immigrants" than at any point in U.S. history.

LIVING ON BORROWED TIME: SOCIAL SECURITY

If you work, you should be regularly getting those official-looking letters about your Social Security benefits. Beginning in 1998, the federal government launched the largest mass mailing in history. The commissioner of Social Security wrote to every single American who pays Social Security taxes. The letter is titled "Your Social Security Statement." The massive computers of the Social Security Administration in Baltimore, Maryland, churned out millions of individualized letters reporting what each individual had paid year by year. The letters also reported estimated benefits. Based on what you had paid in so far, you could expect to receive—if you kept working until the retirement age—so many dollars per month.

About 75 million baby boomers will start retiring in about 2010. Chances are, they will live longer and healthier lives than any generation before—and run up even bigger costs for the Social Security system and its health care cousin, Medicare. (We discuss Medicare in the next chapter.) There are some—including most recent presidents—who think Social Security needs some reform. It is a time bomb, most experts think, ticking away, moving inexorably toward the day when the costs will exceed the income. But what, exactly, is Social Security? Here, we examine its history—and its future.

THE NEW DEAL, THE ELDERLY, AND THE GROWTH OF SOCIAL SECURITY

No event has shaped American social welfare policy more than the Great Depression. Franklin Roosevelt's administration initiated hundreds of New Deal programs in its efforts to help citizens like these jobless men. Government spending on social welfare has continued to grow, even during the Bush administration.

Social Security, the most expensive public policy in the United States, began modestly enough as a "pay-as-you-go" plan during Franklin Roosevelt's New Deal. Its official name is OASDI, for Old Age, Survivors and Disability Insurance. Social Security was designed in part to get older Americans out of the workforce during the Great Depression of the 1930s. At first it was "a deal that couldn't be beat."[29] The idea was that money in payroll taxes would have to come into the federal treasury before money could go out to the beneficiaries. President Roosevelt wanted a plan so fiscally solid that "no damn politician can ever scrap my social security program." Over the years, Americans have tended to believe that their Social Security payments were just getting out what was paid in. But that wasn't true even for the very first Social Security recipient, a woman named Ida May Fuller from Brattleboro, Vermont. Her total contributions were a mere $22.54, but her lifetime benefits were $22,888.92 because she lived to old age. But Ida May Fuller's deal is no longer available. Take a young woman beginning a career today at the age of 22. There will be only about two workers for every one recipient by the time she retires (in contrast to about 25 to 1 when the program began).

Social Security grew over the years, in large part because it worked. More than 90 percent of people polled, year after year, support Social Security. No one gets rich off Social Security. The mean monthly check is about $900. Still, for the cost of a tiny administrative fee to run it, Social Security got the elderly off the bottom of the poverty ladder. In 1965, Congress tacked onto Social Security a new program, Medicare, to assist the elderly with medical costs (see Chapter 19). By the turn of the twenty-first century, Social Security and Medicare had become the most expensive public policies in the history of the world. In a decade, they will consume more than half the federal budget.

Here is how Social Security works: Government taxes workers and their employers a percent of the employee's income up to a maximum. Both employee and employer contributions are paid into the **Social Security Trust Fund**. If you work, you are contributing 6.2 percent of your wages (up to $102,000), and your employer matches it. (If you are making $102,000, you and Bill Gates are paying the same dollar amount into Social Security.) Your contributions, as well as those of more than a hundred million other workers, go into this huge government "bank account." The Trust Fund, of course, is not a literal bank account. As long as there is more money paid in than going out, the Trust Fund stays in the black. Although the sums are huge, the math is not all that complicated. Today's average Social Security payment is equal to about 36 percent of the average worker's wages. Currently, there are about 3.4 workers per recipient. Thus, the cost to each worker is about 10.5 percent of a worker's earnings (36/3.4 = 10.5). Current Social Security payroll taxes are 12.4 percent. Thus, for the moment, more money is going into the Trust Fund than is being paid out. By law, the Trust Fund can do only one thing with these moneys: invest them in U.S. treasury bonds. It cannot buy McDonald's stock or Wal-Mart stock or Joe's Hot New Internet stock. It has been earning about 6 percent a year on its investment.

Essential to this arithmetic is the ratio of workers to beneficiaries. The more retirees, relative to workers, the thinner the Social Security blanket stretches. If instead of 3.4 workers per beneficiaries there are only 2, then the math changes. The cost to each worker rises from 10.5 percent of earnings to 18 percent of earnings (36/2 = 18), and Social Security turns from black to red ink.[30] That will soon happen.

Thus, the Social Security program may be living on borrowed time. Americans are aging. When Social Security was first established, the life expectancy of the average American was lower than the 65 years pegged for the worker to collect benefits. Thus, the "average" American would not even live long enough to collect his or her benefits. Things changed when birthrates began to soar after World War II (the baby boomers) and better medicine kept us alive longer. Of the generation reaching age 65 in 2000, 69 percent of males lived to be 65; those who did will live another 16.2 years. Women have even longer life expectancies.

The Social Security dilemma is this: The number of Social Security contributors (the workers) is growing slowly, while the number of Social Security recipients (the retired) is growing rapidly. As the number of retirees grows, and their average benefit is constantly increased to cover the cost of living (called a cost-of-living allowance), Social Security expenditures are going to increase. The more retirements and the more benefits, the higher the costs. At some point—about 2038 unless something changes—payouts will exceed income.[31] The Trust Fund's accumulated trillions will be gone. If this happens, Congress would have to use regular appropriations to pay out benefits to claimants as they retired. If taxes were not raised, a dollar that would have gone to the military or homeland security or the national parks would have to be diverted to the retirees. No solution is a politically pleasant one. Cutting benefits to retirees is no more popular than raising taxes on working contributors. Hard choices lie ahead. Many young Americans suspect that Social Security is not going to be around for them anyway. (See "Young People and Politics: Social Security and UFOs.")

Where the Money Goes . . .

Social Security Trust Fund
The "bank account" into which Social Security contributions are "deposited" and used to pay out eligible recipients.

YOUNG PEOPLE AND POLITICS

Social Security and UFOs

The story that more young adults believe in UFOs than in the future of Social Security has been repeated so often that it has almost become an urban legend—one of those offbeat, often-told stories that just might be true. President Clinton told an audience at the University of Illinois that "there are polls that say that young people in their twenties think it's more likely that they will see UFOs than that they will ever collect Social Security." The story has been repeated by countless politicians, on ABC, CNN, and elsewhere. How did such an odd "factoid" come into popular lore?

A group called Third Millennium that favors Social Security reform commissioned two surveys in 1994, one of Americans 65 and older and one of young adults. They hired pollster Frank Luntz to conduct the surveys. Luntz asked the young adults if they thought Social Security would exist by the time they retired, and only 28 percent said yes. At the very end of the questionnaire, he asked an out-of-the-blue question: "And one final question, and I ask you to take this seriously—Do you think UFOs exist?" Some 46 percent said yes. That was the basis for the claim that young people believe more in UFOs than in Social Security. (Or, in President Clinton's further embellishment, that "they will see UFOs.")

There was a little more to the survey than that. Interestingly, young people were more likely than seniors themselves (48 to 35 percent) to think that older people were getting "less than their fair share of government benefits." But the quirky finding about UFOs became a part of national lore. Anyone with a complaint about Social Security could trot out the isolated numbers and make something out of them.

Indeed, the "factoid" made so much news that, a few years later, the Employee Benefit Research Institute surveyed people ages 18 to 34 and asked this question: "Which do you have greater confidence in, receiving Social Security benefits after retirement or that alien life from outer space exists?" It found that 63 percent have greater confidence in getting their Social Security and 33 percent thought alien life was more likely.

Americans, even young Americans, remain pretty committed to Social Security. Fay Lomax Cook and Lawrence R. Jacobs examined public opinion about Social Security over the last two decades and found that 90 percent of the population consistently believed that we spend either "too little" or "the right amount" as a nation for Social Security. About half of all Americans were either somewhat confident or very confident about the future of Social Security, and older Americans continue to vote more heavily than younger ones.

QUESTIONS FOR DISCUSSION

▶ In 2008, both candidates promised to protect Social Security benefits for older Americans. What could—or should—we do about younger Americans?

▶ How much do you plan to rely on Social Security?

Sources: The Third Millennium poll is available at their Web site, *www.third.mil. org/*. The Employee Benefit Research Institute Report is "Public Attitudes on Social Security," *EBRI News* 19 (March 1998): 1. The Lomax-Jacobs report is in the National Academy of Social Insurance, "American Attitudes Toward Social Security: Popular Claims Meet Hard Data," March 2001, 1–8.

HOW GEORGE W. BUSH TRIED AND FAILED TO REFORM SOCIAL SECURITY

DEBATE

Welfare Reform

Politicians tread gingerly on the terrain of Social Security, fearing a backlash from elderly Americans.[32] Older Americans vote far more than younger ones. About three-quarters of young people themselves agree with the statement that "voting is something older people do."[33] Elected in a squeaker of an election in 2000, the new president, George W. Bush, was nonetheless determined to behave as if he had a national mandate. Social Security reform was near the top of that mandate. Bush and the Republicans proposed diverting a small portion (the suggested figure was 2 percent—that is a bit less than a third of your contribution of 6.2 percent) of Social Security contributions to private retirement funds. Each individual could, presumably, reduce his or her contribution to the Social Security system and instead put the money into a private account, a stock, a bond, or another investment. They could collect their gains—or perhaps face their losses—when they were eligible to collect Social Security. Or, perhaps, the Social Security system itself would do the investing in the stock market. Chile, Great Britain, Australia, Poland, and Brazil have done just that. Democrats feared what Franklin Roosevelt warned about, that some "damn politicians" were about to scrap the nearly sacred Social Security program.

President Bush appointed a Commission to Strengthen Social Security. The commission was filled with advocates for the "privatization" of Social Security. The late New York Democratic Senator Daniel Patrick Moynihan, one of the few Democrats to favor privatization, and Richard Parsons, AOL-Time Warner's chief executive officer and one of the most prominent African American business leaders, cochaired the commission. Most presidential commissions release their report in the glare of television cameras, often in a showy presentation in the White House. The Moynihan–Parsons commission released its final report on December 21, 2001, while most Americans were Christmas shopping. Its warnings were dire (the warnings of almost every commission to study Social Security are dire).[34] It pushed the idea of limited privatization of Social Security. Workers could put a portion (say a third) of their contributions into the stock or bond market. The problem, the Democrats emphasized, was that permitting people to divert money from the system, even for good reason, would merely hasten its bankruptcy. The report couldn't have come at a worse time for advocates of privatization. Stocks were swooning before the commission reported and slumped further thereafter. One critic called

For years, some economists and many Republicans have advocated the partial "privatization" of Social Security, George W. Bush pushed the idea throughout two terms, never successfully. These protesters in Washington, D.C. want to leave Social Security untouched.

the whole idea of privatizing Social Security the "Trillion Dollar Hustle," a plan only Wall Street could love.[35] The stock slump of the early twenty-first century eroded public and political support of the whole idea.[36]

SOCIAL WELFARE POLICY ELSEWHERE

The future of social welfare policies is just as complex (if somewhat less controversial) in other democratic countries. Most industrial nations not only provide social policy benefits but also are usually more generous with them than the U.S. government. The scope of social benefits in health, child care, parental leave, unemployment compensation, and benefits to the elderly are far greater in European nations than in ours. Europeans often think of their countries as "welfare states," with all the generous benefits—and staggering taxes by U.S. standards—that this implies.[37] European old-age programs are in even bigger trouble than ours are, though, partly because their labor forces are not being replenished by immigration as fast as ours.[38]

Other national governments and their citizens often take quite a different approach to the problems of poverty and social welfare. Americans tend to see poverty and social welfare needs as individual rather than governmental concerns, whereas European nations tend to support greater governmental responsibility for these problems. Also, Europeans often have a more positive attitude toward government, whereas Americans are more likely to distrust government action in areas such as social welfare policy.

Most Americans would be amazed at the range of social benefits in the average European country. French parents, for example, are guaranteed the right to put their toddlers in *crèches* (day care centers), regardless of whether the parents are rich or poor, at work or at home. French unemployment benefits are generous by American standards (and French unemployment rates are two to three times higher than ours). In many European countries, treatments at health spas come with free or low-cost government health care policies.

COMPARATIVE

Comparing Social Welfare Systems

Europeans pay a high price for generous benefits. Taxes in Western European nations far exceed those in the United States (see Chapter 14). There, taxes approach (or even exceed) 50 percent of income. Every problem the United States faces in funding Social Security is even bigger in Europe. In some ways, European social welfare problems are even greater because their populations are shrinking. Fewer babies mean fewer workers. Fewer workers mean fewer taxpayers.

As in the United States, there has been a backlash against the welfare state in Europe. Parties of the Left, advocating generous public benefits, once ruled nearly every European country. Today, conservative parties—like the Republicans in the United States—often win by bashing the welfare state.

UNDERSTANDING SOCIAL WELFARE POLICY

Social welfare policies are going to be controversial in a capitalist, democratic political system. Very few issues divide liberals and conservatives more sharply. Americans struggle to balance individual merit and the rewards of initiative with the reality of systemic inequalities and the need to provide support to many. Citizens disagree on how much government can or should do to even out the competition and protect those who are less able or too old to compete.

SOCIAL WELFARE POLICY AND THE SCOPE OF GOVERNMENT

Nothing more clearly accounts for the growth of government in America than social welfare spending. Americans tend to overestimate how much government spends on the poor. They probably underestimate how much support for the elderly costs, thinking that Social Security is merely "getting back what I paid in." Ever since the New Deal and the invention of Social Security, the growth of government has been driven by the growth of social welfare policies. Conservatives complain about the "welfare state." Even if ours is small relative to those of other nations, the American social welfare system grows generation by generation. American attitudes toward the growth of social welfare often depend on their assessment of what Schneider and Ingram call "target groups."[39] Groups viewed favorably—the elderly who have worked hard or the "deserving poor"—are one thing. The "undeserving poor" are another. Part of the debate about the scope of social welfare policies is a debate about how deserving various groups are and how big they are. We have cut back on aid to the poor, but there is no sign that the elderly will go quietly if political candidates propose cutting back on Social Security.

DEMOCRACY AND SOCIAL WELFARE

There is an extensive social welfare system in every major democracy. Ours, in fact, is the least extensive of all. As with other policies, competing demands have to be resolved by government decision makers, but decision makers do not act in a vacuum. They are aligned with and pay allegiance to various groups in society. These groups include members of their legislative constituencies, members of their electoral coalitions, and members of their political party. Many of these groups provide the financial assistance that the decision makers need to seek and retain political office.

In the social welfare policy arena, the competing groups are often quite unequal in terms of political resources. For example, the elderly are relatively well organized and often have the resources needed to wield significant influence in support of programs they desire. As a result, they are usually successful in protecting and expanding their programs. For the poor, however, influencing political decisions is more difficult. They vote less frequently and lack strong, focused organizations and money. In this unequal battle, cutting welfare benefits is easier than tampering with the Social Security system.

SUMMARY

In the United States—indeed in most countries—social policy goes almost entirely to citizens and those who reside in the country legally. That is one reason why the issue of immigration has soared onto the political agenda. What President Reagan and Congress were able to accomplish in the 1980s—a sort of "grand compromise" on the immigration issue—hasn't been possible in recent decades. Immigration politics have become hostile, even hard, politics.

Our social welfare policies have taken two distinct paths. First are the entitlement policies, dominated by Social Security and Medicare. In the United States, we spend more money on federal entitlements than on any other single thing the government does. Rich or poor, Americans are entitled to Social Security benefits by law. The other road includes the means-tested programs, government's expenditures for poorer Americans.

You have seen in this chapter that government action and inaction can play a major role in affecting the social welfare status of many poor and elderly Americans. Entitlement programs such as Social Security and Medicare have significantly improved the lot of the elderly, but these very costly programs threaten to grow ever larger and more expensive. Programs aimed more specifically at the poor cost less (and perhaps have accomplished less), but they seem likely to remain objects of political controversy for many years to come.

Chapter Test

Multiple Choice

1. Social programs that provide benefits only to people with specific needs are referred to as:
   a. Government handouts
   b. Entitlement programs
   c. Social welfare
   d. Means-tested programs
   e. Government assistance programs

2. Which of the following groups is most likely to be affected by poverty in the United States?
   a. Young men in their 20s
   b. Young men and women in their 20s
   c. Unmarried women with children
   d. The elderly
   e. Foreigners

3. Which of the following takes a higher percentage from those at lower income levels than from the well-to-do?
   a. A progressive tax
   b. A regressive tax
   c. A proportional tax
   d. A low-income tax
   e. A working tax

4. The Earned Income Tax Credit (EITC) refers to:
   a. A special tax category for high-income groups
   b. A special tax for people who make less than $50,000 a year
   c. A tax benefit for the upper class
   d. A tax benefit for the working class
   e. An income tax that everyone has to pay

5. Which of the following is NOT an entitlement program?
   a. Medicaid
   b. Medicare
   c. Unemployment Insurance
   d. Social Security
   e. All of the above

6. All but which of the following were negatively affected by the restrictive 1924 immigration law passed by Congress?
   a. Immigrants from Eastern Europe
   b. Immigrants from Northwestern Europe
   c. Immigrants from Latin America
   d. Immigrants from Asia
   e. Immigrants from Africa

7. Which of the following is NOT an "in-kind" benefit?
   a. The Child Care Assistance Program (CCAP)
   b. Food Stamps
   c. Children's Health Insurance Program (CHIPs)
   d. Earned Income Tax Credit (EITC)
   e. All of the above

8. Which of the following is NOT true about Americans' attitudes toward Social Security?
   a. Younger people are more likely than older people to believe that seniors are getting their "fair share" of benefits
   b. The vast majority of Americans believes that we are paying too little or just enough into Social Security
   c. About half of all Americans are at least fairly confident about the future of Social Security
   d. According to one study, one-third of younger Americans believe it is more likely that aliens exist than that they will receive Social Security benefits
   e. Younger people are more likely than older people to be opposed to paying for Social Security

True/False

9. Singles are more likely to vote Republican than people in traditional families.
   True_____   False_____

10. The government spends much more money on the poor below the poverty line than it does on other citizens.
    True_____   False_____

11. Most of the poor in America work.
    True_____   False_____

12. People making below $50,000 per year receive the highest percentage of tax breaks in this country.
    True_____   False_____

13. Most immigrants have entered the United States legally.
    True_____   False_____

14. Most European nations have far harsher immigration policies than does the United States.
    True_____   False_____

Short Answer

15. What is the definition of "income" as opposed to the definition of "wealth"? Which of the two is more unevenly distributed in the United States?

16. Please explain what is meant by the term "feminization of poverty." Provide examples to illustrate your answer.

17. Explain the two ways in which the government can affect personal income. Provide an example for each.

18. Briefly outline the major provisions in the 1980s Simpson-Mazzoli Act for immigrants in the United States.

19. This textbook quotes Feldman and Steenbergen (2001) as having said that Americans are humanitarians, but not egalitarians. What does this statement mean with regard to Americans' attitudes toward "social insurance" programs?

20. Please explain why the reported median income of over $48,000 per household in America may be misleading as an indicator of how well off Americans are as a whole.

21. How are the poor counted in the United States? Why might this measure underestimate the seriousness of poverty in this country?

22. How do welfare benefits in Europe compare with benefits in the United States? What are the major differences in the types of benefits, including who provides them and who pays for them? Please give specific examples.

Essay

23. In what ways is the upcoming massive retirement wave of baby boomers going to affect the U.S. Social Security system? In your opinion, what should be done in order to "save" Social Security? Outline at least two different strategies you would employ in order to prevent the bankruptcy of this system. What is the biggest obstacle you anticipate for each of your strategies?

24. Review the information presented in the "My State" graph on p. 575 about the percentage of children living in poverty. Please choose one state from the lower end of the spectrum (i.e., with a relatively low percentage of poverty) and one from the higher end of the spectrum (i.e., with a relatively high percentage). In your opinion and based on what you know, what are at least two possible,

context-specific factors that might explain the percentages in your chosen states?

25. Take a look at Table 18.1 on page 573. How has the "middle class" (i.e., the third-fifth and fourth-fifth) developed since the 1960s? Using what you know about the importance of the middle class in upholding democracy (by forming the core of civil society) in the United States, how would you evaluate the developments seen in Table 18.1?

26. The Social Security Act of 1935 could be said to represent a transfer of responsibility for the poor from families to the government. Based on what you know, what are three factors that might explain this shift in perception? In addition, what do you think

is the current perception of most Americans on this issue?

27. What were the three main provisions in the 1996 Personal Responsibility and Work Opportunity Reconciliation Act? Please evaluate these provisions based on (a) how fair you consider them to be and (b) how effectively they deal with the problem of welfare in the long run.

28. The textbook raises the question of the government's role in promoting marriage. Do you believe the government should provide incentives—including monetary ones—to married couples? Why, or why not? Please be specific in your answer and provide substantive pros and cons, rather than merely an opinion.

Answer Key

1. D   2. C   3. B   4. D   5. A   6. B   7. D   8. E   9. False   10. False   11. True   12. False   13. True   14. True

Key Terms

social welfare policies (570)
entitlement programs (571)
means-tested programs (571)
income distribution (572)
income (572)
wealth (572)
poverty line (573)
feminization of poverty (574)

progressive tax (574)
proportional tax (575)
regressive tax (575)
Earned Income Tax Credit (575)
transfer payments (576)
Social Security Act of 1935 (577)

Personal Responsibility and Work Opportunity Reconciliation Act (578)
Temporary Assistance for Needy Families (578)
immigration (579)
Simpson-Mazzoli Act (582)
Social Security Trust Fund (585)

Internet Resources

www.aecf.org
The Annie E. Casey Foundation produces a wealth of information about America's children, including its *Kid's Count* data book.

www.fairus.org
FAIR—the Federation for American Immigration Reform—has data on immigration in the United States.

www.ssa.gov
The official site of the Social Security Administration, where you can learn about the history of the program and find out how to calculate your own benefits.

GetConnected

Insuring Children

Children tend to be the group of Americans least likely to have health insurance coverage. A provision in the Balanced Budget Act of 1997 established the State Children's Health Insurance Program (SCHIP). This program allowed each state to offer health insurance for children, up to age 19, who are not already insured. SCHIP is a state-administered program and each state sets its own guidelines regarding eligibility and services. Let us look a little closer at the State Children's Health Insurance Program.

Search the Web

Go to the U.S. Department of Health and Human Services page on the State Children's Health Insurance Program, *www.cms.hhs.gov/home/schip.asp*. Find the link to your state's program. The department also built a Web site, "Insure Kids Now!," which provides more direct links to information about each state's insurance plan. Visit it at *www.insurekidsnow.gov/* and find the link to the Web site created by your state. Explore your state's Web site. Access some of the pages for other nearby states, and look at the page for a state that is far from your state.

Questions to Ask

- Who determines who is eligible to participate in the Children's Health Insurance Program?
- Who is eligible to participate in the program in your state? How does this compare with the eligibility in surrounding states? How about a state far away from your state?

- Can you see a relationship between who is eligible and the political culture in the states you looked at? For some help identifying the states' political cultures, you may want to consult *http://academic.regis.edu/jriley/421elazar.htm/*.

Why It Matters

The State Children's Health Insurance Program was created because many families cannot afford adequate health insurance coverage. Sick children who are uninsured are often taken to hospital emergency rooms, where the care tends to be more expensive than that received from a family doctor. Usually the American taxpayer pays for the emergency room visit through the Medicaid program because the family can't afford to pay for it.

Get Involved

One of the challenges that has faced the State Children's Health Insurance Program is getting eligible children enrolled in the program. Find out if your state has experienced this problem and think about how to create an outreach plan to reach those children. You can research your state's program by searching the index of the newspaper in your state's capital or your local newspaper. The Web page *www.urban.org/urlprint.cfm?ID=7233* discusses some of the reasons why more children have not enrolled in the insurance program. Look over the items linked on *http://www.financeprojectinfo.org/win/HC_CHIPmisc.asp* for more information on the challenges facing the program. For more exercises, go to *www.longmanamerican.government.com*.

For Further Reading

Campbell, Andrea Louise. *How Policies Make Citizens: Senior Political Activism and the American Welfare State.* Princeton NJ: Princeton University Press, 2003. How Social Security created a new class of political activists.

Diamond, Peter A., and Peter R. Orszag, *Saving Social Security: A Balanced Approach.* Washington, DC: Brookings Institution, 2005. Social Security needs lots of minor surgeries, not major surgery.

Ehrenreich, Barbara. *Nickel and Dimed: On (Not) Getting By in America.* New York: Owl Books, 2001. A well-educated—with

a Ph.D. in biology—journalist experiences the difficulties of getting by in America while working a string of low-wage jobs.

Gilens, Martin. *Why Americans Hate Welfare: Race, Media, and the Politics of Antipoverty Policy.* Chicago: University of Chicago Press, 2000. Gilens argues that public opposition to welfare is fed by a combination of racial and media stereotyping about the true nature of America's poor.

Hacker, Jacob S. *The Great Risk Shift.* New York: Oxford University Press, 2006. Why Americans have to rely more and more on their own resources for health, retirement security, and everything else.

Rodgers, Harrell, Jr. *American Poverty in a New Era of Reform.* 2nd ed. New York: M. E. Sharpe, 2006. Discusses what has happened to poverty since the welfare reforms.

Schieber, Sylvester J., and John B. Shoven. *The Real Deal: The* *History and Future of Social Security.* New Haven, CT: Yale University Press, 2000. An excellent analysis of the past, present and future of Social Security.

Swain, Carol M. (ed.). *Debating Immigration.* New York: Cambridge University Press, 2007. Readable perspectives on the ethics, politics, and policy debates of immigration.

POLICYMAKING
FOR
HEALTH CARE,
THE
ENVIRONMENT,
AND
ENERGY

POLITICS IN ACTION:
HEALTH CARE CRISIS IN THE MEDICAL CAPITAL OF THE WORLD

People come from all over the world to get treated in Houston. Some have a lot of money; some have insurance. Unlike almost every other industrialized nation, the United States relies on private health insurance (sometimes subsidized by employers) to pay for health care. Most of the elderly, though, are insured through government programs, typically Medicare (which we explain in this chapter). People who do not have private health insurance in the United States, however, now number about 46 million. Nationally, that is about 15 percent of the population. In Texas, it is 24 percent, the highest among the states.

*USA Today** took a look at the consequences of uneven health care coverage by focusing on Houston, Texas' largest city. Houston is the site of the world's largest medical complex, where cancer and heart treatments attract the world's elite. But it is also a city where about 30 percent of the population lacks health insurance—about twice the national average.

There are two public hospitals in Houston, Ben Taub and LBJ, to which thousands of sick Houstonians go, especially when they cannot afford health care or are uninsured. Federal law requires emergency rooms to treat all patients. Thus, Ijeoma Onye drove her daughter 45 minutes to Ben Taub Hospital in Houston. Short of breath and with headaches, the girl waited four hours for treatment, but, said the mother, it was faster than getting a regular physician appointment, which

June 19, 2007

could take months. The family did not qualify for state-aided Medicaid assistance. The upper limit for qualifying in Texas was $4822 for a family of three. (In Florida, it was $10,000 for a family of three.) In Texas, emergency room visits had grown by 50 percent over a decade. About half of all emergency room visitors need routine care, and not trauma care. In Houston, patients regularly call 911 trying to get transported from one overcrowded emergency to one less crowded. When a hospital emergency room is over-crowded, it puts itself on "drive by" status; ambulance drivers have to find another hospital for their patient.

And the meter is running on the cost of American medical care, already the highest in the world. Americans spend more on health care than people in any other nation. Still, we are far from the healthiest nation. One reason health care is so expensive is because Americans like high-tech medicine. High-tech medicine is expensive medicine.

This chapter is about two major public policy issues—health care and the environment—that have three things in common. First, unlike many other policies, they both involve life-and-death decisions. Pollution is not merely unsightly or unpleasant; it is also a serious health risk. Second, both health policy and environmental decisions involve sophisticated technologies that are expensive and sometimes controversial. Many of these issues—human cloning and stem cell research, for example—involve moral debates as well. Third, prices for energy, as well as health care, have soared.

HEALTH CARE POLICY

Medical care in the United States differs from that in most other democracies in one important way: the role the government plays. Many nations, both rich and poor, consider health care a basic right. The Italian constitution, for example, says that "the Republic protects individual health care as a basic right." Article 25 of the UN Declaration of Human Rights, which the United States signed, says that basic human rights include a "standard of living adequate for health." We have a medical system driven in large part by a market. And it is a mixed and imperfect market. To a large degree, the goal of most participants in our health care system is to maximize one's health benefits at someone else's expense.

There is a paradox about American health care: As a nation, we spend a far larger share of our national income on health than any other industrialized country, yet we are far from having the healthiest population. There are few things more important to people than their health. It is often said that Americans enjoy the best health care in the world, and some do. Americans, compared to people in other countries, pay a lot for their health care. Yet it is not clear whether they always get their money's worth. Unlike other countries, we do not have a government-run health care system. Nor do we have a completely private one. Like American politics itself, the system is vast, complex, and controversial.

THE HEALTH OF AMERICANS AND THE COST OF HEALTH CARE IN AMERICA

Comparing Health Systems

Although Americans are generally healthy (which is to be expected given the country's wealth), health care statistics show that they still lag behind other countries in some key health care categories (see "America in Perspective: We Pay a Lot for Health Care, but What Do We Get for the Investment?").

The average American has a life expectancy of 77 years—a high number but one surpassed by citizens of most other developed nations. Despite advances in

AMERICA IN PERSPECTIVE

We Pay a Lot for Health Care,
but What Do We Get for the Investment?

The World Health Organization (WHO) compiles a list of health indicators for countries around the world. WHO tabulates what countries spend on their health and measures various health outcomes, mainly how long their citizens live and how healthy children are. We spend 15 percent of our gross domestic product (GDP) on

health care—more than any other nation. On two major indicators of a healthy population—our longevity and the percent of infants and young children who die—our expenditures do not buy better health care. We live shorter lives and have worse childhood mortality. This is the American health care paradox.

Country	Per Capita Spending in U.S. Dollars (2004)	Percent of GDP Spent on Health	Life Expectancy in Years (Men/Women)	Deaths of Children Under 5 (per 1,000)
United States	6,096	15.4	75/80	8
Canada	3,173	9.8	78/83	6
France	3,040	10.5	77/84	5
Germany	3,171	10.6	76/82	5
Japan	2,293	7.8	79/86	4
United Kingdom	2,500	8.1	77/81	6

Source: World Health Organization, Country Statistics, 2007.

medical technology, the average American does not live as long as the average Canadian. Using a measure of healthy longevity, the World Health Organization ranked the United States twenty-fourth among the world's nations. The second common indicator of a healthy population is its infant mortality rate, the chances that a baby will live beyond his or her crucial first year. The chances in the United States of a baby dying in the first year of life are more than 50 percent higher than those of a baby born in Japan. Indeed, the United States ranks only eighteenth among the world's nations in infant mortality. The health care system in the United States may be part of the explanation.

American health care costs are both staggering and soaring. Americans now spend $2.3 *trillion* a year on health care. Health expenditures are one of the largest single components of America's economy, accounting for *one-seventh* of the gross domestic product (GDP). Canada, France, and Germany provide universal health care coverage for their citizens but spend only 8 to 11 percent of their GDPs on health care, and Britain and Japan spend only 8 percent for universal coverage. In America, not only are costs high, but they are increasing faster than any other good or service we purchase. In 1970, we spent a mere 7 percent of our GDP on health care. Today, we spend 15 percent of our GDP on health services.

We will likely be spending 20 percent of our GDP for health care by 2015—about the percent of the GDP now covered by all of government. Because government is so deeply involved in health care, government's burden will soar as well. The two major federal and state health care programs—Medicare and Medicaid—now consume about 4.5 percent of the GDP. By 2050, those two programs alone could amount to 22 percent of the GDP. Since World War II, the *entire federal budget*—defense, social security, parks, the FBI, everything—has never amounted to more than 20 percent of the GDP.

Millions of Americans have had to cope with higher medical costs. Many of them have bought mail-order drugs from Canadian pharmacies. Some states have even encouraged this violation of U.S. law. People in 11 states can even

The United States is the only advanced industrialized Western nation that lacks a system to provide health insurance for all its citizens. Hillary Clinton has long been in the forefront of political efforts to move the USA toward such a system. Here, she is seen speaking about her proposed plan during the 2008 presidential primary campaign.

access state government Web sites to connect with cheaper Canadian pharmacies. Others who can afford it resort to medical migration, outsourcing their medical care to cheaper foreign hospitals. The *Wall Street Journal* reported the story of Amandeep Kaur, whose deteriorating eye stretched her resources far beyond what she made from her newsstand. Ms. Kaur pays far more than most for her eyedrops because she is uninsured; people who are insured get cheaper medicines. In the long run, she will need to have her eye removed at a cost of $12,000. Her best hope at the moment: save enough to get back to her native India, where surgery is cheaper.[1] An estimated 150,000 foreigners travel to India for medical care annually.[2] Just as we outsource computer software jobs to India, we can outsource health care, too. But many Americans do without health care, postpone it, or resort to emergency rooms for minor illnesses.

Why are health care expenditures in the United States so high? Americans do not visit doctors more than people in other countries. Germans, the British, and others spend more nights in the hospital than Americans. Doctor visits per person are actually declining in the United States.[3] American medicine is high-tech medicine. New technologies, drugs, and procedures often add to the cost of health care by addressing previously untreatable conditions or by providing better but more expensive care. Much of the money Americans pay for health care goes to services like organ transplants, kidney dialysis, and other treatments not widely available outside the United States. Americans believe that more care is better care, yet there is little evidence that high costs and more care translate into healthier patients.[4] No one can even imagine the costs of widespread availability of the sort of technologies available from stem cell research and other high-tech medicine. Americans are reluctant to "ration" medicine, at least not openly. Americans were gripped by the story of a young Florida woman named Terri Schiavo, kept alive in a persistent vegetative state. When her husband went to court to terminate her care, even Congress and the president rushed to intervene. Federal courts sided with the husband, the feeding tubes were removed, and Schiavo died. Keeping alive every person like Terri Schiavo could become very expensive.

The economics of health care provide no incentive to keep costs under control. As President Bush's Council of Economic Advisers so bluntly put it, "Buying more health care is not necessarily equivalent to buying more health."[5] When you pay your own money for a new car, you shop and save. When someone else is paying, you want the fanciest, fastest car someone else will pay for. Because insurance companies and government programs pay for most health care expenses, most patients have no reason to ask for cheaper care—they do not directly face the full financial consequences of their care. If someone else pays for your drugs, you are a big drug user. Health care providers, such as physicians, are also insulated from competing with each other to offer less expensive care. In fact, with the rise in medical malpractice suits, doctors may be ordering extra tests, however expensive they may be, to ensure that they cannot be sued—an approach sometimes called "defensive medicine." Such practices drive up the costs of medical care for everyone. Because insurance companies pay the bills, patients do not protest. However, increased costs associated with medical care are making insurance rates skyrocket. In 2007, the average family who could afford health insurance—often with help from an employer plan—was paying $12,100 for it. The level of care varies widely from one group to another in part because money drives the system. The total bill: health economist Laurence J. Kotlikoff estimates that the US now owes $70 trillion for its three major entitlements, Social Security, Medicare and Medicaid.[6] None shows any sign of shrinking in the generations ahead.

UNEVEN COVERAGE, UNEVEN CARE

For American medical care, costs are high, and coverage is spotty. Americans gain access to health care in a variety of ways. The most common means of access is through private insurance plans. These usually come from one's job. The reason is a historical quirk: During World War II, government imposed a wage freeze. Many employers, though, paid health benefits to attract workers. Thus was forged the link between one's job and one's health insurance. About 60 percent of Americans get their health care insurance from their employers. The traditional form of such a plan is a health insurance policy, in which a policyholder pays an annual premium and then is entitled to have the insurance company pay a certain amount of the cost of health care for the year.

Today, many people and their employers contract with a **health maintenance organization** (HMO) that directly provides all or most of a person's health care for a yearly fee. The government-subsidized Medicare program covers older Americans, and many of those living below the poverty line are covered by another government program, Medicaid (discussed in the next section). Some people must pay all health care expenses out of their own pocket. They, of course, are hit the hardest. Because hospitals set a standard rate for each procedure and then bargain for group rates with insurance companies, the uninsured pay the full cost. This makes insurance the ticket to medical care in America.

Health Insurance Most Americans have health insurance of some kind (an individual policy or membership in an HMO), but 46 million people are without health insurance coverage.[7] The most common reason for lacking health insurance is being poor. But the most common reason for losing health insurance is not being poor but losing or changing a job.

Age is one of the biggest predictors of being uninsured. Most of the uninsured are under 65 because nearly everyone 65 and older participates in Medicare, a government-subsidized program. Young adults are the least insured Americans. Children and older people are far more likely to have health insurance than young people. Lacking health insurance, though, matters a lot more than many young Americans think it does. Young Americans think—rightly—that diseases are far more common among older people. What hits them hardest is the most expensive single point in the health care system: the emergency room. (See "Young People and Politics: Health Insurance, Emergency Rooms, and Young Americans.")

health maintenance organization
Organization contracted by individuals or insurance companies to provide health care for a yearly fee. Such network health plans limit the choice of doctors and treatments. About 60 percent of Americans are enrolled in health maintenance organizations or similar programs.

Health Insurance, Emergency Rooms, and Young Americans

In the United States, about 46 million Americans do not have health insurance for some part of a year, and about 20 million lack it all year. Young adults, some people say, see themselves as more or less invincible to illness or death and pay little attention to the unpleasant prospects of getting seriously ill or dying. And, in fact, the uninsured are disproportionately young Americans between the ages of 18 and 35. In contrast, less than 10 percent of children are uninsured, and virtually all Americans over 65 are insured through Medicare.

Young people are certainly right about their fairly low chances of needing medical care for serious illnesses. Chances of getting heart disease or cancer increase with age. Young adults' medical problems come mostly from injuries and accidents—particularly traffic accidents—that require expensive emergency care that is difficult to afford without health insurance coverage.

Indeed, the statistics show that except for the very old (those over 75), young adults are the biggest users of emergency rooms. About 45 out of every 100 young adults aged 15 to 24 visit an emergency room annually, far more than kids under 15 (37 per 100) or even people 65 to 74 (36 per 100). Young people are even more likely than people over 75 to go to an emergency room for an injury. Apparently, those summer jobs can also be hazardous to your health. *Newsweek* reports that 70,000 young people are injured on the job and go to the emergency room each year. Teens are twice as likely as adults to be hurt on the job.

Because of charges of "patient dumping," where some emergency rooms were accused of denying service to desperate patients, Congress passed a 1986 law called EMTALA (Emergency Medical Treatment and Labor Act). EMTALA makes it illegal for emergency rooms to turn away people. The emergency room is therefore the only place in the American health care system that is required by law to treat you. Still, one of the first questions you are likely to be asked on the stretcher is, "What is your insurance situation?" Young adults actually have a harder time answering that question than any other age group, and they can find themselves with big medical debts at the same time they are trying to establish a good credit history and start a family. Emergency rooms provide great care, but they are the most expensive single component of the health care system.

QUESTIONS FOR DISCUSSION

▶ Should young Americans—or all Americans—be required to purchase health insurance, just as they are required to purchase collision insurance on their cars?

▶ Should emergency rooms be required by law to treat everyone who comes in?

Source: The data come from two reports by the Communicable Disease Center: "Early Release of Selected Estimates Based on Data from the January–June 2003 National Health Interview Study," December 12, 2003; and "National Hospital Ambulatory Medical Care: 2001 Emergency Department Survey," *Advance Data*, June 4, 2003. See also *Newsweek*, May 31, 2004, 61.

Access to health insurance in the United States is also closely tied to race and income. The higher a family's income, the more likely that its members are insured.[8] Long-term studies show that people without health insurance face a 25 percent higher risk of dying than those with insurance.[9] Millions of children also lack health insurance, a figure which varies a lot from state to state (see My State: Children's Health Insurance).

Managed Care In recent years, private market forces have transformed the country's health care system dramatically. Insurers choose HMOs or restricted physician lists for the provision of care, negotiate with physician groups and hospitals on fees and costs, and try to monitor most aspects of care to control unnecessary use. At least three-fourths of all doctors have signed contracts, covering at least some of their patients, to cut their fees and accept oversight of their medical decisions. Enrollment in these managed care plans grew slowly in the 1970s but more than tripled in the 1980s and doubled again in the 1990s. Today these plans cover about 60 percent of all Americans, representing about 85 percent of workers who receive health insurance.

My State | Children's Health Insurance

Children without health insurance are more likely to go without medical treatment. Sometimes parents seek out hospital emergency rooms as a medical provider even for minor fevers and ailments, thus adding to the cost of the health care system. There is a joint state–federal program called SCHIPS (State Children's Health Insurance Programs), which covers many poor children. Still, millions of children go without health coverage. Those figures vary a lot from state to state. The Annie E. Casey Foundation's annual report, called *Kids Count*, provides some numbers on the percent of children under 18 uninsured in each state. The map to the right reflects those percentages.

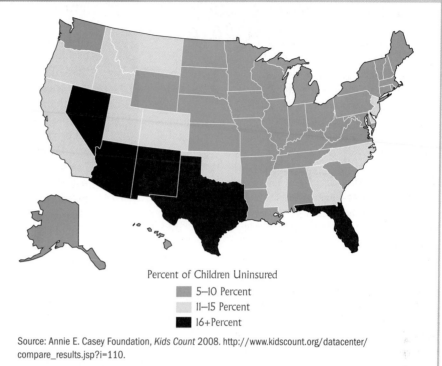

Percent of Children Uninsured

- 5–10 Percent
- 11–15 Percent
- 16+ Percent

Source: Annie E. Casey Foundation, *Kids Count* 2008. http://www.kidscount.org/datacenter/compare_results.jsp?i=110.

THE ROLE OF GOVERNMENT IN HEALTH CARE

The United States has the most thoroughly privatized medical care system in the developed world. National, state, and local governments pay for 46 percent of the country's total health bill, whereas the median for all industrialized countries is about 77 percent. The government also subsidizes employer-provided health insurance with tax breaks worth about $77 billion per year, the benefits of which go disproportionately to affluent, highly paid workers.

Forty-six percent amounts to much more than most Americans realize. Many hospitals are connected to public universities, and much medical research is financed through the National Institutes of Health, for example. Further, the federal government pays for much of the nation's medical bills through the Medicare program for the elderly, the Medicaid program for the poor, and health care for veterans. More than 20,000 physicians work for the federal government, and nearly all the rest receive payments from it. The government thus plays an important health care role in America, although less so than in other countries.

Who pays for the rest of Americans' health care? Private insurance companies cover one-third, and Americans pay nearly one-fifth of their health care costs out of their own pockets. Americans often think insurance companies pay most health care costs, but in fact the government is more heavily involved than the private insurance industry.

More than 50 years ago, Harry S. Truman was the first president to call for **national health insurance**, a compulsory insurance program to finance all Americans'

national health insurance
A compulsory insurance program for all Americans that would have the government finance citizens' medical care. First proposed by President Harry S. Truman, the plan was soundly opposed by the American Medical Association.

ELDON FLAGLER WAS AWARDED the NOBEL PRIZE FOR MEDICINE TODAY FOR DISCOVERING HOW TO GET HIS HMO TO PAY FOR an OVERNIGHT HOSPITAL STAY FOLLOWING QUADRUPLE BYPASS SURGERY.

Medicare

A program added to the Social Security system in 1965 that provides hospitalization insurance for the elderly and permits older Americans to purchase inexpensive coverage for doctor fees and other medical expenses.

Medicaid

A public assistance program designed to provide health care for poor Americans. Medicaid is funded by both the states and the national government.

medical care. The idea was strongly opposed by the American Medical Association, the largest physicians' interest group, which called this program socialized medicine because it would be run by the government. Although every other industrial nation in the world has adopted some form of national health insurance, the United States remains the exception. Today, about two-thirds of Americans support the idea of universal health care even if it involves more taxes. Even among people who call themselves "social conservatives," 59 percent support it.[10]

Politically, a few winds may be blowing toward a national health insurance plan like most other countries have. Even the American Medical Association has done an about-face on the issue. Many American businesses are at a competitive disadvantage in the global economy because they carry hefty health costs for their employees. In other countries, those costs are borne by governments. Businesses that offer health insurance see those who do not (Wal-Mart is a prime target of criticism) as "freeloading"—paying workers and letting someone else pick up their health costs. Business and consumer leaders from 90 organizations created the National Coalition on Health care, which has even explored the possibility of national health care.[11]

In 1965, Congress sought to rectify the special health care problems of elderly Americans by adopting **Medicare**. Medicare is part of the Social Security system and covers 40 million people. You pay for Medicare like you pay for Social Security, as a part of your paycheck. When you become eligible, you can collect. Part A of Medicare provides hospitalization insurance and short-term nursing care; Part B, which is voluntary, permits older Americans to purchase inexpensive coverage for doctor fees and other nonhospital medical expenses.

Like Social Security, Medicare costs are outrunning contributions to the Medicare Trust Fund. While Social Security is likely to last until about 2038, the safe horizon for Medicare is much shorter. It is the most rapidly increasing component of the federal budget. Today it is about 12 percent of the federal budget. Without reform, it will soar to nearly 30 percent by 2030.[12] The cost squeeze, though, is here today. More and more hospitals, physicians, and insurance companies have abandoned Medicare patients because Medicare payments do not cover their costs. To save itself money, Medicare constantly cuts back on the fees it will pay doctors and hospitals. One result: Fewer and fewer doctors treat Medicare patients. If Medicare will pay $1,200 for a $1,400 procedure, the physician loses money. "I have Medicare" is no guarantee that a doctor will treat you at the rate Medicare will reimburse.

Skyrocketing Medicare bills would soar even higher under a Medicare policy announced in February 2006, covering some obesity surgeries. These stomach-reducing surgeries cost $25,000 to $40,000. Nearly 200,000 Americans get them a year. Obesity has about the same health effect as 20 years of aging, a more serious result than smoking or problem drinking.[13] The Centers for Disease Control and Prevention estimates that obesity runs neck in neck with smoking as the nation's leading cause of preventable deaths.[14]

Not to be confused with Medicare is **Medicaid**, a program designed to provide health care for the poor that serves about 42.7 million people. Like other public assistance programs, Medicaid is funded by both the states and the national government (in 2005, the federal and state governments spent $330 billion on Medicaid).

Unlike Medicare, which goes to elderly Americans regardless of their income, Medicaid is a means-tested program. Medicaid is for the poorest of the poor (only 42 percent of people below the poverty line even qualify). Like Medicare, the future of Medicaid is tenuous as costs rise. Insurers and providers who cannot afford Medicare patients cannot afford Medicaid patients either.

POLICYMAKING FOR HEALTH CARE

The Politics of Health Care One reason for uneven government and private health care policies involves the representation of interests. Powerful lobbying organizations representing hospitals, doctors, and the elderly want Medicare to pay for the latest techniques. Politicians hardly feel comfortable denying these lifesaving measures to those who may have voted them into office. On the other hand, many groups are unrepresented in government. Their health needs may not be met simply because no well-organized groups are insisting that the government meet them.

The elderly are now one of the most powerful voting and lobbying forces in American politics. Health care policy that favors the elderly is one of the results of this interest group activity. The American Association of Retired Persons (AARP) has grown from about 150,000 members in 1959 to more than 35 million today, making it the largest voluntary association in the world. This single group now can claim to represent one American in eight, and its numbers may swell as the baby-boom generation reaches retirement. It claims to speak with authority on all questions associated with the elderly. Elderly Americans dependent on Social Security and Medicare are vigorous participators in American elections.[15]

One group that is increasingly active in health care policymaking is business. Conflict between the government (which pays many medical bills) and private employers (who pay much of the insurance premiums for their employees) is increasing. Each side wants the other to assume more of the health care burden. As private insurance rates increase, employers complain that they are paying inflated premiums for their workers to cover the costs of those who cannot pay or whose insurance provides only partial reimbursement for medical care. General Motors pays for medical benefits even for its retirees to supplement their Medicare. Wal-Mart's chief executive officer once sneered that GM was nothing more than a benefits company that had to sell cars in order to pay them. Employers then may attempt to reduce their burden by cutting out benefits that are covered by government programs. More and more employers are doing just that.

Insurance companies are also major players in health care policymaking. They have been making it more difficult for doctors and hospitals to pass along the costs of

Why It Matters
National Health Insurance

The United States is the only industrialized Western nation without a national health insurance system. Health care systems in other countries try to maintain a level of adequate care for everyone, even if it means squeezing high-cost drug expenditures and high-tech medicine. If we had a national health insurance system, we would probably have a higher level of care for the uninsured, but people who could afford it might have to pay more for care beyond the ordinary.

Government funding for stem cell research is controversial, as it raises the same sorts of issues in the public debate over abortion. Those who oppose it view such research as using a potential human being in a research lab. It always help to have a celebrity working on an issue, though. Actor Michael J. Fox, who has Parkinson's disease, has recently campaigned for congressional candidates who support federal funding for stem cell research.

others' unpaid bills to them, causing a cost crunch for some institutions, including inner-city hospitals and trauma centers that serve the poor. In addition, the health insurance industry has a huge stake in the outcome of the debate on national health insurance. A program funded and run by the national government would leave insurance companies without a function (or a profit). All these political fractures came together to defeat President Bill Clinton's major health care reform plan.

Two Presidents, Two Parties, Two Health Care Plans Nothing more starkly divides Democrats and Republicans than their competing health care policies. Both Bill Clinton and George W. Bush tried to tackle health care reform, one with a major national health insurance plan and the other with a market strategy. Neither met with much success in expanding coverage or reducing costs. President Clinton made health care reform the centerpiece of his first administration. His five-pound, 1,342-page Health Security Act proposal was an effort to deal with the two great problems of health care policy: costs and access. The difficulties the president faced with this proposal reveal much about the challenge of reforming health care in America.[16]

Clinton's main concern was guaranteeing health care coverage for all Americans. His plan would particularly have benefited people without any health insurance, but it would also have extended coverage for millions of others with inadequate health insurance.

Paying for the plan would have necessitated either broad-based taxes, which were politically unpalatable, or a requirement that employers provide health insurance for their employees or pay a premium into a public fund (which would also cover Medicaid and Medicare recipients). The president chose the employer insurance option, but the small business community was adamantly opposed to bearing the cost of providing health insurance. The president also proposed raising taxes on cigarettes, which angered the tobacco industry, and imposing a small tax on other large companies.

Because the White House reform plan for health care was bureaucratic and complicated, it was easy for opponents to label it a government takeover of the health care system. Interest groups of all shapes and sizes organized against it. An aggressive advertising campaign mounted by the health insurance industry characterized the president's plan as being expensive and experimental, as providing lower-quality and rationed care, and as killing jobs. The health insurance industry's famous "Harry and Louise" ads—Harry and Louise mull over the Clinton plan around their kitchen table and conclude, "There's got to be a better way"—were one of the most effective policy-oriented campaigns in history. After a long and tortuous battle, the plan died in Congress.

Between Bill Clinton's 1993 health care fiasco and George Bush's reelection in 2004, health costs in America again doubled. Drug prices were soaring. Democrats and older Americans led by the AARP were still clamoring for help meeting their medical costs. Republicans could ill afford to lose the votes of America's most regular voters.

George W. Bush brought the Republican faith in markets to the health care policy agenda. The problem, Bush argued, was that the market for health care—and the discipline markets provide—was alien to the medical care system.[17] The Bush administration supported more health savings accounts, in which individuals (if they could afford them) could set money aside, tax free, to pay for their medical needs or even medical insurance. People could then buy medical care like they buy cars or handbags. Prices would matter because people—not someone else—would have to pay more of their own care. The Bush plan would not come cheap. Government would lose $60 billion in tax breaks over a decade, more than the administration would be able to squeeze from cuts in Medicare and Medicaid benefits.[18]

Republicans and Democrats have long been as bitterly divided on prescription drug coverage for Medicare recipients. Democrats want government to subsidize drugs and control their escalating prices. Republicans want to encourage private plans to get seniors drugs. Finally, in 2003, the Republican-run Congress passed the Medicare Prescription Drug Improvement and Modernization Act. Medicare beneficiaries would be able to get a price reduction on their drugs. Congress and the White House squabbled about the cost, but all agreed it would be high—probably $530 billion over its first decade. Seniors would pay an annual premium of at least $420.

Louisiana's Representative Billy Tauzin steered the drugs-for-seniors bill through Congress (and was rewarded after his

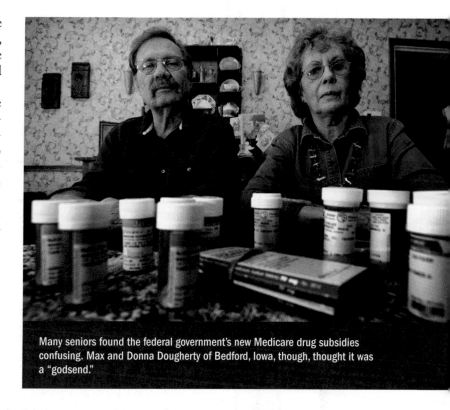

Many seniors found the federal government's new Medicare drug subsidies confusing. Max and Donna Dougherty of Bedford, Iowa, though, thought it was a "godsend."

retirement from Congress with a generous job as a lobbyist for "Big Pharma," the pharmaceutical lobbying group). The goal of the plan was to enroll 42 million elderly Americans in a plan that would reduce their drug costs. Democrats thought that government should buy drugs wholesale and resell them at reduced prices. Republicans, though, thought that "price fixing" by government was market interference. Congress, therefore, forbade the Medicare administration from negotiating with drug companies for wholesale drug pricing as other governments would do or as the Veteran's Administration does.

You Are a State Legislator

HEALTH POLICY: THE ISSUES AHEAD

High-tech medicine is ahead for some, at least. The use of stem cells may revolutionize medical treatments. Stem cells are "master cells" that can grow into virtually any sort of cell in the human body. Using stem cells, many scientists and research advocates are nearly certain that a range of human diseases could be ameliorated, prevented, or even cured. Prominent among them are Parkinson's disease and spinal cord injuries. Congressional hearings on stem cell research has brought out celebrities with various diseases that might be cured by stem cell research (for example, Michael J. Fox for Parkinson's and the late Christopher Reeve for spinal cord injuries).

The stem cell argument is not only political but religious and linguistic as well. Some feared "human cloning." No one was proposing using federal moneys—or even private moneys—to create new human beings. Proponents of stem cell research—Senator Arlen Specter, the moderate Republican from Pennsylvania is one—objected to the very name "cloning" or its milder version, "therapeutic cloning." Stem cell research, he has argued, is not cloning at all because it is not meant to produce a baby. Nancy Reagan, wife of former president Ronald Reagan, has become an advocate for stem cell research. It might, she believes, provide a cure for Alzheimer's disease, which took her husband's life.

Advances in cracking genetic codes have had a downside, however. Employers and insurance companies, critics feared, could use genetic information to deny coverage to employees, or even deny a person a job in the first place. If Mary were genetically susceptible to breast cancer, which might cost an employer and its insurance company a fortune, perhaps Mary would be out of a job. This was "genetic discrimination." Congress passed a law in May, 2008, forbidding this sort of genetic discrimination.

The biggest health care issue—the issue no policymaker would dare to discuss in a campaign speech—is medical rationing. Medical care may not be a constitutional right, but Americans treat it as if it were. We do not like to admit that "rationing" of medical care goes on all the time in our system.[19] Much rationing is informal; physicians and families quietly agree not to provide further care to a loved one. Some of it is formal; medical boards have elaborate rules for allocating donated organs. When we ration openly and publicly, though, conflict erupts. Oregon took the lead on the issue of rationing health care, trying to set priorities for medical treatments under the Medicaid program, which is funded by both the state and the national government. In 1991, the state came up with a list of 709 treatments conditions. The Oregon legislature agreed to fund 587 of these from its tight Medicaid budget. As a result, Oregon does not pay for some costly treatments that might save or merely prolong people's lives, but by doing so it can use its resources to provide medical care to a larger pool of people. Although Oregon's plan was controversial at first, evidence shows that it works well and that patient satisfaction is higher after the plan than it was before.[20] Most Americans continue to believe, though, that they and their loved ones are entitled to all the medical care they—or someone else—can pay for.

ENVIRONMENTAL POLICY

Environmentalists have been telling us for years that our air, water, and land need protection. A generation of environmental policies—started mostly in the 1970s—has targeted dirty air and water. One "skeptical environmentalist," as he calls himself, though, thinks that the world's environmental plight is greatly exaggerated. Danish political scientist Bjorn Lomborg piled on 2,730 footnotes in a 515-page book to argue that environmentalists overlook plenty of improvements in the world's resource supply and environment.[21] Scientists and environmentalists reacted with fury. *Scientific American* headlined a string of rebuttals "Science Defends Itself Against the Skeptical Environmentalist." (One critic gleefully noted Lomborg's own admission that "I am not myself an expert as regards environmental problems.")

One might think that such a cherished national treasure as the natural environment would be above politics. Everyone likes clear water and clean air. Everyone wants plenty of cheap, clean-burning energy with none of the by-products of pollution.

Attempts to control air quality or limit water pollution often affect political choices through their impact on business, economic growth, and jobs. And although Americans may be generally in favor of "doing something" about the environment, specific proposals to limit suburban growth, encourage carpooling, and limit access to national parks have met with strong resistance. (Vice President Cheney once called them mere "personal virtues.") Many Americans think it a stretch to put cans and bottles in a separate container for the garbage truck's recycling. Few are willing to pay more for oil to conserve gasoline; SUVs seem like America's chariots. Yet 60 cents of every dollar put into the gas tank goes to other countries, some of whom are none too friendly. And by mid-2008, Americans were spending $4 a gallon to fuel that car.

Politics puts oil and energy on the nation's front burner. Our oil is running low. Oil refining capacity is almost at its peak. Surging economic growth in China and India increases demand elsewhere. As we went to war with Iraq, Americans learned more about where their oil comes from. Less and less of it comes from our own wells. Two decades ago, President Carter vowed to make the United States energy independent. Yet we are more dependent on foreign oil than when he made the pledge. These days, we debate ferociously over measures that, at best, would extend U.S. oil production by a few years. Soon after taking office, President Bush pushed for further opportunities for oil companies to drill in Alaska's tundra. The Senate defeated it over and over again.

ENVIRONMENTAL POLICIES IN AMERICA

Until the early 1960s, environmental protection was not a prominent element of federal policy. What policy existed then focused largely on conservation and the national parks. It was President Richard Nixon who pressed for most of the nation's first environmental legislation. Spearheading government efforts is the **Environmental Protection Agency** (EPA), now the nation's largest federal regulatory agency. The EPA has a wide-ranging mission; it is charged with administering policies dealing with land, air, and water quality.

Clean Air   One of the most significant pieces of legislation affecting the environment is the **Clean Air Act of 1970**, which charges the Department of Transportation (DOT) with the responsibility of reducing automobile emissions. You have probably met the Clean Air Act if you have bought a new car or even looked at one. Cars today use far cleaner fuels (and less of it) than before the Clean Air Act. For years after the act's passage, fierce battles raged between the automakers and the DOT about how stringent the requirements had to be. Automakers claimed that it was impossible to meet DOT standards; the DOT claimed that automakers were deliberately dragging their feet in hopes Congress would delay or weaken the requirements. In fact, Congress did weaken them, again and again. Still, the smaller size of American cars, the use of unleaded gasoline, and the lower gas consumption of new cars are all due in large part to DOT regulations. In 1990, Congress passed a reauthorization of the Clean Air Act that significantly increased the controls on cars, oil refineries, chemical plants, and coal-fired utility plants.

The Clean Air Act Amendments of 1990 also marked one of the most radical innovations in pollution control policy. Congress permitted utility companies to use emissions trading, essentially the right to buy and trade rights to pollute on the open market (there is even a market for these emissions credits on the Chicago Board of Trade). A utility generating cleaner fuel could "bank" its savings and sell them to other utilities around the country. Some environmentalists were horrified at these "licenses to pollute," but evidence shows the trading program has helped reduce pollution rates.[22]

Clean Water   Congress acted to control pollution of the nation's lakes and rivers with the **Water Pollution Control Act of 1972**. This law was enacted in reaction to the tremendous pollution of northeastern rivers and the Great Lakes. Since its passage, water quality has improved dramatically. In 1972, only one-third of U.S. lakes and rivers were safe for fishing and drinking. Today, the fraction has doubled to

SIMULATION

You Are an Environmental Activist

Environmental Protection Agency
An agency of the federal government created in 1970 that administers much of U.S. environmental protection policy. It is the largest federal independent regulatory agency.

Clean Air Act of 1970
The law aimed at combating air pollution.

Water Pollution Control Act of 1972
A law intended to clean up the nation's rivers and lakes. It requires municipal, industrial, and other polluters to use pollution control technology and secure permits from the **Environmental Protection Agency** for discharging waste products into waters.

two-thirds. Similarly, the number of waterfowl in U.S. waters has increased substantially. But federal laws regulate only "point sources"—places where pollutants can be dumped in the water, such as a paper mill along a river. What is hard to regulate is the most important cause of water pollution, "runoff" from streets, roads, fertilized lawns, and service stations.

Wilderness Preservation   In addition to protecting air and water, environmental policy literally aims to keep some parts of the environment intact. One component of the environment that has received special attention is wilderness—those areas that are largely untouched by human activities. Ever since the founding of the national park system in 1916, the United States has been a world leader in wilderness preservation. Perhaps the most consistently successful environmental campaigns in the postwar era have been those aimed at preserving such wild lands.[23] There are now 378 national parks and 155 national forests. Still, only about 4 percent of the United States is now designated as wilderness, and half of that is in Alaska. The strains of overuse have forced our national parks to consider restricting the public's access to preserve them for future generations. In addition, wilderness areas—with the biological, recreational, and symbolic values they embody—come under increasing pressure from those, such as logging and mining interests, who stress the economic benefits lost by keeping them intact. President Bush and environmentalists were constantly at odds over logging on federal lands. President Clinton had put 60 million acres of federal land beyond the reach of logging. In July 2004, President Bush proposed letting the state governors decide whether there should be roads built—for loggers and others—on federal lands.

In 2006, the Alaska pipeline sprung a leak, causing pipeline operators to shut down the line for repairs and environmentalists to warn again about the conflicts between energy extraction and environmental protection.

Endangered Species Act of 1973

This law requires the federal government to protect actively each of the hundreds of species listed as endangered—regardless of the economic effect on the surrounding towns or region.

Endangered Species   National policy protects wildlife in other, more direct ways as well. One policy—saving endangered species—is among the most controversial. The **Endangered Species Act of 1973** created an endangered species protection program in the U.S. Fish and Wildlife Service. More important, the law required the government to actively protect each of the hundreds of species listed as endangered—regardless of the economic effect on the surrounding towns or region. Later, during the Reagan administration, the act was amended to allow exceptions in cases of overriding national or regional interest. These have been hard to come by, though. There has been plenty of controversy about the implementation of the Endangered Species Act. Bringing back the wolves in Yellowstone has a certain appeal to many Americans but not to neighboring ranchers. In an expanding population, species and people come into conflict. So far, 398 animal and 599 plant species had been listed as endangered. (You can think about the policy issues of saving species in "You Are the Policymaker: How Much Should We Do to Save a Species? The Florida Manatee" on page 610.)

Toxic Wastes   In 1980, Congress reacted to increased pressure to deal with toxic waste by establishing a **Superfund**, funded by taxing chemical products. The law established that those who polluted the land were responsible for paying to clean it up. A controversial retroactive liability provision holds companies liable even for legal dumping prior to 1980. The law also contains strict provisions for liability under which the government can hold a single party liable for cleaning up an entire site that received waste from many sources.

The Comprehensive Environmental Response, Compensation, and Liability Act (the formal name of the Superfund law) has virtually eliminated haphazard dumping of toxic waste, but it has been less successful in cleaning up existing waste. Instead, the law has led to endless rounds of litigation. Large companies facing multi-million-dollar cleanup bills have tried to recover some of their costs by suing small businesses that had contributed to the hazardous waste. They have also been embroiled in protracted court fights with their insurers over whether policies written in the early 1980s cover Superfund-related costs.[24]

Another serious environmental challenge is the disposal of nuclear waste, such as that from nuclear reactors and the production of nuclear weapons. It is necessary to protect not only ourselves but also the people of a distant future from radioactive materials. These wastes must be isolated for 10,000 years. At this point, 30,000 metric tons of highly radioactive nuclear waste are sitting in temporary sites around the country, most of them near nuclear power plants. Congress has studied, debated, and fretted for years over where to store the nation's nuclear waste. In the 1980s, Congress envisioned that spent nuclear fuel would be consolidated and permanently buried. The search was on for the country's least-sought-after public project. Early on, the "winner" appeared to be Nevada, at a site about an hour from Las Vegas called Yucca Flats. Nevada's state government and congressional delegation battled the Yucca Flats site for more than a decade, but in July 2002, President Bush finally signed off on Congress's decision: Yucca Flats would be the nation's home for its nuclear wastes. Those 30,000 tons of nuclear waste would be making their way to Nevada by truck and rail (and these trips, some feared, would be inviting targets for terrorists).

The gray wolf is an endangered species. In 1995–1996, the U.S. Fish and Wildlife Service reintroduced 31 gray wolves into Yellowstone National Park in an effort to reestablish its presence. They number 120 adults today. Environmentalists hail this effort as a great victory, but ranchers and farmers around Yellowstone complain that wolf packs will endanger their livestock.

Superfund
A fund created by Congress in 1980 to clean up hazardous waste sites. Money for the fund comes from taxing chemical products.

ENERGY POLICY

ENERGY SOURCES AND ENERGY POLITICS

Once, the United States produced most of its own oil. Oil, and its most familiar product, gasoline, was the cheapest in the world. No longer. These days, every country in the world competes for oil. Americans once used wood, animals, water, and people power for energy. Today 87 percent of the nation's energy comes from coal, oil, and natural gas (see Figure 19.1 on page 611). Americans search continually for new and more efficient sources of energy both to increase supplies and to reduce pollution. Much of the research on new energy sources and efficiencies comes from the government in Washington.

YOU ARE THE **Policymaker**

How Much Should We Do to Save a Species? The Florida Manatee

The manatee (*Trichechus manatus latirostris*) is a walrus-like freshwater animal weighing in at about 1,000 pounds. Plump and squinty eyed, the Florida manatee is one of the charter members of the Department of Interior's Endangered Species list, first put there in 1967. Being on the Endangered Species list requires that both the federal and state governments enact policies to protect the habitat of the species. Few species have caused such a political conflict as the manatee. One of the major killers of manatees is the propellers on the thousands of boats in Florida's lakes and rivers. Biologists even use scar patterns from the propellers to identify individual manatees. In 2002, more than 95,000 Florida drivers paid an extra $20 for a "Save the Manatee" slogan on their license plates. Singer Jimmy Buffet has been a leader in the campaign to save the manatee, even writing a song ("Growing Older but Not Up") comparing himself to a prop-scarred manatee. Florida first passed a manatee protection law in 1893, making it illegal to kill manatees.

Enshrining an animal or plant as "endangered" puts policy into action. Then politics enters. When the Fisheries and Wildlife Bureau of the Department of Interior lists a species as endangered, it has to design a recovery program. There are even fines and imprisonments for people who kill or injure an endangered species. (Only one person was ever prosecuted, though, and he paid a $750 fine and served a six-month prison term for having a butchered manatee on his boat.) In Florida, nearly one-quarter of the state's canals, rivers, and lakes were designated as manatee protection areas. Any construction project had to come to a halt if a manatee appeared within 100 feet and could resume only if the animal left—as the regulation put it—"of its own volition." Boating was curtailed. Fishing was limited. Canal locks were refitted at a substantial cost.

When the Fish and Wildlife Service proposed reducing the manatee protection areas, environmentalists sued. In December 2002, 3,000 people swarmed into the Fort Myers Convention Center for a hearing on the proposed reduction in the protected habitat. One T-shirt read "Stop the Manatee Insanity." The Coastal Conservation Association of Florida, a profishing group, produced data to show that the manatee population was increasing, and that regulations should be reduced and the habitat restrictions eased. One state legislator there compared environmentalists to watermelons ("green on the outside and red on the inside"). Environmentalists doubted the data.

If the purpose of the Endangered Species Act was to improve the chances of a species surviving, the Coastal Conservation group said, hadn't the act served its purpose? Did the state really need to put a quarter of its waterways off limits to protect the manatee?

Often, the Endangered Species Act collides with other interests—economic growth, protecting property rights, and recreational activities. You be the policymaker. Do we want to save every single species (there may be 100 million of them)? When have we done enough to save a species?

Sources: On the Fort Myers meeting and the debate about the manatee, see Craig Pittman, "Fury over a Gentle Giant," *Smithsonian Magazine*, February 2004, 55–59.

Coal is America's most abundant fuel. (Coal is also China's main fuel—it opens a coal-fired power plant every four days.) An estimated 90 percent of the country's energy resources are in coal deposits—enough to last hundreds of years. Although coal may be the nation's most plentiful fuel, unfortunately it is also the dirtiest. It contributes to global warming (discussed later in this chapter) and smog, and it is responsible for the "black lung" health hazard to coal miners and for the once-soot-blackened cities of the Northeast. In addition, acid rain is traced to the burning of coal to produce electricity. Coal may be abundant, but most Americans do not want to rely on it exclusively for their energy needs. Coal accounts for only 23 percent of the energy Americans use.

Oil, which accounts for 40 percent of the energy Americans use, is one of nature's nonrenewable resources. Some resources, such as the wind and solar energy, are renewable; that is, using them once does not reduce the amount left to be used in the future. These things are constantly renewed by nature. Oil, coal, and other common sources of energy, however, are not renewable. Natural gas and petroleum are somewhat cleaner than coal (though they too contribute to global warming), but petroleum imports inevitably lead to oil dependency.

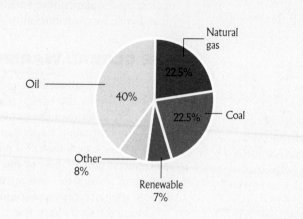

FIGURE 19.1

Sources of America's Energy

Despite the technological advances of society, America still relies on traditional sources for its energy: coal, oil, and natural gas. Coal generates a majority of our electricity; oil fuels our cars, trucks, and planes. Only 6 percent of our energy comes from renewable sources, mainly hydroelectricity and geothermal power.

Note: "Other" consists mostly of nuclear power.
Source: Energy Information Administration, 2007.

Nature did not distribute oil evenly around the world, nor did it bless the biggest users with the most.[25] Compared to its usage, the United States is short of oil. Oil is counted and measured in barrels—whether it is being transported on a massive tanker or refined in Texas or Louisiana.

Table 19.1 shows who has the oil in the world and who consumes it. The United States has about 2 percent of the world's oil but uses a quarter of it. (Even Mexico has more oil reserves than the United States; Russia has twice as much.) Most of the oil—as most Americans know today—is in the Middle East. Nations of the Organization of Petroleum Exporting Countries (OPEC) have 80 percent of the world's reserves. The two nations with the largest oil reserves are Saudi Arabia and Iraq.

The most controversial energy source is nuclear power. During the 1940s and 1950s, Americans were convinced the technology that had ended World War II could be made to serve peaceful purposes. Nuclear scientists spoke enthusiastically about harnessing the atom to produce electricity that would be "too cheap to meter." These claims, however, were met with increasing skepticism in the light of huge cost overruns and the accidents at Three Mile Island in Pennsylvania and

TABLE 19.1

Where Is the Oil? Who Consumes It?

Oil is measured in barrels. The world's reserves of oil are mostly located in OPEC countries (including Iran, Iraq, Kuwait, Qatar, Saudi Arabia, the United Arab Emirates, Algeria, Libya, Nigeria, Indonesia, and Venezuela). The United States, with only 4 percent of the world's population, consumes just exactly a quarter of the world's annual oil production.

	RESERVES		CONSUMPTION	
	Billion Barrels	Reserve Share	Million Barrels Per Day	Share
United States	22.7	2%	19.8	25%
OPEC	826.1	68%	6.6	8%
Rest of world	364.3	30%	51.8	66%

Source: Department of Energy, Energy Fact Sheet, September 6, 2004.

Chernobyl in the former Soviet Union. The wave of environmental concern that developed in the late 1960s devastated the nuclear power industry, and no new nuclear power plants have been built in the United States since 1978. Compared to oil and coal, its contribution to America's energy is tiny.

THE GLOBAL WARMING DEBATE: BEYOND KYOTO?

One of the most intractable and serious issues relating to energy and the environment is global warming. By now, a scientific consensus has emerged that the rising use of fossil fuels has warmed the surface of the Earth. The "greenhouse effect" occurs when energy from the sun is trapped under the atmosphere and warms the Earth as a result, much as in a greenhouse.[26] This is often called global warming, a slow rise in the atmospheric temperature of the earth.[27] Global warming results primarily from the burning of fossil fuels—mainly coal and oil. About a third of it, though, comes from deforestation of trees capable of absorbing pollutants, mainly carbon dioxide.

Many scientists have found that the Earth is warming at a rapid rate and will be between two and six degrees warmer by the year 2100. This may not seem like a major change, but the world is now only five to nine degrees warmer than during the depths of the last ice age, 20,000 years ago. Scientists predict that if the warming trend is not reversed, seas will rise (gobbling up shorelines and displacing millions of people); severe droughts, rainstorms, heat waves, and floods will become more common; and broad shifts in climatic and agricultural zones will occur, bringing famine, disease, and pestilence to some areas. The 15 warmest years on record have happened since 1970. Even that eternal optimist about the conditions of the environment, Danish political scientist Bjorn Lomborg, believes that "global warming is important. Its total costs could be about $5 trillion."[28]

The United States is the leading producer of carbon dioxide. About 23 percent of the entire world's carbon dioxide is generated in the United States, with fast-growing China catching up at 14 percent.[29] The United States, though, is largely alone among the world's nations in international efforts to combat global warming. In 1992, industrialized countries met in Rio de Janeiro and voluntarily agreed to cut greenhouse gas emissions to 1990 levels by the year 2000. The century turned, however, with no country coming close to meeting that goal.

At the end of 1997, 150 nations met in Kyoto, Japan, and agreed in principle to require 38 industrial nations to reduce their emissions of greenhouse gases below 1990 levels by about 2010. (None had come close to succeeding by 2008, however.) The European Union would reduce emissions by 8 percent, the United States by 7 percent, and Japan by 6 percent. The less developed nations argue that rich countries got rich by burning coal and oil and still produce most of the emissions today. Thus, the less developed nations say that developed nations should bear most of the burden in reducing global warming. Besides, less developed nations insist that they are the ones who would be hurt worst by climate changes, and they are hard pressed enough as it is.

The global warming problem has proved to be a hot political issue. Some politicians in the United States seem to believe that scientific support for the global warming hypothesis is weak. Senator James Inhofe of Oklahoma called global warming "the greatest hoax ever perpetrated on the American people." Opponents of the Kyoto treaty in the United States—President Bush was one—fear that

Why It Matters
Global Warming and the Next Generation

Global warming is raising the world's temperatures, and sea levels are likely to rise in the United States and other countries. These changes have precipitated a great debate on what we owe the next generation. Is it acceptable to rely on current technology for transportation and the production of electricity, hoping the next generation will find a technological fix for the problem of global warming?

Global warming is most visible in the form of melting ice in the polar regions. Here, icebergs can be seen floating in a bay off Ammassalik Island, Greenland. A record amount of Greenland's ice sheet melted during the summer of 2008—19 billion tons more than the previous high mark.

cutting greenhouse gases will cost a staggering sum. They also argue that it is unfair that the developed nations should bear the burden of cutting greenhouse emissions. President Clinton never submitted the Kyoto treaty to the Senate. President Bush simply renounced it in 2001. Senators John McCain and Joseph Lieberman, however, proposed a Climate Stewardship Act that would require large companies to reduce their emissions to 1990 levels by 2020. A strong majority of Americans (about 8 in 10) supported that idea, even if it would increase their own energy costs.[30] Meeting in Bali, Indonesia, in 2007, the world's nations again tried their hand at a global warming agreement—this one insisting that developing nations like China and India participate in reducing greenhouse emissions, too.

Because of the gridlock of Washington politics about global warming, political scientist Barry Rabe notes that "perhaps no environmental issue triggers such feelings of hopelessness as global climate change."[31] As so often happens, however, in the American system, what the federal government cannot do, many states try. George W. Bush and Christine Todd Whitman (Bush's first EPA administrator) served as governors of two major states—Texas and New Jersey—which passed major state laws to reduce their states' reliance on energy that produces greenhouse gasses. California's Governor Arnold Schwarzenegger has set a goal of cutting California's emissions to less than their 2000 levels in five years. Republicans and Democrats in Washington, however, continue to feud over the issue.

What the 2008 election brought, though, was a major change in American leadership on global warming. Both Barack Obama and John McCain were firm believers in the reality of global warming. No one imagined that the Kyoto treaty would be ratified by the United States any time soon, however.

GROUPS, ENERGY, AND THE ENVIRONMENT

Nobody is against cleaning up the environment. The issue becomes a political question only because environmental concerns often conflict with equally legitimate concerns about foreign trade, economic growth, and jobs. Those who generate pollution do so in their efforts to make cars, to produce electricity, and to provide food and the consumer products Americans take for granted. On federally owned land, including national parks and forests, there has long been a policy of multiple use whereby mining, lumbering, and grazing leases are awarded to private companies or ranchers at a very low cost. Often the industries supported by these arrangements are important sources of jobs to otherwise depressed areas, and they may also lessen the country's dependence on foreign sources of oil and minerals.

Massive battles pitting lumbering interests against national and local environmental groups have raged in Alaska, where exports of lumber products to Japan provide jobs but decimate large parts of the Tongass National Forest. Similarly, harvesting old-growth timber on public lands has caused great concern in Oregon and Washington. In the Northwest and Alaska, environmentalists have complained that some of the few remaining large tracts of virgin forest, with trees hundreds of years old, are being felled by logging companies operating under generous lease agreements with the U.S. government, which owns the lands. Oil exploration on public lands and offshore in coastal waters also brings the goals of environmental protection and economic growth into conflict. Energy companies and environmentalists have battled over Alaska's reserves.

The 1960s and 1970s saw an explosion in the size and number of environmental interest groups.[32] Bosso and Guber report three environmental groups (the National

Wildlife Federation, the Nature Conservancy, and the World Wildlife Fund) with more than a million members. The Sierra Club, Greenpeace, the National Audubon Society, the Natural Resources Defense Council, and others count more than a half million members each. Everyone loves the environment, but not everyone loves environmentalists. In an age where terrorism trumps every other policy issue, environmental groups face substantial challenges to influencing public policy.[33]

No group proudly announces it is opposed to a clean environment. But there are many groups that oppose self-proclaimed environmentalists ("tree huggers," some sneer). They argue that the effects of environmental regulations on employment, economic growth, and international competitiveness must be part of the policymaking equation. Others, especially ranchers, miners, farmers, and loggers, demand inexpensive access to public land and the right to use their own property as they wish or else be compensated by government for being prohibited from doing so. In the West, groups that oppose the environmentalists often call themselves "wise use" advocates. Western proponents of mining interests formed People for the West. Republicans get a large share of their certain electoral votes from Western states. Ranching, grazing, logging, and mining interests loom large in this coalition. George W. Bush was generous in his appointments of "wise use" Westerners to key environmental posts. (Environmentalists thought this was leaving the fox to watch the henhouse.)

Widening opposition to potentially hazardous industrial facilities (such as toxic or nuclear waste dumps) has further complicated environmental policymaking in recent years. Local groups have often successfully organized resistance to planned development, rallying behind the cry "Not in My Backyard." The so-called NIMBY phenomenon highlights another difficult dilemma in environmental policy: How can government equitably distribute the costs associated with society's seemingly endless demand for new technologies, some of which turn out to be environmentally threatening? If, for example, we are to use nuclear power to keep our lights on, the waste it produces must go in someone's backyard. Whose? Government's answer: Nevada's.

For all these reasons, government policies designed to clean up the environment are sure to be controversial, expensive, and debated for years to come.

Why It Matters
"NIMBY"

Most Americans say "NIMBY"—not in my backyard—when government proposes locating unwanted waste dumps, toxic disposal sites, and other unhealthy land uses near their homes. Would you always oppose the placement of environmental hazards in your neighborhood? Should government give every neighborhood a veto over having to house wastes? If every community, even sparsely populated areas, had a veto, where would society dispose of its hazardous materials?

UNDERSTANDING HEALTH CARE AND ENVIRONMENTAL POLICY

At the beginning of this chapter, we said that environmental issues and health care issues had three things in common. They both have skyrocketing costs—health care costs are the fastest-growing item in the country with gasoline close behind. Both involve health and human welfare. And both are highly technical areas in which ordinary people are ill equipped to make policy. These issues are difficult to understand when discussed in experts' terms, but most Americans do not want to leave them to "experts" to decide.

DEMOCRACY, HEALTH CARE, AND ENVIRONMENTAL POLICY

Would we really want to have national elections about environmental policy? Could anyone imagine voting about health care prices? Very few Americans actually understand how a nuclear power plant operates. Few know much about a stem cell. Does such ignorance mean citizens should not be allowed to participate in the public policy debates concerning complex technologies? High-tech issues, more than any others, strain the limits of public participation in a democracy. Further, the issues associated with high technology are often so complex that many different levels of government—local, state, and national—become heavily involved. Whether it be the new ethical issues raised by machines and devices that can keep patients alive indefinitely—respirators, artificial kidneys, and the like—or whether it be the threats to public safety inherent in an accident at a nuclear power plant, governments are constantly called on to make decisions that involve tremendously complex technologies. Maintaining the right balance between public participation and technological competence is not an easy task.

Policymaking for technological issues seems to rely heavily on group representation. Individual citizens are unlikely to have the information or the resources to participate meaningfully because of the complexity of the debates. Interest groups—associations of professionals and citizens—play an active role in making the complicated decisions that will affect all Americans for generations.

THE SCOPE OF GOVERNMENT AND HEALTH CARE AND ENVIRONMENTAL POLICY

Americans do not hesitate to call for government to play a greater role in high-tech issues, and the scope of the federal government has grown in response to these demands. Medicare for the elderly, Medicaid for the poor, and tax subsidies for employer-provided health insurance are large, expensive public policies. Adding prescription drug coverage for the elderly was a huge increase in the cost of governmentally supported medicine.

The most important single policy difference between the United States and all other industrialized governments is in health care. No country is wildly happy with its health care system, the United States included. We have a mixed, mostly private system; other industrialized democracies have a nearly entirely public one. Creating a national health system would be the biggest domestic policy change since the New Deal. With the parties sharply divided on the scope of government, incremental rather than fundamental change may be all the American political system can produce.

Similarly, in the past three decades, concerns for environmental protection have placed additional demands on the federal government. Volumes of regulations and billions of dollars spent on environmental protection have enlarged the scope of government's environmental policy. Republicans think many of these demands are too onerous on private businesses; Democrats think regulation keeps the environment clean. A new administration in Washington will revisit the world's most pressing environmental issue, global warming.

SUMMARY

Americans live in an age driven by technology. Like so much in human history, technology brings its blessings and its curses. In particular, technology meets public policy in health care and the environment.

Health care already makes up one-seventh of America's GDP, and with increased technology, its costs will almost certainly continue to rise. These advances have improved health care, but tremendous problems also plague health care in America, including inadequate insurance coverage (or no coverage at all) for many people and ever-increasing costs for even routine medical attention. The paradox of health policy in the United States is that it spends more of its national income on health than other nations and is far from the healthiest.

Americans are also increasingly concerned with the environment. Environmental issues will continue to cause the government to become involved in many aspects of daily life, and they often pit citizens' groups against important economic interests. The government has become very active in ensuring the quality of America's air, land, and water and in protecting wildlife. We are dependent on energy, but the most common sources of energy, coal and oil, cause many environmental and health problems. Only a few decades ago, President Carter announced a national policy of energy independence. President Bush, too, called us "addicted to oil." Today, though, 60 percent of our oil still comes from other nations. Two-thirds of the world's oil supply is in the Middle East, fueling foreign policy issues.

In both of these public policy areas, government is and will continue to be at the center of public debate. Furthermore, governmental activities can be expected to grow rather than to decrease in each of these areas. Republicans, not Democrats, were responsible for the most expensive new federal policy in decades, the elderly drug benefit. Finally, citizen participation has profoundly influenced government decisions. Voting and organizing interest group campaigns will continue to be important means of influencing health care and the environment.

Chapter Test

Multiple Choice

1. How does the United States rank worldwide in terms of longevity?
   a. First
   b. In the top 5
   c. In the top 10
   d. In the top 20
   e. Lower than the top 20

2. Roughly what percentage of the GDP do Americans spend annually on health care?
   a. 3 percent
   b. 5 percent
   c. 10 percent
   d. 15 percent
   e. 20 percent

3. Which of the following is one of the two leading causes of preventable deaths in the United States?
   a. Traffic accidents
   b. Heart attacks
   c. Obesity
   d. Cancer
   e. Alcoholism

4. How has the United States dealt with the Kyoto Protocol?
   a. It did not sign the protocol
   b. It signed the protocol, but insisted on exceptions for the U.S.
   c. It signed the protocol and has complied with it
   d. It was introduced into Congress, but never ratified
   e. It was never introduced into Congress and was renounced later

5. According to the Kyoto Protocol, which countries would be primarily responsible for reducing emissions?
   a. Most Asian countries
   b. Middle Eastern countries
   c. Developing countries
   d. Industrialized countries
   e. Both industrialized and developing countries

6. When did environmental protection first become prominent in federal policy?
   a. In the first half of the twentieth century
   b. In the 1950s
   c. In the 1960s
   d. In the 1980s
   e. In the 1990s

7. Whom did the Clean Air Act of 1970 place in charge of reducing automobile emissions?
   a. The Environmental Protection Agency
   b. The Department of Transportation
   c. The State Department
   d. The Department of Clean Air
   e. Greenpeace

True/False

8. The most common reason for losing health insurance in the United States is being poor.
   True_____   False_____

9. President Truman was the first to propose a compulsory national health insurance program.
   True_____   False_____

10. States in the North have the highest percentage of people without health insurance.
    True_____   False_____

11. Today, the majority of Americans supports the idea of universal health care, even if it involves more taxes.
    True_____   False_____

12. Approximately one in six Americans does not have health insurance.
    True_____   False_____

Short Answer

13. How are age, race, and income related to a person's likelihood of having health insurance?

14. What is the difference between Medicare and Medicaid? How is each of these programs funded?

15. In your own words, please explain the so-called paradox of American health care, and illustrate it with examples.

16. The Clean Air Act Amendments of 1990 introduced the concept of "emissions trading." What does this refer to? In your opinion, is emissions trading a useful approach to reducing pollution? Why, or why not?

Essay

17. In your opinion, what is the biggest environmental problem facing us in the 21st century? If you were an adviser to the president, what course of action would you recommend in order to reduce and/or eliminate this problem? Be as specific as possible in your answer and—using your knowledge of American politics and society—try to anticipate possible obstacles to your proposal.

18. Take a look at the "My State" graph on p. 601, which summarizes the percentage of children in each state without health insurance. How would you explain the differences between states with high and those with low percentages of uninsured children?

19. How would you explain the fact that the United States is the only industrialized country in the world without national health insurance? In your answer, please try to consider historical, political, social, economic, and individual factors. What is the current prevailing public opinion on the matter?

20. Compare and contrast the unsuccessful health care reform plans of Bill Clinton and George W. Bush. If you were president of the United States, which plan would you "revive" in order to address the growing health care crisis in this country, and how would you change the plan in order to increase the chances that it would pass? (Alternatively, feel free to propose your own plan!)

21. What does the term "defensive medicine" refer to? What is your own assessment of the increase in this health care practice? What are the causes and what are the consequences? Do you believe the government should intervene in this situation? Why, or why not? And what could the government do?

Answer key

1. E   2. D   3. C   4. E   5. D   6. C   7. B   8. False   9. True   10. False   11. True   12. True

Key Terms

health maintenance
  organization (599)
national health insurance (601)
Medicare (602)
Medicaid (602)

Environmental Protection
  Agency (607)
Clean Air Act of 1970 (607)
Water Pollution Control Act of
  1972 (607)

Endangered Species Act of
  1973 (608)
Superfund (609)
global warming (612)

Internet Resources

www.census.gov/prod/2007pubs/p60-233.pdf
The latest Census Bureau data on health insurance coverage.

www.epa.gov
Official site for the Environmental Protection Agency, which provides information on policies and current environmental issues.

www.sierraclub.org
Web site for the Sierra Club, one of the most active environmental protection organizations.

www.epa.gov/superfund/sites/index.htm
Locate toxic waste sites in your state or city.

Get Connected

Health Care Policy

America spends a large amount on health care yet has a population that is not any healthier than other industrial nations. In addition, about 46 million Americans don't have health insurance. The reason for this seeming paradox is that health care in America is market oriented, meaning it is a profit-making industry. Some argue that health care should not be open to market forces. One group, Physicians for a National Health Program (PNHP), advocates a single-payer system. Let us explore their idea.

Search the Web

Go to *www.pnhp.org/* and read about their single-payer plan.

Questions to Ask

- What is a single-payer plan?
- Who would pay the bill in a single-payer plan?

- Why do these physicians support a single-payer plan? Are there reasons to support the idea?
- Who would be the big winners and big losers if this plan were adopted?

Why It Matters

Health care is important for obvious reasons. The nation's health care system is under severe strain because costs continue to rise and at the same time around 15 percent of the population is not covered by any health insurance.

Get Involved

What kind of plan would you support? Talk to your parents about the cost of your family's health care. What kind of plan would they support? Talk with your doctor about the costs of health care. Would he or she support a single-payer plan? *For more exercises, go to www.longmanamericangovernment.com.*

For Further Reading

Bonnickson, Andrea. *Crafting a Cloning Policy: From Dolly to Stem Cells.* Washington, DC: Georgetown University Press, 2002. Politics and policy issues of cloning.

Casamayou, Maureen Hogan. *The Politics of Breast Cancer.* Washington, DC: Georgetown University Press, 2001. How women's groups and others organized to elevate breast cancer research on the policy agenda.

Kotlikoff, Laurence J. *The Healthcare Fix: Universal Insurance for All Americans.* Cambridge MA: MIT Press, 2007. A conservative health economist tries to devise a plan to cover all Americans.

Lomborg, Bjorn. *The Skeptical Environmentalist: Measuring the Real State of the World.* New York: Cambridge University Press, 2001. Controversial book arguing that the world is a lot better off than environmentalists think.

Rabe, Barry G. *Statehouse and Greenhouse: The Emerging Politics of American Climate Change.* Washington, DC: Brookings Institution, 2004. Many states have taken the policy lead in reducing greenhouse gases even as the federal government has been mired in gridlock about the issue.

Skocpol, Theda. *Boomerang: Health Care Reform and the Turn Against Government.* New York: Norton, 1996. Why Clinton's health care reforms boomeranged.

Vanderheiden, Steve. *Atmospheric Justice: A Political Theory of Climate Change.* New York: Oxford University Press, 2008. An incisive examination of the public policy challenges of global warming via the conceptual frameworks of justice, equality, and responsibility.

Vig, Norman J., and Michael E. Kraft, ed. *Environmental Policy.* 6th ed. Washington, DC: Congressional Quarterly Press, 2006. Useful articles on a range of environmental policy issues.

NATIONAL SECURITY POLICYMAKING

POLITICS IN ACTION:
A NEW THREAT

On September 11, 2001, America trembled. Terrorist attacks on the World Trade Center in New York and the Pentagon in Washington killed thousands and exposed the nation's vulnerability to unconventional attacks.

Less than 12 years after the fall of the Berlin Wall, the United States could no longer take comfort in its status as the world's only superpower. Suddenly the world seemed a more threatening place, with dangers lurking around every corner.

Communism was no longer the principal threat to the security of the United States, and our foreign policy goals suddenly changed to ending terrorism. To achieve this goal, we launched wars against Afghanistan and Iraq. The United States won the battles quite easily, but the aftermath of the wars, especially in Iraq, led to more deaths than the fighting itself and forced America to invest tens of billions of dollars in reconstruction and military occupation. Debate rages as to whether we have dealt terrorists a severe blow or whether U.S. actions have radicalized opponents and recruited new terrorists to their cause. At the same time, "rogue" states like Iran and North Korea have continued their development of nuclear weapons, threatening to make the world even less stable.

The need to answer the question of the appropriate role of the national government in national security policy is more important and perhaps more difficult than ever. America's status in the world makes leadership unavoidable. What should be the role of the world's only remaining superpower? What should we do with our huge defense establishment? Should we go it alone, or should we work closely with our allies on issues ranging from fighting terrorism and stopping nuclear proliferation to protecting the environment and encouraging trade? How should we deal with our former adversaries? Should we aid their transition to democracy?

At the same time, a number of critical areas of the world, most notably the Middle East, exhibit a frightening tendency to conflict. Should the United States get involved in trying to

end conflicts resulting from ethnic, religious, and regional differences? Does the United States have a choice about involvement when the conflict could affect its ability to fight terrorism or prevent the use of nuclear weapons?

And just how should we decide about national security policy? Should the American people delegate discretion in this area to officials who seem at home with complex and even exotic issues of defense and foreign policy? Or should they and their representatives fully participate in the democratic policymaking process, just as they do in domestic policy? Can the public or its representatives in Congress or in interest groups have much influence on the elites who often deal in secrecy with national security policy?

National security is as important as ever. New and complex challenges have emerged to replace the conflict with communism. Some of these challenges, such as the fight against terrorism, are traceable to a malevolent enemy—but many others are not.

AMERICAN FOREIGN POLICY: INSTRUMENTS, ACTORS, AND POLICYMAKERS

foreign policy

A policy that involves choice taking, like domestic policy, but additionally involves choices about relations with the rest of the world. The president is the chief initiator of foreign policy in the United States.

Foreign policy, like domestic policy, involves making choices—but the choices involved are about relations with the rest of the world. Because the president is the main force behind foreign policy, every morning the White House receives a highly confidential intelligence briefing that might cover monetary transactions in Tokyo, last night's events in some trouble spot on the globe, or Fidel Castro's health. The briefing is part of the massive informational arsenal the president uses to manage American foreign policy.

INSTRUMENTS OF FOREIGN POLICY

The instruments of foreign policy are, however, different from those of domestic policy. Foreign policies depend ultimately on three types of tools: military, economic, and diplomatic.

Military   Among the oldest instruments of foreign policy are war and the threat of war. German General Karl von Clausewitz once called war a "continuation of politics by other means." The United States has been involved in only a few full-scale wars. It has often employed force to influence actions in other countries, however. Most of this influence has been close to home, in Central America and the Caribbean.

In recent years, the United States has continued to use force in limited ways around the world: to topple Saddam Hussein's regime in Iraq and the Taliban regime in Afghanistan, to oppose ethnic cleansing in the Kosovo province of Yugoslavia, to prevent the toppling of the democratic government of the Philippines, to assist a UN peacekeeping mission in Somalia, to rescue stranded foreigners and protect our embassy in Liberia, and to launch missile attacks on Baghdad in retaliation for an effort to assassinate former President Bush and for the failure to provide UN weapons inspectors access to suspected weapons sites. The United States also employed military forces to aid the democratic transfer of power in Haiti and for humanitarian relief operations in Yugoslavia, Iraq, Somalia, Bangladesh, Russia, and Bosnia.

Economic   Today, economic instruments are becoming weapons almost as potent as those of war. The control of oil can be as important as the control of guns. Trade regulations, tariff policies, and monetary policies are other economic instruments of foreign policy. A number of studies have called attention to the importance of a country's economic vitality to its long-term national security.[1]

Diplomacy   Diplomacy is the quietest instrument of influence. It is the process by which nations carry on relationships with each other. It often evokes images of ambassadors at chic cocktail parties, but the diplomatic game is played for high stakes. Sometimes national leaders meet in summit talks. More often, less prominent negotiators work out treaties covering all kinds of national contracts, from economic relations to aid for stranded tourists.

You Are the Newly Appointed Ambassador to the Country of Dalmatia

ACTORS ON THE WORLD STAGE

If all the world's a stage, then there are more actors on it than ever before. More than 125 nations have emerged since 1945—nearly two dozen in the 1990s alone. Once foreign relations were almost exclusively transactions among nations in which leaders used military, economic, or diplomatic methods to achieve foreign policy goals. Nations remain the main actors in international politics, but today's world stage is more crowded.

International Organizations   Most of the challenges in international relations, ranging from peacekeeping and controlling weapons of mass destruction to protecting the environment and maintaining stable trade and financial networks, require the cooperation of many nations. It is not surprising that international organizations play an increasingly important role on the world stage.

The best-known international organization is the **United Nations** (UN). Housed in a magnificent skyscraper in New York City, the UN was created in 1945. Its members agree to renounce war and respect certain human and economic freedoms (although they sometimes fail to keep their promises). The UN General Assembly is composed of 192 member nations. Each nation has one vote. Although not legally binding, General Assembly resolutions can achieve a measure of collective legitimization when a broad international consensus is formed on some matter concerning relations among states.

It is the *Security Council,* however, that is the seat of real power in the UN. Five of its 15 members (the United States, Great Britain, China, France, and Russia) are permanent members; the others are chosen from session to session by the General Assembly. Each permanent member has a veto over Security Council decisions, including any decisions that would commit the UN to a military peacekeeping operation. The Secretariat is the executive arm of the UN and directs the administration of UN programs. Composed of about 9,000 international civil servants, it is headed by the secretary-general. In addition to its peacekeeping function, the UN runs a number of programs focused on economic development and on health, education, and welfare.

Since 1948, there have been 63 UN peacekeeping operations, 50 of which were created by the Security Council since 1988. In 2008, there were 17 UN missions under way in Sudan, Haiti, Timor-Leste, the Democratic

United Nations
Created in 1945, an organization whose members agree to renounce war and to respect certain human and economic freedoms. The seat of real power in the United Nations is the Security Council.

The most prominent international organization is the United Nations. Here the General Assembly meets to discuss climate change.

Republic of the Congo, Western Sahara, India/Pakistan, Ethiopia and Eritrea, the Golan Heights, Ivory Coast, Liberia, the Central African Republic and Chad, Lebanon, Cyprus, Georgia, Kosovo, Darfur, and the Middle East generally.

In 1990, the UN Security Council backed resolutions authorizing an embargo on the shipment of goods to or from Iraq in an attempt to force its withdrawal from Kuwait. Later, it authorized the use of force to compel Iraq to withdraw. However, the UN did not support the U.S.-led war in Iraq.

The United States often plays the critical role in implementing UN policies. Although President Clinton envisioned an expanded role for UN peacekeeping operations at the beginning of his term, he later concluded that the UN is often not capable of making and keeping peace, particularly when hostilities among parties still exist. He also backtracked on his willingness to place American troops under foreign commanders—always a controversial policy.

George W. Bush sought but did not receive UN sanction for the war with Iraq and was skeptical of the organization's ability to enforce its own resolutions. Nevertheless, many countries feel the legitimacy of the UN is crucial for their participation in peacekeeping or other operations requiring the use of force.

The UN is only one of many international organizations. The International Monetary Fund, for example, helps regulate the chaotic world of international finance; the World Bank finances development projects in new nations; the World Trade Organization attempts to regulate international trade; and the Universal Postal Union helps get the mail from one country to another.

Regional Organizations   *Regional organizations* have proliferated in the post–World War II era. These are organizations of several nations bound by a treaty, often for military reasons. The **North Atlantic Treaty Organization** (NATO) was created in 1949. Its members—the United States, Canada, most Western European nations, and Turkey—agreed to combine military forces and to treat a war against one as a war against all. During the Cold War, more than a million NATO troops (including about 325,000 Americans) were spread from West Germany to Portugal as a deterrent to foreign aggression. To counter the NATO alliance, the Soviet Union and its Eastern European allies formed the Warsaw Pact. The Warsaw Pact has since been dissolved, however, and the role of NATO has changed dramatically as the Cold War has thawed. In 1999, Poland, Hungary, and the Czech Republic, former members of the Warsaw Pact, became members of NATO. In 2002, NATO invited seven additional Eastern European countries, including Slovakia, Slovenia, Bulgaria, Romania, Latvia, Estonia, and Lithuania, to join the alliance.

Regional organizations can be economic as well as military. The **European Union** (EU) is a transnational government composed of most European nations. The EU coordinates monetary, trade, immigration, and labor policies so that its members have become one economic unit, just as the 50 United States are an economic unit. Other economic federations exist in Latin America and Africa, although none is as unified as the EU. Most EU nations have adopted a common currency, the euro.

Multinational Corporations   Chapter 17 discussed the potent *multinational corporations (MNCs)*. Today, a large portion of the world's industrial output comes from these corporations, and they account for more than one-tenth of the global economy and one-third of world exports.[2] Sometimes more powerful (and often much wealthier) than the governments under which they operate, MNCs have voiced strong opinions about governments, taxes, and business regulations. They have even linked forces with agencies such as the Central Intelligence Agency (CIA) to overturn governments they disliked. In the 1970s, for example, several of

---

North Atlantic Treaty Organization

Created in 1949, an organization whose members include the United States, Canada, most Western European nations, and Turkey, all of whom agreed to combine military forces and to treat a war against one as a war against all.

European Union

A transnational government composed of most European nations that coordinates monetary, trade, immigration, and labor policies, making its members one economic unit. An example of a regional organization.

these corporations worked with the CIA to "destabilize" the democratically elected Marxist government in Chile; Chile's military overthrew the government in 1973. Even when they are not so heavy-handed, MNCs are forces to be reckoned with in nearly all nations.

Nongovernmental Organizations *Groups* are also actors on the global stage. Churches and labor unions have long had international interests and activities. Today, environmental and wildlife groups such as Greenpeace have also proliferated. Ecological interests are active in international as well as in national politics. Groups interested in protecting human rights, such as Amnesty International, have also grown.

Not all groups, however, are committed to saving whales, oceans, or even people. Some are committed to the overthrow of particular governments and operate as terrorists around the world. Airplane hijackings, and assassinations, bombings, and similar terrorist attacks have made the world a more unsettled place. Conflicts within a nation or region may spill over into world politics. Terrorism in the Middle East, for example, affects the price of oil in Tokyo, New York, and Berlin. Civil war in southeastern Europe may strain relations between the West and Russia.

Individuals Finally, *individuals* are international actors. Tourism sends Americans everywhere and brings to America legions of tourists from around the world. Tourism creates its own costs and benefits and thus always affects the international economic system. It may enhance friendship and understanding among nations. However, more tourists traveling out of the country than arriving in the country can create problems with a country's balance of payments (discussed later in this chapter). In addition to tourists, growing numbers of students are going to and coming from other nations; they are carriers of ideas and ideologies. So are immigrants and refugees, who also place new demands on public services.

Just as there are more actors on the global stage than in the past, there are also more American decision makers involved in foreign policy problems.

THE POLICYMAKERS

There are many policymakers involved with national security policy, but any discussion of foreign policymaking must begin with the president.

The President The president, as you know from Chapter 13, is the main force behind foreign policy. As chief diplomat, the president negotiates treaties; as commander in chief of the armed forces, the president deploys American troops abroad. The president also appoints U.S. ambassadors and the heads of executive departments (with the consent of the Senate), and has the sole power to accord official recognition to other countries and receive (or refuse to receive) their representatives.

Presidents make some foreign policy through the formal mechanisms of treaties or executive agreements. Both are written accords in which the parties agree to specific actions. Since the end of World War II, presidents have negotiated thousands of executive agreements but only about 800 treaties. They both have legal standing, but only treaties require Senate ratification. Presidents usually find it more convenient to use executive agreements. Most executive agreements deal with routine and noncontroversial matters, but they have also been used for matters of significance, such as ending the Vietnam War and arms control agreements.

The president combines constitutional prerogatives with greater access to information than other policymakers and can act with speed and secrecy if necessary. The White House also has the advantages of the president's role as a leader of Congress and the public and his ability to commit the nation to a course of action. Presidents do not act alone in foreign policy, however. They are aided (and sometimes thwarted) by a huge national security bureaucracy. In addition, they must contend with the views and desires of Congress, which also wields considerable clout in the foreign policy arena—sometimes in opposition to a president.

The Diplomats   The State Department is the foreign policy arm of the U.S. government. As the department's chief, the **secretary of state** (Thomas Jefferson was the first) has traditionally been the key adviser to the president on foreign policy matters. In over 300 overseas posts from Albania to Zimbabwe, the State Department staffs U.S. embassies and consulates, representing the interests of Americans. Once a dignified and genteel profession, diplomacy is becoming an increasingly dangerous job. The November 1979 seizure of the American embassy in Tehran and the 1998 bombing of the American embassy in Nairobi, Kenya, are extreme examples of the hostilities diplomats can face.

> **secretary of state**
> The head of the Department of State and traditionally a key adviser to the president on **foreign policy**.

The more than 32,000 people working in the State Department are organized into functional areas (such as economic and business affairs and human rights and humanitarian affairs) and area specialties (a section on Middle Eastern affairs, one on European affairs, and so on), each nation being handled by a "country desk." The political appointees who occupy the top positions in the department and the highly select members of the Foreign Service who compose most of the department are heavily involved in formulating and executing American foreign policy.

Many recent presidents have found the State Department too bureaucratic and intransigent. Even its colloquial name "Foggy Bottom," taken from the part of Washington where it is located, conjures up less than an image of cooperation. Some recent presidents have bypassed institutional arrangements for foreign policy decision making and have instead established more personal systems for receiving policy advice. Presidents Nixon and Carter, for example, relied more heavily on their assistants for national security affairs than on their secretaries of state. Foreign policy was thus centered in the White House and was often disconnected from what was occurring in the State Department. Critics, however, charged that this situation led to split-level government and chronic discontinuity in foreign policy.[3] President Reagan, by contrast, relied less on his assistants for national security affairs (six different men filled the job in eight years) and more on Secretary of State George Schultz, who was a powerful player. George Bush continued this pattern, appointing his closest friend, James Baker, as secretary of state. President Clinton also relied heavily on his secretaries of state, Warren Christopher and Madeleine Albright. George W. Bush named Colin Powell, one of the most admired people in America, as secretary of state. Powell was the president's leading foreign policy adviser, but national security assistant Condoleezza Rice also played a prominent role. She replaced Powell as secretary of state in Bush's second term.

The National Security Establishment   Foreign policy and military policy are closely linked. Thus, the Department of Defense is a key foreign policy actor. After World War II, Congress created the Department of Defense, often called "the Pentagon" after the five-sided building in which it is located. The new department collected the U.S. Army, Navy, and Air Force into one giant department, although they have never been thoroughly integrated, and critics contend that they continue to plan and operate too independently of one another. Reforms, made law under the Goldwater-Nichols Defense Reorganization Act of 1986, have increased interservice cooperation and centralization of the military hierarchy, however. The **secretary of defense** manages a budget larger than the entire budget of most nations and is the president's main civilian adviser on national defense matters.

> **secretary of defense**
> The head of the Department of Defense and the president's key adviser on military policy; a key **foreign policy** actor.

The commanding officers of each of the services, along with a chairperson and vice chairperson, constitute the **Joint Chiefs of Staff**. American military leaders are sometimes portrayed as aggressive hawks in policymaking, presumably eager to crush some small nation with a show of American force. Scholar Richard Betts carefully examined the Joint Chiefs' advice to the president in many crises and found them to be no more likely than civilian advisers to push an aggressive military policy. (The most hawkish advice, incidentally, came from the admirals. The most dovish advice came from the army generals and the Marine Corps.)[4] On several occasions during the Reagan administration, the president's uniformed advisers cautioned against aggressive actions—including the use of military force—favored

The secretary of state is typically the president's chief foreign policy adviser, presiding over a global bureaucracy of diplomats. Here, President Bush talks to Secretary of State Condoleezza Rice, a former political science professor.

by the State Department. The military was similarly conservative regarding the use of force against Iraq in 1991[5] and intervention in the civil wars in Eastern Europe. Steeped in the mythology of generals like George Patton and Curtis LeMay, many Americans would be surprised at the cautious attitudes of America's top military leaders.

High-ranking officials are supposed to coordinate American foreign and military policies. Congress formed the *National Security Council (NSC)* in 1947 for this purpose. The NSC is composed of the president, the vice president, the secretary of defense, and the secretary of state. The president's assistant for national security—a position that first gained public prominence with the flamboyant, globe-trotting Henry Kissinger during President Nixon's first term—manages the NSC staff.

Despite the coordinating role assigned to the NSC, conflict within the foreign policy establishment remains common. The NSC staff has sometimes competed with rather than integrated policy advice from cabinet departments—particularly State and Defense. It has also become involved in covert operations. A scandal erupted in November 1986 when officials discovered that NSC staff were involved in a secret operation to sell battlefield missiles to Iran in return for Iranian help in gaining the release of hostages held by Iranian-backed terrorists in Lebanon. Staffers funneled some of the money from the sale secretly to anticommunist rebels (called *Contras*) fighting the Nicaraguan government despite a congressional ban on such aid.

The scandal, termed the Iran-Contra affair, resulted in the resignation of the president's assistant for national security affairs, Vice Admiral John Poindexter, and the sacking of a number of lower-level NSC officials, including Lieutenant Colonel Oliver North. North went from obscurity to national prominence overnight as he described his involvement in the affair before a televised congressional inquiry in 1987. Both Poindexter and North were subsequently convicted of felony charges related to the diversion of funds and misleading Congress, but courts overturned their convictions after concluding that prosecutors used their testimony before Congress, given under conditions of immunity, against them in court.

All policymakers require information to make good decisions. Information on the capabilities and intentions of other nations is often difficult to obtain. As a result, governments resort to intelligence agencies to obtain and interpret such information. Congress created the **Central Intelligence Agency** (CIA) after World War II to coordinate American information- and data-gathering

Joint Chiefs of Staff
The commanding officers of the armed services who advise the president on military policy.

Central Intelligence Agency
An agency created after World War II to coordinate American intelligence activities abroad. It became involved in intrigue, conspiracy, and meddling as well.

The CIA plays a vital role in providing information and analysis to top decision makers. Here CIA Director Michael Hayden addresses a group at CIA headquarters in Langley, Virginia.

intelligence activities abroad and to collect, analyze, and evaluate its own intelligence. Technically, its budget and staff are secret; estimates put them at $5 billion and more than 20,000 people.

The CIA plays a vital role in providing information and analysis necessary for effective development and implementation of national security policy. Most of its activities are uncontroversial because the bulk of the material it collects and analyzes comes from readily available sources, such as government reports and newspapers. However, the CIA also collects information by espionage. Most people accept the necessity of this form of information collection when it is directed against foreign adversaries. However, in the 1970s, Congress discovered that at times the agency had also engaged in wiretaps, interception of mail, and the infiltration of interest groups—in the United States. These actions violated the CIA's charter, and revelations of spying on Americans who disagreed with the foreign policy of the administration badly damaged the agency's morale and external political support.

The CIA also has a long history of involvement in other nations' internal affairs. After the end of World War II, when Eastern European nations had fallen under communism's shadow and Western European nations were teetering, the CIA provided aid to anticommunist parties in Italy and West Germany. It was no less busy in developing countries, where, for example, it nurtured coups in Iran in 1953 and in Guatemala in 1954. The CIA has also trained and supported armies—the most notable, of course, in Vietnam.

In the 1980s, a major controversy surrounded the CIA's activity in Central America, particularly in Nicaragua, where the Marxist government developed close ties with the Soviet Union and Cuba and embarked on a massive military buildup. Determined to undermine the regime, the Reagan administration aggressively supported armed rebels (Contras). Congressional inquiries into the Iran-Contra affair suggested that the CIA, under Director William Casey, was quietly involved in covert operations to assist the Contra rebels.[6]

Reconciling covert activities with the principles of open democratic government remains a challenge for public officials. With the end of the Cold War, there was less pressure for covert activities and a climate more conducive to conventional intelligence gathering. Currently, Congress requires the CIA to inform relevant congressional committees promptly of current and anticipated covert operations. In the meantime, there is substantial debate on the role of the CIA in the post–Cold War era.

The failure to predict the terrorist attack on September 11, 2001, increased the intensity of this debate, with many leaders calling for an increase in covert capabilities. Perhaps more disconcerting was the CIA's conclusion that Iraq possessed weapons of mass destruction. Destroying these weapons became the principal justification for the war, and their absence was a major embarrassment for the agency and the Bush administration.

There are numerous other components of America's intelligence community. For example, the National Reconnaissance Office uses imagery satellites to monitor missile sites and other military activities around the world, and the National Security Agency (NSA) is on the cutting edge of electronic eavesdropping capabilities.

In 2005, debate erupted over the NSA's monitoring of communications between the United States and overseas. Although the interception of communications focused on identifying contacts between those in the United States and terrorists abroad, there was inevitably some slippage. Critics charged the president with violating Americans' privacy and the legal mandate that the NSA obtain a warrant before listening to private messages. The White House claimed that the president possessed the power to authorize the interceptions without a warrant, that the NSA was careful to protect civil liberties, and that the program was necessary to protect Americans against terrorism. As we saw in Chapter 4, in 2008, Congress allowed officials the use of broad warrants to eavesdrop on large groups of foreign targets at once rather than requiring individual warrants for wiretapping purely foreign communications.

To better coordinate the nearly 100,000 people working in 16 agencies involved in intelligence and their more than $50 billion budget, Congress in 2004 created a director of national intelligence. The person filling this position is to be the president's chief adviser on intelligence matters. It is not easy to manage such a large number of diverse agencies, spread across numerous departments, and there are sure to be growing pains in the process.

Congress   The U.S. Congress shares with the president constitutional authority over foreign and defense policy (see Chapters 12 and 13). Congress has sole authority, for example, to declare war, raise and organize the armed forces, and appropriate funds for national security activities. The Senate determines whether treaties will be ratified and ambassadorial and cabinet nominations confirmed. The "power of the purse" (see Chapter 14) and responsibilities for oversight of the executive branch give Congress considerable clout, and each year senators and representatives carefully examine defense budget authorizations.[7]

Congress's important constitutional role in foreign and defense policy is sometimes misunderstood. It is a common mistake among some journalists, executive officials, and even members of Congress to believe that the Constitution vests foreign policy decisions solely in the president. Sometimes this erroneous view leads to perverse results, such as the Iran-Contra affair, which dominated the news in late 1986 and much of 1987. Officials at high levels in the executive branch "sought to protect the president's 'exclusive' prerogative by lying to Congress, to allies, to the public, and to one another." Louis Fisher suggests that such actions undermined the "mutual trust and close coordination by the two branches that are essential attributes in building a foreign policy that ensures continuity and stability."[8]

AMERICAN FOREIGN POLICY: AN OVERVIEW

Throughout most of its history, the United States followed a foreign policy course called **isolationism**. This policy, articulated by George Washington in his farewell address, directed the country to stay out of other nations' conflicts, particularly European wars. The famous *Monroe Doctrine,* enunciated by President James Monroe, reaffirmed America's inattention to Europe's problems but warned European nations to stay out of Latin America. The United States—believing that its own political backyard included Central and South America—did not hesitate to send marines, gunboats, or both to intervene in South American and Caribbean affairs (see Figure 20.1). When European nations were at war, however, Americans relished their distance from the conflicts. So it was until World War I (1914–1918).

isolationism

A foreign policy course followed throughout most of our nation's history whereby the United States tried to stay out of other nations' conflicts, particularly European wars. Isolationism was reaffirmed by the Monroe Doctrine.

FIGURE 20.1

U.S. Military Interventions in Central America and the Caribbean Since 1900

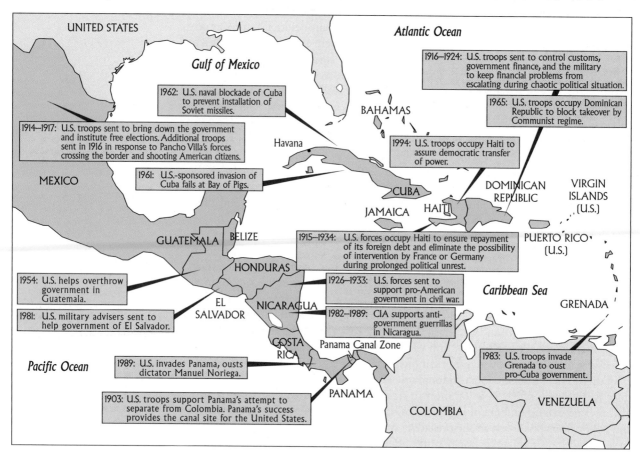

The Evolution of Foreign Policy

In the wake of World War I, President Woodrow Wilson urged the United States to join the League of Nations, a forerunner to the UN. The U.S. Senate refused to ratify the League of Nations treaty, indicating that the country was not ready to abandon the long-standing American habit of isolationism, nor was the Senate ready to turn over its war-making authority to an international body. It was World War II, which forced the United States into a global conflict, that dealt a deathblow to American isolationism. Most nations signed a charter for the UN at a conference in San Francisco in 1945. The United States was an original signatory and soon donated land to house the UN permanently in New York City.

THE COLD WAR

At the end of World War II, the Allies had vanquished Germany and Japan, and much of Europe was strewn with rubble. The United States was unquestionably the dominant world power both economically and militarily. It not only had helped to bring the war to an end but also had inaugurated a new era in warfare by dropping the first atomic bombs on Japan in August 1945. Because only the United States possessed nuclear weapons, Americans looked forward to an era of peace secured by their nuclear umbrella.

After World War II, the United States forged strong alliances with the nations of Western Europe. To help them rebuild their economies, the United

States poured billions of dollars into war-ravaged European nations through a program known as the Marshall Plan—named after its architect, Secretary of State George C. Marshall. A military alliance was also forged; the creation of NATO in 1949 affirmed the mutual military interests of the United States and Western Europe, and NATO remains a cornerstone of American foreign and defense policy.

Containment Abroad and Anticommunism at Home

Although many Americans expected cooperative relations with their wartime ally, the Soviet Union, they soon abandoned these hopes. There is still much dispute about how the Cold War between the United States and the Soviet Union started.[9] Even before World War II ended, some American policymakers feared that their Soviet allies were intent on spreading communism not only to their neighbors but everywhere. All of Eastern Europe fell under Soviet domination as World War II ended. In 1946, Winston Churchill warned that the Russians had sealed off Eastern Europe with an "iron curtain."

Communist support of a revolt in Greece in 1946 compounded fears of Soviet aggression. Writing in *Foreign Affairs* in 1947, foreign policy strategist George F. Kennan proposed a policy of "containment."[10] His **containment doctrine** called for the United States to isolate the Soviet Union—to "contain" its advances and resist its encroachments—by peaceful means if possible but with force if necessary. When economic problems forced Great Britain to decrease its support of Greece, the United States stepped in with the Truman Doctrine of helping other nations oppose communism. The Soviet Union responded with the Berlin Blockade of 1948–1949, in which it closed off land access to West Berlin (which was surrounded by communist East Germany). The United States and its allies broke the blockade by airlifting food, fuel, and other necessities to the people of the beleaguered city.

The fall of China to Mao Zedong's communist-led forces in 1949 seemed to confirm American fears that communism was a cancer spreading over the "free world." In the same year, the Soviet Union exploded its first atomic bomb. The invasion of pro-American South Korea by communist North Korea in 1950 further fueled American fears of Soviet imperialism. President Truman said bluntly, "We've got to stop the Russians now," and sent American troops to Korea under UN auspices. The Korean War was a chance to put containment into practice. Involving China as well as North Korea, the war dragged on until July 27, 1953.

> **containment doctrine**
> A **foreign policy** strategy advocated by George Kennan that called for the United States to isolate the Soviet Union, "contain" its advances, and resist its encroachments by peaceful means if possible but by force if necessary.

In 1963, President John F. Kennedy looked over the Berlin Wall, which the Soviet Union had built to separate communist East Berlin from the western sectors of the city. The wall stood as the most palpable symbol of the Cold War for almost 30 years until it was torn down in 1989.

Cold War

War by other than military means usually emphasizing ideological conflict, such as that between the United States and the Soviet Union from the end of World War II until the 1990s.

You Are President John F. Kennedy

arms race

A tense relationship beginning in the 1950s between the Soviet Union and the United States whereby one side's weaponry became the other side's goad to procure more weaponry, and so on.

The 1950s were the height of the **Cold War**; though hostilities never quite erupted into armed battle between them, the United States and the Soviet Union were often on the brink of war. John Foster Dulles, secretary of state under Eisenhower, proclaimed a policy often referred to as "brinkmanship," in which the United States was to be prepared to use nuclear weapons in order to *deter* the Soviet Union and communist China from taking aggressive actions.

By the 1950s, the Soviet Union and the United States were engaged in an **arms race**. One side's weaponry goaded the other side to procure yet more weaponry, as one missile led to another. By the mid-1960s, the result of the arms race was a point of *mutual assured destruction (MAD)*, in which each side could annihilate the other, even after absorbing a surprise attack. Later sections of this chapter will examine efforts to control the arms race.

The Vietnam War The Korean War and the 1949 victory of communist forces in China fixed the U.S. government's attention on Asian communism. In 1950, President Truman decided to aid France's effort to retain its colonial possessions in Southeast Asia, but the Vietnamese communists finally defeated the French in a battle at Dien Bien Phu in 1954. The morning after the battle, peace talks among the participants and other major powers began in Geneva, Switzerland. Although a party to the resultant agreements, which stipulated that national elections be held in Vietnam in 1956, the United States never accepted them. Instead, it began supporting one noncommunist leader after another in South Vietnam, each seemingly more committed than the last to defeating communist forces in the north.[11]

Unable to contain the forces of the communist guerillas and the North Vietnamese army with American military advisers, President Lyndon Johnson sent in American troops—more than 500,000 at the peak of the undeclared war. He dropped more bombs on communist North Vietnam than the United States had dropped on Germany in all of World War II. These American troops and massive firepower failed to contain the North Vietnamese, however. At home, widespread protests against the war contributed to Johnson's decisions not to run for reelection in 1968 and to begin peace negotiations.

The new Nixon administration prosecuted the war vigorously, in Cambodia as well as in Vietnam, but also negotiated with the Vietnamese communists. A peace treaty was signed in 1973, but few expected it to hold. South Vietnam's capital, Saigon, finally fell to the North Vietnamese army in 1975. South and North Vietnam were reunited into a single nation, and Saigon was renamed Ho Chi Minh City in honor of the late leader of communist North Vietnam.

Looking back on the Vietnam War, most Americans question its worth. It divided the nation and made citizens painfully aware of the government's ability to lie to them—and (perhaps worse) to itself. It reminded Americans that even a "great power" cannot prevail in a protracted military conflict against a determined enemy unless there is a clear objective and unless the national will is sufficiently committed to expend vast resources on the task.

THE ERA OF DÉTENTE

Even while the United States was waging the Vietnam War, Richard Nixon— a veteran fighter of the Cold War—supported a new policy that came to be called *détente*. The term was popularized by Nixon's national security adviser and later secretary of state, Henry Kissinger.

Détente represented a slow transformation from conflict thinking to cooperative thinking in foreign policy strategy. It sought a relaxation of tensions between the superpowers, coupled with firm guarantees of mutual security. The policy assumed that the United States and the Soviet Union had no long-range, irrevocable sources

détente

A slow transformation from conflict thinking to cooperative thinking in **foreign policy** strategy and policy-making. It sought a relaxation of tensions between the superpowers, coupled with firm guarantees of mutual security.

of conflict; that both had an interest in peace and world stability; and that a nuclear war was—and should be—unthinkable. Thus, foreign policy battles between the United States and the Soviet Union were to be waged with diplomatic, economic, and propaganda weapons; the threat of force was downplayed.

One major initiative emerging from détente was the *Strategic Arms Limitation Talks (SALT)*. These talks represented a mutual effort by the United States and the Soviet Union to limit the growth of their nuclear capabilities, with each power maintaining sufficient nuclear weapons to deter a surprise attack by the other. Nixon signed the first SALT accord in 1972, and negotiations for a second agreement, SALT II, soon followed. After six years of laborious negotiations, President Carter finally signed the agreement and sent it to the Senate in 1979. The Soviet invasion of Afghanistan that year caused Carter to withdraw the treaty from Senate consideration, however, even though both he and Ronald Reagan insisted that they would remain committed to the agreement's limitations on nuclear weaponry.

The United States applied the philosophy of détente to the People's Republic of China as well as to the Soviet Union. After the fall of the pro-American government in 1949, the United States refused to extend diplomatic recognition to the world's most populous nation, recognizing instead the government in exile on the nearby island of Taiwan. As a senator in the early 1950s, Richard Nixon had been an implacable foe of "Red China," even suggesting that the Democratic administration had traitorously "lost" China. Nevertheless, two decades later it was this same Richard Nixon who, as president, first visited the People's Republic and sent an American mission there. President Jimmy Carter extended formal diplomatic recognition to China in January 1979. Since then, cultural and economic ties between the United States and China have increased greatly.

Not everyone favored détente, however. Even Carter called for a substantial increase in defense spending after the Soviet Union invaded Afghanistan in 1979. Few people saw more threats from the Soviet Union than did Ronald Reagan, who called it the "Evil Empire." He viewed the Soviet invasion of Afghanistan as typical Russian aggression that, if unchecked, could only grow more common. He hailed anticommunist governments everywhere and pledged to increase American defense spending.

THE REAGAN REARMAMENT

From the mid-1950s to 1981 (with the exception of the Vietnam War), the defense budget had generally been declining as a percentage of both the total federal budget and the GDP. In 1955, during the Eisenhower administration, the government was spending 61 percent of its budget for defense purposes, or about 10 percent of the GDP. By the time President Reagan took office in 1981, the government devoted 23 percent of the federal budget and 5.2 percent of the GDP to defense expenditures. These figures reflected a substantial cut indeed, although the decrease came about more because levels of social spending had increased than because military spending had declined.

According to Reagan, America faced a "window of vulnerability" because the Soviet Union was galloping ahead of the United States in military spending and that the U.S. had to build its defenses before it could negotiate arms control agreements. Determined to reverse the trend of diminishing defense spending, he proposed the largest peacetime defense spending increase in American history: a five-year defense buildup costing $1.5 trillion. Defense officials were ordered to find places to spend more money.[12] These heady days for the Pentagon lasted only through the first term of Reagan's presidency, however. In his second term, concern over huge budget deficits brought defense spending to a standstill. After taking inflation into account, Congress appropriated no increase in defense spending at all from 1985 to 1988.

Strategic Defense Initiative

Renamed "Star Wars" by critics, a plan for defense against the Soviet Union unveiled by President Reagan in 1983. The Strategic Defense Initiative would create a global umbrella in space, using computers to scan the skies and high-tech devices to destroy invading missiles.

In 1983 President Reagan added another element to his defense policy—a new plan for defense against missiles. He called it the **Strategic Defense Initiative** (SDI); critics quickly renamed it "Star Wars." Reagan's plans for SDI proposed creating a global umbrella in space wherein computers would scan the skies and use various high-tech devices to destroy invading missiles. The administration proposed a research program that would have cost tens of billions of dollars over the next decade.

In the face of an onslaught of criticism regarding the feasibility of SDI, its proponents reduced their expectations about the size and capabilities of any defensive shield that could be erected over the next generation. Talk of a smaller system—capable of protecting against an accidental launch of a few missiles or against a threat by some Third World country with nuclear weapons—replaced the dream of an impenetrable umbrella over the United States capable of defeating a massive Soviet nuclear strike.

THE FINAL THAW IN THE COLD WAR

On May 12, 1989, in a commencement address at Texas A&M University, President George Bush announced a new era in American foreign policy. He termed this era one "beyond containment"; the goal of the United States would be more than containing Soviet expansion. Bush declared that it was time to seek the integration of the Soviet Union into the community of nations.

The Cold War ended as few had anticipated—spontaneously. Suddenly, the elusive objective of 40 years of post–World War II U.S. foreign policy—freedom and self-determination for Eastern Europeans and Soviet peoples and the reduction of the military threat from the East—occurred. Forces of change sparked by Soviet leader Mikhail Gorbachev led to a staggering wave of upheaval that shattered communist regimes and the postwar barriers between Eastern and Western Europe. The Berlin Wall, the most prominent symbol of oppression in Eastern Europe, came tumbling down on November 9, 1989, and East and West Germany formed a unified, democratic republic. The former Soviet Union split into 15 separate nations, and noncommunist governments formed in most of them. Poland, Czechoslovakia (splitting into the Czech Republic and Slovakia), and Hungary established democratic governments, and reformers overthrew the old-line communist leaders in Bulgaria and Romania.

Events were unfolding so fast and in so many places at once that no one was quite sure how to deal with them. President Bush declared, "Every morning I receive an intelligence briefing, and I receive the best information available to any world leader today. And yet, the morning news is often overtaken by the news that very same evening."[13]

In 1989, reform seemed on the verge of occurring in China as well as in Eastern Europe. That spring in Tiananmen Square, the central meeting place in Beijing, thousands of students held protests on behalf of democratization. Unable to tolerate challenges to their rule any longer, the aging Chinese leaders forcibly—and brutally—evacuated the square, crushing some protestors under armored tanks. It is still not clear how many students

Beginning in 1989, communism in the Soviet Union and in Eastern Europe suddenly began to crumble. The end of the Cold War between East and West reduced the threat of nuclear war between the superpowers, but it also left a host of difficult new national security issues in its wake. Here, workers dismantle the head from a huge granite statue of Lenin in Berlin in 1991.

were killed and how many others arrested, but the reform movement in China received a serious setback. This suppression of efforts to develop democracy sent a chill through what had been a warming relationship between the United States and the People's Republic of China.

Reform continued elsewhere, however. On June 17, 1992, Boris Yeltsin addressed a joint session of the U.S. Congress. When the burly, silver-haired president of the new Russian republic entered the House chamber, members of Congress greeted him with chants of "Bo-ris, Bo-ris" and hailed him with numerous standing ovations.

Yeltsin proclaimed to thunderous applause,

> The idol of communism, which spread *everywhere* social strife, animosity and unparalleled brutality, which instilled fear in humanity, has collapsed . . . I am here to assure you that we will not let it rise again in our land.

The Cold War that had been waged for two generations had ended, and the West, led by the United States, had won.

THE WAR ON TERRORISM

Perhaps the most troublesome issue in the national security area is the spread of terrorism—the use of violence to demoralize and frighten a country's population or government. Terrorism takes many forms, including the bombing of buildings (such as the attacks on New York and Washington, D.C. on September 11, 2001; on the American embassy in Kenya in 1998; and on the World Trade Center in New York in 1993) and ships (such as the USS *Cole* in Yemen in 2000), the assassinations of political leaders (as when Iraq attempted to kill former president George Bush in 1993), and the kidnappings of diplomats and civilians (as when Iranians took Americans hostage in 1979).

Terrorism takes many forms, including the bombing of buildings and ships. Shown here are terrorist attacks on the World Trade Center in New York in 2001, the American embassy in Kenya in 1998, and the USS *Cole* in Yemen in 2000.

It is difficult to defend against terrorism, especially in an open society. Terrorists have the advantage of stealth and surprise. Improved security measures and better intelligence gathering can help. So, perhaps, can punishing governments and organizations that engage in terrorist activities. In 1986, the United States launched an air attack on Libya in response to Libyan-supported acts of terrorism; in 1993, the United States struck at Iraq's intelligence center in response to a foiled plot to assassinate former president George Bush; and in 1998, the United States launched an attack in Afghanistan on Osama bin Laden, the leader of the terrorist organization al Qaeda.

AFGHANISTAN AND IRAQ

Following the September 11, 2001, attacks on New York and Washington, the United States declared war on terrorism. President George W. Bush made the war the highest priority of his administration, and the United States launched an attack on the Taliban regime that had been harboring terrorists in Afghanistan. The Taliban fell in short order, although many suspected terrorist members of Osama bin Laden's al Qaeda network escaped. In the meantime, the president declared that Iran, Iraq, and North Korea formed an "axis of evil" and began laying plans to remove Iraqi President Saddam Hussein from power. In 2003, a U.S.-led coalition toppled Hussein.

Overthrowing dictators carries with it new problems, however. In the 2000 presidential campaign, George W. Bush spoke of "humility" in foreign affairs and cautioned against overextending America's military. He also warned against "nation building," which involves installing institutions of a national government in a country and often requires massive investment and military occupation. The threat of terrorism, leading to the invasions of both Afghanistan and Iraq, caused the president to rethink these views, and the administration began talking about meeting America's "unparalleled responsibilities." One of those responsibilities has been to rebuild and democratize Iraq.

There is broad consensus that the planning for postwar Iraq was poor. The administration presumed that Americans would be welcomed as liberators, that Iraqi oil would pay for most (if not all) of the necessary reconstruction of the country, and that the Iraqis possessed the necessary skills and infrastructure to do the job. These premises proved to be faulty, and the United States faced first chaos and then a protracted insurrection, especially in the "Sunni triangle" around Baghdad. Five years after the end of the official fighting, 140,000 American troops were still stationed in Iraq, straining our defense resources. As both U.S. expenditures on reconstruction and American casualties mounted in the period since the end of the war with Iraq, the public's support for the effort declined substantially, and the president experienced a corresponding drop in his approval ratings.

President Bush often declared that postwar Iraq was the front line in the global war on terror. The president's critics responded that the war has been a boon for extremists. Muslims consider Iraq, the seat of Islamic power for five centuries, sacred ground. The presence of foreign, non-Muslim occupiers there has become a magnet for militants hoping for an opportunity to kill Americans and other Westerners. Since the war in Afghanistan, al Qaeda has changed from an active source of planning, training, and attacks into an umbrella organization that provides an inspirational focal point for loosely affiliated terrorist groups in dozens of countries worldwide.

Some view this transformed threat as potentially more dangerous than the one posed by the original al Qaeda. A "decapitation" strategy, focusing on the elimination of a small group of senior figures in the original al Qaeda network, may no longer be an adequate or appropriate strategy for dealing with a threat that has, in effect, metastasized.

Formulating a new strategy to defeat al Qaeda and its affiliates will not be easy. The use of military force alone will not neutralize this more dispersed terrorist threat. Because of the increasingly decentralized nature of the threat, the military component of the global counterterrorism campaign is more likely to resemble a war of attrition on multiple fronts than a limited number of surgical strikes against a single adversary. One consequence is that the war on terrorism is likely to persist for many years. There were approximately 14,000 terrorist attacks worldwide during 2006, resulting in over 20,000 deaths. This was a 25 percent increase in incidents over 2005, and deaths from terrorism showed a 40 percent increase.[14] Approximately 45 percent of these attacks occurred in Iraq, and they represented about 65 percent of the worldwide fatalities. (Some of the increase in documented attacks may be explained by improvements in data collection.)

Many observers argue that relying primarily on the use of force to combat terrorism is responding to a tactic (terrorism) rather than to the forces that generate it. Traditionally, winning a war involved defeating an enemy on the battlefield and forcing it to accept political terms. Winning the war on terror, however, will not come when foreign leaders accept certain terms but when political changes erode and ultimately undermine support for the ideology and strategy of those determined to destroy the United States and its allies. It will come not when Washington and its allies kill or capture all terrorists or potential terrorists but when the ideology the terrorists espouse is discredited, when their tactics are seen to have failed, and when they come to find more promising paths to the dignity, respect, and opportunities they crave.

Even conquered territories present problems. Afghanistan is threatened by Taliban insurgents and religious extremists, some of whom are linked to al Qaeda and to sponsors outside the country. A terrorist haven has emerged in Pakistan's tribal belt, and the U.S. military has been unable to conduct the sort of missions that would disrupt terrorist activity there and in similarly ungoverned places. Ensuring legitimate and effective governance in Afghanistan, delivering relief assistance, and countering the surge in narcotics cultivation remain major challenges for the international community.

In 2007, President Bush ordered a troop "surge" in Iraq. It was designed to quell violence and give Iraqis the opportunity to establish a democratic government, train forces to assume police and defense responsibilities, and engage in national reconciliation among the major religious and ethnic groups. The first goal was met, as violence was reduced. Progress on the other goals has been much slower, however. As a result, the U.S. has not been able to reduce its troop levels to those before the surge began.

Whatever the current in the debate over the war on terrorism, there is no doubt that the need to fight terrorists has forced Americans to rethink some of the basic tenets of U.S. national security policy.

RETHINKING NATIONAL SECURITY POLICY

Despite its risks and uncertainties, the Cold War was characterized by a stable and predictable set of relations among the great powers. Now international relations have entered an era of improvisation as nations struggle to develop creative responses to changes in the global balance of power and the new challenges that have emerged.

The threat posed by terrorist groups and the hostile states that support some of them has forced America to reconsider basic tenets of its national security policy. President George W. Bush believed that the strategies and institutions that kept the peace during the Cold War were not suited to a twenty-first-century campaign against terrorism. He concluded that multilateral alliances like NATO and bilateral partnerships like that with South Korea had proven ineffective in dealing with terrorism. Thus, during his presidency the United States maintained its system of formal, structured alliances, but it also emphasized a more fluid system of improvised alignments of nations in which the mission determined the alliance.

The national security strategy doctrine issued by the Bush administration in September 2002 was the most dramatic and far-reaching change in national security policy in a half century. The doctrine moved away from the Cold War pillars of containment and deterrence toward a policy that supported preemptive strikes against terrorists and hostile states to prevent their using chemical, biological, or nuclear weapons against the United States. When the United States found no weapons of mass destruction in Iraq in 2003, the administration expanded its formulation from precluding immediate threats to prevention of the development of threats. The strategic doctrine also explicitly advocated U.S. preeminence in military capabilities and, if necessary, unilateral action in national security policy, contrary to decades of emphasis on grounding defense policy in alliances.

The U.S. invasion of Iraq in 2003 followed directly from these premises. It was a policy designed to preempt future strikes against the United States and its allies. The absence of support from core members of NATO and the potential damage to our most enduring alliances did not deter the president. Nor did the lack of support from the United Nations, which the president felt had failed miserably—in Rwanda, in Kosovo, and most recently in its confrontation with Iraq—and needed to be made anew. Similarly, the president renounced the 1972 Anti-Ballistic Missile Treaty over the objections of Russia and China, refused to participate in the International Criminal Court, and rejected several environmental treaties.

Critics charged that the arrogation of a unilateral right to define threats and use force has squandered America's moral authority and diminished its global credibility. They argue that the United States cannot defend itself without the help of others and thus that American national security is inextricably tied to international security. Success in the war on terror, they believe, will only occur if the U.S. reestablishes its moral authority and ideological appeal, conducts more and smarter diplomacy, and intensifies cooperation with key allies.

In his inaugural address following his reelection in 2005, President George W. Bush spoke to the world, proclaiming that America would stand with those who challenge authoritarian governments and warning those governments to begin liberalizing. Although these exhortations appeared to represent opening another aggressive thrust for U.S. foreign policy, the administration—including a rare press conference held by the president's father—downplayed the significance of the president's statements. For the rest of his tenure, Bush adopted a cautious, diplomatic approach when faced with the inevitable trade-offs between principle and pragmatism in dealing with repressive regimes.

Almost everyone agrees that today's complicated international environment portends an overhaul of the American national security infrastructure. Policymakers are reassessing armed forces and alliances, defense industries, and budgets built up since World War II in light of both the Cold War thaw and the war on terrorism.

THE POLITICS OF DEFENSE POLICY

The politics of national defense involves high stakes—the nation's security, for example. Domestic political concerns, budgetary limitations, and ideology all influence decisions on the structure of defense policy and negotiations with allies and adversaries.

All public policies include budgets, people, and equipment. In the realm of national defense, these elements are especially critical because of the size of the budget and the bureaucracy as well as the destructive potential of modern weapons.

At the core of defense policy is a judgment about what the United States will defend. The central assumption of current American defense policy is that the United States requires forces and equipment sufficient to win decisively a single major conflict, defend American territory against new threats, and conduct a number of holding actions elsewhere around the world. A large military infrastructure is necessary to meet these goals.

DEFENSE SPENDING

Defense spending now makes up about one-fifth of the federal budget. Although this is a much smaller percentage than in earlier years (see Figure 20.2), vast sums of money and fundamental questions of public policy are still involved (see Figure 14.4). Some scholars have argued that America faces a trade-off between defense spending and social spending. A nation, they claim, must choose between guns and butter, and more guns means less butter. Evidence supporting the existence of such a trade-off is mixed, however. In general, defense and domestic policy expenditures appear to be independent of each other.[15] Ronald Reagan's efforts to increase military budgets while cutting back on domestic policy expenditures seem to have stemmed more from his own ideology than from any inevitable choice between the two.

? Why It Matters
The Defense Budget
In the twenty-first century, the United States spends about one-fifth of its national budget on defense to support a large defense establishment. This expenditure contributes to large annual budget deficits, but some argue that we should spend even more to protect the country against terrorism.

FIGURE 20.2

Trends in Defense Spending

John F. Kennedy took office in 1961 at the height of the Cold War. National defense was the dominant public policy for the U.S. government; it accounted for half of all the money ("outlays") the government spent that year. Things have changed dramatically since then, however. Although defense spending continued to increase until the 1990s, spending on other policies increased even more. As a result, defense spending is now only about one-fifth of the budget. Still, at more than $600 billion per year (counting the cost of occupation of Iraq), it remains a significant sum, one over which battles continue to be fought in Congress.

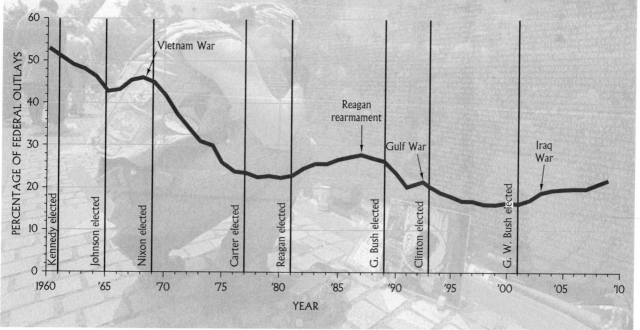

Source: *Budget of the United States Government, Fiscal Year 2009: Historical Tables* (Washington, DC: U.S. Government Printing Office, 2008), Table 3.1.

Evaluating Defense
Spending

Defense spending is a thorny political issue, entangled with ideological disputes. Conservatives advocate increases in defense spending, pointing out that many nations and terrorist organizations retain potent military capability, and insist that America maintain its readiness at a high level. They refer to the Gulf War and the Iraq War as evidence that wars on a significant scale are still possible. In addition, they attribute the collapse of communism in Eastern and Central Europe to Western toughness and the massive increase in defense spending that occurred in the early 1980s. When the Soviet Union saw that it could not outspend the United States, they argue, it finally decided not to continue to allocate so much of its scarce resources to defense and to loosen its grip on Eastern Europe.

Liberals have supported increased defense spending for the war on terrorism. More generally, however, they are skeptical of defense spending, maintaining that the Pentagon wastes money and that the United States buys too many guns and too little butter. The most crucial aspect of national defense, they argue, is a strong economy, which is based on investments in "human capital" such as health and education. Liberals insist that the erosion of the Communist Party's authority was well under way when Gorbachev rose to power. This erosion accelerated as *glasnost* (the Russian term for the new openness of society) made the party's failures a matter of public ridicule as democratization freed new forces to challenge the existing order. They contend that Gorbachev and his fellow reformers were responding primarily to internal, not external, pressures. Inadequacies and defects at the core of the Soviet economy—the inertia, wastefulness, and corruption inherent in the system—were the driving forces that brought change to the Soviet Union, not American defense spending.

In addition, scholars such as Paul Kennedy and David Calleo envision a new world order different from the past bipolar dominance of the United States and the Soviet Union.[16] Kennedy warns of the historical dangers of "imperial overstretch," suggesting that great empires in a stage of relative economic decline compared with emerging powers accelerate their decline by clinging to vast military commitments.

Whatever its cause, the lessening of East–West tensions gave momentum to significant reductions in defense spending in the 1990s, what some called the *peace dividend.* Changing spending patterns was not easy, however. For example, military hardware developed during the early 1980s has proven to be increasingly expensive to purchase and maintain. And when the assembly lines at weapons plants close down, submarine designers, welders, and many others lose their jobs. These programs become political footballs as candidates compete over promises to keep weapons systems such as the *Seawolf* submarine or the Osprey helicopter in production. Ideology plays a crucial role in the basic decisions members of Congress make regarding defense spending, but once these decisions are made, liberal as well as conservative representatives and senators fight hard to help constituencies win and keep defense contracts.[17]

The trend of reductions in defense spending reversed abruptly in 2001 following the September 11 terrorist attacks. Whatever the proper level of spending, there is no question that the United States spends more on defense than the next 15 or 20 biggest spenders combined. It has overwhelming nuclear superiority, the world's dominant air force, the only navy with worldwide operations (which also has impressive airpower), and a unique capability to project power around the globe. No other country in modern history has come close to this level of military predominance, and the gap between the United States and other nations is increasing. Moreover, the military advantages are even greater when one considers the quality as well as the quantity of U.S. defense capabilities. America has exploited the military applications of advanced communications and information technology and has developed the ability to coordinate and process information about the battlefield and to destroy targets from afar with extraordinary precision.

PERSONNEL

The structure of America's defense has been based on a large standing military force and a battery of strategic nuclear weapons. The United States has about 1.4 million men and women on active duty and about 838,000 in the National Guard and reserves (see Figure 20.3). There are about 300,000 active-duty troops deployed abroad, mostly in Europe, Japan, and South Korea;[18] there were about 140,000 troops in Iraq in 2008. This is a very costly enterprise and one that frequently evokes calls to bring the troops home. Many observers believe that America's allies, especially prosperous nations such as Japan and Germany, should bear a greater share of common defense costs.

Other demands on the defense budget have led to reduced numbers of active-duty personnel in the armed services. As a result, the military now relies much more heavily on National Guard and reserve units to maintain national security (the "total force" concept). The president mobilized National Guard units and sent them into active duty in Bosnia, and National Guard and reserve units have served in the war on terrorism, many for extended periods in Iraq.

WEAPONS

To deter an aggressor's attack, the United States has relied on a triad of nuclear weapons: ground-based intercontinental ballistic missiles (ICBMs), submarine-launched ballistic missiles, and strategic bombers. Both the United States and Russia have thousands of large nuclear warheads. These weapons, like troops, are costly (each Stealth bomber costs over $2 *billion*), and they pose obvious dangers to human survival. The total cost of building nuclear weapons has been $5.5 *trillion*.[19]

The rapid drive toward democracy in Eastern Europe, combined with Moscow's economic stagnation and the Pentagon's budgetary squeeze, pushed arms reduction inexorably onto the two superpowers' discussion agenda. Substantial progress has been

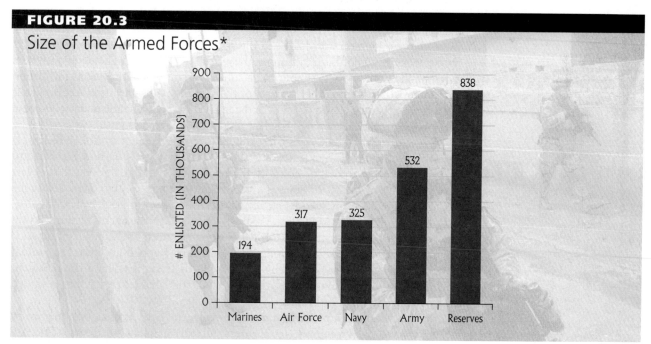

FIGURE 20.3

Size of the Armed Forces*

*2009 estimates

Sources: Office of Management and Budget, *Budget of the United States Government, Fiscal Year 2009: Appendix* (Washington, DC: U.S. Government Printing Office, 2008), 241–242.

President Reagan and Soviet President Mikhail Gorbachev begin their 1988 summit meeting in Moscow. The two presidents later signed a treaty eliminating intermediate-range nuclear missiles from Europe. The INF treaty marked the first time an American president had agreed to reduce current levels of nuclear weapons.

made to end the arms race and what was known as "the balance of terror."

During the May 1988 Moscow summit meeting, President Reagan and Mikhail Gorbachev exchanged ratified copies of a new treaty eliminating *intermediate-range nuclear forces (INF)*. Reagan, who had built his reputation on fervid anticommunism and had denounced earlier arms control efforts (such as Jimmy Carter's SALT II agreement), became the first American president to sign a treaty to reduce current levels of nuclear weapons. Under the terms of the INF treaty, more than 2,500 nuclear weapons with ranges between 300 and 3,400 miles were to be destroyed.

Superpower relations continued to improve at a dizzying pace, accelerated by the dissolution of the Soviet Union. On November 19, 1990, the leaders of 22 countries signed a treaty reducing conventional armed forces in Europe. The treaty slashed forces in Europe by 40 percent—the Soviet Union was called on to remove the most troops. A related change occurred in 1991 as the Warsaw Pact, the military alliance tying Eastern Europe to the Soviet Union, was dissolved.

On July 31, 1991, shortly before Soviet hard-liners attempted a coup to remove President Gorbachev and other reformers from power, he and President Bush signed the *Strategic Arms Reduction Treaty (START)*—after nine years of negotiations. The treaty had the distinction of being the first accord mandating the elimination of strategic nuclear weaponry. (The INF treaty banned a whole class of shorter-range nuclear arms.)

Other events soon overshadowed the significance of these changes, however, as the democratization of Eastern Europe, the restructuring of the Soviet Union, and the deterioration of the Soviet economy substantially diminished both Russia's inclination and potential to threaten the interests of the United States and its allies. President Bush broke ground with his decision in the fall of 1991 to dismantle unilaterally some U.S. nuclear weapons, enticing President Gorbachev to follow suit shortly afterward.

In January 1993, Presidents Bush and Yeltsin signed an agreement (START II) to cut the U.S. and Russian (including those of Ukraine, Belarus, and Kazakhstan) nuclear arsenals to a total of no more than 6,500 weapons by the year 2003—less than one-third of the 20,000 long-range nuclear weapons the two possessed at the time. The agreement banned large, accurate ICBMs with multiple warheads altogether. In 2002, President George W. Bush and Russian President Vladimir Putin signed a treaty to limit strategic nuclear weapons to no more than 2,200 for each country by 2012. At the same time, President Bush stepped up efforts to build a national missile defense. To pursue this system, in December 2001 the president withdrew the United States from the Anti-Ballistic Missile Treaty that it signed with the Soviet Union in 1972.

Nuclear weapons are the most destructive in America's arsenal, but they are by no means the only weapons. Jet fighters, aircraft carriers, and even tanks are extraordinarily complex and equally costly. The perception that space-age technology helped win the Gulf War in "100 hours" and topple the Taliban regime in Afghanistan and Saddam Hussein in Iraq with few American casualties, in addition to the fact that producing expensive weapons provides jobs for American workers, means that high-tech weapons systems will continue to play an important role in America's defense posture.

REFORMING DEFENSE POLICY

Directly related to rethinking national security policy is reforming the nation's military. Reevaluating weapons systems and potentially skipping a generation to produce more technologically advanced systems is part of the effort. So is changing the force structure to make the armed forces lighter, faster, and more flexible. More effectively coupling intelligence with an increasingly agile military and a greater use of Special Forces are also significant breaks from the past. New approaches to military conflict inevitably follow from such transformations.

Although the U.S. has unsurpassed military strength, many international matters clamor for attention. Even the mightiest nation can be mired in intractable issues.

THE NEW GLOBAL AGENDA

The global agenda is changing rapidly. As military competition with communist powers has diminished, economic competition with the world has increased. The gap between domestic and foreign policy is increasingly obscure. Dealing with allies such as Japan and Germany on trade and finance is as crucial as negotiating arms reductions with Russia. Maintaining access to petroleum in the Middle East is more crucial than ever, and determining policy regarding the global environment has taken on new prominence.

Regardless of the standards one uses for measurement, the United States is the world's mightiest military power. Its very strength seems to belie an essential weakness, however. Events on the world stage often appear to counter the American script because countries and groups have their own motivations and agendas that may not match those of the U.S. In the long and controversial Vietnam War, 500,000 American troops were not enough. The economic vulnerability of the United States has increased. Our military might did not protect us from the deadly terrorist attacks on September 11, 2001. Oil supply lines depend on a precarious Middle Eastern peace and on the safe passage of huge tankers through a sliver of water called the Strait of Hormuz. We sometimes appear to be losing the war on drugs to an international network of wealthy drug lords called *narco-traficantes*. Perhaps most important of all, our economy is increasingly dependent on international trade, placing us at the mercy of interest rates in Germany, restrictive markets in Japan, and currency values in China.

There is an interesting paradox to American power: Although the United States is militarily supreme, it is becoming increasingly dependent on other peoples to defeat terrorism, protect the environment, control weapons of mass destruction, regulate trade, and deal with other problems that cross national boundaries.[20] Even the effective use of U.S. military power requires military bases, ports, airfields, fuel supplies, and overflight rights that only its allies can provide.

There is much discussion in governing circles about whether America's military dominance will blind it to the need to cooperate with other nations. The George W. Bush administration has been assertive in acting unilaterally and defending U.S. interests rather than collective international interests. Many critics (including many of America's allies) complain that the United States undermines its ability to obtain the support of other countries when it fails to consult them, refuses to participate in the International Criminal Court, and rejects treaties to eliminate greenhouse gases, restrict antiballistic missile systems, prohibit land mines, and ban biological weapons testing.

THE CHANGING ROLE OF MILITARY POWER

Harvard political scientist Stanley Hoffman likened the plight of the United States to that of Jonathan Swift's fictional character, Gulliver, the traveler seized and bound by the tiny Lilliputians.[21] For Americans, as for Gulliver, merely being big and powerful is no guarantee of dominance. Time after time and place after place, so it seems, the American Gulliver is frustrated by the Lilliputians.

One explanation for America's tribulations is that the nation's strong suit—military might—is no longer the primary instrument of foreign policy. Robert Keohane and Joseph Nye, in describing the diminishing role of military force in contemporary international politics, say that among the developed nations, "the perceived margin of safety has widened: fears of attack in general have declined, and fears of attacks by one another are virtually nonexistent."[22]

Today military power is losing much of its utility in resolving many international issues. "Force," argue Keohane and Nye, "is often not an appropriate way of achieving other goals (such as economic and ecological welfare) that are becoming more important" in world affairs.[23] Economic conflicts do not readily yield to nuclear weapons. America cannot persuade Arab nations to sell it cheap oil by bombing them, nor can it prop up the textile industry's position in world trade by resorting to military might. The United States is long on firepower at the very time when firepower is decreasing in its utility as an instrument of foreign policy.

According to Nye, it is "soft power"—the ability of a country to persuade others to do what it wants without force or coercion—that is often crucial to national security. American culture, ideals, and values have been important in helping Washington attract partners and supporters, and countries require both hard and soft power to shape long-term attitudes and preferences around the globe. Thus, security hinges as much on winning hearts and minds as it does on winning wars.[24]

Conflict among large powers, the threat of nuclear war, and the possibility of conventional war have certainly not disappeared, but grafted onto them are new issues. Former Secretary of State Henry Kissinger described the new era eloquently:

> The traditional agenda of international affairs—the balance among major powers, the security of nations—no longer defines our perils or our possibilities. Now we are entering a new era. Old international patterns are crumbling; old slogans are uninstructive. The world has become interdependent in economics, in communications, in human aspirations.[25]

Despite these changes, military power remains an important element in U.S. foreign policy. The end of the Cold War emboldened local dictators and reignited age-old ethnic rivalries that had been held in check by the Soviet Union. The result: The number of regional crises likely to pose a threat to peace has grown exponentially in the post–Cold War era. Thus, although the end of the Cold War gives the United States unprecedented freedom to act, its status as the only superpower has meant that Washington is the first place people look for help when trouble erupts, even in Europe's backyard, as in the case of the territory of the former Yugoslavia. One of the nation's most difficult foreign policy problems is in deciding when to send U.S. troops to police the world's hot spots.

Humanitarian Interventions   Military interventions are not always designed to increase a country's power or to defeat a threatening foe. In recent years, the United States and its allies have used military force to accomplish humanitarian ends. The most notable examples include the efforts to distribute food and then oust a ruthless and unprincipled warlord in Somalia in 1992 and 1993, restore the elected leader of Haiti in 1994, stop the ethnic warfare in Bosnia by bombing the Serbs in 1995, and protect ethnic Albanians in Kosovo by bombing Serbs in 1999.

Such interventions are often controversial, because they involve violating a nation's sovereignty with the use of force. The United States is usually hesitant to intervene because such an action may cost American lives, and there may be no clear ending point for the mission. Nevertheless, there is a constant demand for U.S. intervention. The Bush administration came under intense pressure in mid-2003 to intervene to quell the violence and relieve suffering in Liberia. The crisis in Darfur in western Sudan—where, since February 2003, more than 250,000 people have been killed and nearly 3 million displaced—prompted new calls for international humanitarian intervention.

"Surely, as the world's only superpower, we're entitled to a little mischief now and then."

Economic Sanctions   An ancient tool of diplomacy, sanctions are nonmilitary penalties imposed on a foreign government in an attempt to modify its behavior. The penalties can vary broadly—a cutoff of U.S. aid, a ban on military sales, restrictions on imports, a denial of aircraft landing rights, or a total trade embargo. The implied power behind sanctions is U.S. economic muscle and access to U.S. markets.

Economic sanctions are often a first resort in times of crises, as they are less risky than sending in troops. Sanctions are often the outgrowth of pressure from well-organized domestic political groups with ethnic, cultural, environmental, human rights, or religious grievances against a foreign regime. These groups and government officials want to curb unfair trade practices, end human rights abuses and drug trafficking, promote environmental initiatives, and stop terrorism.

There are examples of economic sanctions that accomplished the goals of their sponsors, such as the sanctions levied against South Africa in the mid-1980s that contributed to the demise of apartheid. Most experts, however, view these tools as having limited effect. The trade embargo the UN placed on Iraq after its 1990 invasion of Kuwait succeeded in isolating Iraq diplomatically and economically and prevented it from rebuilding its military to its former strength. Yet Saddam Hussein retained a firm grip on power until 2003.

Successful sanctions must often have broad international support, which is rare. Unilateral sanctions are doomed to failure. The barriers of sanctions leak and the real losers are U.S. companies that are forced to abandon lucrative markets. They are quickly replaced by their competitors around the globe. When President Carter imposed a grain embargo on the Soviet Union in 1980 in retaliation for the Soviet invasion of Afghanistan, only U.S. farmers were hurt. The Soviet Union simply bought grain elsewhere.

In addition, critics argue that sanctions are counterproductive because they can provoke a nationalist backlash. The decades-old sanctions against Cuba did not oust Marxist dictator Fidel Castro, and the perennial threats of sanctions against China typically result in a hardening of China's attitude regarding human rights and other matters.

DEBATE

Economic Sanctions and Cuba

NUCLEAR PROLIFERATION

The spread of technology has enabled the creation of nuclear weapons and the missiles to deliver them, encouraging U.S. officials to adopt a more assertive posture in attempting to deny these weapons of mass destruction to rogue states.

American policymakers have sought to halt the spread of nuclear weapons since the signing of the Nuclear Non-Proliferation Treaty in 1968. The primary means of accomplishing this goal has been to encourage nations to agree that they would not acquire—or at least test—nuclear weapons. As you can see in Figure 20.4, only eight countries have declared that they have nuclear weapons capacities: the United States, Russia, Britain, France, China, India, Pakistan, and North Korea. Israel is widely suspected of having nuclear weapons. South Africa and three countries that used to be part of the Soviet Union—Belarus, Kazakhstan, and Ukraine—have given up nuclear weapons. Algeria, Argentina, Brazil, Libya, South Korea, Sweden, and Taiwan have ended their nuclear weapons programs. The United States actively supported the UN weapons inspections of Iraq, which faced continuous harassment and obstruction from Saddam Hussein until he was driven from power. After it invaded Iraq in 2003, it found that only a modest effort to develop nuclear weapons remained.

Currently, policymakers are most concerned about countries that are actively developing nuclear weapons capabilities, principally North Korea and Iran. These nations, frequently branded as "outlaw" states, pose serious threats to their neighbors

You Are the President of the
United States

FIGURE 20.4

The Spread of Nuclear Weapons

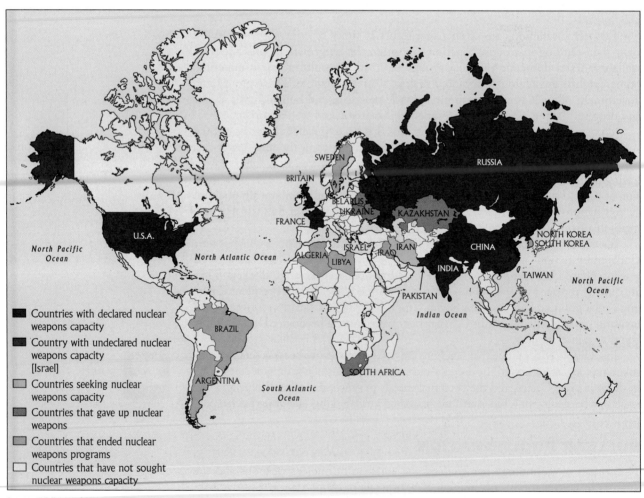

Source: *CQ Weekly*, May 23, 1998, 1,366. Updated by authors.

and perhaps to the United States as well. In the 1990s, the United States provided aid to North Korea in return for a promise to end its nuclear weapons program, but in 2002 North Korea declared its intention to continue the program. It tested a nuclear weapon in 2006, and likely now possesses a few nuclear weapons.

It appears that the unexpected difficulties endured in Iraq since the fall of Saddam Hussein colored the Bush administration's broader efforts against the other members of the axis of evil. Thus, the president favored diplomacy with Iran and North Korean, adopting a decidedly pragmatic turn and irritating some of his conservative supporters in the process. In 2007, the U.S. signed a denuclearization agreement with North Korea in which the latter agreed to shut down its nuclear facility, allow international inspections, and reveal its past efforts at uranium enrichment and any export programs to third parties like Syria. In return, the U.S. promised to move toward normalizing relations, open trade relations, and provide economic, energy, and humanitarian assistance. North Korea began disabling nuclear facilities, but was more hesitant about revealing its past nuclear activity.

Iran does not yet possess nuclear weapons, although it has taken a defiant stance and refused to cooperate fully with international weapons inspectors. In response, the U.S. has aggressively pushed for economic sanctions against Iran to encourage it to ends its pursuit of nuclear weapons, and these efforts have received wide support from its major allies. Other major powers, especially Russia and China, have opposed leveling sanctions. The issue became more complicated in late 2007, when a National Intelligence Estimate concluded that Iran had halted its nuclear weapons program (although it continued to enrich uranium and test-fire ballistic missiles). Such a finding inevitably undermined the push for stricter sanctions. At the same time, the intelligence community was conflicted about Iran's capabilities and intentions, and Director of National Intelligence Mike McConnell declared that he believed Iran was on the path to building a nuclear weapon. Other national intelligence services, such as those in Israel and France, agreed. Iran is likely to occupy a prominent position on the foreign policy agenda for some time (see "You Are the Policymaker: Defanging a Nuclear Threat").

Other nations have serious security concerns when faced with hostile neighbors possessing nuclear weapons. When India resumed testing of nuclear weapons in 1998, neighboring Pakistan quickly tested its first nuclear weapons. Their possession of nuclear weapons is a matter of special concern because of their history of conflict over Kashmir. Ending the proliferation of nuclear weapons will require resolving diplomatic tensions involving undeclared and nonnuclear states. In the meantime, the United States focuses on discouraging the deployment of nuclear weapons that have been developed.

THE INTERNATIONAL ECONOMY

Once upon a time, nations took pains to isolate themselves from the world. They erected high barriers to fend off foreign products and amassed large armies to defend their borders against intruders. Times have changed. One key word describes today's international economy: **interdependency**, a mutual reliance in which actions reverberate and affect other people's economic lifelines. The health of the American economy depends increasingly on the prosperity of its trading partners and on the smooth flow of trade and finance across borders (see "Young People and Politics: Embracing Globalization").

The *International Monetary Fund (IMF)* is a cooperative international organization of 185 countries intended to stabilize the exchange of currencies and the world economy. From 1997 to 1998, the decline of currencies in a number of Asian countries, including South Korea, Thailand, Indonesia, and the Philippines, threatened to force these nations to default on their debts—and throw the international

interdependency
Mutual dependency, in which the actions of nations reverberate and affect one another's economic lifelines.

YOU ARE THE **Policymaker**

Defanging a Nuclear Threat

One of the highest priorities of U.S. foreign policy is stopping the spread of nuclear weapons, especially to countries hostile to America. Some experts estimate that Iran will need only a few more years to build its first nuclear bomb.

Nuclear weapons in Iranian hands is not a comforting thought. The State Department has designated Iran as the world's leading sponsor of terrorism. The mullahs running the country support organizations such as Hamas, Hezbollah, and the Islamic Jihad; may be providing weapons and training to terrorists inside Iraq; and have sheltered senior members of al Qaeda. The current president, Mahmoud Ahmadinejad, has declared that Israel should be "wiped off the map." Iran has missiles that can now reach Israel and U.S. forces in Iraq and Afghanistan and is developing missiles that can reach Western Europe and North America.

How should we deal with this threat? The first response was diplomacy. The United States and its Western European allies sought to convince Iran to stop its nuclear research, and the International Atomic Energy Agency sealed some nuclear research facilities. In 2006, however, Iran removed the seals and declared that it had every right to develop atomic energy.

We could embargo Iran's main export, oil, but that would drive up energy prices everywhere and is unlikely to receive the international support necessary for economic sanctions

to succeed. Curtailing foreign travel will have little impact on a people who currently travel little outside their borders.

Another option is ordering the CIA and other agencies to encourage an overthrow of the government. The chances of succeeding in such a venture are small, however.

There are also military options. In theory, the United States could invade, but the U.S. military is overstretched with its responsibilities in Iraq. That leaves only one serious option—air strikes by Israel or the United States, possibly accompanied by commando raids. It is doubtful that bombs could eradicate Iran's nuclear program (much of which is underground), but it is possible they could set it back for years, possibly long enough for the regime to implode.

Of course, Iran is not likely to react passively to such a strike; the mullahs would almost certainly order terrorist retaliation against the United States and Israel and increase their efforts to sabotage our activities in next-door Afghanistan and Iraq. Iran could also become a rallying point for the Islamic world, which already is deeply suspicious and often disdainful of American policy. One result could be a further radicalization of millions of Muslims and an increase in the pool of potential recruits to terrorism.

As you can see, the president faces a dilemma regarding Iran. If you were president, what would *you* do?

---

economy into turmoil in the process. To stabilize these currencies, the IMF, to which the United States is by far the largest contributor, arranged for loans and credits of more than $100 billion. The IMF's intervention seems to have been successful, but the necessity of making the loans dramatically illustrates the world's economic interdependence.

International Trade   Since the end of World War II, trade among nations has grown rapidly. American exports and imports have increased twenty-fold since 1970 alone. Among the largest U.S. exporters are grain farmers, producers of computer hardware and software, aircraft manufacturers, moviemakers, heavy construction companies, and purveyors of accounting and consulting services. Foreign tourist spending bolsters the U.S. travel, hotel, and recreation industries. American colleges and universities derive a significant portion of their revenue from educating foreign students. The globalization of finances has been even more dramatic than the growth of trade. Worldwide computer and communications networks link financial markets in all parts of the globe instantaneously, making it easier to move capital across national boundaries but also increasing the probability that a steep decline in the Japanese stock market will send prices plummeting on Wall Street— or vice versa.

Coping with foreign economic issues is becoming just as difficult—and increasingly just as important—as coping with domestic ones. In a simpler time, the main instrument of international economic policy was the **tariff**, a special tax added to the cost of imported goods. Tariffs are intended to raise the price of imported goods and thereby protect American businesses and workers from foreign competition. Tariff making, though, is a game everyone can play. High U.S. tariffs encourage other nations

tariff
A special tax added to imported goods to raise the price, thereby protecting businesses and workers from foreign competition.

YOUNG PEOPLE AND POLITICS

Embracing Globalization

The protests that regularly occur during economic summit meetings of the leaders of the world's most economically developed countries might lead you to conclude that young adults are in the forefront of opposition to globalization. Actually, the facts are quite different, according to the Pew *Global Attitudes Project* surveys.

In every country globalization has produced some political tensions. However, strong majorities in all regions believe that increased global interconnectedness is a good thing, and globalization is more popular among the young adults of the world. Everywhere but Latin America, young people are more likely than their elders to see advantages in increased global trade and communication, and they are more likely to support "globalization."

The hesitation among some older citizens to embrace the movement toward globalization may be due in part to national pride. People in all countries and of all ages are proud of their cultures. Yet it is only in the West (North America and Western Europe) where that pride is markedly stronger among the older generations. Younger people tend to be less wedded to their cultural identities. In the United States, 68 percent of those aged 65 and older agree with the statement "our people are not perfect, but our culture is superior," while only 49 percent of those aged 18 to 29 agree. The generation gap in Western Europe is similar. The difference between generations is particularly apparent in France, where only one-fifth of those under age 30 support the notion of cultural superiority, while more than half of those aged 65 and older say French culture is superior.

Despite the general attraction of globalization, solid majorities everywhere think their way of life needs to be protected against foreign influence. In most parts of the world, that desire cuts across all age-groups. However, in the United States and Western Europe, older people are much more worried than the young about defending their country's way of life. In the United States, 71 percent of people aged 65 and older want to shield their way of life from foreign influence, while just 55 percent of those ages 18 to 29 agree. This generation gap is even greater in France, Germany, and Britain, where older people are twice as likely as young people to be worried about erosion of their way of life.

Skepticism about foreign influence is evident in widespread, intense antipathy toward immigration. Majorities in nearly every country surveyed support tougher restrictions on people entering their countries. Immigrants are particularly unpopular across Europe, especially among the older generation, where half of those surveyed *completely agree* with the need for additional immigration controls. The anti-immigrant generation gap is widest in France, where 53 percent of those aged 65 and older *completely agree* that immigration should be restricted. Only 24 percent of younger French men and women shared such strong views. Anti-immigrant sentiment also runs high in the United States, especially among older Americans. Fifty percent of those aged 65 and older strongly support new controls on entry of people into the country. Only 40 percent of young people share that intensity of sentiment.

There are many reasons why young adults may be more supportive of globalization than their elders. Better educated, more widely traveled, and more accustomed to the Internet, young adults seem to be less parochial, have less fear of change, and have more appreciation for the benefits of other cultures. Partially as a result of these attitudes, we should expect the trend toward globalization to accelerate over the coming decades.

QUESTIONS FOR DISCUSSION

▶ Do young people you know fear foreign competition?

▶ Do you agree that education and experience are the best explanations for the greater support of globalization among young people?

---

to respond with high tariffs on American products. The high tariffs that the government enacted early in the Great Depression (and that some say aggravated this economic crisis) were the last of their kind. Since that time, the world economy has moved from a period of high tariffs and protectionism to one of lower tariffs and freer trade.

However, nontariff barriers such as quotas, subsidies, and quality specifications for imported products are common means of limiting imports. In recent decades, the United States has placed quotas on the amount of steel that could be imported and negotiated voluntary limits on the importation of Japanese automobiles. Such policies do save American jobs involved in producing steel and automobiles, but they also raise the price of steel and automobiles that Americans buy, raising the costs of producing yet other products—and costing jobs in the process. American and European subsidies for agricultural products have been an obstacle to negotiating tariff reductions.

Recently, substantial progress has been made in lowering barriers to trade. In 1992, President George Bush signed the *North American Free Trade Agreement*

COMPARATIVE

Comparing Foreign and Security Policy

International trade is a controversial subject. Opponents believe that it undermines U.S. laws that protect the environment and workers' rights, costs some employees their jobs, and encourages the exploitation of foreign workers. Proponents argue that everyone benefits from increased trade. Here Seattle police face protesters during a World Trade Organization meeting in 1999.

(NAFTA) with Canada and Mexico, which would eventually eliminate most tariffs among North American countries. In 1993, after a heated battle, President Clinton obtained congressional passage of the legislation implementing the agreement.

President Clinton submitted an even more important agreement to Congress in 1994. The *General Agreement on Tariffs and Trade (GATT)* is the mechanism by which most of the world's nations negotiate widespread trade agreements. In 1994, 117 nations agreed to (1) reduce tariffs 38 percent for developed countries; (2) eliminate certain nontariff barriers and subsidies; (3) broaden GATT principles to areas such as trade in services, investment, and intellectual property rights; and (4) apply more effective disciplines to agricultural trade. The GATT also included a charter to create the World Trade Organization, which would act as the arbiter of international trade disputes. In its last action, the 103rd Congress passed the legislation necessary to implement this agreement.

In 2005, Congress approved the Central American-Dominican Republic Free Trade Agreement, negotiated by the George W. Bush administration. This agreement lowered tariff barriers to American goods in a number of Central American countries and the Dominican Republic. The president also signed free trade agreements with some individual countries.

A persistent issue for the president is opening up foreign markets for U.S. goods and services. The White House is especially eager to open lucrative Japanese markets in areas such as automobiles, auto parts, telecommunications, insurance, and medical equipment. The United States lacks the influence to *demand* that these markets be opened, however. If we refuse to trade with another nation, that nation will deny *our* exports access to its markets, and U.S. consumers will lose access to its products. In addition, millions of Americans now work in foreign-owned companies in the United States, such as Japanese automobile assembly plants. Although foreign investments and the creation of jobs are good for the United States, a by-product is that Americans have a stake in averting a trade crisis with investing nations. Those benefiting from Japanese investments, for example, may flock to Tokyo's side on some important issues.

Balance of Trade   When Americans purchase foreign products, they send dollars out of the country. When an oil tanker arrives in Houston, dollars travel to Saudi Arabia. If other nations do not buy as many American products as Americans do of theirs, then the United States is paying out more than it is taking in. If the United States puts military bases in Germany, the money that soldiers spend for a night on the town goes into German pockets. When American tourists spend their dollars abroad, they too carry American dollars away. All these instances combine to upset the **balance of trade**: the ratio of what a country pays for imports to what it earns from exports. When a country imports more than it exports, it has a balance-of-trade *deficit.* Year after year, the American balance of trade has been preceded by a minus sign, and the deficit for the balance of trade was $716 billion in 2007[26] (see "A Generation of Change: The Rising Trade Balance Deficit").

balance of trade
The ratio of what is paid for imports to what is earned from exports. When more is imported than exported, there is a balance-of-trade deficit.

A GENERATION OF CHANGE

The Rising **Trade Balance Deficit**

Recently, the United States has imported more than it has exported, resulting in a mounting trade deficit. A generation ago, the deficit in the balance of trade was small, but it grew rapidly and now exceeds $700 billion per year.

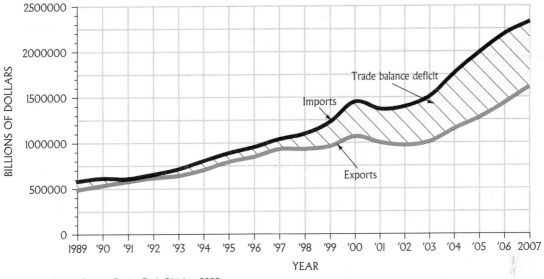

Source: U.S. Census Bureau, Foreign Trade Division, 2008.

The excess of imports over exports decreases the dollar's buying power against other currencies, making Americans pay more for goods that they buy from other nations. This decline in the value of the dollar, however, also makes American products cheaper abroad, thereby increasing our exports. Since the late 1980s, the United States has experienced an export boom, reaching nearly $1.6 trillion in 2007.[27] Exports account for about 10 percent of the GDP.

A poor balance of trade also exacerbates unemployment. About 5 percent of all civilian employment in the United States is related to manufacturing exports. A substantial amount of white-collar employment—in the area of financial services, for example—is also directly tied to exports. The trade imbalance has caused not only dollars but also jobs to flow abroad. Because labor is cheaper in Mexico, Taiwan, Malaysia, and China, products made there can be priced lower than American-made products. Often American firms have shut down their domestic operations and relocated in countries where labor costs are lower. The AFL-CIO claims that hundreds of thousands of American jobs have been lost to foreign competition. Under a special act guaranteeing compensation to American workers who lose their jobs to foreign competition, the Department of Labor has aided thousands of workers. The Labor Department, however, would be the first to note that short-term aid is no substitute for a long-term job.

Even so, a cheaper dollar also makes the cost of American labor more competitive. In response to this and to criticism about the balance of trade, more foreign-owned companies are building factories in the United States—just as American companies have plants around the globe. Thus, many Hondas are made in the United States, and parts for some cars manufactured by General Motors are made abroad. Foreign-owned firms in the United States employ 4.5 percent of the work force and account for 5.7 percent of output, 19 percent of U.S. exports, 13 percent of research-and-development spending, and 10 percent of all U.S. investment in plants and equipment. These firms

Organization of Petroleum Exporting Countries

An economic organization consisting primarily of Arab nations that controls the price of oil and the amount of oil its members produce and sell to other nations.

also pay more than 30 percent higher compensation (wages and benefits) on average than do their counterparts in the rest of the U.S. economy. And 30 percent of these jobs are in manufacturing, compared with fewer than 10 percent of all U.S. jobs.[28] You can see employment by foreign companies in your state in "My State: U.S. Employment of Foreign Multinational Companies." The web of interdependency has become so tangled that it is increasingly difficult to define "imports."

In addition, the stability of the U.S. economy and the low value of the dollar have made the United States attractive to foreign investors, who buy everything from major motion picture studios to the Rockefeller Center. Foreign owners control nearly 20 percent of non-financial U. S. corporations. Although advantages accrue to the United States when investors pour money into the country, some fear that both profits and control will move outside our borders.

Energy   In 1973, the **Organization of Petroleum Exporting Countries** (OPEC) responded to American support of Israel in the short war against Egypt by embargoing oil shipments to the United States and Western European nations. The fuel shortages and long lines at gas stations that resulted from the 1973 oil embargo convincingly illustrated the growing interdependency of world politics.

More than half the world's recoverable reserves of oil lie in the Middle East; Saudi Arabia alone controls much of this resource. States such as Texas, Oklahoma, Louisiana, and Alaska produce considerable amounts of oil within the United States but not enough to meet the country's needs. America imports more than 60 percent of its annual consumption of oil from other countries, particularly from the Middle East. The United States is not as dependent on foreign sources of oil as many European countries, like France or Italy, which have virtually no oil of their

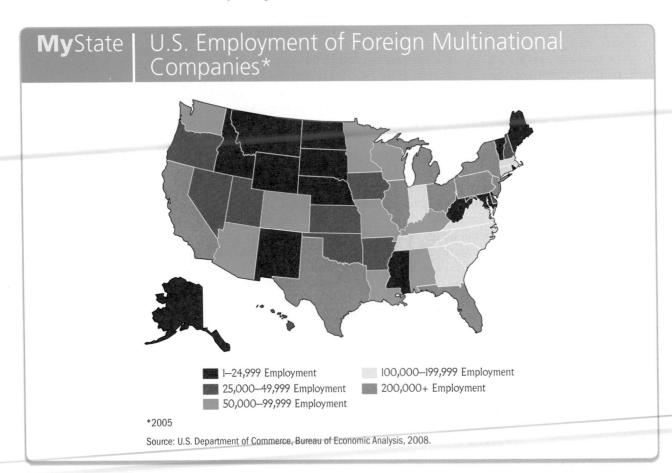

MyState | U.S. Employment of Foreign Multinational Companies*

- ■ 1–24,999 Employment
- ■ 25,000–49,999 Employment
- ■ 50,000–99,999 Employment
- □ 100,000–199,999 Employment
- ■ 200,000+ Employment

*2005

Source: U.S. Department of Commerce, Bureau of Economic Analysis, 2008.

own, or like Japan, which also imports all its oil. On the other hand, America's dependence on foreign oil is growing every year.

America's decision to respond to Iraq's invasion of Kuwait in 1990 was based in large part on this dependence. Kuwait, although a small country, produces about 10 percent of the world's oil; its neighbor, Saudi Arabia, possesses about a quarter of the world's proven oil reserves. Following a UN embargo and ultimatum to Iraq to pull out of Kuwait, the United States and its allies poured forces into Saudi Arabia (more than a half million soldiers from the United States alone). The allied forces quickly defeated the Iraqis and liberated Kuwait.

Circumstances may again restrict the availability of oil, however, and the United States is vulnerable because of its dependence on imported oil. Yet the Middle East—and America's sources of foreign oil—remains unstable.

Foreign Aid   Presidents of each party have pressed for aid to nations in the developing world. Aside from simple humanitarian concern for those who are suffering, presidents have wanted to stabilize nations that were friendly to the United States or that possessed supplies of vital raw materials. Sometimes aid has been given in the form of grants, but often it has taken the form of credits and loan guarantees to purchase American goods, loans at favorable interest rates, and forgiveness of previous loans. At other times, the United States has awarded preferential trade agreements for the sale of foreign goods in the United States.

A substantial percentage of foreign aid is in the form of military assistance and is targeted to a few countries the United States considers to be of vital strategic significance: Israel, Egypt, Turkey, and Greece have received the bulk of such assistance in recent years. Foreign aid programs have also assisted with agricultural modernization, irrigation, and population control. Food for Peace programs have subsidized the sale of American agricultural products to poor countries (and simultaneously given an economic boost to American farmers). Peace Corps volunteers have fanned out over the globe to provide medical care and other services in less developed nations.

Nevertheless, foreign aid has never been very popular with Americans. The president's foreign aid requests lack an electoral constituency to support them, and it is not surprising that Congress typically cuts them. Currently, Congress appropriates less than 1 percent of the federal budget for economic and humanitarian foreign aid. Moreover, many people believe that the provision of economic aid to other nations serves only to further enrich the few without helping the many within a poor nation. Although the United States donates more total aid (both for economic development and military assistance) than any other country, it devotes a smaller share of its GDP to foreign economic development than any other developed nation (see "America in Perspective: Ranking Largesse"). It is important to note, however, that the United States provides a great deal more aid through grants from private voluntary organizations, foundations, religious organizations, corporations, universities, and individuals.[29]

UNDERSTANDING NATIONAL SECURITY POLICYMAKING

National security policy deals with issues and nations that are often far from America's shores, but it is crucially important to all Americans. In addition, the themes that have guided your understanding of American politics throughout *Government in America*—democracy and the scope of government—can also shed light on the topic of international relations.

AMERICA IN PERSPECTIVE

Ranking Largesse

The United States is the largest donor of foreign aid, but it ranks lower than almost all other industrialized nations in the percentage of its gross national income (GNI) it spends on economic development aid for needy nations. American private giving, which is not reflected in these figures, is substantial, however.

DISCUSSION QUESTIONS

▶ Which is the more informative measure of a nation's giving, total aid or percent of GNI?

▶ Should the U.S. be giving more aid to underdeveloped nations?

Source: Organization for Economic Cooperation and Development, *OECD in Figures, 2007 Edition* (Paris: Organization for Economic Cooperation and Development, 2007), 60–61.

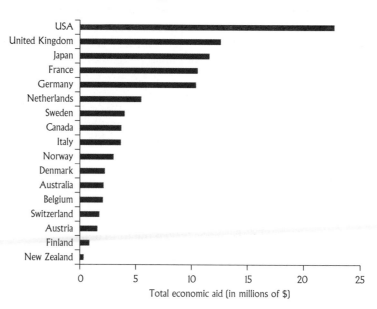

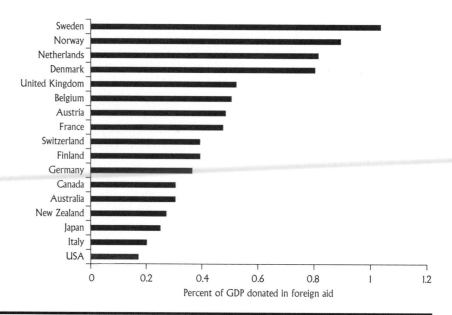

NATIONAL SECURITY POLICYMAKING AND DEMOCRACY

To some commentators, democracy has little to do with America's international relations. Because domestic issues are closer to their daily lives and easier to understand, Americans are usually more interested in domestic policy than in foreign policy. This preference would seem to give public officials more discretion in making national security policy. In addition, some say, those with the discretion are elites in the State Department and unelected military officers in the Pentagon.

There is little evidence, however, that policies at odds with the wishes of the American people can be sustained; civilian control of the military is unquestionable.

When the American people hold strong opinions regarding international relations—as when they first supported and later opposed the war in Vietnam—policymakers are usually responsive. Citizens in democracies do not choose to fight citizens in other democracies, and studies have found that well-established democracies rarely go to war against one another.[30]

In addition, the system of separation of powers plays a crucial role in foreign as well as domestic policy. The president takes the lead on national security matters, but you saw in Chapter 12 that Congress has a central role in matters of international relations. Whether treaties are ratified, defense budgets are appropriated, weapons systems are authorized, or foreign aid is awarded is ultimately at the discretion of Congress—the government's most representative policymaking body. Specific issues such as the proper funding for the Strategic Defense Initiative rarely determine congressional elections, but public demands for and objections to policies are likely to be heard in Washington.

When it comes to the increasingly important arena of American international economic policy, pluralism is pervasive. Agencies and members of Congress, as well as their constituents, all pursue their own policy goals. For example, the Treasury Department and the Federal Reserve Board worry about the negative balance of trade, and the Department of Defense spends billions in other countries to maintain American troops abroad. The Departments of Agriculture and Commerce and their constituents—farmers and businesspeople—want to peddle American products abroad and generally favor freer trade. The Department of Labor and the unions worry that the nation may export not only products but also jobs to other countries where labor costs are low. Jewish citizens closely monitor U.S. policy toward Israel, while Cuban Americans aggressively seek to influence U.S. policy toward Cuba. Even foreign governments hire lobbying firms and join in the political fray. As a result, a wide range of interests are represented in the making of foreign policy.

NATIONAL SECURITY POLICYMAKING AND THE SCOPE OF GOVERNMENT

America's global connections as a superpower have many implications for how active the national government is in the realm of foreign policy and national defense. The war on terrorism, treaty obligations to defend allies around the world, the nation's economic interests in an interdependent global economy, and pressing new questions on the global agenda such as global warming demand government action.

By any standard, the scope of government in these areas is large. The national defense consumes about a fifth of the federal government's budget and requires about 2 million civilian and military employees for the Department of Defense. Although the United States has improved relations with Eastern and Central Europe, it continues to have political, economic, and other interests to defend around the world. As long as these interests remain, the scope of American government in foreign and defense policy will be substantial.

SUMMARY

The world—its politics and its economics—becomes more interdependent each year. This chapter examined America's global connections and the contours of its foreign policy.

The Cold War began shortly after World War II, when the containment doctrine became the basis of American foreign policy. The Cold War led to actual wars in Korea and Vietnam when the United States tried to contain communist advances. With containment came a massive military buildup, resulting in what some people called the *military-industrial complex.* Gradually, containment has been balanced by détente and then friendship with many of our former adversaries. This trend has accelerated with the democratization of Central and Eastern Europe and the dissolution of the Soviet Union. Nevertheless, the United States maintains an enormous defense capability, which it has put to use again in the war on terrorism.

Although the United States has great military power, many of the issues facing the world today are not military issues. Nuclear proliferation and terrorism present new challenges to national security, challenges not easily met by advanced weaponry alone. Global interdependency in economics, energy, the environment, and other areas has also become important, revealing new vulnerabilities and thus additional challenges for national security policy.

Chapter Test
Multiple Choice

1. All but which of the following are permanent members of the UN Security Council?
   a. United States
   b. Great Britain
   c. China
   d. Germany
   e. France

2. The vast majority of UN peacekeeping operations were implemented:
   a. Between 1945 and 1955
   b. Between 1955 and 1965
   c. Between 1965 and 1975
   d. Between 1975 and 1985
   e. Since 1985

3. The sole power to formally recognize other countries lies with:
   a. Congress
   b. The State Department
   c. The president
   d. The House of Representatives
   e. The Senate

4. Which of the following is NOT true of executive agreements?
   a. Presidents have used them much more frequently than treaties
   b. They often deal with routine matters, but can also address very significant issues
   c. They allow for greater speed and efficiency
   d. They need to be ratified by only a simple majority in the Senate
   e. All of the above are true

5. Who originally proposed the containment policy that dominated U.S. foreign policy during the Cold War?
   a. Winston Churchill
   b. George C. Marshall
   c. George F. Kennan
   d. Woodrow Wilson
   e. John Foster Dulles

6. The policy of détente:
   a. Represented a turn toward more cooperative thinking in U.S. foreign policy
   b. Sought a relaxation of tension between the U.S. and the Soviet Union
   c. Assumed that a nuclear war should be unthinkable
   d. Sought firm guarantees of mutual security
   e. All of the above

7. Which of the following is NOT true for the national security strategy doctrine issued by the Bush administration in September 2002?
   a. It moved away from containment and deterrence
   b. It embraced preemptive strikes
   c. It advocated U.S. military preeminence
   d. It called for defensive alliances
   e. It sought to preclude immediate and developing threats

8. Which of the following is NOT a nongovernmental organization?
   a. Greenpeace
   b. Amnesty International
   c. Al Qaeda
   d. Doctors Without Borders
   e. All of the above are NGOs

9. The Monroe Doctrine states that:
   a. Any form of European colonialism is unacceptable
   b. European interference in Latin America is a threat to U.S. interests
   c. The spread of communism to Latin America needs to be stopped
   d. The United States would embark on a policy of democratization of Latin America
   e. The United States would give development aid to Latin America

10. Which of the following is NOT an example of a non-tariff barrier?
    a. A limit on the number of cars a Japanese manufacturer is allowed to bring into the United States
    b. A government subsidy to U.S. farmers
    c. High environmental standards for foreign goods imported into the U.S.
    d. A special tax importers have to pay for their goods
    e. Strict quality control for foreign products

True/False

11. Jimmy Carter was the first U.S. president who visited the People's Republic of China.
    True_____   False_____

12. The United States is the largest donor of foreign aid in terms of percentage of its gross national income (GNI).
    True_____   False_____

13. U.S. foreign aid has typically lacked support from the American people.
    True_____   False_____

14. U.S. private organizations donate more money to foreign aid than the U.S. government.
    True_____   False_____

15. The "coalition of the willing" that supported the United States in the war in Iraq is an example of a formal alliance.
    True_____   False_____

Short Answer

16. Please outline the conservative and the liberal views on defense spending. Provide at least three different arguments for each side, including each side's interpretation of the causes for the fall of the Soviet Union.

17. What are the four components of the GATT trade agreement that 117 nations agreed on in 1994?

18. What is the definition of "balance of trade"? What has the United States' balance of trade looked like in recent years?

19. Briefly describe the purpose and membership of the North Atlantic Treaty Organization (NATO).

20. Explain what President Ronald Reagan meant when he said America was facing a "window of vulnerability" and what policies he proposed as a result.

21. Briefly explain the content and the consequences of the INF treaty of 1988.

22. What are some of the pros and cons of "soft power" as a foreign policy tool? What are concrete examples of soft power?

23. In what ways could the end of the Cold War be considered a "crisis of identity" for U.S. foreign policy? Be as specific as possible in your assessment of U.S. foreign policy prior to and after the collapse of the Soviet Union, and support your arguments with examples.

Short Answer/Essay Questions

24. What role does Congress play in American foreign policy (explain the different areas of responsibility) and what role does the president play? How does this ensure a "balance of power" between the legislative and the executive in theory? Has this always been the case in practice?

25. Given the fact that President George W. Bush believed that the UN had failed miserably in past security situations and that the organization was inefficient in dealing with the threat of terrorism, why do you suppose the U.S. government initially sought the support of the UN in the war against Iraq?

26. This textbook points out that a military response to global terrorism may be of limited value because it addresses the symptoms rather than the causes of terrorism. Based on what you know, what strategy would you recommend to the U.S. government in order to combat both the causes and the symptoms? Be as specific as possible.

27. Given the changes in international politics that have taken place since the end of the Cold War, what specific reforms of the U.S. military would you advocate, and why? Be sure to connect your suggestions to actual changes that have occurred.

28. Please assess the Bush doctrine of using preemptive strikes as a foreign policy tool in the fight against global terrorism. What are the merits of engaging in preemptive warfare? What are the problems? Do you personally agree with preemptive strikes? Why, or why not?

Answer Key

1. D   2. E   3. C   4. D   5. C   6. E   7. D   8. E   9. B   10. D   11. False   12. False   13. True   14. True   15. False

Key Terms

foreign policy (622)	**Joint Chiefs of Staff** (627)	**Strategic Defense Initiative** (634)
United Nations (623)	**Central Intelligence Agency** (627)	**interdependency** (647)
North Atlantic Treaty Organization (624)	**isolationism** (629)	**tariff** (648)
European Union (624)	**containment doctrine** (631)	**balance of trade** (650)
secretary of state (626)	**Cold War** (632)	**Organization of Petroleum Exporting Countries** (652)
secretary of defense (626)	**arms race** (632)	
	détente (632)	

Internet Resources

www.state.gov/
Information about the Department of State and current foreign policy issues.

www.defenselink.mil/
Information about the Department of Defense and current issues in national security policy.

https://www.cia.gov/library/publications/the-world-factbook/index.html
The *CIA World Factbook*.

www.oecd.org/home/
The Organization for Economic Cooperation and Development provides a wealth of economic information on the world's nations.

www.nato.int/
Contains background and activities of NATO.

www.un.org/
Background on the United Nations and its varied programs.

www.cfr.org
The Council on Foreign Relations is the most influential private organization in the area of foreign policy. Its Web site includes a wide range of information on foreign policy.

www.whitehouse.gov/nsc/
Information about the members and functions of the National Security Council.

GetConnected

The Department of State

Congratulations! The president of the United States has just nominated you to be the secretary of state. You have been given advance notice that several members of the Senate Foreign Relations Committee will ask you about the "Palestinian Question" during your confirmation. Although you are aware that the relationship between Arabs and Israel has been a key element of U.S. foreign policy for decades, you want to provide the committee with some new thinking on possible answers to the Palestinian Question. One place you look for ideas is American public opinion.

Search the Web

Go to the "America's Global Role: Quick Takes" page at the Public Agenda Web site *www.publicagenda.org/citizen/issueguides/americas-global-role*. There are several graphs under the heading "Middle East" that show American public opinion about the role the United States should play in the conflict between the Palestinians and Israel. Take a look at all three graphs.

Questions to Ask

- Who do most Americans believe should take the first step in trying to end the bombings and other violence in the region?

- What should the United States do to try to help the two sides find a peaceful resolution to the decades-long conflict?
- Where should the Palestinian–Israeli conflict be on the foreign policy agenda of the United States?

Why It Matters

Israelis and Palestinians have been engaged in varying levels of conflict since Israel became an independent nation in 1948. The conflict has led to large numbers of Palestinian refugees, some of whom become terrorists. Achieving peace in the Middle East has been a foreign policy goal of the United States for decades, partly out of its longstanding support for a Jewish homeland and partly out of concern for the impact of violence in the Middle East on the supply of energy in the United States.

Get Involved

Learn a little more about the U.S. role in seeking answers to the Palestinian Question. What are the current administration's goals? How do your members of Congress feel about the potential for ending conflict between the Palestinians and the Israelis? For more exercises, go to *www.longmanamericangovernment.com*.

For Further Reading

Brzezinski, Zbigniew. *The Choice: Global Domination or Global Leadership.* New York: Basic Books, 2004. An important critique of the Bush administration's national security strategy.

Easterly, William. *The White Man's Burden.* New York: Penguin, 2006. Why the West's efforts to aid the rest of the world have not been more effective.

Gordon, Philip H. *Winning the Right War.* New York: Times Books, 2007. A new way of thinking about the war on terror and a new strategy for winning it.

Howell, William G., and Jon C. Pevehouse. *While Dangers Gather: Congressional Checks on Presidential War Powers.* Princeton, NJ: Princeton University Press, 2007. Shows how Congress can influence the decision to go to war.

Huntington, Samuel P. *The Clash of Civilizations and the Remaking of World Order.* New York: Simon and Schuster, 1996. Argues that civilizational identities built on religious empires of the past will be the source of international turmoil in the next century.

Kagan, Donald. *On the Origins of War and the Preservation of Peace.* New York: Doubleday, 1995. Provides insights gleaned from studying the origins of great wars.

Mandelbaum, Michael. *The Case for Goliath: How America Acts as the World's Government in the Twenty-First Century.*

New York: Public Affairs, 2006. Explains the ways in which the United States provides the world critical services, ranging from physical security to commercial regulation and financial stability.

Mead, Walter Russell. *Power, Terror, Peace, and War.* New York: Alfred A. Knopf, 2004. Analyzes America's grand strategy in national security.

Nye, Joseph S., Jr. *The Paradox of American Power: Why the World's Only Superpower Can't Go It Alone.* New York: Oxford University Press, 2002. Although the United States is militarily and economically supreme, it is increasingly dependent on other nations to accomplish its goals.

Nye, Joseph S., Jr. *Soft Power: The Means to Success in World Politics.* Cambridge, MA: Harvard University Press, 2004. Argues that national security hinges as much on winning hearts and minds as it does on winning wars.

Woodward, Bob. *State of Denial.* New York: Simon and Schuster, 2006. The inside story of decision making regarding the war with Iraq and its aftermath.

Yergin, Daniel. *Shattered Peace: The Origins of the Cold War and the National Security State.* Boston: Houghton Mifflin, 1977. An excellent political history of the early years of the Cold War and containment.

THE
NEW FACE
OF
STATE
AND
LOCAL
GOVERNMENT

POLITICS IN ACTION:
SUBNATIONAL GOVERNMENTS AND HOMELAND SECURITY

Following the terrorist attacks of September 11, 2001, the national government passed laws that created new categories of crime for terrorist acts and increased the power and authority of national law enforcement and intelligence agencies. At the same time, state governments adopted similar laws, consolidated bureaucratic agencies charged with law enforcement and emergency response, and took new steps in attempting to slow the flood of undocumented immigrants. For example, by November 2002, 13 states had adopted laws that provided for the death penalty in cases of murder committed in the furtherance of a terrorist act. New Jersey even adopted a law that carries penalties for recruiting members of a terrorist organization. By 2008, a number of states, including New Mexico, had adopted laws allowing illegal immigrants to obtain a drivers license. In part these laws have been an attempt to document people who cross the border illegally.

Traditionally, state and local governments have been responsible for most criminal justice policy and maintaining the civil order for situations contained within state borders. However, the national government response to September 11 reflects a pattern of growing national involvement in criminal justice policy. The states have been reluctant to forfeit their policymaking role or their role in prosecuting criminals. This competition has led some to suggest that states should maintain

their traditional dominant role in criminal justice policy, but in issues involving national security and defense, state and local governments should defer to the national government, or confusion will abound.[1] Such an example occurred in 2002 as Maryland and Virginia argued with the national government over who would be the first to prosecute the accused in the Washington, D.C.–area sniper case, with Virginia arguing it should go first and make use of its new antiterrorism law that carried the death penalty.

The debate over government jurisdiction in criminal justice policy is important for several reasons. First, maintaining the civil order is a fundamental role for any government. Without civil order, commerce cannot occur and democratic practices, such as elections, cannot take place. Second, the ultimate power of the government comes from its ability to take away the rights and liberties of individuals. Our fear of this power has led us to place limits on the government and to traditionally keep this power close at hand—with state and local governments.

Does increasing national involvement in criminal justice policy, from drug crimes to carjacking to terrorism, threaten our liberties more than traditional state and local government involvement in this area? On the other hand, are state governments threatening the security of our homeland by adopting their own policies and refusing to participate in national intelligence-sharing programs? If we assume that local and state officials are closer to citizens, do we lose some accountability over officials if the states defer to the national government? Clearly there are no simple answers, but the questions reflect the tensions within our federalist system between levels of government and the difficulty of establishing distinct policy jurisdictions.

subnational governments
Another way of referring to state and local governments. Through a process of reform, modernization, and changing intergovernmental relations since the 1960s, subnational governments have assumed new responsibilities and importance.

State and local governments, or **subnational governments**, touch our lives every day. They pick up our garbage; educate us; keep us safe from criminals; protect our critical infrastructure systems, such as the water supply; and perform a myriad of other vital services. Odds are that you are attending a state or city university right now. You will drive home on locally maintained streets (and may perhaps be issued a speeding ticket from a local official). Subnational governments regulate a wide range of business activities, from generating electric power to cutting hair. The state government is also the single largest employer in every state; in aggregate, local governments employ even more people than do the states. So, as a consumer of government services, as a regulated businessperson, and/or as an employee, subnational governments are intimately involved in our lives.

However, not long ago, some political observers predicted that state governments would cease to exist in the near future.[2] The states seemed to some like archaic accidents of history rather than meaningful political entities. For example, how could one possibly equate Wyoming, with fewer than a half million people and fewer than 5 people per square mile, to California with over 34 million people and 217 people per square mile? What do Hawaii and Alaska have in common with Rhode Island and Louisiana as political entities? Some critics in the 1950s and 1960s thought, "Not much." Further, a generation ago, state governments were ridiculed as being "horse and buggy" institutions in an era of space travel.[3] Their institutions were weak, outdated, resource poor, and were simply not up to the task of running a modern government. The states were also seen by social liberals as obstacles to addressing the grievances of racial and ethnic minorities and urban dwellers—witness Governor George Wallace's stand against the racial integration of Alabama schools (Chapter 3). The national government was seen as the driver of progressive policymaking, and the states were encouraged to step aside or get replaced.

But as Mark Twain said about his mistaken obituary, these reports of the death of the states were greatly exaggerated. Through a process of reform, modernization,

MyState | How Have States Responded to Illegal Immigration?

Estimates suggest that more than 11 million people illegally reside in the United States, and that illegal immigration has been on the increase since the 1980s. However, the national government has not adopted any significant policies to address illegal immigration since the late 1980s. As Congress failed to act on this issue in 2006 and 2007, states began to adopt new policies to address local problems stemming from illegal immigration. Some of these policies have tried to address problems faced by the children of illegal immigrants. For example, by early 2008 six states had adopted policies to provide health insurance to the children of illegal immigrants. Other states have tried to discourage illegal immigrants in their states by adopting new policies to require employers to verify employee work status. In sum, during 2007 the 50 states considered over 1,562 bills related to immigration, nearly three times the number of immigration bills considered in 2006. At least 240 of these bills were adopted

The map at right classifies states based on the type of illegal immigration policy adopted in 2007. Many of the uncolored states adopted other legislation related to illegal immigration, but not addressing the issues here.

QUESTIONS FOR DISCUSSION

▶ What immigration legislation has your state considered? What legislation has it adopted?

▶ What problems does immigration pose in your state?

▶ How does your state benefit from immigration?

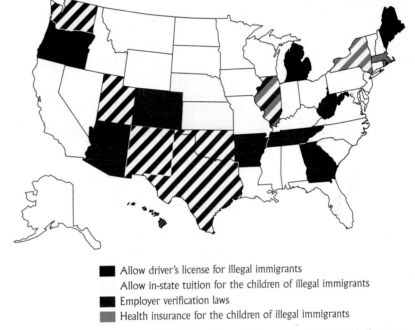

■ Allow driver's license for illegal immigrants
□ Allow in-state tuition for the children of illegal immigrants
■ Employer verification laws
■ Health insurance for the children of illegal immigrants

Source: State of the States, 2008, March 8, 2008, *http://www.stateline.org/live/publications/pdf-request.*

and changing intergovernmental relations since the 1960s, subnational governments have become more vital to our democratic system than ever. They have assumed new and costly responsibilities in areas such as social welfare, education, health, economic development, and criminal justice. States and localities have also gained importance as national policymakers have confronted budgetary limits and policymakers have recognized the virtues of grass-roots democracy—of giving decision-making power to governments closer to the people.

In this chapter, we discuss subnational government with an eye toward two important characteristics: *revitalization* and *diversity*. Since the early 1960s, the states have become revitalized in their institutions, their personnel, and their role in the federal system.[4] State legislatures, governors' offices, courts, and even bureaucracies have undergone dramatic changes that have allowed them to move forward as strong and active players in the U.S. policymaking process. The people involved in governing the states and localities are more representative of their constituents than was previously the case, and they tend to be better educated and more professionalized and have greater policy expertise. With the weight of the philosophical argument about where policymaking power should lie in the

The long, straight, and empty freeways of Montana allowed policymakers there to set a speed limit that would be unthinkable on the crowded highways of New Jersey.

federal system swinging toward the states for the past four decades (Chapter 3), the national government has provided states and localities with increasing control over many policy areas.

The second characteristic important to understanding subnational government in the United States is diversity. As anyone who has ever traveled outside their hometown knows, government, policy, and political behavior differ from place to place. For example, in California citizens can propose and pass laws through the ballot box; in Delaware they can't. On the freeways of New Jersey, you may legally drive no faster than 65 miles per hour, whereas until recently in Montana, the only limit was your own judgment and the power of your car's engine. In South Dakota, almost twice the proportion of eligible voters cast votes as in Louisiana during any given election. To understand this diversity among the states is to understand the politics and history of the United States better. Why do these differences exist and what effects do they have?

STATE CONSTITUTIONS

Each state is governed by a separate and unique constitution that spells out the basic rules of that state's political game. Every state elects a governor as its chief executive officer, and most states have a legislature with two chambers like the Congress (except for Nebraska, which only has a senate). However, the states endow their governors with different powers and organize and elect their legislatures differently. Each state's constitution was written under unique historical conditions and with a unique set of philosophical principles in mind. Each is unique in its length and provisions. Some are modern documents; others were written over 100 years ago. The differences among these documents also reflect the diversity—social, economic, geographic, historic, and political—of the states.[5]

State constitutions are subordinate to the U.S. Constitution and the laws of the United States, but they take precedence over state law. State constitutions share many features in common with the U.S. Constitution. Both provide for separation of powers; the creation of executive, judicial, and legislative branches; and means of taxation and finance, and all include a bill of rights. Figure 21.1 shows how the Texas state constitution arranges the state's governmental structure.

The key difference between the national and state constitutions is that the state documents often provide far more detail about specific policies. The Oklahoma constitution, for example, requires that "stock feeding" be taught in public schools, and the South Dakota constitution authorizes a twine and cordage plant at its state penitentiary.[6] This level of specificity leads to constitutions that are long and sometimes confusing. Whereas the U.S. Constitution is a brief document of 8,700 words, state constitutions can be as long as Alabama's 220,000-word tome. In contrast, a few states try to stick to the point as closely as the national constitution does—Vermont's constitution, adopted in 1793, is a model of brevity with only 6,880 words.

FIGURE 21.1

Government Under the Texas State Constitution

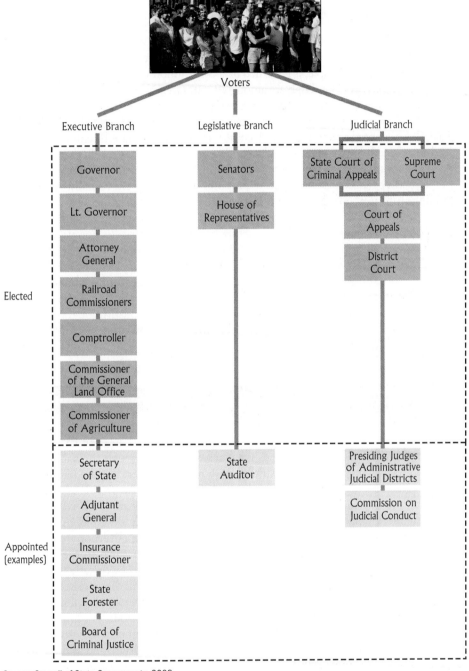

Source: Council of State Governments, 2008.

Why do some states try to embed specific policy into what is supposed to be a document detailing fundamental principles and government organization? It has long been argued that powerful interest groups have encouraged lengthy constitutions in order to protect their interests. It is far more difficult to amend a state constitution than to change a law, so activists try to include policy statements in the constitution in order to guard against their future repeal. In Southern states, where most constitutions were rewritten after the Civil War, state constitutions tend to be longer and more particularistic. Even so, some argue that longer constitutions help limit government interference with Americans' valued individualism.[7]

AMENDING STATE CONSTITUTIONS

Periodically, a state considers changes to the basic rules of its political game. Most avoid the politically difficult process of writing an entirely new constitution. Massachusetts, for example, is governed by a constitution written in 1780. Mississippi, Nebraska, New York, and Utah are among 29 states that have nineteenth-century constitutions. Although a few states have attempted to write entirely new constitutions since World War II (the most recent successful attempt being Georgia in 1983), most states have adapted their governing documents to the late twentieth century by the "cut and paste" method of constitutional amendment.

You Are Attempting to Revise the California Constitution

The most common way that state constitutions are amended is through a two-step process by which the legislature "proposes" an amendment (usually by passing a resolution to this effect by a vote of two-thirds of the legislature and in 12 states doing so in two consecutive sessions) and a majority vote in the next general election "ratifies" it. Although this process is difficult, it is used every election year, typically for taxation and public debt issues. Indeed, California has amended its constitution 493 times since 1879. And across all states between 1898 and 1998, 827 direct (from voters) and indirect (through legislature) initiatives for constitutional amendments were proposed, and voters approved 343 (42 percent) measures.[8] Although rarely used, state constitutions can also be amended through a constitutional convention; Massachusetts used a convention most recently when legislators attempted to ban same-sex marriage in 2004.

STATE ELECTIONS

Most top-level state policymakers are elected to office. To an even greater extent than national officials, state officials must achieve office through the ballot box and respond to the voters' preferences if they wish to remain there. At the national level, voters can elect only one member of the executive branch (the president), while they can elect no one in the judicial branch. However, at the state level, voters usually have far more power to determine who governs them. For example, in California voters select eight statewide executive officers (including the governor, treasurer, and even the insurance commissioner) as well as many judges down to the trial court level.[9] Further, in some states voters are authorized to make law directly through the ballot box by using the direct democracy mechanisms we will discuss shortly.

Historically, state elections have been decided by the general political mood of the country or state, with those running for office having little ability to influence their own electoral fortunes. Voters cared little and knew less about state legislative or even gubernatorial races. But as the states have become more important and as their institutions have become more effective and respected in the past generation, average voters and political activists are more attentive to state elections. As a result, state officials look more like their constituents, in terms of partisanship, ideology, and demographics.

GUBERNATORIAL ELECTIONS

Gubernatorial races have increasingly become focused on individual candidates rather than party affiliations. Political scientists call this the "presidentialization" of gubernatorial elections since they have come to resemble the personality-focused modern campaigns for the White House. This has occurred because of the increasing importance of television (and subsequently money) to gubernatorial campaigns and the decoupling of gubernatorial races from presidential races and state political party organizations.[10]

Historically, most governors were elected during presidential years, either because their term of office was only two years or because their four-year term coincided with that of the presidential term. But since the 1960s, most states have adopted a four-year gubernatorial term and shifted that term so that elections are held during nonpresidential election years. Today, only 11 states hold their gubernatorial elections at the same time as presidential elections.[11]

The change means that the gubernatorial race is the "top of the ticket" in most states, which makes it more likely that voters will pay attention. Races are therefore more likely to be decided on what voters think about the candidates than on any coattail effect from the presidential race. This means that candidates for governor can no longer expect to garner much help from a popular presidential candidate for their party, nor can they assume any candidate's campaign suffers from an unpopular presidential candidate topping the ticket. Political scientists refer to the pattern of running on your own as a "candidate-centered campaign."[12]

In order to run on their own, gubernatorial candidates have taken to television advertising in a big way, just as presidential candidates have, and largely for the same reasons. There are simply too many people in a state for a candidate to meet them all face-to-face. Gubernatorial candidates hire nationally known advertising agencies to develop slick ad campaigns. These campaigns are not cheap. The use of television is one of the main reasons why the costs of gubernatorial campaigns have skyrocketed. For elections between 1977 and 1980, the total cost of gubernatorial elections was $524 million (adjusted for 2006 dollars). That cost increased by 107 percent, to $1,084 million, for elections between 2003 and 2006. Although the largest states have some of the most expensive elections, if we adjust for the cost per general election vote, we find that the 2002 to 2006 election costs were the most in New Hampshire at $47.16 per vote and much less in a larger state like Virginia at $24.03 per vote. However, collectively the elections in California and Texas are the most expensive, with the average costs of the last five races in California at $114 million and in Texas at $59 million through the 2006 election, and the California gubernatorial recall election at nearly $204 million.[13]

Most of this money has to be raised by the candidates themselves. At one time, state political party organizations had a strong hand in funding these campaigns and in selecting the party nominees for the general election. Those days are long gone in most states. With the advent of the direct primary for nominating party candidates, a person who wants to become governor must organize and fund a major campaign in the primary. And by the time a candidate wins the primary, he or she has built a solid campaign organization and has little need for the party's help in the general election.

One result of the personalization of gubernatorial elections has been that parties have a harder time predicting their success. Because voters now become familiar with gubernatorial candidates during campaigns, they more frequently vote based on their attitude toward the candidates rather than resorting to party loyalty. This can lead to ticket splitting and divided government, as citizens vote for less well-known state legislative candidates strictly based on their party affiliation.[14] We see the results of this when states whose voters are predominantly of one party elect governors of the other party. For example, in 2002, Virginia voters elected Democrat Mark R. Warner to the governorship, even though registered Republican voters outnumber registered Democrats and Republicans maintained majorities in the 2004 to 2006 state legislative session. At the extreme, this has led to four Independent governors being elected in recent years. Two of these—Lowell Weicker of Connecticut and Walter Hickel of

Alaska—were politicians formerly associated with a major party who challenged their parties' candidates in the general election due to intraparty squabbles. But the two governors serving in 2002—Angus King of Maine (Independent) and Jesse Ventura of Minnesota (Reform Party)—were truly independent of the Democratic and Republican parties and owed their election completely to the efforts of their personal campaign organizations. However, both of these governors left office in 2003, leaving no Independents in governorships.

STATE LEGISLATIVE ELECTIONS

Of all state- and national-level officials, state legislators face the smallest constituencies, ranging from fewer than 3,000 people in a New Hampshire House of Representatives district to almost 800,000 people in a California Senate district, but with an average size of about 140,000 for state senate districts and 50,000 for state house districts.[15] By comparison, governors (600,000 to 57 million constituents) and members of the U.S. House of Representatives (average 646,952 constituents) need to respond to considerably more constituents.

Throughout much of the twentieth century, state legislatures were horribly malapportioned, giving greater representation to rural areas than their population warranted. One hundred years ago, most state legislators represented rural areas because that was where people lived. However, by the early 1960s the population had become overwhelmingly urban. Since the legislative district boundaries had rarely changed, state legislatures continued to be dominated by rural politicians. The main reason for the underrepresentation of urban areas was that districts were often constructed on the basis of the boundaries of some local government, such as a county, regardless of how many people lived there. This meant that in many states, rural counties with a few thousand residents and urban counties with hundreds of thousands of residents all had the same representation in the state legislature.

In 1962, after decades of avoiding the issue, the U.S. Supreme Court ruled that the districts of the lower chamber of state legislatures must be based on the number of people living in them. This landmark decision in *Baker v. Carr* established the principle of "one person, one vote" in drawing up state house districts. Two years later, the Court ruled in *Reynolds v. Sims* that state senates must also be apportioned in this fashion.

Demonstrators stand on the steps of San Francisco City Hall on the first full day of legal same-sex marriage in San Francisco, California, June 17, 2008.

These cases dramatically changed the face of state legislatures. Gone was the rural dominance of these chambers. New representatives arrived from the central cities and suburbs. Urban and metropolitan area problems became the focus of state legislatures.

Periodic redrawing of legislative districts is required as population shifts. This is now done following every decennial census, further changing the composition of state legislatures. The late twentieth-century migration of citizens to the suburbs has resulted in new voting power for suburban metropolitan interests and a decline in the power of central cities in state capitals.

Ironically, although state legislators have smaller districts than any other state or national elected officials, they are the least well known by voters. This is largely due to the historic lack of media coverage given to state legislatures and the lack of campaign resources of candidates for the office. The result is that races for state legislature, at least in general elections, have been decided on the basis of forces beyond candidates' control—party identification of district voters and the parties' candidates in the race for governor and president.[16]

But with the recent shifting of more policy responsibilities to the states and increases in state legislative salaries (discussed shortly) making the office both more important and attractive, campaigns for the state legislature have started to become more candidate-centered, although not nearly to the extent that gubernatorial campaigns have. This "congressionalization" of state legislative races is encouraged by increased resources (mainly staff and time) for incumbent legislators to retain their seats, and increases in the activities of political action committees (PACs) at the state level willing to fund expensive campaigns.[17] Campaign costs skyrocketed for state legislative campaigns beginning in the 1980s and continue to be high today, with candidates in large states such as California and Illinois finding it necessary to raise at least $200,000; highly competitive races might cost over $2 million. Although it is still possible to run a less closely contested campaign in a less populous state for only several thousand dollars, this is no longer the norm.[18]

The need to raise and spend more money on these campaigns favors incumbent legislators. Incumbents can use the resources and prestige of office both to enhance their visibility with their constituents and to attract campaign contributions from PACs and others interested in garnering favor in the legislature. State legislative leaders also help incumbents through their own PACs and party funds in order to enhance their personal influence as leaders and the prospects of their party retaining or regaining control of their chamber.[19]

Partisan Competition, Legislative Turnover, and Term Limits The 2006–2007 elections continued the 30-year trend in state legislatures of increasing party competition, closer partisan splits, and changing party control (see Table 21.1). Although much of this change has occurred as a result of Republican gains in the South (for example, the South Carolina statehouse now has a majority of Republicans, as do both chambers of the Florida state legislature), even Northern states have been experiencing increasingly close legislative party divisions. Following the 2006–2007 elections Democrats hold 54 percent of all seats in state legislatures, stemming what had been a steady downward trend since the Watergate scandal buoyed the party's fortunes in the mid-1970s.[20]

Although some state legislative chambers have very lopsided partisan splits (for example, in the Idaho state senate Republicans hold 80 percent of the seats, and in the Massachusetts state senate Democrats hold 87 percent), some legislatures are closely divided. In fifteen legislative chambers, there are three or fewer seats separating the parties. The Oklahoma senate is an extreme case, with exactly 24 Republicans and 24 Democrats. And finally, following the 2006–2007 elections, 13 chambers changed majority party control or are now split. This change is consistent with a 20-year trend that indicates a remarkable period of increasing party competition in the state legislatures. However, even as competition has increased in some states, such as Maine, it has declined in others, such as Illinois. And the percentage of contested legislative seats varies widely across the states with some states seeing a large increase in contested seats (Missouri) while others have seen significant declines (Pennsylvania) from the 1970s to 2000s.[21]

Divided government exists when a single party does not control both chambers of the state legislature and the governor's office. With divided government, it is usually much more difficult for coherent policy action to take place because the parties that control the different components of state government have conflicting policy and electoral goals.

TABLE 21.1

The Balance of Power, 2008

STATE BY STATE

THE BALANCE OF POWER

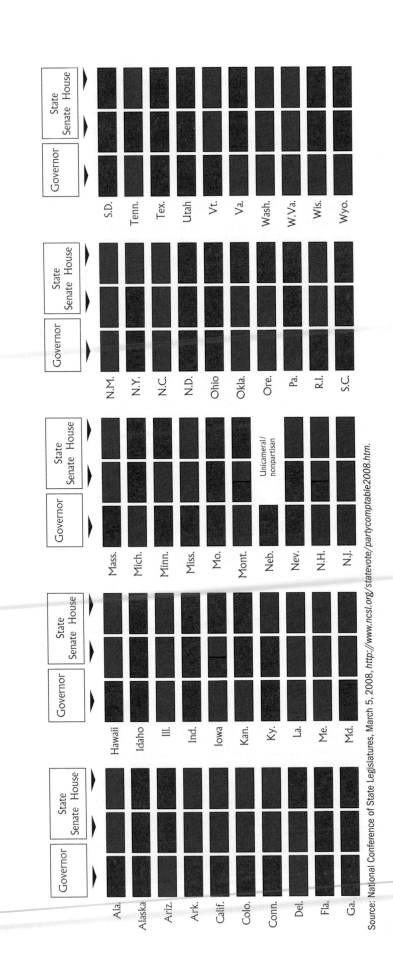

Democratic
Republican
Split

Source: National Conference of State Legislatures, March 5, 2008, http://www.ncsl.org/statevote/partycomptable2008.htm.

Increased switching of party control and party competition has inevitably led to more divided control of state government than in the past, when party affiliation of voters within states was more stable and electorates more homogeneous.[22] After the 2006–2007 elections, 24 states had divided government. In contrast, in 1946 only seven states had divided government. Increased party competition, divided government, and majority party switching in state legislatures has tended to increase legislative partisanship and polarize legislative deliberations, thereby making compromise harder to come by. Further, this sort of swinging from party to party can lead to a lack of policy continuity in a state. On the other hand, high levels of party competition tend to make elected officials more attentive and responsive to voters.[23]

Aside from partisan change, there is the question of turnover in state legislatures. Turnover levels—the rate that state legislators are replaced from election to election—give us an understanding both of how much experience and expertise state legislators have relative to other political actors in the states and how closely they are "connected" to their constituencies and the normal life of a state citizen.

Recent history has shown that in any 10-year period, about 75 percent of state senate and 77 percent of state house legislative seats are turned over.[24] Thus, significant change in the people holding state legislative office is the norm. In 2000, Pennsylvania and Missouri had the lowest average annual percent turnover in their Senates (less than 10 percent). Oregon and Colorado had the highest annual turnover rates, both in their upper chambers, at 48 and 35 percent, respectively.[25] Across all states, the current average annual turnover rate in any election year is about 26 percent in lower chambers and 23 percent in upper chambers.[26]

In recent years, voters in many states have attempted to increase turnover rates by legally restricting the number of terms a member may serve. Increasingly, voters appear to support the argument that professional, career-oriented legislators become so entrenched and difficult to unseat that they lose touch with their constituents and instead pander to special interests. Since 1990, 21 states have adopted term limits for state legislators, almost exclusively through direct democracy mechanisms (discussed shortly). However, four states have seen their term limits overturned in court, or in the case of Idaho and Utah, by the state legislature, leaving only 15 term-limit laws intact.[27] The number of terms permitted varies from state to state. For example, California limits its assembly (its lower house) members to six years and its senators to eight years in office.[28] In the 2002 elections, term-limited states had turnover rates in lower chambers that were 13 percentage points higher than non–term-limited states and almost 9 percentage points higher in upper chambers. In some states the effects of term limits is quite dramatic. For example, 41 percent of Nebraska legislators were term limited out of office in 2006.[29]

THE CHANGING FACE OF STATE ELECTED OFFICIALS

In November 1996, Washington state voters chose Gary Locke, the son of Chinese immigrants, as their governor. Locke became the first Asian American ever to be elected governor of one of the 48 contiguous states. Seven years before, Virginia voters made Douglas Wilder the first elected African American governor. These two governors are exceptions to the rule that governors are White, married men who are often lawyers, and state voters are increasingly electing a wider variety of people to state offices.

Women have made strong inroads into the governors' offices (see Figure 21.2). Before 1974, only a few women had ever been governors, and those were elected because they were married to a former governor who could not run again. But in 1974, Ella Grasso was elected to the governor's office of Connecticut in her own right. Dixie Lee Ray followed her in 1976 in Washington. Since 1925, 29 women have served as governors in states as varied as Delaware, Oregon, Kansas, and

FIGURE 21.2

Female Representation in State Government

Percentage of females in the state legislature in 2008.

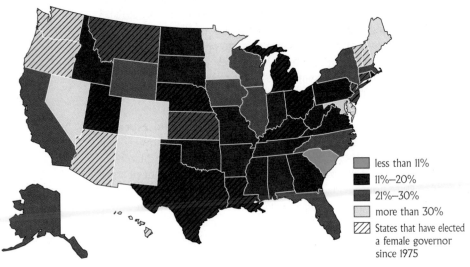

less than 11%

11%–20%

21%–30%

more than 30%

States that have elected
a female governor
since 1975

Source: Center for American Women and Politics, "Facts and Findings," *http://www.cawp.rutgers.edu/Facts.html#leg, March 5, 2008.*

In 1998, women were elected to all five statewide executive offices in Arizona—governor, secretary of state, treasurer, superintendent of public instruction, and attorney general. The so-called Fab Five were sworn into office by another powerful Arizona female—U.S. Supreme Court Justice Sandra Day O'Connor.

Kentucky, representing both the Democratic and Republican parties. At least two prominent female governors—Ann Richards of Texas and Christine Whitman of New Jersey—were mentioned as potential presidential candidates in 2000. In 2006, 36 states held gubernatorial elections, and in 9 of these states women ran for the office. In 2008, there were 8 female state governors and 10 Lieutenant Governors serving in the United States. Being female or a person of color is no longer an insurmountable hurdle to being elected to a state's highest office.

State legislatures too have been looking more and more like the diverse population of the United States.[30] In 2008, 23.6 percent of all state legislators were women, a tremendous increase over 1969, when only about 4 percent of state legislators were women.[31] Women are also taking more leadership roles in state legislatures. In 2007, there were 59 women in legislative leadership positions, serving in positions such as senate or house majority leader. However, state legislatures do vary widely in the percentage of female legislators, from almost 38 percent in Vermont to less than 9 percent in South Carolina during the 2008 legislative session. In 2007, there were 608 state legislators of African American descent—8 percent, a figure that has also been mostly increasing for 30 years. Asians and Hispanics have also been increasing in their state legislative representation, primarily in Florida and the Western states. Indeed, 3 percent of state legislators were Hispanic in 2007.[32]

The less-than-representative percentage of women and ethnic minorities in state elected positions (although at a historic high) shows the slowness with which progress is made in this area, due at least in part to informal qualifications for higher-level offices that can include experience at lower-level offices. Women and minorities are making the inroads today in the state and local offices that may well lead to them being elected more frequently to national positions in the future. For example, the sharp jump in the representation of women in the U.S. Senate and statewide elective office in the 1990s was encouraged by increases in women being elected to state legislative positions in the 1970s and 1980s.

GOVERNORS AND THE EXECUTIVE BRANCH

During his first several months as governor of California in 2003 and 2004, Arnold Schwarzenegger traveled to Israel, Japan, and China to promote investment in California industries, such as biotechnology, and to promote trade between those countries and his state. Schwarzenegger also appeared in television commercials aired oversees that promoted California. Such actions are becoming increasingly common for governors who are interested in creating more economic growth, even though they have no legal capacity to sign formal trade agreements with foreign nations. Governor Kathleen Sebelius of Kansas and former governor of Minnesota Jesse Ventura made similar trips to foreign countries, including Cuba.

The actions of these governors highlight the modern role of the governor. Not only is the governor the chief executive officer of a state, with the responsibility to execute the laws passed by the legislature, but he or she is also the best-known state public official, to whom the public looks for leadership, assurance, conflict resolution, and policy initiatives. If administering public policy is the governor's main constitutional responsibility, then promoting his or her vision of what public policy ought to be is the modern governor's primary responsibility to the public.

THE JOB OF GOVERNOR

Like presidents, governors are expected to wear many hats—sometimes fulfilling constitutionally assigned duties, sometimes performing political tasks. But the powers of governors are not always commensurate with citizens' expectations. State constitutions often hamstring a governor, dividing executive power among many different administrative actors and agencies. But a generation of modernization and reform has resulted in enhanced powers for governors by reducing the number of independently elected officials and independent boards and commissions in the state executive branch, as well as by enhancing governors' other formal powers.[33] These reforms have established clearer lines of authority and enhanced the governor's appointment, reorganization, and budgetary powers. Most states have also raised their governors' salaries and increased the number of years a governor can serve. Nevertheless, the limited formal powers of governors make it very difficult for them to fulfill their responsibilities to the state without resorting to more "informal powers," such as the use of the media and a public relations staff.

How powerful are the nation's governors? Political scientist Thad Beyle has devoted considerable attention to this subject. On the basis of an analysis of gubernatorial powers outlined in state constitutions and statutes and in the strength of their

You Are a Governor

party in their states' legislatures, he has rated each of the states' governor's institutional powers. Figure 21.3 displays this rating, based on the governor's ability to stay in office, make major appointments, prepare the state budget, veto legislation, and direct political parties. Seven states' governors—those in Hawaii, Maryland, New Jersey, New York, Ohio, Pennsylvania, and Utah—have very strong powers. Another 18 governors enjoy strong executive powers. Ten states accord their governors moderate powers. The remaining 15 states, including states as diverse as Massachusetts, California, and Nevada, give only weak powers to their governors.[34]

Two of a governor's most important formal powers for controlling state government are the veto and the executive budget. The governor's veto is similar to that of the president—a governor can refuse to sign a bill passed by the state legislature, blocking it from becoming law. But in most states, the governor's veto power is far more potent than the president's. First, gubernatorial vetoes have been very difficult for state legislatures to override historically, and this remains true today.[35] Although state legislatures have become more aggressive in overriding vetoes in recent years, still less than 10 percent of gubernatorial vetoes are overridden.

Further, 42 state governors have the **line-item veto**, which allows them to veto only certain parts of a bill while allowing the rest of the bill to pass into law. This keeps the legislature from being able to hold a bill hostage, forcing the governor to sign a popular bill even though it contains a provision that the governor thinks is unwise. This is especially useful on appropriations bills, allowing the governor to trim pork barrel spending as he or she sees fit. In Wisconsin, the governor is even allowed to veto individual words and letters from a bill, sometimes changing its basic meaning. In 1987, newly elected Governor Tommy Thompson used this power over 350 times on the budget passed by the Democratic state legislature.[36] With this power, a governor with a sizable minority in the legislature to support him or her can force or cajole the legislature into passing much of his or her agenda. The governor also has the power to initiate the state budget process in almost all states. This allows the governor to set the agenda for what is by far the most important bill(s) of the state legislative session. The budget details how state tax dollars

line-item veto

The power possessed by 42 state governors to veto only certain parts of a bill while allowing the rest of it to pass into law.

FIGURE 21.3

Institutional Powers of the Governors

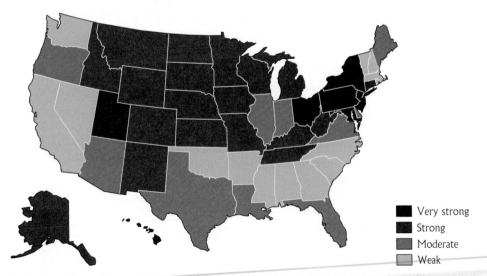

Very strong
Strong
Moderate
Weak

Source: Adapted from Thad Beyle and Margaret Ferguson, "Governors and the Executive Branch," in *Politics in the American States*, 9th ed., ed. Virginia Gray and Russell L. Hanson (Washington, DC: Congressional Quarterly Press, 2008), 192–228.

are going to be spent—it is where state public policy "puts up or shuts up." Although the legislature may amend and must pass the governor's proposal as it does any other bill, the limited staff and session time of most state legislatures, especially compared to that available to the governor, makes the massive budget sent by the governor difficult to change substantially. Further, since the governor has the ability to veto— and sometimes item veto—the budget passed by the legislature, he or she also has the last word in the process. This provides a governor the ability to gain help for his or her policy goals from both state legislators and bureaucrats interested in furthering their own policy goals through state spending.

Illinios Governor Rob Blagojevich speaks to the media after surveying tornado damage April 21, 2004 in Utica, Illinois. Utica, located about 90 miles southwest of Chicago, is home to about 1,000 people and has sustained significant tornado damage leaving eight people dead.

To enhance their influence, governors supplement their formal institutional powers with more "personal powers."[37] A governor's real power depends on the way he or she uses character, leadership style, and persuasive abilities in conjunction with the formal prerogatives of the office. Building public support is an increasingly important part of the policymaking process. This is true as a means for influencing legislative decision making in all states but also applies to influencing citizen behavior directly in states with direct democracy mechanisms. For example, in 2004 California Governor Schwarzenegger expended most of his informal powers in a failed attempt to generate public support for ballot propositions concerning government finances rather than trying to influence legislators.

Not surprisingly, public relations and media experts have become a key part of many governors' staffs. Although press coverage of state politics is intermittent at best, focusing on only the most salient controversies and such predictable events as the governor's State of the State Address, a savvy governor can create media events and opportunities that enhance his or her popularity and political clout. Whether it is Governor Arnold Schwarzenegger visiting the prime minister of Israel or New York Governor George Pataki visiting Ground Zero of the World Trade Center, the media image of a caring, active, busy governor can be parlayed into political clout with the legislature and executive agencies. Likewise, governors are subjected to media frenzies over failures in the bureaucracies they oversee. For example, as Florida Governor Jeb Bush pursued what seemed to be an easy reelection in 2002, the media and Democrats attacked Bush over the unexplained disappearance of a four-year-old girl in the state's foster care system and the system's reputation for being the worst in the country.

After languishing for most of the twentieth century as a political backwater office where political hacks, business leaders, and others went to cap off their careers before retiring to the country club, today's governors are politically savvy and active and have strong policy agendas.[38] Modern governors are likely to highly educated, experienced, and capable of managing the diverse problems of a state. In addition to being better educated than their predecessors, recent governors have often had previous experience as a statewide elected official or held a national position.

Today's governors increasingly have the tools and skills to control state government and guide the state in the policy directions they think are best. Demonstrating

As the state's legal counsel, the attorney general watches out for the state's legal interests. New York Attorney General Eliot Spitzer fought against corporate corruption and greed, even going so far as to sue the former director of the famed New York Stock Exchange.

lieutenant governor

Often the second-highest executive official in state government who is elected with the governor as a ticket in some states and is elected separately in others. She or he may have legislative and executive branch responsibilities.

the esteem in which the modern governorship is held is the fact that in the last quarter of the twentieth century, the U.S. president has been a former governor in all but five years. In each presidential race in this period, at least one of the major party nominees was a sitting or former governor.

OTHER EXECUTIVE OFFICERS

Unlike the U.S. president, most governors must work with an array of independently elected executive branch officials in conducting the affairs of state government. At various times, these officials may assist or oppose the governor. Voters in 43 states choose a **lieutenant governor**. The governor and lieutenant governor are elected as a team in 24 states. In states where the governor and lieutenant governor are chosen independently, it is possible for the two top state executives to be political rivals or even members of different political parties. This can result in some real battles between them. For example, in 1990 when then-Governor (and Democrat) Michael Dukakis of Massachusetts left the state on an international trade mission, Republican Lieutenant Governor Evelyn Murphy initiated major cuts in public employment in an attempt to jump-start her floundering campaign for governor. Perhaps in anticipation of such antics, when Republican Steve Windom became lieutenant governor of Alabama, the Democrat-dominated state legislature and Democratic governor promptly stripped the office of almost all its powers.[40] Most lieutenant governors have few formal duties aside from presiding over the state senate and being in the succession path for governor.

Other major executive positions elected in some states include the following:

- Attorney general—The state's legal counsel and prosecutor (elected in 43 states)
- Treasurer—The manager of the state's bank accounts (elected in 38 states)
- Secretary of state—In charge of elections and record-keeping (elected in 36 states)
- Auditor—Financial comptroller for the state (elected in 25 states)

Other officials elected in fewer states include education secretary and commissioners for land, labor, mines, agriculture, and utilities, among others.[41]

So many independent executives, commissions, and boards work within state governments that many politicians and scholars have called for major state government reorganization to allow governors more control and to increase efficiency generally. Every state has undertaken some kind of reorganization of the executive branch in the past 30 years. However, research shows that the expected benefits of reorganized state governments are not always achieved. Such reorganization only sometimes increases accountability and seldom results in cost saving and efficiency—benefits often promised by its proponents.[42] Although state residents may value smaller governments, they enjoy having electoral control over the leaders of state executive branches.

STATE LEGISLATURES

State legislatures are often easy targets for criticism. Their work is not well understood, and the institution does not typically receive the public attention that the governor's office or national institutions do. Further, up until a generation ago, state legislatures and legislators had a history of poor performance that still haunts them. At that time, they were "malapportioned, unrepresentative, dominated by their governors and/or special interests, and unable and unwilling to deal with the pressing issues of the day."[43]

But between 1965 and 1985, many state legislatures underwent a metamorphosis into more full-time, professional bodies—several like state-level congresses. According to political scientist Alan Rosenthal, "They increased the time they spent on their tasks; they established or increased their professional staffs; and they streamlined their procedures, enlarged their facilities, invigorated their processes, attended to their ethics, disclosed their finances, and reduced their conflicts of interest."[44] As a result, state legislatures are far more active, informed, representative, and democratic today than they were 40 years ago.

State legislatures serve the same basic function in the states as Congress does in the national government, and they do it with the same basic mechanisms. State legislatures make almost all the basic laws of the state by approving identical bills in each of their two-chambered bodies (except in Nebraska's unicameral legislature). They appropriate the money that is needed for a state government to function. They oversee the activities of the executive branch through confirming gubernatorial appointments, controlling the budgets of the agencies, and investigating complaints and concerns of citizens and the press. State legislators themselves attend closely to the needs of their constituents, whether through voting on bills in line with their constituents' interests or chasing down problems a citizen has with a bureaucratic agency.

Members of the state legislature are at the front line of interaction between citizens and government. Because most state legislatures meet for only a limited number of months each year and because state capitals are typically closer to their districts than Washington, D.C., is to the districts of most congresspersons, state legislators usually live among the people they represent. They are closely involved with their constituents not only at election time but also throughout the year. They coach basketball and run restaurants, they teach school and preach at local churches, and they are local attorneys and bankers. In short, the state legislature in almost all states comes closest to the sort of citizen-directed government envisioned by Thomas Jefferson over 200 years ago.

The reforms of the past generation designed to improve the efficiency and effectiveness of state legislatures are collectively called *legislative professionalism*.[45] That is, these are reforms designed "to enhance the capacity of the legislature to perform its role in the policymaking process with an expertise, seriousness, and effort comparable to that of other actors in the process."[46] Changes have been primarily in three areas. First, legislative sessions have been lengthened to give legislators more time to deal with the increasingly complex problems of the states. Before 1965, most state legislatures only met for several weeks each year, and many would only meet every other year. In 2008, 44 state legislatures had annual sessions, usually meeting for between three and five months, with a few (such as in Michigan, Massachusetts, and Wisconsin) meeting year-round.

The second legislative professionalism reform was to increase legislators' salaries so they could devote more of their time to considering the states' business and less to their "regular" job. The idea was also that if service in the state legislature paid a living wage, legislators would have fewer conflicts of interest and a wider variety of people would be willing to serve. For instance, the only people who could afford to serve in the West Virginia state legislature in 1960 for a salary of $1,500 were those with either an outside source of income or who were independently wealthy. In 2008, the roughly $73,613 a Pennsylvania state representative earned could allow him or her to focus full-time on legislative duties.

The third major professionalism reform was the increase in the staff available to help legislators in their duties. Even since 1979 (after many of the big professionalism changes had already occurred), permanent state legislative staff has increased over 60 percent.[47] By increasing their session length, salary, and staff, state legislatures have dramatically increased their ability to have an impact on the state policymaking process.

Not all the effects of this drive toward legislative professionalism are seen as good, and not all states have professionalized their legislatures to the same level. Some argue that professionalism leads to an overemphasis on reelection, inflated campaign costs, and lack of leadership in the lawmaking process.[48] Legislative professionalism threatens the existence of the "citizen legislature," in which people leave their job for a couple of months each year to serve the state and inject some "common sense" into government. The recent spate of state term limits laws indicates the esteem in which many Americans hold this sort of nonprofessional state legislature. There is also some evidence that increased professionalism does not enhance even some of the aspects of the process that proponents argued it would, such as increasing membership diversity in state legislatures.[49]

It is also important to note that not all state legislatures are in any sense full-time, professional bodies. Members of the New Hampshire House of Representatives earn $200 for a two-year term, which consists of only one 30-day period of service in each year. These are clearly not professional legislators. On the other hand, across the border in Massachusetts, state legislators earn over $58,000 and meet virtually the entire year. Figure 21.4 shows which states have professionalized legislatures, which still have citizen legislatures, and which have legislatures that are hybrids, having some characteristics of both. Those states that have developed professional legislatures tend to be those with large and heterogeneous populations that both need and can afford them, although there is a regional effect that may have to do with political preferences for a professional government.[50]

Although this selective process makes it difficult to assess the independent effects of legislative professionalism, there is some evidence that more professionalism leads to more liberal welfare policy and perhaps more divided government in the states.[51]

Explaining Differences in State Laws

FIGURE 21.4

Legislative Professionalism

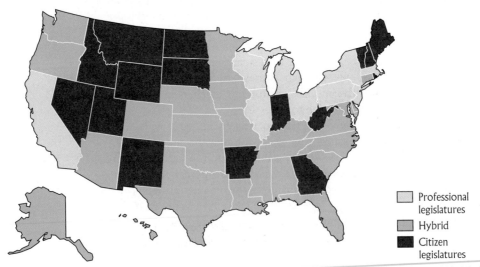

Legend:
- Professional legislatures
- Hybrid
- Citizen legislatures

Source: Adapted from Keith E. Hamm and Gary F. Moncrief, "Legislative Politics in the States," in *Politics in the American States*, 9th ed., ed. Virginia Gray and Russell L. Hanson (Washington, DC: Congressional Quarterly Press, 2008), 154–91.

We may now be seeing the beginning of a "deprofessionalizing" trend in some states, as some hearken back to the Jeffersonian ideal of the citizen legislature. Term limits laws are the most obvious manifestation of this, but recent laws in California limiting legislative staffing and in Colorado limiting the powers of the legislative leadership may also signal that the legislative professionalism movement is cyclical.[52]

STATE COURT SYSTEMS

The organization of the states' courts reflects two major influences: (1) the model of organization set by the national courts and (2) the judicial preferences of each state's citizens as manifested in state constitutions and statutes. State courts are far more involved in administering justice than is the national judiciary. Indeed, 98 percent of all litigation in the United States is settled in state courts. Recent data show that state courts have 52 times the number of criminal cases and 27 times more civil cases than national courts with only 24 times as many judges.[53] In addition, state court workloads have been increasing in both criminal and civil cases, forcing states to experiment with alternatives to trial courts like mediation, arbitration, and plea bargaining, among others. The volume of cases heard by state courts is significant, but courts are also policymaking bodies. Particularly when the highest court in the state rules on a case, judges are doing more than just interpreting the law; they are often making policy in the same fashion as the U.S. Supreme Court.[54]

Since World War II, many state court systems have undergone reforms designed to modernize and rationalize their procedures and structure, much like the reforms undergone in the states' governors' offices and legislatures. These include reforms both of organizational structure and judicial selection.

STATE COURT ORGANIZATION

State court systems often developed as a hodgepodge of individual courts set up at odd times and for odd reasons at the subnational level. Many states have low-level courts, such as justices of the peace or magistrate courts, whose presiding officials may not even be lawyers. Many states developed a variety of specialized courts to deal with specific judicial matters involving traffic, family, or taxes. These systems, which included courts that were completely independent of any higher authority, often led to confusion, duplication of effort, and unfair treatment of cases and people.

Comparing Judicial Systems

In the past generation, efforts have been made to consolidate and coordinate many state courts systems so that they parallel the federal system, discussed in Chapter 16. First, specialized courts have been consolidated and subsumed into trial courts with more general jurisdiction. These courts are usually established for county-sized areas and are the setting for most trials. They are known by a variety of labels—district courts, circuit courts, superior courts, and (in the case of New York) supreme courts. Judges assigned to these trial courts often work in only one county and specialize in criminal, juvenile, or civil litigation. A single judge presides over each case, and citizens may be called on to serve as jurors and members of grand jury panels.

Many states have also moved toward coordinating their court systems through their court of last resort, usually called the state supreme court. Under a coordinated system, the state supreme court not only serves as the court of final appeal for all cases in the state court system but also has the responsibility for administering and regulating the justice system in the state. This usually involves appointing a chief court administrator to handle the day-to-day budgeting, operations, and organization of all the courts in the state, and establishing boards to oversee and deal with complaints against lawyers and judges in the states.

A major innovation adopted by most states in the past 30 years is an *intermediate court of appeal*. Like national appeals courts, states organize these courts on a regional basis and with judges working together in panels of three or more, with a majority deciding each case. No witnesses are called before appellate courts, and juries are not used. Instead, judges read briefs and hear arguments prepared by lawyers that address whether the law was appropriately applied at the trial court level and whether due process of law was followed. The job of judges at this level is not to determine the facts of a case but to interpret the laws and the state or national constitution as they apply to the case.

The organizational purpose of an intermediate court of appeal is to reduce the pressure on the state supreme court of the many "routine" appeals of trial court decisions (see Figure 21.5). These are appeals that have few implications for state policy or procedure; they are appeals that primarily impact only the case at hand. An intermediate appeals court frees up the state supreme court to consider only those cases with statewide policy importance. Twelve states, all with small populations, do not have intermediate courts of appeal,[55] so the appellate work in these states falls solely to the supreme court, reducing its ability to concentrate on making policy through judicial interpretation.

FIGURE 21.5

Prototypical Modern State Court System

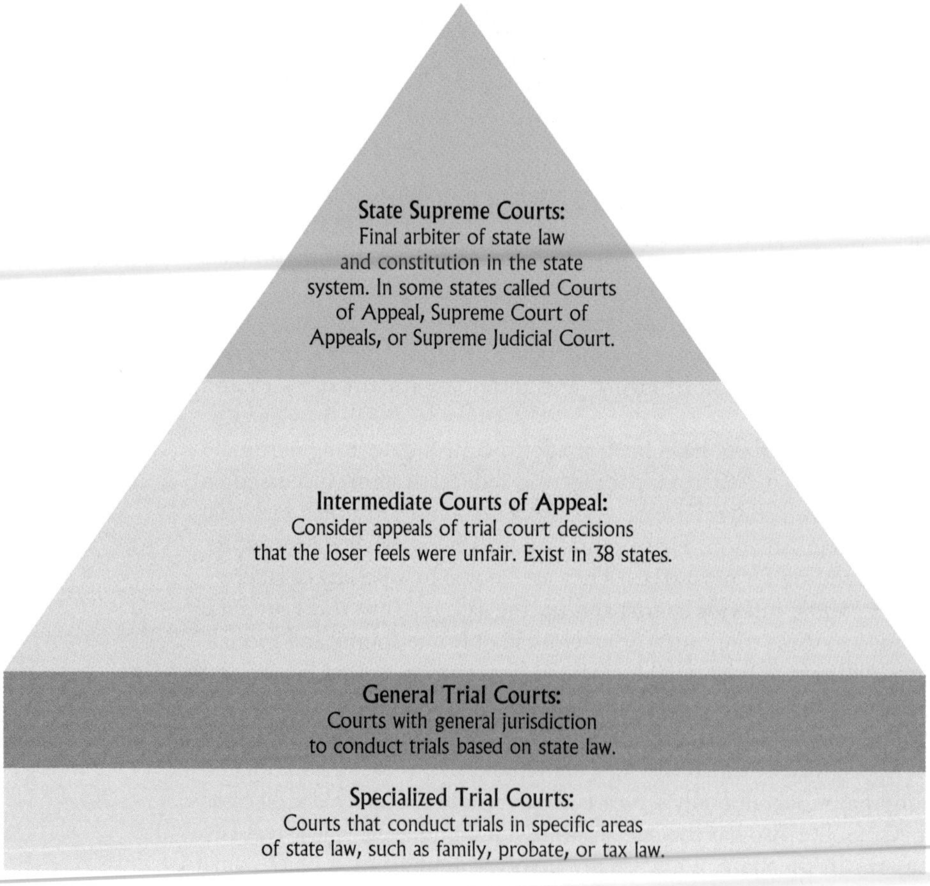

State Supreme Courts:
Final arbiter of state law and constitution in the state system. In some states called Courts of Appeal, Supreme Court of Appeals, or Supreme Judicial Court.

Intermediate Courts of Appeal:
Consider appeals of trial court decisions that the loser feels were unfair. Exist in 38 states.

General Trial Courts:
Courts with general jurisdiction to conduct trials based on state law.

Specialized Trial Courts:
Courts that conduct trials in specific areas of state law, such as family, probate, or tax law.

SELECTING JUDGES

In contrast to national judges, all of whom are appointed by the president for life, judges rise to the bench in the states in a variety of ways (see Table 21.2). These judicial selection mechanisms are each relics of values that were manifested in a series of reform movements over the past 200 years.

At the founding of the country, almost all state judges were appointed, as in the federal system, either by the governor or the state legislature, and 13 states still use this method of judicial selection for some or all their judges. With the Jacksonian democratic impulse of the early to mid-nineteenth century, states began to select their judges by partisan ballot, just as other state officials were selected. Currently, 11 states select some or all of their judges this way. In the Progressive Era (1890–1920), reformers argued that to be administered fairly, justice should be nonpartisan because a judge elected on a party platform might be more biased in his or her decisions. Persuaded by this argument, many states changed their judicial selection mechanism to that of nonpartisan election, where candidates ran against one another but without a party label. Nineteen states still use nonpartisan elections to select some or all their judges. But electing judges remains both common and controversial.[56]

The most recent wave of judicial selection reforms since World War II has been 17 states adopting a hybrid system of appointment and election known as the **Merit Plan**. In this system, the governor appoints the state's judges from a list of persons recommended by the state bar or a committee of jurists and other officials. Each appointed judge then serves a short "trial run" term, usually one year, in which citizens may assess the judge's performance. After this, an election is held in which voters are asked whether the judge should be retained in office—they simply vote yes or no, not for one candidate or another. If voters approve retention by a majority vote (Illinois requires 60 percent), then the judge continues in office for a lengthy term (usually 6 to 12 years), after which another retention election is held if the judge wishes to continue serving. Few judges lose in this type of retention election, which raises the question of whether the Merit Plan's democratic component truly enhances responsiveness to citizens. Indeed, recent research suggests there is little difference between the various selection plans and election outcomes as well as the political responsiveness of judges.[57]

Merit Plan
Method for selecting state judges in which governors appoint persons based on the recommendations of a committee. After serving a short term, the judge then often faces a retention election.

TABLE 21.2

State Judicial Selection Mechanisms

APPOINTMENT	ELECTION	MERIT PLAN
By Governor: DE, ME, MD, MA, NH, NM NJ, NY, RI, VT	**Partisan:** AL, AR, IL, IN, MS, NY, NC, PA, TN, TX, WV	AK, AZ, CA, CO, FL, IN, IA, KS, MD, MO, NE, OK, SD, TN, UT, WY
By Legislature: CT, HI, RI, SC, VA	**Nonpartisan:** AZ, CA, FL, GA, ID, KS, KY, LA, MI, MN, MT, NV, NM, ND, OH, OK, OR, SD, WA	

Note: States may appear more than once, since some states select different types of judges through different mechanisms. Minor local judges, such as justices of the peace, are not considered in this table.

Source: Council of State Governments, *The Book of the States, 2003 Edition* (Washington, DC: Council of State Governments, 2004), 235.

DIRECT DEMOCRACY

direct democracy

Government controlled directly by citizens. In some U.S. states, procedures such as the initiative, the referendum, and the recall give voters a direct impact on policymaking and the political process by means of the voting booth and can therefore be considered forms of direct democracy.

initiative

A process permitted in some states whereby voters may place proposed changes to state law on the ballot if sufficient signatures are obtained on petitions calling for such a vote.

Why It Matters
Direct Democracy

Direct democracy has a special appeal to Americans, who believe in government by the people. But what if all laws passed by a state legislature had to be approved by the voters? We might adopt many policies that infringe on the rights of numerical minorities. We would also have to vote more often and spend more time voting. Extensive voting demands might decrease citizen participation and lead to ill-informed policy choices. At the same time, citizens would likely view government actions as more legitimate.

A method of policymaking that is unique in the United States to subnational governments is **direct democracy**. Three procedures—the initiative, the referendum, and the recall—provide voters with ways they can directly impact policymaking and the political process through the voting booth. One or more of these procedures is available in all but one state (Alabama); the referendum for ratifying constitutional amendments is especially common. The more proactive of these are less widely available—the initiative (24 states) and recall (17 states) (see Table 21.3). These procedures were developed in the Progressive Era largely in the Western and Midwestern states as a way to bring more power to the people by cutting out the middle persons in the policymaking system—political parties, politicians, and interest groups.

The **initiative** is the purest form of direct democracy. Although its details vary from state to state, the basic procedure is as follows. First, a citizen decides that he or she wants to see a law passed. The specific language of that proposal is then registered with a state official (typically the secretary of state), and permission to circulate a petition is given. The advocates of the proposal then try to get a specified number of eligible voters (typically 5 to 10 percent of those voting in the previous election) to sign a petition saying they would like to see the proposal on the ballot. When the appropriate number of signatures has been verified, the proposal is placed on the next general election ballot for an approve/disapprove vote. If a majority of voters approve it, the proposal becomes law. Between 1904 and 2006, at least 2,155 initiatives have been placed on state ballots, and only 41 percent have passed. But both the average number and passage rate of initiatives has increased in the past 15 years.[58]

The initiative allows for the adoption of policy that might otherwise be ignored or opposed by policymakers in the state legislature and governor's offices. The best example of this is the state legislative term-limits movement of the 1990s. Since this policy would directly and negatively affect some state legislators, it is easy to see why such a policy would be difficult to pass through the state legislature. Of the 21 states that have passed such limits, only Louisiana does not have the initiative. Perhaps just as telling, of the 24 states that have the initiative in some form, only four (Alaska, Illinois, Mississippi, and North Dakota) have not passed term limits. Other sorts of ideas become state law through this process that might not otherwise do so, for good or ill. These include everything from a series of property tax limitations in many states in the 1970s and 1980s to recent initiatives allowing marijuana

TABLE 21.3

Direct Democracy Mechanisms

INITIATIVE[a]	LEGISLATIVE REFERENDUM[b]	RECALL
AK, AZ, AR, CA, CO, FL, ID, IL, ME, MA, MI, MS, MO, MT, NE, NV, ND, OH, OK, OR, SD, UT, WA, WY	AZ, AR, CA, DE, ID, IL, KY, ME, MD, MA, MI, MO, MT, NE, NV, NM, ND, OH, OK, OR, SD, UT, WA	AK, AZ, CA, GA, ID, KS, LA, MI, MN, MT, NV, NM, ND, OR, SD, WA, WI

[a] These states have at least one of the several forms of initiative.
[b] All states except Alabama allow or require a referendum for state constitutional amendments. The states listed in this column also allow referenda on the passage of legislative issues that are not constitutional amendments.

Source: Council of State Governments, *The Book of the States, 2003 Edition* (Washington, DC: Council of State Governments, 2004), 281–87.

to be used for medical purposes in California and seven other states. Some research even suggests that legislatures in states with the initiative may pass laws more in line with citizen preferences when the threat of citizen action through the initiative is present,[59] but other research disputes this finding.[60]

Perhaps not surprisingly there is considerable debate over the wisdom of making state law through citizen-initiated proposals. Constitutional amendments and legislation passed through initiative are often poorly drafted and may contain ambiguous or contradictory provisions. As a result, initiatives often create new problems, leading to lawsuits and court interpretation and, often, action by the legislature.

It is also unclear to what extent the initiative process empowers citizens or merely gives new tools to well-financed interest groups. In larger states, special interests can pay professional firms to gather the required number of signatures. Monied interests also have the advantage in mounting expensive television advertising campaigns. These ads can present voters with a biased or incomplete set of facts on an issue they would otherwise know little about. For example, in the 1998 California initiative campaign to legalize Indian tribal casinos, the gambling industry spent more than $71 million on *both sides* of the issue, with advertisements that were often confusing to citizens.[61] In initiative and referendum campaigns, complex public policy questions too often are reduced to simplistic sloganeering. As Ann O' M. Bowman and Richard C. Kearney argue,

> Seldom are issues so simple that a yes-or-no ballot question can adequately reflect appropriate options and alternatives. A legislative setting, in contrast, fosters the negotiation and compromise that produce workable solutions. Legislatures are deliberative bodies, not instant problem solvers.[62]

A hybrid of legislative and direct democratic policymaking is the **referendum**. Unlike the initiative, which is proposed by a citizen or group, the referendum begins life as a legislative resolution. Typically, the state legislature deliberates on and passes the proposal in both chambers in identical form, as required for any bill to become law, but then instead of sending the bill to the governor for his or her approval, the proposal is presented to the voters in a general election. If a majority of voters approve it, it becomes law; otherwise, it does not. In all states (except Alabama), this procedure is required for amendments to the state constitution, and in many subnational governments referenda are required for bond issues (government debt), tax changes, and other fiscal matters.

The **recall** is different than the initiative or referendum because it is about elected officials rather than public policy. In essence, the recall allows voters to call a special election for a specific official in an attempt to throw him or her out of office before the end of his or her term. The process involves gathering signatures on a petition of voters in the jurisdiction of the official being recalled, much like an initiative. Once enough signatures are gathered, a special election is held, usually within three months of official confirmation of the valid number of signatures, in which the official being recalled runs against any forthcoming challenger(s), if he or she desires to do so.

TIMELINE

Initiatives and Referendums

referendum

A state-level method of direct legislation that gives voters a chance to approve or disapprove legislation or a constitutional amendment proposed by the state legislature.

recall

A procedure that allows voters to call a special election for a specific official in an attempt to throw him or her out of office before the end of term. Recalls are permitted in only 17 states, seldom used because of their cost and disruptiveness, and rarely successful.

During the 2004 primary and general elections, 13 states passed constitutional amendments banning same-sex marriage via the referendum process. Here, State Representative Nan Orrock (D-Atlanta) addresses an October 27, 2004, rally against the Georgia referendum (Amendment 1), which passed a week later by 76 to 24 percent.

Needless to say, this is a drastic action and it is infrequently undertaken successfully. It is disruptive of the routine political process and very costly for the jurisdiction having to hold the special election. Because of this, only 17 states allow for the recall, and these states make it difficult to undertake, with the required number of signatures being much higher than that required to place an initiative on the ballot. Historically, those who have been recalled have been accused of a serious breach of propriety, morals, or ethics and often are local officials or judges serving long terms. For example, in 1982 a district judge in Madison, Wisconsin, made the highly publicized and inflammatory statement that he thought a very young victim in a sexual assault case appeared promiscuous; the judge was recalled and removed from office.[63] However, in recent years, some state and local officials have been recalled for more policy-oriented reasons, such as for supporting tax increases in Michigan, a stadium sales tax in Wisconsin, and gun control in California. Most dramatically, California Governor Gray Davis was recalled in 2003 after voters came to believe that he had failed to solve the state's energy and fiscal crisis. California voters elected action-movie star Arnold Schwarzenegger. This was the first successful recall of a governor since North Dakota voters recalled Governor Lynn Frazier in 1921.

STATE AND LOCAL GOVERNMENT RELATIONS

Dillon's Rule
The idea that local governments have only those powers that are explicitly given them by the states. This means that local governments have very little discretion over what policies they pursue or how they pursue them. It was named for Iowa Judge John Dillon, who expressed this idea in an 1868 court decision.

Why It Matters
State Boundaries
State boundaries typically result from historical accidents rather than efforts to define regions that have similar interests and needs. For example, the people of the Florida panhandle probably have more in common with those of southern Alabama and Georgia than those of south Florida. But what if the states were reconstructed so as to make them more homogeneous and therefore more different from one another? How do you think this would affect state policy? For example, would state policies also be more dissimilar? Would citizens be happier with the policies in their state?

In Chapter 3, you read about the concept of federalism and how the nation's Founders tried to strike a balance between the powers of the central government and those of the states. This state–federal *intergovernmental relationship* has evolved in the past 200 years through statutes passed by Congress, constitutional amendments and their interpretation by the U.S. Supreme Court, civil war, and tradition. The relationship between the states and the national government is both contentious and one of the defining characteristics of government in the United States.

The intergovernmental relationship between the states and their inferior governments—local governments—is no less important in defining how our government works. But this relationship is far less ambiguous and involves no balance and little interpretation.

The basic relationship is that local governments are totally subservient to the state government. According to **Dillon's Rule** (after Iowa Judge John Dillon, who expressed this idea in an 1868 court decision), local governments have only those powers that are explicitly given to them by the states. Dillon argued definitively that local governments were "creatures of the state" and that the state legislature gave local governments the "breath of life without which they cannot exist."[64] This means that local governments have very little discretion over which policies they pursue or how they pursue them. In fact, the states have been known to take away policymaking and administrative power from local governments completely, as when the state of Missouri recently took over a school district that state officials felt was being run improperly. An extreme case of state usurpation of local power took place in 1997 when the Massachusetts state legislature actually *abolished* Middlesex County because of mismanagement and corruption.[65]

The basis of this shocking imbalance of power is the U.S. Constitution. Although the Constitution discusses at length the role of the states and the relationship between the states and the central government, local governments are never explicitly mentioned. The establishment and supervision of local government has been interpreted to be one of the "reserve powers" for the states, under the

Tenth Amendment of the Bill of Rights. The idea is that states have certain responsibilities and policy goals they must fulfill, but sometimes the best way to do this is through local units of government they establish. For example, the states have the responsibility to educate children, but all states (except Hawaii) have opted to establish regional school districts to do this for the states.

Although local governments have no constitutional sovereignty, local government officials are certainly not powerless in their efforts to control their own destiny. But the power of local government arises from informal political clout rather than formal powers. First, many people feel more strongly connected to their local governments than to the state. After all, it is the local government officials they see most frequently—the police officer responding to an emergency call, the teacher in the school educating their child, or the city council member helping to get the potholes filled in the street. State officials understand the sympathy (and political clout) these officials have among citizens, so they do not try to rile them without good reason. Further, local government officials of all stripes form interest groups to lobby state officials. In all states, organizations of local officials, such as the Wisconsin League of Municipalities or the Texas Association of Counties, are among the most powerful interest groups in the state capitol.[66]

Many cities have also managed to get state legislatures to grant them a degree of autonomy through a **local charter**. A charter is an organizational statement and grant of authority from the state to a local government, much like a state or national constitution. States sometimes allow cities to write their own charters and to change them without permission from the state legislature, within limits. Today, this practice of **home rule** is widely used to organize and modernize city government.

local charter
An organizational statement and grant of authority from the state to a local government, much like a state or national constitution. States sometimes allow municipalities to write their own charters and to change them without permission of the state legislature, within limits. See also home rule.

home rule
The practice by which municipalities are permitted by the states to write their own charters and change them without permission of the state legislature, within limits. Today this practice is widely used to organize and modernize municipal government. See also local charter.

LOCAL GOVERNMENTS

The U.S. Bureau of the Census counts not only people but also governments. Its latest count revealed an astonishing 89,476 American local governments (see Table 21.4). In addition to being a citizen of the United States and of a state, the average citizen also resides within the jurisdiction of perhaps 10 to 20 local governments. The state of Illinois holds the current record for the largest number of local governments: 6,994 at the latest count. The six-county Chicago metropolitan area alone has more than 1,200 governments.

TABLE 21.4
Local Governments in the United States

TYPE OF GOVERNMENT	1962	2007	% CHANGE, 1962–2007
All local governments	91,186	89,476	−1.1%
General-purpose governments			
County	3,043	3,033	−0.03%
Municipal	18,000	19,492	+7.7%
Township	17,142	16,519	−3.6%
Single-purpose governments			
School district	34,678	13,051	−66.4%
Special district	18,323	37,381	+49.0%

Source: U.S. Bureau of the Census, "Local Governments and Public School Systems by Type and State: 2007," March 7, 2008, *http://www.census.gov/govs/www/cog2007.html.*

The sheer number of governments in the United States is, however, as much a burden as a boon to democracy. Citizens are governed by a complex maze of local governments—some with broad powers, others performing very specialized services. This plethora of local governments creates voter overload and ignorance, thereby defeating the democratic purpose of citizen control.

TYPES OF LOCAL GOVERNMENT

Local governments can be classified into five types based on their legal purpose and the scope of their responsibilities: counties, townships, municipalities, school districts, and special districts.

Counties   The largest geographic unit of government at the local level is the *county* government, although they are called "parishes" in Louisiana and "boroughs" in Alaska. Texas has the most counties with 254, while Delaware and Hawaii have only three. Los Angeles County serves the most people—over 9.5 million residents—whereas Loving County, Texas, serves only 67 residents.

The 3,033 county governments are administrative arms of state government. Typically, counties are responsible for keeping records of births, deaths, and marriages; establishing a system of justice and law enforcement; maintaining roads and bridges; collecting taxes; conducting voter registration and elections; and providing for public welfare and education. Rural residents more often rely on county governments for services because they have fewer local governments to turn to than city dwellers.

County governments usually consist of an elected *county commission*, the legislative body that makes policy, and a collection of "row officers," including sheriffs, prosecutors, county clerks, and assessors, who run county services. Some urban counties, such as Milwaukee County, St. Louis County, and Wayne (Detroit) County, now elect a county executive (like a mayor or governor). In some counties, such as Dade (Miami) County and Sacramento County, the county commission appoints a county administrator to take responsibility for the administration of county policies.

Townships   *Township* governments are found in only 20 states, including Maine, Michigan, New Hampshire, New York, Vermont, and Wisconsin. Most of the 16,519 township governments have limited powers and primarily just assist with county services in rural areas; however, some, such as those in New England, function much like city governments. Voters typically elect a township board, a supervisor, and perhaps a very small number of other executives. Township officers oversee public highways and local law enforcement, keep records of vital statistics and tax collections, and administer elections. However, most lack the power to pass local ordinances since they serve as administrative extensions of state and county governments.

Municipalities   Cities are more formally referred to as municipal governments or *municipalities*, and they supply most local programs and services for 19,492 communities in the United States. Municipalities typically provide police and fire protection, street maintenance, solid waste collection, water and sewer works, park and recreation services, and public planning. Some larger cities also run public hospitals and health programs, administer public welfare services, operate public transit and utilities, manage housing and urban development programs, and even run universities. Citizen satisfaction with the delivery of such services varies greatly. Originally, many municipalities in the United States were run with a special form of direct democracy—the **town meeting**. Under this system, all voting-age adults in a community gathered once a year to make public policy such as passing new local laws,

town meeting

A special form of direct democracy under which all voting-age adults in a community gather once a year to make public policy. Now used only in a few villages in upper New England.

Public Service Through Elective Office

Many young Americans are concerned about particular issues and government policy, and some are inspired to mobilize other young adults to register to vote, attend city council meetings, and sign petitions. However, even though issues such as public spending on education, economic development, and the drinking age have a direct impact on youth, few young people are motivated enough about these issues to run for public office. And because of age restrictions, most national and statewide offices are closed to young adults. However, in most states there are no age requirements for state and local legislative positions, and some young adults successfully run for these offices.

In Kansas, 20-year-old Tanner Fortney ran for the Spring Hill city council in 2001 after becoming interested in public policy through his high school debate team and, later, through an internship with Congressman Dennis Moore (D-Kans.) and through his political science classes at the University of Kansas. Fortney survived the primary election for the city council but lost the general election by 75 votes. After the election, Fortney did not wallow in defeat. Instead, he gained an appointment to the Spring Hill planning commission and immersed himself in the details of zoning and infrastructure.

Fortney's vigor impressed the town's mayor, and when a city council member resigned in October 2001, Mayor Mark Squire appointed Fortney to the council. The appointment made Fortney the council's youngest member ever. Fortney focused his attention on development and economic growth issues, trying to make sure the town balanced residential and commercial development. Fortney's hard work, zeal, and fresh perspective helped to revitalize city government in the sleepy suburb of 3,000 near Kansas City. Voters appreciated Fortney's efforts and reelected him in April 2003 for a four-year term.

Fortney says that he will likely continue in public service, perhaps running for the county commission. In the meantime, he will serve on the council, complete law school, and perhaps dream of serving in the state legislature. Fortney's example clearly demonstrates that young people can become involved and make a difference.

QUESTIONS FOR DISCUSSION

▷ What are the minimum age limits for running for local and state offices in your state? Do you think they are too low or too high?

▷ Would you ever consider running for local or state office? Why or why not? Would a specific issue or desire for a policy change encourage you to run? Explain.

▷ If you did run for office at a young age, what steps would you take to encourage more young people to become involved in politics?

approving a town budget, and electing a small number of local residents to serve as town officials. But as cities became too large for the town meeting style of governance, three modern forms of municipal government developed.

Mayor–Council Government. In a typical mayor–council government (Figure 21.6), local residents elect a mayor and a city council. In "strong mayor" cities, such as New York City, the city council makes public policy, and the mayor and city bureaucrats who report to the mayor are responsible for policy implementation. Strong mayors may also veto actions of the city council. In "weak mayor" cities, most power is vested in the city council, which directs the activities of the city bureaucracy. The mayor serves as the presiding officer for city council meetings and as the ceremonial head of city government. Most mayor–council cities have this weak mayor form of governance because most of the numerous small cities of 10,000 or fewer residents use this system. San Diego is one major city that uses the weak mayor form of government.

Council–Manager Government. In this form of municipal government, voters elect a city council and sometimes a mayor who often acts as both presiding officer and voting member of the council (see Figure 21.7). The council is responsible for setting policy for the city. The implementation and administration of the council's actions are placed in the hands of an appointed **city manager**, who is expected to carry out policy with the aid of city bureaucracy. More than one-third of cities use this form of government, including such major cities as Dallas, Kansas City, and Phoenix.

city manager
An official appointed by the city council who is responsible for implementing and administering the council's actions. More than one-third of U.S. cities use the council-manager form of government.

FIGURE 21.6

Mayor–Council Government

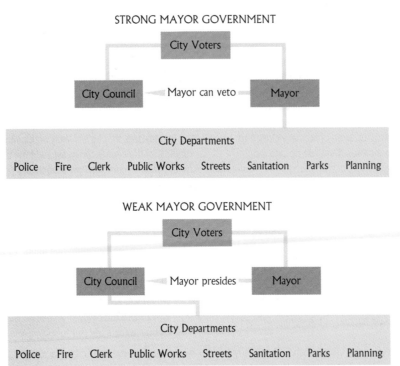

Commission Government. In commission government, voters elect a panel of city commissioners, each of whom serves as both legislator and executive. These officials make public policy just as city council members do in the other two forms of government. However, each member is also elected as a commissioner of a functional area of city government (for example, public safety), and bureaucrats report to a single commissioner. Among the few cities that still use a commission government are Vicksburg, Mississippi, and St. Petersburg, Florida.[67]

Most city council members and many mayors are elected in nonpartisan elections. Traditionally, city council members represented a district or ward of the city—a practice that permitted ward-based machine party bosses to control elections and to try to create public policies that were good for individual wards rather than for the city as a whole. Reformers advocated at-large city elections, with all members of the city council chosen by voters throughout the city. These at-large representatives could not create public policies to benefit only their own neighborhoods because they would have to answer to all the city's voters. A majority of cities use at-large elections today.

A consequence of at-large elections is that they make it more difficult for minority group members to be elected to the city council. This is because African American and other ethnic minorities in U.S. cities have tended to live in more or less homogeneous neighborhoods. Therefore, although they may be a minority of the entire city's population (and so fail to generate a majority in at-large elections), they may be a majority in smaller sections of the city, and so could elect candidates to pursue their interests in district-based electoral systems. Cities that employ district elections may have a greater degree of representational equity for African Americans and Hispanics on city councils than cities that use at-large elections.[68]

FIGURE 21.7

Council–Manager Government

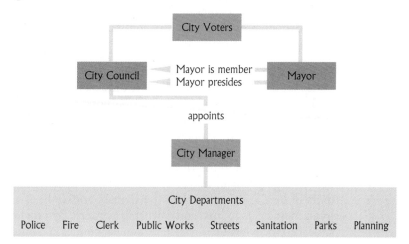

School Districts   The nation's 13,051 *school districts* are responsible for educating children. Although some cities, counties, townships, and one state (Hawaii) operate dependent public school systems (a total of 1,510), school districts are run as independent local governments. Consolidation of small, often rural, districts into larger ones is the major reason for a 66 percent drop in the number of school districts during the past 45 years.

In an independent school district, voters within a geographically defined area are responsible for their own public education system, including electing a board of education, selecting administrators and teachers, building and operating schools, designing and running education programs, and raising the revenues to meet a locally adopted school budget. Because the states are ultimately responsible for public education, state governments adopt general standards for education, mandate certain school programs, and provide a system of state financial assistance to public schools. But within the guidelines of state policy and the parameters of state funding, locally elected school boards and their appointed administrators deliver education services to the nation's children.

School districts have become the focus for many emotionally charged issues at the local level. Prayer in public schools, sex education, equity in school funding, English as a second-language classes, charter schools, gay and lesbian student groups, and lingering racial discrimination are just a few of the more explosive issues surrounding schools in the 2000s. For example, although the Supreme Court declared that states have a responsibility to eliminate discrimination in education in such important decisions as *Brown v. Board of Education* (1954) and *Swann v. Charlotte-Mecklenberg County Schools* (1971) (see Chapter 5), inequities in the public school systems persist, with racial minorities still encountering poorly funded public education in many instances. In fact, political scientists have discovered an extensive pattern of second-generation discrimination—a shortage of minority teachers "which leads to negative outcome for minority students."[69] Furthermore, in 2007 the Supreme Court ruled that public schools cannot use race as a criteria when assigning children to schools. The ruling overturned policies that attempted to create racial diversity across and within schools (*Parents Involved in Community Schools v. Seattle School Dist. No. 1*). How this ruling may influence efforts to prevent racial segregation in the long term is not clear.

This inequity is coupled with a financial crisis in many public school systems. States have widely divergent school aid policies—some states are good providers to their neediest local schools, whereas others leave the financing responsibility largely to local districts. Local revenue sources are disproportionately based on the local property tax—a policy choice that results in wealthier districts having an abundance of resources, while poorer districts have inadequate revenues for their schoolchildren.[70] Schools around the country continue to struggle with providing quality education with limited resources.

Special Districts The fastest-growing form of local government in the United States is the *special district*. The last official U.S. Census Bureau count showed 37,381 of these independent, limited-purpose governments. Generally, special districts provide only a single service, such as flood control, waste disposal, fire protection, public libraries, or public parks. There is no standard model of special district government organization—the types of organizational arrangements are almost as plentiful as the number of districts. Some districts have elected policymaking boards; a governor or mayor appoints others. Special districts are highly flexible units of local government because their boundary lines can be drawn across the usual municipal, county, and township borders. By providing services on a larger scale, they help localities realize certain economies and efficiencies.

However, important questions about democracy are inherent in the growth of special districts. Special districts are, to a great extent, invisible governments; the local press rarely covers their operations, and there is little direct public participation in their decision making. Most citizens do not even know who serves on these district boards or when the boards meet. As a result, the public has great difficulty holding special districts accountable.

FRAGMENTATION, COOPERATION, AND COMPETITION

Each governing body in a fragmented metropolis tends to look at problems from its own narrow perspective. As a result, local bodies fail to cooperate with one another and plan effectively for the region's future needs. For example, the development of an effective mass transit system is often hindered when not all communities are willing to share in financing a new metropolitan bus network or light rail system, or a narrowly focused special district devoted to maintaining the region's road network may not be willing to divert its funds to help finance new rail construction.

Traditionally, regional cooperation on specific policy areas has been undertaken through the use of special districts. For example, local water and sewer needs transcend municipality borders. To address this issue, special sewer and water districts have been set up in most metropolitan areas to coordinate the delivery of this service.

But there are limits to the number of special districts that can be established efficiently and the level of coordination these districts can achieve. What can be done to coordinate a variety of public services in a metropolitan area? A few areas have developed super-locals, institutional arrangements that act almost as general purpose governments for an entire region. Seattle, Miami, and Minneapolis–St. Paul each have a metropolitan council that serves such a function. For example, the Minneapolis–St. Paul Metropolitan Council operates the region's bus service, provides sewer and water services, operates a regional housing and development authority, and funds and plans regional parks and trails, all activities that cut across traditional local governments' physical and policy area boundaries.

But examples of institutionalized regional coordination are the exception rather than the rule. For the most part, the prospects for promoting regional cooperation to correct the inequalities and coordination problems that result from metropolitan fragmentation have been dim. Generally speaking, the United States lacks the strong tradition of regional planning evident in Europe (see "America in Perspective: Urban

? Why It Matters

Local Services

The multitude of local governments with independent authority can make the delivery of public services in a metropolitan area inefficient, contentious, and just plain confusing. If all government services in a metropolitan area were taken over by a single government entity, such as the county, then these services might be provided more effectively and at a lower cost. And inequities in services between wealthy neighborhoods and poor neighborhoods might be resolved. However, such consolidation would allow fewer access points to government, perhaps making it less democratic.

AMERICA IN PERSPECTIVE

Urban Planning in the European Union and the United States

The nations of the European Union play a much stronger role in guiding urban development than does the United States. Europe's strong planning has helped to preserve cities, control the pace of development, protect agricultural land and the environment, and minimize urban sprawl to a degree that is hardly imaginable in the United States. Typically, these urban planning actions are initiated by regional agencies that get their authority from the central government.

In Great Britain, planners prevented the overgrowth of London by encircling the city with a "green belt"—a designated area in which the countryside would be preserved and no new development permitted. The growth of the region's population was absorbed in planned "new towns" that were built some distance from the central city. The result was a mixture of city and countryside in a metropolitan area and the avoidance of American-style urban sprawl.

Faced with the prospect of excessive growth in Paris, France's national agency for development steered new industries into the suburbs and more distant cities. Still the lure of Paris proved attractive. In response, central government and regional planners built two new towns of high-rise office buildings, convention centers, and hotels in different spots just outside the city's borders. These towns became the main office centers of the metropolitan Paris area. High-rise residential new towns were built in a ring around Paris to absorb the area's rapidly growing population. These new commercial and residential centers were connected to the old city by a new commuter rail system.

The Netherlands has also relied on strong government planning and controls over land use to prevent the country's limited supply of land from being eaten up by rapid urbanization. Dutch planners saved valuable agricultural land and recreational space in a "green heart" in the midst of the metropolitan Amsterdam-The Hague-Rotterdam Randstad ("Ring City") area, one of the most densely populated areas in the world. Riding a train through the area today, you can easily see exactly where the city ends and the land designated for agricultural purposes begins. The planning boundaries are extremely clear and well guarded.

European planners now confront new problems. With the globalization of their economies, cities in Europe find that they are increasingly competing with one another for new business. As a result, spatial planning considerations are sometimes sacrificed in order to give a corporation a site it desires. Citizens' demands for individual homes of their own have also led to pressures for continued suburban development, sometimes compromising the integrity of regional land-use plans. Rush-hour traffic jams have become increasingly common in major European metropolises.

Despite these new problems, European nations have been able to ward off the ills of uncontrolled growth. In the United States, by contrast, the private sector and the free market—not government—play the dominant role in deciding where growth will occur. Compared to Europe, regional planning in the United States is essentially toothless.

Sources: Peter Hall, *Urban and Regional Planning*, 4th ed. (Independence, KY: Routledge, 2002); H. V. Savitch, *Post-Industrial Cities: Politics and Planning in New York, Paris, and London* (Princeton, NJ: Princeton University Press, 1988); Hans Thor Andersen and Ronald Van Kempen, *Governing European Cities: Social Fragmentation, Social Exclusion and Urban Governance* (London: Ashgate, 2000).

Planning in the European Union and the United States"). In large part, this reflects the strong localism inherent in American democracy. Americans prefer living in small, autonomous communities. In the United States, there is a tradition (or perhaps a myth) of people being able to "vote with their feet," that is, of people moving to the place where the government's policies best reflect their values.[71] This exacerbates the problem of regional coordination because local governments in different parts of the same metropolitan area will sometimes offer very different services to their citizens. This often manifests itself as a conflict between city dwellers and suburbanites.

A good (if disturbing) example of this is seen in the conflict over the racial integration of the Milwaukee public schools. When its schools were ordered to desegregate in the 1970s and 1980s, many White families moved out of the school district into neighboring suburban districts. In a classic case of "White flight," White student enrollment in the Milwaukee Public Schools dropped rapidly. In response, the federal court that issued the original desegregation order then expanded its order to include other school districts within Milwaukee County, thus attempting to force a regional coordination for educational policy by judicial fiat and with the backing of the national government. But again, many White families voted with their feet and left the county entirely, making the attempt at coordination a failure.

Mass transit is one of the most visible services provided by local government, but the multiplicity of local governments in metropolitan areas makes coordination of service difficult. How would it affect citizens' lives if your local government either eliminated mass transit or began operating a mass transit system?

Other typical conflicts between the preferences and needs of suburbanites and city dwellers involve taxes, roads, and central city services. Many people move to the suburbs because property taxes are lower and land is cheaper. The denser population of an urban area causes a higher need for most local government services and therefore a higher tax burden. Regional coordination often looks to suburbanites to subsidize the taxes of the urban dwellers they left behind. Because suburbanites live more spread out and often far away from their jobs, they need plenty of good roads and highways on which to commute. Meanwhile, urban dwellers would rather that more transportation money be spent on mass transit, which is economical for dense populations. Urban dwellers also complain that suburbanites drive into the central city each workday, using city services like roads, police, water, and so forth, and then take themselves and their tax dollars back to the suburbs at night. These examples offer the barest outline of the differences in preferences and viewpoints of people in different areas of a metropolis. It is easy to understand why coordination and cooperation are hard to come by.

Local governments are also engaged in serious competition for economic development. That is, they try to expand their tax base through commercial and residential development. Some analysts believe that cities are quite limited in their ability to control economic change within their borders, but local officials often believe that development policies are a community's lifeblood.[72] A business owner can simply threaten to leave a community or locate facilities in another town if he or she is unhappy with local policies. Thus, business owners and corporate officials have great leverage to extract concessions from local officials because no local government wants to face the loss of jobs or tax base. As a result, cities compete with one another for desirable business facilities by offering tax reductions, promises of subsidized infrastructure development, and other services demanded by business.

However, local governments can cooperate with one another when they find it in their mutual interest to do so. Central cities and suburbs are often willing, for instance, to share the costs of a new sewage disposal facility. They may also cooperate in ventures to attract a major new employer to the area, or to keep one, as in the case of the massive efforts by local governments in the Chicago metropolitan area to construct a new baseball stadium to keep the White Sox from leaving town in the late 1980s. Sometimes two or more governments may cooperate informally to share equipment and services. In many areas of the country, a **council of governments** (frequently referred to as a COG) exists wherein officials from various localities meet to discuss mutual problems and plan joint, cooperative action. These COGs are often formally very weak, underfunded, poorly staffed, and lacking in any real legislative or taxing power.

SIMULATION

You Are a Restaurant Owner

council of governments
Councils in many areas of the country where officials from various localities meet to discuss mutual problems and plan joint, cooperative action.

STATE AND LOCAL FINANCE POLICY

When a state or local government approves its budget for the next year, the basic policy objectives of the government have also been approved. These objectives are contained in the taxing and spending plans that make up the budget. Lofty speeches

FIGURE 21.8

State Government Revenues and Expenditures

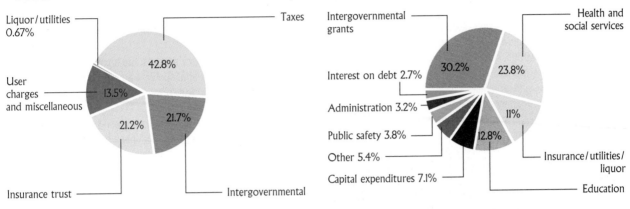

REVENUES   EXPENDITURES

Source: U.S. Bureau of the Census, "State and Local Government Finances, 2004-05," March 7, 2008, *http://www.census.gov/govs/www/estimate05.html.*

can be made and bills passed into law, but without some significant and specific budgetary commitment, a policy will usually have little impact on citizens' lives. Tax-payers increasingly demand more accountability and efficiency from their subnational governments, forcing officials to squeeze services and programs out of limited revenue dollars. Figure 21.8 shows how state governments get their money and how they spend it.

State government revenues are derived from a variety of sources. States receive the largest share of revenue, 42.8 percent, from taxes. States' major sources of tax revenue are sales taxes, income taxes, and motor vehicle and fuel taxes. The second-largest source of state revenue is intergovernmental revenue (21.7 percent)—almost all as grants from the national government. The third major revenue source is state insurance programs (21.2 percent). Charges and fees for services such as state hospitals, college courses, and state parks have become an increasingly important source of revenue for states in the past 20 years (13.5 percent, along with miscellaneous revenue).

Changes in their constitutions over the past 40 years have given states wider access to income and sales taxes and other sources of revenue. Today, 45 states levy a general sales tax; Alaska, Delaware, Montana, New Hampshire, and Oregon are the only holdouts. Only seven states—Alaska, Florida, Nevada, South Dakota, Texas, Washington, and Wyoming—do not have a personal income tax, and New Hampshire and Tennessee have only a limited form of income tax. The modernization of state revenue structures gives the states new money to finance the public programs demanded by citizens.

How do states spend their money? Most of the states' money—about 50 percent—goes to operate state programs (in public safety, education, health and social services, and so on), construct state buildings, and provide direct assistance to individuals. Another 30 percent is allocated as aid to local governments. Since so much of the money that states spend is given to local governments (and since so much of the local governments' revenue comes from the states), the states have even more leverage over the locals than is given to them by Dillon's Rule.

Local government finances can be confusing because of the fragmentation of local governments and the varied ways in which states support and constrain their local authorities. This situation is primarily due to the different ways in which states and their local governments have sorted out the assignment of policy responsibilities

You Are the Mayor and Need to Get a Town Budget Passed

The Fruits of **Devolution**

In the 1980s, President Reagan's revolution of devolving more power and responsibility to the states was well under way. However, few observers foresaw just how important state and local politics and policymaking was becoming.

Throughout the 1990s, state experiments with education, health care, and social welfare policy provided the foundation for national policy change in the late 1990s and 2000s. Meanwhile, governors were increasingly in the national spotlight as potential presidential candidates and possible appointees to executive branch positions. Consider that from 1992 to 2004, voters preferred presidential candidates who were former governors rather than their Washington insider opponents.

Likewise, besides the Iraq War and the war on terrorism, the most prominent national issues have arisen from ongoing debates in the states. From illegal immigration, to abortion, to religion in schools, to same-sex marriage, it has been the actions of state legislatures, state courts, and direct democracy proposals placed on state ballots that have shaped national debate. Meanwhile, state governments have continued to play a primary role in implementing national regulations, including environmental protection, at the same time they have pursued more stringent regulations than those outlined by the national government.

Finally, states have also provided the basis for a gambling revolution in America. Since the 1980s, state governments around the country have increasingly expanded legal gambling in the form of lotteries, tribal casinos, and privately managed casinos. Indeed, there are few areas left in the country where citizens cannot at least buy lottery tickets, and revenues from gambling have given many states new pots of money for spending on basic services, including education. The figure shows that in the state of Indiana, gambling revenues for the state increased from $165.3 million in 1994 to $775 million in 2003. The majority of this revenue goes to the state's Build Indiana Fund, which was created to keep local property taxes down by paying for capital projects in communities across the state.

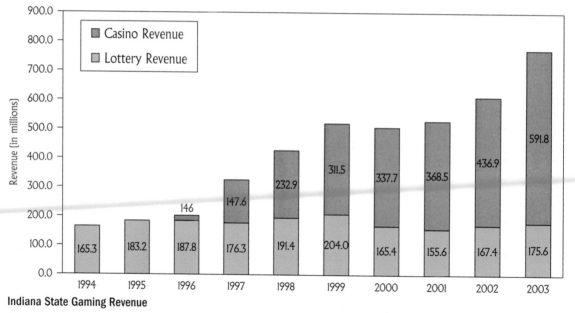

Indiana State Gaming Revenue

Source: Comparative Lottery Analysis: The Impact of Casinos on Lottery Revenues and Total Gaming Revenues, 2004, *www.umassd.edu/cfpa/docs/casinolottery.pdf*.

among local governments. Figure 21.9 offers a snapshot of local government finances—combining county, city, township, school, and special district budgets—across the United States. Local governments receive their revenues from three main sources: taxes, user charges, and intergovernmental aid. Intergovernmental aid (primarily from the states) and "own source" taxes are now about equal in their contribution to local government revenue, again showing the great dependence of local governments on their states. Local taxes are mainly property taxes, but sales and income taxes also contribute to the revenue of some local governments. Charges on the users of certain services, such as libraries and recreation facilities,

FIGURE 21.9

Local Government Revenues and Expenditures

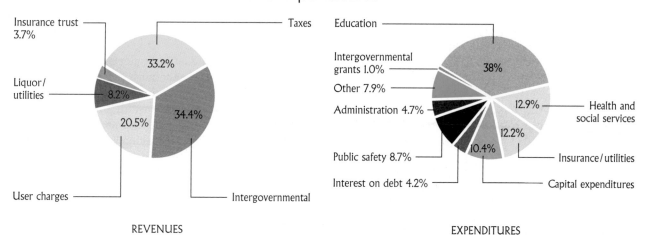

REVENUES   EXPENDITURES

Source: U.S. Bureau of the Census, "State and Local Government Finances, 2004-05," March 7, 2008, *http://www.census.gov/govs/www/estimate05.html.*

YOU ARE THE Policymaker

Should Your State Take a Chance on Gambling?

No one likes taxes, but government services have to be paid for somehow. In the 1980s through 2000s, many states tried to earn money for state programs "painlessly" through legalized gambling. Thirty years ago, only Nevada allowed most forms of gambling; in some states children couldn't even enter a sweepstakes on the back of a cereal box. Today, many states not only allow a variety of types of gambling but even sponsor and earn money from such activities. Various states run lotteries and allow casino and riverboat gambling, horse and dog racing, slot machines, video lottery, bingo, and other forms of what proponents call "gaming."

Suppose you are a state legislator faced with the question of legalizing gambling in your state in order to earn extra revenue without raising taxes. To what extent are you willing to accept the negative aspects of gambling in order to gain its monetary rewards?

States earn money from gambling in two main ways. First, states may run a gambling operation outright. State lotteries are the best example. States skim off as much as 50 percent of the receipts from lottery tickets, offering most of the rest as prize money. Second, states may earn money from gambling by taxing bets and winnings heavily, as is commonly done with casino and racetrack gambling.

This sort of revenue is a very attractive alternative to direct taxation as a way to help states fund public services. First, it is seen as a voluntary source of revenue rather than mandatory taxation. Some characterize it as a tax on stupidity. Second, some forms of gambling are argued to encourage economic development in a local area, thereby being a positive good aside from a

source of revenue. The prosperity that some Native American tribes have gained through opening casinos (allowed by the national government since 1988) is evidence in favor of this position. Third, there are those who view gambling as a harmless recreational activity that the state has no business banning anyway—why not make a little money on it?

Even though dozens of states have legalized and earned money from a wide variety of forms of gambling in the past 20 years, not all states have done so, and not all people are convinced that it is good public policy. One argument against legalized gambling is that it is a regressive form of taxation because the people who gamble the highest proportions of their incomes are those who are relatively poor. There has been increasing concern about compulsive gambling, a psychological disorder akin to alcoholism that drives people to gamble incessantly. Like alcoholism, compulsive gambling can lead to financial ruin and the destruction of families. There are also those who argue that gambling is simply immoral and that legalizing and especially encouraging it (as in state lottery TV commercials) leads people to pursue false hope and a destructive lifestyle. Finally, there is some debate as to just how much money a state can actually earn from gambling, now that it has become so common in the United States.

As a state legislator, you must weigh the benefits of "painless" gambling revenue against the arguments of those who oppose it. Should your state legalize gambling? If so, what form should it adopt? Should it run a lottery? Should it allow casinos and tax them? What difference does it make if neighboring states do or do not have legalized gambling? What would *you* do?

provide another 21 percent of local government revenue. They receive 8 percent of their revenue from the operation of municipally owned utilities and liquor sales.

Local governments allocate their monies to a range of services, but the main areas are public education (38 percent), health and social services (13 percent), and public safety (9 percent). These are services that citizens need on a regular basis and expect local governments to provide.

The difference between state and local expenditures reflects the distribution of public services between these levels of government that has developed over the course of the history of the United States. Local government is expected to provide two of the most important and broadly used services of all government in the United States—education and public safety (police and fire protection). State governments, on the other hand, are mainly in charge of making sure that the poorest of the state's citizens have their basic physical needs met. Further, the state is charged with gathering the state's resources and distributing them where they are most needed via intergovernmental grants. While local governments are busy providing direct citizen service, the state governments can take a broader view to enhance equity in public service.

UNDERSTANDING STATE AND LOCAL GOVERNMENTS

A full understanding of the complexity of subnational government cannot be gleaned from a single textbook chapter, but you should remember a few important points about these 89,476 governments.

DEMOCRACY AT THE SUBNATIONAL LEVEL

The very existence of so many governments to handle complex as well as ordinary—but needed—services, testifies to the health of our democracy. States have been willing to decentralize their governing arrangements to permit the creation of local governments to address citizens' policy demands. Today, local voters choose their own representatives to serve on county commissions, city councils, school boards, and some special district boards. As small legislatures elected from among the community's residents, these governing bodies are usually the policymaking institutions closest and most open to all citizens. In many ways, local governments encourage individual participation in government and promote the value of individualism at the local level.

The states also operate in an open policymaking environment. Many of the most important of state officials are elected to office, far more than in the national government. Direct primaries permit voters to select nominees for state offices. The recall even allows voters to oust an official from office before his or her term is over in about one-third of the states. The initiative and the referendum permit voters in many states to make policy or amend their state constitutions directly. In most states, voters have a far more direct role in selecting judges than is the case in the national court system. And by the 1990s, subnational elections were putting officials into office who are far more representative of the U.S. population demographically than is the case in the national government today or subnational governments in previous years.

Even so, subnational politics may not be as democratic as this initial assessment would seem to indicate. Politics at the state level is poorly covered by the media and, as a result, is relatively invisible to the public. Voters can hardly hold elected officials accountable if they know little about what is going on in the state capital. Even at the local level, there is little press coverage of anything other than the results of city council meetings or a mayor's actions—and that doesn't even happen regularly in smaller communities or in suburbs that lack their own daily newspaper.

When, as is often the case, only 30 to 35 percent of voters participate in statewide elections and fewer than 20 percent turn out for local elections, there are real concerns about the health of our grass-roots governments. In one effort to boost citizen participation, states have begun experimenting with vote-by-mail elections. Instead of having to show up on a specific day to cast a ballot, citizens in Oregon were able to mail in their ballots in 1996, and in 1998 Oregon voters passed an initiative making vote-by-mail the only way to vote for every election. Further, in a small number of cities, including Birmingham, Dayton, Portland, and St. Paul, vigorous programs of neighborhood democracy have been developed where citizen participation in public affairs goes far beyond voting. In these cities, neighborhood boards are given control over meaningful policy decisions and program resources, and their actions are not merely advisory. These cities also reward municipal officials who listen to the views of these neighborhood bodies. The experience in these and other cities shows that citizens will devote the considerable time necessary to participate in public affairs if they are convinced that participation is meaningful and that city officials are not just manipulating them.[73]

Competition between subnational governments for economic development also raises significant questions about democracy. As a result of this competition, state and local governments have subsidized business growth and economic development, often at the cost of slighting redistribution services and human resource needs. Business interests have substantial leverage in state and city affairs as a result of their ability to threaten to leave or locate facilities in another jurisdiction. The increasing importance of money in subnational elections has only added to the influence that special interests exert in state and local affairs.

Comparing State and Local Governments

The workings of democracy are often difficult to see in the judicial branch of government. Because most citizens do not attend trials and only lawyers and judges are directly involved in the appeals process, the proceedings of the judiciary are seldom visible to the public until a significant case or decision is announced. This judicial process is not subject to quite the same scrutiny as the legislative and executive functions of state governments. Even though most state and local judges and justices must face the voters to gain or retain their positions, the lack of information that voters have about the judicial process makes the level of true democracy in this process suspect. Citizens will have to take more interest in the crucial role of courts in our democracy in order for courts to assume the same political importance in states as the other branches of government.

THE SCOPE OF SUBNATIONAL GOVERNMENT

Growth in subnational government employment has proceeded at a pace exceeding that of the national government for most of the past 100 years, as we learned in Chapter 15. Most of this growth has been driven by citizen demand for more government services. Although most American voters want their elected representatives to control the size of government, voters also want government to provide them with more and better programs.

Has the reform and professionalization of subnational government in the past generation made any difference for taxpayers? In most cases, it has not resulted in smaller government. By its very nature, legislative professionalism costs tax dollars and leads to a legislature that is more permanent and continuous. School district consolidation has occurred, reducing the overall number of districts by 66 percent in the past 45 years. This declining number of school districts comes at a time of growing demand for more special district governments, which have increased by over 49 percent in four decades.

Most state governments have experimented with *sunset legislation*, which involves periodically reviewing agencies to control the growth of government and eliminate unneeded programs. States have also empowered their legislatures to review executive branch regulations and rules to ensure that citizens or businesses are not overregulated by government. These practices help limit the scope of governments.

But as citizen demand in the late twentieth century led to growth and development in the areas of technology, communications, and public health and safety, subnational governments have had to grow, not diminish. More police, more health care providers, more computer technicians, and more social welfare caseworkers have been needed to meet the expanding range of problems that confront people daily. Although some local governments are barely able to fulfill their basic responsibilities for public safety and maintenance of the local infrastructure, other cities and counties have become much more competent at managing local affairs. Indeed, recent research suggests that local governments often lead their states and the nation in devising innovative ways to deliver public services.[74]

In sum, with the greater responsibilities thrust on them by the national government and the demands of their citizens, subnational governments have responded by enhancing their capacity to provide services to their citizens. In the past 40 years, the enhanced capacity of democratically elected officials in the states, especially state legislators and governors, and the greater use of direct democracy mechanisms has led to stronger and more effective subnational governments that are also more extensive and expensive.

SUMMARY

Our nation's 50 states and its tens of thousands of local governments are responsible for most public policies with which we are most familiar: education, fire protection, police protection, highway maintenance, public welfare, public health, and trash collection. The states are a diverse group, but each has a government that makes, enforces, and interprets laws for its citizens. The structure for state governments is specified in state constitutions—some very long, others quite short. Citizens may modify these state constitutions when necessary to keep pace with changing demands of government.

State legislatures include elected representatives who make laws, appropriate money, oversee the executive branch, perform casework, and help manage conflict across the state. Legislators are increasingly diverse demographically, but most tend to be from a somewhat higher socioeconomic position than the majority of the people they represent. Significant turnover takes place in state legislatures, and voters in some states have ensured that this will continue by enacting term limits for their public officials.

The governors of our states are elected to administer public policy and to attend to citizen needs. Once in office, a governor directs a complex set of state government institutions and programs, conducts state affairs with other governors and the president, initiates much of the legislation state legislatures will adopt, and helps manage conflict. Governors must often work with a number of other elected executive officials to produce public policy.

The state court systems are similar in organization to national courts. Most states have trial courts, intermediate courts of appeal, and a court of last resort; all have jurisdiction over both civil and criminal cases. Judges may attain office through appointment, election, or a hybrid of both known as the Merit Plan. The actions of state judges, especially those serving on the court of last resort, can affect policy significantly.

Local governments in the United States—counties, municipalities, townships, school districts, and special districts—were established by the states to decide on and administer policy in limited geographic and policy areas. Most cities are run by city councils with either a mayor or a city manager directing the day-to-day affairs of city bureaucracies. Counties and townships help states perform many local functions, such as record keeping and the administration of justice. School districts run public schools, and special districts provide limited services for multiple communities. The existence of nearly 88,000 local governments indicates that democracy truly thrives at the local level in the United States.

Chapter Test

Multiple Choice

1. Which of the following is NOT true for state constitutions?
   a. They provide for separation of power
   b. They create executive, legislative, and judicial branches
   c. They include a bill of rights
   d. They were all written well over 100 years ago
   e. They take precedence over state law

2. Roughly what percentage of proposed amendments to state constitutions was ratified by the voters between 1898 and 1998?
   a. 80 percent
   b. 60 percent
   c. 40 percent
   d. 20 percent
   e. Less than 20 percent

3. Which of the following U.S. Supreme Court decisions required the districts of state legislatures to be based on the number of people who live in the state?
   a. *Baker v. Carr*
   b. *Reynolds v. Sims*
   c. *Simon v. Harris*
   d. Both a and b
   e. None of the above

4. The term "divided government" exists when:
   a. The level of turnover in state legislatures increases
   b. A single party does not control both chambers of the state legislature and the governor's office
   c. When the two parties in a state legislature do not agree on a particular policy
   d. The division of state government into executive, legislative, and judicial branches
   e. The competition for state legislature positions increases

5. According to the so-called "Merit Plan," the process of choosing judges is as follows:
   a. The governor appoints a judge from a list of recommendations by the state bar or a committee; the judge serves a "trial run"; the judge runs against other candidates in a statewide election; the winner serves a 6- to 12-year term
   b. The governor appoints a judge from a list of recommendations by the state bar or a committee; the judge serves a "trial run"; voters are asked to vote for or against the retention of that judge; if retained, the judge serves a 6- to 12-year term
   c. The governor independently appoints a judge s/he deems suitable; the judge serves a "trial run"; voters are asked to vote for or against the retention of that judge; if retained, the judge serves a 6- to 12-year term
   d. Candidates decide to run for the position of judge; in a statewide election, voters choose their preferred candidate; that judge serves a 6- to 12-year term

   e. The governor appoints a judge from a list of recommendations by the state bar or a committee; that judge serves a 6- to 12-year term

6. Which of the following is NOT a procedure of direct democracy?
   a. The initiative
   b. The referendum
   c. The recall
   d. Legislative elections
   e. All of the above are forms of direct democracy

7. All but which of the following are types of local government?
   a. Counties
   b. Townships
   c. Mayor-council government
   d. Municipalities
   e. School districts

8. Which is the largest share of revenue for states?
   a. Intergovernmental revenue
   b. State insurance programs
   c. Traffic and parking tickets
   d. Taxes
   e. Federal grants

9. Local governments spend the largest percentage of their budget on:
   a. Health services
   b. Social services
   c. Public education
   d. Public safety
   e. The local economy

10. The periodic redrawing of legislative districts occurs every:
    a. 15 years
    b. 12 years
    c. 10 years
    d. 6 years
    e. 4 years

11. Which of the following is NOT one of the formal powers of the governor?
    a. The governor has veto power
    b. The governor frequently has line-item veto power
    c. The governor usually initiates the state budget process
    d. The governor can sign trade agreements between his/her state and foreign nations
    e. All of the above are formal powers

True/False

12. Over the past four decades, national power has increased vis-à-vis state power.
    True_____   False_____

13. In Southern states, state constitutions tend to be longer and more particularistic.
    True_____   False_____

14. In terms of ideology, partisanship, and demographics, state officials are much more representative of the general population than national officials.
    True_____   False_____

15. In state legislatures, significant turnover of people holding office is the exception rather than the rule.
    True_____   False_____

16. Ninety-eight percent of all litigation in the United States is settled in state courts.
    True_____   False_____

17. The United States plays a much stronger role in guiding urban development than do the nations of Europe.
    True_____   False_____

18. Due to the nature of the electoral system, state officials can be said to be much more responsive to voter preferences than national officials.
    True_____   False_____

19. By far the best predictor of the outcome of gubernatorial races is the partisanship of the state as a whole.
    True_____   False_____

20. The media is more likely to cover state legislatures than the national legislature.
    True_____   False_____

Short Answer

21. List and briefly explain at least three of a governor's informal (or personal) powers.

22. Define the term "legislative professionalism" and outline the three major areas in which changes have taken place to achieve it.

23. What are intermediate courts of appeal, why have they been established, and how do they work?

24. Explain the process of the initiative, including all the different steps involved.

25. What does "Dillon's Rule" stipulate?

26. What is the so-called "home rule" in the context of state and local government?

27. In your own words, explain what is meant when this textbook states that gubernatorial races have been "presidentialized." How would you personally assess such a development in terms of its implications for state politics?

28. What role has television played in gubernatorial races? Discuss at least three different elements. In your opinion, is this a positive development? Why, or why not?

29. What are the arguments in favor of and against "legislative professionalism" and "citizen legislature," respectively? Which do you favor, and why?

30. This textbook points out that the "power of local government arises from informal political clout rather than formal powers." What are the two main sources of this kind of power?

Short Answer/Essay Questions

31. This textbook states that state officials are more representative of their constituents in terms of demographics, ideology, and partisanship than their national counterparts. Using what you know about state and national politics, what are at least three different explanations for this? In addition, how do you believe this affects policymaking?

32. This textbook refers to the "modern" governor on several occasions. What are the characteristics of such modern governors as opposed to the more traditional roles? Based on what you remember from previous chapters, in what ways does the changing nature of the governor's position resemble the changing nature of the presidency? Please provide examples to illustrate your arguments.

33. What do you know about the ways in which state legislatures regulate term limits? What are the pros and cons of instituting term limits (at least two each)? In your opinion, should state legislatures have term limits? Why, or why not? And what should those term limits be?

Answer Key

1. D   2. C   3. D   4. B   5. B   6. D   7. C   8. D   9. C   10. C   11. D   12. False   13. True   14. True   15. False   16. True   17. False   18. True   19. False   20. False

Key Terms

subnational governments (662)
line-item veto (674)
lieutenant governor (676)
Merit Plan (681)
direct democracy (682)

initiative (682)
referendum (683)
recall (683)
Dillon's Rule (684)
local charter (685)

home rule (685)
town meeting (686)
city manager (687)
council of governments (692)

Internet Resources

http://www.csg.org/
Web site of the Council of State Governments, with information on states and state public policies.

www.ncsl.org/
Web site of the National Conference of State Legislatures, with information on state legislatures, elections, and members.

www.ncsconline.org
Web site of the National Center for State Courts.

www.nga.org/
Web site of the National Governors' Association, with links to Web sites for each state.

www.usmayors.org/
Web site of the U.S. Conference of Mayors.

www.census.gov/
Web site of the U.S. Census Bureau, with links to sites with data on states and local areas.

www.stateline.org/
Web site of the Pew Center on the States, with lots of general and state-specific policy information.

GetConnected

State Legislatures

After reading this chapter, it should be clear to you that state and local government officials regularly make decisions that affect you. And although many citizens can name officials in the national government, such as the president, most of us do not know the names of our representatives in the state legislature. Indeed, in most states each citizen has two representatives in the state legislature, one in a lower chamber (usually called the assembly or house) and one in the upper chamber (usually called the senate). Let us take a closer look at the legislature in your state.

Search the Web

To find your state legislator or to track bills before your state legislature, go to your state's official government Web site or locate your state legislative home page through *www.ncsl.org/* (click on "Legislatures"), a Web site established by the National Council of State Legislatures for this purpose. Once you locate your state legislative home page, select the directory for the lower or upper chamber and enter your address or ZIP code. All of the state Web sites differ, but on most sites you can locate biographical information about your representative, voting records, and his or her committee assignments and sponsored legislation. On most sites you can also track the progress of bills through the legislature by searching under key words, legislative sponsor, or bill number. Often you can find the text of legislative debate on a given bill through the chamber's official journal or calendar. If one issue interests you, state legislative Web sites will allow you to track similar bills in several states during the year.

Questions to Ask

- If your state's Web site is fairly complete, you should be able to develop an opinion about your legislator's voting record. What is your assessment of this record in terms of voting attendance and vote choices?
- In your view, is your legislator representing the views of citizens in your district?
- Does your legislator sponsor legislation or cast votes in a manner that supports your positions on issues?
- Does legislation sponsored by your legislator tend to pass or fail in a vote of the chamber?
- How do your legislator's committee assignments enhance the interests of your district?
- In comparing similar legislation across states, did the outcomes differ (did the legislation pass in one state and fail in another)?

Why It Matters

In a representative democracy, we elect representatives to serve in official positions and to speak for our interests. Each state has a legislature with representatives elected from districts. The expectation is that legislators will serve the constituents of their districts in the legislature. Many constituents may not be concerned about every issue facing the legislature, but each legislator is still expected to discern the district's interests and behave accordingly in the legislature. If a constituent has a specific problem that can be addressed by government, such as a concern about the safety of a nearby prison facility, he or she should have the attention of the state legislator on the issue.

Get Involved

Many constituents contact their legislators over the phone or by mail. As a citizen, you should tell your legislator about the issues you think are important by calling, e-mailing, or mailing your ideas. For more exercises, go to *www.longmanamericangovernment.com.*

For Further Reading

Beyle, Thad L. *Governors and Hard Times.* Washington, DC: Congressional Quarterly Press, 1992. A timely monograph on the modern governor by one of the country's leading experts.

The Council of State Governments. *The Book of the States* (annual). Lexington, KY: Council of State Governments. An overview of annual developments in state government.

Gray, Virginia, and Russell L. Hanson, eds. *Politics in the American States: A Comparative Analysis.* 8th ed. Washington, DC: Congressional Quarterly Press, 2004. A superb collection of essays that review the empirical literature on state politics.

Hedge, David M. *Governance and the Changing American States: Transforming American Politics.* Washington, DC: Congressional Quarterly Press, 1998. An in-depth and balanced assessment of the literature on the resurgence of state government institutions.

Hovey, Hal A., and Kendra A. Hovey. *CQ's State Fact Finder: Rankings Across America* (annual). Washington, DC: Congressional Quarterly Press. A data book with hundreds of state-by-state comparisons on economic, demographic, political, and policy variables.

International City/County Management Association. *The Municipal Year Book.* Washington, DC: ICMA (annual).

Excellent current affairs updates on local governments and informative directories on civic affairs and public officials.

Nelson, Albert J. *Emerging Influentials in State Legislatures: Women, Blacks, and Hispanics.* New York: Praeger, 1991. Explores the power of minority and women legislators by focusing on their representation, turnover, and influence within party leadership and as chairs of committees.

Rosenthal, Alan. *The Decline of Representative Democracy: Process, Participation, and Power in State Legislatures.* Washington, DC: Congressional Quarterly Press, 1998.

A detailed examination and evaluation of the state legislatures at the end of the millennium by the leading analyst of those bodies.

Weber, Ronald E., and Paul Brace, eds. *American State and Local Politics: Directions for the 21st Century.* Chatham, NJ: Chatham House, 1999. A collection of essays by top scholars focusing on recent reforms and their implications.

Welch, Susan, and Timothy Bledsoe. *Urban Reform and Its Consequences: A Study in Representation.* Chicago: University of Chicago Press, 1988. An important review and analysis of urban government today.

APPENDIX

THE DECLARATION OF INDEPENDENCE*

In Congress, July 4, 1776

The Unanimous Declaration of the Thirteen United States of America

When in the Course of human events it becomes necessary for one people to dissolve the political bands which have connected them with another, and to assume among the powers of the earth, the separate and equal station to which the Laws of Nature and of Nature's God entitle them, a decent respect to the opinions of mankind requires that they should declare the causes which impel them to the separation.

We hold these truths to be self-evident, that all men are created equal, that they are endowed by their Creator with certain unalienable Rights, that among these are Life, Liberty and the pursuit of Happiness.— That to secure these rights, Governments are instituted among Men, deriving their just powers from the consent of the governed,—That whenever any Form of Government becomes destructive of these ends, it is the Right of the People to alter or to abolish it, and to institute new Government, laying its foundation on such principles and organizing its powers in such form, as to them shall seem most likely to effect their Safety and Happiness. Prudence, indeed, will dictate that Governments long established should not be changed for light and transient causes; and accordingly all experience hath shewn that mankind are more disposed to suffer, while evils are sufferable, than to right themselves by abolishing the forms to which they are accustomed. But when a long train of abuses and usurpations, pursuing invariably the same Object evinces a design to reduce them under absolute Despotism, it is their right, it is their duty, to throw off such Government, and to provide new Guards for their future security.

Such has been the patient sufferance of these Colonies; and such is now the necessity which constrains them to alter their former Systems of Government. The history of the present King of Great Britain is a history of repeated injuries and usurpations, all having in direct object the establishment of an absolute Tyranny over these States. To prove this, let Facts be submitted to a candid world.

He has refused his Assent to Laws, the most wholesome and necessary for the public good.

He has forbidden his Governors to pass Laws of immediate and pressing importance, unless suspended in their operation till his Assent should be obtained; and when so suspended, he has utterly neglected to attend to them.

He has refused to pass other Laws for the accommodation of large districts of people, unless those people would relinquish the right of Representation in the Legislature, a right inestimable to them and formidable to tyrants only.

He has called together legislative bodies at places unusual, uncomfortable, and distant from the depository of their Public Records, for the sole purpose of fatiguing them into compliance with his measures.

He has dissolved Representative Houses repeatedly, for opposing with manly firmness his invasions on the rights of the people.

He has refused for a long time, after such dissolutions, to cause others to be elected; whereby the

---

*This text retains the spelling, capitalization, and punctuation of the original.

Legislative Powers, incapable of Annihilation, have returned to the People at large for their exercise; the State remaining in the mean time exposed to all the dangers of invasion from without, and convulsions within.

He has endeavored to prevent the population of these States; for that purpose obstructing the Laws for Naturalization of Foreigners; refusing to pass others to encourage their migration hither, and raising the conditions of new Appropriations of Lands.

He has obstructed the Administration of Justice, by refusing his Assent to Laws for establishing Judiciary powers.

He has made Judges dependent on his Will alone, for the tenure of their offices, and the amount and payment of their salaries.

He has erected a multitude of New Offices, and sent hither swarms of Officers to harass our people, and eat out their substance.

He has kept among us, in times of peace, Standing Armies without the Consent of our legislatures.

He has affected to render the Military independent of and superior to the Civil power.

He has combined with others to subject us to a jurisdiction foreign to our constitution, and unacknowledged by our laws; giving his Assent to their Acts of pretended Legislation:

For quartering large bodies of armed troops among us:

For protecting them, by a mock Trial, from punishment for any Murders which they should commit on the Inhabitants of these States:

For cutting off our Trade with all parts of the world:

For imposing Taxes on us without our Consent:

For depriving us in many cases, of the benefits of Trial by Jury:

For transporting us beyond Seas to be tried for pretended offences:

For abolishing the free System of English Laws in a neighboring Province, establishing therein an Arbitrary government, and enlarging its Boundaries so as to render it at once an example and fit instrument for introducing the same absolute rule into these Colonies:

For taking away our Charters, abolishing our most valuable Laws, and altering fundamentally the Forms of our Governments:

For suspending our own Legislatures, and declaring themselves invested with power to legislate for us in all cases whatsoever.

He has abdicated Government here, by declaring us out of his Protection and waging War against us.

He has plundered our seas, ravaged our Coasts, burnt our towns, and destroyed the lives of our people.

He is at this time transporting large Armies of foreign Mercenaries to compleat the works of death, desolation and tyranny, already begun with circumstances of Cruelty & perfidy scarcely paralleled in the most barbarous ages, and totally unworthy the Head of a civilized nation.

He has constrained our fellow Citizens taken Captive on the high Seas to bear Arms against their Country, to become the executioners of their friends and Brethren, or to fall themselves by their Hands.

He has excited domestic insurrections amongst us, and has endeavored to bring on the inhabitants of our frontiers, the merciless Indian Savages, whose known rule of warfare, is an undistinguished destruction of all ages, sexes and conditions.

In every stage of these Oppressions We have Petitioned for Redress in the most humble terms: Our repeated Petitions have been answered only by repeated injury. A Prince, whose character is thus marked by every act which may define a Tyrant, is unfit to be the ruler of a free people.

Nor have We been wanting in attention to our British brethren. We have warned them from time to time of attempts by their legislature to extend an unwarrantable jurisdiction over us. We have reminded them of the circumstances of our emigration and settlement here. We have appealed to their native justice and magnanimity, and we have conjured them by the ties of our common kindred to disavow these usurpations, which would inevitably interrupt our connections and correspondence. They too have been deaf to the voice of justice and consanguinity. We must, therefore, acquiesce in the necessity, which denounces our Separation, and hold them, as we hold the rest of mankind, Enemies in War, in Peace Friends.

We, therefore, the Representatives of the United States of America, in General Congress, Assembled, appealing to the Supreme Judge of the world for the rectitude of our intentions, do, in the Name, and by Authority of the good People of these Colonies, solemnly publish and declare, That these United Colonies are, and of Right ought to be Free and Independent States; that they are Absolved from all Allegiance to the British Crown, and that all political connection between them and the State of Great Britain, is and ought to be totally dissolved; and that as Free and Independent States, they have full Power to levy War, conclude Peace, contract Alliances, establish Commerce, and to do all other Acts and Things which Independent States may of right do. And for the support of this Declaration, with a firm reliance on the protection of divine Providence, we mutually pledge to each other our Lives, our Fortunes and our sacred Honor.

John Hancock

NEW HAMPSHIRE
Josiah Bartlett,
Wm. Whipple,
Matthew Thornton.

MASSACHUSETTS BAY
Saml. Adams,
John Adams,
Robt. Treat Paine,
Elbridge Gerry.

RHODE ISLAND
Step. Hopkins,
William Ellery.

CONNECTICUT
Roger Sherman,
Samuel Huntington,
Wm. Williams,
Oliver Wolcott.

NEW YORK
Wm. Floyd,
Phil. Livingston,
Frans. Lewis,
Lewis Morris.

NEW JERSEY
Richd. Stockton,
Jno. Witherspoon,
Fras. Hopkinson,
John Hart,
Abra. Clark.

PENNSYLVANIA
Robt. Morris,
Benjamin Rush,
Benjamin Franklin,
John Morton,
Geo. Clymer,
Jas. Smith,
Geo. Taylor,
James Wilson,
Geo. Ross.

DELAWARE
Caesar Rodney,
Geo. Read,
Tho. M'kean.

MARYLAND
Samuel Chase,
Wm. Paca,
Thos. Stone,
Charles Caroll of
Carrollton.

VIRGINIA
George Wythe,
Richard Henry Lee,
Th. Jefferson,
Benjamin Harrison,
Thos. Nelson, jr.,
Francis Lightfoot Lee,
Carter Braxton.

NORTH CAROLINA
Wm. Hooper,
Joseph Hewes,
John Penn.

SOUTH CAROLINA
Edward Rutledge,
Thos. Heyward, Junr.,
Thomas Lynch, jnr.,
Arthur Middleton.

GEORGIA
Button Gwinnett,
Lyman Hall,
Geo. Walton.

THE FEDERALIST NO. 10

James Madison

November 22, 1787

To the People of the State of New York.

Among the numerous advantages promised by a well constructed Union, none deserves to be more accurately developed than its tendency to break and control the violence of faction. The friend of popular governments, never finds himself so much alarmed for their character and fate, as when he contemplates their propensity to this dangerous vice. He will not fail therefore to set a due value on any plan which, without violating the principles to which he is attached, provides a proper cure for it. The instability, injustice and confusion introduced into the public councils, have in truth been the mortal diseases under which popular governments have every where perished; as they continue to be the favorite and fruitful topics from which the adversaries to liberty derive their most specious declamations. The valuable improvements made by the American Constitutions on the popular models, both ancient and modern, cannot certainly be too much admired; but it would be an unwarrantable partiality, to contend that they have as effectually obviated the danger on this side as was wished and expected. Complaints are every where heard from our most considerate and virtuous citizens, equally the friends of public and private faith, and of public and personal liberty; that our governments are too unstable; that the public good is disregarded in the conflicts of rival parties; and that measures are too often decided, not according to the rules of justice, and the rights of the minor party; but by the superior force of an interested and over-bearing majority. However anxiously we may wish that these complaints had no foundation, the evidence of known facts will not permit us to deny that they are in some degree true. It will be found indeed, on a candid review of our situation, that some of the distresses under which we labor, have been erroneously charged on the operation of our governments; but it will be found, at the same time, that other causes will not alone account for many of our heaviest misfortunes; and particularly, for that prevailing and increasing distrust of public engagements, and alarm for private rights, which are echoed from one end of the continent to the other. These must be chiefly, if not wholly, effects of the unsteadiness and injustice, with which a factious spirit has tainted our public administrations.

By a faction I understand a number of citizens, whether amounting to a majority or minority of the whole, who are united and actuated by some common impulse of passion, or of interest, adverse to the rights of other citizens, or to the permanent and aggregate interests of the community.

There are two methods of curing the mischiefs of faction: the one, by removing its causes; the other, by controlling its effects.

There are again two methods of removing the causes of faction: the one by destroying the liberty which is essential to its existence; the other, by giving to every citizen the same opinions, the same passions, and the same interests.

It could never be more truly said than of the first remedy, that it is worse than the disease. Liberty is to faction, what air is to fire, an aliment without which it instantly expires. But it could not be a less folly to abolish liberty, which is essential to political life, because it nourishes faction, than it would be to wish the annihilation of air, which is essential to animal life, because it imparts to fire its destructive agency.

The second expedient is as impracticable, as the first would be unwise. As long as the reason of man continues fallible, and he is at liberty to exercise it, different opinions will be formed. As long as the connection subsists between his reason and his self-love, his opinions and his passions will have a reciprocal influence on each other; and the former will be objects to which the latter will attach themselves. The diversity in the faculties of men from which the rights of property originate, is not less an insuperable obstacle to a uniformity of interests. The protection of these faculties is the first object of Government. From the protection of different and unequal faculties of acquiring property, the possession of different degrees and kinds of property immediately results: and from the influence of these on the sentiments and views of the respective proprietors, ensues a division of the society into different interests and parties.

The latent causes of faction are thus sown in the nature of man; and we see them every where brought into different degrees of activity, according to the different circumstances of civil society. A zeal for different opinions concerning religion, concerning Government and many other points, as well of speculation as of practice; an attachment to different leaders ambitiously contending for pre-eminence and power; or to persons of other descriptions whose fortunes have been interesting to the human passions, have in turn divided mankind into parties, inflamed them with mutual animosity, and rendered them much more disposed to vex and oppress each other, than to co-operate for their common good. So strong is this propensity of mankind to fall into mutual animosities, that where no substantial occasion presents itself, the most frivolous and fanciful distinctions have been sufficient to kindle their unfriendly passions, and excite their most violent conflicts. But the most common and durable source of factions, has been the various and unequal distribution of property. Those who hold, and those who are without property, have ever formed distinct interests in society. Those who are creditors, and those who are debtors, fall under a like discrimination. A landed interest, a manufacturing interest, a mercantile interest, a monied interest, with many lesser interests, grow up of necessity in civilized nations, and divide them into different classes, actuated by different sentiments and views. The regulation of these various and interfering interests forms the principal task of modern Legislation, and involves the spirit of party and faction in the necessary and ordinary operations of Government.

No man is allowed to be a judge in his own cause; because his interest would certainly bias his judgment, and, not improbably, corrupt his integrity. With equal, nay with greater reason, a body of men, are unfit to be both judges and parties, at the same time; yet, what are many of the most important acts of legislation, but so many judicial determinations, not indeed concerning the rights of single persons, but concerning the rights of large bodies of citizens, and what are the different classes of legislators, but advocates and parties to the causes which they determine? Is a law proposed concerning private debts? It is a question to which the creditors are parties on one side, and the debtors on the other. Justice ought to hold the balance between them. Yet the parties are and must be themselves the judges; and the most numerous party, or, in other words, the most powerful faction must be expected to prevail. Shall domestic manufactures be encouraged, and in what degree, by restrictions on foreign manufactures? are questions which would be differently decided by the landed and the manufacturing classes; and probably by neither, with a sole regard to justice and the public good. The apportionment of taxes on the various descriptions of property, is an act which seems to require the most exact impartiality; yet, there is perhaps no legislative act in which greater opportunity and temptation are given to a predominant party, to trample on the rules of justice. Every shilling with which they over-burden the inferior number, is a shilling saved to their own pockets.

It is in vain to say, that enlightened statesmen will be able to adjust these clashing interests, and render them all subservient to the public good. Enlightened statesmen will not always be at the helm: Nor, in many cases, can such an adjustment be made at all, without taking into view indirect and remote considerations, which will rarely prevail over the immediate interest which one party may find in disregarding the rights of another, or the good of the whole.

The inference to which we are brought, is, that the causes of faction cannot be removed; and that relief is only to be sought in the means of controlling its effects.

If a faction consists of less than a majority, relief is supplied by the republican principle, which enables the majority to defeat its sinister views by regular vote: It may clog the administration, it may convulse the society; but it will be unable to execute and mask its violence under the forms of the Constitution. When a majority is included in a faction, the form of popular government on the other hand enables it to sacrifice to its ruling passion or interest, both the public good and the rights of other citizens. To secure the public good, and private rights, against the danger of such a faction, and at the same time to preserve the spirit and the form of popular government, is then the great object to which our enquiries are directed: Let me add that it is the great desideratum, by which alone this form of government can be rescued from the opprobrium under which it has so long labored, and be recommended to the esteem and adoption of mankind.

By what means is this object attainable? Evidently by one of two only. Either the existence of the same passion or interest in a majority at the same time, must be prevented; or the majority, having such co-existent passion or interest, must be rendered, by their number and local situation, unable to concert and carry into effect schemes of oppression. If the impulse and the opportunity be suffered to coincide, we well know that neither moral nor religious motives can be relied on as an adequate control. They are not found to be such on the injustice and violence of individuals, and lose their efficacy in proportion to the number combined together; that is, in proportion as their efficacy becomes needful.

From this view of the subject, it may be concluded, that a pure Democracy, by which I mean, a Society, consisting of a small number of citizens, who assemble and administer the Government in person, can admit of no cure for the mischiefs of faction. A common passion or interest will, in almost every case, be felt by a majority of the whole; a communication and concert results from the form of Government itself; and there is nothing to check the inducements to sacrifice the weaker party, or an obnoxious individual. Hence it is, that such Democracies have ever been spectacles of turbulence and contention; have ever been found incompatible with personal security, or the rights of property; and have in general been as short in their lives, as they have been violent in their deaths. Theoretic politicians, who have patronized this species of Government, have erroneously supposed, that by reducing mankind to a perfect equality in their political rights, they would, at the same time, be perfectly equalized and assimilated in their possessions, their opinions, and their passions.

A republic, by which I mean a government in which the scheme of representation takes place, opens a different prospect, and promises the cure for which we are seeking. Let us examine the points in which it varies from pure democracy, and we shall comprehend both the nature of the cure and the efficacy which it must derive from the union.

The two great points of difference, between a democracy and a republic, are, first, the delegation of the government, in the latter, to a small number of citizens, elected by the rest; secondly, the greater number of citizens, and greater sphere of country, over which the latter may be extended.

The effect of the first difference is, on the one hand, to refine and enlarge the public views, by passing them through the medium of a chosen body of citizens, whose wisdom may best discern the true interest of their country, and whose patriotism and love of justice, will be least likely to sacrifice it to temporary or partial considerations. Under such a regulation, it may well happen, that the public voice, pronounced by the representatives of the people, will be more consonant to the public good, than if pronounced by the people themselves, convened for the purpose. On the other hand the effect may be inverted. Men of factious tempers, of local prejudices, or of sinister designs, may by intrigue, by corruption, or by other means, first obtain the suffrages, and then betray the interest of the people. The question resulting is, whether small or extensive republics are most favorable to the election of proper guardians of the public weal, and it is clearly decided in favor of the latter by two obvious considerations.

In the first place, it is to be remarked that, however small the republic may be, the representatives must be raised to a certain number, in order to guard against the cabals of a few; and that however large it may be, they must be limited to a certain number, in order to guard against the confusion of a multitude. Hence, the number of representatives in the two cases not being in proportion to that of the constituents, and being proportionally greatest in the small republic, it follows, that if the proportion of fit characters be not less in the large than in the small republic, the former will present a greater option, and consequently a greater probability of a fit choice.

In the next place, as each Representative will be chosen by a greater number of citizens in the large than in the small Republic, it will be more difficult for unworthy candidates to practise with success the vicious arts, by which elections are too often carried; and the suffrages of the people being more free, will be more likely to center on men who possess the most attractive merit, and the most diffusive and established characters.

It must be confessed, that in this, as in most other cases, there is a mean, on both sides of which inconveniences will be found to lie. By enlarging too much the number of electors, you render the representative too little acquainted with all their local circumstances and lesser interests; as by reducing it too much, you render him unduly attached to these, and too little fit to comprehend and pursue great and national objects. The Federal Constitution forms a happy combination in this respect; the great and aggregate interests being referred to the national, the local and particular, to the state legislatures.

The other point of difference is, the greater number of citizens and extent of territory which may be brought within the compass of Republican, than of Democratic Government; and it is this circumstance principally which renders factious combinations less to be dreaded in the former, than in the latter. The smaller the society, the fewer probably will be the distinct parties and interests composing it; the fewer the distinct parties and interests, the more frequently will a majority be found of the same party; and the smaller the number of individuals composing a majority, and the smaller the compass within which they are placed, the more easily will they concert and execute their plans of oppression. Extend the sphere, and you take in a greater variety of parties and interests; you make it less probable that a majority of the whole will have a common motive to invade the rights of other citizens; or if such a common motive exists, it will be more difficult for all who feel it to discover their own strength, and to act in unison with each other. Besides other impediments, it may be remarked, that where there is a consciousness of unjust or dishonorable purposes, communication is always checked by distrust, in proportion to the number whose concurrence is necessary.

Hence it clearly appears, that the same advantage, which a Republic has over a Democracy, in controlling the effects of faction, is enjoyed by a large over a small Republic—is enjoyed by the Union over the States composing it. Does this advantage consist in the substitution of Representatives, whose enlightened views and virtuous sentiments render them superior to local prejudices, and to schemes of injustice? It will not be denied, that the Representation of the Union will be most likely to possess these requisite endowments. Does it consist in the greater security afforded by a greater variety of parties, against the event of any one party being able to outnumber and oppress the rest? In an equal degree does the increased variety of parties, comprised within the Union, increase this security? Does it, in fine, consist in the greater obstacles opposed to the concert and accomplishment of the secret wishes of an unjust and interested majority? Here, again, the extent of the Union gives it the most palpable advantage.

The influence of factious leaders may kindle a flame within their particular States, but will be unable to spread a general conflagration through the other States: a religious sect may degenerate into a political faction in a part of the Confederacy but the variety of sects dispersed over the entire face of it, must secure the national Councils against any danger from that source: a rage for paper money, for an abolition of debts, for an equal division of property, or for any other improper or wicked project, will be less apt to pervade the whole body of the Union, than a particular member of it; in the same proportion as such a malady is more likely to taint a particular county or district, than an entire State.

In the extent and proper structure of the Union, therefore, we behold a Republican remedy for the diseases most incident to Republican Government. And according to the degree of pleasure and pride, we feel in being Republicans, ought to be our zeal in cherishing the spirit, and supporting the character of Federalists.

PUBLIUS

THE FEDERALIST NO. 51

James Madison

February 6, 1788

To the People of the State of New York.

To what expedient then shall we finally resort for maintaining in practice the necessary partition of power among the several departments, as laid down in the constitution? The only answer that can be given is, that as all these exterior provisions are found to be inadequate, the defect must be supplied, by so contriving the interior structure of the government, as that its several constituent parts may, by their mutual relations, be the means of keeping each other in their proper places. Without presuming to undertake a full development of this important idea, I will hazard a few general observations, which may perhaps place it in a clearer light, and enable us to form a more correct judgment of the principles and structure of the government planned by the convention.

In order to lay a due foundation for that separate and distinct exercise of the different powers of government, which to a certain extent, is admitted on all hands to be essential to the preservation of liberty, it is evident that each department should have a will of its own; and consequently should be so constituted, that the members of each should have as little agency as possible in the appointment of the members of the others. Were this principle rigorously adhered to, it would require that all the appointments for the supreme executive, legislative, and judiciary magistracies, should be drawn from the same fountain of authority, the people, through channels, having no communication whatever with one another. Perhaps such a plan of constructing the several departments would be less difficult in practice than it may in contemplation appear. Some difficulties however, and some additional expense, would attend the execution of it. Some deviations therefore from the principle must be admitted. In the constitution of the judiciary department in particular, it might be inexpedient to insist rigorously on the principle; first, because peculiar qualifications being essential in the members, the primary consideration ought to be to select that mode of choice, which best secures these qualifications; secondly, because the permanent tenure by which the appointments are held in that department, must soon destroy all sense of dependence on the authority conferring them.

It is equally evident that the members of each department should be as little dependent as possible on those of the others, for the emoluments annexed to their offices. Were the executive magistrate, or the judges, not independent of the legislature in this particular, their independence in every other would be merely nominal.

But the great security against a gradual concentration of the several powers in the same department, consists in giving to those who administer each department, the necessary constitutional means, and personal motives, to resist encroachments of the others. The provision for defense must in this, as in all other cases, be made commensurate to the danger of attack. Ambition must be made to counteract ambition. The interest of the man must be connected with the constitutional right of the place. It may be a reflection on human nature, that such devices should be necessary to control the abuses of government. But what is government itself but the greatest of all reflections on human nature? If men were angels, no government would be necessary. If angels were to govern men, neither external nor internal controls on government would be necessary. In framing a government which is to be administered by men over men, the great difficulty lies in this: You must first enable the government to control the governed; and in the next place, oblige it to control itself. A dependence on the people is no doubt the primary control on the government; but experience has taught mankind the necessity of auxiliary precautions.

This policy of supplying by opposite and rival interests, the defect of better motives, might be traced through the whole system of human affairs, private as well as public. We see it particularly displayed in all the subordinate distributions of power; where the constant aim is to divide and arrange the several offices in such a manner as that each may be a check on the other; that the private interest of every individual, may be a sentinel over the public rights. These inventions of prudence cannot be less requisite in the distribution of the supreme powers of the state.

But it is not possible to give to each department an equal power of self defense. In republican government

the legislative authority, necessarily, predominates. The remedy for this inconveniency is, to divide the legislature into different branches; and to render them by different modes of election, and different principles of action, as little connected with each other, as the nature of their common functions, and their common dependence on the society, will admit. It may even be necessary to guard against dangerous encroachments by still further precautions. As the weight of the legislative authority requires that it should be thus divided, the weakness of the executive may require, on the other hand, that it should be fortified. An absolute negative, on the legislature, appears at first view to be the natural defense with which the executive magistrate should be armed. But perhaps it would be neither altogether safe, nor alone sufficient. On ordinary occasions, it might not be exerted with the requisite firmness; and on extraordinary occasions, it might be perfidiously abused. May not this defect of an absolute negative be supplied, by some qualified connection between this weaker department, and the weaker branch of the stronger department, by which the latter may be led to support the constitutional rights of the former, without being too much detached from the rights of its own department?

If the principles on which these observations are founded be just, as I persuade myself they are, and they be applied as a criterion, to the several state constitutions, and to the federal constitution, it will be found, that if the latter does not perfectly correspond with them, the former are infinitely less able to bear such a test.

There are moreover two considerations particularly applicable to the federal system of America, which place that system in a very interesting point of view.

First. In a single republic, all the power surrendered by the people, is submitted to the administration of a single government; and usurpations are guarded against by a division of the government into distinct and separate departments. In the compound republic of America, the power surrendered by the people, is first divided between two distinct governments, and then the portion allotted to each, subdivided among distinct and separate departments. Hence a double security arises to the rights of the people. The different governments will control each other; at the same time that each will be controlled by itself.

Second. It is of great importance in a republic, not only to guard the society against the oppression of its rulers; but to guard one part of the society against the injustice of the other part. Different interests necessarily exist in different classes of citizens. If a majority be united by a common interest, the rights of the minority will be insecure. There are but two methods of providing against this evil: The one by creating a will in the community independent of the majority, that is, of the society itself, the other by comprehending in the society so many separate descriptions of citizens, as will render an unjust combination of a majority of the whole, very improbable, if not impracticable. The first method prevails in all governments possessing an hereditary or self appointed authority. This at best is but a precarious security; because a power independent of the society may as well espouse the unjust views of the major, as the rightful interests, of the minor party, and may possibly be turned against both parties. The second method will be exemplified in the federal republic of the United States. While all authority in it will be derived from and dependent on the society, the society itself will be broken into so many parts, interests and classes of citizens, that the rights of individuals or of the minority, will be in little danger from interested combinations of the majority. In a free government, the security for civil rights must be the same as for religious rights. It consists in the one case in the multiplicity of interests, and in the other, in the multiplicity of sects. The degree of security in both cases will depend on the number of interests and sects; and this may be presumed to depend on the extent of country and number of people comprehended under the same government. This view of the subject must particularly recommend a proper federal system to all the sincere and considerate friends of republican government: Since it shows that in exact proportion as the territory of the union may be formed into more circumscribed confederacies or states, oppressive combinations of a majority will be facilitated, the best security under the republican form, for the rights of every class of citizens, will be diminished; and consequently, the stability and independence of some member of the government, the only other security, must be proportionally increased. Justice is the end of government. It is the end of civil society. It ever has been, and ever will be pursued, until it be obtained, or until liberty be lost in the pursuit. In a society under the forms of which the stronger faction can readily unite and oppress the weaker, anarchy may as truly be said to reign, as in a state of nature where the weaker individual is not secured against the violence of the stronger: And as in the latter state even the stronger individuals are prompted by the uncertainty of their condition, to submit to a government which may protect the weak as well as themselves: So in the former state, will the more powerful factions or parties be gradually induced by a like motive, to wish for a government which will protect all parties, the weaker as well as the more powerful. It can be little doubted, that if the state of Rhode Island was separated from the confederacy, and left to itself, the insecurity of rights under the popular form of government within such narrow limits, would be displayed by such reiterated oppressions of factious majorities, that some power altogether independent of the people would soon be called for by the voice of the very factions whose misrule had proved the necessity of it. In the extended republic of the United States, and among the great variety of interests, parties and sects which it embraces, a coalition of a majority of the whole society could seldom take place on any other principles than those of justice and the general good; and there being thus less danger to a minor from the will of the major party, there must be less pretext also, to provide for the security of the former, by introducing into the government a will not dependent on the latter; or in other words, a will independent of the society itself. It is no less certain than it is important, notwithstanding the contrary opinions which have been entertained, that the larger the society, provided it lie within a practicable sphere, the more duly capable it will be of self government. And happily for the *republican cause*, the practicable sphere may be carried to a very great extent, by a judicious modification and mixture of the *federal principle*.

PUBLIUS

THE CONSTITUTION OF THE UNITED STATES OF AMERICA*

(Preamble)

We the People of the United States, in Order to form a more perfect Union, establish Justice, insure domestic Tranquility, provide for the common defence, promote the general Welfare, and secure the Blessings of Liberty to ourselves and our Posterity, do ordain and establish this Constitution for the United States of America.

ARTICLE I.

(The Legislature)

Section 1. All legislative Powers herein granted shall be vested in a Congress of the United States, which shall consist of a Senate and House of Representatives.

*This text retains the spelling, capitalization, and punctuation of the original. Brackets indicate passages that have been altered by amendments.

Section 2. The House of Representatives shall be composed of Members chosen every second Year by the People of the several States, and the Electors in each State shall have the Qualifications requisite for Electors of the most numerous Branch of the State Legislature.

No person shall be a Representative who shall not have attained to the Age of twenty five Years, and been seven Years a Citizen of the United States, and who shall not, when elected, be an Inhabitant of that State in which he shall be chosen.

Representatives and direct [Taxes][1] shall be apportioned among the several States which may be included within this Union, according to their respective Numbers [which shall be determined by adding to the whole Number of free Persons, including those bound to Service for a Term of Years, and excluding Indians not taxed, three fifths of all other Persons].[2] The actual Enumeration shall be made within three Years after the first Meeting of the Congress of the United States, and within every subsequent Term of ten Years, in such Manner as they shall by Law direct. The Number of Representatives shall not exceed one for every thirty Thousand, but each State shall have at Least one Representative; and until such enumeration shall be made, the State of New Hampshire shall be entitled to chuse three, Massachusetts eight, Rhode-Island and Providence Plantations one, Connecticut five, New-York six, New Jersey four, Pennsylvania eight, Delaware one, Maryland six, Virginia ten, North Carolina five, South Carolina five, and Georgia three.

When vacancies happen in the Representation from any State, the Executive Authority thereof shall issue Writs of Election to fill such Vacancies.

The House of Representatives shall chuse their speaker and other Officers; and shall have the sole Power of Impeachment.

Section 3. The Senate of the United States shall be composed of two Senators from each State [chosen by the Legislature thereof],[3] for six Years; and each Senator shall have one Vote.

Immediately after they shall be assembled in Consequence of the first Election, they shall be divided as equally as may be into three Classes. The Seats of the Senators of the first Class shall be vacated at the Expiration of the second year, of the second Class at the Expiration of the fourth Year, and of the third Class at the Expiration of the sixth Year, so that one third may be chosen every second Year [and if Vacancies happen by Resignation, or otherwise, during the Recess of the Legislature of any State, the Executive thereof may make temporary Appointments until the next Meeting of the Legislature, which shall then fill such Vacancies].[4]

No Person shall be a Senator who shall not have attained to the Age of thirty Years, and been nine Years a Citizen of the United States, and who shall not, when elected, be an Inhabitant of that State for which he shall be chosen.

The Vice President of the United States shall be President of the Senate, but shall have no Vote, unless they be equally divided.

The Senate shall chuse their other Officers, and also a President pro tempore, in the Absence of the Vice President, or when he shall exercise the Office of President of the United States.

The Senate shall have the sole Power to try all Impeachments. When sitting for that Purpose, they shall be on Oath or Affirmation. When the President of the United States is tried, the Chief Justice shall preside: And no Person shall be convicted without the Concurrence of two thirds of the Members present.

Judgment in Cases of Impeachment shall not extend further than to removal from Office, and disqualification to hold and enjoy any Office of honor, Trust or Profit under the United States; but the Party convicted shall nevertheless be liable and subject to Indictment, Trial, Judgment and Punishment, according to Law.

Section 4. The Times, Places and Manner of holding Elections for Senators and Representatives, shall be prescribed in each State by the Legislature thereof; but the Congress may at any time by Law make or alter such Regulations, except as to the Places of chusing Senators.

[The Congress shall assemble at least once in every Year, and such Meeting shall be on the first Monday in December, unless they shall by Law appoint a different Day.][5]

Section 5. Each House shall be the Judge of the Elections, Returns and Qualifications of its own Members, and a Majority of each shall constitute a Quorum to do Business; but a smaller Number may adjourn from day to day, and may be authorized to compel the Attendance of absent Members, in such Manner, and under such Penalties as each House may provide.

[1]See Amendment XVI.
[2]See Amendment XIV.
[3]See Amendment XVII.

[4]See Amendment XVII.
[5]See Amendment XX.

Each House may determine the Rules of its Proceedings, punish its Members for disorderly Behaviour, and, with the Concurrence of two thirds, expel a Member.

Each House shall keep a Journal of its Proceedings, and from time to time publish the same, excepting such Parts as may in their judgment require Secrecy; and the Yeas and Nays of the Members of either House on any question shall, at the Desire of one fifth of those present, be entered on the Journal.

Neither House, during the Session of Congress, shall, without the Consent of the other, adjourn for more than three days, nor to any other Place than that in which the two Houses shall be sitting.

Section 6. The Senators and Representatives shall receive a Compensation for their Services, to be ascertained by Law, and paid out of the Treasury of the United States. They shall in all Cases, except Treason, Felony and Breach of the Peace, be privileged from Arrest during their Attendance at the Session of their respective Houses, and in going to and returning from the same; and for any Speech or Debate in either House, they shall not be questioned in any other Place.

No Senator or Representative shall, during the Time for which he was elected, be appointed to any civil Office under the Authority of the United States, which shall have been created, or the Emoluments whereof shall have been encreased during such time; and no Person holding any Office under the United States, shall be a Member of either House during his Continuance in Office.

Section 7. All Bills for raising Revenue shall originate in the House of Representatives; but the Senate may propose or concur with Amendments as on other Bills.

Every Bill which shall have passed the House of Representatives and the Senate, shall, before it becomes a Law, be presented to the President of the United States; If he approves he shall sign it, but if not he shall return it, with his Objections to that House in which it shall have originated, who shall enter the Objections at large on their Journal, and proceed to reconsider it. If after such Reconsideration two thirds of that House shall agree to pass the Bill, it shall be sent, together with the Objections, to the other House, by which it shall likewise be reconsidered, and if approved by two thirds of that House, it shall become a Law. But in all such Cases the Votes of both Houses shall be determined by yeas and Nays, and the Names of the Persons voting for and against the Bill shall be entered on the Journal of each House respectively. If any Bill shall not be returned by the President

within ten Days (Sundays excepted) after it shall have been presented to him, the Same shall be a Law, in like Manner as if he had signed it, unless the Congress by their Adjournment prevent its Return, in which Case it shall not be a Law.

Every Order, Resolution, or Vote to which the Concurrence of the Senate and House of Representatives may be necessary (except on a question of Adjournment) shall be presented to the President of the United States; and before the Same shall take Effect, shall be approved by him, or being disapproved by him, shall be repassed by two thirds of the Senate and House of Representatives, according to the Rules and Limitations prescribed in the Case of a Bill.

Section 8. The Congress shall have Power To lay and collect Taxes, Duties, Imposts and Excises, to pay the Debts and provide for the common Defence and general Welfare of the United States; but all Duties, Imposts and Excises shall be uniform throughout the United States;

To borrow Money on the credit of the United States;

To regulate Commerce with foreign Nations, and among the several States, and with the Indian Tribes;

To establish a uniform Rule of Naturalization, and uniform Laws on the subject of Bankruptcies throughout the United States;

To coin Money, regulate the Value thereof, and of foreign Coin, and fix the Standard of Weights and Measures;

To provide for the Punishment of counterfeiting the Securities and current Coin of the United States;

To establish Post Offices and post Roads;

To promote the Progress of Science and useful Arts, by securing for limited Times to Authors and Inventors the exclusive Right to their respective Writings and Discoveries;

To constitute Tribunals inferior to the supreme Court;

To define and punish Piracies and Felonies committed on the high Seas, and Offences against the Law of Nations;

To declare War, grant Letters of Marque and Reprisal, and make Rules concerning Captures on Land and Water;

To raise and support Armies, but no Appropriation of Money to that Use shall be for a longer Term than two Years;

To provide and maintain a Navy;

To make Rules for the Government and Regulation of the land and naval Forces;

To provide for calling forth the Militia to execute the Laws of the Union, suppress Insurrections and repel Invasions;

To provide for organizing, arming, and disciplining, the Militia, and for governing such Part of them as may be employed in the Service of the United States, reserving to the States respectively, the Appointment of the Officers, and the Authority of training the Militia according to the discipline prescribed by Congress;

To exercise exclusive Legislation in all Cases whatsoever, over such District (not exceeding ten Miles square) as may, by Cession of particular States, and the Acceptance of Congress, become the Seat of the Government of the United States, and to exercise like Authority over all Places purchased by the Consent of the Legislature of the State in which the Same shall be, for the Erection of Forts, Magazines, Arsenals, dock-Yards, and other needful Buildings;—And

To make all Laws which shall be necessary and proper for carrying into Execution the foregoing Powers, and all other Powers vested by this Constitution in the Government of the United States, or in any Department or Officer thereof.

Section 9. The Migration or Importation of such Persons as any of the States now existing shall think proper to admit, shall not be prohibited by the Congress prior to the Year one thousand eight hundred and eight, but a Tax or duty may be imposed on such Importation, not exceeding ten dollars for each Person.

The Privilege of the Writ of Habeas Corpus shall not be suspended, unless when in Cases of Rebellion or Invasion the public Safety may require it.

No Bill of Attainder or ex post facto Law shall be passed.

[No Capitation, or other direct, Tax shall be laid, unless in Proportion to the Census or Enumeration herein before directed to be taken.][6]

No Tax or Duty shall be laid on Articles exported from any State.

No Preference shall be given by any Regulation of Commerce or Revenue to the Ports of one State over those of another; nor shall Vessels bound to, or from, one State, be obliged to enter, clear, or pay Duties in another.

No Money shall be drawn from the Treasury, but in Consequence of Appropriations made by Law; and a regular Statement and Account of the Receipts and Expenditures of all public Money shall be published from time to time.

No Title of Nobility shall be granted by the United States: And no Person holding any Office of Profit or Trust under them, shall, without the Consent of the Congress, accept of any present, Emolument, Office, or Title, of any kind whatever, from any King, Prince, or foreign State.

[6]See Amendment XVI.

Section 10. No State shall enter into any Treaty, Alliance, or Confederation; grant Letters of Marque and Reprisal; coin Money; emit Bills of Credit; make any Thing but gold and silver Coin a Tender in Payment of Debts; pass any Bill of Attainder, ex post facto Law, or Law impairing the Obligation of Contracts, or grant any Title of Nobility.

No State shall, without the Consent of the Congress, lay any Imposts or Duties on Imports or Exports, except what may be absolutely necessary for executing its inspection Laws: and the net Produce of all Duties and Imposts, laid by any State on Imports or Exports, shall be for the Use of the Treasury of the United States; and all such Laws shall be subject to the Revision and Controul of the Congress.

No State shall, without the Consent of Congress, lay any Duty of Tonnage, keep Troops, or Ships of War in time of Peace, enter into any Agreement or Compact with another State, or with a foreign Power, or engage in War, unless actually invaded, or in such imminent Danger as will not admit of delay.

ARTICLE II.

(The Executive)

Section 1. The executive Power shall be vested in a President of the United States of America. He shall hold his Office during the Term of four Years, and, together with the Vice President, chosen for the same Term, be elected, as follows.

Each State shall appoint, in such Manner as the Legislature thereof may direct, a Number of Electors, equal to the whole Number of Senators and Representatives to which the State may be entitled in the Congress; but no Senator or Representative, or Person holding an Office of Trust or Profit under the United States, shall be appointed an Elector.

[The Electors shall meet in their respective States, and vote by Ballot for two Persons, of whom one at least shall not be an Inhabitant of the same State with themselves. And they shall make a List of all the Persons voted for, and of the Number of Votes for each; which List they shall sign and certify, and transmit sealed to the Seat of the Government of the United States, directed to the President of the Senate. The President of the Senate shall, in the Presence of the Senate and House of Representatives, open all the Certificates, and the Votes shall then be counted. The Person having the greatest Number of Votes shall be the President, if such Number be a Majority of the whole Number of Electors appointed; and if there be more than one who have such Majority, and have an equal Number of Votes, then the House of

Representatives shall immediately chuse by Ballot one of them for President; and if no Person have a Majority, then from the five highest on the List the said House shall in like Manner chuse the President. But in chusing the President, the Votes shall be taken by States, the Representation from each State having one Vote; A quorum for this Purpose shall consist of a Member or Members from two thirds of the States, and a Majority of all the States shall be necessary to a Choice. In every Case, after the Choice of the President, the Person having the greatest Number of Votes of the Electors shall be the Vice President. But if there should remain two or more who have equal Votes, the Senate shall chuse from them by Ballot the Vice President.][7]

The Congress may determine the Time of chusing the Electors, and the Day on which they shall give their Votes; which Day shall be the same throughout the United States.

No Person except a natural born Citizen, or a Citizen of the United States, at the time of the Adoption of this Constitution, shall be eligible to the Office of President; neither shall any Person be eligible to that Office who shall not have attained to the Age of thirty five Years, and been fourteen Years a Resident within the United States.

[In Case of the Removal of the President from Office, or of his Death, Resignation, or Inability to discharge the Powers and Duties of the said Office, the Same shall devolve on the Vice President, and the Congress may by Law provide for the Case of Removal, Death, Resignation or Inability, both of the President and Vice President, declaring what Officer shall then act as President, and such Officer shall act accordingly, until the Disability be removed, or a President shall be elected.][8]

The President shall, at stated Times, receive for his Services, a Compensation, which shall neither be encreased nor diminished during the Period for which he shall have been elected, and he shall not receive within that Period any other Emolument from the United States, or any of them.

Before he enter on the Execution of his Office, he shall take the following Oath or Affirmation:—"I do solemnly swear (or affirm) that I will faithfully execute the Office of President of the United States, and will to the best of my Ability, preserve, protect and defend the Constitution of the United States."

Section 2.   The President shall be Commander in Chief of the Army and Navy of the United States, and of the Militia of the several States, when called into the actual Service of the United States; he may require the Opinion, in writing, of the principal Officer in each of the executive Departments, upon any Subject relating to the Duties of their respective Offices, and he shall have Power to grant Reprieves and Pardons for Offences against the United States, except in Cases of Impeachment.

He shall have Power, by and with the Advice and Consent of the Senate, to make Treaties, provided two thirds of the Senators present concur; and he shall nominate, and by and with the Advice and Consent of the Senate, shall appoint Ambassadors, other public Ministers and Consuls, Judges of the supreme Court, and all other Officers of the United States, whose Appointments are not herein otherwise provided for, and which shall be established by Law: but the Congress may by Law vest the Appointment of such inferior Officers, as they think proper, in the President alone, in the Courts of Law, or in the Heads of Departments.

The President shall have Power to fill up all Vacancies that may happen during the Recess of the Senate, by granting Commissions which shall expire at the end of their next Session.

Section 3.   He shall from time to time give to the Congress Information of the State of the Union, and recommend to their Consideration such Measures as he shall judge necessary and expedient; he may, on extraordinary Occasions, convene both Houses, or either of them, and in Case of Disagreement between them, with Respect to the Time of Adjournment, he may adjourn them to such Time as he shall think proper; he shall receive Ambassadors and other public Ministers; he shall take Care that the Laws be faithfully executed, and shall Commission all the Officers of the United States.

Section 4.   The President, Vice President and all civil Officers of the United States, shall be removed from Office on Impeachment for, and Conviction of, Treason, Bribery, or other high Crimes and Misdemeanors.

ARTICLE III.

(The Judiciary)

Section 1.   The judicial Power of the United States, shall be vested in one supreme Court, and in such inferior Courts as the Congress may from time to time ordain and establish. The Judges, both of the supreme and inferior Courts, shall hold their Offices during good Behaviour, and shall, at stated Times, receive for their Services, a Compensation, which shall not be diminished during their Continuance in Office.

[7]See Amendment XII.
[8]See Amendment XXV.

Section 2. The judicial Power shall extend to all Cases, in Law and Equity, arising under this Constitution, the Laws of the United States, and Treaties made, or which shall be made, under their Authority;—to all Cases affecting Ambassadors, other public Ministers and Consuls;—to all Cases of admiralty and maritime Jurisdiction;—to Controversies to which the United States shall be a Party;—to Controversies between two or more States; [—between a State and Citizens of another State;—][9] between Citizens of different States,—between Citizens of the same State claiming Lands under Grants of different States, [and between a State, or the Citizens thereof, and foreign States, Citizens or Subjects.][10]

In all Cases affecting Ambassadors, other public Ministers and Consuls, and those in which a State shall be Party, the supreme Court shall have original Jurisdiction. In all the other Cases before mentioned, the supreme Court shall have appellate Jurisdiction, both as to Law and Fact, with such Exceptions, and under such Regulations as the Congress shall make.

The Trial of all Crimes, except in Cases of Impeachment, shall be by Jury; and such Trial shall be held in the State where the said Crimes shall have been committed; but when not committed within any State, the Trial shall be at such Place or Places as the Congress may by Law have directed.

Section 3. Treason against the United States, shall consist only in levying War against them, or in adhering to their Enemies, giving them Aid and Comfort. No Person shall be convicted of Treason unless on the Testimony of two Witnesses to the same overt Act, or on Confession in open Court.

The Congress shall have Power to declare the Punishment of Treason, but no Attainder of Treason shall work Corruption of Blood, or Forfeiture except during the Life of the Person attainted.

ARTICLE IV.

(Interstate Relations)

Section 1. Full Faith and Credit shall be given in each State to the public Acts, Records, and judicial Proceedings of every other State. And the Congress may by general Laws prescribe the Manner in which such Acts, Records and Proceedings shall be proved, and the Effect thereof.

Section 2. The Citizens of each State shall be entitled to all Privileges and Immunities of Citizens in the several States.

A Person charged in any State with Treason, Felony, or other Crime, who shall flee from Justice, and be found in another State, shall on Demand of the executive Authority of the State from which he fled, be delivered up, to be removed to the State having Jurisdiction of the Crime.

[No Person held to Service or Labour in one State under the Laws thereof, escaping into another, shall, in Consequence of any Law or Regulation therein, be discharged from such Service or Labour, but shall be delivered up on Claim of the Party to whom such Service or Labour may be due.][11]

Section 3. New States may be admitted by the Congress into this Union; but no new State shall be formed or erected within the Jurisdiction of any other State; nor any State be formed by the Junction of two or more States, or Parts of States, without the Consent of the Legislatures of the States concerned as well as of the Congress.

The Congress shall have Power to dispose of and make all needful Rules and Regulations respecting the Territory or other Property belonging to the United States; and nothing in this Constitution shall be so construed as to Prejudice any Claims of the United States, or of any particular State.

Section 4. The United States shall guarantee to every State in this Union a Republican Form of Government, and shall protect each of them against Invasion, and on Application of the Legislature, or of the Executive (when the Legislature cannot be convened) against domestic Violence.

ARTICLE V.

(Amending the Constitution)

The Congress, whenever two thirds of both Houses shall deem it necessary, shall propose Amendments to this Constitution, or, on the Application of the Legislatures of two thirds of the several States, shall call a Convention for proposing Amendments, which, in either Case, shall be valid to all Intents and Purposes, as Part of this Constitution, when ratified by the Legislatures of three fourths of the several States, or by Conventions in three fourths thereof, as the one or the other Mode of Ratification may be proposed by the Congress; Provided that no Amendment which may be made prior to the Year One thousand eight hundred and eight shall in any Manner affect the first and fourth Clauses in the Ninth Section of the first Article; and that no State, without its Consent, shall be deprived of its equal Suffrage in the Senate.

[9]See Amendment XI.
[10]See Amendment XI.

[11]See Amendment XIII.

ARTICLE VI.

(Debts, Supremacy, Oaths)

All Debts contracted and Engagements entered into, before the Adoption of this Constitution, shall be as valid against the United States under this Constitution, as under the Confederation.

This Constitution, and the laws of the United States which shall be made in Pursuance thereof; and all Treaties made, or which shall be made, under the Authority of the United States, shall be the supreme Law of the Land; and the Judges in every State shall be bound thereby, any Thing in the Constitution or Laws of any State to the Contrary notwithstanding.

The Senators and Representatives before mentioned, and the Members of the several State Legislatures, and all executive and judicial Officers, both of the United States and of the several States, shall be bound by Oath or Affirmation, to support this Constitution; but no religious Test shall ever be required as a Qualification to any Office or public Trust under the United States.

ARTICLE VII.

(Ratifying the Constitution)

The Ratification of the Conventions of nine States, shall be sufficient for the Establishment of this Constitution between the States so ratifying the Same.

Done in Convention by the Unanimous Consent of the States present the Seventeenth Day of September in the Year of our Lord one thousand seven hundred and Eighty seven and of the Independence of the United States of America the Twelfth. IN WITNESS whereof we have hereunto subscribed our Names.

Go. WASHINGTON
Presid't. and deputy from Virginia

ATTTEST
William Jackson
Secretary

DELAWARE
Geo. Read
Gunning Bedford jun
John Dickinson
Richard Basset
Jaco. Broom

MASSACHUSETTS
Nathaniel Gorbam
Rufus King

CONNECTICUT
Wm. Saml. Johnson
Roger Sherman

NEW YORK
Alexander Hamilton

NEW JERSEY
Wh. Livingston
David Brearley
Wm. Paterson
Jona. Dayton

PENNSYLVANIA
B. Franklin
Thomas Mifflin
Robt. Morris
Geo. Clymer
Thos. FitzSimons
Jared Ingersoll
James Wilson
Gouv. Morris

NEW HAMPSHIRE
John Langdon
Nicholas Gilman

MARYLAND
James McHenry
Dan of St. Thos.
Jenifer
Danl. Carroll

VIRGINIA
John Blair
James Madison Jr.

NORTH CAROLINA
Wm. Blount
Richd. Dobbs Spaight
Hu. Williamson

SOUTH CAROLINA
J. Rutledge
Charles Cotesworth
Pinckney
Charles Pinckney
Pierce Butler

GEORGIA
William Few
Abr. Baldwin

Articles in addition to, and amendment of the Constitution of the United States of America, proposed by Congress and ratified by the Legislatures of the several states, pursuant to the Fifth Article of the original Constitution.

(The first ten amendments were passed by Congress on September 25, 1789, and were ratified on December 15, 1791.)

Amendment I—Religion, Speech, Assembly, Petition

Congress shall make no law respecting an establishment of religion, or prohibiting the free exercise thereof; or abridging the freedom of speech, or of the press; or the right of the people peaceably to assemble, and to petition the Government for a redress of grievances.

Amendment II—Right to Bear Arms

A well regulated Militia, being necessary to the security of a free State, the right of the people to keep and bear Arms, shall not be infringed.

Amendment III—Quartering of Soldiers

No Soldier shall, in time of peace be quartered in any house, without the consent of the Owner, nor in time of war, but in a manner to be prescribed by law.

Amendment IV—Searches and Seizures

The right of the people to be secure in their persons, houses, papers, and effects, against unreasonable searches and seizures, shall not be violated, and no warrants shall issue, but upon probable cause, supported by Oath or affirmation, and particularly describing the place to be searched, and the persons or things to be seized.

Amendment V—Grand Juries, Double Jeopardy, Self-incrimination, Due Process, Eminent Domain

No person shall be held to answer for a capital, or otherwise infamous crime, unless on a presentment or indictment of a Grand Jury, except in cases arising in the land or naval forces, or in the Militia, when in actual service in time of War or public danger; nor shall any person be subject for the same offence to be twice put in jeopardy of life or limb; nor shall be compelled in any criminal case to be a witness against himself, nor be deprived of life, liberty, or property, without due process of law; nor shall private property be taken for public use, without just compensation.

Amendment VI—Criminal Court Procedures

In all criminal prosecutions, the accused shall enjoy the right to a speedy and public trial, by an impartial jury of the State and district wherein the crime shall have been committed, which district shall have been previously ascertained by law, and to be informed of the nature and cause of the accusation; to be confronted with the witnesses against him; to have compulsory process for obtaining witnesses in his favor, and to have the assistance of counsel for his defence.

Amendment VII—Trial by Jury in Common-law Cases

In Suits at common law, where the value in controversy shall exceed twenty dollars, the right of trial by jury shall be preserved, and no fact tried by a jury, shall be otherwise re-examined in any Court of the United States, than according to the rules of the common law.

Amendment VIII—Bails, Fines, and Punishment

Excessive bail shall not be required, nor excessive fines imposed, nor cruel and unusual punishments inflicted.

Amendment IX—Rights Retained by the People

The enumeration in the Constitution, of certain rights, shall not be construed to deny or disparage others retained by the people.

Amendment X—Rights Reserved to the States

The powers not delegated to the United States by the Constitution, nor prohibited by it to the States, are reserved to the States respectively, or to the people.

Amendment XI—Suits Against the States (Ratified February 7, 1795)

The Judicial power of the United States shall not be construed to extend to any suit in law or equity, commenced or prosecuted against one of the United States by Citizens of another State, or by Citizens or Subjects of any Foreign State.

Amendment XII—Election of the President and Vice-President (Ratified June 15, 1804)

The Electors shall meet in their respective states, and vote by ballot for President and Vice-President, one of whom, at least, shall not be an inhabitant of the same state with themselves; they shall name in their ballots the person voted for as President, and in distinct ballots the person voted for as Vice-President, and they shall make distinct lists of all persons voted for as President, and of all persons voted for as Vice-President, and of the number of votes for each, which lists they shall sign and certify, and transmit sealed to the seat of the government of the United States, directed to the President of the Senate;—The President of the Senate shall, in the presence of the Senate and House of Representatives, open all the certificates and the votes shall then be counted;—The person having the greatest number of votes for President, shall be the President, if such number be a majority of the whole number of Electors appointed; and if no person have such majority, then from the persons having the highest numbers not exceeding three on the list of those voted for as President, the House of Representatives shall choose immediately, by ballot, the President. But in choosing the President, the votes shall be taken by states, the representation from each state having one vote; a quorum for this purpose shall consist of a member or members from two-thirds of the states, and a majority of all the states shall be necessary to a Choice. [And if the House of Representatives shall not choose a President whenever the right of choice shall devolve upon them, before the fourth day of March next following, then the Vice-President shall act as President, as in the case of the death or other constitutional disability of the President.][12]—The person having the greatest number of votes as Vice-President, shall be the Vice-President, if such number be a majority of the whole number of Electors appointed, and if no person have a majority, then from the two highest numbers on the list, the Senate shall choose the Vice-President; a quorum for the purpose shall consist of two-thirds of the whole number of Senators, and a majority of the whole number shall be necessary to a choice. But no person constitutionally ineligible to the office of President shall be eligible to that of Vice-President of the United States.

Amendment XIII—Slavery (Ratified on December 6, 1865)

Section 1.   Neither slavery nor involuntary servitude, except as a punishment for crime whereof the party shall have been duly convicted, shall exist within the United States, or any place subject to their jurisdiction.

Section 2.   Congress shall have power to enforce this article by appropriate legislation.

---

[12]Amendment XX.

Amendment XIV—Citizenship, Due Process, and Equal Protection of the Laws (Ratified on July 9, 1868)

Section 1. All persons born or naturalized in the United States, and subject to the jurisdiction thereof, are citizens of the United States and of the State wherein they reside. No State shall make or enforce any law which shall abridge the privileges or immunities of citizens of the United States; nor shall any State deprive any person of life, liberty, or property, without due process of law; nor deny to any person within its jurisdiction the equal protection of the laws.

Section 2. Representatives shall be apportioned among the several States according to their respective numbers, counting the whole number of persons in each State, excluding Indians not taxed. But when the right to vote at any election for the choice of electors for President and Vice President of the United States, Representatives in Congress, the Executive and Judicial officers of a State, or the members of the Legislature thereof, is denied to any of the male inhabitants of such State, being twenty-one years of age, and citizens of the United States, or in any way abridged, except for participation in rebellion, or other crime, the basis of representation therein shall be reduced in the proportion which the number of such male citizens shall bear to the whole number of male citizens twenty-one years of age in such State.

Section 3. No person shall be a Senator or Representative in Congress, or elector of President and Vice President, or hold any office, civil or military, under the United States, or under any State, who, having previously taken an oath, as a member of Congress, or as an officer of the United States, or as a member of any State legislature, or as an executive or judicial officer of any State, to support the Constitution of the United States, shall have engaged in insurrection or rebellion against the same, or given aid or comfort to the enemies thereof. But Congress may by a vote of two-thirds of each House, remove such disability.

Section 4. The validity of the public debt of the United States, authorized by law, including debts incurred for payment of pensions and bounties for services in suppressing insurrection or rebellion, shall not be questioned. But neither the United States nor any State shall assume or pay any debt or obligation incurred in aid of insurrection or rebellion against the United States, or any claim for the loss or emancipation of any slave, but all such debts, obligations and claims shall be held illegal and void.

Section 5. The Congress shall have power to enforce, by appropriate legislation, the provisions of this article.

Amendment XV—The Right To Vote (Ratified on February 3, 1870)

Section 1. The right of citizens of the United States to vote shall not be denied or abridged by the United States or by any State on account of race, color, or previous condition of servitude.

Section 2. The Congress shall have power to enforce this article by appropriate legislation.

Amendment XVI—Income Taxes (Ratified on February 3, 1913)

The Congress shall have power to lay and collect taxes on incomes, from whatever source derived, without apportionment among the several States, and without regard to any census or enumeration.

Amendment XVII—Election of Senators (Ratified on April 8, 1913)

The Senate of the United States shall be composed of two Senators from each State, elected by the people thereof, for six years; and each Senator shall have one vote. The electors in each State shall have the qualifications requisite for electors of the most numerous branch of the State legislatures.

When vacancies happen in the representation of any State in the Senate, the executive authority of such State shall issue writs of election to fill such vacancies: *Provided*, That the legislature of any State may empower the executive thereof to make temporary appointments until the people fill the vacancies by election as the legislature may direct.

This amendment shall not be so construed as to affect the election or term of any Senator chosen before it becomes valid as part of the Constitution.

Amendment XVIII—Prohibition (Ratified on January 16, 1919)

Section 1. After one year from the ratification of this article the manufacture, sale, or transportation of intoxicating liquors within, the importation thereof into, or the exportation thereof from the United States and all territory subject to the jurisdiction thereof for beverage purposes is hereby prohibited.

Section 2. The Congress and the several States shall have concurrent power to enforce this article by appropriate legislation.

Section 3. This article shall be inoperative unless it shall have been ratified as an amendment to the Constitution by the legislatures of the several States, as provided in the Constitution, within seven years from the date of the submission hereof to the States by the Congress.[13]

Amendment XIX—Women's Right To Vote (Ratified on August 18, 1920)

The right of citizens of the United States to vote shall not be denied or abridged by the United States or by any State on account of sex.

Congress shall have power to enforce this article by appropriate legislation.

Amendment XX—Terms of Office, Convening of Congress, and Succession (Ratified February 6, 1933)

Section 1. The terms of the President and Vice President shall end at noon on the 20th day of January, and the terms of Senators and Representatives at noon on the 3d day of January, of the years in which such terms would have ended if this article had not been ratified; and the terms of their successors shall then begin.

Section 2. The Congress shall assemble at least once in every year, and such meeting shall begin at noon on the 3d day of January, unless they shall by law appoint a different day.

Section 3. If, at the time fixed for the beginning of the term of the President, the President elect shall have died, the Vice President elect shall become President. If a President shall not have been chosen before the time fixed for the beginning of his term, or if the President elect shall have failed to qualify, then the Vice President elect shall act as President until a President shall have qualified; and the Congress may by law provide for the case wherein neither a President elect nor a Vice President elect shall have qualified, declaring who shall then act as President, or the manner in which one who is to act shall be selected, and such person shall act accordingly until a President or Vice President shall have qualified.

Section 4. The Congress may by law provide for the case of the death of any of the persons from whom the House of Representatives may choose a President whenever the rights of choice shall have devolved upon them, and for the case of the death of any of the persons from whom the Senate may choose a Vice President whenever the right of choice shall have devolved upon them.

Section 5. Sections 1 and 2 shall take effect on the 15th day of October following the ratification of this article.

Section 6. This article shall be inoperative unless it shall have been ratified as an amendment to the Constitution by the legislatures of three-fourths of the several States within seven years from the date of its submission.

Amendment XXI—Repeal of Prohibition (Ratified on December 5, 1933)

Section 1. The eighteenth article of amendment to the Constitution of the United States is hereby repealed.

Section 2. The transportation or importation into any State, Territory, or possession of the United States for delivery or use therein of intoxicating liquors, in violation of the laws thereof, is hereby prohibited.

Section 3. This article shall be inoperative unless it shall have been ratified as an amendment to the Constitution by conventions in the several States, as provided in the Constitution, within seven years from the date of the submission hereof to the States by the Congress.

Amendment XXII—Number of Presidential Terms (Ratified on February 27, 1951)

No person shall be elected to the office of the President more than twice, and no person who has held the office of President, or acted as President, for more than two years of a term to which some other person was elected President shall be elected to the office of the President more than once. But this Article shall not apply to any person holding the office of President when this Article was proposed by the Congress, and shall not prevent any person who may be holding the office of President, or acting as President, during the term within which this Article becomes operative from holding the office of President or acting as President during the remainder of such term.

[13]Amendment XXI.

Amendment XXIII—Presidential Electors for the District of Columbia (Ratified on March 29, 1961)

Section 1. The District constituting the seat of Government of the United States shall appoint in such manner as the Congress may direct:

A number of electors of President and Vice President equal to the whole number of Senators and Representatives in Congress to which the District would be entitled if it were a State, but in no event more than the least populous State; they shall be in addition to those appointed by the States, but they shall be considered, for the purposes of the election of President and Vice President, to be electors appointed by a State; and they shall meet in the District and perform such duties as provided by the twelfth article of amendment.

Section 2. The Congress shall have power to enforce this article by appropriate legislation.

Amendment XXIV—Poll Tax (Ratified on January 23, 1964)

Section 1. The right of citizens of the United States to vote in any primary or other election for President or Vice President, for electors for President or Vice President, or for Senator or Representative in Congress, shall not be denied or abridged by the United States or any State by reason of failure to pay any poll tax or other tax.

Section 2. The Congress shall have power to enforce this article by appropriate legislation.

Amendment XXV—Presidential Disability and Vice Presidential Vacancies (Ratified on February 10, 1967)

Section 1. In case of the removal of the President from office or of his death or resignation, the Vice President shall become President.

Section 2. Whenever there is a vacancy in the office of the Vice President, the President shall nominate a Vice President who shall take office upon confirmation by a majority vote of both Houses of Congress.

Section 3. Whenever the President transmits to the President pro tempore of the Senate and the Speaker of the House of Representatives his written declaration that he is unable to discharge the powers and duties of his office, and until he transmits to them a written declaration to the contrary, such powers and duties shall be discharged by the Vice President as Acting President.

Section 4. Whenever the Vice President and a majority of either the principal officers of the executive departments or of such other body as Congress may by law provide, transmit to the President pro tempore of the Senate and the Speaker of the House of Representatives their written declaration that the President is unable to discharge the powers and duties of his office, the Vice President shall immediately assume the powers and duties of the office as Acting President.

Thereafter, when the President transmits to the President pro tempore of the Senate and the Speaker of the House of Representatives his written declaration that no inability exists, he shall resume the powers and duties of his office unless the Vice President and a majority of either the principal officers of the executive department or of such other body as Congress may by law provide, transmit within four days to the President pro tempore of the Senate and the Speaker of the House of Representatives their written declaration that the President is unable to discharge the powers and duties of his office. Thereupon Congress shall decide the issue, assembling within forty-eight hours for that purpose if not in session. If the Congress, within twenty-one days after receipt of the latter written declaration, or, if Congress is not in session, within twenty-one days after Congress is required to assemble, determines by two-thirds vote of both Houses that the President is unable to discharge the powers and duties of his office, the Vice President shall continue to discharge the same as Acting President; otherwise, the President shall resume the powers and duties of his office.

Amendment XXVI—Eighteen-year-old Vote (Ratified on July 1, 1971)

Section 1. The right of citizens of the United States, who are eighteen years of age or older, to vote shall not be denied or abridged by the United States or by any State on account of age.

Section 2. The Congress shall have power to enforce this article by appropriate legislation.

Amendment XXVII—Congressional Salaries (Ratified on May 18, 1992)

Section 1. No law varying the compensation for the services of the Senators and Representatives, shall take effect, until an election of Representatives shall have intervened.

Presidents of the United States

YEAR	PRESIDENTIAL CANDIDATES	POLITICAL PARTY	ELECTORAL VOTE	PERCENTAGE OF POPULAR VOTE
1789	**George Washington**	–	69	–
	John Adams		34	
	Others		35	
1792	**George Washington**	–	132	–
	John Adams		77	
	Others		55	
1796	**John Adams**	Federalist	71	–
	Thomas Jefferson	Democratic-Republican	68	
	Thomas Pinckney	Federalist	59	
	Aaron Burr	Democratic-Republican	30	
	Others		48	
1800	**Thomas Jefferson**	Democratic-Republican	73	–
	Aaron Burr	Democratic-Republican	73	
	John Adams	Federalist	65	
	C. C. Pinckney	Federalist	64	
	John Jay	Federalist	1	
1804	**Thomas Jefferson**	Democratic-Republican	162	–
	C. C. Pinckney	Federalist	14	
1808	**James Madison**	Democratic-Republican	122	–
	C. C. Pinckney	Federalist	47	
	George Clinton	Independent-Republican	6	
1812	**James Madison**	Democratic-Republican	128	–
	De Witt Clinton	Federalist	89	
1816	**James Monroe**	Democratic-Republican	183	–
	Rufus King	Federalist	34	
1820	**James Monroe**	Democratic-Republican	231	–
	John Q. Adams	Independent-Republican	1	
1824	**John Q. Adams**	Democratic-Republican	84	30.5
	Andrew Jackson	Democratic-Republican	99	
	Henry Clay	Democratic-Republican	37	
	W. H. Crawford	Democratic-Republican	41	
1828	**Andrew Jackson**	Democratic	178	56.0
	John Q. Adams	National Republican	83	
1832	**Andrew Jackson**	Democratic	219	55.0
	Henry Clay	National Republican	49	
	William Wirt	Anti-Masonic	7	
	John Floyd	Independent Democrat	11	
1836	**Martin Van Buren**	Democratic	170	50.9
	William H. Harrison	Whig	73	
	Hugh L. White	Whig	26	
	Daniel Webster	Whig	14	
1840	**William H. Harrison***	Whig	234	53.0
	Martin Van Buren	Democratic	60	
	(John Tyler, 1841)			
1844	**James K. Polk**	Democratic	170	49.6
	Henry Clay	Whig	105	
1848	**Zachary Taylor***	Whig	163	47.4
	Lewis Cass	Democratic	127	
	(Millard Fillmore, 1850)			

Note: Presidents are shown in boldface.
*Died in office, succeeding vice president shown in parentheses.

YEAR	PRESIDENTIAL CANDIDATES	POLITICAL PARTY	ELECTORAL VOTE	PERCENTAGE OF POPULAR VOTE
1852	**Franklin Pierce**	Democratic	254	50.8
	Winfield Scott	Whig	42	
1856	**James Buchanan**	Democratic	174	45.3
	John C. Fremont	Republican	114	
	Millard Fillmore	American	8	
1860	**Abraham Lincoln**	Republican	180	39.8
	J. C. Breckinridge	Democratic	72	
	Stephen A. Douglas	Democratic	12	
	John Bell	Constitutional Union	39	
1864	**Abraham Lincoln***	Republican	212	55.0
	George B. McClellan	Democratic	21	
	(Andrew Johnson, 1865)			
1868	**Ulysses S. Grant**	Republican	214	52.7
	Horatio Seymour	Democratic	80	
1872	**Ulysses S. Grant**	Republican	286	55.6
	Horace Greeley	Democratic	**	
1876	**Rutherford B. Hayes**	Republican	185	47.9
	Samuel J. Tilden	Democratic	184	
1880	**James A. Garfield***	Republican	214	48.3
	Winfield S. Hancock	Democratic	155	
	(Chester A. Arthur, 1881)			
1884	**Grover Cleveland**	Democratic	219	48.5
	James G. Blaine	Republican	182	
1888	**Benjamin Harrison**	Republican	233	47.8
	Grover Cleveland	Democratic	168	
1892	**Grover Cleveland**	Democratic	277	46.0
	Benjamin Harrison	Republican	145	
	James B. Weaver	People's	22	
1896	**William McKinley**	Republican	271	51.0
	William J. Bryan	Democratic	176	
1900	**William McKinley***	Republican	292	51.7
	William J. Bryan	Democratic	155	
	(Theodore Roosevelt, 1901)			
1904	**Theodore Roosevelt**	Republican	336	56.4
	Alton B. Parker	Democratic	140	
1908	**William H. Taft**	Republican	321	51.6
	William J. Bryan	Democratic	162	
1912	**Woodrow Wilson**	Democratic	435	41.8
	Theodore Roosevelt	Progressive	88	
	William H. Taft	Republican	8	
1916	**Woodrow Wilson**	Democratic	277	49.2
	Charles E. Hughes	Republican	254	
1920	**Warren G. Harding***	Republican	404	60.3
	James M. Cox	Democratic	127	
	(Calvin Coolidge, 1923)			
1924	**Calvin Coolidge**	Republican	382	54.1
	John W. Davis	Democratic	136	
	Robert M. LaFollette	Progressive	13	
1928	**Herbert C. Hoover**	Republican	444	58.2
	Alfred E. Smith	Democratic	87	
1932	**Franklin D. Roosevelt**	Democratic	472	57.4
	Herbert C. Hoover	Republican	59	

**Horace Greeley died between the popular vote and the meeting of the presidential electors.

(continues)

Presidents of the United States (continued)

YEAR	PRESIDENTIAL CANDIDATES	POLITICAL PARTY	ELECTORAL VOTE	PERCENTAGE OF POPULAR VOTE
1936	**Franklin D. Roosevelt**	Democratic	523	60.8
	Alfred M. Landon	Republican	8	
1940	**Franklin D. Roosevelt**	Democratic	449	54.7
	Wendell L. Willkie	Republican	82	
1944	**Franklin D. Roosevelt***	Democratic	432	53.4
	Thomas E. Dewey	Republican	99	
	(Harry S Truman, 1945)			
1948	**Harry S Truman**	Democratic	303	49.5
	Thomas E. Dewey	Republican	189	
	J. Strom Thurmond	States' Rights	39	
1952	**Dwight D. Eisenhower**	Republican	442	55.1
	Adlai E. Stevenson	Democratic	89	
1956	**Dwight D. Eisenhower**	Republican	457	57.4
	Adlai E. Stevenson	Democratic	73	
1960	**John F. Kennedy***	Democratic	303	49.7
	Richard M. Nixon	Republican	219	
	(Lyndon B. Johnson, 1963)			
1964	**Lyndon B. Johnson**	Democratic	486	61.0
	Barry M. Goldwater	Republican	52	
1968	**Richard M. Nixon**	Republican	301	43.4
	Hubert H. Humphrey	Democratic	191	
	George C. Wallace	American Independent	46	
1972	**Richard M. Nixon†**	Republican	520	60.7
	George S. McGovern	Democratic	17	
	(Gerald R. Ford, 1974)‡			
1976	**Jimmy Carter**	Democratic	297	50.1
	Gerald R. Ford	Republican	240	
1980	**Ronald Reagan**	Republican	489	50.7
	Jimmy Carter	Democratic	49	
	John B. Anderson	Independent	—	
1984	**Ronald Reagan**	Republican	525	58.8
	Walter Mondale	Democratic	13	
1988	**George Bush**	Republican	426	53.4
	Michael Dukakis	Democratic	112	
1992	**Bill Clinton**	Democratic	370	43.0
	George Bush	Republican	168	
	H. Ross Perot	Independent	—	
1996	**Bill Clinton**	Democratic	379	49.2
	Robert Dole	Republican	159	
	H. Ross Perot	Reform	—	
2000	**George W. Bush**	Republican	271	47.8
	Al Gore	Democratic	266	
	Ralph Nader	Green		
	Patrick J. Buchanan	Reform		
2004	**George W. Bush**	Republican	286	50.7
	John Kerry	Democratic	251	
	Ralph Nader	Independent	—	
2008	**Barack Obama**	Democratic	365	52.7
	John McCain	Republican	173	

†Resigned
‡Appointed vice president

Party Control of the Presidency, Senate, and House of Representatives in the Twentieth and Twenty-first Centuries

CONGRESS	YEARS	PRESIDENT	SENATE			HOUSE		
			D	R	OTHER*	D	R	OTHER*
57th	1901–03	McKinley T. Roosevelt	29	56	3	153	198	5
58th	1903–05	T. Roosevelt	32	58	—	178	207	—
59th	1905–07	T. Roosevelt	32	58	—	136	250	—
60th	1907–09	T. Roosevelt	29	61	—	164	222	—
61st	1909–11	Taft	32	59	—	172	219	—
62d	1911–13	Taft	42	49	—	228‡	162	1
63d	1913–15	Wilson	51	44	1	290	127	18
64th	1915–17	Wilson	56	39	1	230	193	8
65th	1917–19	Wilson	53	42	1	200	216	9
66th	1919–21	Wilson	48	48‡	1	191	237‡	7
67th	1921–23	Harding	37	59	—	132	300	1
68th	1923–25	Coolidge	43	51	2	207	225	3
69th	1925–27	Coolidge	40	54	1	183	247	5
70th	1927–29	Coolidge	47	48	1	195	237	3
71st	1929–31	Hoover	39	56	1	163	267	1
72d	1931–33	Hoover	47	48	1	216‡	218	1
73d	1933–35	F. Roosevelt	59	36	1	313	117	5
74th	1935–37	F. Roosevelt	69	25	2	322	103	10
75th	1937–39	F. Roosevelt	75	17	4	333	89	13
76th	1939–41	F. Roosevelt	69	23	4	262	169	4
77th	1941–43	F. Roosevelt	66	28	2	267	162	6
78th	1943–45	F. Roosevelt	57	38	1	222	209	4
79th	1945–47	Truman	57	38	1	243	190	2
80th	1947–49	Truman	45	51‡	—	188	246‡	1
81st	1949–51	Truman	54	42	—	263	171	1
82d	1951–53	Truman	48	47	1	234	199	2
83d	1953–55	Eisenhower	47	48	1	213	221	1
84th	1955–57	Eisenhower	48‡	47	1	232‡	203	—
85th	1957–59	Eisenhower	49‡	47	—	234‡	201	—
86th†	1959–61	Eisenhower	64‡	34	—	283‡	154	—
87th	1961–63	Kennedy	64	36	—	263	174	—
88th	1963–65	Kennedy Johnson Johnson	67	33	—	258	176	—
89th	1965–67	Johnson	68	32	—	295	140	—
90th	1967–69	Johnson	64	36	—	248	187	—
91st	1969–71	Nixon	58‡	42	—	243‡	192	—
92d	1971–73	Nixon	55‡	45	—	255‡	180	—
93d	1973–75	Nixon Ford	57‡	43	—	243‡	192	—
94th	1975–77	Ford	61‡	38	—	291‡	144	—
95th	1977–79	Carter	62	38	—	292	143	—
96th	1979–81	Carter	59	41	—	277	158	—
97th	1981–83	Reagan	47	53	—	243‡	192	—
98th	1983–85	Reagan	46	54	—	269‡	166	—
99th	1985–87	Reagan	47	53	—	253‡	182	—
100th	1987–89	Reagan	55‡	45	—	258‡	177	—
101st	1989–91	Bush	55‡	45	—	260‡	175	—

*Excludes vacancies at beginning of each session. Party balance immediately following election.

†The 437 members of the House in the 86th and 87th Congresses are attributable to the at-large representative given to both Alaska (January 3, 1959) and Hawaii (August 21, 1959) prior to redistricting in 1962.

‡Chamber controlled by party other than that of the president.

D=Democrat   R=Republican

(continues)

Party Control of the Presidency, Senate, and House of Representatives in the Twentieth and Twenty-first Centuries (continued)

CONGRESS	YEARS	PRESIDENT	SENATE			HOUSE		
			D	R	OTHER*	D	R	OTHER*
102ᵈ	1991–93	Bush	56‡	44	–	267‡	167	1
103ᵈ	1993–95	Clinton	57	43	–	258	176	1
104ᵗʰ	1995–97	Clinton	46	54	–	202	232	1
105ᵗʰ	1997–99	Clinton	45	55	–	206	228	1
106ᵗʰ	1999–01	Clinton	45	55	–	211	223	1
107ᵗʰ	2001–03	G. W. Bush	50	49	1	212	221	2
108ᵗʰ	2003–05	G. W. Bush	48	51	1	205	229	1
109ᵗʰ	2005–07	G. W. Bush	44	55	1	202	232	11
110ᵗʰ	2007–09	G. W. Bush	50	49	1	233	202	–
111ᵗʰ	2009–11	Obama	56	42	2	257	178	–

Supreme Court Justices Serving in the Twentieth and Twenty-first Centuries

NAME	NOMINATED BY	SERVICE
John M. Harlan	Hayes	1877–1911
Horace Gray	Arthur	1882–1902
Melville W. Fuller*	Cleveland	1888–1910
David J. Brewer	Harrison	1890–1910
Henry B. Brown	Harrison	1890–1906
George Shiras, Jr.	Harrison	1892–1903
Edward D. White	Cleveland	1894–1910
Rufus W. Peckham	Cleveland	1895–1909
Joseph McKenna	McKinley	1898–1925
Oliver W. Holmes	T. Roosevelt	1902–1932
William R. Day	T. Roosevelt	1903–1922
William H. Moody	T. Roosevelt	1906–1910
Horace H. Lurton	Taft	1910–1914
Edward D. White	Taft	1910–1921
Charles E. Hughes	Taft	1910–1916
Willis Van Devanter	Taft	1911–1937
Joseph R. Lamar	Taft	1911–1916
Mahlon Pitney	Taft	1912–1922
James C. McReynolds	Wilson	1914–1941
Louis D. Brandeis	Wilson	1916–1939
John H. Clarke	Wilson	1916–1922
William H. Taft	Harding	1921–1930
George Sutherland	Harding	1922–1938
Pierce Butler	Harding	1922–1939
Edward T. Sanford	Harding	1923–1930
Harlan F. Stone	Coolidge	1925–1941
Charles E. Hughes	Hoover	1930–1941
Owen J. Roberts	Hoover	1930–1945
Benjamin N. Cardozo	Hoover	1932–1938
Hugo L. Black	F. Roosevelt	1937–1971
Stanley F. Reed	F. Roosevelt	1938–1957
Felix Frankfurter	F. Roosevelt	1939–1962
William O. Douglas	F. Roosevelt	1939–1975

*Boldface type indicates service as chief justice.

Frank Murphy	F. Roosevelt	1940–1949
Harlan F. Stone	F. Roosevelt	1941–1946
James F. Byrnes	F. Roosevelt	1941–1942
Robert H. Jackson	F. Roosevelt	1941–1954
Wiley B. Rutledge	F. Roosevelt	1943–1949
Harold H. Burton	Truman	1945–1958
Fred M. Vinson	Truman	1946–1953
Tom C. Clark	Truman	1949–1967
Sherman Minton	Truman	1949–1956
Earl Warren	Eisenhower	1953–1969
John M. Harlan	Eisenhower	1955–1971
William J. Brennan, Jr.	Eisenhower	1956–1990
Charles E. Whittaker	Eisenhower	1957–1962
Potter Stewart	Eisenhower	1958–1981
Byron R. White	Kennedy	1962–1993
Arthur J. Goldberg	Kennedy	1962–1965
Abe Fortas	Johnson	1965–1969
Thurgood Marshall	Johnson	1967–1991
Warren E. Burger	Nixon	1969–1986
Harry A. Blackmun	Nixon	1970–1994
Lewis F. Powell, Jr.	Nixon	1971–1987
William H. Rehnquist	Nixon	1971–1986
John Paul Stevens	Ford	1975–
Sandra Day O'Connor	Reagan	1981–2006
William H. Rehnquist	Reagan	1986–2005
Antonin Scalia	Reagan	1986–
Anthony M. Kennedy	Reagan	1988–
David H. Souter	Bush	1990–
Clarence Thomas	Bush	1991–
Ruth Bader Ginsburg	Clinton	1993–
Stephen G. Breyer	Clinton	1994–
John G. Roberts Jr.	G. W. Bush	2005–
Samuel A. Alito Jr.	G. W. Bush	2006–

GLOSSARY

527 groups Independent groups that seek to influence the political process but are not subject to contribution restrictions because they do not directly seek the election of particular candidates. Their name comes from Section 527 of the federal tax code, under which they are governed. In 2004, 52 individuals gave over a million dollars to such groups, and all told they spent $424 million on political messages.

A

activation. One of three key consequences of electoral campaigns for voters, in which the voter is activated to contribute money or ring doorbells instead of just voting. See also **reinforcement** and **conversion**.

actual group. That part of the **potential group** consisting of members who actually join. See also **interest group**.

Adarand Constructors v. Pena. A 1995 Supreme Court decision holding that federal programs that classify people by race, even for an ostensibly benign purpose such as expanding opportunities for minorities, should be presumed to be unconstitutional. Such programs must be subject to the most searching judicial inquiry and can survive only if they are "narrowly tailored" to accomplish a "compelling governmental interest."

administrative discretion. The authority of administrative actors to select among various responses to a given problem. Discretion is greatest when routines, or **standard operating procedures**, do not fit a case.

advertising. According to David Mayhew, one of three primary activities undertaken by members of Congress to increase the probability of their reelection. Advertising involves contacts between members and their constituents between elections. See also **credit claiming** and **position taking**.

affirmative action. A policy designed to give special attention to or compensatory treatment for members of some previously disadvantaged group.

agenda. See **policy agenda**.

agents of socialization. Families, schools, television, peer groups, and other influences that contribute to **political socialization** by shaping formal and especially informal learning about politics.

Americans with Disabilities Act of 1990. A law passed in 1990 that requires employers and public facilities to make "reasonable accommodations" for people with disabilities and prohibits discrimination against these individuals in employment.

amicus curiae **briefs.** Legal briefs submitted by a "friend of the court" for the purpose of raising additional points of view and presenting information not contained in the briefs of the formal parties. These briefs attempt to influence a court's decision.

Anti-Federalists. Opponents of the American Constitution at the time when the states were contemplating its adoption. They argued that the Constitution was a class-based document, that it would erode fundamental liberties, and that it would weaken the power of the states. See also **Federalists** and **U.S. Constitution**.

antitrust policy. A policy designed to ensure competition and prevent monopoly, which is the control of a market by one company.

appellate jurisdiction. The jurisdiction of courts that hear cases brought to them on appeal from lower courts. These courts do not review the factual record, only the legal issues involved. Compare **original jurisdiction**.

appropriations bill. An act of Congress that actually funds programs within limits established by **authorization bills**. Appropriations usually cover one year.

arms race. A tense relationship beginning in the 1950s between the Soviet Union and the United States whereby one side's weaponry became the other side's goad to procure more weaponry, and so on.

Articles of Confederation. The first constitution of the United States, adopted by Congress in 1777 and enacted in 1781. The Articles established a national legislature, the Continental Congress, but most authority rested with the state legislatures.

authorization bill. An act of Congress that establishes, continues, or changes a discretionary government program or an entitlement. It specifies program goals and maximum expenditures for discretionary programs. Compare **appropriations bill**.

B

balance of trade. The ratio of what is paid for imports to what is earned from exports. When more is imported than exported, there is a balance-of-trade deficit.

balanced budget amendment. A proposed amendment to the Constitution that would instruct Congress to hold a national convention to propose to the states a requirement that peacetime federal budgets be balanced. The amendment has been passed in varied forms by the legislatures of nearly two-thirds of the states.

Barron v. Baltimore. The 1833 Supreme Court decision holding that the **Bill of Rights** restrained only the national government, not the states and cities. Almost a century later, the Court first ruled in *Gitlow v. New York* that state governments must respect some **First Amendment rights**.

beats. Specific locations from which news frequently emanates, such as Congress or the White House. Most top reporters work a particular beat, thereby becoming specialists in what goes on at that location.

bicameral legislature. A legislature divided into two houses. The U.S. Congress and every American state legislature except Nebraska's are bicameral.

bill. A proposed law, drafted in precise, legal language. Anyone can draft a bill, but only a member of the House of Representatives or the Senate can formally submit a bill for consideration.

Bill of Rights. The first ten amendments to the **U.S. Constitution**, drafted in response to some of the **Anti-Federalist** concerns. These amendments define such basic liberties as freedom of religion, speech, and press and offer protections against arbitrary searches by the police and being held without talking to a lawyer.

blanket primaries. Elections to select party nominees in which voters are presented with a list of candidates from all the parties. Voters can then select some Democrats and some Republicans if they like. See also **primaries**.

block grants. Federal grants given more or less automatically to states or communities to support broad programs in areas such as community development and social services. Compare **categorical grants**.

broadcast media. Television and radio, as compared with **print media**.

Brown v. Board of Education. The 1954 Supreme Court decision holding that school segregation in Topeka, Kansas, was inherently unconstitutional because it violated the **Fourteenth Amendment's** guarantee of **equal protection**. This case marked the end of legal segregation in the United States. See also *Plessy v. Ferguson.*

budget. A policy document allocating burdens (taxes) and benefits (expenditures). See also **balanced budget amendment**.

budget resolution. A resolution binding Congress to a total expenditure level, supposedly the bottom line of all federal spending for all programs.

bureaucracy. According to Max Weber, a hierarchical authority structure that uses task specialization, operates on the merit principle, and behaves with impersonality. Bureaucracies govern modern states.

C

cabinet. A group of presidential advisers not mentioned in the Constitution, although every president has had one. Today the cabinet is composed of 14 secretaries and the attorney general.

campaign strategy. The master game plan candidates lay out to guide their electoral campaign.

capitalism. An economic system in which individuals and corporations, not the government, own the principal means of production and seek profits. Pure capitalism means the strict noninterference of the government in business affairs. Compare **mixed economy**.

casework. Activities of members of Congress that help constituents as individuals; cutting through bureaucratic red tape to get people what they think they have a right to get. See also **pork barrel**.

categorical grants. Federal grants that can be used only for specific purposes, or "categories," of state and local spending. They come with strings attached, such as nondiscrimination provisions. Compare **block grants**.

caucus (congressional). A group of members of Congress sharing some interest or characteristic. Most are composed of members from both parties and from both houses.

caucus (state party). A meeting of all state party leaders for selecting delegates to the **national party convention**. Caucuses are usually organized as a pyramid.

censorship. Governmental regulation of media content.

census. A valuable tool for understanding demographic changes. The Constitution requires that the government conduct an "actual enumeration" of the population every ten years. See also **demography**.

Central Intelligence Agency (CIA). An agency created after World War II to coordinate American intelligence activities abroad. It became involved in intrigue, conspiracy, and meddling as well.

chains. See **newspaper chains**.

checks and balances. An important part of the Madisonian model designed to limit government's power by requiring that power be balanced among the different governmental institutions. These institutions continually check one another's activities. This system reflects Madison's goal of setting power against power. See also **separation of powers**.

city manager. An offical appointed by the city council who is responsible for implementing and administrating the council's actions. More than one-third of U.S. cities use the council–manager form of government.

civic duty. The belief that in order to support democratic government, a citizen should always vote.

civil disobedience. A form of **political participation** that reflects a conscious decision to break a law believed to be immoral and to suffer the consequences. See also **protest**.

civil law. The body of law involving cases without a charge of criminality. It concerns disputes between two parties and consists of both statutes and **common law**. Compare **criminal law**.

civil liberties. The legal constitutional protections against government. Although our civil liberties are formally set down in the **Bill of Rights**, the courts, police, and legislatures define their meaning.

civil rights. Policies designed to protect people against arbitrary or discriminitory treatment by government officials or individuals.

Civil Rights Act of 1964. The law that made racial discrimination against any group in hotels, motels, and restaurants illegal and forbade many forms of job discrimination. See also **civil rights movement** and **civil rights policies**.

civil rights movement. A movement that began in the 1950s and organized both African Americans and Whites to end the policies of segregation. It sought to establish equal opportunities in the political and economic sectors and to end policies that erected barriers between people because of race.

civil rights policies. Policies that extend government protection to particular disadvantaged groups. Compare **social welfare policies**.

civil service. A system of hiring and promotion based on the **merit principle** and the desire to create a nonpartisan government service. Compare **patronage**.

class action suits. Lawsuits permitting a small number of people to sue on behalf of all other people similarly situated.

Clean Air Act of 1970. The law aimed at combating air pollution.

Clean Water Act of 1972. A law intended to clean up the nation's rivers and lakes. It requires municipal, industrial, and other polluters to use pollution control technology and secure permits from the **Environmental Protection Agency** for discharging waste products into waters.

closed primaries. Elections to select party nominees in which only people who have registered in advance with the party can vote for that party's candidates, thus encouraging greater party loyalty. See also **primaries**.

coalition. A group of individuals with a common interest upon which every political party depends. See also **New Deal Coalition**.

coalition government. When two or more parties join together to form a majority in a national legislature. This form of government is quite common in the multiparty systems of Europe.

coattails. See **presidential coattails**.

Cold War. War by other than military means usually emphasizing ideological conflict, such as that between the United States and the Soviet Union from the end of World War II until the 1990s.

collective bargaining. Negotiations between representatives of labor unions and management to determine acceptable working conditions.

collective good. Something of value (money, a tax write-off, prestige, clean air, and so on) that cannot be withheld from a group member.

command-and-control policy. According to Charles Schultze, the existing system of **regulation** whereby government tells business how to reach certain goals, checks that these commands are followed, and punishes offenders. Compare **incentive system**.

commercial speech. Communication in the form of advertising. It can be restricted more than many other types of speech but has been receiving increased protection from the Supreme Court.

commission government. A form of municipal government in which voters elect individuals to serve as city commissioners who will have legislative responsibilities to approve city policies and executive responsibilities to direct a functional area of city government, such as public safety or public works. See also **mayor-council government** and **council–manager government**.

committee chairs. The most important influencers of the congressional agenda. They play dominant roles in scheduling hearings, hiring staff, appointing subcommittees, and managing committee bills when they are brought before the full house.

committees (congressional). See **conference committees, joint committees, select committees,** and **standing committees**.

common law. The accumulation of judicial decisions applied in **civil law** disputes.

comparable worth. The issue raised when women are paid less than men for working at jobs requiring comparable skill.

conference committees. Congressional committees formed when the Senate and the House pass a particular **bill** in different forms. Party leadership appoints members from each house to iron out the differences and bring back a single bill. See also **standing committees, joint committees,** and **select committees**.

Congressional Budget and Impoundment Control Act of 1974. An act designed to reform the congressional budgetary process. Its supporters hoped that it would also make Congress less dependent on the president's budget and better able to set and meet its own budgetary goals.

Congressional Budget Office (CBO). A counterweight to the president's **Office of Management and Budget (OMB)**. The CBO advises Congress on the probable consequences of budget decisions and forecasts revenues.

Connecticut Compromise. The compromise reached at the Constitutional Convention that established two houses of Congress: the House of Representatives, in which **representation** is based on a state's share of the U.S. population, and the Senate, in which each state has two representatives. Compare **New Jersey Plan** and **Virginia Plan**.

consensus. Agreement. Consensus is reflected by an opinion distribution in which a large majority see eye to eye.

consent of the governed. According to John Locke, the required basis for government. **The Declaration of Independence** reflects Locke's view that governments derive their authority from the consent of the governed.

conservatives. Those who advocate **conservatism**. Compare **liberals**.

constitution. A nation's basic law. It creates political institutions, assigns or divides powers in government, and often provides certain guarantees to citizens. Constitutions can be either written or unwritten. See also **U.S. Constitution**.

constitutional convention. A method of amending a state constitution in which voters may approve the calling of a convention of state citizens to propose amendments to the state constitution; the proposals are submitted to state voters for approval. See also **initiative** and **legislative proposal**.

constitutional courts. Lower federal courts of original jurisdiction created by Congress by the Judiciary Act of 1789. Compare **legislative courts**.

consumer price index (CPI). The key measure of **inflation** that relates the rise in prices over time.

containment doctrine. A **foreign policy** strategy advocated by George Kennan that called for the United States to isolate the Soviet Union, "contain" its advances, and resist its encroachments by peaceful means if possible, but by force if necessary.

continuing resolutions. When Congress cannot reach agreement and pass appropriations bills, these resolutions allow agencies to spend at the level of the previous year.

convention. See **national party convention**.

conversion. One of three key consequences of electoral campaigns for voters, in which the voter's mind is actually changed. See also **reinforcement** and **activation**.

cooperative federalism. A system of government in which powers and policy assignments are shared between states and the national government. They may also share costs, administration, and even blame for programs that work poorly. Compare **dual federalism**.

council–manager government. A common form of government used by municipalities in which voters elect a city council (and possibly an independent mayor) to make public policy for the city. The city council, in turn, appoints a professional city manager to serve as chief executive of the city and to administer public policy. See also **mayor-council government** and **commission government**.

Council of Economic Advisers (CEA). A three-member body appointed by the president to advise the president on economic policy.

council of governments (COG). Councils in many areas of the country where officials from various localities meet to discuss mutual problems and plan joint, cooperative action.

county. A political subdivision of state government that has a set of government officers to administer some local services—often on behalf of the state. Called a *parish* in Louisiana and a *borough* in Alaska. See also **county government**.

county government. A unit of local government that serves as the administrative arm of state government at the local level. It has many social service and record-keeping responsibilities. See also **county**.

court of last resort. The final appeals court in a state, often known as the state "supreme court."

courts. See **constitutional courts, legislative courts, district courts**, and **courts of appeal**.

courts of appeal. Appellate courts empowered to review all final decisions of district courts, except in rare cases. In addition, they also hear appeals to orders of many federal regulatory agencies. Compare **district courts**.

Craig v. Boren. In this 1976 Supreme Court decision, the Court determined that gender classification cases would have a "heightened" or "middle level" of scrutiny. In other words, the courts were to show less deference to gender classifications than to more routine classifications, but more deference than to racial classifications.

credit claiming. According to David Mayhew, one of three primary activities undertaken by members of Congress to increase the probability of their reelection. It involves personal and district service. See also **advertising** and **position taking**.

criminal law. The body of law involving a case in which an individual is charged with violating a specific law. The offense may be harmful to an individual or society and in either case warrants punishment, such as imprisonment or a fine. Compare **civil law**.

crisis. A sudden, unpredictable, and potentially dangerous event requiring the president to play the role of crisis manager.

critical election. An electoral "earthquake" whereby new issues emerge, new coalitions replace old ones, and the majority party is often displaced by the minority party. Critical election periods are sometimes marked by a national crisis and may require more than one election to bring about a new **party era**. See also **party realignment**.

cruel and unusual punishment. Court sentences prohibited by the **Eighth Amendment**. Although the Supreme Court has ruled that mandatory death sentences for certain offenses are unconstitutional, it has not held that the death penalty itself constitutes cruel and unusual punishment. See also *Furman v. Georgia, Gregg v. Georgia,* and *McClesky v. Kemp*.

culture of poverty. Negative attitudes and values toward work, family, and success that condemn the poor to low levels of accomplishment. The view that there is a culture of poverty is most commonly held by **conservatives**.

D

Dartmouth College v. Woodward. The 1819 case in which the Supreme Court held that Dartmouth's charter, as well as the charter of any corporation, is a legalcontract that cannot be tampered with by a government.

dealignment. See **party dealignment**.

debate. See **presidential debate**.

debt. See **federal debt**.

Declaration of Independence. The document approved by representatives of the American colonies in 1776 that stated their grievances against the British monarch and declared their independence.

deficit. An excess of federal **expenditures** over federal **revenues**. See also **budget**.

delegate. See **instructed delegate**.

democracy. A system of selecting policymakers and of organizing government so that policy represents and responds to the public's preferences.

democratic theory. See **traditional democratic theory**.

demography. The science of population changes. See also **census**.

Dennis v. United States. A 1951 Supreme Court decision that permitted the government to jail several American Communist Party leaders under the Smith Act, a law forbidding advocacy of the violent overthrow of the U.S. government.

deregulation. The lifting of restrictions on business, industry, and professional activities for which government rules had been established and that bureaucracies had been created to administer.

détente. A slow transformation from conflict thinking to cooperative thinking in **foreign policy** strategy and policymaking. It sought a relaxation of tensions between the superpowers, coupled with firm guarantees of mutual security.

devolution. Transferring responsibility for policies from the federal government to state and local governments.

Dillon's Rule. The idea that local governments have only those powers that are explicitly given them by the states. This means that local governments have very little discretion over what policies they pursue or how they pursue them. It was named for Iowa Judge John Dillon, who expressed this idea in an 1868 court decision.

direct democracy. Procedures such as the initiative, the referendum, and the recall, by which voters can have a direct impact on policymaking and the political process by means of the voting booth.

direct mail. A high-tech method of raising money for a political cause or candidate. It involves sending information and requests for money to people whose names appear on lists of those who have supported similar views or candidates in the past.

direct primaries. **Primaries** used to select party nominees for congressional and state offices.

district courts. The 91 federal courts of original jurisdiction. They are the only federal courts in which no trials are held and in which juries may be empaneled. Compare **courts of appeal**.

dual federalism. A system of government in which both the states and the national government remain supreme within their own spheres, each responsible for some policies. Compare **cooperative federalism**.

due process clause. Part of the **Fourteenth Amendment** guaranteeing that persons cannot be deprived of life, liberty, or property by the United States or state governments without due process of law. See also *Gitlow v. New York*.

E

earned income tax credit (EITC). A "negative income tax" that provides income to very poor individuals in lieu of charging them federal tax.

efficacy. See **political efficacy**.

Eighth Amendment. The constitutional amendment that forbids **cruel and unusual punishment**, although it does not define this phrase. Through the **Fourteenth Amendment**, this **Bill of Rights** provision applies to the states.

elastic clause. The final paragraph of Article I, Section 8, of the Constitution, which authorizes Congress to pass all laws "necessary and proper" to carry out the enumerated powers. See also **implied powers**.

electioneering. Direct group involvement in the electoral process. Groups can help fund campaigns, provide testimony, and get members to work for candidates, and some form **political action committees (PACs)**.

electoral college. A unique American institution created by the Constitution that provides for the selection of the president by electors chosen by the state parties. Although the electoral college vote usually reflects a popular majority, the winner-take-all rule gives clout to big states.

electoral mandate. A concept based on the idea that "the people have spoken." It is a powerful symbol in American electoral politics, according legitimacy and credibility to a newly elected president's proposals. See also **mandate theory of politics**.

elite. The upper class in a society that utilizes wealth for political power. According to the **elite and class theory** of government and politics, elites control policies because they control key institutions.

elite theory. A theory of government and politics contending that societies are divided along class lines and that an upper-class elite will rule, regardless of the formal niceties of governmental organization. Compare **hyperpluralism, pluralist theory**, and **traditional democratic theory**.

Endangered Species Act of 1973. This law requires the federal government to protect actively each of the hundreds of species listed as endangered—regardless of the economic effect on the surrounding towns or region.

Engel v. Vitale. The 1962 Supreme Court decision holding that state officials violated the **First Amendment** when they wrote a prayer to be recited by New York's schoolchildren. Compare *School District of Abington Township, Pennsylvania v. Schempp*.

entitlement programs. Policies for which expenditures are uncontrollable because Congress has in effect obligated itself to pay X level of benefits to Y number of recipients. Each year, Congress' bill is a straightforward function of the X level of benefits times the Y number of beneficiaries. Social Security benefits are an example.

entrepreneur. See **political entrepreneur**.

enumerated powers. Powers of the federal government that are specifically addressed in the Constitution; for Congress, these powers are listed in Article I, Section 8, and include the power to coin money, regulate its value, and impose taxes. Compare **implied powers**.

environmental impact statement (EIS). A report filed with the **Environmental Protection Agency (EPA)** that specifies what environmental effects a proposed policy would have. The **National Environmental Policy Act** requires that whenever any agency proposes to undertake a policy that is potentially disruptive of the environment, the agency must file a statement with the EPA.

Environmental Protection Agency (EPA). An agency of the federal government created in 1970 and charged with administering all the government's environmental legislation. It also administers policies dealing with toxic wastes. The EPA is the largest federal **independent regulatory agency**.

equal opportunity. A policy statement about equality holding that the rules of the game should be the same for everyone. Most of our **civil rights** policies over the past three decades have presumed that equality of opportunity is a public policy goal. Compare **equal results**.

equal protection of the laws. Part of the **Fourteenth Amendment** emphasizing that the laws must provide equivalent "protection" to all people. As one member of Congress said during debate on the amendment, it should provide "equal protection of life, liberty, and property" to all a state's citizens.

equal results. A policy statement about equality holding that government has a duty to help break down barriers to **equal opportunity**. **Affirmative action** is an example of a policy justified as promoting equal results rather than merely equal opportunities.

Equal Rights Amendment (ERA). A constitutional amendment originally introduced in 1923 and passed by Congress in 1972 and sent to the state legislatures for ratification, stating that "equality of rights under the law shall not be denied or abridged by the United States or by any state on account of sex." Despite substantial public support and an extended deadline, the amendment failed to acquire the necessary support from three-fourths of the state legislatures.

establishment clause. Part of the **First Amendment** stating that "Congress shall make no law respecting an establishment of religion."

European Union (EU). An alliance of the major Western European nations that coordinates monetary, trade, immigration, and labor policies, making its members one economic unit. An example of a regional organization.

exclusionary rule. The rule that evidence, no matter how incriminating, cannot be introduced into a trial if it was not constitutionally obtained. The rule prohibits use of evidence obtained through **unreasonable search and seizure**.

executive agency. See **independent executive agency**.

executive orders. Regulations originating from the executive branch. Executive orders are one method presidents can use to control the bureaucracy; more often, though, presidents pass along their wishes through their aides.

exit poll. Public opinion surveys used by major media pollsters to predict electoral winners with speed and precision.

expenditures. Federal spending of **revenues**. Major areas of such spending are social services and the military.

extradition. A legal process whereby an alleged criminal offender is surrendered by the officials of one state to officials of the state in which the crime is alleged to have been committed.

F

facilitator. According to George Edwards, the effective leader who works at the margin of coalition building to recognize and exploit opportunities presented by a favorable configuration of political forces.

factions. Interest groups arising from the unequal distribution of property or wealth that James Madison attacked in *Federalist Paper No. 10*. Today's parties or interest groups are what Madison had in mind when he warned of the instability in government caused by factions.

federal debt. All the money borrowed by the federal government over the years and still outstanding. Today the federal debt is more than $8 trillion.

Federal Election Campaign Act. A law passed in 1974 for reforming campaign finances. The act created the **Federal Election Commission (FEC)**, provided public financing for presidential primaries and general elections, limited presidential campaign spending, required disclosure, and attempted to limit contributions.

Federal Election Commission (FEC). A six-member bipartisan agency created by the **Federal Election Campaign Act** of 1974. The FEC administers the campaign finance laws and enforces compliance with their requirements.

Federal Regulation of Lobbying Act. Passed in 1946, an act requiring congressional lobbyists to register and state their policy goals. According to the Supreme Court, the law applies only to groups whose "principal" purpose is **lobbying**.

Federal Reserve System. The main instrument for making **monetary policy** in the United States. It was created by Congress in 1913 to regulate the lending practices of banks and thus the money supply. The seven members of its Board of Governors are appointed to 14-year terms by the president with the consent of the Senate.

Federal Trade Commission (FTC). The **independent regulatory agency** traditionally responsible for regulating false and misleading trade practices. The FTC has recently become active in defending consumer interests through its truth-in-advertising rule and the Consumer Credit Protection Act.

federalism. A way of organizing a nation so that two levels of government have formal authority over the same land and people. It is a system of shared power between units of government. Compare **unitary government**.

Federalist Papers. A collection of 85 articles written by Alexander Hamilton, John Jay, and James Madison under the name "Publius" to defend the Constitution in detail. Collectively, these papers are second only to the **U.S. Constitution** in characterizing the framers' intents.

Federalists. Supporters of the **U.S. Constitution** at the time the states were contemplating its adoption. See also **Anti-Federalists** and **Federalist Papers**.

feminization of poverty. The increasing concentration of poverty among women, especially unmarried women and their children.

Fifteenth Amendment. The constitutional amendment adopted in 1870 to extend **suffrage** to African Americans.

Fifth Amendment. The constitutional amendment designed to protect the rights of persons accused of crimes, including protection against double jeopardy, **self-incrimination**, and punishment without due process of law.

filibuster. A strategy unique to the Senate whereby opponents of a piece of legislation try to talk it to death, based on the tradition of unlimited debate. Today, 60 members present and voting can halt a filibuster.

First Amendment. The constitutional amendment that establishes the four great liberties: freedom of the press, of speech, of religion, and of assembly.

fiscal federalism. The pattern of spending, taxing, and providing grants in the federal system; it is the cornerstone of the national government's relations with state and local governments. See also **federalism**.

fiscal policy. The policy that describes the impact of the federal budget—taxes, spending, and borrowing—on the economy. Unlike **monetary policy**, which is mostly controlled by the **Federal Reserve System**, fiscal policy is almost entirely determined by Congress and the president, who are the budget makers. See also **Keynesian economic theory**.

Food and Drug Administration (FDA). The federal agency formed in 1913 and assigned the task of approving all food products and drugs sold in the United States. All drugs, with the exception of tobacco, must have FDA authorization.

foreign policy. A policy that involves choice taking, like domestic policy, but additionally involves choices about relations with the rest of the world. The president is the chief initiator of foreign policy in the United States.

formula grants. Federal **categorical grants** distributed according to a formula specified in legislation or in administrative regulations.

Fourteenth Amendment. The constitutional amendment adopted after the Civil War that states, "No State shall make or enforce any law which shall abridge the privileges or immunities of citizens of the United States; nor shall any state deprive any person of life, liberty, or property, without due process of law; nor deny to any person within its jurisdiction the **equal protection of the laws**." See also **due process clause**.

fragmentation. A situation in which responsibility for a policy area is dispersed among several units within the bureaucracy, making the coordination of policies both time consuming and difficult.

free exercise clause. A **First Amendment** provision that prohibits government from interfering with the practice of religion.

free-rider problem. The problem faced by unions and other groups when people do not join because they can benefit from the group's activities without officially joining. The bigger the group, the more serious the free-rider problem. See also **interest group**.

frontloading. The recent tendency of states to hold primaries early in the calendar in order to capitalize on media attention. At one time, it was considered advantageous for a state to choose its delegates late in the primary season so that it could play a decisive role. However, in recent years, votes cast in states that have held late primaries have been irrelevant given that one candidate had already sewn up the nomination early on.

full faith and credit clause. A clause in Article IV, Section 1, of the Constitution requiring each state to recognize the official documents and civil judgments rendered by the courts of other states.

G

gender gap. A term that refers to the regular pattern by which women are more likely to support Democratic candidates. Women tend to be significantly less conservative than men and are more likely to support spending on social services and to oppose higher levels of military spending.

General Schedule rating. See **GS (General Schedule) rating**.

Gibbons v. Ogden. A landmark case decided in 1824 in which the Supreme Court interpreted very broadly the clause in Article I, Section 8, of the Constitution giving Congress the power to regulate interstate commerce, encompassing virtually every form of commercial activity. The commerce clause has been the constitutional basis for much of Congress' regulation of the economy.

Gideon v. Wainwright. The 1963 Supreme Court decision holding that anyone accused of a felony where imprisonment may be imposed, however poor he or she might be, has a right to a lawyer. See also **Sixth Amendment**.

Gitlow v. New York. The 1925 Supreme Court decision holding that freedoms of press and speech are "fundamental personal rights and liberties protected by the **due process clause** of the **Fourteenth Amendment** from impairment by the states" as well as the federal government. Compare *Barron v. Baltimore*.

government. The institutions and processes through which **public policies** are made for a society.

governmental corporation. A government organization that, like business corporations, provides a service that could be provided by the private sector and typically charges for its services. The U.S. Postal Service is an example. Compare **independent regulatory agency** and **independent executive agency**.

governor. The elected chief executive of state government who directs the administration of state government and the implementation of public policy in the state.

Gramm-Rudman-Hollings. Named for its sponsors and also known as the Balanced Budget and Emergency Deficit Act, legislation mandating maximum allowable deficit levels each year until 1991, when the budget was to be balanced. In 1987, the balanced budget year was shifted to 1993, but the Act was abandoned in 1991.

grandfather clause. One of the methods used by Southern states to deny African Americans the right to vote. In order to exempt illiterate Whites from taking a literacy test before voting, the clause exempted people whose grandfathers were eligible to vote in 1860, thereby disenfranchising the grandchildren of slaves. The grandfather clause was declared unconstitutional by the Supreme Court in 1913. See also **poll taxes** and **White primary**.

grants. See **categorical grants** and **block grants**.

Gregg v. Georgia. The 1976 Supreme Court decision that upheld the constitutionality of the death penalty, stating that "It is an extreme sanction, suitable to the most extreme of crimes." The

court did not, therefore, believe that the death sentence constitutes **cruel and unusual punishment**.

gross domestic product. The sum total of the value of all the goods and services produced in a nation.

GS (General Schedule) rating. A schedule for federal employees, ranging from GS 1 to GS 18, by which salaries can be keyed to rating and experience. See **civil service**.

H

Hatch Act. A federal law prohibiting government employees from active participation in partisan politics.

health maintenance organizations (HMOs). Organizations contracted by individuals or insurance companies to provide health care for a yearly fee. Such network health plans limit the choice of doctors and treatments. About 60 percent of Americans are enrolled in HMOs or similar programs.

Hernandez v. Texas A 1954 Supreme Court decision that extended protection against discrimination to Hispanics.

high-tech politics. A politics in which the behavior of citizens and policymakers and the political agenda itself are increasingly shaped by technology.

home rule. The practice by which municipalities are permitted by the states to write their own charters and change them without permission of the state legislature, within limits. Today this practice is widely used to organize and modernize municipal government. See also **local charter**.

House Rules Committee. An institution unique to the House of Representatives that reviews all bills (except revenue, budget, and appropriations bills) coming from a House committee before they go to the full House.

House Ways and Means Committee. The House of Representatives committee that, along with the **Senate Finance Committee**, writes the tax codes, subject to the approval of Congress as a whole.

hyperpluralism. A theory of government and politics contending that groups are so strong that government is weakened. Hyperpluralism is an extreme, exaggerated, or perverted form of **pluralism**. Compare **elite and class theory**, **pluralist theory**, and **traditional democratic theory**.

I

ideology. See **political ideology**.

impacts. See **policy impacts**.

impeachment. The political equivalent of an indictment in criminal law, prescribed by the Constitution. The House of Representatives may impeach the president by a majority vote for "Treason, Bribery, or other high Crimes and Misdemeanors."

implementation. The stage of policymaking between the establishment of a policy and the consequences of the policy for the people whom it affects. Implementation involves translating the goals and objectives of a policy into an operating, ongoing program. See also **judicial implementation**.

implied powers. Powers of the federal government that go beyond those enumerated in the Constitution. The Constitution states that Congress has the power to "make all laws necessary and proper for carrying into execution" the powers enumerated in Article I. Many federal policies are justified on the basis of implied powers. See also *McCulloch v. Maryland,* **elastic clause**, and **enumerated powers.**

incentive system. According to Charles Shultze, a more effective and efficient policy than **command-and-control;** in the incentive system, market-like strategies are used to manage public policy.

income. The amount of funds collected between any two points in time. Compare **wealth.**

income distribution. The "shares" of the national income earned by various groups.

income tax. Shares of individual wages and corporate revenues collected by the government. The first income tax was declared unconstitutional by the Supreme Court in 1895, but the **Sixteenth Amendment** explicitly authorized Congress to levy a tax on income. See also **Internal Revenue Service.**

incorporation doctrine. The legal concept under which the **Supreme Court** has nationalized the **Bill of Rights** by making most of its provisions applicable to the states through the **Fourteenth Amendment.**

incrementalism. The belief that the best predictor of this year's **budget** is last year's budget, plus a little bit more (an increment). According to Aaron Wildavsky, "Most of the budget is a product of previous decisions."

incumbents. Those already holding office. In congressional elections, incumbents usually win.

independent executive agency. The government not accounted for by **cabinet** departments, **independent regulatory agencies**, and **government corporations**. Its administrators are typically appointed by the president and serve at the president's pleasure. NASA is an example.

independent regulatory agency. A government agency responsible for some sector of the economy, making and enforcing rules supposedly to protect the public interest. It also judges disputes over these rules. Compare **government corporation** and **independent executive agency.**

industrial policy. An economic policy that advocates the federal government's support of key strategic industries, such as the making of computer chips, and protection of these industries from foreign competition by tariffs and other measures.

INF Treaty. The elimination of intermediate range nuclear forces (INF) through an agreement signed by President Reagan and Mikhail Gorbachev during the May 1988 Moscow summit. It was the first treaty to reduce current levels of nuclear weapons.

inflation. The rise in prices for consumer goods. Inflation hurts some but actually benefits others. Groups such as those who live on fixed incomes are particularly hard hit, while people whose salary increases are tied to the **consumer price index** but whose loan rates are fixed may enjoy increased buying power.

initiative. A process permitted in some states whereby voters may put proposed changes in the state constitution to a vote if sufficient signatures are obtained on petitions calling for such a referendum. See also **legislative proposal** and **constitutional convention.**

instructed delegate. A legislator who mirrors the preferences of his or her constituents. Compare **trustee.**

interdependency. Mutual dependency, in which the actions of nations reverberate and affect one another's economic lifelines.

interest group. An organization of people with shared policy goals entering the policy process at several points to try to achieve those goals. Interest groups pursue their goals in many arenas.

intergenerational equity. The issue of the distribution of government benefits and burdens among the generations and over time. Affected groups include children, the working and middle classes, and the elderly, all of whom are beneficiaries of public policies.

intergovernmental relations. The workings of the federal system—the entire set of interactions among national, state, and local governments.

Internal Revenue Service. The office established to collect federal **income taxes**, investigate violations of the tax laws, and prosecute tax criminals.

investigative journalism. The use of in-depth reporting to unearth scandals, scams, and schemes, which at times puts reporters in adversarial relationships with political leaders.

iron triangles. Entities composed of bureaucratic agencies, interest groups, and congressional committees or subcommittees, which have dominated some areas of domestic policymaking. Iron triangles are characterized by mutual dependency, in which each element provides key services, information, or policy for the others.

isolationism. A **foreign policy** course followed throughout most of our nation's history, whereby the United States has tried to stay out of other nations' conflicts, particularly European wars. Isolationism was reaffirmed by the Monroe Doctrine.

issue. See **political issue.**

item veto. The power possessed by 42 state governors to veto only certain parts of a bill while allowing the rest of it to pass into law.

J

Joint Chiefs of Staff. The commanding officers of the armed services who advise the president on military policy.

joint committees. Congressional committees on a few subject-matter areas with membership drawn from both houses. See also **standing committees, conference committees**, and **select committees.**

judicial activism. A judicial philosophy in which judges make bold policy decisions, even charting new constitutional ground. Advocates of this approach emphasize that the courts can correct pressing needs, especially those unmet by the majoritarian political process.

judicial implementation. How and whether court decisions are translated into actual policy, affecting the behavior of others. The courts rely on other units of government to enforce their decisions.

judicial interpretation. A major informal way in which the Constitution is changed by the courts as they balance citizens' rights against those of the government. See also **judicial review.**

judicial restraint. A judicial philosophy in which judges play minimal policymaking roles, leaving that strictly to the legislatures. Compare **judicial activism.**

judicial review. The power of the courts to determine whether acts of Congress, and by implication the executive, are in accord with the **U.S. Constitution**. Judicial review was established by

John Marshall and his associates in *Marbury v. Madison*. See also **judicial interpretation**.

jurisdiction. See **original jurisdiction** and **appellate jurisdiction**.

justiciable disputes. A constraint on the courts, requiring that a case must be capable of being settled by legal methods.

K

Keynesian economic theory. The theory emphasizing that government spending and deficits can help the economy weather its normal ups and downs. Proponents of this theory advocate using the power of government to stimulate the economy when it is lagging. See also **fiscal policy**.

Korematsu v. United States. A 1944 Supreme Court decision that upheld as constitutional the internment of more than 100,000 Americans of Japanese descent in encampments during World War II.

L

labor union. An organization of workers intended to engage in **collective bargaining**.

laissez-faire. The principle that government should not meddle in the economy. See also **capitalism**.

leak. See **news leak**.

legislative courts. Courts established by Congress for specialized purposes, such as the Court of Military Appeals. Judges who serve on these courts have fixed terms and lack the protections of **constitutional court** judges.

legislative oversight. Congress's monitoring of the bureaucracy and its administration of policy, performed mainly through hearings.

legislative proposal. A method of state constitutional revision in which the state legislature offers a proposed change to state voters for approval (or may be used to describe a bill proposed by a legislator). See also **constitutional convention** and **initiative**.

legislative turnover. The rate at which incumbent state legislators leave office by choice or by defeat during a bid for reelection.

legislative veto. The ability of Congress to override a presidential decision. Although the **War Powers Resolution** asserts this authority, there is reason to believe that, if challenged, the Supreme Court would find the legislative veto in violation of the doctrine of separation of powers.

legislators. The elected representatives of state citizens who serve in the state legislature and make public policy.

legitimacy. A characterization of elections by political scientists meaning that they are almost universally accepted as a fair and free method of selecting political leaders. When legitimacy is high, as in the United States, even the losers accept the results peacefully.

Lemon v. Kurtzman. The 1971 Supreme Court decision that established that aid to church-related schools must (1) have a secular legislative purpose (2) have a primary effect that neither advances nor inhibits religion and (3) not foster excessive government entanglement with religion.

libel. The publication of false or malicious statements that damage someone's reputation.

liberalism. A **political ideology** whose advocates prefer a government active in dealing with human needs, support individual rights and liberties, and give higher priority to social needs than to military needs.

lieutenant governor. Often the second-highest executive official in state government, who is elected with the governor as a ticket in some states and is elected separately in others. May have legislative and executive branch responsibilities.

limited government. The idea that certain things are out of bounds for government because of the **natural rights** of citizens. Limited government was central to John Locke's philosophy in the seventeenth century, and it contrasted sharply with the prevailing view of the divine rights of monarchs.

line-item veto. The power possessed by 42 state governors to veto only certain parts of a bill while allowing the rest of it to pass into law.

linkage institutions. The channels or access points through which issues and people's policy preferences get on the government's **policy agenda**. In the United States, elections, **political parties, interest groups**, and the **mass media** are the three main linkage institutions.

litigants. The **plaintiff** and the **defendant** in a **case**.

lobbying. According to Lester Milbrath, a "communication, by someone other than a citizen acting on his own behalf, directed to a governmental decisionmaker with the hope of influencing his decision."

local charter. An organizational statement and grant of authority from the state to a local government, much like a state or federal constitution. States sometimes allow municipalities to write their own charters and to change them without permission of the state legislature, within limits. See also **home rule**.

M

majority leader. The principal partisan ally of the Speaker of the House or the party's wheel horse in the Senate. The majority leader is responsible for scheduling bills, influencing committee assignments, and rounding up votes in behalf of the party's legislative positions.

majority rule. A fundamental principle of **traditional democratic theory**. In a democracy, choosing among alternatives requires that the majority's desire be respected. See also **minority rights**.

mandate. See **electoral mandate** and **mandate theory of elections**.

mandate theory of elections. The idea that the winning candidate has a mandate from the people to carry out his or her platforms and politics. Politicians like the theory better than political scientists do.

Mapp v. Ohio. The 1961 Supreme Court decision ruling that the Fourth Amendment's protection against **unreasonable searches and seizures** must be extended to the states as well as the federal government. See also **exclusionary rule**.

Marbury v. Madison. The 1803 case in which Chief Justice John Marshall and his associates first asserted the right of the **Supreme Court** to determine the meaning of the **U.S. Constitution**. The decision established the Court's power of **judicial review** over acts of Congress, in this case the Judiciary Act of 1789.

mass media. Television, radio, newspapers, magazines, and other means of popular communication. They are a key part of **high-tech politics**. See also **broadcast media** and **print media**.

matching funds. Contributions of up to $250 are matched from the Presidential Election Campaign Fund to candidates for the presidential nomination who qualify and agree to meet various conditions, such as limiting their overall spending.

mayor–council government. One of three common forms of municipal government in which voters elect both a mayor and a city council. In the weak mayor form, the city council is more powerful; in the strong mayor form, the mayor is the chief executive of city government. See also **council–manager government**.

McCarthyism. The fear, prevalent in the 1950s, that international communism was conspiratorial, insidious, bent on world domination, and infiltrating American government and cultural institutions. It was named after Senator Joseph McCarthy and flourished after the Korean War.

McCleskey v. Kemp. The 1987 Supreme Court decision that upheld the constitutionality of the death penalty against charges that it violated the **Fourteenth Amendment** because minority defendants were more likely to receive the death penalty than White defendants.

McCulloch v. Maryland. An 1819 Supreme Court decision that established the supremacy of the national government over state governments. In deciding this case, Chief Justice John Marshall and his colleagues held that Congress had certain **implied powers** in addition to the **enumerated powers** found in the Constitution.

McGovern-Fraser Commission. A commission formed at the 1968 Democratic convention in response to demands for reform by minority groups and others who sought better representation.

means-tested programs. Government programs available only to individuals below a poverty line.

media events. Events purposely staged for the media that nonetheless look spontaneous. In keeping with politics as theater, media events can be staged by individuals, groups, and government officials, especially presidents.

Medicaid. A public assistance program designed to provide health care for poor Americans. Medicaid is funded by both the states and the national government. Compare **Medicare**.

Medicare. A program added to the Social Security system in 1965 that provides hospitalization insurance for the elderly and permits older Americans to purchase inexpensive coverage for doctor fees and other expenses. Compare **Medicaid**.

melting pot. The mixing of cultures, ideas, and peoples that has changed the American nation. The United States, with its history of immigration, has often been called a melting pot.

merit plan. A hybrid system of appointment and election used to select judges in 17 states. In this system the governor appoints the state's judges from a list of recommended persons; an appointed judge then serves a short "trial run" term, after which a retention election is held. If voters approve retention by a majority vote, then the judge continues in office for a lengthy term.

merit principle. The idea that hiring should be based on entrance exams and promotion ratings to produce administration by people with talent and skill. See also **civil service** and compare **patronage**.

Miami Herald Publishing Company v. Tornillo. A 1974 case in which the Supreme Court held that a state could not force a newspaper to print replies from candidates it had criticized, illustrating the limited power of government to restrict the **print media**. See *Red Lion Broadcasting Company v. FCC*.

Miller v. California. A 1973 Supreme Court decision that avoided defining obscenity by holding that community standards be used to determine whether material is obscene in terms of appealing to a "prurient interest."

minimum wage. The legal minimum hourly wage for large employers, currently $5.15 per hour.

minority leader. The principal leader of the minority party in the House of Representatives or in the Senate.

minority majority. The emergence of a non-Caucasian majority, as compared with a White, generally Anglo-Saxon majority. It is predicted that, by about 2060, Hispanic Americans, African Americans, and Asian Americans together will outnumber White Americans.

minority rights. A principle of **traditional democratic theory** that guarantees rights to those who do not belong to majorities and allows that they might join majorities through persuasion and reasoned argument. See also **majority rule**.

Miranda v. Arizona. The 1966 Supreme Court decision that sets guidelines for police questioning of accused persons to protect them against **self-incrimination** and to protect their right to counsel.

mixed economy. An economic system in which the government is deeply involved in economic decisions through its role as regulator, consumer, subsidizer, taxer, employer, and borrower. The United States can be considered a mixed economy. Compare **capitalism**.

monetarism. An economic theory holding that the supply of money is the key to a nation's economic health. Monetarists believe that too much cash and credit in circulation produces inflation. See also **monetary policy**.

monetary policy. Based on **monetarism**, monetary policy is the manipulation of the supply of money in private hands by which the government can control the economy. See also the **Federal Reserve System**, and compare **fiscal policy**.

Motor Voter Act. Passed in 1993, this act went into effect for the 1996 election. It requires states to permit people to register to vote at the same time they apply for driver's licenses.

multinational corporations. Large businesses with vast holdings in many countries. Many of these companies are larger than most governments.

municipalities. Another name for *cities*, also known by the legal term *municipal corporations;* denotes a government created by charter granted from the state government or by home rule charter approved by local voters.

N

NAACP v. Alabama. The Supreme Court protected the right to assemble peaceably in this 1958 case when it decided the NAACP did not have to reveal its membership list and thus subject its members to harassment.

narrowcasting. As opposed to the traditional "broadcasting," the appeal to a narrow, particular audience by channels such as ESPN, MTV, and C-SPAN, which focus on a narrow particular interest.

national chairperson. One of the institutions that keeps the party operating between conventions. The national chairperson is responsible for the day-to-day activities of the party and is usually selected by the presidential nominee. See also **national committee**.

national committee. One of the institutions that keeps the party operating between conventions. The national committee is composed of representatives from the states and territories. See also **national chairperson**.

national convention. The meeting of party delegates every four years to choose a presidential ticket and write the party's platform.

National Environmental Policy Act (NEPA). The law passed in 1969 that is the centerpiece of federal environmental policy in the United States. The NEPA established the requirements for **environmental impact statements**.

national health insurance. A compulsory insurance program for all Americans that would have the government finance citizens' medical care. First proposed by President Harry S Truman, the plan has been soundly opposed by the American Medical Association.

National Labor Relations Act. A 1935 law, also known as the Wagner Act, that guarantees workers the right of **collective bargaining**, sets down rules to protect unions and organizers, and created the National Labor Relations Board to regulate labor management relations.

national party convention. The supreme power within each of the parties. The convention meets every four years to nominate the party's presidential and vice-presidential candidates and to write the party's platform.

national primary. A proposal by critics of the **caucuses** and **presidential primaries** systems who would replace these electoral methods with a nationwide **primary** held early in the election year.

National Security Council. An office created in 1947 to coordinate the president's foreign and military policy advisers. Its formal members are the president, vice president, **secretary of state**, and **secretary of defense**, and it is managed by the president's national security assistant.

NATO. See **North Atlantic Treaty Organization**.

natural rights. Rights inherent in human beings, not dependent on governments, which include life, liberty, and property. The concept of natural rights was central to English philosopher John Locke's theories about government, and was widely accepted among America's Founding Fathers. Thomas Jefferson echoed Locke's language in drafting the Declaration of Independence.

Near v. Minnesota. The 1931 Supreme Court decision holding that the **First Amendment** protects newspapers from **prior restraint**.

necessary and proper clause. See **elastic clause**.

New Deal Coalition. A **coalition** forged by the Democrats, who dominated American politics from the 1930s to the 1960s. Its basic elements were the urban working class, ethnic groups, Catholics and Jews, the poor, Southerners, African Americans, and intellectuals.

New Jersey Plan. The proposal at the Constitutional Convention that called for equal **representation** of each state in Congress regardless of the state's population. Compare **Virginia Plan** and **Connecticut Compromise**.

New York Times v. Sullivan. Decided in 1964, this case established the guidelines for determining whether public officials and public figures could win damage suits for libel. To do so, said the Court, such individuals must prove that the defamatory statements made about them were made with "actual malice" and reckless disregard for the truth.

news leak. A carefully placed bit of inside information given to a friendly reporter. Leaks can benefit both the leaker and the leakee.

newspaper chains. Newspapers published by massive media conglomerates that account for almost three-quarters of the nation's daily circulation. Often these chains control **broadcast media** as well.

Nineteenth Amendment. The constitutional amendment adopted in 1920 that guarantees women the right to vote. See also **suffrage**.

nomination. The official endorsement of a candidate for office by a **political party**. Generally, success in the nomination game requires momentum, money, and media attention.

nonrenewable resources. Minerals and other resources that nature does not replace when they are consumed. Many commonly used energy resources, such as oil and coal, are nonrenewable.

North Atlantic Treaty Organization (NATO). Created in 1949, an organization whose members include the United States, Canada, most Western European nations, and Turkey, all of whom agreed to combine military forces and to treat a war against one as a war against all. Compare **Warsaw Pact**.

O

Office of Management and Budget (OMB). An office that grew out of the Bureau of the Budget, created in 1921, consisting of a handful of political appointees and hundreds of skilled professionals. The OMB performs both managerial and budgetary functions, and although the president is its boss, the director and staff have considerable independence in the budgetary process. See also **Congressional Budget Office**.

Office of Personnel Management (OPM). The office in charge of hiring for most agencies of the federal government, using elaborate rules in the process.

Olson's law of large groups. Advanced by Mancur Olson, a principle stating that "the larger the group, the further it will fall short of providing an optimal amount of a collective good." See also **interest group**.

OPEC. See **Organization of Petroleum Exporting Countries**.

open primaries. Elections to select party nominees in which voters can decide on Election Day whether they want to participate in the Democratic or Republican contests. See also **primaries**.

opinion. A statement of legal reasoning behind a judicial decision. The content of an opinion may be as important as the decision itself.

Organization of Petroleum Exporting Countries (OPEC). An economic organization, consisting primarily of Arab nations, that controls the price of oil and the amount of oil its members produce and sell to other nations. The Arab members of OPEC caused the oil boycott in the winter of 1973–1974.

original intent. A view that the Constitution should be interpreted according to the original intent of the framers. Many **conservatives** support this view.

original jurisdiction. The jurisdiction of courts that hear a case first, usually in a trial. These are the courts that determine the facts about a case. Compare **appellate jurisdiction**.

oversight. The process of monitoring the bureaucracy and its administration of policy, mainly through congressional hearings.

P

PACs. See **political action committees (PACs)**.

parliamentary governments. Governments, like the one in Great Britain, that typically select the political leader from membership in the parliament (the legislature).

participation. See **political participation**.

party. See **political party**.

party competition. The battle of the parties for control of public offices. Ups and downs of the two major parties are one of the most important elements in American politics.

party dealignment. The gradual disengagement of people and politicians from the parties, as seen in part by shrinking **party identification**.

party eras. Historical periods in which a majority of voters cling to the party in power, which tends to win a majority of the elections. See also **critical election** and **party realignment**.

party identification. A citizen's self-proclaimed preference for one party or the other.

party image. The voter's perception of what the Republicans or Democrats stand for, such as **conservatism** or **liberalism**.

party machines. A type of political party organization that relies heavily on material inducements, such as patronage, to win votes and to govern.

party platform. A political party's statement of its goals and policies for the next four years. The platform is drafted prior to the party convention by a committee whose members are chosen in rough proportion to each candidate's strength. It is the best formal statement of what a party believes in.

party realignment. The displacement of the majority party by the minority party, usually during a **critical election period**. See also **party eras**.

patients' bill of rights. A controversial proposal before Congress that would give patients certain rights against medical providers, particularly HMOs, including the right to sue.

patronage. One of the key inducements used by political machines. A patronage job, promotion, or contract is one that is given for political reasons rather than for merit or competence alone. Compare **civil service** and the **merit principle**.

Pendleton Civil Service Act. Passed in 1883, an act that created a federal **civil service** so that hiring and promotion would be based on merit rather than **patronage**.

per curiam **decision.** A court decision without explanation—in other words, without an **opinion**.

Personal Responsibility and Work Opportunity Reconciliation Act (PRWORA). The official name of the welfare reform law of 1996.

Planned Parenthood v. Casey. A 1992 case in which the Supreme Court loosened its standard for evaluating restrictions on abortion from one of "strict scrutiny" of any restraints on a "fundamental right" to one of "undue burden" that permits considerably more regulation.

plea bargaining. A bargain struck between the defendant's lawyer and the prosecutor to the effect that the defendant will plead guilty to a lesser crime (or fewer crimes) in exchange for the state's promise not to prosecute the defendant for a more serious (or additional) crime.

Plessy v. Ferguson. An 1896 Supreme Court decision that provided a constitutional justification for segregation by ruling that a Louisiana law requiring "equal but separate accommodations for the white and colored races" was not unconstitutional.

pluralist theory. A theory of government and politics emphasizing that politics is mainly a competition among groups, each one pressing for its own preferred policies. Compare **elite and class theory, hyperpluralism**, and **traditional democratic theory**.

pocket veto. A veto taking place when Congress adjourns within ten days of having submitted a **bill** to the president, who simply lets it die by neither signing nor vetoing it. See also **veto**.

policy. See **public policy**.

policy agenda. The issues that attract the serious attention of public officials and other people actually involved in politics at any given point in time.

policy differences. The perception of a clear choice between the parties. Those who see such choices are more likely to vote.

policy entrepreneurs. People who invest their political "capital" in an issue. According to John Kingdon, a policy entrepreneur "could be in or out of government, in elected or appointed positions, in interest groups or research organizations."

policy gridlock. A condition that occurs when no coalition is strong enough to form a majority and establish policy. The result is that nothing may get done.

policy impacts. The effects a policy has on people and problems. Impacts are analyzed to see how well a policy has met its goal and at what cost.

policy implementation. See **implementation**.

policymaking institutions. The branches of government charged with taking action on political issues. The U.S. Constitution established three policymaking institutions—the Congress, the presidency, and the courts. Today, the power of the bureaucracy is so great that most political scientists consider it a fourth policymaking institution.

policymaking system. The process by which political problems are communicated by the voters and acted upon by government policymakers. The policymaking system begins with people's needs and expectations for governmental action. When people confront government officials with problems that they want solved, they are trying to influence the government's policy agenda.

policy voting. Electoral choices that are made on the basis of the voters' policy preferences and on the basis of where the candidates stand on policy issues.

political action committees (PACs). Funding vehicles created by the 1974 campaign finance reforms. A corporation, union, or some other interest group can create a PAC and register it with the **Federal Election Commission (FEC)**, which will meticulously monitor the PAC's expenditures.

political culture. An overall set of values widely shared within a society.

political efficacy. The belief that one's **political participation** really matters—that one's vote can actually make a difference.

political ideology. A coherent set of beliefs about politics, public policy, and public purpose. It helps give meaning to political events, personalities, and policies. See also **liberalism** and **conservatism**.

political issue. An issue that arises when people disagree about a problem and a public policy choice.

political participation. All the activities used by citizens to influence the selection of political leaders or the policies they pursue. The most common, but not the only, means of political participation in a **democracy** is voting. Other means include **protest** and **civil disobedience**.

political party. According to Anthony Downs, a "team of men [and women] seeking to control the governing apparatus by gaining office in a duly constituted election."

political questions. A doctrine developed by the federal courts and used as a means to avoid deciding some cases, principally those involving conflicts between the president and Congress.

political socialization. According to Richard Dawson, "the process through which an individual acquires his [or her] particular political orientations—his [or her] knowledge, feelings, and evaluations regarding his [or her] political world." See also **agents of socialization**.

political system. A set of institutions and activities that link together people, politics, and policy.

politics. The process by which we select our governmental leaders and what policies these leaders pursue. Politics produces authoritative decisions about public issues.

poll taxes. Small taxes, levied on the right to vote, that often fell due at a time of year when poor African American sharecroppers had the least cash on hand. This method was used by most Southern states to exclude African Americans from voting registers. Poll taxes were declared void by the **Twenty-fourth Amendment** in 1964. See also **grandfather clause** and **White primary**.

polls. See **exit polls**.

pork barrel. The mighty list of federal projects, grants, and contracts available to cities, businesses, colleges, and institutions available in a congressional district.

position taking. According to David Mayhew, one of three primary activities undertaken by members of Congress to increase the probability of their reelection. It involves taking a stand on issues and responding to constituents about these positions. See also **advertising** and **credit taking**.

potential group. All the people who might be **interest group** members because they share some common interest. A potential group is almost always larger than an actual group.

poverty line. A method used to count the number of poor people, it considers what a family would need to spend for an "austere" standard of living.

power. The capacity to get people to do something they would not otherwise do. The quest for power is a strong motivation to political activity.

precedent. How similar cases have been decided in the past.

presidential approval. An evaluation of the president based on many factors, but especially on the predisposition of many people to support the president. One measure is provided by the Gallup Poll.

presidential coattails. The situation occurring when voters cast their ballots for congressional candidates of the president's party because they support the president. Recent studies show that few races are won this way.

presidential debate. A debate between presidential candidates. The first televised debate was between Richard Nixon and John Kennedy during the 1960 campaign.

Presidential Election Campaign Fund. Money from the $3 federal income tax check-off goes into this fund, which is then distributed to qualified candidates to subsidize their presidential campaigns.

presidential primaries. Elections in which voters in a state vote for a candidate (or delegates pledged to him or her). Most delegates to the **national party conventions** are chosen this way.

press conferences. Meetings of public officials with reporters.

press secretary. The person on the White House staff who most often deals directly with the press, serving as a conduit of information. Press secretaries conduct daily press briefings.

primaries. Elections that select candidates. In addition to **presidential primaries**, there are **direct primaries** for selecting party nominees for congressional and state offices and proposals for **regional primaries**.

print media. Newspapers and magazines, as compared with **broadcast media**.

prior restraint. A government's preventing material from being published. This is a common method of limiting the press in some nations, but it is usually unconstitutional in the United States, according to the **First Amendment** and as confirmed in the 1931 Supreme Court case of *Near v. Minnesota*.

privacy. See **right to privacy**.

privileges and immunities clause. A clause in Article IV, Section 2, of the Constitution according citizens of each state most of the privileges of citizens of other states.

probable cause. The situation occurring when the police have reason to believe that a person should be arrested. In making the arrest, police are allowed legally to search for and seize incriminating evidence. Compare **unreasonable searches and seizures**.

progressive tax. A tax by which the government takes a greater share of the **income** of the rich than of the poor—for example, when a rich family pays 50 percent of its income in taxes and a poor family pays 5 percent. Compare **regressive tax** and **proportional tax**.

project grants. Federal grants given for specific purposes and awarded on the basis of the merits of applications. A type of the **categorical grants** available to states and localities.

proportional representation. An electoral system used throughout most of Europe that awards legislative seats to political parties in proportion to the number of votes won in an election. Compare with **winner-take-all system**.

proportional tax. A tax by which the government takes the same share of income from everyone, rich and poor alike—for example, when a rich family pays 20 percent and a poor family pays 20 percent. Compare **progressive tax** and **regressive tax**.

protectionism. Economic policy of shielding an economy from imports.

protest. A form of **political participation** designed to achieve policy change through dramatic and unconventional tactics. See also **civil disobedience**.

public goods. Goods, such as clean air and clean water, that everyone must share.

public interest. The idea that there are some interests superior to the private interest of groups and individuals, interests we all have in common. See also **public interest lobbies**.

public interest lobbies. According to Jeffrey Berry, organizations that seek "a collective good, the achievement of which will not selectively and materially benefit the membership or activities of the organization." See also **lobbying** and **public interest**.

public opinion. The distribution of the population's beliefs about politics and policy issues.

public policy. A choice that **government** makes in response to a political issue. A policy is a course of action taken with regard to some problem.

R

random digit dialing. A technique used by pollsters to place telephone calls randomly to both listed and unlisted numbers when conducting a survey. See also **random sampling**.

random sampling. The key technique employed by sophisticated survey researchers, which operates on the principle that everyone should have an equal probability of being selected for the sample. See also **sample**.

rational-choice theory. A popular theory in political science to explain the actions of voters as well as politicians. It assumes that individuals act in their own best interest, carefully weighing the costs and benefits of possible alternatives.

realignment. See **party realignment**.

reapportionment. The process of reallocating seats in the House of Representatives every 10 years on the basis of the results of the census.

recall. A procedure that allows voters to call a special election for a specific official in an attempt to throw him or her out of office before the end of his or her term. Recalls are only permitted in 17 states, are seldom used because of their cost and disruptiveness, and are rarely successful.

reconciliation. A congressional process through which program authorizations are revised to achieve required savings. It usually also includes tax or other revenue adjustments.

Red Lion Broadcasting Company v. FCC. A 1969 case in which the Supreme Court upheld restrictions on radio and television broadcasting, such as giving adequate coverage to public issues and covering opposing views. These restrictions on the **broadcast media** are much tighter than those on the **print media** because there are only a limited number of broadcasting frequencies available. See *Miami Herald Publishing Company v. Tornillo.*

Reed v. Reed. The landmark case in 1971 in which the Supreme Court for the first time upheld a claim of gender discrimination.

referendum. A state-level method of direct legislation that gives voters a chance to approve or disapprove legislation or a constitutional amendment proposed by the state legislature.

Regents of the University of California v. Bakke. A 1978 Supreme Court decision holding that a state university could not admit less qualified individuals solely because of their race. The Court did not, however, rule that such **affirmative action** policies and the use of race as a criterion for admission were unconstitutional, only that they had to be formulated differently.

regional primaries. A proposal by critics of the **caucuses** and **presidential primaries** to replace these electoral methods with a series of primaries held in each geographic region.

registration. See **voter registration**.

regressive tax. A tax in which the burden falls relatively more heavily on low-income groups than on wealthy taxpayers. The opposite of a **progressive tax**, in which tax rates increase as income increases.

regulation. The use of governmental authority to control or change some practice in the private sector. Regulations pervade the daily lives of people and institutions.

regulatory agency. See **independent regulatory agency**.

reinforcement. One of three key consequences of electoral campaigns for voters, in which the voter's candidate preference is reinforced. See also **activation** and **conversion**.

relative deprivation. A perception by a group that it is doing less well than is appropriate in relation to a reference group. The desire of a group to correct what it views as the unfair distribution of resources, such as income or government benefits, is a frequent motivator for political activism.

representation. A basic principle of **traditional democratic theory** that describes the relationship between the few leaders and the many followers.

republic. A form of government that derives its power, directly or indirectly, from the people. Those chosen to govern are accountable to those whom they govern. In contrast to a direct democracy, in which people themselves make laws, in a republic the people select representatives who make the laws.

responsible party model. A view favored by some political scientists about how parties should work. According to the model, parties should offer clear choices to the voters, who can then use those choices as cues to their own preferences of candidates. Once in office, parties would carry out their campaign promises.

retrospective voting. A theory of voting in which voters essentially ask this simple question: "What have you done for me lately?"

revenues. The financial resources of the federal government. The individual income tax and Social Security tax are two major sources of revenue. Compare **expenditures**.

right to privacy. The right to a private personal life free from the intrusion of government. The right to privacy is implicitly protected by the **Bill of Rights**. See also **Privacy Act**.

right-to-work law. A state law forbidding requirements that workers must join a union to hold their jobs. State right-to-work laws were specifically permitted by the Taft-Hartley Act of 1947.

Roe v. Wade. The 1973 Supreme Court decision holding that a state ban on all abortions was unconstitutional. The decision forbade state control over abortions during the first trimester of pregnancy, permitted states to limit abortions to protect the mother's health in the second trimester, and permitted states to protect the fetus during the third trimester.

Roth v. United States. A 1957 Supreme Court decision ruling that "obscenity is not within the area of constitutionally protected speech or press."

S

sample. A relatively small proportion of people who are chosen in a survey so as to be representative of the whole.

sampling error. The level of confidence in the findings of a public opinion poll. The more people interviewed, the more confident one can be of the results.

Schenck v. United States. A 1919 decision upholding the conviction of a socialist who had urged young men to resist the draft during World War I. Justice Holmes declared that government can limit speech if the speech provokes a "clear and present danger" of substantive evils.

School District of Abington Township, Pennsylvania v. Schempp. A 1963 Supreme Court decision holding that a Pennsylvania law requiring Bible reading in schools violated the **establishment clause** of the **First Amendment**. Compare *Engel v. Vitale.*

school districts. Units of local government that are normally independent of any other local government and are primarily responsible for operating public schools.

Scott v. Sandford. The 1857 Supreme Court decision ruling that a slave who had escaped to a free state enjoyed no rights as a citizen and that Congress had no authority to ban slavery in the territories.

search warrant. A written authorization from a court specifying the area to be searched and what the police are searching for.

secretary of defense. The head of the Department of Defense and the president's key adviser on military policy; a key **foreign policy** actor.

secretary of state. The head of the Department of State and traditionally a key adviser to the president on **foreign policy**.

Securities and Exchange Commission (SEC). The federal agency created during the New Deal that regulates stock fraud.

select committees. Congressional committees appointed for a specific purpose, such as the Watergate investigation. See also **joint committees, standing committees**, and **conference committees**.

selective benefits. Goods (such as information publications, travel discounts, and group insurance rates) that a group can restrict to those who pay their yearly dues.

selective perception. The phenomenon that people often pay the most attention to things they already agree with and interpret them according to their own predispositions.

self-incrimination. The situation occurring when an individual accused of a crime is compelled to be a witness against himself or herself in court. The **Fifth Amendment** forbids self-incrimination. See also *Miranda v. Arizona.*

Senate Finance Committee. The Senate committee that, along with the **House Ways and Means Committee**, writes the tax codes, subject to the approval of Congress as a whole.

senatorial courtesy. An unwritten tradition whereby nominations for state-level federal judicial posts are not confirmed if they are opposed by the senator from the state in which the nominee will serve. The tradition also applies to courts of appeal when there is opposition from the nominee's state senator, if the senator belongs to the president's party.

Senior Executive Service (SES). An elite cadre of about 11,000 federal government managers, established by the Civil Service Reform Act of 1978, who are mostly career officials but include some political appointees who do not require Senate confirmation.

seniority system. A simple rule for picking **committee chairs**, in effect until the 1970s. The member who had served on the committee the longest and whose party controlled Congress became chair, regardless of party loyalty, mental state, or competence.

separation of powers. An important part of the **Madisonian model** that requires each of the three branches of government—executive, legislative, and judicial—to be relatively independent of the others so that one cannot control the others. Power is shared among these three institutions. See also **checks and balances**.

Shays' Rebellion. A series of attacks on courthouses by a small band of farmers led by revolutionary war Captain Daniel Shays to block foreclosure proceedings.

single-issue groups. Groups that have a narrow interest, tend to dislike compromise, and often draw membership from people new to politics. These features distinguish them from traditional **interest groups**.

Sixteenth Amendment. The constitutional amendment adopted in 1913 that explicitly permitted Congress to levy an **income tax**.

Sixth Amendment. The constitutional amendment designed to protect individuals accused of crimes. It includes the right to counsel, the right to confront witnesses, and the right to a speedy and public trial.

social policies. Policies that manipulate opportunities through public choice. They include policies related to income and policies related to opportunity.

Social Security Act. A 1935 law passed during the Great Depression that was intended to provide a minimal level of sustenance to older Americans and thus save them from poverty.

social welfare policies. Policies that provide benefits to individuals, particularly to those in need. Compare **civil rights policies**.

socialized medicine. A system in which the full cost of medical care is borne by the national government. Great Britain and the former Soviet Union are examples of countries that have socialized medicine. Compare **Medicaid** and **Medicare**.

soft money. Political contributions earmarked for party-building expenses at the grass-roots level (or for generic party advertising). Unlike money that goes to the campaign of a particular candidate, such party donations are not subject to contribution limits.

solicitor general. A presidential appointee and the third-ranking office in the Department of Justice. The solicitor general is in charge of the appellate court litigation of the federal government.

sound bites. Short video clips of approximately 15 seconds, which are typically all that is shown from a politician's speech or activities on television news.

Speaker of the House. An office mandated by the Constitution. The Speaker is chosen in practice by the majority party, has both formal and informal powers, and is second in line to succeed to the presidency should that office become vacant.

special districts. Limited-purpose local governments called *districts* or *public authorities* that are created to run a specific type of service, such as water distribution, airports, public transportation, libraries, and natural resource areas.

standard operating procedures. Better known as SOPs, these procedures are used by bureaucrats to bring uniformity to complex organizations. Uniformity improves fairness and makes personnel interchangeable. See also **administrative discretion**.

standing committees. Separate subject-matter committees in each house of Congress that handle **bills** in different policy areas. See also **joint committees, conference committees,** and **select committees**.

standing to sue. The requirement that **plaintiffs** have a serious interest in a **case,** which depends on whether they have sustained or are likely to sustain a direct and substantial injury from a party or an action of government.

stare decisis. A Latin phrase meaning "let the decision stand." Most cases reaching appellate courts are settled on this principle.

statutory construction. The judicial interpretation of an act of Congress. In some cases where statutory construction is an issue, Congress passes new legislation to clarify existing laws.

Strategic Defense Initiative (SDI). Renamed "Star Wars" by critics, a plan for defense against the Soviet Union unveiled by President Reagan in 1983. SDI would create a global umbrella in space, using computers to scan the skies and high-tech devices to destroy invading missiles.

street-level bureaucrats. A phrase coined by Michael Lipsky, referring to those bureaucrats who are in constant contact with the public and have considerable **administrative discretion**.

subgovernments. A network of groups within the American political system which exercise a great deal of control over specific policy areas. Also known as iron triangles, subgovernments are composed of interest group leaders interested in a particular policy, the government agency in charge of administering that policy, and the members of congressional committees and subcommittees handling that policy.

subnational governments. Another way of referring to state and local governments. Through a process of reform, modernization, and changing intergovernmental relations since the 1960s, subnational governments have assumed new responsibilities and importance.

suffrage. The legal right to vote, extended to African Americans by the **Fifteenth Amendment,** to women by the **Nineteenth Amendment,** and to people over the age of 18 by the **Twenty-sixth Amendment**.

Super Tuesday. Created by a dozen or so Southern states when they held their **presidential primaries** in early March 1988. These states hoped to promote a regional advantage as well as a more conservative candidate.

superdelegates. National party leaders who automatically get a delegate slot at the Democratic **national party convention**.

Superfund. A fund created by Congress in the late 1970s and renewed in the 1980s to clean up hazardous waste sites. Money for the fund comes from taxing chemical products.

supply-side economics. An economic theory, advocated by President Reagan, holding that too much income goes to taxes and too little money is available for purchasing and that the solution is to cut taxes and return purchasing power to consumers.

supremacy clause. Article VI of the Constitution, which makes the Constitution, national laws, and treaties supreme over state laws when the national government is acting within its constitutional limits.

Supreme Court. The pinnacle of the American judicial system. The Court ensures uniformity in interpreting national laws, resolves conflicts among states, and maintains national supremacy in law. It has both **original jurisdiction** and **appellate jurisdiction,** but unlike other federal courts, it controls its own agenda.

symbolic speech. Nonverbal communication, such as burning a flag or wearing an armband. The Supreme Court has accorded some symbolic speech protection under the **First Amendment.** See *Texas v. Johnson*.

T

Taft-Hartley Act. A 1947 law giving the president power to halt major strikes by seeking a court injunction and permitting states to forbid requirements in labor contracts forcing workers to join a union. See also **right-to-work law**.

talking head. A shot of a person's face talking directly to the camera. Because this is visually unappealing, the major commercial networks rarely show a politician talking one-on-one for very long. See also **sound bites**.

tariff. A special tax added to imported goods to raise the price, thereby protecting American businesses and workers from foreign competition.

tax. See **proportional tax, progressive tax,** and **regressive tax**.

tax expenditures. Defined by the 1974 Budget Act as "revenue losses attributable to provisions of the federal tax laws which allow a special exemption, exclusion, or deduction." Tax expenditures represent the difference between what the government actually collects in taxes and what it would have collected without special exemptions.

tax incidence. The proportion of its income a particular group pays in taxes.

Temporary Assistance for Needy Families (TANF). Once called "Aid to Families with Dependent Children," the new name for public assistance to needy families.

Tenth Amendment. The constitutional amendment stating that "The powers not delegated to the United States by the Constitution, nor prohibited by it to the states, are reserved to the states respectively, or to the people."

term limits. Laws to restrict legislators from serving more than a fixed number of years or terms in office.

Texas v. Johnson. A 1989 case in which the Supreme Court struck down a law banning the burning of the American flag on the grounds that such action was **symbolic speech** protected by the **First Amendment**.

third parties. Electoral contenders other than the two major parties. American third parties are not unusual, but they rarely win elections.

Thirteenth Amendment. The constitutional amendment passed after the Civil War that forbade slavery and involuntary servitude.

ticket splitting. Voting with one party for one office and with another party for other offices. It has become the norm in American voting behavior.

town meeting. A special form of direct democracy under which all voting-age adults in a community gather once a year to make public policy. Now only used in a few villages in upper New England, originally many municipalities in the United States were run by town meeting. The growth of most cities has made them too large for this style of governance.

township. A political subdivision of local government that is found in 20 states and often serves to provide local government services in rural areas. It is a particularly strong form of local government—comparable to a municipality—in the Northeast.

traditional democratic theory. A theory about how a democratic government makes its decisions. According to Robert Dahl, its cornerstones are equality in voting, effective participation, enlightened understanding, final control over the agenda, and inclusion.

transfer payments. Benefits given by the government directly to individuals. Transfer payments may be either cash transfers, such as Social Security payments and retirement payments to former government employees, or in-kind transfers, such as food stamps and low-interest loans for college education.

transnational corporations. Businesses with vast holdings in many countries—such as Microsoft, Coca-Cola, and McDonald's—many of which have annual budgets exceeding that of many foreign governments.

trial balloons. An intentional **news leak** for the purpose of assessing the political reaction.

trial courts. The lowest tier in the trial court system, in which the facts of a case are considered. These courts hear both civil and criminal matters.

trustee. A legislator who uses his or her best judgment to make policy in the interests of the people. This concept was favored by Edmund Burke. Compare **instructed delegate**.

Twenty-fifth Amendment. Passed in 1967, this amendment permits the vice president to become acting president if both the vice president and the president's cabinet determine that the president is disabled. The amendment also outlines how a recuperated president can reclaim the job.

Twenty-fourth Amendment. The constitutional amendment passed in 1964 that declared **poll taxes** void.

Twenty-second Amendment. Passed in 1951, the amendment that limits presidents to two terms of office.

U

uncontrollable expenditures. Expenditures that are determined not by a fixed amount of money appropriated by Congress but by how many eligible beneficiaries there are for some particular program or by previous obligations of the government. Three-fourths of the federal **budget** is uncontrollable. Congress can change uncontrollable expenditures only by changing a law or existing benefit levels.

unemployment rate. As measured by the Bureau of Labor Statistics (BLS), the proportion of the labor force actively seeking work but unable to find jobs.

unfunded mandates. When the federal government requires state and local action but does not provide the funds to pay for the action.

union shop. A provision found in some collective bargaining agreements requiring all employees of a business to join the union within a short period, usually 30 days, and to remain members as a condition of employment.

unitary government. A way of organizing a nation so that all power resides in the central government. Most national governments today, including those of Great Britain and Japan, are unitary governments. Compare **federalism**.

United Nations (UN). Created in 1945, an organization whose members agree to renounce war and to respect certain human and economic freedoms. The seat of real power in the UN is the Security Council.

United States v. Nixon. The 1974 case in which the Supreme Court unanimously held that the doctrine of executive privilege was implicit in the Constitution but could not be extended to protect documents relevant to criminal prosecutions.

unreasonable searches and seizures. Obtaining evidence in a haphazard or random manner, a practice prohibited by the Fourth Amendment. Both **probable cause** and a **search warrant** are required for a legal and proper search for and seizure of incriminating evidence.

unwritten constitution. The body of tradition, practice, and procedure that is as important as the written constitution. Changes in the unwritten **constitution** can change the spirit of the Constitution. **Political parties** and **national party conventions** are a part of the unwritten constitution in the United States.

urban underclass. The poorest of the poor in America. These are the Americans whose economic opportunities are severely limited in almost every way. They constitute a large percentage of the Americans afflicted by homelessness, crime, drugs, alcoholism, unwanted pregnancies, and other endemic social problems.

U.S. Constitution. The document written in 1787 and ratified in 1788 that sets forth the institutional structure of U.S. government and the tasks these institutions perform. It replaced the Articles of Confederation. See also **constitution** and **unwritten constitution**.

V

veto. The constitutional power of the president to send a **bill** back to Congress with reasons for rejecting it. A two-thirds vote in each house can override a veto. See also **legislative veto** and **pocket veto**.

Virginia Plan. The proposal at the Constitutional Convention that called for *representation* of each state in Congress in proportion to that state's share of the U.S. population. Compare **Connecticut Compromise** and **New Jersey Plan**.

voter registration. A system adopted by the states that requires voters to register well in advance of Election Day. A few states permit Election Day registration.

Voting Rights Act of 1965. A law designed to help end formal and informal barriers to African American **suffrage**. Under the law, federal registrars were sent to Southern states and counties that had long histories of discrimination; as a result, hundreds of thousands of African Americans were registered and the number of African American elected officials increased dramatically.

W

War Powers Resolution. A law passed in 1973 in reaction to American fighting in Vietnam and Cambodia that requires presidents to consult with Congress whenever possible prior to using military force and to withdraw forces after 60 days unless Congress declares war or grants an extension. Presidents view the resolution as unconstitutional. See also **legislative veto**.

Watergate. The events and scandal surrounding a break-in at the Democratic National Committee headquarters in 1972 and the subsequent cover-up of White House involvement, leading to the eventual resignation of President Nixon under the threat of **impeachment**.

wealth. The amount of funds already owned. Wealth includes stocks, bonds, bank deposits, cars, houses, and so forth. Throughout most of the last generation, wealth has been much less evenly divided than **income**.

whips. Party leaders who work with the **majority leader** or **minority leader** to count votes beforehand and lean on waverers whose votes are crucial to a **bill** favored by the party.

White primary. One of the means used to discourage African American voting that permitted political parties in the heavily Democratic South to exclude African Americans from primary elections, thus depriving them of a voice in the real contests. The Supreme Court declared White primaries unconstitutional in 1944. See also **grandfather clause** and **poll taxes**.

winner-take-all system. An electoral system in which legislative seats are awarded only to the candidates who come in first in their constituencies. In American presidential elections, the system in which the winner of the popular vote in a state receives all the electoral votes of that state. Compare with **proportional representation**.

World Trade Organization (WTO). International organization that regulates international trade.

writ of certiorari. A formal document issued from the **Supreme Court** to a lower federal or state court that calls up a case.

writ of habeas corpus. A court order requiring jailers to explain to a judge why they are holding a prisoner in custody.

writ of mandamus. A court order forcing action. In the dispute leading to *Marbury v. Madison,* Marbury and his associates asked the **Supreme Court** to issue a writ ordering Madison to give them their commissions.

Z

Zelman v. Simmons-Harris. The 2002 Supreme Court decision that upheld a state providing families with vouchers that could be used to pay tuition at religious schools.

Zurcher v. Stanford Daily. A 1978 Supreme Court decision holding that a proper **search warrant** could be applied to a newspaper as well as to anyone else without necessarily violating the **First Amendment** rights to freedom of the press.

NOTES

CHAPTER 1

1. "The Soul of a Senator," *Time*, August 10, 1998.

2. Ganesh Sitaraman and Previn Warren, *Invisible Citizens: Youth Politics After September 11* (New York: iUniverse, Inc., 2003), ix.

3. Because the level of difficulty of the questions differed somewhat, one should only examine the differences within a year and not necessarily infer that political knowledge as a whole has decreased.

4. Stephen Earl Bennett and Eric W. Rademacher, "The Age of Indifference Revisited: Patterns of Political Interest, Media Exposure, and Knowledge Among Generation X," in Stephen C. Craig and Stephen Earl Bennett, eds., *After the Boom: The Politics of Generation X* (Lanham, MD: Rowman & Littlefield, 1997), 39.

5. Michael X. Delli Carpini and Scott Keeter, *What Americans Know About Politics and Why It Matters* (New Haven, CT: Yale University Press, 1996), chap. 6.

6. Samuel Kernell, *Going Public: New Strategies of Presidential Leadership*, 4th ed. (Washington, DC: Congressional Quarterly Press, 2007), 140.

7. Anthony Corrado, "Elections in Cyberspace: Prospects and Problems," in Anthony Corrado and Charles M. Firestone, eds., *Elections in Cyberspace: Toward a New Era in American Politics* (Washington, DC: Aspen Institute, 1996), 29.

8. Harold D. Lasswell, *Politics: Who Gets What, When, and How* (New York: McGraw-Hill, 1938).

9. Randy Shilts, *And the Band Played On: Politics, People, and the AIDS Epidemic* (New York: Penguin Books, 1987).

10. Robert A. Dahl, *Dilemmas of Pluralist Democracy* (New Haven, CT: Yale University Press, 1982), 6.

11. Robert A. Dahl, *A Preface to Democratic Theory* (Chicago: University of Chicago Press, 1956), 137.

12. Robert Putnam, *Bowling Alone: The Collapse and Revival of American Community* (New York: Simon & Schuster, 2000).

13. Kevin Phillips, *The Politics of Rich and Poor: Wealth and the American Electorate in the Reagan Aftermath* (New York: Random House, 1990), 1.

14. Jacob S. Hacker and Paul Pierson, *Off Center: The Republican Revolution and the Erosion of American Democracy* (New Haven, CT: Yale University Press, 2005), 16.

15. American Political Science Association Task Force on Inequality and American Democracy, "American Democracy in an Age of Rising Inequality" (Washington, DC: American Political Science Association, 2004), 2. The entire report can be found at *http://www.apsanet.org/imgtest/taskforcereport.pdf*.

16. Ronald Inglehart and Christian Welzel, *Modernization, Cultural Change, and Democracy: The Human Development Sequence* (New York: Cambridge University Press, 2005), 2.

17. G. K. Chesterton, *What I Saw in America* (New York: Dodd, Mead & Co., 1922), 7.

18. Seymour Martin Lipset, *American Exceptionalism: A Double-Edged Sword* (New York: Norton, 1996), 31.

19. Ibid., 19

20. Louis Hartz, *The Liberal Tradition in America* (New York: Harcourt, Brace, 1955).

21. Frederick Jackson Turner, *The Significance of the Frontier in American History* (New York: Readex Microprint, 1966), 221.

22. John W. Kingdon, *America the Unusual* (New York: St. Martin's/Worth, 1999), 2.

23. Seymour Martin Lipset, *The First New Nation* (New York: Norton, 1979), 68.

24. James Q. Wilson, "How Divided Are We?" *Commentary*, February 2006, 15.

25. Ibid., 21.

26. Morris P. Fiorina, *Culture War? The Myth of a Polarized America*, 2nd ed. (New York: Longman, 2006), 165.

27. Wayne Baker, *America's Crisis of Values: Reality and Perception* (Princeton, NJ: Princeton University Press, 2005).

28. Dick Armey, *The Freedom Revolution* (Washington, DC: Regnery, 1995), 316.

CHAPTER 2

1. Gordon S. Wood, *The Radicalism of the American Revolution* (New York: Vintage, 1993), 4.

2. Garry Wills, *Inventing America: Jefferson's Declaration of Independence* (New York: Doubleday, 1978), 13, 77.

3. Clinton Rossiter, *1787: The Grand Convention* (New York: Macmillan, 1966), 60.

4. On the Lockean influence on the Declaration of Independence, see Carl L. Becker, *The Declaration of Independence: A Study in the History of Political Ideas* (New York: Random House, 1942).

5. Seymour Martin Lipset, *The First New Nation* (New York: Basic Books, 1963).

6. Gordon S. Wood, *The Creation of the American Republic, 1776–1787* (Chapel Hill: University of North Carolina Press, 1969), 3.

7. On the Articles of Confederation, see Merrill Jensen, *The Articles of Confederation* (Madison: University of Wisconsin Press, 1940).

8. Wood, *The Radicalism of the American Revolution*, 6–7.

9. "Federalist #10," in Alexander Hamilton, James Madison, and John Jay, *The Federalist Papers*, 2nd ed., ed. Roy P. Fairfield (Baltimore: Johns Hopkins University Press, 1981), 18.

10. Calvin C. Jillson and Cecil L. Eubanks, "The Political Structure of Constitution-Making: The Federal Convention of 1787," *American Journal of Political Science* 28 (August 1984): 435–58. See also Calvin C. Jillson, *Constitution Making: Conflict and Consensus in the Federal Convention of 1787* (New York: Agathon, 1988).

11. See Arthur Lovejoy, *Reflections on Human Nature* (Baltimore: Johns

Hopkins University Press, 1961), 57–63.

12. "Federalist #10," in Fairfield, *The Federalist Papers*.

13. This representation may have practical consequences. See Frances E. Lee, "Representation and Public Policy: The Consequences of Senate Apportionment for the Geographic Distribution of Federal Funds," *Journal of Politics* 60 (February 1998): 34–62; and Daniel Wirls, "The Consequences of Equal Representation: The Bicameral Politics of NAFTA in the 103rd Congress," *Congress and the President* 25 (Autumn 1998): 129–45.

14. Cecelia M. Kenyon, ed., *The Antifederalists* (Indianapolis: Bobbs-Merrill, 1966), xxxv.

15. Rossiter, *1787*.

16. See Charles A. Beard, *An Economic Interpretation of the Constitution of the United States* (New York: Macmillan, 1913); Robert E. Brown, *Charles Beard and the Constitution* (Princeton, NJ: Princeton University Press, 1956); Forrest B. McDonald, *We the People: The Economic Origins of the Constitution* (Chicago: University of Chicago Press, 1958); and Forrest B. McDonald, *Novus Ordo Seclorum: The Intellectual Origins of the Constitution* (Lawrence: University Press of Kansas, 1986).

17. A brilliant exposition of the Madisonian model is found in Robert A. Dahl, *A Preface to Democratic Theory* (Chicago: University of Chicago Press, 1956).

18. "Federalist #10," in Fairfield, *The Federalist Papers*.

19. "Federalist #51," in Fairfield, *The Federalist Papers*.

20. Quoted in Beard, *An Economic Interpretation of the Constitution of the United States*, 299.

21. The three quotations are from Kenyon, *The Antifederalists*, 195, liv, and 1, respectively.

22. Jackson Turner Main, *The Antifederalists* (Chapel Hill: University of North Carolina Press, 1961). For more on the Anti-Federalists, see Herbert J. Storing, *What the Anti-Federalists Were For* (Chicago: University of Chicago Press, 1981).

23. See "Federalist #78," in Fairfield, *The Federalist Papers*.

24. James MacGregor Burns, *The Deadlock of Democracy* (Englewood Cliffs, NJ: Prentice Hall, 1963), 6.

CHAPTER 3

1. For a study of how different states enforce federal child support enforcement, see Lael R. Keiser and Joe Soss, "With Good Cause: Bureaucratic Discretion and the Politics of Child Support Enforcement," *American Journal of Political Science* 42 (October 1998): 1,133–56.

2. On the states as innovators, see Jack L. Walker, "The Diffusion of Innovations in the American States," *American Political Science Review* 63 (September 1969): 880–99; Virginia Gray, "Innovation in the States: A Diffusion Study," *American Political Science Review* 67 (December 1973): 1,174–85; and Richard P. Nathan and Fred C. Doolittle, *Reagan and the States* (Princeton, NJ: Princeton University Press, 1987).

3. *Alden v. Maine*, (1999). See also *College Savings Bank v. Florida Prepaid Postsecondary Education Expense Board* (1999); and *Florida Prepaid Postsecondary Education Expense Board v. College Savings Bank* (1999).

4. *Federal Maritime Commission v. South Carolina Ports Authority* (2002).

5. The Fourteenth Amendment was passed *after* the Eleventh Amendment.

6. *Monroe v. Pape* (1961); *Monell v. New York City Department of Social Welfare* (1978); *Owen v. Independence* (1980); *Maine v. Thiboutot*, (1980); *Oklahoma City v. Tuttle*, (1985); *Dennis v. Higgins* (1991).

7. The transformation from dual to cooperative federalism is described in Walker, *The Rebirth of Federalism*, chap. 4.

8. The classic discussion of cooperative federalism is found in Morton Grodzins, *The American System: A New View of Governments in the United States*, ed. Daniel J. Elazar (Chicago: Rand McNally, 1966).

9. See Pew Research Center poll, September 25–October 31, 1997, and Craig Volden, "Intergovernmental Political Competition in American Federalism," *American Journal of Political Science* 49 (April 2005): 327–42.

10. Office of Management and Budget, *Budget of the United States Government, Fiscal Year 2009: Analytical Perspectives* (Washington, DC: U.S. Government Printing Office, 2008), Table 8.3

11. On intergovernmental lobbying, see Donald H. Haider, *When Governments Go to Washington* (New York: Free Press, 1974) and Anne, Marie Commisa, *governments as Interest Groups: Intergovernmental Lobbying and the Federal System* (Westport, CT: Praeger, 1995).

12. Michael A. Bailey, "Welfare and the Multifaceted Decision to Move," *American Political Science Review* 99 (February 2005): 125–35; Michael A. Bailey and Mark Carl Rom, "A Wider Race? Interstate Competition Across Health and Welfare Programs," *Journal of Politics* 66 (May 2004): 326–47; Paul E. Peterson and Mark Rom, "American Federalism, Welfare Policy, and Residential Choices," *American Political Science Review* 83 (September 1989): 711–28; Craig Volden, "The Politics of Competitive Federalism: A Race to the Bottom in Welfare Benefits," *American Journal of Political Science* 46 (April 2002): 352–63. But see William D. Berry, Richard C. Fording, and Russell L. Hanson, "Reassessing the 'Race to the Bottom' in State Welfare Policy," *Journal of Politics* 65 (May 2003): 327–49. Some states limit welfare payments to new residents.

13. Office of Management and Budget, *Budget of the United States Government, Fiscal Year 2009: Historical Tables* (Washington, DC: U.S. Government Printing Office, 2008), Table 15.3.

CHAPTER 4

1. James W. Prothro and Charles M. Grigg, "Fundamental Principles of Democracy: Bases of Agreement and Disagreement," *Journal of Politics* 22 (1960): 276–94; John L. Sullivan et al., "The Sources of Political Tolerance: A Multivariate Analysis," *American Political Science Review* 75 (1981): 100–15.

2. Darren W. Davis and Brian D. Silver, "Civil Liberties vs. Security: Public Opinion in the Context of the Terrorist Attacks on America," *American Journal of Political Science* 48 (January 2004): 28–46.

3. *Widmar v. Vincent* (1981).

4. *Westside Community Schools v. Mergens* (1990).

5. *Good News Club v. Milford Central School* (2001).

6. *Lamb's Chapel v. Center Moriches Union Free School* (1993).

7. *Rosenberger v. University of Virginia* (1995).

8. *Locke v. Davey* (2004).

9. *Illinois ex rel McCollum v. Board of Education* (1948).

10. *Zorach v. Clauson* (1952).

11. *Stone v. Graham* (1980).

12. *Lee v. Weisman* (1992).

13. *Santa Fe School District v. Doe* (2000).

14. *Wallace v. Jaffree* (1985).

15. Kenneth D. Wald, *Religion and Politics in the United States*, 4th ed. (Lanham, MD: Rowman & Littlefield, 2003).

16. See, for example, Gallup poll of August 8–11, 2005.

17. *Edwards v. Aguillard* (1987).

18. *Epperson v. Arkansas* (1968).

19. *McCreary County v. American Civil Liberties Union of Kentucky* (2005).

20. *Van Orden v. Perry* (2005).

21. *Lynch v. Donelly* (1984).

22. *County of Allegheny v. American Civil Liberties Union* (1989).

23. *Bob Jones University v. United States* (1983).

24. *Wisconsin v. Yoder* (1972).

25. *Boerne v. Flores* (1997).

26. *Cutter v. Wilkinson* (2005)

27. *Gonzales v. O Centro Espirita Beneficente Uniao do Vegetal* (2006).

28. Charles R. Lawrence III, "If He Hollers Let Him Go: Regulating Racist Speech on Campus," in *Words That Wound: Critical Race Theory, Assaultive Speech, and the First Amendment*, ed. Mari J. Matsuda, Charles R. Lawrence III, Richard Delgado, and Kimberle Crenshaw, (Boulder, CO: Westview, 1993), 67–68.

29. Ira Glasser, "Introduction," in, *Speaking of Race, Speaking of Sex: Hate Speech, Civil Rights, and Civil Liberties*, ed. Henry Louis Gates Jr. (New York: New York University Press, 1994), 8.

30. *R.A.V. v. St. Paul* (1992). However, states may impose longer prison terms on people convicted of "hate crimes" (crimes motivated by racial, religious, or other prejudice) without violating their rights to free speech.

31. See Fred W. Friendly, *Minnesota Rag* (New York: Random House, 1981).

32. *Hazelwood School District v. Kuhlmeier* (1988).

33. *Morse v. Frederick* (2007).

34. The Supreme Court upheld the government's suit in *United States v. Snepp* (1980).

35. *McIntyre v. Ohio Elections Commission* (1995).

36. *Hudgens v. National Labor Relations Board* (1976).

37. *Pruneyard Shopping Center v. Robins* (1980).

38. *City of Ladue v. Gilleo* (1994).

39. *Nebraska Press Association v. Stuart* (1972).

40. *Richmond Newspapers v. Virginia* (1980).

41. Bob Woodward and Scott Armstrong, *The Brethren* (New York: Avon, 1979), 233.

42. *Jenkins v. Georgia* (1974).

43. *Osborne v. Ohio* (1990).

44. *Reno v. ACLU* (1997).

45. *Ashcroft v. Free Speech Coalition* (2002).

46. *Schad v. Mount Ephraim* (1981).

47. *Barnes v. Glen Theater, Inc.* (1991); *Erie v. Pap's A.M.* (2000).

48. Catherine MacKinnon, *Feminism Unmodified* (Cambridge, MA: Harvard University Press, 1987), 198.

49. The story of this case is told in Anthony Lewis, *Make No Law: The Sullivan Case and the First Amendment* (New York: Random House, 1991).

50. Renata Adler, *Reckless Disregard* (New York: Knopf, 1986).

51. *Tinker v. Des Moines Independent School District* (1969).

52. After Congress passed the Flag Protection Act of 1989 outlawing desecration of the American flag, the Supreme Court also found the act an impermissible infringement on free speech in *United States v. Eichman* (1990).

53. *United States v. O'Brien* (1968).

54. *Virginia v. Black* (2003).

55. *Greater New Orleans Broadcasting, Inc. v. United States* (1999).

56. *Central Hudson Gas & Electric Corporation v. Public Service Commission of N.Y.* (1980).

57. *FCC v. Pacifica Foundation* (1978).

58. *Frisby v. Schultz* (1988).

59. *Rumsfeld v. Forum for Academic and Institutional Rights, Inc.* (2006).

60. *Brigham City v. Stuart* (2006).

61. *Michigan v. Sitz* (1990).

62. *Illinois v. Caballes* (2005).

63. *Brendlin v. California* (2007). The police recognized the passenger as a parole violator.

64. *Nix v. Williams* (1984).

65. *United States v. Leon* (1984).

66. *Arizona v. Evans* (1995).

67. *Hudson v. Michigan* (2006)

68. *United States v. Payner* (1980).

69. *Knowles v. Iowa* (1998).

70. *City of Indianapolis v. Edmond* (2000).

71. *Florida v. J.L.* (2000).

72. *Kyllo v. U.S.* (2001).

73. On the *Miranda* case, see Liva Baker, *Miranda: The Crime, the Law, the Politics* (New York: Atheneum, 1983).

74. *Arizona v. Fulminante* (1991).

75. The story of Gideon is eloquently told by Anthony Lewis, *Gideon's Trumpet* (New York: Random House, 1964).

76. *United States v. Gonzalez-Lopez* (2006).

77. David Brereton and Jonathan D. Casper, "Does It Pay to Plead Guilty? Differential Sentencing and the Function of the Criminal Courts," *Law and Society Review* 16 (1981–1982): 45–70.

78. *Batson v. Kentucky* (1986); *Miller-El v. Dretke* (2005).

79. *Apprendi v. New Jersey* (2000); *Blakely v. Washington* (2004); *United States v. Booker* (2005); *Cunningham v. California* (2007).

80. Joe Soss, Laura Langbein, and Alan R. Metelko, "Why Do White Americans Support the Death Penalty?" *Journal of Politics* 65 (May 2003): 397–421.

81. *Baze v. Rees* (2008).

82. Woodward and Armstrong, *The Brethren*, 271–84.

83. Guttmacher Institute, 2008.

84. *Madsen v. Women's Health Center* (1994). In 1997, the Court also upheld a 15-foot buffer zone.

85. *Hill v. Colorado* (2000).

86. *National Organization for Women v. Scheidler* (1994).

87. Although, as Chapter 16 on the judiciary will show, there is indirect accountability.

CHAPTER 5

1. Quoted in Judith A. Baer, *Equality Under the Constitution: Reclaiming the Fourteenth Amendment* (Ithaca, NY: Cornell University Press, 1983), 44–47.

2. For opposing interpretations of the Fourteenth Amendment, see Baer, *Equality Under the Constitution*, and Raoul Berger, *Government by Judiciary: The Transformation of the Fourteenth Amendment* (Cambridge, MA: Harvard University Press, 1977).

3. Desmond King, *Separate but Unequal: Black Americans and the US Federal Government* (Oxford: Oxford University Press, 1995).

4. D. Garth Taylor, Paul B. Sheatsley, and Andrew M. Greeley, "Attitudes Toward Racial Integration," *Scientific American* 238 (June 1978): 42–49; Richard G. Niemi, John Mueller, and John W. Smith, *Trends in Public Opinion* (Westport, CT: Greenwood Press, 1989), 180.

5. There are a few exceptions. Religious institutions such as schools may use religious standards in employment. Gender, age, and disabilities may be considered in the few cases where such occupational qualifications are absolutely essential to the normal operations of a business or enterprise, as in the case of a men's restroom attendant.

6. On the implementation of the Voting Rights Act, see Richard Scher and James Button, "Voting Rights Act: Implementation and Impact," in *Implementation of Civil Rights Policy*, ed. Charles Bullock III and Charles Lamb, (Monterey, CA: Brooks/Cole, 1984); Abigail M. Thernstrom, *Whose Votes Count?* (Cambridge, MA: Harvard University Press, 1987); and Chandler Davidson and Bernard Groffman, eds., *Quiet Revolution in the South:*

The Impact of the Voting Rights Act, 1965–1990 (Princeton, NJ: Princeton University Press, 1994).

7. U.S. Department of Commerce, *Statistical Abstract of the United States, 2008* (Washington, DC: U.S. Government Printing Office, 2008), Table 402. See David Lublin, *The Paradox of Representation: Racial Gerrymandering and Minority Interests in Congress* (Princeton, NJ: Princeton University Press, 1997), on how racial redistricting helped increase the number of minority representatives in Congress.

8. *League of United Latin American Citizens v. Perry* (2006).

9. See Dee Brown, *Bury My Heart at Wounded Knee: An Indian History of the American West* (New York: Holt, Rinehart and Winston, 1970).

10. U.S. Department of Commerce, *Statistical Abstract of the United States, 2008*, Table 403.

11. *White v. Register* (1973).

12. See Eleanor Flexner, *Century of Struggle* (New York: Atheneum, 1971).

13. See J. Stanley Lemons, *The Woman Citizen: Social Feminism in the 1920s* (Urbana: University of Illinois Press, 1973).

14. *Kirchberg v. Feenstra* (1981).

15. *Arizona Governing Committee for Tax Deferred Annuity and Deferred Compensation Plans v. Norris* (1983).

16. *Michael M. v. Superior Court* (1981).

17. *Kahn v. Shevin* (1974).

18. U.S. Department of Labor, Bureau of Labor Statistics, *Women in the Labor Force: A Databook (2007 Edition)*, Tables 1–7; U.S. Department of Commerce, *Statistical Abstract of the United States, 2008*, Tables 58, 570, 571, 573, 578, 579, 580.

19. *Cleveland Board of Education v. LaFleur* (1974).

20. *United Automobile Workers v. Johnson Controls* (1991).

21. *Roberts v. United States Jaycees* (1984); *Board of Directors of Rotary International v. Rotary Club of Duarte* (1987); *New York State Club Association v. New York* (1988).

22. *United States v. Virginia et al.* (1996).

23. U.S. Department of Labor, Bureau of Labor Statistics, *Women in the Labor Force: A Databook (2007 Edition)*, Table 18.

24. U.S. Department of Commerce, *Statistical Abstract of the United States, 2008*, Table 498.

25. *www.eeoc.gov/types/sexual_harassment. html.*

26. *Meritor Savings Bank v. Vinson* (1986).

27. *Burlington Northern Santa Fe Railway Co. v. White* (2006).

28. *Massachusetts Board of Retirement v. Murgia* (1976).

29. *Smith v. City of Jackson* (2005).

30. *Bregdon v. Abbott* (1998).

31. *Sutton v. United Air Lines* (1999); *Albertsons v. Kirkingburg* (1999); *Murphy v. United Parcel Service* (1999).

32. *Boy Scouts of America v. Dale* (2000).

33. Gallup poll, May 10–13, 2007.

34. Kenneth D. Wald, James W. Button, and Barbara A. Rienzo, "The Politics of Gay Rights in American Communities: Explaining Antidiscrimination Ordinances and Policies," *American Journal of Political Science* 40 (November 1996): 1152–78, examines why some communities adopt antidiscrimination ordinances and policies that include sexual orientation and others do not.

35. On the affirmative action issues raised by *Bakke* and other cases, see Allan P. Sindler, *Bakke, De Funis and Minority Admissions* (New York: Longman, 1978).

36. *Richmond v. J.A. Croson Co.* (1989).

37. *Fullilove v. Klutznick* (1980).

38. *Metro Broadcasting, Inc. v. Federal Communications Commission* (1990).

39. *Local Number 93 v. Cleveland* (1986); *United States v. Paradise* (1987).

40. *Local 28 of the Sheet Metal Workers v. EEOC* (1986).

41. *Firefighters v. Stotts* (1984).

42. *Wygant v. Jackson Board of Education* (1986).

43. Harry Holzer and David Newmark, "Assessing Affirmative Action," *Journal of Economic Literature* 38 (September 2000): 483–568.

44. See Barbara S. Gamble, "Putting Civil Rights to a Popular Vote," *American Journal of Political Science* 41 (January 1997): 245–69.

CHAPTER 6

1. John F. Kennedy, *A Nation of Immigrants* (New York: Harper and Row, 1964).

2. See Steven A. Camarota, "Immigrants in the United States, 2007." Center for Immigration Studies, 2007. This report can be found at: *http://www.cis.org/articles/2007/back1007.pdf.*

3. See *Statistical Abstract of the United States, 2007* (Washington, DC: U.S. Government Printing Office, 2007), 255.

4. Harold W. Stanley and Richard G. Niemi, *Vital Statistics on American Politics, 2007–2008* (Washington, DC: Congressional Quarterly Press, 2008), 67–69.

5. On the details of the 1965 Immigration Act and its unintended consequences, see Steven M. Gillon, *That's Not What We Meant to Do: Reform and Its Unintended Consequences in Twentieth-Century America* (New York: Norton, 2000), chap. 4.

6. Ronald T. Takaki, *Strangers from a Different Shore* (Boston: Little, Brown, 1989), chap. 11.

7. Ellis Cose, *A Nation of Strangers: Prejudice, Politics, and the Populating of America* (New York: William Morrow and Company, 1992), 219.

8. Richard Dawson et al., *Political Socialization*, 2nd ed. (Boston: Little, Brown, 1977), 33.

9. See M. Kent Jennings and Richard G. Niemi, *The Political Character of Adolescence: The Influence of Families and Schools* (Princeton, NJ: Princeton University Press, 1981), chap. 2.

10. See M. Kent Jennings and Richard G. Niemi, *Generations and Politics: A Panel Study of Young Adults and Their Parents* (Princeton, NJ: Princeton University Press, 1981).

11. See Martin P. Wattenberg, *Is Voting for Young People?* (New York: Longman, 2008), chs. 1–3.

12. The figure on the average age of the TV news audience can be found in "The State of the Media: 2007." See *http:// www.stateofthenewsmedia.org/ 2007/narrative_networktv_audience. asp?cat=2&media=5* [accessed November 1, 2006]. The figure for a typical prime-time show is cited in Robert D. Putnam, *Bowling Alone: The Collapse and Revival of American Community* (New York: Simon and Schuster, 2000), 221.

13. Quoted in Sabine Reichel, *What Did You Do in the War Daddy? Growing Up German* (New York: Hill & Wang, 1989), 113.

14. David Easton and Jack Dennis, *Children in the Political System* (New York: McGraw-Hill, 1969), 106–7.

15. Jean M. Converse, *Survey Research in the United States: Roots and Emergence, 1890–1960* (Berkeley: University of California Press, 1987), 116. Converse's work is the definitive study on the origins of public opinion sampling.

16. Herbert Asher, *Polling and the Public: What Every Citizen Should Know* (Washington, DC: Congressional Quarterly Press, 1988), 59.

17. Quoted in Norman M. Bradburn and Seymour Sudman, *Polls and Surveys: Understanding What They Tell Us* (San Francisco: Jossey-Bass, 1988), 39–40.

18. Lawrence R. Jacobs and Robert Y. Shapiro, *Politicians Don't Pander* (Chicago: University of Chicago Press, 2000), xiii.

19. John Mueller, "The Iraq Syndrome," *Foreign Affairs*, November/December 2005, 44–54.

20. W. Lance Bennett, *Public Opinion and American Politics* (New York: Harcourt Brace Jovanovich, 1980), 44.

21. E. D. Hirsch Jr., *Cultural Literacy* (Boston: Houghton Mifflin, 1986).

22. Michael X. Delli Carpini and Scott Keeter, *What Americans Know About Politics and Why It Matters* (New Haven, CT: Yale University Press, 1996), chap. 3. For an updated look at this topic, see "Public Knowledge of Current Affairs Little Changed by News and Information Revolutions: What Americans Know: 1989–2007" (report of the Pew Research Center for People and the Press, April 15, 2007). This report can be found online at: *http://people-press.org/reports/display. php3?ReportID=319.*

23. W. Russell Neuman, *The Paradox of Mass Politics: Knowledge and Opinion in the American Electorate* (Cambridge, MA: Harvard University Press, 1986).

24. Mark J. Hetherington, *Why Trust Matters* (Princeton, NJ: Princeton University Press, 2005), 4.

25. See Ronald Inglehart, *Modernization and Postmodernization* (Princeton, NJ: Princeton University Press, 1997), 254–55. Inglehart also shows that the decline of class voting is a general trend throughout Western democracies.

26. See Seymour Martin Lipset and Earl Raab, *Jews and the New American Political Scene* (Cambridge, MA: Harvard University Press, 1995), chap. 6.

27. Angus Campbell et al., *The American Voter* (New York: Wiley, 1960), chap. 10.

28. Norman H. Nie, Sidney Verba, and John R. Petrocik, *The Changing American Voter* (Cambridge, MA: Harvard University Press, 1976), chap. 7.

29. See, for example, John L. Sullivan, James E. Pierson, and George E. Marcus, "Ideological Constraint in the Mass Public: A Methodological Critique and Some New Findings," *American Journal of Political Science* 22 (May 1978): 233–49, and Eric R. A. N. Smith, *The Unchanging American Voter* (Berkeley: University of California Press, 1989).

30. Michael S. Lewis-Beck et al., *The American Voter Revisited* (Ann Arbor, MI: University of Michigan Press, 2008), p. 279.

31. Morris P. Fiorina, *Culture War? The Myth of a Polarized America*, 2nd ed. (New York: Longman, 2006), 127.

32. Ibid., 8.

33. This definition is a close paraphrase of that in Sidney Verba and Norman H. Nie, *Participation in America* (New York: Harper & Row, 1972), 2.

34. See Verba and Nie, *Participation in America*, and Sidney Verba, Kay Lehman Schlozman, and Henry E. Brady, *Voice and Equality: Civic Voluntarism in American Politics* (Cambridge, MA: Harvard University Press, 1995).

35. See Russell J. Dalton, "Citizenship Norms and Political Participation in America: The Good News Is . . . The Bad News Is Wrong" (paper prepared for the conference on Citizenship, Involvement and Democracy at the Center for Democracy and the Third Sector, Georgetown University, December 2005).

36. This letter can be found in Juan Williams, *Eyes on the Prize: America's Civil Rights Years, 1954–1965* (New York: Viking, 1987), 187–89.

37. Verba and Nie, *Participation in America*, 125.

38. Because registration procedures in Louisiana are regulated by the provisions of the Voting Rights Act, registration forms ask people to state their race and the registrars must keep track of this information. Thus, Louisiana can accurately report how many people of each race are registered and voted, which they regularly do. The 2004 data can be found at *http://sos.louisiana.gov/stats/Post_Election_Statistics/Statewide/2004_1102_sta.txt*.

39. See Verba and Nie, *Participation in America*, chap. 10.

40. Campbell et al., *The American Voter*, 541.

41. Morris P. Fiorina, *Retrospective Voting in American National Elections* (New Haven: Yale University Press, 1981), 5.

CHAPTER 7

1. See Darrell M. West, *Air Wars: Television Advertising in Election Campaigns, 1952–2000*, 3rd ed. (Washington, DC: Congressional Quarterly Press, 2001), 67.

2. Stephen Ansolabehere and Shanto Iyengar, *Going Negative* (New York: Free Press, 1995).

3. December 1, 1969, memo from Nixon to H. R. Haldeman in Bruce Oudes, ed., *From: The President—Richard Nixon's Secret Files* (New York: Harper & Row, 1988), 76–77.

4. Mark Hertsgaard, *On Bended Knee: The Press and the Reagan Presidency* (New York: Farrar, Straus & Giroux, 1988), 34.

5. Bob Woodward, *The Agenda: Inside the Clinton White House* (New York: Simon and Schuster, 1994), 313.

6. Quoted in David Brinkley, *Washington Goes to War* (New York: Knopf, 1988), 171.

7. Sam Donaldson, *Hold On, Mr. President!* (New York: Random House, 1987), 54.

8. Marvin Kalb, *One Scandalous Story: Clinton, Lewinsky, and Thirteen Days That Tarnished American Journalism* (New York: Free Press, 2001), 6.

9. Ibid., 20.

10. Ibid., 138.

11. See the classic report by Michael J. Robinson, "Public Affairs Television and the Growth of Political Malaise: The Case of 'The Selling of the Pentagon,'" *American Political Science Review* 70 (June 1976): 409–32. See also Joseph Cappella and Kathleen Hall Jamieson, *Spiral of Cynicism: The Press and the Public Good* (New York: Oxford University Press, 1997).

12. Quoted in Kathleen Hall Jamieson and Paul Waldman, *Electing the President 2000: The Insider's View* (Philadelphia: University of Pennsylvania Press, 2001), 221.

13. William Manchester, *The Last Lion: Winston Churchill, Visions of Glory, 1874–1932* (Boston: Little, Brown, 1984), 225.

14. See, for example, Michael X. Delli Carpini and Scott Keeter, *What Americans Know About Politics and Why It Matters* (New Haven, CT: Yale University Press, 1996), and Ruy A. Teixeira, *The Disappearing American Voter* (Washington, DC: Brookings Institution, 1992).

15. Leonard Downie Jr. and Robert G. Kaiser, *The News About the News: American Journalism in Peril* (New York: Knopf, 2002), 65.

16. Russell Baker, *The Good Times* (New York: William Morrow, 1989), 326.

17. See Walter Cronkite, *A Reporter's Life* (New York: Knopf, 1996), 257–58.

18. Frank Rich, "The Weight of an Anchor," *New York Times*, May 19, 2002.

19. Michael K. Bohn, *Nerve Center: Inside the White House Situation Room* (Dulles, VA: Bassey's, 2003), 59.

20. William and Jane Taubman, *Moscow Spring* (New York: Summit Books, 1989), 286.

21. Project for Excellence in Journalism, *The State of the News Media, 2004*, *www.stateofthenewsmedia.org/index.asp* (accessed August 27, 2004).

22. Thomas Rosenstiel, "The End of Network News," *Washington Post* (September 12, 2004).

23. Bruce Bimber and Richard Davis, *Campaigning Online: The Internet in U.S. Elections* (New York: Oxford University Press, 2003), 145.

24. Doris A. Graber, *Mass Media and American Politics*, 6th ed. (Washington, DC: Congressional Quarterly Press, 2002), 44.

25. Cited in Downey and Kaiser, *The News About the News*, 239.

26. Edward J. Epstein, *News from Nowhere: Television and the News* (New York: Random House, 1973).

27. Downie and Kaiser, *The News About the News*, 137.

28. Steven Ansolabehere, Roy Behr, and Shanto Iyengar, *The Media Game: American Politics in the Television Age* (New York: Macmillan, 1993), 53.

29. For example, see Leon V. Sigal, *Reporters and Officials: The Organization and Politics of News Reporting* (Lexington, MA: D.C. Heath, 1973), 122.

30. This letter can be found in Hedrick Smith, ed., *The Media and the Gulf War: The Press and Democracy in Wartime* (Washington, DC: Seven Locks Press, 1992), 378–80. Smith's book contains an excellent set of readings on media coverage of the war.

31. Stephen J. Farnsworth and S. Robert Lichter, *The Mediated Presidency: Television News and Presidential Governance* (Lanham, MD: Rowman & Littlefield, 2006), 95–96.

32. A *Los Angeles Times* national poll conducted April 2–3, 2003 asked the following question: "Reporters have been assigned to U.S. military units in the region of Iraq and given unprecedented access to military action and personnel. Which of the following statements comes closer to your view: (1) Greater media coverage of the military action and U.S. personnel in Iraq is good for the country because it gives the American people an uncensored view of events as they unfold; or (2) Greater media coverage of the military action and U.S. personnel in Iraq is bad for the country because it provides too much information about military actions as they unfold"? The results were that 55 percent picked the first alternative, 37 percent picked the second, and 8 percent said they didn't know.

33. Jody Powell, "White House Flackery," in *Debating American Government*, 2nd ed., ed. Peter Woll (Glenview, IL: Scott, Foresman, 1988), 180.

34. Dan Rather, quoted in Hoyt Purvis, ed., *The Presidency and the Press* (Austin, TX: Lyndon B. Johnson School of Public Affairs, 1976), 56.

35. Kathleen Hall Jamieson and Joseph N. Capella, "The Role of the Press in the Health Care Reform Debate of 1993–1994," in *The Politics of News, the News of Politics*, ed. Doris Graber, Denis McQuail, and Pippa Norris (Washington, DC: Congressional Quarterly Press, 1998), 118–19.

36. This point is well argued in Kathleen Hall Jamieson, *Eloquence in an Electronic Age* (New York: Oxford University Press, 1988).

37. For a discussion of CBS's failed attempt to lengthen candidate sound bites in 1992, see S. Robert Lichter and Richard E. Noyes, *Good Intentions Make Bad News*, 2nd ed. (Lanham, MD: Rowman & Littlefield, 1996), 246–50.

38. Quoted in Austin Ranney, *Channels of Power* (New York: Basic Books, 1983), 116.

39. Walter Cronkite, *A Reporter's Life*, 376–77.

40. "Campaign 2000 Final: How TV News Covered the General Election Campaign," *Media Monitor* 14 (November/December 2000): 3–4.

41. Ibid.

42. Michael Waldman, *POTUS Speaks: Finding the Words That Defined the Clinton Presidency* (New York: Simon and Schuster, 2000), 267.

43. Project for Excellence in Journalism, *The First 100 Days: How Bush Versus Clinton Fared in the Press* (Washington, DC: Project for Excellence in Journalism, 2001).

44. Stephen J. Farnsworth and S. Robert Lichter, *The Mediated Presidency: Television News and Presidential Governance* (Lanham, MD: Rowman & Littlefield, 2006), 33.

45. David. H. Weaver et al. *The American Journalist in the 21st Century.* (Mahwah, NJ: Lawrence Erlbaum, 2007), 17.

46. Bernard Goldberg, *Bias: A CBS Insider Exposes How the Media Distort the News* (Washington, DC: Regnery, 2002), 5.

47. Ibid., 119.

48. Ibid., 17.

49. Michael J. Robinson and Margaret Petrella, "Who Won the George Bush-Dan Rather Debate?," *Public Opinion* 10 (March/April 1988): 43.

50. Robinson, "Public Affairs Television, and the Growth of Political Malaise," 428.

51. W. Lance Bennett, *News: The Politics of Illusion*, 2nd ed. (New York: Longman, 1988), 46.

52. See Paul F. Lazarsfeld et al., *The People's Choice* (New York: Columbia University Press, 1944).

53. Shanto Iyengar and Donald R. Kinder, *News That Matters* (Chicago: University of Chicago Press, 1987).

54. Ibid., 118–19.

55. Joanne M. Miller and Jon A. Krosnick, "News Media Impact on the Ingredients of Presidential Evaluations: Politically Knowledgeable Citizens Are Guided by a Trusted Source," *American Journal of Political Science* (April 2000): 301–15.

56. Frederick T. Steeper, "Public Response to Gerald Ford's Statements on Eastern Europe in the Second Debate," in *The Presidential Debates: Media, Electoral, and Public Perspectives*, ed. George F. Bishop, Robert G. Meadow, and Marilyn Jackson-Beeck (New York: Praeger, 1978), 81–101.

57. Jamieson and Waldman, *Electing the President 2000*, 5–6.

58. John W. Kingdon, *Agendas, Alternatives, and Public Policies* (Boston: Little, Brown, 1984), 3.

59. Ibid.

60. See the interview with Richard Valeriani in Juan Williams, *Eyes on the Prize* (New York: Viking, 1987), 270–71.

61. For an interesting study of how hiring a public relations firm can help a nation's TV image, see Jarol B. Manheim and Robert B. Albitton, "Changing National Images: International Public Relations and Media Agenda Setting," *American Political Science Review* 78 (September 1984): 641–57.

62. Bernard Cohen, *The Press and Foreign Policy* (Princeton, NJ: Princeton University Press, 1963), 13.

63. "Views of Press Values and Performance" (Pew Research Center for People and the Press, August 9, 2007). This report can be found online at: *http://people-press.org/reports/pdf/348.pdf.*

64. Doris A. Graber, *Mass Media and American Politics*, 6th ed. (Washington, DC: Congressional Quarterly Press, 2002), 275.

65. Ronald W. Berkman and Laura W. Kitch, *Politics in the Media Age* (New York: McGraw-Hill, 1986), 311.

66. Ibid., 313.

67. Matthew Robert Kerbel, *Edited for Television: CNN, ABC, and the 1992 Presidential Campaign* (Boulder, CO: Westview, 1994), 196.

CHAPTER 8

1. E. E. Schattschneider, *Party Government* (New York: Farrar and Rinehart, 1942), 1.

2. Anthony Downs, *An Economic Theory of Democracy* (New York: Harper & Row, 1957).

3. Marjorie Randon Hershey and Paul Allen Beck, *Party Politics in America*, 10th ed. (New York: Longman, 2003), 9.

4. Kay Lawson, ed., *Political Parties and Linkage: A Comparative Perspective* (New Haven, CT: Yale University Press, 1980), 3.

5. The major exception to this rule is nominations for the one-house state legislature in Nebraska, which is officially nonpartisan. In addition, Bernard Sanders has represented Vermont in the House as an Independent since 1990, and in 1994 Angus King was elected governor of Maine as an Independent.

6. Downs, *An Economic Theory of Democracy*.

7. Morris P. Fiorina, *Congress: Keystone of the Washington Establishment*, 2nd ed. (New Haven, CT: Yale University Press, 1989), 101.

8. See Adam Cohen and Elizabeth Taylor, *American Pharaoh* (Boston: Little, Brown, 2000), 155–63.

9. Kay Lawson, "California: The Uncertainties of Reform," *Party Renewal in America*, ed. Gerald Pomper (New Brunswick, NJ: Praeger, 1980), chap. 8.

10. John F. Bibby et al., "Parties in State Politics," in *Politics in the American*

States, 4th ed., ed. Virginia Gray, Herbert Jacob, and Kenneth Vines (Boston: Little, Brown, 1983), 76–79.

11. Hershey and Beck, *Party Politics in America*, 63.

12. John F. Bibby, "State Party Organizations: Coping and Adapting to Candidate-Centered Politics and Nationalization," in *The Parties Respond*, 3rd ed., ed. L. Sandy Maisel (Boulder, CO: Westview, 1998), 34.

13. Comments of Roy Romer and Jim Nicholson at the Bulen Symposium on American Politics, December 1, 1998, as noted by Martin Wattenberg.

14. Gerald M. Pomper, *Elections in America* (New York: Longman, 1980), 161. Another study of presidential promises from Kennedy through Reagan also reaches the conclusion that campaign pledges are taken seriously. See Jeff Fishel, *Presidents and Promises* (Washington, DC: Congressional Quarterly Press, 1985).

15. The term is from V. O. Key. The standard source on critical elections is Walter Dean Burnham, *Critical Elections and the Mainsprings of American Politics* (New York: Norton, 1970).

16. On the origins of the American party system, see William N. Chambers, *Political Parties in a New Nation* (New York: Oxford University Press, 1963).

17. See Richard Hofstader, *The Idea of a Party System: The Rise of Legitimate Opposition in the United States, 1780–1840* (Berkeley: University of California Press, 1969).

18. James W. Ceaser, *Presidential Selection: Theory and Development* (Princeton, NJ: Princeton University Press, 1979), 130.

19. Quoted in James L. Sundquist, *Dynamics of the Party System*, rev. ed. (Washington, DC: Brookings Institution, 1983), 88. Sundquist's book is an excellent account of realignments in American party history.

20. Ibid., 1955.

21. On Boston, see Gerald H. Gamm, *The Making of New Deal Democrats: Voting Behavior and Realignment in Boston, 1920–1940* (Chicago: University of Chicago Press, 1989).

22. See Earl Black and Merle Black, *The Rise of Southern Republicans* (Cambridge, MA: Harvard University Press, 2002).

23. For a good collection of readings on the causes and consequences of divided party government, see Gary W. Cox and Samuel Kernell, eds., *The Politics of Divided Government* (Boulder, CO: Westview, 1991).

24. See Morris P. Fiorina, *Divided Government* (New York: Macmillan, 1992).

25. Steven J. Rosenstone, Roy L. Behr, and Edward H. Lazarus, *Third Parties in America* (Princeton, NJ: Princeton University Press, 1984).

26. For discussion of political ambiguity as a strategy, see Kenneth A. Shepsle, "The Strategy of Ambiguity: Uncertainty and Electoral Competition," *American Political Science Review* 66 (June 1972): 555–68, and Benjamin I. Page, *Choices and Echoes in Presidential Elections* (Chicago: University of Chicago Press, 1978), chap. 6.

27. The classic statement on responsible parties can be found in "Toward a More Responsible Two-Party System: A Report of the Committee on Political Parties, American Political Science Association," *American Political Science Review* 44 (1950): supplement, number 3, part 2.

28. David R. Mayhew, *Divided We Govern: Party Control, Lawmaking, and Investigations, 1946–1990* (New Haven, CT: Yale University Press, 1991), 199.

29. See Evron M. Kirkpatrick, "Toward a More Responsible Party System: Political Science, Policy Science, or Pseudo-Science?," *American Political Science Review* 65 (1971): 965–90.

30. Leon Epstein, *Political Parties in the American Mold* (Madison: University of Wisconsin Press, 1986), 346.

CHAPTER 9

1. Karl Rove, "The Endless Campaign," *Wall Street Journal*, December 20, 2007, A17.

2. Anthony King, *Running Scared* (New York: Free Press, 1997).

3. R. W. Apple Jr., "Foley Assesses Presidential Elections and Tells Why He Wouldn't Run," *New York Times*, November 4, 1998, A12.

4. Paul Taylor, "Is This Any Way to Pick a President?" *Washington Post National Weekly Edition*, April 13, 1987, 6.

5. See Hugh Winebrenner, *The Iowa Precinct Caucuses: The Making of a Media Event* (Ames: Iowa State University Press, 1987).

6. David Yepsen, "Brows Wrinkle, Yet Expect to See a Record Turnout." *Des Moines Register*, January 2, 2008.

7. See Byron Shafer, *Quiet Revolution: The Struggle for the Democratic Party and the Shaping of Post-Reform Politics* (New York: Russell Sage Foundation, 1983).

8. Theodore White, *America in Search of Itself: The Making of the President 1956–1980* (New York: Harper & Row, 1982), 285.

9. This tradition extends back to 1916. The early primary date was chosen then to coincide with the already existing town meetings. Town meetings were held in February prior to the thawing of the snow, which in the days of unpaved roads made traveling extremely difficult in the spring. In 1916 no one could have dreamed that by holding the state's primary so early they were creating a mass media extravaganza for New Hampshire.

10. Harold W. Stanley and Richard G. Niemi, *Vital Statistics on American Politics*, 6th ed. (Washington, DC: Congressional Quarterly Press, 1998), 173. The same research also showed that New Hampshire received just 3 percent of the TV coverage during the general election—a figure far more in line with its small population size.

11. Robert Farmer, quoted in Clifford W. Brown Jr., Lynda W. Powell, and Clyde Wilcox, *Serious Money: Fundraising and Contributing in Presidential Nomination Campaigns* (New York: Cambridge University Press, 1995), 1.

12. Frank Bruni, *Ambling into History: The Unlikely Odyssey of George W. Bush* (New York: HarperCollins, 2002), 5.

13. Larry M. Bartels, *Presidential Primaries and the Dynamics of Public*

Choice (Princeton, NJ: Princeton University Press, 1988), 269.

14. "CQ Vote Studies—Participation: A Numbers Game," *CQ Weekly*, January 14, 2008, 156.

15. See *www.stateofthemedia.org/2005/ chartland.asp?id=470&ct=line&dir= &sort=&col1_box=1&col2_box=1.*

16. R. W. Apple, "No Decisions, No Drama," *New York Times*, August 1, 2000, A14.

17. Barack Obama, *The Audacity of Hope* (New York: Three Rivers Press, 2006), 358.

18. Thomas E. Patterson, *The Mass Media Election* (New York: Praeger, 1980), 3.

19. Obama, *The Audacity of Hope*, 121.

20. "The Internet and the 2008 Election." Report of the Pew Internet and American Life Project, June 15, 2008 [*http:// www.pewinternet.org/pdfs/PIP_2008_election. pdf*].

21. See R. Kenneth Godwin, *One Billion Dollars of Influence: The Direct Marketing of Politics* (Chatham, NJ: Chatham House, 1988).

22. Jonathan S. Krasno and Daniel E. Seltz, "Buying Time: Television Advertising in the 1998 Congressional Elections," *www.brennancenter. org/programs/cmag_temp/download. html.*

23. David R. Runkel, ed., *Campaign for President: The Managers Look at '88* (Dover, MA: Auburn, 1989), 136.

24. Project for Excellence in Journalism, "The Invisible Primary—Invisible No Longer: A First Look at Coverage of the 2008 Presidential Campaign." Report released October 29, 2007. See *http://www. journalism.org/files/The%20Early% 20Campaign%20FINAL_0.pdf.*

25. *Federal Election Commission v. Wisconsin Right to Life, Inc.* (2007).

26. Steve Weissman and Ruth Hassan, "BCRA and the 527 Groups," in *The Election After Reform: Money, Politics and the Bipartisan Campaign Reform Act*, ed. Michael J. Malbin (Lanham, MD: Rowman & Littlefield, 2006), chap. 5.

27. Frank J. Sorauf, *Inside Campaign Finance: Myths and Realities* (New Haven, CT: Yale University Press, 1992), 229.

28. Ibid., 162–63.

29. Archibald Cox and Fred Wertheimer, "The Choice Is Clear: It's People vs. the PACs," in *Debating American Government*, 2nd ed., ed. Peter Woll (Glenview, IL: Scott, Foresman, 1988), 125.

30. This is discussed in Jeffrey M. Berry, *The Interest Group Society*, 3rd ed. (New York: Longman, 1997), 172.

31. Frank J. Sorauf, *Money in American Elections* (Glenview, IL: Scott Foresman, 1988), 312.

32. Bradley A. Smith, *Unfree Speech: The Folly of Campaign Finance Reform* (Princeton, NJ: Princeton University Press, 2001), 173.

33. Gary C. Jacobson, "The Effects of Campaign Spending in Congressional Elections," *American Political Science Review* 72 (June 1978): 469. For an updated analysis of this argument, see Gary C. Jacobson, "The Effects of Campaign Spending in House Elections: New Evidence for Old Arguments," *American Journal of Political Science* 34 (May 1990): 334–62.

34. Herbert E. Alexander, *Financing Politics: Money, Elections, and Political Reform*, 4th ed. (Washington, DC: Congressional Quarterly Press, 1992), 96.

35. See Dennis J. McGrath and Dane Smith, *Professor Wellstone Goes to Washington: The Inside Story of a Grassroots U.S. Senate Campaign* (Minneapolis: University of Minnesota Press, 1995).

36. Dan Nimmo, *The Political Persuaders* (Englewood Cliffs, NJ: Prentice Hall, 1970), 5.

37. Sidney Blumenthal, *The Permanent Campaign* (New York: Simon and Schuster, 1982).

38. See Martin P. Wattenberg, *The Rise of Candidate-Centered Politics: Presidential Elections of the 1980s* (Cambridge, MA: Harvard University Press, 1991).

39. James W. Ceaser, *Presidential Selection: Theory and Development* (Princeton, NJ: Princeton University Press, 1979), 83.

CHAPTER 10

1. Quoted in Stanley G. Kelley Jr., *Interpreting Elections* (Princeton, NJ: Princeton University Press, 1983), 3–4.

2. See Thomas E. Cronin, *Direct Democracy* (Cambridge, MA: Harvard University Press, 1989), chap. 7.

3. Daniel A. Smith, *Tax Crusaders and the Politics of Direct Democracy* (New York: Routledge, 1998).

4. Morton Grodzins, "Political Parties and the Crisis of Succession in the United States: The Case of 1800," in *Political Parties and Political Development*, ed. Joseph LaPalombara and Myron Weiner (Princeton, NJ: Princeton University Press, 1966), 319.

5. In 1804, the Twelfth Amendment to the Constitution changed the procedure to the one we know today, in which each elector votes separately for president and vice president.

6. A summary of these survey results can be found at *www.census.gov/ population/www/socdemo/voting.html.*

7. See Martin P. Wattenberg, "Should Election Day Be a Holiday?," *Atlantic Monthly*, October 1998, 42–46.

8. Anthony Downs, *An Economic Theory of Democracy* (New York: Harper & Row, 1957), chap. 14.

9. See *http://www.sos.state.ia.us/pdfs/ 2006Statewidestats.pdf.*

10. See George C. Edwards III, *At the Margins* (New Haven, CT: Yale University Press, 1989), chap. 8.

11. Richard G. Niemi and Herbert F. Weisberg, eds., *Controversies in Voting Behavior*, 2nd ed. (Washington, DC: Congressional Quarterly Press, 1984), 164–65.

12. See Martin P. Wattenberg, *The Decline of American Political Parties, 1952–1996* (Cambridge, MA: Harvard University Press, 1998).

13. Shawn W. Rosenberg with Patrick McCafferty, "Image and Voter Preference," *Public Opinion Quarterly* 51 (Spring 1987): 44.

14. Arthur H. Miller, Martin P. Wattenberg, and Oksana Malanchuk, "Schematic Assessments of Presidential Candidates," *American Political Science Review* 80 (1986): 521–40. For more recent data, see Martin P. Wattenberg, "Personal Popularity in U.S. Presidential Elections," *Presidential Studies Quarterly* 34 (2004): 119–31.

15. Paul R. Abramson, John H. Aldrich, and David W. Rohde, *Change and Continuity in the 2004 Elections* (Washington, DC: Congressional Quarterly Press, 2006), chap. 6.

16. See Gary C. Jacobson, *A Divider, Not a Uniter: George W. Bush and the American People* (New York: Longman, 2007).

17. American Bar Association, *Electing the President* (Chicago: American Bar Association, 1967), 3.

18. The Twenty-third Amendment (1961) permits the District of Columbia to have three electors even though it has no representatives in Congress.

19. In both Maine and Nebraska, an elector is allocated for every congressional district won, and whoever wins the state as a whole wins the two electors allotted to the state for its senators.

20. Benjamin Page, *Choices and Echoes in American Presidential Elections* (Chicago: University of Chicago Press, 1978), 153.

21. See Morris P. Fiorina, *Retrospective Voting in American National Elections* (New Haven, CT: Yale University Press, 1981).

22. V. O. Key, *The Responsible Electorate* (New York: Random House, 1966), 76.

23. Benjamin Ginsberg, *Consequences of Consent* (Reading, MA: Addison-Wesley, 1982), 194.

24. Ibid., 198.

CHAPTER 11

1. Kay L. Schlozman and John T. Tierney, *Organized Interests and American Democracy* (New York: Harper & Row, 1986), 1.

2. The classic work is David B. Truman, *The Governmental Process*, 2nd ed. (New York: Knopf, 1971).

3. Thomas R. Dye, *Who's Running America?*, 5th ed. (Englewood Cliffs, NJ: Prentice Hall, 1990), 170.

4. Robert Engler, *The Brotherhood of Oil* (Chicago: University of Chicago Press, 1977).

5. Theodore J. Lowi, *The End of Liberalism*, 2nd ed. (New York: Norton, 1979).

6. See Lee Fritschler, *Smoking and Politics: Policy Making and the Federal Bureaucracy* (Englewood Cliffs, NJ: Prentice Hall, 1983).

7. Morris P. Fiorina, *Congress: Keystone of the Washington Establishment*, 2nd ed. (New Haven, CT: Yale University Press, 1989), 122.

8. E. E. Schattschneider, *The Semisovereign People* (New York: Holt, Rinehart and Winston, 1960), 35.

9. Truman, *The Governmental Process*, 511.

10. Mancur Olson, *The Logic of Collective Action* (Cambridge, MA: Harvard University Press, 1965), especially 9–36.

11. Ibid., 35.

12. Jeffrey H. Birnbaum and Alan S. Murray, *Showdown at Gucci Gulch: Lawmakers, Lobbyists, and the Unlikely Triumph of Tax Reform* (New York: Vintage, 1987).

13. Ibid., 235.

14. Christy Swartout, ed., *Encyclopedia of Associations*, 44th ed. (Detroit: Gale Research Company, 2007).

15. See Frank R. Baumgartner and Beth L. Leech, *Basic Interests: The Importance of Groups in Politics and in Political Science* (Princeton, NJ: Princeton University Press, 1998), 109; data for 2006 posted at *http://library.dialog.com/bluesheets/html/bl0114.html*.

16. Jack L. Walker, "The Origins and Maintenance of Interest Groups in America," *American Political Science Review* 77 (June 1983): 390–406.

17. Andrew S. McFarland, *Common Cause: Lobbying in the Public Interest* (Chatham, NJ: Chatham House, 1984), 1.

18. Lester W. Milbrath, *The Washington Lobbyists* (Chicago: Rand McNally, 1963), 8.

19. See "Congressional Revolving Doors: The Journey from Congress to K Street," Public Citizen Congress Watch, July 2005. This report can be found at *www.lobbyinginfo.org/* (accessed January 4, 2006).

20. See *http://www.columbiabooks.com/servlet/the-26/Washington-Representatives-2008-Package/Detail*.

21. Norman Ornstein and Shirley Elder, *Interest Groups, Lobbying, and Policymaking* (Washington, DC: Congressional Quarterly Press, 1978), 59–60.

22. Peter H. Stone, "Friends, After All," *National Journal*, October 22, 1994, 2440.

23. Rogan Kersh, "The Well-Informed Lobbyist: Information and Interest Group Lobbying." In Allan J. Cigler and Burdett A. Loomis, eds., *Interest Group Politics*, 7th ed. (Washington, DC: Congressional Quarterly Press, 2007), 390.

24. Richard L. Hall and Alan V. Deardorff, "Lobbying as Legislative Subsidy," *American Political Science Review* 100 (February 2006): 69.

25. For a summary of recent studies on the influence of lobbying, see Baumgartner and Leech, *Basic Interests*, 130.

26. See Kelly Patterson and Matthew M. Singer, "Targeting Success: The Enduring Power of the NRA." In Allan J. Cigler and Burdett A. Loomis, eds., *Interest Group Politics*, 7th edition (Washington, DC: Congressional Quarterly Press, 2007): 37–64.

27. See *http://www.opensecrets.org/pacs/lookup2.asp?strid=C00368142&cycle=2006*.

28. Frederic J. Frommer, "Baseball PAC Gives Thousands to Parties," Associated Press, May 13, 2003.

29. See *http://www.fec.gov/press/press2007/20071009pac/20071009pac.shtml*.

30. R. Kenneth Godwin and Barry J. Seldon, "What Corporations Really Want from Government: The Public Provision of Private Goods," in Cigler and Loomis, *Interest Group Politics*, 6th ed., 219.

31. The Sovern story is told in "Taking an Ax to PACs," *Time*, August 20, 1984, 27.

32. Karen Orren, "Standing to Sue: Interest Group Conflict in Federal Courts," *American Political Science Review* 70 (September 1976): 724.

33. Gregory A. Caldeira and John R. Wright, "*Amici Curiae* Before the Supreme Court: Who Participates, When, and How Much," *Journal of Politics* 52 (August 1990): 782–804.

34. Ronald J. Hrebenar and Ruth K. Scott, *Interest Group Politics in America*, 2nd ed. (Englewood Cliffs, NJ: Prentice Hall, 1990), 201.

35. Ken Kollman, *Outside Lobbying: Public Opinion and Interest Group*

Strategies (Princeton, NJ: Princeton University Press, 1998), 33.

36. Quoted in Jeffrey M. Berry, *The Interest Group Society*, 2nd ed. (Glenview, IL: Scott, Foresman, 1989), 103.

37. Paul Edward Johnson, "Organized Labor in an Era of Blue-Collar Decline," in *Interest Group Politics*, 3rd ed., ed. Allan J. Cigler and Burdett A. Loomis (Washington, DC: Congressional Quarterly Press, 1991), 33–62.

38. See Pat Choate, *Agents of Influence: How Japan Manipulates America's Political and Economic System* (New York: Simon and Schuster, 1990).

39. Christopher J. Bosso, "The Color of Money: Environmental Groups and the Pathologies of Fund Raising," in *Interest Group Politics*, 4th ed., ed. Allan J. Cigler and Burdett A. Loomis (Washington, DC: Congressional Quarterly Press, 1995), 102.

40. For an interesting analysis of how changes in the regulatory environment, congressional oversight, and public opinion altered the debate on nuclear power, see Frank R. Baumgartner and Bryan D. Jones, *Agendas and Instability in American Politics* (Chicago: University of Chicago Press, 1993).

41. See *www.naacp.org/departments/programs/economy/economy_index.html*.

42. Dona C. Hamilton and Charles V. Hamilton, *The Dual Agenda: Race and Social Welfare Policies of Civil Rights Organizations* (New York: Columbia University Press, 1997), 2.

43. Jeffrey M. Berry, *Lobbying for the People* (Princeton, NJ: Princeton University Press, 1977), 7.

44. Robert H. Salisbury, "The Paradox of Interest Groups in Washington—More Groups, Less Clout," in *The New American Political System*, 2nd ed., ed. Anthony King (Washington, DC: American Enterprise Institute, 1990), 204.

45. Mark J. Rozell, Clyde Wilcox, and David Madland, *Interest Groups in American Campaigns: The New Face of Electioneering*, 2nd ed. (Washington, DC: Congressional Quarterly Press, 2006), 87.

46. Alexis de Tocqueville, *Democracy in America*, vol. 2 (New York: Vintage, 1945), 114.

47. Hrebenar and Scott, *Interest Group Politics in America*, 234.

48. Steven V. Roberts, "Angered President Blames Others for the Huge Deficit," *New York Times*, December 14, 1988, A16.

49. William M. Lunch, *The Nationalization of American Politics* (Berkeley: University of California Press, 1987), 206.

50. Salisbury, "The Paradox of Interest Groups in Washington," 229.

CHAPTER 12

1. See Craig Schultz, ed., *Setting Course: A Congressional Management Guide* (Washington, DC: Congressional Management Foundation, 1994); and David E. Price, *The Congressional Experience: A View from the Hill* (Boulder, CO: Westview Press, 1999).

2. David T. Canon, *Race, Redistricting, and Representation: The Unintended Consequences of Black Majority Districts* (Chicago: University of Chicago Press, 1999).

3. Susan A. Banducci, Todd Donovan, and Jeffrey A. Karp, "Minority Representation, Empowerment, and Participation," *Journal of Politics* 66 (May 2004): 534–56.

4. There is some evidence that women state legislators in states with the highest percentage of female representatives are more likely than men to introduce and pass legislation dealing with women, children, and families. See Sue Thomas, "The Impact of Women on State Legislative Policies," *Journal of Politics* 53 (November 1991): 958–76. See also Arturo Vega and Juanita M. Firestone, "The Effects of Gender on Congressional Behavior and the Substantive Representation of Women," *Legislative Studies Quarterly* 20 (May 1995): 213–22, and Leslie A. Schwindt-Bayer and Renato Corbetta, "Gender Turnover and Roll-Call Voting in the U.S. House of Representatives," *Legislative Studies Quarterly* 29 (May 2004): 215–29.

5. On various views of representation, see Hanna Pitkin, *The Concept of Representation* (Berkeley: University of California Press, 1967).

6. Sally Friedman, "House Committee Assignments of Women and Minority Newcomers, 1965–1994," *Legislative Studies Quarterly* 21 (February 1996): 73–81; Alan Gerber, "African Americans' Congressional Careers and the Democratic House Delegation," *Journal of Politics* 58 (August 1996): 831–45.

7. These data were calculated from "Women Candidates-Election 2006," Center for American Women and Politics.

8. Sarah A. Fulton, Cherie D. Maestas, L. Sandy Maisel, and Walter J. Stone, "The Sense of a Woman: Gender, Ambition and the Decision to Run for Congress," *Political Research Quarterly* 59 (June 2006): 235–248.

9. A review of congressional campaign costs and spending can be found in Paul S. Herrnson, *Congressional Elections: Campaigning at Home and in Washington*, 5th ed. (Washington, DC: Congressional Quarterly Press, 2008).

10. John L. Sullivan and Eric Uslaner, "Congressional Behavior and Electoral Marginality," *American Journal of Political Science* 22 (August 1978): 536–53.

11. Thomas Mann, *Unsafe at Any Margin* (Washington, DC: American Enterprise Institute, 1978).

12. Glenn R. Parker, *Homeward Bound* (Pittsburgh: University of Pittsburgh Press, 1986); John R. Johannes, *To Serve the People* (Lincoln: University of Nebraska Press, 1984).

13. Patricia Hurley and Kim Q. Hill, "The Prospects for Issue Voting in Contemporary Congressional Elections," *American Politics Quarterly* 8 (October 1980): 446.

14. Mann, *Unsafe at Any Margin*, 37.

15. That presidential elections and congressional elections are not closely related is an argument made in Lyn Ragsdale, "The Fiction of Congressional Elections as Presidential Events," *American Politics Quarterly* 8 (October 1980): 375–98. For evidence that voters' views of the president affect their voting for senators, see Lonna Rae Atkeson and Randall W. Partin, "Economic and Referendum Voting: A Comparison of Gubernatorial

and Senatorial Elections," *American Political Science Review* 89 (March 1995): 99–107.

16. John R. Owens and Edward C. Olson, "Economic Fluctuations and Congressional Elections," *American Journal of Political Science* 24 (August 1980): 469–93; Benjamin Radcliff, "Solving a Puzzle: Aggregate Analysis and Economic Voting Revisited," *Journal of Politics* 50 (May 1988): 440–58; Robert S. Erikson, "Economic Conditions and the Congressional Vote: A Review of the Macrolevel Evidence," *American Journal of Political Science* 34 (May 1990): 373–99; James E. Campbell, *The Presidential Pulse of Congressional Elections* (Lexington: University Press of Kentucky, 1993), 119; Gary C. Jacobson, "Does the Economy Matter in Midterm Elections?," *American Journal of Political Science* 34 (May 1990): 400–404.

17. David R. Mayhew, *Congress: The Electoral Connection* (New Haven, CT: Yale University Press, 1974).

18. Richard F. Fenno Jr., *Home Style* (Boston: Little, Brown, 1978), 32.

19. Ibid., 106–7.

20. The "service spells success" argument is made in Morris P. Fiorina, *Congress: Keystone of the Washington Establishment*, 2nd ed. (New Haven, CT: Yale University Press, 1989), and, with a slightly different emphasis, in Glenn R. Parker, "The Advantages of Incumbency in Congressional Elections," *American Politics Quarterly* 8 (October 1980): 449–61.

21. Fiorina, *Congress*, 43.

22. Gary C. Jacobson, *The Politics of Congressional Elections*, 7th ed. (New York: Longman, 2007), 122–33; Stephen Ansolabehere, James M. Snyder Jr., and Charles Stewart III, "Old Voters, New Voters, and the Personal Vote: Using Redistricting to Measure the Incumbency Advantage," *American Journal of Political Science* 44 (January 2000): 17–34.

23. See, for example, Paul Feldman and James Jondrow, "Congressional Elections and Local Federal Spending," *American Journal of Political Science* 28 (February 1984): 147–63; Glenn R. Parker and Suzanne L. Parker, "The Correlates and Effects of Attention to District by U.S. House Members," *Legislative Studies Quarterly* 10 (May 1985): 223–42; and John C. McAdams and John R. Johannes, "Congressmen, Perquisites, and Elections," *Journal of Politics* 50 (May 1988): 412–39.

24. On strategies of challengers, see Gary C. Jacobson and Samuel Kernell, *Strategy and Choice in Congressional Elections*, 2nd ed. (New Haven, CT: Yale University Press, 1983), and Gary C. Jacobson, "Strategic Politicians and the Dynamics of U.S. House Elections, 1946–1986," *American Political Science Review* 83 (September 1989): 773–94. See also Steven D. Levitt and Catherine D. Wolfram, "Decomposing the Sources of Incumbency Advantage in the U.S. House," *Legislative Studies Quarterly* 22 (February 1997): 45–60.

25. See Gary C. Jacobson, *Money in Congressional Elections* (New Haven, CT: Yale University Press, 1980).

26. On the importance of challenger quality and financing, see Alan I. Abramowitz, Brad Alexander, and Matthew Gunning, "Incumbency, Redistricting, and the Decline of Competition in U.S. House Elections," *Journal of Politics* 68 (February 2006): 75–88; Alan I. Abramowitz, "Explaining Senate Election Outcomes," *American Political Science Review* 82 (June 1988): 385–403; and Donald Philip Green and Jonathan S. Krasno, "Salvation for the Spendthrift Incumbent," *American Journal of Political Science* 32 (November 1988): 884–907.

27. Jacobson, *The Politics of Congressional Elections*, 45–51, 133–35. See also Gary C. Jacobson, "The Effects of Campaign Spending in House Elections: New Evidence for Old Arguments," *American Journal of Political Science* 34 (May 1990): 334–62; Christopher Kenny and Michael McBurnett, "An Individual-Level Multiequation Model of Expenditure Effects in Contested House Elections," *American Political Science Review* 88 (September 1994): 699–707; Robert S. Erikson and Thomas R. Palfrey, "Campaign Spending and Incumbency: An Alternative Simultaneous Equation Approach," *Journal of Politics* 60 (May 1998): 355–73; and Alan Gerber, "Estimating the Effect of Campaign Spending on Senate Election Outcomes Using Instrumental Variables," *American Political Science Review* 92 (June 1998): 401–12.

28. Center for Responsive Politics (*www. opensecrets.org*).

29. Gary C. Jacobson and Michael A. Dimock, "Checking Out: The Effects of Bank Overdrafts on the 1992 House Elections," *American Journal of Political Science* 38 (August 1994): 601–24. See also Marshal A. Dimock and Gary C. Jacobson, "Checks and Choices: The House Bank Scandal's Impact on Voters in 1992," *Journal of Politics* 57 (November 1995): 1143–59, and Carl McCurley and Jeffrey J. Mondak, "Inspected by #1184063113: The Influence of Incumbents' Competence and Integrity in U.S. House Elections," *American Journal of Political Science* 39 (November 1995): 864–85.

30. John G. Peters and Susan Welch, "The Effects of Corruption on Voting Behavior in Congressional Elections," *American Political Science Review* 74 (September 1980): 697–708; Susan Welch and John R. Hibbing, "The Effects of Charges of Corruption on Voting Behavior in Congressional Elections, 1982–1990," *Journal of Politics* 59 (February 1997): 226–39.

31. For a discussion of the politics and process of reapportionment, see Thomas E. Mann, *Redistricting* (Washington, DC: Brookings Institution Press, 2008).

32. On term limits, see Gerald Benjamin and Michael J. Malbin, eds., *Limiting Our Legislative Terms* (Washington, DC: Congressional Quarterly Press, 1992).

33. Said former House Speaker Jim Wright in *You and Your Congressman* (New York: Putnam, 1976), 190. See also Donald R. Matthews and James Stimson, *Yeas and Nays: Normal Decision-Making in the House of Representatives* (New York: Wiley, 1975),

and John L. Sullivan et al., "The Dimensions of Cue-Taking in the House of Representatives: Variations by Issue Area," *Journal of Politics* 55 (November 1993): 975–97.

34. Nelson W. Polsby et al., "Institutionalization of the House of Representatives," *American Political Science Review* 62 (1968): 144–68.

35. John R. Hibbing, "Contours of the Modern Congressional Career," *American Political Science Review* 85 (June 1991): 405–28.

36. See Bernard Grofman, Robert Griffin, and Amihai Glazer, "Is the Senate More Liberal Than the House? Another Look," *Legislative Studies Quarterly* 16 (May 1991): 281–96.

37. See Sarah A. Binder and Steven S. Smith, *Politics or Principle? Filibustering in the United States Senate* (Washington, DC: Brookings Institution, 1997).

38. Robert L. Peabody, *Leadership in Congress* (Boston: Little, Brown, 1976), 4.

39. On the increasing importance of party leadership in the House, see David W. Rohde, *Parties and Leaders in the Postreform House* (Chicago: University of Chicago Press, 1991); Barbara Sinclair, "The Emergence of Strong Leadership in the 1980s House of Representatives," *Journal of Politics* 54 (August 1992): 657–84; and Gary W. Cox and Matthew D. McCubbins, *Legislative Leviathan* (Berkley: University of California Press, 1993).

40. For more on congressional oversight, see Christopher H. Foreman Jr., *Signals from the Hill* (New Haven, CT: Yale University Press, 1988), and Diana Evans, "Congressional Oversight and the Diversity of Members' Goals," *Political Science Quarterly* 109 (fall 1994): 669–87.

41. Joel D. Aberbach, *Keeping a Watchful Eye: The Politics of Congressional Oversight* (Washington, DC: Brookings Institution, 1990).

42. Aberbach, *Keeping a Watchful Eye;* Joel D. Aberbach, "What's Happened to the Watchful Eye?," *Congress and the Presidency* 29 (spring 2002): 3–23.

43. Thomas E. Mann and Norman J. Ornstein, *The Broken Branch* (New York: Oxford University Press, 2006).

44. Richard F. Fenno Jr., *Congressmen in Committees* (Boston: Little, Brown, 1973), 1.

45. Useful studies of committee assignments include Kenneth Shepsle, *The Giant Jigsaw Puzzle* (Chicago: University of Chicago Press, 1978), and Cox and McCubbins, *Legislative Leviathan*, chaps. 1, 7, and 8.

46. Richard F. Fenno Jr., "If, as Ralph Nader Says, Congress Is the 'Broken Branch,' How Come We Love Our Congressmen So Much?," in *Congress in Change*, ed. Norman Ornstein (New York: Praeger, 1975), 282.

47. For more on congressional reform, see Leroy N. Rieselbach, *Congressional Reform* (Washington, DC: Congressional Quarterly Press, 1986).

48. See Susan Webb Hammond, *Congressional Caucuses in National Policy Making* (Baltimore: Johns Hopkins University Press, 1998).

49. For a thorough discussion of rule changes and the impact of procedures, see Steven S. Smith, *Call to Order: Floor Politics in the House and Senate* (Washington, DC: Brookings Institution, 1989).

50. Barbara Sinclair, *Unorthodox Lawmaking*, 3rd ed. (Washington, DC: Congressional Quarterly Press, 2007).

51. George C. Edwards III and Andrew Barrett, "Presidential Agenda Setting in Congress," in *Polarized Politics: Congress and the President in a Partisan Era*, ed. Jon R. Bond and Richard Fleisher (Washington, DC: Congressional Quarterly Press, 2000).

52. George C. Edwards III, *At the Margins: Presidential Leadership of Congress* (New Haven, CT: Yale University Press, 1989).

53. James M. Snyder Jr. and Tim Groseclose, "Estimating Party Influence in Congressional Roll-Call Voting," *American Journal of Political Science* 44 (April 2000): 187–205; Aage Clausen, *How Congressmen Decide: A Policy Focus* (New York: St. Martin's Press, 1973).

54. Quoted in Peter G. Richards, *Honourable Members* (London: Faber and Faber, 1959), 157.

55. See Roger H. Davidson, *The Role of the Congressman* (New York: Pegasus, 1969), and Thomas E. Cavanaugh, "Role Orientations of House Members: The Process of Representation" (paper delivered at the annual meeting of the American Political Science Association, Washington, DC, August 1979).

56. John L. Sullivan and Robert E. O'Connor, "Electoral Choice and Popular Control of Public Policy: The Case of the 1966 House Elections," *American Political Science Review* 66 (December 1972): 1256–68.

57. The *New York Times*/CBS News Poll cited in "Voters Disgusted with Politicians as Election Nears," *New York Times*, November 13, 1994, A10.

58. Robert A. Bernstein, *Elections, Representation, and Congressional Voting Behavior* (Englewood Cliffs, NJ: Prentice Hall, 1989), 99.

59. Patricia A. Hurley and Kim Quaile Hill, "Beyond the Demand-Input Model: A Theory of Representational Linkages," *Journal of Politics* 65 (May 2003): 304–26; Christopher Wlezien, "Patterns of Representation: Dynamics of Public Preferences and Policy," *Journal of Politics* 66 (February 2004): 1–24.

60. Larry M. Bartels, however, found that members of Congress were responsive to constituency opinion in supporting the Reagan defense buildup. See "Constituency Opinion and Congressional Policy Making: The Reagan Defense Buildup," *American Political Science Review* 85 (June 1991): 457–74.

61. Kim Quaile Hill and Patricia A. Hurley, "Dyadic Representation Reappraised," *American Journal of Political Science* 43 (January 1999): 109–37.

62. On the importance of ideology, see Bernstein, *Elections, Representation, and Congressional Voting Behavior*.

63. *Washington Representatives 2008* (Washington, DC: Columbia Books, 2008); *PoliticalMoneyLine*.

64. Center for Responsive Politics, 2008; *PoliticalMoneyLine*.

65. Richard L. Hall and Alan V. Deardorff, "Lobbying as Legislative Subsidy," *American Political Science*

Review 100 (February 2006): 69–84.

66. John W. Kingdon, *Congressmen's Voting Decisions*, 3rd ed. (Ann Arbor: University of Michigan Press, 1989), 242.

67. See M. Darrell West, *Congress and Economic Policymaking* (Pittsburgh: University of Pittsburgh Press, 1987).

CHAPTER 13

1. Quoted in Thomas E. Cronin, *The State of the Presidency*, 2nd ed. (Boston: Little, Brown, 1980), 223.

2. Richard E. Neustadt, *Presidential Power and the Modern Presidents* (New York: Free Press, 1990).

3. On the public's expectations of the president, see George C. Edwards III, *The Public Presidency* (New York: St. Martin's Press, 1983), chap. 5.

4. Office of the White House Press Secretary, *Remarks of the President at a Meeting with Non-Washington Editors and Broadcasters*, September 21, 1979, 12.

5. Samuel P. Huntington, *American Politics: The Promises of Disharmony* (Cambridge, MA: Belknap, 1981), 33.

6. On the creation of the presidency, see Donald L. Robinson, *To the Best of My Ability* (New York: Norton, 1987), and Thomas E. Cronin, ed., *Inventing the American Presidency* (Lawrence: University Press of Kansas, 1989).

7. A good example is Clinton Rossiter, *The American Presidency*, rev. ed. (New York: Harcourt, 1960).

8. Arthur Schlesinger, *The Imperial Presidency* (Boston: Houghton Mifflin, 1973).

9. The titles of chapters 5 and 11 in Thomas E. Cronin, *The State of the Presidency*, 2nd ed. (Boston: Little, Brown, 1980).

10. On the factors important in the presidential nominee's choice of a running mate, see Lee Sigelman and Paul J. Wahlbeck, "The 'Veepstakes': Strategic Choice in Presidential Running Mate Selection," *American Political Science Review* 91 (December 1997): 855–64.

11. See Paul C. Light, *Vice Presidential Power* (Baltimore: Johns Hopkins University Press, 1984).

12. For a study of the backgrounds of cabinet members, see Jeffrey E. Cohen, *The Politics of the U.S. Cabinet* (Pittsburgh: University of Pittsburgh Press, 1988).

13. For background on the Executive Office, see John Hart, *The Presidential Branch*, 2nd ed. (Chatham, NJ: Chatham House, 1995).

14. Two useful books on the history and functions of the White House staff are Hart, *The Presidential Branch*, and Bradley H. Patterson Jr., *The White House Staff* (Washington, DC: Brookings Institution, 2000).

15. For a discussion of presidential party leadership in Congress, see George C. Edwards III, *At the Margins: Presidential Leadership of Congress* (New Haven, CT: Yale University Press, 1989), chaps. 3–5.

16. Jimmy Carter, *Keeping Faith* (New York: Bantam, 1982), 80.

17. For a review of these studies and an analysis showing the limited impact of presidential coattails on congressional election outcomes, see Edwards, *The Public Presidency*, 83–93.

18. For evidence of the impact of the president's campaigning in midterm elections, see Jeffrey E. Cohen, Michael A. Krassa, and John A. Hamman, "The Impact of Presidential Campaigning on Midterm U.S. Senate Elections," *American Political Science Review* 85 (March 1991): 165–78. On the president's effect on congressional elections more broadly, see James E. Campbell, *The Presidential Pulse of Congressional Elections* (Lexington: University Press of Kentucky, 1993).

19. Quoted in Sidney Blumenthal, "Marketing the President," *New York Times Magazine*, September 13, 1981, 110.

20. Quoted in "Slings and Arrows," *Newsweek*, July 31, 1978, 20.

21. Edwards, *At the Margins*, chaps. 6–7.

22. Lawrence J. Grossback, David A. M. Peterson, and James A. Stimson, *Mandate Politics* (New York: Cambridge University Press, 2006).

23. For an analysis of the factors that affect perceptions of mandates, see Edwards, *At the Margins*, chap. 8.

24. David Stockman, *The Triumph of Politics* (New York: Harper & Row, 1986), 251–65; William Greider, "The Education of David Stockman," *Atlantic*, December 1981, 51.

25. George C. Edwards III and Andrew Barrett, "Presidential Agenda Setting in Congress," in *Polarized Politics*, ed. Jon R. Bond and Richard Fleisher (Washington, DC: Congressional Quarterly Press, 2000).

26. John Kingdon, *Agendas, Alternatives, and Public Policies* (Boston: Little, Brown, 1984), 25. On presidential agenda setting, see Paul C. Light, *The President's Agenda* (Baltimore: Johns Hopkins University Press, 1991), and George C. Edwards III and B. Dan Wood, "Who Influences Whom? The President, Congress, and the Media," *American Political Science Review* 93 (June 1999): 327–44.

27. Edwards, *At the Margins*, chaps. 9–10; Jon R. Bond and Richard Fleisher, *The President in the Legislative Arena* (Chicago: University of Chicago Press, 1990), chap. 8.

28. See David Auerswald and Forrest Maltzman, "Policymaking Through Advice and Consent: Treaty Considerations by the United States Senate," *Journal of Politics* 65 (November 2003): 1097–110.

29. For an analysis of war powers and other issues related to separation of powers, see Louis Fisher, *Constitutional Conflicts Between Congress and the President*, 4th ed. rev. (Lawrence: University Press of Kansas, 1997), and Louis Fisher, *Presidential War Power* (Lawrence: University Press of Kansas, 1995).

30. See William G. Howell and Jon C. Pevehouse, *While Dangers Gather: Congressional Checks on Presidential War Powers* (Princeton, NJ: Princeton University Press, 2007).

31. See Barbara Hinckley, *Less than Meets the Eye* (Chicago: University of Chicago Press, 1994).

32. The phrase was originated by Aaron Wildavsky in "The Two Presidencies," *Trans-Action* 4 (December 1966): 7–14. He later determined that the two presidencies applied

mostly to the 1950s. See Duane M. Oldfield and Aaron Wildavsky, "Reconsidering the Two Presidencies," in *The Two Presidencies: A Quarter Century Assessment*, ed. Steven A. Shull (Chicago: Nelson-Hall, 1991), 181–90.

33. Edwards, *At the Margins*, chap. 4.

34. Samuel Kernell, *Going Public*, 4th ed. (Washington, DC: Congressional Quarterly Press, 2004.

35. Edwards, *The Public Presidency*, chap. 6; George C. Edwards III, *Presidential Approval* (Baltimore: Johns Hopkins University Press, 1990).

36. Mueller also included the inaugural period of a president's term as a rally event. See John E. Mueller, *War, Presidents and Public Opinion* (New York: Wiley, 1973), 208–13.

37. Kernell, *Going Public*, 169.

38. On presidents' efforts to build policy support, see Jeffrey K. Tulis, *The Rhetorical Presidency* (Princeton, NJ: Princeton University Press, 1987).

39. Evan Parker-Stephen, "Campaigns, Motivation, and the Dynamics of Political Learning." *Working Paper*, 2008.

40. Steven Kull, Clay Ramsay, and Evan Lewis, "Misperceptions, the Media, and the Iraq War," *Political Science Quarterly* 118 (Winter 2003–2004): 569–598.

41. Useful comparisons over Reagan's and Clinton's tenures can be found in George C. Edwards III, *On Deaf Ears: The Limits of the Bully Pulpit* (New Haven, CT: Yale University Press, 2003), chaps. 2–3.

42. George C. Edwards III, *Governing by Campaigning: The Politics of the Bush Presidency*, 2nd ed. (New York: Longman, 2007).

43. The best source for the White House's relations with the press is Martha Kumar, *Managing the President's Message: The White House Communications Operation* (Baltimore, MD: Johns Hopkins University Press, 2007).

44. Sam Donaldson, *Hold On, Mr. President!* (New York: Random House, 1987), 196–97.

45. Two of the leading studies are found in Michael J. Robinson and Margaret A. Sheehan, *Over the Wire and on TV* (New York: Russell Sage Foundation, 1983), and Daniel C. Hallin, *"The 'Uncensored War': the Media and Vietnam* (New York: Oxford University Press, 1986).

46. Carter, *Keeping Faith*, 179–80.

47. See Mark J. Rozell, *The Press and the Ford Presidency* (Ann Arbor: University of Michigan Press, 1992).

48. Doris A. Graber, *Mass Media and American Politics*, 5th ed. (Washington, DC: Congressional Quarterly Press, 1997), 277. On the 1992 presidential campaign, see "Clinton's the One," *Media Monitor* 6 (November 1992): 3–5.

49. Thomas E. Patterson, *Out of Order* (New York: Knopf, 1993), chap. 3.

50. Ibid., 113.

51. *Media Monitor*, May/June 1995, 2–5; Thomas E. Patterson, "Legitimate Beef: The Presidency and a Carnivorous Press," *Media Studies Journal*, spring 1994, 21–26; "Sex, Lies, and TV News," *Media Monitor* 12 (September/October 1998); "TV News Coverage of the 1998 Midterm Elections," *Media Monitor* 12 (November/December 1998). See also Andras Szanto, "In Our Opinion . . . : Editorial Page Views of Clinton's First Year," *Media Studies Journal*, spring 1994, 97–105; Lichter and Noyes, *Good Intentions Make Bad News*, p. 214.

52. See, for example, *Media Monitor*, June/July 1998.

53. Stephen J. Farnsworth and S. Robert Lichter, T*he Mediated Presidency: Television News and Presidential Governance* (Lanham, MD: Rowman and Littlefield, 2006), pp. 40–45, chap. 4; Stephen J. Farnsworth and S. Robert Lichter, *The Nightly News Nightmare: Television's Coverage of U.S. Presidential Elections, 1988–2004*, 2nd ed. (Lanham, MD: Rowman & Littlefield, 2007), chap. 4. See also Jeffrey E. Cohen, *The Presidency in the Era of 24-Hour News* (Princeton, NJ: Princeton University Press), chaps. 5–6.

54. Katherine Graham, *Personal History* (New York: Vintage, 1998).

55. Michael Baruch Grossman and Martha Joynt Kumar, *Portraying the President: The White House and the News Media* (Baltimore: Johns Hopkins University Press, 1981), chaps. 10–11.

56. Donaldson, *Hold On, Mr. President!*, 237–38.

57. Quoted in Eleanor Randolph, "Speakes Aims Final Salvo at White House Practices," *Washington Post*, January 31, 1987, A3.

58. George C. Edwards III, Andrew Barrett, and Jeffrey S. Peake, "The Legislative Impact of Divided Government," *American Journal of Political Science* 41 (April 1997): 545–63.

59. David R. Mayhew, *Divided We Govern* (New Haven, CT: Yale University Press, 1991).

CHAPTER 14

1. Aaron Wildavsky and Naomi Caiden, *The New Politics of the Budgetary Process*, 5th ed. (New York: Longman, 2004), 2.

2. *Budget of the United States Government, Fiscal Year 2009: Historical Tables* (Washington, DC: U.S. Government Printing Office, 2008), Tables 3.1 and 7.1.

3. Quoted in Gerald Carson, *The Golden Egg: The Personal Income Tax, Where It Came From, How It Grew* (Boston: Houghton Mifflin, 1977), 12.

4. Statistics on the number of returns and audits come from the U.S. Department of Commerce, *Statistical Abstract of the United States, 2008* (Washington, DC: U.S. Government Printing Office, 2008), Tables 467 and 479.

5. Tax Foundation, 2008.

6. An exception is Robert Eisner, who argues that if the government counted its debt as families and business firms do—that is, by balancing assets against liabilities—the government would be in pretty good shape. See *How Real Is the Federal Deficit?* (New York: Free Press, 1986).

7. An excellent discussion of such issues is Bryan D. Jones and Walter Williams, *The Politics of Bad Ideas* (New York: Pearson Longman, 2007).

8. Carson, *The Golden Egg*, 181–82.

9. Carson, *The Golden Egg*, 181–82.

10. For some perspectives on the rise of government expenditures, see David Cameron, "The Expansion of the Public Economy: A Comparative

Analysis," *American Political Science Review* 72 (December 1978): 1243–61, and William D. Berry and David Lowery, *Understanding United States Government Growth* (New York: Praeger, 1987).

11. E. E. Schattschneider, *Two Hundred Million Americans in Search of a Government* (New York: Holt, Rinehart and Winston, 1969), 29–30.

12. Berry and Lowery, *Understanding United States Government Growth*.

13. Paul Light, *Artful Work: The Politics of Social Security Reform* (New York: HarperCollins, 1992), 82.

14. *Budget of the United States Government, Fiscal Year 2009: Historical Tables* (Washington, DC: U.S. Government Printing Office, 2006), Tables 15.2 and 15.4.

15. Aaron Wildavsky and Naomi Caiden, *The New Politics of the Budgetary Process*, 3rd ed. (New York: Longman, 1997), 45.

16. John R. Gist, *Mandatory Expenditures and the Defense Sector* (Beverly Hills, CA: Russell Sage Foundation, 1974).

17. Paul R. Schulman, "Nonincremental Policymaking: Notes Toward an Alternative Paradigm," *American Political Science Review* 69 (December 1975): 1354–70.

18. For an extensive examination of incrementalism in federal budgeting, see Bryan D. Jones and Frank R. Baumgartner, *The Politics of Attention* (Chicago: University of Chicago Press, 2005).

19. A good description of budgetary strategies is in Wildavsky and Caiden, *The New Politics of the Budgetary Process*, chap. 3.

20. Ibid., 2.

21. For a discussion of the ways in which bureaucracies manipulate benefits to gain advantage with members of Congress, see Douglas Arnold, *Congress and the Bureaucracy* (New Haven, CT: Yale University Press, 1979), and the articles in Barry S. Rundquist, ed., *Political Benefits* (Lexington, MA: D.C. Heath, 1980).

22. A good review of the formation of the budget is Allen Schick, *The Federal Budget: Politics, Policy, Process* (Washington, DC: Brookings Institution, 2000).

23. An important work on congressional budget making is Wildavsky and Caiden, *The New Politics of the Budgetary Process*.

24. Allen Meltzer and Scott F. Richard, "Why the Government Grows (and Grows) in a Democracy," *The Public Interest* 52 (summer 1978): 117.

25. *Budget of the United States Government, Fiscal Year 2009* (Washington, DC: U.S. Government Printing Office, 2008), Department of Defense. Accessed at *www.whitehouse.gov/omb/budget/fy2009/defense.html*.

26. See James D. Savage, *Balanced Budgets and American Politics* (Ithaca, NY: Cornell University Press, 1988), for a study of the influence the principle of budget balancing has had on politics and public policy from the earliest days of U.S. history.

CHAPTER 15

1. This example is based on Allan Freedman, "Battles over Jurisdiction Likely to Block Merger of Agencies," *Congressional Quarterly Weekly Report*, May 30, 1998, 1440; Marian Burros, "F.D.A. Inspections Lax, Congress Is Told," *New York Times*, July 18, 2007; Stephen J. Hedges, "How Imports Swamp FDA Thin Line of Defense Against Tainted Food," *Chicago Tribune*, September 2, 2007; Gardiner Harris, "Advisers Say F.D.A.'s Flaws Put Lives at Risk," *New York Times*, December 1, 2007.

2. H. H. Gerth and C. Wright Mills, *From Max Weber: Essays in Sociology* (New York: Oxford University Press, 1958), chap. 8.

3. See Charles T. Goodsell, *The Case for Bureaucracy*, 4th ed. (Washington, DC: CQ Press, 2004), chap. 2. See also Daniel Katz et al., *Bureaucratic Encounters* (Ann Arbor: Institute for Social Research, University of Michigan, 1975).

4. See Paul C. Light, *The True Size of Government* (Washington, DC: Brookings Institution, 1999), 1, 44.

5. Office of Personnel Administration, "Federal Civilian Personnel Summary," 2008.

6. See Herbert Kaufman, *Red Tape* (Washington, DC: Brookings Institution, 1977).

7. See Goodsell, *The Case for Bureaucracy*, 48–54.

8. Ibid., chap. 5.

9. Hugh M. Heclo, *A Government of Strangers: Executive Politics in Washington* (Washington, DC: Brookings Institution, 1977).

10. On the transient nature of presidential appointees, see G. Calvin Mackenzie, ed., *The In-and-Outers* (Baltimore: Johns Hopkins University Press, 1987).

11. David E. Lewis, "Testing Pendleton's Premise: Do Political Appointees Make Worse Bureaucrats?" *Journal of Politics* 69 (November 2007): 1073–1088; George C. Edwards III, "Why Not the Best? The Loyalty–Competence Trade-Off in Presidential Appointments," in G. Calvin Mackenzie, ed., *Innocent Until Nominated* (Brookings Institution, 2000).

12. On the independent regulatory agencies, see the classic work by Marver Bernstein, *Regulating Business by Independent Commission* (Princeton, NJ: Princeton University Press, 1955). See also, on regulation, James Q. Wilson, ed., *The Politics of Regulation* (New York: Basic Books, 1980), and A. Lee Fritschler and Bernard H. Ross, *Business Regulation and Government Decision-Making* (Cambridge, MA: Winthrop, 1980).

13. Bernstein, *Regulating Business by Independent Commission*, 90. For a partial test of the capture theory that finds the theory not altogether accurate, see John P. Plumlee and Kenneth J. Meier, "Capture and Rigidity in Regulatory Administration," in *The Policy Cycle*, ed. Judith May and Aaron Wildavsky (Beverly Hills, CA: Russell Sage Foundation, 1978). Another critique of the capture theory is Paul J. Quirk, *Industry Influence in Federal Regulatory Agencies* (Princeton, NJ: Princeton University Press, 1981).

14. George C. Edwards III, *Implementing Public Policy* (Washington, DC: Congressional Quarterly Press, 1980), 1.

15. Lineberry, *American Public Policy*, 70–71.

16. For another dramatic example, see Martha Derthick, *New Towns*

In-Town (Washington, DC: Urban Institute Press, 1972).

17. Eugene Bardach, *The Implementation Game* (Cambridge, MA: MIT Press, 1977), 250–51.

18. A good discussion of how policymakers ignored the administrative capacity of one important agency when assigning it new responsibilities can be found in Martha Derthick, *Agency Under Stress* (Washington, DC: Brookings Institution, 1990).

19. The implementation of the athletics policy is well documented in two articles by Cheryl M. Fields in the *Chronicle of Higher Education*, December 11 and 18, 1978, on which this account relies.

20. James Q. Wilson, *Bureaucracy* (New York: Basic Books, 1989), 158.

21. Kenneth J. Meier and Laurence J. O'Toole, *Bureaucracy in a Democratic State* (Baltimore, MD: Johns Hopkins University Press, 2006).

22. Report of the DOD Commission on Beirut International Airport Terrorist Act, October 23, 1983, December 20, 1983, 133.

23. *The 9/11 Commission Report* (New York: Norton, 2004), 17–18.

24. Quoted in M. S. Eccles, *Beckoning Frontiers* (New York: Knopf, 1951), 336.

25. On administrative discretion, see Gary S. Bryner, *Bureaucratic Discretion* (New York: Pergamon Press, 1987).

26. Michael Lipsky, *Street-Level Bureaucracy* (New York: Russell Sage Foundation, 1980).

27. Quoted in Seymour Hersh, *The Price of Power: Kissinger in the Nixon White House* (New York: Summit, 1983), 235–36.

28. Albert Gore, *From Red Tape to Results: Creating a Government That Works Better and Costs Less* (New York: Times Books, 1993), 11.

29. For a careful analysis of efforts to reorganize the federal bureaucracy, see Peri E. Arnold, *Making the Managerial Presidency*, 2nd ed. (Princeton, NJ: Princeton University Press, 1996).

30. On the implementation and impact of the Voting Rights Act, see Charles S. Bullock III and Harrell R. Rodgers Jr., *Law and Social Change: Civil Rights Laws and Their Consequences*

(New York: McGraw-Hill, 1972), chap. 2; Richard Scher and James Button, "Voting Rights Act: Implementation and Impact," in *Implementation of Civil Rights Policy*, ed. C. S. Bullock and C. M. Lamb (Monterey, CA: Brooks/ Cole, 1984), chap. 2; and Abigail M. Thernstrom, *Whose Votes Count?* (Cambridge, MA: Harvard University Press, 1987).

31. Light, *The True Size of Government*.

32. Scott Shane and Ron Nixon, "In Washington, Contractors Take on Biggest Role Ever," *New York Times*, February 4, 2007.

33. Based on a more elaborate account by James Worsham, "A Typical Day Is Full of Rules," *Chicago Tribune*, July 12, 1981, 1ff, with updating by the authors.

34. See Martha Derthick and Paul J. Quirk, *The Politics of Deregulation* (Washington, DC: Brookings Institution, 1985).

35. See, for example, Susan J. Tolchin and Martin J. Tolchin, *Dismantling America: The Rush to Deregulate* (New York: Oxford University Press, 1983).

36. Evan J. Ringquist, "Does Regulation Matter? Evaluating the Effects of State Air Pollution Control Programs," *Journal of Politics* 55 (November 1993): 1022–45.

37. Michael Lewis-Beck and John Alford, "Can Government Regulate Safety? The Coal Mine Example," *American Political Science Review* 74 (September 1980): 745–56.

38. Paul Sabatier and Dan Mazmanian, *Can Regulation Work? Implementation of the 1972 California Coastal Initiative* (New York: Plenum, 1983).

39. Gary Copeland and Kenneth J. Meier, "Gaining Ground: The Impact of Medicaid and WIC on Infant Mortality," *American Politics Quarterly* 15 (April 1987): 254–73.

40. See B. Dan Wood and Richard W. Waterman, *Bureaucratic Dynamics: The Role of Bureaucracy in a Democracy* (Boulder, CO: Westview, 1994).

41. A good work on this point is Richard P. Nathan, *The Administrative Presidency* (New York: Wiley, 1983).

42. See Kenneth R. Mayer, *With the Stroke of a Pen, Executive Orders and*

Presidential Power (Princeton, NJ: Princeton University Press, 2001), and William G. Howell, *Power Without Persuasion* (Princeton, NJ: Princeton University Press, 2003).

43. Andrew B. Whitford and Jeff Yates, "Policy Signals and Executive Governance: Presidential Rhetoric in the War on Drugs," *Journal of Politics* 65 (November 2003): 995–1012; Matthew Eshbaugh-Soha, *The President's Speeches: Beyond Going Public* (Boulder, CO: Lynne Rienner, 2006).

44. Morris Fiorina, *Congress: Keystone of the Washington Establishment*, 2nd ed. (New Haven, CT: Yale University Press, 1989).

45. Richard A. Rettig, *Cancer Crusade* (Princeton, NJ: Princeton University Press, 1977).

46. Hugh M. Heclo, "Issue Networks and the Executive Establishment," in *The New American Political System*, ed. Anthony King (Washington, DC: American Enterprise Institute, 1978), 87–124. See also William P. Browne and Won K. Paik, "Beyond the Domain: Recasting Network Politics in the Postreform Congress," *American Journal of Political Science* 37 (November 1993): 1054–78, and John P. Heinz, Edward O. Laumann, Robert L. Nelson, and Robert L. Salisbury, *The Hollow Core: Private Interests in National Policy Making* (Cambridge, MA: Harvard University Press, 1993).

47. Frank R. Baumgartner and Bryan D. Jones, *Agendas and Instability in American Politics* (Chicago: University of Chicago Press, 1993).

48. Ibid.

CHAPTER 16

1. Quoted in Lawrence C. Baum, *The Supreme Court*, 4th ed. (Washington, DC: Congressional Quarterly Press, 1992), 72.

2. U.S. Department of Commerce, *Statistical Abstract of the United States, 2008* (Washington, DC: U.S. Government Printing Office, 2008), Table 598.

3. Administrative Office of the United States Courts.

4. Administrative Office of the United States Courts.

5. Administrative Office of the United States Courts.

6. Sarah Binder and Forrest Maltzman, "The Limits of Senatorial Courtesy," *Legislative Studies Quarterly* 29 (February 2004): 5–22.

7. Quoted in J. Woodford Howard Jr., *Courts of Appeals in the Federal Judicial System: A Study of the Second, Fifth, and District of Columbia Circuits* (Princeton, NJ: Princeton University Press, 1981), 101.

8. Lauren Cohen Bell, "Senatorial Discourtesy: The Senate's Use of Delay to Shape the Federal Judiciary," *Political Research Quarterly* 55 (September 2002): 589–607.

9. See Gary King, "Presidential Appointments to the Supreme Court: Adding Systematic Explanation to Probabilistic Description," *American Politics Quarterly* 15 (July 1987): 373–86.

10. Charles R. Shipan and Megan L. Shannon, "Delaying Justice(s): A Duration Analysis of Supreme Court Confirmations," *American Journal of Political Science* 47 (October 2003): 654–68.

11. Quoted in Nina Totenberg, "Will Judges Be Chosen Rationally?," *Judicature* 60 (August/September 1976): 93.

12. See John Schmidhauser, *Judges and Justices: The Federal Appellate Judiciary* (Boston: Little, Brown, 1978).

13. One study found, however, that judicial experience is not related to the congruence of presidential preferences and the justices' decisions on racial equality cases. See John Gates and Jeffrey Cohen, "Presidents, Supreme Court Justices, and Racial Equality Cases: 1954–1984," *Political Behavior* 10 (November 1, 1988): 22–35.

14. On the importance of ideology and partisanship considerations in judicial retirement and resignation decisions, see Deborah J. Barrow and Gary Zuk, "An Institutional Analysis of Turnover in the Lower Federal Courts, 1900–1987," *Journal of Politics* 52 (May 1990): 457–76.

15. Quoted in Henry J. Abraham, *Justices and Presidents: A Political History of Appointments to the Supreme Court*, 3rd ed. (New York: Oxford University Press, 1992), 266.

16. Ibid., 70.

17. See, for example, the important role that African American support played in the confirmation of Clarence Thomas even though he was likely to vote against the wishes of leading civil rights organizations. L. Marvin Overby, Beth M. Henschen, Julie Walsh, and Michael H. Strauss, "Courting Constituents: An Analysis of the Senate Confirmation Vote on Justice Clarence Thomas," *American Political Science Review* 86 (December 1992): 997–1003.

18. On the impact of the background of members of the judiciary, see Robert A. Carp and C. K. Rowland, *Policymaking and Politics in the Federal District Courts* (Knoxville: University of Tennessee Press, 1983); Thomas G. Walker and Deborah J. Barrow, "The Diversification of the Federal Bench: Policy and Process Ramifications," *Journal of Politics* 47 (May 1985): 596–617; and C. Neal Tate, "Personal Attribute Models of the Voting Behavior of United States Supreme Court Justices: Liberalism in Civil Liberties and Economics Decisions, 1946–1978," *American Political Science Review* 75 (June 1981): 355–67.

19. Quoted in Nina Totenberg, "Behind the Marble, Beneath the Robes," *New York Times Magazine*, March 16, 1975, 37.

20. H. W. Perry Jr., *Deciding to Decide: Agenda Setting in the United States Supreme Court* (Cambridge, MA: Harvard University Press, 1991); Doris Marie Provine, *Case Selection in the United States Supreme Court* (Chicago: University of Chicago Press, 1980); Stuart H. Teger and Douglas Kosinski, "The Cue Theory of Supreme Court Certiorari Jurisdiction: A Reconsideration," *Journal of Politics* 42 (August 1980): 834–46.

21. Sidney Ulmer, "The Supreme Court's Certiorari Decisions: Conflict as a Predictive Variable," *American Political Science Review* (December 1984): 901–11.

22. On the solicitor general's *amicus* briefs, see Rebecca E. Deen, Joseph Ignagni, and James Meernik, "Executive Influence on the U.S. Supreme Court: Solicitor General *Amicus* Cases, 1953–1997," *American Review of Politics* 22 (spring 2001): 3–26, and Timothy R. Johnson, "The Supreme Court, the Solicitor General, and the Separation of Powers," *American Politics Research* 31 (July 2001): 426–51.

23. See Rebecca Mae Salokar, *The Solicitor General* (Philadelphia: Temple University Press, 1992).

24. Each year, data on Supreme Court decisions can be found in the November issue of the *Harvard Law Review*.

25. On the influence of oral arguments on the Supreme Court, see Timothy R. Johnson, Paul J. Wahlbeck, and James F. Spriggs II, "The Influence of Oral Arguments on the U.S. Supreme Court," *American Political Science Review* 100 (February 2006): 99–113.

26. A useful look at attorneys practicing before the Supreme Court is Kevin McGuire, *The Supreme Court Bar: Legal Elites in the Washington Community* (Charlottesville: University Press of Virginia, 1993).

27. See, for example, Forrest Maltzman and Paul J. Wahlbeck, "Strategic Policy Considerations and Voting Fluidity on the Burger Court," *American Political Science Review* 90 (September 1996): 581–92; Paul J. Wahlbeck, James F. Spriggs II, and Forrest Maltzman, "Marshalling the Court: Bargaining and Accommodation on the United States Supreme Court," *American Journal of Political Science* 42 (January 1998): 294–315; and James F. Spriggs II, Forrest Maltzman, and Paul J. Wahlbeck, "Bargaining on the U.S. Supreme Court: Justices' Responses to Majority Opinion Drafts," *Journal of Politics* 61 (May 1999): 485–506.

28. A. P. Blaustein and A. H. Field, "Overruling Opinions in the Supreme Court," *Michigan Law Review* 57, no. 2 (1957): 151; David H. O'Brien, *Constitutional Law and Politics*, 3rd ed. (New York: Norton, 1997), 38.

29. See, for example, Jeffrey A. Segal and Harold J. Spaeth, *The Supreme Court and the Attitudinal Model* (Cambridge: Cambridge University Press,

1993); Jeffrey A. Segal and Albert O. Cover, "Ideological Values and the Votes of U.S. Supreme Court Justices," *American Political Science Review* 83 (June 1989): 557–66; Tracey E. George and Lee Epstein, "On the Nature of Supreme Court Decision Making," *American Political Science Review* 86 (June 1992): 323–37; and Jeffrey A. Segal and Harold J. Spaeth, "The Influence of *Stare Decisis* on the Votes of United States Supreme Court Justices," *American Journal of Political Science* 40 (November 1996): 971–1003.

30. Doris Graber, *Mass Media and American Politics*, 6th ed. (Washington, DC: Congressional Quarterly Press, 2002), 312–13.

31. Charles A. Johnson and Bradley C. Canon, *Judicial Policies: Implementation and Impact*, 2nd ed. (Washington, DC: Congressional Quarterly Press, 1999), chap. 1. See also James F. Spriggs II, "The Supreme Court and Federal Administrative Agencies: A Resource-Based Theory and Analysis of Judicial Impact," *American Journal of Political Science* 40 (November 1996): 1122–51.

32. See Richard L. Pacelle Jr. and Lawrence Baum, "Supreme Court Authority in the Judiciary," *American Politics Quarterly* 20 (April 1992): 169–91, and Donald R. Songer, Jeffrey A. Segal, and Charles M. Cameron, "The Hierarchy of Justice: Testing a Principal-Agent Model of Supreme Court-Circuit Court Interactions," *American Journal of Political Science* 38 (August 1994): 673–96.

33. For an excellent overview of the Warren period by former Watergate special prosecutor and Harvard law professor Archibald Cox, see *The Warren Court* (Cambridge, MA: Harvard University Press, 1968).

34. William Rehnquist, "The Notion of a Living Constitution," in *Views from the Bench*, ed. Mark W. Cannon and David M. O'Brien (Chatham, NJ: Chatham House, 1985), 129. One study found, however, that judicial experience is not related to the congruence of presidential preferences and the justices' decisions on racial equality cases.

See John Gates and Jeffrey Cohen, "Presidents, Supreme Court Justices, and Racial Equality Cases: 1954–1984," *Political Behavior* 10 (November 1, 1988): 22–35.

35. Richard Funston, "The Supreme Court and Critical Elections," *American Political Science Review* 69 (1975): 810; John B. Gates, *The Supreme Court and Partisan Realignment* (Boulder, CO: Westview, 1992); Thomas R. Marshall, "Public Opinion, Representation, and the Modern Supreme Court," *American Politics Quarterly* 16 (July 1988): 296–316; William Mishler and Reginald S. Sheehan, "The Supreme Court as a Countermajoritarian Institution? The Impact of Public Opinion on Supreme Court Decisions," *American Political Science Review* 87 (March 1993): 87–101; William Mishler and Reginald S. Sheehan, "Public Opinion, the Attitudinal Model, and Supreme Court Decision Making: A Micro-Analytic Perspective," *Journal of Politics* 58 (February 1996): 169–200; Roy B. Flemming and B. Dan Wood, "The Public and the Supreme Court: Individual Justice Responsiveness to American Policy Moods," *American Journal of Political Science* 41 (April 1997): 468–98; Kevin T. McGuire and James A. Stimson, "The Least Dangerous Branch: New Evidence on Supreme Court Responsiveness to Public Preferences," *Journal of Politics* 66 (November 2004): 1018–35.

36. Mario Bergara, Barak Richman, and Pablo T. Spiller, "Modeling Supreme Court Strategic Decision Making: The Congressional Constraint," *Legislative Studies Quarterly* 28 (May 2003) 247–80.

37. David G. Barnum, "The Supreme Court and Public Opinion: Judicial Decision Making in the Post-New Deal Period," *Journal of Politics* 47 (May 1985): 652–62.

38. Gregory A. Caldeira and John R. Wright, "Organized Interests and Agenda Setting in the U.S. Supreme Court," *American Political Science Review* 82 (December 1988): 1109–28.

39. On group use of the litigation process, see Karen Orren, "Standing

to Sue: Interest Group Conflict in the Federal Courts," *American Political Science Review* 70 (September 1976): 723–42; Karen O'Connor and Lee Epstein, "The Rise of Conservative Interest Group Litigation," *Journal of Politics* 45 (May 1983): 479–89; and Lee Epstein and C. K. Rowland, "Debunking the Myth of Interest Group Invincibility in the Courts," *American Political Science Review* 85 (March 1991): 205–17.

40. "Federalist #78," in Hamilton, Madison, and Jay, *The Federalist Papers*.

41. However, see Gerald N. Rosenberg, *The Hollow Hope: Can Courts Bring About Social Change?* (Chicago: University of Chicago Press, 1991). Rosenberg questions whether courts have brought about much social change.

42. Examples of judicial activism are reported in a critical assessment of judicial intervention by Donald Horowitz, *The Courts and Social Policy* (Washington, DC: Brookings Institution, 1977).

43. Paul Gerwitz and Chad Golder, "So Who Are the Activists?," *New York Times*, July 6, 2005.

44. William N. Eskridge, "Overriding Supreme Court Statutory Interpretation Decisions," *Yale Law Journal* 101 (1991): 331–455; Joseph Ignagni and James Meernik, "Explaining Congressional Attempts to Reverse Supreme Court Decisions," *Political Research Quarterly* 10 (June 1994): 353–72. See also R. Chep Melnick, *Between the Lines: Interpreting Welfare Rights* (Washington, DC: Brookings Institution, 1994).

45. Kirk A Randazzo, Richard W. Waterman, and Jeffrey A. Fine, "Checking the Federal Courts: The Impact of Congressional Statutes on Judicial Behavior," *Journal of Politics* 68 (November 2006): 1006–1017.

CHAPTER 17

1. Tom Friedman, *The World Is Flat: A Brief History of the 21st Century* (New York: Ferrar, Straus and Giroux, 2005), 24.

2. The Fortune 500 is annually updated and accessible at *www.fortune.com*.

3. "The 400 Richest People in America," *Forbes*, November 28, 2005, 100.

4. "The Wal-Mart You Don't Know," *Fast Company* 77 (December 2003): 68 ff.

5. Greg Schneider and Din El Boghdady, "Stores Follow Wal-Mart's Lead in Labor," *Washington Post*, November 6, 2003, A1.

6. These data are from C. Fred Bergsten, director of the Institute for International Economics, writing in *Foreign Affairs* (March/April, 2004), 89.

7. "The Long Arm of Bentonville Arkansas," *Business Week*, October 6, 2003, 103.

8. "The Wal-Martization of America," *New York Times*, November 15, 2003, A12.

9. Although political folklore recounts the sign as "It's the economy, stupid," the actual complete sign read as follows: "Change vs. more of the same. The economy, stupid. Don't forget health care."

10. George Stephanopoulos, *All Too Human: A Political Education* (Boston: Little, Brown, 1999), 88.

11. Brad T. Gomez and J. Matthew Wilson, "Political Sophistication and Economic Voting in the American Electorate: A Theory of Heterogeneous Attribution," *American Journal of Political Science* 45 (October 2001): 899.

12. Robert S. Erikson, Matthew MacKuen, and James L. Stimson, *The Macro Polity* (New York: Cambridge University Press, 2002), 59.

13. Gomez and Wilson, "Political Sophistication and Economic Voting in the American Electorate."

14. For a summary of economic conditions and voting choice, see Michael S. Lewis-Beck and Mary Stegmaier, "Economic Determinants of Electoral Outcomes," *Annual Review of Political Science* (Palo Alto, CA: Annual Reviews, 2000), 183–219.

15. "The Political (and Economic) Origins of Consumer Confidence," *American Journal of Political Science* 48 (October 2004): 633–49.

16. Erikson et al., *The Macro Polity*, 445.

17. Benjamin I. Page and Robert Y. Shapiro, *The Rational Public: Fifty Years of Trends in America's Policy Preferences* (Chicago: University of Chicago Press, 1992), 122.

18. For frequently asked questions about the CPI, see the Bureau of Labor Statistics Web site, *www.bls.gov/cpi*.

19. See William Greider, *Secrets of the Temple: How the Federal Reserve Runs the Country* (New York: Simon and Schuster, 1987); Nathaniel Beck, "Elections and the Fed: Is There a Political Monetary Cycle?," *American Journal of Political Science* 20 (February 1987): 194–216; and Manabu Saeki, "Explaining Federal Reserve Monetary Policy," *Review of Policy Research* 19 (summer 2002): 129–50.

21. Conrad Black, *Franklin Delano Roosevelt: Champion of Freedom* (New York: Public Affairs Press, 2003), 1133–34.

22. Sidney Milkis, *The President and the Parties* (New York: Oxford University Press, 1993), 263.

23. Ibid.

24. The classic supply-side theory can be found in George Gilder, *Wealth and Poverty* (New York: Basic Books, 1981).

25. John W. Sloan, *The Reagan Effect: Economics and Presidential Leadership* (Lawrence: University Press of Kansas, 1999), 63.

26. "A Phony Jobs Debate," *Washington Post*, February 25, 2004, A25.

27. The most ardent proponent of this view is Edward Tufte. See his *Political Control of the Economy* (Princeton, NJ: Princeton University Press, 1978).

28. In 12 elections studied by Erikson, MacKuen, and Stimson, real income growth grew in a strict linear pattern rather than in a short spurt just before the election. *Macro Policy*, 248.

29. The standard and very readable book on globalization is Daniel Yergin and Joseph Stanislaw, *The Commanding Heights* (New York: Touchstone, 2002). See also Benjamin Barber, *Jihad vs. McWorld: How Globalism and Tribalism Are Reshaping the World* (New York: Ballantine, 1996).

30. Beth A. Simmons and Zachary Elkins, "The Globalization of Liberalization," *American Political Science Review* 98 (February 2004): 171.

31. Doug Henwood, *After the New Economy* (New York: New Press, 2003), 159.

32. Catherine Mann, "Globalization of IT Services and White Collar Jobs: The Next Wave of Productivity Growth" (Washington, DC: Institute for International Economics, 2004).

33. Friedman, *The World Is Flat*, 38–39.

34. Wendy L. Hansen and Neil J. Mitchell, "Disaggregating and Explaining Corporate Political Activity: Domestic and Foreign Corporations in National Politics," *American Political Science Review* 94 (December 2000): 891.

35. Carol Graham, Robert Litan, and Sandip Sukhtankar, "The Bigger They Are, the Harder They Fall: An Estimate of the Costs of the Crisis in Corporate Governance" (Washington, DC: Brookings Institution Working Papers, August 30, 2002).

CHAPTER 18

1. On the decline of social insurance in the United States, see Jacob S. Hacker, "Privatizing Risk Without Privatizing the Welfare State: The Hidden Politics of Social Policy Retrenchment in the United States," *American Political Science Review* 98 (May 2004): 243–60.

2. *The Great Risk Shift: The Assault on American Jobs, Families, Health Care and Retirement* (New York: Oxford, 2006).

3. Ibid., p. 98.

4. Stanley Feldman and Marco R. Steenbergen, "The Humanitarian Foundation of Public Support for Social Welfare," *American Journal of Political Science* 45 (July 2001): 658–77.

5. Janie Calmes, "Budget Wish Lists Come and Go, but 'Entitlements' Outweigh All," *Wall Street Journal*, February 3, 2006, 1.

6. Alan Weil and Kenneth Finegold, "Introduction," *Welfare Reform: The*

Next Act, ed. Alan Weil and Kenneth Finegold (Washington, DC: Urban Institute Press, 2002), xiii.

7. Timothy M. Smeeding, "Public Policy, Income Inequality, and Poverty: The United States in Comparative Perspective," *Social Science Quarterly* 86 (2005): 955. See also Lane Kenworthy and Jonas Pontusson, "Rising Inequality and the Politics of Redistribution in Affluent Countries," *Perspectives on Politics* 3 (September 2005): 449–72.

8. Nolan McCarty, Keith T. Poole, and Howard Rosenthal, *Income Distribution and the Realignment of American Politics* (Washington, DC: American Enterprise Institute, 1977), 1. See also their *Polarized America: The Dance of Ideology and Unequal Riches* (Cambridge, MA: MIT Press, 2006).

9. An economic analysis and explanation of the workings of the old adage can be found in Thomas Piketty and Emmanuel Saez, "Income Inequality in the United States 1913–1998," *Quarterly Journal of Economics* 113 (February 2003): 1–39.

10. Arthur Kennickell, "A Rolling Tide; Changes in the Distribution of Wealth in the United States, 1989–2001," Federal Reserve Board, May 3, 2003.

11. Hacker, *The Great Risk Shift*, 24 and 32.

12. Barbara Ehrenreich, *Nickel and Dimed: On (Not) Getting By in America* (New York: Owl Books, 2002).

13. See David K. Shipler, *The Working Poor: Invisible in America* (New York: Knopf, 2004).

14. Harrell Rodgers, *Poor Women, Poor Children*, 3rd ed. (New York: M. E. Sharpe, 1996).

15. Harrell Rodgers, *American Poverty in a New Era of Reform* (New York: M. E. Sharpe, 2000), 207.

16. "The Real State of the Budget," *Atlantic*, January/February 2003, 81.

17. Alan Berube and Benjamin Forman, "Rewarding Work: The Impact of the Earned Income Tax Credit." Brookings Institution Report, June 2001.

18. See, for example, Francis Fox Piven and Richard Cloward, *Regulating the Poor* (New York: Pantheon, 1971). For an empirical analysis of theories of the rise of welfare that finds some support for the Piven and Cloward thesis, see Richard Fording, "The Political Response to Black Insurgency: A Critical Test of Competing Theories of the State," *American Political Science Review* 95 (March 2001): 115–30.

19. Charles Murray, *Losing Ground: American Social Policy, 1950–1980* (New York: Basic Books, 1984). Marvin Olasky, the guru of "compassionate conservatism," makes a similar argument in his *Tragedy of Human Compassion* (Chicago: Regnery, 1992). Doing good for people, especially through government, Olasky argues, is bad for them. For a contrary argument, see Benjamin Page and James R. Simmons, *What Government Can Do: Dealing with Poverty and Inequality* (Chicago: University of Chicago Press, 2000).

20. Martin Gilens, *Why Americans Hate Welfare: Race, Media, and the Politics of Antipoverty Policy* (Chicago: University of Chicago Press, 2000).

21. Martin Gilens, "Race Coding and White Opposition to Welfare," *American Political Science Review* 90 (December 1996): 593–604.

22. Gilens, *Why Americans Hate Welfare*, chap. 5.

23. Aristide Zolberg, *A Nation By Design* (Cambridge MA: Harvard University Press, 2006), 1.

24. Rudolfo de la Garza, Angela Falcon and F. Chris Garcia, "Will the Real Americans Please Stand Up?" *American Journal of Political Science* 40 (May 1996): 535–51; Jack Citrin, et al., "Testing Huntington: Is Hispanic Immigration a Threat to American Identity?" *Perspectives on Politics* 5 (March 2007).

25. Jon Butler, *Becoming America* (Cambridge MA: Harvard University Press, 2000), 32.

26. Daniel J. Tichenor, *Dividing Lines: The Politics of Immigration Control in America* (Princeton, NJ: Princeton University Press, 2002), p. 19.

27. Lou Dobbs, *War on the Middle Class* (New York: Viking, 2006), chap. 8.

28. Congressional Budget Office, "The Impact of Unauthorized Immigrants on the Budgets of State and Local Governments," December 2007.

29. Sylvester J. Schieber and John B. Shoven, *The Real Deal: The History and Future of Social Security* (New Haven, CT: Yale University Press, 1999), chap. 7. The Ida May Fuller story is also from Schieber and Shoven.

30. The math on Social Security is from the President's Commission to Strengthen Social Security, *Interim Report*, August 2001, 13.

31. Worse, President Bush's Commission to Strengthen Social Security argues that in about 2016, the Social Security Commission will have to begin calling in its IOUs from the federal treasury or cashing in its bonds. Social Security funds are not kept in what politicians have come to call a "lockbox." In 2016, Social Security claims would compete for regular budget dollars against national defense, homeland security, school aid, and other federal expenditures. See their *Interim Report*, August 2001.

32. Andrea Louise Campbell explains how Social Security has energized one of America's most important interest groups in her *How Policies Make Citizens* (Princeton, NJ: Princeton University Press, 2002).

33. Martin Wattenberg, *Is Voting for Young People?* (New York: Pearson Longman, 2006), 4.

34. For one rare but dissenting view that argues that the Social Security "crisis" is exaggerated, partly by people who would profit from more private investment, see Dean Baker and Mark Weisbrot, *Social Security: The Phony Crisis* (Chicago: University of Chicago Press, 2000).

35. Thomas Frank, "The Trillion Dollar Hustle: Hello Wall Street, Goodbye Social Security," *Harper's*, January 2002.

36. Greg Hitt, "Social Security Plan Stalls," *Wall Street Journal*, July 23, 2002, A4.

37. Political scientist Benjamin Radcliff developed some empirical data to show that the extent of government welfare provisions is in fact positively related to people's sense of well-being from country to country. See his "Politics, Markets

and Life Satisfaction: The Political Economy of Human Happiness," *American Political Science Review* 95 (December 2001): 939–52.

38. The United States, emphasizes Jacob Hacker, is not as niggardly about social benefits as liberals often think. Social spending in the United States is close to social spending levels in Europe. The major difference is that social expenditures—for health care, pensions, and other benefits—are often provided by private employers in the United States. See his *The Divided Welfare State* (New York: Cambridge University Press, 2002).

39. Anne Schneider and Helen Ingram, "The Social Construction of Target Populations," *American Political Science Review* 87 (1993): 334–47.

CHAPTER 19

1. Lucette Lagnado, "Uninsured and Ill, a Woman Is Forced to Ration Her Care," *Wall Street Journal*, November 12, 2002, 1.

2. John Lancaster, "Surgeries, Side Trips for 'Medical Tourists,'" *Washington Post*, October 21, 2004, A1.

3. Council of Economic Advisers, *Annual Report 2006*, 88.

4. Gina Kolata, "More May Not Mean Better in Health Care, Studies Find," *New York Times*, July 21, 2002, 1.

5. Council of Economic Advisers, *Annual Report 2006*, 87.

6. *The Health Care Fix* (Cambridge MA: MIT Press, 2007), p. 10.

7. Census Bureau, *Income, Poverty and Health Insurance Coverage in the United States, 2004*, October 2005, 16.

8. John Budetti et al., *Can't Afford to Get Sick: A Reality for Millions of Working Americans* (New York: Commonwealth Fund, 2000).

9. "Care Without Coverage," Institute of Medicine, May 2002, 6.

10. Kotlikoff, "More May Not Mean Better in Health Care, Studies Find," p. 53.

11. Mary Agnes Carey, "Hidden Costs of the Uninsured," *CQ Weekly*, August 8, 2004, 2178–83.

12. On Medicare's future, see Ronald Lee and Jonathan Skinner, "Will Aging Baby Boomers Bust the Federal Budget?," *Journal of Economic Perspectives* 13 (winter 1999): 117–40.

13. Roland Sturm, "The Effects of Obesity, Smoking and Drinking on Medical Problems and Costs," *Health Affairs* 21 (2002): 245–53.

14. Rob Stein, "Obesity Rivals Tobacco for Most US Deaths," *Washington Post*, March 9, 2004, 1.

15. Andrea Louise Campbell, "Self-Interest, Social Security, and the Distinctive Political Participation Patterns of Senior Citizens," *American Political Science Review* 96 (September 2002): 565–74.

16. The story of the Clinton health care plan is told in Theda Skocpol, *Boomerang: Health Care Reform and the Turn Against Government* (New York: Norton, 1996).

17. See the Bush administration positions argued in Council of Economic Advisers, 2006, *Economic Report of the President 2006*, chap. 4.

18. Sarah Lueck, "Tax Breaks to Boost Cost of Bush's Health Budget," *Wall Street Journal*, February 6, 2006, A1.

19. Robert Blank, *Rationing Medicine* (New York: Columbia University Press, 1988).

20. Howard M. Leichter, "The Poor and Managed Care in the Oregon Experience," *Journal of Health Politics, Policy and Law* 24 (October 1999): 1172–84.

21. Bjorn Lomborg, *The Skeptical Environmentalist: Measuring the Real State of the World* (New York: Cambridge University Press, 2001).

22. See the January 2002 issue, 61 f.

23. Robert Stavins, "What Can We Learn from the Grand Policy Experiment? Positive and Normative Lessons from SO2 Allowance Trading," *Journal of Economic Perspectives* 12 (summer 1998) 69–88; see also A. Denny Ellerman et al., *Markets for Clean Air: The U.S. Acid Rain Program* (Cambridge, MA: Cambridge University Press, 2000).

24. Samuel Hays, *Beauty, Health, Permanence* (New York: Cambridge University Press, 1987), 99.

25. On toxic waste and its politics, see Robert Nakamura and Thomas Church, *Taming Regulation* (Washington, DC: Brookings Institution, 2003).

26. A classic study of oil is Daniel Yergin, *The Prize: The Epic Quest for Oil, Money and Power* (New York: Simon and Shuster, 1991).

27. The global warming issue and the politics of climate are discussed in Lamont C. Hemple, "Climate Policy on the Installment Plan," in *Environmental Policy*, 5th ed., ed. Norman J. Vig and Michael E. Kraft (Washington, DC: CQ Press, 2003), chap. 13.

28. A good summary of the politics of global warming is Steve Vanderheiden, *Atmospheric Justice: A Political Theory of Climate Change* (New York: Oxford University Press, 2008).

29. Lomborg, *The Skeptical Environmentalist*, 318.

30. Jeff Tollefson, "Getting a Grip on Carbon," *CQ Weekly*, December 5, 2005, 3263.

31. Program on International Policy Attitudes, University of Maryland, "Americans on Climate Change," June 25, 2004.

32. Barry Rabe, *Statehouse and Greenhouse: The Emerging Politics of American Climate Change Policy* (Washington, DC: Brookings Institution, 2004), ix. The Bush and Whitman stories are from Rabe.

33. On environmental groups, see Christopher Bosso and Deborah Lynn Guber, "The Boundaries and Contours of American Environmentalism," in Kraft and Vig, *Environmental Policy*, chap. 4. The data on group size are from Bosso and Guber.

34. Ibid., 97.

CHAPTER 20

1. See, for example, Paul Kennedy, *The Rise and Fall of the Great Powers* (New York: Random House, 1987).

2. Raymond Vernon, *In the Hurricane's Eye: The Troubled Prospects of Multinational Enterprises* (Cambridge, MA: Harvard University Press, 1998); United Nations, *World Investment Report, 2005* (New York: United Nations, 2005).

3. I. M. Destler, "National Security Management: What Presidents Have Wrought," *Political Science Quarterly* 95 (winter 1980–1981): 573–88.

4. Richard Betts, *Soldiers, Statesmen, and Cold War Crises* (Cambridge, MA: Harvard University Press, 1977), 216, Table A.

5. For more on decision making regarding the Gulf War, see Bob Woodward, *The Commanders* (New York: Simon and Schuster, 1991).

6. See Bob Woodward, *Veil: The Secret Wars of the CIA, 1981–1987* (New York: Simon and Schuster, 1987).

7. A good study of the role of Congress in setting U.S. foreign policy is James M. Lindsay, *Congress and the Politics of U.S. Foreign Policy* (Baltimore: Johns Hopkins University Press, 1994). Congress's role in the defense budget process is discussed in Ralph G. Carter, "Budgeting for Defense," in *The President, Congress, and the Making of Foreign Policy*, ed. Paul E. Peterson (Norman: University of Oklahoma Press, 1994).

8. Louis Fisher, "Executive-Legislative Revelations in Foreign Policy" (paper presented at the United States-Mexico Comparative Constitutional Law Conference, Mexico City, June 17, 1998), 1.

9. An excellent treatment of the origins of the Cold War is Daniel Yergin, *Shattered Peace: The Origins of the Cold War and the National Security State* (Boston: Houghton Mifflin, 1977).

10. The article was titled "Sources of Soviet Conduct" and appeared in *Foreign Affairs* (July 1947) under the pseudonym X.

11. Stanley Karnow, *Vietnam: A History* (New York: Penguin Books, 1983), 43. Karnow's book is one of the best of many excellent books on Vietnam. See also Frances Fitzgerald, *Fire in the Lake* (Boston: Little, Brown, 1972), and David Halberstam, *The Best and the Brightest* (New York: Random House, 1972).

12. Nicholas Lemann, "The Peacetime War," *Atlantic Monthly*, October 1984, 72.

13. Quoted in Andrew Rosenthal, "Striking a Defensive Tone, Bush Sees Virtue in Caution," *New York Times*, February 8, 1990, A10.

14. National Counterterrorism Center, 2008.

15. See, for example, Bruce Russett, "Defense Expenditures and National Well-Being," *American Political Science Review* 76 (December 1982): 767–77; William K. Domke, Richard C. Eichenberg, and Catherine M. Kelleher, "The Illusion of Choice: Defense and Welfare in Advanced Industrial Democracies, 1948–78," *American Political Science Review* 77 (March 1983): 19–35; and Alex Mintz, "Guns Versus Butter: A Disaggregated Analysis," *American Political Science Review* 83 (December 1989): 1285–96.

16. Kennedy, *The Rise and Fall of the Great Powers*; David Calleo, *Beyond American Hegemony: The Future of the Western Alliance* (New York: Basic Books, 1987). For a different view, see Joseph S. Nye, *Bound to Lead* (New York: Basic Books, 1990).

17. On the importance of ideology, see studies discussed in Robert A. Bernstein, *Elections, Representation, and Congressional Voting Behavior* (Englewood Cliffs, NJ: Prentice Hall, 1989), 70–76.

18. U.S. Department of Commerce, *Statistical Abstract of the United States, 2008* (Washington, DC: U.S. Government Printing Office, 2008), Tables 497, 499.

19. Stephen I. Schwartz, ed., *Atomic Audit: The Costs and Consequences of U.S. Nuclear Weapons Since 1940* (Washington, DC: Brookings Institution, 1998).

20. Joseph S. Nye Jr., *The Paradox of American Power: Why the World's Only Superpower Can't Go It Alone* (New York: Oxford University Press, 2002).

21. Stanley Hoffman, *Gulliver's Troubles, or the Setting of American Foreign Policy* (New York: McGraw-Hill, 1968).

22. Robert O. Keohane and Joseph S. Nye, *Power and Interdependence*, 2nd ed. (New York: HarperCollins, 1989), 27.

23. Ibid., 27–28.

24. Joseph S. Nye Jr., *Soft Power: The Means to Success in World Politics* (Cambridge, MA: Harvard University Press, 2004).

25. Ibid., 3.

26. U.S. Census Bureau, Foreign Trade Division, 2008.

27. Ibid.

28. Robert M. Kimmit, "Public Footprints in Private Markets," *Foreign Affairs* 87 (January/February 2008), 126.

29. Carol C. Adelman, "The Privatization of Foreign Aid," *Foreign Affairs* 82 (November/December 2003): 9–14.

30. See Bruce M. Russett, *Controlling the Sword* (Cambridge, MA: Harvard University Press, 1990), chap. 5; Thomas Hartley and Bruce M. Russett, "Public Opinion and the Common Defense: Who Governs Military Spending in the United States?" *American Political Science Review* 86 (December 1992): 905–15; Bruce M. Russett, *Grasping the Democratic Peace* (Princeton, NJ: Princeton University Press, 1993); Spencer R. Weart, *Never at War* (New Haven, CT: Yale University Press, 1998); Michael D. Ward and Kristian S. Gleditsch, "Democratizing Peace," *American Political Science Review* 92 (March 1998): 51–62; and Paul R. Hensel, Gary Foertz, and Paul F. Diehl, "The Democratic Peace and Rivalries," *Journal of Politics* 62 (November 2000): 1173–88.

CHAPTER 21

1. Laura K. Donohue and Juliette N. Kayyem, "Federalism and the Battle over Counterterrorist Law: State Sovereignty, Criminal Law Enforcement, and National Security," *Studies in Conflict and Terrorism* 25 (2002): 1–18.

2. Luther H. Gulick, "Reorganization of the State," *Civil Engineering* (August 1933): 420–21.

3. James N. Miller, "Hamstrung Legislatures," *National Civic Review* (May 1965): 178–87.

4. Ann O'M. Bowman and Richard C. Kearney, *The Resurgence of the States* (Englewood Cliffs, NJ: Prentice Hall, 1986). For other important statements of the improved capacity of state governments to undertake innovative action, see David Osborne, *Laboratories of Democracy* (Boston: Harvard Business School Press, 1988); David B. Walker, *The Rebirth of Federalism* (Chatham, NJ: Chatham House, 1995); and David

M. Hedge, *Governance and the Changing American States* (Boulder, CO: Westview, 1998).

5. See Daniel J. Elazar, "The Principles and Traditions Underlying American State Constitutions," *Publius: The Journal of Federalism* 12 (winter 1982): 11–25.

6. Mavis Mann Reeves, *The Question of State Government Capability* (Washington, DC: Advisory Commission on Intergovernmental Relations, 1985), 38.

7. Christopher W. Hammons, "Was James Madison Wrong? Rethinking the American Preference for Short, Framework-Oriented Constitutions," *American Political Science Review* 93 (December 1999): 837–50.

8. Initiative and Referendum Institute, *I & R Usage, 2000* (Washington, DC: Initiative and Referendum Institute, 2000).

9. Council of State Governments, *The Book of the States, 2003 Edition* (Washington, DC: Council of State Governments, 2004), 235.

10. Thomas M. Carsey, *Campaign Dynamics: The Race for Governor* (Ann Arbor: University of Michigan Press, 1999).

11. Council of State Governments, *The Book of the States, 2003 Edition*, 176.

12. Thomas M. Carsey and Gerald C. Wright, "State and National Factors in Gubernatorial and Senatorial Elections," *American Journal of Political Science* 42 (July 1998): 994–1002.

13. Data are from Thad Beyle and Margaret Ferguson, "Governors and the Executive Branch," in *Politics in the American States*, 9th ed., ed. Virginia Gray and Russell L. Hanson (Washington, DC: Congressional Quarterly Press, 2008), 198–99.

14. Carsey, *Campaign Dynamics*.

15. Note that not all lower chambers of state legislatures are called the "house of representatives," although most are; we refer to them as such in this chapter to avoid confusion. Council of State Governments, *The Book of the States, 2003 Edition*, 108.

16. Alan Rosenthal, *The Decline of Representative Democracy: Process, Participation, and Power in State Legislatures* (Washington, DC: Congressional Quarterly Press, 1998).

17. Sarah McCally Morehouse and Malcolm E. Jewell, *State Politics, Parties, and Policy*, 2nd ed. (Lanham, MD: Rowman & Littlefield, 2003), 197–201.

18. Rosenthal, *The Decline of Representative Democracy*, 179–80; Keith E. Hamm and Gary F. Moncrief, "Legislative Politics in the States," in *Politics in the American States*, 9th ed., ed. Virginia Gray and Russell L. Hanson (Washington, DC: Congressional Quarterly Press, 2008), 154–91; Institute on Money in State Politics, *State Elections Overview 2004* (Helena, MT: The Institute on Money in State Politics, 2005).

19. Morehouse and Jewell, *State Politics, Parties, and Policy*, 199–200.

20. National Conference of State Legislatures, "2008 Partisan Composition of State Legislatures," March 5, 2008, *http://www.ncsl.org/statevote/partycomptable2008.htm.*

21. Keith E. Hamm and Gary F. Moncrief, "Legislative Politics in the States," 154–91.

22. Morris P. Fiorina, "Divided Government in the States," in *The Politics of Divided Government*, ed. Gary Cox and Samuel Kernell (Boulder, CO: Westview, 1991).

23. Thomas M. Holbrook and Raymond J. La Raja, "Parties and Elections," in *Politics in the American States*, 9th ed., ed. Virginia Gray and Russell L. Hanson (Washington, DC: Congressional Quarterly Press, 2008), 61–97.

24. Hamm and Moncrief, "Legislative Politics in the States," 154–91.

25. Gary Moncrief, Richard G. Niemi, and Lynda W. Powell, "Time, Turnover and Term Limits: Trends in Membership Turnover in U.S. State Legislatures" (paper presented at the Annual State Politics and Policy Conference, Tucson, Arizona, March 2003).

26. Hamm and Moncrief, "Legislative Politics in the States," 154–91.

27. National Conference of State Legislatures, "Legislative Term Limits: An Overview," June 9, 2004, *www.ncsl.org/programs/legman/ABOUT/Termlimit.htm.*

28. Alan Rosenthal, "The Legislature: Unraveling of Institutional Fabric," in *The State of the States*, 3rd ed., ed. Carl E. Van Horn (Washington, DC: Congressional Quarterly Press, 1996), 128.

29. Moncrief et al., "Time, Turnover and Term Limits," 17; National Conference of State Legislatures, "The Effect of Term Limits on the 2006 Elections," March 7, 2008. *http://www.ncsl.org/programs/legismgt/about/effects0tl-2006.htm.*

30. Charles E. Menifield, ed., *Representation of Minority Groups in the U.S.: Implications for the Twenty-First Century* (Lanham, MD: Austin & Winfield, 2001).

31. Center for American Women and Politics, "Women in Elective Office 2008," March 5, 2008, *http://www.cawp.rutgers.edu/Facts/Officeholders/elective.pdf.*

32. National Conference of State Legislatures, "Legislator Demographics," March 5, 2008, *http://www.ncsl.org/Programs/legismgt/about/Demographic_Overview.htm.*

33. Nelson C. Dometrius, "Governors: Their Heritage and Future," in *American State and Local Politics: Directions for the 21st Century*, ed. Ronald E. Weber and Paul Brace (Chatham, NJ: Chatham House, 1999).

34. Thad Beyle and Margaret Ferguson, "Governors and the Executive Branch," in *Politics in the American States*, 9th ed., ed. Virginia Gray and Russell L. Hanson (Washington, DC: Congressional Quarterly Press, 2008), 192–228.

35. Beyle and Ferguson, "Governors and the Executive Branch," 192–228.

36. Dennis Farney, "When Wisconsin Governor Wields Partial Veto, the Legislature Might as Well Go Play Scrabble," *Wall Street Journal*, July 1, 1993.

37. Beyle and Ferguson, "Governors and the Executive Branch," 192–228.

38. Carsey, *Campaign Dynamics*, 1999.

39. Ann O' M. Bowman and Richard C. Kearney, *State and Local Government*, 4th ed. (Boston: Houghton-Mifflin, 1999), 203–4.

40. Associated Press, "Alabama Lt. Governor Finds Nothing to Do," *New York Times*, February 17, 1999.

41. Council of State Governments, *The Book of the States, 2003 Edition* (Washington, DC: Council of State Governments, 2004), 199–208.

42. Kenneth J. Meier, "Executive Reorganization of Government: Impact on Employment and Expenditures," *American Journal of Political Science* 24 (1980): 396–412.

43. Hedge, *Governance and the Changing American States*, 111.

44. Alan Rosenthal, "The Legislative Institution: Transformed and at Risk," in *The State of the States*, ed. Carl Van Horn (Washington, DC: Congressional Quarterly Press, 1989), 69.

45. Joel A. Thompson and Gary E. Moncrief, "The Evolution of the State Legislature: Institutional Change and Legislative Careers," in *Changing Patterns in State Legislative Careers*, ed. Gary E. Moncrief and Joel A. Thompson (Ann Arbor: University of Michigan Press, 1992).

46. Christopher Z. Mooney, "Measuring U.S. State Legislative Professionalism: An Evaluation of Five Indices," *State and Local Government Review* 26 (spring 1994): 70–71.

47. National Conference of State Legislatures, "Size of State Legislative Staff: 1979, 1988, 1996, and 2003—Permanent Staff (November 2003)," July 7, 2004, *www.ncsl.org/programs/ legman/about/staffcount2003.htm.*

48. Alan Rosenthal, *The Decline of Representative Democracy.*

49. Peverill Squire, "Legislative Professionalization and Membership Diversity in State Legislatures, *Legislative Studies Quarterly* 17 (February 1992): 69–79.

50. Christopher Z. Mooney, "Citizens, Structures, and Sister States: Influences on State Legislative Professionalism," *Legislative Studies Quarterly* 20 (February 1995): 47–68.

51. Phillip W. Roeder, "State Legislative Reform: Determinants and Policy Consequences," *American Politics Quarterly* 7 (January 1979): 51–70; Morris P. Fiorina "Further Evidence of the Partisan Consequences of Legislative Professionalism,"

American Journal of Political Science 43 (July 1999): 974–77.

52. James King, "Changes in Professionalism in U.S. State Legislatures," *Legislative Studies Quarterly* 25 (2000): 327–43.

53. Robert C. LaFountain, Richard Y. Schauffler, Shauna M. Strickland, William E. Raftery, and Chantal G. Bromage, eds. *Examining the Work of State Courts: A National Perspective from the Court Statistics Project.* (Washington, DC: A joint project of the Conference of State Court Administrators, the Bureau of Justice Statistics, and the National Center for State Courts, 2006).

54. Paul Brace, Melinda Gann Hall, and Laura Langer, "Placing State Supreme Courts in State Politics," *State Politics and Policy Quarterly* 1 (spring 2001): 81–108.

55. Delaware, Maine, Mississippi, Montana, Nevada, New Hampshire, North Dakota, Rhode Island, South Dakota, Vermont, West Virginia, and Wyoming.

56. Melinda Gann Hall, "State Supreme Courts in American Democracy: Probing the Myths of Judicial Reform," *American Political Science Review* 95 (June 2001): 315–30.

57. Ibid.

58. Initiative and Referendum Institute, *Initiative Use* (Washington, DC: Initiative and Referendum Institute, 2006), *www.iandrinstitute.org/Usage.htm.*

60. Elisabeth R. Gerber, "Legislative Response to the Threat of Popular Initiatives," *American Journal of Political Science* 40 (February 1996): 99–128.

61. Edward L. Lascher Jr., Michael G. Hagen, and Steven A. Rochlin, "Gun Behind the Door? Ballot Initiatives, State Policies, and Public Opinion," *Journal of Politics* 58 (August 1996): 760–75.

62. Brett Pulley, "The 1998 Campaign: Special Interests; Gambling Proponents Bet $85 Million on Election," *New York Times*, October 31, 1998.

63. Bowman and Kearney, *State and Local Government*, 125.

64. Thomas E. Cronin, *Direct Democracy* (Cambridge, MA: Harvard University Press, 1989), 143.

65. *City of Clinton v. Cedar Rapids and Missouri RR Co.*, 24 Iowa 475 (1868), as quoted in Richard P. Nathan, "The Role of the States in American Federalism," in *The State of the States*, 2nd ed., ed. Carl E. Van Horn (Washington, DC: Congressional Quarterly Press, 1993).

66. Don AuCoin and William F. Doherty, "House Votes to Pull Plug on Middlesex," *Boston Globe*, June 13, 1997, B12.

67. Nownes, Thomas, and Hrebenar, "Interest Groups in the States," in Gray and Hanson, *Politics in the American States*, 98–126.

68. *The Municipal Year Book, 1996* (Washington, DC: International City/County Management Association, 1996).

69. David Brockington, Todd Donovan, Shaun Bowler, and Richard Brischetto, "Minority Representation Under Cumulative and Limited Voting," *Journal of Politics* 60 (November 1998): 1108–25.

70. Kenneth J. Meier, Robert D. Wrinkle, and J. L. Polinard, "Representative bureaucracy and Distributional Equity: Addressing the Hard Question," *Journal of Politics* 61 (November 1999): 1025–39.

71. Kenneth K. Wong, "The Politics of Education," in Gray and Hanson, *Politics in the American States*, 365–71.

72. Thomas R. Dye, *American Federalism* (Lexington, MA: D. C. Heath, 1990).

73. Paul E. Peterson, *City Limits* (Chicago: University of Chicago Press, 1981).

74. Jeffrey Berry, Kent Portney, and Ken Thomson, *The Rebirth of Urban Democracy* (Washington, DC: Brookings Institution, 1993).

75. David Osborne and Ted Gaebler, *Reinventing Government: How the Entrepreneurial Spirit Is Transforming the Public Sector* (Reading, MA: Addison-Wesley, 1992).

KEY TERMS IN SPANISH

A

activation—acción y efecto de activar

actual group—grupo actual

administrative discretion—discreción administrativa

affirmative action—acción afirmativa

Americans with Disabilities Act of 1990—disposición legal de 1990 para ciudadanos americanos minusválidos

amicus curiae **briefs**—instrucciones, informes, de la competencia de amigos del senado.

Anti-Federalists—anti-federalistas

antitrust policy—política antimonopolio

appellate jurisdiction—jurisdicción apelatoria

appropriations bill—proyecto de ley de apropiación

arms race—carrera armamentista

Articles of Confederation—Artículos de la Confederación

authorization bill—estatuto de autorización

B

balance of trade—balance de intercambio comercial

beats—v. derrotar; recorrido de vigilancia policiaca

bicameral legislature—legislatura bi-camaral

Bill of Rights—proyecto de ley de derechos

bill—proyecto de ley; moción; cuenta

blanket primaries—cubiertas primarias

block grants—otorgamientos en conjunto

broadcast media—medios de transmisión

budget—presupuesto

budget resolution—resolución de presupuesto

bureaucracy—burocracia

C

cabinet—gabinete

campaign strategy—estrategia de campaña

capitalism—capitalismo

casework—trabajo de asistencia social

categorical grants—concesiones categorizadas

caucus—reunión del comité central o asamblea local de un partido

censorship—censura

census—censo

Central Intelligence Agency (CIA)—Agencia Central de Inteligencia

chains (newspaper chains)—cadena (cadenas periodísticas)

checks and balances—cheques y balances

city manager—aministrador de la ciudad

civic duty—deber cívico

civil disobedience—desobediencia civil

civil liberties—libertades civiles

civil rights—derechos civiles

Civil Rights Act of 1964—ley de Derechos Humanos de 1964

civil rights movement—movimiento de derechos civiles

civil service—administración pública

class action lawsuits—demanda colectiva

Clean Air Act of 1970—ley contra la contaminación del aire de 1970

closed primaries—primarias cerradas

coalition—coalición

coalition government—coalición de gobierno

cold war—guerra fría

collective bargaining—negociación colectiva

collective good—bienestar colectivo

command-and-control policy—política de ordenamiento y control

commercial speech—discurso comercial

committee chairs—presidentes de comité

comparable worth—valor comparable

conference committees—comités de conferencias

Congressional Budget and Impoundment Control Act of 1974—Ley del Presupuesto e Incautación del Congreso de 1974

Congressional Budget Office (CBO)—Oficina de Presupuesto del Congreso

Connecticut Compromise—Compromiso de Connecticut

consent of the governed—consentimiento del gobernado

conservatives—conservadores

Constitution—constitución

consumer price index (CPI)—índice de precios del consumidor

containment doctrine—doctrina o política de contención

continuing resolutions—resoluciones continuas

conversion—conversión

cooperative federalism—federalismo cooperativo

Council of Economic Advisers (CEA)—Consejo de Asesores Económicos

council of governments—consejo de gobiernos

courts of appeal—corte de apelación

crisis—crisis

critical election—elección crítica

cruel and unusual punishment—castigo cruel e inusual
culture of poverty—cultura de pobreza

D

Declaration of Independence—Declaración de Independencia
deficit—déficit
democracy—democracia
demography—demografía
deregulation—desregular, liberalizar
détente—relajación
Dillon's Rule—Regla de Dillon
direct democracy—democracia directa
direct mail—correo directo
district courts—juzgado de distrito
dual federalism—federalismo dual

E

Eighth Amendment—Octava Enmienda (constitucional)
elastic clause—cláusula flexible
electioneering—campaña electoral
electoral college—colegio electoral
elite theory—teoría de la élite
Endangered Species Act of 1973—Ley de Especies en Peligro de Extinción de 1973
entitlements—derechos
enumerated powers—poderes enumerados
Environmental Protection Agency (EPA)—Agencia de Protección al Ambiente
environmental impact statement (EIS)—declaración de impacto sobre el ambiente
Equal Rights Amendment—Enmienda de Igualdad de Derechos
equal protection of the laws—igualdad de protección de la ley
establishment clause—cláusula de instauración
European Union (EU)—Unión Europea
exclusionary rule—regla de exclusión
executive orders—órdenes ejecutivas
exit poll—conteo de salida de votación
expenditures—gastos
extradition—extradición

F

factions—facciones
Federal Election Campaign Act—Ley de la Campaña Federal de Elección
Federal Election Commission (FEC)—Comisión Federal Electoral
Federal Reserve System—Sistema Federal de Reserva
Federal Trade Commission (FTC)—Comisión Federal de Comercio

federal debt—deuda federal
federalism—federalismo
Federalist Papers—Documentos Federalistas
Federalists—federalistas
Fifteenth Amendment—Quinceava Enmienda
Fifth Amendment—Enmienda Quinta
filibuster—intervención parlamentaria con objeto de impedir una votación
First Amendment—Enmienda Primera
fiscal federalism—federalismo fiscal
fiscal policy—política fiscal
Food and Drug Administration (FDA)—Departamento Administrativo de Alimentos y Estupefacientes
foreign policy—política extranjera
formula grants—fórmula de concesión
Fourteenth Amendment—Catorceava Enmienda
free exercise clause—cláusula de ejercicio libre
free-rider problem—problema de polizón
frontloading—carga frontal
full faith and credit—fe y crédito completo

G

gender gap—disparidad de género
government—gobierno
government corporations—corporaciones gubernamentales
gross domestic product—producto doméstico bruto
GS (General Schedule) rating—prorrateo programático general

H

Hatch Act—Ley Hatch
health maintenance organization (HMO)—Organización para el Mantenimiento de la Salud
high-tech politics—política sobre alta tecnología
home rule—regla de casa (local)
House Rules Committee—Comité de Reglas de la Cámara
House Ways and Means Committee—Comité de Formas y Medios de la Cámara
hyperpluralism—hiperpluralismo; pluralismo en exceso

I

impeachment—juicio de impugnación
implied powers—poderes implícitos
incentive system—sistema de incentivos
income—ingresos de enlace
incorporation doctrine—doctrina de incorporación
incrementalism—incrementalismo
incumbents—titular en función
independent executive agencies—agencias ejecutivas independientes

independent regulatory agency—agencia regulatoria independiente
industrial policy—política industrial
inflation—inflación
initiative—iniciativa
initiative petition—iniciativa de petición
interdependency—interdependencia
interest group—grupos de interés
intergovernmental relations—relaciones intergubernamentales
investigative journalism—periodismo de investigación
iron triangles—triángulos de acero
isolationism—aislacionismo
item veto—artículo de veto

J

Joint Chiefs of Staff—Junta de Comandantes de las Fuerzas Armadas (Estado Mayor)
joint committees—comisiones
judicial activisim—activismo judicial
judicial implementation—implementación judicial
judicial restraint—restricción judicial
judicial review—revisión judicial
justiciable disputes—conflictos enjuiciables

K

Keynesian economic theory—teoría económica keynesiana

L

laissez-faire—liberalismo económico
legislative oversight—descuido legislativo
legislative veto—Veto legislativo
legitimacy—legitimidad
libel—difamación, calumnia
liberals—liberales
lieutenant governor—lugarteniente del gobernador
limited government—gobierno limitado
linkage institutions—instituciones de enlace
lobbying—cabildeo
local charter—estatutos locales; fuero local

M

majority leader—líder de la mayoría
majority rule—gobierno de la mayoría
mandate theory of elections—mandato teórico de elecciones
mass media—medios de difusión (comunicación) masiva
McCarthyism—macartismo
McGovern-Fraser Commission—Comisión *McGovern-Fraser*

media event—evento de los medios de difusión (comunicación)
Medicaid—programa de asistencia médica estatal *Medicaid* para personas de bajos ingresos
Medicare—programa de asistencia médica estatal *Medicare* para personas mayores de 65 años
melting pot—crisol
merit plan—plan meritorio (por méritos)
merit principle—principio de mérito
minority leader—líder de la minoría parlamentaria
minority majority—majoria de la minoría
minority rights—derechos de las minorías
mixed economy—economía mixta
monetarism—monetarismo
monetary policy—política monetaria
Motor Voter Act—Ley para promoción del voto

N

narrowcasting—transmisión cerrada; monitoreo cerrado
National Environmental Policy Act (NEPA)—Ley de la Política Ambiental Nacional
National Labor Relations Act—Ley Nacional de Relaciones Laborales
National Security Council (NSC)—Consejo Nacional de Seguridad
national chairperson—director/a de comité nacional
national committee—comité nacional
national convention—convención nacional
national health insurance—seguro de salud nacional
national party convention—convención nacional del partido
national primary—primaria nacional
natural rights—derechos naturales
New Deal coalition—coalición para el Nuevo Tratado
New Jersey Plan—Plan de New Jersey
Nineteenth Amendment—Enmienda Diecinueve
nomination—nominación
North Atlantic Treaty Organization (NATO)—Tratado de las Organizaciones del Atlantico Norte

O

Office of Management and Budget (OMB)—Oficina de Gestión y Presupuesto
Office of Personnel Management (OPM)—Oficina de Gestión de Personal
Olson's law of large groups—ley de Olson de grandes grupos
open primaries—primarias abiertas
opinion—opinión

Organization of Petroleum Exporting Countries (OPEC)—Organización de Países Exportadores de Petróleo
original intent—intento original
original jurisdiction—jurisdicción original

P

party competition—competencia de partido
party dealignment—desalineamiento del partido
party eras—épocas del partido
party identification—identificación partidista
party image—imágen del partido
party machines—maquinaria partidista
party platform—plataforma del partido
party realignment—realinación del partido
patronage—patrocinio
Pendleton Civil Service Act—Ley del Servicio Público de Pendleton
plea bargaining—negociación fiscal-defensa
pluralist theory—teoría pluralista
pocket veto—veto indirecto del presidente al no firmar dentro de los diez días establecidos
policy agenda—agenda política
policy entrepreneurs—política empresarial
policy gridlock—parálisis política
policy implementation—implementación política
policy voting—política de votación
policymaking institutions—instituciones de normatividad política
policymaking system—sistema de normatividad política
political action committees (PACs)—comités de acción política
political culture—cultura política
political efficacy—eficacia política
political ideology—ideología política
political issue—asunto político
political participation—participación política
political party—partido político
political questions—cuestiones políticas
political socialization—socialización política
politics—política
poll taxes—votación para impuestos
pork barrel—asignación de impuestos estatales para el beneficio de una cierta zona o grupo
potential group—grupo potencial
poverty line—límite económico mínimo para sobrevivencia
precedent—precedente
presidential coattails—acción a la sombra presidencial
presidential primaries—elecciones primarias presidenciales
press conferences—conferencias de prensa

print media—medios de comunicación impresos
prior restraint—restricción anterior
privileges and immunities—privilegios e inmunidades
probable cause—causa probable
progressive tax—impuesto progresivo
project grant—proyecto de concecsión
proportional representation—representación proporcional
proportional tax—impuesto proporcional
protest—n. protesta; v. protestar
public goods—bienes públicos
public interest lobbies—cabildeo por intereses públicos
public opinion—opinión pública
public policy—política pública

R

random sampling—muestreo aleatorio
random-digit dialing—llamadas con números aleatorios
rational-choice theory—teoría de selección racional
reapportionment—nueva distribución en la representación del congreso
recall—retirar
reconciliation—reconciliación
referendum—referendum
regional primaries—elecciones primarias regionales
regressive tax—impuesto regresivo
regulation—norma, regla
reinforcement—refuerzo
relative deprivation—privación relativa
representation—representación
republic—república
responsible party model—modelo de partido responsable
retrospective voting—votación retrospectiva
revenues—ingresos
right to privacy—derecho a la privacidad
right-to-work laws—leyes del derecho al trabajo

S

sample—muestra
sampling error—error de muestreo
search warrant—orden de cateo
secretary of defense—secretario de la defensa
secretary of state—secretario de estado
select committees—comités seleccionados
selective benefits—beneficios selectivos
selective perception—percepción selectiva
self-incrimination—auto incriminación
Senate Finance Committee—Comité Senatorial de Finanzas
senatorial courtesy—cortesía senatorial
Senior Executive Service—el de más alto rango en el servicio del ejecutivo

seniority system—sistema de antigüedad
separation of powers—separación de poderes
Shays' Rebellion—Rebelion de Shays
single-issue groups—grupos para una sola causa
Sixteenth Amendment—Enmienda Dieciséis
Sixth Amendment—Enmienda Sexta
Social Security Act—Ley de Seguridad Social
social welfare policies—políticas para el bien social
soft money—moneda débil, sin garantía
solicitor general—subsecretario de justicia
sound bites—segmentos de sonido
Speaker of the House—presidente de la cámara
standard operating procedures (SOPs)—procedimientos normales de operación
standing committees—comités permanentes
standing to sue—en posición de entablar demanda
stare decisis—variación de "decisión firme" o "decisión tomada"; la decisión se fundamenta en algo ya decidio.
statutory construction—construcción establecida por ley
Strategic Defense Initiative (SDI)—Iniciativa de Defensa Estratégica
street-level bureaucrats—burócratas de bajo nivel
subnational government—gobierno subnacional
subgovernments—subgobiernos
suffrage—sufragio
Super Tuesday—Super martes: día de votación en varios estados importantes.
superdelegates—superdelegados
Superfund—superfondo; fondo de proporciones mayores
supply-side economics—economía de la oferta
supremacy clause—cláusula de supremacía
Supreme Court—Suprema Corte
symbolic speech—discurso simbólico

T

Taft-Hartley Act—Ley de Taft-Hatley
talking head—busto parlante; presentador, entrevistador
tariff—tarifa
tax expenditures—gastos de impuesto
Tenth Amendment—Enmienda Décima
term limits—periodo límite
third parties—terceras personas
Thirteenth Amendment—Enmienda Treceava

ticket splitting—votación de candidatos de diferentes partidos para diferentes cargos
town meeting—consejo municipal de vecinos
transfer payments—transferencia de pagos
transnational corporations—corporaciones transnacionales
trial balloons—globo de prueba; proponer algo para conocer la reacción de alguien
Twenty-fifth Amendment—Enmienda veiticincoava
Twenty-fourth Amendment—Enmienda veiticuatrava
Twenty-second Amendment—Enmienda veintidoava

U

U.S. Constitution—Constitución de los Estados Unidos
uncontrollable expenditures—gastos incontrolables
unemployment rate—nivel de desempleo; porcentaje de desempleo
union shop—empresa que emplea sólo trabajadores sindicalizados
unitary governments—estados/gobiernos unitarios
United Nations (UN)—Naciones Unidas
unreasonable searches and seizures—cateos y detenciones/embargos irrazonables
urban underclass—urbanita de clase baja

V

veto—veto
Virginia Plan—Plan Virginia
voter registration—registro de votantes
Voting Rights Act of 1965—Ley de Derechos del Elector de 1965

W

War Powers Resolution—Resolución de Poderes de Guerra
Water Pollution Control Act of 1972—Ley para el Control de la Contaminación de Aguas de 1972
wealth—riqueza
whips—miembro de un cuerpo legislativo encargado de hacer observar las consignas del partido
white primary—primaria blanca/ sin novedad
winner-take-all system—sistema en el que el ganador toma todos los votos
writ of habeas corpus—un recurso de hábeas corpus

ACKNOWLEDGMENTS

TEXT ACKNOWLEDGMENTS

Chapter 2, p.45: Jackson Turner Main, "Government by the People: The American Revolution and the Democratization of the Legislatures," *The William and Mary Quarterly*, 3rd ser., 23 (July 1966). Reprinted by permission of the Omohundro Institute of Early American History and Culture.

Chapter 4, p.136: Abortion Chart, Gallup Poll, May 8-11, 2007. Used by permission.

Chapter 7, p.221: Adapted from *The American Journalist in the 21st Century* by David H. Weavere. Copyright © 2007 by Taylor & Francis Group LLC - Books. Reproduced with permission of Taylor & Francis Group LLC - Books in the format Textbook and Other Book via Copyright Clearance Center.

Chapter 7, p.225: "How Network News Broadcasts Are Going the Way of the Dinosaurs," State of the News Media, 2007, from http://www.stateofthenewsmedia.org/2007.

Chapter 7, p.230: "Press Freedom Around the World" from Reporters Without Borders, "Worldwide Press Freedom Index." Used by permission of Reporters Without Borders.

Chapter 8, p.262: Courtesy of Pew Research Center, from http://people-press.org/commentary/display.php3?AnalysisID=95.

Chapter 9, p.290: From *The Nightly News Nightmare Revisited: Network Television's Coverage of U.S. Presidential Elections, 1988–2004*, Second Edition, by Stephen J. Farnsworth and S. Robert Lichter, Lanham, MD: Rowman & Littlefield, 2007.

Chapter 9, p.296: Copyright Center for Responsive Politics, www.opensecrets.org.

Chapter 11, p.337: Washington Power 25 listing from "Fat&Happy in D.C.," May 28, 2001, Vol. 143, No. 11, U.S. Edition, Fortune. Copyright © 2001 Time Inc. All rights reserved. Used by permission.

Chapter 12, p.368: "Incumbency Factor in Congressional Elections" adapted from Harold W. Stanley and Richard G. Niemi, *Vital Statistics on American Politics*, 2007–2008, CQ Press, 2008.

Chapter 12, p.392: David Samuels and Richard Snyder, "The Value of a Vote: Malapportionment in Comparative Perspective," *British Journal of Political Science* 31, October 2001. Reprinted with the permission of Cambridge University Press.

Chapter 16, p.540: *The Judicial Process: An Introductory Analysis of the Courts of the United States, England and France*, 7th Edition, 1998, by Henry J. Abraham. Used by permission of Oxford University Press, Inc.

Chapter 19, p.601: Kids Count 2008. Courtesy of the Annie E. Casey Foundation.

Chapter 20, p.646: Congressional Quarterly Weekly Report by Congressional Quarterly. Copyright © 1998 by Congressional Quarterly Inc. Reproduced with permission of Congressional Quarterly Inc. in the format Textbook and Other Book via Copyright Clearance Center.

Chapter 21, p.663: State of the States, 2008, March 8, 2008 courtsey of Stateline.org.

PHOTO ACKNOWLEDGMENTS

Page abbreviations are as follows: (T) top, (C) center, (B) bottom, (L) left, (R) right.

Chapter 1, page 2: ROGER L. WOLLENBERG/UPI/Landov; **3:** TAP/Wide World Photos; **3TC:** AFP/Getty Images; **3BC:** Getty Images; **3B:** Joseph Sohm/ChromoSohm Inc./Corbis; **5:** ColorBlind Images/Getty Images; **7:** AFP/Getty Images; **8:** AP/Wide World Photos; **9:** AP/Wide World Photos; **10:** AFP/Getty Images; **13:** AFP/Getty Images; **14TR:** AP/Wide World Photos; **17:** Getty Images; **19:** Joseph Sohm/ChromoSohm Inc./Corbis; **21:** Robert Trippett/Sipa Press; **23:** GLEN MCCOY © 2001 Belleville News-Democrat. Reprinted with permission of UNIVERSAL PRESS SYNDICATE. All rights reserved.

Chapter 2, page 30: AP/Wide World Photos; **31L:** AP/Wide World Photos; **31T:** U.S. Capitol Historical Society; **33:** Joe Griffin/Hulton Archive/Getty Images; **34:** U.S. Capitol Historical Society; **36L:** Brown Brothers; **36R:** National Archives and Records Administration; **40:** Scribner's Popular History of the US, 1897; **41:** Yale University Library, Sterling Memorial Library; **42:** The New York Public Library, Astor, Lenox and Tilden Foundations; **44:** DOONSBURY © G.B. Trudeau. Reprinted with permission of Universal Press Syndicate. All rights reserved.; **45:** New York Library Picture Collection; **52:** National Geographic Photographer George Mobley/US Capitol Historical Society; **57:** Hulton Archive/Getty Images; **62:** By permission of Mike Luckovich and Creators Syndicate, Inc.; **64:** Luke Frazza/AFP/Getty Images

Chapter 3, page 70: AP/Wide World Photos; **71TR:** Joe Raedle/Getty Images; **71L:** AP/Wide World Photos; **71CR:** Hulton Archive/Getty Images; **71BR:** Michael Newman/PhotoEdit, Inc.; **74:** Joe Raedle/Getty Images; **80:** Hulton Archive/Getty Images; **80:** AP/Wide World Photos; **85:** AP/Wide World Photos; **86:** AP/Wide World Photos; **88:** Michael Newman/PhotoEdit, Inc.; **89:** Ron Sachs-Pool/Getty Images

Chapter 4, page 100: Brendan Smialoski/AFP/Getty Images; **101CR:** AP/Wide World Photos; **101L:** Brendan Smialoski/AFP/Getty Images; **101BR:** Jean-Yves Rabeuf/The Image Works; **102:** AP/Wide World Photos; **107:** Annie Griffiths Belt/Corbis; **109:** AP/Wide World Photos; **113:** AP/Wide World Photos; **114:** AP/Wide World Photos; **115:** Corbis; **120:** Getty Images; **121:** Jean-Yves Rabeuf/The Image Works; **125:** Michael Newman/PhotoEdit, Inc.; **127:** Mobile Press Register/Corbis; **128:** By permission of the John L. Hart LP, and Creators Syndicate, Inc.; **130:** AP/Wide World Photos

Chapter 5, page 144: Francis Miller/Time & Life Pictures/Getty Images/Getty Images; **145L:** Francis Miller/Time & Life Pictures/Getty Images/Getty Images; **145BR:** Justin Sullivan/Getty Images; **145BCR:** Steven Rubin/The Image Works; **145TCR:** Reuters/Corbis; **148:** AP/Wide World Photos; **150:** The Granger Collection, NY; **152:** Bettmann/Corbis; **153:** Bettmann/Corbis; **154:** John Elk III/Alamy; **157:** AP/Wide World Photos; **159:** Reuters/Corbis; **161:** Corbis; **164:** Bettmann/Corbis; **165:** AP/Wide World Photos; **168:** Mark Wilson/Getty Images; **170:** Steven Rubin/The Image Works; **172:** Justin Sullivan/Getty Images

Chapter 6, page 182: Mark Wilson/Getty Images; **182TBR:** Sven Hagolani/Corbis; **182L:** Mark Wilson/Getty Images; **183CTR:** Rebecca Cook/Reuters/Landov; **183T:** Allan J. Barnes; **185:** Allan J. Barnes; **187:** Bob Daemmrich/The Image Works; **187:** Rebecca Cook/Reuters/Landov; **189:** author photo; **194:** AP/Wide World Photos; **196:** Sven Hagolani/Corbis; **207:** AP/Wide World Photos; **208:** AP/Wide World Photos; **209:** John Filo/Getty Images

Chapter 7, page 216: AP/Wide World Photos; **217TCR:** AP/Wide World Photos; **217BCR:** AP/Wide World Photos; **217L:** AP/Wide World Photos; **217TR:** Ron Sachs/CNP/Corbis; **219:** AP/Wide World Photos; **220:** Ron Sachs/CNP/Corbis; **222:** Kevin Lamarque/Reuters/Corbis; **226:** AP/Wide World Photos; **232:** © Tribune Media Services, Inc. All Rights Reserved. Reprinted with permission.; **235:** © Tribune Media Services, Inc. All Rights Reserved. Reprinted with permission.; **236:** AP/Wide World Photos; **238:** Reuters/Corbis; **239:** barelypolitical.com

Chapter 8, page 246: DANIEL ACKER/Bloomberg News/Landov; **247TCR:** Bettmann/Corbis; **247L:** DANIEL ACKER/Bloomberg News /Landov; **247TR:** Jean-Claude Lejeuen/STOCKPHOTO; **250:** Matt Browner-Hamlin; **254:** Jean-Claude Lejeuen/STOCKPHOTO; **257:** TOLES © 2000 The Washington Post. Reprinted with permission of Universal Press Syndicate. All rights reserved.; **261:** Bettmann/Corbis; **263:** The Granger Collection, New York; **266:** Ron Wurzer/Polaris Images

Chapter 9, page 276: Bruce Ely/The Oregonian; **277TR:** Jim Ruyman/UPI/Landov; **277L:** Bruce Ely/The Oregonian; **277BR:** Howell/Getty Images; **277TBR:** AP/Wide World Photos; **280:** Jim Ruyman/UPI/Landov; **281:** AP/Wide World Photos; **282:** AP/Wide World Photos; **287:** Howell/Getty Images; **290:** Courtesy the authors; **294:** AUTH © 2002 The Philadelphia Inquirer. Reprint with permission of Universal Press Syndicate. All rights reserved.; **295:** Reuters/HO/Swiftvets.com/Landov; **299:** AP/Wide World Photos

Chapter 10, page 304: Robert King/Zuma Press, Inc.; **305L** Robert King/Zuma Press, Inc.; **305TR:** Reproduced from the collections of the Library of Congress; **305BCR:** Bettmann/Corbis; **305TCR:** AP/Wide World Photos; **307:** www.jankenphoto.com; **308:** Reproduced from the collections of the Library of Congress; **312:** Dennis Renault/Renault; **317:** AP/Wide World Photos; **321:** © The New Yorker Collection 2002 Mike Twohy from cartoonbank.com. All rights reserved.; **322:** TOLES © 2004 The Washington Post. Reprinted with permission of UNIVERSAL PRESS SYNDICATE. All rights reserved.; **324:** Bettmann/Corbis

Chapter 11, page 330: AP/Wide World Photos; **331:** AP/Wide World Photos; **331TCR:** AP/Wide World Photos; **331BCR:** AP/Wide World Photos; **331BR:** Carlo Allegri/Getty Images; **334:** © Tribune Media Services, Inc. All Rights Reserved. Reprinted with permission.; **339:** Jim Borgman/Reprinted with special permission of King Features Syndicate; **344:** AP/Wide World Photos; **345:** Jim Borgman/Reprinted with special permission of King Features Syndicate; **348:** Jeffrey Markowitz/Corbis; **349:** AP/Wide World Photos; **352:** AP/Wide World Photos; **353:** AP/Wide World Photos; **354:** Carlo Allegri/Getty Images

Chapter 12, page 362: Stefan Zaklin/epa/LandovCorbis; **363L:** Stefan Zaklin/epa/LandovCorbis; **363BR:** National Cable Satellite Corporation/C-SPAN; **363BCR:** Carol T. Powers/The New York Times/Redux; **363TR:** Mark Wilson/Getty Images; **363TCR:** Gunther/Sipa Press; **365:** Lifetime Television; **367:** Gunther/Sipa Press; **373:** Reprinted with permission from David Horsey, Seattle Post-Intelligencer; **377L:** AP/Wide World Photos; **377C:** Brendan Hoffman/Getty Images; **377R:** Alex Wong/Getty Images; **380:** Mark Wilson/Getty Images; **383:** AP/Wide World Photos; **384:** Dominic Bracco II/UPI/Landov; **391:** Carol T. Powers/The New YorkRedux Times/Redux; **393:** National Cable Satellite Corporation/C-SPAN

Chapter 13, page 399TC: AP/Wide World Photos; **399BR:** Stephen Jaffe; **399TR:** Alex Webb/Magnum Photos, Inc.; **399BCR:** Tim Sloan/AFP/Getty Images; **401:** AP/Wide World Photos; **402a:** Courtesy of the Eisenhower Library; **402b:** AP/Wide World Photos; **402c:** AP/Wide World Photos; **402d:** AP/Wide World Photos; **402e:** AP/Wide World Photos; **402f:** AP/Wide World Photos; **402g:** AP/Wide World Photos; **402h:** AP/Wide World Photos; **403:** AUTH © 2002 The Philadelphia Inquirer. Reprint with permission of Universal Press Syndicate. All rights reserved.; **403i:** Getty Images; **404:** Alex Webb/Magnum Photos, Inc.; **414:** AP/Wide World Photos; **421:** Stephen Jaffe; **422:** Tim Sloan/AFP/Getty Images; **423:** Corbis; **424:** Bettmann/Corbis; **426:** AP/Wide World Photos; **428:** AP/Wide World Photos; **431:** Wayne Miller/Magnum Photos, Inc.; **433:** AP/Wide World Photos

Chapter 14, page 440: AP/Wide World Photos; **441L:** AP/Wide World Photos; **441BCR:** Phillip Wallick/Corbis; **441TCR:** Time Life Pictures/Getty Images; **441TR:** AP/Wide World Photos; **441BR:** AP/Wide World Photos; **442:** AP/Wide World Photos; **445:** KEVIN LAMARQUE/Reuters/Landov; **450:** Time Life Pictures/Getty Images; **453:** Phillip Wallick/Corbis; **454:** AP/Wide World Photos; **459:** Dennis Brack/Bloomberg News/Landov; **465:** Ted Korodny/Corbis

Chapter 15, page 470: AP/Wide World Photos; **471L:** AP/Wide World Photos; **471TR:** Syracuse Newspapers/Dennis Cantrell/The Image Works; **471TCR:** Chuck Nacke/Woodfin Camp & Associates; **471BCR:** AP/Wide World Photos; **471BR:** Jack KurtzThe Image Works; **474:** AP/Wide World Photos; **478:** DOONSBURY © G.B. Trudeau. Reprinted with permission of Universal Press Syndicate. All rights reserved.; **482:** Syracuse Newspapers/Dennis Cantrell/The Image Works; **483:** Chuck Nacke/Woodfin Camp & Associates; **486:** AP/Wide World Photos; **488:** Jack KurtzThe Image Works; **491:** Bettmann/Corbis; **497:** Reuters/Corbis

Chapter 16, page 508: Joe Sohm/The Image Works; **509L:** Joe Sohm/The Image Works; **509TR:** Carol Iwasaki/Time & Life Pictures/Getty Images; **509TCR:** Reuters NewMedia Inc./Corbis Reuters/Corbis; **509BCR:** Getty Images; **509BR:** David Hume Kennerly/Getty Images; **512:** Carol Iwasaki/Time & Life Pictures/Getty Images; **521:** Reuters NewMedia Inc./Corbis Reuters/Corbis; **524:** Corbis; **526:** Getty Images; **529:** David Hume Kennerly/Getty Images; **530:** © The New Yorker Collection 1992 J.B. Handelsman from cartoonbank.com. All rights reserved.; **532:** Bettman/Corbis; **534:** Supreme Court Historical Society; **537:** Alex Wong/Getty Images; **538:** Paul Conklin/PhotoEdit, Inc

Chapter 17, page 546: Ethan Miller/Getty Images; **547:** Lethan Miller/Getty Images; **547TR:** Scott Olson/Getty Images; **547CR:** AP/Wide World Photos; **547BR:** Wally McNamee/Corbis; **549:** Scott Olson/Getty Images; **555:** AP/Wide World Photos; **556:** AP/Wide World Photos; **558:** Romeo Ranoco/Reuters/Landov; **558:** Wally McNamee/Corbis; **562:** AP/Wide World Photos

Chapter 18, page 568: AP/Wide World Photos; **569L:** AP/Wide World Photos; **569TR:** Brooks Kraft/Corbis Sygma; **569BR:** Bettmann/Corbis; **569CR:** Mario Tama/Getty Images; **571:** Brooks Kraft/Corbis Sygma; **574T:** Mario Tama/Getty Images; **574B:** Varley Charlie/Sipa Press; **578:** Carmel Zucka/The New York Times/Redux; **579:** Bettmann/Corbis; **581:** Daniel Barry/Bloomberg News/Landov; **583:** Chip Somodveilla/Getty Images; **587:** Alex Wong/Getty Images

Chapter 19, page 594: Todd Bigelow/Aurora Photos; **595L:** Todd Bigelow/Aurora Photos; **595TR:** AP/Wide World Photos; **595TCR:** AP/Wide World Photos; **595BCR:** AP/Wide World Photos; **595BR:** Pienee Lynn/Getty Images; **598:** AP/Wide World Photos; **602:** Art by Jim Borgman. Reprinted with special permission of King Features Syndicate; **603:** AP/Wide World Photos; **605:** AP/Wide World Photos; **608:** AP/Wide World Photos; **609:** Pienee Lynn/Getty Images; **612:** AP/Wide World Photos

Chapter 20, page 620: Robert Clark/Aurora Photos; **621L:** Robert Clark/Aurora Photos; **621TR:** STAN HONDA/AFP/Getty Images; **621TCR:** AFP/Getty Images; **621BCR:** LARRY DOWNING/Reuters /Landov; **621BR:** AP/Wide World Photos; **623:** STAN HONDA/AFP/Getty Images; **627:** AFP/Getty Images; **628:** LARRY DOWNING/Reuters/Landov; **631L:** Bettmann/Corbis; **631R:** AP/Wide World Photos; **634:** AP/Wide World Photos; **635L:** Matthew McDermott/Corbis; **635C:** AP/Wide World Photos; **635R:** AFP/Getty Images; **639:** Trippet/Sipa Press; **641:** DAVID FURST/AFP/Getty Images; **642:** Bettmann/Corbis; **645:** © The New Yorker Collection 1993 Joseph Farris from cartoonbank.com. All rights reserved; **650:** Corbis Sygma

Chapter 21, page 660: AP/Wide World Photos; **661L:** AP/Wide World Photos; **661TR:** Steven Starr/Stock Boston; **661CR:** Erin Siegal/Reuters/Landov; **661BR:** AP/Wide World Photos; **664:** Steven Starr/Stock Boston; **668:** Erin Siegal/Reuters/Landov; **672:** AP/Wide World Photos; **675:** Tasos Katopodis/Getty Images; **676:** AP/Wide World Photos; **683:** R.O. Youngblood/Southern Voice; **692:** Bryan Smith/Zuma Press

INDEX

Chapter 1: Introducing Government in America

Multiple-Choice Questions

1. Which of the following statements is the best indication of pluralism in American politics?
   (A) The American Association of Retired Persons has the largest membership of any interest group.
   (B) Third parties often endorse candidates for office, but rarely do they win elections.
   (C) The federal bureaucracy is expanding as more and more citizens are hired for federal jobs.
   (D) Numerous interest groups lobby Congress each year.
   (E) Citizens are able to vote in local, state, and national elections.

2. According to traditional democratic theory, all of the following are characteristics of an ideal democracy EXCEPT
   (A) freedom of speech.
   (B) a bill of rights.
   (C) equality of voting.
   (D) citizens have collective control over the government's policy agenda.
   (E) government extends rights to everyone who is subject to its laws.

3. According to elite and class theorists, which of the following statements describe the American political system?
   I. Political action committees translate the financial power of large corporations into political influence.
   II. Interest groups fairly shape the public agenda by representing the interests of all Americans.
   III. The wealthiest 1 percent of the public is in some way responsible for most policymaking.
   IV. Policymaking relies heavily on compromise because interest groups receive equal access to the policy arena.
   (A) I only
   (B) II only
   (C) I and III only
   (D) II and IV only
   (E) I, II, and IV only

4. The following functions are shared by all governments EXCEPT
   (A) maintaining a national defense.
   (B) ensuring social equality.
   (C) preserving order.
   (D) providing public services.
   (E) socializing the young.

5. Which of the following concepts is fundamental to democracies?
   (A) Economic equality
   (B) Tyranny of the majority
   (C) Majority rule with minority rights
   (D) Bicameralism
   (E) Seniority

6. On which of the following indicators of democratic health does American democracy do poorly?
   (A) Political equality
   (B) Majority rule
   (C) Minority rights
   (D) Voter turnout
   (E) Freedom of speech

7. Linkage institutions are mechanisms through which citizens can influence the policy agenda. All of the following are linkage institutions EXCEPT
   (A) the Constitution.
   (B) political parties.
   (C) interest groups.
   (D) the media.
   (E) elections.

8. According to pluralists, a wealthy interest group would
   (A) have more access to policymakers.
   (B) compete with other interest groups for an equal share of influence.
   (C) buy all of the votes on a piece of legislation.
   (D) manipulate public opinion to support legislations proposed by Congress.
   (E) have no influence on the policy agenda.

9. Which of the following statements most accurately summarizes Figure 1.2?
   (A) The gap in political knowledge between the young and the old has narrowed between 1964 and 2004.
   (B) While political knowledge has decreased for all age groups between 1964 and 2004, the decrease has been the largest for younger Americans.
   (C) In 1964 the young were considerably more politically knowledgeable than the elderly; in 2004 the elderly were considerably more politically knowledgeable than the young.
   (D) Older Americans are more likely to vote than younger Americans.
   (E) The advent of cable television and the Internet helps explain why Americans were more politically knowledgeable in 2004 than they were in 1964.

10. Hyperpluralists differ from pluralists in their belief that
    (A) the representation of too many interests is detrimental to policymaking.
    (B) only the wealthiest lobbyists are heard in Congress.
    (C) power should be centralized in one branch of government.
    (D) competition among groups leads to compromise and, hence, stronger policy.
    (E) political groups get their funds exclusively from big business.

Free-Response Questions

1. Democracy is a key feature in the United States political system. Democracy is instilled and maintained through a set of values referred to as political culture. Many scholars believe that in spite of this shared culture, the United States is experiencing a culture war.
   a) Identify and describe three aspects of the American political culture.
   b) Define "culture war" and identify one issue that is divisive to the American people.

2. The framers of the Constitution established a representative democracy. Political scientists have developed at least three theories of American democracy—pluralism, elitism, and hyperpluralism.
   a) Briefly describe each of these three theories.
   b) Include in your description of each theory a description of how the average citizen is to play a role in politics.
   c) Choose one of the above theories. For that theory, explain one way in which it would support representative democracy and one way in which it would retard representative democracy.

Chapter 2: The Constitution

Multiple-Choice Questions

1. Which of the following institutions was specifically outlined in the Constitution?
   - (A) The Federal Reserve System
   - (B) The Cabinet
   - (C) Federal district courts
   - (D) The Electoral College
   - (E) The Department of State

2. The Seventeenth Amendment changed the nature of senatorial elections by
   - (A) prohibiting PACs from contributing to senatorial campaigns.
   - (B) establishing a group of electors from each state to nominate senators.
   - (C) permitting senatorial debates to be aired on television.
   - (D) scheduling them to be held every two years.
   - (E) requiring senators to be elected directly by the public.

3. Which of the following statements accurately describe the system of checks and balances?
   - I. The system of checks and balances limits tyranny of the majority because one institution cannot gain total power over the others.
   - II. The power to veto bills allows the president to check Congress.
   - III. The system of checks and balances grew out of a long political tradition but is not defined by the Constitution.
   - IV. Congress checks the power of the judicial branch by nominating Supreme Court justices.
   - (A) I only
   - (B) III only
   - (C) I and II only
   - (D) III and IV only
   - (E) I, II, and III only

4. Which of the following statements best summarizes the Supreme Court's decision regarding flag burning?
   - (A) Flag burning is an unconstitutional desecration of a venerated object.
   - (B) Laws that prohibit flag burning infringe on citizens' freedom of speech.
   - (C) A democratic society can restrict flag burning if there is clear majority sentiment against the practice.
   - (D) The government has an obligation to protect revered symbols and icons of American democracy.
   - (E) Only Congress has the authority to prohibit flag burning; states cannot prohibit the practice.

5. Which of the following concepts guided both the Articles of Confederation and the Constitution?
   - (A) Exclusionary rule
   - (B) Limited government
   - (C) Checks and balances
   - (D) State supremacy
   - (E) Direct democracy

6. The Bill of Rights was added to the Constitution to
   - (A) clarify the Supreme Court's power of judicial review.
   - (B) ensure equal voting rights.
   - (C) protect individual liberties.
   - (D) define all powers reserved for the federal and state governments.
   - (E) prevent the supremacy of one faction of government over another.

7. Which of the following statements are true about the Declaration of Independence?
   - I. The Declaration contains important statements about the philosophy that undergirds American government.
   - II. The bulk of the Declaration is a list of grievances against King George III.
   - III. The Declaration outlines the basic institutions and processes of American government.
   - IV. The Declaration implores the Netherlands to aid the colonies in their revolt against the British Empire and the "merciless Indian savages."
   - (A) I only
   - (B) IV only
   - (C) I and II only
   - (D) II and IV only
   - (E) I, II, and III only

8. Which of the following arguments did the Anti-Federalists make against ratifying the Constitution?
   - (A) It entrusted too much power in the king of England.
   - (B) It prohibited political parties.
   - (C) It made the states too powerful.
   - (D) It neglected to protect important liberties.
   - (E) It destroyed the mercantile class.

9. Which of the following conclusions is supported by Table 2.1?
   - (A) The Constitution creates a limited government the preserves natural rights while promoting equality.
   - (B) John Locke eloquently expressed the virtues of liberty when he drafted the Constitution.
   - (C) John Locke eloquently expressed the virtues of liberty when he drafted the Declaration of Independence.
   - (D) The Declaration of Independence establishes a new nation and outlines its governing structure.
   - (E) The Declaration of Independence borrows heavily from the John Locke's writings.

10. In which of the following ways does the Constitution protect the rights of individuals?
    - (A) It gives Congress the power to impeach the president.
    - (B) It invests the president with the powers of commander in chief.
    - (C) It prevents Congress from passing bills of attainder.
    - (D) It allows states to collect taxes.
    - (E) It divides government into the national and state levels.

Free-Response Questions

1. The Constitution has been amended over time to reflect changes in the American political system. No issue has received more attention among these amendments than that of voting rights.
   a) Describe three amendments that had an impact on voting rights.
   b) Describe how each amendment has changed the nature of the electorate.

2. The Declaration of Independence states "Governments are instituted among men, deriving their just powers from the consent of the governed."
   a) Describe one way in which this ideal of government was implemented into a state constitution during the Revolutionary period.
   b) Describe one way in which this ideal of government was neglected from a state constitution during the Revolutionary period.
   c) Describe one way in which this ideal of government was implemented into the United States Constitution in 1787.
   d) Describe one way in which this ideal of government was neglected in the United States Constitution in 1787.

Chapter 3: Federalism

Multiple-Choice Questions

1. Which of the following powers are given to both the national and state governments?
   (A) Coin money
   (B) Tax
   (C) Establish post offices
   (D) Declare war
   (E) Conduct foreign relations

2. In *United States v. Darby*, the Supreme Court ruled that the Tenth Amendment
   (A) violates the supremacy clause in Article VI.
   (B) cannot be interpreted to assert state supremacy over the national government.
   (C) can bestow unlimited implied powers to state governments.
   (D) denies states the power to regulate intrastate commerce.
   (E) authorizes the state governments to overturn federal laws.

3. The elastic clause gives Congress the authority to
   (A) overrule the president's veto.
   (B) pass laws necessary to carry out its enumerated powers.
   (C) overturn state laws.
   (D) check the power of the Supreme Court by approving the president's nominees for justices.
   (E) dismiss members of the federal judiciary for making unpopular decisions.

4. Which of the following statements about federalism is true?
   (A) Power is concentrated in a central government that oversees policymaking and the enforcement of laws.
   (B) Power is shared among state governments in such a way that all states have identical laws.
   (C) Power is divided among levels of government.
   (D) Power is relegated primarily to local governments.
   (E) Power is vested mostly in state governments.

5. Which of the following statements is supported by the evidence presented in the map included as part of the feature titled, "My State: State and Local Spending on Public Education"?
   (A) An advantage of federalism is that some states are able to provide quality public education at substantially lower costs than do other states.
   (B) The states that spend the least amount of money on each student's education are concentrated in the Midwest and the Northeast.
   (C) The District of Columbia spends a higher percentage of its budget on education than do any of the states.
   (D) Mississippi spends less money per student than does any other state.
   (E) Some states spend less than half as much money per student as other states spend.

6. The full faith and credit clause would require all of the following EXCEPT
   (A) that a marriage performed in Las Vegas be valid in other states.
   (B) that a driver's license be valid in other states.
   (C) that a divorced parent pay child support even if his or her children reside in another state.
   (D) that a birth certificate issued by any state be recognized by other states.
   (E) that something against the law in one state be against the law in all other states.

7. What is the difference between block grants and categorical grants?
   (A) Block grants are given by the federal government to the states. Categorical grants are given by the states to the federal government.
   (B) States have greater flexibility over how to use block grants.
   (C) Block grants are always smaller than categorical grants.
   (D) States prefer categorical grants to block grants because they come with fewer strings attached.
   (E) Categorical grants are prohibited by the constitutional requirement that each state receives block grants according to its population.

8. A resident of New Mexico is threatened by an angry mob while visiting relatives in Texas. The local police must provide the New Mexico resident with the same protection it provides the Texas relatives. This is an example of
   (A) the Tenth Amendment.
   (B) the supremacy clause.
   (C) the rights of the accused.
   (D) the privileges and immunities clause.
   (E) dual federalism.

9. Which of the following statements accurately describe public participation in a federal system?
   I. Multilevel elections allow voters to influence more government bodies.
   II. Concerned citizens may join both state and national political groups to try to influence policymaking.
   III. People are more likely to participate in state-level politics because state governments are always more responsive.
   IV. Political parties offer voters more choice among candidates.
   (A) I only
   (B) III only
   (C) I and II only
   (D) I, II, and III only
   (E) II, III, and IV only

10. When there is a dispute about whether an issue falls under
the jurisdiction of the federal or a state government
    (A) the president decides and issues an executive order.
    (B) a court rules on the matter.
    (C) Congress votes to determine who has the authority.
    (D) the state legislatures must decide whether to overrule
the federal government.
    (E) the issue falls to the jurisdiction of local governments.

Free-Response Questions

1. The Federalist system in the United States was intended to divide power between the
federal government and state governments. Since the creation of the federal system,
however, power has tended to gravitate from the states to the federal government.
    a) Explain how TWO of the following have shifted power to the federal government.
       - *McCulloch v. Maryland*
       - Federal grants to states
       - The civil rights movement
    b) Explain how ONE of the following Supreme Court cases from the Rehnquist Court
reverted power back to the states from the federal government.
       - *United States v. Lopez*
       - *United States v. Morrison*
       - *Printz v. United States*

2. Several parts of the Constitution have important implications for federalism. Describe the
relevance of these for federalism.
    - Supremacy clause
    - Tenth Amendment
    - Necessary and proper, or "elastic," clause

3. Explain how federalism has affected federal/state relations in ONE of the following areas:
    - Environmental policy
    - International relations
    - Elections

Chapter 4: Civil Liberties and Public Policy

Multiple-Choice Questions

1. In which of the following cases did the Supreme Court enforce the use of the exclusionary rule in state trials?
   (A) *Near v. Minnesota*
   (B) *Miranda v. Arizona*
   (C) *Miller v. California*
   (D) *Mapp v. Ohio*
   (E) *Gregg v. Georgia*

2. *Roth v. United States* and *Texas v. Johnson* are Supreme Court cases that address the
   (A) Sixth Amendment rights of defendants.
   (B) definition of obscenity.
   (C) right of free speech.
   (D) definition of probable cause.
   (E) right to privacy.

3. Which of the following statements accurately describe(s) the exercise of religious freedom in public schools and universities?
   I. A nondenominational prayer required in schools is constitutional and does not violate the First Amendment.
   II. Schools must allow student religious groups to meet if other student groups are permitted to do so.
   III. Federal funding may be used by religious schools to construct buildings and acquire educational supplies.
   IV. States can forbid all types of prayer in school.
   V. The separation of church and state is clearly stated in the elastic clause of the Constitution.
   (A) I and IV only
   (B) II and V only
   (C) II and III only
   (D) II, III, and IV only
   (E) III, IV, and V only

4. Under reasonable time, place, and manner restrictions, all of the following are protected under the First Amendment EXCEPT
   (A) picketing.
   (B) libel.
   (C) flag burning.
   (D) political demonstrations.
   (E) criticizing government officials.

5. Approximately 90 percent of criminal cases in the United States
   (A) are cases in which the defendants' rights have been abused by law enforcement officials.
   (B) are appealed to the Supreme Court.
   (C) involve First Amendment rights.
   (D) are closed to the public during the trial.
   (E) are resolved by plea bargaining and do not go to trial.

6. The Supreme Court has regularly cited the due process clause of the Fourteenth Amendment to
   (A) extend the protection of the Bill of Rights to be binding on the states.
   (B) assert its power of judicial review.
   (C) allow the executive branch to infringe on civil liberties.
   (D) ensure the right to bear arms.
   (E) impose limitations on the exercise of defendants' rights.

7. In which of the following cases did the Supreme Court rule that the death penalty is not a form of cruel and unusual punishment?
   (A) *Gregg v. Georgia*
   (B) *Gideon v. Wainwright*
   (C) *Barron v. Baltimore*
   (D) *Engel v. Vitale*
   (E) *Gitlow v. New York*

8. Which of the following generalizations about the Supreme Court's stance on abortion is true?
   (A) In *Roe v. Wade*, the Supreme Court ruled that abortions infringe on the constitutional rights of the unborn.
   (B) The Supreme Court is usually conservative and therefore favors the right to life in all situations unless the mother's health is at risk.
   (C) The Supreme Court has always been distinctly pro-choice and has struck down state laws that attempted to interfere with the performing of abortions.
   (D) The Supreme Court permitted the right to an abortion in certain circumstances in *Roe v. Wade*, but it has since upheld several restrictions on abortions.
   (E) The Supreme Court has consistently upheld a woman's right to an abortion, even if she is in her third trimester or if she is a minor.

9. Which of the following statements about Americans' abortion attitudes is supported by Figure 4.1?
   (A) More Americans believe abortion should be legal under any circumstances than believe it should be illegal in all circumstances.
   (B) A majority of Americans consider themselves to be pro-life.
   (C) A majority of Americans believe that abortions should be legal only in the case of rape or incest.
   (D) A majority of Americans believe that some abortions should be legal.
   (E) A majority of Americans have strong opinions about abortion.

10. Under reasonable time, place, and manner restrictions, the right to assemble extends to groups in all of the following situations EXCEPT
    (A) a hate group such as the Ku Klux Klan holding a rally.
    (B) "right-to-life" advocates blocking access to abortion clinics.
    (C) an antiwar demonstration that threatens to harm the morale of American troops.
    (D) a religious group holding a public prayer meeting.
    (E) a labor union starting a picket line.

Free-Response Questions

1. Define *plea-bargaining*. Why do prosecutors agree to use this method rather than a full trial? Why do defendants agree to use this method rather than a full trial?

2. a) Identify and describe two provisions in the First Amendment which pertain to the issue of religion.
   Choose ONE of the Supreme Court cases listed below.
   Lemon v. Kurtzman
   Engel v. Vitale
   Employment Division v. Smith
   b) For the case you choose above, identify which part of the first Amendment pertains to this case.
   c) For the case you choose in (b), describe the ruling the Supreme Court made in this case.

Chapter 5: Civil Rights and Public Policy

Multiple-Choice Questions

1. The Civil Rights Act did all of the following EXCEPT
   - (A) create the Equal Employment Opportunity Commission.
   - (B) deny federal funding to businesses and schools that practiced racial discrimination.
   - (C) prevent racial discrimination in housing.
   - (D) prohibit racial discrimination in hotels, in restaurants, and on public transportation.
   - (E) outlaw job discrimination.

2. According to Figure 5.1, which of the following statements about school integration is accurate?
   - (A) By the early 1970s, most Southern schools had large numbers of Black students.
   - (B) School integration in the South increased dramatically immediately following the Supreme Court's decision in *Brown v. Board of Education*.
   - (C) In the 1950s, most Southern Black students attended schools without any White students. In the 1970s, most Southern Black students attended schools with some White students.
   - (D) By the 1970s, more than 80 percent of Southern schools were fully integrated.
   - (E) During the 1968–1969 school year, about 15 percent of American Blacks attended schools with White students.

3. Which of the following generalizations accurately describe the advancement of civil rights in the twentieth century?
   - I. The Fourteenth Amendment served as the foundation on which the Supreme Court based many of its decisions regarding civil rights.
   - II. The national government has opted to pursue civil rights at the expense of limited government.
   - III. The Supreme Court typically finds laws that racial classifications are unconstitutional.
   - IV. The Supreme Court has outlawed all laws that classify citizens by race, gender, sexual orientation, ethnicity, and disability.
   - (A) II only
   - (B) IV only
   - (C) I and II only
   - (D) III and IV only
   - (E) I, II, and III only

4. The Equal Rights Amendment has not become a part of the Constitution because
   - (A) it was not ratified by enough states.
   - (B) the Senate voted against it after the House had passed it.
   - (C) the women's rights movement has focused primarily on preserving protectionist laws.
   - (D) the Supreme Court found it unconstitutional.
   - (E) feminists decried it for neglecting to take a firm position on women's rights.

5. Opponents of affirmative action claim that it
   - (A) violates the First Amendment freedom of speech.
   - (B) fails to sufficiently compensate minorities for past discrimination.
   - (C) encourages reverse discrimination.
   - (D) excuses the federal government from having to enforce civil rights.
   - (E) favors certain minority groups over other minority groups.

6. Which of the following statements accurately describes the relationship between *Plessy v. Ferguson* and *Brown v. Board of Education*?
   - (A) *Plessy* reinforced the advancement of civil rights begun by the Supreme Court in *Brown*.
   - (B) The Supreme Court overturned its decision in *Plessy* with its *Brown* ruling.
   - (C) Both *Plessy* and *Brown* extended voting rights to disenfranchised African Americans in the South.
   - (D) Both *Plessy* and *Brown* made desegregation in public schools compulsory.
   - (E) The Supreme Court extended the precedent established in *Plessy* with its *Brown* decision.

7. Which of the following groups has focused on ensuring civil rights for Hispanic Americans and Latinos?
   - (A) MALDEF
   - (B) AIM
   - (C) NAACP
   - (D) EEOC
   - (E) ADA

8. Where is the guarantee of "equal protection of the laws" found?
   - (A) in the Bill of Rights
   - (B) in the Supreme Court's decision in *Korematsu v. United States*
   - (C) in the Supreme Court's decision in *Brown v. Board of Education*
   - (D) in the Fourteenth Amendment
   - (E) in the preamble to the Constitution

9. In which of the following cases did the Supreme Court first declare gender discrimination unconstitutional?
   - (A) *Faragher v. City of Boca Raton*
   - (B) *Reed v. Reed*
   - (C) *Stanton v. Stanton*
   - (D) *Craig v. Boren*
   - (E) *Dothard v. Rawlinson*

10. All of the following were methods used by Southern states to reduce the electoral voice of African Americans EXCEPT
    - (A) tests about the Constitution.
    - (B) white primaries.
    - (C) literacy tests.
    - (D) poll taxes.
    - (E) the Fifteenth Amendment.

Free-Response Questions

1. Civil rights has been an issue that has affected the United States since the founding of the nation. All branches of government have been involved in the civil rights arena.
   a) Do TWO of the following:
      - Identify and describe one Supreme Court case in the twentieth century that affected civil rights.
      - Identify and describe one law passed by Congress in the twentieth century that affected civil rights.
      - Identify and describe one presidential action in the twentieth century that affected civil rights.
   b) Identify ONE nongovernmental institution that has helped advance civil rights and describe the actions it has taken.

2. The civil rights movement of the 1950s and 1960s was successful in part due to strong individual leadership. Choose TWO of the following:
   - Earl Warren
   - Martin Luther King Jr.
   - Lyndon Johnson

   For each person you have chosen:
   a) Identify and describe one specific action through which this individual helped advance civil rights for Black Americans.
   b) Describe the opposition these people faced while trying to advance civil rights for African Americans.

Chapter 6: Public Opinion and Political Action

Multiple-Choice Questions

1. Reapportionment of seats in the House of Representatives occurs
   (A) every four years after a presidential election.
   (B) when the minority party wins a majority in the House.
   (C) after every four congressional election cycles.
   (D) every 10 years as a result of the census.
   (E) when the president requests it through an executive order.

2. Which of the following statements is supported by the evidence presented in "A Generation of Change: Attitudes Toward Gays and Lesbians by Political Ideology"?
   (A) Since 1988, attitudes toward gays and lesbians have remained fairly constant.
   (B) Since 1988, liberals and conservatives have grown more positive about gays and lesbians.
   (C) Since 1988, liberals have grown more positive about gays and lesbians, while the attitudes of conservatives have grown more negative.
   (D) Since 1988, liberals have grown more positive about gays and lesbians, while the attitudes of conservatives have remained fairly constant.
   (E) Since 1988, the gap between liberals and conservatives in opinions about gays and lesbians has increased sharply.

3. All of the following influence the formation of political beliefs EXCEPT
   (A) schooling.
   (B) the family.
   (C) religion.
   (D) the mass media.
   (E) the month in which you were born.

4. Recent immigrants to the United States have tended to come from
   (A) Central America and Asia.
   (B) southern and eastern Europe.
   (C) northern and western Europe.
   (D) the former Soviet republics.
   (E) the Middle East and Scandinavia.

5. How are older Americans different from younger Americans?
   I. Older Americans are more likely to vote.
   II. Older Americans are more conservative.
   III. Older Americans are more supportive of investing Social Security funds in the stock market.
   IV. Older Americans are more likely to favor spending money on national defense.
   (A) III only
   (B) I and II only

   (C) I, II, and III only
   (D) II, III, and IV only
   (E) I, II, and IV only

6. Which of the following are liberals most likely to endorse?
   (A) military intervention
   (B) tax cuts
   (C) free-market solutions to public policy problems
   (D) increased spending on the poor
   (E) increased defense spending

7. According to recent research by Jacobs and Shapiro, politicians use public opinion polls to
   (A) decide whether to change party affiliation.
   (B) shape their platform for the next election.
   (C) determine how to craft their policy proposals so that they will win public support.
   (D) know if they should run for re-election.
   (E) solicit campaign contributions.

8. According to the prediction of the gender gap, women are more likely to
   (A) vote for a Democratic candidate.
   (B) support military spending.
   (C) vote for an Independent candidate.
   (D) disapprove of increased social spending.
   (E) vote for a Republican candidate.

9. The U.S. is expected to have a minority majority population by 2050. What does this mean?
   (A) Hispanic Americans will outnumber African Americans.
   (B) Female conservatives will outnumber male conservatives.
   (C) Asian Americans will outnumber Hispanic Americans.
   (D) Voters under the age of 30 will outnumber senior citizens.
   (E) The minority populations will outnumber the Caucasian population.

10. Which of the following statements is a reason why young Americans are typically the least politically active?
   (A) They have little political experience.
   (B) They spend too much time watching television news.
   (C) They have been socialized through their formal education to distrust the government.
   (D) They pay higher taxes than older Americans, making them especially cynical.
   (E) Young voters are more mobile than older voters, but most states require that citizens live at the same address for a full year before they are allowed to participate.

Free-Response Questions

1. Political socialization is a major process for developing public opinions.
   a) Define political socialization.
   b) Explain how two of the following agents affect political socialization.
      - Mass media
      - School
      - Religion
   c) Explain why the family is considered to have the greatest influence on political socialization.

2. Refer to Figure 6.2. After reviewing the maps:
   a) Describe one demographic change that has taken place in the United States between 1940 and 2000.
   b) Explain one cause of the shift you described in (a).
   c) Describe one political ramification of the shift you described in (b).

Chapter 7: The Mass Media and the Political Agenda

Multiple-Choice Questions

1. Which of the following is a consequence of investigative journalism?
   (A) More stringent requirements for becoming a journalist
   (B) Increased news coverage of scandals
   (C) A better informed citizenry
   (D) The increased reliance of television news
   (E) A more in-depth understanding of political issues by typical Americans

2. Who is most likely to receive media coverage?
   (A) Congress
   (B) The House of Representatives
   (C) The Senate
   (D) The president
   (E) The Supreme Court

3. Which of the following statements about journalists is accurate?
   (A) Journalists consider themselves more liberal than does the general public.
   (B) Journalists have a liberal bias in their coverage of politics.
   (C) Journalists have a conservative bias in their coverage of politics.
   (D) Journalists have a Democratic bias in their coverage of politics.
   (E) Journalists have a Republican bias in their coverage of politics.

4. Which of the following statements is supported by the table accompanying the feature, "Young People and Politics: How the Under-30 Crowd Learns from Different Media Sources Compared to Older Americans"?
   (A) In 2007, young Americans were more likely to regularly learn something about the presidential campaign from the Internet than from any other source.
   (B) In 2007, older Americans were more informed about the presidential campaign than were younger Americans.
   (C) In 2007, younger Americans were more informed about the presidential campaign than were older Americans.
   (D) In 2007, younger Americans learned more about the presidential campaign from the cable news networks than from the nightly network news.
   (E) In 2007, 40 percent of older Americans learned all of their information about the presidential campaign from the nightly network news.

5. Which of the following statements are true about the media's agenda-setting effect?
   I. The agenda-setting effect influences the criteria by which citizens evaluate political leaders.
   II. The agenda-setting effect is particularly strong among uninformed citizens.

III. The agenda-setting effect is the media's direct impact on how Americans vote.
   IV. The agenda-setting effect rewards investigative journalism.
   (A) I and II only
   (B) III and IV only
   (C) I, II, and III only
   (D) I, III, and IV only
   (E) II, III and IV only

6. What is one foreseeable political consequence of narrowcasting?
   (A) The print media will appeal to a greater percentage of the public.
   (B) Politicians will have more freedom to act according to their own agenda because they will be able to avoid the public eye.
   (C) Journalists will be forced to concentrate more on political issues than on politicians.
   (D) The gap between the political elite and the politically uninformed majority will increase.
   (E) The public will become more informed about politics.

7. What is the primary objective of the American media?
   (A) Enriching democracy
   (B) Informing the public
   (C) Accurately depicting public policy debates
   (D) Providing a means for the government to communicate with the people
   (E) Making a profit

8. A journalist who regularly reports on predictions about interest rates would probably be on which of the following beats?
   (A) White House
   (B) Senate Appropriations Committee
   (C) Department of the Interior
   (D) Congress
   (E) Federal Reserve Board

9. Which of the following statements about sound bites is accurate?
   (A) The news media have had to narrow their scope of coverage because they have only a limited amount of material to broadcast.
   (B) The news media have tended to report longer and longer sound bites because they decrease the amount of time they must spend researching and reporting stories.
   (C) The complexity of most sound bites is not fully understood by the general public.
   (D) The media's tendency to focus on sound bites allows politicians to avoid an in-depth discussion of issues.
   (E) Politicians avoid using sound bites because it makes them sound trite.

10. If a political candidate wanted to deliver his or her message to the most politically informed Americans in the electorate, through which medium would he or she be most likely to reach them?
    (A) Television
    (B) Radio
    (C) Mass mailings
    (D) Newspapers
    (E) Internet

Free-Response Questions

1. In his role as leader, the president communicates with the public on many occasions.
    a) Explain how the president uses the strategy of "going public" to try to achieve his goals.
    b) Explain how three of the following might help the president "go public":
       • Press conferences
       • The State of the Union address
       • Trial balloons
       • Sound bites
    c) Explain why the President may prefer to use one of the following methods to "go public" more than the others:
       • Press conferences
       • The State of the Union address
       • Trial balloons
       • Sound bites

2. In the past 20 years, the media in the United States has undergone a transformation from "broadcasting" to "narrowcasting."
    a) Explain the difference between broadcasting and narrowcasting.
    b) Describe how narrowcasting effects bias in the media.
    c) Describe how narrowcasting can affect the media's ability to influence public opinion.

Chapter 8: Political Parties

Multiple-Choice Questions

1. According to Figure 8.3, members of which group are most likely to be Democrats?
   (A) Jews
   (B) White Catholics
   (C) White Evangelicals
   (D) Women
   (E) Those under 30 years old

2. Which of the following best explains why the United States has a two-party system?
   (A) The Constitution mandates a two-party system.
   (B) Federal laws mandate a two-party system.
   (C) In every state except California, state laws mandate a two-party system.
   (D) Seats in Congress are awarded on a winner-take-all basis.
   (E) Seats in Congress are awarded according to the principles of proportional representation.

3. Which of the following statements are generally true of third parties?
   I. Third-party officeholders threaten the political standing of the United States in the eyes of other nations.
   II. Third parties expand the political agenda.
   III. Third parties rarely gain enough support in the electorate to win.
   IV. Third-party success may indicate popular discontent.
   (A) I only
   (B) III only
   (C) II and III only
   (D) I and IV only
   (E) II, III, and IV only

4. Political parties play an important role in democracy because they
   (A) guarantee voters radically different choices of policy outcomes.
   (B) offer politicians unique identities.
   (C) connect the public with policymaking institutions.
   (D) contribute to a centralized federal government.
   (E) control each of the three branches of government.

5. Who is most likely to engage in ticket splitting?
   (A) Nonvoters
   (B) Primary election voters
   (C) Democrats
   (D) Republicans
   (E) Independents

6. The process that parties use to nominate their candidate for the presidency is called
   (A) a critical election.
   (B) a national convention.
   (C) an open primary.
   (D) a closed primary.
   (E) a national committee.

7. Which of the following can be seen as an advantage of divided government?
   (A) Divided government creates clear lines of accountability for policy failures and successes
   (B) Political parties are better able to enact their policy platforms
   (C) Divided government encourages compromise between the parties
   (D) The president maintains the upper hand in negotiations with Congress
   (E) Increased voter turnout

8. When were local party organizations strongest?
   (A) When party machines controlled large cities
   (B) During the New Deal Coalition
   (C) During a realignment
   (D) During a dealignment
   (E) Immediately after a presidential election

9. Which of the following statements accurately describe critical elections?
   I. Critical elections are often associated with significant political or social events.
   II. After a critical election, the previously existing minority party usually collapses and a new party forms.
   III. A critical election ensures that the previously existing majority party will maintain its position of power.
   IV. Critical elections usually signal the beginning of a new political era.
   (A) II only
   (B) IV only
   (C) I and IV only
   (D) II and III only
   (E) I, II, and IV only

10. All of the following were part of the New Deal Coalition EXCEPT
    (A) urbanites.
    (B) bankers.
    (C) labor unions.
    (D) Southerners.
    (E) Jews.

Free-Response Questions

1. Please refer to Table 8.1. According to the chart, the Republican Party has had fewer members than the Democratic Party in every election since 1952. Yet, Republicans have been able to win the presidential election in 9 out of 14 elections. Explain THREE reasons why Republicans are able to win the presidency in spite of having fewer members than the Democratic Party.

2. Political parties are linkage institutions in American politics, helping convert public preferences into governmental action.
   a) Describe THREE ways in which parties serve as linkage institutions.
   b) Explain one reason political parties have been weakening since the 1960s.

Chapter 9: Nominations and Campaigns

Multiple-Choice Questions

1. The Federal Election Campaign Act established all of the following EXCEPT
   (A) a fund to partially fund presidential campaigns.
   (B) rules for the disclosure of all campaign financing and spending information.
   (C) limits on personal contributions to presidential and congressional candidates.
   (D) a fund for public donations to congressional campaigns.
   (E) the Federal Election Commission to regulate campaign financing.

2. Which of the following conclusions may be drawn from the data in Table 9.1?
   (A) Labor groups did not give a high percentage of their contributions to Republicans.
   (B) Single-issue groups divided their contributions equally between the two parties.
   (C) Overall, Republicans received more campaign contributions than did Democrats.
   (D) Microsoft made the biggest contribution to the Republican Party.
   (E) All of the business groups listed were more supportive of Republicans, whereas all of the labor groups listed were more supportive of Democrats.

3. Which state's presidential primary traditionally receives the most media coverage?
   (A) Florida
   (B) Ohio
   (C) Iowa
   (D) Pennsylvania
   (E) New Hampshire

4. All of the following are criticisms raised against the nomination system EXCEPT
   (A) few citizens are permitted to participate in the nomination process.
   (B) too much weight is placed on early primaries in unrepresentative states.
   (C) the campaign process is too long.
   (D) it discourages many qualified politicians from running.
   (E) the media have too much power to shape the presidential campaigns.

5. Which of the following statements is true concerning the use of PACs in political campaigns?
   (A) The Constitution requires businesses to finance campaigns.
   (B) Businesses can channel an unlimited amount of money through a PAC to a given candidate.
   (C) The president officially established PACs in a 1974 executive order.

   (D) PACs must be registered with and monitored by the FEC.
   (E) The Supreme Court has struck down all efforts to regulate campaign finance.

6. In addition to officially nominating a party's candidate for the presidency, national conventions perform which of the following tasks?
   (A) Select the new chairs of the party's national committee
   (B) Raise funds for the general election
   (C) Determine the party's platform
   (D) Elect delegates to the next convention
   (E) Organize new party coalitions in Congress

7. Primaries and caucuses are unrepresentative of the electorate's preferences because
   (A) they occur in only a few states.
   (B) voters in primary elections are usually less politically knowledgeable than the majority.
   (C) only college graduates are allowed to vote in them.
   (D) they take place early, before voters have a chance to learn about the candidates.
   (E) voters in primary elections are usually older and more affluent than the majority.

8. Which of the following factors contributes most to the cost of a presidential campaign?
   (A) Direct-mail campaigns
   (B) Television advertising
   (C) Hiring a campaign coordinator
   (D) Soliciting donations via the Internet
   (E) Printing posters and campaign paraphernalia

9. Presidential campaigns in the United States differ most from most European campaigns in which of the following ways?
   (A) American campaigns cost candidates less in personal contributions.
   (B) Candidates in other countries are not allowed to appear on television.
   (C) Campaigns in the United States are geared toward a general election.
   (D) American campaigns are much longer than other campaigns.
   (E) Candidates in the United States are selected by party elites.

10. Media coverage of campaigns tend to focus on
    (A) foreign and military policy.
    (B) social and environmental policy.
    (C) candidate biographies and background.
    (D) campaign strategies and the horse race.
    (E) accusations of media bias and wrongdoing.

Free-Response Questions

1. The United States holds some of the longest and most expensive political campaigns in the world. To finance their campaigns, candidates rely heavily on contributions from the following:
   - PACs
   - Soft money
   - Matching funds
   - Individual contributions
     a) Define each of the above sources of campaign contributions.
     b) Choose two of these sources and describe the positive impact that each has on political campaigns.
     c) Choose two of these sources and describe the negative impact that each has on political campaigns.
     d) Choose two of these sources and describe TWO legal restrictions that have been placed on them.

2. Please refer to Figure 9.3.
   a) Why do Iowa and New Hampshire receive more media attention than any other state?
   b) How could the system of nominating candidates be changed to decrease the importance of Iowa and New Hampshire?
   c) What obstacles keep the changes from taking place that you mentioned in (b)?

Chapter 10: Elections and Voting Behavior

Multiple-Choice Questions

1. The electoral votes of most states are allocated by which of the following methods?
   (A) Each party's candidate receives electoral votes based on his or her percentage of the state's popular vote.
   (B) Each elector chooses the candidate whom he or she feels is best suited to represent the needs of the state.
   (C) The winner of the popular election in the state receives 75 percent of the state's electoral votes and the loser receives 25 percent.
   (D) All of the state's electors cast their votes for whichever candidate won the state's popular vote.
   (E) The loser in the popular election receives one electoral vote and the winner receives the rest of the state's electoral votes.

2. Which of the following groups usually has the highest voter turnout in a presidential election?
   (A) Women
   (B) People aged 25 to 44
   (C) Members of minority groups
   (D) Single people
   (E) People with a college education

3. Policy voting requires all of the following conditions EXCEPT
   (A) the person must be familiar with each candidate's policy positions.
   (B) the person must have developed a pattern of policy voting over several elections.
   (C) the person must know his or her own position on policy issues.
   (D) the person must vote for the candidate whose policy positions coincide with her or her own preferences.
   (E) the person must be able to determine policy differences among the candidates.

4. Suffrage is most likely to be denied to a citizen who is
   (A) African American.
   (B) disabled.
   (C) 18 years old.
   (D) a convicted felon.
   (E) a pauper.

5. According to Figure 10.1, which of the following most accurately describes states won by the Democratic presidential candidate in the 2004 presidential election?
   (A) The Mountain West and the South
   (B) The West Coast and the Northeast
   (C) The Frostbelt and the Deep South
   (D) The Mountain West and parts of the Midwest
   (E) The Pacific Northwest and the Deep South

6. Which of the following statements help to explain why voter turnout is lower in the United States than in most other democracies?
   I. Citizens in other democracies vote more often and, therefore, have developed stronger voting habits.
   II. Citizens in most other democracies are required by law to vote.
   III. Citizens in most other democracies are not required to register to vote
   IV. Citizens in other democracies face starker differences between the viable political parties.
   (A) I and II only
   (B) I and III only
   (C) II and III only
   (D) II and IV only
   (E) III and IV only

7. What is political efficacy?
   (A) The chance that you will cast the deciding vote in an election
   (B) The belief that one vote can make a difference
   (C) The distance between your preferred policy position and the position of the nearest candidate
   (D) The belief that good citizens should vote
   (E) Any reason a voter gives for failing to vote

8. Which of the following statements about young voters is accurate?
   (A) Young voters are more likely to support third-party candidates.
   (B) Young citizens are more likely to vote than older citizens.
   (C) Young voters typically vote through the mail.
   (D) Young citizens do not need to register to vote if they live with at least one parent.
   (E) Young voters typically vote for president but do not vote for Congress.

9. The Motor Voter Act was intended to
   (A) expand suffrage to minorities.
   (B) lower the voting age.
   (C) redistribute states' electoral votes.
   (D) increase voter registration.
   (E) raise the voting age.

10. How are Oregon's elections different from most other elections in the United States?
    (A) All Oregon elections are nonpartisan.
    (B) All Oregon elections are conducted through the mail.
    (C) Oregon revokes the driver's licenses of nonvoters.
    (D) Oregon allows citizens to vote at 16 years old.
    (E) Election Day in Oregon is a state holiday and only emergency or essential employees are allowed to work.

Free-Response Questions

1. Table 10.2 illustrates how different groups in the United States voted in the 1960 and 2004 elections. The percentages are of the people in each group who voted, *not* of the total number of people in that group.
   a) Describe the change that has occurred in attendance to religious services and the party for which a person is more likely to vote.
   b) Explain ONE reason this change has occurred.
   c) Describe the change that has occurred in the way Catholics vote.
   d) Explain ONE reason for this change. (Note: Both Kennedy and Kerry were Catholics; both Nixon and Bush were Protestants.)

2. The Electoral College, not the voters, elects the President in the United States.
   a) Describe ONE way in which the Electoral College system affects the way Presidential candidates campaign, and give an example.
   b) Describe ONE way in which the Electoral College is undemocratic, and give an example.
   c) Explain ONE reason the Electoral College has not been abolished.

Chapter 11: Interest Groups

Multiple-Choice Questions

1. What do elite theorists believe about the influence of interest groups?
   (A) Each interest group has equal access to the government.
   (B) Interest groups counterbalance each other, so that no one group becomes too powerful.
   (C) Interest groups with large memberships are always more influential than those with smaller memberships.
   (D) Interest groups help create a more democratic government.
   (E) A few wealthy groups have the most influence.

2. Smaller interest groups often meet with more success because
   (A) they have highly developed methods of fundraising.
   (B) their members have a great incentive to actively pursue their collective good.
   (C) they make large campaign contributions.
   (D) they have more resources with which to mobilize the public.
   (E) they pursue only less politicized issues.

3. Citizens concerned about a proposal to redistribute federal funding to public schools would form which of the following groups?
   (A) Public interest group
   (B) Economic interest group
   (C) Consumer interest group
   (D) Elite interest group
   (E) Class action group

4. Lawmakers often rely on lobbyists for all of the following reasons EXCEPT
   (A) to come up with new policy ideas that they can introduce in Congress.
   (B) for advice on strategies to advance or prevent a piece of legislation.
   (C) for money that can legally supplement a lawmaker's salary.
   (D) to encourage group members to vote for them during re-election.
   (E) for expertise on a certain issue.

5. Iron triangles are composed of
   (A) a cabinet department, a legislative committee, and a federal judge.
   (B) a corporate board, an interest group, and the Speaker of the House.
   (C) a PAC, an interest group, and a congressional candidate.
   (D) an interest group, a legislative committee, and a federal agency.
   (E) a local civic group, a state legislator, and a federal department.

6. Proponents of the pluralist theory argue that power is nearly evenly distributed among interest groups because
   (A) the public participates equally in different types of interest groups.
   (B) all interest groups receive the same amount of federal funds.
   (C) each policy area is assigned a limited number of related interest groups.
   (D) interest groups each get the same attention from politicians.
   (E) competition prevents any one group from becoming more influential.

7. Which of the following statements accurately describe methods interest groups employ to influence policymaking?
   I. Class action lawsuits allow interest groups to sue in the name of a larger section of the public.
   II. Interest groups meet with judges about cases that affect their policy area.
   III. Interest groups make more PAC contributions to incumbents rather than challengers.
   IV. Lobbyists provide policy expertise to lawmakers.
   V. Interest groups pay committee members to introduce favorable legislation.
   (A) III only
   (B) I and IV only
   (C) II and V only
   (D) I, III, and IV only
   (E) II, IV, and V only

8. According to the map included in the feature titled, "My State: Labor Union Membership as Percentage of State Workforce," which state has the higher percentage of union members?
   (A) Wisconsin
   (B) New York
   (C) Ohio
   (D) Kentucky
   (E) There is not enough information presented in this map to answer the question.

9. Interest groups differ from political parties in which of the following ways?
   (A) Interest groups link the public to the political process.
   (B) Interest groups pursue general policy goals in the political arena.
   (C) Interest groups try to shape specific policy goals.
   (D) Interest groups are not allowed to play any part in political campaigns.
   (E) Interest groups unite politicians with the same political ideology.

10. Which of the following causes would most likely be taken up by a single-issue group?
    (A) Abortion
    (B) Corporate taxation
    (C) International trade
    (D) Workers' rights
    (E) Social justice

Free-Response Questions

1. Interest groups play an important role in the American political system, helping the concerns of the electorate with policymakers. Choose ONE interest group from the following list:
   - National Association for the Advancement of Colored People (NAACP)
   - Health Insurance Association of America (HIAA)
   - National Rifle Association (NRA)
   - National Education Association (NEA)

   For the group you selected, complete the following tasks:
   a) Identify a government institution to which this group would appeal to pursue its policy interests.
   b) Identify two resources that the group has at its disposal and explain how it uses these resources to influence policymaking.

2. The United States has a pluralistic governmental system, in which people have multiple points of access to the government. Interest groups serve an important function, connecting citizens with their government.
   a) Differentiate between an interest group and a political party.
   b) Choose TWO topics from the following list and identify a specific interest group that is concerned with this issue.
      - Environmental interests
      - Economic interests
      - Equality interests
      - Public interests
   c) Choose ONE of the groups you picked in (b) and describe one method it has used to influence policymaking.

Chapter 12: Congress

Multiple-Choice Questions

1. Conference committees
   (A) register bills to be introduced on the floor and schedule debate.
   (B) handle proposed legislation that deals with more than one area of policy.
   (C) work out compromises between House and Senate versions of bills.
   (D) combine members of both the House and Senate to consider overlapping policy areas.
   (E) educate the public about the activities of Congress.

2. Incumbents have all of the following advantages over their challengers EXCEPT
   (A) incumbents spend more money than do challengers.
   (B) incumbents can brag about federal spending projects in their districts.
   (C) incumbents can increase visibility among their constituents by using the franking privilege.
   (D) incumbents provide casework for their constituents.
   (E) challengers have a clean political record, and incumbents do not.

3. In which of the following ways does Congress conduct legislative oversight?
   I. Appointing conference committees to investigate the actions of the bureaucracy
   II. Determining the federal budget
   III. Holding hearings to question agency officials
   IV. Inspecting government offices
   (A) I and III only
   (B) II and III only
   (C) III and IV only
   (D) I, II, and III only
   (E) I, III, and IV only

4. Which of the following statements accurately describe legislative committees?
   I. Committees are in session only when preparing bills to be introduced onto the floor.
   II. Junior members of Congress have few opportunities to sit on committees.
   III. The Speaker of the House has a great deal of influence in appointing committee chairs.
   IV. Conference committees are composed of senators whose task is to amend bills that are in danger of being killed in Congress.
   (A) III only
   (B) I and III only
   (C) II and III only
   (D) I, II, and IV only
   (E) I, III, and V only

5. A senator can often prevent the Senate from voting on the bill being debated on the Senate floor by
   (A) conducting oversight.
   (B) filibustering.
   (C) introducing another bill.
   (D) holding hearings.
   (E) logrolling.

6. Which of the following claims can be made from an examination of Figure 12.1?
   I. Since 1958, re-election rates for Senate have typically been higher than re-election rates for the House.
   II. In every year since 1958, a majority of House incumbents have been reelected.
   III. In every year since 1958, a majority of Senate incumbents have been reelected.
   IV. Since 1958, re-election rates for House incumbents have frequently been higher than 90 percent.
   (A) I and II only
   (B) I and IV only
   (C) II and IV only
   (D) II, III, and IV only
   (E) I, I, III, and IV

7. On a bill with high visibility, members of Congress are most likely to vote
   (A) along party lines.
   (B) according to their personal ideology.
   (C) in a presidential coalition.
   (D) in keeping with the needs of their constituency.
   (E) according to the pressures of lobbyists.

8. After a House committee reviews a bill and writes its report, the bill typically goes to the
   (A) Senate.
   (B) House appropriate subcommittee.
   (C) president.
   (D) House floor for debate.
   (E) House Rules Committee.

9. Which of the following is a difference between the House and Senate?
   (A) Power is more decentralized in the Senate.
   (B) The filibuster is more common in the House than in the Senate.
   (C) The Senate allows twice as much time for debate on a bill than does the House.
   (D) Members of the House have large constituencies.
   (E) The legislative process starts in the House; the Senate can only debate bills once the House has passed them.

10. Which of the following statements about Congressional parties is accurate?
   (A) The majority party controls all of the seats on a majority of the committees.
   (B) Both political parties became more became more extreme and more homogenous.
   (C) Both political parties moderated, taking policy positions closer to the median voter.
   (D) The House operates on a nonpartisan basis while the Senate is heavily partisan.
   (E) Political parties are much weaker and disjointed than they were 30 years ago.

Free-Response Questions

1. Please refer to Figure 12.1.
    a) Describe TWO trends from the graph.
    b) Choosing ONE of the trends you identified in part (a), explain TWO reasons for this trend.
    c) Choosing the other trend you identified in part (a), explain TWO reasons for this trend.

2. Congress is organized in such a way that its leaders have important roles.
    a) Describe how the Speaker of the House of Representatives is selected and describe that position's power.
    b) Discuss how the president of the Senate is selected and describe that position's power.
    c) Explain how the powers of the two positions reflect the differences in the two houses of Congress.
    d) Identify another leader, other than the Speaker of the House or President of the Senate, and describe that position's power.

Chapter 13: The Presidency

Multiple-Choice Questions

1. A bill that is vetoed by the president
   (A) goes to a conference committee for revision.
   (B) must be rewritten by the representative who authored it.
   (C) will never become law.
   (D) goes to a federal court for approval of the veto.
   (E) can become law if Congress overrides the veto.

2. Which of the following statements accurately describe a step in the process of removing a president from office?
   I. The accused president is tried by the Senate.
   II. The chief justice of the Supreme Court decides if the president is guilty of the crime with which he is charged.
   III. The House of Representatives votes to impeach the president.
   IV. A two-thirds vote in the Senate is required to remove the president from office.
   V. A conference committee holds hearings to consider public opinion of the president's performance.
   (A) I and II only
   (B) I and IV only
   (C) I, III, and IV only
   (D) II, III, and V only
   (E) III, IV, and V only

3. The War Powers Resolution checks the president's power by
   (A) prohibiting him from issuing executive agreements that engage the country in war.
   (B) increasing the power of Congress to control the military budget.
   (C) preventing him from sending troops into crisis situations without congressional approval.
   (D) mandating that Congress approve the president's decision to use weapons of mass destruction.
   (E) requiring troops to be withdrawn in 60 days unless Congress declares war or issues an extension.

4. Presidents attempt to influence policymaking in all of the following ways EXCEPT by
   (A) appealing directly to the public for support.
   (B) proposing legislation in congressional committees.
   (C) offering favors such as backing during re-election.
   (D) exchanging support for policies with representatives.
   (E) building coalitions among party members.

5. Which of the following tasks falls to the vice president?
   (A) Leading Cabinet meetings
   (B) Presiding over the Senate
   (C) Commanding the military
   (D) Determining the federal budget
   (E) Overseeing congressional elections

6. Which of the following factors is the greatest influence on a citizen's approval of the president?
   (A) The citizen's party affiliation
   (B) The president's success in working with Congress
   (C) The citizen's state of residence
   (D) The president's success in diplomacy
   (E) The president's understanding of the Constitution

7. According to Figure 13.4, which of the following presidential pairs had similar average approval ratings?
   (A) Clinton and Carter
   (B) George H. W. Bush and Reagan
   (C) Kennedy and Johnson
   (D) George W. Bush and Nixon
   (E) Kennedy and Reagan

8. Which of the following statements about the presidential veto is true?
   (A) Presidents frequently veto legislation.
   (B) Congress rarely overrides a veto.
   (C) The pocket veto has been declared unconstitutional by the Supreme Court.
   (D) Presidents can use a line-item veto to reject only part of a bill.
   (E) Presidents are more likely to veto Supreme Court decisions than congressional legislation.

9. All of the following are powers of the president EXCEPT
   (A) conducting diplomatic relations.
   (B) granting pardons.
   (C) dismissing Supreme Court justices.
   (D) negotiating treaties.
   (E) appointing top-level administrators to serve in the bureaucracy.

10. As set forth in the Constitution, the order of presidential succession is the vice president, then the
    (A) Speaker of the House.
    (B) secretary of state.
    (C) Senate majority leader.
    (D) attorney general.
    (E) chief justice of the Supreme Court.

Free-Response Questions

1. The president has to make instant decisions regarding war making.
   a) Identify a military power of the legislative branch and a military power of the executive branch.
   b) Describe how the Wars Powers Resolution (1973) tried to curtail the President's power in foreign affairs.
   c) Describe one action taken by a president involving foreign affairs since the passage of the Wars Powers Resolution and explain Congress's reaction to it.

2. Along with the roles assigned to the president by the Constitution, the president also serves as leader of his political party.
   a) Explain TWO ways the president's role as party leader can make him a more effective legislative leader.
   b) Explain TWO reasons presidents do not exercise more authority over members of Congress.

Chapter 14: The Congress, the President, and the Budget: The Politics of Taxing and Spending

Multiple-Choice Questions

1. A progressive income tax system requires the wealthiest people to
   (A) pay taxes according to how much they consume.
   (B) pay the same amount in taxes as people in other income brackets.
   (C) pay taxes at the same rate as people in other income brackets.
   (D) pay taxes at a higher rate than people in other income brackets.
   (E) pay taxes at a slightly lower rate than people in the middle income bracket.

2. Which of the following institutions is responsible for compiling the president's budget proposal?
   (A) Department of the Treasury
   (B) Congressional Budget Office
   (C) Senate Appropriations Committee
   (D) Office of Management and Budget
   (E) Council of Economic Advisers

3. Which of the following are accurate statements about the federal debt?
   I. The rising cost of public education has contributed significantly to the federal debt.
   II. The debt shifts the cost of current policies onto the shoulders of future generations.
   III. President Reagan's major tax cuts in the 1980s caused the national debt to grow to an unprecedented size.
   IV. The government will erase the national debt as soon as it succeeds in balancing the fiscal budget.
   (A) II only
   (B) IV only
   (C) I and II only
   (D) II and III only
   (E) I, III, and IV only

4. Which of the following is considered an uncontrollable expenditure?
   (A) National security
   (B) Federal subsidies for public education
   (C) Entitlement programs
   (D) Highway systems
   (E) Energy research

5. All of the following are steps in the budgetary process EXCEPT
   (A) the Congressional Budget Office works closely with the president to finalize the budget that he will propose to Congress.
   (B) the House Ways and Means Committee and the Senate Finance Committee work together to write the tax codes.
   (C) the Office of Management and Budget reviews and assesses the budget proposals submitted by each agency.
   (D) Congress passes a budget resolution to set a cap on expenditures for the fiscal year.
   (E) the Appropriations Committee decides how to divide federal resources among the departments and agencies.

6. The federal government borrows money from citizens through
   (A) income taxes.
   (B) bonds.
   (C) Social Security.
   (D) authorization bills.
   (E) entitlement programs.

7. Which of the following programs account for the largest chunk of the federal budget?
   (A) Bridges and highways
   (B) Welfare and unemployment
   (C) Law enforcement and corrections
   (D) Social Security and Medicare
   (E) Foreign aid and espionage

8. The government receives most of its revenues from
   (A) excise taxes.
   (B) social income taxes.
   (C) personal income taxes.
   (D) public bonds.
   (E) sales taxes.

9. Examine Figure 14.1 to determine which of the following statements can accurately be made from the information provided in the graph.
   I. The federal government is projected to spend about $2.9 trillion in 2010.
   II. The two biggest revenue sources for the federal government are individual income taxes and social insurance taxes and contributions.
   III. In 1998, corporate income taxes contributed about $1 trillion in federal revenue.
   IV. In 2006, individual income taxes contributed about $1 trillion in federal revenue.
   (A) I only
   (B) II and IV only
   (C) I, II, and IV only
   (D) II, III, and IV only
   (E) I, II, III, and IV

10. Which of the following is a tax expenditure?
    (A) The Social Security trust fund
    (B) Deductions for interest paid on home mortgages
    (C) Social insurance taxes
    (D) The interstate highway system
    (E) The war in Iraq

Free-Response Questions

1. Since the 1970s, the national debt has growth from $1 trillion to over $9 trillion. Two factors that have contributed to this growth are incrementalism and "uncontrollable" expenditures.
   a) Define incrementalism and "uncontrollable" expenditures.
   b) Describe how each contribute to the increasing national debt of the past 40 years.
   c) Describe one other factor that has contributed to the growing national debt of the past 40 years.

2. The president and the Congress are both very important in the passage of the federal budget each year.
   a) Explain the significance of the House Ways and Means Committee on the budget.
   b) Explain the significance of the Office of Management and Budget on the budget.
   c) Explain the significance of the Congressional Budget Office on the budget.

Chapter 15: The Federal Bureaucracy

Multiple-Choice Questions

1. Which of the following statements accurately describes the size of the federal bureaucracy?
   (A) Homeland Security is the largest department in the bureaucracy.
   (B) The State Department is the largest department in the bureaucracy.
   (C) The size of the federal bureaucracy has remained relatively stable in recent years.
   (D) The size of the federal bureaucracy has doubled since the 9/11 terrorist attacks.
   (E) The percentage of the workforce employed by the federal government has increased slightly in recent years.

2. Most federal bureaucrats are hired in which of the following ways?
   (A) They are awarded positions by the political party in power.
   (B) They take an examination to prove their qualifications.
   (C) They are appointed to a position by the president.
   (D) They work in the legislative branch and then move to the bureaucracy.
   (E) They get their positions in exchange for campaign contributions.

3. Which of the following best describes the role of the bureaucracy?
   (A) To implement policies
   (B) To maintain order
   (C) To promote the general welfare
   (D) To secure the blessings of liberty to ourselves and our posterity
   (E) To ensure domestic tranquility

4. According to Table 15.1, which federal bureaucracy has the most civilian employees?
   (A) Department of Defense
   (B) Veterans Affairs
   (C) The armed forces
   (D) Department of Homeland Security
   (E) U.S. Postal Service

5. Which of the following reasons accurately describe why it may be difficult for the bureaucracy to implement laws passed by Congress?
   I. Laws are often written in terms of broad policy goals.
   II. Laws are often unclear about the details of a policy.
   III. Congress frequently fails to give the bureaucracy enough money to effectively implement policies.
   IV. Bureaucracies often lack the necessary authority necessary to meet their responsibilities.
   (A) I and II only
   (B) II and IV only

(C) I, II, and IV only
(D) II, III and IV only
(E) I, II, III and IV

6. Which of the following is a government corporation?
   (A) The Department of the Interior
   (B) The Food and Drug Administration
   (C) The Bureau of Engraving
   (D) General Motors
   (E) Amtrak

7. The president exercises his influence over the federal bureaucracy in which of the following ways?
   (A) By hiring interest groups to influence certain agencies
   (B) By appointing administrators sympathetic to the president's policy agenda
   (C) By creating new Cabinet-level agencies
   (D) By frequently removing administrators from office
   (E) By having federal judges disband ineffective agencies

8. Which of the following is the most likely effect of administrative discretion?
   (A) Administrative discretion is a major contributor to skyrocketing implementation costs.
   (B) Laws are implemented in ways that are consistent with bureaucrats' personal preferences.
   (C) High job turnover results from poorly crafted public policies.
   (D) Fewer bureaucrats gain necessary job skills because administrative discretion encourages laziness.
   (E) Administrative discretion results in poorly crafted public policies.

9. The Department of Homeland Security was created to address which of the following concerns?
   (A) The free-rider problem
   (B) Administrative discretion
   (C) The proliferation of constituency service and casework
   (D) Fragmentation of responsibility among various bureaucracies
   (E) Standard operating procedures

10. A citizen would best express his or her concern about airport safety in which of the following ways?
    (A) Filing a complaint with the National Transportation Safety Board
    (B) Voting for a new secretary of the Department of Transportation
    (C) Abstaining from voting in the next congressional election
    (D) Writing a letter to the Supreme Court
    (E) Hiring someone to inspect aircraft manufacturing plants

Free-Response Questions

1. Iron triangles, or subgovernments, often form around a specific policy area to shape and administer relevant policies. Select ONE of the following policy areas and complete the tasks below.
   - Agriculture
   - The environment
   - Product safety
   - Oil
   a) Identify the participants in the iron triangle.
   b) Describe something each participant would receive from each of the other participants in the triangle.

2. In the first half of the United States history, bureaucracies tended to act in a client-oriented role. However, since the early 1900s, the bureaucracy has become more of a regulator.
   a) Identify TWO agencies that serve in a regulatory capacity and give an example of a regulation they have made.
   b) Describe ONE complaint made about the federal bureaucracy acting in the role of a regulator.

Chapter 16: The Federal Courts

Multiple-Choice Questions

1. A plaintiff cannot bring suit unless he or she has fulfilled which of the following requirements?
   (A) Paid bail
   (B) Filed an *amicus curiae* brief
   (C) Appealed the case
   (D) Hired a public defender
   (E) Established standing to sue

2. Which of the following statements are true about the cases on the Supreme Court's docket?
   I. The Supreme Court tries to hear every case that is appealed to it.
   II. Cases pertaining to civil liberties are more likely to be placed on the docket.
   III. The U.S. solicitor general decides which cases the Supreme Court will hear.
   IV. The Supreme Court has original jurisdiction in cases involving civil disputes among residents of a particular state.
   (A) II only
   (B) IV only
   (C) I and II only
   (D) II and III only
   (E) III and IV only

3. Courts with appellate jurisdiction focus their attention on which aspect of a case?
   (A) The facts presented by both parties in the original case
   (B) The *amicus curiae* briefs registered with the court
   (C) The backgrounds of the jury members in the original case
   (D) The legal issues involved in the original case
   (E) The testimonies of both sides given before the Supreme Court

4. Congress influences the ideology of the Supreme Court by
   (A) passing laws to limit judicial review and prohibit judicial activism.
   (B) issuing recommendations on pending cases through the Senate Judiciary Committee.
   (C) approving or rejecting the president's nomination of Supreme Court justices.
   (D) choosing which cases the Supreme Court will hear.
   (E) nominating justices for the president's approval.

5. All of the following statements accurately describe the federal court system EXCEPT
   (A) very few federal cases actually go to trial.
   (B) federal courts only handle cases involving federal laws.
   (C) all federal judges must be nominated by the president and confirmed by the Senate.
   (D) lower courts are expected to adhere to the precedents set by higher courts.
   (E) some federal courts have original jurisdiction, whereas others have appellate jurisdiction.

6. Which of the following statements is supported by the evidence presented in Table 16.3?
   (A) Bill Clinton nominated more district court judges than any other president.
   (B) George W. Bush nominated 92 Republican judges to the appeals courts as of January 1, 2007.
   (C) George W. Bush nominated a higher percentage of women to the district courts than did Carter.
   (D) Across the presidents included in Table 16.3, politics/government is the most common occupation of appeals and district court nominees.
   (E) A majority of district court judges were appointed by Republican presidents.

7. Which of the following is the most frequent outcome of a case on the Supreme Court's docket?
   (A) It significantly alters current policies.
   (B) The justices vote unanimously.
   (C) It reverses the decision of the lower court.
   (D) It overrules the Court's own precedent.
   (E) The lower court's decision stands.

8. The decision of a federal court is most likely determined by
   (A) the argument put forth by the prosecution.
   (B) the argument put forth by the defense.
   (C) precedents set in similar cases.
   (D) which law school the judge attended.
   (E) briefs submitted by the federal government.

9. Which of the following methods is an interest group most likely to use to influence the federal judiciary?
   (A) running advertisements endorsing a Supreme Court nominee
   (B) giving campaign contribution to prospective federal judges
   (C) filing *amicus curiae* briefs
   (D) contributing money to the Federal Judiciary Retirement Fund
   (E) recruiting candidates to run against disliked federal judges

10. What is the significance of the Supreme Court's decision in *Marbury v. Madison?*
    (A) It articulated the doctrine of *habeas corpus.*
    (B) It established the Supreme Court's power to exercise judicial review.
    (C) It limited the influence and authority of the Supreme Court.
    (D) It established the doctrine of implied powers.
    (E) It established the principle of equal protection of the laws as the cornerstone for expanding civil rights.

Free-Response Questions

1. When presidents appoint judges to the federal courts, judges go to the bench for a term of "good behavior," which means they can serve for life.
   a) Identify and describe two advantages of having judges on the bench without fear of being removed.
   b) Identify and describe two disadvantages of having judges on the bench without fear of being removed.

2. Many of the writers of the Constitution believed that the federal judiciary would be the weakest of the three branches of government. Today, however, many consider the Supreme Court to be the most powerful of the three branches. This is due mainly to the use of judicial review and the theory of judicial activism.
   a) Define "judicial review" and describe a case in which judicial review was used.
   b) Describe "judicial activism."
   c) Describe TWO reasons the federal courts can be considered undemocratic.
   d) Explain ONE way in which one of the other branches of the federal government can reign in the power of the federal courts.

Chapter 17: Economic Policymaking

Multiple-Choice Questions

1. According to Keynesian economic theory, increasing government spending
   - (A) threatens the economy by raising the federal deficit.
   - (B) stimulates the economy by creating demand among consumers.
   - (C) does little to curb unemployment.
   - (D) creates a supply among consumers and encourages them to save.
   - (E) prevents the Federal Reserve System from managing banks.

2. All of the following factors indicate that the United States has a mixed economy EXCEPT
   - (A) the federal government determines monetary policy.
   - (B) the Justice Department can sue monopolistic companies.
   - (C) Congress sets tariffs on imported goods.
   - (D) the federal government owns the means of production.
   - (E) there is a federal minimum age requirement for employment.

3. Which of the following statements is one reason why Republican presidents usually focus their attention on controlling inflation?
   - (A) Controlling inflation is a bigger concern to investors than is unemployment.
   - (B) They hope to attract the votes of the middle- and lower-class Americans.
   - (C) They endorse Keynesian economics.
   - (D) Controlling inflation keeps people from buying too much.
   - (E) They want to avoid having to solve the problem of high unemployment.

4. Some believe that inflation occurs when there is too much money in circulation. To overcome this problem, the government could do which of the following?
   - (A) Decrease loan rates to make them more available to the public
   - (B) Increase the amount of credit available to the public
   - (C) Decrease the amount of money in banks, thus raising loan rates and discouraging people from borrowing
   - (D) Limit the number of bonds sold to the public to discourage people from buying
   - (E) Increase the amount of money in banks to help people borrow money

5. Which of the following individuals were proponents of supply-side economics?
   - I. John Maynard Keynes
   - II. Franklin D. Roosevelt
   - III. Ronald Reagan
   - IV. George W. Bush
   - (A) I only
   - (B) III only
   - (C) I and II only
   - (D) III and IV only
   - (E) I, III, and IV only

6. Which of the following government institutions has the greatest impact on the economy?
   - (A) Senate Economic Committee
   - (B) Federal Reserve Board
   - (C) Office of Management and Budget
   - (D) Council of Economic Advisers
   - (E) House Allocations Committee

7. Which of the following statements is supported by the map included with the feature titled, "My State: Unemployment Rates by State, 2008"?
   - (A) The unemployment rate is higher in the District of Columbia than it is in any of the states.
   - (B) There are more unemployed people in Alaska than there are in Pennsylvania.
   - (C) In the past decade, the unemployment rate has increased more in Michigan than in any other state.
   - (D) A smaller percentage of South Dakotans are unemployed than in any other state.
   - (E) Fewer than 4 percent of Americans are unemployed.

8. Antitrust policies are designed to prevent
   - (A) a company from having a monopoly over a specific good or service.
   - (B) the expansion of large multinational corporations.
   - (C) the government from interfering in international business transactions.
   - (D) the spread of dot-com businesses into traditional economic spheres.
   - (E) the Federal Reserve Board from gaining too much power over economic policy.

9. The government could exercise fiscal policy in which of the following ways?
   - (A) Increasing agricultural subsidies
   - (B) Buying bonds from banks
   - (C) Selling bonds to banks
   - (D) Establishing the federal funds rate
   - (E) Setting the interest rate banks charge each other for overnight loans

10. Which of the following statement about the Federal Reserve Board is accurate?
    - (A) Its members are elected directly by the public.
    - (B) Its members serve at the discretion of the president, meaning the president can dismiss them at any time.
    - (C) It is part of the judicial branch, but its members are appointed by the legislative branch.
    - (D) Democrats and Republicans are prohibited from serving on the Federal Reserve Board.
    - (E) Its members are appointed for 14-year terms to remain isolated from politics.

Free-Response Questions

1. Define "global economy." Describe one aspect of the global economy that is helpful to the economy of the United States and one aspect of the global economy that is detrimental to the economy of the United States.

2. The federal government and its agencies have several tools for trying to control the economy. Two of the primary tools are monetary and fiscal policy.
   a) Describe ONE way monetary policy is used to control the economy.
   b) Describe ONE way fiscal policy is used to try to control the economy.
   c) Describe TWO reasons the federal government and its agencies are not always successful in their attempts to control the economy.

Chapter 18: Social Welfare Policymaking

Multiple-Choice Questions

1. The federal government spends the most money on social welfare programs that benefit
   (A) African Americans.
   (B) Hispanics.
   (C) those whose income is below the official poverty line.
   (D) the unemployed.
   (E) the elderly.

2. Who benefits from the Earned Income Tax Credit?
   (A) the unemployed
   (B) the working poor
   (C) all employees
   (D) all employers
   (E) the self-employed

3. Which of the following statements best describes income distribution in the United States in recent decades?
   (A) Most Americans belong to the middle class because income is distributed fairly equally.
   (B) A rising tide lifts all boats.
   (C) The U.S. has narrower extremes of income than do European countries.
   (D) From each according to his ability, to each according to his need.
   (E) The rich get richer, and the poor get poorer.

4. Which of the following best describes the employment of illegal immigrants in the United States?
   (A) The federal government has passed strict laws that prevent most illegal immigrants from working; these laws have proven to be very effective.
   (B) Employers are not permitted to hire illegal immigrants, but they are also not permitted to challenge the authenticity of documents presented for employment.
   (C) Illegal immigrants are permitted to work in the United States if they are employed in agriculture or have an IR-3 visa.
   (D) Employers are prohibited from withholding income taxes from the paychecks of illegal immigrants but many do so anyway.
   (E) Employers in the construction and hospitality industries have strong economic incentives not to hire illegal immigrants.

5. According to Figure 18.1, where does child poverty tend to be most concentrated?
   (A) In New England
   (B) In the Mid-Atlantic states
   (C) West of the Mississippi River
   (D) In the South
   (E) Along the Canadian border

6. The poor are largely at a disadvantage in the political process because they
   (A) are represented by too many antipoverty interest groups that are competing for influence.
   (B) have been denied access to policymakers by an executive order from the president.
   (C) are less likely to vote.
   (D) tend to prefer egalitarian policies that benefit all citizens equally.
   (E) do not pay enough in income tax to gain the attention of policymakers.

7. Which of the following factors is expected to put a financial strain on Social Security?
   (A) People are retiring earlier.
   (B) The cost of living is stagnant.
   (C) The number of retirees is growing.
   (D) Revenue is expected to exceed expenditures by 2010.
   (E) Rising unemployment will drain the program's income.

8. Which of the following is an accurate comparison of social welfare in the United States and welfare in European countries?
   (A) Americans pay higher taxes to fund social welfare programs.
   (B) Americans receive greater benefits from social welfare programs.
   (C) Americans are less supportive of social welfare programs.
   (D) The American government spends more per capita resources to reduce poverty.
   (E) The American government is more actively involved in addressing social welfare concerns.

9. A member of which of the following groups is the least likely to live in poverty?
   (A) African Americans
   (B) Female-headed families
   (C) Two-parent families
   (D) Hispanics
   (E) The elderly

10. What change to Social Security did George W. Bush propose?
    (A) Turning over the entire Social Security system to a private corporation that would invest in the stock market.
    (B) Raising taxes on current workers to pay for current retirees.
    (C) Raising taxes on current workers to build up the Social Security Trust Fund to pay for future retirees.
    (D) Devolving Social Security to the states and giving each state a block grant to cover 90 percent of the cost.
    (E) Allowing workers to invest part of their Social Security taxes into a private investment account.

Free-Response Questions

1. Social Security, once a very popular program in the United States, is now a major concern to the American public. Estimates are that by 2038 the Social Security Trust Fund will run out of money.
   a) Explain TWO reasons that Social Security, as is currently operated, may go bankrupt by 2038.
   b) Explain TWO reasons why attempts to reform Social Security in recent years have failed.

2. Social welfare in the United States consists of two kinds of policy: entitlement programs and means tested programs.
   a) Define entitlement programs and identify one such program.
   b) Define means tested programs and identify one such program.
   c) Explain the changes that ONE of the following Presidents has brought to a means tested program
      - Ronald Reagan
      - Bill Clinton
      - George W. Bush

Chapter 19: Policymaking for Health Care and the Environment

Multiple-Choice Questions

1. Which of the following most accurately summarizes the map presented as part of the feature titled, "My State: Children's Health Insurance"?
   (A) The percentage of uninsured children ranges from 5 percent in Michigan to 20 percent in Texas.
   (B) The highest concentration of uninsured children can be found in the Pacific Northwest.
   (C) All Southern states have high percentages of uninsured children.
   (D) Children in Michigan are healthier than in any other state.
   (E) The percentage of uninsured children is greater in Arkansas than it is in Utah.

2. The cost of health care in the United States is very high for all of the following reasons EXCEPT
   (A) modern medicine can treat more illnesses.
   (B) malpractice suits lead to higher insurance rates.
   (C) Americans often lack incentive to keep costs low because they do not directly pay the bill.
   (D) more people are getting sick than ever before.
   (E) new medical technologies are expensive.

3. The biggest portion of total health care costs in the United States is paid for by
   (A) individuals.
   (B) employers.
   (C) doctors and hospitals.
   (D) insurance companies.
   (E) national, state, and local governments.

4. Which of the following statements best describes Americans' heath compared with other industrialized Western democracies?
   (A) Americans live longer and have one of the lowest infant mortality rates.
   (B) Americans have a shorter life expectancy but one of the lowest infant mortality rates.
   (C) Americans live longer but have a very high infant mortality rate.
   (D) Americans have a shorter life expectancy and a higher infant mortality rate than many other democracies.
   (E) Despite the money Americans spend on health care, the life expectancy and mortality rate of Americans is comparable to that in other democracies.

5. Which of the following statements accurately describes coal?
   I. Coal is a dirtier fuel than oil.
   II. Coal is a more abundant natural resource in the United States than oil.
   III. More of the energy America uses comes from coal than from oil.
   IV. Coal contributes to global warming.
   V. America imports more coal than oil.

   (A) I and III only
   (B) II and V only
   (C) II, IV, and V only
   (D) I, II, III, and IV only
   (E) I, II, IV, and V only

6. A member of which of the following is the least likely to have health insurance?
   (A) The elderly
   (B) Children
   (C) Young adults
   (D) Full-time employees
   (E) The poorest of the poor

7. Which of the following statements about the American health care system is accurate?
   (A) The American health care system is run by the federal government instead of state and local governments.
   (B) All Americans receive the same quality health care.
   (C) The American health care system covers more people at a lower per capita cost than in other democracies.
   (D) American doctors are required to treat all patients regardless of their ability to pay.
   (E) The American health care system costs more and covers a smaller percentage of the population.

8. How did George W. Bush's proposal to reform health care differ from Bill Clinton's proposal?
   (A) Bush's proposal relied on market mechanisms while Clinton's proposal ensured universal coverage.
   (B) Bush's proposal rationed health care while Clinton's proposal created health savings accounts.
   (C) Bush's proposal encouraged health savings accounts while Clinton's proposal relied on market mechanisms.
   (D) Bush's proposal required all Americans to purchase catastrophic health insurance coverage while Clinton's program created a fee-for-service health care system.
   (E) Bush's proposal would be paid for by cuts in welfare spending while Clinton's program would be paid for by massive tax increases.

9. Which of the following best describes where Americans believe toxic waste dumps should be located?
   (A) On military instillations
   (B) In municipal landfills
   (C) In urban areas
   (D) In whatever place scientists have determined to be the safest
   (E) Not in my backyard

10. Which of the following is a benefit of multiple-use policies that allow mining, logging, and grazing interests to use public lands at very low costs?
    (A) The federal government maximizes revenue.
    (B) Mining, logging, and grazing improve the overall health of the environment by creating clearings and meadows for wildlife.
    (C) Mining, logging, and grazing bring people to public lands that would otherwise receive few visitors.
    (D) The multiple use policy promotes jobs in otherwise depressed areas.
    (E) The multiple use policy increases America's dependence on imported natural resources.

Free-Response Questions

1. Figure 19.1 shows the sources of energy used by the United States. Choose ONE form of energy from the chart. For the one you have chosen
   a) explain ONE way in which using this form of energy is beneficial to the United States.
   b) explain TWO ways in which using this form of energy is detrimental to the United States.
   Choose a second source of energy from the chart. For the second one you have chosen
   a) explain ONE ways in which using this form of energy is beneficial to the United States.
   b) explain TWO ways in which using this form of energy is detrimental to the United States.

2. Environmental policies have been an increasingly important topic in American politics. Three major areas of concern are
   • Pollution
   • Wilderness preservation
   • Global warming
   Select ONE of the environmental concerns listed above. For each
   a) identify and describe specific legislation that has been passed by the federal government to deal with one of these concerns.
   b) evaluate the effectiveness of the legislation you choose in (a).
   c) explain a reason that some groups oppose the policy you listed in (a).

Chapter 20: National Security Policymaking

Multiple-Choice Questions

1. Which of the following institutions would be most likely to press for international environmental regulations?
   - (A) Multinational corporations
   - (B) NATO
   - (C) Congress
   - (D) Nongovernmental organizations
   - (E) Joint Chiefs of Staff

2. Which of the following statements best explains why the United States got involved in the Vietnam War?
   - (A) NATO membership required the U.S. to treat a war against one member country as a war against all.
   - (B) UN membership required the U.S. to treat a war against one member country as a war against all.
   - (C) The U.S. commitment to the isolationism doctrine.
   - (D) The U.S. commitment to the containment doctrine.
   - (E) The U.S. commitment to the Monroe Doctrine.

3. Economic sanctions typically are the least effective when
   - (A) they are unilateral.
   - (B) the economy of the targeted nation is weak.
   - (C) the nation imposing sanctions is not part of NATO.
   - (D) the oil market is doing well.
   - (E) they are proposed by human rights groups.

4. Congress influences foreign policy by
   - I. declaring war.
   - II. ratifying treaties.
   - III. appropriating money for foreign and military policies.
   - IV. commanding the armed forces.
   - V. confirming ambassadors.
   - (A) I and IV only
   - (B) II and V only
   - (C) III, IV, and V only
   - (D) I, II, III, and V only
   - (E) I, III, IV, and V only

5. Which of the following statements best explains why defense spending decreased in the 1990s?
   - (A) Most resources were channeled into increasing the standing army, which costs less to maintain than military equipment does.
   - (B) Weapons could be produced more cheaply as a result of new technology.
   - (C) The U.S. succeeded in containing all world threats.
   - (D) The U.S. decided to scrap its nuclear program and focus on conventional weapons which are better suited to fight terrorism.
   - (E) East–West tensions had lessened with the end of the Cold War.

6. All of the following are characteristic of foreign policy during the Cold War EXCEPT
   - (A) increased military spending.
   - (B) an end to détente.
   - (C) the arms race.
   - (D) isolationism.
   - (E) the rise of the military-industrial complex.

7. George W. Bush's foreign policy tenets include all of the following EXCEPT
   - (A) preemptive strikes against terrorists.
   - (B) prevention of developing threats against American interests.
   - (C) unilateralism if necessary.
   - (D) U.S. military preeminence.
   - (E) elimination of the military-industrial complex.

8. Which of the following claims can be made from the figures included in the feature titled, "America in Perspective: Ranking Largesse"?
   - I. U.S. foreign aid accounts for about 2 percent of its gross domestic product.
   - II. Sweden gives more economic aid than any of the other countries mentioned.
   - III. Most U.S. foreign aid goes Sweden.
   - IV. The U.S. gives more money in economic aid than any of the other countries mentioned.
   - V. The U.S. gives a smaller percentage of its gross domestic product in foreign aid than any of the other countries mentioned.
   - (A) I and IV only
   - (B) IV and V only
   - (C) I, IV, and V only
   - (D) I, III, IV and V only
   - (E) I, II, III, IV, and V

9. Which of the following bureaucratic institutions is primarily responsible for coordinating American intelligence activities abroad?
   - (A) The Department of Defense
   - (B) The Federal Bureau of Investigation
   - (C) The Federal Communications Commission
   - (D) The Central Intelligence Agency
   - (E) The State Department

10. Which of the following was a major consequence of the Vietnam War?
   - (A) The United States failed to stop the spread of communism throughout Asia.
   - (B) The Cold War came to an end, leaving the United States as the sole superpower.
   - (C) NATO was created to protect the United States and Western nations from the threat of communism.
   - (D) The United States abandoned the doctrine of détente as the cornerstone of its foreign policy.
   - (E) American citizens lost faith in the government after being lied to about the war.

Free-Response Questions

1. In the post World War II era, the United States has been involved in two extended global conflicts: the Cold War and the War on Terror.
   a) Identify ONE armed conflict the United States was involved in during the Cold War and describe the rationale for this conflict.
   b) Identify ONE armed conflict the United States was involved in during the War of Terror and describe the rationale for this conflict.
   c) Choose ONE of the above conflicts you have chosen. For this conflict, explain the arguments used against this war.

2. The President is responsible for leading the nation in foreign policy, as commander in chief, and in war making.
   a) Identify and describe TWO Constitutional powers the president has in foreign policy-making and/or commander in chief.
   b) Identify and describe ONE non-Constitutional power the president has in foreign policymaking and/or commander in chief.
   c) Describe TWO limits on the president's foreign policymaking powers and/or powers as commander in chief.

Chapter 21: The New Face of State and Local Government

Multiple-Choice Questions

1. Which of the following powers is given to most state governors but not the president of the United States?
   (A) The line-item veto
   (B) Assigning members to legislative committees
   (C) Determining the budget
   (D) Issuing pardons
   (E) Declaring laws unconstitutional

2. Which of the following statements about state constitutions is accurate?
   (A) All state constitutions contain a bill of rights.
   (B) All state constitutions give executive power to a governor and legislative power to a bicameral legislature.
   (C) Most state constitutions are shorter than the U.S. Constitution.
   (D) State constitutions typically provide fewer details about specific policies than does the U.S. Constitution.
   (E) State constitutions supersede the U.S. Constitution.

3. Which of the following best summarizes the most common method states use to amend their constitutions?
   (A) The state senate proposes amendments which must be ratified by the state house of representatives.
   (B) The state house of representatives proposes amendments which must be ratified by the state senate.
   (C) The state legislature proposes amendments which must be ratified the voters.
   (D) The voters propose amendments which must be ratified by the state legislature.
   (E) The governor proposes amendments which be ratified by the state legislature.

4. Which of the following best describes gubernatorial elections?
   (A) Gubernatorial campaigns are candidate-centered.
   (B) Gubernatorial campaigns are party-centered.
   (C) The winner of gubernatorial elections is heavily influenced by the coattail effect.
   (D) Gubernatorial races are seldom at the top of the ticket.
   (E) Governors are usually elected during presidential election years.

5. The recent trend towards legislative professionalism in state government includes
   I. increasing legislators' salaries.
   II. reducing the influence of interest groups.
   III. lengthening legislative sessions.
   IV. reducing the power of the state executive branch.
   V. limiting the number of professional staff members employed by the legislature.
   (A) I and III only
   (B) II and V only
   (C) II, IV, and V only
   (D) I, II, III, and IV only
   (E) I, III, IV, and V only

6. According to Table 21.4, the increase in the number of governments in the United States is mostly attributable to the growth in what type of government?
   (A) County
   (B) Municipal
   (C) Township
   (D) School district
   (E) Special district

7. What was the impact of the U.S. Supreme Court's decision in *Baker v. Carr*?
   (A) All states had to have an equal number of state house districts.
   (B) State senate districts had to be the same size as state house districts.
   (C) Rural interests began to dominate urban interests in state legislatures.
   (D) The influence of rural interests in state legislatures declined.
   (E) States could not discriminate on the basis of race in local and state elections.

8. Which of the following best describes how most state laws are created?
   (A) The governor proposes bills that become law once ratified by both houses of the legislature.
   (B) Both houses of the legislature pass identical versions of a bill and the governor signs it.
   (C) Both houses of the legislature pass identical versions of a bill that becomes law when the state supreme court determines that is does not violate the state constitution.
   (D) The state house of representatives passes a bill which must then be approved by the U.S. Congress.
   (E) The state legislature passes a bill which must then be ratified by the state's voters in the next general election.

9. Which of the following are common methods for selecting state judges?
   I. Partisan elections
   II. Nonpartisan elections
   III. Appointment
   IV. Appointment followed by retention elections
   (A) I and IV only
   (B) II and III only
   (C) I, III, and IV only
   (D) II, III, and IV only
   (E) I, II, III, and IV

10. All of the following are forms of direct democracy EXCEPT
    (A) town meetings.
    (B) line-item vetoes.
    (C) recall elections.
    (D) initiatives.
    (E) referenda.

Free-Response Questions

1. Both presidents and governors serve as leaders of their respective governments. Describe two formal legislative powers that can make governors more effective legislative leaders than the president. Describe two non-formal abilities that both the president and governors need in order to be effective leaders.

2. While the Constitution only allows individual citizens to vote directly for three offices (one representative and two senators), states are able to give their citizens a much more active voice. Identify and describe TWO ways in which a state has broader power of the electorate, either through direct policymaking or through elective offices.

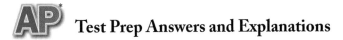 **Test Prep Answers and Explanations**

Chapter 1: Introducing Government in America

Multiple-Choice Questions

1. (D) is correct. Pluralist theory holds that numerous groups participate in politics to represent a wider variety of public concerns. Interest groups are usually a good example of pluralism in American politics. The fact that there are thousands of them would indicate, according to pluralists, that these groups are speaking on behalf of many different public needs. The political agenda would therefore be determined by the people.

2. (B) is correct. Although a bill of rights often reinforces a democracy, it is not necessarily indicative of a democracy. The essential elements of a democracy can be specified in a constitution. The Bill of Rights does protect the freedoms guaranteed under this democratic form of government, but it does not itself establish a democracy.

3. (C) is correct. Elite and class theorists believe that the government is mainly controlled by an elite and wealthy minority, most of whom are involved in big business. Statement I is therefore correct because political action committees are one method by which the elite influence politics during elections. Statement III mentions the wealthy, so there is a good chance this statement is in keeping with elite theory. Only choice (C) lists statement III as well as statement I.

4. (B) is correct. All governments share certain functions, such as maintaining a national defense, preserving order, providing public services, and socializing the young. All governments also collect taxes. Ensuring social equality, however, is not typically a function of government. While some governments may try to reduce social inequality, very few attempt to eliminate it. Democratic governments attempt to ensure political equality, but not social or economic equality.

5. (C) is correct. A democracy must listen to the will of the people, as expressed by a majority of its citizens. At the same time, democracies must ensure that the rights of the minority are respected. Thus, democracies operate under majority rule, but protect minority rights.

6. (D) is correct. When compared with other democracies, voter turnout in the United States is very low. American democracy does reasonably well at ensuring majority rule with minority rights. Political equality, or "one person, one vote," is a hallmark of American democracy. The First Amendment guarantees freedom of speech, another essential element of democracy.

7. (A) is correct. The Constitution establishes and limits the powers of government. It is not considered a linkage institution because it is not a mechanism for citizens to influence the policy agenda. Linkage institutions include parties, interest groups, the media, and elections—each of which enables citizens to affect the policy agenda.

8. (B) is correct. Pluralists believe that all groups have access to policymaking, thereby representing a wide range of public needs. Elite theorists, not pluralists, believe that there is a connection between wealth and influence. A pluralist would expect all interest groups, regardless of their financial resources, to vie for influence. If a group fails to influence policy on one issue, it might still succeed on another. Competition among groups ultimately balances out inequities among them.

9. (B) is correct. Figure 1.2 examines how political knowledge has changed by age group from 1964 to 2004. In 2004, every age group had less political knowledge than the same age group had in 1964. At the same time, the drop in political knowledge is the largest for those under 30 years old (from about 66 percent to about 36 percent) and smallest for those over 65 (from about 61 percent to about 55 percent). In addition, the variation in political knowledge by age is fairly small in 1964, but quite large in 2004. Figure 1.2 does not address voter turnout.

10. (A) is correct. Hyperpluralists agree with pluralists in asserting that a number of groups represent the interests of the public in the political arena, but they contend that so many groups are essentially glutting the whole policymaking system. Representatives who are eager to appease as many groups as possible end up producing conflicting or diluted policies.

Free-Response Questions

This question has an 8-point rubric; 3 points for identifying aspects of the American political culture, 3 points for describing the aspects of political culture, and 1 point each for defining and describing the culture war. This response has 3 points for identifying the three aspects in the first sentence. It is also a good habit to underline your main points when writing for the Advanced Placement U.S. Government exam. This will help insure the reader will find and award you your points.

1. Three major aspects of American political culture are liberty, individualism, and populism. Americans' belief in liberty is their desire to live freely with minimum interference from the government. Examples can be seen in the Declaration of Independence or the Civil War, fought to free the slaves. Individualism, another aspect of political culture, is the belief that people should succeed or fail based on their own merits and efforts. Americans have always resented a privileged class, and prefer the self-made man. A sign that populism is important to the American political culture is the fact that both Democrats and Republicans try to claim that they represent the ordinary people. Both parties say that they are the ones who help the voice of the people to be heard.

The student receives 1 point for the description of liberty. The examples given would not be needed to earn the point. The examples on their own, without the description given in the preceding sentence, would not be enough to earn the point.

Again, the student earns the point in the first sentence. The second sentence does not detract from this, but is not needed to earn the point.

The student stumbles into an answer here, but "the voice of the people being heard" is enough of a definition to earn the point.

The student need only name the issue to receive the 8th point. Although the student names several issues, all of which are acceptable, only one point is awarded.

Stating that there are two opposing groups and using any wording which indicates the strong dislike, mistrust, or hatred between the two groups is enough to award a point for the definition of "culture war." One point awarded.

In spite of having a common political culture, many people believe that the United States is in the midst of a culture war. A culture war is where Americans divide into two camps, liberal Democrats and conservative Republicans. The two camps see each other not just as political opponents, but as fools or scoundrels whose election could mean the downfall of our nation. Abortion, gun rights, and gay marriage are all examples of issues that are part of the culture war in the United States.

This paragraph briefly describes a central feature of pluralist theory and gives an example that reconfirms an understanding. The example is not necessary but is useful to confirm for the reader that you understand the concept. (1 point)

This paragraph briefly describes a central feature of pluralist theory and gives an example that reconfirms an understanding. The example is not necessary but is useful to confirm for the reader that you understand the concept. (1 point)

This paragraph briefly describes a central feature of hyperpluralism. (1 point)

This paragraph gives both a positive and negative aspect of the question. (2 points)

2. a. There are at least three common theories of democracy put forward by political scientists. Pluralist theory argues that the people may have influence on what government does by gathering into groups of people with similar interests, organizing, and pressing their positions to public policymakers. For example, the National Rifle Association (NRA) might pool its resources to help support a member who hopes to get a Supreme Court ruling that the Second Amendment applies to the states.
    - Elitist theory argues that there is an economic elite that makes all of the important decisions. In fact, left to their own devices, average citizens would vote away some of their basic rights, such as freedom of press.
    - Hyperpluralism argues that groups are so strong and there are so many points of access that it is hard to get anything done.
    - Whatever victory one group can achieve in one part of government can be undone by the efforts of another group in another part of government.

    b. In pluralism and hyperpluralism, the average citizen can play a role in politics by joining and participating in groups. In elitism, the average citizen does not play a role in politics.

    c. The theory of pluralism would allow for the most representative democracy. Citizens could join groups, such as the National Rifle Association, which would then represent them to their elected representatives in government. Others argue that as Americans became more isolated from one another, participation in interest groups often times means little more than contributing money. Many Americans don't really know what the group they belong to really stands for.

    > *This paragraph could have been woven into the paragraphs above, but the student has chosen to use the outline explicit in the question to organize the response. The role of the average citizen in each of the three theories is correctly described. (3 points earned in two simple sentences)*

Chapter 2: The Constitution

Multiple-Choice Questions

1. **(D) is correct.** All but one of the answer choices evolved out of interpretations of the Constitution. Bear in mind that the Constitution is really only a blueprint for government—it lays out only the basic structure and powers of the three branches and defines the powers of the federal and state governments. Most governmental bodies have resulted from particular needs neither specified nor denied in the Constitution. However, the authors of the Constitution did create the Electoral College to choose the president as a means of keeping government out of the hands of the poor and uneducated majority.

2. **(E) is correct.** The Seventeenth Amendment allows voters to elect directly their own senators. Previously, as stated in Article I of the Constitution, senators had been selected by states' legislatures. This was another way the framers attempted to distance government from the populace.

3. **(C) is correct.** Madison devised the system of checks and balances primarily to prevent any one branch, if it came under the control of a majority faction, from dominating the whole government. Thus, checks and balances help prevent tyranny of the majority. These checks include the ability of the president to veto laws passed by Congress and the president's authority to nominate Supreme Court justices. The system is clearly defined in the first three articles of the Constitution; it is not merely a part of the unwritten body of tradition that has evolved.

4. **(B) is correct.** While Americans generally disdain flag burning, the Supreme Court has determined that the Constitution protects the practice as an exercise of free speech. Therefore, the Texas law against "desecration of a venerated object" was unconstitutional. This means that neither Congress nor the states can pass laws that prohibit flag burning because it is a protected form of political expression.

5. **(B) is correct.** The authors of the Articles of Confederation were so determined to minimize the power of the federal government that ultimately they created one that was not politically or economically viable. The challenge they faced in writing the Constitution was to create a more centralized government without risking giving it too much power. The concept of limited government is therefore the correct answer.

6. **(C) is correct.** Recall the debate surrounding the ratification of the Constitution: Anti-Federalists feared that it favored the elite over the majority, whose individual freedoms were not sufficiently addressed. The promise of a bill of rights was necessary to win over those states that hesitated to vote for adoption of the Constitution. Think also about what rights are guaranteed by the first 10 amendments: free speech, freedom of religion, freedom to petition, protection against unlawful searches and seizures, and the right to a trial by jury. All of these address personal liberty and assert the basic natural rights of citizens.

7. **(C) is correct.** While the bulk of the Declaration of Independence is a list of grievance against King George, it is also a political and philosophical treatise about American political beliefs. The basic institutions and processes of government, however, are outlined in the Constitution, not the Declaration.

8. **(D) is correct.** Anti-Federalists feared that the Constitution did not give significant protection to individual liberties, such as freedom of speech and freedom of the press. They were concerned that such omissions indicated that citizens would not retain these liberties under the Constitution. To alleviate these concerns, the Federalists agreed that the first order of business under the new government would be the addition of a bill of rights to the Constitution to ensure that these fundamental liberties were protected. The Constitution did not give any powers to the king of England, weakened the authority of the states, and was silent about political parties. The Anti-Federalists also feared that the Constitution was a class-based document that would increase the power of the mercantile class.

9. **(E) is correct.** The evidence presented in Table 2.1 suggests that when Thomas Jefferson wrote the Declaration of Independence, he borrowed heavily from the ideas (and words) of John Locke. The governing structure for the new nation is outlined in the Constitution, not the Declaration of Independence. The Constitution is not addressed in Table 2.1.

10. **(C) is correct.** The Constitution prohibits Congress from infringing on individual rights by passing bills of attainder. Every citizen is entitled to the right of due process by law—no one may be found guilty without first being tried. This idea of justice forms the cornerstone of the American judiciary system.

Free-Response Questions

1. These amendments would serve as appropriate examples for this question:
   - **Fifteenth Amendment (1870):** extended voting rights to freed slaves (male) after the Civil War
   - **Nineteenth Amendment (1920):** gave women the right to vote
   - **Twenty-third Amendment (1961):** granted the residents of Washington, D.C., the right to vote
   - **Twenty-fourth Amendment (1964):** prohibited states from using poll taxes or tests to prevent the poor from voting
   - **Twenty-sixth Amendment (1971):** changed the voting age from 21 to 18

Identifies an amendment that had an impact on voting rights. (1 point)

The Constitution largely left voting rights up to the states, which generally granted voting rights only to free males. Over time, amendments such as the Fifteenth, Nineteenth, and Twenty-fourth have been added to the Constitution to extend voting rights to all Americans.

Describes how the Fifteenth Amendment changed the nature of the electorate. (1 point)

The Civil War ended slavery in the South, but it would take government intervention to ensure that newly freed slaves would be treated as citizens. Southern states held out against the Fourteenth Amendment, which extended citizenship to freed slaves, so it became necessary to add a new amendment, the Fifteenth, which would specifically allow these disenfranchised Americans to vote. For the first time, African Americans were able to vote legally and to hold public office. The Fifteenth Amendment was not wholly successful, but it did act as a first step toward righting the wrongs of slavery.

Identifies an amendment that had an impact on voting rights. (1 point)

Describes how the Twenty-fourth Amendment changed the nature of the electorate. (1 point)

It took 100 years and another amendment for the Fifteenth Amendment to be fully realized. Southern states sidestepped the Fifteenth Amendment by imposing poll taxes on voters. Most freed slaves were poor, so these measures prevented them from voting. The civil rights movement of the 1960s brought to light such injustices. The Twenty-fourth Amendment was passed to prohibit southern states from using the poll tax to prevent African Americans from voting. Today people of all races are able to vote without the imposition of any tax.

American women, too, were denied the right to vote for more than a century. The Nineteenth Amendment extended the vote to them. Since then, not only have women been able to serve as senators, representatives, mayors, and governors, but also women's issues have found a place in the political arena. Politicians, to win the votes of half the electorate, now address such issues as abortion, family leave, and equal opportunity in the workplace. The Nineteenth Amendment, therefore, both doubled the number of eligible voters and changed the political landscape of the United States.

This response identifies three valid amendments and offers adequate descriptions of how they changed the nature of the electorate. (6 of 6 points)

2. Americans like to have a say in their government. Before the Constitution was written, however, this was not always the case. Although the state and national governments did give considerable voice to the American people, there were several instances where the people were shortchanged on democracy.

    a. During the Revolutionary period, the state of <u>New York expanded voting rights</u>, allowing farmers of moderate means to vote, not just wealthy landowners. This is an example of governing by consent.

    b. Most states <u>only allowed White males to vote</u>. This was not very democratic since women, Native Americans, and Blacks were barred from having any say in elections.

    c. Under the Constitution, people could elect the <u>president, senators, and members of the House of Representative</u>. This was a very democratic notion.

    d. Under the Constitution, <u>the people did not elect federal judges</u>. Rather, they received lifetime appointments.

The appointment, rather than election of federal judges, would qualify for a point in (d). Total score on this question, 3 out of 4.

Chapter 3: Federalism

Multiple-Choice Questions

1. **(B) is correct.** The federal government has sole authority to conduct foreign relations, establish post offices, coin money, and declare war. The only listed power that is shared by both the national and state governments is the power to tax. This is why citizens pay a variety of state, local, and federal taxes.

2. **(B) is correct.** The Tenth Amendment reserves all powers not specifically relegated to the federal government or denied in the Constitution to the states. This does not mean that state governments have unlimited powers, however. In fact, the Supreme Court ruled that even though the Tenth Amendment bestows a fair amount of freedom to the states, it should not be too heavily interpreted in favor of the states. This 1941 case confirmed federal supremacy.

3. **(B) is correct.** This clause in Article I of the Constitution gives Congress the authority to "make all laws which shall be necessary and proper for carrying into execution the foregoing Powers, and all other Powers vested by [the] Constitution." That is, it gives Congress implied powers beyond those specifically listed in the Constitution. The elastic clause allows flexibility for the federal government to change and adapt over time.

4. **(C) is correct.** This question simply asks you to identify the basic premise of federalism, which is that the government is divided between various levels of government. In the United States, government is divided into local, state, and national levels.

5. **(E) is correct.** According to Figure 3.5, some states spend less than half as much per student as do other states. For example, Arizona and Utah spend under $6,000 per student, while Massachusetts, Connecticut, New York, New Jersey, and Vermont spend more than $12,000 per student. Figure 3.5 does not address the quality of education, so there is no way to know if some states are able to provide quality education and lower costs than other states. Likewise, Figure 3.5 does not provide information about the percentage of a state's budget that is used for education. We cannot assume that high-cost states devote a larger percentage of their budget to education than do low-cost states. Both Utah and Arizona spend less per student than does Mississippi.

6. **(E) is correct.** The full faith and credit clause requires that a state's public acts, records, and civil judicial proceedings be recognized in all other states. These include driver's licenses, birth and death certificates, and marriage licenses. However, each state passes its own laws, which might be different from another state's law on the same topic. For example, each state sets its own speed limits, which do not automatically apply elsewhere.

7. **(B) is correct.** The federal government often encourages states to assist with federal policy priorities through grants. Categorical grants often come with strings attached. One of the most common requirements is that the state must follow specific federal regulations to receive the money. Block grants, however, have fewer strings attached and allow greater discretion to a state to decide how to spend the money. It is no surprise, then, that states much prefer block grants to categorical grants.

8. **(D) is correct.** The privileges and immunities clause gives residents of any state equal protection under the law, no matter what state they happen to be in. This clause serves to unite the states by extending equal national citizenship regardless of state lines.

9. **(C) is correct.** In a federal system, the electorate chooses local, state, and national representatives. This gives them the potential to influence government at each level. Similarly, a government divided into levels offers more points of access for political groups; a citizen concerned about gun control can join either a state or a national advocate group, or both. State governments are not necessarily more responsive. Even if political parties do offer more choice, they are not exclusive to a federal system—many unitary governments have multiparty systems.

10. **(B) is correct.** It is the role of the courts to settle disputes between the federal and state levels of government. A court, through its interpretation of the Constitution, determines whether a particular issue falls under the scope of the federal or state level of government. This is one reason why the court system has grown more extensive over the course of American history.

Free-Response Questions

Notice the student does not give any introduction in the answer. None is needed. In the AP Government exam, no points are awarded for style, only for content. This response correctly explains how the McCulloch case and the federal grant system have given the federal government more power. 2 points awarded.

In section (b), the student both describes the case and explains how it has shifted power from the federal government back to the states. 2 points awarded. Total score, 4 out of 4.

1. a. _McCulloch v. Maryland_—In this case, the state of Maryland tried to place a tax on a federal bank located in Baltimore. The Supreme Court ruled that national laws are supreme to state laws. Therefore, states cannot set up laws that go against national laws. This helped make the federal government more powerful.

   b. The federal grant system has also increased the power of the federal government. The federal government will give money to states for different projects, such as the building of highways. The states, however, are required to abide by the conditions of aid that the federal government puts on these grants, such as speed limits.

   c. _United States v. Lopez_—The Supreme Court ruled that a federal law outlawing guns in a school zone was unconstitutional. Guns, the court ruled, had nothing to do with commerce. This gave more power to the states to create their own laws about guns.

   d. _Printz v. United States_—In this case, the court struck down a federal mandate that states conduct background check on people who wanted to purchase a handgun. Again, this gave more power to the states to create their own laws regulating guns.

This paragraph sets the stage and is a good introductory paragraph, but earns no points.

This paragraph provides an excellent description of the Supremacy Clause and its relevance for federalism. (1 point)

This paragraph describes the Tenth Amendment and its relevance for federalism. (1 point)

This paragraph gives an explanation of the impact of international relations (the Cold War) to federalism (control over education) for 1 point. Total score on this question: 4 of 4.

2. The Founding Fathers had a difficult task. They had to concentrate power more than it had been concentrated under the Articles of Confederation, and they had to make sure power was not too concentrated. One of the ways they dealt with this issue was with federalism—the division of power between levels of government. Some powers were put in the national government, some were put in state governments, and some were shared by both.

    The Supremacy Clause is the part of the Constitution that the framers included at the end of the Constitution that says that the Constitution, the laws made by the national government that do not violate the Constitution, and treaties made by the national government override conflicting state laws. By this provision, the framers sought to solve one of the major problems of the Articles—the lack of power for the national government.

    The Tenth Amendment is the part of the Constitution that attempts to reserve to the states powers not given to the national government nor denied to the states. In essence, the states have powers of their own, but the states and the national government continue to argue over exactly what these are.

    During the 1950s and 60s, the United States became very fearful that the Soviets had surpassed us in military technology. The launching of *Sputnik* made the federal government much more concerned with education in the United States. Up until this time, education had been primarily in the hands of the state governments. But with the passage of the National Defense Education Act, federal aid started pouring into schools to boost their math and science departments. Federal money still goes into the schools, but now with more strings attached. This gives the federal government more control over what had been a state institution.

Chapter 4: Civil Liberties and Public Policy

Multiple-Choice Questions

1. **(D) is correct.** In *Mapp v. Ohio,* the Supreme Court extended the protection of the Fourteenth Amendment to defendants in state trials. Specifically, as in federal cases, state courts must adhere to the exclusionary rule: prosecutors cannot use evidence acquired through unreasonable search and seizure to convict a person.

2. **(C) is correct.** In *Roth,* the Court ruled that obscenity is not protected under the Constitution as a form of free speech. In *Texas v. Johnson,* it decided that flag burning is protected as an act of symbolic speech. These two cases clarify the First Amendment right of free speech.

3. **(C) is correct.** The Supreme Court ruled that student religious groups should have the same right to assemble as any other extracurricular group and, in *Lemon v. Kurtzman,* that parochial schools may receive federal funding as long as they use it for educational rather than religious purposes. Of course, it is always permissible for students to pray silently in school.

4. **(B) is correct.** Only libel is not protected by the First Amendment because it represents an intentional misconstruing of the truth. However, libel is difficult to prove in court because the plaintiff must present evidence of malicious intent. Furthermore, the negative attention generated by a libel suit often dissuades public officials from pursuing claims.

5. **(E) is correct.** Most criminal cases are resolved through plea bargaining. The prosecutor and the defendant's attorney work out a deal in which the defendant receives a lighter sentence for pleading guilty. This saves the public considerable money by minimizes court costs, while guaranteeing a conviction.

6. **(A) is correct.** Throughout the twentieth century, the Supreme Court has gradually extended the protection of the Bill of Rights to citizens of the states. It has done so by citing the due process clause of the Fourteenth Amendment. Previously, the Supreme Court had ruled that the Bill of Rights did not apply to the states. Now, citizens can be assured that state, local, and national governments can not infringe on most of the protections guaranteed by the Bill of Rights.

7. **(A) is correct.** In the 1976 case of *Gregg v. Georgia,* the Supreme Court dismissed Gregg's argument that the death penalty constitutes cruel and unusual punishment. The court allowed capital punishment, citing it as "an extreme sanction, suitable to the most extreme of crimes." This case set the precedent for excluding the death penalty from the definition of cruel and unusual punishment.

8. **(D) is correct.** In *Roe v. Wade,* the Supreme Court allowed abortion in the first trimester—and allowed it in the second trimester with some state regulation.

However, the Court has also upheld several state laws that limit abortion, such as parental notification laws.

9. **(D) is correct.** The only statement supported by the evidence in Figure 4.1 is that a majority of Americans believe that some abortions should be legal. Fifty-five percent of Americans think abortion should be legal under certain circumstances and another 26 percent think it should be legal under any circumstance. While it *may* be true that that a majority of American have strong opinions on abortions, believe abortion should be legal only in the case of rape or incest, or consider themselves pro-life, these opinions are not addressed in Figure 4.1.

10. **(B) is correct.** The right to assemble clearly is protected by the First Amendment; even a hate group may convene as long as it is not endorsing or performing any crime against an individual. However, according to a 1994 Supreme Court decision, right-to-life advocates who block access to an abortion violate the right of women to enter the clinic. This was then endorsed by Congress, which passed the Freedom of Access to Clinic Entrances Act. Thus, governments can pass laws that ensure access to abortion clinics, such as laws restrict protestors from a specified buffer zone around abortion clinics.

Free-Response Questions

This sentence correctly describes a plea bargain for 1 point.

The cost and time are two major considerations. 1 point earned.

1. In the United States justice system, plea bargains are commonly used. A plea bargain occurs when a person charged with a crime agrees to plead guilty to a lesser crime, or fewer crimes, in exchange for a lighter sentence. Prosecutors agree to plea bargains because they speed up the process of incarcerating a criminal. Plea bargaining is also much less expensive than going to trial, which could take months to complete and cost thousands of dollars. Defendants often prefer to plea bargain because it will help them to spend less time in jail. Sometimes a plea bargain will involve no jail time at all.

The hope of lesser jail time for a defendant is correct for the third point. Total score on question: 3 of 3.

There are no points to be found in this section. Introductions are not needed in the free response section of the AP Government exam.

The writer gets 2 points for identifying the establishment clause and the free exercise clause. The writer also gets 2 points for the description of the establishment clause and free exercise clause. The paragraph, however, could have been shortened considerably.

2. Freedom of religion holds a special place in the hearts and minds of the Americans people. From the Pilgrims sailing to America to escape the Church of England and to worship freely, to the Mormons crossing the desert pulling handcarts to establish a new community in Utah, Americans yearn for religious freedom. That is one reason religion is mentioned in the First Amendment. The Founding Fathers wanted everyone to know how important it was. Today, we take these freedoms for granted. But it was only through the hard-fought battles of the Revolutionary War that America truly became a free nation.

   The First Amendment has two parts that pertain to religion. One is called the establishment clause, which states that there cannot be a national church, one supported by tax money or endorsed by the federal government. The Founders didn't want what they had in England, where the Anglican Church was the official state church. We had many churches in the United States: Congregationalists in New England, Lutherans, Catholics, Quakers in the Middle Colonies, Anglicans and Baptists in the South. How could we have decided on one state church? The free exercise clause stated that the federal government couldn't keep people from practicing their religion as they saw fit. Now this doesn't mean that we can practice *anything,* such as human sacrifices or multiple marriages. But the government cannot stop you from being a Catholic or a Jew.

One point for linking the establishment clause to the Lemon *case.*

One point for describing the Court's ruling in Lemon. *The total score is 6 of 6, but the writer could have written a much more concise answer.*

The Supreme Court hears cases on religion all the time. One such case was *Lemon v. Kurtzman.* This case involved states giving money to private religious schools. Some people complained that it went against the establishment clause. The Supreme Court disagreed. It said a state can give money to a religious school as long as the money is not to be used for religious purposes and doesn't get the government too involved in religion. The Court also said the money could not help advance the religion.

All in all, the Founders did a pretty good job of setting up the First Amendment, which still protects our freedoms today.

Chapter 5: Civil Rights and Public Policy

Multiple-Choice Questions

1. **(C) is correct.** The Open Housing Act of 1968 eliminated housing discrimination. Since housing is not a form of public accommodation, the Civil Rights Act did not address this form of discrimination. It did, however, prohibit many other types of discrimination.

2. **(C) is correct.** According to Figure 5.1, almost no Southern Blacks attended school with White students in the immediate wake of the Supreme Court's 1954 mandate to integrate. By 1970 this had changed completely, with most Black students attending schools with some Whites. Figure 5.1 does not indicate the size of the Black or White student populations or how many schools were fully integrated. Furthermore, Figure 5.1 is silent about integration outside of the South.

3. **(E) is correct.** The Supreme Court has developed different standards to determine if classification systems are permissible. For example, the Supreme Courts considers classification based on race to be *inherently suspect* and, therefore, usually impermissible. Classification based on gender, however, is considered under an intermediate standard. Other classification systems (e.g., disability, age, sexual orientation), most only be considered reasonable for achieving a legitimate government goal. The Fourteenth Amendment is regularly cited in civil rights cases, and the preference for limited government has been ignored in the pursuit of civil rights. Thus, only answers I, II, and III are correct.

4. **(A) is correct.** The Equal Rights Amendment was first introduced in Congress in 1923 and finally passed both houses in 1972. It was not ratified by enough states, however, to become part of the Constitution. Some people (including some women) opposed the amendment because they viewed it as an attack on the family.

5. **(C) is correct.** Some critics of affirmative action see it as a mechanism of reverse discrimination. One such example is the case of *Regents of the University of California v. Bakke*, in which the Supreme Court found the university's quotas for enrolling minorities unconstitutional. Allan Bakke was denied enrollment in favor of a minority applicant to fulfill the university's quota.

6. **(B) is correct.** In *Plessy v. Ferguson*, the Supreme Court judged segregation to be constitutional, as long as races were allowed facilities of equal quality. More than 50 years later, the Warren court struck down segregation in its *Brown* ruling, therefore, overturned the Court's earlier ruling in *Plessy*.

7. **(A) is correct.** The Mexican American Legal Defense and Education Fund (MALDEF) has a long history of fighting for the civil rights of Hispanic Americans. The American Indian Movement (AIM) and the National Association for the Advancement of Colored People (NAACP) have fought for the rights of Native Americans and Blacks, respectively. While the Equal Employment Opportunity Commission (EEOC) may help to ensure equal job opportunities for Hispanic Americans, this is not necessarily its focus. The Americans with Disabilities Act (ADA) protects the civil rights of disabled Americans and does not specifically address Hispanic Americans.

8. **(D) is correct.** Nowhere does the Constitution or the Bill of Rights endorse equality for all citizens. Rather, the requirement for "equal protection of the laws" can be found in the Fourteenth Amendment, which was passed in the wake of the civil war. In many cases, the Fourteenth Amendment has been the foundation of important advancements in civil rights.

9. **(B) is correct.** The Supreme Court first ruled against gender discrimination in the case of *Reed v. Reed*. It struck down an Idaho law that granted men automatic preference over women in determining which parent would be administrator of their daughter's estate. The court ruled that gender cannot be used as the sole qualification for determining the winner of such a case.

10. **(E) is correct.** The Fifteenth Amendment guaranteed African Americans the right to vote. Despite this written guarantee, Southern states employed various instruments to prevent or diminish the ability of African Americans to meaningfully participate in elections. Literacy tests, often about the national or state constitution, were administered in such a way as to prevent Blacks from voting. Poll taxes fell disproportionately on African Americans. White primaries excluded Blacks from the main election for determining officeholders, as the winner of the Democratic primary was virtually assured a victory in the general election.

Free-Response Questions

1. a. The civil rights era from 1954 to 1968 brought about great changes in the rights of African Americans in the United States. The federal government was involved at several levels.

    The identification of the Supreme Court is worth 1 point. The description that follows is worth the second point.

    The Supreme Court ruled in the case of *Brown v. Board of Education* that the equal protection clause of the Fourteenth Amendment required that schools could no longer be desegregated. The next year, the Court said that schools needed to be desegregated "with all deliberate speed."

    Congress and the president got into the act as well. Congress passed two very important bills in 1964 and 1965. The Civil Rights Act of 1964 was a broad, sweeping bill that made private businesses serve Black Americans in the same way that they served others. The next year, Congress expanded voting rights through the passage of the Voting Rights Act of 1965.

    The identification of Congress is worth 1 point. The description that follows is worth a second point.

    b. Churches were also important in the civil rights movement. Martin Luther King Jr. headed up the Southern Christian Leadership Conference, which was instrumental in helping organize boycotts, marches, and petition drives throughout the South in the 1950s and 60s.

    The identification of churches is worth 1 point. The description that follows is worth a second point. Total score on this question: 6 of 6.

2. a. <u>Earl Warren</u> took over as chief justice of the U.S. Supreme Court when the case of <u>*Brown v. Board of Education*</u> was being discussed. Warren helped the Court reach a unanimous decision to end the federal policy of segregation. <u>Lyndon Johnson</u> took over as president when Kennedy was assassinated. Johnson was <u>*able to get the Civil Rights Act of 1964*</u> through Congress. The act struck down discrimination in the workplace and public accommodations such as hotels.

   b. Although the Brown case required that public schools desegregate their student population, <u>few did so either quickly</u> or willingly. <u>Central High School in Little Rock</u>, Arkansas, for example, went so far as to have the National Guard surround the school to keep Black students from attending. And while the Civil Rights Act of 1964 brought about swift changes to ensuring civil rights for Blacks, President Johnson had to work very hard to get the bill through a hostile Senate, where Southerners such as Strom Thurmond tried to block its passage with a filibuster.

Chapter 6: Public Opinion and Political Action

Multiple-Choice Questions

1. **(D) is correct.** The apportionment of seats in the House is based on the population of each state. The Constitution specifically requires that a national census be taken every 10 years to determine how seats in the House of Representatives should be reapportioned.

2. **(B) is correct.** The figure shows that since 1988, ratings of gays and lesbians have increased by up to 20 points among liberals, conservatives, and moderates. The gap between liberals' attitudes and conservatives' attitudes remained fairly constant from 1988 to 2004.

3. **(E) is correct.** People learn about government and form their beliefs primarily through their family, what they are taught in school, and what they see and hear on television. Factors such as a religious upbringing can also influence a person's political ideology. However, the month in which a person was born has no bearing on his or her political beliefs.

4. **(A) is correct.** While early immigrants typically came from Europe, recent immigrants have tended to come from Central American countries such as Mexico and Asian countries such as Vietnam, Korea, and the Philippines.

5. **(E) is correct.** Because older Americans are more conservative than your younger counterparts, they are also more likely to favor greater military spending. However, older Americans are less likely to favor investing Social Security funds in the stock market. These differences are important because senior citizens are more likely to vote than younger Americans, suggesting that government policies may be disproportionately tilted toward older Americans and away from younger Americans.

6. **(D) is correct.** Liberals typically support increased spending to aid the poor. This may require higher taxes on the wealthy to achieve. Conservatives, however, favor lower taxes, greater defense spending, and greater military intervention around the world.

7. **(C) is correct.** Despite the perception that politicians use polls to help them determine what policy positions will best get them re-elected, Jacobs and Shapiro find evidence of a very different use of polls. Rather than pandering to the public, politicians use polls to determine how to craft their message to best support those policy positions the politicians already desire to enact.

8. **(A) is correct.** The gender gap predicts that women are more likely to vote for a Democratic candidate than a Republican. The gender gap is a significant predictor because women outnumber men in the United States.

9. **(E) is correct.** A minority majority means that more than half the population of the United States would be nonwhite. Hispanic Americans have become the largest minority group, recently surpassing African Americans. If the percentages continue to change at the same rate, the United States will reach a minority majority sometime in the middle of the twenty-first century.

10. **(A) is correct.** Young people do not vote primarily because they have not had enough experience to develop political awareness and form their beliefs about government. In school, students are taught the virtues of a federal government, not distrust of it.

Free-Response Questions

Very thorough definition. (1 point)

1. Political socialization is the process through which people learn their political values and orientations. It is a process that begins very early and continues throughout life. Political socialization is one way that people become loyal to their nation.

   A good explanation of the role of the family in political socialization. (2 points)

   Two of the primary agents of political socialization are family and school. Families have the earliest and perhaps longest-lasting impact on political views. From their very earliest memories, children learn about politics through the discussions about politics that their parents have. Most children learn their parents' political party affiliation at an early age. Usually, children become members of the same party as their parents. This shows how important family is in political socialization.

   A good explanation of how schools play a role in political socialization. (2 points)

   School is another important agent of socialization. In school, students learn about American politics and history. Through teaching and learning, American students learn to value the capitalistic economic system and democratic political system enjoyed in America. Through reciting the Pledge of Allegiance and singing patriotic songs, students become patriotic themselves. As a result, one can readily see the importance of school in political socialization.

   A good explanation of why the family is such an important factor. Total score on question: 4 of 4.

   Of all the factors that will influence an individual's socialization, family is the most controlling variable. There are a couple of reasons for this. First, children tend to be of the same class and ethnic group as their parents. Also, parents are with their children from the time they are born until they first enter the voting booth. Along with all the social values that a parent gives to their child come political values.

   Of course, other important agents of socialization include the mass media and people with whom one works. But family and school are perhaps the most important.

2. a. California is much more populated in 2000 than it was in 1940.

   A short response, but it does answer the question and earns a point.

   b. People moved to California during World War II to get jobs.

   Another short answer, but it is accurate and earns a second point.

   c. California has more representatives in Congress than any other state does. This makes California much more powerful. California also has more electoral votes than any other states, making it an important state when it comes to electing the president.

   Either one of these answers, more powerful due to more congressmen or more Electoral voters, would have been enough to earn the third point. Total score: 3 of 3.

Chapter 7: The Mass Media and the Political Agenda

Multiple-Choice Questions

1. **(B) is correct.** Investigative journalism often seeks to root out political scandal. Scandals are more likely to achieve higher ratings than, say, an in-depth analysis of an issue. Scandals therefore receive more air time.

2. **(D) is correct.** The president is the most likely politician to be featured in the media. This is because, visually, it is easier to focus on one person than on the 535 members of Congress. As a result, presidents have been able to gain significant political power through public opinion.

3. **(A) is correct.** While 40 percent of journalists indicated that they leaned to the left, only 25 percent indicated that they leaned to the right. Studies show, however, that news stories contain no systematic ideological or partisan bias.

4. **(A) is correct.** Americans were more likely to regularly learn something about the campaign from the Internet than from any other source. The key to understanding this question is to realize that the table tells us *how often* Americans got their campaign news from each source; it does not tell us *how much* information they received. Answer (A) is the only option that discusses

how often Americans of various ages got their campaign news from various sources.

5. **(C) is correct.** Research on media effects has largely determined that the media has no direct effect on citizens' political attitudes. However, the media may have an indirect effect on attitudes by influencing the importance Americans assign to a particular policy issues. That is, the media do not influence what Americans think, but they influence what Americans think about. The agenda-setting effect is strongest for citizens who are informed about politics and who trust the media. The agenda-setting effect is not directly related to investigative journalism.

6. **(D) is correct.** People who choose to watch news stations like CNN and C-SPAN will have direct access to congressional proceedings and in-depth political analysis. They will gain more political knowledge than was ever available to the public before. However, the majority of Americans will choose to watch other specialized stations instead and will become even less politically knowledgeable.

7. **(E) is correct.** The main objective of the American media is to make a profit. While the media may also strive to accurately

portray news events and inform the public, these are all secondary to making money. In other countries, the public may own the major networks; in the U.S., most major media outlets are private businesses.

8. **(E) is correct.** Journalists typically stick to one beat and become familiar with that policy area. A journalist covering interest rates would most likely get his or her information from the spokespeople for the Federal Reserve Board, which helps regulate the economy by influencing interest rates.

9. **(D) is correct.** Sound bites result in very little substantive news coverage and allow candidates to avoid an in-depth discussion of important issues. Why talk about an issue in depth when the media will relegate your words to a simple sound bite?

10. **(D) is correct.** Studies have shown that newspaper readers possess the most political knowledge and usually are the more active members of the electorate. The print media generally analyze issues in greater depth than do the other media, which instead tend to rely on sound bites and other visual information.

Free-Response Questions

A thorough explanation of how the president uses the "going public" strategy. (1 point)

This response explains how the president might use press conferences to "go public." (1 point)

This response explains how the president might use the State of the Union Address to "go public." The last sentence is crucial to linking the address to the strategy. Otherwise, there is a description of the address but no explanation. (1 point)

This response explains how the president might use trial balloons to "go public." (1 point)

This would be a strong and well-written explanation for when and why a president would use a sound bite. The student could have earned the point with less detail. Total score on this question: 5 of 5.

1. In his role as leader of the United States and the world, the president often uses the strategy of "going public."

   Going public means that the president attempts to persuade the American people about his view of government and what policies ought to be made. By persuading the public, the president hopes also to be seen as the leader of Congress and other agencies of government. If Congress feels pressure from the people, it may enact the president's agenda. Even the Supreme Court might be affected by the president's popularity, along with the Federal Reserve Board or other executive agencies who might otherwise be isolated from presidential influence.

   The president often uses the media to take his message public. One way he does that is to hold a press conference and call the Washington news media to the White House. The president often begins press conferences with a statement designed to persuade the American public to share the president's perspective. However, there is a risk in press conferences because the president may be asked questions that he would rather not answer, or that might show him in a negative light.

   Another way that the president might "go public" is when he addresses Congress each year in his state of the union message.

   The State of the Union Address is a constitutional power that the president has to go before the Congress each year to tell them what he would like for them to do in the coming year. Because the address is televised, he tells the American people of his goals in hopes that they will communicate with their representatives to support him.

   Finally, sometimes a president has an idea about something he would like to accomplish, but he does not know if the idea will be popular. In that case, the president may "leak" an idea to the media without using his name. These leaks are called "trial balloons." If the idea is popular, the president will then pursue it. On the other hand, if it looks to be unpopular, the president may never mention the idea himself and it will go away.

   Of all the methods mentioned above, sound bites are used by presidents when they want to drum up public support for an issue. If President Bush wanted to rally public support for a position he holds strongly, such as keeping American forces in Iraq, this would be the best method. However, the State of the Union address only takes place once a year, and he might not want to wait that long. Trial balloons are good for judging the public mood, but they are not that good for directing the mood. At a press conference, a president might have to answer difficult questions for reporters that would erode the support he was trying to build. A sound bite, well written and spoken, can put a positive view into the minds of the American people. Some presidents, such as Reagan or Clinton, were very good at using sound bites. Others, like Bush and Bush, have found it very difficult.

Response gives a strong definition of broadcasting and narrowcasting. Major points are underlined to help the reader easily find the points, with examples given to further support the response. 2 points earned.

2. a. Broadcasting dominated the electronic media from the 1950s through the 1980s when there were only three major networks: NBC, ABC, CBS. In order to attract as many viewers as possible, <u>these stations would air stories with broad interest</u>. They did not want to appear too liberal or too conservative for fear of losing voters. With the rise of cable television, stations look to attract a niche audience. This is sometimes done through entertainment programming (i.e., ESPN, the Cooking Network) or with news programs. Rather than having a news programs that is written to cover all spectrums of viewers, from liberal to conservative, narrowcasting will have some shows slanted with a conservative bias (such as Fox News) and some with a liberal bias (such as CNN).

A good description of the media bias and, again, good examples in case the reader does not consider the description strong enough. 1 point earned.

   b. To attract a conservative audience, Fox News will give a more conservative view on the news. For example, a story about illegal immigration is more likely to talk about violent crime rates among Latinos than the contributions Latinos make to the U.S. economy. <u>Narrowcasting tends to make the news stories either more conservative or more liberal</u>.

A clear explanation of the impact of bias. The explanation is not needed to earn the point, but again serves as a safety net in case the reader is unsure of the answer. 1 point earned. Total score: 4 of 4.

   c. <u>Narrowcasting causes the media to reinforce the views people already have on an issue</u>. With people choosing to only hear their own side of an argument repeated over and over on the news, the American people have become more extreme.

Chapter 8: Political Parties

Multiple-Choice Questions

1. **(A) is correct.** While more than 50 percent of Jews identify themselves as Democrats, fewer than 40 percent of women and White Catholics are Democrats, and fewer than 30 percent of White Evangelicals and those under 30 years old are Democrats.

2. **(D) is correct.** Congressional seats are awarded on a winner-take-all basis. This means that a party is not rewarded unless that party wins the election, because only the winner has a say in Congress. Since small parties will almost never have a voice in Congress, they have an incentive to join with other groups in the hopes of forming a majority coalition that will result in their victory. This helps encourage a two-party system. In contrast, if seats are allocated according to proportional representation, parties can have votes in the legislature according to their electoral strength. Under this system, small parties do not have the same incentive to merge with other parties, encouraging a multiparty system. Neither the Constitution nor statutes mandate political parties.

3. **(E) is correct.** While third parties seldom win elections, they nonetheless have an important influence on American politics. Third parties bring new issues into the political arena and they offer an alternative to voters who are displeased with the two major parties.

4. **(C) is correct.** Political parties are important to democracy because they link the American people with their government. Voters, members of Congress, and even the president may share the same party affiliation. By electing the candidate of their preferred party, voters are able to advance their own policy preferences in the political arena.

5. **(E) is correct.** Ticket splitting is voting for one party for one office and for another party for other offices. Independents are most likely to engage in ticket splitting. Nonvoters do not engage in ticket splitting because they do not vote. Primary election voters are given a slate of candidates who all belong to the party running the primary (except in the relatively rare blanket primaries).

6. **(B) is correct.** A political party officially nominates its candidate for the presidency at a national convention. It is attended by party delegates from all 50 states.

7. **(C) is correct.** Divided government occurs when the party controlling the presidency does not control both houses of Congress. Under divided government, it is nearly impossible for one party to enact its legislative agenda. The parties must reach a compromise in order to get things done. Such compromises help to prevent extreme public policies and force the parties to reach a mutually agreeable solution.

8. **(A) is correct.** From the late nineteenth century through the 1930s, local parties were often incredibly powerful in large cities such as New York and Chicago. These cities were controlled by party machines whose bosses used the patronage system to reward people who supported the party. Today, staffing city government is much more professionalized, and local parties have declined significantly.

9. **(C) is correct.** Critical elections reveal fissures in each party's coalition of supporters and results in a realignment of supports behind each party. This realignment may propel what used to be the minority party to power, though the coalition forming the new majority party is likely to be considerably different. Therefore, critical elections usher in a new political era in American politics.

10. **(B) is correct.** The New Deal Coalition was comprised of urbanites, labor unions, Catholics, Jews, the poor, Southerners, and African Americans. Bankers, however, remained with the Republican Party. This successful coalition kept Democrats dominant for decades.

Free-Response Questions

Remember, you do not need an essay response on the AP Government exam. Bullet point responses are acceptable. In this response, the student does a good job of describing two ways in which parties serve as linkage institutions. Coordinating policymaking is not clearly connected to a party's role as a linkage institution, and therefore does not earn a point. 2 of 3 points awarded in part (a).

1. a. Three ways in which political parties serve as linkage institutions are:

   1. <u>Running campaigns</u>—Political parties poll voters to find out what issues the people are concerned about and then organize the campaign to highlight their candidates' stance on these issues.

   2. <u>Recruiting candidates</u>—Parties choose candidates whose views they believe are in line with the public's. A candidate whose stand on issues is seen as too extreme is not likely to get nominated by one of the major parties.

   3. Parties coordinate policymaking—Political leaders in the House and Senate work to make sure their party members vote in support of party issues.

   b. Political parties are not as strong today as they were 50 years ago, in part <u>because of television</u>. Television gives candidates direct access to the people, without the help of their party. Arnold Schwarzenegger of California has a much more liberal stance on issues than the Republican Party in that state. Zell Miller, a democrat, spoke at the Republican National Convention in 2004. Both men retained their offices, in spite of their tweaking their parties' noses, because they can directly access the voters.

Identifying television as a cause of the weakening of political parties is good, but it does not earn a point without an explanation.

A good explanation of how television has weakened parties. The examples that follow insure the earning of the point. Total score for this response: 3 of 4.

The role of independent voters is important in presidential elections. 1 point.

A strong explanation of the role of third-party candidates. 1 point.

Not much discussion here, but enough to earn a third point. Total score: 3 of 3.

2. Since 1952, there have been more self-proclaimed Democrats in the United States than Republicans. Yet the Democrats find it much harder to win presidential elections. There are three reasons for this. First, Independent voters, who make up almost 40 percent of all voters today, tend to vote Republican in presidential elections. This is one reason why both Democrat and Republican candidates tend to drift toward the center in the general election.

   Second, third-party candidates can have an impact on elections. In 1968 and 1972, George Wallace pulled votes away from the Democratic Party, allowing Republican Richard Nixon to win both times. In 2000, Ralph Nadar pulled enough votes away from Al Gore to allow Bush to become president. Of course, the knife cuts both ways. Third-party candidate Ross Perot caused George H. W. Bush to lose his election to Democrat Bill Clinton. Still, Democrats are hurt more often by third-party candidates than Republicans.

   Finally, Republicans tend to vote more than do Democrats. A 10 percent lead in self-identified voters doesn't help the Democrats if that 10 percent doesn't go to the polls and cast their votes.

Chapter 9: Nominations and Campaigns

Multiple-Choice Questions

1. **(D) is correct.** All of the other choices were established. Not surprisingly, members of Congress were reluctant to provide any funds to the campaigns of their future opponents.

2. **(A) is correct.** The only conclusion that may be drawn strictly from the information given is that the labor groups listed did contribute significantly to non-Republican candidates. This is confirmed by the fact that only a small percentage of their large donations went to Republicans. The rest must have gone to other candidates, most likely to Democrats.

3. **(E) is correct.** During the presidential nomination season, the media tend to focus their attention on Iowa and New Hampshire. Of these two states, only New Hampshire holds a primary, while Iowa holds a caucus. Every four years, the media flock to New Hampshire to cover their first-in-the-nation primary. Thus, media coverage of presidential primaries is heavily skewed toward New Hampshire.

4. **(A) is correct.** While the nomination system has many faults, exclusivity is not one of them. All registered voters can participate in open primaries and all registered partisans can participate in closed parties. Under the current nomination system, the door is wide open to participation by ordinary citizens, and about one-fourth of Americans weigh in with their candidate preferences. The days of candidates being selected by a small group of political elites are long over.

5. **(D) is correct.** For a business to make contributions through a PAC, it must register the PAC with the Federal Election Commission (FEC). The PAC then must report on all of its activities and spending so that the FEC can closely monitor it to ensure that it is not making illegal contributions directly to candidates.

6. **(C) is correct.** National committees meet and decide on the party's official platform for the next four years. The platform is the best available statement of a party's policy positions.

7. **(E) is correct.** Voter turnout in primaries and caucuses is unrepresentative because those who vote tend to be older and wealthier. In addition, participants in caucuses need to be willing and able to devote a significant amount of time and effort to have their voice heard. This, too, helps make the process unrepresentative.

8. **(B) is correct.** Television time is expensive and consumes more than half of the budget for a presidential or senatorial campaign. Most candidates apparently believe that their policy positions are a crucial part of their campaign, and they are willing to pay substantial sums to communicate them to voters.

9. **(D) is correct.** The United States often receives criticism for its long campaign season. In most European countries, for example, campaigns last only a few months. As a result, European campaigns are also less expensive than American campaigns.

10. **(D) is correct.** Rather than a discussion of issues, the media tend to focus on campaign strategies and the horse race. That is, the media are more likely to report the candidate who is ahead in the polls than to discuss the candidates' differences on important policy issues. In fact, a study by the Project for Excellence in Journalism found that that 63 percent of news stories dealt with the horse race and campaign strategies; only 32 percent dealt with the substance of the campaign, including issues, policies, and the candidates' backgrounds.

Free-Response Questions

None of this is applicable to the question. Be sure to keep your answer focused on the specifics of the question.

This phrase defines (1 point)

This phrase somewhat defines PACs. (1 point)

Within the context, the reader is able to infer that the student sees this as a negative impact of PACs on campaigns. (1 point)

The student briefly describes two regulations: good for 2 points.

This response presents an interesting argument, which, unfortunately, addresses only part of the question. Two sources of campaign funding go totally undefined, and without definitions, it is impossible to describe either a positive or a negative impact. (5 of 10 points)

1. Today's political campaigns are long, drawn-out media extravaganzas that cost millions of dollars. To reach voters, candidates must spend large sums of money on television advertising, travel, and a professional campaign staff. The difficulties of financing such an event and the ways in which these difficulties are overcome ultimately infringe on the practice of democracy.

    To run for office, a candidate must have hundreds of thousands of dollars at his or her disposal. This money is necessary to buy a candidate exposure—it allows the candidate to convey his or her political beliefs to the public through television and even just to maintain a constant presence in the minds of the public. The more money you can spend, the more visible you will be, and ultimately the more successful you'll be in the race. Any candidates who cannot afford to spend such large sums on campaigning are instantly at a disadvantage. Some qualified people interested in running are not able to because of the impossibility of acquiring such funds. In a true democracy, anyone with political knowledge and experience should be able to run for office. However, very few Americans can, thus putting wealthy people and incumbents at a distinct advantage. Furthermore, third-party candidates who represent the middle and lower classes or who have innovative new ideas are not able to spread their message and compete against wealthier politicians. The cost of campaigns therefore limits political participation and discourages the introduction of innovative policies from different sectors of the electorate.

    Expensive campaigns also act as a deterrent to democracy because they often allow businesses to gain a foothold in the political arena. Candidates are able to finance their campaigns only with the help of soft money and PACs. Soft money includes all the donations to a party for its general use, most of which go indirectly to campaigning, and PACs are funding vehicles established by businesses to channel money into campaigns. Candidates, then, receive a great deal of campaign support indirectly from businesses, to which they are somewhat beholden when they reach office. Campaigns therefore allow business interests to play a role in the election process. Rather than being elected by the will of the people and taking office with their needs in mind, politicians shape the political agenda around the needs of those businesses, which helped them get to Capitol Hill.

    In an effort to curb abuses in campaign funding, Congress has set up regulations for how PACs operate. PACs must register with the Federal Election Commission if they contribute more than $1,000 to candidates. The McCain-Feingold bill worked to get rid of soft money altogether in 2002. This regulation, however, has only seemed to push the money in a new direction (527 groups).

    By enacting campaign finance reforms that limit soft money and PAC donations, campaigns might become more democratic. Moreover, if all candidates were guaranteed the same amount of money with which to run their campaigns and free, equal airtime, as is done in many other countries, all people who wanted to run for office would have a fair chance, and businesses would not be able to influence politics so easily.

*This one sentence is enough informa-
tion to earn a point. The examples
that follow are not required, but they
do help reinforce the point.*

*The question only asks for one change.
In giving two, the student insures
that if one of the answers they give is
deemed unacceptable for some reason,
they may still earn the point for (b).*

2. Iowa and New Hampshire receive more media attention than any other state because they are the first two contests in the process of nominating candidates for the Presidency. If a candidate does well in these two states, they can use that momentum to start winning the bigger primaries and caucuses that follow. Jimmy Carter in 1976 and Barak Obama in 2008 were both able to use upset wins in Iowa as momentum to capture the Democratic nomination. Rudy Giuliani, once considered a frontrunner for the Republican nomination in 2008, ignored Iowa and New Hampshire and concentrated instead on Florida. By the time the Florida nomination came around, he was so out of the news cycle, he failed miserably and soon had to abandon his campaign.

   The influence of Iowa and New Hampshire could be lessened if other states held earlier primaries. The parties could lessen the influence of these two states if they assigned the dates for primaries and caucuses rather than allowing the states to decide their own dates (with some restrictions).

   The parties themselves are fearful of upsetting Iowa or New Hampshire and losing their votes. Therefore, the parties discourage other states from moving their primaries earlier. This is what happened to Florida and Michigan. They moved their primaries earlier, and were punished by the Democratic National Convention (but not by the Republicans).

*A weak explanation, but enough to earn a point. The student would have
been safer to explain why the parties are fearful of upsetting Iowa and New
Hampshire. Total score on this question: 3 of 3.*

Chapter 10: Elections and Voting Behavior

Multiple-Choice Questions

1. **(D) is correct.** Most states award their electoral votes in a "winner-take-all" system. Whichever candidate wins the popular vote in the state receives all of that state's electoral votes.

2. **(E) is correct.** Americans with a college education are the most likely group to vote in a presidential election. In 2004, 74 percent of those with a college education voted. In contrast, 60 percent of women, 47 percent of singles, 56 percent of African Americans, and 54 percent of those 25 to 44 voted.

3. **(B) is correct.** While many people who vote according to policy preferences probably have developed certain voting habits over the course of several elections, this is not necessarily a requirement for choosing candidates in this manner. Well-informed first-time voters could also vote according to those policies on which they agree with a particular candidate.

4. **(D) is correct.** Suffrage, or the right to vote, has gradually expanded in the United States. Laws or constitutional amendments have extended suffrage to those who don't own property, women, African Americans, Native Americans, and those at least 18 years old. However, suffrage can be denied to those in prison and even those who have completed their sentences. Thus, a convicted felon would be the person most likely to be denied suffrage.

5. **(B) is correct.** Figure 10.1 shows that the Democratic presidential candidate won on the West Coast (Washington, Oregon, and California) and the Northeast (Maine, New Hampshire, Vermont, New York, Massachusetts, Rhode Island, Connecticut, New Jersey, Delaware, Maryland, and Pennsylvania).

6. **(E) is correct.** In most other democracies, governments take the effort to register citizens to vote. In the United States, however, this is an individual responsibility and a prerequisite for voting. This works to lower voter turnout. In addition, the differences between the Democratic candidate and the Republican candidate are likely to be smaller than the differences between the various candidates in multiparty European democracies. This also works to lower American turnout compared with other democracies. However, American voters are asked to vote more frequently; this leads to voter fatigue, not the development of good voting habits. Finally, only a handful of democracies require their citizens to vote.

7. **(B) is correct.** Political efficacy is the belief that your voter matters. Those with political efficacy are more likely to vote. Those who lack efficacy are more likely to stay home on Election Day.

8. **(A) is correct.** Young voters are less likely to have strong attachments with political parties, partly because they have less experience with political parties. Without partisan attachments, young voters are more likely to support independent or third-party candidates. One of the biggest distinctions about young citizens, however, is that they are much less likely to vote than older Americans.

9. **(D) is correct.** The Motor Voter Act allows people to register to vote when they get or renew a driver's license. This increases voter registration by making it easier for people to register. However, while more people have registered, voter turnout has not been significantly affected by the Motor Voter Act.

10. **(B) is correct.** Oregon has been conducting elections by mail since 1998, when voters passed a referendum to eliminate polling places and conduct all elections through the United States Postal Service.

Free-Response Questions

The student identifies two changes that have occurred. The maximum points possible is only one, which the student earns.

1. a. In 1960, those who regularly attended religious services were very evenly split between Democrats (49 percent) and Republican (50 percent). By 2004, Democrats lost much support (39 percent) while Republican increased among those who regularly attended services (60 percent). Another group that showed strong patterns of change was those who never attended religious services; Democrats going from 51 percent support in 1960 to 62 percent in 2004. Republicans showed a loss among this group, dropping from 49 percent vote for Nixon to a 36 percent support for Bush in 2004.

The issue of abortion is a religiously divisive one. 1 point earned.

   b. One reason for the change in support is the issue of abortion. In 1960, it was a state matter and was not given much attention by the national parties. Following *Roe v. Wade*, the Republicans made a pro-life plank in their platform and begun attracting more Evangelicals and Catholics to their party.

The students gives a correct explanation of the changing Catholic vote. 1 point.

   c. Catholics went from strongly supporting democratic candidate Kennedy in 1960 to strongly supporting Bush in 2004.

The writer again identifies abortion as a cause of party realignment. 1 point. Total score on question: 4 of 4.

   d. The big change for Catholics was the abortion issue. As the Republican Party became more religious, the Democratic Party became more secular.

The writer could have argued the reverse as well, that candidates will focus more on states where they are competitive. The example of Bush in California (or Kerry in Texas) is good for another point.

2. a. Since most states have a winner-take-all system, candidates <u>will not focus on states where they are not likely to win</u>. For example, George W. Bush did not campaign much in California in either 2000 or 2004 because he was so far behind in the polls.

   b. The Electoral College is undemocratic because a candidate <u>could lose the popular vote and still be elected</u> president if he or she has a majority of electoral votes. George W. Bush was able to do this in 2000. Likewise, Bill Clinton was able to win the presidency twice without ever having won a majority of popular votes.

Losing the popular election and still being elected president is worth one point. The example of Bush in 2000 is worth another point. Although Clinton did not receive a majority of popular votes in either of his elections, he still had more popular votes than any of his competitors. This example would not have been awarded a point. Fortunately, the student had already earned two points for this section.

   c. The reason that the Electoral College system has not changed is that it is found in the Constitution. And to change the Constitution, it would take three-quarters of the states to approve the change. <u>Small states, which are overrepresented in the Electoral College system, are unlikely to vote to change this system.</u>

Small states supporting the Electoral College is worth the third point. In fact, the student could have simply extended the argument that amending the Constitution is a difficult enough barrier to keep the system from being changed. Total score: 5 of 5.

Chapter 11: Interest Groups

Multiple-Choice Questions

1. **(E) is correct.** Elite theorists believe that power, influence, and access are not distributed evenly among interest groups. Only those with money to promote themselves and to contribute to campaigns have any significant influence on policymaking. Elite theorists point to the proliferation of business PACs as evidence of more interest group corruption in American politics. For example, in 2004, a quarter of all PAC contributions came from just 48 PACs.

2. **(B) is correct.** In a small interest group, members' share of a collective good is large enough that they are more likely to participate actively to maintain the group's success. In contrast, the success of a large group is divided among many more people and might be less apparent to them. Therefore, large groups are more likely to suffer from the free-rider problem.

3. **(A) is correct.** Public education is an issue that affects all Americans, not just those who are members of an interest group. An interest group that focuses on public education would therefore be a public interest group. Any successes achieved by the group would benefit the public as a whole.

4. **(C) is correct.** Lobbyists are forbidden by law from contributing any money directly to lawmakers for any reason. They must establish a PAC to make campaign contributions, and this money, in theory, can be used only for general party purposes; it cannot go to a specific candidate. All interest group donations, moreover, are monitored by the Federal Election Commission.

5. **(D) is correct.** An iron triangle, or subgovernment, is composed of an interest group, the federal agency, and the legislative committee, which all handle a specific policy. They work together closely to create policies in the given policy area that benefit those involved.

6. **(E) is correct.** Pluralists believe that interest groups have about the same amount of power because they must compete with each other for influence. If, for example, one group increases its efforts to reach politicians, other groups will quickly follow suit to catch up and will, therefore, balance the system again.

7. **(D) is correct.** Interest groups frequently file class action lawsuits in an attempt to reverse policy decisions. They also solidify their relationships with members of Congress by channeling the bulk of their campaign contributions to incumbents. Interest groups also share their policy expertise with lawmakers when they believe it will encourage lawmakers to pass favorable legislation. Of course, it is illegal for interest groups to pay for legislative favors and unethical for judges to meet with interest group representatives.

8. **(E) is correct.** The map indicates relative differences between the states; the information is not specific enough to ascertain which state has the highest percentage of its workforce in unions. We know that New York and Wisconsin have a higher percentage of union members than do Kentucky and Ohio, but this does not bring us any closer to being able to answer the specific question asked.

9. **(C) is correct.** Interest groups concentrate most of their efforts on shaping policy during the political process. They maintain frequent contact with lawmakers while Congress is in session. Political parties, on the other hand, try to shape the policy agenda by having their candidates elected to office. They therefore apply their efforts mostly to campaigns.

10. **(A) is correct.** Single-issue groups have a narrow focus. Members of single-issue groups usually feel incredibly strongly about the issue that concerns them. Such issues often appeal to their emotions. Abortion is one such issue about which some voters feel strongly.

Free-Response Questions

Chooses one group from list.

Identifies an institution to which the NAACP would appeal. (1 point)

This sentence hints at a resource, but a more direct statement would assure the point.

This is a clear statement identifying a resource of the NAACP. (1 point)

This section, in conjunction with the discussion of concentrating on certain congressional committees in the previous paragraph, constitutes an explanation of how the NAACP would use the resource of black population to influence policymaking. (1 point)

1. The National Association for the Advancement of Colored People has been an influential interest group since the early twentieth century, when it formed to fight for the rights of African Americans. It has become a powerful and prestigious interest group.

   This group works with the Department of Justice to make sure civil rights are enforced, but otherwise it pursues its interests primarily in the legislative arena. It is most likely to win the attention and cooperation of members of Congress whose constituencies include a high percentage of African Americans. It would also be most likely to concentrate its efforts on a few key committees in the House and Senate that handle urban housing, education, and labor policy. For example, the NAACP might lobby members of the Senate Labor and Human Resources Committee about the minimum wage or the House Education and the Workforce Committee about after-school programs in low-income school districts. With the help of the NAACP, in fact, Congress passed the Civil Rights Act of 1964, the Voting Rights Act of 1965, and the Fair Housing Act of 1968. These legislative victories also demonstrate the success of the NAACP in pursuing its interests and representing a major group of Americans.

   The most powerful resource of the NAACP is the body of people whom it represents, African Americans. They are one of the largest minority groups in the United States and, when organized under the NAACP, have had significant political successes. However, only about half of all African Americans vote. To encourage African Americans to exercise this right and thus wield their power, the NAACP has initiated voter registration and education efforts. If voter turnout were higher among this portion of the electorate, more African Americans might be elected to influential governmental positions to work directly for the group. They would also gain political clout because politicians, to win their votes, would have to pay attention to their concerns. An interest group is, in part, as powerful as its members are vocal.

   This is a somewhat rambling discussion of the NAACP, a target to which it would appeal, a resource at its disposal, and how that resource might be used. No second resource is identified. (3 of 5 points)

The student correctly defines political parties.

The explanation for interest groups, coupled with the definition of a political party, is enough to earn a point in part (a).

The student correctly identifies the NAACP and the AFL-CIO for the 2 identification points in part (b).

2. a. Political parties and interest groups both play important roles in the American political system. Parties work to control the government by getting their members elected to office. Once in office, these politicians can help make the laws that their party favors. Interest groups, on the other hand, do not nominate people to run for office. They may support a candidate who is running, but they do not run their own candidate. Instead, interest groups put pressure on the government (both elected officials and nonelected officials) to try to get their agenda put into action. For example, the NRA doesn't nominate anyone to run for office, buy it strongly endorses candidate who are pro-gun. The NRA may also bring cases before the courts to try to protect gun rights.

   b. The NAACP would be a group concerned with equality interests. The AFL-CIO would be an interest group concerned with economic interests.

   c. The NAACP has successfully challenged segregation in the court system. In the case of *Brown v. Board of Education* the NAACP was able to have the Supreme Court rule that segregation was unconstitutional.

The use of courts has been one of the strongest methods of the NAACP. Total score on this question: 4 of 4.

Chapter 12: Congress

Multiple-Choice Questions

1. **(C) is correct.** Conference committees are composed of House and Senate members who seek a compromise when the House and Senate pass different versions of the same bill. After the conference committee reaches a compromise, the bill returns to the House and Senate where it must be passed without amendments before it is sent to the president.

2. **(E) is correct.** Challengers do not necessarily have a clean record just because they are new to the potential governmental position. Many challengers have held other posts, and ones who have not would have no record at all. Furthermore, incumbents, just because they have already served in Congress, do not necessarily have a poor record. In fact, it is to their advantage to demonstrate to the public their record of service to the constituency.

3. **(B) is correct.** Standing committees conduct legislative oversight primarily by holding hearings in which they question bureaucrats. Each committee conducts oversight of the federal departments that fall within its policy area. The budgets of these departments are controlled by Congress, a strong form of oversight.

4. **(C) is correct.** The speaker has a great deal of influence in the House, guiding the party leaders in assigning positions on House committees. Congressional committees have other duties besides referring bills to the floor, including oversight and numerous legislative tasks.

5. **(B) is correct.** In the Senate, there is no limit to debate over a piece of legislation. A senator who has the floor is free to talk for as long as he wishes. He or she may attempt to stall by talking a bill to death. This tactic, called a filibuster, prevents senators from calling for a vote. The Senate may simply adjourn without voting.

6. **(D) is correct.** According to Figure 12.1, while Senators have slightly lower re-election rates than members of the House, all members of Congress are re-elected at fairly high rates. That is, House incumbents are often re-elected more than 90 percent of the time, and Senators fare only slightly worse.

7. **(D) is correct.** A number of different factors may influence a representative's vote on a bill concerned with a highly publicized issue. With re-election in mind, members of Congress would *most likely* vote as their constituency would want them to on high-profile issues. On issues that receive less public visibility, members are more likely to vote in accordance with their personal ideology.

8. **(E) is correct.** After a bill has been reviewed by a committee in the House, it is not yet ready to be debated on the floor of the House. Most bills must first be submitted to the House Rules Committee (revenue, budget, and appropriations bills are the exceptions). The Rules Committee sets a limited time for debate and may set rules for amending the bill. This gives the House Rules Committee a significant degree of influence over proposed legislation.

9. **(A) is correct.** Power in the Senate is more decentralized than in the House. The House is headed by the Speaker, who exerts considerable influence over the legislative process. In the Senate, the filibuster gives individual senators considerable power, resulting in a more decentralized chamber. Only the Senate provides for unlimited debate and, therefore, enables the filibuster.

10. **(B) is correct.** In recent years, congressional parties have strengthened. Congressional Democrats have become more consistently liberal and congressional Republicans have become more consistently conservative, while the distance between the political parties has increased.

Free-Response Questions

On a graph or table question, the sometimes obvious answers count as much as the more difficult parts of the question. Even if you did not know the answers to parts (b) and (c), you could still earn two points for correctly reading the graph. Both descriptions are correct here, earning 2 points.

1. a. One trend shown in the graph is that House incumbents are more likely to get re-re-elected than are Senators. A second trend is that House incumbents get re-elected at a very high rate (usually over 90 percent of the time).

A good explanation followed with strong support

   b. One reasons House incumbents get re-elected at such a high rate is that their names are well known in their home districts. People will know who their Congressmen is. Being a Congressman carries a certain prestige that can earn votes come November. The challenger usually does not have the same amount of name recognition. Also, incumbents have a record they can run on. They can point to bills they have supported which have helped their home district. This can sway voters as well. Finally, in a piece of self-fulfilling prophecy, donors are more likely to give money to incumbents, because incumbents are more likely to win an election. This extra money also gives the incumbent an edge in the election.

Another good example. In both answers for part (b), the students needs to do more than just list the answer. Had the student only written "an incumbent has a record they can run on," they would not have earned the point. Be sure to explain when the question asks for an explanation.

This would be true except in the cases of states such as North or South Dakota, where the Congressional district is the entire state.

   c. House incumbents may get re-elected more often than senators for a couple of reasons. First, House incumbents come from smaller districts than senators, so it is easier to represent the needs of their constituency. For example, a representative from Cleveland, Ohio, can be an advocate for the needs of the urban poor, and win many votes in this way. Whereas a senator from Ohio doesn't represent just the urban poor, but also farmers, factory workers, and many other interests. Needless to say, the more people you try to please, the more difficult it becomes to win. Another reason House incumbents are more likely to win is that they run against weaker competition than do senators. In a senatorial race, the challenger may be a former member of the House of Representatives, a governor, or even or former presidential candidate. House incumbents don't usually have to face such powerful opponents, and are thus more likely to win re-election.

It is said that every representative wants to be a senator and every senator wants to be president. Total score on this question: 6 of 6.

Describes how the Speaker is chosen. (1 point)

Describes the powers of the Speaker. (1 point)

Describes how the president of the Senate is chosen. (1 point)

Describes the powers of the president of the Senate. (1 point)

Explains chamber leadership differences. (2 points)

Identifies and describes a third congressional office. 2 points. Total score on response: 8 of 8.

2. The leaders in the two chambers of Congress are very important and they are selected in different ways. In the House of Representatives, the leader is the Speaker of the House and is elected by the members of the House. Because one party has the majority, in fact the Speaker is always selected in an election in that party. When the whole House votes, all members of the majority party vote for their candidate for Speaker, ensuring his election. For example, since the Republican Party had a majority in the House of Representatives in 1999, that party met in caucus to agree to support Dennis Hastert for the Speaker position. When the whole House voted, he won election.

    Once elected, the Speaker is a very powerful leader. He presides over the House and therefore can help control debate. He plays a major role in making assignments to standing committees. Because of these powers, the Speaker is the most powerful member of the House.

    In the Senate, things are quite different. The president of the Senate is the vice president of the United States. He is elected to the office by the Electoral College and not by the members of the Senate. Traditionally, the president of the Senate serves mostly a symbolic role in leadership. His only real power comes in voting when there is a tie in the Senate.

    The Senate is smaller than the House of Representatives, with only 100 members compared to the 435 in the House. Because of the sizes of the two houses, leaders play a different role. In the House, the Speaker is a very important leader because committees are more important in the House and rules of debate are much stricter. In the Senate, there is more of a debating society, and the leader is much less important. Often, amendments are made to bills during floor debate in the Senate and the leader is not important. All the leader does is recognize the speakers. He cannot control debate as the Speaker can in the House.

    In the House of Representative, each party has a Whip. The job of the party Whip is to make sure the party members vote with the party on important issues. Although he or she has no constitutional function in the Congress, the Whip's ability to influence important positions within the party makes him or her a powerful force.

Chapter 13: The Presidency

Multiple-Choice Questions

1. **(E) is correct.** While a presidential veto usually effectively kills proposed legislation, Congress can override the veto and has done so in about four percent of the vetoes. The Constitution gives the president the power to veto as a means to check Congress, and it gives Congress the power to override a veto as a means of checking the president. Veto overrides, however, require a supermajority of each chamber.

2. **(C) is correct.** As sanctioned by the Constitution, the process of removing a president from office is as follows: 1) the House votes to impeach the president; 2) the Senate carries out the impeachment trial, over which the Chief Justice presides; and 3) the Senate must have a two-thirds vote to convict and remove the president. Statements I, III, and IV describe these steps.

3. **(E) is correct.** The War Powers Resolution maintains a president's ability to act quickly and decisively by sending troops to a troubled spot, but it prevents him from sidestepping Congress's power to declare war by requiring that those troops be withdrawn after 60 days. Congress is, by virtue of its size, a slow institution. The time limit gives Congress time to debate and declare war if it chooses to. If it does not, the president must withdraw the troops.

4. **(B) is correct.** If the answer does not leap out at you, try eliminating those ways that you know presidents *do* try to influence policy decisions. They do appeal directly to the electorate through public appearances or televised addresses. They also offer to support the legislation of a representative in exchange for that representative's vote, and they do work closely with party leaders in Congress to build coalitions. There is also an understanding between presidents and Congress that representatives who support the president's agenda receive small favors. While presidents often do push their own proposals through Congress, they cannot introduce a bill themselves—they must find a member of Congress to endorse it for them. This enforces the separation of powers set forth in the Constitution.

5. **(B) is correct.** The vice president has few official responsibilities, other than presiding over the Senate and assuming the presidency if there is a vacancy. Commanding the military and heading the Cabinet are duties that fall to the president, creating the federal budget falls to the Congress, and running congressional elections belongs to the states.

6. **(A) is correct.** A citizen's approval of the president is often derived from party affiliation. A president of his or her preferred party most likely acts in keeping with the platform of which the citizen already approves. By relying on party identification, a person is able to make a judgment about the president, even if he or she is not well informed about the president's performance. Historically, those who identify with the president's party give the president approval more than 40 percentage points higher than do those who identify with the opposition party.

7. **(D) is correct.** According to Figure 13.4, Nixon's average approval rating was 48 percent and George W. Bush's average approval rating was 49 percent—a difference of only one percentage point. The differences in the approval ratings of the other pairs are all considerably larger. The differences for the remaining pairs are as follows: Clinton and Carter, 8 points; George H. W. Bush and Reagan, 9 points; Kennedy and Johnson, 15 points; and Kennedy and Reagan, 19 points.

8. **(B) is correct.** Recent presidents have vetoed an average of 35 bills in each term. However, it is fairly unusual for Congress to override a president's veto. Fewer than 5 percent of vetoed bills are overridden, largely because it is difficult to achieve a two-thirds vote in both houses of Congress.

9. **(C) is correct.** Presidents can nominate justices, but they cannot remove them from their seats on the Supreme Court. In fact, justices, once they have been nominated by the president and approved by Congress, hold their positions for life. The Constitution specifies that justices have no term limit. Justices can be impeached, but this has happened only once.

10. **(A) is correct.** The Constitution authorizes the vice president to take over the office of the presidency if the president dies, resigns, is impeached, or is otherwise unable to perform his duties. If the vice president is also unable to serve for any of these reasons, the Speaker of the House assumes the presidency until the next election.

Free-Response Questions

Explains one power the President has. 1 point.	1. The Founding Fathers had intended to make the president stronger in foreign affairs than Congress. But in keeping with the ideals of checks and balances, they also gave Congress some power over foreign relations. One power the president has in foreign relations is to dispatch troops. As commander in chief, the president can order the military to strike at America's enemies or defend America's interest overseas. But the president cannot declare war. Only Congress can declare war.
Explains one power Congress has. 1 point.	Following a long conflict in Vietnam, which was never declared a war, Congress decided to reign in the power of the president as commander in chief. The War Powers Act, passed in 1973, required the president to consult with Congress before dispatching troops. Once the troops were deployed, the president had to seek congressional approval for these actions within 30 days.
Explains the War Powers Act. 1 point	Since the passage of the War Powers Act, there have been numerous military actions ordered by presidents without congressional approval. George H. W. Bush ordered Operation Shield and Operation Desert Storm to remove the Iraqis from Kuwait. American troops were stationed in Saudi Arabia for months before Congress finally gave official sanction to the action.
Describes an action taken by the president since the passage of this act and Congress' reaction. 2 points. Total score on this question: 5 of 5 points.	

Presidential coattails are one way to earn support.

While a veto is a powerful tool used by presidents, it is not specific to their role as party leader, and therefore not worth a point.

Only the more popular presidents are able to use coattails. Lame duck presidents often have a difficult time campaigning on behalf of their fellow party members. Total score on question: 3 of 4 points.

2. a. The Presidency is considered the highest office in the land. The presidency is the only office that is elected by all Americans. One role the president plays in politics is that of party leader. The president is able to use the position of party leader to become a more effective national leader in two ways. First, a popular president can help <u>members of his own party get re-elected</u>. A president can campaign in a congressman's district and help him or her get more votes. In exchange for this, the president can expect the congressman to support the president's legislative program. Second, a president can veto to <u>strike down bills</u> he does not support, giving him a strong hand in making Congress pass legislation of which he approves.

   b. While presidents do have some tools to try to keep their party in line, helping them pass laws, congressmen do not always listen to the president. <u>First</u>, congressmen do not owe their office to the president; their constituents elect them to the House or Senate. If a congressman has to choose between upsetting the president or upsetting his or her constituency in an election year, the congressman would rather upset the President. <u>Second</u>, a president's ability to help a congressmen get re-elected is not guaranteed. In mid-term elections, the president's party often loses seats. Or if a president is unpopular, a congressman may actually avoid being linked to the president.

Chapter 14: The Congress, the President, and the Budget: The Politics of Taxing and Spending

Multiple-Choice Questions

1. **(D) is correct.** People in the lowest income bracket pay taxes at about a rate of 15 percent. People in the highest income bracket pay taxes at a rate of about 36 percent. Under a progressive tax system, the wealthy pay at a higher rate because they can better afford to do so.

2. **(D) is correct.** The Office of Budget and Management was established to coordinate the budget proposals of all government agencies into the president's final proposal. It has a significant amount of budgetary power, but this is checked by Congress's approval of the president's nominee for its director.

3. **(D) is correct.** Ronald Reagan instituted enormous tax cuts while dramatically increasing defense spending at the same time. During his eight years as president, the national debt soared. This debt allows the government to spend more money now, but obligates future generations to repay the largess. Eliminating the deficit, also called balancing the budget, will not reduce the national debt. The national debt can only be reduced through budget surpluses.

4. **(C) is correct.** Entitlement programs are a form of mandatory spending because everyone entitled to the benefits of the program must be paid. Congress cannot control these expenditures unless it changes the eligibility requirements of the program, which it is unlikely to do unless such measures are absolutely necessary.

5. **(A) is correct.** The president works closely with the Office of Management and Budget, an executive office, to formulate his budget proposal. The Congressional Budget Office works with congressional committees to review and amend the president's proposal. The tax codes determine how much money the government has to spend, a necessary first step in budgeting.

6. **(B) is correct.** Bonds function like loans—people buy them from the government, and the government must pay them back with interest. Bonds are usually a good source of income for the federal government.

7. **(D) is correct.** Social Security and Medicare consume more of the federal budget than any other social programs. More than one out of every three tax dollars is spent for these programs. Furthermore, as entitlement programs, the costs of these programs are considered uncontrollable and have increased significantly in recent years. Congress has also added prescription drug coverage to Medicare, further contributing to its costs.

8. **(C) is correct.** The federal government receives the biggest portion of its revenue from income taxes levied on individuals. Social Security revenues have been increasing and also count for a large portion of federal revenues. Corporate income tax revenue has decreased, however. Congress borrows whatever money it needs so that revenues match expenses.

9. **(B) is correct.** Figure 14.1 describes the sources of federal revenue, not spending.

Due to the ability of the government to borrow money, the federal government spends considerably more than it earns in revenue. Thus, response I can be eliminated. It is also important to notice that the y-axis provides total government revenue. Thus, in 1998, corporate income taxes accounted for only about $200 billion in revenue. In 2006, individual income taxes account for about $1 trillion in federal revenue. Thus, response III is inaccurate, while response IV is accurate. It is clear from Figure 14.1 that individual income taxes and social insurance taxes are the biggest revenue sources for the federal government. In fact, this fact is summarized in words included in the graph itself. Thus, the correct responses are II and IV, which is answer (B).

10. **(B) is correct.** Tax expenditures occur when the government decides to lower the tax burden on citizens or businesses to encourage various behaviors. For example, by excluding interest on home mortgages from income taxes, the government foregoes more than $100 billion every year. Tax expenditures add up to more than one-third of the government's total revenue. This is money that the government could collect, but has decided not to in order to encourage behaviors the government believes to be beneficial.

Free-Response Questions

Incrementalism is defined well here for one point. The writer also answers part of question (b) here, but still only receives the point for the definition.

Social Security is the government's largest uncontrollable expenditure. This definition is worth a point.

This is not an explanation of the impact of incrementalism. The writer did give an explanation in part (a), but readers will not flip points from one section to another. The section of uncontrollable expenditures is worth one point, however.

1. a. When making the budget each year, the CBO and OMB ask executive departments for estimates of how much money they will need for the upcoming year. Most departments will calculate that they will need as least the same amount as they received in the previous year, plus a little bit more. The "little bit more" that is tacked on each year isn't much; however, it is significant when it is added up over 10 or so years. This is called incrementalism. Uncontrollable expenditures are monies that are set aside by Congress for specific programs such as Social Security. The U.S. government has made a social contract of sorts with the American people. The people pay into Social Security while they are working, and they will collect back when they retire. Because it would take a major change in the relationship between the government and the people to get rid of a program like Social Security, it is considered an uncontrollable expenditure.

   b. Incrementalism increases the national debt because Congress won't stop it. Congress just keeps on passing the bills without much thought. Uncontrollable expenditures increase the national debt because there is no easy way to slow them down and they take up such a large portion of the budget.

   c. Wars have also contributed to the national debt. George W. Bush and the war on terror have caused the United States to borrow billions of dollars for the conflicts in Iraq and Afghanistan.

   Reagan also increased the national debt in fighting the Cold War. Total score on this question: 4 of 5 points.

Correctly explains the role of the Ways and Means Committee. 1 point.

Describes the role of the OMB. 1 point.

Explains the role of the CBO. 1 point. Total score: 3 of 3 points.

2.   The budget process is very important each year because it is the way that the government can set priorities in government programs. Both the president and Congress are important in the process.

Congress plays a major role in the budget because it must agree to all taxes passed by the government. In fact, the most important committee in Congress regarding taxes is the House Ways and Means Committee. The Constitution says that all bills raising revenue must originate in the House, and the Ways and Means Committee is the committee in the House responsible for tax policy. As a result, the government is dependent on the Ways and Means Committee to make tax policy that will give the government the right amount of revenue to pay for its programs.

The working budget is submitted to Congress each year by the Office of Management and Budget, an agency that works for the president. The OMB budget becomes the working document from which Congress proceeds. Because the OMB proposal is a coordinated effort with the major cabinet departments, it is a dominant document in preparing the budget.

The Congressional Budget Office was created in the 1970s. Congress grew weary of relying on the budgetary numbers produced by the executive branches OMB. The CBO plays a similar role to the OMB; helping to make predictions about the best way to raise and spend money. Deciding which numbers to rely on, those produced by the OMB or those produced by the CBO (which can differ dramatically) can produce major battles between the legislative and executive branches.

Chapter 15: The Federal Bureaucracy

Multiple-Choice Questions

1. **(C) is correct.** Despite the common misconception, the federal bureaucracy actually has *not* grown. In fact, the American population has grown and the social responsibilities of the government have increased without the size of the federal bureaucracy changing much. State and local bureaucracies, however, have grown considerably.

2. **(B) is correct.** Civil service is based on the merit system. Applicants must take an exam, and those individuals in the highest scoring group are hired. Most bureaucratic positions are filled this way, though the president does appoint some people to high-level positions.

3. **(A) is correct.** Bureaucracies are essentially implementers of policies crafted by Congress, the president, and sometimes the courts.

4. **(E) is correct.** Table 15.1 is limited to the number of civilian employees. By excluding members of the armed forces, the Department of Defense comes in behind the U.S. Postal Service in terms of the number of employees (677,200 verses 762,305, respectively).

5. **(E) is correct.** Bureaucracies are often faced with daunting tasks. They are expected to implement policies that frequently lack important details. They may be tasked with achieving an important goal, but given neither the authority nor the money to do so effectively. Thus, it is not surprising that Americans are frequently frustrated with the bureaucracy, even though many of the problems are beyond their control.

6. **(E) is correct.** Government corporations perform tasks that could be done by private enterprise and charge fees for their services. Amtrak is such a government corporation. The Department of the Interior is a Cabinet-level department, the Food and Drug Administration is an independent regulatory commission, the Bureau of Engraving is an independent executive agency, and General Motors is a private business.

7. **(B) is correct.** Each new president has the task and the privilege of filling countless bureaucratic posts. He therefore solicits individuals who not only are well qualified but also are likely to endorse the president's policy proposals and work to advance his agenda. The constitutional system of checks and balances, however, requires that all appointees be confirmed by Congress.

8. **(B) is correct.** Administrative discretion is the ability of bureaucrats to select among several viable alternatives when implementing policies crafted by Congress. Because such policies are frequently vague, administrative discretion can be considerable. This freedom to mold policy outcomes allows bureaucrats to select courses of action that are most consistent with their personal policy beliefs.

9. **(D) is correct.** Responsibility for a single policy area is often split between various federal bureaucracies. The fragmentation can lead to overlap and inefficiency. The Department of Homeland Security was created after the 9/11 terrorist attacks revealed weaknesses caused by the fragmentation of authority over domestic security among 46 federal agencies.

10. **(A) is correct.** One of the ways federal agencies assess the effectiveness of their policy implementation is by gauging public reaction. Citizens' complaints also help agencies enforce regulations and prosecute violators.

Free-Response Questions

Correctly identifies all three participants in an iron triangle. (3 points)

The agency receives information from the interest group. (1 point)

Congressional committee members receive information and campaign support from the interest group (1 point)

Congressional committee members receive help with constituents' complaints from the agency. (1 point)

The interest group receives legislation it desires from the congressional committee. (1 point)

The agency receives additional funding from the congressional committee. (1 point)

1. Iron triangles often form among an interest group, a federal agency, and a legislative committee or subcommittee to shape policies in a particular policy area. One example of an iron triangle that deals with environmental issues might include an interest group such as Greenpeace, the Environmental Protection Agency, and the Senate Environment and Public Works Committee or one of its subcommittees.

   For example, suppose hundreds of residents near a few different power plants have developed chronic asthma from the plants' emissions. They may take their case to the EPA and seek assistance from Greenpeace, which has the resources to draw attention to their cause. Greenpeace brings the issue into the political arena by demanding tighter federal regulation of plant emissions. It issues many reports to the EPA showing a link between the chemicals emitted by the plants and the illnesses of the residents. The EPA may also become involved if citizens register their complaints directly with the agency. As a result of these claims, the EPA may send inspectors to test the air quality in the neighborhoods around each plant. The EPA, with the help of Greenpeace, has gathered enough information to prompt the need for new regulations. However, suppose federal law prohibits the EPA from making certain industry changes to power plants. The EPA and Greenpeace then must enlist the help of a sympathetic committee, such as the Senate Environment and Public Works Committee.

   The interest group now lobbies the committee—it provides information about the effects of plant emissions and pledges support for committee members in the next congressional election. The EPA also appeals to the committee and can argue that it has already done its best to shoulder the complaints of the public, thereby shielding committee members from angry voters. The committee, to appease the voters and Greenpeace, may revise the law to allow further regulation by the EPA. Alternatively, it may increase the budget of the EPA so that the agency can develop some kind of solution on its own.

   Either way, each member of the iron triangle benefits. The interest group has succeeded in influencing policy. The agency, with the help of Greenpeace's resources, has done its job of enforcing regulations or may have increased its budget to do so. The members of the committee are allowed to remain out of the fray; voters are not likely to take out their anger on the committee members at the polls, and the committee is absolved of most of the responsibility of resolving the issue by handing the practicalities over to the EPA. Finally, by working together, these three participants have solidified their relationships with each other in case another issue arises.

   This response identifies the participants in an environmental iron triangle and describes how the iron triangle forms during various steps of the policy process. The student successfully applies a theoretical concept to a real-world situation to demonstrate a knowledge of iron triangles and the way they operate in politics. The only link missing is an explicit expression of something the interest group might receive from the agency. (8 of 9 points)

The writer both identifies an agency and gives an example. 2 points.

Another identification and example. 2 points.

The writer correctly explains a complaint. Total score on question: 5 of 5.

2. a. The Securities and Exchange Commission is responsible for regulating the sales of stocks. The SEC makes sure that the stock market is operating fairly. One requirement the SEC has made is for companies selling stocks to submit a report every three months showing how well they are doing economically. The Environmental Protection Agency regulates the amount of pollution that is in the air. If a locality, such as Los Angeles, is allowing too much pollution, the EPA can fine the city (usually by withholding federal highway funds).

   b. One major complaint about the bureaucracy acting as a regulator is the cost. Many small businesses cannot afford to meet all the provisions established by an agency of an act like the Americans with Disabilities Act. When an agency comes in and insists they replace all their desks to make them wheelchair accessible, some small businesses cannot afford it and simply shut down.

Chapter 16: The Federal Courts

Multiple-Choice Questions

1. **(E) is correct.** A plaintiff must have sufficient standing to sue. This means that he or she has a legitimate personal stake in the case. It must be evident that the plaintiff has suffered as a result of another person's actions or of a government action. A citizen cannot simply bring a suit against a law with which he or she disagrees.

2. **(A) is correct.** The Supreme Court justices, not the solicitor general, select the cases they will hear. However, very few appeals are chosen. Cases involving civil liberties are more likely to draw the attention of the Supreme Court.

3. **(D) is correct.** Courts with appellate jurisdiction do not become directly involved with the facts of a case. Rather, they review how a case was handled in a lower court—how the ruling was decided and whether or not that ruling appropriately applied the law to the case.

4. **(C) is correct.** The Constitution authorizes Congress to confirm the president's nominees for federal judgeships as part of the system of checks and balances. The Senate Judiciary Committee is fairly active in this role; about one-fifth of the nominees have been denied a position on the bench.

5. **(B) is correct.** Federal courts sometimes interpret state laws. In some cases, the Supreme Court must decide if a state law violates the Constitution. Federal courts also have jurisdiction over "diversity of citizenship" cases in which the litigants reside in different states; federal judges weigh the appropriate state laws.

6. **(C) is correct.** According to Table 16.3, 20 percent of George W. Bush's nominees to the district courts were women, while only 14 percent of Carter's nominees were women. The scope of Table 16.3 is limited to presidents serving since Carter, which eliminates (A) and (E) as possible correct answers because they make much broader claims that are not addressed in this table. Answer (B) is incorrect because the table uses percentages to describe nominees' traits, whereas answer (B) refers to an absolute number. Finally, answer (D) is incorrect because the most common occupation is the judiciary.

7. **(E) is correct.** Most Supreme Court rulings uphold the decision made by the lower court. This is the principle of *stare decisis,* meaning "let the decision stand."

8. **(C) is correct.** Most court rulings are based on precedents set by previous cases that addressed a similar issue. Judges are not required to rule by precedent, but precedents do serve as a guide and help to make the law more uniform.

9. **(C) is correct.** While state judges may be elected, all federal judges are appointed. Therefore, interest groups cannot influence elections for federal judges. It would also be illegal for interest groups to contribute money to a federal judge's retirement account. While interest groups do sometimes run advertisements in support or opposition to a Supreme Court appointee or a high-profile case (such as abortion), this is very rare. It is very common, however, for interest groups to file *amicus curiae* briefs in which they try to persuade the Supreme Court to decide a case a certain way.

10. **(B) is correct.** Under Chief Justice John Marshall, the Supreme Court used *Marbury v. Madison* to establish the principle of judicial review. Judicial review allows the Supreme Court to determine if laws passed by Congress are consistent with the Constitution. By extension, this principle also allows the Supreme Court to determine if executive branch actions are constitutional.

Free-Response Questions

Two identifications of advantages. (1 point each)

1. When the framers of the Constitution set up the judicial branch, they wanted a branch where judges could make decisions about law without worrying about the political consequences of their decisions. However, that also meant that judges did not have to pay attention to public opinion when they made their decisions. That is a disadvantage in a democracy.

Description of first advantage. (1 point)

Description of second advantage. (1 point)

Two advantages of the independence of the judiciary are that the judges can make decisions about law without having to worry about whether their decisions are popular and they can overrule actions of the president or Congress that step outside of the Constitution. Because judges do not have to worry about elections, they can simply look at the Constitution and make decisions based on the rule of law. When the Warren Court handed down the *Miranda* decision, many Americans opposed it because Miranda was such a terrible criminal. However, the Court was able to look past the single case and make a decision that protected the rights of all Americans. The Court might not have made that decision if they had to run for reelection. The power of judicial review gives the Court the ability to declare acts of the president or Congress unconstitutional. Because the president is popularly elected, it would be difficult to check his power if the Court was elected. But on many occasions in the past, the Court has done so.

Two identifications of disadvantages. (1 point each)

Description of first disadvantage. (1 point)

Description of second disadvantage. (1 point)

Two disadvantages of judicial independence are that they can ignore public opinion and they can make "activist decisions." In a democracy, the government should make decisions that reflect the public will. When the Court makes choices about the law that are unpopular, that can hurt the respect that the government has. Also, the court is not limited to just interpreting the Constitution. Sometimes they can make decisions that are outside of the meaning of the Constitution. For example, in the *Roe v. Wade* case, the Supreme Court made a decision that gave Roe a right to abortion based on the right to privacy when privacy is not even mentioned in the Constitution.

This response identifies advantages and disadvantages in the first sentences of the respective paragraphs, quickly earning one-half of the points for the entire question. The descriptions are adequate and follow. (8 of 8 points)

Defines judicial review. 1 point.

Gives an example of a case involving judicial review. 1 point.

Defines judicial activism. 1 point.

Gives an example of a case involving judicial activism. 1 point.

Describes two ways in which federal judges could be considered undemocratic. 2 points.

Explains how a president could contain the power of the courts. 1 point. Total score on question: 7 of 7.

2. a. <u>Judicial review</u> is when a federal court rules on the constitutionality of a law or governmental action. When the Taney Court ruled in the Dred Scott case that slaves were property and could therefore be taken into free territories, they were using judicial review.

    b. <u>Judicial activism</u> is the belief that judges should not be bound by a strict interpretation of the Constitution; instead, they must be willing to make decisions to meet the pressing needs of society, or to make a just decision that may not be found in the Constitution. The case of <u>*Brown v. Board of Education*</u> would be one such example. In this case, the Warren Court struck down segregation laws, not based on a provision of the Constitution, but because they said it was wrong and detrimental to treat Black children differently than White children.

    c. Judges are <u>appointed to federal courts, not elected</u>. This is not very democratic. It would be more democratic to have the judges elected, but then that might influence the way in which they decided cases. Also, federal judges are mainly from prestigious, expensive law schools. This is elitism, which is also undemocratic.

    d. The President can restrain the courts by the <u>type of person they appoint</u> to serve as judges. Of course, there is no guarantee that the person the president appoints is going to act in the manner in which the president predicted he or she would. But a candidate who appears to be a strict constructionist is more likely to act this way than a person who everyone knows is liberal is.

Chapter 17: Economic Policymaking

Multiple-Choice Questions

1. **(B) is correct.** Keynesian economic theory endorses an active government because government spending creates demand among consumers. The government spending can create jobs for the unemployed and help businesses expand.

2. **(D) is correct.** In a communist system, the government owns the means of production; in a capitalist system, the government plays no part at all in the economy. The United States has a mixed economy that falls between these two extremes. The private sector is large, but the government has established many measures to regulate and influence it.

3. **(A) is correct.** Republican presidents focus on keeping inflation down because this helps the investor class, which is worried that inflation will erode their savings. Democrats, however, are more concerned with the interests of the working class, and thus focus their attention on minimizing unemployment.

4. **(C) is correct.** The Federal Reserve Board controls how much money is issued from the Federal Reserve Bank to all other banks. When it limits those available funds, banks are forced to offer loans at higher rates. This discourages people from applying for loans, which are one cause of the overcirculation of money.

5. **(D) is correct.** According to supply-side economics, government policies should stimulate the economy by increasing the supply of goods and services. Both Ronald Reagan and George W. Bush were strong advocates for supply-side economic policies. In contrast, economist John Maynard Keynes argued that government policies should stimulate the economic by influencing the demand for goods. Thus, to pull the U.S. out of the Great Depression, Franklin D. Roosevelt advocated massive government spending programs.

6. **(B) is correct.** The Federal Reserve Board has the most direct influence over the economy because it controls the money supply. It is also able to act quickly and decisively because it is a relatively nonpartisan government institution. Some even claim that the chair of the Federal Reserve Board is the second most powerful politician in the country.

7. **(D) is correct.** The state with the lowest unemployment rate is South Dakota, where only 2.5 percent of the population is unemployed. The scope of this table is limited and does not indicate how many people are unemployed in any given state, how unemployment has changed over time, or how what the national unemployment rate is. While unemployment in the District of Columbia is high, it is not as high as in Michigan or Alaska.

8. **(A) is correct.** Antitrust laws were developed at the turn of the twentieth century to check the power of such business magnates as John D. Rockefeller. These laws prevent any one company from monopolizing a particular market.

9. **(A) is correct.** The government exercises fiscal policies through its taxing, spending, and borrowing policies. Increasing agricultural subsidies is a form of government spending. On the other hand, monetary policy is the government's efforts to influence the money supply. All of the other response options are form of monetary policy.

10. **(E) is correct.** Long terms for members of the Federal Reserve Board allow them greater independence. They do not have to appeal to anyone to be re-elected, and they do not necessarily have to please the president or Congress once they have been guaranteed a 14-year post on the Board.

Free-Response Questions

Definition of global economy, good for 1 point.

An example of a positive impact of the global economy on the United States. 1 point.

An example of a negative impact of the global economy on the United States. 1 point. Total score on this essay: 3 of 3 points.

1. Once, the fight in the United States over the economy was between Thomas Jefferson's view of small farmers and Alexander Hamilton's view of an industrial giant protected by high tariffs. Neither man's visions would accurately portray the modern economy of the United States. Today we live in a global economy, one in which we trade freely with other nations, and where industries and corporations are no longer bound by geographical and political borders. "Japanese" cars are made in California and Tennessee; McDonald's restaurants are open in China and Russia. NAFTA allows the United States, Mexico, and Canada to trade freely, with no tariffs at all between these nations. With growing technology, even jobs can be exported with having to move people around. An X-ray taken at a local hospital is oftentimes sent to India to be looked at.

The global economy has had both positive and negative effects on the United States. On the positive side, Americans can buy many items at a lower price. Many household goods from shoes to televisions are now sold for much lower prices than they were 20 years ago. With low labor costs in places like China and Indonesia, imported goods are much more affordable. But on the negative side, there is a question of product safety. Last year, a high level of lead was found in many products made in China. These goods had not been properly inspected, and the factories where they were made would not have been allowed to open in the United States due to safety issues. There are also moral questions involved in this global economy. Is it right to pay a company for a product made by political prisoners?

For better or worse, the global economy is here to stay.

Correct explanation of monetary policy. 1 point.

1 point for an explanation of how monetary policy can be used.

A correct description of fiscal policy. 1 point.

Taxing and spending are the two main tools of fiscal policy. 1 point.

An explanation of one difficulty in trying to control the economy. 1 point.

2. a. <u>Monetary policy</u> is when the government (the Federal Reserve) tries to control the economy by controlling the availability of money. One way monetarism works is through <u>interest rates</u>. The Fed can raise interest rates to discourage people from borrowing money, or lower them to encourage borrowing. This will then affect the availability of money.

    b. <u>Fiscal policy</u> is when the government tries to control the economy through taxing and spending. <u>Low taxes and high spending</u> will stimulate the economy (but also drive a nation into debt). High taxes and low spending will slow the economy.

    c. One reason it is so difficult for the government to control the economy is that the <u>budget is created months ahead of time</u>. Say the government is trying to stimulate the economy by spending more money. Six months later, when the spending takes place, the economy might have already recovered. <u>Another reason the government has a difficult time controlling the economy is that government spending only accounts for about 20 percent of the economy</u>. The other 80 percent comes from the private sector, which may be taking the opposite actions of the government. For example, if the government gives tax breaks to stimulate the economy, but businesses increase their prices, the tax breaks won't have much of an impact.

A second point earned for this example. Total score on this questions: 6 of 6.

Chapter 18: Social Welfare Policymaking

Multiple-Choice Questions

1. **(E) is correct.** The most expensive social welfare programs are Social Security and Medicare, both of which primarily benefit the elderly. Programs for the poor account for only 17 percent of social welfare spending.

2. **(B) is correct.** Instead of paying taxes, the working poor receive money from the government through a program called the Earned Income Tax Credit. This program distributes $20 billion to poor families.

3. **(E) is correct.** In recent decades, income inequality has continued to grow. Thus, the adage that the rich get richer, and the poor get poorer accurately describes income distribution in the United States in recent decades. Income distribution in European democracies is more equal than in the United States.

4. **(B) is correct.** The Simpson-Mazzoli Act tried to discourage illegal immigration by forbidding employers to hire illegal immigrants. However, in order to prevent discrimination against Hispanics, the law also forbade employers from scrutinizing the documents employees present to prove citizenship. Thus, the law has not been a strong deterrent for hiring illegal immigrants, as long as they present reasonable evidence of citizenship. Nor has the law helped to slow the flow of illegal immigrants to the United States.

5. **(D) is correct.** Childhood poverty is concentrated in the South, with Alabama, Arkansas, Georgia, Kentucky, Louisiana, Mississippi, North Carolina, South Carolina, Tennessee, Texas, and West Virginia, where at least 40 percent of children live in poverty. Childhood poverty is also reasonably high in Florida at 39 percent. The only Southern state without high childhood poverty is Virginia (31 percent). Where there is considerable childhood poverty in some other states primarily west of the Mississippi, it is not as concentrated as in the South.

6. **(C) is correct.** Because people in poverty do not vote in very high numbers, they do not have a significant political voice. Politicians are more likely to respond to the needs of those people who elect them to office, such as senior citizens. It is not surprising, then, than the largest social welfare programs are Social Security and Medicare—both of which benefit the elderly.

7. **(C) is correct.** Because the number of retirees is growing, Social Security cannot remain solvent without cutting benefits or earning additional revenue, either through tax increases or cuts in other government programs. Of course, none of these solutions is politically palatable. Social Security also faces financial challenges associated with the increasing cost of medical care.

8. **(C) is correct.** Americans view social welfare with a greater degree of skepticism than do Europeans, who pay as much as 50 percent of their income in taxes to fund a wealth of social programs. Americans are generally more suspicious of big government and also tend to believe that poverty is more the fault of the individual than of society at large.

9. **(C) is correct.** Unmarried women with children have about a 30 percent chance of living in poverty, whereas African Americans and Hispanics have about a 40 percent chance of living in poverty. Two-parent families have only about a 6 percent chance of living in poverty. While poverty used to be concentrated among the elderly, programs like Social Security and Medicare have drastically reduced poverty among older Americans.

10. **(E) is correct.** Social Security is facing financial challenges due to increasing costs associated with increased longevity, advancements in medical technology, and an increasing number of retirees. George W. Bush proposed changing the Social Security program to allow current workers to invest part of their Social Security contributions into a personal investment account that might contain stocks or bonds. However, the pay-as-you-go nature of Social Security means that the transition costs for such a program would actually hasten Social Security's bankruptcy. A slumping stock market also reminded Americans of the pitfalls of investing in the stock market. Thus, Bush was unable to marshal enough support for his proposal.

Free-Response Questions

The student describes one cause; point earned. The student should remember to underline their main points to help the reader find them easily.

This explanation of the baby boom generation is worth a second point.

The "leaky bucket" explanation is worth one point.

The stock market fears are worth a second point here. Total score: 4 of 4 points.

1. a. One reason that Social Security cannot continue to operate as it has been is due to rising life expectancy. People are living longer, much longer than the age (65) at which they can collect Social Security. Therefore, they are drawing more money out than they had in years past. A second reason is the baby boomers. This generation, born in the 1950s, is much larger than the generation born in the 1960s and 70s. The way Social Security operates, the generation that is working pays in and the generation that retired collects that money. When you have fewer and fewer people paying in and more and more people collecting, you soon run out of money.

   b. President Bush had proposed that Social Security could be saved if people were allowed to put some of their Social Security money into private accounts for retirement. There were two reasons this plan failed. First, allowing people to divert some of their money away from Social Security would have caused it to run out of money even sooner. There would have been less money paid in at the same time as more people (the baby boomers) were trying to collect. Second, people were worried about putting their retirement accounts into the stock market or other investments. Bush's plan was announced just as the stock market took a dive in 2001, making people nervous about investing their retirement there.

A very brief answer, but it both defines entitlement and gives an example. 2 points.

Again short, but on target. A definition and an example. 2 points.

2. a. Entitlement programs are government-run programs that pay money out to <u>individuals who qualify, regardless of any neediness.</u> <u>Social Security</u> is an entitlement program.

   b. Means-tested programs are programs that <u>give aid only to those people who qualify</u>, such as those living below the poverty line. <u>Food stamps</u> is a means-tested program.

   c. Clinton wanted to change the means-tested programs of Johnson's Great Society. Clinton moved the nation from welfare to what he called "workfare." Limits were put on how much money the federal government would give to the states for their welfare programs. Individuals were also limited as to how much they were able to collect from welfare and how long they were able to stay on welfare.

Strongly supported by Republicans, Clinton brought about more welfare reform then the far more conservative Reagan was able to. Correct response, 1 point. Total score: 5 of 5.

Chapter 19: Policymaking for Health Care and the Environment

Multiple-Choice Questions

1. **(A) is correct.** The percentage of uninsured children varies considerably from state to state, even between bordering states in the same geographic region. Thus, the only accurate claim that can be made from the map is that the percentage varies by state, but is highest in Texas and lowest in Michigan.

2. **(D) is correct.** More people are undergoing medical treatment because more types of illnesses can be treated today, but people are not actually getting sick in greater numbers. Yet cutting-edge medical treatments are extremely expensive. In addition, patients have little incentive to seek out less expensive treatments because they often are not paying the bill themselves. Instead, the government and insurance companies pick up the bulk of the tab.

3. **(E) is correct.** Despite the common misconception that the American health care system is entirely privatized, the government is actually the greatest financial contributor. It funds nearly 50 percent of health care, while insurance companies pay about 30 percent and individuals pay about 20 percent.

4. **(D) is correct.** Americans have a life expectancy of about 77 years, which is shorter than those in most other democracies. The United States does not do well in infant mortality either. Seventeen other democracies have a lower infant mortality rate than the United States. For example, the infant mortality rate in the United States is twice that of Japan. Even though American health care costs more than in other countries, the United States rates poorly in these two key indicators of a populations health.

5. **(D) is correct.** Coal is America's most plentiful resource but also its dirtiest and a contributor to global warming. Although the United States has significant coal deposits, it relies more heavily on oil for its energy. Because domestic supplies of oil are insufficient to meet demand, the U.S. is a net importer of oil.

6. **(C) is correct.** Those without health insurance are disproportionately young Americans between the ages of 18 and 35. More than 90 percent of children are insured through a parent's health insurance or a government program such a CHIP. Virtually all elderly Americans are insured through Medicare, while Medicaid insures the poorest of the poor. Going without health insurance is risky for young adults, however, as they make up a disproportionate number of emergency room visitors.

7. **(E) is correct.** Most other democracies have nationalized health care systems in which everyone has equal access to health care at virtually no cost, while still spending a smaller percentage of their gross domestic product than the United States. Many Americans lack insurance, either through the government or their employer, and cannot afford to buy insurance or pay for medical treatment.

8. **(A) is correct.** Bill Clinton proposed reforms that would have insured all Americans. Under his proposal, most employers would be required to provide health insurance for their employees and the government would not have to increase taxes significantly to pay the cost. George W. Bush, on the other hand, favored market-based reformed, such as policies that rewarded Americans for creating health savings accounts to pay for their medical care. Bush's proposal did not ration care nor mandate that Americans purchase health insurance.

9. **(E) is correct.** While everyone agrees that it is important to have a safe place to keep toxic wastes, everyone also follows the mantra, "not in my backyard!" That is, everyone wants toxic waste to be disposed somewhere else—preferably a long way away from here. This is known as the NIMBY problem, or not in my backyard! When it comes to public opinion about the location of toxic waste dumps, NIMBY trumps scientific opinion about the optimal site.

10. **(D) is correct.** Environmental groups often spar with "wise use" advocates who believe that public lands should be managed so as to allow conservation and recreation along with economic uses such as grazing, mining, and logging. In the West, these industries are often the lifeblood of communities that would otherwise have very little economic opportunity.

Free-Response Questions

The abundance of coal is one of its major benefits. 1 point earned.

Black lung would score one point as an example, and global warming would score the second point.

Student explanation of the benefits of nuclear power. 1 point.

Student correctly explains the concerns of nuclear safety and toxic disposal. 2 points earned on this section. Total score for the question: 6 of 6.

1. a. Coal is beneficial to the United States because it is in such abundant supply within the United States. It makes up nearly 90 percent of our domestic energy resources. Coal does not need to be transferred in from other nations, and therefore it is not part of our foreign policy.

   b. Coal is also very dirty. Burning coal and the pollution it releases can cause black lung in people who breathe in its soot. A second problem is that coal pollution contributes to global warming.

   c. Nuclear power is once again gaining attention because it is a clean, relatively cheap form of power. Nuclear power stations are used throughout much of Europe, but are only beginning to be considered again for use in the United States.

   d. Nuclear power is controversial because of safety issues. In 1978, the United States experienced a near meltdown at Three Mile Island nuclear facility. A meltdown would have sent radioactive materials into the atmosphere and could have potentially killed thousands. The tragedy was avoided, but Americans became fearful of another such meltdown occurring. The toxic waste created by nuclear power stations is also a problem. This waste can remain radioactive for hundreds of years, and no community wants to have it buried nearby.

The student gives a specific act (the Clean Air Act) and gives a strong and specified explanation of it. 2 points earned.

A simple explanation, but enough to earn a point.

The student gives two examples. Either would suffice. Only one was necessary to earn the point. Total score: 4 of 4.

2. From the time the first smokestacks begun to rise around Pittsburgh, America has been pumping pollutants into the air. In 1970, Congress passed the <u>Clean Air Act</u> in an effort to cut back on this environmental problem. The Clean Air Act required fuels (<u>especially gasoline) to have produce fewer pollutants</u>. This act also required <u>manufacturers to cut back on the amount of particle waste</u> that they released into the air.

    The Clean Air Act has been weakened over the years. But air <u>pollution levels are lower today because of it</u>. The smog in LA is still the worst in the nation, but it is better than what it was in the 1960s before the Clean Air Act.

    <u>Automakers and manufacturers have both found problems with the Clean Air Act</u>. Automakers do not like the increased expense of making a cleaner-burning engine, and have fought Congress over this bill for years. Manufacturers likewise do not like the increased cost of filtering their smokestacks, and argue it makes them less competitive with foreign industries that do not have such regulations.

Chapter 20: National Security Policymaking

Multiple-Choice Questions

1. **(D) is correct.** Nongovernmental organizations such as Greenpeace and Amnesty International form to advance particular causes across nations.

2. **(D) is correct.** U.S. membership in NATO or the UN did not compel the United States to war. Rather, the Vietnam War was fundamentally about the U.S. desire to contain the spread of communism. The U.S. had abandoned isolationism (and the Monroe Doctrine) after World War II.

3. **(A) is correct.** Sanctions brought by only one country against another are doomed to failure because the sanctioned country can simply divert its trade elsewhere. When the U.S. imposed a grain embargo on the Soviet Union for invading Afghanistan, the Soviets simply bought grain from other countries; thus, only U.S. farmers were hurt by the embargo. Sanctions are thus effective only when a group of countries agrees to impose trade restrictions on a country together.

4. **(D) is correct.** Congressional foreign policy powers include declaring war, ratifying treaties, and confirming ambassadors. Perhaps most importantly, Congress has the power of the purse, which means it controls how much money will be appropriated for foreign and military policies. While Congress raises, organizes, and funds the military, the Constitution specifically states that the president will be commander in chief of the armed forces.

5. **(E) is correct.** The end of the Cold War opened the door for lower spending for national defense. However, defense spending increased once again after the terrorist attacks of 9/11 to provide improved homeland security and to fight the war on terrorism.

6. **(D) is correct.** Isolationism is the doctrine that the United States should stay out of military conflicts in other countries. Isolationism was a central part of American foreign policy prior to World War II. The Cold War is notable for the doctrine of containment, not isolationism.

7. **(E) is correct.** George W. Bush pursued an aggressive foreign policy doctrine to counter terrorism. The Bush Doctrine relied on preemptive attacks against terrorists and was later expanded to preemptive attacks against developing threats. The aggressiveness was evident in Bush's belief in unilateralism and American military preeminence. The military-industrial complex consists of the U.S. military and defense contractors; it would not have made sense for Bush to eliminate these entities.

8. **(B) is correct.** While the United States spends more money in foreign aid than any of the other countries mentioned, America does not appear nearly as generous when our largesse is measured as a percentage of the gross domestic product. While Sweden invests less money in foreign aid, it is much more generous as a percentage of its gross domestic product—more than five times as generous as the U.S. American foreign aid accounts for less than one-half of one percent of its GDP (about 0.18 percent).

9. **(D) is correct.** Although the CIA has a somewhat glorified image of conducting espionage and covert operations, it actually collects most of its data from legitimate sources, such as foreign governmental reports. This information is then used to help make foreign policy decisions.

10. **(E) is correct.** The Vietnam War had a great impact on American attitudes toward government. Americans came to realize that the federal government is capable of lying when it suits the interests of those in power. It also reminded Americans that the U.S. is not invincible.

Free-Response Questions

The Korean War would be a correct identification. 1 point.

Containment would count as a rationale for the Korean War. 1 point.

The war in Iraq is part of the war on terror. 1 point.

Explaining the causes of the war in Iraq is not easy, but the student's explanation of the continuing conflict is worth a point.

1. a. A conflict the United States was involved in during the Cold War was the Korean War. The United States became involved in Korea as part of Truman's Containment Policy. Truman believed the United States needed to keep communism from spreading past its current borders, and that meant keeping communist North Korea out of South Korea.

b. The war in Iraq would be a conflict the United States was involved in during the war on terror. The causes of the war in Iraq are a bit confusing. President Bush said that the U.S. invaded Iraq to remove any weapons of mass destruction, but few have been found since the invasion. However, the continuing American military presence in Iraq, according to many, is considered the frontline for fighting terrorist organizations.

c. Those who oppose the war in Iraq argue that using force in the Middle East simply creates more rather than fewer terrorists. They would argue that the United States would be better off fighting the causes of terrorism instead of the already established terrorists.

Another point awarded for this description of an argument against the war in Iraq. Total score on this question: 5 of 5.

2. The Constitution gives the president a great amount of power when it comes to foreign policy. One power the President has is to appoint ambassadors. An ambassador represents the United States to another nation. If the president wants to work to improve America's relation with another nation, the president might send a more diplomatic ambassador. If the president feels he must take a hard-line stance, an ambassador with a different set of skills might be needed. The president can also send the military to strike at an enemy. Reagan used this power to strike at terrorist in Libya. Bush I invaded Panama. Clinton attacked terrorist bases in Afghanistan. Bush II launched invasions of Afghanistan and Iraq.

Along with his constitutional powers, the President can also use nonconstitutional powers in conducting foreign affairs. Executive agreements allow the president to make pacts with the leaders of other nations. These agreements do not need congressional approval, and therefore are often used instead of treaties.

But there are limits to a president's powers. Presidents cannot declare war. Only Congress is able to do this. The president also relies upon Congress to fund military actions. In theory, if the president were acting in a manner that Congress did not like, (such as the invasion of a small nation), it could stop the action simply by halting the flow of money. This is unlikely to occur, however. Congress does not want to be seen as unsupportive of our troops when they are in harm's way.

Chapter 21: The New Face of State and Local Government

Multiple-Choice Questions

1. **(A) is correct.** The line-item veto is a powerful tool that 42 governors have. With it, governors often have the final say in the budget because they can simply remove parts of it with which they disagree. State legislatures often accept the governor's final version of the legislation since they seldom have the votes to override it.

2. **(A) is correct.** State constitutions are subordinate to the U.S. Constitution. They are also different from the U.S. Constitution in that they are typically longer and include many details about specific public policies. Each state has a different constitution and, therefore, a different way of organizing the state's government. For example, Nebraska's constitution establishes a unicameral legislature, where the other 49 states have bicameral legislatures. One similarity between the state constitution and the U.S. Constitution is that all 51 documents contain a bill of rights.

3. **(C) is correct.** While the specific process for amending state constitutions varies from state to state, the most common method is for state legislatures to propose amendments which must then be approved by voters in the next general election. In some states, the legislature must propose the amendment in two consecutive sessions.

4. **(A) is correct.** Many states have moved their gubernatorial elections from presidential election years so that the governor's race will be at the top of the ticket. Thus, gubernatorial elections are determined less by party (and coattail) influences and more by the characteristics of the candidates.

5. **(A) is correct.** In recent years, state legislatures have undergone reforms to make them more efficient and effective. These reforms are known collectively as legislative professionalism and include longer sessions, better pay for legislators, and an increase in the number of staff members who assist legislators.

6. **(E) is correct.** In 1962, there were 13,381 special districts; by 2007 this number had mushroomed to 18,323—a staggering increase of 49 percent. At the same time, the number of other types of government often shrank.

7. **(D) is correct.** *Baker v. Carr* established the principle of "one person, one vote" and required that states draw their house districts so that each had equal population. Prior to this decision, a state's house districts varied considerably in size with rural districts being heavily overrepresented in the legislature. After *Baker v. Carr,* states redrew their district lines, increasing the influence of urban areas so that representation matched their population; this decreased the influence of rural areas.

8. **(B) is correct.** Most lawmaking at the state level is parallel to lawmaking at the federal level. Both houses of the state legislature must pass identical versions of the same bill, which then becomes law when the president signs it. The other procedures for making state laws are relatively rare, but include a legislative override of the governor's veto, citizen initiatives, and citizen referenda.

9. **(E) is correct.** States vary considerably in how judges are selected and all of the methods mentioned are common. Judges are appointed in 13 states, compete in partisan elections in 11 states, compete in nonpartisan elections in 19 states, and are appointed but must sit for retention elections in 17 states.

10. **(B) is correct.** Direct democracy occurs when citizens play a direct role in politics and policymaking. States can be outlets for direct democracy in many different ways. Initiatives and referenda allow citizens to have a direct influence on public policies. Recall elections allow citizens to end an elected official's term early. Town meetings are still used in some parts of New England to create local laws. While many state governors have line-item veto authority, it is not an example of direct democracy.

Free-Response Questions

The student distinguishes between the power of a gubernatorial veto and a presidential veto to earn one point here.

The line item veto is a second legislative power. The description earns the student a second point in this section.

Building public support, coupled with the examples, is good for one point.

An executive need for media skills is worth a second point. Total score for this question: 4 of 4 points.

1. One power that makes many governors stronger than the president is the veto. Although both a governor and the president have the power to veto, it is usually more difficult for a state legislature to override a governor's veto than it is for Congress to override the president's. The line-item veto is a power that many governors have that the president does not. This veto allows a governor to strike a specific clause from legislation. This was designed to allow governors to remove wasteful spending from bills. Congress gave President Clinton the power of the line-item veto, but the Supreme Court ruled it unconstitutional.

   Both presidents and governors need to build public support if their programs are going to be successful. When the public is not backing a plan by a governor or a president, it is much less likely that it will receive legislative support. For example, when George W. Bush tried to reform Social Security, it was not received well by the public, and went nowhere with Congress. Likewise, when Governor Schwarzenegger failed to get the California voters to pass a package of reform legislative propositions, he had a much more difficult time getting the state legislature to support his programs.

   Creating a good media-image goes hand in hand with building public support for presidents and governors. From a press conference, where an executive must answer sometimes difficult questions from reporters, to a media event, where the executive's mere presence becomes newsworthy, executives need good skills in dealing with the press.

The question on democracy in the states was prefaced with a comparison to the federal government. Legislators are also elected at the federal level (representatives, senators), and therefore, this response would not warrant any points. The students would have done better to write about either the initiative process, the referendum, or the recall. No points for the first section.

2. Many states have direct election of their legislature. This gives the people a stronger say in the laws that are made. If the state's legislature passes an unpopular bill, or continues to raise taxes, its members can be voted out of office. This would be one way in which states have given the people a greater say in elections.

   Other states have allowed for the election of judges. While all federal judges are appointed for life, some states allow the people to vote for a judge like they would for any other elected office. Some argue that elected judges may feel pressured to decide cases in a way that would please their constituency, but little evidence has been found to support this argument.

The election of judges is allowed at the state but not the national level. 2 points earned here, one for the identification and one for the explanation. Total score: 2 of 4 points.